Client/Server

Programming with

OS/2 2.0

2ND ED.

Robert Orfali • Dan Harkey

Library of Congress Catalog Card Number 92-7802
ISBN 0-442-01219-5

Van Nostrand Reinhold
115 Fifth Avenue
New York, N.Y. 10003

Chapman and Hall
2-6 Boundary Row
London, SE1 8HN, England

Thomas Nelson Australia
102 Dodds Street
South Melborne 3205
Victoria, Australia

Nelson Canada
1120 Birchmount Road
Scarborough, Ontario M1K 5G4, Canada

16 15 14 13 12 11 10 9 8 7 6 5 4 3 2 1

Library of Congress Cataloging-in-Publication Data

Orfali, Robert
     Client/Server Programming with OS/2 2.0 / by Robert Orfali, Dan Harkey
     —2nd Edition
     p.   cm.
     Includes Index
     ISBN 0-442-01219-5
     1. OS/2 (Computer operating system) 2. Local area networks
(Computer Networks) I. Harkey, Dan II. Orfali, Robert, Client/Server
Programming with OS/2 2.0. III. Title.
QA76.76.O634O74 1992
005.4'469—dc20
                                           92-7802
                                         CIP

Dedication

This book is dedicated to my wife and daughter, Michiko and Tomomi, and to my parents, Howard and Barbara. Their support and encouragement were invaluable.

Dan Harkey

This book is dedicated with love to my wife Jeri and my mother Mimi.

Robert Orfali

Trademarks

Apollo—NCS
Apple Computer, Inc.—Macintosh and Hyper-card
Arcadia Technologies, Inc.—CUA Workbench
Ashton-Tate Corporation—Ashton-Tate
AT&T—OPEN LOOK, Tuxedo
Banyan Systems—VINES, SMP
Borland International, Inc.—Paradox, Borland C++, Application FrameWorks, Borland International
CASEWORKS, Inc.—CASE:PM
Club Med Sales, Inc—CLUB MED
COMPAQ Computer Corporation—COMPAQ
CompuServe—CompuServe
Cooperative Solutions, Inc.—Ellipse
Digital Equipment Corporation—DECdns, DECtds, Concert Multithread Architecture, Ultrix, VMS
Dow Jones & Company, Inc.—Dow Jones
Enfin Software Corp.—Enfin/3
FTP Software Inc.—PC/TCP Plus
Guidance Technologies, Inc.—Choreographer
Gupta Technologies, Inc.—SQLBase and SQLWindows
Hewlett-Packard—OpenView, NetLS, HP NCS, HP/UX, Domain
Horn Abbot Ltd—Trivial Pursuit
IBM Corporation—IBM, OS/2, Netview, AS/400, Personal System/2, PS/2, Presentation Manager, Database Manager, Query Manager, Dialog Manager, Communications Manager, C/2, GDDM, NETBIOS, OfficeVision, DB2, SQL/400, SQL/DS, OS/400, CICS, System 370, CUA, BookMaster, Systems Application Architecture, SAA, AIX, Information Warehouse C Set/2, WorkFrame/2, DDCS/2, DRDA, Extended Services, CPI-C, Workplace Shell, SOM, DDCS/2, Data Engine, RISC System/6000, PowerPC

Information Builders, Inc.—Focus
Interactive Images, Inc.—EASEL
International Institute of Engineers (IEEE)—POSIX
Lotus Development Corporation—Lotus Notes, cc:Mail
Massachusetts Institute of Technology—X Window
mdbs, Inc.—Object/1 and mdbs
Microformatic U.S.A, Inc.—Gpf
Microsoft Corporation—Microsoft, MS, MS-DOS, CodeView, Microsoft Windows, NT, LAN Manager, SQL Server
Miramar System's Inc.—MACLAN Connect
NCR Corporation—Top End
Network General Corporation—The Sniffer
Neuron Data Inc.—Open Interface
Novell Corporation—Netware, IPX, SPX
Objective Solutions, Inc.—ObjectPM
Open Software Foundation, Inc.—Motif, DCE, DFS
Oracle Corporation—Oracle
The Regents of California—Berkeley Unix (BSD)
The Santa Cruz Operation, Inc.—SCO Unix, SCO
Siemens—DIR-X X.500, SINIX
Sun Microsystems—Sun Sparcserver, SunSoft Solaris, ONC, Sun Microsystems, Sparc, NFS, RPC
Sybase, Inc.—Sybase and Transact-SQL
Tandem Computers, Inc.—Nonstop SQL, Pathway, Guardian
Tivoli—WizDOM
Transarc—Encina, AFS
Ungermann-Bass, Inc.—Ungermann-Bass
Unix Systems Laboratories, Inc.—UNIX
Wang—Network Event Logger (NeL)
Xerox Corporation—Ethernet, Xerox Star
3Com Corporation—3Com

What's New in This Edition?

This short list of what's new is for the brave souls (and by now friends) who survived the 16-bit OS/2 edition of our book, and are now contemplating joining us again for the 32-bit Odyssey. As you will soon discover, there are major changes in this book. What started as a mere upgrade became a major new production. This second edition contains 600 new pages. We spent nine hectic months playing catch up with OS/2 2.0 and the fast moving client/server market. Here's what's new in this edition:

- We present a new model of the client/server market, how it is evolving, and where OS/2 2.0 fits in.

- We added the NetWare Requester for OS/2 2.0, TCP/IP, and CPI-C to our repertoire of FX client/server programs. You will see how these "big name" newcomers perform in our famous BLOB Olympics.

- We introduce the new OS/2 2.0 features, including the new semaphore services, the flat memory model, and the MMPM/2 multimedia extensions.

- We develop our code using the superb OS/2 2.0 WorkFrame/2 environment and the superfast 32-bit C Set/2 compiler.

- We converted all our code to 32-bit OS/2. Comparing some of the code from the previous edition with this one may help you in your conversion efforts. Many of the programs, however, are entirely new.

- We provide in-depth coverage of CUA'91, the OS/2 Workplace Shell, and Object-Oriented User Interfaces (OOUIs).

- We use OS/2 2.0's Object Oriented System Object Model (SOM) and the Workplace Shell class libraries to create our graphical user interfaces.

- We gave an OOUI facelift to our Club Med application. You will be pleased with "pizzaz" added by the new PM controls such as containers and notebooks.

- We explain how Extended Edition became Extended Services, and what it all means in terms of new functions.

- We introduce the new Extended Services database features and, of course, incorporate them into RSQL. You will be pleased with the new rollforward feature.

- We cover Distributed Relational Database Access (DRDA) using DDCS/2.

- We describe the new SAA features, including the Distributed Computing Environment (DCE).

- We added over 100 new illustrations that add some life (and humor) to the arcane technical jargon.

Preface

The new generation of *client/server* business solutions combines the intuitive user interface of the PC with multiuser server capabilities for transaction processing previously found only on superminis or mainframes. Client/Server makes it possible to create industrial strength software solutions on low-cost, network-attached PCs. These solutions promise to maintain the PC's traditional autonomy and ease of use and at the same time overcome the "stand-alone" isolation of PC software.

To create these new solutions, you must learn how to use and integrate the *extended* services provided by a new breed of PC operating systems. The services that "extend" the PC include: preemptive multitasking, interprocess communication, peer-to-peer LAN protocols, SQL database, and an advanced graphical user interface (GUI). This book teaches you how to develop client/server solutions using OS/2 2.0 and five complementary products that help complete the platform. These products include a Database Manager, a LAN Operating System, and a set of protocol stacks that allow you to communicate with "almost everything."

Why did we pick OS/2 2.0? Because it is a modern operating system that was designed from the ground up for personal computer technology and client/server environments. OS/2 2.0 provides a very complete platform on which you can build working software on both the client and the server.

What You Will Learn

In this book we will go beyond merely describing the client/server architecture; we will create working client/server systems that demonstrate *how the pieces play together*. These working systems will give you a practical understanding of how to exploit the synergy (and avoid the pitfalls) inherent in distributed applications. OS/2 2.0 is the operating system package that comes closest to providing all the necessary platform ingredients needed to create these systems.

While you learn how to program OS/2 2.0 and its extensions, you will cover almost the entire curriculum of applied computer science. By the time you have finished this book, you will be able to use the C-language to create multitasking applications that communicate with other applications over a Local Area Network (LAN). Your applications will be able to use the full power of the Standard Query Language (SQL) to interface to a database. Your user interfaces will be able to take advantage of the new object-oriented graphic features provided by OS/2 2.0's Workplace Shell.

Client/Server is primarily a relationship between programs running on separate machines. The separation of the client and server tasks became feasible with the advent of low-cost and robust peer-to-peer communications over LANs and Wide Area Networks (WANs). We assume that you will want your client/server platform to communicate with the largest number of machines. With that in mind, we will develop code using NetBIOS, LAN Server, Named Pipes, and Novell, the PC world's most predominant protocols. You will learn how to program Berkeley sockets on TCP/IP, which will give you access to the Unix world in all its variants. At the other end of the spectrum, you may want to communicate with mainframes. You will learn how to write peer-to-peer applications using the SAA Common Programming Interface-Communications (CPI-C) over APPC. With CPI-C, you can treat the mainframe as just another server.

Once you master communications, you will have the capability to provide useful services to remote clients. In this book, you will learn to combine this capability with the power of a network-based relational database. OS/2 2.0 provides up to 512 MBytes of memory per process. As a result, you will have plenty of memory space available to write powerful server applications that support large multimedia object types such as image and voice. You will find that OS/2 2.0 provides a powerful platform for creating intelligent network objects. These objects may be combined into "ensembles" that cooperate to provide increasingly more sophisticated functions. OS/2 2.0 provides many of the pieces that you'll need to create client/server "killer apps."

How hard will it be for you to learn all these technologies and build working systems out of them? We wrote this book with the intention of getting you there by the shortest route possible. We also want you to enjoy the process. We believe that studying working code is probably the most effortless way to demystify the arcane terminology of operating systems, database, data communications, and graphical user interface programming.

We will start you off with simple C programs that become building blocks in creating complete client/server applications. You will see ensembles come together from diverse elements. Most importantly, you will understand which of the different techniques provides the best fit for a job. In many instances, we will program the same function using different OS/2 Application Programming Interfaces (APIs) and then compare the cost benefits of each approach. The programming examples will be accompanied by in-depth tutorials that provide you with the necessary background on a particular topic.

Who Is This Book For?

This book is for anyone interested in creating client/server software solutions as well as learning how to program OS/2 2.0. If you are a novice, the book will serve as a crash course in computer science in addition to teaching OS/2. If you are a seasoned professional programmer, then you can dive straight into the examples. Here, you will find a wealth of working code that may save you hundreds of hours of debugging and wading through stacks of manuals. If you are a manager, system architect, or planner, this book will address issues such as:

- When do you use processes and when do you use threads?
- What are the relative merits of the different peer-to-peer communication protocols?
- What do you look for in a Graphical User Interface (GUI) for Online Transaction Processing (OLTP)?
- How hard is it to put together an Object-Oriented User Interface?
- What is the most effective way to provide network services?
- What is the best strategy for developing client/server software using an SQL database as a platform?

To get the most out of this book, you should have a working knowledge of the C language and be somewhat familiar with PCs. Prior experience with networks and databases can be helpful, but we will help you get by without it.

How the Information Is Organized

Part I introduces the client/server model and presents a detailed overview of OS/2 2.0 and its extensions. You get to see the whole picture before plunging into the details. We situate OS/2 2.0 in relation to other server platforms such as Unix, NT, and NetWare 3.1. We conclude with an overview of distributed architectures that starts with simple client/server and evolves to multiservers and heterogeneous servers in multivendor environments. We examine some of the great "intergalactic" architectures proposed by SAA and "open systems" to bring order out of chaos in the universe.

Part II covers the important core services needed for the creation of multitasking clients and servers. Many of the OS/2 2.0's kernel strengths—including preemptive multitasking, multithreading, and the hardware enforced protection between applications—are invisible to the end user. Nevertheless, these strengths are critical to build LAN-based, mission critical, client/server applications. When you combine these elements with the Database, Communications, and LAN Managers, you are very close to having a "world-class" server platform on a PC. OS/2 is the first commonly available operating system to provide threads that allow you to multitask very effectively from within a process. We will develop a benchmark program that demonstrates how to effectively use multitasking and multithreading. We will then explore Named Pipes, OS/2's most powerful and elegant method for interprocess communication. The expertise you develop with processes, threads, semaphores, and Named Pipes will serve you well with the programs in the book.

Part III covers protocols for LAN-based client/server communications. We will develop a client/server repository for Binary Large Objects (BLOBs) using a layered software approach. The client/server implementation uses a generic file transfer program that runs on top of CPI-C, APPC, NetBIOS, Named Pipes, TCP/IP, NetWare, and the LAN Server. We will run benchmarks that compare the performance of these six protocols and the ease of programming them. We will show you how to package these communications programs as Dynamic Link Libraries (DLLs). This area should especially interest providers of commercial software.

Part IV covers the OS/2 Extended Services Database Manager. This component is the heart of the *Database Server* platform. We will show you how to use SQL to program the Database Manager. You will learn how to invoke the Database Manager's environment, configuration, and system utilities directly through the C language API. We will use this knowledge to create an "all-in-one" utility that runs scripts of SQL and Database Administration commands. This utility teaches you how to use SQL effectively and how to measure the performance of the various commands.

Part V introduces benchmarks that compare the performance of *Database Servers* and *Transaction Servers*. We will develop a standard TP1 benchmark toolkit that measures raw OLTP performance in units of transactions per second (tps). We will use the TP1 benchmark to measure the performance of different client/server architectures. We will answer questions like: How slow is Dynamic SQL? How much faster are Transaction Servers than Database Servers? What is the effect of CPU speed on server performance? What is the effect of the network?

Part VI is about creating interactive front-end clients using the Presentation Manager and the Object-Oriented User Interface (OOUI) features of the OS/2 2.0 Workplace Shell. OOUIs invite users to manipulate objects on the Workplace Shell. They present an opportunity to create new front-ends for networked database and transaction servers that simulate the look and feel of real-life business objects. The Workplace Shell integrates the various business objects and provides a seamless visual space where users conduct their day-to-day business with information literally appearing at their fingertips. We will show how to program the Workplace Shell using the *System Object Model's* language-independent, Object Oriented (OO) facilities. We will build our OOUI programs by inheriting functions from the Workplace Shell's SOM class libraries. Our emphasis will be on how to use Object Libraries rather than low-level Presentation Manager programming. SOM allows you to get the benefits of OO classes from within standard C programs. We will use this introduction to OOUIs, GUIs, and OO classes to discuss the principles of *human computer interaction* as embodied by the CUA '91 standard. We will also examine what kind of tools are needed to create highly graphical front-ends in client/server environments.

Part VII is the grand finale that brings together all the client/server elements developed in this book. We will develop a fun client/server application called Club Med. In this adventurous example, the multithreaded Club Med clients use a OOUI-based graphical user interface. The clients communicate with a Club Med *Transaction Server* through Named Pipes.

Acknowledgements

- To our managers at IBM: Ken Ouchi and Dick Luedtke. They gave us six challenging years to learn client/server technology as it is used in the "real world." Their client/server vision is reflected in this book.

- To Jeri Edwards, who created *all* the illustrations. She brought life and humor to this thick book with her incredible gift for making the most complicated system concepts "obvious" through images and icons. Jeri is an expert in client/server computing and has taught us a lot.

- To Dick Conklin, Editor of the IBM **Personal Systems Developer.** He was there when we needed him and was instrumental in making this book happen.

- To the OS/2 2.0 developers in Boca, Austin, Raleigh, and Toronto for a superb operating system. They worked many long hours to make it happen.

- To the grassroots movement that is known as *Team OS/2*. This formidable movement of free spirits decided it was time to "do the right thing," then *did it*.

- To Lee Reiswig, John Soyring, Jim Cannavino, Art Olbert, and Tommy Steele. They created a vision and are now teaching the elephant how to dance.

- To the team of programmers who are helping us make TxE into a world-class client/server platform. This book was inspired by the ongoing TxE effort.

- To Jim Gray for his helpful review of the book and for the deep insights he provided. Jim pioneered this field and has remained its guru.

- To Lori Gauthier at Novell for her ongoing support.

- To Dianne Littwin, the Senior Editor at Van Nostrand Reinhold. She is a pleasure to work with. We also thank the members of Dianne's staff.

- We thank our tireless copy editor Larry Mackin for keeping us honest.

- We thank cartoonist Frank Brown for the *Mon People* on the cover and Dave Coffman for his special effects.

- The entire book was created on OS/2 2.0 using Ventura Publisher and Corel Draw.

You forgot me! They bought the book because they think I'm cute!

All the views expressed in this book are solely the Authors' and should not be attributed to IBM or any other IBM employee. The two authors contributed equally to the production of this book and are still alive to see it published.

Contents

Part I

The Big Picture

The OS/2 2.0 platform provides the raw building blocks we will use to develop working examples of client/server business solutions. So the first order of the day will be to understand these building blocks and their functions. We will then examine what business solutions can be provided using these building blocks as our platform. Finally, we will develop an architectural framework that helps us better understand how the building blocks and the business solutions come together. Here's the road map we will follow in Part I:

- In Chapter 1, "Welcome to Client/Server Computing," we introduce the concept of client/server. We explain what client/server computing is and what makes a product "client/server." We also explain the importance of client/server software for the next generation of PC applications.

- In Chapter 2, "Clients, Servers, and Operating Systems," we describe what each side of the client/server equation needs from an operating system.

- In Chapter 3, "OS/2: The Client/Server Platform," we introduce OS/2 2.0 in a general way. Among other things we explain where OS/2 fits into the scheme of things and why we chose it as a base for a client/server platform. We then review the database, communications, and network operating system products we chose to create an OS/2-based client/server platform.

- In Chapter 4, " OS/2 Servers: Reaching For The Limits," we continue our exploration of OS/2 as a client/server platform. Here, we consider the question of server upward scalability. We answer the question by looking at Intel processor trends, multiprocessor architectures for superservers, and multiservers.

- In Chapter 5, " Server Platforms: OS/2's Competition," we review OS/2 2.0's main competitors on the server front. The server platform you choose will directly influence what software systems you can build, how fast can you build them, and at what cost. A platform is like a long-term marriage; think through it carefully before you jump into it. Competing server platforms include Unix and NetWare

1

today, and future platforms such as NT and Taligent. The comparisons will help you situate OS/2 in the context of other operating systems present and future.

- In Chapter 6, "OS/2 2.0: A Grand Tour," we provide an overview of OS/2 2.0. This is the first of five chapters that provide the bird's eye view of the OS/2 client/server platform. A first encounter with this client/server platform is like looking at a very long buffet table filled with hundreds of exotic food dishes, most of which you do not recognize. Where do you start? Ideally you should take a quick tour of the buffet and then return to make your choice of dishes at a more leisurely pace. We will take such a tour starting with this chapter and continue into the next four chapters.

- In Chapter 7, "Communications Manager: The SAA Connection," we discuss the platform's mainframe connectivity functions. The Communications Manager, a well-endowed component of OS/2's Extended Services, provides virtually everything a PC needs to interoperate with the world of SAA. This includes IBM's traditional mainframes and the AS/400 superminis.

- In Chapter 8, "TCP/IP for OS/2: The Unix Connection," we describe what the platform provides to interoperate with the world of Unix. Since this is another very "well-endowed" product prepare yourself for a long, but interesting, tour.

- In Chapter 9, "LAN Server and NetWare: The NOS Dimension," we describe the network operating system extensions to OS/2. These two products allow you to distribute resources and functions on a PC LAN and make them look as if they were part of the local PC's environment. Between the IBM LAN Server (Microsoft's LAN Man sibling) and NetWare, we almost cover the entire spectrum of PC LAN Connectivity.

- In Chapter 10, "Database Manager and DDCS/2," we cover the database server components of our platform. The Database Manager, also part of Extended Services, provides a powerful SQL-based DBMS Server for PC LANs. DDCS/2 allows the Database Manager to interoperate with IBM's other SAA database platforms (this includes the AS/400 SLQ/400, and DB2 and SQL/DS on mainframes). All these components work together using IBM's DRDA architecture for distributed database.

- In Chapter 11, "Architectures for Client/Server Computing," we introduce a set of distributed architecture models that should help you make sense out of the seemingly overabundant software technology introduced by our client/server platform elements. These models will also help you identify the technology components that provide the best fit for a particular business solution. If the last five chapters provided an overview of hundreds of exotic dishes, then this chapter teaches the principles of good dieting and how to be selective in the food you eat. Architecture provides a framework in which we can organize our thinking. It teaches us how to create systems from individual components. The client/server model is an example of an architectural construct that can be used to create cost-efficient business solutions using the OS/2 platform. Architecture, however, is also used to develop a vision of future systems. We will first look at what OS/2 can do for us today as a server for low-cost ("skinny") clients on a network. We will then look at how OS/2 allows us to play in the distributed intergalactic world of SAA, DCE, and "open systems" architecture.

Chapter 1

Welcome to
Client/Server Computing

"The massive shift toward client/server is incredible. This shift is not a revolution, and it is not an evolution. It's an explosion! For the past 30 years, the computer industry has been moving in the direction of the hierarchical mainframe-centric approach, but in the last 5 years the industry has virtually turned on its heels toward a distributed network-centric approach."

Business Research Group, January 1992[1]

At times, it seems as if everyone associated with computing has an opinion on the client/server relationship. In this chapter, we will give one more "definitive" opinion of what this all means. We will first look at the market forces that are driving the client/server industry today. We then peek through our crystal ball at the computer industry in the advanced stages of the client/server era. After coming this far, we feel we can handle even more danger in our lives, so we tackle the issue of *what is client/server*. We end this chapter with a lively diatribe on fat clients versus fat servers.

THE MARKET FORCES DRIVING CLIENT/SERVER

Client/Server computing is an irresistible movement that is reshaping the way computers are being used. This is a relatively young movement that is already in full force and is not leaving any facet of the computer industry untouched. Big transformations in the computer industry are usually driven by new technologies and needs. The technologies and needs pushing client/server computing comes from three directions: *downsizing*, *upsizing*, and *rightsizing* (Figure 1-1).

---

[1] Source: **Client/Server Computing Study,** Business Research Group (January, 1992). The BRG study covered 300 Fortune 1000 and mid-sized companies.

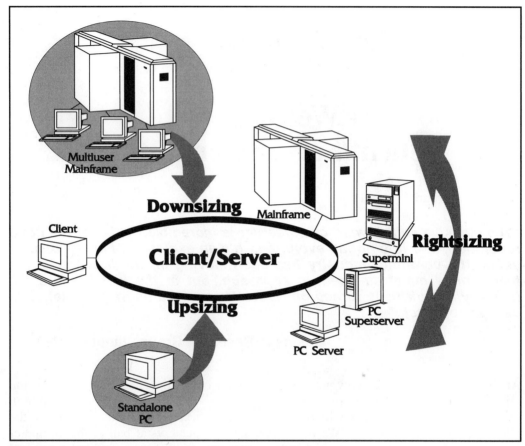

Figure 1-1.   The Forces Driving the Client/Server Market.

Downsizing

Downsizing is the downward migration of business applications from superminis and mainframes to PCs, PS/2s, Macintoshes, and Unix workstations.   The downsizing process breaks up large supermini and mainframe-type applications into program modules that run on one or more network servers. User-interface functions move to the client workstations and replace the "green screen uglies" with state-of-the-art graphical user interfaces. The centralized processors with time-shared terminals are replaced by networked client/server machines.

Client/Server software solutions on low-cost standard hardware are the driving force behind downsizing. Today's low-cost desktop machines are as powerful as last decade's top-of-the-line mainframes. Client/Server software solutions allow us to create coherent environments out of these autonomous desktop machines. By doing this, client/server computing combines the best of two worlds: the cost-effective and almost addictive power of desktop computers with multiuser access to shared resources and data.

Upsizing

Upsizing is the bottom-up trend of networking standalone PCs at the departmental or workgroup level. By 1993, the majority of PCs will no longer be living in isolation. In 1985, only 5.5% of all business PCs were connected to a LAN. By 1991, the percentage of LAN-attached business PCs rose to 44.2% percent. IDC predicts that 60% of PCs will be on LANs by the end of 1992.[2] The vast majority of PCs were originally attached to LANs for sharing expensive peripheral devices such as laser printers and scanners. The LANs are now used primarily for electronic mail and for sharing databases and files (including repositories of images and documents). In addition, a new generation of client/server workflow software promises to introduce finely tuned levels of interaction in the workgroup.

PC LAN connections are growing equally among all types of environments. Growth is particularly strong in small (PC only), business environments: "the forgotten one million." According to the IDC 1992 Annual Briefing, Intel-based PCs accounted for 94% of the 389,000 servers shipped worldwide in 1991.

Rightsizing

Rightsizing moves applications to the most appropriate server platform. Clients request services over the network and the server best suited for the job provides it. In this open model, a server can be a PC, a supermini, or a mainframe. Servers from different vendors can happily coexist: *the network is the system*. This is especially important for large companies, where this *enterprise network* articulates the business. Rightsizing moves information and server power to the points of impact. It matches the job to the server without having to resort to "islands of automation."

Personal computers and LANs are now equipped with the technology to support enterprise networking. Mainframes and superminis are learning how to compete on the enterprise network. Open standards for enterprise client/server interoperability are now in place that define exactly what it takes to become "just another server." Computer system vendors, such as IBM, DEC, HP, and Tandem are embracing client/server open standards as the strategic platform that ties together their disparate product lines (workstations, superminis, and mainframes). For their customers, client/server standards finally enable cost-effective, multi-vendor integration at the enterprise level.[3]

---

[2] Source: **IDC's 27th Annual Computer Industry Briefing** (March 5, 1992). The Gartner Group's LAN penetration predictions for the US are even higher: 67% by the end of 1992.

[3] IDC found that 60% of IBM mainframe sites and 50% of DEC Vax sites are developing new client/server applications. Source: **IDC's 27th Annual Computer Industry Briefing** (March 5, 1992).

According to the Gartner Group, the *Enterprise Server Platform (ESP)* will allow large corporations to leverage the benefits of personal, workgroup, and mainframe resources. Instead of centralized enterprise megaservers, Gartner envisions "a collection of services, which will typically be distributed across a variety of computers for price/performance, high availability, and platform specialization advantages." The critical services provided will include mail routing, file and print sharing, OLTP and decision support, network and systems management, resource brokering, software distribution and license management, security, and inter-enterprise gateways.[4]

THE CLIENT/SERVER COMPUTING ERA

What will the brave new world of client/server computing look like? What effect will it have on MIS shops? What does it mean to compete in an open client/server computing market? What new opportunities does it create for software developers?

Which Client/Server Vision?

Client/Server computing has the unique distinction of having strong champions across the entire spectrum of the computer industry. For the "PC can do it all" crowd, client/server computing means scrapping every mainframe that can't fit on the desktop and the demise of host-centric computing. For mainframe diehards, client/server computing means unleashing a new breed of "born-again" networked mainframes that will bring every PC in the enterprise back to the fold. For the middle of the roaders, client/server is "computer glasnost," which really means a new era of coexistence and openness in which all can play.

---

[4] Source: **Client/Server Computing: Exploiting the Inevitable**, Gartner Group (February 12, 1992).

There is some truth in all these visions. Client/Server computing provides an open and flexible environment where mix and match is the rule. The client applications will run predominantly on PCs and other desktop machines that are at home on LANs. The successful servers will also feel at home on LANs and know exactly how to communicate with their PC clients. Beefy PCs make natural superservers. For mainframes to succeed as servers, however, they will have to learn how to meet PCs as equals on the LAN. In this world of equals, mainframe servers cannot treat PCs as dumb terminals. They need to support peer-to-peer protocols, interpret PC messages, service their PC clients' files in their native formats, and provide data and services to PCs in the most direct manner. Ultimately, the server platform with the best cost/performance and services wins.

Client/Server and the "New MIS"

Client/Server solutions almost always result in lower development and maintenance costs and higher productivity solutions. Through open standards (and de facto ones such as SAA) client/server computing may also provide the seamless integration of PCs and mainframes. Most new applications will follow the client/server model. Client/Server application development requires hybrid skills that include transaction processing, database design, communications experience, and graphical user interface savvy. Mastering these skills will require renaissance programmers who can combine the best of "big-iron" reliability-driven thinking with the PC LAN traditions. Where will these renaissance programmers come from? Will MIS shops be able to provide solutions and services in this new computing environment? Or will that service be provided by consultants and system integrators who have taken the time to learn these new skills?

Most client/server solutions today are PC LAN implementations that are personalized for the group that uses them. Everything from LAN directories to security requirements must be properly configured, often by the users themselves. MIS departments have the skills to not only manage and deploy large networks but also to provide interoperability standards. They also know how to fine-tune applications, distribute fixes, and ensure data integrity. MIS traditionally caters to the large data centers and not the line departments that own the PCs and LANs. The key is for them to do what they do well in a distributed client/server environment where they share the power, responsibility, computing know-how, and financial budgets with the line business managers (the end users). Consequently, distributing the MIS function is essential.

Client/Server computing may be best served by two-tiered MIS organizations: a *line MIS* for managing and deploying departmental systems, and an *enterprise MIS* for managing the internet and setting interoperability standards. This type of organization will not only preserve departmental autonomy but also allow the local LANs to be part of the multiserver, multivendor enterprise internet.

Competition in the Client/Server Market

Client/Server, the *great equalizer* of the computer business, encourages openness and provides a level playing field in which a wide variety of client and server platforms can participate. The open client/server environment serves as the catalyst for commoditizing hardware and system software. The PC is a good example of a computer commodity; it can be obtained from multiple suppliers and is sold in very price-competitive market situations. LAN adapters, LAN protocol stacks, network routers, and bridges are also becoming commodities. On the software side, workstation operating systems, SQL DBMSs, and imaging software are approaching commodity status. The Distributed Computing Environment (DCE) will make instant commodities out of remote procedures, network directory software, security services, and system management. These trends are good news for computer users.

But, where are the *great differentiators* that will set vendors apart in this highly competitive commodity environment? What will happen to the computer vendors when commodity-priced client/server computing power satisfies the needs for computerization as we know it today?

Computer vendors will in the short run differentiate themselves by the power of the superservers they provide. This will last until commodity operating systems start to routinely support multiprocessor hardware platforms. We anticipate that the most sustained differentiation will be in the area of new client/server software and not hardware platforms. Low-cost, easy to deploy client/server solutions will unleash a massive new wave of computerization. For example, image and multimedia enhanced client/server solutions have ravenous appetites for storage, network bandwidth, and processing power. These solutions will easily consume the new supply of low-cost client/server systems as long as software providers (like ourselves) can create enough applications.

We foresee a brave new era of ubiquitous client/server computing. Clients will be everywhere. They will come in all shapes and forms including desktops, palmtops, pen tablets, intelligent appliances, mobile personal communicators, electronic clipboards, TV sets, intelligent books, robots, automobile dashboards, and myriads of yet-to-be-invented information hungry devices. These clients, wherever they are, will be able to obtain the services of millions of other servers. This bullish view of the industry puts us in the camp of those who believe that *the supply of low-cost MIPs creates its own demand.*

WHAT IS CLIENT/SERVER?

Even though client/server is the leading industry buzzword, there is no agreed upon definition of what that term means. This provides us with the opportunity to create our own definition. As the name implies, clients and servers are separate logical entities that work together over a network to accomplish a task. So what makes client/server different from other forms of distributed software? We propose that all client/server systems have the following distinguishing characteristics:

- *Service:* Client/Server is primarily a relationship between processes running on separate machines. The server process is a provider of services. The client is a consumer of services. In essence, client/server provides a clean separation of function based on the idea of service.

- *Shared Resources:* A server can service many clients at the same time and regulate their access to shared resources.

- *Asymmetrical protocols:* There is a many-to-one relationship between clients and server. Clients always *initiate* the dialog by requesting a service. Servers are passively waiting on requests from the clients.

- *Transparency of location:* The server is a process which can reside on the same machine as the client or on a different machine across a network. Client/Server software usually masks the location of the server from the clients by redirecting the service calls when needed. A program can be a client, a server, or both.

- *Mix and match:* The ideal client/server software is independent of hardware or operating system software platforms. You should be able to mix and match client and server platforms.

- *Message-based exchanges:* Clients and servers are loosely coupled systems which interact through a message-passing mechanism. The message is the delivery mechanism for the service requests and replies.

- *Encapsulation of services:* The server is a "specialist." A message tells a server what service is requested and it is then up to the server to determine how to get the job done. Servers can be upgraded without affecting the clients as long as the published message interface is not changed.

- *Scalability:* Client/Server systems can be scaled horizontally or vertically. Horizontal scaling means adding or removing client workstations with only a slight performance impact. Vertical scaling means migrating to a larger and faster server machine or multiservers.

- *Integrity:* The server code and server data is centrally maintained, which results in cheaper maintenance and the guarding of shared data integrity. At the same time, the clients remain personal and independent.

The client/server characteristics described here allow intelligence to be easily distributed across a network and provide a framework for the design of loosely coupled network based applications.

WILL THE REAL CLIENT/SERVER PLEASE STAND UP?

Many systems with very different architectures have been called "client/server." System vendors often use "client/server" as if the term can only be applied to their specific packages. For example, file server vendors swear they first invented the term, and database server vendors are known in some circles solely as *the* client/server vendors. To add to the confusion, we make the claim that this book teaches you how to write client/server applications. So who is right? Which of these packages is the real client/server? The answer is all of the above.

The idea of splitting an application along client/server lines has been used over the last ten years to create various forms of Local Area Network software solutions. Typically these solutions sell as shrink-wrapped software packages, and many are sold by more than one vendor. Each of these solutions, however, is distinguished by the nature of the service it provides to its clients as shown in the examples below.

File Servers

With a file server, the client (typically a PC) passes requests for file records over a network to the file server (Figure 1-2). This is a very primitive form of data service that necessitates many message exchanges over the network to find the requested data. File servers are useful for sharing files across a network. They are indispensable for creating shared repositories of documents, images, engineering drawings, and other large data objects.

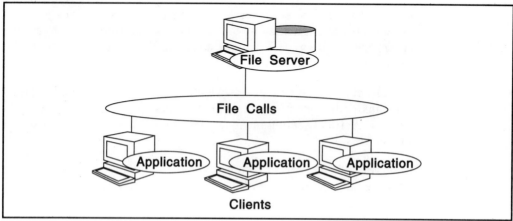

Figure 1-2.   Client/Server with File Servers.

Database Servers

With a database server, the client passes SQL requests as messages to the database server (Figure 1-3). The results of each SQL command are returned over the network. The code that processes the SQL request and the data reside on the same machine. The server uses its own processing power to find the requested data, rather than pass all the records back to a client and let it find its own data as was the case for the file server. The result is a much more efficient use of distributed processing power. With this approach, the server code is shrink-wrapped by the vendor; but you often need to write code for the client application (or you can buy shrink-wrapped clients like Query Manager, Enfin/3, or Paradox). Database servers provide the foundation for decision-support systems that require ad hoc queries and flexible reports.

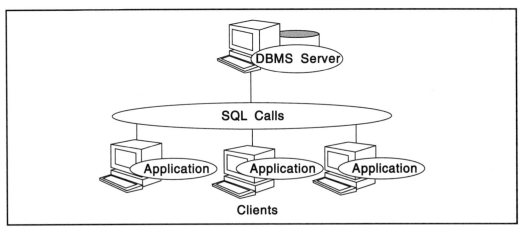

Figure 1-3. Client/Server with Database Servers.

Transaction Servers

With a transaction server, the client invokes *remote procedures* that reside on the server with an SQL database engine (Figure 1-4). These remote procedures on the server execute a group of SQL statements. The network exchange consists of a single request/reply message (as opposed to the database server's approach of one request/reply message for each SQL statement in a transaction). You will need to use a peer-to-peer protocol to issue the call to the remote procedure and obtain the results. The SQL statements either all succeed or fail as a unit. These grouped SQL statements are called *transactions*. You create the client/server application by writing the code for both the client and server components. The client component usually includes a graphical user interface. The server component usually consists of SQL transactions against a database. These applications have a name, "Online Transaction Processing" or *OLTP*. They tend to be mission-critical applications that require a 1-3 second response time 100% of the time. OLTP applications also require tight controls over the security and integrity of the database.

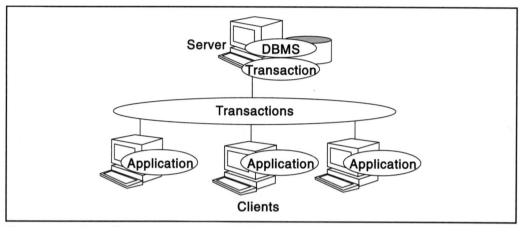

Figure 1-4. Client/Server with Transaction Servers.

Application Servers

With an application server, you also supply the code for both the client and the server (Figure 1-5). Unlike transaction servers, however, application servers are not necessarily database centered. For example, an application server can control a device such as an optical jukebox, or it can serve as an inference engine with download capabilities from Dow Jones. Application servers can also be built on top of databases to create new types of client/server applications. For example, Lotus Notes is an application server that manages semi-structured information (such as text and graphics) in a bulletin-board workgroup environment. Database augmented application servers form the basis for the new generation of image and document workflow servers. In a nutshell application servers are used to roll-your-own general-purpose network applications using the client/server model.

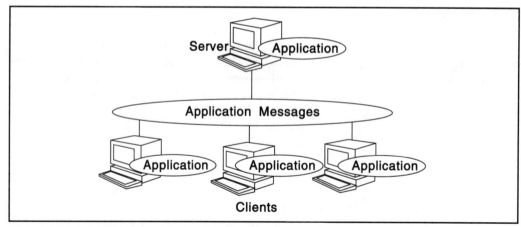

Figure 1-5. Client/Server with Application Servers.

FAT SERVERS OR FAT CLIENTS?

We've shown that client/server models can be distinguished by the service they provide. Client/Server applications can also be differentiated by how the distributed application is split between the client and the server. The *fat server model* places more function on the server (see Figure 1-6). The *fat client model* model does the reverse. Application and transaction servers are examples of fat servers; database and file servers are examples of fat clients.

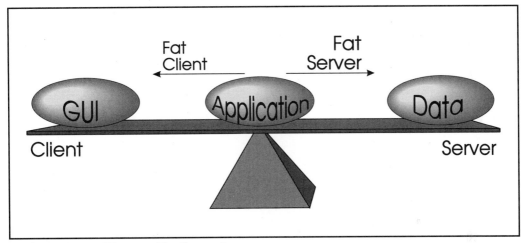

Figure 1-6. Fat Clients or Fat Servers?

Fat clients are the more traditional form of client/server. The bulk of the application runs on the client side of the equation. In both the file server and database server models, the clients are cognizant of how the data is organized and stored on the server side. Fat clients are used for decision support and personal software. They provide flexibility and opportunities for creating front-end tools that let end users create their own applications.

Fat server applications are easier to manage and deploy on the network because most of the code runs on the servers. Fat servers try to minimize network interchanges by creating more abstract levels of service. Transaction servers, for example, encapsulate the database. Instead of exporting raw data, they export the procedures (or methods in object-oriented terminology) that operate on that data. The client in the fat server model provides the GUI and interacts with the server through remote procedure calls. We will show in this book that fat servers are faster than fat clients.

Each client/server model has its uses. In many cases, the models complement each other and it is not unusual to have them coexist in one application. For example, an imaging groupware application could require an all-in-one server that combines file, database, transaction, and application services. Fat servers represent the new growth area for PC-based client/server computing. They require people like us creating *custom* applications that use the client/server model and build on top of shrink wrapped system components. The idea is to create vertical mission-critical applications packages that provide total business solutions using low-cost commodity type hardware and LANs.

Chapter 2

Clients, Servers, and
Operating Systems

This chapter starts with a brief description of what typical clients and servers do in life. We then examine what each side of the client/server equation needs from an operating system. We close by discussing how OS/2 2.0 fits these requirements and how we came to choose OS/2 as the platform for this book. By the time you reach the end of this chapter, you should be better prepared to know what to look for in a client/server platform.

THE ANATOMY OF A SERVER PROGRAM

The role of a server program is to *serve* multiple clients who have an interest in a shared resource owned by the server. This section describes a day in the life of a typical server. Here's what a typical server program does:

- *Waits for client-initiated requests*. The server program spends most of its time passively waiting on client requests, in the form of messages, to arrive over a communication session. Some servers assign a dedicated session to every client. Others create a dynamic pool of reusable sessions. Some also provide a mix of the two environments. Of course, to be successful, the server must always be responsive to its clients and be prepared for *rush hour traffic* when many clients will request services at the same time.

- *Executes many requests at the same time*. The server program must do the work requested by the client promptly. Clearly a client should not have to depend on a single-threaded server process. A server program that does will run the risk of having a client hog all the system's resources and starve out its fellow clients. The server must be able to concurrently service multiple clients while protecting the integrity of shared resources.

- *Takes care of VIP clients first*. The server program must be able to provide different levels of service priority to its clients. For example, a server can service a request for a report or batch job in low priority while maintaining OLTP-type responsiveness for high priority clients.

- *Initiates and runs background task activity*. The server program must be able to run background tasks triggered to perform chores unrelated to the main program's thrust. For example, it can trigger a task to download records from a host database during non-peak hours.

- *Keeps running*. The server program is typically a mission-critical application. If the server goes down it impacts all the clients that depend on its services. The server program and the environment on which it runs must be very robust.

- *Grows bigger and fatter*. Server programs seem to have an insatiable appetite for memory and processing power. The server environment must be upwardly scalable and modular.

WHAT DOES A SERVER NEED FROM AN OS?

In distributed computing environments, operating system functions become either *base* or *extended* services. The base services are part of the standard operating system, while the extended services are add-on modular software components that are layered on top of the base services. Functionally equivalent extended services are usually provided by more than one vendor. There is no hard rule that determines what gets bundled in the base operating system and what goes into the extensions. Today's extensions are usually good candidates for tomorrow's base system services.

Base Services

It should be apparent from the description above that server programs exhibit a high level of concurrency. Ideally, a separate task will be assigned to each of the clients the server is designed to concurrently support. Task management is best done by a multitasking operating system. Multitasking is the natural way to simplify the coding of complex applications that can be divided into a collection of discrete and logically distinct, concurrent tasks. It improves the performance, throughput, modularity, and responsiveness of server programs. Multitasking also implies the existence of mechanisms for intertask coordination and information exchanges.

Servers also require a high level of concurrency within a single program. Server code will run more efficiently if tasks are allocated to parts of the same program rather than to separate programs (these tasks are called coroutines or threads). Tasks within the same program are faster to create, faster to context switch, and have easier access to shared information. Figure 2-1 shows the type of support that servers require from their operating system. Let's go over these server requirements starting with the bottom layer and working our way up.

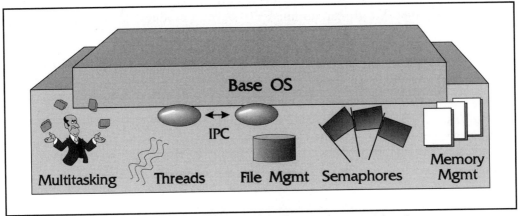

Figure 2-1. What Server Programs Expect From Their Base Operating System.

- *Task Preemption*. An operating system with preemptive multitasking must allot fixed time slots of execution to each task. Without preemptive multitasking, a task must voluntarily agree to give up the processor before another task can run. It is much safer and easier to write multitasking server programs in environments where the operating system automatically handles all the task switching.

- *Task Priority*. An operating system must dispatch tasks based on their priority. This feature allows servers to differentiate the level of service based on their client's priority.

- *Semaphores*. An operating system must provide simple synchronization mechanisms for keeping concurrent tasks from bumping into one another when accessing shared resources. These mechanisms, known as semaphores, are used to synchronize the actions of independent server tasks and alert them when some significant event occurs.

- *Interprocess Communications (IPC)*. An operating system must provide the mechanisms that allow independent processes to exchange and share data.

- *Local/Remote Interprocess Communications*. An operating system must allow the transparent redirection of interprocess calls to a remote process over a network without the application being aware of it. The extension of the interprocess communications across machine boundaries is key to the development of applications where resources and processes can be easily moved across machines (i.e., they allow servers to grow bigger and fatter).

- *Threads*. These are units of concurrency provided within the program itself. Threads are used to create very concurrent event-driven server programs. Each waiting event can be assigned to a thread that blocks until the event occurs. In the meantime, other threads can use the CPU's cycles productively to perform useful work.

- *Intertask Protection*. The operating system must protect tasks from interfering with each other's resources. A single task must not be able to bring down the entire system. Protection also extends to the file system and calls to the operating system.

- *Multiuser High Performance File System*. The file system must support multiple tasks and provide the locks that protect the integrity of the data. Server programs typically work on many files at the same time. The file system must support large number of open files without too much deterioration in performance.

- *Efficient Memory Management*. The memory system must efficiently support very large programs and very large data objects. These programs and data objects must be easily swapped to and from disk preferably in small granular blocks.

- *Dynamically Linked Runtime Extensions*. The operating system services should be extendable. A mechanism must be provided to allow services to grow at run time without recompiling the operating system.

Extended Services

The extended services must provide the advanced system software that will exploit the distributed potential of networks, provide flexible access to shared information, and make the system easier to manage and maintain. It should also make it easier for independent software vendors (ISVs) and system integrators to create new server applications. Figure 2-2 shows some of the extended services server programs expect from their operating system. We will go over these expectations starting from the bottom layer and working our way up. Some of these expectations read more like wish lists. They will eventually find their way into most operating systems.

- *Ubiquitous Communications*. The operating system extensions must provide a rich set of communications protocol stacks that allow the server to communicate with the greatest number of client platforms. In addition the server should be able to communicate with other server platforms in case it needs assistance in providing services.

- *Network Operating System Extensions*. The operating system extensions must provide facilities for extending the file and print services over the network. Ideally, the applications should be able to transparently access any remote device (such as printers and files) as if they were local.

- *Database and Transaction Services*. The operating system extensions must provide a robust multiuser database management system (DBMS). This DBMS should ideally support SQL for decision support and server-stored procedures for transaction services. The server-stored procedures are created outside the operating system

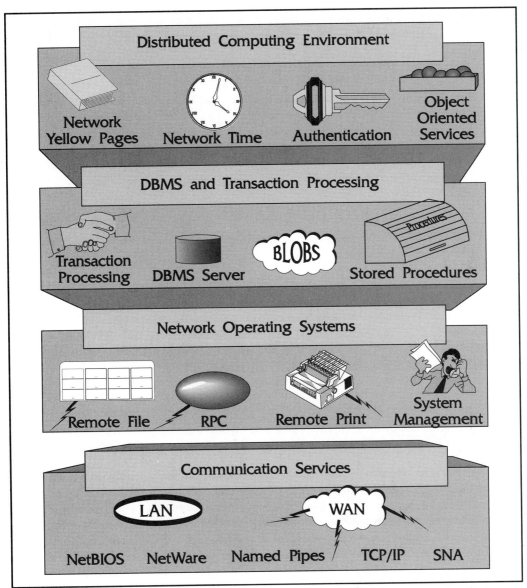

Figure 2-2.   What Server Programs Hope To Get From Their Extended Operating System.

by programmers like us. More advanced functions include a *Transaction Monitor (TM)* for managing stored procedures (or transactions) as atomic units of work that execute on one or more servers.

* *Naming and Network Yellow Pages*. The operating system extensions must provide a way for clients to locate servers and their services on the network using a network directory yellow page type of service. Network resources must be found by name. Servers must be able to dynamically register their services with the directory provider.

- *Authentication and Authorization Services*. The operating system extensions must provide a way for clients to prove to the server that they are who they claim to be. The authorization system determines if the authenticated client has the permission to obtain a remote service.

- *System Management*. The operating system extensions must provide an integrated network and system management platform. The system should be managed as a single server or as multiple servers assigned to domains. An enterprise view that covers multiple domains must be provided for servers that play in the big leagues. System management includes services for configuring a system, facilities for monitoring the performance of all elements, generating alerts when things break, distributing and managing software packages on client workstations, checking for viruses and intruders, and metering capabilities for pay-as-you-use server resources.

- *Network Time*. The operating system extensions must provide a mechanism for clients and servers to synchronize their clocks. This time should be coordinated with some universal time authority.

- *Object Oriented Services*. This is an area where extended services will flourish for a long time to come. Services are becoming more object-oriented. The operating system will be required to provide "object broker" services that allow any object to interact with any other object across the network. The operating system will also have to provide object interchange services and object repositories. Client/server applications of the future will be between communicating objects (in addition to communicating processes). Object groups will come together in loose associations to provide a service. The Object Management Group (OMG) is working on an architecture that allows objects to communicate across networks, hardware platforms, and operating systems.

- *Binary Large Objects (BLOBs)*. Images, video, graphics, intelligent documents, and database snapshots are about to test the capabilities of our operating systems, databases, and networks. These large objects (affectionately called BLOBs) require operating system extensions such as intelligent message streams and object representation formats. Networks must be prepared to move and transport these large BLOBs at astronomic speeds. Databases must be prepared to store those BLOBs and provide access to them. Protocols are needed for the exchange of BLOBs across systems and for associating BLOBs with programs that know what to do when they see one.

As you can see extended does mean "extended." It covers the universe of current and future services needed to create distributed client/server environments.

THE ANATOMY OF A CLIENT PROGRAM

All client applications have this in common: they request the services of a server. What makes client applications different is what triggers the requests and what graphical user interface (GUI), if any, is needed. Based on these differences, we can classify clients into three categories: *Non-GUI Clients*, *GUI Clients*, and *OOUI Clients* (see Figure 2-3).

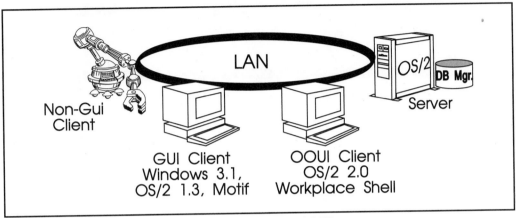

Figure 2-3.   Three Client Types: Non-GUI, GUI, and OOUI.

Non-GUI Clients

Non-GUI client applications generate server requests with a minimal amount of human interaction (see Figure 2-4). Non-GUI clients fall into two sub-categories:

1. *Non-GUI clients that do not need multitasking.* Examples include: automatic teller machines (ATMs), barcode readers, cellular phones, fax machines, smart gas pumps, and intelligent clipboards (future). These clients may provide a simple human interface in the request generation loop.
2. *Non-GUI clients that need multitasking.* Examples include robots, testers, and daemon programs. These clients often require very granular, real-time, event-driven multitasking services.

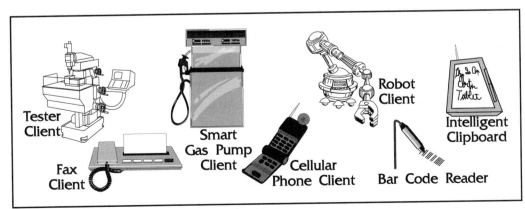

Figure 2-4.   The Many Faces of Non-GUI Clients.

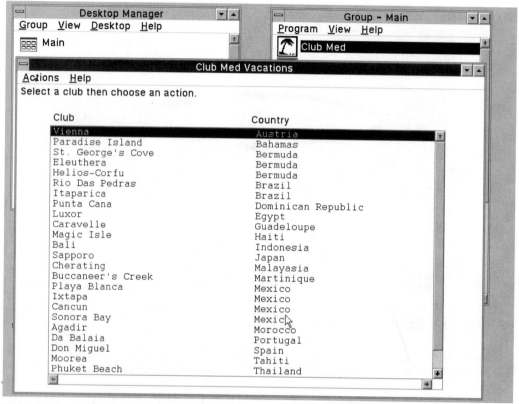

Figure 2-5. A Club Med GUI Application "Look and Feel."

GUI Clients

Simple GUI Clients are applications where occasional requests to the server result from a human interacting with a GUI. The simple GUI interface is a good fit for mainstream, OLTP-type business applications with repetitive tasks and high volumes. They also make good front-end clients to database servers. Simple GUI client applications are graphical renditions of the dialogs that previously ran on dumb terminals. GUIs replace the "green screen uglies" with graphic dialogs, color, menu bars, scroll boxes, and pull-down and pop-up windows (see Figure 2-5). Simple GUI dialogs use the object/action model where users can select objects and then select the actions to be performed on the chosen objects. Most dialogs are serial in nature. This model of user interaction is predominantly used in Windows 3.X, OS/2 1.X, and OSF Motif applications. It is also known as the CUA 89 graphical model.[1]

---

[1] This model is described in the SAA **Common User Access Advanced Guide**, IBM publication SC26-4582 (June, 1989).

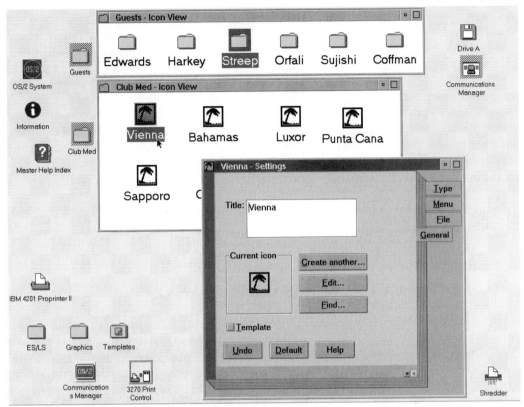

Figure 2-6. A Club Med OOUI Application "Look and Feel."

Object Oriented User Interface (OOUI) Clients

The *Object Oriented User Interface (OOUI)* metaphor is used to provide what Microsoft Chairman, Bill Gates, calls *information at your fingertips*. This "universal client" interface is a highly-iconic, object-oriented user interface that provides seamless access to information in very visual formats.[2] OOUIs will be used by information workers doing multiple, variable tasks whose sequence cannot be predicted. Examples include executive and decision-support applications, multimedia based training systems, operations consoles, and stockbroker workstations. OOUIs have an insatiable appetite for communications. OOUI desktop objects need to communicate among themselves and with external servers. The communications are, by necessity, real-time, interactive, and highly concurrent.

---

[2] The term "Universal Client" was coined by Gartner Group. They define it as "a personal information appliance that helps people get and understand information they need, wherever it may be, and to communicate it with other people." Source: **Client/Server Computing: Exploiting the Inevitable**, Gartner Group (February 12, 1992).

An example of an OOUI is the OS/2 2.0 Workplace Shell.[3] The Workplace Shell provides a visual space (think of it as a container) where related objects and programs can be brought together to perform a task. The desktop can contain multiple workplaces running concurrently (see Figure 2-6). Each workplace may be running parallel dialogs, also called *modeless dialogs*, over parallel sessions with the server. With advanced multimedia-type applications, these parallel dialogs may be used to display images, video, multiobject folders, and voice annotated mail. Information is displayed to the user in the foreground windows, while background tasks are constantly moving information to and from servers. For example, the first page from a multimedia document is displayed in a window while a background task is busy prefetching the rest of the document from the server. The workplace must provide support for:

- The direct manipulation of iconic objects through mouse *drag and drop* techniques
- Advanced interobject communications
- Parallel dialogs over concurrent information channels

WHAT DOES A CLIENT NEED FROM AN OS?

Each of the three types of clients described here place a different set of requirements on the operating system. These requirements are listed in Table 2-1. As you can see, all client applications need some mechanism to communicate service requests and files to a server. All three client categories will function best in a robust, multitasking environment. It is particularly important for the client environment to be robust because it is impossible for system providers to test the client software on all possible hardware/software combinations (you can't dictate what people run on their PCs). It is important to use an operating system that can protect programs from clashing and crashing. No client program should cause the system to hang (requiring a reboot).

GUI and OOUI clients work best with a thread-like mechanism for handling the background requests. By using separate threads for the user interface and background processing, the program can respond to user input while a separate thread handles the interaction with the server. This is how GUIs avoid the notorious "hourglass" icon, a sure sign that the computing environment is not keeping up with the human. Priority-based preemptive multitasking is also required to respond to multimedia devices and to create client applications where multiple dialogs are displayed in parallel.

---

[3] The workplace metaphor is described in the SAA **CUA Guide To User Interface Design**, IBM publication SC34-4289 (October, 1991). Also see the OS/2 2.0 Multimedia Specifications.

Table 2-1. What Does a Client Need From an Operating System?

Requirement from an OS	Non-GUI Client		Simple GUI Client	OOUI Client
	Without Multitasking	With Multitasking		
Request/reply mechanism (preferably with local/remote transparency)	Yes	Yes	Yes	Yes
File transfer mechanism to move pictures, text, database snapshots	Yes	Yes	Yes	Yes
Preemptive multitasking	No	Yes	Desirable	Yes
Task Priorities	No	Yes	Desirable	Yes
Interprocess communications	No	Yes	Desirable	Yes
Threads for background communications with server	No	Yes	Yes (unless you like the hourglass icon)	Yes
OS robustness including intertask protection and reentrant OS calls	No	Yes	Desirable	Yes
Window 3.X GUI (CUA '89 vintage) with menus, scroll bars, and so on.	No	No	Yes	Yes
Advanced GUI with parallel interactive dialogs, drag and drop, multimedia support, Workplace Shell or Macintosh vintage.	No	No	No	Yes

BETTING YOUR BUSINESS ON AN OS PLATFORM

Picking a client/server platform is not an easy task. New operating systems for the desktop seem to be sprouting like weeds, while older operating systems are fragmenting into mutant "sibling" variants. This is not necessarily bad news for the client/server architecture model, which thrives on diversity. However, it can be bad news if you're trying to develop a software product and you end up picking the wrong client/server platform.

As authors of a client/server book with over three hundred pages of working code, we're faced with a very similar business decision. We must create that code on top of a popular system platform for our book to sell. Like you, we need to ensure our client/server product sells in large numbers. Like you, we also need to make sure our product is leading-edge and incorporates the most advanced client/server features that will make our product competitive.

As you can see from this the title of this book, we decided that OS/2 was our client/server platform of choice. This section gives you a marketing synopsis of why we picked OS/2. But, you will have to read the rest of the book for the in-depth details.

Which Mass Market Will You Choose?

To choose an operating system platform, you must first decide which computer mass computer market (or culture) you're going to play in. A computer mass market provides distribution channels, a support infrastructure, user groups, mass publications, trade shows, complementary products, and large installed bases of users that are potential customers for your product. Here are the leading contenders:

- **The PC world**, which includes all types of Intel 80X86-based machines that run DOS (and its variants), Windows 3.X, OS/2, and NetWare. PCs are ubiquitous in the business world.
- **The Macintosh world**, which is strongly entrenched in certain sectors of the business world (among writers, illustrators, and marketing departments).
- **The Unix world**, in all its variants and hardware platforms; it is the world of engineering workstations and power users.
- **The supermini world**, which is dominated by DEC hardware and VMS based solutions.
- **The mainframe world**, which is dominated by IBM's mainframes and its SAA standards. Parts of SAA have also been adopted as de facto standards by many non-IBM system vendors (such as Tandem Computers). OS/2 and OS/400 are non-mainframe members of the SAA family.

Like the cartoon character, we decided to write our applications for the *PC world*, which provides by far the largest market, with an installed base of sixty million machines and growing at twenty million a year.[4] This is a world of highly commoditized software that boasts thousands of high-quality, low-cost, shrink-wrapped applications that users can buy off a retailers shelf and easily install and run on millions of PCs.

With OS/2 2.0, we are in the doubly fortunate position of being able to create solutions for the PC mass market that build on top of a state-of-the-art platform. OS/2 and its extensions come close to providing the industry's most complete platform for handling both the client and server needs, as defined in this chapter. OS/2 has the advantage of playing well with SAA mainframes, as well as interoperating with the Unix world. And, as a result of the Apple/IBM agreements, OS/2 will soon become a server platform of choice for Macintosh.

Our choice of a platform may not suit your needs if you're dealing with customers who have exclusive Macintosh or Unix shops, or if you're writing a client/server application that works with an existing piece of software that does not run on PCs (a rare occurrence given the huge number of DOS, Windows 3.X, and OS/2 applications that are on the market).

What OS/2 2.0 Brings to Client/Server

A client/server platform on PCs must meet most of the requirements we listed earlier in this chapter. The PC platform must provide a robust operating system that supports multitasking, a multiuser database engine, and LAN communications. The server should be able to handle concurrent requests from clients with minimal performance degradations. The client must be robust, capable of running concurrent tasks, and provide a highly graphical user interface. The bottom line is that client/server solutions on PCs must provide the same level of service as multiuser superminis while maintaining the autonomy of the client PCs.

"The dominant MS-DOS environment at the desktop is technologically impoverished. Building a client/server architecture on MS-DOS is like building a house on sand. Microsoft Windows version 3 does not solve the problem because it relies upon the MS-DOS foundation."[5] This is where OS/2 2.0 comes into the picture:

- OS/2 2.0 servers provide minicomputer power at PC prices. The 32-bit OS/2 running on a PC with an 80486 processor has the power of a minicomputer, both in terms of brute processor speed and system software sophistication through features like preemptive multitasking, multithreading, and built-in memory protection.

---

[4] Source: Lee Reiswig, Assistant General Manager of IBM's Entry Systems Division, as quoted in **Windows and OS/2 Magazine** (October, 1991).

[5] Source: **Client/Server Computing: Exploiting the Inevitable**, Gartner Group (February 12, 1992).

- OS/2 supports a rich multivendor set of database server platforms and communications stacks that make it possible to create "mission-critical" systems using personal computers.

- OS/2 is an "open" commercial platform, which means it provides a choice of vendor products and services at competitive prices. These translate into enormous savings in hardware and software system costs, especially when compared to an equivalent, proprietary supermini solution.

- OS/2 servers, unlike minicomputers, were designed from the ground up to communicate "seamlessly" with MS-DOS and OS/2 clients. The client and server use the same file types, commands, and internal data representations. Operating system calls can be transparently "redirected" to the server via a network operating system.

- OS/2 provides a very complete and robust client platform. It lets multiple applications run concurrently while providing the necessary protection so that they don't bump into each other.

- OS/2 provides an integrated environment for running DOS, Windows, and OS/2 applications. The Workplace Shell makes the desktop appear seamless to the end user; it even supports cut and paste between MS-DOS, MS-Windows, and OS/2 applications. The 32-bit Presentation Manager engine provides a state-of-the-art GUI services (see Figure 2-7).

- OS/2 2.0 supports more shrink-wrapped applications than any other operating system. It does that by running MS-DOS, MS-Windows, and 16-bit OS/2 applications unchanged. In addition, over 1500 new OS/2 2.0 applications are being targeted for 1992 (see Figure 2-7).

- OS/2 2.0 extends the Workplace Shell to the LAN. Users can manipulate network resources such as shared files and printers by simply clicking on a network object's icon and performing whatever action is required. The local and network environments are seamless. Currently, the Workplace Shell supports Novell's NetWare and the IBM LAN Server (see Figure 2-7). Banyan's Vines is expected to join the club soon.

- OS/2 2.0 eliminates the need for minicomputers to act as the middle tier between PC clients and hosts in three-tiered networks. OS/2 Extended Services makes it possible for PCs to seamlessly interoperate with SAA mainframes.

In short, OS/2 2.0 comes fully loaded with the hooks that make it possible to design client/server systems around personal computers. Any discussion of client/server architecture that goes beyond the "armchair design" phase will need working programs to demonstrate the design trade-offs involved. In the chapters that follow, we will explain the hooks OS/2 2.0 provides and how they can be used to effectively create working client/server solutions.

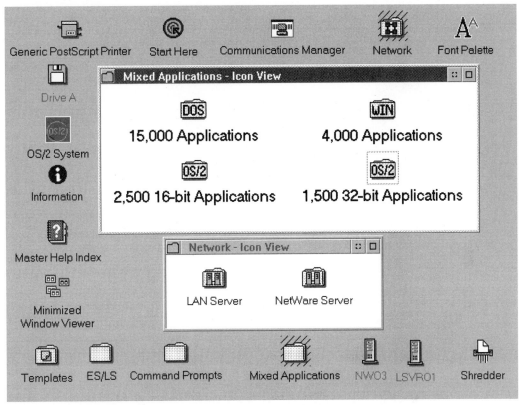

Figure 2-7. OS/2 2.0 Workplace Shell: The Universal Client.

Chapter 3

OS/2: The Client/Server Platform

This chapter introduces OS/2 2.0 and its system software "extensions." It gives you the bird's eye view of the software components used to create this book's OS/2-based client/server platform. We will use whatever system software it takes to put together a platform that meets the needs of both clients and servers as described in the last chapter. As part of the general introduction, we situate OS/2 as a client platform. We explain the close affinity between DOS, MS-Windows, and OS/2. We also discuss OS/2's intergalactic positioning through its affiliation with club SAA.

A SHORT HISTORY OF OS/2

In spite of its recent introduction, OS/2 has already gone through several major versions and one major reincarnation as a 32-bit operating system. OS/2 is transforming the standalone PC of the MS-DOS world into a powerful multitasking workstation endowed with an advanced graphic subsystem, a distributed database engine, and a rich set of communications capabilities. The various OS/2 components collectively provide the most advanced operating system platform in existence for the creation of client/server solutions while retaining the much cherished standalone autonomy of the PC.

We present a short history of OS/2 that may help clarify the different packaging schemes of the extended services. If you followed OS/2's history, you may have noticed that the current marketing trend is to unbundle the extended system software. With OS/2 2.0, the "Extended Edition" was unbundled from the base operating system and renamed "Extended Services." We will start the history with the 16-bit flavors of OS/2 and take you all the way to the current 32-bit version and "Extended Services." Some of the acronyms and products we'll introduce may not be familiar to you. Be patient; this is just a top level overview. The gory details and in-depth explanations will appear in later chapters.

OS/2 1.X: Standard and Extended Editions

Figure 3-1 shows the progression of the 16-bit OS/2 1.X **Standard** and **Extended Editions** and the features they introduced to the operating system. The OS/2 1.X

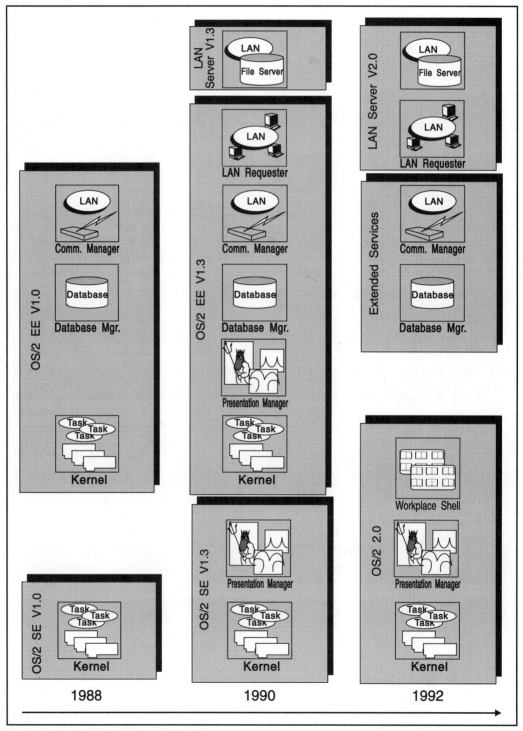

Figure 3-1.   The Evolution of OS/2.

Standard Edition, developed jointly by Microsoft and IBM, is still available from IBM and Microsoft as well as from many manufacturers of IBM PC compatibles. The OS/2 1.X Extended Edition includes all the features of the Standard Edition; it also provides a Database Manager and an integrated Communications Manager.

OS/2 **Standard Edition (SE)** version 1.0, unveiled by IBM and Microsoft in December 1987, provides the base operating system functions such as multitasking, file services, memory management, keyboard services, and character-mode output. This base system, consisting of over 250 system calls, is commonly called the OS/2 "kernel." In October 1988, IBM and Microsoft released OS/2 Standard Edition version 1.1, which enhanced OS/2 with the Presentation Manager, an advanced windowing and graphic subsystem with a repertoire of approximately 500 new system calls. The OS/2 Standard Edition version 1.2, introduced in September 1989, introduced a High Performance File System. The OS/2 Standard Edition version 1.3, also known as "OS/2 lite," was introduced in November 1990 as a slimmer and faster version of OS/2. OS/2 lite is still being sold today and can be used as a 16-bit low-cost, low-memory client platform for Intel 80286 class machines that cannot run OS/2 2.0.

OS/2 **Extended Edition (EE)** Version 1.0 introduced by IBM in July 1988, enhances the base OS/2 with two additional subsystems: the Communications Manager and the Database Manager. Extended Edition Version 1.1, shipped in November 1988, added support for Local Area Network (LAN) protocols including NetBIOS, 802.2, and the LAN Requester. OS/2 EE version 1.2, which shipped in March 1990, enhanced the Communications Manager with X.25 support for packet switching data networks (PSDN); it also added an SNA LAN gateway server. The Database Manager was also enhanced with remote SQL access, which enabled an OS/2 EE workstation to become a networked database server for OS/2 or MS-DOS clients. OS/2 EE version 1.3, which shipped in December 1990, fixed many of the bugs of the previous releases. Extended Edition is still available from IBM for OS/2 1.X users. However, we believe that most high-powered servers that use Extended Edition will migrate to the more powerful OS/2 2.0 32-bit platform where Extended Edition was transformed into Extended Services.[1]

OS/2 2.0: The 32-bit Operating System

OS/2 2.0 introduced by IBM in March 1992, is a robust operating system for Intel 80386 and 80486 PCs. It provides an all-in-one operating platform that can run multiple DOS, Windows, and 16 bit and 32 bit OS/2 applications concurrently from a single operating system (Figure 3-2). OS/2 2.0 comes with a Macintosh-like interface, the Workplace Shell, that serves as a launching pad for OS/2, Windows, and DOS applications. The Workplace Shell supports the "cut and paste" of graphics and text

---

[1] This edition of our book does not cover OS/2 EE. Copies of the first edition, which discusses OS/2 EE, may be obtained through the publisher.

information between Windows, Presentation Manager (PM), and DOS applications using the clipboard. OS/2 2.0 also supports Dynamic Data Exchange (DDE) between Windows and PM applications. Object Linking and Embedding (OLE) is currently only supported between Windows applications.

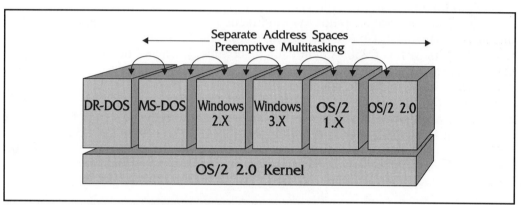

Figure 3-2. OS/2 2.0: The All-In-One Operating System.

The Workplace Shell is integrated with the LAN environment. It provides iconic views of LAN-based resources which can be manipulated through "drag and drop" techniques like any other desktop resource. Shared network directories appear as simple Workplace Shell folders. Files may be moved across the network by simply dragging an icon and dropping it into the network destination folder. The current version of the Workplace Shell supports the IBM LAN Server and NetWare simultaneously. This high level of visual integration across network operating systems (NetWare and LAN Server) and operating systems (DOS, Windows, and OS/2) makes OS/2 an ideal platform for running client applications. It makes it possible to link information from multiple application sources across networks and operating systems.

OS/2 2.0 has evolved into a very robust server platform. It is very hard for any program to bring the system down. If any of the DOS, Windows, or OS/2 applications "crashes," only that single application quits, leaving the operating system stable and other applications running. When software failures occur, they are isolated, traced, and reported, thereby minimizing the need to duplicate error scenarios.

The OS/2 2.0 file system performs much faster than its OS/2 1.3 or DOS counterparts while still maintaining full compatibility. The file system uses smarter caching and better techniques for laying out files so that fragmentation is kept to a minimum. The file system now has enough smarts to exploit the enhanced performance features of SCSI disk drives.

From a programmer's perspective, OS/2 2.0 has finally abandoned the segmented memory model in favor of a more efficient 32-bit flat model that now makes it possible to manipulate huge objects in memory. This model should be good news to designers of imaging and multimedia applications. The 32-bit API significantly increases the system performance over OS/2 1.3. OS/2 2.0 supports a total of 4096 threads and processes, as opposed to OS/2 1.3's support for 511 of each. OS/2 2.0 uses a much simpler semaphore model and has raised the semaphore ceiling to 64,000 per process.

OS/2 2.0 runs "right out of the box" on most PC vendors' hardware platforms (386SX and higher). The new installation facility is relatively fast and graphic. You can choose to install only the functions you need and save on disk space. The installation facility will automatically register with the Workplace Shell any DOS, Windows, or OS/2 applications it finds on the disk. A very useful feature from a client/server perspective is the ability to install OS/2 2.0 from any logical drive including a LAN drive. This feature makes it possible to install from a central remote location. Installation options can be preselected through a "response file," which automatically answers any questions, making it easier to automate the entire process. This last feature will make LAN administrators very happy.

OS/2 2.0's Extended Services

Extended Services with Database Server for OS/2 was introduced by IBM in April 1992 as the repackaged successor of OS/2 Extended Edition. The new package offers the same Database Manager and Communications Manager functions as OS/2 Extended Edition. But, it does not include the base operating system (OS/2 1.3 or OS/2 2.0) and the LAN Requester, which is now provided with the **IBM OS/2 LAN Server Version 2.0**. Repackaging has made it easier to create low-cost database clients because the database requester is now sold as a separate low-cost program called the **Database Client Application Enabler**. This program enables MS-DOS, MS-Windows, and OS/2 clients to access any Extended Services database server on a LAN. This same client software provides read/write access to IBM's relational database servers on mainframes (DB2 and SQL/DS) and on AS/400s through another OS/2 server product called **Distributed Database Connection Services/2 Version 1.0**, or **DDCS/2** for short. The good news is that the repackaged programs can now work on most PC vendors' hardware.

The **Communications Manager** was greatly improved. All its protocol stacks now run on top of the industry's standard NDIS interface, which allows non-IBM vendors to extend the product with new protocol stacks and network adapters. The transport layer was totally rewritten to improve performance. Both the IEEE 802.2 and NetBIOS protocol stacks are new and provide greatly improved performance. The APPC stack now supports the Advanced Peer-to-Peer Network (APPN) function, which provides simplified configuration, improved performance, dynamic routing, and easier network maintenance. The stack can be accessed using IBM's strategic Common Programming Interface-Communications (CPI-C).

The **Database Manager** offers new enhanced SQL capabilities and roll-forward recovery, which helps a database recover from a systems failure. A new set of graphical tools will help you manage and configure the database and its directories. A SQL command line interface was added to provide users familiar with SQL the ability to enter SQL statements to access the Database Manager and mainframe-based databases directly from the OS/2 command line. For improved performance, Remote Data Services now support NetBIOS as well as the APPC/APPN protocol. The term "Extended Services" will be used for the remainder of this book to refer to Extended Services with Database Server for OS/2.

Extended Services runs on either OS/2 1.3 or OS/2 2.0. In its current release, it is still a 16-bit application. This is the bad news. The good news is that your 32-bit OS/2 applications created using the IBM C Set/2 Version 1.0 compiler can work with all the Extended Services API sets.

EXTENDING THE EXTENDED SERVICES

The combination of OS/2 and **Extended Services with Database Server for OS/2** fulfills many client/server platform requirements. Together, they provide a robust multitasking operating system, a database server, and two very general-purpose communications protocol stacks: NetBIOS, the ubiquitous protocol of PC LANs; and APPC/APPN, the protocol of choice in the world of SAA and mainframes (see Figure 3-3). So what else do we need to get a complete client/server platform?

A File Server and Network Operating System

We will definitely need a file server. In this book, we will use the **IBM OS/2 LAN Server 2.0** product, which is IBM's beefed up version of the Microsoft LAN Manager 2.0. This product extends OS/2's file, printer, and Named Pipes services over networks. It also provides a rich set of application services such as the remote IPL of DOS, MS-Windows, and OS/2 clients and network management functions. IBM sells two versions of this product: a low-cost *entry* server, and a fault-tolerant *advanced* server. The DOS or OS/2 client code is sold separately at a very minimal cost. The term "LAN Server" will be used to refer to the IBM OS/2 LAN Server Version 2.0.

Novell Connectivity

OS/2 clients and servers need to extend their reach into the world of Novell, which has the largest installed base of departmental networks. The product that will give us this connectivity is the **NetWare Requester for OS/2 2.0**. This very useful and low-cost product can be obtained from either Novell or IBM. The difference is that Novell ships it in a red box and IBM ships it in a blue box. You get to pick the color!

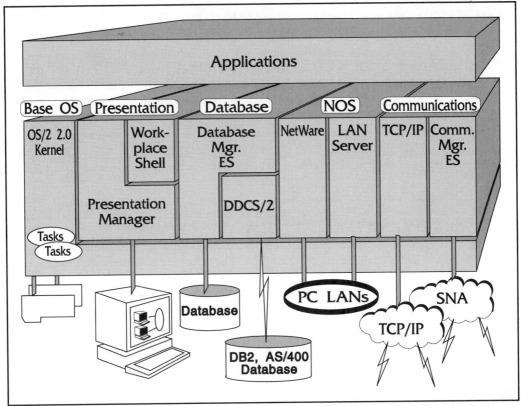

Figure 3-3.   The Components of an Advanced OS/2-based Client/Server Platform.

Unix Connectivity

We will also need to extend OS/2's reach into the world of Unix networks. The product that will allow us to play beautifully in this world, as either a client or server of Unix machines, is **TCP/IP Version 1.2 For OS/2**. This IBM product provides connectivity functions for both Local Area Networks and Wide Area Networks. It also includes a large suite of network application services such as remote procedure calls, file transfer, X Windows, network file server (NFS), remote job execution, authentication, and network management.

Mainframe Database Access

The final product in our repertoire is one already introduced: the **Distributed Database Connection Services/2 Version 1.0**, or **DDCS/2**. This gateway product allows an OS/2, MS-DOS, or MS-Windows database client to work with a database server on either OS/2, AS/400, or a mainframe running DB2 or SQL/DS. This product will allow our database server to grow "as big and fat" as necessary. It partially fulfills our platform's requirement for server scalability.

HOW THE PIECES COME TOGETHER

You will need OS/2 2.0, Extended Services, and the LAN Server to run the bulk of the software developed in this book. You will need NetWare and TCP/IP to run the communications benchmarks. Figure 3-3 shows how the pieces of the OS/2 client/server jigsaw come together. We will go over each of the components in great detail in later chapters. Your applications can obtain the services of any of those subsystems, as well as those of the OS/2 kernel, through API calls. In the case of the Database Manager, the API is supplemented with a SQL precompiler that allows you to embed SQL statements directly into a C program.

ALTERNATIVES TO AN ALL IBM PLATFORM

It may be easier for you to start programming client/server solutions on OS/2 with a single vendor solution where all the pieces are guaranteed to work together. This is no small feat in a complex client/server system environment. For example, we need to make sure that the TCP/IP, NetWare, NetBIOS, and APPC stacks happily coexist on the same Token Ring or Ethernet adapter. By using a single vendor's products, we know who to call when something goes wrong.

The products from IBM provide a common focus for installation, programming APIs, configuration, documentation, administration, system management, LAN adapter coexistence, and education. This common focus makes it easier for us to explain general client/server principles without getting bogged down into vendor differentiations. Most importantly, we can compare protocols, run benchmarks, and describe programming principles without getting involved in marketing holy wars because all the pieces are provided by a single vendor.

However, once you understand the principles of client/server design and the various trade-offs involved, then you may want to look at other vendor offerings for missing components or for extensions that suit your particular needs. The all-IBM platform we put together uses *de facto* industry standards, which makes it an excellent base for comparison shopping. For example, once you have mastered SQL using the IBM's Database Manager and the examples in this book, you may decide to switch database engines to Microsoft's SQL Server, Oracle, or Gupta's SQLBase. For database front-end tools, you may prefer to use Borland, Oracle, or Gupta tools. You may want to develop your own graphic interfaces using Enfin/3 or Choreographer. Microsoft's LAN Manager is almost a plug compatible replacement for IBM's LAN Server. FTP Software Inc's PC/TCP Plus can be used as a substitute for IBM's TCP/IP for OS/2.

With OS/2 2.0, you're dealing with a commodity 32-bit operating system with an open environment for client/server platform tools and extensions. In this open market, "mix and match" is the rule once you know what you're doing. So first get a good working understanding of the principles of client/server design; then shop for the vendor platform that best meets your preferences.

CREATING YOUR OWN OS/2 EXTENSIONS

OS/2 was designed to be "piecemeal extensible out in the field," which means a user can add new functions to the operating system or upgrade and replace existing system components without a new release from IBM. Each component of OS/2 was designed so that it does not restrict new features and can be supported by a new version of OS/2 even if the internals are dramatically changed. OS/2's modular operating system design is a radical departure from MS-DOS's monolithic COMMAND.COM. In MS-DOS, almost any change or improvement to the operating system requires a modification of COMMAND.COM, as shown in the top half of Figure 3-4. This is an impediment to MS-DOS's ability to grow or change as an operating system.

In contrast, extensions are a way of life for OS/2. The key to understanding OS/2's extensions is in the layered approach to OS/2's design, as shown in the bottom half of Figure 3-4. Between the application and the hardware, OS/2 provides three interacting yet modular layers: the Dynamic Link Library (DLL) layer, the resident kernel, and the device drivers.

The Dynamic Link Libraries provide a call-based interface to the operating system services in place of the MS-DOS number-based interrupts. When a program runs under OS/2, the resident portion of the operating system kernel determines which DLLs are required and loads them into memory at run time or at load time. Now your program can call any of the functions provided by the DLLs. Most of OS/2—including much of the file I/O, keyboard, mouse and screen systems, and all of the Presentation Manager—consists of a collection of DLLs.

Independent software and hardware vendors can provide their "extended" OS/2 versions by supplying their own DLLs and functions. For example, hardware vendors may want to extend the operating system to work with an optical jukebox. Software vendors may want to add operating system calls for an expert system inference engine. These new functions would then have to be documented and may need to become part of an industry "standard" before they become de facto extensions.

Vendors may choose to go with the DLL interface published by IBM, but they will probably want to extend it with some new features. For example, a database vendor may want to replace IBM's Database Manager with their own database engine while retaining the IBM supplied SQL interface. To make their product more attractive, those vendors could presumably add new functionality to the existing DLLs such as triggers or rules-based referential integrity.

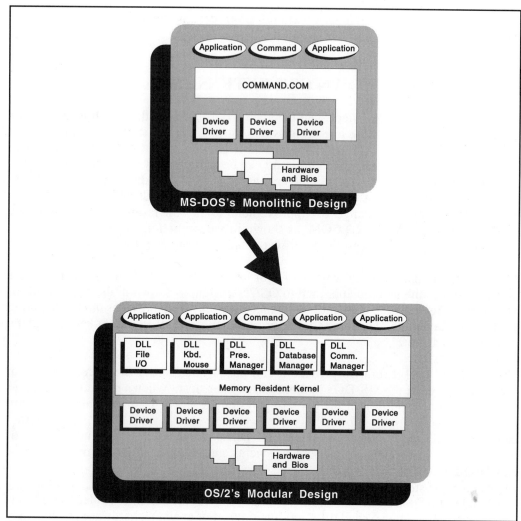

Figure 3-4.   From Monolithic To Modular.

OS/2 AND IBM'S SAA

OS/2 is an integral part of Systems Application Architecture (SAA), IBM's strategic plan to provide seamless connectivity and interfaces across the spectrum of its major product lines. To comply with SAA, the Extended Services Database Manager running under OS/2 must provide the same functionality as IBM's best-selling mainframe-based DB2 offering. The Database Manager does that quite successfully by incorporating 95% of DB2's function. The Query Manager is very similar to its mainframe counterpart. OS/2 2.0's Presentation Manager is the first IBM product to fully demonstrate the new workplace-based Common User Access (CUA 91). The Extended Services Communications Manager incorporates IBM's latest communications technology. It was designed to meet IBM's large customers' expectations of a *total network solution* that includes connectivity between products, peer-to-peer protocols between PCs and mainframes, centralized network management, SNA compliance, Token Ring support, and distributed database.

In view of OS/2's special "show case" role in the context of SAA, it is not surprising that IBM has created a "fully loaded" OS/2, which it will replenish with new extensions for a long time to come. OS/2 will be used as the leading-edge platform for the majority of IBM's new software introductions throughout the 1990s. The incorporation of OS/2 into SAA provides software developers with a stable set of API services that allows their code to run on a multiplicity of operating systems and hardware platforms. In theory, you should be able to port the code developed in this book to any member of IBM's SAA family of computers by just recompiling (we're not quite there yet!). This means your application is upwardly scalable; and when you consider that IBM's product line ranges from an IBM PC to the ES/9000, you are talking about a rather large spread in performance.

C is an SAA language. Many of the C library calls, and most of the OS/2 Extended Services APIs, are part of what IBM calls the Common Programming Interface (CPI) standard of SAA. You can think of the CPI as the operating system interface to a generic SAA machine that has a full range of network, database, and graphic capabilities. As new forms of computing emerge, IBM will define corresponding application-enabling interfaces and add them to the list of CPI calls. These calls will also be supported by all the SAA-compliant compilers and be made to work across SAA platforms.

WINDOWS AND OS/2: A FAMILY AFFAIR

MS-DOS, PC-DOS, DR-DOS, Windows 3.X, and OS/2 are all part of the same family of operating systems. If you have any doubts, take a look at the OS/2 2.0 workplace shell and get a first-hand look at how it integrates *all* flavors of DOS, MS-Windows, and OS/2 applications, including device drivers (see Figure 3-5). OS/2 allows PC users to leverage their investment in DOS and Windows 3.X software. The potent 32-bit OS/2 platform allows PC users to take full advantage of multimedia and client/server technologies.

Microsoft's May 1990 introduction of Windows 3.0 sparked a debate that pitted Windows against OS/2. The phenomenal acceptance of Windows and the continued popularity of MS-DOS was seen by some as a rebuff of OS/2. Far from being a rival to OS/2, we see Windows 3.X as providing the foundation for the mass acceptance of OS/2. Here's why:

- Windows 3.X running on DOS helped introduce a sizeable portion of the 60-million plus DOS community to the wonders of a graphical user interface and multitasking. These applications can now run unchanged on OS/2 2.0 with better multitasking,

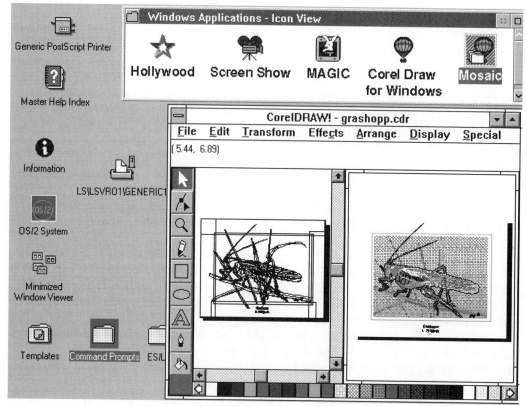

Figure 3-5. The Workplace Shell: Seamless Windows on OS/2.

better performance, better memory management and protection, better integration with DOS applications, and better file services.

- OS/2 runs Windows and DOS applications unchanged. These applications run directly on top of the OS/2 kernel; not in emulation mode. Unlike Windows and other DOS extenders, OS/2 is not just a GUI running on top of DOS real-mode; it is a protected-mode operating system that provides exceptional stability. OS/2 provides an almost bullet-proof environment for running ordinary DOS and Windows PC applications.

- Windows 3.X applications can easily be migrated into OS/2 2.0's PM using the Micrografx Mirrors Toolkit. The porting can be done by programmers without much PM experience. Ported applications will typically run much faster under 32-bit PM. Micrografx also provides a second toolkit for porting Windows 3.0 drivers into PM.

- Millions of PCs were upgraded to run Windows 3.X. These PCs usually have enough memory, disk space, and processing power to run OS/2. This large installed base of well endowed PCs makes the transition to OS/2 easier.

- Presentation Manager versions of Windows programs can be made more reactive by using OS/2's powerful multithreaded capabilities. A PM application designer can schedule computational or I/O bound activities as separate threads to ensure crisp user interaction at all times. The multithread PM versions of Windows applications may entice power users to migrate to OS/2.

- OS/2 provides preemptive multitasking, while Windows 3.X provides cooperative multitasking (a form of task switching). Peter Lewis of the New York Times explains the difference: "OS/2 can walk and chew gum at the same time. Windows takes a step, chews, takes another step, chews some more."[2] Preemptive multitasking (some call it "true" multitasking) is needed for multimedia and networked applications.
- Windows 3.X served as a training ground for many developers of graphical user interface (GUI) programs. These GUI implementation skills can then be applied to PM.
- Windows 3.X made GUI "addicts" out of masses of PC users. Once hooked on GUIs, users will always want more and more graphical sizzle. The PM object-oriented Workplace Shell provides the next level of sizzle. It transforms the GUI into the OOUI (pronounced "oooey") for Object Oriented User Interface.
- Windows 3.X is introducing multimedia to thousands of PC users. OS/2 2.0—with its advanced multithreading, interprocess communications, and support for very large memory objects—provides a superior platform for multimedia. Both OS/2 2.0 and Windows 3.X support the same multimedia API extensions that make it easy to convert a Windows 3.X multimedia application to PM.

In short, we see Windows as a low-end version of the OS/2 operating system. It's still "all in the family." OS/2 2.0 embraces DOS and Windows and provides a smooth upgrade path. You only need to install and purchase OS/2 2.0 to get support for OS/2, Windows, and DOS applications. We see OS/2's competition as coming from Unix and the Macintosh, not from DOS or Windows. The strength of Windows will help make OS/2 the top contender for the replacement of DOS on personal computers.

MS-DOS: THE OS THAT WON'T GO AWAY

It will take a long time before OS/2 completely supplants MS-DOS in the business environment for the following reasons:

- MS-DOS machines, when not running Windows 3.X, are significantly less expensive than OS/2 machines. They require a lot less memory, a lot less disk, and may run on low-cost 8086-type machines.
- MS-DOS is an acceptable operating system for many applications that do not require multitasking or large amounts of memory.
- There is a large inventory of 8086 type machines that cannot run OS/2 or Windows 3.X.

---

[2] Peter Lewis, "How the New OS/2 and Windows Stack Up," **New York Times** (April 26, 1992).

- There is a huge investment in MS-DOS application software. OS/2 2.0, however, allows users to salvage this software investment while providing a migration path for those who can afford the hardware upgrades.
- MS-DOS is familiar to large numbers of users, and there may be a reluctance to migrate away from a familiar base. Again, OS/2 2.0 helps alleviate that problem.

Paradoxically, these reservations do not carry over to OS/2 as a server for DOS machines in a networked environment. In such an environment, OS/2 machines can cost-effectively provide shared services to DOS client machines on a network. Networks give DOS clients access to the advantages of OS/2 servers without requiring an all-at-once switch from DOS. The same organizations that find it too costly to put OS/2 on every workstation will find that OS/2 servers can help them leverage their existing MS-DOS machine base. Such organizations will accept OS/2 in network servers long before putting OS/2 or Windows 3.0 on every machine.

OS/2 AS A SUPERSERVER FOR DOS MACHINES

As we explained in the section "What OS/2 2.0 Brings to Client/Server," on page 29, OS/2 is a natural server for MS-DOS machines. OS/2 servers blend well with the MS-DOS environment and at the same time provide minicomputer power at PC prices. The OS/2 server can replace both the overworked DOS server machines and the minicomputers in the PC environment.

The real change in personal computing will be brought about by the new breed of client/server applications on LANs. As you will discover later in this book, the action is in the networked *Transaction Servers* and the client/server model that ties it all together. Anyone putting together a client/server application on a PC LAN will almost have to run OS/2 on the server machine. So, it appears that one of OS/2's primary roles will be to provide a robust platform for the creation of the next generation of LAN-based personal software.

The client/server platform allows us to "mix and match" clients and servers almost seamlessly. Figure 3-6 shows a mixed operating system network environment where an application is split between "skinny" clients running the application front-end and an OS/2 Superserver, which runs the application's back-end. We anticipate that the bulk of clients may initially be DOS and Windows machines and that these will be replaced with OS/2 2.0 providing a robust integration platform. We will need to design software solutions for an environment that will remain "mixed" for a long time. The client/server platform we develop in this book fully takes into account this mixed client reality. We will be using standard peer-to-peer protocols such as NetBIOS, Named Pipes, TCP/IP, NetWare, and APPC/APPN, which allow servers to communicate with practically every form of client.

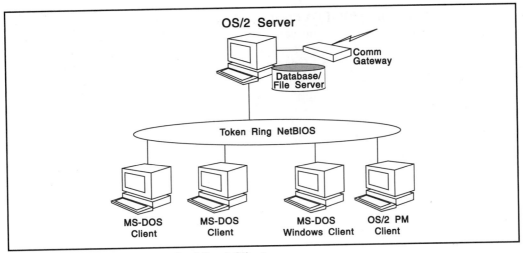

Figure 3-6. OS/2 As a Server for Mixed Clients.

OS/2 FUTURE DIRECTIONS

Yes, there will be newer versions of OS/2, followed shortly after by a "newer" version of OS/2 extensions. And, yes, these new versions will always have something "newer and better" to offer.[3] The following should give you a feel for OS/2's future directions:

- *Portable Kernel.* IBM intends to provide a portable kernel for OS/2 that will run on Intel and non-Intel RISC processors. New file system technologies, symmetric multiprocessing, and POSIX compliance are being explored for this kernel. The kernel is to be designed to B level security and will be certified at the C2 level.

- *Object OS/2.* IBM intends to extend OS/2's support for object-based technologies to include multimedia and future objects. The object extensions will be provided as class libraries that build on the *System Object Model* (SOM) that was used to create OS/2 2.0's workplace shell. SOM will evolve to comply with the Object Management Group (OMG) **Common Object Request Broker Architecture (CORBA)** and will provide multiple inheritance. SOM will also support distributed objects along the lines of OMG's architecture. IBM also intends to migrate pieces of Taligent's object-oriented technology into the OS/2 environment using SOM.

- *Multimedia.* IBM intends to continue to extend PM (and MMPM/2) with new multimedia types. The next multimedia type to be introduced will be digital video,

---

[3] The information in this section was adapted from **OS/2–The Bigger Picture,** IBM White Paper (March 26, 1992). We also incorporated more recent public statements of direction—that appeared in the press—made by Lee Reiswig, John Soyring, and James Cannavino.

using the exciting Intel/IBM DVI technology (among others). For the longer term, the IBM-Apple multimedia joint venture (Kaleida) should produce fruits for OS/2.

- *PM WorkGroup Manager and Open Message Interface (OMI).* IBM will support the Lotus OMI APIs in a future release of OS/2 Extended Services. OMI makes it easy to develop mail-enabled applications, especially in the areas of office automation and workflow. OMI provides C API calls for sending documents, notification of new mail, reading mail from an inbox, browsing mail from a message store, and interfacing to an address book. OMI will provide gateways to other mail providers. The **Workgroup Manager**, a proposed OS/2 extension, will provide the Workplace Shell user objects for mail (using Lotus Notes, cc:Mail, and OMI technology). Extended Services will provide the gateways to the various mail transports.

- *Database.* IBM will provide a 32-bit version of the Database Manager and support distributed database technology across heterogeneous SAA and AIX database engines based on DRDA.

- *LAN Solutions.* IBM will continue to enhance LAN Server and integrate it with Novell's NetWare through partnerships and cross-licensing agreements. The two companies will focus on network interoperability, common management, software distribution, and selective backup/archive.

- *Distributed Computing Environment (DCE).* IBM will port the OSF DCE on the OS/2 2.0 platform. This will make it possible for OS/2 clients and servers to interoperate with other machines in heterogeneous enterprise networks. OS/2 will include the following key DCE technologies: Remote Procedure Call (RPC), Distributed Naming Service, Network Security, Threads, and the OSF Distributed File System.

- *Pen-Based Computing (Pen/PM).* IBM will extend PM and OS/2 to support pen-based computing. The Workplace Shell will be extended to support a noteclip metaphor and handwritten input. Pen-based also requires sophisticated communications over mobile radio links that will put OS/2's multitasking capabilities to good use. Support for pen-based computing will extend OS/2's reach as a client platform.

- *PM OLE.* IBM will provide an advanced version of the *Object Linking and Embedding (OLE)* in PM. It is currently only supported in Windows on OS/2. PM and Windows application will be able to use the same OLE facilities.

- *Client/Server Packaging.* IBM will repackage OS/2 into a slimmed-down client version and a superserver version. The client OS/2 will include built-in Multimedia, Pen, and Mail technologies. The superserver OS/2 will support Symmetric Multiprocessing (SMP), RISC, and C2 level security. The enhancements to the client OS/2 will be incremental changes to the OS/2 2.0 base. The server enhancements will be more fundamental.

Chapter 4

OS/2 Servers:
Reaching for the Limits

In this chapter, we continue our exploration of OS/2 as a client/server platform by looking at the question of server upward scalability. Most LANs in operation today have less than 50 clients. A normal PC server can handle these situations without too much effort. The trend, however, is to put more PCs on the LAN. At some point, we will have to answer the question: When does an OS/2 server run out of steam?

SERVER SCALABILITY

OS/2's support for multiple LAN adapters, in theory, allows 1000 clients to be in session with a single server machine. If datagrams or non-persistent sessions are used, a single server machine could, again in theory, talk to hundreds of thousands of clients. What are the upper limits of PC servers running OS/2? The limits depend on the type of service required by these clients. If they require simple services such as, "give me the time," then a single server could probably handle thousands of clients. On the other hand, if they're each asking the server to perform a complicated weather report, then there will only be a small number of satisfied clients. We will look at some of the factors affecting the scalability of the PC running OS/2 as a server platform. Figure 4-1 shows the different levels of escalation in server power. It starts with a single PC server that reaches its limits with the top-of-the-line processor and I/O power. The next level of server power is provided by superservers populated with multiprocessors. If that is not enough power, the client/server model allows you to divide the work among different servers. These multiservers know no upper limits to power provided they know how to work together.

RISC VERSUS INTEL

At the heart of each PC is at least one Intel microprocessor that is a key factor in determining how fast that machine will run. Will Intel deliver enough power to fuel servers? Or, is it time to move on to *RISC* technology? Reduced Instruction Set

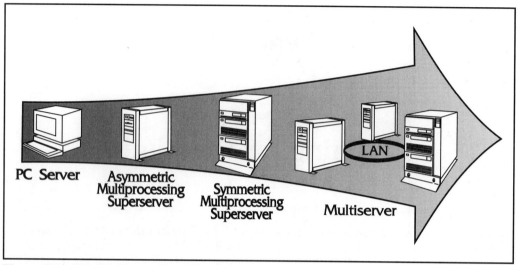

Figure 4-1. The PC Server Scalability Story.

Computers (RISC) have traditionally been available only in the Unix workstation market such as Sun's SPARC and IBM's RS/6000 series. Microsoft's NT operating system will support Intel as well as the RISC R4000 and Alpha. Taligent's "Pink and Blue" OS will also run on an Intel and RISC PowerPC platform. RISC provides a very steep price/performance improvement curve. RISC architectures place only the most used instructions in hardware. This results in smaller chips that allow the introduction of a new generation of processors with double the performance every sixteen months, on average. Vendors of RISC microprocessors believe that they have an insurmountable advantage over Intel's Complex Instruction Set Computer (CISC) 80X86 family.

Intel, however, claims that it is working on three generations of microprocessors at the same time. Its 80586 processor, due in late 1992, uses a *superscalar RISC* technology. The 80586 will perform 100 Dhrystone (million instructions per second), which is as good or better than any traditional RISC machine.[1] Intel, which is outshipping any competitive microprocessors at a ratio of one hundred to one, is known for its continuous breakthroughs in process technology. The numbers in Table 4-1 show that the firm is accelerating the rate of its performance upgrades and should be able to keep up with most of its RISC competitors.

Intel's promise to deliver RISC performance on the 80X86 gives PC servers the best of all worlds. They get the benefits of RISC performance and at the same time maintain backward compatibility with the large base of existing PC software. Most importantly, they avoid the pitfalls associated with multihardware OS platforms.

---

[1] "The 50 MHz 80586 will be about four times faster than a 40 MHz SPARC chip and about twice the speed of the first 50 MHz version of the MIPS R4000." **PC Week** (November 25, 1991).

Table 4-1. Intel Processor Speeds.

Intel Micro Name	Introduction Date	Clock Speed	Processor Speed	Comments
8086	1978	10 MHz	0.7 Mips	First IBM PCs
80286	1982	12 MHz	2.6 Mips	AT class machine
386SX	1988	20 MHz	4.2 Mips	Entry level 386
386DX	1987	20 MHz	7 Mips	Used in this book's benchmarks
486DX	1989	25 MHz	20 Mips	Single clock technology. Also used in this book's benchmarks.
	1990	33 MHz	27 Mips	
	1991	50 MHz	40 Mips	
486DX (double)	1992	50 MHz	40 Mips	Double clock technology
	1992	66 MHz	54 Mips	
586	1992	50 MHz	100 Mips	More than two instructions per clock cycle
	1993	66 MHz	135 Mips	
	1993	100 MHz	200 Mips	
786	2000	250 MHz	2000 Mips	Compatible with 80386

Source: *Intel Corp. (Intel uses the code name P5 for the 586. The performance projection for the year 2000 was made in 1990 by David House of Intel).*

PC servers have, indeed, come a long way. The power of an 80486 today is equivalent to that of a 3090E, a top-of-the-line mainframe circa 1987. The 80586 will help create even more formidable PC-based server platforms. But this is not the entire story. We can do better than wait for future speed improvements in processor technology by exploiting multiprocessing and parallel architectures which are the topics of the next section.

SUPERSERVERS

If you need more server power, you'll be looking at a new generation of PC-based *superservers*. These are fully-loaded Intel PCs equipped with multiprocessors, high-speed disk arrays for intensive I/O, and fault-tolerant features. Machines that run OS/2 with different levels of asymmetric multiprocessing support include the IBM Model 95, Compaq SystemPro, NetFrame NF400, Parallan 290, and Tricord PowerFrames. These machines are rapidly coming down in price. They provide a grow path for OS/2 servers without moving to multiservers.

Operating systems can enhance the server hardware by providing support for multi-processors in a single machine. With the proper division of labor, multiprocessors should improve job throughput and server application speeds. A multiprocessor server is upwardly scalable. Users can get more performance out of their servers by simply adding more processors instead of additional servers. Multiprocessing comes in two flavors: asymmetric and fully symmetric (Figure 4-2).

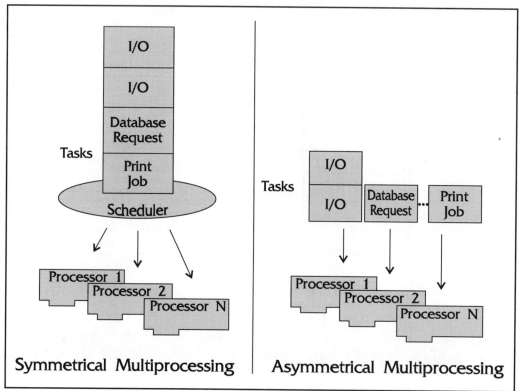

Figure 4-2. Symmetric and Asymmetric Multiprocessing.

Asymmetric Multiprocessing

Asymmetric multiprocessing imposes hierarchy and a division of labor among processors. Only one designated processor, the master, can run the operating system at any one time. The master controls (in a tightly-coupled arrangement) slave processors dedicated to specific functions such as disk I/O or network I/O. For example, the OS/2 LAN Server allows a master 80486 to run OS/2 and all the application tasks in parallel with a peripheral 80486 that executes the LAN protocol. The multiprocessing version of Microsoft's LAN Manager MP allows the slave processor to run LAN Manager and OS/2's HPFS file system.[2]

Symmetric Multiprocessing

Symmetric multiprocessing treats all processors as equals. Any processor can do the work of any other processor. Applications are broken down into threads which can run concurrently on any available processor. Any processor in the pool can run the operating system kernel and execute user-written threads. Symmetric multiprocessing improves the performance of the application itself as well as the total throughput of the server system. Ideally, the operating system supports symmetric multiprocessing by supplying three basic functions: a reentrant OS kernel, a global scheduler that assigns threads to available processors, and shared I/O structures. Symmetric multiprocessing requires multiprocessor hardware with some form of shared memory and local instruction caches. Most importantly, symmetric multiprocessing requires new applications that can exploit multithreaded parallelism. There are very few of these applications on the market, with the exception of some SQL database managers.

OS/2 Multiprocessing

IBM has stated that future versions of OS/2 will support symmetric multiprocessing.[3] Microsoft has made similar statements about NT. The Unix world is awaiting AT&T's UNIX System V Release 4 with multiprocessing extensions (SVR4MP), which will provide threads for parallel processing. OSF, the other major Unix standard provider, is working on a Mach-based multiprocessor Unix microkernel. Many proprietary or hardware-specific Unix multiprocessor offerings are currently available such as: Sun's Sparcserver 600MP series, Banyan's VINES SMP, SCO's Unix MPX, Sequent Computers, and Pyramid Technology.

---

[2] A coprocessor is an extreme form of codependency where one processor completely controls a slave processor through interlocked special purpose instructions. The coprocessor has unique special-purpose hardware that is not identical to the main processor. An example is a graphic coprocessor.

[3] A good discussion of the issues involved in creating a multiprocessor version of OS/2 is provided by Deitel and Kogan, **The Design of OS/2**, Addison Wesley (1992).

MULTISERVERS: UNLIMITED SERVER POWER

Multiservers are used in environments that require more processing power than that provided by a single OS/2 server. The client/server model is upwardly scalable. When more processing power is needed, more servers can be added (thus creating a pool of servers). Or, the existing server machine can be traded up to the latest generation of PC superserver machine. Multiservers remove any upward limits to the growth of server power. This power can be provided by ordinary PC servers working in all kinds of ensembles. Operating system extensions like the *Distributed Computing Environment (DCE)* will provide OS/2 some of the plumbing needed to participate in these ensembles. We will return to DCE and how to get the most out of multiservers in Chapter 11, "Architectures for Client/Server Computing."

Chapter 5

Server Platforms: OS/2's Competition

Ironically, it is on the server front that OS/2 2.0 faces some stiff competition. This chapter reviews OS/2 2.0's competition from current server platforms such as Unix and NetWare, and from future platforms such as NT and Taligent. We will discuss OS/2's server competitors in broad terms. The comparisons will help you situate OS/2 in the context of other operating systems present and future. It will also give us a chance to get on the soapbox and present some opinions and biases. "Yes Virginia, there is an operating system war."

MAY THE BEST CLIENT WIN

OS/2 2.0 is the *ideal client platform for the PC world.* It is hard (if not impossible) for any operating system platform to beat OS/2 2.0's robust and seamless integration of all DOS, MS-Windows, and OS/2 environments in its Workplace Shell. OS/2 creates a client desktop environment where all the network services—including Printers, E-Mail, File Server Directories, and Decision Support Tools—appear as groups of *smart icons.* Network services are obtained by simply clicking on icons. Users can move business objects across networks by simply grabbing an icon and dropping it on the appropriate destination icon. The network, essentially, becomes an arcade game. Users are encouraged to directly interact with objects. How much friendlier can it be?

The large installed base of PCs creates a high-quality, shrink-wrapped, software commodity market for DOS, Windows and OS/2 application software. Bad products cannot survive for long in the mass market because they will face a costly maintenance nightmare; it takes a lot of resource to support thousands of irate customers. The software that survives on the open market is usually of very high quality, and it sells at rock-bottom commodity prices.

OS/2 2.0 can run more shrink-wrapped applications than any other operating system and provides a better environment for running existing PM and DOS applications. Its advanced 32-bit features and page-based virtual memory are ideal for multimedia applications. OS/2 2.0 packs a formidable amount of power, yet it is easy to use and install. It provides that "friendly feel" associated with PCs. All this helps make OS/2 2.0 an irresistible client platform.

The Macintosh is also a powerful desktop client machine, but the size of its installed base and market is dwarfed by that of the PC. Macintosh has its own obvious "niche" of the client market.

Unix is too fragmented to be a strong contender as a desktop client. You can't call an 800 number or walk into the local Egghead store and buy standard Unix. DOS, Windows, and OS/2 2.0 are much more available, applications-rich, and entrenched on the desktop. OS/2 2.0 is about 20% the cost of a comparable Unix platform. It also requires half the disk and memory. OS/2's threads provide more responsive user interfaces than the various Unix GUIs. Of course, OS/2 runs DOS and Windows natively, a tough act for Unix machines to follow.

Microsoft is positioning NT as an advanced server platform. It requires at least 8 MBytes of memory and a 486 class machine. This leaves out most of the laptops, notebooks, and 386-SX desktops. NT is certainly not the migration platform for your average MS-Windows user. OS/2 2.0, with its Workplace Shell and seamless Windows, is the more logical choice. OS/2 2.0 provides each 16-bit Window application its own address space, as opposed to NT, which runs all 16-bit Window applications in the same address space (like Windows 3.X does today). This protected environment makes OS/2 2.0 a more reliable platform because both the kernel and other applications are protected from misbehaved applications. NT will not support PM applications in its first release, which further limits NT's effectiveness as an integrating client platform.

OS/2's competition as a client platform comes from the extreme low-end of the PC spectrum: DOS machines that cannot afford the upward migration and the large base of 80286-class machines. DOS and Windows will continue to rule supreme on low-end machines (80286 and below). So, we will end this diatribe and propose that OS/2 2.0 is the client platform of choice for 80386-class machines (and above).

THE SERVER WARS

OS/2 2.0's two most serious competitors on the server front are Unix and NetWare 3.1. Future competition is anticipated from Microsoft's NT and, possibly, Taligent's "Pink and Blue" operating systems. All these systems are 32-bit OSs (or higher) that run on PCs and other hardware. There is also room for other server platforms to thrive in the "mix and match" world of client/server. For example, almost any mainframe or supermini worth its salt can act as a server to PCs.

Servers that are not members of the PC family of operating systems will have a hard time beating OS/2 on its home turf. OS/2 as a server platform makes it possible to create homogeneous LANs where clients and servers run the same operating system family (OS/2, DOS, and Windows). Homogenous LANs are simple to administer, and you can easily move programs (and function) between clients and servers. In addition, the installation procedures, the file systems, and the interfaces to the operating system are the same on both the clients and the server. This familiar setting makes it easy for departments and small organizations to introduce client/server solutions.[1]

Unix and mainframe servers for PCs result in heterogeneous client/server solutions, which is not good for the small shops. NetWare does not own the client but it more than compensates for that by owning the network operating system on more than fifty percent of PC LAN installations. NT is part of the PC family and will fiercely compete with OS/2 as a server platform. Taligent's impact is still unclear.

NOVELL's NETWARE 3.1

Version 3.11 of NetWare released in mid-1991 offers an attractive 32-bit server platform for Intel 386 and 486 machines. In addition to Novell's very popular file server, communications protocols, and LAN administration services, NetWare sets aside special name spaces on the server that allow programmers to extend the system services. The server modules you create get loaded by NetWare to manage these name spaces. These modules, called *NetWare Loadable Modules* or NLMs, become part of the NetWare operating system kernel. Novell provides tools and a programming environment for the development of NLMs.

In 1991, six popular database servers were ported to the NetWare 386 environment. Oracle reported that the 32-bit NetWare product was significantly faster than its 16-bit

---

[1] The majority of client/server installations are in single locations consisting of less than twenty clients. These are predominantly PC LAN installations.

OS/2 version. Database benchmarks tend to cache in memory the bulk of the database (NetWare 3.11 supports 4 GBytes of RAM address space to 16-bit OS/2's 16 MBytes). Of course, OS/2 2.0 does not have the 16-bit limitation and supports very large memory objects (up to 512 MBytes in size). Here is a list of other features that make OS/2 2.0 a better general-purpose server platform than NetWare:

- *Memory protection.* NLM applications are not memory protected. They operate in Ring 0, which is reserved for the operating system. A bug in an application can bring the whole system down.

- *Virtual Memory.* NetWare does not support paging code in and out of memory, which limits the number of NetWare applications that can run on a server.

- *Preemptive multitasking.* NetWare will not interrupt a running application to allow one with higher priority to run. A misbehaved application that runs for a long time (such as a batch job) can cause problems for everybody else.

- *Threads.* NLMs do not support threads, which is a key requirement for supporting remote procedure calls on servers.

- *Programming tools.* With NLMs, you are dependent on a Novell-specific programming environment. OS/2 supports a very rich general-purpose programming environment. Compilers are available from all major vendors.

- *Versatility.* NLMs will run only on NetWare networks. OS/2 server applications will run on anyone's network, including Novell.

In summary, NLMs grew as ad hoc tools to allow non-Novell vendors to extend the NetWare platform. They do not provide the robustness you expect from a general-purpose operating system such as OS/2 or Unix. According to Richard Finkelstein, NetWare's non-preemptive status puts too much of the burden on the application developer because it requires applications to be bug free, "a virtual impossibility with the complexity of software we are talking about."[2]

But there is some good news on the horizon: *NetWare 3.2 will run on OS/2 2.0.*[3] NetWare 3.2 will provide a true marriage of NetWare and OS/2, very much like the IBM LAN Server does today. You should be able to run your favorite NetWare software and any OS/2 2.0 created software on the same machine.

---

[2] Richard Finkelstein is president of Performance Computing Inc, a Chicago-based database consulting firm.

[3] IBM/Novell Announcement (February 1991). NetWare 3.2 to expected to ship by 4Q 1992.

UNIX

Can a Unix server platform beat OS/2 2.0 on its own turf? What can Unix offer PC clients running DOS, Windows and OS/2 beyond what OS/2 2.0 can? Unix proponents claim three advantages for their platform: it is open, it provides a function-rich operating system, and it is scalable from the desktop to the supercomputer.[4] We will briefly look at each of these issues form the viewpoint of how Unix compares to OS/2 2.0 as a server platform.

How Open Is Unix?

Open can mean different things to different people. The PC industry has its own cult of openness. In the PC world, open means a market with hundreds of PC vendors, shrink-wrapped commodity software selling at highly competitive prices, and a cutthroat competition for every conceivable type service. Open means designing a new operating system with the help of 20,000 beta testers, a Blue Ninja, and daily headlines in the computer press and occasionally in the mass tabloids. If OS/2 2.0 is not the better system that the market expects, there is NT on the horizon. If NT cannot do it, there is Pink and Blue. This is an open, fiercely competitive environment where innovation and the "market" rules.

For all its talk of "openness," the Unix world is different from the PC world where software comes in low-cost, shrink-wrapped floppy packages that can run on any PC clone that runs MS-DOS or OS/2 2.0. There is still no single Unix standard. There are

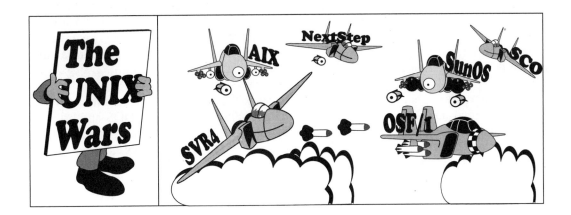

---

[4]The case for Unix is very well presented by Ed Dunphy in **The Unix Industry**, QED (1991).

hundreds of Unix variants that are converging on two Unix standards: OSF and AT&T's System V Release 4 (SVR4). At best, Unix variants may some day achieve the elusive goal of *conditional portability*. There is no inexpensive, easy to install, run-time Unix version that can be used as an application platform. As Gartner puts it, "Unix is not really open. Most Unix vendors currently ship what we have dubbed a *closed Unix system strategy with an Open rhetoric disguise. Caveat Emptor.*"[5]

Interoperability is another form of "openness." It means that various operating systems can continue doing what they each do best, as long as they can "plug and play" together like the components of a stereo system. OS/2 is very well equipped to interoperate with the Unix world (and almost everything else). Its advanced TCP/IP services include most of Berkeley Unix's network extensions (BSD), Sun's RPC and NFS, and the Apollo NCS distributed environment. In the future, OS/2 will support OSF's Distributed Computing Environment (DCE), the ultimate standard for interoperability. These acronyms will be fully explained in future chapters.

Is Unix More Advanced Than OS/2 2.0?

Unix is the melting pot of the computer industry. Its close connection with universities makes it a great incubator of new ideas. Most of these ideas first appear on the commercial market as Unix extensions and variants. The Unix mainstream, on the other hand, moves a lot more cautiously. Because of debt to history, multiple platform portability issues, and getting many vendors to agree on the least common denominator, it takes much longer to bring extensions into the commercial offerings of Unix standards. Unix's continuing usability problems stem from its debt to history (i.e., backward-compatibility issues). Revamping Unix completely is out of the question; too much Unix software relies on the old text-mode environment and utilities. Motif and OpenLook sit on top of X Windows, which run on top of the Unix kernel. This layering may help mask some of the ugliness, but it introduces more overhead and bulk. And, there is still no standard Unix GUI to write to.

OS/2 is in many ways is a modern variant of Unix; however, it is not encumbered by a debt to history. OS/2 combines the best of Unix, Windows 3.X, and DOS and brings it to the market as a shrink-wrapped operating system package. It incorporates, and in many cases surpasses, many of the most advanced features in SVR4 and OSF/1, including dynamic link libraries, demand-paged virtual memory, multitasking, interprocess communications, and an installable file system. Advanced OS/2 features, such as threads, are now slowly making their way into the Unix mainstream. With OS/2 2.0, Unix loses its 32-bit advantage. OS/2 programming APIs are better architected, more consistent, and less cumbersome (they carry less luggage) than their Unix counterparts.

---

[5] Gartner Group (June, 1991).

OS/2 is not burdened with thousands of cryptic commands from the era of text-based computing.

OS/2's communications and database offerings are very similar to their Unix counterparts. They are almost always easier to install, use, and manage. And, as a rule, they are much less expensive.

Arguments are frequently made that OS/2 is multitasking but not multiuser. Unix is both. Is this a problem for OS/2? The multiuser feature is a remnant of the old timeshare, terminal-based paradigm of Unix. It was only a few years ago that Unix systems with dumb terminals were positioned as the alternative to PC LANs. Because of these origins, Unix comes standard with a security system that lets systems administrators restrict access to files, directories, and other system resources. Unix's multiuser administrative features are cumbersome and complex for single user client machines. In multiuser client/server environments, Unix's administrative features compete with the server software's own multiuser facilities.

The client/server architecture is multiclient rather than multiuser. The client is usually on a remote machine. The server does not manage the client's workstation; it simply provides concurrent services to multiple clients using its multitasking facilities. Different OS/2 services, like the database manager and the file server, provide their own very sophisticated multiuser paradigm on top of the base operating system. Other services, like remote procedure calls, may not even require the notion of a user or a session (authentication and security may be provided at the call level).

In general, OS/2 provides operating system functions that are at least as good as those of Unix while remaining within the PC paradigm. OS/2 servers use the same file system, device drivers, and presentation services as their MS-DOS and Windows clients.

How Scalable Is Unix?

Because Unix is a hardware independent operating system, an application should, in theory, be able to run on any machine that supports Unix from a PC to a Cray supercomputer. This server scalability story is very attractive, but it is not realistic. In real-world situations what keeps that from happening are three factors: binary incompatibility, Unix variants, and applications that are optimized for a particular operating system platform.

We already discussed the Unix variants and the binary incompatibilities between the various machines. The third factor is probably the Achilles heel of scalability: operating systems are usually optimized for the hardware they manage. Portable Unix applications rarely outperform applications that are optimized for a native operating system. For example, it is very hard for a database application ported to IBM's S/370

Unix (AIX) to outperform a DB2 or CICS application running on MVS the S/370's native operating system.

Unix applications are at a price/performance disadvantage against applications that were designed to take advantage of an optimized solutions-oriented operating system with a supporting hardware platform. For example, Unix OLTP applications on RISC cannot provide the overall price/performance of OLTP applications running on Tandem Computers' Guardian, an operating system that is designed to exploit a loosely-coupled RISC multiprocessor network optimized for OLTP and high availability (no shared memory anywhere).

Likewise, the AS/400, a recent vintage non-Unix IBM midrange computer, generated $14 billion worth of sales in 1990, which is more than the combined Unix sales of the top five Unix vendors.[6] The OS/400 operating system was designed specifically to exploit the AS/400. It offers a turn-key solutions environment with excellent price/performance.

Unix's niche is in technical workstations where it provides unchallenged leadership and price/performance. The new generation of workstations from Apollo, Sun, and IBM were designed for Unix as their primary operating system. The networking requirements of these workstations were fed into Unix and became part of the operating system. Today, as these workstations start to exploit symmetrical multiprocessing, they feed their advanced new requirements into Unix. This synergy between the hardware and the operating system on workstations is similar to what happens on other operating system platforms such as OS/2 or DEC VMS.

The SAA Scalability Alternative

We're comparing OS/2 and Unix in terms of scalability, so we will take a short detour and explain the SAA alternative model of scalability. Remember that OS/2 is a *bona fide* member of the SAA clan. One of the benefits of this membership is upward (and downward) scalability. The SAA model represents an alternative to the Unix "single operating system" scalability story. SAA does not require a single operating system on all computer platforms. Instead, SAA provides scalability by publishing a set of APIs that can be ported to different operating systems. SAA is similar in spirit to POSIX, except that it provides a much wider range of specifications.[7] SAA applications

---

[6] In 1991 the Unix revenue of the top five vendors was: Sun $3.63 billion, HP $3.6 billion, IBM $2 billion, DEC $1.64 billion, and AT&T $915.5 billion. Source: **UNIXWORLD** (December, 1991).

[7] POSIX stands for **Portable Operating System Interface**; it is a set of ISO and IEEE standards for "open" operating systems. The POSIX 1003.1 standard is a watered down subset of AT&T's Unix SVR4 operating system interface. Because it is so watered down, POSIX compliance can easily be

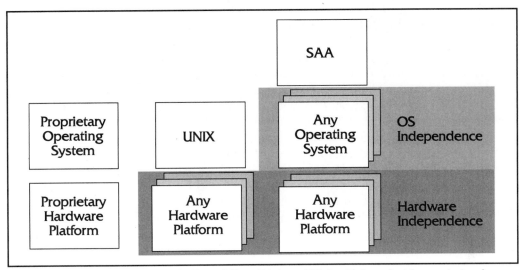

Figure 5-1.   Two Approaches To Portability: SAA and Unix. *(Adapted with permission from Randesi and Czubeck, SAA IBM's Systems Application Architecture, VNR, 1991).*

running on OS/2 PCs, could in theory, be scaled upwards by a source-level recompile to an AS/400 running OS/400, or a S/370 running MVS or VM. In the SAA model, each operating system is optimized for its respective platform (see Figure 5-1).

The main drawback of SAA is that it is controlled by a single vendor, IBM. This reliance presents the same drawbacks as AT&T's control of Unix in the pre-Unix International days. However, IBM has more disparate computer platforms than any other vendor, and it needs SAA to create an "open" environment among its own operating systems. For IBM and its customers SAA is an economic necessity. Cross-platform commonality relieves IBM of considerable development and marketing resources. Because of this vested interest in using common solutions across its product lines, IBM is probably spending more money and efforts developing an open heterogeneous operating system environment than all the standard bodies combined. IBM publishes the SAA APIs, many of these are built on industry standards or have become de facto standards, such as SQL and APPC. Vendors with superior operating systems and hardware platforms can "out-SAA" IBM and participate in the cost/performance scalability derby.

provided on non-Unix operating systems such as DEC VMS, OS/2, NT, and OS/400.

MICROSOFT WINDOWS NT

Microsoft Windows NT (New Technology) poses the greatest challenge to OS/2 2.0 as the premier server platform for PCs. This is not surprising since NT started out as OS/2 3.0. It was designed to be the portable OS/2 kernel that would run on multiple hardware platforms (Intel and RISC), and support symmetric multiprocessing. It was to be a "better OS/2 than OS/2 2.0" by supporting Windows, DOS, OS/2, and POSIX-compatible applications. Building such a full featured operating system is enormously complex. Today, both IBM and Microsoft are creating their own versions of OS/2 3.0. Byte Magazine's editor, Michael Nadeau, finds it worth cheering about that "two strong companies competing fiercely to develop a 32-bit OS ensures that OS/2 and NT will evolve rapidly in response to one another and that end-user concerns will be quickly addressed."[8] Nadeau feels that this contest will energize the PC market and create operating systems that support features such as multimedia and object-based technologies.

As we go to press, NT stands for "not there." From publicly available information it appears that NT, like OS/2, is a thread-based preemptive multitasking operating system. NT supports multiprocessing (not in the first release) and a portable kernel that will support Intel 80386/80486 and the MIPS and Alpha RISC platforms. The NT kernel will run 16-bit Windows, 32-bit Windows, POSIX, and OS/2 (without PM in first release) applications (see Figure 5-2). NT will provide C2 security certification (not in the first release). It will provide fault tolerance through a transaction-oriented recoverable file system and disk mirroring (not in the first release). NT will support memory-mapped files that allows disk-based files to be assigned a range of virtual memory addresses. NT will provide built-in LAN support, including Named Pipes, and Mailslots.[9]

NT is positioned to be an advanced server platform. It requires at least 8 MBytes of memory, 100 MBytes of disk space, and an Intel 486 class machine. When it comes to advanced server features, NT appears to be OS/2's most serious competitor if Microsoft delivers on all the promised features. Of course, OS/2 2.0 has a head start as a server platform. It is here now, which means it will have a much larger base of server code. NT will be able to run the subset of that code that is not PM-based. Of course, we agree with the Byte editorial that IBM will not stand still either. The NT microkernel was, after all, co-developed by IBM and Microsoft when both companies were working together on OS/2 3.0 in the fall of 1988. IBM also has rights to Microsoft's NT, and it can choose to implement any portions of it. IBM is also looking at the Carnegie Mellon Mach kernel that is used in the OSF microkernel (OSF/1 MK).

---

[8] **Byte**, editorial, December 1991.

[9] A good overview of NT's technical features is provided by Paul Yao, in **Microsoft Systems Journal** (Nov/Dec 1991).

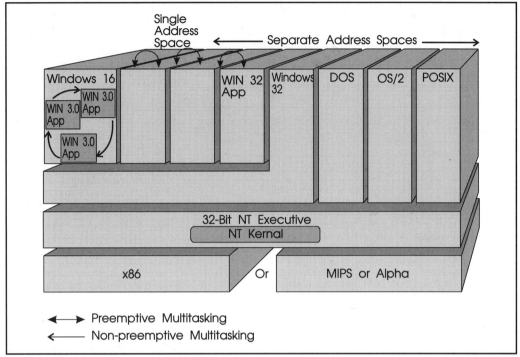

Figure 5-2. Windows NT Architecture.

TALIGENT'S PINK AND BLUE

Taligent, a joint venture of IBM and Apple, is developing an object-based operating system that some call "Pink and Blue." This new operating system is targeted for the mid 90's and will be introduced in stages. IBM will integrate some of the "Pink and Blue" technology into OS/2. Taligent will run OS/2, MacOS, and AIX applications in the new environment. These applications will run on Intel 80X86s, Motorola 680X0s, and IBM PowerPC RISC chips (see Figure 5-3).

It is still too early to assess Taligent's strengths as a client/server platform for PCs. OS/2 2.0, with its Workplace Shell, is already moving PCs in the direction of object-based GUIs. Competitive market pressures, from NT primarily, will cause new object-oriented extensions for multimedia, image, and voice to first appear on OS/2. Taligent and OS/2 will both benefit from each other in the next few years. OS/2 will benefit by incorporating early releases of the Taligent object technology in toolkit form. Taligent will benefit by trying out its technology on a widely used commercial platform. After that, whichever company has the best product will win.

For developers, Taligent must provide OS/2 compatibility at the API and class library level, in addition to being able to run OS/2 programs unchanged (binary compatibility). This level of compatibility will fully protect your current investment in software development on an OS/2 platform. If Taligent succeeds in providing this level of compatibility; we can then call it OS/2 X.0.

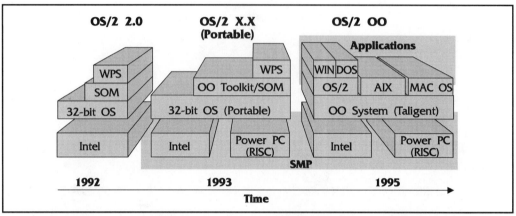

Figure 5-3. OS/2 2.0 to Taligent: An Artist's Rendition of IBM's Direction Statements.

THE OS/2 CHALLENGE

From a technical viewpoint it appears that OS/2 has the potential to win both the desktop client and server. OS/2 2.0's market potential is as large as the population of installed 80386, 80486, and 80586 systems, which will be over 23 million 32-bit Intel personal computers worldwide by year end 1992. Even if OS/2 2.0 is successful in penetrating only 10 percent of this installed base in 1992, it provides independent software developers with a substantial base of OS/2 users for which to write native OS/2 applications.[10]

Proper marketing will determine whether OS/2 can live up to its potential. OS/2 will face stiff marketplace competition from Windows on the client side. On the server side, the competition will be from Windows-NT and many of the smaller Unix desktop variants, including NeXTStep for Intel 80486 computers, SunSoft Solaris on Intel 32-bit processors and Sparc, DEC's OSF/1, SCO's Unix (as part of the ACE initiative), and IBM's own AIX. So far, the desktop has been almost a *Unix-free* zone. The lack of Unix compatibility with existing desktop applications may keep it that way forever. One of OS/2's major strengths is its ability to unify the desktop, and it is here now. In the unlikely event that OS/2 fails, a major showdown will result between desktop Unix and NT. The winners will then face Taligent's Pink and Blue. Yes, it appears we are "condemned" to live in fascinating, and fiercely competitive, times.

---

[10] Source: **OS/2 2.0...Well Worth The Wait**, Workgroup Technologies (February, 1992).

Chapter 6

OS/2 2.0: A Grand Tour

We will start our overview of the OS/2 client/server platform by reviewing the services provided by OS/2 2.0, the base operating system (see the light area in Figure 6-1). The shrink-wrapped OS/2 2.0 package consists of two major components: the OS/2 Kernel and the Presentation Manager. This chapter reads like a feature, function, and benefit list of what OS/2 2.0 offers programmers. Remember, we're now painting the big picture and building a common vocabulary. The gory details come later in the book.

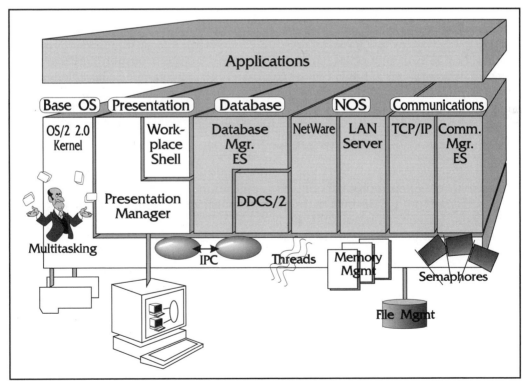

Figure 6-1. Base OS/2: The Kernel, PM, and the Workplace Shell.

THE OS/2 2.0 KERNEL SERVICES

OS/2 2.0 is the first major single-user, multitasking operating system developed specifically for personal computers. Unix, for example, runs on personal computers and provides multitasking. It does this, however, by creating a time-share multiuser environment that is not optimized for single-user situations. The OS/2 2.0 kernel provides multitasking, interprocess communications, memory management, device I/O, and support for running DOS and Windows applications. Large portions of the OS/2 2.0 kernel were written in C for portability. This section presents the major features and functions provided by the OS/2 2.0 kernel.

Multitasking

Multitasking, or the ability to run multiple programs concurrently, is OS/2's most powerful feature. OS/2 provides a very granular level of multitasking that is optimized for concurrency on a single-user machine. The architecture builds on a three-tiered tasking model: the thread, the process, and the session (or screen group). Threads run within processes which in turn run within screen groups. Figure 6-2 shows the relationships in the hierarchy. The *thread* is the basic unit of concurrency and CPU allocation in OS/2. The *process* provides a level of multitasking which roughly corresponds to a running program. A process consists of one or more threads, which means that in addition to having multiple programs execute at the same time, a single program may have multiple threads that are executing concurrently. OS/2 controls multitasking by using a preemptive priority-based scheduler. A thread can be assigned to one of four priority classes, and within each class the scheduler recognizes 32 priority levels. The *priority classes* are:

- *Time-critical* for threads that require immediate attention. Time-critical threads are used in communications and real-time applications.
- *Fixed-high* for threads that require good responsiveness without being critical.
- *Regular* for normally executing threads.
- *Idle-time* for very low priority threads.

OS/2 uses time-slicing to ensure that threads of equal priority are given equal chances to execute. OS/2 can preempt a thread when its time slice expires if a thread with a higher or equal priority is ready to execute. If not defined otherwise, the default minimum time-slice is 32 milliseconds. You can configure the timeslice from 32 to 65,536 milliseconds. The elaborate OS/2 scheduling capabilities make it possible to create real-time applications that have almost deterministic response times. The system guarantees that time-critical threads are dispatched within 6 milliseconds of becoming ready to run. The maximum interrupt disable time is 400 milliseconds.

In addition, OS/2 makes available an even higher level of multitasking: the *session* or *screen-group*. The session represents a logically separate unit of screen, keyboard, and mouse, and the group of processes associated with those resources. You can think of

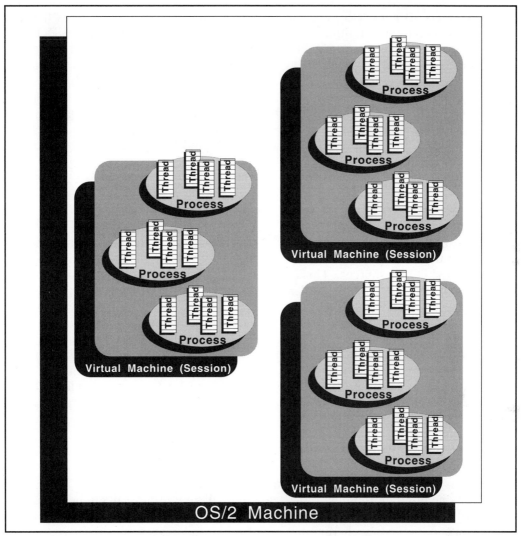

Figure 6-2. OS/2 2.0's Multitasking Model.

the session as providing a virtual personal computer. OS/2 also provides the capability to start a process in the background. A *background process* will not have its own screen and it will continue executing in the background even if you exit from your OS/2 screen group (background processes should be self-terminating). You can start a background process using the DETACH command.

This three-level hierarchy of multitasking control: sessions, processes, and threads addresses the user's need to control concurrent execution and the developer's need to design applications whose activities can be controlled at a very granular level.

OS/2 2.0 treats all applications in the system as protected mode processes that are provided full preemptive multitasking and memory protection. This includes DOS and MS-Windows applications. OS/2 2.0 supports a total of 4096 threads and processes. Threads are more easily created, controlled, synchronized, and terminated than under previous versions of OS/2.

We will look at OS/2's multitasking capabilities in great detail by developing a program that compares the overheads of processes and threads. This program will help us develop a framework for how best to exploit OS/2's powerful concurrency features in client/server applications.

Virtual Resources

The basis for multitasking is to manage the physical resources of the computer in such a way that multiple programs can run at the same time without bumping into each other as they use the PC's resources. This is where the OS/2 kernel comes in; it sits between the programs and the hardware and regulates the access to memory, disks, printers, screens, and modems. Applications interact with virtual memory and devices which OS/2 then maps to the real device. OS/2 maintains order when many programs go after the same resource. It also serializes access from the virtual device to the actual physical device automatically without user intervention. This ability of OS/2 to *redirect* output (without the application knowing it) is essential for networked environments. Resources can be mapped across a LAN to remote machines, thus extending OS/2's *virtual* reach.

Interprocess Communication

Interprocess communication is a corollary of multitasking. Now that PCs can have more than one program running at the same time, there will most likely be a need for those programs to exchange information and commands. OS/2 provides the facilities for separate programs, each running in their own address space, to communicate information through system supported interprocess communication protocols (*IPCs*). Some of the IPCs can operate across machine boundaries and are key to the development of LAN-based client/server applications. OS/2 provides a rich set of IPCs. These include Anonymous Pipes, Named Pipes, Queues, and Shared Memory.

An **Anonymous Pipe** is a fixed length circular buffer in memory that can be accessed like a file of serial characters through a write handle and a read handle (handles are pointers into the file). Anonymous pipes are used mostly by a parent process to communicate with its descendants by passing the pipe handles through inheritance.

Named Pipes provide two-way communications among unrelated processes either locally or remotely. The server side of an OS/2 process creates the pipe and waits for the clients to access it. Clients use the standard OS/2 file services to gain access to the

Named Pipe. Multiple clients can be serviced concurrently over the same pipe. The elegance of Named Pipes and their support for *remote* interprocess communication makes them the IPC of choice for client/server software development.

A **Queue** allows byte stream packets written by multiple processes to be read by a single process. The exchange does not have to be synchronized. The receiving process can order the access to the packets or messages in one of three modes: first-in/first-out (FIFO), last-in/first-out (LIFO), or priority. Items can be retrieved from the queue either sequentially or by random access. The OS/2 queues contain pointers to messages, as opposed to a copy of the data itself.

Shared Memory is another interprocess communication protocol. OS/2 provides facilities for creating named objects in shared memory. Any process that knows the memory object's name has automatic shared access to it. Processes must coordinate their access to shared memory objects through the use of semaphores.

Interprocess Synchronization

Interprocess synchronization is another corollary of multitasking. It consists of the mechanisms for keeping concurrent processes or threads from interfering with one another when accessing shared resources. The idea is to serialize the access to the shared resource by using a protocol that all parties agree to follow. OS/2, like most operating systems, provides an atomic service called the *semaphore*, which applications may use to synchronize their actions.

OS/2 2.0 provides significantly improved semaphore facilities. Gone are RAM semaphores of 16-bit OS/2, which don't lend themselves well to portability across hardware platforms and multiprocessing. Semaphores are now fully protected, portable, easier to use, and more abundant. All semaphores now reside in the system kernel and can only be manipulated through API calls. OS/2 2.0 provides two classes of semaphores: private and shared. *Private semaphores* are used to synchronize threads within a process. A process may have up to 64K private semaphores. *Shared semaphores* are available to all processes in the system. OS/2 2.0 supports up to 64K shared semaphores. This is abundance! We will learn how to use semaphores to synchronize processes and threads.

Dynamic Linking

Dynamic linking allows a program to gain access at run time to functions that are not part of its executable code. These functions are packaged in *Dynamic Link Libraries (DLLs)* that contain executable code but cannot be run as applications. Instead, your application can load the appropriate DLLs and execute the functions in the libraries by linking to them dynamically. Your applications are linked with library routines at load time (or at run time) instead of at compile time. Dynamic linking solves two problems:

1. It allows functions to be added to a program without having to relink the entire program, which makes it easier to add new extensions to a system. As described earlier, OS/2 uses Dynamic Linking to provide its system extensions.
2. It removes the need to store on disk and load in memory multiple copies of the same code, which is especially important in a multiprogram environment where each application may require the same library code. Without dynamic linking, each program would have to load its own copy of the system library in memory, even if some other executable program has already loaded a copy of the library in memory. Dynamic linking allows an application to load a DLL only when it needs to execute a function in the library. Once a DLL is loaded it can be shared with other applications. Only one copy of the DLL is in memory at any one time.

The performance of calls to DLL functions has been greatly improved with OS/2 2.0's flat memory model. All the calls are *near*, which means they do not require segment register reloading as was previously the case. You should be aware of the benefits of DLLs and how they are used to extend system code. You may want to consider the benefits of packaging your programs as DLLs for commercial distribution.

The File Systems

OS/2 has two file systems: the **File Allocation Table (FAT)** and the **High Performance File System (HPFS)**. The FAT system is the default file system and does not need to be installed. HPFS can be installed during system initialization. OS/2 manages its disk files and devices in the same way. For example, an application uses the same API calls to open and read from a disk file as it uses to open and read from a serial port.

The OS/2 file system is compatible with that of MS-DOS. Both file systems represent a hierarchy of files on physical disk. The disk can also be subdivided into logical disks or partitions; each has its own hierarchy. Using the CONFIG.SYS file, OS/2 allows you to specify the number of KBytes allocated to a cache in RAM. The system then uses a Least Recently Used (LRU) algorithm to manage the cache. The file system can accommodate 64,000 file handles, with a maximum of 32,000 handles per process.

OS/2 provides *locking and sharing* facilities to support concurrent file access in a multitasking environment. A process can open a file in exclusive mode (not allowing other processes access), or it can provide read access while denying write, or it can opt to share the file for read/write access with other processes. A process can lock any contiguous range of bytes within a shared file. These services allow multiple processes to share information at the byte level on a single file. This sharing also applies to devices that a process might open.

The **High Performance File System (HPFS)** is optimized for the management of large disk media in a fast and consistent manner. The HPFS under OS/2 2.0 supports disk partitions with capacities of up to 512 Gigabytes. The maximum file size supported is 2 Gigabytes. HPFS maintains compatibility with FAT at the API level. However, it is less performance sensitive as file sizes or directories get very large. The HPFS also supports new long file names (up to 254 characters), but can still work with the traditional eleven character file names (the infamous 8.3 format). Fully qualified path names can be up to 260 characters. The HPFS makes it possible for OS/2 to support very large databases on personal computers.

OS/2 2.0 provides a new HPFS device driver that is designed to optimally exploit the power of SCSI devices. The file system and the device driver now communicate through *command chains* that contain lists of prioritized commands. The device driver may choose to reorder the execution of commands to optimize disk access. After the completion of the I/O, the device driver calls the notification procedure specified in the command chain. A feature called *scatter/gather* is now supported, allowing data to be transferred to and from discontiguous memory buffers in a single operation. This allows multiple page-in and page-out requests to be supported in a single logical operation. The caching is also improved, allowing the HPFS driver to recognize devices that have outboard caches and incorporate them into the total caching scheme (for example, it may send them data prefetch requests).

The FAT system under OS/2 2.0 is also greatly improved. The maximum size of a FAT disk partition is 2 Gigabytes, which is also the maximum file size. The caching is now moved from the device driver to the FAT, where more intelligence resides. FAT is also optimized to exploit the capabilities of the new SCSI adapters and disks. The FAT driver, like its HPFS counterpart, supports command chaining and scatter/gather. FAT provides faster allocation of free space on the logical drive, using a bitmap to track free clusters. It also automatically bypasses bad sectors on reads.

Previous versions OS/2 required that you get the correct SCSI driver from the card (or device) vendor. The SCSI drivers in OS/2 2.0 are generic and designed to work with all SCSI drives. The generic driver also supports CD-ROM, Adaptec, and Future Domain SCSI devices.

OS/2 introduces an important feature in both of its file systems: the *Extended Attributes*. This feature allows each file to have up to 64 KBytes of file-related descriptive information, which can be used to create object-oriented file systems.

Memory Management

With OS/2 2.0, PCs finally have a world-class memory management facility that fully supports DOS, Windows, and OS/2 applications. All applications, regardless of their OS origin, run as OS/2 processes. OS/2 processes really get to enjoy the good life, when it comes to superabundant memory. Perhaps, this is to compensate for the many years of starvation under DOS's 640 KByte limitation. Here's a list of memory management features that each of OS/2's 4095 processes get to enjoy:

- OS/2 provides each process with its own *virtual address space*, which is up to 512 MBytes for application processes and 4 GBytes for privileged system processes.[1] OS/2 provides protection against memory violations by misbehaved programs, and will prevent concurrently executing programs from clobbering each other's memory. If a program attempts to access memory outside its address space, a general protection fault is generated by the hardware. OS/2 is notified of the fault and terminates the process that caused it.

- OS/2 uses the paging feature of the Intel 80386 (and above) machines to provide a *demand-paged virtual memory* environment. The 512 MByte per/process virtual memory system allows you to run programs that are much larger than the available physical memory on your machine. Memory is allocated in 4 KByte blocks called *pages*. OS/2 creates a virtual memory environment by giving each process its own set of page tables. A process can *overcommit* the memory of the system. If a page is not in memory, OS/2 will automatically swap to the disk some of the least-used pages to make room for the newly requested page.[2] The overflow memory goes to a swap file on disk. The sum of the space required by all your active applications must not exceed the available RAM plus the disk space available for the swap file (SWAPPER.DAT). The swap file is now *elastic*; it grows and shrinks as needed. In previous versions it only grew. The fixed size pages make OS/2 2.0's swapping algorithms much simpler and faster (less calculations and smaller I/O blocks) than OS/2 1.X's segmented memory scheme.

- OS/2 provides APIs that let you create *memory objects* whose size can vary up to 512 MBytes. Memory objects consist of one or more pages. When you allocate your memory objects you can tag them with attributes such as: read, read/write, execute, etc. These tagged objects are protected by the hardware at the page level. OS/2 also lets you share memory objects with other processes. *Shared objects* reside in a reserved address range that starts at the top of every process's address space and grows downward. Figure 6-3 shows the OS/2 2.0 process address space. Notice that the system sits on top of the process address space. Shared memory allocations grow down from the top and private memory grows up from the bottom.

- OS/2, in conjunction with the 80386 hardware, ensures that less privileged code stays within its address boundaries and uses a carefully restricted *call gate* to police access to more privileged code. Likewise, the 80386 controls access to input/output

---

[1] OS/2 2.0 supports a variety of DOS memory expanders without added hardware. In addition to Windows, it supports the Expanded Memory Specification (EMS), with up to 32 MBytes of memory per DOS process; the Lotus-Intel-Microsoft (LIM) and Expanded Memory Specifications (XMS), with up to 16 MBytes of memory; and the DOS Protected Mode Interface (DPMI), with up to 512 MBytes of memory.

[2] The 80386 architecture, which OS/2 2.0 fully exploits, provides a total of virtual address space of 64 Terabytes. In comparison, the 80286 is limited to 1 Gigabyte.

and interrupt instructions using a program's I/O privilege level (IOPL for short). The privilege level mechanisms prevent a program from accessing any part of OS/2 in an uncontrolled manner. The 80386 supports four privilege levels (or rings), which are arranged hierarchically from level 0 (maximum protection) to level 3 (minimum protection). The OS/2 core runs in level 0, level 1 is not used by OS/2, level 2 is used by programs that directly manipulate I/O devices (have IOPL privilege level), and level 3 is where your normal OS/2 programs run.

In summary, OS/2 2.0's flat memory model makes life easier for programmers writing new 32-bit applications. Gone are the calls that manipulate segment selectors. Large objects are easier to create and manipulate, and performance is better because all calls are near. The near and far keywords are not needed. The complications associated with the different memory models and their corresponding function libraries are gone. Programs that use the 32-bit model are also easier to port to non-Intel platforms. The OS/2 2.0 memory management also makes life easier for DOS and MS-Windows programs. It allows multiple DOS and Windows applications to run simultaneously; each has more virtual memory (512 MBytes) and more protection than was ever available through DOS memory extenders such as Window 3.X.

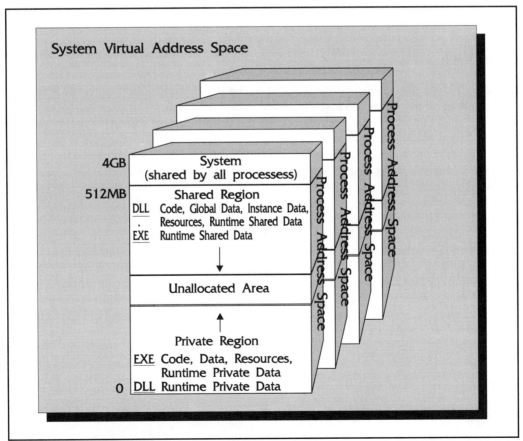

Figure 6-3. OS/2 2.0's Process Address Spaces.

Exception Handling

In a multitasking environment, a serious error occurring in one application must not be allowed to damage other applications that are running in the system. Unexpected errors, such as memory violations, are called *exceptions*. When OS/2 detects an exception, it will usually end the application unless the application has registered its own exception-handler function. This function allows an application to correct the error and continue. Four new API calls have been defined for creating exception handlers on a "per-thread" basis. Unlike previous versions of OS/2, these exception handlers can be written in a high-level language like C (no more assembler).

The OS/2 2.0 PRESENTATION MANAGER (PM)

The Presentation Manager (PM) provides a powerful Graphical User Interface (GUI) subsystem for OS/2 2.0. The new PM provides six Macintosh-like controls to help you create CUA'91 applications. Perhaps this is the cure for "Macintosh GUI envy" that some PC programmers have long been having.

PM's Origins

The core Presentation Manager window services are similar to the Microsoft Windows environment under DOS. This similarity is not surprising because much of PM's windowing technology, user interface, raster graphics, and bitmap support comes directly from Microsoft Windows. IBM's contribution to PM is the powerful vector-graphics draw commands called the Graphic Programming Interface (GPI). The GPI is largely derived form the Graphical Data Display Manager (GDDM) mainframe graphics system.

The PM graphics engine was almost completely rewritten in portable C code by a joint team from Micrografx and IBM. The new code takes full advantage of 32-bit flat memory model, resulting in noticeably improved performance. Some of PM's more sluggish features, such as area fills and polygons, are performing much better. A new, bitmap-stretcher will help you create highly recognizable reduced-size images. OS/2 1.X PM programmers can recompile their existing applications for the 32-bit environment and watch them run at least twenty percent faster (the PM 1.x API was essentially 32-bit from the very start).

New Graphic Features

With OS/2 2.0, PM added considerable support for new graphical features, including two standard dialogs for opening files and selecting fonts (these are features most applications had to constantly reinvent), and six nifty new controls (see Figure 6-4 and Figure 6-5). The *Notebook* control allows an application to create hypercard-like pages organized in a notebook. The *Container* control can display objects in various formats and views. This super-powerful control supports direct manipulation and allows users to move objects between containers. The *Value Set*, another powerful control, allows a user to select from a group of icons or images. A *slider* enables a user to change or view a value by moving a slider arm. Figure 6-4 shows some of these new controls. We will show you, in Part VI, how to give your applications a "new look and feel" using these new controls.

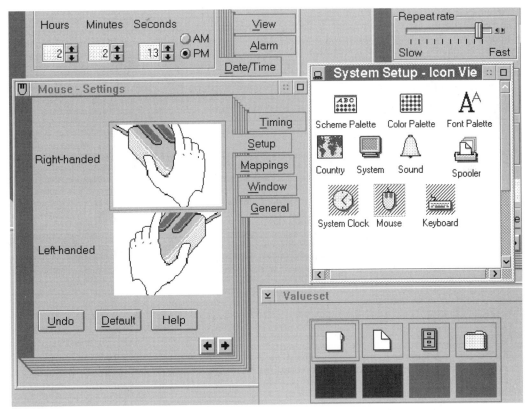

Figure 6-4. OS/2 2.0's New CUA '91 Controls.

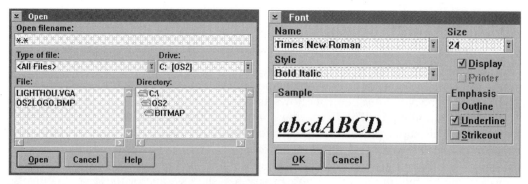

Figure 6-5. OS/2 2.0's Standard File and Font Dialogs.

Messages and Object Orientation

PM enforces an *object-oriented*, message-based style of programming. The core of a Presentation Manager program is a set of window procedures that you write to process outside events such as the mouse or keyboard input associated with a particular window. Presentation Manager will call the appropriate window procedure and pass it parameters in the form of a message (see Figure 6-6).

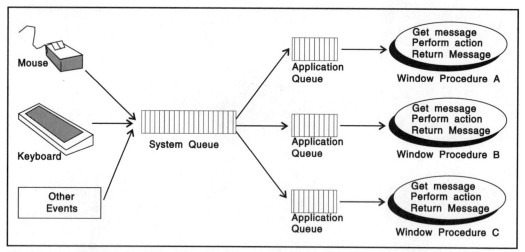

Figure 6-6. Presentation Manager's System and Window Procedures Queues.

PM and SAA

PM fully conforms to the SAA *Common User Access 1991 (CUA'91)* programming standard for structuring a workplace application. This includes how the application's objects are displayed on the screen, how messages are handled, and how pictures are exchanged. The Presentation Manager's pre-registered window classes (containers, notebooks, sliders, standard windows, menus, scroll bars, and dialog boxes) embody the CUA'91 vintage architecture. The PM API fully conforms to the Common Programming Interface (CPI) of SAA, which facilitates the portability of your applications to other SAA platforms. IBM uses the PM platform to bring to market its large body of advanced CUA research on how people and computers graphically interact. PM, with some help from PC hardware, will be the first IBM platform to embody new multimedia features such as video, voice, and three-dimensional graphics.

PM's Programming Services

The following is a list of PM's most important API services:

- *Managing windows:* PM provides a large set of API calls for controlling windows. This includes calls to allow an application to create, size, move, and control windows and their contents.

- *Graphic primitives*: The PM GPI primitives allow you to create lines, markers, areas, arcs, and character fonts. Using these primitives, you can construct complete graphic objects that can then be displayed, printed, or stored. You can invoke the primitive set with specific attributes such as color, type of line, shape to fill, or shading levels.

- *Graphic object management*: PM provides a set of API calls to manage graphic objects. The PM API allows you to place the graphic objects you construct (known as graphic segments) in libraries. It allows you to reuse your stored segments by drawing the same segment repeatedly into a single picture or on many graphic devices.

- *Graphic object manipulation*: PM provides a set of API calls through which you can transform a graphic object by scaling it in size, rotating it, translating its position, or changing its slant. PM will also clip the parts of an object that lie outside a specified boundary.

- *Presentation spaces*: PM provides a set of API calls to manage the presentation space while assembling an object from world coordinates to the coordinates of your display device or printer. PM allows you to draw in a virtual space and then associate your drawing with a device context. You can then switch your associations to a different device context. For example, you assemble your drawing in a virtual space, then you can choose to associate that space with a printer, display, or plotter. Consequently, PM provides a device-independent graphic system. The presentation drivers virtualize the display environment (screen, printer, and plotter). Your API calls interact with the virtual driver (a device independent interface), which then translates the request into commands for a specific device driver when you request an association.

- *Metafiles*: PM provides a set of API calls to import or export an image object. Pictures created with the PM API can be packaged in a metafile that conforms to

IBM's Mixed Object Document Content Architecture (MODCA) interchange standard. This allows another application to run the metafile and recreate the picture. The metafile contains all the PM API instructions to create the final version of the picture.

- **Bitmaps**: PM provides a set of API calls for bitmap manipulation. Bitmap operations are very useful for animation and when areas of a screen need to be filled, moved, or restored. The PM API supports high-speed operations on bitmap representations of a screen.

- **Clipboard**: PM provides a set of API calls that enable the user-initiated exchange of data between applications using the clipboard. A user first copies selected data into the clipboard, deletes (cut) it from the source application, and then inserts it (paste) into the target application from the clipboard. The cut, copy, and paste commands must be supported by an application. They are implemented as a set of PM API calls.

- **Dynamic Data Exchange (DDE)**: PM provides a set of API calls that support the DDE protocol for message-based exchanges of data among applications. DDE can be used to construct *hot links* between applications where data can be fed from window to window without operator intervention. For example, the changes in an inventory table in a database window can be fed directly into another window where a spreadsheet is dynamically displaying inventory in graphical bar-chart format. As the inventory changes in the database, the changes get automatically reflected on the bar charts. Hot links provide a level of integration between PM applications that goes beyond the Clipboard's "cut and paste." The hot link ties the data in an application to its source. When the source data changes, the pasted data is updated automatically via the hot link. DDE defines the data format and control sequences of the message exchange. The data is exchanged using the OS/2's shared memory services. Through a DDE API call, an application can automatically be advised by way of a message if some data of interest has changed. Two DDE compliant applications having no prior knowledge of each other can negotiate (in theory) an interchange format and exchange details such as the length of each message.

- **Drag and Drop**: PM provides a set of API functions that support protocols for the direct manipulation of objects. These protocols allow a user to visually drag a *source object* and drop it on a *target object*. The drag causes a message exchange, which may be accompanied by a data exchange, to take place between the two objects.

System Object Model (SOM)

The OS/2 2.0 Toolkit includes an object-oriented programming facility called the *System Object Model* or SOM. This new facility includes a compiler that lets you create class libraries with any language you choose (although in the current release only C is supported). SOM is not a language; it is a system for defining, manipulating, and releasing class libraries. You use SOM to define object-oriented classes and their inter-relationships (including inheritance, encapsulation, and method overrides). The methods themselves are written in C.

You can think of SOM as an object-oriented environment for C programs. You create an application by defining your classes using the SOM *Object Interface Definition Language (OIDL)*. The OIDL is then processed by a SOM precompiler to create a set of language-specific binding files (currently C only). SOM, of course, provides functions that help you debug and work with your object. SOM's claim to fame is that it provides a set of canned classes that allow you to inherit the Workplace Shell's capabilities in your own applications.

The OS/2 2.0 Workplace Shell was created using SOM classes. In fact, every object in the Workplace Shell is an instance of a SOM class. Your applications can use the Workplace class library "as is" to create containers, context menus, folders, and notebooks. You can also create new classes that inherit characteristics from existing Workplace classes. If this is not enough, you can extend and modify the functions of any SOM class by substituting (overriding) the class-provided methods with your own. We will show you later how to take advantage of SOM in your applications.

IBM is working with Borland and Digitalk to provide SOM bindings for C++ and Smalltalk. SOM provides the hooks for exchanging class libraries with other object-oriented languages. SOM's language neutrality makes it possible for a Smalltalk object written in SOM to inherit attributes from a C or C++ object. This also means that objects written in different languages can communicate using SOM's common object interface. IBM has offered SOM to both Taligent and OSF.

Information Presentation Facility

The Information Presentation Facility (IPF) is a useful tool that you can use to provide context-sensitive help from within PM applications. You can also use the IPF to create separate online documentation that can be viewed independently of your application. The IPF viewer is shipped with every copy of OS/2. OS/2 2.0 lets you create very sophisticated PM presentations using IPF. You can create hypertext links from within text, bitmaps, or metafiles. You can use these hypertext (or "hypergrahic") links to display additional textual or pictorial information, send a message to an application, or start a new process. The links may extend across multiple files which makes it easy to update information. A link may be defined for either the entire bitmap or individual parts. This is a splendid way to hotspot pictures.

The new OS/2 2.0 IPF facilities allow you to create multiple split screens within a PM window. This is useful for displaying related information in separately scrollable PM window areas called *viewports*. You can use split screens to select a hypertext or hypergrahic link in one viewport and simultaneously watch the target information displayed in another viewport inside the same window. IPF also allows you to specify application controlled viewports. You do that by specifying the name of a DLL function and the parameters to be passed to it. You can use these DLL functions to create special graphic effects such as displaying a video clip in a target viewport in response to a link being selected in an adjoining viewport. IPF also supports multiple text fonts and sizes.

PM Resources

PM allows you to create resources that are defined apart from your source code in a resource script (.RC) file. You may place in the resource files existing PM resources or create your own using the **IBM OS/2 Developer's Toolkit 2.0** (we will cover the Toolkit in the Development Platform section below). The Toolkit supplies font, icon, and dialog box editors together with the RC utility, which allows you to compile and bind resources to your applications. Resources can also be put in a DLL and accessed by your application at run time.

Converting Windows 3.X Applications to 32-bit PM

Converting 16-bit Windows 3.X applications to 32-bit PM is easy with the Mirrors and Oasis Toolkits from Micrografx and IBM. The tool is compatible with the Windows API, which it emulates with 32-bit PM code. Windows developers can produce native looking PM applications with minimum effort and no performance degradation (some claim improved performance). The Oasis toolkit makes it easy to port Windows 3.X device drivers into OS/2.

OS/2 2.0 runs Windows applications directly, so what does a 32-bit PM version of the application buy you? For starters, you can add the Macintosh look and make your application participate in the Workplace Shell drag/drop environment. We will show in Part VI how the Workplace Shell's Object Oriented User Interface (OOUI) can be used to create new categories of graphical business applications. A 32-bit PM application has full use of OS/2's advanced features, including HPFS extended file attributes, interprocess communications, semaphores, multithreading, and PM's powerful graphics repertoire. These features can be used to enhance your application with more robust and responsive client features. Threads, for example, can be used to handle communications with a server on the network. Background tasks (daemons) can be used to create client agents that are always ready to accept calls from a server—such as "are you alive?" Last but not least, you can market your product as a true 32-bit application.

OS/2 2.0: Development Platform

To develop OS/2 software professionally, you will need the **IBM C Developer's WorkSet/2**, a kit that provides a self-contained, 32-bit OS/2 C language application development environment. The WorkSet/2 includes the following:

- *The WorkFrame/2* provides a graphical environment for developing programs. The environment allows you to plug in your favorite tools and organize your application development environment according to projects. A project consists of source files, object files, and one target (.EXE) or (.DLL). Each project is associated with a compiler, debugger, make, and a linker.

- *The Developer's Toolkit* provides language-independent build tools, PM tools, productivity tools, sample programs, IPF tools, SOM tools, online reference information, and a kernel debugger. These tools can be integrated into the WorkFrame/2. The online help supports hypertext links, which let you find information quickly. You can copy API statements directly into your programs using the clipboard.

- *C Set/2 compiler kit* provides a 32-bit C compiler with its run-time libraries, and a fully interactive, full-function, source-level Presentation Manager debugger. PM windows can be displayed during the debug process. The compiler supports calling 16-bit libraries or APIs from 32-bit OS/2 and provides a migration switch that helps migrate applications written for the IBM C/2 and Microsoft C 6.0 compilers. The compiler also supports the SAA C *Common Programming Interface (CPI)*, which makes it possible to port code to and from other SAA compilers such as the IBM C/370 and C/400 SAA compilers and the AIX C compiler for the RS/6000 machines.

We will show you how to use these tools in the programming sections. We wanted to let you know, early on, that OS/2 2.0 provides a very attractive programming environment. The environment is definitely "first class" all the way. Extraordinary discounts are available: IBM offered the entire WorkSet/2 package for $295 from May through September 1992; the regular price is $895. Always look for special offers provided by the OS/2 Developer Assistance Program. You can usually get this information on CompuServe's IBMOS2 forum.

GUI Tools

There is a wide selection of PM application development tools on the market. Most of these tools allow your applications to also run on Windows 3.0. Here's a sample of what tools are available:

- **EASEL** from Interactive Images, Inc.
- **Enfin/3** from Enfin Software Corp.
- **Choreographer** from GUIdance Technologies, Inc.
- **CASE:PM** from CASEWORKS, Inc.
- **Object/1** from mdbs, Inc.
- **Extensible Virtual Toolkit** from XVT Software, Inc.
- **Open Interface** from Neuron Data, Inc.
- **Applications Manager** from Intelligent Environments, Inc.
- **Arcadia Workplace Vision** from Arcadia Technologies, Inc.
- **VZ Programmer** from VZCorp, Inc.

- **Gpf** from Microformatic U.S.A, Inc.
- **Borland C++ with Application FrameWorks** from Borland International Inc.
- **ObjectPM** from Objective Solutions, Inc.
- **Ellipse** from Cooperative Solutions, Inc. This tool is more than a GUI generator; it creates complete client/server applications.

Even with this excellent choice of tools, you will need to program the Presentation Manager for applications that require animation or need to take full advantage of multimedia. In addition, most tools cannot handle the direct manipulation of objects through mouse "drag and drop" techniques. Many of the tools do not even provide support for multiple fonts, bitmaps, metafiles, and DDE.

As a *rule of thumb*, if you're producing the normal window type of PM graphics, then a tool will greatly increase your productivity. However, if you're producing leading-edge graphic applications, you'll have to learn PM at an intimate level. But even with advanced applications, you can still use a tool to create the more mundane graphics and handcode the rest.

Multimedia Presentation Manager/2 (MMPM/2)

In June 1992, IBM introduced MMPM/2, the first multimedia extensions for OS/2. MMPM/2 Version 1.0 is a foundation product that provides API support, a run-time environment, and new CUA '91 controls for multimedia. The product provides a consistent programming interface across OS/2 and Windows. The API is based on the *Multimedia Programming Interface and Data Specifications* that was issued jointly by IBM and Microsoft in August 1991. These extensions allow you to use common multimedia APIs and file formats across OS/2 and Windows. OS/2's multitasking and support for large memory objects makes PM the better platform for the development of advanced multimedia applications.

MMPM/2 is a noisy product: *it talks and it sings*. Luckily, it also comes with a set of visual knobs that allow you to control the volume. The new multimedia controls (see Figure 6-7), include a volume knob (also called a circular slider), an animated push button, and a two-state push button. With these standardized controls, you should be able to provide consistent interfaces to any multimedia device no matter which product is being used.

MMPM/2 provides some very exciting architecture extensions to OS/2. Some of these extensions can be very useful to programs that have nothing to do with multimedia. A quick overview of the MMPM/2 architecture will provide you some insight into what this product can do for you. MMPM/2 (see Figure 6-8) consists of three components: the Media Control Interface (MCI), the Synchronization/Streaming Programming Interface (SPI), and the Multimedia I/O Programming Interface (MMIO). What a mouthful! The explanation follows.

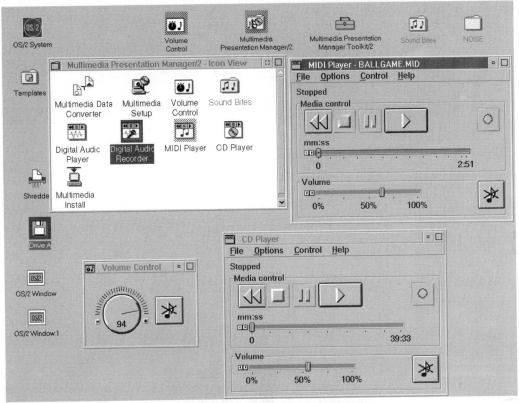

Figure 6-7. MMPM/2: The New CUA'91 Controls for Multimedia.

MMPM/2: The Media Control Interface (MCI)

The IBM/Microsoft MCI interface provides the heart of multimedia programming support. MCI provides a well thought-out, consistent, and device-independent interface to different media devices. It masks the complexity and variety of multimedia devices—including CD audio, waveform audio, MIDI, audio amp/mixer, and videodisc—by creating a "logical device," patterned after a tape drive. Commands supported by most devices include open, play, pause, stop, record, seek, and close. The first two are all that's required to get most multimedia devices to play (or display) their output.

The interface consists of two API calls: **MCISendCommand** and **MCISendString**. **MCISendCommand** is a procedural interface; while **MCISendString** allows the application to send a textual string representing the command. Here is an example of a three-command string that plays a CD: *open cdaudio alias bob; play bob; close bob.* Playing any other media is just as easy, and the same format will be used with future media such as digital video.

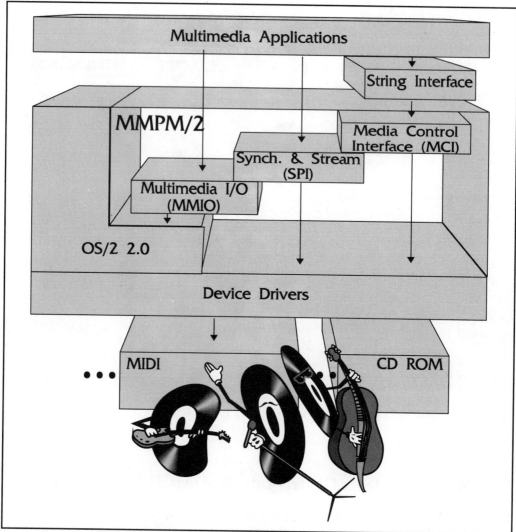

Figure 6-8. MMPM/2: The Architectural Components.

The MCI interface allows two or more applications to share the same device, either serially or in parallel, depending on the capabilities of the device. This is an area where OS/2's preemptive multitasking provides more granular levels of device sharing than the Windows alternative.

MMPM/2: The Synchronization Programming Interface (SPI)

The SPI component controls the synchronization of multimedia data streams such as audio and video. SPI provides a low-level interface that can be used by applications or subsystems within MMPM/2 to stream (i.e., move) data from a source device to a target device—for example, from memory to an audio adapter—without interruptions. SPI also allows applications to synchronize multiple data streams and receive notifications of real-time events. This is done by defining synchronization groups consisting of collections of streams with one data stream acting as the master. The master sends synchronization pulses to the slave streams at predefined intervals.

The SPI service really takes advantage of the preemptive multitasking capabilities of OS/2. For example, with the synchronization services you can be playing music in the background while a voice is narrating in the foreground. Or you can mix different audio tracks. In the future, you will be able to create sound tracks for digital video streams. The SPI service uses OS/2's threads to provide a fine degree of real-time control over the flow of data streams to media devices. The flat memory of OS/2 is essential for handling very large data streams.

MMPM/2: The Multimedia I/O Programming Interface (MMIO)

The MMIO is an extension of the OS/2 file services. It provides a powerful mechanism for accessing and manipulating multimedia data files. These files may contain a variety of media elements, including digital audio, digital video, images, graphics, and others. MMIO provides standard methods for applications to manipulate—open, read and write data, query the contents, and close—multimedia files.

The MMIO manager provides the following services:

- Buffered file I/O.
- Functions that locate, create, enter, exit, and access RIFF data chunks ("RIFF" is the IBM/Microsoft Resource Interchange File Format for multimedia).
- Memory File I/O that makes a block of memory look like a file to an application.
- Installable I/O procedures that allow you to supply your own functions, such as open, read, write, seek, and close on non-RIFF multimedia files (such as TIFFs).
- User-written data handlers through which you can provide additional MMIO controls for data format translations.

MMPM/2: Packaging

MMPM/2 wasn't ready on time to be part of the base OS/2 2.0 package. The MMPM/2 run-time extensions sell for $125. An MMPM/2 Programmer's Toolkit is available for

$199 (it includes the runtime). You will also need additional hardware depending on your multimedia tastes:

- A digital audio board that can be used to play (.WAV) files. These files can store representations of any sound and they tend to be very large (compared to MIDI files). Many public bulletin boards have (.WAV) files containing everything from the sound of jets taking off to Clint Eastwood's "Go ahead...make my day!"
- A digital audio board that supports the Musical Instrument Device Interface (MIDI) will let you record and play (.MID) files. These files contain music scores such as the sounds of guitars, drums, horns, and thundering applause.
- Boards for other supported media types, including audio CD, videodisc, audio amp/mixer, and video overlay. Each of these types requires additional hardware and drivers from vendors.
- Future media types will include support for full motion digital video using the "digitalvideo" media type (expected shortly), and other future media types, such as scanner and VCR.

In Summary

This concludes our "short" introduction to the base OS/2 system platform, which provides most of the ingredients needed to create a new generation of super-client applications. In the next few chapters we will go over the OS/2 extensions that will help you create server applications on top of the base platform.

Chapter 7

Communications Manager:
The SAA Connection

This is the first of three chapters in which we introduce the communications component of the OS/2 client/server platform. As we explained earlier, communications will be provided by four products: Extended Services' Communications Manager, TCP/IP, NetWare LAN Requester for OS/2, and LAN Server. Collectively, these products transform a PC running OS/2 into a formidable communications machine that can handle both local and remote networking with almost every conceivable type of client or server machine. This includes PCs running Novell or Microsoft network protocols, almost any type of Unix machine, and most mainframes. This chapter introduces the Extended Services Communications Manager (see light area in Figure 7-1). We pro-

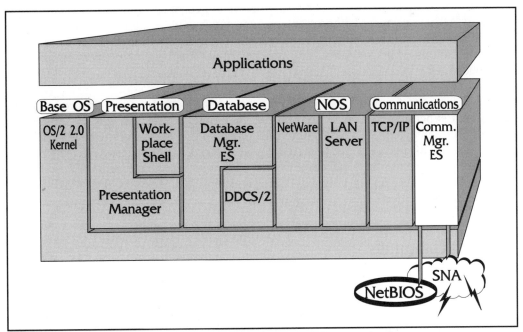

Figure 7-1. Client/Server Platform: Extended Services' Communications.

vide a bird's eye view of the product, enough to introduce you to the awesome amount of communication power that is made available to your client/server applications. It may be hard to believe, but this is a minimum size "architectural overview" that goes one step beyond the marketing literature.

COMMUNICATIONS MANAGER: OVERVIEW

The **Communications Manager** component of OS/2's Extended Services provides an *all-in-one* subsystem for communicating with almost everything in the mainframe world. It also provides a minimal subset of communications for the PC world. The intent was to provide a fully integrated and tested product that provides a "superset" of communications functions. These functions can then be *scaled downwards* to meet a particular machine's communications needs.

"All-In-One" Communications

The Communications Manager supports a variety of communication protocols and communication hardware that can all run concurrently on the same machine. The product consists of modular building blocks with well-defined APIs to many of the popular protocols. The APIs are reentrant, meaning that they can be used simultaneously by more than one user. The support of concurrent communications and the reentrant APIs is a marked improvement over comparable protocols in the MS-DOS environment. In addition, network management support is built into all the elements of Communications Manager, providing another major improvement over similar MS-DOS packages.

The packaging of Communication Manager as a single subsystem ensures that the constituent subcomponents will not interfere with one another, as was so common in the MS-DOS environment. The single package also offers a single user interface for installation, configuration, network management, and common services. From this interface, you can start or stop a communication service, send and receive files, display status and messages, remap your keyboard, and look at traces and alert messages for problem determination.

When to Unbundle

The bundled Communications Manager package provides a large amount of function at a price significantly lower than a comparable system of separately purchased applications. However, these improvements incur a price in terms of hardware. The communication software alone requires 5 MBytes of hard-disk space. The runtime requires 200 KBytes of RAM for the Communication Manager base and 100 KBytes to 400 KBytes for each of the protocols. Most probably, you will only need a small subset of the communication offerings. Make sure to exclude the functions that you do not need in order to save memory. One of your minor challenges when using Communications Manager will be learning how to configure your machines to fit your particular mix of communication needs.

The Layered View

One glance at Figure 7-2 should help convince you that Communications Manager makes available a kaleidoscope of Application Programming Interfaces (APIs). These APIs sit on top of layers of communication protocols and services. Each layer builds on top of the services provided by the layers below it. The APIs allow you to tap into the system at selective interfaces. To understand the layers of Communications Manager, we will start at the bottom of Figure 7-2 and work our way upwards.

The lowest layer of software belongs to the device drivers that provide an interface to several types of communication hardware adapters. The OS/2 kernel sits on top of the device drivers. On top of the OS/2 kernel, there are several layers of protocol functions implemented as Dynamic Link Libraries (DLLs). The DLLs provide protocol stacks for SNA, NetBIOS, Asynchronous communications, and X.25. The functions provided by some of the protocol stacks are roughly equivalent to the OSI Link, Network, Transport, Session, and to some degree Presentation layers. Some of the protocol stacks are far more complete than others; X.25, for example, only partially covers the OSI Physical, Link, and Network layers, while SNA covers all the OSI layers.

The terminal emulators provide user level presentation services that allow you to run your OS/2 machine as a dumb terminal attached to a multiuser host. The screen-driven common services enable you to interactively manage the communications environment. The Network Management functions that are necessary to monitor and control a communication network are present in all the layers.

Connectivity Options

The first requirement of a communication subsystem is to be able to physically link up with other machines. This rudimentary linkup, or *connectivity*, is the prerequisite for all communications; it forms the platform on which more meaningful forms of information exchange are constructed. Communications Manager provides connectivity through its device drivers and the link layer protocols shown at the bottom of Figure 7-2. The large selection of connectivity options provided by Communications Manager can be divided into three categories: LAN attachment, remote connectivity, and direct attachment to IBM mainframes.

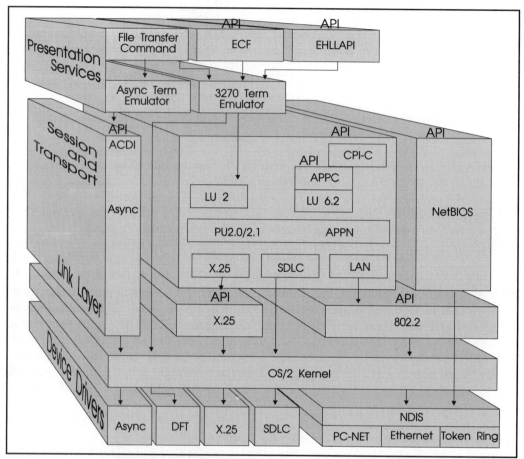

Figure 7-2. Communications Manager Functional Layers and Programming.

LAN Attachments

LAN attachments provide high-speed local connectivity over a shared LAN cable that serves as the broadcast medium. The media access link layer, which is built into the hardware, arbitrates the access to the cable and allows packets of information to be exchanged reliably over the medium. The Communications Manager provides built-in driver support for the IEEE 802.5 Media Access Control protocol, otherwise known as Token Ring, and the IEEE 802.3 Media Access Control, otherwise known as Ethernet. In terms of connectivity hardware, the following networks are supported:

1. IBM Token Ring (IEEE 802.5)
2. IBM PC Network broadband (a low-cost variation of IEEE 802.3)
3. IBM PC Network baseband (a very low-cost variation of IEEE 802.3)
4. The original Ethernet V2 protocol (a variation of IEEE 802.3)
5. The new Ethernet protocol (IEEE 802.3)

Communications Manager supports *Network Driver Interface Spec (NDIS)*. This is the Microsoft/3Com standard for interfacing protocol stacks to network adapter device drivers. NDIS creates a "logical network board" that makes it easy to interface different LAN adapters with multiple protocol stacks. NDIS network adapters are readily obtainable from vendors such as Ungermann-Bass, 3Com, and Western Digital. A workstation can support a maximum of four NDIS LAN adapters. NDIS allows multiple protocol stacks to access the same adapter. Since NDIS is a standard interface fewer drivers need to be installed and maintained. All the OS/2 LAN adapters and protocol stacks, including NetWare, now support NDIS. This support is an enhancement over the previous versions of Communications Manager, which provided NDIS-compatible communications only for Ethernet.

The various LAN adapters provide a wide choice of physical layer cabling options. The Token Ring LAN adapter from IBM supports low-cost telephone twisted-pair cable at 4Mb/s bandwidth. The more reliable shielded twisted-pair cable supports 16Mb/s bandwidth, and the fiber-optic cable can be used for wiring long segments (up to 2 KM). The PC Network Broadband LAN adapter from IBM works with cable TV technology and in theory can support multiple (2 Mb/s) LAN channels over the same cable. The PC Network Baseband LAN adapter, also from IBM, provides low-cost, low-bandwidth communication over ordinary telephone cables. The various OEM Ethernet adapters usually work with baseband coax cable that come in a variety of cable thickness and prices.

Remote Connectivity

The remote connectivity options enable your machine to communicate with the world-at-large. Communications Manager supports remote connectivity over telephone lines through public or private networks using a variety of link protocols, including Asynchronous (ASYNC), Synchronous Data Link Control (SDLC), and CCITT's X.25 standard for packet switching. Figure 7-3 shows the various options provided by Communication Manager for programs to "reach out and talk" to other programs over long-distance carriers.

The term *DTE* stands for Data Terminal Equipment in telephony jargon. The DTE is your OS/2 machine, including the adapter hardware. DTE's connect to the Data Communications Equipment (or *DCE*), which provides the long-distance connectivity service through communication carriers.[1] The DCE consists of the modem and the carrier facilities. ASYNC adapters require asynchronous modems. SDLC and X.25 require synchronous modems. The long-distance carrier may be your ordinary telephone service (switched lines), or it can be a dedicated leased line (where speed,

---

[1] This telephony jargon use of the term DCE should not be confused with the OSF's Distributed Communications Environment (also called DCE).

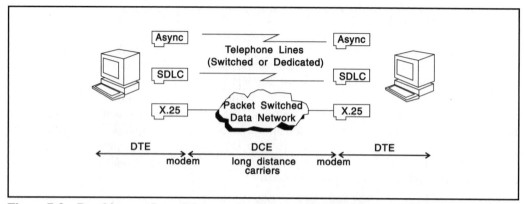

Figure 7-3. Reaching out Long Distance the Communications Manager Way.

connection availability, and noise immunity are requirements); it can also be an X.25 Packet Switched Data Network (PSDN).

*PSDN*s provide reliable long-distance service over a shared network of connected computers and provide an alternative to networks made up of lines dedicated to pairs of users. Packet switching technology allows multiple users to use the same network paths by breaking the information transmitted into intelligent packets that are routed through a network and re-assembled at the destination. PSDNs create permanent or switched virtual circuits between network subscribers and offer various ways of paying for network bandwidth, including schemes where you can literally *pay by the packet*. The term "virtual" in the X.25 context means that you can have multiple logical connections (virtual circuits) over a single physical link. Communications Manager supports up to 128 virtual circuits that can be used concurrently by up to 40 X.25 applications. To use a PSDN, you connect your equipment (the DTE) to the network through a modem (the DCE), as shown in Figure 7-3. The X.25 driver works with up to eight concurrent Micro Channel IBM X.25 Coprocessor/2 adapters, which provide bit-synchronous attachment to the DCE.

Direct Attachment to IBM Mainframes

Direct attachment to IBM mainframes is another form of connectivity that is supported by Communications Manager. In fact, Communications Manager transforms a PC into a "great communicator" in the world of IBM host networks. This transformation is accomplished by supporting the old terminal networks as well as the new *peer-to-peer* host/PC connectivity strategies, which are typically LAN-based.

A PC can attach directly through point-to-point coax cable to System/370 terminal controllers (the 3174, 3274, 3X74 series) and the 9370 workstation controller. This type of attachment is called *Distributed Function Terminal (DFT)*. Most IBM customer shops have miles of coax cables on their premises. DFT support can help leverage some of that coax base. The new 3174 Peer Communications network, also known as

LAN over coax, provides peer-to-peer communications for PCs attached to a 3174 Control Unit using existing coax cable or telephone twisted pair wire. This network allows PCs to communicate with other PCs using APPC, IEEE 802.2, or NetBIOS. It requires the LAN over Coax driver running in the OS/2 workstation and the 3174 Peer Communication Program running in the 3174 Control Unit.

PCs can now be connected to most IBM hosts and their front-end processors (the 37XX series) through Token Ring and Ethernet LANs, ASYNC, SDLC, and X.25.

Upper-Layer Protocol Support

It takes more than link layer connectivity for two entities to communicate. Additional layers of protocol are required on top of the link. An upper-layer protocol should provide:

- Reliable end-to-end service across multiple networks.
- Logical names for network entities.
- Session-based rules of exchange. This is the protocol that is followed after a session is established. It includes agreements on who talks first, on how to gracefully end conversations, and who does what in case of error. It also includes some convention for establishing checkpoints during a conversation.
- Common data structures for the representation of information that gets exchanged over a network. This includes protocols for mail, documents, folders, and images.
- Common network services such as file transfers, terminal emulation, network management, network authentication and security, network directory services, network time, and electronic mail.

As you can see, the list of upper-layer services is extensive and open-ended. Communications software vendors have tackled the problem by offering the upper-layer protocols as a *stack* of offerings that is architected to work together to provide system solutions. Some of the protocol stacks are more complete than others. Examples of the more complete protocol stacks are SNA, TCP/IP, and OSI. Communications Manager supports a variety of upper-layer protocol stacks over the connectivity links that were described. Each protocol stack opens up a communication universe in which your programs can participate. The upper-layer protocol stacks provided by Communications Manager are SNA, X.25, and LAN peer-to-peer protocols. The three other products covered in the next chapters all provide stacks that complement Communications Manager and further extend OS/2's reach.

System Network Architecture (SNA)

The Communications Manager implements IBM's System Network Architecture (SNA) in both its old and new forms. The *old SNA* is a hierarchical terminal controller network. This is a network in which hosts reside at the center of the universe and are surrounded by dumb terminals. All the processing power in the network resides at the top of the hierarchy in mainframes running VTAM (in SNA parlance a Physical Unit 5 or PU 5 node). Mainframes are front-ended by communication controllers running the NCP program (a PU 4 node), which in turn is front-ended by terminal cluster controllers (PU 2 nodes). Terminals talk to the host through terminal controllers. Communications Manager allows the PC to look like a dumb terminal (a Logical Unit type 2 or LU 2 in SNA terminology). A logical unit type describes the characteristics of an SNA session. In an LU 2 session, the entire application runs in the host. The PC can attach to hosts by looking like a terminal through a coax cable or Token Ring. Another option is to have the PC look like a terminal combined with a terminal controller (a PU 2 node) and talk to the host through SDLC.

The New SNA: APPC, APPN, and CPI-C

The *new SNA* is a network of peers where PC programs can talk to the host programs at a program-to-program level through the use of well-defined *verb* commands (this type of session is called an LU 6.2 type in SNA terminology). Physically, the PCs are endowed with local intelligence to provide parallel session initiation services without VTAM host involvement. A node with those attributes is an SNA PU 2.1 node.

IBM is evolving SNA into a true distributed operating system that supports: cross network directory services, transparent network access to resources (such as servers, applications, displays, printers, and data), common data streams, and integrated network management. *Advanced Peer-to-Peer Network* or *APPN* is the network infrastructure responsible for this "true distribution." APPN creates an SNA internet without the mainframe-centric hierarchy of traditional SNA configurations. The mainframe is just another node on the internet. APPN allows LU 6.2 SNA applications, using APPC or CPI-C APIs, to take full advantage of peer networks. It also greatly simplifies SNA configuration, provides better availability through dynamic routing, makes it easier to maintain SNA networks, and meets the flexibility requirements of modern networks.

The Communications Manager provides a very complete APPN implementation. It allows OS/2 PCs configured as *Network Nodes (NN)* to act as smart routers that know how to reach any other node on the SNA internet using the best route for a particular class of service. Intermediate routing is supported for nodes that are not on the same physical network. This means that an SNA session can traverse one or more intermediate nodes (these are called mesh networks). The Network Nodes know how to reroute traffic if part of the network is down. For example, the Network Node in Chicago (see Figure 7-4) will get to Montreal via Hong Kong if the direct route is down.

With APPN, all an application needs to know to communicate is its partner's LU name, but not the location. APPN provides a dynamic directory service that discovers, through message exchanges, the destination address and the best routes for getting there. Previously, this information had to be configured manually (a real nightmare).

APPN almost makes it a snap to add a new workstation to an SNA network. Programs are not affected any more when machines are moved or when a network adapter's physical address changes.

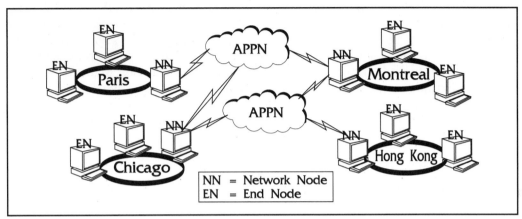

Figure 7-4. The New SNA's APPN Network Layer.

X.25

X.25 is an international standard that defines how to connect computers to either public or private packet switching data networks (PSDNs). X.25 support is provided by IBM to primarily extend SNA communications across packet-switched networks and to communicate with equipment from other vendors. X.25 is an SAA supported protocol that provides an alternative network service to SNA's VTAM/NCP. There are no indications, however, that X.25 will replace SNA's VTAM/NCP backbone networks.

LAN Protocols

The Communications Manager supports two Local Area Network Protocol stacks: NetBIOS and IEEE 802.2. NetBIOS is an excellent peer-to-peer protocol that is very useful in client/server applications. We defer the in-depth discussion of the LAN upper-layer protocols to the API section.

Terminal Emulation and File Transfers

The Communications Manager includes the following terminal emulation programs:

- IBM 3270 terminal emulation
- IBM 3101 and DEC VT100 terminal emulation
- IBM 5250 terminal emulation

IBM 3270 Terminal Emulation

IBM 3270 terminal emulation provides interactive access to IBM System/370 host computers. The IBM 3270 terminal models that are emulated include the 3178, 3278, and 3279. As many as ten 3270 terminal emulation sessions can be active at any one time. This includes up to five sessions multiplexed over a single DFT coaxial cable link and up to five more sessions multiplexed over either an SDLC, X.25, or a Token Ring network. Each logical terminal appears in a separate Presentation Manager window. You can start and stop sessions, and you can move the session windows using the Presentation Manager controls. Multiple sessions can be viewed simultaneously on the screen, and PM functions such as Mark, Cut, Paste, Copy can be used to transfer simple text or bitmaps between windows.

In addition to terminal emulation, an active 3270 session can be used to move files to and from an IBM/370 host on which the 3270-PC file transfer program (IND$FILE) is installed. File transfer to and from IBM hosts running MVS/TSO, VM/CMS, or CICS is supported over any active 3270 session. You can initiate a file transfer from the OS/2 command line with the SEND or RECEIVE command. An OS/2 workstation can also access and display during a 3270 emulation session host GDDM graphics (the GDDM-OS/2 link program must be installed on the host). This support allows a host GDDM picture to be downloaded to an OS/2 PC, where it can be displayed, printed, or plotted. The GDDM picture may also be saved as a Presentation Manager or PIF Metafile.

IBM 3101 and DEC VT100 Terminal Emulation

The IBM 3101 and DEC VT100 terminal emulation options provide interactive access to hosts that support ASCII terminals via an asynchronous link. Multiple ASCII terminal emulations may be configured, but only one may be active at any time. With the asynchronous services, a user can access a range of data services such as Dow Jones News, CompuServe, MCI Mail, and Prodigy. Three types of file transfers are supported over an asynchronous link:

*   With an IBM host (VM/CMS or MVS/TSO) using the 3270-PC File Transfer Program (IND$FILE). ALMCOPY, a superfast multifile transfer program is provided on an "as is" basis.
*   With any host that supports the XMODEM file transfer protocol.
*   With any partner that supports a simple Send ASCII Text File function. This works well with systems like MCI Mail.

IBM 5250 Terminal Emulation

The IBM 5250 terminal emulation option provides interactive access to IBM AS/400 hosts via SDLC, X.25, Twinax, or LAN connections. Up to five concurrent 5250 sessions can be supported; each 5250 session being a separate APPC session.

SNA Gateway

The SNA Gateway is a non-dedicated server PC which provides its clients a shared link to an IBM System/370 host. Each client workstation thinks it is directly connected to the host, while the host thinks it is communicating with a single terminal controller. The gateway uses a single host communication link to get data from the host and route it to the appropriate workstation. In the other direction, it accepts data from workstations, appends the appropriate control headers, and routes the data to the host. The gateway code emulates the SNA cluster controller 3X74 family with the gateway PC made to appear to the host as a single PU 2 in SNA terminology.

Up to 256 client PCs can be configured on the LAN supported by the SNA gateway. Each client can have several active host sessions (not all the clients can be active at the same time). The gateway can transparently extend a 3270 emulation (LU 2) or an APPC (LU6.2) session. The gateway must be linked to the host via SDLC, X.25, or Token Ring. The clients may attach to the gateway via Token Ring, PC Network,

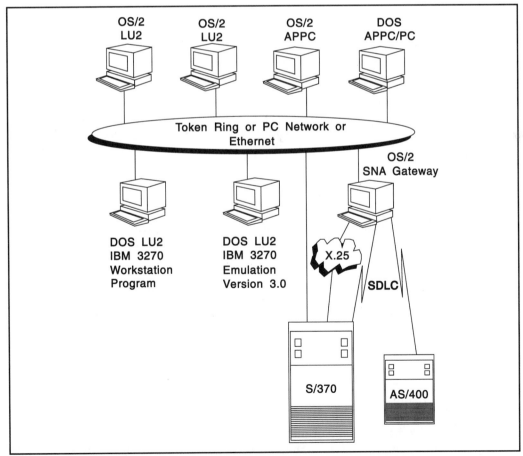

Figure 7-5. The Communications Manager SNA Gateway.

Ethernet, SDLC switched links, or X.25 networks. Figure 7-5 shows some of the connectivity options the gateway makes available to workstations. In addition to OS/2 clients, the gateway can support DOS clients running any of the following programs:

- IBM 3270 Emulation Program Version 3.0
- IBM 3270 Workstation Program
- IBM APPC/PC

PROGRAMMING INTERFACES (APIs)

In this section we describe the programming interfaces Communications Manager brings to the C programmer. The Communications Manager makes its whole repertoire of network services and protocols available to the C programmer through API sets. Each of the API sets has a specific purpose making it possible to create programs that can communicate with many host and PC environments across Local Area Networks, Wide Area Networks, and telephone lines. The APIs are accessible from C applications running concurrently under OS/2 user sessions or within the windows of a Presentation Manager session.

Communication API Types

The Communications Manager provides eight sets of protocol APIs in addition to an API set to obtain common services. The protocol APIs can be classified into three categories:

- **Peer-to-Peer APIs** are used to create both cooperative and client/server applications. The term "peer-to-peer" indicates that the two sides of a communication link use the same protocol interface to conduct a networked conversation. Any computer can initiate a conversation with any other computer. The protocol tends to be quite symmetric and is sometimes called "program-to-program." The peer-to-peer APIs fall into two categories:

  1. Higher-level APIs that mask the communications and provide associations between two logical programs. The APIs that fall into this category include NetBIOS and APPC.
  2. Lower-level APIs that do not quite mask the communications and require that you get more involved with the mechanics of networking, message buffer allocation, session management, and sometimes the direct control of the communication adapter. Protocols that fall into this category include IEEE 802.2, Asynchronous Communications Device Interface (ACDI) and X.25. Both ACDI and X.25 are interface protocols, as opposed to end-to-end protocols. This means that a portion of the API has only local significance and is involved with interfacing to the communications equipment, as opposed to the remote partner.

- **Client/Server APIs** are used for the remote invocation of services. Communications Manager provides an API for remote host services through the Server-Requester Programming Interface (SRPI), which makes it easier for a PC to share resources on S/370 hosts. The Extended Services remote database services are also an example of a client/server API which uses SQL over the network (more on that when we discuss database services).
- **Emulation service APIs** are used to automate and simplify the interaction between a PC user and a terminal-based mainframe application. Unlike the more modern application-to-application protocols (like APPC and CPI-C), emulation service APIs do not require any changes to the numerous mainframe programs designed to work with terminals. APPC, on the other hand, is a more general protocol that provides communications among cooperating programs, but it requires writing new software on the mainframe. Communications Manager supports the Emulator High-Level Language Application Interface (EHLLAPI).

The Communications Manager APIs

In this section, we provide a brief overview of the Communications Manager APIs. Refer to Figure 7-2 to understand the underlying protocol stacks on which the APIs build their services.

NetBIOS

NetBIOS is currently the premier protocol for LAN-based program-to-program communications. Introduced by IBM and Sytek in 1984 for the IBM PC Network, NetBIOS now runs with almost no changes on Ethernet, Token Ring, ARCnet, StarLAN, and even low-cost serial-port LANs. NetBIOS interfaces to TCP/IP, XNS, OSI, and IEEE 802.2 protocol stacks. Support for a NetBIOS platform exists on many operating systems including MS-DOS, OS/2, Unix, and some host environments such as Tandem Computers. NetBIOS is currently the de facto portable standard for network application providers.

One of the many reasons for NetBIOS's success is its intuitive simplicity, which makes it easy to master. NetBIOS provides a naming service that allows a LAN adapter card to have multiple logical names. Through NetBIOS, you can write LAN applications that can exchange information between named entities on the network. NetBIOS provides two classes of network transmission services: sessions and datagrams.

Sessions provide a reliable two-way connection service in which each packet is tracked and acknowledged in sequenced message exchanges. *Datagrams* provide a simple, but unreliable, service with powerful broadcast capabilities. You can send datagrams to a named entity, to a select group of entities (multicast), or to all entities on a network (broadcast). Datagrams are unreliable in the sense that they are not acknowledged or tracked through a sequence number. You "transmit and pray" that your datagram gets received.

The NetBIOS API consists of about 20 commands which are grouped into four categories: general purpose (such as reset, cancel, adapter status), name support (such as add name, add group name), datagram support (such as send datagram, send broadcast datagram), and session support (such as call, listen, hang up, send, receive). NetBIOS does have some weaknesses; it does not support an internetwork naming convention, and it does not provide authentication and security mechanisms.

APPC

Using APPC, an OS/2 program can converse through one of SNA's 50,000 installed networks with peers located anywhere in the world. These peers can run on PCs, RS/6000s, AS/400s, S/38s, and S/370s, as well as on many non-IBM host platforms.

APPC is IBM's architected solution for program-to-program communication, distributed transaction processing, and remote database access across the entire IBM product line. An application program, called a Transaction Program (TP) uses the APPC or CPI-C APIs to communicate with other TPs on systems that support APPC/SNA. This includes MS-DOS/APPC, OS/400s, System/370 (MVS/XA, TSO-E, VM/APPC, and CICS/MVS environments). APPC is also supported by many non-IBM host vendors. APPC supplies a variety of advanced communication functions such as: password validation, starting a remote program and sending it Program Initialization Parameters (PIP), and distributed checkpoints. The checkpoint function can be used to synchronize distributed applications; in the future, it will be used synchronize distributed databases using a two-phase commit protocol.

APPC's weaknesses include the lack of support for datagrams, broadcast, and multicast services. The APPC model is inherently conversational. In addition, the APPC protocol is half-duplex over a session, which means that it requires two sessions for full-duplex operation. APPC's other weakness is the lack of a consistent API across all platforms (see next section).

Common Programming Interface-Communications (CPI-C)

CPI-C, SAA's official *Common Programming Interface for Communications*, builds on top of APPC and masks its complexities and irregularities. Every product that supports APPC has a slightly different API. CPI-C fixes that problem. Writing to the CPI-C API allows you to port your programs to other SAA platforms such as S/370 and AS/400. Networking Services/DOS (NS/DOS), available 3Q '92, provides CPI-C/APPC for DOS and Windows using less than 140 KBytes of memory. From a programmer's perspective, APPC provides a *verb with control-block* API while CPI-C provides a consistent *call-based* API on top of APPC (see Figure 7-6).

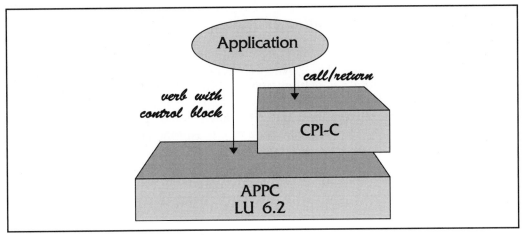

Figure 7-6.   CPI-C on Top of APPC.

The CPI-C API is common across different operating systems and programming languages. IBM provides CPI-C language bindings for all its SAA compilers. APPC offers interoperability and platform-specific optimizations. CPI-C offers *both* portability and interoperability, but it gives up some of the platform-specific features. These trade-offs will become clearer when we compare the APPC and CPI-C features in Part III.

The X/Open consortium has licensed the CPI-C interface from IBM, so have several companies (including Novell and Apple). CPI-C is becoming an important "de facto" (and possibly "de jure") API standard for peer-to-peer communications. When IBM delivers its multiprotocol common transport, CPI-C applications will be able to run unchanged on a broad selection of transport stacks including TCP/IP, OSI, IPX/SPX, SNA, and NetBIOS (see Figure 7-7). In the meantime, CPI-C applications can only run on an APPC foundation, which in turn is built on top of SNA.

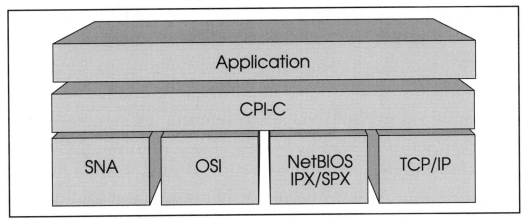

Figure 7-7.   CPI-C: A Stack-Independent API (Source: *IBM Blueprint for Networking, March 1992*).

Server-Requester Programming Interface (SRPI)

SRPI provides an API that allows an OS/2 client application to request host services through an active 3270 session (LU 2) with a System/370 host server running VM/CMS or MVS/TSO. The calling application first specifies a server name, a function ID, request parameters, and data, and then issues a SEND_REQUEST API call. Communications Manager ensures that the request is routed to the appropriate 3270 session according to the profile you configured. You also must logon to the appropriate 3270 session and start the host router programs (CMSSERV and/or MVSSERV), before using SRPI. Multiple applications can use SRPI concurrently; however, each 3270 session can handle only one call at a time. Calls are queued if a session is busy; however, if SRPI is active you cannot use the session for interactive work or file transfers.

SRPI's limitation is that it uses 3270 terminal emulation, instead of a peer-to-peer protocol such as APPC. Terminal emulation is a very clumsy protocol in unattended client/server environments (that do not have a human sitting at a terminal). The reason for this clumsiness is that your application has to anticipate all the hung-terminal conditions and recover from them without human intervention. IBM made a statement of direction that SRPI will eventually run on APPC. When this happens, SRPI will become a useful client/server protocol for requesting mainframe services (SRPI's design is protocol independent).

IEEE 802.2

IEEE 802.2 API provides a low-level interface to the 802.2 Local Area Network Logical Link Control (LLC) layer. 802.2 is the ISO standard that defines the protocol for accessing LAN link layer services in a media-access independent manner. The LLC interfaces to the Media Access Control (MAC) link protocols such as Token Ring (IEEE 802.5) and CSMA/CD (IEEE 802.3). Communications Manager provides NDIS drivers for IBM Token Ring, Ethernet V 2.0 (also known as Ethernet DIX for DEC, Intel, and Xerox), IEEE 802.3 (the new Ethernet), and the IBM PC Network.

The 802.2 API provides a set of commands for directly controlling the LAN adapters, such as Open and Close. The API supports two types of service: *Connectionless* and *Connection-oriented*. The Connectionless service provides datagram-like "unreliable" frame transmissions between Service Access Points (SAPs). The Connection-oriented service provides reliable sequenced packet exchanges over a session between link station interfaces. The number of link stations that can be supported is adapter dependent. For example, an IBM Token Ring Adapter/A supports 64 link stations.

You should program to the IEEE 802.2 API only if you have serious memory constraints and cannot afford NetBIOS or APPC, or if you need to provide special network utilities that require an intimate control of the communication facilities (it's like programming in assembler versus a high-level language).

Asynchronous Communications Device Interface (ACDI)

The Asynchronous Communications Device Interface (ACDI) provides a low-level programming interface to asynchronous serial ports. ACDI can perform concurrent communications over multiple serial ports (three on a PS/2), although only one application at a time can use a particular port. However, if an application is waiting for a call-in or call-back, ACDI will give control of that port to another waiting application.

ACDI supports modem commands including AutoDial and AutoAnswer, which you can use to customize and automate dialing procedures, such as redialing a busy number. ACDI provides device-independent services for setting line parameters and for device connection control. For example, ACDI allows you to set and read the following parameters: bit rate, word length, flow control, parity, time-outs, stop bits, modem command strings, and AutoAnswer controls. An application can send and receive data through a buffered (block I/O) interface.

ACDI provides a useful LAN redirection feature. Instead of attaching modems to every PC, the ACDI redirection API allows a LAN-attached client machine to use serial ports COM1, COM2, and COM3 on a server as if they were located on the local machine. The *async gateway server* is a non-dedicated PC which provides serial ports, modems, and telephone line connection services to its clients. In addition, the server machine must run IBM's **LAN Asynchronous Connection Server (LANACS)** program. The ACDI redirector communicates with the LANACS server using NetBIOS.

The main benefit of ACDI is that it makes it easy to develop an asynchronous communications program without requiring detailed knowledge of the hardware, device drivers, or the multitasking environment. An ACDI application should work without requiring modification if the hardware or device drivers are changed.

ACDI's main weakness is that it does not provide a reliable session service, such as that provided by NetBIOS, APPC, and 802.2. You will have to code your own packet sequencing and control protocol if you need such a service. However, ACDI does provide some limited error-detection services. It can detect the following error conditions: parity errors, framing errors, overflow and overrun errors, device errors, and line errors. Another ACDI weakness is that LANACS is a DOS program. You can, of course, run it from within OS/2 and share the server with other functions.

X.25

X.25's API service provides a low-level interface to packet switched networks. Much of the X.25 interface is concerned with interfacing the local data communication equipment to the packet switched network. Through the API service, you request a virtual-circuit and, from then on, you can send and receive information on your virtual circuit. The virtual circuit can be permanent or switched. X.25 allows you to multiplex virtual circuits over the same communication interface (Communications Manager limits you to 128 virtual circuits; the X.25 standard supports 4095). The virtual circuits provide a reliable end-to-end service. Communications Manager allows up to forty X.25 applications to run concurrently. Incoming calls are routed to the appropriate X.25 application. X.25 provides two facilities for recovering from errors: reset and restart. Reset is used to reinitialize a virtual circuit (the sequence counts are reset). Restart causes all virtual circuits to be cleared.

Communications Manager's implementation of X.25 conforms to CCITT's 1980 and 1984 recommendations. Two complementary types of X.25 are provided by Communication Manager:

1. *For SNA applications*, the Qualified Link Level Control (QLLC) allows up to 128 SNA switched or virtual circuits. A virtual circuit has a maximum bandwidth of 64 Kb/s. SNA applications such as APPC, 3270 terminal emulation, SRPI, and EHLLAPI may use X.25 through the SNA QLLC protocol to communicate with other SNA remote applications.
2. *For non-SNA applications*, the API can be used to support multiple concurrent applications across X.25 virtual network sessions. The X.25 API provides verbs that enable an application to interact with a PSDN. Functions are provided to make and receive calls, allocate and clear virtual circuits, transfer data, and reset the virtual circuit.

Both the SNA and non-SNA applications require, and may share, the same IBM X.25 Interface Co-Processor/2 adapter (the C2X adapter card) to attach to one or more X.25 packet-switched networks. The C2X outboard adapter code is loaded onto the co-processor when X.25 is started as a Communications Manager task. The X.25 DLL can control and manage multiple adapter cards, and it routes incoming calls to the target programs and outgoing calls to the appropriate X.25 virtual circuit.

EHLLAPI

EHLLAPI (pronounced "ee-ha-lap-pee") was introduced by IBM in 1986 as a generic API for accessing terminal emulation functions. EHLLAPI is mainly used by PCs to communicate with existing mainframe applications without altering the code on the mainframe side. It is a cost-effective way to extend the capabilities and lifetimes of the huge inventory of existing IBM 3270 applications. EHLLAPI was designed to be terminal emulator independent. The Communications Manager implementation of EHLLAPI works with 3270 terminal emulators for S/370 mainframes, and with the 5250 terminal emulators for AS/400 minicomputers. Prior to EHLLAPI, programs had to be tediously written in assembler to manipulate the host data streams, and a program written for a particular terminal emulator would not work with another terminal emulator.

Generally speaking, EHLLAPI applications are not difficult to develop. The API consists of over 30 function calls that handle an assortment of terminal operator functions, from simple automatic host logon to the complexities of starting and monitoring an unattended host task. Developers can create OS/2 applications to take on tasks formerly performed by a human operator, such as sending keystrokes to the host or capturing information from a 3270 or 5250 "screen."

When writing an EHLLAPI program, you should think of yourself as an operator interacting with a host through a 3270 or 5250 terminal emulation session. Your program should be able to automate tasks performed by an operator, such as sending keystrokes to the host, requesting host update information, and copying to and from a screen. EHLLAPI API provides calls that perform these functions. You should be able to write applications that automate console operations, filter host messages, and monitor host response time and availability. You can use EHLLAPI to customize PC screens to display only certain fields from a host screen, or you can make a single screen from many screens. You can also run multiple host sessions and display the results on a single composite screen. The data received from the host by EHLLAPI is in the PC memory and is not necessarily displayed on the screen. The EHLLAPI API verbs can be categorized as follows:

1. Operator Services that provide you with controls such as query the system and session status, set session parameters, send_key, wait, pause, reset system, query host update, and start/stop host notification.
2. Presentation Services that allow you to manipulate a block of memory on the PC (the *presentation space*), which represents what the host displays on a terminal screen. It is up to your application to display any, all, or none of the received data. You can use the presentation services to query and set the cursor location, query field attributes, position, and length. You can copy field contents or the presentation space to/from a string. You can search fields or the entire presentation space for string matches or updates.
3. Device Services that allow you to intercept key strokes and to reserve or release a device.
4. Communication Services that allow you to send and receive files.

You should consider EHLLAPI as a useful tool that allows you to work with existing host applications. It is by no means a reliable peer-to-peer protocol that could be used by serious cooperative or client/server applications.

NETWORK MANAGEMENT

Network Management features are built into all the levels of Communication Manager (see Figure 7-8). Errors are detected, logged and can be forwarded as network alerts to an IBM host running Netview. Netview allows a network to be remotely managed from a central location and provides tools that allow an operator to stay current on error conditions and monitor network performance. Communications Manager supports the TRANSFER_MS_DATA API call that allows an application to send its own alerts and messages to Netview. Hardware-related errors from SDLC, ASYNC, IBM Token Ring, PC Network, Ethernet, and the X.25 co-processor can be recorded in a local error log and also sent to Netview as a generic alert if a host connection is provided. The generic alert contains information about the type of error detected, probable causes of failure, and recommended action.

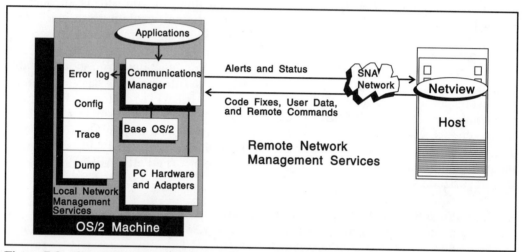

Figure 7-8. Communications Manager Network Management Facilities.

The Communications Manager also supports the receipt of remote commands from Netview. The commands are passed to the program that requests them. For example, a command may be sent to run remote diagnostics on a device and to send back the results to Netview. Netview can also query vital PC data such as machine type, model number, and the name, version, and release of the installed Extended Services software. The **Service Point Application Router (SPA Router)** is the Communications Manager component that receives commands from a NetView Host and routes them to the appropriate application (any OS/2 program on that machine). The router allows the same command to be broadcast to multiple applications.

A companion process, the **Remote Operations Service (ROP)**, receives OS/2 requests from the SPA Router and executes them on the local OS/2 machine. Currently, ROP executes any OS/2 Command Line Interface program that does not require user input.

The Communications Manager also provides local utilities for problem determination, running traces of the flow of commands and data across interfaces, and for displaying and printing error information. The utilities can be run under program control, allowing user written programs to monitor error incidents selectively and then to take appropriate action. Message pop-ups on the screen can be suppressed making it easy to run unattended diagnostics.

Common Services API

The Common Services API provides general services that can be used with any of the communication APIs. You would use Common Services to gather, process, and send problem determination data. For example, you can use the CONVERT API verb to translate a character string from/to ASCII and EBCDIC. The DEFINE_TRACE verb turns on or off the Communications Manager trace. The LOG_MESSAGE verb allows you to append a message to the Communications Manager's system log file; this message can be displayed through the message services. The TRANSFER_MS_DATA verb allows you to send alerts to a System/370 host running Netview or you could have the alert stored in the Communications Manager error log for local display.

Communcations Manager Packaging

The Communications Manager is packaged with the Database Manager as part of OS/2 **Extended Services**. The product comes in two flavors:

1. *Extended Services*—a low-cost product that only supports a standalone Database Manager together with Communications Manager. This product sells for $595.
2. *Extended Services with Database Server*—a more costly product that provides a networked Database Manager server function for MS-DOS, MS-Windows, and OS/2 clients. This server product also includes the Communications Manager and sells for $1995.

Chapter 8

TCP/IP for OS/2:
The Unix Connection

In this second chapter of the communications trilogy, we explore TCP/IP for OS/2, a product that opens up our client/server platform to the Unix world (see light area in Figure 8-1). This product goes far beyond mere communications. The very rich protocol suite extends the reach of OS/2 deep inside the world of Unix and provides many levels of *interoperability* with Unix in all its variants.

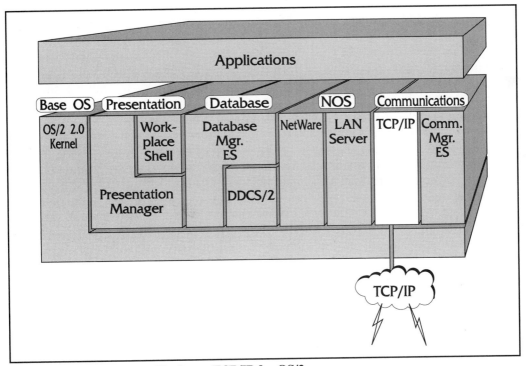

Figure 8-1. Client/Server Platform: TCP/IP for OS/2.

The reach of TCP/IP for OS/2 extends beyond the world of Unix. The product, for example, interoperates with IBM's TCP/IP products for VM, MVS, MS-DOS, AS/400, the RS/6000, and the AIX family. TCP/IP is also the protocol of choice in heterogeneous internet environments that include universities and government agencies. Over two hundred vendors sell TCP/IP communications products, and that market is rapidly growing.

TCP/IP FOR OS/2

TCP/IP Version 1.2 for OS/2, shipped by IBM in October 1991, provides a complete TCP/IP protocol suite on an OS/2 platform. In addition, the product incorporates a number of Unix network services such as the Berkeley sockets, SunOS RPC, HP/Apollo's NCS, and MIT's Kerberos authentication services. The TCP/IP product allows OS/2 to play both a client and server role in Unix networks. Figure 8-2 shows the OS/2 TCP/IP stack components.

The TCP/IP for OS/2 Stack

When dealing with communications, you'll always be staring at a layered diagram that shows a protocol stack resembling a wedding cake (Figure 8-2). Unfortunately, the analogy ends there. Instead of chocolate, coconut, and vanilla, you get layers of strange sounding names and acronyms that form the common language of a communication subculture. TCP/IP provides an exotic subculture that has been evolving since the pioneer days of networking. This is the good news. The bad news is that when it comes to acronyms, TCP/IP makes even SNA look pale by comparison. So how do we tell you all there is to know about TCP/IP and its extended network services?

We will present the broad features of TCP/IP for OS/2 by dividing the product into five functional layers: physical network, internet services, transport services, session services, and application services (see Figure 8-2). As usual, we will start at the bottom of the stack and work our way upwards. By the end of this overview, you will be a master of TCP/IP acronyms. Programmers, of course, are mostly interested in the APIs that give their programs access to the services of a particular communications layer. We will cover these APIs after we explain the major TCP/IP features.

The Physical Network

The TCP/IP protocol does not specify the physical or link layers. These are typically provided by vendor-specific implementations. The OS/2 TCP/IP product provides a very rich set of link layer and physical connectivity options. It does that by using the same physical and link layer protocols that were developed for the Communications

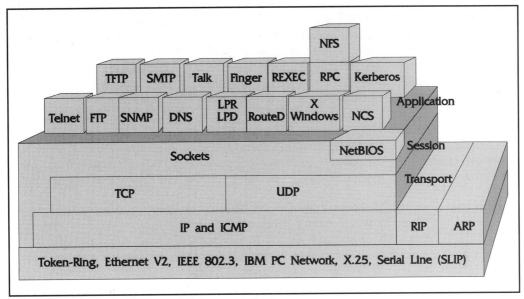

Figure 8-2.   The TCP/IP for OS/2 Protocol Stack.

Manager and LAN Server. The TCP/IP stack interfaces with NDIS drivers and the 802.2 logical link layer. This means TCP/IP will work over any NDIS compliant Token Ring or Ethernet LAN adapter. And, because NDIS allows multiple protocol stacks to access the same adapter, TCP/IP can happily coexist with OS/2's other protocol stacks. TCP/IP, like Communications Manager, can concurrently support up to four LAN adapters on a single machine. The product also supports IBM's PC Network.

The **Serial Line Internet Protocol (SLIP)** is a TCP/IP specific ASYNC protocol that lets you to set up a point-to-point connection over a serial line using an RS-232 modem connection over a telephone line. You can use SLIP to access a remote TCP/IP network from your local host, or to route datagrams between two TCP/IP networks. The maximum ASYNC speed is 19.2 Kb/s.

TCP/IP also provides Wide Area Network support using the X.25 protocol. It uses the same X.25 driver as Communications Manager and requires the X.25 Coprocessor/2 adapter. The maximum line speed over X.25 is 64 Kb/s.

The Internet Services

The TCP/IP network layer creates a logical network called an *internet* out of one or more physical networks. Each computer on the internet is assigned at least one unique 32-bit internet address consisting of two parts: a network number and a local address. A unique network number is assigned to each network when it connects to the internet. Packets are routed through the internet using this global addressing scheme. A *port* is an end point for communication between applications; it provides queues for sending and receiving data. Each port has a port number for identification. A *socket* is a unique address that combines a port number with an internet address. The TCP/IP programs you develop will most likely communicate at the socket level. TCP/IP provides several protocols that support the internet and feed it routing information. Most of these protocols are totally transparent to your applications. But we still should quickly review them since some of the acronyms are culturally significant.

- **Internet Protocol (IP)** provides the basic mechanism for routing packets in the internet. IP is not a reliable communication protocol. It does not understand the relationships between packets and does not perform retransmissions. IP requires higher-level protocols such as TCP or UDP to provide a reliable class of service.

- **Internet Control Message Protocol (ICMP)** is an internal protocol for passing control messages between gateways, routers, and workstations.[1] ICMP provides general feedback about problems in the internet environment. For example, ICMP messages are used when a packet cannot reach its destination, or when a workstation PINGs to check if another workstation is available.

- **Routing Information Protocol (RIP)** is a dynamic routing protocol for passing routing messages between gateways, routers, and workstations. This is the information that is used to dynamically maintain routing tables that reflect the state of the internet. It is the job of routers to discover the best path from one point to another within an internet. A router must know the location of every node within its domain. This knowledge is obtained dynamically through periodic RIP packet exchanges between the router and the nodes in its domain (every 30 seconds or so). RIP maintains only the path to the next router; it does not store the entire network path to a destination. RIP allows an OS/2 machine to function as a non-dedicated IP internet router.

- **Address Resolution Protocol (ARP)** is another internal protocol used by TCP/IP to maintain and refresh its internet address mapping tables. When an application sends an internet packet, IP requests the appropriate address mapping. If the mapping is not in the mapping table, an ARP broadcast packet (*where is?*) is sent to all the nodes on the network requesting the physical address of the target IP address. The ARP response maps the IP target address to a physical address such

---

[1] Some background information can be helpful here. *Bridges* are computers (or devices) that interconnect LANs using link layer routing information and physical addresses; protocols that do not support a network layer, like NetBIOS, are bridged. *Routers* interconnect LANs using protocol-dependent network layer routing information. Routers create and maintain dynamic routing tables of the destinations they know about. They are typically used with protocols such as: TCP/IP, IPX/SPX, APPN, XNS, AppleTalk, and OSI. *Multiprotocol Routers* support different combinations of network layer protocols. *BRouters* provide both bridging and multiprotocol routing functions; they are quite popular today.

as that of a Token Ring or Ethernet adapter. ARPs require network hardware that supports broadcasts. Bridges repeat ARPs, while routers act as "firewalls" that block the flow of ARPs.

The Transport Services

The transport services of TCP/IP consists of two protocols that provide end-to-end transport services.

- **User Datagram Protocol (UDP)** provides a datagram service. Like the NetBIOS datagrams, TCP/IP datagrams are unreliable but fast. Applications that require reliable delivery of streams of data should use TCP instead of datagrams.

- **Transmission Control Protocol (TCP)** provides a reliable, session-based service for the delivery of sequenced packets across an internet.

The Session Services

The Session services provide a friendly environment for programs that use the TCP/IP transport services. The TCP/IP standard does not specify how application programs interact with the transport protocols. TCP/IP for OS/2 provides two interfaces to the transport services: Berkeley Sockets and NetBIOS.

- **Berkeley Sockets** provide a friendly API interface to the services of TCP, UDP, ICMP, and IP. Sockets are TCP/IP's premier peer-to-peer API, they were introduced in 1981 as the Unix BSD 4.2 generic interface that would provide UNIX-to-UNIX communications over networks. In 1985, SunOS introduced NFS and RPC over sockets. Sockets are also part of UNIX SVR4. Sockets define how an operating system provides network I/O using, whenever possible, a Unix file read/write paradigm. Sockets allow data to be transmitted and received simultaneously (they are duplex) and provide a peer-to-peer communications service.

- **NetBIOS** provides a send/receive type of interface to the transport services. The NetBIOS interface makes it easy to port to the TCP/IP environment communications programs that are popular in the PC world. The TCP/IP NetBIOS implementation is essentially an emulation layer that sits on top of sockets. It is not native to the TCP/IP protocol.

The TCP/IP Application Layer

The application layer of TCP/IP for OS/2 includes a long list of network applications and utilities. These applications usually reside on well-known sockets that are reserved for them.

- **Telnet** is the TCP/IP standard protocol for remote terminal connection. An OS/2 machine can be configured as a Telnet terminal emulator (client) or as a Telnet terminal server. Over seven terminal emulator protocols are supported including 3270, dumb ASCII, and VT100. PMANT is a PM 3270 terminal emulator. Telnet uses TCP as its transport mechanism.

- **File Transfer Protocol (FTP)** is the TCP/IP standard protocol for transferring files from one machine to another. FTP supports the transfer of both binary and ASCII files. FTP also supports the OS/2's HPFS file system and its long file names. An OS/2 TCP/IP node can be an FTP client, or server, or both. An FTP client includes a PM front-end that graphically supports functions such as listing remote directories, changing the current remote directory, creating and removing remote directories, and transferring one or more files in a single request. The client also allows simultaneous connections to FTP servers within a single session. The FTP server provides security features such as user account and password validation. FTP uses TCP as its transport mechanism. FTP services can be invoked through API calls.

- **Trivial File Transfer Protocol (TFTP)**, like FTP, provides a file transfer protocol. Unlike FTP, however, TFTP cannot be used to list or change directories and does not support client authentication. TFTP builds on top of the UDP transport layer.

- **Simple Mail Transfer Protocol (SMTP)** provides an E-mail protocol for transferring electronic mail messages from a client (sender) to a server (receiver). You do not interface directly with SMTP in the OS/2 environment. Instead, you use **LaMail**, a PM application that provides a user interface to **SendMail** which, in turn, uses SMTP to send the mail to its destination. The LaMail program allows you to view, create, edit, spell check, sort, and send mail. It also allows you to organize mail in folders and provides an icon that changes when it receives mail.

- **BOOTP** allows a client machine that knows its hardware address to get an internet address from a server. Both the BOOTP client and server are supported by TCP/IP for OS/2.

- **Domain Name System (DNS)** is an online "distributed database" system used to map human-readable, symbolic names into IP addresses. DNS servers throughout the IP internet implement a hierarchical naming convention that gives local network administrators the freedom to assign machine names and addresses within their domains. An internet name consists of domain labels separated by periods; each label to the right of a period represents an increasingly higher domain level: *machine.subdomain.subdomain.rootdomain.* You must provide an ETC\HOSTS file, containing entries that map symbolic names to internet addresses. You can override that by placing a RESOLV file in the ETC subdirectory. When the name resolver program finds the RESOLV file, it sends the name resolution request to a foreign name server before using the local HOSTS file. The HOSTS file is used on small internets to avoid the hierarchical naming system. The NSLOOKUP function allows a user to interactively query a Domain Name Server for information.

•   **Simple Network Management Protocol (SNMP)** is the de facto standard for managing TCP/IP multivendor networks. SNMP separates the job of network management into two types of tasks: agents and managers. The *agent* tasks monitor the network nodes on which they reside and execute remote commands. The agent tasks act on behalf of the network managers. The *manager* tasks run on a network management station and communicate with the distributed agents through remote commands (called sets) to provide an overall view of the network's status. The manager tasks are the clients. However, agents can also send unsolicited alerts, called traps, to the manager to inform it of important events such as errors, cold starts, and authentication failures (see Figure 8-3). **SNMPTRAP** is a PM program that displays SNMP alerts received from any agent on the network. **PMPING**, another PM program, can graphically display the status of all workstations defined in a user table. It does that by "pinging" each workstation. **PING**, the acronym for Packet InterNet Groper, is an echo protocol used in "Are you alive?" type of queries. SNMP defines the protocol for communications between agents and managers. OS/2 SNMP can act as both a managing system and a managed system.

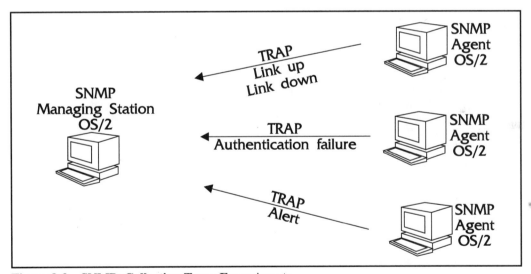

Figure 8-3. SNMP: Collecting Traps From Agents.

The heart of SNMP open management is the **Management Information Base (MIB)**. The MIB defines groups of information fields that the SNMP agents use to store device status. The standard defines the data items that the managed workstation must collect and the operations that are allowed on that data. The information from each agent is kept in the agent's MIB database. The MIB variables are grouped as objects. For example, an Ethernet adapter (agent) may collect statistics on network utilization, CRC errors, and collisions, and then save them in a MIB object. The manager task can query the appropriate MIB objects on the agent to create a report. MIB allows any vendor's management station to access statistics and parameters of any device, regardless of its maker, as long as it supports MIB.

Most SNMP vendors today, including TCP/IP for OS/2, implement the MIB II standard, which specifies 57 additional managed objects. An OS/2 manager task has the ability to obtain values of individual MIB variables using SNMP (see Figure 8-4). The values include performance related statistical variables, network device status, and many others.

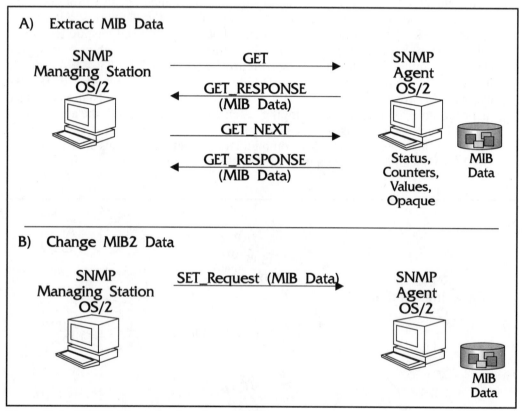

Figure 8-4.   SNMP: Manager, Agents, and MIBs.

- **Kerberos Authentication System** provides additional levels of security on client/server networks by checking authorization at the user level rather than at the node level. The Kerberos server identifies clients and authenticates connection requests. It then grants an encrypted ticket to the client for a particular service. The key provides a way for authenticated clients to prove their identity to other servers across the network. The client must present its key to the provider of the requested service. Clients must obtain a separate ticket from the Kerberos authentication server for each specific service. Kerberos clients and servers never transmit passwords on the network. They use their password, however, to decode enciphered tickets.

- **Remote Printing (LPR and LPD)** provides both client and server support for remote printing. This application allows you to spool files remotely to a line printer daemon (LPD). The line printer client (LPR) sends the file to be printed to a specified printer on the server station.

- **X Windows** is a client/server presentation services protocol. A "server," in X Windows terminology, is a workstation that allows its display screen and mouse events to be monitored by a remote X Windows client. An X server provides a way for remote programs on the network to share the real estate on the server workstation's screen (see Figure 8-5). In this respect, X Windows provides a modern version of the traditional host/terminal arrangement. You can think of the X Window server as a terminal with GUI-like graphics, and the X Window client as the terminal monitoring application. Unlike a traditional terminal, the X server is an intelligent PC that can service many clients at the same time. One client may display a bar chart in a window, another may interact with a user through a menu, and a third client may display an icon to inform the user that the meeting with the boss was rescheduled. TCP/IP for OS/2 provides server support to X Windows client applications. The X server function uses PM as the window manager. IBM will provide X Window client capability in a future release of OS/2.

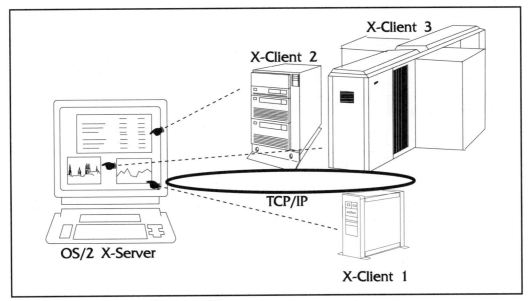

Figure 8-5. X Windows Clients and Servers.

- **Talk** allows end users to send interactive messages, as opposed to the asynchronous mail capabilities of SMTP. When a local node sends a Talk request to a target node, the user of that machine is immediately notified of the connection request. If it is accepted, the two partners can engage in an electronic conversation. This is a synchronous form of conversation.

- **FINGER** provides an interface for querying the current status of a remote host or a user ID on a remote host. FINGER uses TCP as the underlying protocol.

- **RouteD**, pronounced "Route-Dee," is a routing server program (a daemon) that uses RIP to dynamically create and maintain network routing tables. The RIP protocol arranges to have gateways and routers periodically broadcast their routing tables to neighbors. Using this information, an OS/2 RouteD server can update its routing tables. RouteD can determine if a new route has been created, if a route is temporarily unavailable, or if a more efficient route exists.

- **Sun Remote Procedure Call (SunRPC)** is a programming interface that allows programs to invoke remote functions on a server machine. With SunRPC, the combination of a server address, program number, version number, and a procedure number specifies a remote procedure. A client makes a procedure call to send a request to the server. The RPC software collects values for the parameters, forms a message, and sends it to the remote server. The server receives the request, unpacks the parameters, calls the procedure, and sends the reply back to the client. The procedure call then returns to the client. The SunRPC uses the *eXternal Data Representation (XDR)*, a machine-independent protocol for representing data. Sun-RPC, like all RPCs, hides most of the details of the network and extends the local procedure call to distributed environments. The SunRPC is used by NFS and is freely licensed by Sun Microsystems as part of its *Open Network Computing (ONC)* environment. Over 90 vendors offer ports of SunRPC, XDR, and NFS. ONC has been around for quite some time (since 1985) and has an installed base of over a million nodes. The OS/2 implementation of SunRPC is almost identical to the SunRPC, except for some very minor differences that will be explained in the sockets programming chapter.

- **Network Computing System (NCS)** is the Apollo (now HP) RPC toolkit. This toolkit (with extensions and enhancements from DEC) was chosen as the foundation for OSF's DCE RPC implementation. The NCS toolkit consists of three components: the RPC run-time library, the Location Broker, and the Network Interface Definition Language (NIDL) stub compiler.[2]

  NIDL allows programmers to specify the procedures and parameters that a server exports to clients using an *interface definition language*. You run the definition file through the NIDL compiler to produce C source code stubs and header files for both the client and server (Figure 8-6). These stubs can then be compiled and linked with the client and server code. The client stub packages the parameters in an RPC packet, converts the data, calls the *RPC run-time library*, and waits for the server's reply. On the server side, the server stub unpacks the parameters, calls the remote procedure, packages the results, and sends the reply to the client.

---

[2] This is not the OS/2 DCE product. DCE RPC contains many added features. Any product that uses the DCE label must go through the OSF validation cycle.

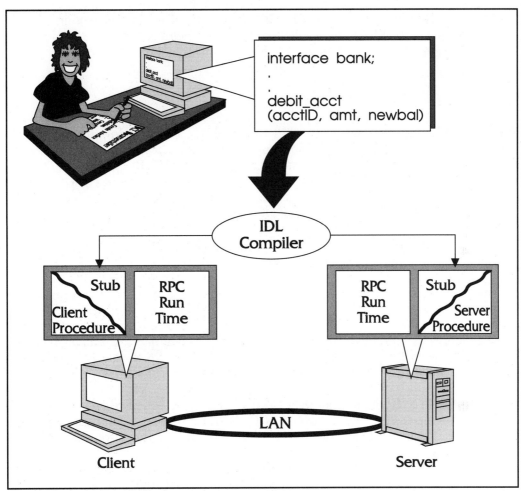

Figure 8-6.   **The Mechanics of an RPC Stub Compiler.**

The *Location Broker* provides clients with run-time information about the locations of objects and interfaces, including procedure names and calling syntax. The NCS RPC uses sockets for interprocess communications. The location broker makes it possible to bind the address of the RPC server at run time. Servers must register their sockets, objects, and interfaces with the location broker. Clients can issue requests for the location of objects by object ID, type, or interface.

- **Network File System (NFS)** is the OS/2 implementation of Sun Microsystems' very popular distributed file system. NFS uses SunRPC to communicate between the client and the server. NFS supports a hierarchical file structure. OS/2 provides both a full client and server implementation of the NFS system. It allows users to share files with each other, much the same way that LAN Server/Requester works. It also allows a Unix machine, or any NFS client, to share files with an OS/2 machine. The product also supports software that translates between OS/2 and Unix text file formats (mostly end-of-line format differences).

- **Remote Execution Protocol (REXEC)** is a protocol for the invocation of commands (and getting back the results) on a remote machine. The OS/2 implementation of REXEC provides automatic logon and authentication.

The TCP/IP APIs

It should be evident by now that TCP/IP for OS/2 is a well endowed product. Its services and protocols transcend simple connectivity, and they allow OS/2 to interoperate with the various operating systems that use the TCP/IP environment. Your programs can take advantage of all this good stuff by plugging into the right APIs. The product provides seven API interfaces that you can tap into: Berkeley Sockets, NetBIOS, FTP, SunRPC, NCS RPC, SNMP DPI, and Kerberos.

Berkeley Sockets API provide the least common denominator for writing portable communications programs in the TCP/IP environment. OS/2 supports three socket types: stream, datagram, and raw. Stream and datagram sockets interface to the transport layer, and raw sockets interface to the network layer. In addition to peer-to-peer communications, the OS/2 socket API also provides network service APIs that allow you to obtain internet addressing information, and to convert symbolic names to internet addresses (or domain name resolution). The socket interface can be expanded to provide new socket types for additional services. The OS/2 socket API consists of 57 function calls. We will be covering the socket peer-to-peer services in Part III.

NetBIOS for TCP/IP requires an IBM Corrective Service Diskette update to run with TCP/IP V1.2 for OS/2. The **NetBIOS/TCP** control program is compatible with the IBM/Microsoft NetBIOS specifications and also provides facilities for internet operations (these extensions are compatible with RFC 1001 and RFC 1002). The TCP/IP NetBIOS interface supports naming services, datagrams, and sessions. Sessions use TCP; datagrams use UDP. The main weakness of NetBIOS/TCP is that it is an emulation layer not integrated into Ring 0 like the rest of the TCP/IP transports.

FTP API allows you to transfer files between FTP clients and servers and between two FTP servers without sending the file to a local machine. You can append information to a remote file and delete files from a remote machine. You can manipulate the remote directory. And, you can use two flavors of ping to determine whether a machine is alive before attempting a file transfer. Your applications can use this API to talk to up to 256 FTP servers at the same time. The FTP API consists of 19 function calls.

SunRPC and NCS RPC both provide APIs that facilitate writing client/server applications. The bad news is that you must choose between SunRPC and NCS RPC; whatever services you create will not interoperate across those two environments. Your choice of RPC will lock you into an RPC compiler environment. The "good news" is that the industry is currently standardizing around a third RPC, called **DCE**. The DCE

RPC is a derivative of NCS.[3] So, if you care about portability and interoperability, we recommend that you write to sockets for now, and use the DCE RPC when it becomes available. If you do not have interoperability requirements, you may find that the OS/2 implementation of NCS provides a more complete set of services with its NIDL compiler and Location Broker. The NCS RPC API set consists of 26 function calls. The combined SunRPC and XDR API sets consists of 83 function calls.

SNMP DPI API, a short for *Distributed Programming Interface*, is used to dynamically add, delete, or replace network management variables in the local MIB without recompiling the SNMP agent. This lets you create subagents that extend the function provided by the OS/2 SNMP agent. Your subagents can define their own MIB variables and register them with the SNMP agent. When requests for these variables are received from managing stations, the SNMP agent passes the request to the subagent. The subagent returns a response to the agent, which is sent back in a reply packet to the requesting station. The SNMP DPI API consists of 7 function calls.

Kerberos API includes calls that can be used by both your client and server programs. Kerberos provides API calls for creating and reading authentication requests using encrypted or unencrypted messages. The API calls also provide the ticketing services. The Kerberos API consists of 12 function calls.

TCP/IP for OS/2 Packaging

The TCP/IP for OS/2 Version 1.2 is packaged as a base kit with optional function kits. The *Base Kit* sells for $200. It includes the functions described in this section minus X.25, X Windows, NFS, the Programmer's Toolkit, and NetBIOS. The *Total Kit*, which includes all the functions described here, sells for $650. The *Programmer's Toolkit* sells for an additional $500. NetBIOS for TCP/IP is a separate product.

---

[3] Sun is, of course, aggressively backing its own RPC standard, which is available on over one million computers (mostly because of NFS). The Unix International consortium backs SunRPC but also supports the DCE RPC. Netwise offers SunRPC tools on almost every hardware platform.

Chapter 9

LAN Server and NetWare: The NOS Dimension

This chapter concludes our communications trilogy by discussing the network operating system extensions of the OS/2 client/server platform. This function is provided by two products: the IBM LAN Server and the NetWare LAN Requester for OS/2 (see light area in Figure 9-1). You will rarely use both products on the same network since they provide an equivalent set of functions. We must, however, discuss both products to give you the broadest set of choices.

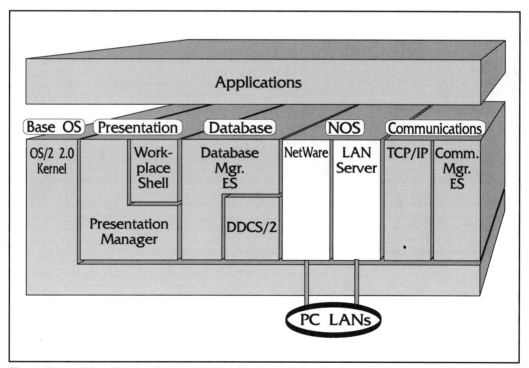

Figure 9-1. Client/Server Platform: The Network Operating System Component.

IBM LAN SERVER VERSION 2.0

The IBM LAN Server program transforms OS/2 into a full-fledged *Network Operating System (NOS)*, which allows applications to become "networked" without being rewritten. The beauty of a Network Operating System is that it lets you get all this network power through your standard OS/2 commands and APIs. The reach of the OS/2 application programmer is now extended beyond the physical boundaries of a single machine, while the network is transparent to the application.

LAN Server and LAN Man

The IBM LAN Server is the most widely used OEM variant of Microsoft's LAN Manager, popularly known as *LAN Man*. LAN Man makes the network an integral part of OS/2 and provides interoperability with MS-NET and PC-LAN workstations running MS-DOS and Windows. LAN Manager/X extends the platform to UNIX System V (the first release provides fairly complete support for Named Pipes interoperability). Microsoft also plans to integrate LAN Man's functions into NT (as NT Server) as well as support its current OS/2 version of the product. The IBM LAN Server is fully compatible with LAN Man at the API level and functional levels. LAN Server supports LAN Man clients (and vice versa), both utilize the same security system, and the same applications will run on both platforms. The LAN Server product is functionally a superset of LAN Man 2.0.[1]

With LAN Man and LAN Server, you can write your own network servers as simple OS/2 programs. Your programs can use OS/2's native Named Pipes protocol to communicate with MS-DOS, MS-Windows, OS/2, and Macintosh clients.[2] Your programs can also take advantage of all the built-in server features such as network security, audit trails, single domain multiserver management, and fault-tolerance. We explain what this all means later in this section. NetWare 3.2 will provide a similar kind of environment for OS/2 programs when it becomes available.

IBM's contractual rights to Microsoft's LAN Man code ends with the current version of the code. IBM intends to continue to evolve LAN Server toward full interoperability with NetWare. In addition, LAN Server will continue to interoperate with its LAN Man sibling, Windows, and NT when it is available. Most importantly, LAN Server will

---

[1] IBM owns the LAN Server 2.0 code and has developed in-house skills by adding new features such as network aliases and dynamic resource sharing. LAN Server is IBM's "strategic" network operating system product and will be developed independently from Microsoft.

[2] Macintosh support is provided by Miramar System's **MACLAN Connect**. IBM is also working on Macintosh clients with Apple as part of the Apple/IBM agreements.

implement the powerful OSF Distributed Computing Environment (DCE) on the OS/2 platform.

NetWare interoperability will be delivered in three phases. The first phase (today) provides client coexistence with NetWare. LAN Server and NetWare clients can use the same adapter at the same time. The second phase (very soon) will provide a single client for both NetWare and LAN Server. That client can access either NetWare or LAN Server services. The third phase will provide the transparent integration of LAN Server and NetWare; both will probably use features of the Distributed Computing Environment (DCE) for interoperability.

IBM has stated that LAN Server will be its DCE-based enterprise server. Future versions of the product will be portable and platform-independent. LAN Server will be ported to IBM's other SAA and AIX platforms and used to create a heterogeneous network operating system layer. The DCE LAN Server will adhere to open systems standards for network naming (by providing multidomain hierarchies), implement the DCE Distributed File System, and provide three-way authentication using Kerberos. It will also support the DCE RPC and adhere to OSF's DME standard for system management. This will become clearer after we explain the DCE and SAA architectures in Chapter 11. [3]

The Network Operating System

The LAN Server is a classic implementation of a client/server architecture. The server machine acts as a *central hub* that fulfills work requests from requesters (i.e., clients) all over the network (see Figure 9-2). The server forms the core of the LAN Server application. At least one machine on the network must run the server function before requesters can perform anything useful. Network Servers can be added to the network to provide more resources, remove bottlenecks, and scale an application upward (or downward). Network devices, programs, and data can be centralized on a single server or distributed on multiple servers as the environment dictates. Your LAN Server machines can be dedicated or they can be running other programs concurrently with the server function. The modular capabilities of LAN Server appear to be limited only by checkbook constraints.

From a programmer's viewpoint, LAN Server offers flexibility and the capability to distribute an application easily, without having to learn a communication API. In essence, it transforms OS/2 into a powerful Network Operating System. This aug-

---

[3] This public information was provided in **LAN Server Directions**, IBM White Paper (April, 1991). More details were provided by Jeanine J. Roadhouse, IBM senior planning manager, in **DATAMATION** (December 15, 1991).

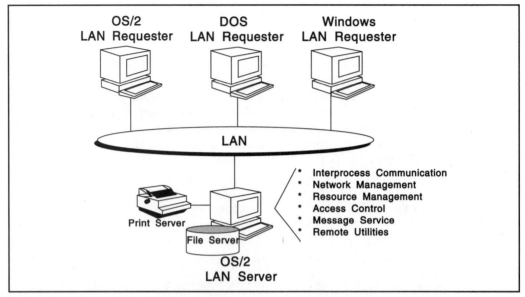

Figure 9-2.   The OS/2 LAN Server.

mented OS/2 opens up a universe of network services. The repertoire of network functions falls into the following categories:

- Transparent access to remote resources
- Network device and queue management
- Remote network applications support
- Single systems image
- Network services
- Network management and administration
- Network security and access controls
- Remote Named Pipes
- Fault tolerant features
- Open NDIS adapter support
- An open network API

Together these functions provide a very complete Network Operating System. We explain the Network Operating System enhancements in the sections that follow.

Transparent Access to Remote Resources

A client workstation can access the resources of an OS/2 LAN Server workstation as if they were locally attached. The requests are routed from the client workstation to the server by a piece of code called the **LAN Requester**. In Version 2.0, all requesters and LAN transport facilities are packaged with the LAN Server product. The LAN Requester makes the physical location of resources (over a network), transparent to an application. Resources that can be shared on a LAN Server include: disk directories, disk files, printers and printer queues, serially attached devices and queues, network services, application programs, and Named Pipes. The LAN Requester *redirects* (over the network) API calls for resources that reside on an OS/2 LAN Server; it then passes back the response to the application as if the call were locally serviced. The LAN Server thus extends OS/2's virtual device support across the network. Practically anything that can be done on a local OS/2 PC can be done remotely in a transparent fashion. Basic file sharing is done using logical drives. Users map their own virtual drives to drives and directories on various file servers. Printer sharing is done with virtual printer ports. Users can redirect their serial or parallel printer ports to logical ports on various servers. The network operating system thus transparently extends OS/2 and allows applications written for DOS, Windows 3.x, or OS/2 to become networked without changing a line of code.

Network Device and Queue Management

The OS/2 LAN Server allows an application to send its network job to a printer when it is busy. The jobs get queued at the printer and executed in the order received, or in the order set by the network administrator. Print jobs can be routed to the first available printer or to a specific printer. Printing can be scheduled for a specific time of day, such as after peak-use hours. Users can be notified of job status with messages. LAN Server also allows you to share character I/O devices such as modems, scanners, and plotters. These devices can be accessed over the network with optional pooling and queuing so that a client will automatically wait for access to the first available device.

Remote Network Application Support

The LAN Server program allows workstations to execute programs that reside on the server. Such programs include standard OS/2 commands, utilities supplied with the LAN Server, or user supplied programs. You could, for instance, offload compiles, backups, and other processor or disk intensive tasks to the LAN Server machines on the network. The remote program runs on the server with the standard input, output, and error streams redirected back to the requester station that invoked the program. This makes it possible to interactively control a remote program and to receive its output. LAN Server allows you to classify applications as either public or private. *Public* applications can be used by other users in the network; *private* applications are maintained and used solely by the owner of the application. When a user logs on to the network, the OS/2 Workplace Shell network folder is updated automatically with the icons of available network applications (both public and private). The network applications are invoked just like any other application on the Workplace Shell.

Single System Image

The LAN Server allows multiple OS/2 LAN Servers to be managed as a single logical system. This capability allows users and administrators to view the network as a single server instead of as a collection of separate resources attached to specific servers. A *domain* consists of the set of servers whose resources are configured as a single logical system. There may be one or more servers in each domain. One server within a domain is designated as the domain controller; this machine provides the view of the OS/2 LAN Server domain to the users. Multiple OS/2 LAN Server domains may coexist on the same LAN. User and machine names can be defined in several domains as long as they maintain unique names. Domain controllers take away some of the headaches associated with managing a growing multiserver LAN. A new user account is added once on the domain controller instead of on each server. The new account automatically becomes available on all servers in the domain. The administrators can control all network resources from a central point. Clients need only one password to access all the resources for which they have permissions within the domain.

Network Services

The bulk of the LAN Server code consists of configurable *services*. These are programs that can be started (installed), stopped (uninstalled), paused, or resumed through LAN Server commands. You can also create your own services by writing programs to a set of simple specifications, which makes it possible to extend the core of LAN Server. You can also individually configure the functional components to provide a certain level of service. Here's a brief description of the standard LAN Server services:

- The *Workstation Service* enables the redirection of system calls. This service and the operating system work closely together. The redirector packages and passes system calls from the operating system and sends them to a remote server. The server software reissues the call against a local resource, packages the results, and returns them to the redirector. This basic service must be started before any other services can be installed on a client workstation.

- The *Server Service* handles network requests for disk, printer, and serially attached device services. These primary services can only be provided by servers.

- The *Message Service* supports the sending and receiving of synchronous messages.

- The *Netpopup Service* displays received messages as pop-up panels on a user's screen.

- The *Alerter Service* runs in the server and sends alert notifications to designated users.

- The *Netrun Service* lets a workstation execute a program on a remote server. This service must also be installed on the servers where the programs execute.

- The ***Remoteboot Service*** runs in the server and supports the remote IPL of MS-DOS, Windows, and OS/2 client machines on all the networks supported by LAN Server. This service is particularly important to users, such as financial institutions, who require diskless PCs. Network administrators can specify through a graphic utility a Remote Initial Program Load (RIPL) *file information table* on the server that describes each diskless workstation's remote-boot requirements. Diskless workstations can have their own individual requirements or the network administrator can specify that multiple machines share the same configuration information.

- The ***Time Server Service*** allows a domain controller to be designated as the network time server. Clients can then synchronize their time with a designated time server.

- The ***Replicator Service*** enables a set of files stored on one server to be selectively replicated to other client or server machines. The Replicator service makes it easy to distribute files and programs across the network. It's a great way to propagate new versions of programs and to maintain bulletin boards. A LAN administrator can control the frequency of file replication. For example, the system could be set to replicate at short intervals if the files to be replicated are constantly changing. If the files change infrequently, the system could be set to replicate once a day after everybody goes home.

Other Network services include the network copy and move utilities, as well as extensive online network help.

Network Management and Administration

The administrative and network management facilities of LAN Server are extensive. An administrator can *logon* to LAN Server from any OS/2 requester workstation. A user interface, with context-based help and online hypertext documentation, allows the administrator to control installation and configuration facilities. It also allows the administrator to support daily operations such as Startup, Shutdown, Audit Control, and LAN Usage monitoring. An administrator may browse or update user, group, or resource profiles. The administrator can also manage server print queues, close files, and terminate user sessions. Additionally, the OS/2 LAN Server allows administrators to see at a glance who is using a server, how long they have been connected, what resources they are using, and when they were last active. The new operator rights facility allows an administrator to delegate management capabilities to any user.

In a network environment, it is important to track who has used or misused what resource and when. The LAN Server can capture in an audit trail almost everything that is happening on a network: every file accessed, every attempted access, every connection made, every resource used, every logon and logoff, changes in server states (start, pauses, continued, stopped), and violations in sharing limits or access permission. The network administrator can configure the audit system to only track exceptional events. Audit information may be displayed by the administrator.

Administrators and operators can choose which events are written to the network audit log. For example, to ensure that only pertinent information is captured, an operator can choose to have only failed file-access attempts recorded in the audit log instead of all the file-access attempts.

The LAN Server maintains a set of in-memory statistics that track all network activity. These statistics provide valuable information that help an administrator configure, monitor, and tune the network. LAN Server also provides a disk-based error log that includes comprehensive diagnostic information of errors. A LAN Server can send automatic administrative alert messages to designated users or groups of users when errors that require immediate attention are encountered. Such alerts are generated in case of disk or printer problems—for example if a printer is out of paper or the server disk is almost full—and when incorrect passwords or excessive error occurrences exceed a threshold. When alerts are sent all pertinent data is recorded, including the server name, date, and time of the alert. Alerts also provide a description of the problem and the recommended action.

The OS/2 LAN Server provides time scheduled execution through an **AT** command for automating scheduled functions under time controls. The AT command can run any OS/2 command periodically at a specified date and time. A schedule for periodically executed commands is saved on disk and loaded when the server starts. For example, an AT command may be used to automate a disk backup on a time-scheduled basis.

Network Security: Who Can Do What?

The network security and access controls provided by LAN Server allow practically every aspect of a user's network activity to be defined by the network administrator. The network administrator defines a user's login script and privileges, the files they may use, the resources they may share, the programs they may execute, and the mode in which they perform these activities. Users may belong to groups and are assigned various privilege levels.

The *User Profile Management (UPM)* provides a facility for user and group validation that is common to both the OS/2 LAN Server and the Database Manager. LAN Requester and database clients use the same UPM-defined user and group IDs to control access to resources on a LAN. The passwords for these user IDs are also administered through UPM. A PM interface is provided to help the network administrator maintain all these security features.

OS/2 LAN Server provides two facets of system access controls: logon control and resource protection. A system administrator controls whether a password is required at logon for a specific user and the interval of password expiration. The administrator can specify permitted logon times weekly intervals and hourly intervals, such as Monday and Friday between 8 AM and 5 PM. A user, by default, can logon from any workstation on the network; however, the administrator can specify one to eight workstations to which a user is restricted.

LAN Server is smart when it comes to passwords. All passwords are doubly encrypted. Passwords are encrypted at the workstation before being sent to the server for validation. LAN Server uses the U.S. Government *Data Encryption Standard (DES)* for encrypted passwords and an equally sophisticated authentication algorithm. The logon dialog is different for every logon attempt. The first time a user enters an incorrect password an *intruder prevention mechanism* is activated to delay password validation for three seconds. This scheme effectively defeats password-finding programs, known as dictionary attacks, that repeatedly try to logon using random passwords.

Resources are controlled by identifying the relationship between the user and the resource. For example, files and directories may be made accessible to a particular user, group of users, or all users. Access authority may be granted to a single user or group of users for a single resource or for a generic resource profile. Access authorities include None, Read, Update, Alter, and Execute. Execute privileges prevent users from copying a program while allowing them to run it. An administrator can specify the maximum number of users who can concurrently execute a program to enforce network license agreements. The category of resources that can be protected using access rights include disk directories, individual files, groups of files (specified with wild cards), application programs, print queues, Named Pipes, and serial device queues.

A new local security feature provides file protection for servers that are not be locked away in a fortress behind barbed wire. A local PC file on a 386 HPFS partition can be protected against unauthorized access. An intruder cannot get around this protection by rebooting the server. The protection is active even if the LAN Server code is not running. Even local applications on the server machine cannot use these protected files without the proper authorization. This local file protection complements other OS/2 local security features such as the power-on password facility, which disables the machines on startup until a proper password is provided, and the *Server Mode* function that automatically disables input at startup but allows the machine to come to full readiness without operator interaction.

Remote Named Pipes

Remote Named Pipes extend the OS/2 Interprocess Communication (IPC) mechanism across the network. Most LAN vendors now support Named Pipes on MS-DOS, Windows, and OS/2. This includes Novell's NetWare, Banyan's Vines, and the LAN Manager/LAN Server family of products from IBM, Microsoft and 3Com. Unix support for Named Pipes is provided by LAN Manager/X. Named Pipes provide highly reliable, two-way communications between clients and a server. Named Pipes applications benefit from the network controls provided by LAN Server. For example, access to your server application through a Named Pipe can be controlled by the LAN Server security system so that only specified users can gain access to it. A very important benefit of Named Pipes is that they're part of the base OS/2 interprocess communications service. The Named Pipes interface is identical whether the processes are running on an individual machine or distributed across the network.

Named Pipes provide a high-level abstraction that hides the network from your applications. The LAN Server handles the low-level details of communications, making it much easier to write sophisticated distributed applications. A single Named Pipe function call equates to many low-level NetBIOS calls. Named Pipes are an abstraction of a full-duplex session. Processes can read and write streams of messages as well as byte-streams. Named Pipes employ a file naming convention as well as file-like semantics (such as open, close, read, write).

Named Pipes provide a convenient mechanism for writing request/response transactions such as RPCs. The powerful **DosCallNPipe** call combines a connect, send, receive, and disconnect. Another feature of Named Pipes is that they allow messages to queue in the pipe. When a process reads from a Named Pipe, it gets one completed message per read. Named Pipes build their services using NetBIOS primitives. They provide *value-added* by making it easy to code communication functions using file-like metaphors to obtain network services. The main drawback of Named Pipes is that you must have the LAN Server program installed to use the service over the network.

Fault-Tolerant Features

The LAN Server provides many new fault-tolerant features that keep your server running and protect your data (Figure 9-3). The product provides many levels of storage subsystem fault tolerance. At the lowest level, the product detects errors that occur while performing hard disk read-and-write operations, and then issues alerts and provides error correction that helps recover and restore data. At the next level, the HPFS file system maps all the defective disk sectors on its hard disks and assigns them "on the fly" to alternate disk sectors. *Disk mirroring* provides the next level of fault tolerance by writing dual copies of the data on separate disk drives. If the primary drive fails, the backup drive takes over and protects against any data loss or interruption of service. *Disk duplexing* extends fault tolerance to the disk drive controller itself. Two disk drive controllers are paired with two hard drives to provide added protection against failure of the controller components.

A complete set of tools is available to help the LAN administrator configure and monitor errors on a server with disk mirroring or disk duplexing. These errors can be monitored and corrected from any workstation on the LAN. For example, a failed mirrored disk can be repaired by the administrator using the FTADMIN PM-based utility.

LAN Server also provides protection against server crashes due to power failures by integrating *Uninterruptible Power Supply (UPS)* support into the product. Depending on the capabilities of the UPS unit, an alert can be sent when the battery first takes over,

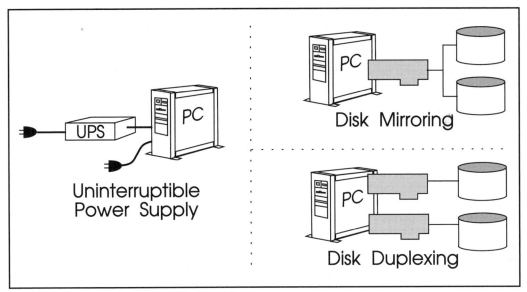

Figure 9-3. The LAN Server's Fault-Tolerant Features.

when battery power gets low, and when server shutdown is about to begin. These alerts can be sent to users, administrators, and to your programs. If power is not restored before the battery runs down, the server flushes its cached data, logs the event, and closes all the open files before shutting down. In the area of communications, LAN Server keeps track of established sessions and rebuilds them automatically if they're lost because of a failure.

Open NDIS Adapter Support

LAN Server, like TCP/IP and Communications Manager, works with NDIS-compliant LAN adapters and supports up to four LAN adapters per machine. This support means that LAN Server's "Named Pipes over NetBIOS" stack can happily coexist on the same adapter with Communications Manager and TCP/IP stacks. The multiple adapter support allows LAN Server to provide shared services to clients on four logical networks. Remember, the four adapters can be a combination of PC Network, Ethernet, or Token-Ring types. The maximum number of NetBIOS sessions supported is the total available for all adapters installed in the machine (254 x 4 = 1016).

The Network API

The publication of the OS/2 LAN API creates an open architecture for OS/2 and DOS LAN applications. The product provides over 150 API functions; most of these are available to DOS, Windows, and OS/2 clients. With the network API, a C programmer can now explicitly control many of the already described Network Operating System functions through programming interfaces. This makes it easy for your programs to control almost every aspect of LAN administration. Through the DOS Requester component, the API also allows DOS/Windows programmers to use the interprocess communication facilities to exchange data and event signals with OS/2 servers. The DOS Requesters support a subset of the API calls in all the categories except Alerts and Error Logging. Table 9-1 provides a quick reference of what these calls do by functional category.

Table 9-1 (Part 1 of 2). LAN Server APIs.

Service	Description
Named Pipes	This service consists of the same 13 Named Pipe API calls that are part of the native OS/2 interprocess communication. They are included here because you must have a running copy of the LAN Server to use Named Pipes remotely. Most of the OS/2 Named Pipe API calls are extended to DOS and MS-Windows Requesters through the LAN Server (or Microsoft LAN Manager).
MailSlots	This service consists of 6 API calls that provide one-way interprocess communications. These calls can come in handy for remote data collection and "I'm alive" heartbeats. Mailslots use NetBIOS datagrams to provide their services. The server side of the communication creates a mailslot for receiving messages (NetBIOS *add name*). The client writes messages to the mailslot. The server side can block waiting for messages to arrive. Mailslots are inherently fast because they do not need to be opened or closed. A process can write to a remote Mailslot with a class and priority attribute. Priority controls the order in which messages are read. *First-class messages* on Mailslots are abstractions of acknowledged datagrams. A sending process blocks (or waits) until its first-class message is delivered and acknowledged or an error occurs. *Second-class messages* are simple datagrams of the "transmit-and-pray" variety. An important feature of second class messages is that they can be broadcast to all workstations in a domain. The full repertoire of Mailslot API calls is available to DOS/Windows Requesters.
Alerts	This service consists of 3 API calls that notify applications of the occurrence of certain network events.
Network Management	This service consists of 23 API calls that do the following: • Control the server's Audit log file • Control the Error log • Collect and reset network statistics on both servers and requesters • Control network sessions, requesters, and servers • Read remote configuration information from the IBMLAN.INI file
Resource Management	This service consists of 23 API calls that do the following: • Control the sharing of server resources • Establish controls and connections between requesters and servers • Control the sharing of serial devices and their associated queues • Monitor the open file, device, and pipe resources on a server • Set or obtain information on a per-handle basis

Table 9-1 (Part 1 of 2). LAN Server APIs.

Service	Description
Access Control	This service consists of 27 API calls that do the following: • Examine or modify user or group access permissions for server resources • Control user and group accounts
Network Services	This server consists of 19 API calls that do the following: • Send, forward, and log messages • Copy and move files • Execute remote programs • Obtain time-of-day from a server • Start and control network service programs

LAN Server Packaging

The LAN Server 2.0 comes in two packages: Entry and Advanced.

- The **OS/2 LAN Server Version 2.0 - Entry** sells for $795 and runs on OS/2 2.0. This product provides all the functions described in this section, except for the 32-bit HPFS 386 file system, local security, and the disk mirroring and duplexing fault tolerant capability.
- The **OS/2 LAN Server Version 2.0 - Advanced** sells for $2,295 and supports all the functions described in this section; it also provides a highly optimized, Ring 0, 32-bit HPFS file system. It is recommended for servers in high-workload environments where prime performance is critical. It is also recommended for servers that support a large number of remote IPL requesters or that require optimal reliability and security. Here's the unfortunate news (other than price): this server product will only run on OS/2 1.3 (an OS/2 2.0 version is in the works).

This choice of server packaging presents us with a dilemma: Should we write 16-bit OS/2 applications on the server that supports the 32-bit HPFS file system? Or should we write 32-bit applications on the server that supports the 16-bit HPFS file system? This book is about programming 32-bit OS/2 applications. So the decision is a no-brainer: We will develop our 32-bit OS/2 applications on the *entry* level server and wait for IBM to deliver the 32-bit HPFS on a 32-bit OS/2 platform.

LAN Requesters are available for DOS 3.3, DOS 4.01, DOS 5.0, Windows 3.0, OS/2 1.3, and OS/2 2.0. The LAN Requesters work with both entry or advanced LAN Server products. The client programs are distributed with both server packages mentioned here. The client code sells for $75 per client workstation.

NETWARE REQUESTER FOR OS/2 2.0

Novell has the distinction of providing the world's most popular file server, and network operating system. The NetWare Requester for OS/2 opens up the vast world of Novell LAN servers to an OS/2 client, and also allows OS/2 servers to service NetWare clients. There is one major limitation: OS/2 and NetWare services cannot reside on the same server machine. This is a serious shortcoming for departmental and small business LANs that can only afford a single server solution. NetWare 3.2, when it becomes available, will fix that shortcoming by running NetWare on top of OS/2 2.0. In the meantime, we can still get plenty of mileage from the NetWare Requester; it is one of the key ingredients of our OS/2 client/server platform.

NetWare 3.1 and LAN Server

NetWare 3.1, as a server platform, offers the same kind of services as LAN Server. Both server platforms are more or less equivalent in the following areas: file and print services, disk duplexing, disk mirroring, UPS support, multiserver domain administration, audit trails, alerts, security features, login scripts, multiple adapter support, Named Pipes support, and remote IPL capabilities for DOS, Windows, and OS/2 clients. Both platforms can support, in theory, a maximum of 1000 clients.

So what does NetWare 3.1 do better than LAN Server? For starters, it allows you to create monstrous files that can span across multiple disk drives. NetWare can work with a gargantuan amount of total disk storage: 32 Terabytes versus LAN Server's, not too shabby, 48 Gigabytes. NetWare directly supports Macintosh and Unix clients, while LAN Server relies on third parties. NetWare can be installed and upgraded remotely. Bean counters are in love with NetWare's meticulously built-in accounting services, which can be used to charge clients for any service used.

The feature that really makes NetWare wonderful is its multifaceted, chameleon-like file server that can be made to look like everybody else's favorite file system. The NetWare file server stores everybody's files in its own a "private-label" Novell format. But depending on what the client wants, NetWare can apply the right magic to make its files look like: MS-DOS FAT, OS/2 HPFS, Sun NFS, or Macintosh AFP. This is how NetWare allows OS/2, Mac, Unix, DOS, and Windows clients to access the same source files. Novell is even going one step further with its "Switzerland of the computer world" strategy. It is in the process of creating portable versions of NetWare that can reside on everybody's favorite operating system and hardware.[4] This is how Novell won the West.

---

[4] Novell seems to be announcing a new alliance every other week. IBM, DEC, and HP have all declared their solemn allegiance to Novell, and they are all providing guest quarters for NetWare on their operating systems.

So what does LAN Server do better than NetWare 3.1? It provides some unique features—such as the file replication service, the network time service, and the remote execution of commands—and it is able to accept commands from Netview. Its system management and network administration features are in some ways better than Net-Ware's.

But, what makes LAN Server really *great* is its programming platform. It is safe to say that most of the world's great server applications have yet to be written. LAN Server, because of its affinity to OS/2, provides an ideal platform for creating those applications (perhaps by you, the reader of this book). When you're programming in the LAN Server environment, you can use any of the software packages described in this book and thousands of others. LAN Server applications can use OS/2's preemptive multi-tasking, threads, interprocess communications, memory protection, dynamic link library facilities, and demand-paged virtual memory. The LAN Server API package has very consistent semantics, since it was designed from the outset as an extension of the OS/2 API set. NetWare, by contrast, added functions piecemeal as the product matured. The OS/2 connection also gives you access to dozens of compilers, programmer productivity tools, CASE tools, DBMSs, image and multimedia application enablers, communication stacks, and device drivers for almost anything that can be controlled by a computer.

In summary, LAN Server may not be the world's most ubiquitous server platform, but it gives you everything you need to create 32-bit server "killer apps" on a commodity hardware platform.[5] Of course, NetWare 3.2 will take away some of that advantage, depending on how much affinity it has with the OS/2 API environment.

What is a NetWare Requester for OS/2 2.0?

The NetWare LAN Requester for OS/2 2.0 provides OS/2 clients transparent access to all features of NetWare, including advanced file, print and communication services, comprehensive security, fault tolerance, and resource accounting. The Requester supports NetWare 2.X, NetWare 3.X, and the NetWare for UNIX environments. Like the OS/2 LAN Requester, the NetWare Requester is integrated into the OS/2 Workplace Shell. This means you can manipulate files and printers that reside on a remote NetWare Server using the familiar PM and Workplace OS/2 interfaces. You can copy files from one server to another by simply dragging them between containers. Likewise, you can print documents on NetWare or LAN Server network printers by

---

[5] In terms of popularity, LAN Server (and Microsoft LAN Manager) are second-place to NetWare. This situation could change if Microsoft bundles the client software with every copy of Windows it ships.

simply dragging the document and dropping it on the appropriate icon. This is a good example of how the Workplace creates a cohesive online view of distributed resources.

NetWare Requester/IBM LAN Requester Coexistence

DOS, Windows, and OS/2 clients can access services on both NetWare and LAN Server concurrently using the same adapter card. In this release, IBM and Novell solved the NDIS and ODI coexistence issue. *Open Data-Link Interface (ODI)*, is Novell's version of a "logical network board." ODI, like Microsoft's NDIS standard, allows multiple protocol stacks to use the same network adapter. The good news is that NetWare and LAN Server requesters can now coexist in memory without conflict. The NetWare Requester for OS/2 2.0 now makes available two miracle pieces of code, affectionately called "shims," for translating between NDIS and ODI and vice versa (see Figure 9-4). The **LANSUP** shim translates ODI to NDIS, and allows the Novell OS/2 Requester to use the same NDIS drivers and adapters as the rest of the IBM OS/2 LAN products. The **ODINSUP** shim, translates NDIS to ODI, and allows the rest of the IBM OS/2 LAN products to share a NetWare ODI driver and adapter; you'll have to do some strange things in your CONFIG.SYS file, but it does work. Regardless of which shim you use, you do not have to reboot your machine (like in the old days) to access NetWare when running LAN Server and vice versa. You can have your LAN Server and NetWare too.

NetWare Requester for OS/2 2.0: API Categories

We will present a brief overview of the NetWare APIs available to OS/2 applications through the NetWare Requester for OS/2 2.0. Like the IBM LAN Server, NetWare opens up through its APIs a whole universe of LAN services. The purpose of this section is to give you a feel for what you can do with these APIs.[6]

From a programmer's perspective (see Figure 9-5), the NetWare Requester for OS/2 2.0 provides the following API services:

- **Peer-to-Peer Communications**, including Novell's native IPX/SPX protocol and the ubiquitous NetBIOS protocol. These protocols allow your OS/2 programs to communicate at the peer-to-peer level with other DOS, Windows, and OS/2 NetWare Requesters as well as Novell servers.

---

[6] The full description of these APIs is in the Novell **NetWare OS/2 API Developer's Guide**. This is a thick 400-page document that is part of the NetWare Client SDK.

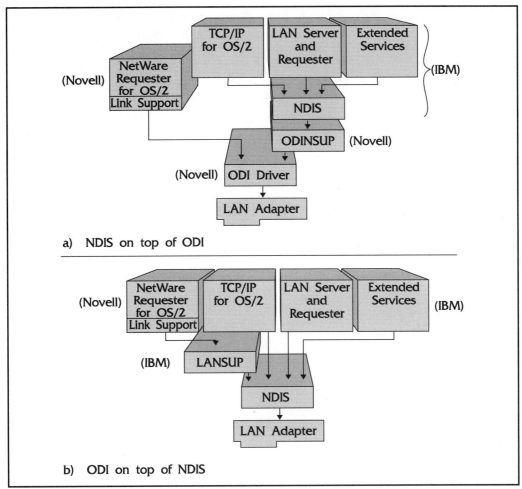

a)   NDIS on top of ODI

b)   ODI on top of NDIS

Figure 9-4.   Shim: ODI to NDIS or NDIS to ODI.

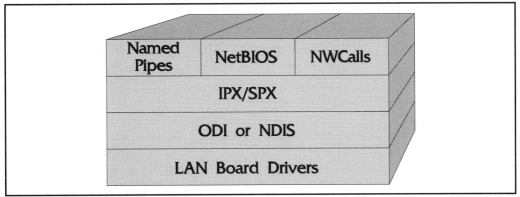

Figure 9-5.   NetWare's LAN Requester for OS/2 Protocol Stack.

- **Network Named Pipes** provide both client and server Named Pipes services without requiring a NetWare server on the network (see Figure 9-6). In theory, this function allows up to 1000 simultaneous Named Pipes connections. This means 1000 DOS, Windows, or OS/2 NetWare clients can simultaneously communicate with an OS/2 NetWare Named Pipes server. Windows and DOS NetWare Requesters do not support the Named Pipes server calls; only the OS/2 NetWare Requesters support those APIs.[7]

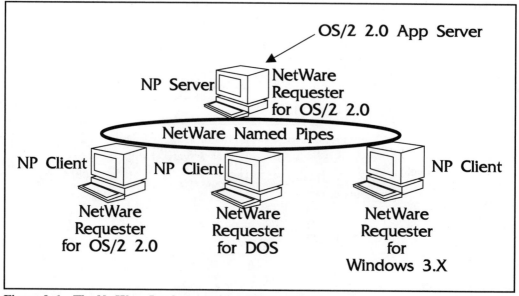

Figure 9-6.   The NetWare Implementation of Named Pipes.

- **NetWare Services**, also known as "NWCalls," provide APIs to NetWare's services like shared file and printer services, login, the bindery, queues, and semaphores. Your programs can use these APIs to access services that run on NetWare 3.X server machines. The APIs cover any service that can be invoked interactively using the NetWare Requester's Workplace Shell user interface.

Table 9-2 provides a quick reference to the NetWare Requester for OS/2 2.0 API categories. These services collectively provide a little under 300 API calls.

---

[7] The NetWare Named Pipes are an ISV's dream come true in terms of pricing and packaging. All you pay for is one $200 site license. You can use the product to create very sophisticated client/server applications using shrink-wrapped copies of DOS, Windows, and OS/2 2.0. You don't even need a NetWare file server!

NetWare Requester for OS/2 2.0: API Services

Table 9-2 (Part 1 of 4). NetWare Requester for OS/2 2.0 API Categories.

Service	Description
Peer-to-Peer APIs	
IPX	This service consists of 12 API calls that provide a datagram service over Novell's native Internet Packet Exchange (IPX) protocol. This is a "send and pray" type of protocol with no guarantees. It is used as a foundation protocol by sophisticated network applications for sending and receiving low-overhead datagram packets over the internet. Novell's SPX builds a reliable protocol service on top of IPX.
SPX	This service consists 16 API calls that provide a reliable, guaranteed delivery service over IPX. SPX stands for Sequenced Packet Exchange. It enables two client processes to exchange messages over a sequenced packet stream. Duplicate packets are detected and suppressed. SPX provides automatic time-outs and retransmissions over a connection-based service. SPX APIs allow two partners to establish a connection, exchange sequenced packets, and terminate the connection. SPX, like IPX, is native to NetWare.
NetBIOS	This service consists 5 API calls that emulate the NetBIOS interface over IPX/SPX. The actual NetBIOS commands are passed using the NCB control block. The NCBs are submitted using NetWare's **NetBiosSubmit** calls. NetWare supports all the standard NetBIOS commands. This includes general commands, name support commands, session commands, and the datagrams commands. NetBIOS combines the functions of both IPX and SPX and is widely used in PC LAN applications. NetBIOS does not require the presence of a NetWare Server. OS/2 NetWare Requesters can communicate with DOS and Windows NetWare Requesters using NetBIOS.
Client/Server APIs: Network Named Pipes	
Named Pipes	This service consists of 16 API calls. This includes the 13 API calls that are part of OS/2's native interprocess communication and 3 calls that are specific to NetWare. OS/2 NetWare Requesters support both client and server Named Pipes calls. DOS and Windows NetWare Requesters only support the client Named Pipes calls. In theory, an OS/2 NetWare Requester can simultaneously service up to 1000 clients (DOS, Windows, and OS/2). The Named Pipes service does not require a NetWare server on the network. The NetWare-specific Named Pipes calls are used to obtain Named Pipes server names on the network.
NetWare Services: NWCalls	
Apple File Services (AFP)	This service consists of 14 API calls that follow Apple Computer's **AppleTalk Filing Protocol (AFP)**. AFP allows a NetWare file server to store both OS/2 and Apple data files. You can write applications to create, access, and delete Macintosh-format directories and files on a NetWare file server.

Table 9-2 (Part 2 of 4).   NetWare Requester for OS/2 2.0 API Categories.

Service	Description
Bindery Services	This service consists of 23 API calls that maintain information about objects allowed to access a NetWare Server. Each NetWare server maintains a database, implemented as two hidden files, of bindery objects. This special purpose database is called the *bindery*. A bindery object can be a user, user group, network server, print server, or any other named entity that can access a NetWare server. NetWare records information about each bindery object. The API service allows you to manipulate and query object attributes such as: security, password, id, name, and properties (id identifies an objectname.objecttype). **Note:** NetWare 3.2 will replace the proprietary bindery service with a distributed *NetWare Directory Services(NDS)* that provides a global view of the network. This service will be object-based (i.e., it will support class inheritance) and will comply with the X.500 syntax and naming definitions. The IBM LAN Server naming services will also migrate to X.500.
Connection Services	This service consists of 11 API calls that provide information on the status of connections between client workstations and NetWare servers. The server maintains a table that includes connection id and passwords for all connected objects. An OS/2 client can obtain information on a connection's id, number, and status. It can query the maximum number of connections available at the requesting workstation (the default is 8). It can obtain the internet address of the connection. This is the address (adapter id and network id) that uniquely identifies the client on a NetWare internet. The service also allows a client to set the primary connection id (this is the connection to the server to which the client originally logged into).
Directory Entry Services	This service consists of 8 API calls that allow a client to obtain directory entry information; modify a directory entry's maximum rights mask, add and delete directory trustees, move directory entries, and get effective rights. The directory structure and the bindery structure are independent. The bindery provides a database for network resources and clients to be identified and maintains information about these objects. The directory entries provide information about volumes and directories including users (or "trustees") and their rights. Directory structures are stored in the file system. **Note:** *This service is not the same as NetWare 3.2's Network Directory Services (NDS).* The NDS is the bindery replacement.
Extended Attributes	This service consists of 6 API calls that allow a client to read and write Extended Attributes associated with OS/2 files and to open and close extended attribute files.
File Server Environment	This service consists of 10 API calls that allow a client to "login" and "logout" to a file server and attach or detach from a server. Attach creates a connection id (session) with the server. The API calls can also be used to obtain information such as server type, name, and description. An API call returns the network date and time maintained on a specified server. *Warning:* Since date and time are not automatically synchronized across NetWare servers, they may differ on the internet.
File Systems Services	This service consists of 48 API calls that provide NetWare-specific file service functions. These include create, delete, and rename a directory; get, release, and clear file locks and file lock sets; set file and extended file attributes; and copy, rename, and erase a file. **Note:** You may be better off using the native OS/2 file APIs and have your calls transparently redirected to a NetWare file server.

Table 9-2 (Part 3 of 4). NetWare Requester for OS/2 2.0 API Categories.

Service	Description
Message Services	This service consists of 8 API calls that enable clients to send broadcast messages to up to 256 specified target workstations. The sending workstation and the target workstations must be attached to the same NetWare file server. The maximum message size is 254 bytes (NetWare 3.11c and above).
Miscellaneous Services	This service consists of 2 API calls that enable clients to obtain the OS/2 Requester version they are running, and to determine whether long names are supported on a specified volume.
Name Space Services	This service consists of 17 API calls that enable DOS, OS/2, Unix, FTAM, and Macintosh clients to create files on a NetWare Server using their own familiar naming conventions. The primary name space is DOS. For example, if you have a DOS file and you load OS/2 (HPFS), Unix, and Mac name spaces the file would have four entries. The APIs allow you to create name space entries, scan name space entries, and write name space entries.
Path and Drive Services	This service consists of 7 API calls that enable clients to delete or map a logical network drive to a specified directory path; obtain information about specific drives, such as the connection id, path, and drive handle; and parse path strings.
Print Services	This service consists of 12 API calls that enable clients to redirect data sent to a local LPT device to a specified NetWare server's print queue. Clients can query the server for the status of the network printer. They can specify the number of copies, tab size, form type, banner page, and so on.
Queue Management Services (QMS)	This service consists of 39 API calls that create, manage, and control network queues. These queues are maintained in special directories on a NetWare file server. One queue can hold up to 250 jobs. Queues are implemented on a server as a Bindery object (they're secure). Clients submit work requests on a queue in first-in, first-out order. Job server applications remove work from the queue and execute it (these applications can also run on an OS/2 client). One queue may be serviced by as many as 25 job servers at a time. Once a job is serviced, its associated file is deleted from the queue directory. Using the API calls, an OS/2 client can create, manipulate, abort, verify the status, and remove queue entries.
Salvage and Purge	This service consists of 5 API calls that scan for deleted files, purge deleted files, recover deleted files, purge erased files, and restore erased files.
Synchronization Services	This service consists of 5 API calls that allow clients to create semaphores on a NetWare server to protect a shared resource, wait on semaphores, and signal on semaphores when they finish using the resource. Wait decrements the semaphore count, and signal increments it. The creator of a semaphore can configure the number of applications that can access the semaphore at one time (1 to 127). If access is restricted to 1, only serial access will be allowed on the resource. A client must first open a semaphore and check its count before using it. If the resource is unavailable, the client is placed in a wait queue for a specified timeout interval or until the resource frees up.

Table 9-2 (Part 4 of 4). NetWare Requester for OS/2 2.0 API Categories.

Service	Description
Transaction Tracking Services (TTS)	This service consists of 11 API calls that allow NetWare file servers to track file-based transactions and ensure file integrity by backing out or erasing interrupted or partially completed transactions. Only transactional files are affected. A file is made transactional by setting an extended attribute for transactions. Client applications can explicitly issue begin/end transaction calls to bracket a specific transaction. If the file server fails before all updates to transactional files are committed to disk, the transaction will be backed out when the file server is rebooted. A file server can monitor a maximum of 200 transactions at a time, and only one for each client session.
Volume Services	This service consists of 4 API calls that allow clients to obtain information such as the number of volumes mounted on a file server (64 maximum) and the name and sizes of each volume, the total number of blocks per volume, the number of sectors per block, and the number of available blocks and directory entries.

The NetWare Management Map for the OS/2 Workplace

The **NetWare Management Map (NMM)** creates graphic displays of a Novell internet using the OS/2 Workplace Shell's object-oriented display facilities. NMM is used primarily by network administrators. It works by automatically discovering all the NetWare servers on network and then creating a graphic display of the NetWare internet including the largest NetWare networks (see Figure 9-7). Icons are used to represent all the servers, cable segments, routers, and workstations running NetWare. The display continuously updates itself to reflect the status of each node. The interface allows a network administrator to directly manipulate each graphic object by selecting its icon. NMM conducts point-to-point packet transmit/receive tests to isolate communication faults, and it provides online, context-sensitive help that includes probable cause of errors.

The NetWare Requester for OS/2 2.0: Packaging

The purchase of a single $200 NetWare Services for OS/2 license from IBM entitles you to create: "as many copies of the NetWare Requester for OS/2 as required within the customer's corporation to access appropriate NetWare network Servers."

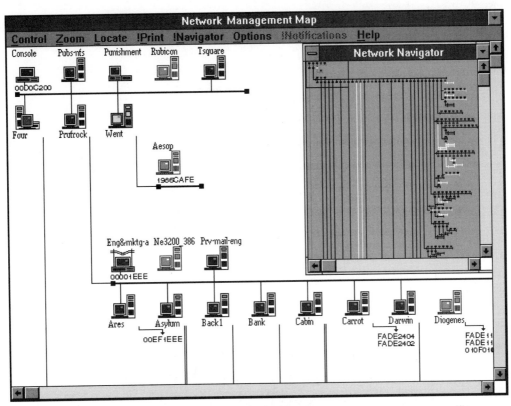

Figure 9-7. The OS/2 Workplace Shell NetWare Management Map (NMM).

Conclusion

This concludes our "brief" overview of the communications services to be used in our OS/2 client/server platform. At the risk of sounding sadistic, this was only the "gentle" introduction to the terminology and functions provided by those products. In later chapters, we will show you how some of that power can be harnessed and put to productive uses by your client/server applications.

Chapter 10

Database Manager and DDCS/2

This chapter introduces the database server component of the OS/2 client/server platform. This function is provided by two complementary products: the **Database Manager** and **DDCS/2** (see light area in Figure 10-1). The Database Manager is the heart of our LAN-based client/server platform. We will go over the main features, functions, and benefits of that product. We then introduce DDCS/2, a product that extends the OS/2 Database Manager's reach and makes it interoperate with IBM's other SAA DBMSs: DB2, SQL/DS, and SQL/400. You will need DDCS/2 if your OS/2 Database Manager runs out of steam, or if you're operating in a heterogeneous server environment where the data is spread across PCs, AS/400s, and mainframes.

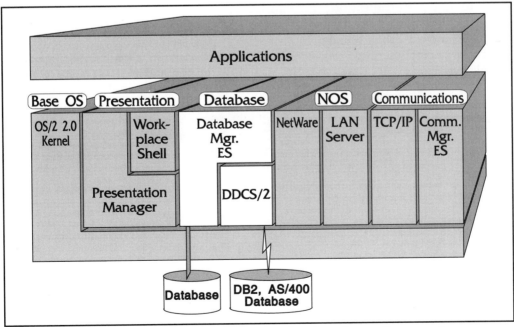

Figure 10-1. OS/2 2.0 Client/Server Platform: The Database Server Components.

THE DATABASE MANAGER

The **Database Manager** component of OS/2's Extended Services is more than just a multiuser Database Management System (DBMS) on a PC. It is a DBMS on a network, a member of a new breed of PC software, popularly referred to as *SQL Database Servers*. But this is only the tip of the iceberg. The Database Manager is also being groomed for playing a "kingpin" role in IBM's SAA platform for distributed databases. It is the designated front-end to IBM's SAA databases, which means that most of IBM's database tools will run on the OS/2 platform.

Because what is offered today is really an embryonic form of what is yet to come, we will start this section by positioning the Database Manager in the dual contexts of IBM's SAA architecture and that of an SQL LAN Database Server. Having done this, we can then proceed with the description of the three major sub-components of the system: *Database Services*, *Database Tools*, and *Remote Data Services*.

The Database Manager as a SQL Server

Perhaps the most important trend among database servers of any size is the emergence of **SQL** as the standard Lingua Franca for the manipulation, definition, and control of data. SQL, originally developed at IBM's San Jose Research Lab and now an ANSI standard, is a powerful set-oriented language consisting of 12 commands. SQL was created as a language for databases that adhere to the *relational model*. Relational Databases have a strong foundation in set theory and predicate logic; the model calls for a clear separation of the physical aspects of data from their logical representation. Data is made to appear as simple tables that mask the complexity of the storage access mechanisms. The SQL language can then be used to perform complex data operations with a few simple commands in situations that would have required hundreds of lines of conventional code. Physicists might call SQL "the grand unified theory of database" because of the multifaceted roles it plays. Here is a partial list of roles:

- SQL is an interactive Query Language for ad hoc database queries.
- SQL is a database programming language; it can be embedded in languages such as C and Cobol to access data.
- SQL is a data definition and data administration language; it is used for security and access control and for defining complex data integrity constraints and rules.
- SQL is the language of networked database servers.

SQL is the predominant database language of mainframes and minicomputers, where it provides the focus for a market-share battleground. The emergence of SQL on OS/2, offers many of the advantages of mainframe and minicomputer Database Management Systems (DBMSs) at PC prices, and with intuitive PC front-ends.

The Database Manager in the SAA DRDA Context

The OS/2 Database Manager is a vital part of IBM's long-term distributed database strategy and SAA direction. This strategy is known as the *Distributed Relational Database Architecture*, or simply *DRDA*. IBM is promoting DRDA as the standard for multivendor database interoperability. A number of influential database vendors, including Oracle, Sybase, Novell, and Gupta, have announced support for DRDA. The DRDA architecture is the vehicle for the interoperation of IBM's four strategic relational database managers:

1. Database Manager for OS/2 workstations[1]
2. SQL/400 Database Manager for the AS/400 mid-range processors
3. SQL/DS for the S/370 VM Operating System
4. DB2 for IBM's high end S/370 MVS Operating System

While the implementation of each product is tuned for its environment, the commonality of the interfaces is key in realizing the SAA distributed database goal. This goal is to make it possible for the end user to access any SAA database from an OS/2 machine as if it were a local OS/2 Database Manager. To realize this goal, IBM has stated it will provide the following:

- The OS/2 environment will serve as the primary window for end users to access any of the IBM SAA databases, including those on the S/370s and the AS/400s.
- The OS/2 Database Manager will be cognizant of multisite data and provide a logical view of the distributed data that makes the location transparent.
- The OS/2 Database Manager will handle the multisite synchronization, security, and data integrity functions on behalf of its users and in cooperation with other SAA Database Managers. This means locating the remote data sites and coordinating requests (including the update of data) at several locations in a single transaction. It also means servicing of single requests that span multiple sites, such as a *multisite JOIN*.

The current implementation of the OS/2 Database Manager is an embryonic version of the fully distributed DRDA goal described here. DRDA calls this embryonic level the *Remote Unit of Work (RUOW)*. This means that an application can connect to a remote OS/2 Database Manager and process multiple SQL statements against that database, issue a commit to make the work permanent, and then switch to another OS/2 Database Manager to start a subsequent unit of work. The DDCS/2 product extends the RUOW function to heterogeneous (or unlike) SAA DBMSs. In the RUOW model offered today, transactional integrity is only provided on a per site basis. It is up to the application to coordinate the multisite integrity and access of data. However, with the

---

[1] IBM also plans to provide a common 32-bit AIX and OS/2 version of the Database Manager.

RUOW capability, an OS/2 machine can be used as a *Database Server* that can provide centralized data storage services to multiple users. These multiuser services include security and data integrity.

Why Should I Care?

In summary, the OS/2 Database Manager uses SQL, the language of choice for DBMSs on mainframes, superminis, and the high end of the PC market. The Database Manager is an integral part of IBM's SAA DRDA strategy, both as a database front-end tool and as a Database Server. IBM customers can scale up their server applications with the OS/2 Database Manager at the low end, and DB2 at the high end. Thus, the SQL code you develop on the OS/2 Database Manager can be ported to DB2 with very minor changes. More importantly, OS/2 and other DRDA machines will eventually all be able to coexist on a network and provide a single logical view of distributed data, with all the necessary integrity and controls that this entails.

The Components of Database Manager

The Database Manager consists of three components: Database Services, Database Tools, and Remote Data Services (see Figure 10-2).

Database Services

The heart of OS/2's Database Manager is *Database Services*, which in industry jargon is typically referred to as an *SQL Engine*. This is the component that controls all accesses to the database, manages the logical and physical views of the data, generates optimized access plans to the data, and provides the transaction management, data integrity, data security, and concurrency support that allow multiple applications to access the same database at the same time. The Referential Integrity feature provides a consistent level of data integrity similar to DB2. The Database Services is a multiuser database that can be configured either in *standalone* mode or as a network *Database Server* machine. A user application can access multiple local or remote SQL Engines serially.

The Database Services also includes a wide repertoire of service calls for maintaining and fine-tuning a database. These services include import and export of bulk data, backup and restore a database, table reorganization, statistics for query optimization, and operations on database directories. Service calls are also provided to create and delete databases and for connecting to databases on local or remote machines. IBM includes a precompiler with the Database Services that allows applications written in procedural languages such as C to invoke the Database Manager API. Through the API, you can submit SQL statements, invoke the database utilities, or trigger the execution of stored procedures. IBM also includes the REXX procedures language with OS/2,

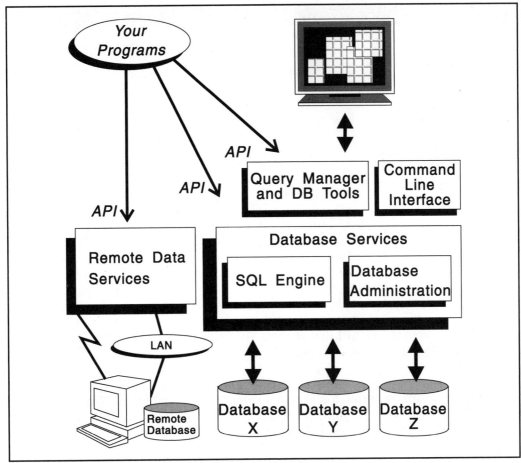

Figure 10-2. The Components of the Database Manager.

which requires no precompiler to access the database services available to the programmer. The REXX interpreter can be used in prototyping situations.

Database Tools

Complementing the SQL engine is a suite of Database Manager tools that are shipped with the product and can be selectively installed on your machine. These tools (see Figure 10-3) collectively allow you to configure the Database Manager, backup and restore a database, perform forward recovery, and catalog databases and workstations for client/server and DDCS/2 connections. All the database administration tools have fancy graphical user interfaces that make database administration chores less painful.

The most venerable of these tools, the *Query Manager*, is an interactive end-user tool, used to execute database functions and utilities. The Query Manager uses Presentation

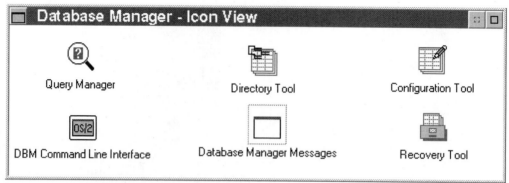

Figure 10-3. The Database Manager Tools.

Manager to provide a front-end for creating database elements, submitting SQL queries, editing and entering table data, and for generating reports and procedures. The
Query Manager can also be used to create customized applications with forms, menus,
queries, reports, and procedures. The customized application can then be executed
without the user ever knowing of Query Manager's involvement. Query Manager is the
most direct route between an end user and the Database Manager. Via the Remote Data
Services, it can serve as a window on either local or remote databases. The Query
Manager also provides an API that enables you to call Query Manager functions and
commands from within your C programs.

Database administration functions previously executed only through the Query Manager are now available through a separate suite of graphical tools. This unbundling
makes it easier for users to replace Query Manager with some of the excellent Database
Manager front-end tools on the market, such as Enfin/3. Functions that are still in the
Query Manager are import/export, runstats, reorg, operational status, manage authori-
zations, restore defaults, and open/erase printer name. Forward recovery (also known
as roll-forward) is not supported within the Query Manager.

Another new feature provided with the Database Manager is the *Database Command
Line Interface*, which lets you create and run SQL statements, database environment
commands, and database utilities from the OS/2 command prompt or from OS/2
command files. The Command Line Interface also includes a REORG check feature
that lets you know when your database tables need to be reorganized to improve system
performance.

Remote Data Services (RDS)

This is the component of the Database Manager that provides distributed database
capabilities to OS/2, MS-Windows, or MS-DOS clients on a LAN. Here's what these
capabilities currently include:

- *Transparent SQL access:* This means that your SQL call is automatically routed to either a local or remote database (see Figure 10-4). This form of remote access is useful for ad hoc SQL calls over networks.

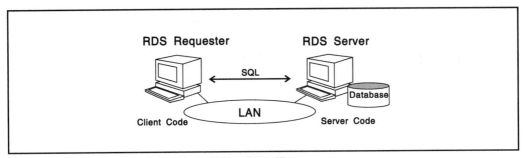

Figure 10-4.   Remote Data Services: SQL Client/Server.

- *Remote Procedure Calls:* This capability allows you to invoke remote procedures (DLLs) that are stored on the database machine (see Figure 10-5). This form of remote invocation cuts down on network traffic and is typically used for transaction processing.

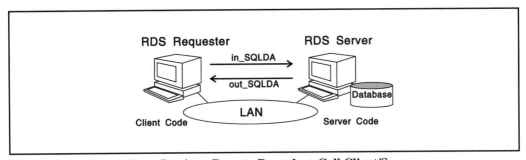

Figure 10-5.   Remote Data Services: Remote Procedure Call Client/Server.

- *Database consistency across the network:* This means that if a remote site fails, the transaction for that application is rolled back and the database is returned to its last consistent state.
- *Network directory services:* The current method for achieving local/remote transparency consists of manually adding information about the physical location of the databases to the system directories. These directories are consulted when an application first connects to the database. The RDS requester routes the non-local database calls to the RDS server where the database resides. The application is not cognizant whether the database being accessed is local or remote, and the same code can be run in both situations.

Database Manager Packaging

The Database Manager is packaged with the Communications Manager as part of OS/2 **Extended Services**. The product comes in two flavors:

1. **Extended Services**, a low-cost product that only supports a standalone Database Manager together with Communications Manager. This product sells for $595.
2. **Extended Services with Database Server**, a more costly product that provides a networked Database Manager server function for MS-DOS, MS-Windows, and OS/2 clients (see Figure 10-6). This product also includes the Communications Manager and sells for $1995.

Figure 10-6. The Database Manager's Client/Server Configurations.

The database clients only require a separate, skinny, low-cost program that sells for $75, called the **Database Client Application Enabler**. This program includes a Net-BIOS communications protocol stack. The NetBIOS support for OS/2 database clients is a new feature of Database Manager. NetBIOS is the default LAN protocol for OS/2, DOS, and MS-Windows database clients. NetBIOS greatly simplifies the installation and configuration of database clients and servers. It keeps the clients "skinny" by using up less memory than APPC/APPN, the other protocol stack option for database clients. You will need APPC/APPN if your database clients require internet routing capabilities, SNA management, non-LAN attached communications, or direct access to mainframe DBMSs through DDCS/2. The APPC/APPN stack is a component of the Extended Services Communications Manager.

DDCS/2: OS/2's DRDA PRODUCT

DDCS/2, which stands for *Distributed Database Connection Services/2 Version 1.0*, is a new SAA gateway product that allows the OS/2 Database Manager to interoperate with DB2, SQL/DS, and the AS/400 SQL/400. With DDCS/2, any of those DBMS platforms can become Database Servers to DOS, MS-Windows, and OS/2 clients (see Figure 10-7).

DDCS/2 is the first PC product to implement the RUOW subset of DRDA. What this mouthful of acronyms means, in a nutshell, is that you can write database server applications on OS/2's Database Manager and then run them on either OS/2, DB2, SQL/DS, or SQL/400. You decide where the application runs with a simple directory entry without having to change (or recompile) the code on either the client or server. The choice of a database platform is totally transparent to your application. You just flip the switch by changing a directory entry; you're then connected to DB2, SQL/400, SQL/DS, or OS/2's Database Manager.

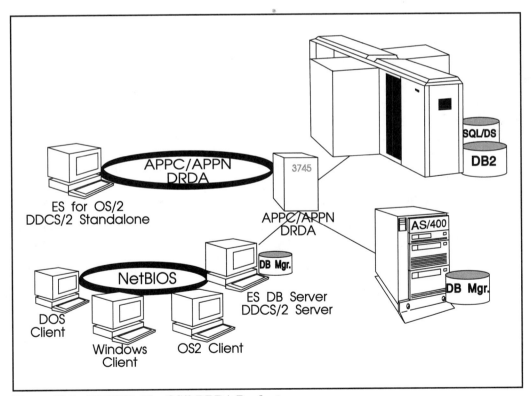

Figure 10-7. DDCS/2: The OS/2 DRDA Product.

There are a few caveats with DDCS/2, as we will point out in the next section. However, once you get over the caveats and the maze of acronyms, you may discover that DDCS/2 offers radically new client/server possibilities for environments where the data resides on both PCs and mainframes. With some modification, a mainframe application can be moved to an OS/2 platform, and an OS/2 application can access data without regard to location.

What DRDA Currently Provides

The DRDA architecture, as we explained earlier, will eventually result in a fully distributed heterogeneous relational database environment. In its current RUOW incarnation, DRDA addresses the issues of SQL interoperability across heterogeneous database servers. DRDA handles many of the thorny network and code portability issues, including:

- **SQL Message Content and Exchange Protocol:** DRDA handles the negotiations between clients and servers for supported server attributes. It uses DDM, an intermediate messaging language, to mediate SQL exchanges across unlike machines. DRDA takes care of dissimilar data representations, catalog structures, and command syntax conversions.

- **Client/Server Communications:** DRDA uses APPC/APPN for client/server communications. APPC/APPN handles network routing, data blocking, security, authentication, and generates alerts for both network and database failures.

- **Multiplatform Program Preparation:** DRDA supports under-the-cover multiplatform program preparation. A program is created locally; its output can be distributed to multiple servers using a remote BIND utility. The BIND process produces executable SQL code (called packages or plans) on the servers.

- **Static or Dynamic SQL Support:** A DRDA client can invoke the SQL statements on the server one at a time by identifying a package and the statement within it. In addition to dynamic SQL, packages make it possible to execute precompiled static SQL statements on the servers (including support for cursors).

- **Common Diagnostics:** DRDA provides returns status information upon completion of each SQL command. DRDA provides a standard set of return codes in the SQLSTATE field (based on the ISO-ANSI working draft). Database specific return codes are still provided in the SQLCODE field.

- *Common SAA SQL Syntax:* DRDA recommends the use of SAA SQL for application portability across platforms. SAA SQL is a superset of ANSI SQL and a subset
of the OS/2 Database Manager SQL described in this book.[2] We will point out the
differences in the SQL chapters. DRDA also supports target-specific SQL commands for situations when it is more efficient to use SQL extensions. Who says you
can't have your cake and eat it too?

- *Open Platform:* DRDA is one of the industry's two leading "standards" for
heterogeneous database connectivity. The other proposed standard is being developed by the SQL Access Group (SAG), a consortium of 42 vendors. IBM stated
that it will license DRDA specifications (and possibly the code) to interested parties
for a nominal fee. At least nine major vendors have joined the DRDA bandwagon.
The good news is that some of those vendors belong to both groups and are working
on "gateways" between DRDA and SQL Access. Yes, this business always has at
least two standards for everything![3]

Programming DDCS/2

DDCS/2 does not introduce any new programming constructs or functional APIs,
except for a couple of APIs used to manipulate the DCS directory (this is better done
with a database administration tool). DDCS/2, however, does introduce a programming for portability discipline. Other than that minor caveat, DDCS/2 is totally
transparent to programmers. This is quite a feat for a program that provides so much
added value at the system level.

DDCS/2 does not support the Query Manager; instead, it lets you submit queries
interactively through the Database Command Line interface. You can submit import
and export commands to the host DBMSs (but only the PC/IXF data format is supported). Other administrative functions should be done from the host platform.

DDCS/2 Installation

DDCS/2 installation is PM based. The program fits on a single diskette. DDCS/2 is
always installed on top of the OS/2 Extended Services Database Manager. On the other
IBM platforms, DRDA is part of the DBMS itself. DDCS/2 connects to the following
DBMS products: DB2 Version 2 Release 3, SQL/DS Version 3 Release 3, and SQL/400
Version 2 Release 1.1. You should make sure that the proper host-based software is
installed and that the required communications links and hardware are in place.

---

[2] See SAA CPI Database Reference, IBM Order Number SC26-4798.

[3] A spirited comparison of SQL Access and DRDA is provided by Scott Newman and Jim Gray,
"Which Way to Remote SQL?" **Database Programming and Design** (December, 1991).

DDCS/2 Packaging

So what's left to know about DDCS/2? We need to understand how the program is packaged, how it is installed and configured, and what tools are provided. The DDCS/2 product, like everything else it seems, comes in two flavors:

1. *DDCS/2 Single User*, a low-cost product that provides single user access to a host database from a LAN-attached OS/2 workstation with Extended Services installed on it (see Figure 10-7). This product retails for $500.
2. **DDCS/2 Multiuser**, a more costly gateway server product that provides concurrent, multiuser access to a host DBMS from LAN-attached DOS, MS-Windows, and OS/2 clients (see Figure 10-7). The DDCS/2 gateway server runs on top of the Extended Services Database Manager server and OS/2. You can think of it as an ordinary Database Manager server that has the added capability of being able to redirect requests to the appropriate host database server. This product retails for a hefty $4950. Welcome to mainframe prices!

There is some good news on the pricing front. The clients use the same software that is used by Database Manager clients, which is the $75 *Database Client Application Enabler* program we introduced earlier in the chapter. This means that DDCS/2 does not introduce new costs on the client workstation, if you already own (or are planning) a Database Manager client/server installation.

Chapter 11

Architectures for Client/Server Computing

In this chapter, we examine the architectural principles that can be used to create powerful system solutions on low-cost hardware. We will start with the client/server model and show how it can be extended to play in the intergalactic world of SAA and the Distributed Computing Environment (DCE). OS/2 brings to the personal computer the power of network communications and SQL databases and makes it possible to write highly robust applications that can control huge amounts of data. OS/2's preemptive multitasking allows you to modularize your code based on processes and to add services where needed, when needed. When we add the graphics environment of the Workplace Shell and the Presentation Manager, we have all the major ingredients to create powerful new distributed systems on low-cost hardware.

THE POWER OF ARCHITECTURE

What are you able to build with your blocks?
Castles and palaces, temples and docks.

R. L. Stevenson
A Child's Garden of Verses

We are all familiar with the concept of *architecture* as applied in the construction of buildings. Architectures help us identify structural elements that may be used as building blocks in the construction of ever more complex systems. The purpose of this chapter is to identify some durable architectural concepts and structures which can be used in the design of distributed systems. We will discuss system building using OS/2 in the following architectural contexts:

- *Client/Server:* where we examine OS/2 as a server for networked DOS machines and other *skinny* clients. We then introduce the concept of OS/2 multiservers.

161

- *Cooperative processing:* where we examine OS/2's role in a post-scarcity computing environment. We will look at the concept of the network agent and the personal agent.

- *SAA cooperative environment:* where we examine OS/2's role in a heterogeneous host-PC environment. We also define what SAA means to distributed processing.

- *Distributed Computing Environment:* where we examine OS/2's role in "open" heterogeneous multivendor, multiserver, client/server environments.

In the sections that follow, we explain each architectural model. These models will help guide our software development strategy. They also help us identify what system provides the best fit for a particular business solution.

THE CLIENT/SERVER ARCHITECTURE MODEL

Over 80% of LAN-based client/server solutions are deployed on PC LANs. They run in departmental-sized establishments consisting of twenty (or less) clients talking to a single PC server that provides database, file, and mail services. The other 20% run on mixed LANs, involve one or more servers (PCs, workstations, superminis, and mainframes), support thirty or more clients, and are more likely to be attached to an enterprise backbone.

We will start this section with a design of servers that are front-ended by *skinny clients*. A *skinny client* is a low-cost client machine that runs MS-DOS (with or without Windows) or a *bare bones* base OS/2 machine. The skinny client architecture is particularly well-suited for the LAN-based single server establishments (the 80%). We then introduce a multiserver architecture that demonstrates the upward scalability of the client/server model. The multiserver model starts to address the needs of mixed LAN establishments (the 20%). The larger heterogeneous mixed LANs will require the additional support of architectures such as SAA and DCE, also covered in this chapter.

How to Create Servers for "Skinny" Clients

Generally, users do not buy architectures; they buy solutions to business problems. The million dollar question is: how is the application split between the client and the server? What function goes in the client and what function goes in the server? Here's a set of "rules of thumb" for the design of client/server applications that use OS/2 servers for skinny clients:

1. Run the bulk of your application code on the OS/2 server. This is where all the system extensions, such as the OS/2 Database Manager and LAN Server, reside. A well-endowed server can provide the following to its clients: database services, gateway services, and shared file access. Since the OS/2 server is not memory-bound, you can also use it to "roll-your-own" server applications.

2. The client machines, also known as the *front-end*, manage the user interface portion of a distributed application. The server machine provides the *back-end* of an application. The back-end typically provides shared services to the front-end clients.

3. Use a transaction discipline to code your back-end database services. A *transaction* is an *all or nothing* set of operations. Either all the operations succeed and the transaction gets recorded on the database, or the entire transaction gets rolled back if any step fails. A failed transaction leaves the database in its pre-transaction state.

4. Partition and fine-tune your server applications to take advantage of OS/2's multi-tasking.

5. Buy a *superserver* machine if you can afford it. A single OS/2 server helps you leverage dozens of lower cost client machines. So it makes business sense that your server should be the fastest machine you can afford (load the machine with extra memory for caching, an extra disk for backup, and all the communication boards you may need for gateway services).

6. Provide the highest level of interface possible to the server's services. The client should be shielded from the inner workings of the resources a server controls. For example, if a server controls a database, then it should not surface the table structures to the clients. Instead, the interface should consist of requests for actions to be applied against the database.

7. Use a LAN for local communications between the clients and the server. LANs provide high-speed, low-cost, reliable communications.

8. Use NetBIOS or Named Pipes as your LAN protocol. NetBIOS requires less than 30 KBytes of memory address space on the MS-DOS PC. This is close to ideal for a low-cost front-end node.

9. Publish the message protocol for requesting services. Use it as the requester interface to your network services.

10. Invest in maintenance and configuration tools. Client/Server products, being inherently distributed, are complex to install and maintain. You will need tools to distribute new versions of the client code over the network and to add new services as required. Where possible, build your tools using the services of LAN Server and the Database Manager. For example, a configuration management tool could maintain a list of client workstations and their attributes in the database. A workstation's attributes may include: the version of code it is running, its network address, its hardware components, the logon IDs of its users, etc. A maintenance tool should periodically fine-tune the database, log errors, maintain statistics, and *call home* (to some central maintenance organization) when a machine starts to act funny.

11. Buy off-the-shelf "shrink wrapped" solutions wherever they exist. If you can't find an off-the-shelf package, invest in a client/server enabler tool.[1]

A "Widget" Server

An example should help clarify the anatomy of a *Transaction Server* application and will introduce some common terminology that will be used throughout this book. Figure 11-1 shows a mixed operating system network environment where an application is split between skinny clients running the application front-end and an OS/2 server running the application's back-end. The back-end manages a hypothetical object-type called "widgets." It provides "widget retrieval and filing" services to its front-end clients. The back-end OS/2 server controls a database consisting of multiple tables that are used to represent an application-created object type: "widget." The details of the database implementation of the widget object are hidden from the clients.

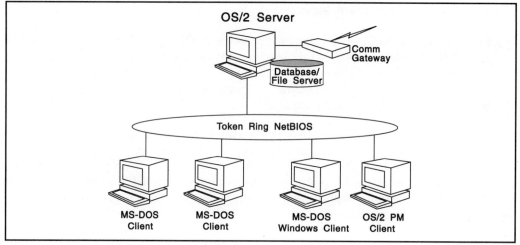

Figure 11-1. OS/2 Single Server Configuration.

A client only needs to know the set of commands that can be issued to manipulate widget objects. The commands are issued over a network in the form of messages. A widget object is only known to its clients by its behavior. For example, the widget object type is defined by such higher level actions as *move to another operation*, *rework*, *scrap from inventory*, and *ship to customer*. The set of actions a server is

---

[1] Many of the industry's most innovative client/server tools first make their appearance on the OS/2 platform. Cooperative Solution's Ellipse is a good example. Ellipse provides a graphic outliner for creating both the client and server code, a run-time facility for deploying the client/server software on networks, and an automatic version control feature.

capable of performing on object types get published in the form of network request and reply message formats. These are the messages eligible clients can send to a network server to request remote services. For example, the receipt of a *scrap from inventory* request message may trigger a procedure (or transaction) on the server that performs the following operations:

1. · Checks the authority of the client against a table of authorized users of widgets.
2. Sends a copy of the widget record to archive.
3. Deletes the widget from the active database.
4. Removes the entry for this widget from a directory table.
5. Executes any *triggers* or *alerters* that are associated with this transaction.
6. Commits the transaction to the database.
7. Sends an "OK" reply to the client.

In essence, widgets are database-centered creations. Real world examples of widgets are: parts on a manufacturing floor, CAD folders, bank accounts, airline seats, or plain old widgets. What these entities have in common is that they can be implemented on servers as encapsulated database object types that respond to certain messages. Servers become a collection of persistent data objects and the programs that control them. Instead of exporting data, these application servers export the procedures that act on the data. This design is a good first step toward creating Object-Oriented back-ends with off-the-shelf SQL database servers.

Extending Client/Server With Multiservers

Multiservers are used in environments that require more processing power than that provided by a single OS/2 server. The client/server model is upwardly scalable. When more processing power is needed, more servers can be added (thus creating a pool of servers), or the existing server machine can be traded up to the latest generation of PC superserver machine. In this section we focus on multiservers, an area that's becoming a hot topic in the industry as solutions are moving from a few large computers to LAN-based servers. The applications are broken up into program modules that run on one or more network servers.

How to Mix and Match?

We can partition servers based on the function they provide, the resource they control, or the database they own. In addition, we may choose to replicate servers for fault tolerance or for performance considerations. There can be as many servers combinations as your budget will tolerate. Multiserver capability when properly used, can provide an awesome amount of computing power and flexibility, in many cases rivaling that of mainframes. A topology of OS/2 multiservers front-ended by MS-DOS machines and skinny OS/2 clients is depicted in Figure 11-2.

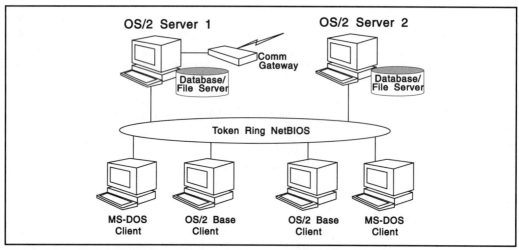

Figure 11-2. OS/2 Multiserver Configuration.

What New Functions Are Needed?

To exploit the full power of OS/2 multiservers, we will have to supplement our architecture with the following features:

- We need a *network resource locator* so that clients can find their servers wherever they may be. One way to accomplish that is through a "network yellow pages" service. In this approach, a server process whose network address is known to all will provide the yellow page service. We will call that server the "location broker." This broker maintains a yellow pages database of known services and supplies service related information to network subscribers when they ask for it. Providers of services will advertise their services through the location broker. Later in this chapter, we describe the DCE implementation of a location broker.

- We need a method for *partitioning work among the servers.* One such method is to partition work based on object managers. An object manager accepts message based requests to perform actions against the object it controls. Examples of objects are files, databases, transactions, communication lines, printers, inference engines, and video libraries. A server machine may provide more than one service using OS/2's multitasking facilities.

- We need to design our servers so that they can *delegate work* to their fellow object managers. We shouldn't always have to re-invent the wheel. A complex request may involve a *task force* of object servers working together on the request. Preferably, the client should not be made aware of this *behind-the-scenes* collaboration. The object server that the client first contacted should be in charge of orchestrating the object manager task force and returning its findings to the client. This last constraint should be balanced against the need to keep interfaces generic and modular; in this case the client, may be required to act as the integrator. Later in this chapter discuss how DCE (and the proposed Transarc extensions) will help orchestrate multiserver, distributed transactions.

Good software architecture is all about creating system "ensembles" out of modular building blocks. With some practice, you may develop creative skills akin to those of a composer in the articulation of OS/2 servers.

BEYOND CLIENT/SERVER: COOPERATIVE SOFTWARE

In this section we up the ante. We will investigate what new systems can be created on a distributed PC platform when memory and hardware become *incredibly affordable*? A network of OS/2 machines opens the door to a whole new class of cooperative software. We will assume that each OS/2 machine is fully loaded with Communications Manager, Database Manager, LAN Server, NetWare LAN Requester, and TCP/IP. In other words, every PC comes fully equipped with the ingredients we chose for our server platform. We will name this plentiful environment *post-scarcity personal computing*. What new architecture opportunities are created by post-scarcity personal computing?

Programming Your Way to Tahiti

The post-scarcity paradigm opens new vistas for network-based transactions. For example, OS/2 may be used in a small business environment or in branch offices of large companies to create a new generation of business software packages. The best way to describe the capabilities of the technology is to work our way through an imaginary application: *the Automated Travel Agent*. The following scenario will explain the features of this imaginary application.

You walk into travel agency **"Paradise OS/2"** to discuss your vacation plans. You are greeted by the Automated Travel Agent, an OS/2 computer with a Workplace Shell OOUI (perhaps like the one in Figure 2-6). You start a friendly conversation with the Automated Agent, a few dialog windows later, the Automated Agent knows that you have ten days of vacation coming in March, you want to spend them on a nice beach, and you have at most $2000 to spend on your vacation.

The Automated Agent searches its local database for a vacation strategy that fits your needs and offers you a set of alternative choices in the form of icons placed on a map. The choices for this time of the year are Tahiti, Hawai, Cancun, and other "paradises." You click your mouse on Tahiti and the Automated Travel Agent displays a set of resort choices that include the Club Meds at Bora Bora and Morea. You choose to explore the Club Med alternative, and then ask for more information about the Club Med Villages in Tahiti. You are now placed in a Hypermedia-like environment that allows you to explore the sports offered, the beaches, the room accommodations, and so on. Embedded in the Hypermedia displays are *links* that allow you to view and zoom in on pictures of beaches, lagoons, huts on the water, romantic restaurants with views of the sunset, water sports, and tennis. After spending a delightful 30 minutes or so browsing through screens of dreamland and imagining what your vacation will be like, you decide to book your vacation now!

The Automated Agent presents you with more choices, and by the time you are finished you've decided you want to spend six days in Bora Bora and four in Morea. You want a hut on the lagoon with a double bed, and you opt for low-cholesterol dinners. You may even decide to make table reservations in the romantic restaurant with the view of the sunset.

The Automated Agent now has all the information it needs from you to carry out the transaction. Consequently, it starts a background process that places a call to Club Med's mainframe computer. It also starts another background process that calls your credit card company's mainframe computer. While all this activity is happening in the background, the Automated Agent keeps you occupied by listing information in a window that may be relevant to your trip, like what kind of clothes to bring, passport requirements, and so on.

A few seconds elapse. Now all the parties are ready to carry out the transaction. We have established a rendezvous between the Club Med computer, the credit card company's computer, and the Automated Agent who is your broker. The transaction is electronically prepared. You have your reservation, Club Med has your money, the Automated Agent has the commission, and you are set for a wonderful vacation. You are asked one last time if you want to confirm the transaction. Click OK and you will be in Morea next March.

Implementing Paradise OS/2

The Hardware Base

Figure 11-3 shows a possible implementation of the "Paradise OS/2." The machines in the bottom half of the figure run the Automated Travel Agent application and those in the top half are dedicated file servers that run the off-the-shelf LAN Server Program. The first file server in our hypothetical implementation controls two 500 MByte drives that are designated as network drives E: and F: that store small objects such as text files and graphic metafiles. The second server controls eight optical disk drives that are each 1000 MBytes in size. These will be known as drives G: through N: and will store large objects. We now have nine Gigabytes of shared storage on the LAN, which is used to store travel brochures, airline-schedules, images of distant sunsets, and so on.

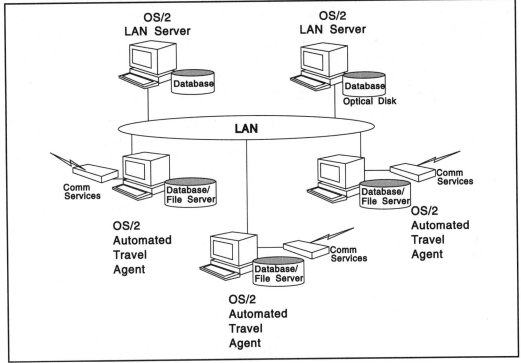

Figure 11-3. A Configuration of The Paradise OS/2 Travel Agency.

The Software Base

The Automated Travel Agent application maintains, in its private database cache, the list of available files (viewing objects) and a reference to the network drive on which they reside. The application may maintain a local copy of some of the files using its own hard disk as a cache. The network files are, of course, viewed through the Presentation Manager's display services which allow you to manipulate both vector and bitmap graphics.

In the implementation, the Automated Travel Agent may access remote mainframes through either an SDLC card or through an Asynchronous RS232 port (with their respective modems). These two gateways to the outside world allow us to talk to service providers such as the airlines, Club Med, and the credit card services. The protocol on top of SDLC could be APPC, and the one on top of the Async line could be X-Modem. The handshake with the mainframe may range from a simple file download or upload, to a series of requests and replies that lead to the commitment of a transaction. Authentication and network security are essential in this environment.

The Automated Travel Agent and the mainframes cooperate to perform business transactions. During non-peak hours, the Automated Travel Agent, having a ravenous appetite for information, downloads price lists and other related information from the mainframes and caches it on its local database server. This downloading allows the Automated Travel Agent to provide extensive searches against local data to find the best rates for a given function. The Automated Travel Agent is an example of a cooperative type of application that makes full use of OS/2's advanced features. The transactions involved several parties with the OS/2 machine (the Automated Travel Agent) acting as the transaction coordinator.

From an architectural viewpoint, we've gone past the concept of client/server where every event is generated by the client. We've augmented this architectural paradigm with the concept of *autonomous agents* that reside in the network machines and perform background tasks. In our example, an agent downloads the price lists from the hosts during non-peak hours. These agents can be augmented to analyze data and perform some actions based on a set of rules. In other words, the agents are always on *fact-finding* missions working on your behalf.

A More Personal Version of Paradise

It is easy to imagine that the next step is to have a personal version the Automated Agent run on your own OS/2 PC. You will have your own personal agent to take care of your vacations. Your agent will know your vacation schedule and preferences. It has also kept a history of your previous vacations in the database and has learned from it your likes and dislikes. Your personal agent knows you like to take your vacations in March, so it started a search sometime in December to find you the best bargains. Your agent is of course always negotiating with other agents all over the world, always "wheeling and dealing" on your behalf. The best part is that you do not have to babysit your agent while it's out there doing all this work on your behalf. You get the picture?

Distributed Data: Client/Server Agents versus Distributed Database

What does "post-scarcity" mean to database servers? With disk prices being reduced every day and with the database software running on every PC, we can now enjoy the luxury of storing large amounts of data in our personal databases. This luxury will make life very pleasant for personal software providers; however, the question which we must ask is: *how is shared data handled in a post-scarcity data storage world?* There are two strategies to shared data:

1. Keep all shared data on servers using the technology developed for servers and multiservers. This is the straight client/server model we previously discussed.

2. Allow outsiders to access the public parts of your shared data and obtain, when you require it, access to other people's data. There are two ways of providing this type of service in a distributed data sharing environment:

- Through a standard *distributed database package*
- Through a *network of agents* that use the client/server model to exchange services and data

We will now compare the distributed database and network agent approaches to shared data.

The Distributed Database Model

Standard *off-the-shelf* commercial distributed database packages will provide, when they fully blossom, transparent access to data on a network. The distributed database keeps track of the location of data on the network, and will route your requests to the right database nodes, making their location transparent. OS/2's remote SQL provides a rudimentary distributed database function. To be fully distributed, a database should allow you to join data from tables that reside on several machines. It should also *atomically* update data in tables that reside on several machines.

Distributed databases make it easy to write distributed applications without having to first decompose your applications (as we had to do for client/server). With *true* distributed database, the location of the data is completely transparent to the application. The chief advantage of a distributed database is that it allows access to remote data transparently while keeping most of the data local to the locations that actually use it. The disadvantages of a distributed database are:

1. They currently do not work in heterogeneous database environments. As a result, you are locked into a single vendor solution.
2. They poorly encapsulate data and services. You cannot change a local database table if it is being used by other nodes.
3. They require too many low-level message exchanges to get work done. Distributed databases exchange messages at the SQL level. This is not as efficient as the distributed transaction server alternative, which uses RPCs.

Network Agents

In the Network Agents approach, each machine on the network contains an agent that runs in the background and performs useful tasks, such as dealing with requests for remote information both outgoing and incoming. The agents communicate with one another using the client/server RPC exchanges described in the previous sections. These include OS/2's native Named Pipes, and TCP/IP for OS/2's Sun and NCS RPCs.

Agents are better suited than distributed database management systems to handle heterogeneous databases from multiple vendors. The local agent acts as a client to a remote agent server when it needs data from the server's database and vice versa. The agent client/server paradigm provides better local autonomy. A node can change its database designs without affecting clients. The database design and structure does not have to be known to the outside world. The only thing that cannot easily change are the RPC service interfaces (or the request and reply message formats for applications that issue their own messages).

The network shown in Figure 11-4 shows a Personal Agent application running on every machine. These agents are more than just background tasks; they have to cooperate with other agents on the network through the client/server interface to get their work done. They also need to be programmed to understand their user's personal information needs. In other words, we're creating a brave new world of *agents* that are programmed to have a ravenous appetite for information on a list of topics. These agents control the private information on your machine. Your machine's agent is always operating on your behalf in the background accumulating and sorting information on topics which interest you. It does that by conducting constant negotiations and fact-finding missions with fellow information agents on remote machines. The background agent is always ready to immediately service any request for information from either a foreground process on your machine or from a *cooperative* network agent.

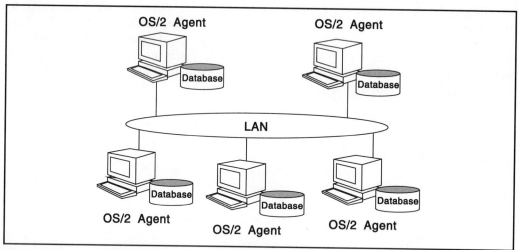

Figure 11-4. An OS/2 Network With Personal Agents.

OS/2 IN THE SAA ENVIRONMENT

SAA, as you recall, is the architecture that promises to seamlessly integrate IBM's four mainstream, commercial operating-system platforms (OS/2, OS/400, MVS, and VM). SAA addresses three specific needs: 1) to migrate an application across SAA machine platforms, 2) to split up an application across SAA machines, and 3) to communicate data between different SAA machine types independent of location. More recently, IBM extended the SAA vision to include multivendor interoperability through the Distributed Computing Environment (DCE). The DCE standard is supported by most Unix vendors, DEC, HP, Tandem Computers, and many others.

If it succeeds, IBM's SAA will remove the present distinction between mainframes, minicomputers, and PCs. Everyone will write to a Common Programming Interface (CPI) and no one will know (or care) about target machines, about where data comes from, or how information gets passed over networks. SAA is IBM's most strategic architectural blueprint since the unveiling of the System/360 in 1964. It promises to have an immense impact on how PCs are used on enterprise networks. SAA defines a "standard" operating environment for executing cooperative software solutions. At a client/server level, SAA defines standards for clients to transparently access resources and services at the enterprise level. It also provides a blueprint for total system management in heterogeneous environments. The *Information Warehouse* strategy, announced in September 1991, promises to provide an environment in which data on all IBM and non-IBM platforms can be accessed and managed regardless of format, database, or geographic location.[2]

Since OS/2 is so fundamentally linked to SAA, you will need to understand SAA architecturally so that you can understand OS/2's present and future distributed processing capabilities. In the following sections, we will first outline the architecture of a virtual distributed SAA machine. We will then demonstrate, through two futuristic scenarios, how OS/2 can be used in a distributed SAA architecture context.

What Does an SAA Machine Look Like?

To navigate in the world of SAA, you will need to familiarize yourself with its many acronyms. This section will serve as a "gentle" guide to SAA. We will create the architectural framework for an idealized SAA machine. This machine will look very much like an extended OS/2 machine. This is not too surprising, since IBM has chosen to support SAA across three major systems: System/370, AS/400, and Personal System/2 (PS/2). OS/2 and its Extended Services are the embodiment of SAA for the PS/2s. You will note that the System/370 supports two SAA operating systems: VM and MVS.

SAA is a collection of selected software interfaces, conventions, and protocols that collectively provide the framework for the development and execution of consistent

---

[2] Since its inception in 1987, SAA was declared, on more than one occasion, "dead" by pundits. It was seen as an architecture without a product base. In September 1991, IBM unleashed a blitz of products which delivered a message that SAA was alive and well. The announcement included implementations of DRDA and CPI-C on every SAA platform, a clearer view of SystemView, the Information Warehouse, and a pledge to support DCE. Following the announcement, columnist Anura Guruge wrote the following: "Since I was responsible for dismissing SAA as the Hubble Telescope of the computer industry, it's only appropriate that I take the lead in admitting that where SAA is concerned IBM has regained its focus." **Data Communications** (November, 1991).

distributed applications. Figure 11-5 presents a layered representation of the SAA components from a programmer's perspective. We will start from the top of the figure and introduce the various SAA components.

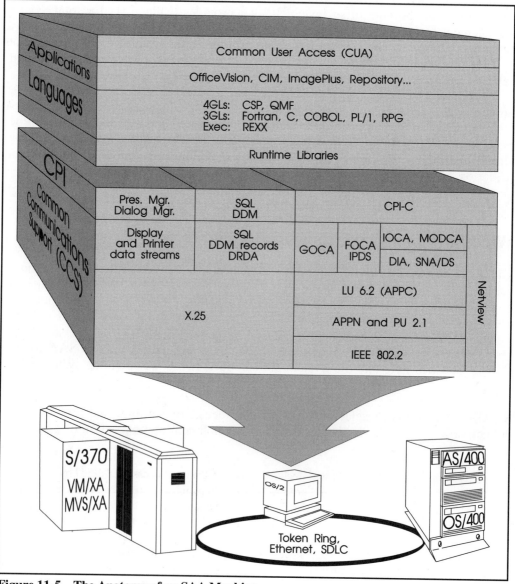

Figure 11-5. The Anatomy of an SAA Machine.

Common User Access (CUA)

Common User Access (CUA) is a set of rules and guidelines for providing a consistent user *look and feel* across all SAA machines. Both Windows 3.X and OS/2 1.3's Presentation Manager embody the CUA'89 Graphical User Interface (GUI) standard. The OS/2 2.0 Workplace Shell embodies the CUA'91 Object Oriented User Interface (OOUI) standard. We will have a lot more to say about CUA'91, PM, OOUI's, and the Workplace Shell in Part VI.

SAA Applications

SAA applications have the following attributes:

1. They provide a CUA look and feel to the user.
2. They use SAA languages, system interfaces, and protocols, which make it easy to port applications across SAA machines.
3. They store data in SQL databases.
4. They should be able to share function and data with related SAA applications.
5. They preferably use a PC to provide the user interface (ideally the workstation would run OS/2's Presentation Manager).

IBM's **ImagePlus** provides an example of a current vintage SAA application. Image-Plus provides document and image management services that run on the OS/400, OS/2, MVS, and VM. It uses common interchange formats for displaying, storing, and retrieving images across the SAA platforms.

SAA Languages

SAA languages provide the interface to the SAA Common Programming Interface (CPI) through run-time libraries of SAA services and precompilers (where applicable). IBM offers a Fourth Generation Language (4GL), the Application Generator based on CSP. The Query Manager may also be considered to be an SAA-supported 4GL. The third-generation languages (3GLs) SAA supports are Cobol, C, Fortran, RPG, and PL/1. Finally, the command language of choice for SAA environments is REXX. The SAA languages, with the exception of RPG and PL/1, run on all of IBM's SAA compliant operating systems.

Common Programming Interface (CPI)

The Common Programming Interface (CPI) specifies the APIs to the key "system enablers" that allow you to write portable SAA applications. This is the part of SAA that is most relevant to programmers. Through the CPI, you have access to the SAA's major services in an operating system-independent manner. Currently, SAA specifies the CPI to the following services:

1. **SAA Data Services** are provided through Relational Databases and network file systems. The SAA Relational Database Manager's CPI is SQL. DRDA, when it is fully implemented, will provide a single view of the database throughout a network of SAA machines. The SAA network file system's CPI is based on the Distributed Data Manager (DDM) architecture, which allows an application to access file records transparently over an SAA network. DDM provides a network directory of files and handles the translation of record formats between dissimilar file systems. The DDM CPI is the standard file I/O on the various SAA operating systems. When the local file system determines that a file is not in its directory, it passes the call to a DDM agent. This agent translates the local file call to a generic DDM request that it sends to the target file system. The results of the request are returned in a similar manner.

2. **SAA Presentation Services** are provided through an SAA Dialog Manager CPI and an SAA Presentation Manager CPI. The Dialog Manager CPI provides a high-level programming capability for defining and displaying CUA compliant screens and windows. The Presentation Manager CPI (which is OS/2's PM), provides lower-level graphic controls of screens and printers.[3]

3. **SAA Communication Services** provide a consistent high-level programming interface to the SAA communication and network facilities, referred to as the Common Communication Support (CCS) services. CPI-C, the SAA Communications API, provides an interface to the SNA LU Type 6.2 protocol for program-to-program communications (also known as APPC). CPI-C includes the APIs to network management services (IBM's Netview). CPI-C may eventually include APIs to generic remote services such as the Document Interchange Architecture (DIA) for the retrieval, processing, and distribution of documents.

Common Communication Support (CCS)

Common Communication Support (CCS) specifies the protocols for the interconnection and data interchange among the SAA systems. Over time, CCS will allow applications to be executed cooperatively across SAA systems and will provide transparent access to distributed data. The following summarizes what is provided today:

---

[3] The OS/2 Dialog Manager is part of the OS/2 1.3 Toolkit. It was not enhanced for OS/2 2.0. Perhaps, this is one CPI you should avoid writing to.

- CCS defines the *contents and structure* of network objects. The Mixed Object Document Content Architecture (MODCA) specifies the structure of multimedia documents. The Image Object Content Architecture (IOCA) specifies image interchanges. The Graphics Object Content Architecture (GOCA) specifies graphic interchanges. The Font Object Content Architecture (FOCA) specifies font interchanges. DRDA and its underlying protocols (such as FDOCA) specify the format of tabular relational data exchanges. DDM describes the format of records and files. The SAA 3270 data stream specifies a virtual screen protocol. The SAA Intelligent Printer Data Stream (IPDS) specifies a protocol for all-points-addressable printing.

- CCS defines *Remote Services*, such as remote SQL, remote file access, and electronic mail. In an SAA office system, DCA-structured documents may be interchanged with other SAA office systems using the Document Interchange Architecture (DIA). DIA uses the SNA Distribution Services (SNADS), a store-and-forward service.

- CCS defines *Peer-to-Peer* services for establishing sessions and conversations between SAA programs. The SAA architecture specifies the use of System Network Architecture (SNA) Logical Unit Type 6.2 (LU 6.2), which specifies the handshakes and message formats used during a peer-to-peer SNA session. LU 6.2 roughly corresponds to the International Standard's Organization's (ISO's) Open System Interconnection (OSI) framework for the Presentation, Session, and Transport layers.

- CCS defines an *Internet Packet Service* based on SNA's Advanced Peer-to-Peer Networking (APPN) architecture and SNA's PU 2.1 protocol for node control. This corresponds roughly to OSI's network Layer.

- CCS defines the *Data Link and Physical layers* for the interconnection of SAA machines. SAA systems may be interconnected using LANs, telecommunication links, or packet-switched networks. SAA specifies four data-link protocols, namely X.25, SDLC, Ethernet, and Token Ring.

The OSI SAA Stack

In 1989 IBM added support for the OSI stack to SAA. So, you can implement either the SNA or OSI protocol stacks and still be *SAA-compliant*. The OSI stack replaces the SNA CCS layer and is compliant with the government's GOSIP OSI interoperability profile. The SAA OSI stack provides networking functions from the application layer down to the physical layer (see Figure 11-6). The application layer supports the FTAM file access protocol and the X.400 message handling system (for electronic mail). The session layer supports the OSI Session protocol Versions 1 and 2. The transport layer supports the OSI Transport Protocol, including the reliable Class 4 service and the less reliable Classes 0 and 2. The network layer supports both OSI's Connectionless (CLNS) and Connection-oriented (CONS) network protocols. At the physical and link layers, the OSI stack supports X.25, Ethernet, and Token Ring.

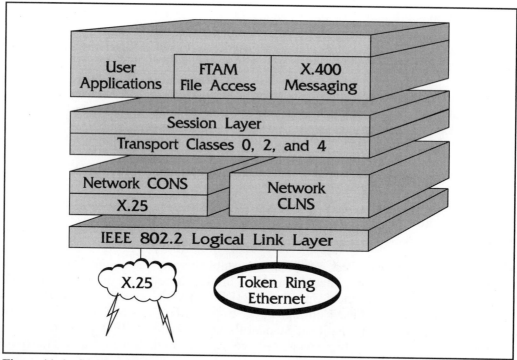

Figure 11-6. SAA's OSI Stack.

The OSI stack is implemented on all the SAA platforms. There are still some holes in the different implementations. The OS/2 implementation, provided by the OSI/CS and OSI FS/2 products, does not include X.400 support. The OS/400 platform does not provide LAN support; it supports only X.25. The MVS and VM platforms, surprisingly, do not provide Token Ring LAN support; they support only Ethernet using the 3172 controller.

OS/2 Extended Services: The "Ideal" SAA Machine

You may have noticed some of the "incredible" similarities between the SAA virtual machine and elements of the OS/2 client/server platform we described in previous chapters. This is not a coincidence. OS/2 with Extended Services is being built from the ground up as the "ideal" SAA machine. OS/2's "Managers" for Presentation, Dialog, Database, Query, and Communications closely match the structure of the SAA model. If you're still not comfortable with SAA after this concentrated and acronym-intensive explanation, do not despair. Most of this book is about SAA in one form or another. The code we develop is mostly SAA-compatible. You will have every opportunity to explore CUA 91, CPI-C, APPC, and SQL in great depth; we will provide many in-depth tutorials and hands-on programming examples.

SystemView

IBM's September 1991 **SystemView** announcements describe the framework of the SAA *System Management Architecture*. When this architecture is totally specified, it will provide an all-encompassing blueprint for total network and systems management that cuts across vendor lines. SystemView, in its current form, provides an embryonic framework of what it takes to provide systems management in a distributed computing environment. It builds on top of the OSI *Manager/Agent* model. *Managers* are applications that interact with a human and with agents in a client/server relationship. *Agents* are pieces of software on a remote node that are able to respond to manager requests and translate them into internal calls to the object being managed.

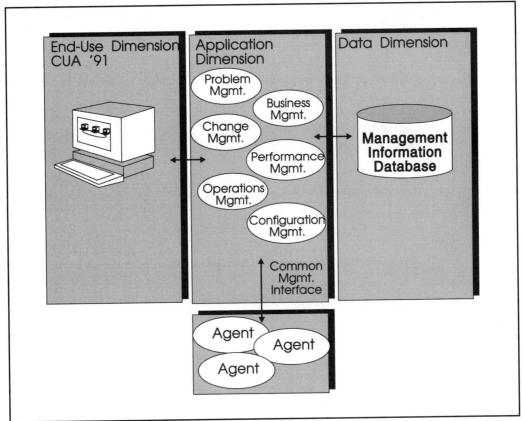

Figure 11-7. SAA's SystemView Framework for Systems Management.

SystemView assumes the existence of the Manager/Agent infrastructure on top of which it provides a framework for writing management applications. The framework consists of three *dimensions*: end-use, application, and data (see Figure 11-7). The *end-use dimension* describes an object-based CUA'91 Workplace Shell front-end that represents iconically the objects to be managed. This interface will be implemented using the OS/2 based GraphicsView/2 product. The *application dimension* specifies the APIs for system management applications (on heterogeneous platforms). System-View applications are grouped into six management categories: business, operations, change, configuration, performance, and problem. The *data dimension* defines the data (in a relational format) and the operations on that data. The data model will conform with the ISO's 10165 guideline for the definition of managed objects.

The SystemView framework introduces well-defined boundaries between the various system management components. These open boundaries will encourage the creation of object-oriented system management components that will work together to provide a total system management solution. Code from IBM and third parties will plug-and-play on the SystemView platform. The SystemView framework will, over time, create a new generation of distributed system management software that can run on any SAA platform. SystemView will become a reality when IBM publishes its System Management Architecture (due in 1992).[4]

OS/2 in a Distributed SAA World

Now that we know what constitutes an SAA machine, we will put together two somewhat futuristic scenarios that help situate OS/2 architecturally in the distributed world of SAA. These scenarios should help you understand the total system solution that SAA will provide across the IBM product line and beyond. In fact, if you think about it, SAA is a de facto standard that specifies in abundant detail how any set of *heterogeneous* computer systems from IBM or any other vendor may interoperate architecturally.

In the previous section we pointed out that a distributed SAA environment provides:

- Distributed database
- Distributed application management
- Cooperative processing
- Network management
- Location-transparent application run-time environment
- A single system image to the application programmer

When it comes to building SAA system solutions, the OS/2 workstation lies at the *center of the universe*. The OS/2 workstation is not only SAA's primary user interface device; it is also the primary gateway between SAA environments and provides a single image of the SAA system.

---

[4] Some analysts speculate that the new architecture, originally to be announced in 1991, was delayed to make SystemView fully conform with OSF's DME architecture for heterogeneous system management. DME was announced in September, 1991.

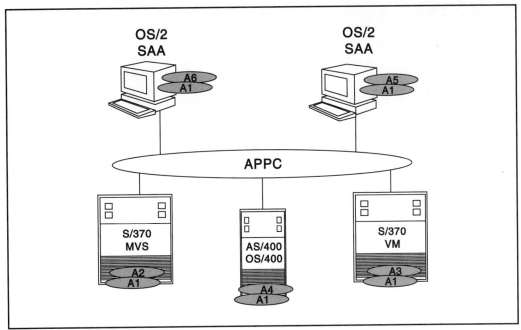

Figure 11-8. A Distributed SAA Application.

Futuristic Scenario 1: An SAA Cooperative Environment

This scenario will help clarify the workings of SAA and more specifically will clarify the key role OS/2 will play in that environment. Figure 11-8 shows a network of distributed applications running on a variety of SAA machines.

Application *A1* runs on all the machines in the network. *A1* is an example of a cooperative SAA application, parts of which run on various SAA machines. In our scenario, *A1* could be accessing data from various SAA machines and then pre-process the data before it gets delivered to the end user. *A2* is an application that runs on an IBM S/370 under MVS. *A3* is an application that runs on an IBM S/370 under VM. *A4* is an application that runs on an IBM AS/400 under OS/400. Finally, *A5* and *A6* are applications that run on OS/2 machines.

We assume that the OS/2 machine with *A6* provides a front-end to all the applications. In this futuristic scenario, this front-end looks very much like the Workplace Shell (see Figure 11-9). When users first sign on to the *A6* OS/2 machine, they will be asked for a logon id; this single id will be used "under-the-covers" to connect to a variety of remote applications. This implies a common authentication service across SAA machines. The Workplace Shell presents an iconic view of the objects that are available to the user. The fact that some of these objects are handled by the remote applications *A1* through *A5* is totally transparent to the user, who only sees a single object-based image of the entire system.

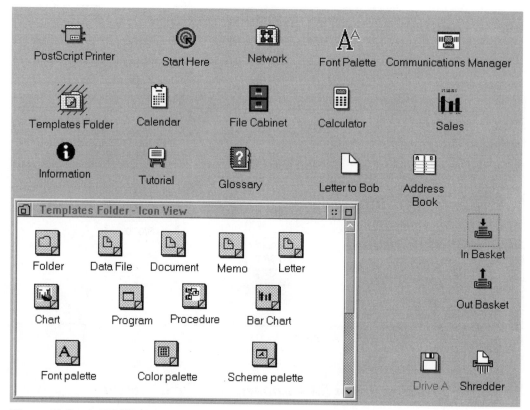

Figure 11-9. A CUA'91 View of a Distributed SAA Application.

The user clicks on an icon to start a particular application. This causes a frenzy of under-the-covers network activity as APPC sessions get established with the remote applications. Because all the applications are SAA-compliant, each object will have its window or view; the user can move from application to application by clicking the mouse. More interestingly, the user can use the clipboard or *drag and drop objects* with a mouse between windows to exchange data between applications. Thus, a user can move data from an AS/400 to a S/370 and vice versa through cut-and-paste and drag-and-drop operations.

This scenario shows that through the OS/2 front-end, the user is at the control of a vast universe of SAA applications all of which appear to run locally under the Workplace Shell. The user is totally oblivious as to where those applications actually reside or on which machines they are running. If application *A4* is too slow when it runs on an AS/400 machine, there is no architectural reason why it cannot be moved to an IBM S/370. From the user's perspective, when the application gets moved to the S/370, nothing changes except the response time, which should improve substantially.

Futuristic Scenario 2: An SAA Lifecycle Repository

Future SAA applications will be managed through their entire lifecycle from conception to run time. We will explain the implications of this by introducing the concept of a *network repository*. The *repository* in our scenario is an application that supports network applications from build time to run time. It does this by controlling objects in a repository database. The repository is used in the creation, distribution, and management of networked SAA applications.

The scenario starts with business planners and modelers who use an Upper CASE tool on a repository to design an enterprise-wide distributed application. A Lower CASE tool then uses the specifications stored by the Upper CASE tool in the repository to build visual forms and objects, tables, and transactions that will make up the application. Once built, the transactions, tables, and visual objects will be versioned and stored in the repository.

A run-time manager application then uses the repository to download the transaction code, the tables, and the visual forms to the network machines that will do the actual work. A run-time network manager uses the repository to control the code versions and to provide security and configuration services. It will measure application performance and, if necessary, migrate the applications to faster SAA machines, or it may simply redirect client requests to faster servers. All this is done by consulting the repository for topological information. The repository is also kept informed of changes on the network and of significant events.

As you can see, a "brave new world" is evolving that operates without programmers like us. The business planners are at the controls. Don't panic though. It will require millions of hours of programmer time to create the intelligent repository tools that will make this scenario a reality. So plan your retirement accordingly.

Moving Through Virtual SAA Space

These two examples are architectural renditions of what an SAA foundation should be able to provide in the not too distant future. The first scenario demonstrates the SAA run time. You should get the picture that SAA provides a machine-independent and location-transparent environment to its applications and users. Think of it as a *virtual SAA space* in which applications float. The front-end and entry-point to this brave new world is our friendly OS/2 Workplace Shell. The second scenario demonstrates how future SAA applications can be created and managed. Applications will live in repositories and move back and forth between repositories and virtual SAA space.

SAA is a foundation for the creation of distributed architectures on heterogeneous computer systems. The good news is that SAA is an *open* architecture of sorts (more on that later). Any computer vendor that adheres to the SAA virtual machine standard can play in this game. PCs using OS/2 Extended Services are fully equipped to become major players in the SAA scheme of things. Most importantly, the software you create is what brings "life" to this architectural space. You can see an embryonic form of that life in the software we will create in this book.

OS/2 IN THE OPEN SYSTEMS WORLD

The dominance of single-vendor hardware and software architectures is fading as corporations move into the multivendor world of client/server and enterprise networks. *Open Systems* is the current buzzword for creating a new world order in distributed computing. We will close this chapter by looking at how OS/2 (and SAA) will participate in this open systems movement.

What Is an Open System?

Given all the hype about open systems, it may come as a surprise that there is no consensus in the industry about what is an *open system*. Everyone agrees that open is desirable. Users seem to equate open with interoperability, freedom of choice, integrated multivendor solutions, and the disintegration of the Soviet Union. Vendors equate open with standards and focus on portability. Users do not trust the vendors or standard groups. There is obviously a mismatch in perceptions. Let's work our way through some of the open mythology:

- **Myth #1: Open systems means Unix.** Open systems are not about any single technology. Unix-derived systems were first to use the open systems code-phrase in advertising their products. But Forrester Research discovered in an extensive user survey that Unix got a 71% open rating, AIX got 29%, and SunOS only got 17%. The conclusion is that users see Unix as open, but perceive its commercial implementations as being proprietary.[5] In contrast, MS-DOS got a 42% rating and OS/2 got 32%. Forrester concluded that users accept the reality that multiple operating systems will forever be the norm. A consensus seems to be emerging that "open" has to encompass more than just Unix, or else 90% of the computer industry will be left out.[6]

- **Myth #2: Open means application portability.** Portability seems to be the primary issue on vendor-dominated "standards" groups. Forrester discovered that portability ranked low on users' agenda. X/Open's **Xtra** 1991 Open System Directive came to the same conclusion. The **Xtra** survey lists the five top strategic

---

[5] The users are right. Unix SVR4 is a technology; not a standard or a product. Each company that sells SVR4 does something different with it. Sun added a thousand person-years of value-added effort to its SVR4 product.

[6] Source: **Open Systems Agony,** Forrester Research, Inc. (July, 1991).

priorities as: 1) interoperability across heterogeneous systems, 2) an overall architecture for enterprise open systems computing, 3) heterogeneous networked database access, 4) integrated open and proprietary network management, and 5) open access to proprietary mainframe applications.

- **Myth #3: Open means the arrival of standards.** The Forrester survey detects a deep user mistrust of standards. Users perceive standards bodies as just vendors in disguise. They think that vendors actively resist the shift to openness and create confusion by subsidizing competing standards, consortia, and technology frameworks. In the "open wars," there are as many standards as consortia attempting to define them.

The best way to explain this situation is by walking you through an example of how two consortia come to life. Early in 1988, AT&T, the godfather of Unix, acquired equity in Sun Microsystems. In May 1988, a group of large system vendors (including DEC, HP, and IBM) set aside their differences and created the **Open Software Foundation (OSF)**, a consortium whose purpose was to coordinate the development of "open systems" software. OSF's initial goal was to wrest control of Unix from AT&T (and Sun) and provide a vendor-neutral, hardware-independent Unix. They were afraid that Sun would have a disproportionate influence in determining the future of Unix System V. In the view of Scott McNealy, Sun Microsystem's CEO, "OSF" stands for "Oppose Sun Forever." The OSF group developed an alternative Unix, OSF/1—based on the Mach kernel technology from Carnegie Mellon University and IBM's AIX—that vendors could create products around without paying licensing fees to AT&T. Soon after, vendors who supported System V formed a new consortium called the *Friends of AT&T*, which in December 1988 became **Unix International (UI)**.

All attempts to create a merger between UI and OSF have since failed. Aside from dissimilar kernels, the two Unix standards promote dissimilar GUIs and multiprocessor standards. Now both UI and OSF are broadening their charters to encompass the entire spectrum of "open" distributed computing. The result is two more standards: DCE from OSF and Atlas from UI. The standard makers are also busily working two different object broker and system management standards.

The Open Catch-22

So what does "open" really mean? For the purposes of this book, "open" means standards that facilitate the creation of flexible distributed solutions between dissimilar platforms. We subscribe to the *open is choice* and *open is interoperability* viewpoints. Interoperability, of course, has several dimensions: network connectivity, data sharing, multiclient support, and integrated system management. These are all areas where standards, both de facto and de jure, are essential.

In areas, such as portability, we feel standards should be used only when they are already available (one of the authors got badly burnt waiting for MAP standards to materialize many years ago). Be warned, standards are literally designed by commit-tees. The process tends to produce mediocrity and does not easily keep up with new technology. The various consortia try to speed up the process by offering working technologies. But, they also end up creating a proliferation of competing "standards." This multiplicity of standards leads to more bodies (and consortia) that form to pick out groups of "correct" standards.

How Open Is SAA?

How does the SAA effort to standardize software and network computing environments across dissimilar hardware platforms compare to Unix? The Unix approach is to standardize on a single operating system that can run on multiple hardware platforms. The SAA approach is to create a system-independent environment that can run on existing hardware platforms and operating systems, but mask the underlying differ-ences from users, programs, and programmers. If you subscribe to the view that no one operating system is best across all platforms, then you will love SAA.[7]

Is SAA open? The answer is actually yes and no. The real answer depends on your perception of what is open. Open must bring to its fold all of the world's operating systems. SAA is providing the links that will make OS/400, OS/2, and MVS interop-erate with the Unix "open" world. Yet, SAA is definitely a proprietary architecture created and owned by IBM. However, the SAA standards are published and can be implemented on any platform. Many of the SAA standards (such as SQL) were adopted as international standards. Other SAA standards—such as APPC, CPI-C, APPN, CUA, and DRDA—are de facto industry standards that are implemented on many non-IBM platforms.

SAA is IBM's attempt to create an open environment across its own platforms. SAA succeeded in the "mission impossible" task of opening up the MVS and VM mainframe operating systems and bringing them into the client/server era. This is good news for anybody with an interest in the incredible amounts of information held in IBM main-frames. It is also good news for IBM customers who found in SAA a way to fully exploit PCs while protecting their investments in existing systems, applications, and people. SAA makes it possible for IBM shops to gradually move from where they are into the next generation of client/server software.

---

[7] This is closer to the IEEE *Posix Open Systems Environment* definition of "open," which is based on the specification of interfaces, services, and supporting formats.

The SAA Open Interoperability Layer

The OSI protocol stack is supported on every SAA platform. Unix network extensions such as TCP/IP, NFS, and SNMP are now available on all the SAA platforms. NetView was enhanced to manage mixed SAA and TCP/IP networks, and SystemView promises seamless system management in a heterogeneous distributed environment. So we can say that there is no shortage of connectivity options between the Unix and SAA worlds. TCP/IP, is for all practical purposes, a de facto SAA standard. IBM has announced its intentions to port the OS/2 Database Manager and DRDA to AIX. This will create very intimate data links between Unix platforms and the SAA platforms. IBM announced a Network Blueprint in March 1992 that demonstrates a lot of "openness" with its new multiprotocol transport layer. CPI-C applications will be able to use TCP/IP and Berkeley Sockets applications will be able to use SNA/APPN, and so on (see Figure 11-10). IBM has already suggested that this common transport layer be standardized by X/Open as an extension the X/Open Transport Interface.

SAA is also being augmented with an "official" *open interoperability layer* that conforms to the Open Software Foundation's (OSF) DCE standards. The DCE layer allows operating systems to remain proprietary, but at the same time provides open interfaces, distributed services, and communications. When it is fully implemented this layer will provide total interoperability between SAA and Unix platforms (of the OSF variant). If you buy into this "open means interoperability" model, then SAA is fast becoming a leader in open platforms. So, SAA can be open at the interop level while at the same time allowing its various operating systems to exploit new technologies and hardware at a rapid pace.[8]

---

[8] The authors also believe that an "open SAA" consortium could definitely help the SAA cause.

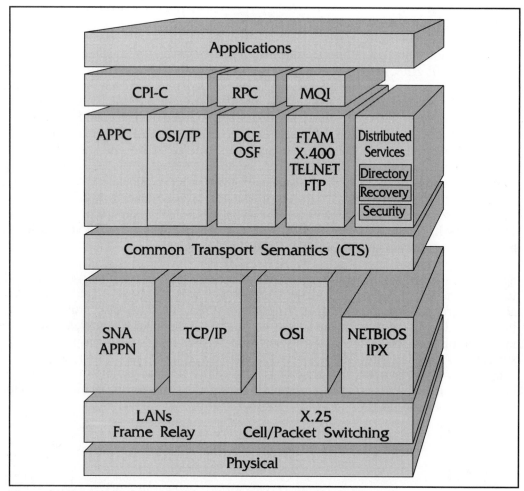

Figure 11-10.   IBM's Open Network Blueprint (circa March 1992).

What Is DCE?

The Distributed Computing Environment (DCE) from the Open Software Foundation (OSF) is probably the most significant open systems standard for heterogeneous client/server interoperability. DCE consists of an integrated set of technologies that make it easy to create, use, and maintain applications in a distributed environment. DCE provides the plumbing that enables secure access to distributed resources wherever they are and on whatever operating system they run. In essence, DCE creates a *distributed open environment* that spans multiple architectures, protocols, and operating systems. The importance of DCE is that almost every computer manufacturer is planning to support it. Even UI plans to coexist with some elements of DCE. [9]

DCE is the result of a multitechnology and multivendor open selection process. OSF identifies requirements and solicits technologies from the computer industry at large through an open bidding process. The OSF staff then picks the best submissions and integrates the technology into core software layers for resale by others. OSF member companies receive the core code in "snapshots" that can be integrated into their products. The DCE Release 1.0 package contains more than 1.1 million lines of C code, documentation, and a set of functional tests. Note that DCE is not just for Unix. Its purpose is to facilitate the creation of distributed applications and to enable the transparent sharing of resources across a variety of networks, operating systems, and vendors.

DCE provides key distributed technologies including a remote procedure call, a distributed naming service, a timestamp synchronization service, a distributed file system, network security service, and a threads package (see Figure 11-11). The following is a brief summary of the main DCE components including their origins:

- **Remote Procedure Call (RPC):** OSF adopted the Apollo RPC with some enhancements from DEC (the multithread server). To the application programmer, a remote call almost looks like a local procedure call. DCE provides an *Interface Definition Language (IDL)* and compiler that facilitate the creation of RPCs. The IDL compiler creates portable C code stubs for both the client and server sides of an application. The stubs are compiled and linked to the RPC run-time library, which is responsible for finding servers in a distributed system, performing the message exchanges, packing and unpacking message parameters, and processing any errors that occur. The DCE RPC can be integrated into the security services and the name services. This integration makes it possible to authenticate each procedure call and to dynamically locate servers at run time. Servers can concurrently service RPCs

---

[9] As we go to press, Sun, whose RPC was rejected by OSF, has not endorsed DCE. Sun is enhancing its RPC and offering its Open Network Computing (ONC) as the alternative to the OSF DCE. UI's Atlas will support both the ONC and DCE RPCs. A number of third parties are planning DCE ports to Sun platforms.

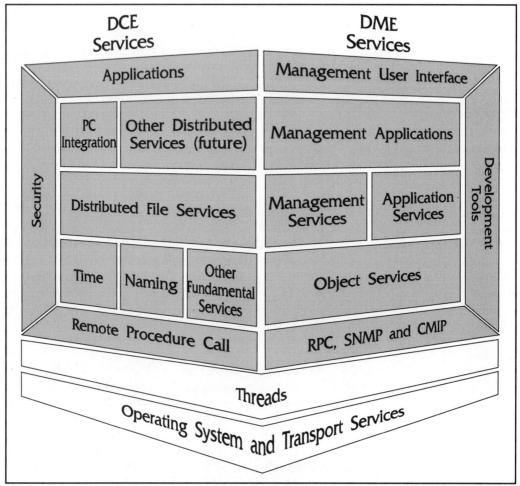

Figure 11-11. The DCE and DME Architecture Stacks.

using threads. The RPC mechanism provides protocol and network independence. DCE supports both datagrams and session-based transports. DCE tags the client data types and leaves it up to the server to perform any data conversions. This "server makes it right" approach speeds up client/server interactions on like-machines since data is not always converted into an intermediate network format.[10]

- **Distributed Naming Service:** OSF adopted this technology from DEC's DECdns product and Siemens' DIR-X X.500 services. The DCE naming services allow

---

[10]Transarc provides a transactional RPC component including a precompiler. This component adds context information in the RPC messages that identify the transaction on behalf of which the RPC is doing the work. It also encodes the transaction's status.

resources such as servers, files, disks, or print queues to be identified by user-oriented names in a special-purpose distributed database that describes the objects of interest. DCE divides the distributed environment into administrative units called *cells*. Object names are independent of their location on the network. The DCE directory service consists of two elements: Cell Directory Service (CDS) and Global Directory Service (GDS). This two-tier hierarchy provides local naming autonomy (at the cell level) and global interoperability (at the intercell level). Global access is provided using X.500's "intergalactic" naming system or with TCP/IP's Internet Domain Name Service (DNS).

DCE provides replication services that allow administrators to maintain copies of critical data on multiple name servers. Caching services are provided to improve lookup speeds. The directory supports yellow pages (attributes to names), *white pages* (name to attributes), *aliases* (name to different names), and *groups* (name to distribution lists).

- **Time Service:** OSF adopted this technology from DEC's DECtds time server product. The Time Service provides a mechanism for synchronizing each computer in the network to a recognized time standard. The DCE Time Service provides APIs for manipulating time stamps and for obtaining universal time from public sources such as the Traconex/PSTI radio clock.

- **Security Services:** OSF adopted MIT's Kerberos authentication system augmented with some HP security features. DCE's network security services provide authentication, authorization, and user account management. *Authentication* validates that a client, typically a user or program, is who or what it claims to be. This validation is accomplished through the secure communications capability provided by the RPC and the Kerberos ticketing mechanism. Kerberos is a protocol that is based on mutual distrust (it could have been designed by Machiavelli). Both the client and the server mutually authenticate one another by exchanging tickets (little secrets) with a trusted third party (the Kerberos server). *Authorization* comes after authentication; it determines whether the authenticated client has permission to access a resource. DCE supports authorization through Access Control Lists.

- **Distributed File System (DFS):** OSF chose the Andrew File System (AFS) from Transarc (and Carnegie Mellon University) and the diskless client from HP (also based on AFS protocols). The DCE Distributed File System (DFS) provides a uniform name space, file location transparency, and high availability. DFS is log-based and thus offers the advantage of a fast restart and recovery after a server crash. Files and directories can be replicated (invisibly) on multiple servers for high availability. A cache-consistency protocol allows a file to be changed in a cache. The changes are automatically propagated to all other caches where the file is used as well as on the disk that owns the file. DFS file system APIs are based on the POSIX 1003.1a (portable OS interface).

- **Threads:** OSF chose the Concert Multithread Architecture (CMA) from DEC. This portable thread package runs in the user space and includes small wrapper routines to translate calls to a native kernel-based thread package (like OS/2 or Mach threads). Threads are an essential component of client/server applications and are used by the other DCE components. The DCE thread package makes it possible to provide granular levels of multitasking on operating systems that do not provide kernel-supported threads. The DCE thread APIs are based on the POSIX 1003.4a (Pthreads standard). The DCE threads also support multiprocessor environments using shared memory.

These six key technologies will be incorporated by IBM (into MVS, AIX, and OS/2), DEC (into VMS, Ultrix, OSF/1, and ACE), HP (into HP/UX, Domain, and OSF/1), Gradient (into MS-DOS), Cray (into Unicos), Siemens (into SINIX), and Tandem (into Guardian). DCE will also interoperate (at the RPC level) with **Atlas**, the competing open standard for distributed computing from Unix International. The Gartner group predicts that DCE will become the dominant client/server industry standard by 1993.[11]

The Distributed Management Environment (DME)

Who provides system and network management in a heterogeneous multivendor environment? This is where OSF's **Distributed Management Environment (DME)** comes to the rescue sometime in 1994. DME, like SAA's SystemView, addresses all aspects of system management (see Figure 11-11). This includes the relationships between agents of managed resources and the manager applications, the common management database, common management services, and the user interface. DME will provide three management applications: software distribution and installation, distributed print services, and a distributed license server.

What makes DME exciting is the pervasive use of object-oriented technologies. A management request broker facilitates the communication between applications and object servers (agents). The broker accepts requests on objects, locates the objects, and forwards requests. Management applications collect information from agents (including event notifications and alerts) via DCE RPC requests and then act on this information. A special broker supports standard network management protocols such as TCP/IP's SNMP and ISO's CMIP. DME provides a data repository for storing information generated by managed objects. An object-oriented graphical user interface represents the managed objects in iconic form and allows them to be directly manipulated. Views show the interiors of objects. DCE's directory and security services will be used for naming and locating objects and services.

For the developer, DME will provide a toolkit for compiling object definitions and event templates. The templates are used to filter event notifications and associate

---

[11] Source: **Client/Server Computing: Exploiting the Inevitable**, Gartner Group (February 12, 1992).

events with user prescribed actions. The toolkit will also provide a dialog scripting language, user interface services, and services needed to write object servers and management applications using C++ or C.

DME is a very ambitious project. Instead of just adopting an existing framework (the DEC proposal), OSF decided to stretch the technology by integrating multiple products from multiple vendors using the object-oriented framework. DME will combine elements from HP's OpenView, Tivoli's WizDOM, IBM's Data Engine, Groupe Bull's CMIP and SNMP network interfaces, Wang's Network Event Logger (NeL), MIT Project Athena's Palladium Print System, the Network License System (NetLS) from HP, and the PC Client agent from Gradient. And, when it all comes together it will taste like good Minnestrone soup.

How to Profit From SAA and DCE

Brave new architectural possibilities are opening up for PCs in the MIS shops of the future. There are no limits to the possible system ensembles that can be built on top of an architectural base, such as the ones SAA and DCE provide. The winners in the software development game will be those who learn how to harness that architectural power and use it to create exciting new software packages. Just think of all the personal agents and network gnomes that can roam through the SAA with DCE universe and do all kinds of interesting stuff.

You can think of "intergalactic" distributed architectures (such as SAA and DCE) as large shopping malls who will rent you space on which to run your software. You create the shops, boutiques, and even department stores that physically reside in the mall and depend on the mall owners to provide parking, common grounds, and a pleasant environment for shoppers. The key is to figure out what services and boutiques will thrive in that mall. You'll have to discover the software server equivalents of bookstores, restaurants, record stores, jewellers, clothing boutiques, hairdressers, and large department stores.

All you need to open shop in this client/server shopping mall is a PC running software components, such as the ones described in this book. Some of the pieces, such as DCE and DME, are yet to come; but there is still enough to get you started. The point we're making is that there is a very low barrier to entry in this business. Anybody with a fully-loaded PC can play in it and compete effectively. So now that you don't have to worry about the plumbing, lighting, or parking, you have more time to concentrate on what the shoppers in the mall (the clients) really need in terms of services and goods.

Part II

Multitasking Fundamentals

The chapters in Part II teach you how to effectively make use of multitasking in your programs. Using multitasking effectively will enable you to develop increasingly sophisticated client/server programs that are limited only by your imagination. OS/2's processes, threads, and interprocess communications services provide a state-of-the-art platform for understanding what multitasking can do for you. You will need to acquire a working knowledge of these fundamental OS/2 services before you can write programs that use OS/2's Database, Communications, and Presentation Managers.

In client/server applications, the server uses multitasking to service multiple clients concurrently. The clients use multitasking to provide highly responsive and non-modal user interfaces. Multitasking is the natural way to simplify the coding of complex applications that can be divided into a collection of discrete and logically distinct, concurrent tasks. Multitasking can increase the performance, throughput, and responsiveness of your programs. However, there is no "free lunch." To use multitasking *effectively*, it is not enough just to learn how to use the OS/2 kernel services. You will also need to develop some good design techniques that enable you to:

- Decompose a program effectively into tasks and threads.
- Control the access to critical shared resources.
- Synchronize the execution of independent threads and processes.
- Create protocols for passing data and information between processes.
- Avoid deadlocks by programming defensively.
- Use priorities effectively to enhance performance.
- Write event-driven code that avoids *busy looping* by suspending execution (i.e., blocking) while waiting on events.
- Debug programs in a concurrent non-sequential environment.

We will develop a framework that will help you understand these concepts. The time that you invest in learning OS/2's multitasking is time well spent. The payoff is sharpened programming skills and better performing programs.

The approach we'll take in presenting the OS/2 multitasking services is to avoid simply rehashing the OS/2 Programmer's Manual. What we do instead is provide the necessary background information in tutorial form, and then develop a set of useful program examples that bring together the most important OS/2 API calls in a realistic setting. In addition to serving as production-quality OS/2 template programs, the examples also serve as learning tools that you can use to understand and measure the performance trade-offs of the OS/2 kernel services. In short, the program examples teach you how to program OS/2 and at the same time serve as tools that you can use to better understand OS/2's real-time performance attributes.

To provide realistic programs, we chose to write our code using standard C library calls where possible. The OS/2 API calls are *only* used where they can provide added function and performance, or in situations where the equivalent C library function is not available. You will find that this approach lets you explore OS/2 from a familiar C base, and that when you see an OS/2 call in the program it provides a new or improved service over what is already available in C. With your C background, you are already in a position to put together some working OS/2 programs that make use of the kernel's services. Your C programs only need to call the OS/2 kernel to obtain multitasking services, to write to the screen, and to invoke new services that are not in the C library. Here is the road map we will follow in Part II:

- In Chapter 12, "Processes, Threads, and Semaphores," we provide a tutorial on OS/2 2.0's services for threads and processes. We also explain the use of semaphores for task control and inter-task coordination.

- In Chapter 13, "Daemons and Killers," we introduce our first OS/2 programs, DAEMON.C and KILLER.C, which serve as a gentle introduction to the **C Developer's WorkSet/2** and the **C Set/2** compiler.

- In Chapter 14, "MULTI.C - Multitasking Can Be Fun," we introduce a longer program, MULTI.C, whose effect is to give a visual demonstration of multithread and multiprocess performance. Users are able to interactively change the running priorities and levels of the executing threads or processes, as well as control their execution dynamically by setting or clearing semaphores. The MULTI.C program is a tool that lets you learn, through experimentation and immediate feedback, how to fine-tune an OS/2 multitasking program. MULTI is used again in Part V to study the effects of multitasking on the performance of client/server architectures for OLTP.

- In Chapter 15, "Named Pipes," we present a tutorial on Named Pipes, OS/2's *top-of-the-line* Interprocess Communication (IPC) mechanism. IPCs are mostly used for managing the exchange of data between processes. OS/2 offers a rich set of IPC mechanisms, including Named Pipes, Anonymous Pipes, Queues, Shared Memory, and PM's Dynamic Data Exchange (DDE). Each IPC protocol has some strengths and weaknesses, as well as appropriate uses. These IPC protocols were briefly covered in Chapter 6, "OS/2 2.0: A Grand Tour". This book focuses exclusively on Named Pipes because it is the only IPC that provides communications between processes running on the same computer or on different computers. This intercomputer IPC is used to create multiprocess applications that can be configured to work over networks. The tutorial provides the prerequisite background information on Named Pipes you will need to understand the programs in this book.

- In Chapter 16, "A Generic Client/Server File Transfer Service," we introduce the concept of "layering" as it applies in the design of distributed client/server programs. We then create the topmost layer of an application that is used to measure the performance of various interprocess communication techniques. This topmost layer provides a generic file transfer protocol that is used to move data or files between two processes. The protocol is generic in the sense that it is independent of the underlying IPC or LAN communication protocol service. The same calls will execute on top of Named Pipes (on both LAN Server and NetWare), NetBIOS, TCP/IP sockets, and APPC/CPI-C. The generic file transfer is performed by two programs, FXREQ.C and FXSVR.C, which respectively implement the client and server portions of the client/server application. This application also measures the performance of the file transfer and displays the results. The actual file transfer is done using the underlying IPC and LAN protocols. In Part II, the underlying IPC is provided by local Named Pipes. In Part III, the underlying IPC is provided by the LAN protocols: APPC/CPI-C, Sockets, NetBIOS, remote Named Pipes, and the LAN Requester/Server.

- In Chapter 17, "FX Using Named Pipes," we develop FXNPIPE.DLL. This is a Dynamic Link Library package that we provide to execute data movement commands using Named Pipes. The Dynamic Link Library is linked at run time to the FXREQ and FXSVR processes, which in this chapter, run on the same machine. In Part III, the FXREQ and FXSVR will execute on separate machines and will be used to measure the comparative performance of file transfers using Named Pipes, NetBIOS, TCP/IP sockets, APPC/CPI-C, and the LAN Requester/Server. You will then be in the remarkable position of having in front of you a consistent set of benchmarks that compare local and remote process-to-process communications using OS/2's most popular communication protocols. In the process, you will also have gained valuable knowledge on the mechanics of implementing those protocols. This is the in-depth comparative knowledge you will need to help you make decisions such as which protocol provides the best fit for a particular application? Most importantly, you will have some good code skeletons on which to build your future applications.

Chapter 12

Processes, Threads, and Semaphores

The term *tasks* is used in this book to include both processes and threads. This chapter starts us in our exploration of OS/2's tasking repertoire with a tutorial on processes, threads, and the basic semaphore services used for synchronizing them.

ABOUT PROCESSES AND THREADS

We'll start out the tutorial on processes and threads with a sanity check: Do you really need multitasking? Next, we define what is a thread and what is a process? We then offer some guidelines for determining when to use threads and when to use processes in your multitasking programs. We conclude with a brief exposition on how to use OS/2's tasking API services.

Do You Really Need Multitasking?

So when do you need multitasking? It would be tempting to answer "you'll know when you need it." In general, you need multitasking if you have interspersed code throughout the main body of your application that waits on events to happen. Multitasking can also help you maintain context for multiple users in a Server type of application. You can also benefit from multitasking if your code can be divided into logically distinct simultaneous tasks.

There are many applications that do not fall into these categories. This is not too surprising; after all, the predominant thinking paradigm is sequential. We usually do not think in parallel; our spoken languages are "sequential" and most of our computer architectures and computer languages are sequential. The result is that few of our programs are written to exploit concurrency. If your application does not need multitasking and can be coded easily using sequential code, then the KISS principle (Keep It Simple and Stupid) dictates *not* using multitasking. Don't be tempted to introduce processes and threads over sequential code purely because it provides a more elegant structure or style. You should be aware that multitasking is no panacea. Concurrent programs are difficult to design and debug. Multitasking introduces side effects such as "deadlocks." In some cases, multitasking may slow down an application that is highly sequential in nature. If these dire warnings have not persuaded you otherwise, then read on because multitasking may be what you really need. If nothing else, it's a lot of fun.

What Type of Multitasking?

Once you've determined to go with a multitasking solution, then the rule of thumb is to use processes to implement functions that are loosely coupled, require a minimum amount of shared resources, and can be packaged to run independently as well as concurrently. Processes should be used to implement independent programs that can run concurrently. With processes the size of the multitasking unit is the program itself.

On the other hand, use threads to implement functions that are closely coupled, require the use of shared resources, and are the size of a typical C procedure. You are generally better off under OS/2 if you can allocate tasks (i.e., concurrently executing units of code) to parts of the same program rather than allocate them to separate programs. You use threads when you want to run many functions at the same time within a single program. Threads can be thought of as separate procedures within the same program, except that they are procedures that execute concurrently. The term *coroutines* is synonymous with threads, if that means something to you. Threads have also been called *lightweight processes*.

OS/2 2.0 can handle a theoretical maximum of 4095 processes or threads for the entire system. The number of threads that can be started by one process is 4095. You will need to learn how to manage these resources effectively to obtain a reasonable level of performance. To work successfully with multitasking, you clearly need to understand the differences between processes and threads.

What Is a Process?

A process is simply an OS/2 program that has been loaded into memory and prepared for execution. A process consists of code, data, and other resources such as open files and open queues. The OS/2 kernel considers every program that gets loaded through **CMD.EXE**, **DosExecPgm**, and **DosStartSession** to be a process. Creating a new process is relatively slow and requires a substantial amount of overhead, since the program files must be read from disk and loaded into memory. How do processes that are self-contained programs, each in its own isolated address space, communicate with each other? This is done through the Interprocess Communication services—such as Named Pipes, Queues, and Shared Memory—provided by OS/2.

What Is a Thread?

A thread provides a unique way of sharing the processor within an application, as opposed to between applications. OS/2 is one of the few commercial operating systems that provides the power of multithreading. So what is a thread? A thread is a dispatchable piece of code that merely owns a stack, registers, and its priority. It shares everything else with all the other active threads in a process. The OS/2 multitasking model is thread-based, which means that the scheduler allocates CPU time to threads, not processes. Every process must have at least one thread. A program executes when the system scheduler gives the thread execution control.

Creating a thread requires much less system overhead than creating a process. The overhead is comparable to calling a C function, where the function is in the same file as the calling program. Threads, like functions, are loaded into memory as part of the calling program; so no disk access is necessary when a thread is invoked by another thread. It is much easier to share data between threads than it is between processes. Threads use variables the same way C functions do, and any thread in a process can access global variables. Threads, therefore, can communicate easily using global variables. On the negative side, threads require elaborate protocols based on semaphores to protect all shared resources. You must design these protocols carefully to avoid deadlocks. Debugging threads can be quite tricky.

Processes or Threads?

So, which is the preferred multitasking method? The answer to this question is, of course, "all of the above." The choice of method will depend on the nature of your application. It will depend on how much time you can afford between task switches, how long it takes to create a task, and how easy it is for tasks to share information. Other factors that may affect your choice are the ease of debugging and the required level of intertask isolation and protection.

Use *processes* if your application:

- Is to be packaged as independent cooperating processes that can be sold as separate and even interchangeable modules. An example is a Computer Integrated Manufacturing (CIM) offering.
- Is oversized and needs to make more efficient use of memory. A process then becomes the unit of memory swapping which gives you a lot more control then relying on OS/2 to do the swapping on your behalf.
- Needs to protect its resources from indiscriminate access. Processes provide better encapsulation than threads and should be used as object managers.
- Needs to be ported to other operating systems. Threads are a leading-edge OS/2 construct.

Use *threads* if your application:

- Spends a lot of time waiting on things to happen. You can assign each waiting event to a thread that blocks until the event occurs. In the meantime, other threads can use the CPU's cycles productively to perform useful work. The use of threads can considerably improve the performance and responsiveness of such applications.
- Manipulates a lot of devices at the same time. The handling of each device should be assigned to a separate thread.
- Requires background tasks that get put on timers to perform chores that are unrelated to the main program's thrust. As an example, you could have a background thread wake up every 24 hours and backup a database.
- Requires an interactive user interface that supports CPU intensive background processing. By using separate threads for the user interface and background processing, you can keep the program responsive to user input.
- Requires a high level of concurrency within a single program. Threads provide a very economical form of multitasking. They are faster to create, less expensive to maintain, and share data more naturally than processes.

HOW TO MULTITASK WITH PROCESSES

The Life of a Process

OS/2 allows you to start a process using **DosExecPgm**, self-terminate a process using **DosExit**, kill a child process using **DosKillProcess**, synchronize with a child process using **DosWaitChild**, and prepare a process for premature death using **DosExitList**. The application that starts the process is called the *parent process*. Processes can find out find out all sorts of information about themselves using **DosGetInfoBlocks**. This call returns a pointer to a *Process Information Block (PIB)* that contains per process information such as the *Process Identifier (PID)*, the parent process ID (PPID), and a pointer to the process environment block. Using **DosSetPriority**, a process can change the priority of all the threads of any process, or all the threads of the current process. A process can also change the priority of a single thread within the current process.

Processes and Their Children

Processes form close parental bonds with their child processes. Typically, a child process will inherit all the resources owned by the parent process unless the parent specifies otherwise, through the inheritance flag, when it creates the resource. When a thread or child process is created, it is initially dispatched with the same priority as the thread of the parent that created it. Child processes typically execute in the same Virtual Screen group (or session) as the parent. An interesting part of the relationship between a parent and its child processes is how they will manage this common session without corrupting the display.

A parent can choose to pass command line arguments to its child process at invocation time. The child process also inherits the parent's environment; the parent has the option to enhance or change this legacy at invocation time. Environment strings contain values for system variables such as PATH and any variables defined using the SET command. You can access these variables and the process environment through the *Process Information Block*.

When a parent process is terminated, all its children are terminated as well, unless the parent specifies otherwise (as a parameter of **DosExit**). A parent can also abort a child's execution through **DosKillProcess**, or it can wait for the child to terminate through **DosWaitChild**. The parent also has the option of blocking its execution until the child process completes, or it can run in parallel with its child processes. The blocking option, called the *synchronous* execution mode, is provided mainly for compatibility with MS-DOS's EXEC function (interrupt 21, function 4BH), and it does not particularly take advantage of OS/2's multitasking. The parallel execution option, officially called *asynchronous* execution, is what you will need to develop "true" multiprocessing applications.

The Children Are Not All Equal

Under OS/2, not all the child processes are created equal. With OS/2, not unlike the real world, a child process can be born *ordinary*, *deprived*, or *spoiled rotten*. We've already discussed the parental bonds with the ordinary children; we now present how the process deals with its deprived and spoiled rotten children.

The *deprived* children, officially called *background* processes, are detached asynchronous processes that are disinherited by the parent. Thus, the background processes do not inherit resources from the parent, and are not allowed access to the parent's virtual screen group. To interact with the outside world, they use special constructs called **VioPopUps** that overlay information on the parent's screen temporarily. To receive keyboard input, they need another special construct, *Device Monitors*, which monitor the input stream. Thus, when the appropriate sequence of keys is entered, the monitor can activate the background process, which can then pop-up into the foreground and momentarily take control of the screen and keyboard.[1]

---

[1] The DosMon and VIO calls are 16-bit API calls with no 32-bit equivalent functions. The idea is that everybody should use PM and that "background" tasks should remain in the background (i.e., they should not interact with the user). We feel these services are still needed, especially for server programs. PM is a luxury they may not be able to afford. So, we will show you how to obtain these services from a 32-bit program using "thunks."

Background processes do not terminate when their parents *die*; instead, they continue to run forever long after the parent is gone. You cannot stop them by issuing Control-C or Control-Break. The parent has to explicitly kill its background children (if the application dictates it) as part of the clean up it performs before termination. Creating a background process has the same effect as issuing the **DETACH** command at the OS/2 prompt. Background processes are used to implement Daemon programs under OS/2 and provide a very useful construct in the design of multitasking applications.

The *spoiled rotten* children processes are created and given their own session, i.e., virtual screen group, through **DosStartSession**. The new session can be run in either a controlled *related* mode or in an autonomous *unrelated* mode. If the session is run in a controlled mode, then the creating process can select, set, or stop the child session using **DosSelectSession, DosSetSession, or DosStopSession**, respectively. Developers will mainly use threads and processes as opposed to session services. When you want one process to cause the execution of another, related process, you will use **DosExecPgm**, instead of **DosStartSession**. This causes the child to be run in the parent's session. It should be noted that even Presentation Manager, with its rich window environment, only consumes one OS/2 session.

OS/2 2.0 supports up to 255 concurrent sessions, which can be subdivided into processes and threads. Sessions help the user move from one application to another (by pressing Alt/Esc or clicking the mouse in the session window) without disrupting the contents of the screen. The session services are used mostly by unrelated processes, and they can be used to run DOS, Windows, or PM applications.

HOW TO MULTITASK WITH THREADS

The Life of a Thread

OS/2 provides a rich set of tasking functions for working with threads. The first thread of execution, the *primary thread* of a process, gets created automatically by OS/2 when a process is first executed. This primary thread can create other threads, which in turn can create threads of their own. You create a new thread by issuing **DosCreateThread** and pass it the address of the code to execute and the size of the stack. OS/2 2.0 will allocate the stack space and dynamically resize it as necessary during the thread's life. You can pass one parameter to the thread when you start it or the address of a data structure if you need to pass more than one parameter.

You can also create threads using the powerful C library call: **_beginthread**. Using either method makes threads as easy to create and invoke as procedures. However, you will find that threads are, in general, harder to debug than procedures. [2]

A thread continues to run until it terminates itself by returning control to the operating system or by explicitly issuing a **DosExit** call. The C library includes a special thread termination API, **_endthread**; however, we recommend you use **DosExit** instead because it returns a termination code that may be useful to your application. A thread can kill another thread within the same process using **DosKillThread**.

Once created, each thread is assigned a thread ID, which is used as a handle for identifying the particular thread. Threads can find out find out all sorts of information about themselves using **DosGetInfoBlocks**. This call returns a pointer to a *Thread Information Block (TIB)* that contains useful information about the current thread such as its *Thread Identifier (TID)*, priority, stack limit, stack base, and the exception handlers associated with it.

Controlling Threads

OS/2 allows a thread to suspend other threads in a program (i.e., within the same process) by issuing the **DosSuspendThread** call. The suspended thread will stop execution until a **DosResumeThread** call is issued. OS/2 provides an even more drastic thread control mechanism, the **DosEnterCritSec** call, whose effect is to suspend all running threads in the current process, except for the thread that issued the call. The calling thread must issue **DosExitCritSec** very soon after, or you will not have any kind of working system left. A thread may even suspend itself waiting for another thread in the same process to complete using **DosWaitThread**.

OS/2 provides a full range of very handy interval timers that can be used for timing a thread's execution. The **DosSleep** API call causes a thread to suspend its execution for a specified time interval (a thread cannot use **DosSuspendThread** to suspend itself). The **DosAsyncTimer** call will notify a running thread, through the clearing of a semaphore, when a specified time interval elapses. The **DosStartTimer** call creates a repeatable timer that can be used by threads to perform an operation on a regular basis.

In general, the thread control mechanisms just discussed are too blunt to provide a fine level of control. For example, **DosEnterCritSec**, is overkill in most situations and its effect of suspending all threads is quite arbitrary. In the next section, we will introduce

---

[2] The **DosCreateThread** function provides some stack-overflow protection using a guard page. However, it is possible for an errant application to allocate memory beyond the guard page boundary and cause an OS/2 exception. The **_beginthread** C function issues a **DosCreateThread** on your behalf and handles any exceptions that are generated by stack overflows.

semaphores; you will find that they provide a much finer scalpel-like level of control for thread execution and for the coordination of interthread activity.

Thread Priorities

Threads within a process can change their execution priority (i.e., how often they get a CPU execution time-slice) using **DosSetPriorty**. A thread can change the priority of all the threads within the process, or for a particular thread. A thread can also change the priority of a single thread within the current process. A thread may run in one of four priority classes: Idle-time, Regular, Fixed-high, and Time-critical. *Idle-time* threads have the lowest priority and receive the least amount of scheduling attention. *Time-critical* threads have the highest and get scheduled ahead of other threads. *Regular* priority is the default priority OS/2 assigns to a new process (and primary thread). The *Fixed-high* priority assists in the synchronization of a background thread that is expected to run at a certain priority in relation to a foreground thread.

Within each priority class, OS/2 supports 32 distinct priority levels. When a thread is created, it is initially dispatched with the same priority as the creating thread. Your code will then adjust the priorities of the various threads in a program using **DosSet-Priority** to meet the variety in demand for performance. For example, to satisfy a time-critical requirement, you can raise the priority of a thread temporarily during its critical processing, or you can assign the critical processing to a separate dedicated thread. The best use of high priority, in general, is to assign it to threads in a program that are part of the critical-path that other threads depend on for their execution.

Thread Coexistence

Each thread inherits all the common resources of the process of which it is a part. Thus, all threads that are part of a process share the same memory address space and resources such as environmental strings, open file and semaphore handles, and global data. This common environment is both a blessing and a curse. The blessing is that threads can easily communicate with each other, invoke common procedures, and have unlimited access to global data. The curse is that the unrestricted access can cause threads to interfere with each other and corrupt common data. Of course, OS/2's rich semaphore service is there to solve this problem and turn threads (and processes) into blessings you can count on.

ABOUT SEMAPHORES

This section provides a tutorial on OS/2 2.0's elaborate set of semaphore services. We start by explaining what a semaphore is and what semaphores can do for your programs. We then introduce OS/2's semaphore types. You will need to understand what each type does best. Following that, we go over the semaphore API calls, emphasizing how to combine API calls to perform different services. We end the section with some scenarios that explain how semaphores are used in typical multitasking situations.

What Is a Semaphore?

Semaphores are OS/2-managed software flags used to coordinate the actions of concurrent threads and processes. You can think of semaphores as "stop and go" traffic lights that synchronize the flow of independently executing pieces of software. Without traffic lights, our roads would look more like non-intersecting straight lines or circles instead of the complex street-grids we are used to. Presumably, without traffic lights and driving conventions, anarchy would prevail on the roads, leading to traffic accidents and more traffic jams. For traffic conventions to work, motorists need to abide by the traffic laws and voluntarily "stop on red" and "go on green," as well as respect the various signals and signs. In a similar vein, the use of semaphores in programs implies some form of voluntary cooperation between processes and threads. The trick is to write "law-abiding," yet highly autonomous, programs that strictly adhere to a set of mutually agreed upon semaphore rules that enable the different pieces to work together when necessary while staying out of each other's way.

The OS/2 2.0 Semaphore Types

OS/2 2.0 semaphores reside in the kernel and are manipulated through the semaphore service API calls. All semaphores are controlled by the system. OS/2 2.0 provides two classes of semaphores: private and shared. *Private semaphores* are used to synchronize threads within a process and are only valid within the process where they are created. A process may have up to 64K private semaphores. *Shared semaphores* are used for interprocess synchronization and are available to all processes in the system. OS/2 2.0 supports up to 64K shared semaphores. Private semaphores are always unnamed and are identified by their handles. Shared semaphores can either be named or unnamed (when they are created). If named, they can be opened using either the name or handle. OS/2 semaphores, private or shared, belong to one of three *types* based on the nature of the service they provide:

- **Mutual Exclusion (Mutex) semaphores** are used to regulate access to shared resources. By mutual agreement among consenting tasks, a mutex semaphore must first be *owned* before any operations are performed on a shared resource (such as a file or data structure). The code that manipulates that resource is called a *critical region* because it is serially executed by one task at a time. When the task exits the critical region, it relinquishes its ownership of the semaphore by releasing it. Using this protocol, tasks wait for their turn to use a critical resource; only one task is unblocked when a semaphore is released. The effect of this protocol is to enforce a "this is mine, stay out" agreement while a task is in the critical region.
- **Event semaphores** are used by one task to signal other tasks that an event ("the house is on fire") occurred. The *posting* of an event semaphore signals the occur-

rence of an event. All the interested tasks *block* their execution, waiting for the event to happen (i.e., for the semaphore to post). The semaphore is posted by a separate event-handling task (for example: the task that's monitoring the fire alarm).

- **Multiple Wait (Muxwait) semaphores** enable a task to wait on several event or mutex semaphores simultaneously. A task can block waiting on multiple events to occur: "an incoming message" or "a timer pop." In the *wait-any* mode, any semaphore on a list that gets posted or released will cause the task to unblock. In the *wait-all* mode, all the semaphores in the list must simultaneously be posted or released for the waiting task to unblock. This kind of signaling is extremely useful in real-time, event-driven systems where a task may be monitoring hundreds of asynchronous events. The alternative is to go into a polling loop looking for things to happen. Polling loops use up CPU cycles *busy-waiting*, which is not very good practice in multitasking systems. The muxwait semaphore scheme must be able to identify which of the various multiplexed semaphores cleared. OS/2 does that by returning an index number to indicate which semaphore on the list got posted or released.

Using Semaphores

OS/2 2.0 provides a different set of API functions to manipulate each semaphore type: EventSem APIs, MutexSem APIs, and MuxWaitSem APIs. This is unlike previous releases of OS/2 where the same set of API calls were used to create different types of semaphore effects. In general, semaphores are less ambiguous and easier to use under OS/2 2.0 than in previous releases.

Common Semaphore Mechanics

All semaphores, regardless of their type, need to be created. OS/2 provides three calls for creating semaphores: **DosCreateMutexSem**, **DosCreateEventSem**, and **DosCreateMuxWaitSem**. If the created semaphore is shared, you may optionally use a name parameter with the create call. OS/2 maintains a pseudo-directory called *SEM32* in RAM to keep track of named semaphores. Semaphore names must include the prefix *SEM32* and must conform to OS/2 file naming conventions. No actual file is created for the semaphore. Instead, OS/2 simply returns a handle for the semaphore.

The creating process and all its threads can subsequently use the handle to manipulate a semaphore. However, threads in other processes must first *open* the shared semaphore before they can use it. OS/2 provides three calls for opening semaphores: **DosOpenMutexSem**, **DosOpenEventSem**, and **DosOpenMuxWaitSem**. If the semaphore is named, the name is used as an input parameter. Otherwise, the semaphore is anonymous and must be identified by the handle returned from the create API.

Semaphores are then manipulated using API calls. We will describe the calls for each semaphore type in the next sections. When a thread no longer requires access to a semaphore, it must *close* it. OS/2 provides three calls for closing semaphores: **DosCloseMutexSem**, **DosCloseEventSem**, and **DosCloseMuxWaitSem**. If a thread ends without closing an open semaphore, OS/2 will close it automatically. When all threads that use a semaphore close it, OS/2 automatically deletes the semaphore.

OS/2 provides three calls for *querying* the state of a semaphore. **DosQueryMutexSem** will return information on the current owner of a mutex semaphore and a count of waiting requests. **DosQueryEventSem** will return information such as the *post count*, which is used to track number of times that semaphore has been posted since the last time it was reset. **DosQueryMuxWaitSem** will return information about the semaphores in the muxwait list.

Using Mutex Semaphores

A mutex semaphore can be in one of two states: *owned* or *unowned*. Mutex semaphores are created to protect critical regions. Before a thread can enter a critical region, it must first gain ownership of the mutex semaphore guarding that region. A thread gains ownership by issuing **DosRequestMutexSem**. If the mutex is unowned, the call will set it to owned and immediately return control to the caller. If the mutex is already owned, the calling thread is blocked until the semaphore is released, or until a specified timeout is reached. Once a thread owns the mutex, it can then execute the code in the critical region and operate on a protected resource. When it finishes, it must immediately release ownership of the mutex semaphore by calling **DosReleaseMutexSem**.

Using Event Semaphores

An event semaphore can be in one of two states: *reset* or *posted*. Applications block on an event semaphore that is in the reset state. When the event semaphore gets posted, all threads or processes waiting on the semaphore resume execution. **DosResetEventSem** resets an event semaphore if it is not already reset, and then returns the number of times the semaphore was posted since it was last reset. All threads that subsequently call **DosWaitEventSem** for the semaphore will be blocked. **DosPostEventSem** posts the semaphore if it is not already posted, and then unblocks all waiting threads and processes. The event semaphore is *edge-triggered*, meaning that all waiting threads are immediately enabled when a semaphore posts. It does not matter if the event semaphore gets reset before the thread gets a chance to run. The edge trigger is ideal for broadcasting signals to waiting threads.

Using Muxwait Semaphores

The muxwait is a compound semaphore that allows threads to wait on a list consisting of up to 64 event or mutex semaphores (the two semaphore types cannot be mixed). Muxwait semaphores are created with either *wait-any* or *wait-all* semantics. The

DosWaitMuxWaitSem call will be used in four different ways, depending on whether the list consists event or mutex semaphores and whether they are waiting on all or any:

1. *Threads can wait for any one mutex semaphore in the list to be released.* Waiting threads will block until one of the the mutex semaphores in the muxwait list is released. Ownership of the released semaphore is given to the highest-priority blocked thread. OS/2 detects if a mutex semaphore is used simultaneously on an individual basis and as part of a muxwait and gives precedence to the thread with the muxwait.

2. *Threads can wait for all the mutex semaphores in the list to be released.* Waiting threads will block until all of the mutex semaphores in the muxwait list are released. Ownership of all the released semaphores is given to the highest-priority blocked thread.

3. *Threads can wait for any one event semaphore in the list to be posted.* Waiting threads will block until one of the event semaphores in the muxwait list is posted. When the post occurs, all waiting threads are unblocked.

4. *Threads can wait for all the event semaphores in the list to be posted.* The waiting threads will block until all the event semaphores are in the posted state at the same time (it does not count if the event was posted and then reset). This makes the event semaphores in the muxlist *level-triggered*, unlike individual event semaphores which are *edge-triggered*.

An application can use **DosAddMuxWaitSem** to add semaphores to a muxwait list for a semaphore that has already been created. This call will work even while threads are waiting on the muxwait semaphore. A maximum of 64 semaphores can be included in the list. All of the semaphores must be of the same type (i.e., either event or mutex). A shared muxwait semaphore can contain only shared semaphores in its list. A private muxwait semaphore can contain both private and shared semaphores. An application can delete semaphores from a muxwait list by using **DosDeleteMuxWaitSem**. Semaphores can be deleted from the muxwait list even while threads are currently waiting for the semaphore. If the deleted semaphore in the muxwait list is the only one still pending, then OS/2 will unblock all waiting threads.

Semaphore Fail-safe Features

Semaphores are made "safe" by OS/2, in the following sense:

- If a process "dies" or exits while still owning a semaphore, OS/2 will notify any waiting threads in other processes that the owner died leaving the protected resource in an indeterminate state. All applications receiving this premature death notification should close the semaphore so that it can be deleted by OS/2 and take appropriate action concerning the shared resource.
- OS/2 maintains a request count for all mutex semaphores that allows a thread that owns a semaphore to issue a request for that semaphore again without first releasing the semaphore. This type of nesting helps in the writing of reentrant

threads. OS/2 guarantees that the nested calls (64K deep) will not result in a deadlock. That is, the thread will not block on the second request for the semaphore waiting on itself to release the semaphore. OS/2 counts how many times the owning thread has requested the semaphore without a corresponding release. The semaphore is not released to another thread until the count is zero.

- OS/2 maintains a *post count* for event semaphores that keeps track of post attempts against an already posted semaphore.
- OS/2 2.0 semaphores rely on the kernel to provide atomic nonpreemptible operations. A single wakeup mechanism is used to ensure that the system wakes up the waiting thread with the highest priority, and thus ensures that there are no race conditions.

Semaphore Scenarios

We now present some scenarios that choreograph the use of semaphores in typical multitasking environments. Once you grasp the mechanics of semaphore usage, you can create your own repertoire of API sequences using our scenarios as a starting point.

Scenario 1: Mutual Exclusion

Scenario 1 demonstrates how semaphores can be used to provide mutual exclusive access to shared resources. We implement the mutual exclusion scenario using shared semaphores (Figure 12-1).

Scenario 2: Signaling Events

Scenario 2 demonstrates the use of semaphores to signal events between tasks (Figure 12-2). The scenario shows how a semaphore is used to organize a race between threads. Such a race could be used to measure the performance of a set of threads (or processes). The start-of-execution is synchronized by posting a semaphore.

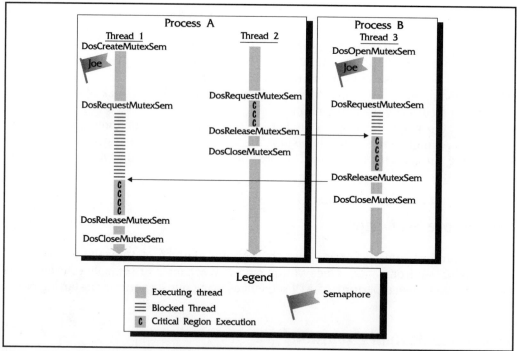

Figure 12-1. Scenario 1: Serializing Access With a Mutex Semaphore.

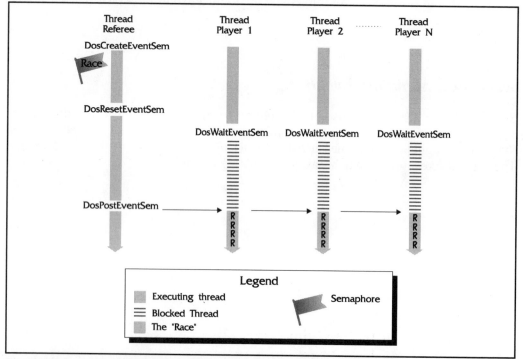

Figure 12-2. Scenario 2: Using a Semaphore to Broadcast an Event, START Running!

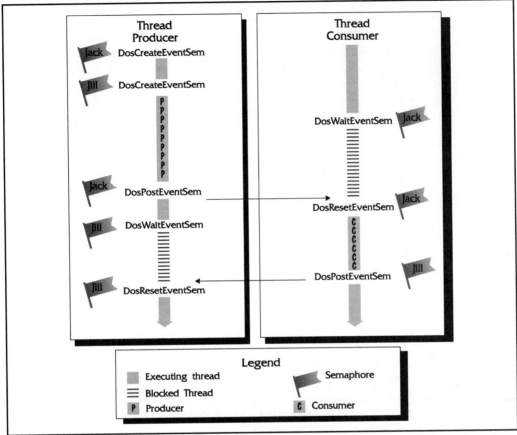

Figure 12-3. Scenario 3: Producer/Consumer Lock-Step Synchronization of Two Threads.

Scenario 3: Producer/Consumer

Scenario 3 demonstrates how semaphores can be used to synchronize two threads into lock-step for producer/consumer types of situations (Figure 12-3). The scenario imposes more stringent synchronization requirements than any of the methods discussed so far. It imposes an ordered alternating access to the shared resource, the producer always going first. The producer and consumer also need to wait for each other when the resource is busy. This kind of lock-step is used in situations where tasks are assigned different functional responsibilities but still have a need to synchronize their production in the style of an assembly line.

To accomplish this, we will use two semaphores, *Jack* and *Jill*; each indicates the beginning of a particular state. The posting of *Jack* indicates that the buffer is full, and the posting of *Jill* indicates that the buffer is empty. Why do we need two semaphores? Because we have two events; the buffer becoming full and the buffer becoming empty. So we need to have one semaphore for each event we're waiting on.

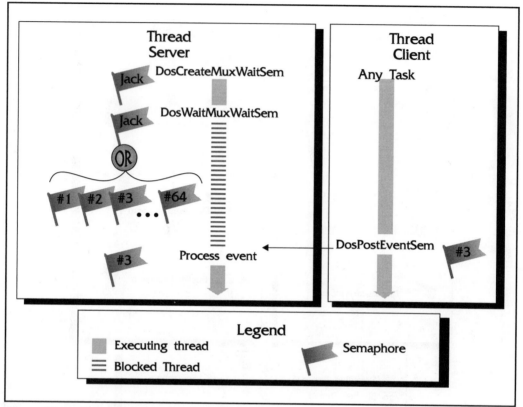

Figure 12-4. Scenario 4: The Event-Dispatcher Thread Blocks Waiting for Any Event.

Scenario 4: A Multiple-Event Handler

Scenario 4 demonstrates how semaphores can be used in creating event-driven systems (Figure 12-4). The multiple-event scenario shows an event-dispatcher task blocked waiting for any of the several semaphores on its muxwait list to post. Eventually, some event posts a semaphore and the event-dispatcher task comes to life and does its thing!

Chapter 13

Daemons and Killers

This chapter provides a gentle introduction to writing, compiling, and debugging an OS/2 2.0 program. It has become customary for programming books to start with a *do nothing* program that just writes "Hello World" to the screen. The purpose of such programs is to introduce the compiler, the MAKE utility, the development environment, and the operating system's programming interface. Our version of the "Hello World" is a Daemon program that wakes up every day at a set time and says hello to the world.

A *Daemon* is an ominous-sounding name for a parentless background process that sleeps inside a machine waiting for some event to trigger it. When a Daemon comes to life, it does whatever it was programmed to do and may then put itself back to sleep waiting for the next event to trigger it. Clearly, a Daemon may be put to good uses such as backing up your database, notifying you of your next appointment with the dentist, or executing a batch file of commands at a set time. As a public service, we also provide KILLER, a daemon-killer program. If you get a chance to run DAEMON, you may be thankful to have KILLER, which gets rid of the Daemons without forcing you to reboot your machine.

The plan for this chapter is to take you through a panoramic grand tour that starts out with what you'll need in terms of software to program the OS/2 client/server platform. We'll then walk you through the code listings of DAEMON.C and KILLER.C, your "gentle" introductions to program-writing under OS/2 2.0. Once we have a program in hand, we'll want to compile and run it. This will serve as our chance to introduce you to the joys of *making* programs using the OS/2 **NMAKE** utility. We'll walk through a *make* file that automates the production of DAEMON and KILLER. We then briefly touch on the topic of debugging multithreaded programs using the symbolic debugger that comes with IBM's 32-bit **C Set/2** compiler. This takes us to the last leg of our grand tour where we introduce OS/2 2.0's **WorkFrame/2**, a PM-based integrated development environment that helps you produce, run, debug, and maintain code.

WHAT YOU NEED TO GET STARTED

This is a good time to create the environment on your machines for running the programs in this book. Even though most programs will run on a single machine, what you really need to get the most benefit are two machines connected via a Token Ring or Ethernet LAN.

Installing the OS/2 Client/Server Platform

Each of the software packages we used for our Client/Server platform comes with an installation utility and detailed install instructions. The installation programs will guide you step-by-step through the installation of each package. Installtion options will be presented for you to tailor your system to your specific needs. Cookbook style documentation is provided with each package for added detail. All of the packages also have context-specific help built into their install programs. Just hit F1 anywhere in the install process for help. For the purposes of this book, configure one of your machines as a server and the other one as a client (or, you can configure a single machine as a client/server).

Here's what you install on the *client* machine:

• OS/2 2.0
• LAN Requester
• Extended Services
• Database Client Application Enabler
• TCP/IP for OS/2
• NetWare Requester for OS/2 2.0

Here's what you install on the *server* machine:

• OS/2 2.0
• LAN Server
• OS/2 Extended Services with Database Server
• TCP/IP for OS/2
• NetWare Requester for OS/2 2.0

Now you're all set up to run the programs in this book in a luxurious style. If you plan to modify and recompile the programs, you'll also need a 32-bit C compiler and the IBM OS/2 2.0 Developer's Toolkit.[1] You may, optionally, want to install the **Work-Frame/2** if you need a powerful development environment with all your tools at your fingertips. If you find development environments too wimpy, you can always use the "true programmer's" favorite interface, *the command line*. We provide MAKE files that allow you to go either way. If you're going to create a development environment,

---

[1] Borland C++ provides an alternative integrated environment for the development of 32-bit OS/2 code. Borland supplies its own Toolkit and PM tools (due 4Q '92).

then do your installation in the following order: 1) Workframe/2, 2) IBM OS/2 2.0 Developer's Toolkit, and 3) C Set/2.

Installing the C Set/2 32-bit Compiler

Our programs were compiled using the IBM C Set/2 32-bit compiler. The compiler includes 32-bit C run-time libraries and a very powerful PM-based, source-level debugger. C Set/2 allows you to call 16-bit OS/2 APIs or code libraries and to make 16-bit call backs to 32-bit code. Without that, we would need to create *thunks* to place calls between those two environments (there will be more on thunks later). C Set/2 also provides comprehensive migration support for applications written in IBM C/2 or Microsoft C 6.0. C Set/2 provides SAA (level 2) and ANSI C conformance. This may be important for those of you who plan to write code that can be exported to other platforms, including AIX C, SAA C/400, and SAA C/370. C Set/2 comes with a graphical installation program that walks you through installation and allows you to add new options later.

Installing the IBM OS/2 2.0 Developer's Toolkit

You must use the OS/2 Toolkit along with C Set/2 primarily because it contains the **LINK386** system linker, and the **NMAKE** utility. In addition, the Toolkit includes all the OS/2 2.0 C-language header files that contain the function prototypes, data types, and the structures and constants needed to program the OS/2. The Toolkit also contains the PM resource editors and the SOM precompiler. We will make use of all these facilities in the code we develop. Use the INSTALL utility to install the package. While you're at it, make sure to install the C language sample programs and the online documentation for the OS/2 API calls.

Installing the WorkFrame/2

The PM-based Workframe/2 is complementary to C Set/2. It is really a project-oriented, language-independent development environment. You can customize it with your set of OS/2 (32-bit or 16-bit) tools as well as DOS and Windows tools. If you install the WorkFrame before C Set/2, the installation program will create some sample C Set/2 project control files under the WorkFrame home directory.

OS/2 Client/Server Platform Memory Requirements

Table 13-1 gives you a feeling for OS/2 and the client/server platform software's memory requirements. You can start out with a 4 MByte client machine, and quickly work your way to a 16 MByte fully loaded server machine that runs Database Manager,

DDCS/2, and LAN Server. It all depends on your server's requirements. Make sure you refer to IBM's **Information and Planning Guide** for the latest official numbers.

Table 13-1. OS/2 2.0 Client/Server Platform Memory Requirements.

Client/Server Component	Recommended Memory (MBytes)
Operating System	
Base (required)	2.5
DOS compatibility	0.5
Windows compatibility	1.0
High Performance File System	0.5
Active spooling (while printing)	0.5
System Performance Buffer	0.5
Communications Manager	
Base and NetBIOS (required)	0.2
APPC/APPN	0.4
Database Manager	
OS/2 Database Client (NetBIOS)	0.5
Database Services (stand-alone)	1.4
Database Server (with 1 MByte buffer pool)	2.6
add for each concurrent client	0.2
Query Manager	1.6
DDCS/2	
DDCS/2 Single User	0.1
DDCS/2 Server	1.8
add for each concurrent client	0.2
LAN Server	
OS/2 LAN Requester	0.6
DOS LAN Requester	0.13
OS/2 LAN Server V 2.0 Entry	4.4
OS/2 LAN Server V 2.0 Advanced	9.9
TCP/IP For OS/2	
Base Product	0.7
NetWare	
NetWare Requester for OS/2 2.0	0.15

Table 13-2. OS/2 2.0 Client/Server Platform Disk Requirements.

Client/Server Component	Required Disk Space (MBytes)
Operating System Base (required) Base (optional) Swap Area	 15.0 15.0 8.0
Extended Services Base (required for CM or DB)	 4.5
Communications Manager Base (required) APPC/APPN LAN Communications Config Services API Libraries	 3.2 0.8 0.6 2.2 1.1
Database Manager OS/2 Database Client (NetBIOS) Database Services (stand-alone) Database Server add for each additional database Query Manager	 3.2 3.6 3.8 1.1 2.8
DDCS/2 DDCS/2 all configurations	 0.3
LAN Server OS/2 LAN Requester OS/2 LAN Server V 2.0 Entry OS/2 LAN Server V 2.0 Advanced	 5.5 9.4 10.4
TCP/IP For OS/2 Base Product	 5.0
NetWare NetWare Requester for OS/2 2.0	 0.5

OS/2 Client/Server Platform Disk Requirements

Table 13-2 gives you a feeling for OS/2 and the client/server platform software's hard disk requirements. You can start out with a 20 MByte disk on a client machine and quickly work your way to a 100 MByte fully loaded Database Manager and LAN Server machine. Again, it all depends on your requirements. Make sure you refer to IBM's **Information and Planning Guide** for the latest official numbers.

Your Roadmap for Reading the Programs in This Book

Due to size limitations, there will be little opportunity in this book to explain C language programming basics. To understand the program listings, you should be reasonably familiar with C. On the other hand, we do not assume that you are familiar with OS/2 and the client/server platform, so we will explain each new function when it is first encountered in a program and then reference it from there on.

Our explanation of the API will focus on the *essential* elements in each function. A book has the advantage over a technical reference, of not having the burden of presenting every last feature in a function. Because of the broad nature of OS/2 and our emphasis on client/server systems, we do not always have the luxury of grouping related API functions. An API function will be introduced at the point where it is first encountered in the development of a program. The advantage of this approach is that each function will be explained within the context of where it is first used. The disadvantage, of course, is that not all related functions are grouped in one place. We compensate for this inconvenience by indexing all API references which, in itself, is a convenient way of reminding you of where you first encountered a function. The tutorials, however, cover the APIs by related area and, in many cases, present scenarios that show the interrelationships between the calls.

In most cases, we will present you with the complete set of listings you will need to compile the programs. We also include the *make* file that is used to build the program. To follow a program, first take a quick look at the *make* file to understand what set of modules make up the code. Then, move straight to the **main()** procedure, which we've written in the form of an outline for the program. From the outline, you can follow the top-level functions that are usually listed in the order in which they appear within **main()**. Common functions that provide an underlying service are usually grouped together under a **helper** function subheading.

We are the first to admit that some chapters have listings that seem to go on forever. Much of those listings consist of header files, error recovery code, and the normal stuff that makes "real life" production programs fat. Remember that this is a book about OS/2 as it gets used in production-level code. The tab you may have to pay for obtaining this level of code completeness is an occasional lengthy program listing. When you encounter one of those programs, you can avoid letting the "fat" get in your way by setting your focus on the overall workings of the program, while taking an occasional dip into the detail where you think you may need it. The programs were designed to provide you this kind of two-tier navigation into the code; so make sure you use it!

The OS/2 2.0 Application Programming Interface (API)

From the programmer's point of view, OS/2 and the related client/server software packages should be looked at as one giant, massively documented toolkit with a well designed programming interface. OS/2's interface is much more consistent than MS-DOS's. For example, to obtain MS-DOS's services you had to place your parameters in registers and then issue an interrupt to the operating system. Error status from MS-DOS was returned through a variety of irregular schemes. In the place of the chaotic DOS interface, OS/2 offers an Application Programming Interface (API for short) written to work seamlessly with high-level languages like C. You invoke OS/2 services much the same way you call your procedures or functions. In both cases, parameters are passed through the stack and the error status is returned by the function call.

The base OS/2 API functions begin with a three-letter prefix that identifies the general operating system category to which the function belongs. The OS/2 kernel functions have prefixes of **DOS** (OS/2 system), **VIO** (16-bit video I/O), and **KBD** (16-bit keyboard). The Presentation Manager adds new prefixes such as **WIN** (Windows), **GPI** (Graphics Program Interface), and so on.

In general, you will not have to concern yourself with OS/2 function declarations. IBM supplies C header files with the OS/2 Toolkit. Including the appropriate header files with your programs will take care of your OS/2 function prototype definitions, as well as the definitions of constants, data types, structures, and macros. In this book, we will generally include header files that come with the Toolkit. Occasionally we will introduce our own types to improve readability while referring you to the IBM originals.

The OS/2 2.0 Data Types

When programming OS/2, you must bite the bullet and follow the OS/2 data type conventions originally introduced by IBM and Microsoft. These are derived data types that replace the standard C types, as shown in Table 13-3. So why are we introducing these new types instead of sticking to the familiar C types? Here's the benefits of using the OS/2 types:

- They are consistent with the OS/2 technical documentation and, more importantly, the OS/2 supplied header files.
- They provide more information regarding the purpose of an item than the C data type. This is especially the case for the Presentation Manager APIs.

- They make your programs more portable across system platforms: for example, your data types will remain valid whether you're using the current version or a RISC version of OS/2.
- They shorten the function descriptions.
- They sometimes begin with letters that identify what the type is used for. For example, **P** identifies a 32-bit pointer; **U**, an unsigned variable; and **H**, a handle.

Table 13-3.   A Sample of the Most Commonly Used OS/2 Data Types.

OS/2 Type	C Language Equivalent	Meaning
BOOL	unsigned long	32-bit Boolean value
BYTE	unsigned char	8-bit unsigned value
CHAR	char	8-bit signed value
UCHAR	unsigned char	8-bit unsigned value
SHORT	short	16-bit signed value
USHORT	unsigned short	16-bit unsigned value
LONG	long	32-bit signed value
ULONG	unsigned long	32-bit unsigned value
PBYTE	unsigned byte far *	32-bit pointer to a BYTE value
PSZ	unsigned char far *	32-bit pointer to a null-terminated string
PCHAR	char far *	32-bit pointer to a string
PSHORT	int far *	32-bit pointer to a SHORT value
PLONG	long *	32-bit pointer to a LONG value
PVOID	void far *	32-bit pointer to a void value
TRUE	1	Predefined constant set to one
FALSE	0	Predefined constant set to zero
NULL	0	Predefined pointer set to zero
APIENTRY	_System	Type identifier for OS/2 2.X API call linkage
APIRET	unsigned long	Type identifier for OS/2 2.0 API return values
APIENTRY16	_Far16 _Pascal	Type identifier for OS/2 1.X API call linkage. Thunking is implied.
APIRET16	unsigned short	Type identifier for OS/2 1.X API return values

Here's an example of the API prototype call to obtain the date and time using the OS/2 data types:

```
APIRET DosGetDateTime(PDATETIME ppdatetime);
```

Here's how you read this. The function **DosGetDateTime** has one parameter, *pp-datetime*, which is the address (a 32-bit pointer) to a DATETIME data structure. The function returns an unsigned long integer which, OS/2 typedefs as APIRET. If this all looks strange and unfamiliar don't despair: you'll soon get used to it. You will find it easier to simply use the OS/2 types without paying attention to the equivalent basic C types.

OS/2 1.X Compatibility: Thunks

OS/2 2.0 allows you to mix 16-bit and 32-bit APIs in the same program using "glue" code called *thunks*. A *32-to-16 thunk* allows a 32-bit OS/2 application to invoke 16-bit APIs. A *16-to-32 thunk* allows a 16-bit OS/2 application to call 32-bit APIs. OS/2 and the C Set/2 header files provide extensive thunking support that make thunking transparent to the application. Most of the system thunks are of the 32-to-16 variety. Many OS/2 functions are still in 16-bit code, but that's hidden from your 32-bit API calls by an OS/2 thunking layer. Thunking involves converting flat 0:32 addresses to 16:16 segmented addresses (and vice versa), copying parameters, converting pointers, checking for segment boundary crossings, converting the stack, calling the function, restoring the context, and returning to caller.

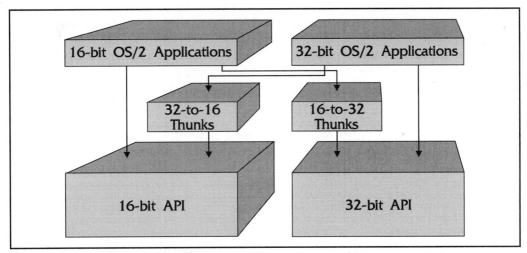

Figure 13-1. OS/2's Thunking Infrastructure.

This book is about programming OS/2 2.0. If it's as good as we've been saying, what do 16-bit OS/2 API calls buy us? They buy us access to functions that have vanished altogether from the 32-bit API set. These include the *Vio*, *Kbd*, *Mou*, and *DosMon* functions. IBM dropped support for these functions in OS/2 2.0 because it wants us to create "true PM" applications that promote a consistent user interface. We, of course, share this noble goal, and we will do our part to help create true PM applications on client machines. However, we find that there is a definite need for the *Vio* and *Kbd* functions in server programs. Servers are typically unattended (according to the folklore they reside in closets); they require a minimum user interface (more than **printf**), and they may not be able to afford the PM overhead. This is what got us into mixed APIs and thunking. We also encounter thunking when we call 16-bit APIs in programs such as TCP/IP for OS/2. Luckily, most of the thunking is handled by the compiler and system providers. They provide thunked headers and translations that make the 16-bit API calls almost totally transparent to our code. The best thunk is the one you don't know about (in a few cases, we will not be that lucky).

DAEMON: OUR FIRST OS/2 PROGRAM

Now that we have spelled out the rules we're going to code by, let's move on and work our way through some live OS/2 program examples. We will start by exploring **DAEMON.C**, followed by **KILLER.C**. DAEMON.C is a simple OS/2 program that illustrates the workings of a time of day activated background task. It also illustrates the **VioPopUp** mechanism that it uses to communicate information to the foreground screen.

DAEMON.C: main()

DAEMON's **main()** function, listed in Figure 13-2, will serve as the outline for the program. Like any good C program, DAEMON starts out by including the various C library header files. Like any good OS/2 program, DAEMON needs to include header material from **OS2.H**, which serves as the *master file* for a set of IBM provided include files that contain definitions for specific groups of OS/2 functions. These definitions include the OS/2 API declarations and OS/2 defined data types and structures.

To minimize the time required to process some of the header files, each function group can be *conditionally* included on the basis of whether a corresponding constant is defined within the program source file. To use a function within your program, you simply define the corresponding include constant using the **#define** directive before you include OS2.H. In DAEMON.C, we define the following include constants before including OS2.H:

```
#define INCL_VIO            /* include VIO api calls    */
#define INCL_KBD            /* include KBD api calls    */
#define INCL_DOSDATETIME    /* include timer api calls  */
#define INCL_DOSPROCESS     /* for DosSleep, DosExitList */
```

```
/*********************************************************************/
/*    PROGRAM NAME: DAEMON - a background task example             */
/*                                                                 */
/*    PROGRAM DESCRIPTION:  This program demonstrates the use of a background  */
/*       task to tell the world Hello!                             */
/*                                                                 */
/*    PROGRAM INVOCATION:                                          */
/*                                                                 */
/*       DAEMON time                                               */
/*                                                                 */
/*********************************************************************/
#include <process.h>                /* For exit()                 */
#include <stdio.h>                  /* For sprintf()              */
#include <string.h>                 /* For string functions       */

#define INCL_VIO                    /* include VIO calls          */
#define INCL_KBD                    /* include KBD calls          */
#define INCL_DOSDATETIME            /* include timer      api calls  */
#define INCL_DOSPROCESS             /* for DosSleep, DosExitList   */
#include <os2.h>
#include "daemon.h"

/*_____*/
/* Main routine.                                                 */
/*_____*/
VOID main(USHORT argc, PCHAR argv[], PCHAR envp[])
{
  get_args(argc, argv);       /* read time information from command line  */

  initialize_daemon();

  do
    {
    wait_to_display_hello(); /* calculate time to wait, then sleep  */

    tell_the_world_hello();   /* show a pop-up, tell the world hello  */
    } while (TRUE); /* enddo */

} /* end main */
```

Figure 13-2. DAEMON.C: main().

The final file to be included is **daemon.h**, listed in Figure 13-3. This file contains DAEMON's forward function declarations, the definitions of constants and data types, and the program's global variables.

The **main()** DAEMON procedure follows. DAEMON really is a simple program:

1. It starts out by invoking **get_args()**, listed in Figure 13-4, which obtains the time of day when "Hello" is to be displayed.
2. It then calls **initialize_daemon()**, listed in Figure 13-5, to perform some initialization chores.
3. This is followed by a "do forever" loop that does the following:

    1. It calculates how long to wait before saying hello.

2. It takes a nap for that duration of time. The function **wait_to_display_hello**(), listed in Figure 13-6, calculates how long DAEMON is to sleep and then puts the program to sleep for that time duration.

3. It says "Hello World" whenever the time is right to do so. When the time is right, **tell_the_world_hello**(), listed in Figure 13-7, announces "Hello World" on the foreground screen via a pop-up.

Aside from the top level functions just mentioned, the DAEMON program also contains a set of common helper routines. The **print_error**() helper function, listed in Figure 13-8, is a pop-up adaptation of a generic print error function. The **daemon_exit**(), listed in Figure 13-9, is an illustration of the use of OS/2's **Exit Lists** for program termination.

DAEMON.H: The daemon.h Include File

The **daemon.h** include file is your garden variety C include file that contains the declarations of constants, forward declarations of procedures, and the global variables used in the program. The only strange encounter in **daemon.h** may be the special OS/2 types **PTIB** and **PPIB**. The OS/2 types will be explained when we encounter the functions that use them.

```
/****************************************************************************/
/*   INCLUDE NAME: DAEMON - declarations for DAEMON program                */
/****************************************************************************/

/*_____*/
/* defines                                                                 */
/*_____*/
                    /*_____*/
                    /* function return values                         */
                    /*_____*/
#define GOOD              0
#define WARNING           1
#define FAILED           -1

/*_____*/
/* Forward declarations of procedures in this module                       */
/*_____*/
                    /*_____*/
                    /* top level routines                             */
                    /*_____*/
VOID    get_args(USHORT, PCHAR []);
VOID    initialize_daemon(VOID);
VOID    wait_to_display_hello(VOID);
VOID    tell_the_world_hello(VOID);
```

Figure 13-3 (1 of 2). Daemon Program Include File.

```
                    /*————————————————————*/
                    /* Miscellaneous helper routines      */
                    /*————————————————————*/
VOID    print_error(USHORT, PCHAR , PCHAR , USHORT);
VOID    FAR daemon_exit(USHORT);

/*——————————————————————————————————————*/
/* Global variables/type definitions for this module         */
/*——————————————————————————————————————*/
ULONG    hello_hours,
         hello_minutes,
         hello_seconds;           /* time to display hello          */

PTIB     ptib;                     /* pointer to thread info block   */
PPIB     ppib;                     /* pointer to process info block  */

USHORT   rc;                       /* return code variable           */
USHORT   i;                        /* loop counter variable          */
```

Figure 13-3 (2 of 2). Daemon Program Include File.

DAEMON.C: get_args()

The **get_args()** procedure listed below uses the C library **sscanf** function to format and set the time of day variables based on the command line argument that is passed when the DAEMON program is invoked.

```
/*————————————————————————————————————————*/
/* read time from command line                                  */
/*————————————————————————————————————————*/
VOID get_args(USHORT argc, PCHAR argv[])
{
  if ((argc != 2) ||
      (sscanf(argv[1]," %lu:%lu:%lu ",
       &hello_hours, &hello_minutes, &hello_seconds) != 3))
      { printf("Enter command as follows: DAEMON hh:mm:ss \n");
       exit(FAILED);
      }
} /* end get_args */
```

Figure 13-4. The get_args() Procedure.

DAEMON.C: initialize_daemon()

The **initialize_daemon()** function, listed in Figure 13-5, introduces our first two OS/2 API calls: **DosExitList** and **DosGetInfoBlocks**. The **DosExitList** function is used here to add the **daemon_exit()** function to the exit list. DAEMON, being an independent background task, is acutely aware that it can be killed at any time by a DAEMON killer or through natural causes. By registering **daemon_exit()** with OS/2, DAEMON will be notified of its pending death and will be given a chance to run one last procedure **daemon_exit()** before it is put to eternal rest. Obviously, exit functions can be put to good uses, such as program clean-up. We recommend that you make it a practice, under OS/2, to register a "last will" at the start of every program. We explain the workings of **DosExitList** API in detail in the section below.

The **DosGetInfoBlocks** API call is used by DAEMON to obtain its process ID or **PID**. The **PID** is like a "passport number" that is used to uniquely identify a process. The API for that call is described on page 229. We recommend you read the API descriptions carefully *before and after* you've gone through the code because this is where you'll find the detailed information on how to use OS/2's programming services.

DosExitList

The **DosExitList** API specifies a list of exit procedures used for process clean-up. Exit lists allow you to set up procedures that are run just before a process terminates (either normally or abnormally). You could set up exit lists to free semaphores, deallocate memory, write to a trace log, reset hardware, etc. Exit lists will run even if your process gets killed unexpectedly. They are part of the *defensive* programming you should provide in a multitasking environment where you need to protect yourself from others. The prototype for this call is:

```
DosExitList(ULONG action_flag,             /* 1=add, 2=delete, 3=exit*/
            PVOID proc(ULONG term_code));  /* Exit routine address   */
```

A description of the parameters follows:

- The *action_flag* parameter specifies the action to perform on the exit list. This parameter can be one of the following values:

Value	Meaning
1	Add procedure to exit list.
2	Remove procedure from exit list.
3	Current exit procedure executed; move on to the next exit list procedure or terminate program if none are left.

- The *proc* parameter points to an exit list procedure, which has one input parameter, no return value. The input parameter to the procedure contains a termination code that indicates the reason why the process terminated. The termination code values mean the same as those for **DosExecPgm** and **DosCWait**, and they can be any of the following: normal exit, hard error, trap, and process killed. The exit list procedure should carry out its tasks and then call **DosExitList** with the action_flag parameter set to the value 3. This directs OS/2 to call the next procedure on the list. When all procedures are executed the process terminates. Here are some ground rules for writing exit list procedures:

1. Keep your procedures short and fail-safe, and take into account that OS/2 has already terminated all the other threads in the process except for your current thread.

2. An incorrectly constructed exit procedure will not necessarily crash the operating system; but you may not be able to exit from the process, thereby causing a degradation in performance.

3. Do not issue a return or call **DosExit** from your exit procedure. You should always end your procedure by issuing a call to **DosExitList** with the action_flag set to 3; then, OS/2 can transfer control to the next exit list procedure.

4. Do not issue calls from an exit procedure to **DosExecPgm** or to **DosCreateThread**.

5. All exit procedures must be declared as VOID APIENTRY to ensure the integrity of the stack.

DosGetInfoBlocks

The **DosGetInfoBlocks** API call is used by processes and threads to find out all sorts of information, some of it quite useless, about themselves. The information is maintained by OS/2 2.0 on a per-process and per-thread basis in corresponding **PIB** and **TIB** data structures. Each process virtual address space contains one PIB, and as many TIBs as there are threads within that process. The prototype for this call is:

```
DosGetInfoBlocks(PTIB  *threadinfo,    /* pointer to a TIB structure */
                 PPIB  *processinfo); /*pointer to a PIB structure  */
```

A description of the parameters follows:

- The *threadinfo* parameter returns a pointer to a **TIB** structure that contains information about the calling thread. The TIB structure has the following form:

```
typedef struct _TIB {
   PVOID   exception_chain; /* Pointer to head of thread exception handlers*/
   PVOID   stack_base;      /* Pointer to the base of the thread's stack   */
   PVOID   stack_limit;     /* Pointer to the end of the thread's stack    */
   PTIB2   more_info;       /* Pointer to the TIB2 structure (see below)   */
   ULONG   version;         /* Version number of the TIB structure         */
   PVOID   userdata;        /* Unused field that is available for your use  */
   } TIB;
```

Notice that OS/2 2.0 allows you to assign to each thread one or more termination exception handlers. These handlers are registered using the exception management APIs. They are invoked by the OS/2 trap manager when a user-mode exception occurs. The **TIB2** structure contains more thread information and has the following form:

```
typedef struct _TIB2 {
   ULONG    tid;        /* Current thread ID, also known as TID  */
   ULONG    priority;   /* Current thread priority               */
   ULONG    version;    /* Version number of TIB2 structure      */
   USHORT   count;      /* Must complete counts (used by OS/2)   */
   USHORT   forceflag;  /* Must complete forceflag (used by OS/2)*/
   } TIB2;
```

• The *processinfo* parameter returns a pointer to a **PIB** structure that contains information about the current process. The PIB structure has the following form:

```
typedef struct _PIB {
   ULONG pid;              /* Current process ID, also known as PID   */
   ULONG ppid;             /* Parent Process ID, also known as PPID   */
   ULONG module_handle;    /* Program (.EXE) module handle            */
   PCHAR command_line;     /* Pointer to the command line parameters  */
   PCHAR environment;      /* Pointer to the process environment block */
   ULONG process_status;   /* Process' status bits (used by OS/2)     */
   ULONG process_type;     /* Process' type code (used by OS/2)       */
   } PIB;
```

```
/*-------------------------------------------------------------------*/
/* initialize daemon program                                         */
/*-------------------------------------------------------------------*/
VOID initialize_daemon(VOID)
{
  rc = DosExitList(1,(PFNEXITLIST) daemon_exit);
  if (rc)
     { print_error(rc,"establishing DosExitList",__FILE__,__LINE__);
       exit(FAILED);
     }

  rc = DosGetInfoBlocks(&ptib, &ppib);
  if (rc)
     { print_error(rc,"getting DosGetInfoBlocks",__FILE__,__LINE__);
       exit(FAILED);
     }

} /* end initialize_daemon */
```

Figure 13-5. The initialize_daemom() Procedure.

DAEMON.C: wait_to_display_hello()

The **wait_to_display_hello()** function, listed in Figure 13-6, first calculates the difference in milliseconds between the time when DAEMON is to make its "Hello" statement to the world and the current time. It then puts DAEMON to sleep for that entire time duration. Two new OS/2 API calls are introduced: **DosGetDateTime** and **DosSleep**. The **DosGetDateTime** API call, described below, is used to obtain the current date and time. The **DosSleep** API call, also described below, is used to suspend the execution of DAEMON until the time comes to say "Hello."

DosGetDateTime

The **DosGetDateTime** API call, returns the current date and time maintained by the operating system. The prototype for this call is:

```
DosGetDateTime(DATETIME far *datetime);  /* pointer to structure    */
```

A description of the parameters follows:

- The *datetime* parameter points to the **DATETIME** structure that receives the date and time information. The DATETIME structure has the following form:

```
typedef struct _DATETIME {
   UCHAR    hours;           /* current hour                      */
   UCHAR    minutes;         /* current minute                    */
   UCHAR    seconds;         /* current second                    */
   UCHAR    hundredths;      /* current hundredths of a second    */
   UCHAR    day;             /* current day                       */
   UCHAR    month;           /* current month                     */
   USHORT   year;            /* current year                      */
   SHORT    timezone;        /* minutes of time west of GMT       */
   UCHAR    weekday;         /* current day of week               */
   } DATETIME;
```

The day of week value is based on Sunday being zero.

```
/*_____*/
/* calculate time to wait before Hello is to appear, wait that time  */
/*_____*/
VOID wait_to_display_hello(VOID)
{
  DATETIME date_time;                   /* structure for DosGetDateTime   */
  ULONG     current_time_seconds;       /* current time in seconds        */
  ULONG     hello_time_seconds;         /* time to display hello in seconds*/
  ULONG     wait_time_seconds;          /* time to wait in seconds        */
  ULONG     wait_time_msecs;            /* time to wait in milliseconds   */

  DosGetDateTime(&date_time);

  current_time_seconds = date_time.hours * 3600 + date_time.minutes * 60
                   + date_time.seconds;

  hello_time_seconds = hello_hours * 3600 + hello_minutes * 60 + hello_seconds;

  if (hello_time_seconds > current_time_seconds)
     wait_time_seconds  = hello_time_seconds - current_time_seconds;
  else
     { wait_time_seconds = 24 * 3600      /* seconds in 1 day             */
                   - (hello_time_seconds - current_time_seconds);
     } /* endif */

  wait_time_msecs = wait_time_seconds * 1000;

  rc = DosSleep(wait_time_msecs);
  if (rc)
     { print_error(rc,"during DosSleep", __FILE__,__LINE__);
       exit(FAILED);
     }

} /* end wait_to_display_hello */
```

Figure 13-6. The wait_to_display_hello() Procedure.

DosSleep

The **DosSleep** API call suspends the current thread for the specified time period. The actual sleep time may be off by a clock tick or two, depending on the execution status of other threads running in the system. The prototype for this call is:

```
DosSleep(ULONG delay);              /* delay time in milliseconds */
```

A description of the parameters follows:

- The *delay* parameter specifies the sleep interval in milliseconds. If the time is set to zero, the thread gives up the remainder of its current time slice, allowing other ready threads of equal priority to run.

DAEMON.C: tell_the_world_hello()

The **tell_the_world_hello**() procedure, listed in Figure 13-7, uses OS/2 1.3's highly efficient **VIO** subsystem to write to the screen. The efficiency of **VIO** services are such that they have removed the need for an application to manipulate the video hardware directly, as was the case with MS-DOS. The efficiency of the 16-bit **VIO** calls could have been further enhanced had they been incorporated into 32-bit OS/2 (without thunks). But the good news is that you get to see, first hand, how easy it is to call 16-bit APIs from an OS/2 2.0 application. The OS/2 Toolkit makes it easy by defining all VIO and KBD calls as APIENTRY16, an indication to the C Set/2 compiler that thunking is required.

In the current situation, we are faced with the problem of finding a way to allow DAEMON (a background task that does not have its own screen group) to gain access to a screen and keyboard to say "hello." Fortunately, **VIO** offers a means by which the background process can temporarily pop up in the foreground using the VIO API calls **VioPopUp** and **VioEndPopUp**, for activating a pop-up program. Those two API calls are described shortly. Once the pop-up mode is activated, **tell_the_world_hello**() uses the **VioWrtCharStrAtt** API call to write to the screen. This call, which is also described in this section, offers considerable control over how text is written to the screen, including control over the color attribute and the position.

While we're on the subject of pop-ups, you may be tempted to think of a pop-up as being comparable to an MS-DOS terminate-stay-resident program, or *TSR*. This is not quite the case. Under MS-DOS, TSRs provide a multitasking element in a single-tasking environment. Under OS/2, you don't need TSRs because you can run applications in different screen groups and switch between screen groups whenever you like. This is even more the case under PM, where a single screen group can simultaneously display and run multiple windows. In this sense, every OS/2 program can be thought of as a TSR. Pop-ups, on the other hand, should be used only in exceptional conditions, since other OS/2 processes cannot be switched into the foreground during the pop-up.

The pop-up must be designed to perform its action and relinquish control of the screen as quickly as possible. The best use of pop-ups is for displaying error alerts and for DETACHED daemon programs that otherwise make very little use of the screen and keyboard facilities.

The **KbdCharIn** API call used by **tell_the_world_hello**() is a good example of the power OS/2 packs into its **KBD** subsystem. Not only does this function return the ASCII code of the character, it also tells you the status of the shift keys and the time the key was pressed. The **KbdCharIn** API call is described on page 235. The **tell_the_world_hello**() procedure calls the **DosExit** OS/2 API for terminating DAEMON. This exit function can be used to return information to a parent process. The capabilities of **DosExit** are explained on page 236.

VioPopUp

The **VioPopUp** API call allocates a pop-up display screen. It is used primarily by background processes to temporarily take over the screen and keyboard. When the interaction is complete, the previous screen is restored by issuing **VioEndPopUp**. While a video pop-up is in effect, all video calls from the previous foreground session are blocked until the process that issued VioPopUp issues VioEndPopUp. If you're thinking of using pop-ups, don't forget to take into account the disrupting effect frequent interruptions may have on the foreground application. The prototype for this call is:

```
VioPopUp(USHORT   *wait_flags,   /* pointer to flag word    */
         USHORT    handle);      /* video handle            */
```

A description of the parameters follows:

- The *wait_flags* parameter points to a flag variable. The flag contents specify whether the pop-up is to be opaque or transparent, and whether the function should wait for an open pop-up to close or return immediately with an error code if a pop-up screen already exists. There can be only one pop-up in existence at any time. The flag word bits are defined as follows:

```
Bits   Description
  0    0 = No-wait- return with an error code if pop-up already exists.
       1 = Wait- if a pop-up screen already exists.

  1    0 = Opaque Mode.  Sets the screen to 25 lines by 80 columns of
           text, clears the screen, and positions the cursor at the upper-
           left corner.
       1 = Transparent Mode.  If the video mode of the outgoing fore-
           ground session is text the screen remains unchanged.
           Otherwise the pop-up request is refused.

           OS/2 is responsible for saving and restoring the display buffer
           of the foreground session.  This is true for both modes.

2-15   Reserved, set to zero.
```

- The *handle* parameter is a presentation handle used by PM applications. It is NULL otherwise.

DosExecPgm cannot be issued by a process during a pop-up, and the process must not access or modify the physical video buffer.

VioEndPopUp

The **VioEndPopUp** API call closes a pop-up screen and restores the physical video buffer to its previous contents. The pop-up may only be closed by the process that opened it. The prototype for this call is:

```
VioEndPopUp(USHORT  handle);        /* video handle              */
```

A description of the parameters follows:

- The *handle* parameter is a presentation handle used by PM applications. It is NULL otherwise.

VioWrtCharStrAtt

The **VioWrtCharStrAtt** call writes a character string to a screen location using the specified attribute. The prototype for this call is:

```
VioWrtCharStrAtt(PCHAR    charstr,   /* character string          */
                 USHORT   length,    /* length of string          */
                 USHORT   row_x,     /* row to start writing       */
                 USHORT   column_y,  /* column to start writing    */
                 PCHAR    attr,      /* pointer to attribute byte  */
                 USHORT   handle);   /* video handle               */
```

A description of the parameters follows:

- The *charstr* parameter points to the character string you want to write. If the string is longer than the current line, the function continues writing at the start of the next line, but it does not go past the end of the screen.
- The *length* parameter specifies the length of the string in bytes.
- The *row_x* parameter specifies the row at which to start writing the string.
- The *column_y* parameter specifies the column at which to start writing the string.
- The *attr* parameter points to the display attribute of the string. Here's the structure of the attribute byte:

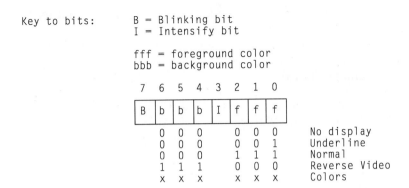

```
Key to bits:      B = Blinking bit
                  I = Intensify bit

                  fff = foreground color
                  bbb = background color

                  7  6  5  4  3  2  1  0

                 │B │b │b │b │I │f │f │f │

                     0  0  0     0  0  0    No display
                     0  0  0     0  0  1    Underline
                     0  0  0     1  1  1    Normal
                     1  1  1     0  0  0    Reverse Video
                     x  x  x     x  x  x    Colors
```

- The *handle* parameter is a presentation handle used by PM applications. It is NULL otherwise.

KbdCharIn

The **KbdCharIn** API call reads the character and scan-code information from a logical keyboard. The keystroke information includes the ASCII value of the key, the scan code, the state of the various shift keys, and the system time when the key was pressed. The function does not echo the characters it reads. The prototype for this call is:

```
KbdCharIn(KBDKEYINFO    *kbdinfo,   /* pointer to KBDKEYINFO structure */
          USHORT        wait_flag,  /* 0=wait for character, 1=no wait */
          USHORT        hkbd);      /* keyboard handle, usually 0      */
```

A description of the parameters follows:

- The *kbdinfo* parameter points to a **KBDKEYINFO** structure where the keyboard information is placed. Here's what the structure looks like:

```
typedef struct _KBDKEYINFO {
        UCHAR    chChar;     /* ASCII character code                   */
        UCHAR    chScan;     /* Scan Code                              */
        UCHAR    fbStatus;   /* State of the character for NLS         */
        UCHAR    bNlsShift;  /* Reserved (must equal 0)                */
        USHORT   fsState;    /* state of the shift keys                */
        ULONG    time;       /* time stamp of key stroke (ms since ipl) */
        }KBDKEYINFO;
```

The *chChar* field returns the ASCII value of the key pressed by translating the *chScan* field. The field is set to zero when it retrieves an extended ASCII code, such as when the ALT key and a character key are pressed simultaneously or when a non-shift special key (such as a function key) is pressed. In such situations, the scan code should be read to get the extended ASCII or special key value. The *chScan* field returns the scan code provides an unambiguous indication of the key that was pressed based on its position on the keyboard. But it does not report the state of the shift keys. The *fbStatus* field is used in National Languages. The *fsState* field returns the status of the various shift keys. The *time* field returns the time in milliseconds when a key was pressed and can be used to measure the time duration between characters typed.

- The *wait_flag* parameter specifies if the API is to wait for keystroke information if there is no character information. Wait suspends the thread until a key is pressed. The *no wait* option causes the API call to return immediately with whatever keystroke information is present. The value of the *fbstatus* field returns zero if no keystroke is received in the no wait option. Warning: A thread in the foreground session that repeatedly polls the keyboard with KbdCharIn (with no wait) can prevent all regular priority class threads from executing. If polling must be used and a minimal amount of other processing is being performed, the thread should periodically yield to the CPU by issuing a DosSleep call.

- The *hkbd* parameter identifies the logical keyboard. It is usually set to zero unless your application makes use of the **KbdOpen** function.

DosExit

The **DosExit** API is used to end a thread or a process and all its threads. When a process terminates, all its resources are closed and its buffers are flushed. When a thread or process terminate their execution, they do not return to a caller; they just stop running. The prototype for this call is:

```
DosExit(ULONG     terminate_action,   /* Current thread or process  */
        ULONG     exit_code);         /* Any exit code for parent   */
```

A description of the parameters follows:

- The *terminate_action* parameter specifies what to terminate. It is set to zero to terminate the current thread only. It is set to one to terminate the current process and all its threads.
- The *exit_code* parameter specifies the program's completion status. This is an arbitrary number sent to the parent process. If there is any interest, the parent process can retrieve the exit code through **DosCWait**. By convention, use zero to indicate an OK return and use positive numbers to indicate an error type. And if you really want to get fancy, use negative numbers to indicate warnings!

```
/*_____*/
/* Create popup, display hello message, wait for user key press, then end.  */
/*_____*/
VOID tell_the_world_hello(VOID)
{
  USHORT wait_flags = 0;
  BYTE   attribute  = 0x71;              /* blue on grey            */
  USHORT row        = 7;
  USHORT column     = 27;
  static CHAR  *hello_msg[] = {"                                        ",
                               "        Hello World!!                   ",
                               "                                        ",
                               "        The time is                     ",
                               "                                        ",
                               "        Daemon PID =                     ",
                               "                                        ",
                               "        Press Q/q to quit.              ",
                               "        Press any other key to          ",
                               "        enable Daemon again.            ",
                               "                                        ",
                               ""};
  CHAR    hello_time[10];
  CHAR    pid[12];
  KBDKEYINFO key;

  /*_____*/
  /* create the popup     */
  /*_____*/
  rc = VioPopUp(&wait_flags, 0L);

  /*_____*/
  /* display the message  */
  /*_____*/
  i = 0;
  do
    {VioWrtCharStrAtt(hello_msg[i], strlen(hello_msg[i]),
                      row+i, column, &attribute, 0);
     ++i;
    } while ( strcmp(hello_msg[i],"") != 0  ); /* enddo */
  sprintf(hello_time,"%lu:%lu:%lu",hello_hours, hello_minutes, hello_seconds);
  VioWrtCharStrAtt(hello_time, strlen(hello_time),
                   row + 3, column + 15, &attribute, 0);
  sprintf(pid,"%lu",ppib->pib_ulpid);
  VioWrtCharStrAtt(pid, strlen(pid), row + 5, column + 15, &attribute, 0);

  /*_____*/
  /* wait for a key press */
  /*_____*/
  KbdCharIn(&key,0,0);
  /*_____*/
  /* end the popup        */
  /*_____*/
  VioEndPopUp(0);
  /*_____*/
  /* re-enable or not?    */
  /*_____*/
  if ((key.chChar == 'Q') || (key.chChar == 'q'))
     DosExit(1,1);                       /* kill all threads, return code=1 */

} /* end tell_the_world_hello */
```

Figure 13-7. The tell_the_world_hello() Procedure.

DAEMON.C: print_error()

The **print_error()** helper function, listed in Figure 13-8, records useful debug information such as the error number, the error description, and the name and line number of the source code file where the error occurred. Both the IBM C Set/2 and Microsoft 6.0 C compilers maintain two predefined preprocessor symbols, __FILE__ and __LINE__, which refer to the current input file name and the current line number being processed by the compiler. A failing procedure uses the preprocessor symbols to obtain the source code file and line number where the error occurs; it then passes these numbers to **print_error()** as parameters.

We introduce a new OS/2 API call that extends our **VIO** repertoire, **VioWrtTTY**. Since error messages are variable in length, the **VioWrtTTY** is a better fit in this situation than the previously encountered **VioWrtCharStrAtt** call, which requires a row/column location. The **VioWrtTTY** uses the cursor as its starting point and carries the cursor along with it. This leaves the cursor in the correct position for the next screen call. The description of **VioWrtTTY** is given below.

VioWrtTTY

The **VioWrtTTY** call writes a character string to a screen starting at the current cursor position. At the completion of the write, the cursor is at the first position beyond the end of the string. The prototype for this call is:

```
VioWrtTTY(PCHAR    string,      /* pointer to string   */
          USHORT   length,      /* length of string    */
          USHORT   handle);     /* video handle        */
```

A description of the parameters follows:

- The *string* parameter points to the character string that will be written to the screen.
- The *length* parameter specifies the length in bytes of the character string.
- The *handle* parameter is a presentation handle used by PM applications. It is NULL otherwise.

```
/*_____*/
/* Error Display Routine                                              */
/*_____*/
VOID print_error(USHORT Error, PCHAR msg, PCHAR file, USHORT line)
{
  CHAR    error_msg[80];
  USHORT  wait_flags = 0;
  BYTE    attribute  = 0x47;           /* grey on red           */
  USHORT  row        = 0;
  USHORT  column     = 0;
  KBDKEYINFO key;
```

Figure 13-8 (Part 1 of 2). The print_error() Helper Routine.

```
/*_____*/
/* display the error message  */
/*_____*/
VioPopUp(&wait_flags, 0);
sprintf(error_msg, "Error %d detected while %s at line %d in file %s.\n",
        Error, msg, line, file);
VioWrtTTY(error_msg, strlen(error_msg), 0);

/*_____*/
/* wait for a key press       */
/*_____*/
KbdCharIn(&key,0,0);

/*_____*/
/* end the popup              */
/*_____*/
VioEndPopUp(0);

} /* end print_error */
```

Figure 13-8 (Part 2 of 2). The print_error() Helper Routine.

DAEMON.C: daemon_exit()

The **daemon_exit()** function, listed below, gets executed as part of the previously setup **DosExitList**. This is DAEMON's "last will" that gets executed by OS/2 just before it terminates DAEMON. Not unexpectedly, this is a sentimental occasion for which DAEMON uses most of the **VIO** calls we have just learned to say "Good bye World." The grand exit gets performed by issuing a **DosExitList** (as described on page 228) with the action_flag set to 3. This tells OS/2 that it can now transfer control to the next exit list procedure, which in this case is non-existent: so in effect, DAEMON gets terminated.

```
/*_____*/
/* Exit Routine                                       */
/*_____*/
VOID FAR daemon_exit(ULONG exit_type)
{
  USHORT wait_flags = 0;
  BYTE   attribute  = 0x71;          /* blue on grey            */
  USHORT row        = 10;
  USHORT column     = 27;
  static CHAR    *exit_msg[] =  {"",
                "Good-bye world!",
                "",
                "  Press any key...",
                "",
                ""};

  KBDKEYINFO key;

  /*_____*/
  /* display the error message  */
  /*_____*/
  VioPopUp(&wait_flags, 0);
```

Figure 13-9 (Part 1 of 2). The daemon_exit() Helper Routine.

```
/*_____*/
/* display the exit message    */
/*_____*/
i = 0;
do
  {
   VioWrtCharStrAtt(exit_msg[i], strlen(exit_msg[i]),
                    row+i, column, &attribute, 0);
   ++i;
  } while ( strcmp(exit_msg[i],"") != 0  ); /* enddo */

/*_____*/
/* wait for a key press        */
/*_____*/
KbdCharIn(&key,0,0);

/*_____*/
/* end the popup               */
/*_____*/
VioEndPopUp(0);

DosExitList(3, (void far *) 0);
} /* end daemon_exit */
```

Figure 13-9 (Part 2 of 2). The daemon_exit() Helper Routine.

KILLER: OUR SECOND OS/2 PROGRAM

We are now ready for our second OS/2 program, **KILLER.C**, a program whose sole purpose in life is to kill daemon programs. DAEMON by now is an old and intimate friend, so you may ask why are we introducing this killer? Well, we too like DAEMON and are not too fond of homicidal maniac program killers, but there may come a time when you may want to clear your machine of some unwanted DETACHED daemons. So, we offer you KILLER. The good news is that killer is a very short program, which should take less than five minutes of your reading time.

KILLER.C: main()

As usual, we start with the **main()** program listing, see Figure 13-10. At the top, we have the usual C and OS/2 include files. Notice that we've introduced a new *include flag*:

```
#define INCL_DOSPROCESS         /* for DosSleep, DosExitList         */
```

As is to be expected, we have a **killer.h** include file, which is listed in Figure 13-11, and which does not contain any startling new information.

The KILLER **main()** procedure, which serves as our program outline, consists of two functions: **get_args()**, listed in Figure 13-12, and **kill_the_process()**, listed in Figure 13-13. The first function, **get_args()**, simply obtains the **PID** of the process we're trying to kill. The actual killing gets done by **kill_the_process()**, which introduces the one new OS/2 call in the program. Finally, KILLER makes use of a new **print_error()**, listed in Figure 13-14, which uses the **printf()** C library function. This is because KILLER executes as a foreground task and has the screen to itself; the need for pop-ups has been removed. We said it would take less than five minutes of reading, and we're almost there!

```
/**********************************************************************/
/*   PROGRAM NAME: KILLER - a kill process example                  */
/*                                                                   */
/*   PROGRAM DESCRIPTION:  This program demonstrates the use of      */
/*      DosKillProcess to kill a process.                            */
/*                                                                   */
/*   PROGRAM INVOCATION:                                             */
/*                                                                   */
/*      KILLER process-id                                           */
/*                                                                   */
/**********************************************************************/
#include <process.h>              /* For exit()                      */
#include <stdio.h>                /* For sprintf()                   */
#include <string.h>               /* For string functions            */

#define INCL_DOSPROCESS           /* for DosSleep, DosExitList        */
#include <os2.h>
#include "killer.h"

/*_____*/
/* Main routine.                                                     */
/*_____*/
VOID main(USHORT argc, PCHAR argv[], PCHAR envp[])
{
    get_args(argc, argv);        /* read process id from command line */

    kill_the_process();          /* kill the process                 */

} /* end main */
```

Figure 13-10. KILLER.C main().

KILLER.C: The killer.h Include File

```
/*****************************************************************************/
/*   INCLUDE NAME: KILLER - declarations for KILLER program                  */
/*****************************************************************************/

/*_____*/
/* defines                                                                   */
/*_____*/
                    /*_____*/
                    /* function return values                    */
                    /*_____*/
#define GOOD            0
#define WARNING         1
#define FAILED         -1


/*_____*/
/* Forward declarations of procedures in this module                         */
/*_____*/
                    /*_____*/
                    /* top level routines                        */
                    /*_____*/
VOID    get_args(USHORT, PCHAR []);
VOID    kill_the_process(VOID);

                    /*_____*/
                    /* Miscellaneous helper routines             */
                    /*_____*/
VOID    print_error(USHORT, PCHAR , PCHAR , USHORT);

/*_____*/
/* Global variables/type definitions for this module                         */
/*_____*/
                    /*_____*/
                    /* process variable                          */
                    /*_____*/
USHORT      process_id;                 /* time to display hello             */
RESULTCODES term_result;                /* termination result code           */
PID         term_processid;             /* terminating process id            */

                    /*_____*/
                    /* misc. variables                           */
                    /*_____*/
USHORT  rc;                             /* return code variable              */
USHORT  i;                              /* loop counter variable             */
```

Figure 13-11.   KILLER.H Include File.

KILLER.C: get_args()

```
/*_____*/
/* read process ID from command line                          */
/*_____*/
VOID get_args(USHORT argc, PCHAR argv[])
{
   if (argc != 2)
      { printf("Enter command as follows: KILLER process-id \n");
        exit(FAILED);
      }

   process_id = atoi(argv[1]);

} /* end get_args */
```

Figure 13-12. KILLER.C: get_args().

KILLER.C: kill_the_process()

This is the function that contains the new OS/2 API call that KILLER introduces. Not too surprising given the context, it is called **DosKillProcess**. A full explanation of its workings is given below.

DosKillProcess

The **DosKillProcess** API call kills the specified process with the option of terminating all of its descendants. The prototype for this call is:

```
DosKillProcess(ULONG     scope_flag,    /* Scope of killing    */
               ULONG     processID);    /* ID of process to kill */
```

A description of the parameters follows:

- The *scope_flag* parameter specifies what to kill. Setting it to zero kills the specified process and all of its descendants. Setting it to one only kills the specified process.
- The *processID* parameter specifies the ID of the process to be killed.

```
/*————————————————————————————————————*/
/* kill the process number indicated by the user.                    */
/*————————————————————————————————————*/
VOID kill_the_process(VOID)
{
  rc = DosKillProcess(1,                /* only this process        */
                  process_id);    /* process id number        */
  if (rc)
      { print_error(rc,"killing a process",__FILE__,__LINE__);
        exit(FAILED);
      }

} /* end kill_the_process */
```

Figure 13-13.   KILLER.C: kill_the_process().

KILLER.C: print_error()

```
/*————————————————————————————————————*/
/* Error Display Routine                                             */
/*————————————————————————————————————*/
VOID
print_error(USHORT Error, PCHAR msg, PCHAR file, USHORT line)
{
 printf("Error %u (0x%x) detected while %s at line %u in file %s.\n",
        Error, Error, msg, line, file);
} /* end print_error */
```

Figure 13-14.   KILLER.C: print_error().

NMAKE: A BRIEF TUTORIAL

This short tutorial covers some of the key constructs that will be used by the *make* files in this book. The **OS/2 2.0 Developer's Toolkit** provides a **NMAKE** utility that is used to automate the code production process. You will discover NMAKE to be a great time saver for programs that consist of several source files. This is because the utility only performs those steps that are necessary to produce an up-to-date version of a program. NMAKE is smart enough to build the program using only the components that changed since the last time the program was compiled. NMAKE takes a text file as its input. The input file contains a series of commands, rules, and macros. NMAKE's goal is to create one or more executable files from one or more source code files using the rules it was given.

Target Rule Blocks

The heart of the *make* file are the target rule blocks that specify the conditions for something to happen, followed by what is to happen. The syntax for these target rule blocks is:

```
target-list: dependent-list
        [command]
        [command]
```

The first line consists of a list of *target* file names, followed by a colon, followed by a list of dependent files. If one of the dependent files is older than any of the target files, the rule fires and the associated commands get executed. A command usually specifies an action to be taken to generate the target. An action is the execution of an operating system command or a program.

Inference Rules

If you do not specify any commands, NMAKE searches for an *inference rule* to build the target files. An inference rule is a way of telling NMAKE how to produce a file with one type of extension from a file with the same name and a second type of extension. It's a lazy way out of having to specify explicit commands for each target list. The following format is used to specify an inference rule:

```
.dependent-ext.target-ext:
        command
        [command]
```

Inference rules start with a period in column one, followed by the dependent extension, followed by a period, followed by the target extension, followed by a colon, followed by the command to be executed on the dependent files to produce the "target" file. More than one command can be given, but each must be listed on a separate line. Commands cannot start in the first column.

Comments

You can place **comments** in a *make* file by starting them with the comment character #. The following samples show how to use comments:

```
daemon.exe:  daemon.obj       #valid comment
# valid comment starts in first column
        link daemon.obj;       # invalid, comments cannot be in command line
```

Macros

NMAKE supports *macro definitions*, which associate a symbolic name on the left side of an equal sign with the value on the right side of the equal sign. Macros can be used to change values in a *make* file without editing every line that uses the particular value. A macro is invoked by preceding the macro name with a **$** sign. Macro names longer than one character require parentheses around them. The following is an example of the use of macro called **program**:

```
program = daemon
    $(program).obj = $(program).c
      ICC $(program),$(program),$(program),$(program)
```

NMAKE recognizes some special macros, two of which we use extensively in our *make* files. The first macro symbol (you'll see a lot of symbols) is **$***, which means "substitute the target file name without an extension." The second ubiquitous macro symbol is **$****, which means "substitute the complete list of dependents."

Build Goals

The NMAKE utility uses metarules for determining what needs to be built. Traditional make utilities search through the *make* file sequentially and evaluate each target rule-block in order. With NMAKE, the targets you specify in the command line are updated regardless of their positions in the file. If you do not specify a target, NMAKE updates or builds the first target in the file. If you need to build multiple targets, then you must either pass the name of each target in the command line, or you can make your first target rule block a pseudo-target with all the other targets as its dependents list. The following is an example of a pseudo-target rule:

```
all: daemon.exe killer.exe
```

Here, **all** is the name of a dummy file that does not exist, and daemon.exe and killer.exe are the names of the two separate programs that we want to build with this one *make* file. This is how NMAKE goes about executing this rule: in order to build **all**, NMAKE has to first instantiate the build rules for daemon.exe and killer.exe, which is exactly what we want it to do for us. In this manner, you can specify all the files you want to build and the order in which you want them built.

MAKE as a Documentation Tool

We find that *make* files serve as an excellent source of program documentation. A good practice when looking at a new program, is to start with its *make* file, and use it to understand the relationship between the different modules that make up a program. We will encourage this practice by starting all our programming chapters with the *make* file for that particular program. Our *make* files have the same name as the program they create, with the extension (.MAK). If more than one program is produced, the name will be that of the first program created.

DAEMON.MAK

DAEMON.MAK, see Figure 13-15, is the *make* file used to create DAEMON.EXE and KILLER.EXE. You can invoke the MAKE program from the OS/2 command line by entering:

```
NMAKE DAEMON.MAK
```

DAEMON.MAK contains many of the constructs you will encounter in the *make* files presented in this book. We will walk very carefully through this *make* file in the next section. The idea is to take an exhaustive look at the NMAKE constructs, so as not to have to explain them again in subsequent chapters.

```
#***********************************************************************
# Make File for DAEMON program
#***********************************************************************

#** MACROS ************************************************************
cflags=/C+ /Q+ /Sm /Ti+ /Gm- /Ge+ /Gd-
lflags=/CO /NOLogo
linklibs=

#** INFERENCE RULES **************************************************
.obj.exe:
        echo LINKING    $*.exe
        link386 $(lflags) $**,$*.exe,,$(linklibs),;

.c.obj:
        echo COMPILING $*.c
        ICC $(cflags) $*.c

#** BUILD STATEMENTS ************************************************
all: daemon.exe killer.exe

daemon.exe:             daemon.obj
daemon.obj:             daemon.c      daemon.h

killer.exe:             killer.obj
killer.obj:             killer.c      killer.h
```

Figure 13-15. Daemon Make File.

DAEMON.MAK: WALKING THROUGH A MAKE FILE

We will walk through the *make* file in Figure 13-15 in great detail. It will serve as the "Rosetta Stone" for deciphering all the *make* files in this book.

DAEMON.MAK starts off with some comment lines, that are followed by macro definitions for three symbols: **cflags**, **lflags**, and **linklibs**. The contents of the three macros provide some insight into how to compile and link in the OS/2 2.0 environment. We will take a short detour in our exploration of DAEMON.MAK to understand what these symbols mean:

- The **cflags** macro defines the flags used to control and modify the operation of the C Set/2 compiler. The flags are preceded by a slash "/". The following is a "flag by flag" description of what it all means:

  /C+   This is the "compile and link" option. C+ suppresses linking during compilation. C- (the default) performs compile and link. We chose C+ because we want a separate link step.

  /Q+   This flag suppresses writing the logo and copyright lines in the compiler output stream.

  /Sm   This flag specifies the standard you want to impose on your C language. /Sa allows only ANSI C conforming code. /S2 allows only SAA Level 2 conforming code (you'll need this level of adherence for porting code across SAA platforms). /Se (the default) allows SAA, ANSI, and standard C Set/2 extensions. /Sm, the most tolerant level, supports IBM C/2 and Microsoft C 6.0 extensions. We chose /Sm because much of our code was migrated from a Microsoft C environment.

  /Ti+   This flag causes the compiler to generate debugger information. The default is /Ti-. Make sure that optimization is turned off (/O- the default) when you're debugging. You should enable code optimization once you have stable code.

  /Gm-   This flag specifies single or multithreading libraries. The default is /Gm- for the single thread library. Daemon and killer are single-threaded. In later chapters, we will specify /Gm+ to link with multithreaded, reentrant, C libraries that serialize access to resources. The compiler flags will cause the correct library to be linked by default.

  /Ge+   This flag allows you to specify the type of code that the compiler will produce. /Ge+ (the default) specifies the creation of an .EXE. /Ge- specifies the creation of a .DLL. Both Daemon and Killer are (.EXEs).

/Gd-   This flag allows you to specify the static or dynamic linking of the run-time library. /Gd- (the default) specifies static linking. /Gd+ specifies dynamic linking.

- The **lflags** macro defines the link flags or options which are used to control and modify the operation of the **LINK386** linker. The flags or options are preceded by a slash "/" symbol. The following is a "flag by flag" description of what it all means:

  /CO   This flag directs LINK386 to include symbolic debug information for the OS/2 32-bit PM Debugger. No, it's not Codeview.

  /NOLogo This flag directs LINK386 not to include logo and copyright lines.

- The **linklibs** macro defines the run-time libraries we need to link with. In the present case, we do not have to specify the library since the C Set/2 will choose it for us based on the option flags. If you do not specify options, C Set/2 will choose the default library that produces single-thread executable modules that are statically linked. Later in the book, we will be linking to NetBIOS, CPI-C, TCP/IP, and SQL run-time libraries.

Continuing with our walk through DAEMON.MAK, we encounter our first inference rule, **.obj.exe**, whose effect is to produce an **.exe** file from an **.obj** file of the same name. NMAKE does not execute the inference rule at this point because it still does not know what is to be built. So, NMAKE skips over the next two lines and encounters a second inference rule, **.c.obj**, whose effect is to produce an **.obj** file from a **.c** file of the same name. But NMAKE still has no idea of what needs to be built, so it also skips over this inference rule and the two lines that follow it.

Finally, NMAKE finds something it can build when it encounters the "dummy" condition list statement:

```
all: daemon.exe killer.exe
```

Here's how it works:

1. When NMAKE encounters the dummy, it says, "Aha! they want me to build **all**." So off it goes looking for **all**, which it will not find, because it's just a dummy name we are using to get it to build the other two programs.
2. NMAKE eventually gives up looking for **all** and decides to build it from scratch. So it looks at the right side and says, "In order to build **all**, I will need the most recent versions of daemon.exe and killer.exe. So let me start with daemon.exe, and then I'll come back and do killer.exe."
3. Before NMAKE can determine that daemon.exe is up-to-date, it must first check for a target-dependent rule where daemon.exe appears as a target. Any rule with daemon.exe as a target could potentially update daemon.exe, so it needs to be executed first. In fact, the NMAKE utility builds a tree of interrelated target-de-

pendent rules before it executes any commands. The bottom part of the tree contains rules where the dependents are existing files and have no references as targets in any target-dependent rule in the *make* file. The following shows the tree for daemon.exe:

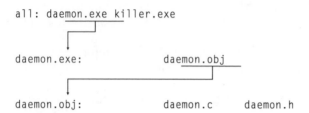

```
all: daemon.exe killer.exe


daemon.exe:            daemon.obj


daemon.obj:            daemon.c      daemon.h
```

4. Once the tree has been determined, the build process begins starting from the bottom of the tree and working upward. If any of the dependents have a later time-stamp than the targets for the rule, the commands or the inference rule commands for the target-dependent rule are executed. In our example, the rule

    ```
    daemon.obj:            daemon.c      daemon.h
    ```

    is checked first. If daemon.c or daemon.h is of a later time-stamp than daemon.obj or daemon.obj doesn't exist, then the **.obj.c** inference rule commands are executed. In our example the line

    ```
    ICC /C+ /Q+ /Sm /Ti+ /Gm- /Ge+ /Gd-  daemon.c
    ```

    is executed. This line causes NMAKE to invoke the C Set/2 compiler and pass it the flags and the source file daemon.c. Remember, we've disabled the link part of compile-link by using the **C+ flag**. We do that because we want the much finer level of link control that is obtained by invoking the **link** command separately.

5. So now, NMAKE has an up-to-date **daemon.obj**, and it is ready to examine the next higher target-dependent rule in the tree:

    ```
    daemon.exe:   daemon.obj
    ```

6. Again, if daemon.obj has a later time-stamp than daemon.exe, or if daemon.exe doesn't exist, then the commands or inference rule commands associated with the rule are executed. In our example, the inference rule commands are executed. Before producing the **.exe** file. The inference rule then echoes **LINKING daemon.exe**. The name, of course, is obtained through the $* macro.

7. The real action, once more, takes place in the next line which, after all the macro substitutions reads:

    ```
    LINK386 /CO /NOLogo daemon.obj, daemon.exe,,,;
    ```

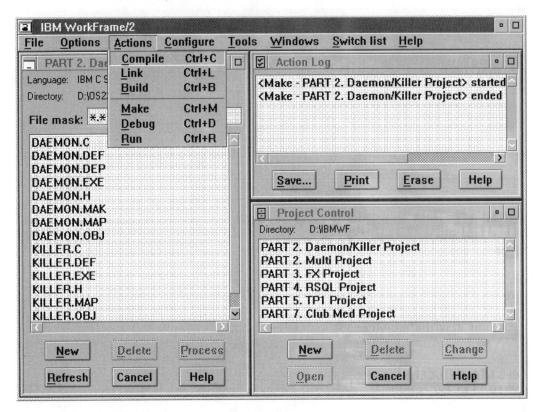

Figure 13-16. Workframe/2: The Project Organizer.

You are essentially linking daemon.obj with the specified libraries and creating daemon.exe (using the specified link option flags).

8. The NMAKE has now successfully either created or found an up-to-date version of daemon.exe.

9. The NMAKE now works on the second goal, which is to create or find an up-to-date version of killer.exe. The last two lines of DAEMON.MAK are, thankfully, the rules for creating killer.exe, which leads to the execution of the following two commands associated with our inference rules:

```
ICC /c+ /Q+ /Sm /Ti+ /Gm- /Ge+ /Gd-  killer.c
LINK386 /CO /NOLogo killer.obj, killer.exe,,,;
```

10. At this point, NMAKE has up-to-date versions of both daemon.exe and killer.exe, so it can go about building **all**, its primary goal for this *make* file. Unfortunately for NMAKE and fortunately for us, there are no further rules that apply to **all**, so NMAKE terminates, and we've got what we were looking for.

The key then to reading any of our *make* files is to first look for the dummy rule for building **all**. The left side of the rule tells you what it is that we're trying to build and

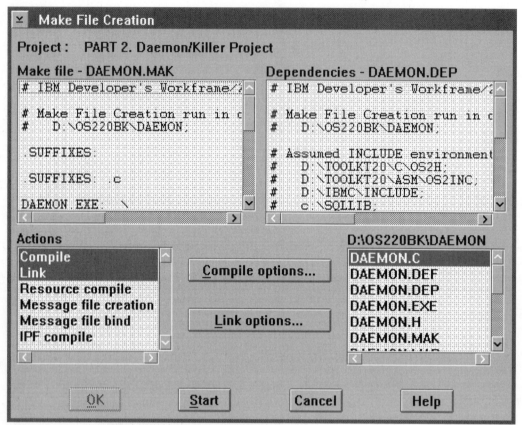

Figure 13-17. Workframe/2: The Make Builder.

in which order. From there, you can follow the various dependency lists and get a good understanding of how the programs are put together.

PUTTING WORKFRAME/2 TO WORK

You can use **WorkFrame/2** to create the make file for you and help manage your code. WorkFrame/2 organizes your code by grouping related files into logical units called *projects*. Figure 13-16 shows how we organized the code in this book into projects using WorkFrame. Notice that a project such as *Part 2. Daemon/Killer* (see top of the screen) contains all the source, object, and resource files, as well as targets such as (.EXE) and (.DLL) files. The menu gives you an idea of what actions can be performed on your project objects. WorkFrame provides an open environment that lets you plug-and-play your choice of edit, compile, debug tools, resource compilers, precompilers, and so on. These tools can be integrated with online help to provide you with a completely integrated and self-contained environment for the production of code.

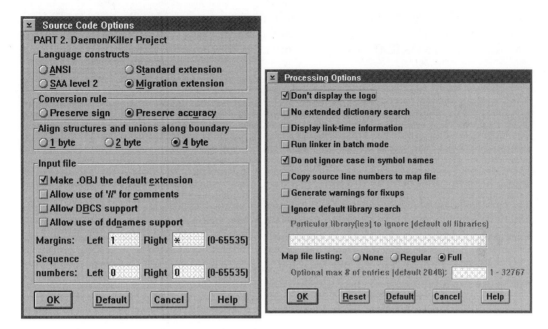

Figure 13-18.   Sample Make Dialogs.

Figure 13-17 and Figure 13-18 show some of the dialogs associated with creating a make file from within the WorkFrame. These dialogs are provided by **MAKEDEP**, a WorkFrame supplied utility. MAKEDEP works seamlessly with NMAKE, the C Set/2 compiler, LINK386, and the PM tools from the OS/2 Toolkit. The WorkFrame allows you to provide your own make file for a project. But why do that when WorkFrame can build one for you? The answer is that the current version of MAKEDEP is self-sufficient when it comes to building regular OS/2 2.0 programs and DLLs. However, when we get into the SQL and SOM precompilers there will be a need to "doctor" the make files to add the additional build steps. We will make those make files available to you. You then have the choice to plug-and-play the make files from the WorkFrame, or to run them from the command line. We found that after using the WorkFrame for a while there was no return to the command line interface. Who says "real programmers" cannot get hooked on GUI?

RUNNING DAEMON AND KILLER

You can run DAEMON by either invoking it from the command line, or running it as a background process using the DETACH command. If you run it from the command line, your screen will remain frozen until DAEMON comes to life. So, you may want to consider running the program in a separate screen group. If you run DAEMON using the DETACH command, OS/2 will display the program's **process ID** and then return control to you while DAEMON executes in the background. In all cases, DAEMON will interrupt whatever screen group you are in and tell you "Hello" when the right time comes. To invoke DAEMON from the command line, type:

```
C>DAEMON hh:mm:ss
```

To invoke it as a background process, type:

```
C>DETACH DAEMON hh:mm:ss
```

where hh:mm:ss is the time in hours, minutes, and seconds when you want DAEMON to wake-up and say Hello on a daily basis. As an example, if you were to enter:

```
C>DETACH DAEMON 15:30:30
```

You should expect to see on your screen, every day, at 3:30 in the afternoon, the following greeting:

```
Hello World!!

The time is 15:30:30

Daemon PID = 8

Press Q/q to quit.
Press any other key to
enable Daemon again.
```

You can kill DAEMON by pressing **Q** to quit at the time the greeting appears on the screen, or you can invoke from the command line, at any time:

```
KILLER 8
```

where **8** is the process ID that OS/2 returned when DAEMON was first created. DAEMON also tells you its process ID when it displays Hello!

THE C SET/2 PM DEBUGGER

C Set/2 provides a wonderful PM-based symbolic debugger. Caveat Emptor: *this debugger is so much fun that it's addictive. It might make you want to add bugs into your programs just so that you can play with it.* Figure 13-19 gives you the gestalt of how this debugger looks and feels. Like all debuggers, it allows you to set break-points, single-step through the code, view variables, evaluate expressions, and so on.

Now, take a closer look at Figure 13-19. Notice that we are able to view any variable in the Daemon Program by just clicking on it in the source view (the top window). We clicked on *&ptib*, a parameter of the DosGetInfoBlocks call, and its structure and contents magically appeared in the window (on the bottom right). You can follow the execution of a program in the compiler source view, find errors, and correct them in the source. "Step" and "Go" allows you to bypass previously debugged code and focus on problem areas. The stack window shows you what functions were called to get to the point where you stopped. And who says "real programmers" don't like GUI?

There is more to this debugger's story. Figure 13-20 shows a debugging session for MULTI, a multithreaded OS/2 program we will develop in the next chapter. Notice that each thread has its own window and can be controlled individually. You can set breakpoints on individual threads, view the thread's variables and stacks, and follow the execution of the thread using the source view. The top three windows in Figure 13-20 show three of MULTI's threads. The bottom left window shows the status of all the threads in the MULTI program. The bottom right window shows the stack for one of the threads.

In summary, the debugger can trace the program through multiple source files, multiple threads, and through an executable in several DLLs. "It's a very powerful debugger.

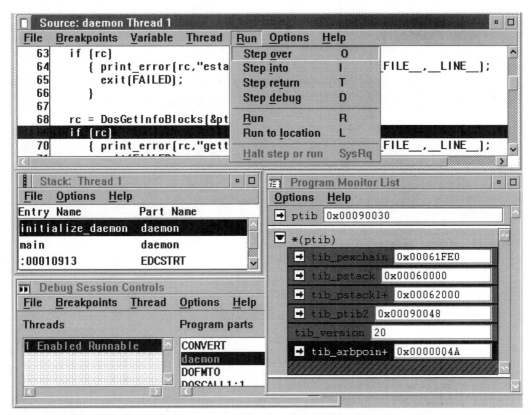

Figure 13-19. C Set/2 PM Debugger: A Debugger That Makes You Love Bugs.

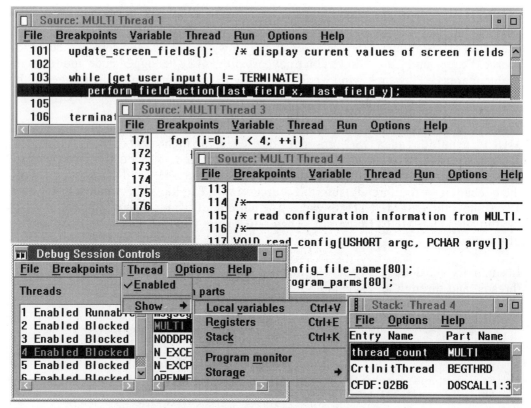

Figure 13-20. C Set/2 PM Debugger: The Multithread Debugging Facilities.

Anywhere you can go we can trace it there. You can't get away." [2] The debugger also provides very powerful facilities for debugging PM applications. You can view and manage your application's PM windows concurrently with the debugger windows.

The purpose of this brief introduction is to make you aware that tools do exist to help you debug programs in a multitasking environment. To obtain more details on how to use them, you should consult the documentation that comes with C Set/2, Work-Frame/2, and the OS/2 Toolkit.

This concludes our panoramic grand tour of the C programming environment under OS/2 2.0. If you've survived that far, the rest of the book should be a piece of cake. It's just more code, more APIs, and more functions.

---

[2] Source: Dave Mooney, IBM Toronto Lab. Dave is one of the people who created the C Set/2 compiler and tools. If you get lost in your code, you know who to call.

Chapter 14

MULTI.C - Multitasking Can Be Fun

This chapter is about MULTI.C, a program that lets you organize "races" between tasks. In this chapter, we make use of MULTI's facilities to run races between four threads, or four processes. The processes and threads will perform the same counting function. This will give us a chance to compare threads versus processes from two angles: ease of programming and execution speeds. After going through the program, you should be able to get a good feel for the relative merits of OS/2's two multitasking approaches. MULTI.C also lets you experiment with multitasking performance. For example, you can vary the number of concurrently executing tasks or change the priority level of individual tasks and get immediate feedback on how these effect system performance.

MULTI.C is easy to follow and understand. A good portion of MULTI's bulk comes from familiar C function calls whose sole purpose is to provide us with a working set of dialog tools to be used until we get to the fancy graphics and windowing pizzaz of the Presentation Manager. You can skip over MULTI's screen and keyboard interaction code, if you choose to, without detracting from your understanding MULTI's treatment of multitasking. The "long walk" through MULTI.C code and the time you spend playing with the program will count heavily towards your "accreditation" as an OS/2 multitasking guru.

OFF TO THE RACES WITH MULTI THREADS

To run MULTI, first edit MULTI.CFG, a configuration file that specifies what threads or processes you want MULTI to run. Then invoke the program by entering MULTI at the command line and off you go into the world of multitasking. Once MULTI is up and running, you are at the controls.

Creating a Config File for Threads

We will first run MULTI in **THREADS** mode by creating the entries in the MULTI.CFG file shown in Figure 14-1.

Let's take a look at what the entries in this file mean:

```
PROGRAM_TYPE    =  THREADS
STOP_TIME_MS    =  20000
TASK_NAME       =  THREAD_1
TASK_NAME       =  THREAD_2
TASK_NAME       =  THREAD_3
TASK_NAME       =  THREAD_4
```

Figure 14-1. A MULTI.CFG File for Running Four Threads.

- The PROGRAM_TYPE entry tells MULTI that it will be racing threads as opposed to processes.
- The STOP_TIME_MS entry specifies the duration of the race in units of milliseconds. In this example, we've specified that our races will be 20 seconds long.
- The TASK_NAME entries contain the names of the contending tasks. In the case of processes, these are the names of separately compiled programs that will be run. Threads, on the other hand, are compiled as part of the MULTI program. So in effect, we're telling MULTI to run in THREADS mode for 20 seconds after we say GO.

How to Read a MULTI Screen

We will now go through some screen capture sequences of MULTI races that were obtained on an IBM PS/2 Mod 80. Figure 14-2 shows the MULTI screen that gets displayed when the program first comes up. You can think of the MULTI screen as a control panel for running races between tasks.

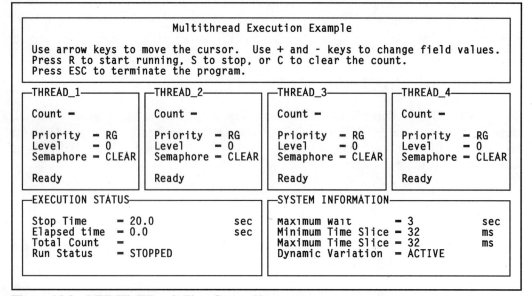

Figure 14-2.   MULTI: When it First Comes Up.

The MULTI control panel is organized into several window areas:

- We start with the top window, whose current title indicates that MULTI is running threads as opposed to processes. Remember, this is exactly what we told MULTI to do in the MULTI.CFG file for this run. Below the title are the instructions you will need to manipulate MULTI's control knobs.
- In the middle of the screen are four windows, one for each of the tasks (in this case threads) that we told MULTI to run in MULTI.CFG. Notice that all four tasks first come up with their task semaphore in the CLEAR state, indicating that they are ready to run. You can START or STOP a particular task by moving the cursor to the semaphore knob in the task's window, and then use the + or - keys to CLEAR or SET the task's control semaphore. Even with the semaphore CLEAR, the task will not run so long as MULTI itself is STOPPED.
- Currently, MULTI is in a STOPPED state as shown in the bottom left window. You can start MULTI by pressing **R** for RUN.
- The parameters displayed in the lower right-hand window display the maximum and minimum **time-slices** of CPU time allocated to a running thread before it gets preempted. The other two parameters, *Max Wait* and *Dynamic Variation*, specify the maximum wait interval that a thread waits without being executed. OS/2 automatically boosts the priority of a thread that has waited longer than maxwait seconds when the Dynamic Variation parameter is enabled. This is to prevent a low-priority task from starving when it shares the CPU with higher-priority tasks. You specify all four of these parameters in your OS/2 *config.sys* file.

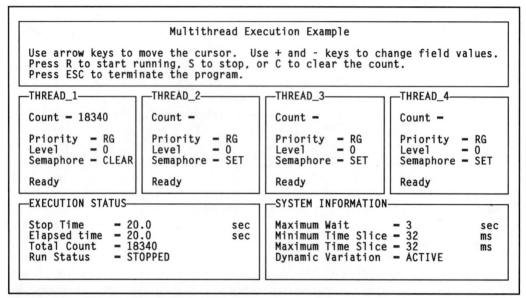

Figure 14-3.   One Regular Priority Thread.

Our First Race: One Thread Running Solo

We will now bring MULTI to life by first running a race with a single task contender. We do this by moving the cursor to the windows of THREAD_2, THREAD_3, and THREAD_4, and SET their respective semaphores. Having set up the conditions for the race, we are now ready to hit **R**, our signal to start the race. When we do so, MULTI will run for 20 seconds, after which our display looks like Figure 14-3.

The display shows that THREAD_1 accumulated a count of 18,340 during the 20 second run interval. The other three threads didn't budge since their semaphores were in the SET state.

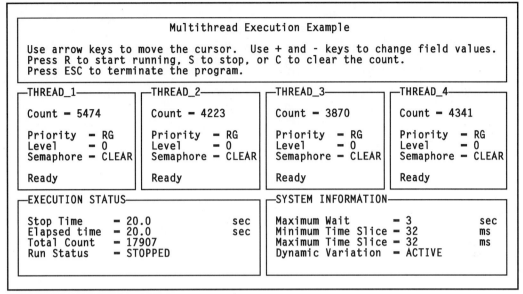

Figure 14-4.   Four Regular 0 Priority Threads.

Our Second Race: Four Regular Threads

Here's what you do to organize a race between all four threads:

1. Clear all four thread semaphores. CLEAR should appear in all four thread windows.
2. Clear all the counters by entering **C**.
3. Give the Go signal to start the race by entering **R** to run MULTI.

Observing MULTI run during this 20 second race is interesting in its own right. You get to see different tasks come to life during short time durations. Unfortunately, providing animated output is beyond the display capabilities of this book's pages. So we're counting on you to run the program to observe all the special effects.

What we can do is show you a screen capture of the MULTI display at the end of the 20 seconds (see Figure 14-4). What the screen shows is that all four threads produced a cumulative count of 17,907. We also observe a sizeable deviation in the counts produced by *equal priority* threads. The first thread ran a better race. In theory, all four threads should have produced the same count since they were all set to run at the same priority. Should we expect a closer race by making the STOP_TIME_MS parameter longer than 20 seconds?

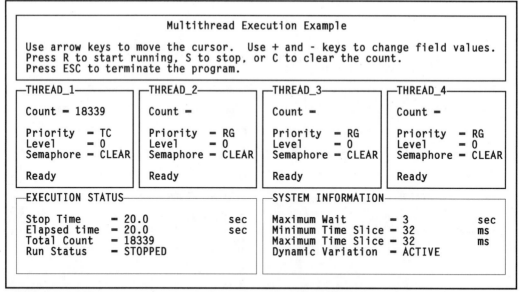

```
┌──────────────────────────────────────────────────────────────────────────────┐
│  ┌──────────────────────────────────────────────────────────────────────────┐ │
│  │                   Multithread Execution Example                          │ │
│  │  Use arrow keys to move the cursor.  Use + and - keys to change field    │ │
│  │  values.                                                                 │ │
│  │  Press R to start running, S to stop, or C to clear the count.           │ │
│  │  Press ESC to terminate the program.                                     │ │
│  └──────────────────────────────────────────────────────────────────────────┘ │
│  ┌THREAD_1────────┐ ┌THREAD_2────────┐ ┌THREAD_3────────┐ ┌THREAD_4────────┐   │
│  │                │ │                │ │                │ │                │   │
│  │ Count = 18339  │ │ Count =        │ │ Count =        │ │ Count =        │   │
│  │                │ │                │ │                │ │                │   │
│  │ Priority  = TC │ │ Priority  = RG │ │ Priority  = RG │ │ Priority  = RG │   │
│  │ Level     = 0  │ │ Level     = 0  │ │ Level     = 0  │ │ Level     = 0  │   │
│  │ Semaphore = CLEAR│ Semaphore = CLEAR│ Semaphore = CLEAR│ Semaphore = CLEAR│  │
│  │                │ │                │ │                │ │                │   │
│  │ Ready          │ │ Ready          │ │ Ready          │ │ Ready          │   │
│  └────────────────┘ └────────────────┘ └────────────────┘ └────────────────┘   │
│  ┌EXECUTION STATUS────────────────────┐ ┌SYSTEM INFORMATION────────────────┐   │
│  │                                    │ │                                  │   │
│  │ Stop Time    = 20.0         sec    │ │ Maximum Wait       = 3      sec   │   │
│  │ Elapsed time = 20.0         sec    │ │ Minimum Time Slice = 32     ms    │   │
│  │ Total Count  = 18339               │ │ Maximum Time Slice = 32     ms    │   │
│  │ Run Status   = STOPPED             │ │ Dynamic Variation  = ACTIVE      │   │
│  │                                    │ │                                  │   │
│  └────────────────────────────────────┘ └──────────────────────────────────┘   │
└──────────────────────────────────────────────────────────────────────────────┘
```

Figure 14-5.   One Time Critical 0 Thread, Three Regular 0 Threads.

Our Third Race: Introducing Extreme Priorities

Now, let's try to make this race more uneven by varying the priority levels. Priorities determine how often a task gets assigned a CPU execution time-slice by the OS/2 scheduler. As a review, under OS/2 a thread may run in one of four priority classes: *Idle-time, Regular, Fixed-high,* and *Time-critical.* Idle-time threads have the lowest priority and receive the least amount of scheduling attention. Time-critical threads have the highest priority and get scheduled ahead of all others. OS/2 assigns regular priority to a new process (and its primary thread) as the default. You can assign any of OS/2's four priority levels to a MULTI task by moving the cursor to the task's Priority field, and then using the + or - keys to "sequence" to the priority class you want to assign. You'll see the field change from BG (for background or idle-time) to RG (for regular) to FH (for fixed-high) to TC for (time-critical).

Within each priority class, OS/2 supports 32 distinct priority levels. When a thread is created, it is initially dispatched with the same priority as the creating thread. MULTI starts you out at level 0, but you can sequence through 32 levels by placing your cursor on a task's level field and then hitting + or - keys to increment or decrement the level until you're at the level you want to assign to a task.

So now that we know something about priorities, let's apply this new knowledge to some practical undertaking, like rigging the race between our four tasks. We can do that by placing the cursor on Thread_1's Priority field and hitting + twice. The display indicates **TC** for time-critical. Having done this, we hit **C** to clear the counters and then enter **R**, our signal to start a new race. Once more, the race will last 20 seconds, after which the MULTI screen would look like Figure 14-5.

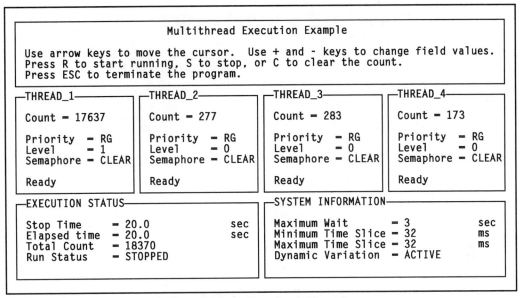

Figure 14-6. One Regular 1 Thread, Three Regular 0 Threads.

The results displayed in Figure 14-5 show that our race rigging was an absolute success! Thread_1, our time-critical winner, was able to starve off the competition and deliver all 18,339 counts. The OS/2 *Dynamic Variation* feature did not help because it cannot boost a thread past its current priority level.

Our Fourth Race: Introducing the Smallest Priority

In our next variation of a rigged race, we will apply the smallest level of rigging and see what OS/2 can do with its automatic boosts of priority to help out the starving tasks. The plan for this new race is to demote Thread_1 to the Regular Priority class, but raise its level by a notch to 1 (of 32). In so doing, we are applying the smallest increment of priority that OS/2 provides. The display indicates **RG** for all threads, and Level 1 for Thread_1.

Once again, we hit **C** to clear the counters and then enter **R** to start the minimally rigged race. The race lasts 20 seconds, after which the MULTI screen looks like Figure 14-6.

The results shown in Figure 14-6 are worthy of note. Once again, Thread_1, is the undisputed winner. However, this time the OS/2 *Dynamic Variation* feature was able to throw a few crumbs of CPU time-slices at the other starving contenders, and they were able to do much better than in the previous race. The question is what made OS/2 manifest so much generosity this time around? The answer is that after 3 seconds (the Maximum Wait), OS/2 was able to raise the priority of some threads to level 1, where they were able to get some CPU time-slices.

OFF TO THE RACES WITH MULTI PROCESSES

In this section, we organize a race between four processes. We do this by running MULTI in the **PROCESS** mode. This is easily done by creating the new MULTI.CFG file shown in Figure 14-7.

```
PROGRAM_TYPE    = PROCESS
STOP_TIME_MS    = 20000
TASK_NAME       = COUNT.EXE 0
TASK_NAME       = COUNT.EXE 1
TASK_NAME       = COUNT.EXE 2
TASK_NAME       = COUNT.EXE 3
```

Figure 14-7.   A MULTI.CFG File for Running Four Processes.

The first line entry tells MULTI that it will be dealing with processes as opposed to threads. The STOP_TIME_MS parameter, specified in the second line, tells MULTI to run the races in 20 second intervals. The last four lines are the names of the processes to run. Since processes are separately compiled programs, we need to specify the name of the executable file. The example in Figure 14-7 will be running four instances of the same program, COUNT.EXE, each of which is a separate process. The number following COUNT.EXE in the MULTI.CFG file gives each process a unique identifier.

The COUNT.EXE program, which is described later in this chapter, is designed to provide the same COUNT function as the threads we've been running. The idea is to get a feel for the relative performance of threads versus processes, and more importantly, we want to demonstrate how to code the same function using either method.

Our Fifth Race: Four Regular Processes

We will run this race between four REGULAR processes. Once again, we hit **C** to clear the counters and then enter **R** to give the Go signal to start the new race. At the end of 20 seconds, the MULTI screen looks like Figure 14-8.

Not too surprisingly, we observe in Figure 14-8 that, all things being equal, there are still some minor variations in the performance of "equal" processes. More importantly, if we compare the results of Figure 14-8 with the corresponding run for threads shown in Figure 14-4, we show 17,988 counts for processes versus 17,907 counts for threads. What do these numbers seem to indicate? They seem to indicate that threads and processes perform equally well under OS/2 2.0.[1]

---

[1] When we ran the same benchmarks for OS/2 1.3 in the first edition of our book threads were slightly faster.

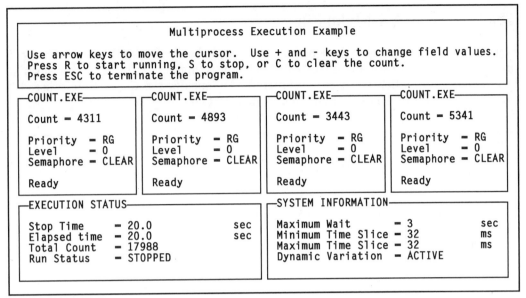

Figure 14-8. Four Regular Processes.

Run Your Own Races

MULTI is a tool for running empirical experiments. It is up to you to set up the experiments and draw the appropriate conclusions. The numbers we've shown so far were for demonstrative purposes only. We caution you to run your own experiments before you start quoting them. You should also be getting the idea, by now, that in addition to running benchmarks, MULTI can be a useful learning tool. We will be returning to MULTI in future chapters to run some database benchmark tests.

DISSECTING THE MULTI.C PROGRAM

The purpose of MULTI in the context of the current chapters is to learn how to write multitasking programs using the OS/2 kernel. Now that we know what MULTI does, we are ready to dive into the code and find out how it gets done.

The MULTI.MAK Make File

Figure 14-9 is the listing of the make file used to build the **MULTI** and **COUNT** programs (you will learn about COUNT later in this chapter). The only new surprise in this make file is that we used the **Gm+** flag to specify the C Set/2 multithreaded run-time library. MULTI is our first multithreaded OS/2 program.

```
#************************************************************************
# Make File for MULTI and COUNT programs
#************************************************************************

#** MACROS *************************************************************
cflags=/C /Ti /Q+ /Sm /Gs- /Gm+ /Ge+ /Gd+
lflags=/ST:24000/CO/NOLOGO/NOI/L/M:FULL/PM:VIO
linklibs=

#** INFERENCE RULES ****************************************************
.obj.exe:
        echo LINKING    $*.exe
        link386 $(lflags) $**,$*.exe,,$(linklibs),;

.c.obj:
        echo COMPILING $*.c
        icc $(cflags) $*.c

#** BUILD STATEMENTS ***************************************************
all: multi.exe  count.exe

multi.exe:              multi.obj
multi.obj:              multi.c    const.h multi.h

count.exe:              count.obj
count.obj:              count.c    const.h count.h
```

Figure 14-9. The MULTI.MAK Make File.

MULTI.C: main()

The **main()** function, listed in Figure 14-10, will serve as the MULTI.C program outline. This means that whenever you feel you're getting lost in the detail of the code, you should come back to **main()** to refresh your top-down perspective on what the program does. This section also provides a good index into the different code listings. We will walk through MULTI's code components with the idea of demonstrating OS/2's kernel functions in the context of a fairly realistic program setting. We are especially interested in how the different multitasking elements come together in programming ensembles. So, stay alert during this long exposition on how the new OS/2 kernel services can be put to work, and avoid getting hung up on the more mundane aspects of MULTI, like **get_user_input()** or **update_screen_fields()**.

Like most C programs, MULTI starts out by including the various header files. Starting from the top, we include headers for the C library functions. This is followed by a list of **#define** directives whose purpose is to define the OS/2 header material that gets included through **OS2.H**. The OS/2 API functions we include with this program are VIO display, shared memory, process control, semaphores, date/time, and query system information. Following the OS/2 include files are two MULTI specific header files: const.h and multi.h. The first file, **const.h**, listed in Figure 14-11, contains the declarations of constants used by both the MULTI.C and COUNT.C programs. The second file, **multi.h**, listed in Figure 14-12, contains the forward declarations of the procedures and global variables used in the MULTI.C program.

The main program starts right after the include files and is mostly self-explanatory. The first six functions are involved in setting up the environment for running the task "races." This is followed by the code that starts the four tasks. From then on the program is under interactive user control and consists of running the races and displaying results. Eventually, the user gets tired of watching threads and processes chase each other, and terminates the program. Let's first take a look at the six functions involved in setting up the races:

1. The first of the set up functions is **read_config()**, listed in Figure 14-13. This function simply obtains the race setup information and the list of task contenders from MULTI.CFG.
2. The **create_semaphores()** function, listed in Figure 14-15, sets up the control mechanisms for the races.
3. The, **create_timer_thread()** function, listed in Figure 14-16, creates the **elapsed_time_thread()**, which serves as the referee for the race and keeps track of elapsed time. The **elapsed_time_thread()** is listed in Figure 14-17.
4. The next function, **set_thread_priorities()**, listed in Figure 14-18, assigns time-critical priority class to **main()** and the **elapsed_time_thread()** so that the organizers of the race and the referee can remain in control at all times.
5. The **create_counter_memory()** function, listed in Figure 14-19, creates a global memory area where all the task contenders record their output counts.
6. Finally the **paint_screen()** function, listed in Figure 14-20, displays the control panel from which the races are run.

Having set up the conditions for the races, **main()** now lines up and starts four task contenders. If the contenders are processes, **main()** invokes **create_processes()**, listed in Figure 14-22, and starts four processes specified in MULTI.CFG. Otherwise, **main()** invokes **create_threads()**, listed in Figure 14-21, and starts four threads. For the purposes of this chapter, the four processes started are four instances of **COUNT.EXE**, and the four threads are four instances of the **thread_count()** thread. For comparison purposes, both the threads and the processes perform the same *counting* function. The source code listing for the **COUNT** process is given in Figure 14-32 and Figure 14-33. The code for the **thread_count()** thread is listed in Figure 14-31. **Main()** updates the screen to reflect the state of the contenders by invoking **update_screen_fields()**, listed in Figure 14-23.

From this point on, the races are run under user control and **main()** obtains its input through **get_user_input()**, listed in Figure 14-24, and performs the requested actions through **perform_field_action**(), listed in Figure 14-25. Eventually, the user puts out a TERMINATE request, which causes **main**() to invoke **terminate_program**(), listed in Figure 14-30. The MULTI program also contains four sets of helper routines:

1. The screen helper functions listed in Figure 14-26.
2. The OS/2 **DOS** helper functions listed in Figure 14-27.
3. The **VIO** helper functions listed in Figure 14-28.
4. The miscellaneous helper functions listed in Figure 14-29.

```
/*************************************************************************/
/*  PROGRAM NAME: MULTI - a multitasking execution example              */
/*                                                                      */
/*  PROGRAM DESCRIPTION:  This program gives a visual demonstration of  */
/*     the execution of 4 processes or 4 threads.   The user can        */
/*     interactively control the task execution environment.            */
/*************************************************************************/
#include <process.h>                    /* For exit()                   */
#include <conio.h>                       /* For kbhit()                  */
#include <stdio.h>                       /* For printf() & NULL          */
#include <stdlib.h>                      /* For printf                   */
#include <stddef.h>                      /* For _beginthread             */
#include <string.h>                      /* For printf                   */

#define INCL_VIO                         /* include VIO calls            */
#define INCL_DOSMEMMGR                   /* for shared segment functions */
#define INCL_DOSPROCESS                  /* include priority api calls   */
#define INCL_DOSSEMAPHORES               /* include semaphore api calls  */
#define INCL_DOSDATETIME                 /* include timer     api calls  */
#define INCL_DOSMISC                     /* include DosQuerySysInfo      */
#include <os2.h>
#include "const.h"
#include "multi.h"
/*---------------------------------------------------------------------*/
/* Main routine.                                                       */
/*---------------------------------------------------------------------*/
VOID main(USHORT argc, PCHAR argv[])
{ read_config(argc, argv);   /* read configuration information from MULTI.CFG */

  create_semaphores();       /* Create semaphores for task control     */

  create_timer_thread();     /* Start a time critical referee thread   */

  set_thread_priorities();   /* Increase timer and main thread priorities */

  create_counter_memory();   /* Create shared memory segment for count values */

  paint_screen();            /* Draw screen with title, task status etc.. */

  if (program_type == PROCESSES)
     create_processes();     /* Start processes                        */
  else
     create_threads();       /* Start threads                          */

  update_screen_fields();    /* display current values of screen fields */
  while (get_user_input() != TERMINATE)
     perform_field_action(last_field_x, last_field_y);

  terminate_program();       /* At user request, kill tasks and clean up */
} /* end main */
```

Figure 14-10.   MULTI main() Function.

MULTI.C: Include Files

MULTI.C is packaged with two separate include files: CONST.H and MULTI.H. The **CONST.H** file, listed in Figure 14-11, contains the symbolic names of constants that are used by the MULTI.C and COUNT.C programs. The main purpose of the constant **#defines** is to make the programs easier to read, especially in the sections that deal with screen display attributes and task priorities.

The **MULTI.H** include file, listed in Figure 14-12, is your garden variety C include file. We first pre-declare all the procedures that will be used by the program to make the compiler happy. We then declare, and in many cases initialize, the program's global variables. One look at the include file variables shows a heavy usage of 4-element arrays. We have 4-element arrays of: task_names, task_status, thread_stack, thread_id, fields, etc. This magic number *four* comes from the fact that MULTI keeps track at all times of four tasks. The arrays maintain the necessary information on those tasks.

The most formidable looking of these arrays, **field**, uses a home-made **FIELD** structure to keep track of information pertinent to each screen field such as: screen location, length, minimum and maximum values, and current field value. Notice that the MULTI control panel, shown in Figure 14-2, contains four task windows, each consisting of multiple fields such as PRIORITY, LEVEL, and SEMAPHORE. An array of arrays of structures is used for this occasion.

The only other "unfamiliar" occurrences in MULTI.H are the OS/2-defined types. We will be explaining the new OS/2 types when we get to the OS/2 calls that use them. Likewise, we explain a new OS/2 function the first time we encounter it in a program.

```
/*****************************************************************************/
/*  INCLUDE NAME: CONST - constants for MULTI and related programs         */
/*****************************************************************************/

/*_____*/
/* defines                                                                 */
/*_____*/
                    /*_____*/
                    /* box characters                       */
                    /*_____*/
#define HORIZONTAL_LINE     "\0xC4"
#define VERTICAL_LINE       "\0xB3"
#define BOX_UL_CORNER       "\0xDA"
#define BOX_UR_CORNER       "\0xBF"
#define BOX_LL_CORNER       "\0xC0"
#define BOX_LR_CORNER       "\0xD9"
#define BLANK               " "

                    /*_____*/
                    /* foreground color values              */
                    /*_____*/
#define BLACK               0x00
#define BLUE                0x01
#define GREEN               0x02
```

Figure 14-11 (Part 1 of 3). CONST.H Include File.

```
#define CYAN                    0x03
#define RED                     0x04
#define MAGENTA                 0x05
#define BROWN                   0x06
#define LT_GRAY                 0x07
#define GRAY                    0x08
#define LT_BLUE                 0x09
#define LT_GREEN                0x0A
#define LT_CYAN                 0x0B
#define LT_RED                  0x0C
#define LT_MAGENTA              0x0D
#define YELLOW                  0x0E
#define WHITE                   0x0F

                    /*_____*/
                    /* background color values                */
                    /*_____*/
#define BGND_BLACK              0x00
#define BGND_BLUE               0x10
#define BGND_GREEN              0x20
#define BGND_TURQ               0x30
#define BGND_RED                0x40
#define BGND_MAGENTA            0x50
#define BGND_BROWN              0x60
#define BGND_LT_GRAY            0x70
#define BGND_GRAY               0x80
#define BGND_LT_BLUE            0x90
#define BGND_LT_GREEN           0xA0
#define BGND_LT_CYAN            0xB0
#define BGND_LT_RED             0xC0
#define BGND_LT_MAGENTA         0xD0
#define BGND_YELLOW             0xE0
#define BGND_WHITE              0xF0

                    /*_____*/
                    /* panel color attributes                 */
                    /*_____*/
#define BOX_ATTR             ((CHAR)CYAN    | BGND_BLACK)
#define BOX_TITLE_ATTR       ((CHAR)GREEN   | BGND_BLACK)
#define FIELD_TEXT_ATTR      ((CHAR)BROWN   | BGND_BLACK)
#define IO_FIELD_ATTR        ((CHAR)LT_GRAY | BGND_BLACK)
#define OUTPUT_FIELD_ATTR    ((CHAR)WHITE   | BGND_BLACK)
#define CURSOR_FIELD_ATTR    ((CHAR)BLACK     BGND_LT_GRAY)
#define PANEL_TITLE_ATTR     ((CHAR)YELLOW  | BGND_BLACK)
#define PANEL_HELP_ATTR      ((CHAR)LT_RED  | BGND_BLACK)
#define PANEL_STATUS_ATTR    ((CHAR)RED     | BGND_BLACK)

                    /*_____*/
                    /* key definitions                        */
                    /*_____*/
#define UP_ARROW                (256 + 72)
#define DOWN_ARROW              (256 + 80)
#define LEFT_ARROW              (256 + 75)
#define RIGHT_ARROW             (256 + 77)
#define PLUS_KEY                '+'
#define MINUS_KEY               '-'
#define ESC_KEY                 27

                    /*_____*/
                    /* panel field limits                     */
                    /*_____*/
#define FIELD_X_MAX             3
#define FIELD_Y_MAX             2
```

Figure 14-11 (Part 2 of 3). CONST.H Include File.

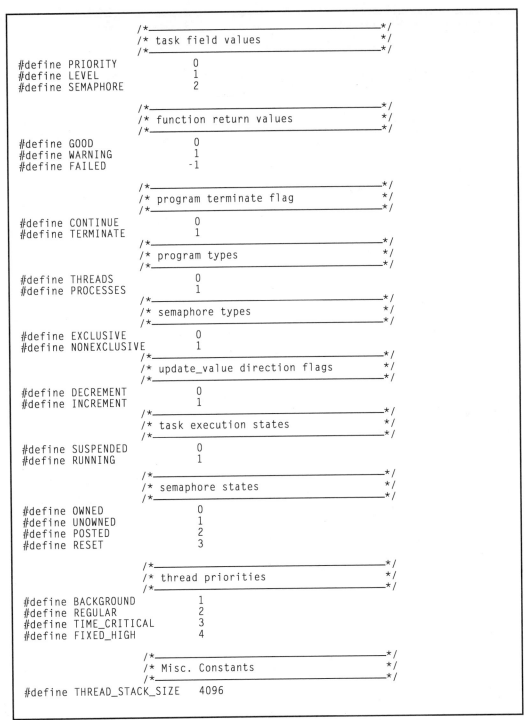

```
                    /*────────────────────────────────*/
                    /* task field values              */
                    /*────────────────────────────────*/
#define PRIORITY             0
#define LEVEL                1
#define SEMAPHORE            2

                    /*────────────────────────────────*/
                    /* function return values         */
                    /*────────────────────────────────*/
#define GOOD                 0
#define WARNING              1
#define FAILED              -1

                    /*────────────────────────────────*/
                    /* program terminate flag         */
                    /*────────────────────────────────*/
#define CONTINUE             0
#define TERMINATE            1
                    /*────────────────────────────────*/
                    /* program types                  */
                    /*────────────────────────────────*/
#define THREADS              0
#define PROCESSES            1
                    /*────────────────────────────────*/
                    /* semaphore types                */
                    /*────────────────────────────────*/
#define EXCLUSIVE            0
#define NONEXCLUSIVE         1
                    /*────────────────────────────────*/
                    /* update_value direction flags   */
                    /*────────────────────────────────*/
#define DECREMENT            0
#define INCREMENT            1
                    /*────────────────────────────────*/
                    /* task execution states          */
                    /*────────────────────────────────*/
#define SUSPENDED            0
#define RUNNING              1

                    /*────────────────────────────────*/
                    /* semaphore states               */
                    /*────────────────────────────────*/
#define OWNED                0
#define UNOWNED              1
#define POSTED               2
#define RESET                3

                    /*────────────────────────────────*/
                    /* thread priorities              */
                    /*────────────────────────────────*/
#define BACKGROUND           1
#define REGULAR              2
#define TIME_CRITICAL        3
#define FIXED_HIGH           4

                    /*────────────────────────────────*/
                    /* Misc. Constants                */
                    /*────────────────────────────────*/
#define THREAD_STACK_SIZE  4096
```

Figure 14-11 (Part 3 of 3). CONST.H Include File.

```
/***********************************************************************/
/*  INCLUDE NAME: MULTI.H  - declarations for MULTI program            */
/***********************************************************************/

/*_____*/
/* Forward declarations of procedures in this module                   */
/*_____*/
                    /*_____*/
                    /* top level routines                    */
                    /*_____*/
VOID    read_config(USHORT argc, PCHAR argv[]);
VOID    create_semaphores(VOID);
VOID    create_timer_thread(VOID);
VOID    set_thread_priorities(VOID);
VOID    create_counter_segment(VOID);
VOID    paint_screen(VOID);
VOID    create_processes(VOID);
VOID    create_threads(VOID);
VOID    update_screen_fields(VOID);
USHORT  get_user_input(VOID);
VOID    perform_field_action(USHORT, USHORT);
VOID    terminate_program(VOID);

                    /*_____*/
                    /* thread routines                       */
                    /*_____*/
VOID    thread_count(PVOID);
VOID    elapsed_time_thread(PVOID);

                    /*_____*/
                    /* screen helper routines                */
                    /*_____*/
VOID    move_cursor(USHORT);
VOID    update_value(PUSHORT, USHORT, USHORT, USHORT);

                    /*_____*/
                    /* DOS call helper functions             */
                    /*_____*/
VOID    request_mutex_semaphore(HMTX, PUSHORT);
VOID    release_mutex_semaphore(HMTX, PUSHORT);
VOID    post_event_semaphore(HEV, PUSHORT);
VOID    reset_event_semaphore(HEV, PUSHORT);
VOID    set_priority(USHORT);

                    /*_____*/
                    /* VIO call helper functions             */
                    /*_____*/
VOID    clear_screen(VOID);
VOID    draw_title_box(USHORT, USHORT);
VOID    draw_task_box(PCHAR, USHORT, USHORT);
VOID    display_sys_info(USHORT, USHORT);
VOID    display_exec_status(USHORT, USHORT);
VOID    draw_box(PCHAR, CHAR, USHORT, USHORT, USHORT, USHORT, CHAR);
VOID    hide_cursor(VOID);
VOID    restore_cursor(VOID);
VOID    draw_cursor(BYTE, USHORT, USHORT, USHORT);
VOID    write_str(PCHAR, CHAR, USHORT, USHORT);
VOID    fill_area(PCHAR, CHAR, USHORT, USHORT, USHORT, USHORT);
VOID    draw_horizontal_line(USHORT, USHORT, USHORT, CHAR);
VOID    draw_vertical_line(USHORT, USHORT, USHORT, CHAR);
```

Figure 14-12 (Part 1 of 4). MULTI.H Include File.

```
                        /*_____*/
                        /* Miscellaneous helper routines  */
                        /*_____*/
VOID    print_error(USHORT, PCHAR , PCHAR , USHORT);
VOID    FAR multi_exit(USHORT);

/*_____*/
/* Global variables/type definitions for this module       */
/*_____*/
                        /*_____*/
                        /* configuration variables        */
                        /*_____*/
USHORT    program_type;                 /* threads or processes?        */
ULONG     stop_time_msecs;              /* number of ms to run a test    */
UCHAR     task_names[4][15] =
          { "              ",           /* program names go in this      */
            "              ",           /*   array and are used for      */
            "              ",           /*   DosExecPgm                   */
            "              " };


                        /*_____*/
                        /* variables for run all semaphore */
                        /*_____*/
HEV     runall_sem_handle;              /* semaphore handle              */
USHORT  runall_sem_status;              /* is the semaphore set or clear */

                        /*_____*/
                        /* variables and typedefs for task */
                        /*   execution control.            */
                        /*_____*/
typedef struct STATUS { USHORT active;
                        USHORT semaphore;} STATUS;

STATUS task_status[4] = {{RUNNING, UNOWNED},
                         {RUNNING, UNOWNED},
                         {RUNNING, UNOWNED},
                         {RUNNING, UNOWNED}};

HMTX    run_sem_handle[4];
USHORT  threadid[4];                    /* thread IDs                      */
SHORT   thread_parm[4]                  /* array of parameters, one for each */
          = {0, 1, 2, 3};               /*   executing thread              */
                        /*_____*/
                        /* variables for stop time/elapsed */
                        /* time update and control         */
                        /*_____*/
ULONG   elapsed_time_msecs;             /* ms elapsed from beginning of test */
ULONG   current_msecs;                  /* current ms counter value from    */
                                        /*   DosGetInfoSeg                  */


ULONG   start_msecs;                    /* beginning of current time interval*/
ULONG   delta_msecs;                    /* current time interval            */
USHORT  test_running;                   /* flag to indicate a test is running*/

TID     elapsed_time_threadid;          /* id of timer thread               */
```

Figure 14-12 (Part 2 of 4).   MULTI.H Include File.

```
                      /*_____*/
                      /* count variable definition          */
                      /*_____*/
typedef struct _COUNT
        { ULONG count[8];
        } COUNT;
COUNT    *count_ptr;
ULONG    total_count = 0;

                      /*_____*/
                      /* variables and typedefs for screen  */
                      /*  paint and cursor control.          */
                      /*_____*/
typedef struct FIELD { USHORT x;         /* column location         */
                       USHORT y;         /* row location            */
                       USHORT cx;        /* field length            */
                       USHORT min;       /* field minimum value     */
                       USHORT max;       /* field maximum value     */
                       USHORT value;     /* current field value     */
                     } FIELD;

     /* x   y   cx  min   max   value */
FIELD field[4][3] =
    {{
        {14, 11 , 2,   1,    4,     2},  /* task 1, PRIORITY field  */
        {14, 12 , 2,   0,   31,     0},  /* task 1, LEVEL field     */
        {14, 13 , 5,   0,    1,     0}   /* task 1, SEMAPHORE field */
     },
     {
        {34, 11 , 2,   1,    4,     2},  /* task 2, PRIORITY field  */
        {34, 12 , 2,   0,   31,     0},  /* task 2, LEVEL field     */
        {34, 13 , 5,   0,    1,     0}   /* task 2, SEMAPHORE field */
     },
     {
        {54, 11 , 2,   1,    4,     2},  /* task 3, PRIORITY field  */
        {54, 12 , 2,   0,   31,     0},  /* task 3, LEVEL field     */
        {54, 13 , 5,   0,    1,     0}   /* task 3, SEMAPHORE field */
     },
     {
        {74, 11 , 2,   1,    4,     2},  /* task 4, PRIORITY field  */
        {74, 12 , 2,   0,   31,     0},  /* task 4, LEVEL field     */
        {74, 13 , 5,   0,    1,     0},  /* task 4, SEMAPHORE field */
     }};

VIOCURSORINFO cursor_data;            /* used for hiding cursor      */
VIOCURSORINFO save_cursor_data;       /* used for restoring the cursor */

USHORT field_x      = 0;              /* variables                   */
USHORT field_y      = 0;              /*   for tracking              */
USHORT last_field_x = 0;              /*      cursor                 */
USHORT last_field_y = 0;              /*         movement            */

                      /*_____*/
                      /* variables for child processes      */
                      /*_____*/
USHORT processid[4];                  /* thread IDs                  */
UCHAR object_name[13];                /* buffer for failure name     */
RESULTCODES ExecResult;               /* structure for child proc. results */
UCHAR programs[4][80] =
     {"        0",                    /* program names go in this    */
      "        1",                    /*    array and are used for   */
      "        2"};                   /*    DosExecPgm               */
      "        3"};
```

Figure 14-12 (Part 3 of 4). MULTI.H Include File.

```
RESULTCODES term_result;            /* termination result code     */
PID         term_processid;         /* terminating process id      */
                  /*_____*/
                  /* misc. variables           */
                  /*_____*/
USHORT   i,x,y;                     /* for loop indices            */
USHORT   rc;                        /* return code variable        */
```

Figure 14-12 (Part 4 of 4). MULTI.H Include File.

MULTI.C: read_config()

The **read_config()** code, listed in Figure 14-13, is straightforward C code that consists of reading a MULTI.CFG file and obtaining from it the parameters that govern the running of a race. Figure 14-1 contains an example of MULTI.CFG for running a race between threads, while Figure 14-7 provides an example of a MULTI.CFG file for processes.

```
/*_____*/
/* read configuration information from MULTI.CFG          */
/*_____*/
VOID read_config(USHORT argc, PCHAR argv[])
{
  CHAR config_file_name[80];
  CHAR program_parms[80];
                /*_____*/
                /* configuration file variables   */
                /*_____*/
  FILE    *config_file;          /* Input file control block       */
  CHAR    line[80];              /* one line of config file        */
  CHAR    prog_type[15];

  /*_____*/
  /* determine config file name     */
  /*_____*/
  if (argc == 2)
     strcpy(config_file_name, argv[1]);
  else
     strcpy(config_file_name, "multi.cfg");

  /*_____*/
  /* open the configuration file    */
  /*_____*/
  if (NULL == (config_file = fopen(config_file_name,"r")))
     { print_error(rc,"opening configuration file",__FILE__,__LINE__);
       exit(FAILED);
     }
```

Figure 14-13 (Part 1 of 2). The read_config() Function.

```
/*_____*/
/* read program type                      */
/*_____*/
fgets(line, sizeof(line), config_file);
if (sscanf(line,"PROGRAM_TYPE    = %s ", prog_type) != 1)
   { print_error(rc,"reading program type from configuration file",
                 __FILE__,__LINE__);
     exit(FAILED);
   }
if  (strcmp(strupr(prog_type),"THREADS") == 0)
    program_type = THREADS;
else
    program_type = PROCESSES;

/*_____*/
/* read stop time                         */
/*_____*/
fgets(line, sizeof(line), config_file);
if (sscanf(line,"STOP_TIME_MS    = %lu ", &stop_time_msecs) != 1)
   { print_error(rc,"reading stop time from configuration file",
               __FILE__,__LINE__);
     exit(FAILED);
   }

/*_____*/
/* read task names for 4 tasks            */
/*_____*/
for (i=0; i < 4; ++i)
   {
     /*_____*/
     /* read a line from config file           */
     /*_____*/
     fgets(line, sizeof(line), config_file);
     if (sscanf(line,"TASK_NAME      = %s %[^;] ",
               &task_names[i][0], program_parms) == 0)
        { print_error(rc,"reading program name from configuration file",
                    __FILE__,__LINE__);
          exit(FAILED);
        }
     sprintf(programs[i],"%s%c%s", task_names[i], '\0', program_parms);
   }
/*_____*/
/* all done with the config file          */
/*_____*/
fclose(config_file);

} /* end read_config */
```

Figure 14-13 (Part 2 of 2). The read_config() Function.

MULTI.C: create_semaphores()

Semaphores provide the controls for MULTI's races. Figure 14-14 shows how MULTI uses semaphores to control and referee the race. We will use both a shared event semaphore and mutex semaphores. The shared event semaphore, \SEM32\RUNALL, is the broadcast signal to start the race. The mutex semaphores, SEM32\RUN1 through \SEM32\RUN4, each control an individual task's execution. The design goal was to use the two types of OS/2 semaphores in the program.

Now let's carefully walk through Figure 14-14 to understand how MULTI's sema-phores work. The MULTI program initially starts with the **main()** thread running. As part of its setup, **main()** calls the **create_semaphores()** function, listed in Figure 14-15. This function creates the shared event semaphore, \SEM32\RUNALL, in the *reset* state. It also creates the four shared mutex semaphores, \SEM32\RUN1 through \SEM32\RUN4, in the *unowned* state.

Main() then invokes **elapsed_time_thread()**. This is the function that creates the referee and broadcasting thread. The race has not yet started, so **elapsed_time_thread()** blocks its execution and waits on \SEM32\RUNALL to post. **Main()** then starts the four race contenders, which may be either threads or processes, and they too are blocked waiting for \SEM32\RUNALL to post. In the case where the four tasks are processes, they need to first issue a **DosOpenEventSem** before using the semaphores (this is not shown in the figure).

At this point, everybody is blocked waiting for \SEM32\RUNALL to post while **main()** itself is blocked waiting for keyboard input. MULTI is in a state, like that shown in Figure 14-2, waiting for you to give the GO! signal to start the race. You, of course, do that by hitting **R** (see left-hand side of figure). Your action brings **main()** back to life long enough to issue a **DosPostEventSem** on \SEM32\RUNALL.

This time, **main()** itself goes back to sleep waiting for your next keyboard input. The **elapsed_time_thread()** starts the countdown and periodically updates the elapsed_time and total_count values. When the elapsed time is equal to the race stop_time, the **elapsed_time_thread()**, like any good referee, stops the race by reset-ting \SEM32\RUNALL. As for our racing contenders, as long as \SEM32\RUNALL is not reset they will keep on racing, incrementing their COUNTs as fast as the CPU will let them do so. The first race eventually ends (see left-hand side of figure) when the **elapsed_time_thread()** resets \SEM32\RUNALL. Notice that all the tasks are, once again, blocked waiting. The loop is linearly represented in Figure 14-14 (that's the best we can do without inserting a video clip in the text).

We're not done yet! The user, in the example of Figure 14-14, now decides to start another race with only one task contending. The user does that by moving the cursor to the different task windows and setting the semaphores of the tasks that will not run. The user decides to set all the semaphores, except for \SEM32\RUN1. This causes **main()** to request the mutex semaphores, RUN2 through RUN4, and put them in an "owned" state (meaning the task can't own them now).

So what happens next? When the user hits **R** to start a second race, all the tasks first come to life when \SEM32\RUNALL is posted. However, for most this life is short. Except for task1, they go back to sleep blocked on their respective RUNx semaphore (remember main owns those mutexes in this race). This leaves us with task 1 as the sole contender in the second race. The task will run until the **elapsed_time_thread()** stops the race by resetting \SEM32\RUNALL.

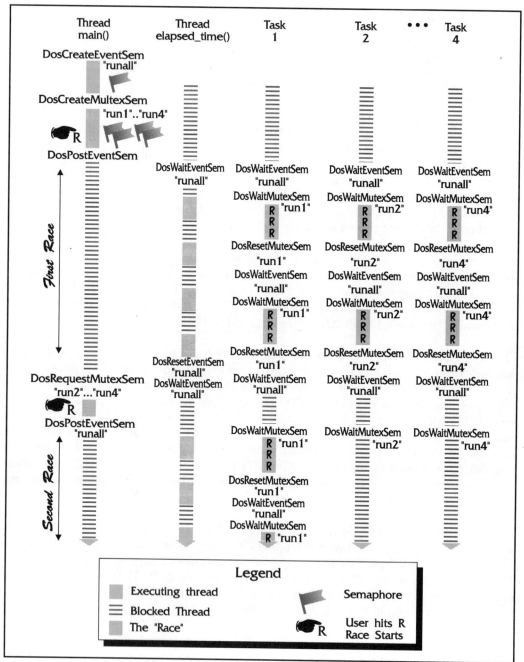

Figure 14-14. MULTI's Semaphore Structure.

The **create_semaphores()** function, listed in Figure 14-15, introduces the use of two new OS/2 calls: **DosCreateEventSem** and **DosCreateMutexSem**. A description of these calls follows.

DosCreateEventSem

The **DosCreateEventSem** API call is used to create an event semaphore. The effect of the call is to establish the semaphore, initialize it, and return a handle to it. The prototype for this call is:

```
DosCreateEventSem(PSZ       sem_name,        /* pointer to semaphore name   */
                  PULONG    sem_handle,      /* pointer to semaphore handle */
                  ULONG     attribute_flag,  /* shared/not shared           */
                  ULONG     initial_state);  /* 0= reset    1= posted       */
```

A description of the parameters follows:

- The *sem_name* parameter points to a null-terminated string where you provide the semaphore name. The format of the string is **\SEM32\name**, where the name must be unique and follow OS/2 file-naming conventions. The SEM32 pathname is fictitious and does not exist on disk. A maximum of 255 characters is allowed. If this field is NULL, the semaphore is unnamed. By default, a named semaphore is shared (also see the attribute_flag parameter below).
- The *sem_handle* parameter points to a semaphore handle, which is returned by the system when the call succeeds. The handle returned is only available to threads that are part of the calling process.
- The *attribute_flag* parameter is used with unnamed semaphores to specify whether the semaphore is private or shared. If the DC_SEM_SHARED bit is set, the semaphore is shared. Named semaphores are always shared, so set the parameter to NULL (i.e., 0L).
- The *initial_state* parameter is used to specify the initial state of the semaphore. The value is Boolean: FALSE creates the semaphore in the "reset" state, TRUE creates the semaphore in the "posted" state.

DosCreateMutexSem

The **DosCreateMutexSem** API call is used to create a mutex semaphore. The effect of the call is to establish the semaphore, initialize it, and return a handle to it. The prototype for this call is:

```
DosCreateMutexSem(PSZ       sem_name,        /* pointer to semaphore name   */
                  PULONG    sem_handle,      /* pointer to semaphore handle */
                  ULONG     attribute_flag,  /* shared/not shared           */
                  ULONG     initial_state);  /* 0= unowned  1= owned        */
```

A description of the parameters follows:

- The *sem_name* parameter points to a null-terminated string where you provide the semaphore name. The format of the string is **\SEM32\name**, where the name must be unique and follow OS/2 file-naming conventions. The SEM32 pathname is fictitious and does not exist on disk. A maximum of 255 characters is allowed. If this field is NULL, the semaphore is unnamed. By default, a named semaphore is shared (also see the attribute_flag parameter below).

- The *sem_handle* parameter points to a semaphore handle, which is returned by the system when the call succeeds. The handle returned is only available to threads that are part of the calling process.

- The *attribute_flag* parameter is used with unnamed semaphores to specify whether the semaphore is private or shared. If the DC_SEM_SHARED bit is set, the semaphore is shared. Named semaphores are always shared, so set the parameter to NULL (i.e., 0L).

- The *initial_state* parameter is used to specify the initial state of the semaphore. The value is Boolean: FALSE creates the semaphore in the "unowned" state and TRUE creates the semaphore in the "owned" state.

```
/*_____*/
/* Create semaphores for task control                        */
/*_____*/
VOID create_semaphores(VOID)
{
  CHAR sem_name[30];

  /*_____*/
  /* create the run all semaphore       */
  /*_____*/
  sprintf(sem_name,"\\SEM32\\RUNALL");
  if (rc = DosCreateEventSem(sem_name,           /* semaphore name       */
                        &runall_sem_handle, /* semaphore handle     */
                        0l,                 /* shared by default    */
                        FALSE))             /* RESET initially      */
      { print_error(rc,"excuting DosCreateEventSem", __FILE__,__LINE__);
        exit(FAILED);
      }
  runall_sem_status = RESET;

  /*_____*/
  /* create task specific semaphores    */
  /*_____*/
  for (i=0; i < 4; ++i)
      {
        sprintf(sem_name,"\\SEM32\\RUN%d",i);
        if (rc = DosCreateMutexSem(sem_name,            /* semaphore name       */
                              &run_sem_handle[i], /* semaphore handle     */
                              0l,                 /* shared by default    */
                              FALSE))             /* UNOWNED initially    */
            { print_error(rc,"executing DosCreateMutexSem", __FILE__,__LINE__);
              exit(FAILED);
            }
      }
} /* end create_semaphores */
```

Figure 14-15.   The create_semaphores() Function.

MULTI.C: create_timer_thread()

The **create_timer_thread()** function, listed in Figure 14-16, creates the **elapsed_time_thread**. This is the famous race referee thread you've already heard so much about. The listing for the thread itself can be found in Figure 14-17. Notice that a thread looks like any ordinary procedure. However, you just can't call a thread the way you do an ordinary procedure. Instead, you create the thread, and from then on it runs concurrently with your code. The newly created thread begins to execute immediately after it is successfully created.

To create the thread, we'll be using the C-language **_beginthread()** function. This function must be used instead of OS/2's **DosCreateThread** when using the C Set/2 multithread library. This is obtained by using the **/Gm+** compiler option. The C Set/2 compiler does not limit the number of threads you create within the OS/2 system limits. The C Set/2 compiler performs certain initializations when the thread is started that ensure that resources and data are handled correctly between threads. It also makes the C calls within a thread reentrant. Threads that use the **DosCreateThread** API do not have access to the resource management facilities or to C Set/2's exception handling.[2]

_beginthread()

The **_beginthread()** C-language function creates and starts the execution of a new thread. The function returns a thread's identifier number if it is successful. If it fails, it returns -1. The prototype for this function is:

```
_beginthread(VOID     (*thread) (void *), /* thread address          */
             PVOID    stack_bottom,        /* not used                */
             USHORT   stack_size,          /* stack size              */
             PVOID    args);               /* arguments to be passed  */
```

A description of the parameters follows:

- The *thread* parameter points to the starting address of a far routine the newly created thread will execute. This is the name of the thread you want to execute. The thread does not return a parameter.
- The *stack_bottom* parameter is ignored, but is retained to ease the migration of 16-bit OS/2 program. OS/2 2.0, unlike previous versions, will allocate the thread stack itself.
- The *stack_size* parameter is the length in bytes of the stack you're providing. It must be a non-zero multiple of 4 KBytes since memory is used when needed, one page at a time. The minimum is 4 Kbytes, but you must specify more stack if your

---

[2] Source: **IBM C Set/2 User's Guide**.

thread uses lots of local storage or makes multiple C library calls. For example, the C function **printf** requires more than 500 bytes of stack space.

- The *args* parameter points to an argument you want passed to the newly created thread. It is usually the address of a data item, such as a **char** string. It may be NULL if not needed.

```
/*_____*/
/* Create a time critical thread for maintaining elapsed time   */
/*_____*/
VOID create_timer_thread(VOID)
{
    /*_____*/
    /* start the elapsed timer thread     */
    /*_____*/
    if ((elapsed_time_threadid =
         _beginthread(elapsed_time_thread,        /* name of function     */
                      NULL,                        /* stack ptr (not used) */
                      THREAD_STACK_SIZE,           /* size of stack        */
                      NULL) ) == -1)               /* no parms             */
      { print_error(elapsed_time_threadid,"creating a thread", __FILE__,__LINE__);
        exit(FAILED);
      }

} /* end create_timer_thread */
```

Figure 14-16.   The create_timer_thread() Function.

MULTI.C: elapsed_time_thread()

We now get a chance to explore the code that makes our famous referee thread tick. The listing for the thread in Figure 14-17 looks like any ordinary procedure. No parameters were passed to the thread by **_beginthread()**, even though the thread is capable of accepting one. The thread code consists of a do-forever loop that blocks itself waiting until the semaphore \SEM32\RUNALL clears. This happens when the **R** key is pressed to indicate the start of a given race. As soon as the thread comes to life, it obtains the current time by issuing a **DosQuerySysInfo** call; then it goes into another loop which executes throughout the duration of the race. So, what does the referee do while looping?

Well, first it takes a short 100 millisecond nap! Now, before you jump to conclusions and imply that our referee is lazy, you should realize that the "nap" is really an act of great generosity! By going to sleep and doing nothing for a while, our referee gives up its share of machine time. This means that the actual contenders for the race can run a little faster! At the end of the nap, however, the referee goes back to work and performs the following:

- It calculates the current elapsed time for the race and displays it on the MULTI control panel.
- It calculates the running total count by adding the counts produced by each contender. It then displays the current total on the MULTI control panel. Notice

how the referee adds counts, which in the case of processes are produced by four separate programs. This is done through the use of shared memory, which the referee can access through the use of a pointer named **count_ptr** (more on this later).

- It checks to see if the time for the race is up, in which case it stops the race by resetting the semaphore \SEM32\RUNALL. Otherwise, it's time for another round through the loop. Yes, this means another well-deserved nap and a repeat perform-ance of the work. An interesting tid-bit is how the code handles timer rollover.

So what is new and exciting in this code? Well, we have two new OS/2 2.0 calls: **DosWaitEventSem** and **DosQuerySysInfo**. We will explore these calls shortly. We also introduce two of our helper routines: reset_event_semaphore() and write_str(). The helper routine reset_event_semaphore(), listed in Figure 14-27, resets semaphores. The write_str() helper, listed with the other VIO helper routines in Figure 14-28, writes a string with a display attribute to an x,y location on the screen. The OS/2 API call, **DosSleep**, was previously encountered and explained (see page 232). We will now explain the two new OS/2 calls.

DosWaitEventSem

The **DosWaitEventSem** API call is used in "wait-until-semaphore-posts" situations for synchronizing the execution of processes or threads. The thread blocks until the event semaphore is posted, or until a time-out occurs. The API is level-triggered, meaning that a thread may have to wait through multiple changes of the semaphore before it continues. This may happen if another waiting thread grabs the semaphore before it. The prototype for this call is:

```
DosWaitEventSem(PULONG    sem_handle,  /* semaphore handle          */
                ULONG     timeout);    /* -1L= wait, 0=nowait, 0=msecs */
```

A description of the parameters follows:

- The *sem_handle* parameter points to the handle of the event semaphore to wait for. This handle must have been previously created using **DosCreateEventSem** or **DosOpenEventSem**.
- The *timeout* parameter specifies how long to wait. Setting the value to zero causes the call to return immediately. Setting the value to -1L will cause the call to wait indefinitely until the semaphore clears. Otherwise, a positive value specifies the number of milliseconds to wait before returning.

DosQuerySysInfo

The **DosQuerySysInfo** API call is used to extract a wealth of OS/2 maintained system information. The call returns a single system variable or a range of system variables in a buffer you provide. You can request a single system variable by setting the *StartIndex* equal to the *LastIndex*. You can request a range of variables by setting the *StartIndex* less than the *LastIndex*. Each system variable returned is double-word. Table 14-1 shows the type of system variable returned by each index number. There's a lot of good system information! The prototype for the call that brings it to you is:

```
DosQuerySysInfo(ULONG StartIndex,     /* index of first variable to return */
                ULONG LastIndex,      /* index of last variable to return  */
                PVOID Buffer,         /* address of buffer you provide     */
                ULONG BufferLength);  /* length of the buffer              */
```

A description of the parameters follows:

- The *StartIndex* parameter is an ordinal index that specifies the first system variable to return (see Table 14-1).
- The *LastIndex* parameter is an ordinal index that specifies the last system variable to return (see Table 14-1).
- The *Buffer* parameter points to the data buffer where you want OS/2 to place the returned system variables.
- The *BufferLength* parameter specifies the length in bytes of the buffer you provide.

Table 14-1 (Part 1 of 2). DosQuerySysInfo Information Index.

Index	System Variable Constant	Description
1	QSV_MAX_PATH_LENGTH	Maximum length, in bytes, of a path name. The path length includes the drive specifier (d:)
2	QSV_MAX_TEXT_SESSIONS	Maximum number of text sessions.
3	QSV_MAX_PM_SESSIONS	Maximum number of PM sessions.
4	QSV_MAX_VDM_SESSIONS	Maximum number of DOS sessions.
5	QSV_BOOT_DRIVE	Drive from which the system was started 1 = Drive A, 2 = Drive B, etc.
6	QSV_DYN_PRI_VARIATION	Dynamic priority variation flag (0 = absolute priority, 1 = dynamic priority).
7	QSV_MAX_WAIT	Maximum wait in seconds.
8	QSV_MIN_SLICE	Minimum CPU allocation time slice in milliseconds.
9	QSV_MAX_SLICE	Maximum CPU allocation time slice in milliseconds.
10	QSV_PAGE_SIZE	Memory page size in bytes. This value is 4096 for the 80386 and 80486 processors.
11	QSV_VERSION_MAJOR	Major OS/2 version number.
12	QSV_VERSION_MINOR	Minor OS/2 version number.
13	QSV_VERSION_REVISION	OS/2 Revision letter.

Table 14-1 (Part 2 of 2). DosQuerySysInfo Information Index.

Index	System Variable Constant	Description
14	QSV_MS_COUNT	Value of a 32-bit, free-running millisecond counter. This value is zero when the system is started.
15	QSV_TIME_LOW	Low-order 32 bits of the time in seconds since January 1, 1970 at 0:00:00.
16	QSV_TIME_HIGH	High-order 32 bits of the time in seconds since January 1, 1970 at 0:00:00.
17	QSV_TOTPHYSMEM	Total number of pages of physical memory in the system. One page is 4KB.
18	BQSV_TOTRESMEM	Total number of pages of resident memory in the system.
19	QSV_TOTAVAILMEM	Maximum number of pages of memory that can be allocated by all processes in the system. This number is advisory and is not guaranteed, since system conditions change constantly.
20	QSV_MAXPRMEM	Maximum number of bytes of memory that this process can allocate in its private address space. This number is advisory and is not guaranteed.
21	QSV_MAXSHMEM	Maximum number of bytes of memory that a process can allocate in the shared address space. This number is advisory and is not guaranteed.
22	QSV_TIMER_INTERVAL	Timer interval in tenths of a millisecond.
23	QSV_MAX_COMP_LENGTH	Maximum length, in bytes, of one component in a path name.

```
/*_____*/
/* thread to keep elapsed timer up to date, and determine when to stop   */
/*_____*/
VOID elapsed_time_thread(PVOID parm)
{
  CHAR time_str[20];
  CHAR value_str[20];

  while (TRUE)
    {/*_____*/
     /* wait for execution control semaphore*/
     /* to post                           */
     /*_____*/
     rc = DosWaitEventSem(runall_sem_handle,          /* semaphore handle */
                          -1L);                         /* infinite timeout */
     if (rc)
        { print_error(rc,"excuting DosWaitEventSem", __FILE__,__LINE__);
          exit(FAILED);
        }

     /*_____*/
     /* get ms value from DosQuerySysInfo, */
     /* save for later use                */
     /*_____*/
     rc = DosQuerySysInfo(QSV_MS_COUNT,
                          QSV_MS_COUNT,
                          &start_msecs,
                          sizeof(start_msecs));
     if (rc)
        { print_error(rc,"excuting DosQuerySysInfo", __FILE__,__LINE__);
          exit(FAILED);
        }

     while (test_running)
       {
        /*_____*/
        /* sleep for a while                 */
        /*_____*/
        DosSleep(100L);
        /*_____*/
        /* get ms value from DosQuerySysInfo */
        /*_____*/
        rc = DosQuerySysInfo(QSV_MS_COUNT,
                             QSV_MS_COUNT,
                             &current_msecs,
                             sizeof(current_msecs));
        if (rc)
           { print_error(rc,"executing DosQuerySysInfo", __FILE__,__LINE__);
             exit(FAILED);
           }
        if (current_msecs >= start_msecs)    /* was there a timer rollover?  */
           delta_msecs  = current_msecs - start_msecs;
        else
           {delta_msecs = delta_msecs +      /* compensate for rollover      */
                 (0xFFFFFFFF - start_msecs)
                 + current_msecs;
           }
        start_msecs   = current_msecs;
```

Figure 14-17 (Part 1 of 2).   The elapsed_time_thread() Thread.

```
/*_____*/
/* update elapsed time value        */
/*_____*/
elapsed_time_msecs = elapsed_time_msecs + delta_msecs;
if (elapsed_time_msecs >= stop_time_msecs)
    {
        reset_event_semaphore(runall_sem_handle, &runall_sem_status);
        elapsed_time_msecs = stop_time_msecs;
        write_str("STOPPED", OUTPUT_FIELD_ATTR,
                    18, 22);
        test_running = FALSE;
    }
sprintf(time_str,"%lu.%-4lu",
        elapsed_time_msecs / 1000, elapsed_time_msecs % 1000);
write_str(time_str, OUTPUT_FIELD_ATTR, 18, 20);

/*_____*/
/* update total count value         */
/*_____*/
total_count = 0;
for (i=0; i < 4; ++i)
    total_count = total_count + count_ptr->count[i];
sprintf(value_str,"%lu", total_count);
write_str(value_str, OUTPUT_FIELD_ATTR, 18, 21);

    } /* end while */
  } /* end while */

} /* elapsed_time_thread */
```

Figure 14-17 (Part 2 of 2). The elapsed_time_thread() Thread.

MULTI.C: set_thread_priorities()

The set_thread_priorities() function, listed in Figure 14-18, sets the priority of **main()** and all of its threads to *time-critical*. As the comment in the listing points out, we want the referee and the race organizers to be in control and responsive to user input at all times. This function introduces the OS/2 API call **DosSetPriority** described below:

DosSetPriority

The **DosSetPriority** API call is used to change the priority level and the priority class of the specified process or thread. You may recall that OS/2 supports 4 priority classes and 32 distinct priority levels within each class. Most programs are regular class and they start out at level 0. These are default values that can be changed using DosSetPriority. The prototype for this call is:

```
DosSetPriority(ULONG    scope_flag,     /* change process or thread? */
               ULONG    priority_class, /* class to be set  0-4      */
               LONG     priority_delta, /* add to level (-31 to +31) */
               ULONG    id);            /* process or thread ID      */
```

A description of the parameters follows:

- The *scope_flag* parameter specifies the scope (i.e., the extent) of the priority change. This parameter can be one of the following values:

```
Value  Meaning
  0    The specified process (any process) and all its threads
  1    The current process (or a child) and all its descendants
  2    A single thread in the current process
```

- The *priority_class* parameter specifies the requested priority class of the process or thread. This parameter can have one of the following values:

```
Value  Meaning
  0    No change to priority class (leave as is)
  1    Idle-time priority class (lowest priority)
  2    Regular priority class (default)
  3    Time-critical priority class (highest priority)
  4    Fixed-high priority class (second highest priority)
```

Most threads should run at regular priority. Time-critical priority is reserved for those threads that cannot tolerate interruption. The fixed-high priority assists in the synchronization of a background thread that is expected to run at a certain priority in relation to a foreground thread. You must be careful not to arbitrarily use the higher-level priorities if you share the system with other tasks that have time-critical requirements of their own.

- The *priority_level* parameter specifies the delta change to apply to the current priority level (i.e., the base). Since there are 32 priority levels, numbered from 0 through 31, delta can range from -31 to +31 to accommodate a change in either direction.
- The *id* parameter is the PID if the scope_flag is set to 0 or 1, or is a thread_ID if the scope_flag is set to 2. If you set the this parameter to 0, it indicates the current thread or process.

```
/*_____*/
/* Set timer and main thread priority to time critical        */
/*_____*/
VOID set_thread_priorities(VOID)
{
    /*_____*/
    /* Make threads in this process time   */
    /* critical.  We want user input and   */
    /* timer management to be done         */
    /* responsively regardless of what the */
    /* user sets in the other tasks.       */
    /*_____*/
    if (rc = DosSetPriority(PRTYS_PROCESS,      /* this process, all threads */
                            PRTYC_TIMECRITICAL, /* time critical  */
                            10,                 /* level          */
                            0))                 /* this thread    */
        {print_error(rc,"excuting DosSetPriority",__FILE__,__LINE__);
        exit(FAILED);
        }

} /* end set_thread_priorities */
```

Figure 14-18.   The set_thread_priorities() Function.

MULTI.C: create_counter_memory()

The **create_counter_memory**() function, listed in Figure 14-19, creates a shared area in memory where different tasks can output their counts to. If MULTI's only involvement was running races between threads, then a regular global variable would have been used instead. However, MULTI is also in the business of organizing races between processes, which tend to be far more isolated from one another. One of the means OS/2 provides for interprocess communication is through **shared memory objects**, where any process can randomly access shared data.

The **create_counter_memory**() function uses the OS/2 2.0 API call **DosAllocShared-Mem** to allocate a shared memory object named **\SHAREMEM\TASK**. Once this object is created, any process that knows its name can access it. The *count_ptr-* points to the start of the shared area. This is the same pointer the referee thread used to add the counts. We now introduce the OS/2 API call **DosAllocSharedMem**.

DosAllocSharedMem

The **DosAllocSharedMem** API call allocates a shared memory object within the virtual-address space. This causes the creation of an object that describes a region of shared memory that is reserved in the virtual address space of every process. This allows any process to gain access to the shared object at the virtual address location where it was originally allocated. The prototype for this call is:

```
DosAllocSharedMem(PVOID   *BaseAddress, /* pointer to address object*/
                  PSZ     Name,         /* pointer to object name   */
                  ULONG   ObjectSize,   /* number of bytes          */
                  ULONG   Flags);       /* allocation attributes    */
```

A description of the parameters follows:

- The *BaseAddress* parameter points to a variable that receives the object's address. This is the base address of an allocated range of pages.
- The *Name* parameter points to a null-terminated string, which is the optional name to be given to the object. The string must include the fictitious subdirectory name **\SHAREMEM**, and the name must be unique. Set the parameter to NULL if your object is unnamed.
- The *ObjectSize* parameter specifies the number of bytes to be allocated. The size is rounded up to the next page-size boundary. The committed memory allocated is movable and can be swapped. So don't worry about creating large objects.
- The *Flags* parameter consists of a set of flags that describe the allocation attributes and desired access protection for the shared memory object. OR those flags to get the desired combination of attributes:

```
Allocation Flags   Meaning
PAG_COMMIT         All object pages are initially committed to memory
OBJ_GIVEABLE       Access to object can be given to other processes
OBJ_GETTABLE       Allow access to object by any process that knows address
OBJ_TILE           16-bit selector mapping, for OS/2 1.X compatibility

Access
Protection Flags   Meaning
PAG_EXECUTE        Provide execute access to object
PAG_READ           Provide read access to object
PAG_WRITE          Provide write access to object
PAG_GUARD          Access to object causes a "guard page violation"
```

```
/*_____*/
/* Create shared memory for count values                                */
/*_____*/
VOID create_counter_memory(VOID)
{
  CHAR      shared_mem_name[40];        /* variable for building ascii names  */

    /*_____*/
    /* Create a shared memory object for  */
    /*    the count arrays            */
    /*_____*/
    sprintf(shared_mem_name,"\\SHAREMEM\\TASK");
    rc = DosAllocSharedMem((PVOID)&count_ptr,      /* count structure pointer  */
                           shared_name,            /* name of shared memory    */
                           sizeof(COUNT),          /* size of count structure  */
                           PAG_COMMIT | PAG_READ | /* attribute flags          */
                           PAG_WRITE);             /*                          */
    if (rc)
       { print_error(rc,"allocating count buffer",__FILE__,__LINE__);
         exit(FAILED);
       }

    /*_____*/
    /* initialize the count array     */
    /*_____*/
    for (i=0; i<8; ++i)
        count_ptr->count[i] = 0;

} /* end create_counter_memory */
```

Figure 14-19.   The create_counter_memory() Function.

MULTI.C: paint_screen()

The **paint_screen()** function paints and fills in the information for the different windows that make up MULTI's control panel. The procedures used in **paint_screen()** are part of the VIO helper routines, listed in Figure 14-28. These are the helper routines that provide value-added services, such as drawing boxes and centering titles, using 16-bit OS/2 VIO API calls for writing to the screen and controlling the cursor.

Thus, **paint_screen()**, through the use of its helpers, clears the screen, hides the cursor, draws the top window that contains MULTI's instructions, draws the four task windows, and finally draws the bottom two windows that display the status of the race and the system information.

```
/*_____*/
/* Draw screen with title, task, execution status, and system blocks  */
/*_____*/
VOID paint_screen(VOID)
{
  clear_screen();
  hide_cursor();

  /*_____*/
  /* paint the title at column  0, row  0              */
  /*_____*/
  draw_title_box(0,0);

  /*_____*/
  /* draw 4 task boxes with titles read from configuration file  */
  /*_____*/
  for (i=0; i < 4; ++i)
      draw_task_box(task_names[i], i*20, 7);

  /*_____*/
  /* display execution status at column 0, row 17      */
  /*_____*/
  display_exec_status(0,17);

  /*_____*/
  /* display system info box at column 40, row 17      */
  /*_____*/
  display_sys_info(40,17);

} /* end paint_screen */
```

Figure 14-20. The paint_screen() Function.

MULTI.C: create_threads() and create_processes()

This is the section where we create our four task contenders. We do that by calling either **create_threads()** or **create_processes()**, depending on whether the contenders are threads or processes. The **create_threads()** function, listed in Figure 14-21, uses the _beginthread C library function, previously described on page 281. We want to use the same thread, **thread_count** (see listing in Figure 14-31) to run as Thread 1 through Thread 4. But how does a thread know its race contender number? An argument is passed to it specifying its contender number. This number is then used by the thread to index into the global arrays and to identify the task window it will interact with.

The **create_processes()** function, listed in Figure 14-22, uses the OS/2 **DosExecPgm** call to create the four processes that were specified in MULTI.CFG. The parameter passed to each process is its process name, which in this case is very helpful since we are running four instances of the program COUNT.C, listed in Figure 14-32. We do not have to worry about re-entrancy with processes or providing them with a stack.

Processes are independent entities and do not share global variables, except through the shared object. Each instance of COUNT.EXE will know where to write its output based on the contender number that was passed to each process at creation time.

DosExecPgm

The **DosExecPgm** API call starts a process from a currently running program. The target program is located and loaded into storage (if necessary). Then a process is created for it and placed into execution. The new process is created with an address space separate and distinct from its parent. The prototype for this call is:

```
DosExecPgm(PCHAR        object_name,          /* Name of failing object */
           LONG         sizeof_object_name,   /* Size of object buffer  */
           ULONG        exec_mode,            /* Sync or async or trace */
           PSZ          args,                 /* Command line string    */
           PSZ          env,                  /* Environment string     */
           RESULTCODES  *results,             /* PID or termination code*/
           PSZ          child_program_name);  /* Name of program to run */
```

A description of the parameters follows:

- The *object_name* parameter is the address of a buffer that receives the name of an object that contributed to the failure of the API call. The named object could be a nonexistent program file or a missing dynamic link library module.
- The *sizeof_object_name* parameter is the length (in bytes) of the buffer that contains the object_name.
- The *exec_mode* parameter specifies how the child program should execute in relation to the parent. You can set it to one of the following values:

Value	Meaning
0	EXEC_SYNC: Child executes synchronously to the parent process. The parent waits for child to terminate, and obtains the child's result code in the structure pointed to by the results parameter.
1	EXEC_ASYNC: Child executes asynchronously to parent; no result code.
2	EXEC_ASYNCRESULT: Child executes asynchronously to parent; the result code is saved for DosWaitChild.
3	EXEC_TRACE: Child executes under conditions for tracing used by parent to debug the child. An example of such a parent is the C Set/2 debugger.
4	EXEC_BACKGROUND: Child executes as a background process.
5	EXEC_LOAD: The child is loaded into storage and will not execute until the session manager dispatches the threads belonging to the process.
6	EXEC_ASYNCRESULTDB: Same as 2 with the addition of debug.

The asynchronous processes in exec_modes 1 or 2 can be brought back into synchronization with the caller process when the latter issues a **DosWaitChild**. This suspends the parent thread until the child process terminates. When the exec_mode is set to 2, it directs OS/2 to save a copy of the child process's termination code and result codes. The result code is supplied by the terminating process using **DosExit** and can contain any mutually agreed upon values. The OS/2 termination codes can have the following values:

```
Value     Meaning
  0       TC_EXIT: Normal exit.
  1       TC_HARDERROR: Unrecoverable or hard error.
  2       TC_TRAP: System trap error for a 16-bit child process.
  3       TC_KILLPROCESS: Unintercepted DosKillProcess.
  4       TC_EXCEPTION: Exception operation for a 32-bit child process.
```

These values can be obtained by the parent process using **DosWaitChild**.

- The *args* parameter points to the string of command line arguments that get passed to the child process. The string can be NULL (no command line arguments passed) or can have any format, but must end with two NULL characters. A conventional format is the program name, a NULL, and the program arguments (separated by spaces) followed by a double NULL termination. A command line string may look like this:

```
"parent.exe\0arg1 arg2 arg3 argN\0\0"
```

- The *env* parameter points to the environment double NULL terminated string. If left NULL, the child inherits the parent process's environment "as is." The parent has the option of augmenting or modifying the environment it passes to the child through the environment string. An environment string has the following format:

```
"variable1=value1\0variable2=value2\0variable3=value3\0\0"
```

An example of an environment variable is the PATH and the value can be any string, which then gets copied into the process's environment segment. A C-language program can access both the environment and the command line arguments through the familiar **main**() function prototype declaration:

```
main(argc, argv, envp)
```

- The *results* parameter points to the **RESULTCODES** structure, which has the following form:

```
struct  _RESULTCODES
    { ULONG    codeTerminate; /* Term code for SYNC or PID for ASYNC */
      ULONG    codeResult;    /* Exit code for SYNC or 0 for ASYNC   */
    } RESULTCODES;
```

The *codeTerminate* field returns the OS/2 process termination code if the child executes synchronously, or it returns the child's process identifier (PID) if the child executes asynchronously. The PID can be used to control the child and change its priority. The *codeResult* field returns the child's exit code for synchronous operation and is not used otherwise.

- The *child_program_name* parameter points to a NULL terminated string that specifies the file name and extension of the program (process) to start.

```
/*_____*/
/* Start processes based on configuration information      */
/*_____*/
VOID create_threads(VOID)
{
  for (i=0; i<4; ++i)
      {
          /*_____*/
          /* start the threads                  */
          /*_____*/
          if ((threadid[i] =
               _beginthread(thread_count,              /* name of function      */
                        NULL,                          /* stack ptr. (not used) */
                        THREAD_STACK_SIZE,             /* size of stack         */
                        &thread_parm[i]) ) == -1)      /* pointer to parm       */
                                                       /*  passed to thread     */
                                                       /*  function             */
              { print_error(threadid[i],"creating a thread", __FILE__,__LINE__);
                exit(FAILED);
              }
      }
} /* end create_threads */
```

Figure 14-21.   The create_thread() Function.

```
/*_____*/
/* Start processes based on configuration information      */
/*_____*/
VOID create_processes(VOID)
{
    /*_____*/
    /* start the process                  */
    /*_____*/
    for (i=0; i<4; ++i)
      {
          rc = DosExecPgm(object_name,            /* failing object if progam fails*/
                      sizeof(object_name),        /* the object size       */
                      EXEC_ASYNCRESULT,           /* async. program execution */
                      programs[i],                /* program parameters    */
                      NULL,                       /* inherit environment   */
                      &ExecResult,                /* termination reason code */
                      programs[i]);               /* program name          */
          if (rc)
              { print_error(rc,"creating a process", __FILE__,__LINE__);
                exit(FAILED);
              }
          processid[i] = ExecResult.codeTerminate;  /* save process id       */
      }
} /* end create_processes */
```

Figure 14-22.   The create_processes() Function.

MULTI.C: User Interaction Functions

The functions described in this section perform the user interaction and field update portions of the MULTI program. The **update_screen_fields()** function, listed in Figure 14-23, is used to display information in the four task windows when the MULTI control panel first comes up. The function simply invokes **perform_field_action()** twelve times, since we have four task windows each containing a PRIORITY field, a LEVEL field, and a SEMAPHORE field.

The **perform_field_action**() function, listed in Figure 14-25, specializes in performing the operations specified in the fields located in the four task windows. It knows which field to update by the task/task_field parameter pair that gets passed to it. The function maintains information on each of the task fields in the **field** array that we introduced in Figure 14-12. It will display a string on the control panel, which is derived from the current field value.

The **get_user_input**() function, listed in Figure 14-24, blocks on **getch**() waiting for the user to enter something. When this happens, the function comes to life, and with the assistance of its helper routines, it performs some work. Here's what the different keys do:

- The ARROW keys result in moving the cursor to an adjacent task window field and updating the field focus.
- The **+** and **-** keys increment and decrement the value of the field with the focus. The action itself gets executed when **perform_field_action**() is invoked.
- The ESC key terminates MULTI.
- The **R** and **S** keys are used to start or terminate a race.
- The **C** key is used to reset the race counters.

No new OS/2 API calls are introduced here; we will encounter new calls when we get into the helper routine listings.

```
/*-----------------------------------------------------------*/
/* Update fields on the screen that the user can modify      */
/*-----------------------------------------------------------*/
VOID update_screen_fields(VOID)
{
  for (x = 0; x <= FIELD_X_MAX; ++x)
    {for (y = 0; y <= FIELD_Y_MAX; ++y)
       perform_field_action(x, y);
    }
} /* end update_screen_fields */
```

Figure 14-23.   The update_screen_fields() Function.

```
/*-----------------------------------------------------------*/
/* get keystrokes from user, act on input                    */
/*-----------------------------------------------------------*/
USHORT get_user_input()
{
  USHORT ch;                      /* input char from keyboard     */
  CHAR   time_str[10];            /* for formulating a time  to display*/
```

Figure 14-24 (Part 1 of 3).   The get_user_input() Function.

```
/*_____*/
/* get the user key strokes and    */
/* process them.                    */
/*_____*/
draw_cursor(CURSOR_FIELD_ATTR, field[field_x][field_y].x,
                              field[field_x][field_y].y,
                              field[field_x][field_y].cx);

ch = (USHORT)getch();
if (ch == 0)
   ch = (USHORT)getch() + 256;

last_field_x = field_x;            /* set the current task field focus  */
last_field_y = field_y;            /*    ..                             */

switch (ch)
  {
   case LEFT_ARROW :
   case RIGHT_ARROW:
   case UP_ARROW   :
   case DOWN_ARROW : move_cursor(ch);
                     break;

   case PLUS_KEY    : update_value(&field[field_x][field_y].value,
                                   INCREMENT,
                                   field[field_x][field_y].min,
                                   field[field_x][field_y].max);
                      break;

   case MINUS_KEY   : update_value(&field[field_x][field_y].value,
                                   DECREMENT,
                                   field[field_x][field_y].min,
                                   field[field_x][field_y].max);
                      break;

   case ESC_KEY     : return(TERMINATE);

   case 'c'         : /*_____*/
   case 'C'         : /* reset and redisplay the count fields*/
                      /*_____*/
                      for (i=0; i<4; ++i)
                        {
                         count_ptr->count[i] = 0;
                         count_ptr->count[i+4] = 0;
                         write_str("      ", OUTPUT_FIELD_ATTR,
                                   (i * 20) + 10, 9);
                         write_str("      ", OUTPUT_FIELD_ATTR,
                                   (i * 20) + 10,10);
                        }

                      /*_____*/
                      /* reset elapsed time msecs            */
                      /*_____*/
                      elapsed_time_msecs = 0;
                      sprintf(time_str,"%lu.%-4lu",
                              elapsed_time_msecs / 1000,
                              elapsed_time_msecs % 1000);
                      write_str(time_str, OUTPUT_FIELD_ATTR, 18, 20);

                      /*_____*/
                      /* reset total count                   */
                      /*_____*/
                      write_str("      ", OUTPUT_FIELD_ATTR, 18, 21);
```

Figure 14-24 (Part 2 of 3).   The get_user_input() Function.

```
                       break;
    case 'r'        : /*——————————————————————————*/
    case 'R'        : /* start execution                     */
                      /*——————————————————————————*/
                      post_event_semaphore(runall_sem_handle,
                                            &runall_sem_status);
                      test_running = TRUE;
                      write_str("RUNNING", OUTPUT_FIELD_ATTR, 18, 22);
                      break;

    case 's'        : /*——————————————————————————*/
    case 'S'        : /* stop execution                      */
                      /*——————————————————————————*/
                      reset_event_semaphore(runall_sem_handle,
                                            &runall_sem_status);
                      test_running = FALSE;
                      write_str("STOPPED", OUTPUT_FIELD_ATTR, 18, 22);
                      break;

    default         :
                      break;
  } /* end switch */

  return(CONTINUE);
} /* end get_user_input */
```

Figure 14-24 (Part 3 of 3).   The get_user_input() Function.

```
/*——————————————————————————————————————————————*/
/* write IO field value to screen, perform action                  */
/*——————————————————————————————————————————————*/
VOID perform_field_action(USHORT task, USHORT task_field)
{
  CHAR       field_str[20];

  switch(task_field)
    {
    case PRIORITY : switch(field[task][task_field].value)
                    {case BACKGROUND   : strcpy(field_str,"BG");
                                         break;
                     case REGULAR      : strcpy(field_str,"RG");
                                         break;
                     case TIME_CRITICAL: strcpy(field_str,"TC");
                                         break;
                     case FIXED_HIGH   : strcpy(field_str,"FH");
                                         break;
                    }
                    set_priority(task);
                    break;

    case LEVEL    : sprintf(field_str, "%-2d", field[task][task_field].value);
                    set_priority(task);
                    break;

    case SEMAPHORE : if (field[task][task_field].value == 0)
                     {strcpy(field_str,"CLEAR");
                      release_mutex_semaphore(run_sem_handle[task],
                                              &task_status[task].semaphore);
                     }
                     else
```

Figure 14-25 (Part 1 of 2).   The perform_field_action() Function.

```
                              {strcpy(field_str,"SET  ");
                               request_mutex_semaphore(run_sem_handle[task],
                                                   &task_status[task].semaphore);
                              }
                         break;

      default             : break;
      }

  write_str(field_str, IO_FIELD_ATTR,
            field[task][task_field].x,
            field[task][task_field].y);

} /* end perform_field_action */
```

Figure 14-25 (Part 2 of 2).   The perform_field_action() Function.

MULTI.C: Screen Helper Routines

The two screen helper routines listed below are used primarily by **get_user_input()**.
They consist of straight C code that does not introduce new OS/2 functions.

```
/*_____*/
/* Update cursor location                                         */
/*_____*/
VOID move_cursor(USHORT key)
{
  switch (key)
    {
      case DOWN_ARROW : update_value(&field_y, INCREMENT, 0, FIELD_Y_MAX);
                        break;
      case UP_ARROW   : update_value(&field_y, DECREMENT, 0, FIELD_Y_MAX);
                        break;
      case RIGHT_ARROW: update_value(&field_x, INCREMENT, 0, FIELD_X_MAX);
                        break;
      case LEFT_ARROW : update_value(&field_x, DECREMENT, 0, FIELD_X_MAX);
                        break;
    } /* endswitch */

} /* end move_cursor */

/*_____*/
/* Update value of a a variable                                   */
/*_____*/
VOID update_value(PUSHORT value,    USHORT direction,
                  USHORT  min_value, USHORT max_value)
{
  if (direction == INCREMENT)
      if (*value == max_value)
          *value = min_value;
      else
          ++*value;
  else
      if (*value == min_value)
          *value = max_value;
      else
          --*value;
} /* end update_value */
```

Figure 14-26.   The Screen Helper Routines.

MULTI.C: DOS Helper Routines

The helper functions, listed in Figure 14-27, invoke some of the more frequently used OS/2 calls and take care of the error handling associated with them. We've already encountered one of the OS/2 calls used in this section: **DosSetPriority**, described on page 287. We are encountering four new OS/2 semaphore calls: **DosRequestMutex-Sem**, **DosReleaseMutexSem**, **DosPostEventSem**, and **DosResetEventSem**. A description of the APIs follows.

DosRequestMutexSem

The **DosRequestMutexSem** API call is used in "wait until the mutex semaphore is released then try and grab it" mutual exclusion situations. The call grabs the semaphore in one uninterruptible *atomic* operation. The calling thread blocks until the semaphore is released or a time-out occurs. If multiple calls to **DosRequestMutexSem** are issued, they must be matched by a corresponding number of **DosReleaseMutexSem** calls to clear the semaphore. The API is level-triggered, meaning that a thread may have to wait through multiple changes of the semaphore before it continues. This may happen if another waiting thread grabs the semaphore before it. The prototype for this call is:

```
DosRequestMutexSem(PULONG    sem_handle,  /* semaphore handle          */
                   ULONG     timeout);    /* -1L= wait, 0=nowait,  0=msecs */
```

A description of the parameters follows:

- The *sem_handle* parameter is the handle of the mutex semaphore to request. This handle must have been previously created using **DosCreateMutexSem** or **DosOpenMutexSem**.
- The *timeout* parameter specifies how long to wait on the semaphore. If you set this parameter to zero, the call returns immediately. A positive value specifies the number of milliseconds to wait before returning. Most probably, you will be setting this value to -1L, which means "wait indefinitely until the semaphore is available."

DosReleaseMutexSem

The **DosReleaseMutexSem** API call is used to free a mutex semaphore ("I don't own it any more"). Only the thread that owns the semaphore can issue this call. The prototype for this call is:

```
DosReleaseMutexSem(PULONG   sem_handle); /* semaphore handle          */
```

A description of the parameters follows:

- The *sem_handle* parameter is the handle of the mutex semaphore to be released.

DosPostEventSem

The **DosPostEventSem** API call is used to post an event semaphore. This is like a "wake up call" for all the threads blocked waiting for that event to be posted. The prototype for this call is:

```
DosPostEventSem(PULONG    sem_handle); /* semaphore handle              */
```

A description of the parameters follows:

- The *sem_handle* parameter is the handle of the event semaphore to post.

DosResetEventSem

The **DosResetEventSem** API call is used to reset an event semaphore, causing all subsequent DosWaitEventSem calls to block. The prototype for this call is:

```
DosResetEventSem(PULONG    sem_handle,   /* semaphore handle           */
                 PULONG    post_count);  /* outstanding post counts    */
```

A description of the parameters follows:

- The *sem_handle* parameter is the handle of the event semaphore to reset.
- The *post_count* parameter points to a variable that receives the semaphore's post count. These are the number of calls to DosPostEvent that were made since the semaphore was last reset.

```
/*---------------------------------------------------------------------*/
/*request a MUTEX semaphore which controls a thread's execution        */
/*---------------------------------------------------------------------*/
VOID request_mutex_semaphore(HMTX sem_handle, PUSHORT status)
{
 if (*status == UNOWNED)
    {if (rc = DosRequestMutexSem(sem_handle,-1L))
       { print_error(rc,"executing DosRequestMutexSem", __FILE__,__LINE__);
         exit(FAILED);
       }
     *status = OWNED;
    }
} /* end request_mutex_semaphore */
```

Figure 14-27 (Part 1 of 3). The DOS Call Helper Routines.

```
/*_____*/
/* release a MUTEX semaphore which controls a thread's execution   */
/*_____*/
VOID release_mutex_semaphore(HMTX sem_handle, PUSHORT status)
{
 if (*status == OWNED)
    {if (rc = DosReleaseMutexSem(sem_handle))
        { print_error(rc,"executing DosReleaseSem", __FILE__,__LINE__);
          exit(FAILED);
        }
      *status = UNOWNED;
     }
} /* end release_mutex_semaphore */

/*_____*/
/* post an EVENT semaphore which controls a thread's execution     */
/*_____*/
VOID post_event_semaphore(HEV sem_handle, PUSHORT status)
{
 if (*status == RESET)
    {if (rc = DosPostEventSem(sem_handle))
        { print_error(rc,"executing DosPostEventSet", __FILE__,__LINE__);
          exit(FAILED);
        }
      *status = POSTED;
     }
}   /* end set_semaphore */

/*_____*/
/* reset an EVENT semaphore which controls a thread's execution    */
/*_____*/
VOID reset_event_semaphore(HEV sem_handle, PUSHORT status)
{
 ULONG post_count;

 if (*status == POSTED)
    {if (rc = DosResetEventSem(sem_handle, &post_count))
        { print_error(rc,"executing DosResetEventSem", __FILE__,__LINE__);
          exit(FAILED);
        }
      *status = RESET;
     }
} /* end reset_event_semaphore */


/*_____*/
/* set the priority of a task                                       */
/*_____*/
VOID set_priority(USHORT task_number)
{
   /*_____*/
   /* set the the priority, level       */
   /*_____*/
   if (program_type == PROCESSES)
      rc = DosSetPriority(PRTYS_PROCESS,            /* id is a process id      */
                    field[task_number][PRIORITY].value,    /* priority*/
                    field[task_number][LEVEL   ].value,    /* level   */
                    processid[task_number]);               /* thread  */
   else
```

Figure 14-27 (Part 2 of 3). The DOS Call Helper Routines.

```
        rc = DosSetPriority(PRTYS_THREAD,              /* id is a thread id       */
                     field[task_number][PRIORITY].value,       /* priority*/
                     field[task_number][LEVEL  ].value,        /* level   */
                     threadid[task_number]);                   /* thread  */
    if (rc)
       {print_error(rc,"executing DosSetPriority",__FILE__,__LINE__);
        exit(FAILED);
       }
   }  /* end set_priority */
```

Figure 14-27 (Part 3 of 3). The DOS Call Helper Routines.

MULTI.C: VIO Helper Routines

In this section, we introduce a number of screen helper routines that build on top of the OS/2 **VIO** API calls. The helper routines, listed in Figure 14-28, fall into the following two categories:

- Application specific helper routines that are used to paint the MULTI control panel windows.
- Generic helper routines which provide a set of screen primitives which you may want to use in future programs.

Application Specific Helper Routines

These are the helper routines which paint the MULTI control panel window. They use the generic help routines to provide their services, and they are written using ordinary C; so, they should be easy to follow:

- The **draw_title_box()** routine draws the top window.
- The **draw_task_box()** routine is used to draw the four task windows.
- The **display_exec_status()** routine draws the lower left window that displays the execution status.
- The **display_sys_info()** routine displays the lower right window that contains system information.

Generic Helper Routines

These helper routines provide a set of reusable screen primitives. You can tell by their names what they do:

- clear_screen()
- write_str()
- fill_area()

- draw_box()
- draw_horizontal_line(), draw_vertical_line()
- draw_cursor(), hide_cursor(), restore_cursor()

The generic routines use the OS/2 1.X VIO services. This service provides a convenient set of API functions for writing text to the screen and for controlling the cursor. You will find that these API functions can be used effectively to supplement the standard C library functions you are familiar with. You should still use C functions, such as **sprintf()**, to format complex string output. However, you can now supplement those functions with the OS/2 VIO API calls to add color, manipulate display attributes, control the cursor, or write to a particular location on the screen.

The generic helper routines make use of a total of five OS/2 VIO calls, on top of which they create their services:

VioWrtCharStrAtt: This 16-bit API call is used for placing a character string at a specified screen location with video attributes such as: bold, color, reverse video, blinking, and underline. It is used by **write_str()**. We previously encountered this API in Chapter 13, on page 234.

VioWrtNAttr: This API call is issued to change the color or display attributes of portions of the screen. It is used by **draw_cursor()** to create a custom cursor. This API call is described in Chapter 14, on page 303.

VioScrollDn: This API call is the preferred method for clearing the screen and may be used, of course, for scrolling down the screen. It is used by **fill_area()**. This API call is described in Chapter 14, on page 304.

VioGetCurType and VioSetCurType: These API calls are used to change the cursor format interactively. We can for example, choose to hide the cursor entirely when we do not expect any user input, and this is precisely how it is used by **hide_cursor()**. These API calls are described in Chapter 14, on page 305.

A description of the newly introduced VIO calls follows.

VioWrtNAttr

The **VioWrtNAttr** API call writes a character attribute string to a screen a specified number of times. The prototype for this call is:

```
VioWrtNAttr(PCHAR    attr,         /* pointer to fill char/attrib  */
            USHORT   times,        /* number of times to write     */
            USHORT   row_x,        /* row to start writing         */
            USHORT   column_y,     /* column to start writing      */
            USHORT   handle);      /* video handle                 */
```

A description of the parameters follows:

- The *attr* parameter points to the display attribute that will be used to write to the screen. For a description of the character attribute, see Chapter 13 on page 234.
- The *times* parameter specifies the number of times to write the character attribute. If the number is larger than the current line, the function continues writing at the start of the next line but does go past the end of the screen.
- The *row_x* parameter specifies the row at which to start writing attributes.
- The *column_y* parameter specifies the column at which to start writing attributes.
- The *handle* parameter is the presentation handle used by PM applications, and is otherwise NULL.

VioScrollDn

The **VioScrollDn** API call scrolls an area of the screen downward a specified number of lines. The prototype for this call is:

```
VioScrollDn(USHORT    top_x,      /* top row of scrolled area      */
            USHORT    left_y,     /* left column of scrolled area  */
            USHORT    bottom_x,   /* bottom row of scrolled area   */
            USHORT    right_y,    /* right column of scrolled area */
            USHORT    lines,      /* number of lines               */
            PCHAR     fill,       /* pointer to fill char/attrib   */
            USHORT    handle);    /* video handle                  */
```

A description of the parameters follows:

- The *top_x* parameter specifies the top row of the scroll area.
- The *left_y* parameter specifies the leftmost column of the scroll area.
- The *bottom_x* parameter specifies the bottom row of the scroll area.
- The *right_y* parameter specifies the rightmost column of the scroll area.
- The *lines* parameter specifies the number of blank lines to be inserted at the top of the screen area, which gets scrolled.
- The *fill* parameter points to a character/attribute array, also called a cell, that fills the screen area left blank by scrolling. The first array element contains the character. The second array element contains an attribute byte such as that described in Chapter 13 on page 234.
- The **handle** parameter is the presentation handle used by PM applications, and is otherwise NULL.

VioGetCurType

The **VioGetCurType** API call retrieves information about the cursor, including its height and width, and whether it is currently visible. The prototype for this call is:

```
VioGetCurType(VIOCURSORINFO *curdata,  /* pointer to cur info struct*/
              USHORT        handle);   /* video handle            */
```

A description of the parameters follows:

*   The *curdata* parameter points to the **VIOCURSORINFO** structure, which receives the information about the cursor. The structure has the following form:

```
struct   _VIOCURSORINFO
     {USHORT yStart; /* Top scan line in cursor 0=top              */
      USHORT cEnd;   /* Bottom scan line in cursor max=cell height */
      USHORT cx;     /* Width of cursor columns in pels or chars
                        0 =default i.e., 1 char or cell width in pels*/
      USHORT attr;   /* 0xFFFF = hides the cursor                  */
     } VIOCURSORINFO;
```

*   The *handle* parameter is a presentation handle used by PM applications. It is set to NULL by non-PM applications.

VioSetCurType

The **VioSetCurType** API call sets the cursor type for all processes in a screen group. The prototype for this call is:

```
VioSetCurType    (VIOCURSORINFO far *curdata,  /* pointer to cur info struct*/
                  USHORT             handle);   /* video handle            */
```

A description of the parameters follows:

*   The *curdata* parameter points to the **VIOCURSORINFO** structure, which specifies the characteristics of the cursor. The structure is defined in VioGetCurType on page 305.
*   The *handle* parameter is a presentation handle used by PM applications. It is set to NULL by non-PM applications.

Now that we have a description of the VIO calls, it becomes easy to follow the code for the generic helper functions. Note that the **hide_cursor**() helper routine uses **DosExitList** (see Chapter 13 on page 228) with the action_flag set to 1 to add the function **multi_exit**() to the exit list. The **multi_exit**() function, among other things, invokes **restore_cursor**(), which re-enables the cursor for the screen group when MULTI terminates.

```
/*----------------------------------------------------------------------*/
/* draw a MULTI panel title box window                                  */
/*----------------------------------------------------------------------*/
VOID draw_title_box(USHORT x, USHORT y)
{
  #define TITLE_BOX_CX 80
  #define TITLE_BOX_CY 7

  draw_box("", BOX_TITLE_ATTR, x, y,
           TITLE_BOX_CX, TITLE_BOX_CY, BOX_ATTR);
  if (program_type == THREADS)
    write_str("Multithread Execution Example", PANEL_TITLE_ATTR, x+25, y+1);
  else
    write_str("Multiprocess Execution Example", PANEL_TITLE_ATTR, x+25, y+1);
  write_str("Use arrow keys to move the cursor.  "
            "Use + and - keys to change field values.",
            PANEL_HELP_ATTR, x+2, y+3);
  write_str("Press R to start running, S to stop, or C to clear the count.",
            PANEL_HELP_ATTR, x+2, y+4);
  write_str("Press ESC to terminate the program.",
            PANEL_HELP_ATTR, x+2, y+5);
}  /* end draw_title_box */

/*----------------------------------------------------------------------*/
/* draw MULTI task display window                                       */
/*----------------------------------------------------------------------*/
VOID draw_task_box(PCHAR title, USHORT x, USHORT y)
{
  #define TASK_BOX_CX 20
  #define TASK_BOX_CY 10

  draw_box(title, BOX_TITLE_ATTR,
           x, y, TASK_BOX_CX, TASK_BOX_CY, BOX_ATTR);

  write_str("Count = ",     FIELD_TEXT_ATTR, x+2, y+2);
  write_str("Priority  = ", FIELD_TEXT_ATTR, x+2, y+4);
  write_str("Level     = ", FIELD_TEXT_ATTR, x+2, y+5);
  write_str("Semaphore = ", FIELD_TEXT_ATTR, x+2, y+6);

  /*------------------------------------------*/
  /* display task status                      */
  /*------------------------------------------*/
  write_str("Initializing", PANEL_STATUS_ATTR,
            x+2, y+8);                      /* calculate display loction  */
                                            /*  based on thread number    */
}  /* end draw_task_box */

/*----------------------------------------------------------------------*/
/* display MULTI system configuration window                            */
/*----------------------------------------------------------------------*/
VOID display_sys_info(USHORT x, USHORT y)
{
  #define SYSTEM_BOX_CX 40
  #define SYSTEM_BOX_CY  8
  struct { ULONG  fDynamicSched;
           ULONG  csecMaxWait;
           ULONG  cmsecMinSlice;
           ULONG  cmsecMaxSlice;
         } global_info;
  CHAR value_str[20];                       /* format string for displaying values*/
```

Figure 14-28 (Part 1 of 5). The VIO Call Helper Functions.

```
/*———————————————————*/
/* get system values from        */
/* DosQuerySysInfo               */
/*———————————————————*/
rc = DosQuerySysInfo(QSV_DYN_PRI_VARIATION,
                     QSV_MAX_SLICE,
                     &global_info,
                     sizeof(global_info));
if (rc)
   { print_error(rc,"executing DosQuerySysInfo", __FILE__,__LINE__);
     exit(FAILED);
   }

/*———————————————————*/
/* draw the box, display the info   */
/*———————————————————*/
draw_box("SYSTEM INFORMATION", BOX_TITLE_ATTR,
         x, y, SYSTEM_BOX_CX, SYSTEM_BOX_CY, BOX_ATTR);

write_str("Maximum Wait         =            sec", FIELD_TEXT_ATTR, x+2, y+2);
sprintf(value_str, "%u", global_info.csecMaxWait);
write_str(value_str, OUTPUT_FIELD_ATTR, x+23, y+2);

sprintf(value_str, "%u", global_info.cmsecMinSlice);
write_str("Minimum Time Slice =         ms ", FIELD_TEXT_ATTR, x+2, y+3);
write_str(value_str, OUTPUT_FIELD_ATTR, x+23, y+3);

sprintf(value_str, "%u", global_info.cmsecMaxSlice);
write_str("Maximum Time Slice =         ms ", FIELD_TEXT_ATTR, x+2, y+4);
write_str(value_str, OUTPUT_FIELD_ATTR, x+23, y+4);

write_str("Dynamic Variation  =           ", FIELD_TEXT_ATTR, x+2, y+5);
if (global_info.fDynamicSched)
   write_str("ACTIVE", OUTPUT_FIELD_ATTR, x+23, y+5);
else
   write_str("INACTIVE", OUTPUT_FIELD_ATTR, x+23, y+5);

} /* end display_sys_info */

/*————————————————————————*/
/* .display MULTI execution status data window         */
/*————————————————————————*/
VOID display_exec_status(USHORT x, USHORT y)
{
   #define SYSTEM_BOX_CX 40
   #define SYSTEM_BOX_CY  8

   CHAR value_str[20];                  /* format string for displaying values*/

   /*———————————————————*/
   /* draw the box, display the info   */
   /*———————————————————*/
   draw_box("EXECUTION STATUS", BOX_TITLE_ATTR,
            x, y, SYSTEM_BOX_CX, SYSTEM_BOX_CY, BOX_ATTR);

   write_str("Stop Time      =             sec", FIELD_TEXT_ATTR, x+2, y+2);
   sprintf(value_str,"%lu.%-4lu", stop_time_msecs/1000, stop_time_msecs % 1000);
   write_str(value_str, OUTPUT_FIELD_ATTR, x+18, y+2);

   write_str("Elapsed Time  =             sec", FIELD_TEXT_ATTR, x+2, y+3);
   sprintf(value_str,"%lu.%-4lu", elapsed_time_msecs/1000,
           elapsed_time_msecs % 1000);
   write_str(value_str, OUTPUT_FIELD_ATTR, x+18, y+3);
```

Figure 14-28 (Part 2 of 5). The VIO Call Helper Functions.

```
    write_str("Total Count   =                              ", FIELD_TEXT_ATTR, x+2, y+4);

    write_str("Run Status    =                              ", FIELD_TEXT_ATTR, x+2, y+5);
    write_str("STOPPED", OUTPUT_FIELD_ATTR, x+18, y+5);


} /* end display_exec_status */
/*_____*/
/* draw a generic box with a title.                                    */
/*_____*/
VOID draw_box(PCHAR title, CHAR title_attribute,
         USHORT x, USHORT y, USHORT cx, USHORT cy, CHAR box_attribute)
{
    draw_horizontal_line(x+1   , y     , cx-2 , box_attribute); /* top        */
    draw_horizontal_line(x+1   , y+cy-1, cx-2 , box_attribute); /* bottom     */
    draw_vertical_line  (x     , y+1   , cy-2 , box_attribute); /* left side  */
    draw_vertical_line  (x+cx-1, y+1   , cy-2 , box_attribute); /* right side */

    write_str(BOX_UL_CORNER, box_attribute,  x     , y     );   /* update     */
    write_str(BOX_UR_CORNER, box_attribute,  x+cx-1, y     );   /*   the      */
    write_str(BOX_LL_CORNER, box_attribute,  x     , y+cy-1);   /*    corners */
    write_str(BOX_LR_CORNER, box_attribute,  x+cx-1, y+cy-1);   /*            */

    write_str(title, title_attribute,  x+2, y);                 /* box title  */
}  /* end draw_box */


/*_____*/
/* hide the cursor                                                     */
/*_____*/
VOID hide_cursor(VOID)
{

    if (rc = VioGetCurType(&save_cursor_data,      /* cursor definition    */
                      0))                           /* reserved             */
        print_error(rc,"executing VioGetCurType",__FILE__,__LINE__);

    cursor_data.yStart = 0;
    cursor_data.cEnd   = 0;
    cursor_data.cx     = 0;
    cursor_data.attr   = -1;

    if (rc = VioSetCurType(&cursor_data, /* cursor definition             */
                      0))                /* reserved                      */
        print_error(rc,"executing VioSetCurType",__FILE__,__LINE__);

    /*_____*/
    /* exit routine to restore cursor  */
    /*    when program ends            */
    /*_____*/
    if (rc = DosExitList(1,(PFNEXITLIST) multi_exit))
       { printf("Error establishing error exit routine.\n");
         exit(FAILED);
       }
}  /* end hide_cursor */
```

Figure 14-28 (Part 3 of 5).   The VIO Call Helper Functions.

```
/*_____*/
/* restore the cursor                                                 */
/*_____*/
VOID restore_cursor(VOID)
{
   if (rc = VioSetCurType(&save_cursor_data,      /* cursor definition    */
                          0))                      /* reserved             */
      print_error(rc,"executing VioSetCurType",__FILE__,__LINE__);
} /* end restore_cursor */

/*_____*/
/* draw field cursor                                                  */
/*_____*/
VOID draw_cursor(BYTE attribute, USHORT x, USHORT y, USHORT cx)
{
   if (rc = VioWrtNAttr(&attribute,      /* attribute            */
                        cx,              /* number of times      */
                        y, x,            /* screen position      */
                        0))              /* reserved             */
      print_error(rc,"executing VioWrtNAttr",__FILE__,__LINE__);

} /* end draw_cursor */

/*_____*/
/* write a character strimg to the screen.                            */
/*_____*/
VOID write_str(PCHAR charstr, CHAR attribute, USHORT x, USHORT y)
{
   if (rc = VioWrtCharStrAtt(charstr,                    /* character string */
                             (USHORT)strlen(charstr),    /* number of times  */
                             y, x,                        /* screen position  */
                             &attribute,                  /* attribute        */
                             0))                          /* reserved         */
      print_error(rc,"executing VioWrtCharStrAtt",__FILE__,__LINE__);
} /* end write_str */

/*_____*/
/* fill an area with a specified char and attribute                   */
/*_____*/
VOID fill_area(PCHAR ch, CHAR attribute, USHORT x,  USHORT y,
                                         USHORT cx, USHORT cy)
{
   CHAR fill[2];
   fill[0] = ch[0];

   fill[1] = attribute;
   /*_____*/
   /* Scroll cy lines to fill an area                                    */
   /*_____*/
   if (rc = VioScrollDn(y, x,                   /* upper left of scroll area  */
                        y+cy-1, x+cx-1,         /* lower right of scroll area */
                        cy,                     /* lines to scroll            */
                        fill,                   /* fill char/attrib pair      */
                        0))                     /* reserved word of 0's       */
      print_error(rc,"executing VioScrollDn",__FILE__,__LINE__);
} /* end fill_area */
```

Figure 14-28 (Part 4 of 5).   The VIO Call Helper Functions.

```
/*—————————————————————————————————*/
/* clear the screen                                          */
/*—————————————————————————————————*/

VOID clear_screen()
{
   fill_area(BLANK, FIELD_TEXT_ATTR, 0, 0, 999, 999);
}  /* end clear_screen */

/*—————————————————————————————————*/
/* draw a horizontal line.                                   */
/*—————————————————————————————————*/
VOID draw_horizontal_line(USHORT x, USHORT y, USHORT cx, CHAR attribute)
{
   fill_area(HORIZONTAL_LINE, attribute, x, y, cx, 1);
}  /* end draw_horizontal_line */

/*—————————————————————————————————*/
/* draw a vertical line.                                     */
/*—————————————————————————————————*/
VOID draw_vertical_line(USHORT x, USHORT y, USHORT cy, CHAR attribute)
{
   fill_area(VERTICAL_LINE, attribute, x, y, 1, cy);
}  /* end draw_vertical_line */
```

Figure 14-28 (Part 5 of 5).   The VIO Call Helper Functions.

MULTI.C: Miscellaneous Helper Routines

The miscellaneous helper routines, **print_error()** and **multi_exit()**, are listed in Figure 14-29. The **print_error()** function records useful debug information such as the error number, the error description, and the source code file and line number where the error occurred. The IBM C Set/2 compiler maintains two predefined preprocessor symbols, __FILE__ and __LINE__, which refer to the current input file name and the current line number being processed by the compiler. A failing program uses the preprocessor macros to obtain the source code file and line number where the error occurs. It then passes these numbers to **print_error()** as parameters.

The **multi_exit()** function simply restores the cursor and issues a **DosExitList**, (see Chapter 13, "DosExitList" on page 228) with the action_flag set to 3. This indicates that OS/2 can transfer control to the next exit list procedure.

```
VOID print_error(USHORT Error, PCHAR msg, PCHAR file, USHORT line)
{
 printf("Error %d detected while %s at line %d in file %s.\n",
         Error, msg, line, file);
} /* end print_error */

/*_____*/
/* Exit Routine                                                      */
/*_____*/
VOID FAR multi_exit(USHORT exit_type)
{
   restore_cursor();
   DosExitList(3, (PVOID) 0);
} /* end multi_exit */
```

Figure 14-29. Miscellaneous Helper Routines.

MULTI.C: terminate_program()

The **terminate_program**() function, listed in Figure 14-30, kills the four process contenders, clears the screen, and returns to OS/2. Notice that we only kill processes; threads terminate automatically with the program. Killing processes is a two-step affair. First, the OS/2 **DosKillProcess** call (see Chapter 13, on page 243) is issued to kill the process, followed by a **DosWaitChild** call, which performs a post-mortem. The following is a description of **DosWaitChild**.

DosWaitChild

The **DosWaitChild** API call blocks the calling process until a specified child process (or processes) terminate. It is used when the parent is asynchronously executing with a child process and the parent has to wait at some point in the program for the child to finish processing. The prototype for this call is:

```
DosWaitChild(ULONG        scope_flag,      /* Process or descendants too*/
             ULONG        wait_flag,       /* Wait or no wait           */
             RESULTCODES  far *results,    /* Result codes              */
             PPID         processID,       /* Pointer to returned PID   */
             PID          waitprocessID);  /* 0 = any or PID to wait for*/
```

A description of the parameters follows:

- The *scope_flag* parameter specifies how many processes to wait for. If it is 0 (DCWA_PROCESS), the parent waits only for the specified process. If it is 1 (DCWA_PROCESSTREE), the function waits for the specified process and all its child processes to end.
- The *wait_flag* parameter specifies whether or not to wait for processes to end. If it is 0 (DCWW_WAIT), the function waits for a child process to terminate. If it is 1 (DCWW_NOWAIT), the function returns immediately with the resultcodes of the most recent process to end; however, an error message is returned if the specified process is still running.

- The *results* parameter points to the RESULTCODES structure, previously described for **DosExecProgram** (see Chapter 14, on page 292). The structure is filled with a termination code supplied by OS/2 and the result code supplied by the terminating process when it invokes **DosExit**
- The *processID* parameter is a pointer to the PID returned by OS/2 for the terminating process. This is used to identify which of the descendants just terminated.
- The *waitprocessID* parameter specifies the PID of the process to wait for. If it is NULL and the scope flag specifies all descendants, then the first child to terminate causes the function to return. This option requires **DoWaitChild** to be called repeatedly for each child process of the specified PID.

```
/*_____*/
/* User requested program terminate, kill tasks and clean up          */
/*_____*/
VOID terminate_program(VOID)
{
  if (program_type == PROCESSES)
    {
     for (i=0; i<4; ++i)
       {
         /*_____*/
         /* display process status       */
         /*_____*/
         write_str("Terminating ", PANEL_STATUS_ATTR,
                   (i * 20) + 2, 15);        /* calculate display loction  */
                                             /*  based on process number   */

         rc = DosKillProcess(1, /* only kill one process */
                    processid[i]);
         if (rc)
           { print_error(rc,"killing a process",
                    __FILE__,__LINE__);
             exit(FAILED);
           }

         rc = DosWaitChild(DCWA_PROCESSTREE, /* wait for child, descendants  */
                    DCWW_WAIT      , /* wait for child termination  */
                    &term_result,
                    &term_processid,
                    processid[i]);/* id to wait for   */
         if (rc)
           { print_error(rc,"waiting for a process to end",
                    __FILE__,__LINE__);
             exit(FAILED);
           }

         write_str("Terminated   ", PANEL_STATUS_ATTR,
                   (i * 20) + 2, 15);        /* calculate display location */
                                             /*  based on process number   */
       }
    }
  clear_screen();
  exit(GOOD);
} /* end terminate_program */
```

Figure 14-30. The terminate_program() Function.

MULTI.C: thread_count

Up until this point, the MULTI program was involved with setting up the infrastructure for running races. In the remaining sections of this chapter, we examine the code that gets executed by the race contenders. The listing in Figure 14-31, is that of our representative thread champion, **thread_count**. Remember that we will be running races between four thread instances of the code listed here, which we do by passing a thread_number parameter. A thread first clears its counter in the shared memory and then goes into a do forever loop. Before getting into the details of the loop, you should refer to Figure 14-14 for a quick refresher on the semaphore structure that was put in place by MULTI to control the races.

This is how a racing thread champion loops through life:

• The champ first waits on the \SEM32\RUNALL event semaphore to post indicating a race just started.
• The champ then waits on the \SEM32\RUNn mutex semaphore to be released (where "n" is the particular champ's number). If the semaphore is "unowned," then this champ was asked to participate in the race. The champ then sets the semaphore to "owned" and starts racing.
• The champ then increments its race counter by 1, and updates the task window on MULTI's control panel, with the new count.
• The champ then releases the \SEM32\RUNn mutex.
• The champ is now ready for another round through the loop...

Our champion's life, as you see, literally revolves around updating its counters. In later chapters, we will introduce other champions that perform more interesting types of additional activity that we will want to measure in a race setting.

The **thread_count** does not introduce any new OS/2 functions. The **DosWaitEvent-Sem** call was described on page 283, the **DosRequestMutexSem** call was described on page 299, and the **DosReleaseMutexSem** call was described on page 299.

```
/*———————————————————————————————————————————————*/
/* Thread routine. This routine continuously 1) requests a semaphore, */
/*    2) increments and displays a count, 3) clears the semaphore. The user */
/*    can disable counting by setting the semaphore from the display panel. */
/*———————————————————————————————————————————————*/
VOID thread_count(PVOID thread_number)
{
  CHAR    count_str[10];
  USHORT  rc;
  USHORT  task_number;
  HMTX    sem_handle;
```

Figure 14-31 (Part 1 of 2). The thread_count() Thread.

```
      task_number = *(PUSHORT)thread_number;
      sem_handle  = run_sem_handle[task_number];
      count_ptr->count[task_number] = 0;

      /*————————————————————————————————*/
      /* display thread status                  */
      /*————————————————————————————————*/
      write_str("Ready        ", PANEL_STATUS_ATTR,
                (task_number * 20) + 2, 15);    /* calculate display location  */
                                                /* based on thread number      */

      /*————————————————————————————————*/
      /* continuous count loop                  */
      /*————————————————————————————————*/
      while (TRUE)
         {
            /*————————————————————————————————*/
            /* wait for control sem to post       */
            /*————————————————————————————————*/
            if (rc = DosWaitEventSem(runall_sem_handle,      /* semaphore handle */
                         -1L))                               /* infinite timeout */
               { print_error(rc,"executing DosWaitEventSem",
                         __FILE__,__LINE__);
                  exit(FAILED);
               }

            /*————————————————————————————————*/
            /* request the semaphore              */
            /*————————————————————————————————*/
            if (rc = DosRequestMutexSem(sem_handle,          /* semaphore handle */
                         -1L))                               /* infinite timeout */
               { print_error(rc,"executing DosRequestMutexSem",
                         __FILE__,__LINE__);
                  exit(FAILED);
               }
            /*————————————————————————————————*/
            /* increment the count                */
            /*————————————————————————————————*/
            ++(count_ptr->count[task_number]);
            /*————————————————————————————————*/
            /* display the count value            */
            /*————————————————————————————————*/
            sprintf(count_str, "%-7lu", count_ptr->count[task_number]);
            write_str(count_str, OUTPUT_FIELD_ATTR,
                      (task_number * 20) + 10,  9);   /* calculate display loction */
                                                      /* based on thread number    */
            /*————————————————————————————————*/
            /* Release the semaphore              */
            /*————————————————————————————————*/
            if (rc = DosReleaseMutexSem(sem_handle))
               { print_error(rc,"executing DosReleaseMutexSem", __FILE__,__LINE__);
                  exit(FAILED);
               }
         }/* end while */
} /* end thread_count */
```

Figure 14-31 (Part 2 of 2).   The thread_count() Thread.

COUNT.C: THE PROCESS CHAMPION

This section describes **COUNT.C**, our representative process champion. As you can see from the listing in Figure 14-32, a process is just a separate program. This program performs the same counting function as the representative **thread_count** thread (see listing in Figure 14-31). The purpose of this exercise is to compare OS/2's thread and process tasking services. So, we'll run races, using MULTI's racing infrastructure, between four process champions that all execute the same **COUNT.EXE** code.

Dissecting the COUNT.C Program

The **main()** program starts with the OS/2 and C library include files. The **const.h** include file is identical to the one used in MULTI.C and is listed in Figure 14-11. The **count.h** include file contains the forward procedure declarations and global variables for **COUNT.C**; it is listed in Figure 14-33.

The first piece of code **main()** executes is to decode the champion number it will run the race under. This is needed, of course, because we will be using the same code for the four process contenders. The next pieces of code in **main()** are very important because they distinguish the way processes do things from threads:

- A process needs to issue **DosOpenEventSem** to access **\SEM32\RUNALL**, the shared event semaphore, and **DosOpenMutexSem** to access the **\SEM32\RUNn** shared mutex (where "n" is the champion's number for the race). Threads don't have to issue open calls because they run in the same address space as MULTI and have direct access to the semaphore handles. For processes, the following semaphore protocol is followed:

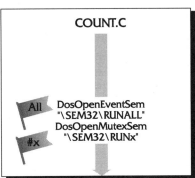

- A process issues **DosGetNamedSharedMem** to obtain a pointer to the shared memory object **\SHAREMEM\TASK**, which was previously allocated by MULTI. This is the area in memory where each champion writes its count. The protocol between MULTI.C and COUNT.C for sharing memory is as follows:

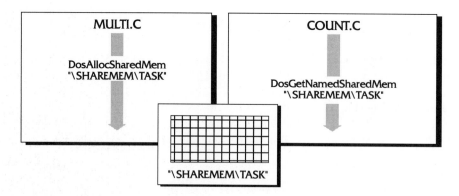

With the exceptions noted, the **main()** process champion code is identical to its thread champion. You can convince yourself of this by noting that the last thing **main()** does is invoke **thread_count()**, a procedure that runs code that is functionally identical to the **thread_count** champion thread code we presented in Figure 14-31. You should consult the explanation given in that section to find out what a champion process does as it loops through life.

The three new OS/2 2.0 API calls introduced in this section are **DosOpenEventSem**, **DosOpenMutexSem**, and **DosGetNamedSharedMem**; their description follows.

DosOpenEventSem

The **DosOpenEventSem** API call allows a process to obtain access to a shared event semaphore that was created by another process. The effect of the call is to return the handle to the semaphore; it does not test or change the status of the semaphore. The prototype for this call is:

```
DosOpenEventSem (PSZ    sem_name,     /* pointer to semaphore name  */
                 PULONG sem_handle);  /* semaphore handle           */
```

A description of the parameters follows:

- The *sem_name* parameter points to a null-terminated string that provides the semaphore name. This is the same name that was provided originally by the process that created the semaphore. Set this field to NULL if the semaphore is unnamed. The unnamed semaphore is identified by supplying a pointer to the event semaphore handle (see the following parameter).
- The *sem_handle* parameter is a handle that points to a semaphore variable. OS/2 will return the handle for a named semaphore. If name is NULL (i.e., the semaphore is unnamed), you must point to the event semaphore handle to open.

DosOpenMutexSem

The **DosOpenMutexSem** API call allows a process to obtain access to a shared mutex semaphore that was created by another process. The effect of the call is to return the handle to the semaphore; it does not test or change the status of the semaphore. The prototype for this call is:

```
DosOpenMutexSem(PSZ     sem_name,     /* pointer to semaphore name */
                PULONG  sem_handle);  /* semaphore handle          */
```

A description of the parameters follows:

- The *sem_name* parameter points to a null-terminated string that provides the semaphore name. This is the same name that was provided originally by the process that created the semaphore. Set this field to NULL if the semaphore is unnamed. The unnamed semaphore is identified by supplying a pointer to the mutex semaphore handle (see the following parameter).
- The *sem_handle* parameter is a handle that points to a semaphore variable. OS/2 will return the handle for a named semaphore. If name is NULL (i.e., the semaphore is unnamed), you must point to the mutex semaphore handle to open.

DosGetNamedSharedMem

The **DosGetNamedSharedMem** API call obtains access to a named shared memory object, which was previously allocated by another process. The call allocates the virtual address of the shared memory object in the address space of the calling process. The prototype for this call is:

```
DosGetNamedSharedMem(PVOID *BaseAddress, /* pointer to address object*/
                     PSZ    Name,        /* pointer to object name   */
                     ULONG  Flags);      /* allocation attributes    */
```

A description of the parameters follows:

- The *BaseAddress* parameter points to a variable that receives the object's address. This is the base address of an allocated range of pages.
- The *Name* parameter points to a null-terminated string, which is the optional name to be given to the object. The string must include the fictitious subdirectory name **\SHAREMEM**, and the name must be unique.
- The *Flags* parameter consists of a set of flags that describe the desired access protection for the shared memory object. OR those flags to get the desired combination of attributes:

Access Protection Flags	Meaning
PAG_EXECUTE	Provide execute access to object.
PAG_READ	Provide read access to object.
PAG_WRITE	Provide write access to object.
PAG_GUARD	Access to object causes a "guard page violation."

```
/*********************************************************************/
/*  PROGRAM NAME: COUNT - A process program that MULTI starts        */
/*                                                                   */
/*  PROGRAM DESCRIPTION:  This program is run as a child task of the MULTI  */
/*     program to illustrate multiprocess interaction.               */
/*                                                                   */
/*********************************************************************/
#include <process.h>              /* For exit()                      */
#include <string.h>               /* For printf                      */
#include <stdlib.h>               /* For atoi                        */
#include <stdio.h>                /* For sprintf, printf             */

#define INCL_VIO                  /* include VIO calls               */
#define INCL_DOSMEMMGR            /* for shared segment functions    */
#define INCL_DOSSEMAPHORES        /* include semaphore api calls     */
#include <os2.h>
#include "const.h"
#include "count.h"

/*-----------------------------------------------------------------*/
/* Main routine.                                                   */
/*-----------------------------------------------------------------*/
INT
main(USHORT argc, PCHAR argv[], PCHAR envp[])
{
   CHAR sem_name[30];

   /*------------------------------------*/
   /* validate and get arguments         */
   /*------------------------------------*/
   if (argc <= 1)
      { printf("Incorrect number of arguments (argc = %u).\n", argc);
        exit(FAILED);
      }

   process_number = atoi(argv[1]);
   if ((process_number < 0) || (process_number > 3))
      { printf("Process Number out of range.\n");
        exit(FAILED);
      }

   /*------------------------------------*/
   /* open the semaphores                */
   /*------------------------------------*/
   sprintf(sem_name,"\\SEM32\\RUN%d", process_number);
   if (rc = DosOpenMutexSem(sem_name,       /* handle to semaphore returned*/
                         &sem_handle)) /* ASCIIZ name of semaphore     */
      { print_error(rc,"during DosOpenMutexSem", __FILE__,__LINE__);
        exit(FAILED);
      }
```

Figure 14-32 (Part 1 of 3). COUNT Program Listing.

```
    sprintf(sem_name,"\\SEM32\\RUNALL");
    if (rc = DosOpenEventSem(sem_name,              /* handle to semaphore returned*/
                             &control_sem_handle))/* ASCIIZ name of semaphore    */
       { print_error(rc,"during DosOpenEventSem", __FILE__,__LINE__);
         exit(FAILED);
       }

    /*————————————————————————*/
    /* get a shared segment for the count  */
    /*   values                            */
    /*————————————————————————*/
    sprintf(name,"\\SHAREMEM\\TASK");
    rc = DosGetNamedSharedMem((PVOID)&count_ptr, name, PAG_READ | PAG_WRITE);
    if (rc)
       {print_error(rc,"allocating count buffer",__FILE__,__LINE__);
        return(FAILED);
       }

    thread_count(process_number);
} /* end main */

/*——————————————————————————————————————————————*/
/* Thread routine. This routine continuously 1) requests a semaphore,    */
/*   2) increments and displays a count, 3) clears the semaphore.  The user */
/*   can disable counting by setting the semaphore from the display panel.  */
/*——————————————————————————————————————————————*/
VOID
thread_count(USHORT process_number)
{
  CHAR    count_str[10];
  USHORT  rc;
  USHORT  task_number;

  task_number = process_number;
  count_ptr->count[task_number] = 0;

  /*————————————————————————*/
  /* display process status            */
  /*————————————————————————*/
  write_str("Ready       ", PANEL_STATUS_ATTR,
            (task_number * 20) + 2, 15);    /* calculate display location  */
                                            /*   based on thread number    */

  /*————————————————————————*/
  /* continuous count loop             */
  /*————————————————————————*/
  while (TRUE)
     {
       /*————————————————————————*/
       /* wait for control sem to clear      */
       /*————————————————————————*/
       if (rc = DosWaitEventSem(control_sem_handle,      /* semaphore handle */
                                -1L))                    /* infinite timeout */
          { print_error(rc,"executing DosSemWait",
                        __FILE__,__LINE__);
            exit(FAILED);
          }
```

Figure 14-32 (Part 2 of 3). COUNT Program Listing.

```
        /*─────────────────────────────────────────*/
        /* request the semaphore                   */
        /*─────────────────────────────────────────*/
        if (rc = DosRequestMutexSem(sem_handle,            /* semaphore handle */
                               -1L))                       /* infinite timeout */
            { print_error(rc,"executing DosSemRequest",
                        __FILE__,__LINE__);
              exit(FAILED);
            }
        /*─────────────────────────────────────────*/
        /* increment the count                     */
        /*─────────────────────────────────────────*/
        ++(count_ptr->count[task_number]);

        /*─────────────────────────────────────────*/
        /* display the count value                 */
        /*─────────────────────────────────────────*/
        sprintf(count_str, "%-7lu", count_ptr->count[task_number]);


        write_str(count_str, OUTPUT_FIELD_ATTR,
                (task_number * 20) + 10,  9);    /* calculate display loction */
                                                 /*  based on thread number   */
        /*─────────────────────────────────────────*/
        /* clear the semaphore                     */
        /*─────────────────────────────────────────*/
        if (rc = DosReleaseMutexSem(sem_handle))
            { print_error(rc,"executing DosReleaseMutexSem", __FILE__,__LINE__);
              exit(FAILED);
            }
   }/* end while */
} /* end thread_count */

/*───────────────────────────────────────────────────────────────────────────*/
/* write a character string to the screen.                                     */
/*───────────────────────────────────────────────────────────────────────────*/
VOID
write_str(PCHAR charstr, CHAR attribute, USHORT x, USHORT y)
{
   CHAR cell[2];
   BYTE attr;

   if (rc = VioWrtCharStrAtt(charstr,    /* character string       */
                     strlen(charstr),/* number of times        */
                     y, x,           /* screen position        */
                     &attribute,     /* attribute              */
                     0))             /* reserved               */
       print_error(rc,"during VioWrtCharStrAtt",__FILE__,__LINE__);
}

/*───────────────────────────────────────────────────────────────────────────*/
/* Error Display Routine                                                       */
/*───────────────────────────────────────────────────────────────────────────*/
VOID
print_error(USHORT Error, PCHAR msg, PCHAR file, USHORT line)
{
 printf("Error %d detected while %s at line %d in file %s.\n",
        Error, msg, line, file);
} /* end print_error */
```

Figure 14-32 (Part 3 of 3). COUNT Program Listing.

```
/****************************************************************************/
/*   INCLUDE NAME: COUNT - declarations for COUNT program                   */
/****************************************************************************/

/*_____*/
/* Forward declarations of procedures in this module                       */
/*_____*/
                    /*_____*/
                    /* top level routines                     */
                    /*_____*/
VOID thread_count(USHORT);

                    /*_____*/
                    /* VIO call helper functions              */
                    /*_____*/
VOID write_str(PCHAR, CHAR, USHORT, USHORT);

                    /*_____*/
                    /* Error display routine                  */
                    /*_____*/
VOID print_error(USHORT, PCHAR, PCHAR, USHORT);

/*_____*/
/* Global variables/type definitions for this module                      */
/*_____*/
USHORT process_number;                 /* number of this process           */
HMTX   sem_handle;                     /* semaphore handle                 */
HEV    control_sem_handle;             /* semaphore handle                 */
USHORT rc;                             /* return code variable             */

                    /*_____*/
                    /* count variable definition              */
                    /*_____*/
typedef struct _COUNT
        { ULONG count[4];
        } COUNT;
COUNT   *count_ptr;

CHAR    name[80];                      /* variable for building ascii names */
```

Figure 14-33.   COUNT Include File.

Chapter 15

Named Pipes

This chapter presents a tutorial on *Named Pipes*, OS/2's most complete service for interprocess communications (*IPC*). In previous chapters, we covered the *semaphore services*, which are OS/2's most primitive IPC service. Semaphores are used to synchronize the actions of independent processes and regulate their access to shared resources. The information carried in semaphores consists, at most, of simple signals and flags. Clearly, a form of IPC is needed that goes beyond semaphores and allows independent processes to exchange and share data. This function is provided by OS/2's advanced IPC services for interprocess data transfer.

The interprocess data transfer services are the most complex and sophisticated form of IPC provided by an operating system. OS/2, being a late-model operating system, is endowed with several state-of-the-art IPC data exchange mechanisms namely: Named Pipes, Shared Memory, Anonymous Pipes, Queues, and PM's Dynamic Data Exchange.

In this book, we focus on Named Pipes because it is the most powerful and complete IPC OS/2 offers. It is also the only IPC that allows communicating processes to be distributed on different computers on a network. The communicating processes can even be MS-DOS or UNIX (through LAN Manager/X) applications on the network.

The plan for this chapter is to first define the "ideal" interprocess data transfer IPC. We then explore how Named Pipes measure-up against the check-list of "ideal" IPC features by way of the tutorial. We conclude the tutorial with scenarios that demonstrate the use of the Named Pipes IPC protocol in typical application environments. The tutorials provide the prerequisite background information on IPCs for the programming examples in the chapters that follow.

WHAT SHOULD THE "IDEAL" IPC PROVIDE?

The "ideal" IPC for interprocess data transfer should provide the following services:

- A built-in protocol for coordinating the sending and receiving of data between processes.

- A mechanism for pacing the data interchange so that new data does not over-write old data before it gets consumed. An example of such a mechanism is a queue.
- Support for data transfers that may involve many-to-one exchanges. An example of a many-to-one exchange is a server process that concurrently services several client processes.
- Support for the interprocess exchange of data over a network. The location of processes should be made transparent to the programmer. Network security and network recovery should be integrated into the protocol.
- A Remote Procedure Call-like mechanism to facilitate the creation of transaction-based applications between processes.
- Support for the exchange of data using a variety of data structures.
- A familiar programming interface that does not require learning a large number of new commands or a new programming metaphor.
- A protocol that can be implemented using a minimum amount of code. Interprocess communications in a multitasking environment should be "natural" and easy to use.
- A protocol that does not introduce a heavy performance overhead.

So, this is really a checklist of what to expect from a well designed interprocess data transfer protocol. In the tutorial that follows, we evaluate how Named Pipes, OS/2's *best of breed* IPC protocol, measures up to this "ideal" wish list.

NAMED PIPES: THE "IDEAL" IPC?

Named Pipes are the OS/2 IPC mechanism that comes closest to providing the "ideal" interprocess data transfer protocol. For starters, Named Pipes are the only OS/2 IPC mechanism that can transfer data across a network. They provide a file-like program-ming API for the two-way exchange of data. Using Named Pipes, processes can exchange data as if they were writing to, or reading from, a sequential file.

Named Pipes are especially suitable for implementing server programs which require many-to-one pipelines. A server application can set up a pipeline where the receiving end of the pipe can exchange data with several client processes and have OS/2 handle all the scheduling and synchronization issues. Named Pipes also provide a very strong platform for the development of client/server applications. Here is what they offer:

- They provide a method for exchanging data and control information between processes running on different computers.
- They hide the interface to the network.
- They provide API calls that are optimized for the implementation of *Remote Procedure Calls*, which are request/reply message pairs that can be used for building client/server applications using procedure-like calls. The invocation of a remote procedure will result in a request/reply exchange over the Named Pipe. The incoming request may be used to trigger a procedure on a server and pass it the required parameters. The results will be returned by the server in a reply message over the same pipe.

USING NAMED PIPES

Creating a Named Pipe: What's in a Name?

To establish a Named Pipe, a server process has to first create the pipe by issuing a **DosCreateNPipe** call, which returns a handle that identifies the pipe. A Named Pipe is identified by a unique name that conforms to the OS/2 file naming convention, although no actual file is created. Pipes are named **\PIPE\name**, and local pipes are referenced by that name. Remote pipes are referenced as **\\server\PIPE\name**, where "server" is the network name of a server machine. A local pipe can only be used by processes on the same machine; a remote pipe can be used by processes connected over a local area network. This network-naming capability is one of Named Pipes' most important features. It means a client application can communicate with a Named Pipe from any machine on the network.

How Do You Like Your Pipe?

When a server process first creates a Named Pipe, it specifies several parameters that will determine the nature of that Named Pipe and how it can be used. Here is a list of what can be specified:

Which direction?   Although Named Pipes are bidirectional, you have the option of putting constraints on the direction of data through the pipe. You can specify that a pipe be *in-bound*, *out-bound*, or *duplex*. An *in-bound* pipe can only read data from a client process. An *out-bound* pipe can only write data to a client process. A *duplex* pipe supports bidirectional data exchanges between clients and the server.

Byte stream or message stream?   You can specify whether the pipe will be used in byte stream or message stream mode. In byte stream mode, the processes read and write bytes; in message stream mode, they read and write messages with OS/2 providing a system-supplied length header. The size and content of the individual messages is determined by the application.

How many concurrent clients?   What happens when many clients all want to open the same Named Pipe? You can specify through an *instance count* the number of times a Named Pipe can be opened by clients at the same time. Pipe instances are actually separate pipes that share the same name. Each instance of the pipe has its own handle and file buffer. Pipe instances allow a server to communicate with multiple clients at the same time. When clients connect to the same pipe, each connection is assigned its own instance (handle) of the pipe.

Will the pipe be inherited?   You can specify whether the Named Pipe handle is to be inherited by child processes.

Flushing versus blocking?   You can specify for remote pipes whether the data is to be sent over the remote pipe immediately (flushed) as it is written, or whether it gets blocked and then sent when an internal buffer fills up. Blocking reduces the message traffic over a network and improves performance. The cost, however, is the loss of the immediate acknowledgement that the data arrived at its destination.

Wait or immediate return?   You can specify whether all subsequent operations on a pipe will block waiting when no data is available or will return immediately.

Making the Connection

Once the pipe is created on the server, it must be in a listening state before a client can connect to it. The server does that by issuing **DosConnectNPipe**. The pipe is now in a *LISTENING* state waiting for a client process to open it. At this point, any client process that knows the fully qualified path name of a Named Pipe can open the pipe by issuing a **DosOpen**. This is the same OS/2 call that is used for opening a regular file. If **DosOpen** succeeds, it returns a handle and the pipe is then in the *CONNECTED* state.

If the call fails and returns ERROR_PIPE_BUSY, the client may issue **DosWaitNPipe**, which will block the process until the first pipe instance becomes available. What happens when many clients are waiting on the same pipe? OS/2 will wake up the process that has waited the longest when an instance of the pipe becomes available. The *unblocked* process should then reissue **DosOpen** to connect to the pipe.

Information Exchange Using File Semantics

Once a pipe is in the *CONNECTED* state, server and client processes can use the regular OS/2 file-subsystem calls to communicate over it as follows:

- **DosWrite** or **DosWriteAsync** are issued to write data to a pipe.
- **DosRead** or **DosReadAsync** are issued to read data from a pipe.
- **DosBufReset** is used to synchronize read and write dialogs. It does this by blocking the calling process at one end of the pipe until all the data it has written has been read at the other end of a pipe.

Transaction Processing With Named Pipes

Named Pipes support two API calls that are ideally suited for transaction processing: **DosTransactNPipe** and **DosCallNPipe**. These two calls can only be issued on a duplex message pipe that is setup for the message-stream mode.

DosTransactNPipe: This API call writes a message and receives a reply in one single operation. The request/reply pair can be used to trigger a transaction or a Remote Procedure Call. If the pipe contains unread data or is not a message pipe, the call fails. The call will not return until a complete message is read. **DosTransactNPipe** is typically issued over "persistent" connections. In this type of connection, several transactions are usually issued over an open pipe before the connection is terminated. The persistent connection is appropriate for remote pipes because their overhead for establishing connections is high.

DosCallNPipe: This API call combines a **DosOpen**, **DosTransactNPipe**, and a **DosClose** in a single operation. It is used in "non-persistent" connections that get established and terminated just to issue a single Remote Procedure Call. Non-persistent connections are ideal for simple request/reply transactions.

Terminating a Named Pipe Dialog

When a client process is through using a Named Pipe, it closes the pipe by issuing a **DosClose**. This is the same OS/2 call that is used for closing regular files. The pipe is now in the *CLOSING* state. The server process can then issue a **DosDisConnectNPipe**, which puts the pipe in a *DISCONNECTED* state. The server can then issue another **DosConnectNPipe** and wait for the next client. This allows the server to create the Named Pipe and reuse it to communicate with many clients without having to recreate the pipe each time. The server can always close the Named Pipe for good by using issuing **DosClose**. A server may also issue a **DosClose** without a preceding **DosDisConnectNPipe**. This will free the pipe handle and still enable the client to read any data remaining in the buffer. However, a closed pipe cannot be reused again without reissuing **DosCreateNPipe**.

If the client end of the pipe is open when **DosDisConnectNPipe** is issued, it is forced to close and the client gets an error code on its next operation. Forcing the client end to close prematurely may cause data to be discarded that has not yet been read by the client. A client that gets forced off a pipe by a **DosDisConnectNPipe** must issue **DosClose** to free the handle resource.

Although **DosDisConnectNPipe** makes the client's handle invalid, it does not free the resource. Any threads that are blocked on the pipe are awakened by **DosDisConnectN-Pipe**. A thread blocked on the pipe by a **DosWrite** returns ERROR_BROKEN_PIPE.

A thread blocked on the pipe by a **DosRead** returns an **EOF** indicator. In general, forced disconnects should be avoided. You can do that by providing a user enforced protocol for gracefully shutting down a pipe.

Using Semaphores With Named Pipes

Event semaphores can be used with a local Named Pipe to notify a process that data has arrived or that write space has become available. A reading process can use **DosWaitE-ventSem** or **DosWaitMuxWaitSem** to wait for data to arrive on one or more pipes. This avoids more costly methods, such as dedicating a thread for each incoming pipe or polling each pipe with no-wait mode. The **DosSetNPipeSem** call is used to associate a semaphore with an instance of a local Named Pipe. But, first make sure you create the event semaphore using **DosCreateEventSem** with the semaphore in the *reset* state. If an attempt is made to attach a semaphore to a remote Named Pipe, ERROR_INVA-LID_FUNCTION is returned. Up to two event semaphores may be attached to a pipe, one for the server and one for the client. If there is already a semaphore associated with one end of the pipe, that semaphore is replaced. OS/2 will clear the semaphore whenever new data is available, whenever buffer space is available for a write, or whenever either side closes the pipe. An application is notified of this event through the regular semaphore calls (examples include DosWaitMuxWaitSem or DosWaitE-ventSem).

A server process can monitor multiple pipes by: 1) creating an event semaphore for each pipe, 2) attaching the event semaphore to the pipe by issuing **DosSetNPipeSem**, 3) calling **DosCreateMuxWaitSem** specifying that it will wait on *any* of the event semaphores, and 4) calling **DosWaitMuxWaitSem** to be notified the next time data is read or written on the other end of any of the pipes.

A process can check the state of the Named Pipe semaphores by issuing **DosQueryN-PipeSemState**. This call returns information about local Named Pipes attached to a specific system semaphore, as well as additional information about the I/O that can be performed on the set of pipes. This information can be scanned to determine which pipes can be read or written. In addition, this call provides all the information about the event that triggered the clearing of a semaphore associated with a particular pipe handle (through DosSetNPipeSem).

Obtaining and Modifying Pipe Information

A process can peek at data from a Named Pipe without removing the data by issuing **DosPeekNPipe**. This call also returns the state of the pipe. A process can obtain general information about a pipe by issuing **DosQueryNPipeInfo**. The information returned includes the input and output buffer sizes, the maximum number of allowed pipe instances, the current number of pipe instances, and the name of the pipe including the server's computer name if the pipe is remote.

By issuing **DosQueryNPHState**, a process can obtain information on the current state of the pipe, the current number of pipe instances, the pipe's direction, and what type of pipe it is.

A process can modify the state of a pipe through the **DosSetNPHState** call. This call is issued to change the mode of a pipe from byte stream to message stream or vice versa, and to change the wait/no-wait mode. This call will be used mostly by clients to modify the default **DosOpen** which always opens Named Pipes with the wait mode enabled and sets the pipe to read the pipe in byte stream mode.

Named Pipes State Transitions

Named Pipes may be in one of several states depending on the actions that have been taken on it by the server and client ends. The state/action diagram in Table 15-1 summarizes the valid state transitions.

Table 15-1. The Named Pipes State Transition Table.

Current State	Action		Next State
	From	**API Call**	
none	server	DosCreateNPipe	DISCONNECTED
DISCONNECTED	server	DosConnectNPipe	LISTENING
LISTENING	client	DosOpen	CONNECTED
CONNECTED	server	DosDisConnectNPipe	DISCONNECTED
CONNECTED	client	DosClose	CLOSING
CLOSING	server	DosDisconnectNPipe	DISCONNECTED
CONNECTED	server	DosClose	CLOSING

THE ANATOMY OF A NAMED PIPES PROGRAM

This section summarizes how Named Pipes are used by describing the anatomy of a typical Named Pipe program:

1. *Create the Named Pipe*. The server side of an application creates a Named Pipe by issuing DosCreateNPipe. The instances parameter specifies how many clients can use this pipe concurrently.

2. *Wait for the clients to connect*. The server application creates as many threads as the number of simultaneous clients it wants to service. Each "server" thread issues a DosConnectNPipe and blocks waiting for a client to connect to the other end of the pipe instance.

3. *Establish the connection with the clients*. The clients connect to their end of the pipe by issuing a DosOpen or DosCallNPipe (which performs the DosOpen auto-

matically). Each successful DosOpen returns a unique handle to the pipe. On the server side, the DosConnectNPipe succeeds.

4. ***Conduct your business***. After both sides of a pipe are connected, they can begin to conduct their business using one of two dialog styles:

   • By maintaining a *persistent* pipe connection. Here the client and the server conduct multiple message exchanges over the pipe. This is like carrying out a long conversation over the telephone. A *conversational dialog* typically uses calls like DosWrite, DosRead, and DosTransactNPipe.
   • By maintaining a *non-persistent* pipe connection. Here the client and the server conduct a *transactional dialog*, which typically consists of a single request/reply exchange after which both parties disconnect from their end of the pipe. A transactional dialog is conducted by issuing calls such as DosCallNPipe on the client side and DosTransactNPipe on the server side. Non-persistent pipes cost you setup time, but the benefit is that the pipe instance can be serially reused by other clients. This is useful in situations where one server may be required to talk to hundreds of clients.

5. ***Disconnect and take the next call***. When the business is completed, the server side of the pipe issues a DosDisconnectNPipe and the client issues a DosClose (DosCallNPipe performs a DosClose automatically). The server can then execute another DosConnectNPipe and wait on the next client to call.

6. ***Terminate the pipe***. When the server thread wants to stop accepting calls from clients it issues a DosClose to delete that instance of the Named Pipe. When the last instance is closed, the pipe no longer exists.

NAMED PIPES SCENARIOS

The scenarios that follow will help demonstrate the use of Named Pipes in environments that require interprocess data exchanges. Once you grasp the mechanics of Named Pipe usage, you can create your own repertoire of API sequences using our scenarios as a starting point.

Scenario 1: A Simple Transaction Involving Two Processes

Scenario 1 consists of a simple transaction which results in a single request/reply data exchange. A typical example is a simple banking transaction to query an account, such as:

```
What is Bob's Balance?      ──────→

                     ←──────      $300
```

We implement this simple transaction three different ways:

- The first implementation of Scenario 1 uses file-oriented Named Pipe calls exclusively (see Figure 15-1).
- The second implementation of Scenario 1 refines the client by introducing the use of **DosTransactNPipe** (see Figure 15-2).
- The third implementation of Scenario 1 further refines the client by introducing the use of **DosCallNPipe** (see Figure 15-3).

Clearly, the third implementation of scenario 1 is the most elegant and economical way to design simple *transactional dialogs*. The **DosCallNPipe** was designed specifically for a single request/reply exchange over a non-persistent connection. This call is sometimes referred to in the OS/2 literature as the *Remote Procedure Call*. What this means is that DosCallNPipe can be used to implement a request/reply exchange using the semantics of a procedure call. To get Bob's account, you would call a local procedure stub with "Bob" as the argument. The local stub, in turn, creates a message and issues DosCallNPipe. On the server side, the arrival of the message results in the invocation of a server procedure that calculates Bob's balance and returns the result: $300. The result is returned to the client stub over the Named Pipe. The client stub *unblocks* and returns the result to its caller.

The effect of this Remote Procedure Call is to introduce procedure-like semantics for interprocess communications. From the point of view of Named Pipes, however, it does not really matter how the interface is presented to the user or what data gets passed on the pipe. The pipe is simply a super-efficient delivery mechanism which can be used either "raw" or through a presentation forms such as the Remote Procedure Call.

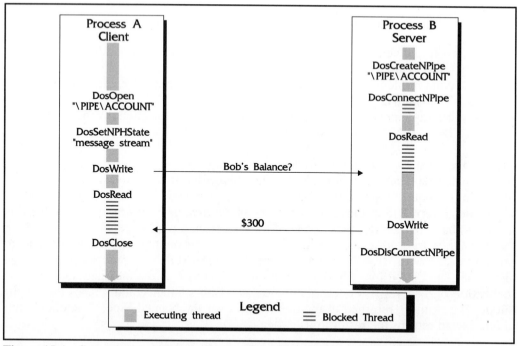

Figure 15-1. Scenario 1a: A Simple Transaction Using File Service Named Pipe Calls.

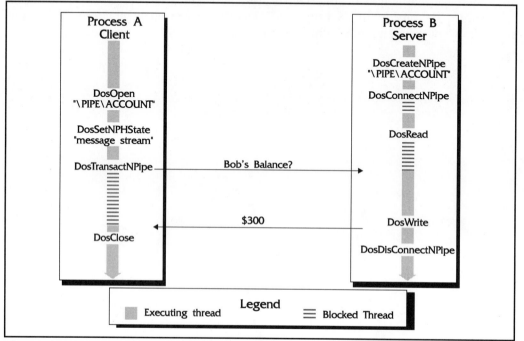

Figure 15-2. Scenario 1b: A Simple Transaction Using DosTransactNPipe.

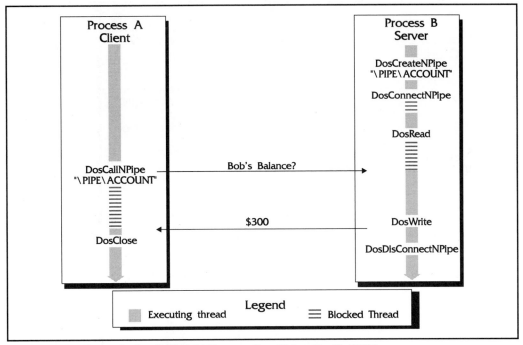

Figure 15-3. Scenario 1c: A Simple Transaction Using DosCallNPipe.

Scenario 2: One Server Multiple Clients Using a Single Pipe Instance

Scenario 2 shows how a single pipe instance may be used to serially service two clients (see Figure 15-4). The scenario can easily be expanded to "n" clients. We assume that all the clients will be executing simple transactions, such as the one described in Scenario 1. The key point to notice in the scenario is how the server reconnects the Named Pipe to allow other clients to use it. In Scenario 2, the server services Process 1 followed by Process 2. We assume that the time-out values on **DosCallNPipe** are large enough to keep a process blocked until the server frees up.

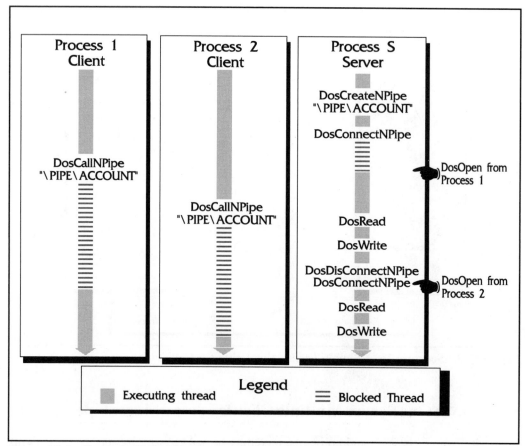

Figure 15-4. Scenario 2: Serially Reusing a Named Pipe Instance.

Scenario 3: A Multithreaded Server Using Multiple Pipe Instances

Scenario 3 shows how a single pipe with multiple instances can be used to accommodate two clients (see Figure 15-5). The scenario can easily be extended to "n" clients. We will assume in the scenario that the client transactions are persistent, meaning that multiple simple transactions will be issued over a single pipe connection. The server must also be capable of providing simultaneous service for up to two clients over the well-known pipe: \PIPE\ACCOUNT. Here are some observations that are pertinent to how this scenario plays out:

1. The scenario starts out with the server process creating two server threads; each handles an instance of the pipe. Each pipe instance will be used to service a client process, meaning that up to two clients can open \PIPE\ACCOUNT simultaneously.

2. Each server thread issues a **DosCreateNPipe** to create the pipe \PIPE\ACCOUNT with two instances specified. OS/2 returns a separate handle for each pipe instance.

The server thread will then use the returned handle to manage its instance of the pipe and connect to a client through **DosConnectNPipe**.

3. In Scenario 3, all the threads execute concurrently. At any one time, only one thread is running and only one message is going through the pipe. OS/2 will make sure that all messages get to their appropriate thread. A thread need not be aware that it is sharing the pipe with other threads. If there are more clients than there are server threads, then the additional clients will get a busy return when they try to do a **DosOpen**. For systems that need to support large number of clients, you may want to implement a non-persistent server thread pool in addition to the persistent server thread pool shown in Scenario 3.

4. A non-persistent thread is similar to the server thread in Scenario 2. It conducts its business with a client and disconnects as soon as it is able to do so.

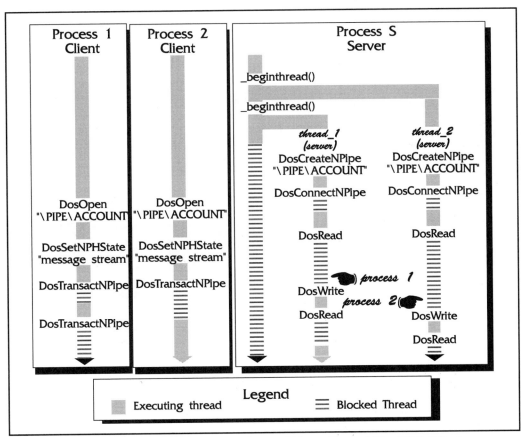

Figure 15-5. Scenario 3: A Multithreaded Server Using a Named Pipe With 2 Instances.

Scenario 4: Sending Bulk Data Over a Named Pipe

Scenario 4 shows how moving bulk data, such as a file transfer, can be implemented over a Named Pipe (see Figure 15-6). Initially, the server is blocked waiting for the client. The client starts the file transfer by telling the server, through a **DosTransactN-Pipe** transaction that it is about to receive a file and gives it the name of the file and its size. The server says "OK" and issues a **DosRead** waiting on the first file segment to arrive. The file copy gets done through a series of exchanges. Eventually, the server finishes consuming the file and sends a message to the client saying the file got there OK; then both sides break their end of the pipe.

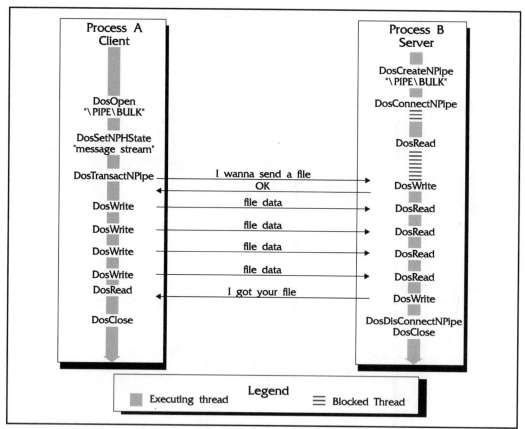

Figure 15-6. Scenario 4: Moving Bulk Data Over a Named Pipe.

Chapter 16

A Generic Client/Server File Transfer Service

By the time you finish this chapter, you will have accomplished five worthy goals:

1. You will have learned how to design and build communicating programs using layered software techniques.
2. You will have learned how to create a server program that provides a file repository service to its clients. Clients will be able to store and retrieve files using the server.
3. You will have learned how to use Dynamic Link Libraries (DLLs) to provide flexible run-time services and operating system extensions.
4. You will have walked through the design of a *protocol independent interface* to the service layer that moves the data between processes.
5. You will have walked through **FXREQ.C** and **FXSVR.C**, the code for the protocol-independent client and server components of a generic file transfer service. These two programs will be used to benchmark the performance of IPC and LAN protocols.

In this chapter, we create the topmost layers of an application that is used to measure the performance of various interprocess communication techniques. These topmost layers provide a generic file transfer protocol that can be used to move data or files between two processes. The protocol is *generic* in the sense that it is independent of the underlying IPC or LAN communication service. The same calls will execute on top of Named Pipes, NetBIOS, APPC/CPI-C, TCP/IP Sockets, LAN Server, and NetWare. They will serve as our level playing field for running BLOB Transfer Olympics. But we can't say anymore right now about these Olympics—we don't want to ruin the suspense!

The generic file transfer is performed by two programs, **FXREQ.C** and **FXSVR.C**, which respectively implement the client and server portions of the distributed application. These programs also measure the performance of the file transfer and display the results. The actual file transfer is done using the underlying IPC and LAN protocols. In Part II, the underlying IPC is provided by local Named Pipes. In Part III, the underlying IPC is provided by the LAN peer-to-peer protocols, the Network Operating Systems, and remote Named Pipes.

LAYERING AND CLIENT/SERVER SOFTWARE DESIGN

Layering is a software design technique used to break down complex programs into a hierarchy of services. Powerful new services can be provided by adding new layers on top of more primitive service layers. A service interface defines the services provided by an underlying layer to the layers above it.

Layering also provides an ideal framework for explaining and organizing the communications between two independent programs. Program-to-program communications is broken down into exchanges between the corresponding peer layers in each program. The following three concepts form the basis for the layered approach:

1. At each layer, client and server peers cooperate jointly to provide a service. Of course, one peer can end up doing all of the work, but the service is still considered to be a joint effort by the peers for that layer. The *protocol* is the contract the peers abide by. It specifies how the work is divided among the peers, the semantics of the message exchanges for that layer, and the handshake sequences.
2. Each layer builds on top of the services provided by the layers beneath it. A *service interface* specifies how a layer can obtain access to the services of the layer directly below it. The interface should hide all the nasty details of the workings of the underlying layer while providing a complete set of services.
3. Services become more abstract the higher the layer. For example, the lower layers may be concerned with the interfaces to the hardware or the operating system, while the higher layers may provide a more application-specific type of service, such as a file transfer.

We will apply layering techniques to the design of a client/server file repository. The server can be used to store all kinds of large data objects such as: documents, images, video, voice, metafiles, and database snapshots. We will use the file transfer service to compare how the IPC and LAN protocols perform when it comes to moving large data objects.

Our layered model of the file transfer service breaks the client and server programs into three layers (see Figure 16-1). We now discuss the function each layer provides starting with the top layer.

The Application Layer

This layer provides timers which calculate and display the performance of the file transfers. The timers calculate and display the overhead for establishing a connection between the client and server, the total number of bytes transferred, the average transfer rate in KBytes/sec, and the overhead for closing a connection. The application layer is provided jointly by two programs: **FXREQ.C** on the client side and **FXSVR.C** on the server side.

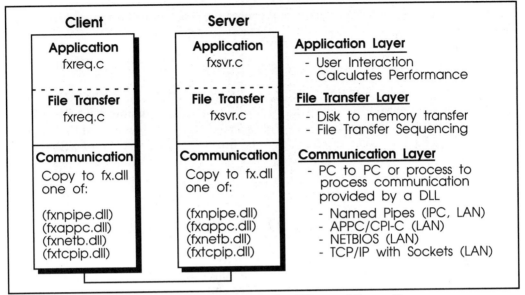

Figure 16-1. A Layered Model of the File Transfer Client and Server Programs.

The File Transfer Layer

This layer provides a logical file transfer protocol for moving the file from a client to the server and vice versa. The protocol includes a method for requesting a remote service as well as an implementation of the requested service. Of course, the only services we currently provide are *Send* and *Receive* a file, both of which use the same interprocess file transfer protocol. This protocol specifies how a service is requested, the handshaking for transferring the file, and the message structures used. The file transfer layer only provides the logical protocol. It *delegates* the actual moving of the data to the layers below it. The requests to the layer below are communicated through a generic service interface which we will define later in this chapter. The file transfer layer function is provided jointly by **FXREQ.C** on the client side, and **FXSVR.C** on the server side.

The Communication Layer

This layer performs the actual movement of data between processes. If the client and server processes are in the same machine, the communications is provided by the Named Pipes IPC. If the client and server processes are on separate machines, the communications is provided using one of OS/2's LAN-based protocols. The communication layer implements the generic interface calls using either **Named Pipes**, **NetBIOS**, **APPC/CPI-C**, **TCP/IP**, etc. Each of these implementations will be packaged as a Dynamic Link Library (DLL). Before running a benchmark test, the appropriate (.DLL) file gets copied into FX.DLL. Both FXREQ.EXE and FXSVR.EXE will be linked dynamically to FX.DLL to create the client process and server processes of the benchmark program. The code that implements the DLLs will be introduced as follows:

- In Chapter 17, "FX Using Named Pipes," we develop **FXNPIPE.DLL** which will move the data using Named Pipes.
- In Part III, we introduce **FXAPPC.DLL**, **FXNETB.DLL**, and **FXTCPIP.DLL** to move the data across the network. We will also be introducing **FXNPIPE.DLL** again to perform the remote Named Pipe service over both Novell and LAN Server networks. Each of these programs will be linked dynamically with **FXSVR.EXE** and **FXREQ.EXE** to produce the respective server and client versions of the program.

A PROTOCOL-INDEPENDENT GENERIC INTERFACE

This section defines the service level interface between the File Transfer layer and the Communications Layer (see Figure 16-2). This interface will drive the different IPC and LAN protocols and will be used to measure and compare the performance of the various protocols. This interface should mask the details of the underlying layer while providing the required service. We also have an additional design challenge: how to package this interface so that it can work with the different underlying protocols? As you can see in Figure 16-2, we face quite a challenge. The generic interface should work for Named Pipes, APPC/CPI-C, TCP/IP Sockets, and NetBIOS. This means the same set of calls can be issued from the upper layer and still work transparently on any of those protocols. So where do we start with our design?

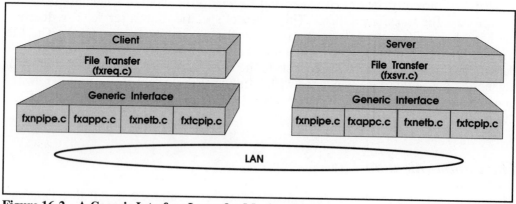

Figure 16-2. A Generic Interface Layer for Moving Data.

The Art of Defining a Service Level Interface

We first have to decide which services will be offered by the communication layer, while keeping in mind that:

1. The communication layer exists to service the file transfer layer.

2. The services required should be supported by the underlying IPCs or LAN protocols.

The approach we take is to look at the interface from both a top-down and bottom-up perspective and then balance the set of requirements. The top-down perspective defines the set of services required by a generic file transfer layer to do its job. The bottom-up perspective introduces the constraints that are specific to IPCs or LAN protocols.

What Is Required From the Top Down?

Looking at the service requirements top-down, the file transfer layer consists of two communicating peers: a client and a server. These peers first need to establish some kind of a connection or "rendezvous." The client needs to indicate to the server what type of service it needs performed. Then the two sides need to send and receive the file data. Finally, there should be some way to break a connection.

What Is Required Bottom-Up?

Looking at the service requirements bottom-up, the IPC or LAN protocol needs to be initialized with parameters that are going to be different for each LAN protocol or IPC. In addition, the LAN protocol or IPC has to be told what to connect to and when. The implementation of a connection will be different for each of the protocols. Servers need to be told to listen for incoming requests. Data needs to be exchanged. Finally, the IPC or LAN protocol has to be told when to break the connection.

Choosing the "Right" Interface Calls

You do not have the necessary background, at this point, to determine the specifics of what each IPC and LAN protocol needs to do its job. This means you will have to trust us to come up with a solution. We get to specify the interface without having to justify all "the wisdom" that went behind our choice! So after many aborted efforts at combining the top-down and bottom-up requirements, we propose the following generic interface which we name **FX**:

*   fx_Initialize(buffer_pointer, size)
*   fx_MakePipe()*
*   fx_ConnectPipe()*
*   fx_DisconnectPipe()*
*   fx_Open()**
*   fx_Write(Buffer, Bufferlength, BytesWritten)
*   fx_Read(Buffer, Bufferlength, BytesRead)
*   fx_Transact(InBuffer, InBufferLength, OutBuffer, OutBufferLength, BytesRead)

- fx_Close()

Note: Calls with an * are server-specific. Calls with ** are client-specific. The remaining calls can be issued by either servers or clients.

How Does the FX Interface Compare With Named Pipes?

The FX interface consists of general-purpose service calls that *emulate* the functions of the very flexible and state-of-the-art Named Pipes API. The FX interface can support almost any form of interprocess data transfer. It can be used for transaction processing as well as for the bulk movement of data required by file transfer protocols. You should already be familiar with the FX calls; if not, please take a few minutes to review the Named Pipes tutorial in Chapter 15. We borrowed the *flavor and function* of the Named Pipes protocol. But make no mistake, this is our own private FX service call interface. Our calls look like the Named Pipes API, but in fact, they all start with **fx_**, meaning that they are special procedures that we've implemented.

Notice that many of the FX calls do not pass parameters, but their Named Pipes counterparts do. This is because most of the required parameters are specific to the underlying protocols. Rather than making the interface overly complicated, we are passing the required information through a protocol-specific configuration file when we issue **fx_Initialize**. The Named Pipes API does not support a counterpart of **fx_Initialize**. We introduced **fx_Initialize** to initialize the various protocols by having them read a protocol-specific configuration. Each protocol will then do whatever it takes to obtain its required resources based on the user-specified configuration parameters. The service layer will also allocate a communication buffer of a size specified in the configuration file as part of **fx_Initialize**. A pointer to that buffer, as well as the buffer size, is returned to the caller.

Does this choice of interface give Named Pipes a competitive advantage over the other protocols? Perhaps a very slight one, and we may have to take that into account when we come up with our final verdict on which protocol wins.

How to Package a Service Layer?

We have to determine how the program layers are going to be packaged, because it will influence the method by which the services get invoked. We made the choice to package the various implementations of the FX functions in DLLs, which get linked to **FXREQ.EXE** and **FXSVR.EXE** at run time. It may be instructive, however, to walk through the thought process that got us there. We had three packaging options to choose from:

1. The communication layer could be packaged as a *separate process*. In this case, the communications between layers would take place through an IPC.

2. The communication layer could be packaged as a *module of code* that gets combined with the other modules that form the program through static linking. The invocation of services in this case is through calls to external procedures that get resolved at link time.

3. The communication layer could be packaged as a *Dynamic Link Library*. With standard libraries, such as the C-language run-time library, the code is combined with the program code when the program is created. With DLLs, the code is not combined. Instead, the program contains an import record of the function and the name of the DLL which implements it. The function is not linked until the program needs it. The invocation of services would work very much like OS/2's API. We could even advertise our "added services" as an operating system extension!

Packaging FX Using Dynamic Link Libraries

The choice was made to go with the third option for the following reasons:

*   DLLs provide new opportunities for packaging and distributing software. Our project will serve as an excellent example on how DLLs can be used to package OS/2 programs.
*   Dynamic Link Libraries permit library functions to be changed without recompiling or relinking the programs that call them. This is very important to us because our project requires us to run **FXREQ** and **FXSVR** on a multiplicity of IPC and LAN platforms. One easy way to provide this function is to link to the different libraries that implement the protocols at run time. We can then change the underlying protocol or IPC by just using a different DLL.
*   Dynamic Link Libraries make it possible for common functions to be shared by different programs while maintaining a single copy of the function in memory. This means that both **FXREQ** and **FXSVR** can use the same copy of the DLL when their code runs in the same machine.
*   The operation of dynamic linking is largely transparent to the user. A function in a Dynamic Link Library is declared like any other external call. You call a DLL function like you would call any ordinary procedure in a statically linked library. The only immediate visible difference is smaller (.EXE) files since the procedure is not copied to your executable file as in static linking.

A TUTORIAL ON DYNAMIC LINK LIBRARIES

What Is a DLL?

Dynamic linking lets a program gain access to functions at run time that are not part of its executable code. DLLs make it possible for you to use the same code without making it part of any single application. DLLs can be bound to an (.EXE) file when the application loads, or later on demand, during the execution of an application. Once a

DLL is loaded, it can be shared with any other program that needs it. A function in a DLL library is called like any statically linked procedure in your code. The DLL code executes as part of the calling thread or process and the DLL function gets its arguments from the calling program's stack. Dynamic Linking has become the standardized mechanism for attaching add-ins to OS/2.

The Module-Definition File

Each DLL library must provide some mechanism to make its functions directly available to other modules. The vehicle provided by OS/2 to do that is a module-definition (.DEF) file. This is a plain text file that describes the name of the DLL the functions it exports and other attributes.

The IMPLIB Utility

Once you've created the (.DEF) file, the **IMPLIB** utility is used to create a (.LIB) file which can be added to the list of library files a module can link to. The (.LIB) file does not contain the code for the library functions. However, it does contain the information that tells the (.EXE) file which (.DLL) is to be invoked to perform a function.

Creating the DLL

The source code for the function that provides the DLL is first compiled normally into an (.OBJ) file. You must specify the **/Ge-** compile flag that tells C Set/2 you're creating DLLs (and not EXEs). C Set/2 will then figure out which of its run-time libraries to include in the link step. You then use the LINK386 linker to create the (.DLL) file from the (.OBJ).

Loading and Executing an Application That Uses DLLs

OS/2 examines an application's (.EXE) file at load time for the special records that indicate references to DLLs. If such records are found, the operating system finds the (.DLL) file on disk and loads it into memory *if it is not already there*. It also puts the addresses for the DLL functions in the special records so that the application can place its calls. The DLLs will stay in memory until all the applications that use its services are terminated.

DLLs That Are Managed by an Application at Run Time

The tutorial has so far focused on DLLs that are loaded by OS/2 and made available to the application at run time. The whole DLL process is totally invisible to your programs. A DLL function is called just like any other function. It is OS/2's responsibility to make sure the function is there when you need it. All this is very convenient, but what happens if you want to add a new function to the system at run time? This is where OS/2's super flexible *run time dynamic linking* service comes to play.

Here's what this service allows you to do:

1. Your application can be created without any prior knowledge of the DLL.
2. At run time, your application can issue a **DosLoadModule** call to tell OS/2 to load a DLL module.
3. Your application then issues a **DosQueryProcAddr** call to obtain the address of a DLL function in that module.
4. Your application then invokes the DLL function.
5. Your application can then unload from memory the DLL module by issuing a **DosFreeModule** call. Or, you can choose not to do that and leave the DLL in memory for performance reasons.

What this means is that you can have it both ways. You can let OS/2 manage DLLs on your behalf; or, you can do it all yourself. If you know ahead of time which functions are going to execute, then you're better off letting OS/2 manage the DLLs for you. If you need maximum flexibility (for example you may be adding new commands at run time), then you're better off managing the DLLs yourself.

HOW THE FX DLLS ARE BUILT

The plan is to build each of our IPC and LAN implementations of FX as a separate (.DLL) file. Thus, in future chapters, we will build the following (.DLL) files out of corresponding (.C) files: fxnpipe.dll, fxnetb.dll, fxtcpip.dll, and fxappc.dll. The **FXREQ.EXE** and **FXSVR.EXE** programs we create in this chapter dynamically link to **FX.DLL** at run time to obtain the FX services. We know ahead of time what our FX functions look like, so we'll let OS/2 load and manage the FX DLLs. The **FX.DLL** file will contain a copy of the IPC or LAN protocol (.DLL) file needed to run a particular benchmark. So what do we need to do to build our system?

The FX.DEF Import Library

The first thing we need to create is the **FX.DEF** file, which provides the name of the DLL and the functions it exports. This file is shown in Figure 16-3. The first line says that this a DLL library named FX and that we want it to be initialized each time it is called by a different application. The next nine lines specify the name of the FX

```
LIBRARY FX INITINSTANCE
EXPORTS fx_Initialize
EXPORTS fx_MakePipe
EXPORTS fx_ConnectPipe
EXPORTS fx_DisconnectPipe
EXPORTS fx_Open
EXPORTS fx_Write
EXPORTS fx_Read
EXPORTS fx_Transact
EXPORTS fx_Close
DATA MULTIPLE NONSHARED
```

Figure 16-3.   The FX.DEF Import Library.

functions which will be exported by FX to other applications. The last line specifies that a different data segment needs to be loaded for each application that uses FX. We do this to maintain separate copies of the FX variables and stack for each running program that uses FX.DLL.

Making the FX Programs

We are now ready for the make process. We will build the FX programs using two separate make files: **FXEXE.MAK**, which creates the (.EXE) programs, and **FXDLL.MAK**, which creates the DLLs. We could have combined those two files into one make file but it would have been harder to follow.

FXEXE.MAK

Let's first walk through **FXEXE.MAK** (see Figure 16-4). From the ALL statement you can tell that this make file is responsible for building one (.LIB) library file and three (.EXE) programs:

```
all:    fx.lib fxsvr.exe fxreq.exe fxlsvr.exe
```

The ALL statement specifies that FX.LIB is the first thing to be built. NMAKE obliges by applying the **.def.lib** inference rule which runs FX.DEF through IMPLIB to generate FX.LIB. The next thing on the ALL agenda is to build FXSVR.EXE, FXREQ.EXE, and FXLSVR.EXE. NMAKE does that by compiling the (.C) files into (.EXE) files. Note that the FX.LIB, which was built in the previous step, is now included with the link libraries for creating (.EXE) files. Remember from the tutorial that FX.LIB does not contain any code; it just provides the stubs to access the services of a FX.DLL.

```
#*********************************************************************
# Make File for FX Program .EXEs
#*********************************************************************

#** MACROS ***********************************************************
cflags=/C /Ti /Q+ /Sm /Gs- /Gm+ /Ge+ /Gd+
exe_lflags=/ST:15000/SE:1024/CO/NOLOGO/NOI/L/M:FULL/PM:VIO
exe_libs=fx

#** INFERENCE RULES **************************************************
.SUFFIXES: .lib .def              # non-default extensions need definition

.obj.exe:
      echo LINKING   $** to create $*.exe
      link386 $(exe_lflags) $**,, nul, $(exe_libs),;

.c.obj:
      echo COMPILING $*.c
      icc $(cflags) $*.c

.def.lib:
      echo CREATING  $*.lib import library
      implib /NOLOGO $*.lib $*.def

#** BUILD STATEMENTS *************************************************
all: fx.lib fxsvr.exe fxreq.exe fxlsvr.exe

fx.lib:      fx.def                    # create library for fx dll

fxsvr.exe:   fxsvr.obj                 # create server executable module
fxsvr.obj:   fxsvr.c
fxreq.exe:   fxreq.obj                 # create requester executable module
fxreq.obj:   fxreq.c

fxlsvr.exe:  fxlsvr.obj                # create LAN Server file transfer
fxlsvr.obj:  fxlsvr.c                  #  program
```

Figure 16-4.   The FXEXE.MAK Make File.

FXDLL.MAK

Let's now walk through **FXDLL.MAK** (see Figure 16-5). From the ALL statement, you can tell that this make file is responsible for building four (.DLL) modules:

```
all: fxnpipe.dll fxnetb.dll fxappc.dll fxtcpip.dll
```

These are the (.DLL) files for the various protocols and IPCs. Of course, we first have to develop the (.C) code in the upcoming chapters before anything can be built.

We tell C Set/2 that we're creating DLLs by enabling the **Ge-** flag. C Set/2 will then figure out which of its run time libraries to include. The only other odd step involved in building DLLs is that they have their own link libraries (see the **dll_libs** macro definition in Figure 16-5). The **ACS** library is needed by the NetBIOS LAN protocol, the **CPIC** library is needed by APPC/CPI-C, and the **TCPIPDLL** library is needed by TCP/IP sockets. These libraries are provided by the respective products. The C Set/2 run time for DLLs is provided automatically by setting the **/Gd+** compiler flag. Notice that the **FX.DEF** file is included in the link step.

```
#******************************************************************************
# Make File for FX program .DLLs
#******************************************************************************

#** MACROS ********************************************************************
cflags=/C /Ti /Q+ /Sm /Gs- /Gm+ /Ge- /Gd+
dll_lflags=/ST:15000/SE:1024/CO/NOLOGO/NOI/L/M:FULL/PM:VIO
dll_libs=acs cpic tcpipdll  # standard libraries for NetBIOS, APPC, and TCP/IP

#** INFERENCE RULES ***********************************************************

.obj.dll:
      echo LINKING   $** to create $*.dll
      LINK386 $(dll_lflags) $**,$*.dll, nul, $(dll_libs), fx.def;

.c.obj:
      echo COMPILING $*.c
      icc $(cflags) $*.c

#** BUILD STATEMENTS **********************************************************
all: fxnpipe.dll fxnetb.dll fxappc.dll fxtcpip.dll

fxnpipe.dll: fxnpipe.obj              # create named pipe dll
fxnpipe.obj: fxnpipe.c
fxnetb.dll:  fxnetb.obj               # create NETBIOS dll
fxnetb.obj:  fxnetb.c
fxappc.dll:  fxappc.obj               # create APPC dll
fxappc.obj:  fxappc.c
fxtcpip.dll: fxtcpip.obj              # create TCP/IP dll
fxtcpip.obj: fxtcpip.c
```

Figure 16-5. The FXDLL.MAK Make File.

THE GENERIC FILE TRANSFER PROTOCOL

The best way to explain the workings of the file transfer layer is by demonstrating
through two scenarios how a file gets sent to the server (see Figure 16-7) and how a file
gets retrieved from the server (see Figure 16-8). The scenarios depict the exchange
from the perspective of file transfer layer (see Figure 16-6), and do not deal with the
mechanics of how the data gets moved between processes. We leave that for later
chapters. The scenarios describe the handshake part of the protocol: "who does what
and when." Protocols also specify the structure and meaning (or semantics) of the

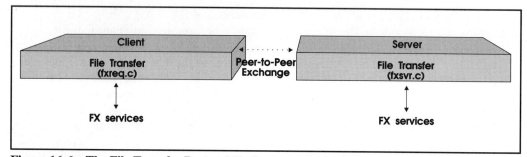

Figure 16-6. The File Transfer Protocol Exchange as Seen by the File Transfer Layer.

messages exchanged. So, we provide the message specifications for FX in the sections that follow the scenarios.

Walking Through the File Send Scenario

1. When the server first comes up, it issues **fx_Initialize**, which, initializes the underlying service layer (see Figure 16-7). It then calls **fx_MakePipe** to create an **FX PIPE**, followed by an **fx_ConnectPipe**, which waits for a client to connect to this instance of the pipe.
2. A client program is started by a user and told to send the file "test.txt" to the server.
3. The client program issues **fx_Initialize** to initialize its underlying service layer, followed by **fx_Open** to start a connection with the server.
4. Once the connection is made, the client prepares a FILE_SEND_TO_SERVER request packet, whose format is shown in Figure 16-9, and then issues **fx_Transact**, which sends the request packet and obtains the reply from the server all in one

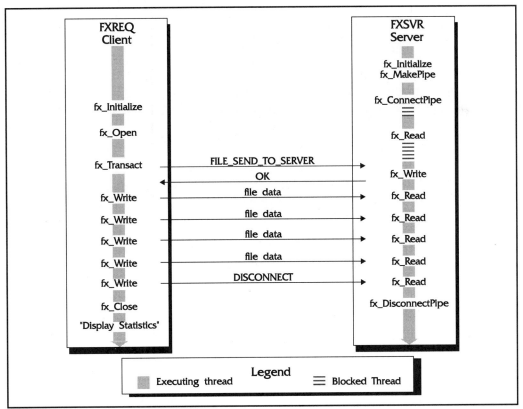

Figure 16-7. Sending a File Using FX.

operation. The reply packet format is shown in Figure 16-10. This request/reply exchange is an example of how FX may be used for simple transaction processing.

5. The server accepts the request for a file transfer and issues a **fx_Read**, which waits for the first packet of file data to arrive.

6. The client reads the file from disk and prepares a data packet which it sends to the server using **fx_Write**. This operation will be repeated until the entire file has been read from the disk and sent to the server. The data packet format is shown in Figure 16-11.

7. After the entire file is sent, the client prepares a DISCONNECT request packet (see Figure 16-9) and sends it to the server using **fx_Write**.

8. After receiving the DISCONNECT packet, the server issues **fx_DisconnectPipe** which frees the pipe for the next client.

9. The client issues **fx_Close** to close its end of the pipe. It then displays the file transfer performance statistics on the screen.

Walking Through the File Receive Scenario

This scenario is very similar to the file send scenario, with the following exceptions:

1. A client program is started by a user and told to *receive* the file "test.txt" from the server.

2. After the connection, the client sends a FILE_RECEIVE_FROM_SERVER request packet, whose format is shown in Figure 16-9, and then issues **fx_Transact**.

3. The direction of the file transfer is reversed.

The File Receive Scenario

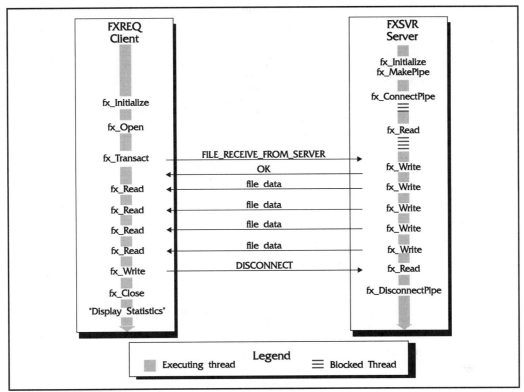

Figure 16-8.   **Retrieving a File From the Server Using FX.**

REQUEST_PACKET Format

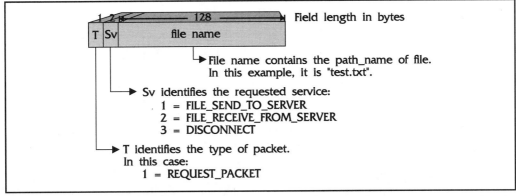

Figure 16-9.   **Format of the Request Packet.**

RESPONSE_PACKET Format

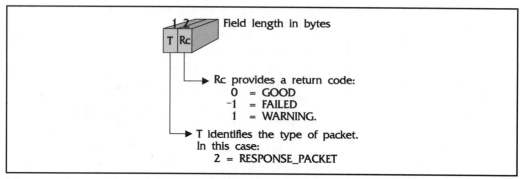

Figure 16-10.   Format of a Response Packet.

FILEDATA_PACKET Format

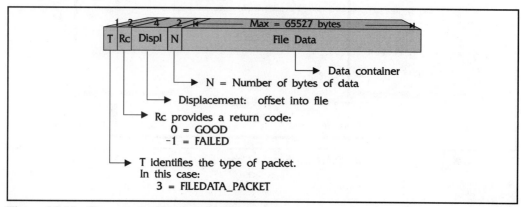

Figure 16-11.   Format of a File Data Packet.

The fields in the FILEDATA_PACKET (see Figure 16-11) require further explanation:

T   The **type** field specifies the format of the message (or packet). Our protocol supports three types of packets: request, response, and filedata. The type field acts as a signature that identifies the type of packet received.

Rc   This field contains the **return code**. You may wonder why a return code is sent with a data packet. The answer is that it provides an easy way to abort a file transfer. If, for example, the sender reads bad data from the file in the middle of a file transfer, it sends a FILEDATA_PACKET with a FAILED return code. This will cause the receiver to discontinue the file transfer. If we didn't have this field, we would need to add a new type of packet that provides an ABORT function.

Displ   The **displacement** field specifies the offset in bytes inside a file where the receiver is to write the data. Having the sender specify explicitly where to write the data protects against corrupting the received file. This can happen, for example, if a packet gets inadvertently retransmitted and the duplication is not recognized by the underlying protocol. Without the displacement field, the duplicate data gets written in the file starting at the current location. On the other hand, if the sender specifies the displacement, the worse that can happen is that the same information gets rewritten in the same file locations.

N   This field specifies the actual *number* of bytes of file data sent. This number will depend on how many bytes of data are read from the disk, which in turn depends on the disk read *block size*. The block size is specified by the user in the configuration file (see the following chapters). The file transfer layer obtains this block size when it calls **fx_Initialize**.

File Data This field can contain up to 65,527 bytes of *file data*. The actual number of bytes sent is specified by the **N** parameter.

HOW TO READ FXREQ.C

FXREQ.C, listed in Figure 16-12, is an implementation of the application and file transfer layers (see Figure 16-1) of a file client program. The file client program in conjunction with a file server program will be used for benchmarking the OS/2 LAN and IPC protocols.

FXREQ.C shares, with **FXSVR.C**, the use of the common include file: **FXFER.H**, listed in Figure 16-13. It also uses **FXREQ.H** a custom include file, listed in Figure 16-14.

The following is a list of general observations about the code:

- No OS/2 calls are used in this module. We have included **OS2.H** only to obtain the OS/2 data type definitions.
- The FX calls are not implemented in this module. They get implemented in the DLLs. The FX calls make extensive use of the OS/2 IPC and LAN APIs.
- Since there is no new OS/2 material to introduce, we assume that walking through the code will be a straightforward exercise in reading C listings. However, here are some simple directions that can help you in your reading:

  1. Start with **main()**, which serves as the outline for the program.
  2. Use the scenarios (see Figure 16-7 and Figure 16-8) as your protocol guide. The code is no more than the implementation of the scenarios.
  3. Use the message structures (see Figure 16-9 through Figure 16-11) as your guide to the data structures used in the program.

- Make sure you read the sections of the code that implement the gathering and display of file transfer performance statistics. The end goal of this project is to come up with an equitable benchmark, and it's your job to keep us honest!
- Make sure you understand how the FX calls are used. It is important to develop a user's perspective of FX to better understand the implementations of FX in the chapters that follow.

FXREQ.C LISTING

```c
/*****************************************************************************/
/*  PROGRAM NAME: FXREQ - File Transfer example,  requester module (client)  */
/*                                                                           */
/*  PROGRAM DESCRIPTION:  This module is the requester portion of a file     */
/*     transfer program.  This module uses communication functions modeled   */
/*     after named pipe functions to perform the file transfer.  The services*/
/*     are implemented in separate modules using NETBIOS, APPC, or named pipe*/
/*     communication for PC-PC communication.  Named pipes is used to        */
/*     implement a local file transfer between two processes.                */
/*                                                                           */
/*     A summary report is displayed showing how long it took to transfer    */
/*     the file.                                                             */
/*                                                                           */
/*  PROGRAM INVOCATION:                                                      */
/*                                                                           */
/*  FXREQ direction file-name                                                */
/*                                                                           */
/*     where:                                                                */
/*          direction is either SEND or RECV.                                */
/*                                                                           */
/*          file-name is the name of the file to transfer.  If a path is     */
/*                    specified the path must exist on the client and        */
/*                    server machines.                                       */
/*                                                                           */
/*          NOTE: The DLL for the protocol you wish to test must be copied    */
/*                to PROTOCOL.DLL in a subdirectory in your LIBPATH.          */
/*                                                                           */
/*                                                                           */
/*  EXAMPLE INVOCATIONS:                                                     */
/*                                                                           */
/*     FXREQ SEND MYFILE.TMP                                                 */
/*     FXREQ RECV MYFILE.TMP                                                 */
/*                                                                           */
/*****************************************************************************/
#include <process.h>               /* For exit()                           */
#include <stdio.h>                 /* For printf() & NULL                  */
#include <stdlib.h>                /* For printf                           */
#include <string.h>                /* For printf                           */
#include <sys\types.h>             /* For time()                           */
#include <sys\timeb.h>             /* For time()                           */
#include <sys\stat.h>              /* For stat()                           */
#include <io.h>                    /* For file I/O                         */
#include <fcntl.h>                 /* For file I/O                         */
#include <sys\types.h>             /* For file I/O                         */

#include <os2.h>                   /* for types only                       */
```

Figure 16-12 (Part 1 of 8). File Transfer Requester Program.

```
#include "fxfer.h"
#include "fxreq.h"

/*_____*/
/* Main routine. Performs a file transfer and calculates statistics.    */
/*_____*/
VOID main(SHORT argc, PCHAR argv[], PCHAR envp[])
{
    /*_____*/
    /* get command line arguments      */
    /*_____*/
    if (get_args(argc, argv))
       { print_help();
         exit(FAILED);
       }

    /*_____*/
    /* initialize requester            */
    /*_____*/
    initialize_requester();

    /*_____*/
    /* request service                 */
    /*_____*/
    switch (service)
       {
       case FILE_SEND_TO_SERVER:       open_file();
                                       request_file_transfer();
                                       send_file();
                                       break;

       case FILE_RECEIVE_FROM_SERVER:  open_file();
                                       request_file_transfer();
                                       receive_file();
                                       break;

       } /* end switch */

    /*_____*/
    /* end the service request         */
    /*_____*/
    terminate_service_request();

    /*_____*/
    /* print the statistics            */
    /*_____*/
    printf("File transfer completed.\n");
    file_size = get_file_size(file_name);
    print_statistics();

    exit(GOOD);

} /* end main */


/*_____*/
/* Initialize program variables from command line.            */
/*_____*/
USHORT get_args(SHORT argc, PCHAR argv[])
{
    /*_____*/
    /* are there the right number of args? */
    /*_____*/
```

Figure 16-12 (Part 2 of 8).   File Transfer Requester Program.

```
  if (argc != 3)
    return(FAILED);

  /*_____*/
  /* send or receive??               */
  /*_____*/
  if (strcmp("SEND", strupr(argv[1])) == 0)
    service = FILE_SEND_TO_SERVER;
  else
    if (strcmp("RECV", strupr(argv[1])) == 0)
      service = FILE_RECEIVE_FROM_SERVER;
    else return(FAILED);

  /*_____*/
  /* get the file name               */
  /*_____*/
  strcpy(file_name, argv[2]);

  /*_____*/
  /* everything is OK!               */
  /*_____*/
  return(GOOD);
} /* end get_args */

/*_____*/
/* Initialize requester from config file data.                       */
/*_____*/
VOID initialize_requester(VOID)
{
  /*_____*/
  /* perform initialization          */
  /*    -get configuration data      */
  /*    -allocate a buffer for       */
  /*      communication (pointer to buffer*/
  /*      and size are returned)     */
  /*_____*/
  printf("Initializing...\n");
  open_bgn_time = save_time();
  if (fx_Initialize(&packet_ptr, &filedata_packet_size))
    { printf("Error Initializing.\n");
      exit(FAILED);
    }

  /*_____*/
  /* calculate header and data sizes of */
  /* packet used for file transfer   */
  /*_____*/
  filedata_header_size = (sizeof(packet_ptr->filedata) -
                          sizeof(packet_ptr->filedata.Data));

  filedata_data_size = filedata_packet_size - filedata_header_size;

  /*_____*/
  /* open the pipe                   */
  /*_____*/
  if (fx_Open())
    { printf("Error Opening Communication Pipe.\n");
      exit(FAILED);
    }

  printf("Initialization complete.\n\n");
} /* end initialize_requester */
```

Figure 16-12 (Part 3 of 8).   File Transfer Requester Program.

```
/*_____*/
/* Function to open an existing file or create a new file.           */
/*_____*/
VOID open_file(VOID)
{
   /*_____*/
   /* open the file                              */
   /*_____*/
   printf("Starting file transfer...\n");
   if (service == FILE_SEND_TO_SERVER)
      {if (-1 == (FileHandle = open(file_name, O_BINARY | O_RDONLY )))
          {print_error(errno,"opening a file",__FILE__,__LINE__);
           exit(FAILED);
          }
      }
   else
      {if (-1 == (FileHandle = open(file_name,
                          O_BINARY | O_WRONLY | O_CREAT, S_IREAD | S_IWRITE)))
          {print_error(errno,"opening a file",__FILE__,__LINE__);
           exit(FAILED);
          }
      }
} /* end open_file */

/*_____*/
/* Function to request the file transfer service.                    */
/*_____*/
VOID request_file_transfer(VOID)
{
   /*_____*/
   /* send file transfer parms to server         */
   /* and get response                           */
   /*_____*/
   xfer_bgn_time = save_time();
   packet_ptr->request.packet_type = REQUEST_PACKET;
   packet_ptr->request.service     = service;
   strcpy(packet_ptr->request.file_name, file_name);

   if (fx_Transact(packet_ptr,                        /* packet to be sent     */
                   sizeof(packet_ptr->request),  /* packet size           */
                   packet_ptr,                        /* packet to be received */
                   sizeof(packet_ptr->response),/* packet size           */
                   &PipeBytesRead))                   /* number of bytes received */
      {printf("Error starting file transfer.\n");
       exit(FAILED);
      }

   if (packet_ptr->response.rc != 0)
      {printf("Server Error when starting file transfer.\n");
       exit(FAILED);
      }
} /* end request_file_transfer */

/*_____*/
/* Function to receive a file from the server.                       */
/*_____*/
VOID receive_file(VOID)
{
   /*_____*/
   /* receive file data from requester           */
   /*_____*/
```

Figure 16-12 (Part 4 of 8). File Transfer Requester Program.

```
  do {
      /*_____*/
      /* receive a block of file data        */
      /*_____*/
      if (fx_Read(packet_ptr,
                  filedata_packet_size,
                  &PipeBytesRead))
        break;

      /*_____*/
      /* seek to file location for the block */
      /*_____*/
      if (-1L == lseek(FileHandle,

                     packet_ptr->filedata.offset,
                     SEEK_SET))
        {print_error(errno,"performing a LSEEK",__FILE__,__LINE__);
         break;
        }

      /*_____*/
      /* write the block to the file         */
      /*_____*/
      if (-1 == write(FileHandle,
                  packet_ptr->filedata.Data,
                  packet_ptr->filedata.length))
        {print_error(errno,"writing to a file",__FILE__,__LINE__);
         break;
        }

  } while ((packet_ptr->filedata.rc == 0)
        && (packet_ptr->filedata.length != 0));/*enddo*/

  /*_____*/
  /* end the file transfer               */
  /*_____*/
  close(FileHandle);                /* close the file            */

} /* end receive_file */

/*_____*/
/* Function to send a file to the server.                       */
/*_____*/
VOID send_file(VOID)
{
  /*_____*/
  /* send file data to server            */
  /*_____*/
  packet_ptr->filedata.offset = 0;
  do {
      /*_____*/
      /* read a block of file data           */
      /*_____*/
      packet_ptr->filedata.length = read(FileHandle,
                                     packet_ptr->filedata.Data,
                                     filedata_data_size);
      if (packet_ptr->filedata.length == -1)
        {print_error(errno,"reading file data",__FILE__,__LINE__);
         packet_ptr->filedata.rc = FAILED;
         packet_ptr->filedata.length = 0;
        }
```

Figure 16-12 (Part 5 of 8).   File Transfer Requester Program.

```
          /*_____*/
          /* send the block of file data, drop   */
          /*   out of loop if send error or file */
          /*   error.                            */
          /*_____*/
          packet_ptr->filedata.packet_type = FILEDATA_PACKET;
          if (fx_Write(packet_ptr,
                       filedata_header_size +
                       packet_ptr->filedata.length,
                       &PipeBytesWritten)
             | packet_ptr->filedata.rc)
             break;
          packet_ptr->filedata.offset = packet_ptr->filedata.offset +
                                        packet_ptr->filedata.length;

       } while ((packet_ptr->filedata.rc == 0) &&
               (packet_ptr->filedata.length != 0)); /* enddo */

   /*_____*/
   /* end the file transfer          */
   /*_____*/
   close(FileHandle);               /* close the file          */

} /* end send_file */

/*_____*/
/* close the file, terminate service request, close the comm. pipe  */
/*_____*/
VOID terminate_service_request(VOID)
{
   /*_____*/
   /* Send disconnect request        */
   /*_____*/
   packet_ptr->request.packet_type = REQUEST_PACKET;
   packet_ptr->request.service     = DISCONNECT;
   if (fx_Write(packet_ptr,
                sizeof(packet_ptr->request),
                &PipeBytesRead))
      { printf("Error terminating service.",__FILE__,__LINE__);
        exit(FAILED);
      }

   /*_____*/
   /* end the pipe session           */
   /*_____*/
   close_bgn_time = save_time();
   if (fx_Close())
      {printf("Error Closing communication pipe.");
       exit(FAILED);
      }
   end_time = save_time();

} /* end terminate_service_request */

/*_____*/
/* Start timing an event.                                  */
/*_____*/
double save_time(VOID)
{
   ftime(&timebuff);
```

Figure 16-12 (Part 6 of 8). File Transfer Requester Program.

```
    return((double)timebuff.time+((double)timebuff.millitm)/(double)1000);
  } /* end save_time */

  /*_____*/
  /* Print Statistics.                                                 */
  /*_____*/
  VOID print_statistics(VOID)
  {
    if (service == FILE_SEND_TO_SERVER)
      printf("\n%s sent to the server.\n", file_name);
    else
      printf("\n%s received from the server.\n",file_name);

    printf("Communication link open time was %f seconds.\n",
           xfer_bgn_time-open_bgn_time);
    printf("%ld bytes transferred in %f seconds.\n",
           file_size, close_bgn_time-xfer_bgn_time);
    printf("The average transfer rate was %.2f kilobytes/second.\n",
           file_size/((close_bgn_time-xfer_bgn_time)*1000));
    printf("Communication link close time was %f seconds.\n",
           end_time-close_bgn_time);
  } /* end print_statistics */

  /*_____*/
  /* Print Help.                                                       */
  /*_____*/
  VOID print_help(VOID)
  {

    printf("\nIncorrect command invocation.  Enter as follows:\n");
    printf("\n");
    printf("FXR  direction file-name                                \n");
    printf("                                                        \n");
    printf(" where:                                                 \n");
    printf("     direction is either SEND or RECV.                  \n");
    printf("                                                        \n");
    printf("     file-name is the name of the file to transfer.  If a  \n");
    printf("               path is specified the path must exist on the \n");
    printf("               requester and server machines.          \n");
    printf("                                                        \n");
    printf("     NOTE: The DLL for the protocol you wish to test must \n");
    printf("           be copied to PROTOCOL.DLL in a subdirectory in  \n");
    printf("           your LIBPATH.                                \n");
    printf("\n\n");
  } /* end print_help */

  /*_____*/
  /* Get File Size                                                     */
  /*_____*/
  ULONG get_file_size(PCHAR name)
  {
    SHORT fhandle;
    ULONG size;

    if (-1 == (fhandle = open(name, O_BINARY | O_RDONLY )))
       {print_error(errno,"opening a file",__FILE__,__LINE__);
        return(FAILED);
        }
    size = filelength(fhandle);
    close(fhandle);
```

Figure 16-12 (Part 7 of 8). File Transfer Requester Program.

```
  return(size);
} /* end get_file_size */
/*_____*/
/* Error Display Routine                                                  */
/*_____*/
VOID print_error(USHORT Error, PCHAR msg, PCHAR file, USHORT line)
{
 printf("Error %u (0x%x) detected while %s at line %u in file %s.\n",
        Error, Error, msg, line, file);
} /* end print_error */
```

Figure 16-12 (Part 8 of 8).   File Transfer Requester Program.

FXFER.H INCLUDE FILE

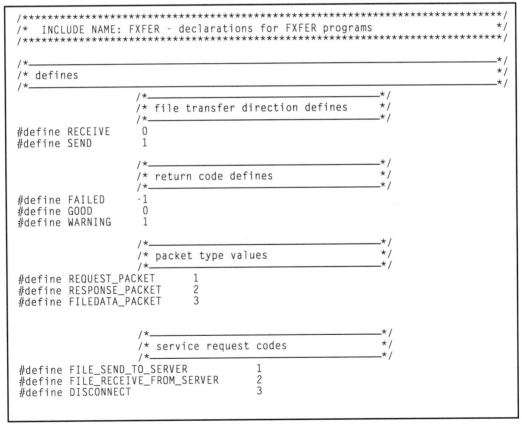

```
/****************************************************************************/
/*   INCLUDE NAME: FXFER - declarations for FXFER programs                 */
/****************************************************************************/
/*_____*/
/* defines                                                                */
/*_____*/
                     /*_____*/
                     /* file transfer direction defines         */
                     /*_____*/
#define RECEIVE       0
#define SEND          1

                     /*_____*/
                     /* return code defines                     */
                     /*_____*/
#define FAILED       -1
#define GOOD          0
#define WARNING       1

                     /*_____*/
                     /* packet type values                      */
                     /*_____*/
#define REQUEST_PACKET        1
#define RESPONSE_PACKET       2
#define FILEDATA_PACKET       3

                     /*_____*/
                     /* service request codes                   */
                     /*_____*/
#define FILE_SEND_TO_SERVER        1
#define FILE_RECEIVE_FROM_SERVER   2
#define DISCONNECT                 3
```

Figure 16-13 (Part 1 of 2).   FXFER.H Include File.

```
/*_____*/
/* Structure declarations                                         */
/*_____*/
                    /*_____*/
                    /* service request packet             */
                    /*_____*/
typedef struct
    { BYTE    packet_type;              /* packet type = REQUEST_PACKET    */
      USHORT service;                   /* service being requested         */
                                        /*     FILE_SEND                   */
                                        /*     FILE_RECEIVE                */
                                        /*     DISCONNECT                  */
      CHAR    file_name[128];           /* file name for file transfer     */
    } REQUEST;

                    /*_____*/
                    /* response packet                    */
                    /*_____*/
typedef struct
    { BYTE    packet_type;              /* packet type = RESPONSE_PACKET   */
      USHORT rc;                        /* service being requested         */
    } RESPONSE;

                    /*_____*/
                    /* filedata packet                    */
                    /*_____*/
typedef struct
    { BYTE    packet_type;              /* packet type = FILEDATA_PACKET   */
      USHORT rc;                        /* return code                     */
      ULONG  offset;                    /* filedata offset                 */
      USHORT length;                    /* filedata length                 */
      BYTE    Data[65526];              /* file data                       */
    } FILEDATA;

                    /*_____*/
                    /* union of all packet types          */
                    /*_____*/
typedef union PACKET
    { REQUEST  request;                 /* request  packet                 */
      RESPONSE response;                /* response packet                 */
      FILEDATA filedata;                /* filedata packet                 */
    } PACKET, *PPACKET;


/*_____*/
/* Forward declarations of communication functions                */
/*_____*/
ULONG fx_Initialize(PPACKET *, PUSHORT);
ULONG fx_MakePipe(VOID);
ULONG fx_ConnectPipe(VOID);
ULONG fx_DisconnectPipe(VOID);
ULONG fx_Open(VOID);
ULONG fx_Write(PVOID, USHORT, PUSHORT);
ULONG fx_Read(PVOID,  USHORT, PUSHORT);
ULONG fx_Transact(PVOID, USHORT, PVOID, USHORT, PUSHORT);
ULONG fx_Close(VOID);
```

Figure 16-13 (Part 2 of 2).   FXFER.H Include File.

FXREQ.H INCLUDE FILE

```
/***************************************************************/
/*  INCLUDE NAME: FXREQ - declarations for FXREQ program       */
/***************************************************************/
/*_____*/
/* Forward declarations of functions in this module           */
/*_____*/
USHORT get_args(SHORT, PCHAR *);
VOID   initialize_requester(VOID);
VOID   open_file(VOID);
VOID   request_file_transfer(VOID);
VOID   receive_file(VOID);
VOID   send_file(VOID);
VOID   terminate_service_request(VOID);
double save_time(VOID);
VOID   print_statistics(VOID);
VOID   print_help(VOID);
ULONG  get_file_size(PCHAR);
VOID   print_error(USHORT, PCHAR, PCHAR, USHORT);

/*_____*/
/* Global variables for this module                           */
/*_____*/
                        /*_____*/
                        /* command line argument variables */
                        /*_____*/
USHORT   service;
CHAR     file_name[128];

                        /*_____*/
                        /* timing variables                */
                        /*_____*/
double   open_bgn_time    = 0.0;        /* Begin fx_Open              */
double   xfer_bgn_time    = 0.0;        /* Begin start of data transfer */
double   close_bgn_time   = 0.0;        /* Begin fx_Close             */
double   end_time         = 0.0;        /* fx_Close complete          */
struct   timeb  timebuff;               /* Timer buffer               */

                        /*_____*/
                        /* file size variable              */
                        /*_____*/
ULONG    file_size;

                        /*_____*/
                        /* file transfer variables         */
                        /*_____*/
PACKET   *packet_ptr;                   /* pointer to packet          */
USHORT    filedata_packet_size;         /* size of packet for file transfer */
USHORT    filedata_data_size;           /* size of data area for file transfer*/
USHORT    filedata_header_size;         /* size of header area for file xfer */

USHORT    PipeBytesRead;                /* number of bytes read from pipe  */
USHORT    PipeBytesWritten;             /* number of bytes written to pipe */
ULONG     FileHandle;                   /* handle for File            */

                        /*_____*/
                        /* misc                            */
                        /*_____*/
ULONG     rc;                           /* variable to receive return codes */
```

Figure 16-14. FXREQ.H Include File.

HOW TO READ FXSVR.C

FXSRV.C, listed in Figure 16-15, is an implementation of the application and file transfer layers (see Figure 16-1) of a file server program. The file server program, in conjunction with a file requester program, will be used for benchmarking the OS/2 LAN and IPC protocols. **FXSVR.C** shares, with **FXREQ.C**, the use of the common include file: **FXFER.H**, listed in Figure 16-13. It also uses **FXSVR.H**, a custom include file, listed in Figure 16-16. The following is list of general observations about the code:

- The only OS/2 call used in this module is **DosExitList**, which you've already encountered in Chapter 13 on page 228. The call is used to set up a routine that is run just before the server terminates. We use it for file cleanup.
- The FX calls are not implemented in this module. They get implemented in the DLLs. The FX calls make extensive use of OS/2 IPC and LAN APIs.
- There is no new OS/2 material to introduce, so we assume that walking through the code will be a straightforward exercise in reading C listings. The same directions we recommended for **FXREQ.C** apply here:
  1. Start with **main**(), which serves as the outline for the program.
  2. Use the scenarios (see Figure 16-7 and Figure 16-8) as your protocol guide. The code is no more than the implementation of the scenarios.
  3. Use the message structures (see Figure 16-9 through Figure 16-11) as your guide to the data structures used in the program.

- The file transfer itself, as implemented by **send_file**() and **receive_file**(), is identical to its counterpart in **FXREQ.C**. After all, this part of the protocol is totally symmetrical.
- Make sure you understand how the FX calls are used. It is important to develop a user's perspective of FX to better understand the implementations of FX in the chapters that follow.

If you've already gone through the **FXREQ.C** code, you're almost at the finishing line for this chapter. What remains is the implementation of the other side of the protocol. It should be quick and easy reading!

FXSVR.C LISTING

```
/**********************************************************************/
/*   PROGRAM NAME: FXSVR - A File Transfer example, server module     */
/*                                                                    */
/*   PROGRAM DESCRIPTION:  This module is the server portion of a file*/
/*     transfer program.  This module uses communication functions modeled */
/*     after named pipe functions to perform the file transfer. The services */
/*     are implemented in separate modules using IEEE 802.2, NETBIOS, */
/*     APPC, or named pipe communication for PC-PC communication.  Named */
/*     pipes, queues, and shared segments are used to implement a local file */
/*     transfer between two processes.                                */
/*                                                                    */
/*     Refer to the FXREQ module for a more detailed description of the file */
/*     transfer programs.                                             */
/*                                                                    */
/*   PROGRAM INVOCATION:    FXSVR                                     */
/**********************************************************************/
#include <process.h>                    /* For exit()                 */
#include <stdio.h>                       /* For printf() & NULL        */
#include <stdlib.h>                      /* For printf                 */
#include <string.h>                      /* For printf                 */
#include <io.h>                          /* For file I/O               */
#include <fcntl.h>                       /* For file I/O               */
#include <sys\types.h>                   /* For time()                 */
#include <sys\timeb.h>                   /* For time()                 */
#include <sys\stat.h>                    /* For stat()                 */

#define INCL_DOSPROCESS                  /* for DosExit function call  */
#include <os2.h>

#include "fxfer.h"
#include "fxsvr.h"
/*_____*/
/* Main routine. Performs file transfer.                              */
/*_____*/
VOID main(VOID)
{
    initialize_server();

    /*_____*/
    /* loop which continuously services requests      */
    /*_____*/
    do
    {
      if (get_service_request() == GOOD)
         {
           switch (packet_ptr->request.service)
              {
                case FILE_SEND_TO_SERVER:      receive_file();
                                               break;
                case FILE_RECEIVE_FROM_SERVER: send_file();
                                               break;
                default : printf("Request for unknown service received.\n");
              } /* end switch */
```

Figure 16-15 (Part 1 of 6). File Transfer Server Program.

```
            terminate_service_request();
        }
    } while (TRUE); /* enddo */

} /* end main */

/*_____*/
/* Initialize server from config file data               */
/*_____*/
VOID initialize_server(VOID)
{
  printf("Initializing Server...\n");

  /*_____*/
  /* exit routine to close pipe if           */
  /*    server terminates                    */
  /*_____*/
  if (rc = DosExitList(1,(PFNEXITLIST) fxsvr_exit))
      { print_error(rc,"establishing DosExitList",__FILE__,__LINE__);
        exit(FAILED);
      }

  /*_____*/
  /* perform initialization                  */
  /*    -get configuration data              */
  /*    -allocate a buffer for               */
  /*      communication (pointer to buffer*/
  /*      and size are returned)             */
  /*_____*/
  if (rc = fx_Initialize(&packet_ptr, &filedata_packet_size))
      { print_error(rc,"during fx_Initialize",__FILE__,__LINE__);
        exit(FAILED);
      }

  /*_____*/
  /* calculate header and data sizes of      */
  /* packet used for file transfer           */
  /*_____*/
  filedata_header_size = (sizeof(packet_ptr->filedata) -
                          sizeof(packet_ptr->filedata.Data));
  filedata_data_size = filedata_packet_size - filedata_header_size;

  /*_____*/
  /* Establish the server                    */
  /*_____*/
  if (rc = fx_MakePipe())
      { print_error(rc,"during fx_MakePipe",__FILE__,__LINE__);
        exit(FAILED);
      }

  printf("Server Initialization complete.\n\n");
} /* end initialize_server */

/*_____*/
/* receive client request                                */
/*_____*/
USHORT get_service_request(VOID)
{
  /*_____*/
  /* Wait for requester to open the pipe */
  /*_____*/
  printf("\nWaiting for service request...\n");
  if (fx_ConnectPipe())
```

Figure 16-15 (Part 2 of 6). File Transfer Server Program.

```
          return(FAILED);
     /*———————————————————————*/
     /* Receive the file transfer parameters*/
     /*———————————————————————*/
     if (fx_Read(packet_ptr,              /* read file xfer parms        */
                 sizeof(packet_ptr->request),
                 &PipeBytesRead))
         return(FAILED);

} /* end get_service_request */

/*————————————————————————————————————————*/
/* Server program function which receives a file using the following steps:  */
/*   1) create file,  2) respond to request, 3) receive file data            */
/*————————————————————————————————————————*/
VOID receive_file(VOID)
{
  printf("File Send Request received.\n");
  /*———————————————————————*/
  /* create file                          */
  /*———————————————————————*/
  FileHandle = open(packet_ptr->request.file_name,
                    O_BINARY | O_WRONLY | O_CREAT,
                    S_IREAD | S_IWRITE);
  if (FileHandle == -1)
     {print_error(errno,"opening a file",__FILE__,__LINE__);
      packet_ptr->response.rc = FAILED;
     }
  else packet_ptr->response.rc = GOOD;
  packet_ptr->filedata.packet_type = RESPONSE_PACKET;

  /*———————————————————————*/
  /* respond to request                   */
  /*———————————————————————*/
  if ( (fx_Write(packet_ptr,
                 sizeof(packet_ptr->response),
                 &PipeBytesWritten) == 0)
      && (packet_ptr->response.rc == 0))

  /*———————————————————————*/
  /* receive file data from requester     */
  /*———————————————————————*/
  do {
      /*———————————————————————*/
      /* Receive a block of data              */
      /*———————————————————————*/
      if (fx_Read(packet_ptr,
                  filedata_packet_size,
                  &PipeBytesRead))
          break;

      /*———————————————————————*/
      /* seek to file location for the block */
      /*———————————————————————*/
      if (-1L == lseek(FileHandle,
                       packet_ptr->filedata.offset,
                       SEEK_SET))
         {print_error(errno,"performing a LSEEK",__FILE__,__LINE__);
          break;
         }
```

Figure 16-15 (Part 3 of 6). File Transfer Server Program.

```
        /*_____*/
        /* write the block to the file      */
        /*_____*/
        if (-1 == write(FileHandle,
                        packet_ptr->filedata.Data,
                        packet_ptr->filedata.length))
          {print_error(errno,"writing to a file",__FILE__,__LINE__);
           break;
           }

      } while ((packet_ptr->filedata.rc == 0)
            && (packet_ptr->filedata.length != 0));/*enddo*/

  /*_____*/
  /* close the file                   */
  /*_____*/
  close(FileHandle);
 } /*end receive_file */

 /*_____*/
 /* Server program function which sends a file using the following steps:    */
 /*   1) open file,  2) respond to request, 3) send file data                */
 /*_____*/
VOID send_file(VOID)
{
   printf("File Receive request received.\n");

    /*_____*/
    /* open existing file              */
    /*_____*/
    FileHandle = open(packet_ptr->request.file_name,
                      O_BINARY | O_RDONLY );
    if (FileHandle == -1)
       {print_error(errno,"opening a file",__FILE__,__LINE__);
        packet_ptr->response.rc = FAILED;
        }
    else packet_ptr->response.rc = GOOD;
    packet_ptr->filedata.packet_type = RESPONSE_PACKET;

    /*_____*/
    /* respond to request              */
    /*_____*/
    if ( (fx_Write(packet_ptr,
                   sizeof(packet_ptr->response),
                   &PipeBytesWritten) == 0)
        && (packet_ptr->response.rc == 0))
       {packet_ptr->filedata.offset = 0L;

        /*_____*/
        /* send file data to requester      */
        /*_____*/
        do {
            packet_ptr->filedata.packet_type = FILEDATA_PACKET;
            packet_ptr->filedata.length = 0L;
            /*_____*/
            /* read a block of data from the file  */
            /*_____*/
            packet_ptr->filedata.length = read(FileHandle,
                                               packet_ptr->filedata.Data,
                                               filedata_data_size);
            if (packet_ptr->filedata.length == -1)
```

Figure 16-15 (Part 4 of 6). File Transfer Server Program.

```
                     {print_error(errno,"reading file data",__FILE__,__LINE__);
                      packet_ptr->filedata.rc = -1;
                      packet_ptr->filedata.length = 0;
                     }

             /*_____*/
             /* send the block of file data         */
             /*_____*/
             if (fx_Write(packet_ptr,
                          filedata_header_size +
                          packet_ptr->filedata.length,
                          &PipeBytesWritten)
                 | packet_ptr->filedata.rc)
                 break;
             packet_ptr->filedata.offset =
                          packet_ptr->filedata.offset +
                          packet_ptr->filedata.length;

           } while ((packet_ptr->filedata.rc == 0) &&

                 (packet_ptr->filedata.length != 0)); /* enddo */

       } /* end if */
    /*_____*/
    /* close the file                      */
    /*_____*/
    close(FileHandle);
} /* end send_file */

/*_____*/
/* function to end a service request                                   */
/*_____*/
USHORT terminate_service_request(VOID)
{
    /*_____*/
    /* Receive disconnect request          */
    /*_____*/
    if (fx_Read(packet_ptr,
               filedata_packet_size,
               &PipeBytesRead))
       { print_error(rc,"receiving request disconnect",__FILE__,__LINE__);
         return(FAILED);
       }

    if (!((packet_ptr->request.packet_type == REQUEST_PACKET) &&
          (packet_ptr->request.service      == DISCONNECT)))
       printf("Incorrect protocol. Disconnect request expected.\n");

    /*_____*/
    /* end the pipe session                */
    /*_____*/
    if (fx_DisconnectPipe())              /* prepare for next request     */
       { print_error(rc, "during fx_DisconnectPipe",__FILE__,__LINE__);
         return(FAILED);
       }

    printf("Service Request completed.\n");
```

Figure 16-15 (Part 5 of 6).   File Transfer Server Program.

```
} /* end server_send_receive_file */

/*─────────────────────────────────────────────────────*/
/* Error Display Routine                                 */
/*─────────────────────────────────────────────────────*/
VOID print_error(ULONG Error, PCHAR msg, PCHAR file, USHORT line)
{
 printf("Error %lu (0x%x) detected while %s \
        at line %lu in file %s.\n",
        Error, Error, msg, line, file);
} /* end print_error */

/*─────────────────────────────────────────────────────*/
/* Exit Routine                                          */
/*─────────────────────────────────────────────────────*/
VOID APIENTRY fxsvr_exit(ULONG exit_type)
{
  if (fx_Close())
    printf("Error encountered will terminating the file transfer server.");
  else
    printf("File transfer server terminated normally.\n");

  DosExitList(3, (void far *) 0);
} /* end fxsvr_exit */
```

Figure 16-15 (Part 6 of 6).   File Transfer Server Program.

FXSVR.H INCLUDE FILE

```
/**********************************************************************/
/*   INCLUDE NAME: FXSVR - declarations for FXSVR program            */
/**********************************************************************/
/*------------------------------------------------------------------*/
/* Forward declarations of functions in this module                 */
/*------------------------------------------------------------------*/
VOID   initialize_server(VOID);
USHORT get_service_request(VOID);
USHORT terminate_service_request(VOID);
VOID   send_file(VOID);
VOID   receive_file(VOID);
VOID   print_error(ULONG, PCHAR, PCHAR, USHORT);
VOID   APIENTRY fxsvr_exit(ULONG);

/*------------------------------------------------------------------*/
/* Global variables for this module                                 */
/*------------------------------------------------------------------*/
                    /*----------------------------------------*/
                    /* file transfer variables                */
                    /*----------------------------------------*/
PACKET    *packet_ptr;              /* pointer to packet                  */
USHORT    filedata_packet_size;     /* size of packet for file transfer   */
USHORT    filedata_data_size;       /* size of data area for file transfer*/
USHORT    filedata_header_size;     /* size of header area for file xfer  */

USHORT    PipeBytesRead;            /* number of bytes read from pipe     */
USHORT    PipeBytesWritten;         /* number of bytes written to pipe    */
ULONG     FileHandle;               /* handle for File                    */

                    /*----------------------------------------*/
                    /* miscellaneous variables                */
                    /*----------------------------------------*/
ULONG     rc;
```

Figure 16-16. FXSVR.H Include File.

Chapter 17

FX Using Named Pipes

This chapter presents an implementation of the communication layer of the FX protocol using OS/2 2.0's *Named Pipes* Interprocess Communication (IPC) protocol. The interface will be packaged as a Dynamic Link Library (FXNPIPE.DLL). The DLL is created from **FXNPIPE.C** using the FX make file introduced in Chapter 16.

The Named Pipes communication DLL makes it possible to transfer files using FXREQ and FXSVR, the client and server programs developed in Chapter 16. We will use this setup to collect benchmark numbers on the performance of Named Pipes. The program we develop in this chapter will serve as the Named Pipes representative champion in the *Great FX LAN Derby* of Part III. We will run the champion on a single machine, and across NetWare and IBM LAN Server LANs.

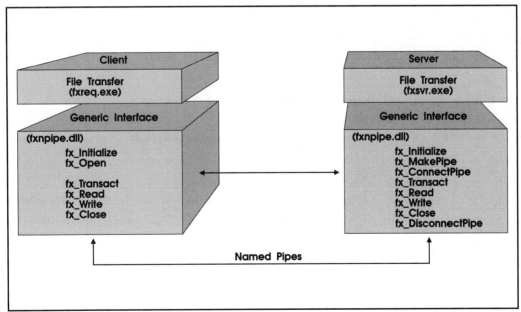

Figure 17-1. Implementing the FX Interface Using the Named Pipes DLL.

The plan for this chapter is to make use of whatever mechanisms are provided by the OS/2 2.0 Named Pipes protocol to implement the nine **FX** interface calls shown in Figure 17-1. Figure 17-2 demonstrates how each of the FX calls is implemented by the FXNPIPE.DLL using OS/2 2.0's Named Pipes services. It also shows the effect each call has on the partner transaction.

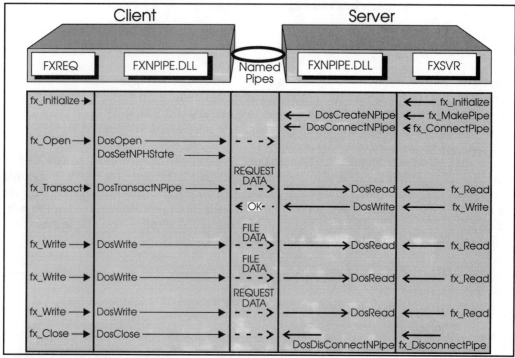

Figure 17-2. Sending a File Using the FXNPIPE.DLL.

HOW THE FXNPIPE.DLL USES NAMED PIPES

Figure 17-2 demonstrates how *send file* gets implemented at the DLL level. Notice that, with two exceptions, there is a one-to-one correspondence between the FX calls and their Named Pipes counterparts. The two exceptions are **fx_initialize**, for which there is no counterpart, and **fx_open**, which gets implemented using two Named Pipes API calls: **DosOpen** and **DosSetNPHState**.

The FX protocol is an emulation of Named Pipes; consequently the implementation of **FXNPIPE.C** should be a "piece of cake." The C code is certainly the most straightfor-ward (almost one-for-one) implementation of any of the FX DLLs. But we will not let you get off the hook that easily; in this chapter, we introduce nine new OS/2 API calls. Some of these new API calls are "feature-packed" and can be applied to files and devices as well as Named Pipes. This all leads to some lengthy API descriptions. So, once again, please make sure you understand the material in the Named Pipes tutorial in Chapter 15 on page 323, before you immerse yourself in the details of this chapter.

By the end of this chapter, you will know both OS/2's Named Pipe and file service APIs, and you will probably notice the similarities between these two services. One of the design goals of Named Pipes was to extend the familiar file service paradigm to the LAN and IPC services. You'll find that obtaining LAN and IPC services is just as easy as issuing calls to the file system. Remember that Named Pipes provide a very complete set of IPC and LAN services. By the time you get through this straightforward chapter, you will have a greatly expanded programming repertoire.

FXNPIPE.C: THE NAMED PIPE FX DLLS

The code we present in this section does *not* contain a **main()** procedure. The FX DLLs are simply functions that get linked to a (.EXE) file at run time. The **main()** procedure is provided by the program that calls the DLL functions. This means **FXNPIPE.C** is not a separate program; it contains a list of functions that get packaged in a DLL.

FXNPIPE.C: General Stuff

The following listing (see Figure 17-3) contains all the miscellaneous header "stuff" that will be used by the FX procedures. The first thing to notice is the enabled INCL_DOSNMPIPES flag. By enabling this flag, we include the Named Pipes services from **OS2.H**. We follow that with the usual declarations of constants, global variables, and forward declarations of functions. With the exception of **print_error()**, the nine new functions we introduce are all one-for-one implementations of the **FX** interface services. The **print_error()** helper function is similar to the functions with the same name that were introduced in previous chapters.

```
/****************************************************************************/
/*   MODULE NAME: FXNPIPE - Named pipe communication.                      */
/*                                                                         */
/*   PROGRAM DESCRIPTION:                                                  */
/*     This module implements the FX services using OS/2 named pipes.      */
/*     The FXNPIPE.C code will be packaged as the FXNPIPE.DLL Dynamic link */
/*     library.                                                            */
/****************************************************************************/
#include <stdio.h>                      /* For printf() & NULL             */
#include <stdlib.h>                     /* For conversion routines         */
#include <string.h>                     /* For string functions            */

#define INCL_DOSNMPIPES                 /* for named pipe function declares */
#include <os2.h>
#include "fxfer.h"                      /* For FX functions                */
```

Figure 17-3 (Part 1 of 2). FXNPIPE.C: General Header Stuff and print_error().

```
/*-----------------------------------------------------------------*/
/* forward declarations                                            */
/*-----------------------------------------------------------------*/
VOID print_error(ULONG, PCHAR, PCHAR, USHORT);

/*-----------------------------------------------------------------*/
/* Configuration variables, initialized after fx_Initialize()      */
/* function call.                                                  */
/*-----------------------------------------------------------------*/
CHAR    PipeName[128];
CHAR    ComputerName[128];
USHORT  OutBufSize;                /* out buffer size for DosMakeNmPipe */
USHORT  InBufSize;                 /* in buffer  ,,    ,,     ,,        */
USHORT  FileBufferSize;            /* file and message buffer           */

/*-----------------------------------------------------------------*/
/* global variables for this module.                               */
/*-----------------------------------------------------------------*/
HPIPE   PipeHandle;                /* handle from DosOpen or DosMakeNmPipe*/
ULONG   rc;                        /* return code                       */
ULONG   ActionTaken;               /* DosOpen action                    */

/*-----------------------------------------------------------------*/
/* Error Display Routine                                           */
/*-----------------------------------------------------------------*/
VOID print_error(ULONG Error, PCHAR msg, PCHAR file, USHORT line)
{
 printf("Named Pipe Error %lu (0x%x) detected \
        while %s at line %lu in file %s.\n",
        Error, Error, msg, line, file);
} /* end print_error */
```

Figure 17-3 (Part 2 of 2).   FXNPIPE.C: General Header Stuff and print_error().

FXNPIPE.C: fx_Initialize()

The **fx_Initialize()** function (see Figure 17-5) reads a protocol-specific configuration file to obtain the parameters required to initialize the system.   The name of the user-specified configuration file for Named Pipes is **fxnpipe.cfg**.   Here is an example of a such a file:

```
PIPE_NAME          = \PIPE\filesvr
COMPUTER_NAME      =
OUT_BUFFER_SIZE    = 4096
IN_BUFFER_SIZE     = 4096
FILE_BUFFER_SIZE   = 16384
```

Figure 17-4.   FXNPIPE.CFG: The Configuration File for the FX Named Pipes DLL.

PIPE_NAME   This parameter defines the pipe name.   \PIPE\ refers to a pseudo subdirectory name.

COMPUTER_NAME   This parameter defines the network name of the server computer. It is used for remote Named Pipes. We left it blank because we are using Named Pipes as a local IPC in this chapter.

OUT_BUFFER_SIZE   This parameter defines the output buffer size (in bytes) and is used in DosCreateNPipe.

IN_BUFFER_SIZE   This parameter defines the input buffer size (in bytes) and is used in DosCreateNPipe.

FILE_BUFFER_SIZE   This parameter defines the size (in bytes) of the message buffer. This is the buffer we will use for reading and writing data to the disk and for exchanging messages across the LAN or the IPC. The memory space for this parameter will be dynamically allocated. The **fx_Initialize** function returns a pointer to this buffer and its size to the application. One of the factors we will measure in our benchmarks is the effect of the message buffer size on performance.

No new OS/2 calls are introduced in the implementation of this function. This should come as no surprise, because the OS/2 Named Pipes service does not provide an "initialize" API call. We introduced this call in the FX protocol as a "catch-all" for performing protocol-specific start-up actions.

```
/*_____*/
/* function to read communication specific parameters and allocate a buffer */
/* for communication.  A pointer to the buffer and the buffer size is        */
/* returned.                                                                  */
/*_____*/
ULONG fx_Initialize(PPACKET *buffer_p , PUSHORT size)
{
  FILE    *config_file;                   /* Input file control block         */
  CHAR    line[80];                       /* one line of config file          */

  printf("Reading configuration parameters.\n");
    /*_____*/
    /* open the configuration file       */
    /*_____*/
  if (NULL == (config_file = fopen("fxnpipe.cfg","r")))
      {print_error(rc,"opening configuration file",__FILE__,__LINE__);
       return(FAILED);
      }
  else
      /*_____*/
      /* read the configuration parameters. */
      /* The parameters are expected to be: */
      /*    - in the form <name = value>    */
      /*    - in the order read below       */
      /*_____*/
      {
```

Figure 17-5 (Part 1 of 2). FXNPIPE.C: fx_Initialize().

```
          fgets(line, sizeof(line), config_file);
          if (sscanf(line,"PIPE_NAME = %s ", PipeName) != 1)
              {print_error(rc,"reading PipeName from configuration",
                          __FILE__,__LINE__);
               return(FAILED);
               }
          printf("PIPE_NAME = %s \n", PipeName);

          fgets(line, sizeof(line), config_file);
          if (sscanf(line,"COMPUTER_NAME = %s ", ComputerName) == EOF)
              strcpy(ComputerName,"");
          printf("COMPUTER_NAME = %s \n", ComputerName);

          fgets(line, sizeof(line), config_file);
          if (sscanf(line,"OUT_BUFFER_SIZE = %u ", &OutBufSize) != 1)
              {print_error(rc,"reading OutBufSize from configuration",
                          __FILE__,__LINE__);
               return(FAILED);
               }
          printf("OUT_BUFFER_SIZE = %u \n", OutBufSize);

          fgets(line, sizeof(line), config_file);
          if (sscanf(line,"IN_BUFFER_SIZE = %u ", &InBufSize) != 1)
              {print_error(rc,"reading InBufSize from configuration",
                          __FILE__,__LINE__);
               return(FAILED);
               }
          printf("IN_BUFFER_SIZE = %u \n", InBufSize);

          fgets(line, sizeof(line), config_file);
          if (sscanf(line,"FILE_BUFFER_SIZE = %u ", &FileBufferSize) != 1)
              {print_error(rc,"reading FileBufferSize from configuration",
                          __FILE__,__LINE__);
               return(FAILED);
               }
          printf("FILE_BUFFER_SIZE = %u \n", FileBufferSize);
          } /* end if */

     fclose(config_file);

     /*─────────────────────────────────────*/
     /* allocate buffer, return pointer      */
     /* and size                             */
     /*─────────────────────────────────────*/
     if ((*buffer_p = (PPACKET)malloc(FileBufferSize)) == NULL)
         {print_error(rc,"allocating file buffer",__FILE__,__LINE__);
          return(FAILED);
          }
     *size = FileBufferSize;

     return(GOOD);
} /* end fx_Initialize */
```

Figure 17-5 (Part 2 of 2). FXNPIPE.C: fx_Initialize().

FXNPIPE.C: fx_MakePipe()

The **fx_MakePipe()** function (see Figure 17-6) is as straightforward as functions get.
All it does is turn around and issue the equivalent OS/2 **DosCreateNPipe** call described
here:

DosCreateNPipe

The **DosCreateNPipe** API call creates a Named Pipe and returns its handle. If the Named Pipe is to be used over a network, it must be created by a server process running on the IBM LAN Server, Microsoft LAN Manager, or NetWare. The prototype for this call is:

```
DosCreateNPipe(PSZ     name,      /* Pipe Name                        */
               PHPIPE  handle,    /* Pointer to returned pipe handle  */
               ULONG   OpenMode,  /* Open mode of pipe                */
               ULONG   PipeMode,  /* Pipe-specific mode               */
               ULONG   OutBuf,    /* Output buffer size in bytes      */
               ULONG   InBuf,     /* Number of bytes in input buffer  */
               ULONG   TimeOut);  /* Timeout value                    */
```

A description of the parameters follows:

- The *name* parameter points to a null-terminated string that contains the name of the pipe. Pipes are named **\PIPE\PipeName**, where **\PIPE** is the name of a virtual subdirectory in memory. The rest of the name can use any valid file system characters including a backslash.
- The *handle* parameter points to a variable that receives the Named Pipe identifier (a file system handle). If multiple instances of the pipe are created, each DosCreateNPipe call returns a different handle.
- The *OpenMode* parameter consists of a set of bits which specify the mode with which to open the Named Pipe. More specifically, this parameter specifies when to flush the data, inheritance, and the direction of the pipe. The OpenMode parameter contains the following bit fields:

```
Bits     Value
31-16    Reserved.
15       Reserved must be zero.
14       Flush buffer flag (for remote pipes):
         0 = (NP_WRITEBEHIND); Multiple-writes may be blocked before
             data is sent over LAN.
         1 = (NP_NOWRITEBEHIND); Send data over LAN after each write.
13-8     Reserved, must be zero.
7        Inheritance Flag:
         0 = (NP_INHERIT); Pipe handle is inherited by child process
         1 = (NP_NOINHERIT); Pipe handle is private to the current
             process.
6-3      Reserved, must be zero.
2-0      Access mode flags:
         000 = (NP_ACCESS_INBOUND);  In-bound Pipe, from client to server
         001 = (NP_ACCESS_OUTBOUND); Out-bound Pipe, from server
             to client
         010 = (NP_ACCESS_DUPLEX); Duplex Pipe, server to/from client
```

- The *PipeMode* parameter is a set of bits which specify wait/nowait, the message type, and the instance count. Here is a more detailed description of the bit fields:

```
Bits      Value
31-16     Reserved.
15        Wait flag:
          0 = (NP_WAIT); Wait (i.e.block) if no data available.
          1 = (NP_NOWAIT); Return immediately if no data available.
14-12     Reserved.
11-10     Type flag:
          00 = (NP_TYPE_BYTE); Pipe is a byte stream.
          01 = (NP_TYPE_MESSAGE); Pipe is a message stream.
          All writes to message stream pipes record the length of the write
          along with the Message Data.  In message stream mode the first
          two bytes of each message represents the length of that message
          is called the message header.
9-8       Read-Mode Flag:
          00 = (NP_READMODE_BYTE); Read pipe as a byte stream.
          01 = (NP_READMODE_MESSAGE); Read pipe as a message stream.
          Message pipes can be read as byte or message streams,
          Byte pipes can only be read as byte streams.
7-0       Instance count:  Byte wide (8-bit) count to which specifies how
          many instances of the pipe can be created.  A value of 1 through
          254 can be specified.  A -1 (NP_UNLIMITED_INSTANCES)
          value specifies unlimited value specifies unlimited instances,
          0 is reserved. Attempts to make a pipe fail if the maximum
          instances already exists.  This parameter is ignored when making
          any other than the first instance of a pipe.  When multiple
          instances are allowed, multiple clients can simultaneously
          issue the same pipe name and get handles to distinct
          pipe instances.
```

```c
/*-----------------------------------------------------------------*/
/* function to establish the server end of the communication pipe. */
/*-----------------------------------------------------------------*/
ULONG fx_MakePipe(VOID)
{
                        /*-----------------------------------*/
                        /* defines for DosMakeNmPipe         */
                        /*-----------------------------------*/
  #define PIPE_OPENMODE     0x4002    /* no write-behind allowed, duplex  */
  #define PIPEMODE          0x0501    /* message pipe, one instance only  */
  #define TIMEOUT           0L        /* wait forever timeout value       */

  rc = DosCreateNPipe(PipeName,       /* PipeName from fx_Initialize      */
                      &PipeHandle,     /* pipe handle returned             */
                      PIPE_OPENMODE,
                      PIPEMODE,
                      OutBufSize,      /* OutBufSize set during fx_Initialize*/
                      InBufSize,       /* InBufSize set during fx_Initialize */
                      TIMEOUT);
  if (rc)
     {print_error(rc,"Making a named pipe",__FILE__,__LINE__);
      return(FAILED);
      }

  return(GOOD);

} /* end fx_MakePipe */
```

Figure 17-6.   FXNPIPE.C: MakePipe().

- The *OutBuf* parameter specifies the number of bytes to allocate for the outgoing buffer. This is a hint to the operating system.
- The *InBuf* parameter specifies the number of bytes to allocate for the incoming buffer. This is a hint to the operating system.
- The *TimeOut* parameter specifies how long DosWaitNPipe should wait (in milliseconds) for the next available instance of a Named Pipe. This value may be set only at the creation of the first instance of the pipe name. If the value is set to zero, a default value of 50 milliseconds is chosen. Your programs will be more readable if you specify the timeout directly when issuing a DosWaitNPipe instead of relying on the default timeout value from DosCreateNPipe.

FXNPIPE.C: fx_ConnectPipe()

The **fx_ConnectPipe()** function (see Figure 17-7) is also very straightforward. All it does is turn around and issue the equivalent OS/2 **DosConnectNPipe** IPC call described here:

DosConnectNPipe

The **DosConnectNPipe** API call is issued by a server process to wait on a client to open a Named Pipe. If the client end is already open, this call returns immediately and has no effect. If the client end is not open, the behavior of this call depends on the pipe's blocking mode:

- If the blocking mode is active, the call "blocks" until the client issues a DosOpen.
- If blocking is not set, the call returns immediately with an error value and the pipe enters a listening state, permitting a client to issue a successful DosOpen. A DosOpen to a pipe that is not in a listening state fails.

The prototype for this call is:

```
DosConnectNPipe(HPIPE   handle);      /* Pipe Handle               */
```

A description of the parameters follows:

- The *handle* parameter is the pipe instance identifier returned by DosCreateNPipe.

```
/*————————————————————————————————————————————————*/
/* function to enable the server end of the communication pipe.          */
/*————————————————————————————————————————————————*/
ULONG fx_ConnectPipe(VOID)
{
  rc = DosConnectNPipe(PipeHandle);    /* handle from DosMakeNmPipe          */
  if (rc)
     {print_error(rc,"Connect to a named pipe",__FILE__,__LINE__);
      return(FAILED);
     }
  return(GOOD);
} /* end fx_ConnectPipe */
```

Figure 17-7. FXNPIPE.C: fx_ConnectPipe().

FXNPIPE.C: fx_DisconnectPipe()

The **fx_DisconnectPipe()** function (see Figure 17-8) is also very straightforward. All it does is turn around and issue the equivalent OS/2 **DosDisConnectNPipe** API call described here:

DosDisConnectNPipe

The **DosDisConnectNPipe** API call is issued by the server side of a Named Pipe to close a Named Pipe instance. This call will force the client end off the pipe. This forced closure may cause data to be discarded, in which case the client will get an error code on the next operation. The DosDisConnectNPipe must be issued before a new client is allowed to connect to the pipe. The prototype for this call is:

```
DosDisConnectNPipe(HPIPE    handle);      /* Pipe Handle              */
```

A description of the parameters follows:

- The *handle* parameter is the pipe's instance identifier returned by a DosCreateN-Pipe.

```
/*————————————————————————————————————————————————*/
/* function to disable the server end of the communication pipe.         */
/*————————————————————————————————————————————————*/
ULONG fx_DisconnectPipe(VOID)
{
  rc = DosDisConnectNPipe(PipeHandle);
  if (rc)
     {print_error(rc,"Disconnecting from a named pipe",__FILE__,__LINE__);
      return(FAILED);
     }
  return(GOOD);
} /* end fx_DisconnectPipe */
```

Figure 17-8. FXNPIPE.C: fx_DisconnectPipe().

FXNPIPE.C: fx_Open()

The **fx_Open()** function (see Figure 17-9) does a little bit more work than its predecessors. First, it appends the computer network name to the pipe name (for cases where the pipe is remote). It then issues an OS/2 **DosOpen** API call. This is followed by a **DosSetNPHState** call, which changes the pipe from a byte-stream pipe (the default for open) to a message-pipe. These two new OS/2 API calls are described below. It may seem like the description of **DosOpen** goes on forever because, in addition to Named Pipes, this important function is used for opening files and devices. It contains all the sharing hooks required by a file system to operate in a multitasking environment.

DosOpen

The **DosOpen** API call opens an existing file, device, or Named Pipe. It can also create a new file. The call returns a handle which can be used to read from and write to a file, device, or Named Pipe. The prototype for this call is:

```
DosOpen(PSZ       Name,        /* path name of file, pipe, device*/
        PHFILE    Handle,      /* handle (returned )            */
        PULONG    Action,      /* action taken (returned)       */
        ULONG     Size,        /* file's new size               */
        ULONG     Attr,        /* attributes                    */
        ULONG     OpenFlags,   /* action take if file exists    */
        ULONG     OpenMode,    /* open shared/access mode       */
        PEAOP2    EABuff);     /* pointer to Extended Attr buffer*/
```

A description of the parameters follows:

- The *Name* parameter points to a null-terminated string that contains the name of the file, device, or Named Pipe to be opened. Named Pipes are named **\PIPE\PipeName**, where **\PIPE** is the name of a virtual subdirectory in memory.
- The *Handle* parameter points to a variable that receives the Named Pipe, device or file handle.
- The *Action* parameter points to a variable that specifies the action returned by the API if successful. It is one of the following three values:

```
Value      Action Taken
  1        (FILE_EXISTED); File, device or Named Pipe already exists.
  2        (FILE_CREATED); File, device or Named Pipe created.
  3        (FILE_TRUNCATED); File existed and was replaced.
```

- The *Size* parameter specifies the file's new size in bytes. It is significant only when creating a new file or replacing an existing file and is otherwise ignored. This is only a recommended size for the file. The file system makes a reasonable attempt to allocate the new size in as nearly contiguous an area as possible on the medium.
- The *Attr* parameter specifies the file attributes. It can be a combination (the OR) of the following values:

```
Value                    Meaning
FILE_NORMAL              File is read/write
FILE_READONLY            File is read only
FILE_HIDDEN             File does not appear in directories
FILE_SYSTEM             System file
FILE_ARCHIVED           File has been archived
FILE_DIRECTORY          File is a subdirectory
```

- The *OpenFlags* parameter specifies what to do when opening a file which exists or does not exist. Choices of actions are:

```
Value                        Meaning
OPEN_ACTION_FAIL_IF_EXISTS   Create new file;  fail if file exists
OPEN_ACTION_FAIL_IF_NEW      Open existing file; fail if does not exist
OPEN_ACTION_CREATE_IF_NEW    Open existing file; create if does not exist
OPEN_ACTION_OPEN_IF_EXISTS   Open existing file; if it exists
OPEN_ACTION_REPLACE_IF_EXISTS Open existing file; replace if existed
```

- The *OpenMode* parameter specifies, among other things, how file sharing is enforced in a multiprocess environment. File sharing requires interprocess cooperation, which gets communicated through the sharing and access modes. Any sharing restrictions placed on a file opened by a process are removed when the process closes the file with a DosClose request. The *Sharing Mode* specifies the type of access other processes may have to the file. For example, if you will allow other processes to read the file after your process opened it, then specify Deny Write. This sharing mode prevents other processes from writing to the file, but still allows them to read it. The *Access Mode* specifies the type of access to the file needed by your process. For example, if your process requires Read/Write access, and another process has already opened the file with a sharing mode of Deny None, your DosOpen request succeeds. However, if the file is open with a sharing mode of Deny Write, your process is denied access. All the sharing and access restrictions are inherited. They will also apply to duplicated handles. The *OpenMode* parameter must contain one access mode choice and one shared mode choice. The other options can be given in any combination:

```
Value                        Meaning
OPEN_ACCESS_READONLY         Caller will only read from file
OPEN_ACCESS_READWRITE        Caller will read/write
OPEN_ACCESS_WRITEONLY        Caller will write only

OPEN_SHARE_DENYNONE          Other processes can open file for any access
OPEN_SHARE_DENYREAD          Other processes can open file for write only
OPEN_SHARE_DENYWRITE         Other processes can open file for read only
OPEN_SHARE_DENYREADWRITE     Caller has exclusive access to file

OPEN_FLAGS_DASD              FileName is "Drive:" and represents a mounted
                             disk or diskette volume to be opened for
                             direct access.
OPEN_FLAGS_FAIL_ON_ERROR     Report media errors to caller via return code.
                             Don't display error popup
OPEN_FLAGS_NOINHERIT         File is private and not inheritable.
OPEN_FLAGS_WRITE_THROUGH     No file buffering.
OPEN_FLAGS_NO_CACHE          No file caching
```

- The *EABuff* parameter is a pointer to an *extended attribute* buffer. You can use this buffer to set extended attributes when creating a file or replacing an existing file, but not when opening an existing file. Set this parameter to zero if you're not going to define or modify extended attributes.

Named Pipe Considerations

* DosOpen opens the client end of a pipe by name and returns a handle. The open succeeds only if the pipe is in a listening state.
* Once a given instance has been opened by a client, that same instance cannot be opened by another client at the same time.
* Pipes can only be two-ended; however, the opening process can duplicate the open handle as many times as desired.
* The access and sharing modes specified on the open must be consistent with those specified by the DosCreateNPipe.

DosSetNPHState

The **DosSetNPHState** API call is issued to change the read or wait modes of a Named Pipe handle. This call will be used mostly by clients to modify the default DosOpen. The default always opens the Named Pipe with the wait and byte stream message modes activated. The client can change these modes by calling **DosSetNPHState** if desired. The prototype for this call is:

```
DosSetNPHState(HPIPE    handle,            /* Pipe Handle    */
               ULONG    state_flag);       /* State flag     */
```

A description of the parameters follows:

* The *handle* parameter is the Named Pipe instance identifier returned by DosCreateNPipe or DosOpen.
* The *state_flag* parameter specifies the updated mode of the Named Pipe handle; it consists of the following bit fields:

```
Bits                        Value
31-16    Reserved.
15       Wait flag:
         0 = (NP_WAIT); Wait (i.e block) if no data available.
         1 = (NP_NOWAIT); Return immediately if no data available.
14-10    Reserved, must be zero.
9-8      Read-Mode Flag:
         00 = (NP_READMODE_BYTE); Read pipe as a byte stream.
         01 = (NP_READMODE_MESSAGE);Read pipe as a message stream.
         Message pipes can be read as byte or message streams,
         Byte pipes can only be read as byte streams.
7-0      Reserved, must be zero.
```

```
/*————————————————————————————————————————————————*/
/* function a requester uses to prepare a pipe for communication.    */
/*————————————————————————————————————————————————*/
ULONG fx_Open(VOID)
{ CHAR RemotePipeName[128];

                        /*———————————————————————————*/
                        /* defines for DosOpen           */
                        /*———————————————————————————*/
#define PIPE_HANDLE_STATE  0x0100    /* blocking, message stream          */

    /*————————————————————————*/
    /* create a remote pipe name from    */
    /*    parameters read during         */
    /*    fx_Initialize                  */
    /*————————————————————————*/
    strcpy(RemotePipeName, ComputerName);
    strcat(RemotePipeName, PipeName);

    rc = DosOpen(RemotePipeName,      /* name of pipe to open, may include  */
                                      /*    the name of a remote computer   */
            &PipeHandle,              /* handle returned                    */
            &ActionTaken,             /* open action returned               */
            0L,                       /* File size for name pipe            */
            FILE_NORMAL,              /* File is read/write                 */
            FILE_OPEN,                /* open if pipe exists, otherwise fail */
            OPEN_FLAGS_FAIL_ON_ERROR |
            OPEN_SHARE_DENYNONE
            OPEN_ACCESS_READWRITE,    /* open mode flags                    */
            0L);
    if (rc)
        {print_error(rc,"Opening a named pipe",__FILE__,__LINE__);
         return(FAILED);
        }

    /*————————————————————————*/
    /* change to a message pipe          */
    /*————————————————————————*/
    rc = DosSetNPHState(PipeHandle,    /* pipe handle returned from DosOpen  */
                    PIPE_HANDLE_STATE);
    if (rc)
        {print_error(rc,"setting a named pipe handle state",__FILE__,__LINE__);
         return(FAILED);
        }

    return(GOOD);
} /* end fx_Open */
```

Figure 17-9. FXNPIPE.C: fx_Open().

FXNPIPE.C: fx_Write()

The **fx_Write()** function (see Figure 17-10) falls in the very straightforward category.
All it does is turn around and issue the equivalent OS/2 **DosWrite** IPC call described
next. Notice that Named Pipes use the ULONG type for the number of bytes transferred. We use the USHORT type for the fx_ variable byte counts because some of
protocols that we will use later can only accept maximum message sizes of 64 KBytes.
The variable **bytes** is used for the ULONG to USHORT conversion.

DosWrite

The **DosWrite** API call transfers the specified number of bytes from a buffer to the specified file, pipe, or device. The prototype for this call is:

```
DosWrite(HFILE    handle,        /* file, device or pipe handle        */
         PVOID    OutBuf,        /* output buffer                      */
         ULONG    count,         /* number of bytes to be written      */
         PULONG   BytesWritten); /* number of bytes written (returned) */
```

A description of the parameters follows:

- The *handle* parameter identifies the file, device, or Named Pipe instance to be read. The handle must have been previously created using DosOpen.
- The *OutBuf* parameter points to the buffer that contains the data to be written.
- The *count* parameter specifies the number of bytes to write.
- The *BytesWritten* parameter points to a variable that receives the count of the number of bytes written. If BytesWritten is different from count, this usually indicates insufficient disk space.

Named Pipe Considerations

- Each write to a *message* pipe writes a message whose size is the length of the write. DosWrite automatically encodes message lengths in the pipe, so applications need not encode this information in the buffer being written.
- In the case of a *byte* pipe, if the number of bytes to be written exceeds the space available in the pipe, DosWrite writes as many bytes as it can and returns with the number of bytes actually written.
- Writes in blocking mode always write all the requested bytes before returning. If the pipe buffer can't hold all the data, this call will block until the other end reads the data off the pipe and makes room in the buffer. Message mode pipes will block if the pipe can't hold the entire message.
- In non-blocking mode, if the message size is bigger than the buffer size, the write blocks. If the message size is smaller than the pipe but not enough space is left in the pipe, the write returns immediately with a value of zero, indicating no bytes were written.
- An attempt to write to a pipe whose other end has been closed returns ER-ROR_BROKEN_PIPE.

```
/*_____*/
/* function both requester and server use to write to a pipe.      */
/*_____*/
ULONG fx_Write(PVOID BufferArea, USHORT BufferLength, PUSHORT BytesWritten)
{
  ULONG bytes;

  rc = DosWrite(PipeHandle,            /* handle returned from DosOpen or  */
                                       /* DosMakeNmPipe                    */
               BufferArea,
               BufferLength,
               &bytes);
  if (rc)
     {print_error(rc,"Writing to a named pipe",__FILE__,__LINE__);
      return(FAILED);
      }

  *BytesWritten = bytes;
  return(GOOD);
} /* end fx_Write */
```

Figure 17-10.   FXNPIPE.C: fx_Write().

FXNPIPE.C: fx_Read()

The **fx_Read()** function (see Figure 17-11) is also in the very straightforward category. All it does is turn around and issue the equivalent OS/2 **DosRead** IPC call described below:

DosRead

The **DosRead** API call reads the specified number of bytes from a file, pipe, or device to a buffer location. The function may read fewer than the specified number of bytes if it reaches the end of the file or if it is in Named Pipe message mode. The prototype for this call is:

```
DosRead(HFILE   handle,      /* file, device or pipe handle    */
        PVOID   InBuf,       /* input buffer                   */
        ULONG   count,       /* number of bytes to be read     */
        PULONG  BytesRead);  /* number of bytes read (returned) */
```

A description of the parameters follows:

- The *handle* parameter identifies the file, device, or Named Pipe instance to be read. The handle must have been previously created using DosOpen.
- The *InBuf* parameter points to the buffer that receives the data.
- The *count* parameter specifies the number of bytes to read.
- The *BytesRead* parameter points to a variable that receives the count of the number of bytes actually read. This parameter is 0 if the file pointer is positioned at the end of the file prior to the DosRead call.

Named Pipe Considerations

- A Named Pipe in *byte* read mode reads all currently available data, up to the size requested.
- A message pipe in *message* read mode returns only the next available message even if more bytes are requested than are in the message (the BytesRead argument will be set appropriately). If the read request is for fewer bytes than the size of the message, the bytes requested are read into the buffer and an ERROR_MORE_DATA is also returned. Subsequent DosRead calls will continue to read the message where the last call left off, but without crossing over to the next message.
- A message pipe is read as if it were a byte stream, skipping over message headers. This is like reading a byte pipe in byte read mode. A read size that is smaller than the next available message returns with the number of bytes requested and an ERROR_MORE_DATA return code. When resuming the reading of a message after ERROR_MORE_DATA is returned, a read always blocks until the next piece (or the rest) of the message can be received. DosPeekNPipe may be used to determine how many bytes are left in the message.
- When blocking mode is set for a Named Pipe, a read blocks until data is available. The read never returns with BytesRead = 0, except at EOF. In message read mode, messages are always read in their entirety except in the case where the message is bigger than the size of the read.
- When non-blocking mode is set, BytesRead = 0 is returned when no data is available at the time of the read.

```
/*————————————————————————————————————————————————*/
/* function both requester and server use to read from a pipe.          */
/*————————————————————————————————————————————————*/
ULONG fx_Read(PVOID BufferArea, USHORT BufferLength, PUSHORT BytesRead)
{
  ULONG bytes;

  rc = DosRead(PipeHandle,               /* handle returned from DosOpen or  */
                                         /* DosMakeNmPipe                    */
              BufferArea,
              BufferLength,
              &bytes);
  if (rc)
     {print_error(rc,"Reading from a named pipe",__FILE__,__LINE__);
      return(FAILED);
     }

  *BytesRead = bytes;
  return(GOOD);
} /* end fx_Read */
```

Figure 17-11. FXNPIPE.C: fx_Read().

FXNPIPE.C: fx_Transact()

The **fx_Transact()** function (see Figure 17-12) is also very straightforward. All it does is turn around and issue the equivalent OS/2 **DosTransactNPipe** IPC call described below:

DosTransactNPipe

The **DosTransactNPipe** API call performs, in one step, a write followed by a read. This call can only be used on duplex message pipes and allows you to implement transaction-oriented dialogs. **DosTransactNPipe** writes the entire InBuffer to the pipe and then reads a response from the pipe into the OutBuffer and does not return until a message has been read into the OutBuffer. The transaction fails if the Named Pipe contains any unread data. The prototype for this call is:

```
DosTransactNPipe(HPIPE    handle,      /* Pipe handle                   */
                 PVOID    OutBuf,      /* Write buffer address          */
                 ULONG    OutLength,   /* Write buffer length           */
                 PVOID    InBuf,       /* Read buffer address           */
                 ULONG    InLen,       /* Read buffer length            */
                 PULONG   BytesRead);  /* Actual number of Bytes read   */
```

A description of the parameters follows:

- The *handle* parameter identifies a the Named Pipe instance. It is the handle returned by DosCreateNPipe or DosOpen.
- The *OutBuf* parameter points to the buffer containing the data to be written to the pipe.
- The *OutLength* parameter specifies the size in bytes of the output buffer.
- The *InBuf* parameter points to the input buffer.
- The *InLen* parameter specifies the size in bytes of the input buffer.
- The *BytesRead* parameter points to a variable that receives the actual number of bytes read into the input buffer.

```
/*_____*/
/* function requester uses to request a service.                  */
/*_____*/
ULONG fx_Transact(PVOID InBufferArea,  USHORT InBufferLength,
                  PVOID OutBufferArea, USHORT OutBufferLength,
                  PUSHORT BytesRead)
{
  ULONG bytes;

  rc = DosTransactNPipe(PipeHandle,    /* handle returned from DosOpen    */
                        InBufferArea,
                        InBufferLength,
                        OutBufferArea,
                        OutBufferLength,
                        &bytes);
  if (rc)
     {print_error(rc,"executing a pipe transaction",__FILE__,__LINE__);
      return(FAILED);
      }

  *BytesRead = bytes;
  return(GOOD);
} /* end fx_Transact */
```

Figure 17-12. FXNPIPE.C: fx_Transact().

FXNPIPE.C: fx_Close()

The **fx_Close()** function (see Figure 17-13) is the last of a streak of very straightforward to implement functions. All it does is turn around and issue the equivalent OS/2 **DosClose** IPC call described below:

DosClose

The **DosClose** API call closes a handle to a file, pipe, or device. The call causes the system to write the contents of the file's internal buffers to the device, and to update directory information where applicable. If one or more additional handles to a file have been created with DosDupHandle, the directory is not updated and all internal buffers are not written to the medium until DosClose has been issued for the duplicated handles. The prototype for this call is:

```
DosClose(HFILE   handle);        /* file handle              */
```

A description of the parameters follows:

- The first *handle* parameter identifies the file, device, or Named Pipe instance to be closed. The handle must have been previously created using DosOpen.

Named Pipe Considerations

- When all handles referencing one end of a pipe are closed, the pipe is considered broken.
- If the client end closes, no other process can reopen the pipe until the serving end issues a DosDisConnectNPipe followed by a DosConnectNPipe.
- If the server end closes when the pipe is already broken, it is deallocated immediately; otherwise, the pipe is not deallocated until the last client handle is closed.

```
/*————————————————————————————————————————————*/
/* function reqester uses to end communication with a server.          */
/*————————————————————————————————————————————*/
ULONG fx_Close(VOID)
{
  rc = DosClose(PipeHandle);        /* handle from DosOpen or DosMakeNmPipe */
  if (rc)
    {print_error(rc,"Closing a named pipe",__FILE__,__LINE__);
     return(FAILED);
     }
  else return(GOOD);
} /* end fx_Close */
```

Figure 17-13.   FXNPIPE.C: fx_Close().

Part III

Communication Protocols for Client/Server

Part III covers peer-to-peer protocols for client/server exchanges over Local Area Networks (LANs). We will develop programs that use OS/2's extensive LAN protocols. As was explained in Part I, OS/2 provides an overwhelming offering of communication services. We will focus our attention on those offerings that are of interest to a client/server programming platform. These are primarily the *peer-to-peer* facilities required for the exchange of data and services between clients and servers. Peer-to-peer protocols allow you to create your *own* intercomputer message exchanges. As you will soon discover, message exchanges provide the lifeblood of client/server systems.

In Part III, we also cover the LAN Requester/Server types of "canned" exchanges that transform OS/2 into a "Network Operating System". The LAN Server provides a powerful repertoire of services, including file server, print server, remote Named Pipes, and network management. In Part IV, we will add the power of a network database server to our repertoire of canned client/server services. This is when you'll have at your disposal all the distributed software ingredients needed to provide your client/server applications access to data and services wherever they are.

The approach we take in Part III is to provide you with the necessary background information in the form of tutorials and then focus on developing a set of peer-to-peer program examples that use these LAN protocols: **NetBIOS**, **CPI-C/APPC**, and **Sockets on TCP/IP**. We will also cover **Named Pipes** as a client/server protocol on NetWare and LAN Server LANs. Named Pipes extend OS/2's Interprocess Communication (IPC) services across the network without your programs ever being aware of it (the network is made transparent). We will also be covering the important **LAN Requester/Server** service, even though it does not fall into the category of a general-purpose LAN protocol. We will look at this service from the viewpoint of how it performs compared to the "do-it-yourself" types of communications schemes we will be introducing.

The programming examples that are introduced in Part III extend the **FX DLL** services to work across machines using the OS/2 LAN protocols. In addition to serving as production-quality template programs, the examples double as learning tools that can be used to understand and measure the performance trade-offs of the LAN protocols.

Here is the "road map" we will follow in Part III:

- In Chapter 18, "A Tutorial on NetBIOS," we cover all you need to know about the NetBIOS LAN protocol.

- In Chapter 19, "FX Using NetBIOS," we develop FXNETB.C, which implements the **FX DLL** interface for file transfer using NetBIOS.

- In Chapter 20, "A Tutorial on TCP/IP Sockets," we cover all you need to know about the Sockets interface to TCP/IP.

- In Chapter 21, "FX Using TCP/IP Sockets," we develop FXTCPIP.C, which implements the **FX DLL** interface for file transfer using Berkeley Sockets on TCP/IP.

- In Chapter 22, "A Tutorial on CPI-C and APPC," we cover all you need to know about CPI-C, APPC, and SNA.

- In Chapter 23, "FX with CPI-C," we develop FXAPPC.C, which implements the **FX DLL** interface for file transfer using CPI-C/APPC.

- In Chapter 24, "FX Using LAN Server, NetWare, and Remote Named Pipes," we perform the file transfers using *remote* Named Pipes on NetWare and LAN Server. We also implement a version of FX using LAN Server's canned NOS facilities.

- In Chapter 25, "The Great FX LAN Derby," we compare the performance of the LAN protocols. We are in the remarkable position of having in front of us a consistent set of benchmarks that compare local and remote process-to-process communications using the wide range of standard protocols. This is where we will publish the results of our LAN protocol Derby and the BLOB Olympics.

Chapter 18

A Tutorial on NetBIOS

This chapter presents a tutorial on NetBIOS, a *peer-to-peer* LAN protocol. We start by defining peer-to-peer protocols. We then examine what makes distributed software so different, and in the process develop a set of requirements for an "ideal" peer-to-peer protocol. This should provide us with a framework for evaluating the LAN protocols that OS/2 provides. It tells us what to look for when we do our comparison shopping for protocols. We then look in some detail at NetBIOS and the services it provides. We conclude the tutorial with scenarios that demonstrate how NetBIOS is used in typical network applications.

PEER-TO-PEER PROTOCOLS

In this section, we will answer questions such as: What is a peer-to-peer protocol? When do I need to use one? What are the pitfalls of network software? What should I be looking for in an "ideal" peer-to-peer protocol?

What Is a Peer-to-Peer Protocol?

A *Peer-to-peer* protocol, as the name implies, is the communication between equals. This is in contrast to the older hierarchical *master-slave* type of network protocols where all the communications is initiated by the master. A peer-to-peer protocol provides the primitives to perform process-to-process communications across network nodes. This kind of communication is required to synchronize the nodes involved in a client/server network application and to pass work requests back and forth. You would typically use the peer-to-peer protocols to create your own LAN exchanges, with message structures and semantics that are customized to your application's needs.

Do I Need a Peer-to-Peer Protocol?

Typically, a large percentage of your network services can be provided by an "off-the-shelf" client/server package with built-in network communications. Here are some examples:

- The **LAN Requester/Server** and the **NetWare Requester for OS/2**, which can be used "as is" to obtain remote file and printer services that extend the operating system.
- The Database Manager's **Remote Data Services** provide transparent access to remote tables and stored procedures.
- Off-the-shelf products with built-in communications services and the APIs to access them. Examples include **Lotus Notes and CC:Mail**, which provide access to electronic mail and document distribution services.

However, there are times when "off-the-shelf" solutions may not do a job. This is when you will need to program a peer-to-peer protocol. The peer-to-peer protocol is the general-purpose communication toolkit that you can always rely on to perform almost any "network job."

OS/2's Peer-to-Peer Protocols

There are four peer-to-peer protocol offerings in the OS/2 client/server platform we selected: NetBIOS, CPI-C/APPC, Named Pipes (on NetWare and LAN Server), and Sockets on TCP/IP. These protocols are, in a sense, competing for the endorsement of network application developers. One of the purposes of the material in Part III is to provide a level playing field that lets you judge how these protocols stack up in the following areas:

- The systems they connect to
- The communications features they provide
- Performance
- Ease of programming

It is imperative that you understand the trade-offs involved before we go too far down the path of software development. Ideally, you will want to invest time and energy understanding and keeping up with, at most, one LAN protocol. It should be there, ready to be used when needed, like a hammer or a screwdriver in a toolbox.

Cooperative Network Software

As we said in the introduction to Part III, OS/2 provides the platform to create software that goes beyond the "stand-alone put it on your desk" type of application. We can now create the tools to develop new categories of distributed software that can access data and services wherever they are. Data in particular tends to start its life in many strange locations, and eventually may need to be collected and assembled from different sources and repositories. Local Area Networks are making it possible to use PCs in shared applications while retaining their autonomy for personal computing. The number of different ways applications and data can come together over networks is only limited by the imagination. So, how can we talk meaningfully about network software?

Client/Server Transaction Processing

The approach we'll take is to concentrate on a particular kind of *cooperative* network software and use it as a generic model for establishing a common framework. Applications in distributed environments can be partitioned in several different ways. One of the more popular partitions is the *client/server* model where applications are broken into front-end and back-end entities. We will use the client/server model as our network software paradigm because most of the distributed software developed in this book falls into that category. This book is on applications where the front-end clients and the back-end servers work together on executing a *cooperative transaction*. These applications are characterized as real-time, multiuser, shared database applications that alter the state of a business entity. *Transactions* are business activities that transform a database from one state to another (for example, monitor the movement of a part on a shop floor, make an airline reservation, or custom order an automobile).

In a distributed application, the *front-end clients* typically provide an interactive GUI interface, data validation, error-reporting, varying amounts of local computation, and message communication with the back-end nodes that provide shared services. The *back-end server* typically provide shared services to the front-ends. Back-end servers may be PCs, hosts, clusters of hosts, or combinations of the above. Back-end nodes may operate either singly or in some form of cooperative arrangement.

The Cooperative Transaction

The cooperative synergy between the back-end and front-end nodes over the LAN introduces a new form of architecture that replaces the traditional terminal/host paradigm of computing with a new form of *cooperative computing*.

The fundamental building block of cooperative applications is the *cooperative transaction*. Unlike transactions in traditional host/terminal environments, cooperative transactions span multiple nodes. As an example, a cooperative transaction may start when the end user first enters or selects data on the screen of the front-end node. The transaction ends when all nodes have completed all of the work for the transaction, and control is back to the front-end node. This time span may be short, with a simple request resulting in a single response. Or it may be long and complex, and require many front-end interactions with the user and several exchanges between the front-end and back-end nodes. Transaction management is a distributed task in which the front-end and back-end processes must cooperate to provide the services and synchronization necessary for success or recovery in the case of a failure.

LAN technology is a requirement for these kinds of applications. LANs not only provide low-error high-bandwidth communications, but also provide new functionality such as broadcast facilities, group names, and multiple sessions per PC. These facilities enable new types of applications that are far richer and more cost effective than their "stand-alone" counterparts.

The Pitfalls of Distributed Software

However, all these gains come at a price. The distributed software introduces some new levels of complexity in application design. For example, consider the following design implications introduced by the client/server category of software:

- The front-end and back-end processes are autonomous entities connected via a network. They must be able to fail and recover independently. Each must be robust despite failures of the other.
- Communication failures may look like hardware or software failures. The communicating processes must be able to detect the error and resynchronize after a network failure, regardless of the cause.
- The number of messages to maintain global state across a network must be minimized to enhance performance.
- Peer-to-peer symmetrical protocols create more complex situations and more subtle errors than the centralized master/slave protocols of host/terminals.
- Clients must be able to find servers over LANs, and they must have a way to identify themselves, and prove their identity, on an open network.

Is distributed software still worth pursuing? The answer is absolutely yes; the potential benefits far outweigh the costs.

So What Should the "Ideal" Peer-to-Peer Protocol Do?

From a network application programmer's perspective, an "ideal" peer-to-peer protocols should, at the very least, provide the same list of functions as the "ideal" IPC (see Chapter 15). We add to the IPC list the following "wish list" of network-specific functions:

- Any-to-any protocols that provide program-to-program communications independent of operating systems, hardware, programming languages, transport and link protocols, data representation, etc.. In short, these protocols must provide a wide choice of connectivity options. If nothing else, the protocol should connect whatever your application requires to have connected.
- Logical naming of network entities. There should be a mechanism to provide unique names and group names or "aliases."
- Broadcast of messages to all nodes on a network.
- Multicast of messages to named groups.
- Reliable end-to-end sequenced transmissions between two named entities. We will refer to this form of reliable transmission as a session-based service.
- Concurrent multiple-session support on a given node. This allows for multiple conversations to take place at the same time.
- Support multiple conversations on a single session. A conversation provides a way for applications to take turns using a shared session.

- Datagram commands for low overhead short messages. Datagram is required for broadcast and multicast transmissions.
- Execution of the network commands in "wait" or "no-wait" modes so that processing may continue while communication occurs.
- Cancelling a network command.
- Stacking multiple network commands for execution to enable several LAN-related tasks at the same time.
- Support for the generation and processing of network events. A network event may be the receipt of a message, a datagram alert, a session connect request, the abnormal termination of a session, a high-priority message, or a communication from a particular named entity. Support for conditional event triggering should be provided as a feature, allowing us to trigger on the receipt of a combination of events. At the least, the recipient program should be started if it is not already running by the arrival of a request to start a session.
- An authentication mechanism such as encrypted passwords for secure sessions.
- Support for *transaction processing,* which includes the following:

  1. *Recoverable sessions* that support the logging of messages on fixed media. A recoverable message queue can be used to reconstitute the system after a network crash.
  2. *Remote invocation of procedures*. that should be loaded, invoked, and passed parameters. This invocation is triggered by the arrival of a message.
  3. *Sync-points* that allow programs to establish mutually agreed upon points at which programs or data can be verified. In case of error, work can be backed up to the last sync-point rather than starting all over from scratch. Sync-point commands may be useful to delineate units of recovery provided work can be rolled back at the application level up to the last communication sync-point. This means a network sync-point and a database commit should be simultaneously issued. If the database commit will be surfaced at the peer-to-peer level, then it requires additional primitives, such as abort and prepare-to-commit (i.e., the full implementation of a two-phase commit protocol).

NETBIOS: A PEER-TO-PEER LAN PROTOCOL

In this section of the tutorial, we answer the following questions: Where does NetBIOS fit into the scheme of things? What services are provided by NetBIOS? How is NetBIOS used? The intimate details on how to program NetBIOS will appear in a later chapter.

Situating NetBIOS

As you may recall from the introduction to Communications Manager in Part I, NetBIOS is the premier protocol for LAN-based program-to-program communications. Introduced by IBM and Sytek in 1984 for the IBM PC Network, NetBIOS now runs with almost no changes on Ethernets, Token Rings, ARCnets, StarLANs, and even low-cost serial-port LANs. NetBIOS interfaces to IBM/Microsoft LANs, TCP/IP, XNS, OSI, and IPX/SPX protocol stacks. Support for a NetBIOS platform exists on a multiplicity of operating system environments, including MS-DOS, OS/2, UNIX, and some mainframe environments. NetBIOS is currently the de facto portable standard for network application providers. One of the many reasons for NetBIOS's success is its intuitive simplicity which makes it easy to master.

Providing Services the NetBIOS Way

The NetBIOS services are provided through a set of **commands**, specified in a structure called the Network Control Block, or **NCB**. The structure also contains the parameters associated with the command and the fields in which NetBIOS will return information to the program. The NCB can be viewed as a general-purpose command container that gets passed to a NetBIOS DLL by invoking the **NETBIOS()** Communications Manager API call. So technically speaking, the NetBIOS API consists of a single OS/2 call.

The NetBIOS DLL can handle multiple commands concurrently. A command can be issued in either wait or no-wait mode. In the *wait* mode, the requesting thread is blocked until the command completes. In the *no-wait* mode, control is returned to the calling thread at the earliest time possible, usually before the command completes. When the command completes, the NetBIOS DLL places a return code in the NCB. You may request, through the NCB, to have a "post-routine" executed when a command completes. An NCB is owned by the NetBIOS DLL until the command completes. The NetBIOS DLL creates a thread for each active no-wait command; so if you have too many outstanding commands, you may eventually run out of system resources.

NetBIOS's Four Command Categories

The NetBIOS commands (see Table 18-1) can be placed into the following four categories:

- General services commands
- Name support commands
- Session support commands
- Datagram support commands

NetBIOS: General Purpose Commands

The general purpose commands provide miscellaneous types of networking services. Table 18-2 presents a quick summary of the function each general service command provides, as well as the command codes for both wait and no-wait modes where applicable.

Table 18-1. NetBIOS: Command Categories.

General Services	Name Services	Session Services	Datagram Services
Reset Status Cancel Alert Unlink	Add Name Add Group Name Delete Name Find Name	Call Listen Send Chain Send Send No-Ack Chain Send No-Ack Receive Receive Any Hang Up Session Status	Send Datagram Send-Broadcast Datagram Receive Datagram Receive-Broadcast Datagram

Table 18-2. NetBIOS: General Purpose Commands.

Command Name	Command Code		Function Description
	Wait (Hex)	No-Wait (Hex)	
Reset	32		Under OS/2 a process issues Reset to request resources for its use from the NetBIOS resource pool. A process should also issue a Reset to deallocate its resources and return them to the NetBIOS pool for subsequent use by other processes. When a process terminates, OS/2 implicitly issues a NetBIOS Reset to deallocate the resources the process owns. The resources that can be requested include: the number of sessions, number of commands, names, etc..
Status	33	B3	This command is used to obtain information on the status of a local or remote network adapter. A wealth of information gets returned, including the adapter's burned-in address.
Cancel	35		This command is used to cancel a pending command. This is useful when you are using no-wait commands. Cancellation always ends a session.
Alert		F3	This command is used by applications that want to be notified of soft error conditions at the adapter level that last over one minute.
Unlink	70		This command is provided for compatibilty with previous NetBIOS versions. Under OS/2 it is treated as a "no-operation."

NetBIOS: Name Support Commands

Why Logical Naming?

With NetBIOS's name services, a LAN adapter card can have multiple logical names, each consisting of 16 bytes. Logical naming is a way to make your programs independent from burned-in adapter numbers. Not having to rely on a stream of digits makes communications programs clearer and less error-prone. It is much more convenient (and more personal) to call a remote adapter by a logical nickname, such as "Bob," instead of a burned-in address like X'444221113355'.

NetBIOS Naming Services

Here is a summary of the naming services NetBIOS provides:

* It maintains a list of logical names assigned to an adapter in a local name table. This table is volatile and needs to be recreated dynamically when an application program is started.
* It supports both unique names and group names. If a name is unique, NetBIOS will make sure no such name already exists on the network before it gets added to the name table. If the name is a group name, NetBIOS will make sure that nobody else on the LAN is claiming that name as unique. Group names are used for sending messages to a group of workstations.
* It returns a name handle that identifies successfully registered names.
* It allows you to deregister a name when it is no longer needed.

Table 18-3 provides a quick summary of the function each NetBIOS name support command provides as well as the command codes for both wait and no-wait modes.

NetBIOS: Session Support Commands

What Is a Session?

NetBIOS sessions provide a reliable logical connection service over which a pair of network applications can exchange information. Each packet of information that gets exchanged over a session is given a sequence number through which it gets tracked and individually acknowledged. The packets are received in the order sent and blocked into user messages. Duplicate packets are detected and discarded by the session services. The price you pay for this reliable class of service is the overhead associated with creating and managing the session.

Table 18-3. NetBIOS: Name Support Commands.

Command Name	Command Code		Function Description
	Wait (Hex)	No-Wait (Hex)	
Add Name	30	B0	This command allows you to add a unique name to the local name table. This is the name an application on this machine will be known by.
Add Group Name	36	B6	This command allows you to add a group name to the local name table. This is the name this application and other applications are known by.
Delete Name	31	B1	This command deletes a name from the local name table. This name must not be associated with active sessions when the command is issued.
Find Name	78	F8	This command is issued to find the location on the network of a given name. NetBIOS broadcasts a query and returns whether the name is a unique name or group name; it also returns the list of adapters that responded to the query.

NetBIOS's Session Services

Here is what NetBIOS provides to help you get this class of service:

- Applications can create sessions between two adapter names. You tell NetBIOS through a listen command who you want to talk to, and NetBIOS will inform you when you've been called. Using an asterisk (*), you can specify that you will accept a connection from *any* adapter that calls you. Once the two applications are *matched*, NetBIOS will provide a handle number that is used to identify this session.
- Once a session is in place, applications can receive information from a particular partner or from any partner that is in session with a specified name, or from any partner to any name for which a session was created.
- Applications can send messages, up to 64 KBytes (contiguous in memory), with a single send command. If this is not enough, the Chain Send command can be used to send two buffers of user data for up to 128 KBytes. On the receiver end, the receive command will treat the two buffers as a contiguous single message if the combined size of the two messages does not exceed 64 KBytes. Otherwise, a second receive is issued to accept the remaining data.
- Applications can find out the status of a session and determine if it is still active or if it got cancelled. In addition, a wealth of other information is provided for a particular session or for all sessions, including the number of sessions with this local name, the name of the remote partners, the number of NCBs outstanding, etc.

Table 18-4 provides a quick summary of the function each NetBIOS session support command provides, as well as the command codes for both wait and no-wait modes.

Table 18-4. NetBIOS: Session Support Commands.

Command Name	Command Code		Function Description
	Wait (Hex)	No-Wait (Hex)	
Call	10	90	This command attempts to open a session with another name. The caller's name and the partner's name are both specified in the NCB. The destination station must have an outstanding Listen so that the session can be established. Multiple sessions may be established with the same pair of names.
Listen	11	91	This command allows you to accept a session call. You can specify whether you will accept calls from a named partner or from any name that calls.
Send	14	94	This command sends data to the session partner as defined in the lsn NCB field. You will supply the data to send in a separate buffer pointed to by the buffer_address field in the NCB. You must supply the message size length, which can be between 0 and 65,535 bytes long.
Chain Send	17	97	This command is like Send, except that you can point to two data buffers that get sent as a single message. The message size must be between 0 and 131,070 bytes long.
Send Ack	71	F1	This command is like Send, except that no data acknowledgement is required at the NetBIOS level. This will speed up the send and you'll still get some reliability from the link layer sequencing.
Chain Send No-Ack	72	F2	This command is like Chain Send, except that no data acknowledgement is required at the NetBIOS level.
Receive	15	95	This command receives data from a session partner, which sends data using any of the session send commands. A return code will tell you if the receive buffer you specified is not large enough for the incoming message. Issue another Receive to read the rest of the message.
Receive Any	16	96	This command is like Receive, except that data can be received from any partner that is in session with the specified name.
Hang Up	12	92	This command closes an open session identified by the lsn field in the NCB.
Session Status	34	B4	This command obtains information about all the sessions with a local name or for all local names.

NetBIOS: Datagram Support Commands

What Is a Datagram?

NetBIOS's datagrams provide a simple but unreliable transmission service with powerful broadcast capabilities. You can send datagrams to a named entity, to a select group of entities (multicast), or to all entities on a network (broadcast). Datagrams are unreliable in the sense that their information packets are not acknowledged or tracked through a sequence number. You "transmit and pray" that your datagram gets received. The recipient may not be there or may not be expecting a datagram, and you will never know. You may, of course, design your own acknowledgement schemes on top of the datagram service.

Creating Electronic Bazaars With Datagrams

Datagrams are very useful to have in "discovery" types of situations. These are situations where you discover things about your network environment by broadcasting queries and learning who is out there from the responses. Broadcast can be used to obtain bids for services or to advertise the availability of new services. Broadcast datagrams provide the capability of creating electronic "bazaars." They support the creation of very dynamic types of environments where things can happen spontaneously. In situations where the name of the recipient is not known, broadcast datagrams are the only way to get the message out. The cost of broadcast datagrams is that, in some cases, recipients may get overloaded with "junk mail" that they have to sift through. The multicast facility helps alleviate that somehow, because broadcast mail can then be sent only to "special interest" groups. The alternative to broadcast is the network "yellow pages." These are well-known names on the network that specialize in giving out information.

Sending Control Information With Datagrams

Datagrams are very useful in situations where there is a need to send a quick message, without the world coming to an end if the message is not received. The typical situation is sending control-like information, such as telling a network manager "I'm alive." It doesn't make sense to go through all the overhead of creating a session with the network manager just to say "I'm alive," and what if there are 500 nodes on the network? The manager will need 500 permanent sessions, an exorbitant cost in resources. This is where the datagram alternative comes in. With datagrams you can send your "I'm alive" message, and if the manager misses your message once, it will get another one when you next send your next heartbeat (provided you're still alive).

NetBIOS's Datagram Services

Here is what NetBIOS provides in terms of datagram services:

- Datagrams are very fast small messages; they consume much less time and system overhead resources than the session service.
- Simple datagrams are sent to a recipient name; this may either be a unique name or a group name (multicast).
- Broadcast datagrams are sent to all adapters, including the sending machine's adapter.
- Applications can receive simple datagrams or broadcast datagrams for a specific name or for any name.
- The default size of a datagram is 512 bytes; the maximum size of the datagram is based on the size of the LAN adapter's transmit buffer.
- Datagrams cannot be received and filtered based on specific sender names.

Table 18-5 provides a quick summary of the function each NetBIOS datagram support command provides, as well as the command codes for both wait and no-wait modes.

Table 18-5. NetBIOS: Datagram Support Commands.

Command Name	Command Code		Function Description
	Wait (Hex)	No-Wait (Hex)	
Send Datagram	20	A0	This command sends a datagram message to any unique name or group name on the network.
Send Broadcast Datagram	22	A2	This command sends a datagram to every station on the network that has an outstanding Receive Broadcast Datagram command.
Receive Datagram	21	A1	This command receives a datagram from any name on the network that issues a send datagram to the local name. You can also specify by putting X'FF' in the NCB num field that you'll accept datagrams directed to any local adapter name. This command will not receive a broadcast datagram. If the receive buffer is not large enough, you will get notified, but the overflow data is lost.
Receive Broadcast Datagram	23	A3	This command receives a datagram from any name that issues a Send Broadcast Datagram. If the receive buffer is not large enough, you will get notified, but the overflow data is lost.

The Anatomy of a NetBIOS Program

A NetBIOS program goes through the following sequence of operations:

1. ***Allocate the Resources***. Every process must issue a *Reset* as its first NetBIOS command. The *Reset* is used to allocate resources for the process's exclusive use from the NetBIOS environment. The three important resources you need to allocate on a per process basis are sessions, names, and commands. You can specify the NetBIOS environment's resource pool through the Communications Manager configuration services. The following table should give you an idea of the valid range of parameters that constitute the NetBIOS pool.

Table 18-6. NetBIOS: Load Parameters System Defaults and Valid Ranges.

Load Parameter	Default	Valid Values
SESSIONS	32	0 - 254
COMMANDS	32	0 - 255
NAMES	17	0 - 254

You can change the NetBIOS defaults through the Communications Manager's Installation and Configuration facilities. You will also need to check on the maximum numbers of sessions, commands, and names supported by your LAN adapter hardware. (Note that you will be sharing the resource pool with other processes that are running concurrently on your PC. So make sure that NetBIOS has enough resources to satisfy all of the concurrent process needs.)

2. ***Add the adapter names***. The next thing a process does is issue *Add Name* and *Add Group Name* commands to create the unique and group logical names that identify an adapter to the network.

3. ***Start the persistent sessions***. The process then issues a *Listen* command for each session which will be initiated by an incoming *Call*. The application can accept a *Call* from a particular name; or by specifying (*), it can accept calls from any name on the network. The application will also issue a *Call* for each session it needs to initiate. The sessions are persistent in the sense that they will persist for the duration of an application, or until they are explicitly terminated through a *Hang Up* command.

4. ***Conduct network business***. The network business can be conducted in the following NetBIOS environments:

   • Using **persistent sessions**. Here the sender and receiver exchange messages over existing sessions using NetBIOS's session-based send and receive commands (see Table 18-4).

   • Using **non-persistent sessions**. Here the sender and receiver first establish a session and then exchange messages using NetBIOS's session-based send and receive commands (see Table 18-4). When they're through conducting their business, each party issues a *Hang Up* command. Non-persistent sessions cost you setup time, but the benefit is that they get around the limitation placed on the number of sessions. Non-persistent sessions are especially useful in situations where one server may be required to talk to hundreds of clients.

- Using **Datagrams**. Here the sender and receiver exchange messages using datagrams (see Table 18-5). The sender and receiver may create their own protocol for acknowledging the datagrams.

5. *Log off the Network*. A well-behaved network citizen "logs off the network" by issuing a NetBIOS *Reset* with the deallocate option (a non-zero in the lsn NCB field). This returns all the processes's resources to the NetBIOS pool. A deallocating *Reset* also performs the following terminating actions on behalf of the process:

- All current NetBIOS names are deleted.
- All current sessions are aborted.
- All pending commands are cancelled.
- All outstanding NCBs are purged.

If your process terminates at the same time as it stops using the network, then it need not issue an explicit *Reset*; OS/2 automatically issues a *Reset* on behalf of a terminating process that has open NetBIOS resources.

NETBIOS SCENARIOS

The scenarios that follow will help demonstrate the use of NetBIOS in typical peer-to-peer exchanges.

Scenario 1: A Simple Transaction Involving Two Processes

Scenario 1 is the NetBIOS version of the simple transaction:

```
What is Bob's Balance? ─────────────────▶

        ◀───────────────── $300
```

We show two implementations of this simple transaction (or Remote Procedure Call):

1. Using a NetBIOS session (see Figure 18-1)
2. Using a NetBIOS datagram exchange (see Figure 18-2)

Note that in both implementations we issued receive commands before issuing the sends. We can do this because NetBIOS allows us to issue multiple outstanding commands in no-wait mode. Issuing a receive before the send is a way to make sure that the reply will not get lost. This may happen, for example, if the server code runs on a very fast machine and the client runs on a very slow machine.

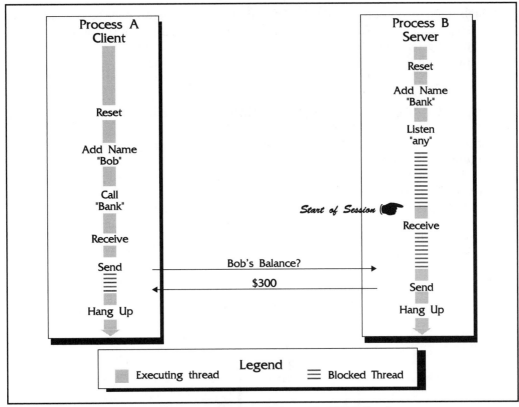

Figure 18-1. Scenario 1a: Simple Transaction Using a NetBIOS Session.

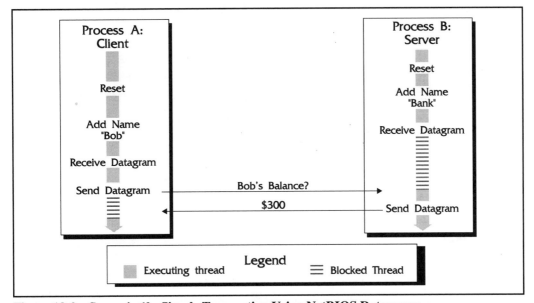

Figure 18-2. Scenario 1b: Simple Transaction Using NetBIOS Datagrams.

So which implementation is better? It's a tossup. The session may be overkill for a two-message exchange. It does, however, provide all the built-in sequencing and error recovery. The datagram requires a lower setup overhead, but you have to include information with the data that uniquely identifies each message.

Scenario 2: One Server With a Serially Reusable Session

Scenario 2 shows how a single NetBIOS session is used to serially service two clients (see Figure 18-3). The scenario can easily be expanded to "n" clients. We assume that all the clients will be executing simple transactions such as the one described in Scenario 1. The cost of establishing a NetBIOS session is usually under 50 milliseconds. The benefit of the non-persistent session server scheme is that it removes the ceiling on how many clients can be serviced using sessions. Another benefit is that the boundaries for the transaction execution and session coincide. This is goodness from an error-recovery viewpoint.

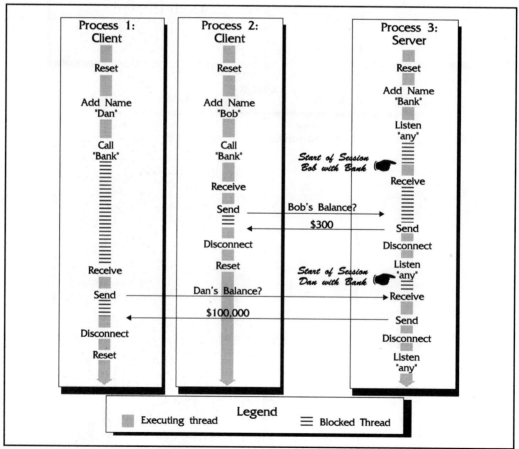

Figure 18-3.   Scenario 2: Obtaining Services Using a Single NetBIOS Session.

The time-out values on the *call* command should be made large enough to keep the calling thread blocked until the server frees up. We expect that only the thread that issued the *call* command will block; other threads in the process can continue to do useful work. An application that attempts to *call* a name on the network that is registered, but for which there is no outstanding *Listen*, will retry 12 times in 1/2 second intervals (i.e., the default time-out is six seconds). If no *Listen* response is obtained after this period, a "session open rejected" is returned. You can change the default values through the Communications Manager's Installation and Configuration facilities. You do that by modifying the TRANSMIT_TIMEOUT and TRANSMIT_COUNT parameters.

Scenario 3: Sending Bulk Data Over a NetBIOS Session

Scenario 3 shows how moving bulk data, such as a file transfer, may get implemented over a NetBIOS session (see Figure 18-4). Initially, the server is blocked waiting for the client. The client starts the file transfer by telling the server that it is about to receive a file, and gives it the name of the file and its size. The server says "OK" and issues a *Receive* waiting on the first file segment to arrive. The file copy gets done through a series of exchanges. Eventually, the server finishes consuming the file and sends a message to the client saying the file got there OK; then both sides break their end of the session.

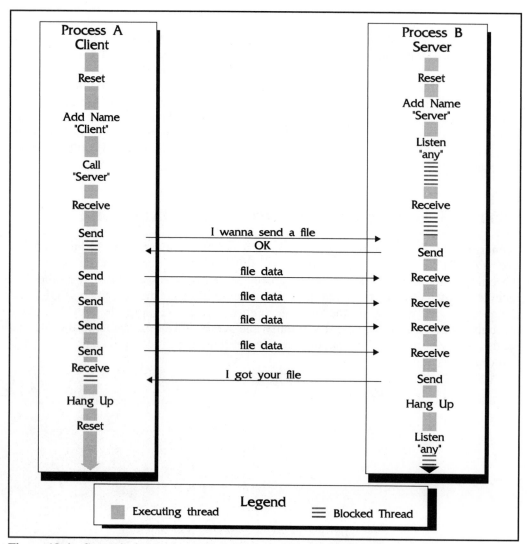

Figure 18-4. Scenario 3: Moving Bulk Data Over a NetBIOS Session.

Chapter 19

FX Using NetBIOS

This chapter presents an implementation of the communication layer of the FX protocol using OS/2's **NetBIOS** LAN protocol. The interface will be packaged as a Dynamic Link Library (FXNETB.DLL). The DLL will be created from **FXNETB.C** using the FX make file introduced in Chapter 16.

The NetBIOS communication DLL makes it possible to transfer files using FXREQ and FXSVR, the client/server programs developed in Chapter 16. Figure 19-1 shows how this all comes together. We will use this setup to collect benchmark numbers on the performance of NetBIOS by measuring the time it takes to exchange files between the client and the server.

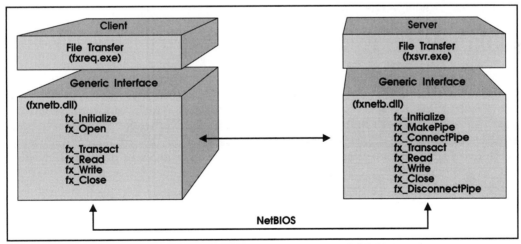

Figure 19-1. Implementing the FX Interface Using the NetBIOS DLL.

The plan for this chapter is to make use of whatever mechanisms are provided by the OS/2's NetBIOS LAN protocol to implement the nine **FX** interface calls shown in Figure 19-1. Figure 19-2 demonstrates how each of the FX calls is implemented by the FXNETB.DLL using OS/2's NetBIOS LAN services. It also shows the effect each call has on the partner transaction.

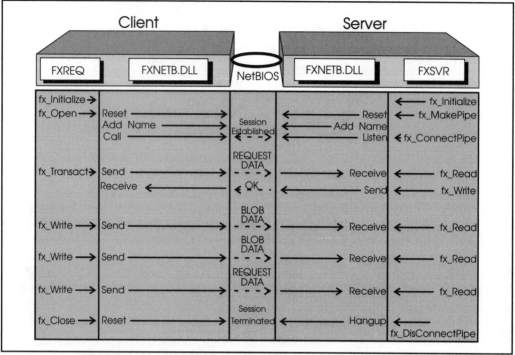

Figure 19-2. Sending a File Using the FXNETB.DLL.

PROGRAMMING NETBIOS

NetBIOS uses a *command with a control block* style of programming that is popular in the communications world. A single control block, the Network Control Block or **NCB** (see Figure 19-3), is used by all the NetBIOS commands. With a couple of exceptions, the fields in the NCB mean the same thing across all the NetBIOS commands. Different commands, of course, use different NCB fields based on the parameters required to perform an action. In this section, we describe the mechanics of programming NetBIOS's command interface. Once you understand the general principles that are described here, the rest of this chapter is a piece of cake.

How to Invoke a NetBIOS Command

The NetBIOS functions are defined by a set of commands or verbs. The verb to be executed is specified in an NCB, which gets passed to an OS/2 API call. Thus, technically speaking, the NetBIOS API consists of a single OS/2 call. Here is how you submit a NetBIOS command in the OS/2 environment:

1. Allocate a 64-byte NCB control structure.
2. Zero out all 64 bytes of the NCB, regardless of whether the fields are used or not. This prevents residual data from interfering with NetBIOS's operation.

3. Fill in the required NCB fields. This always includes the *command* field, which tells NetBIOS what command to execute. It also includes the relevant parameter fields for that command.
4. Invoke the OS/2 NetBIOS DLL, which handles the LAN adapter, by issuing the following API call where the parameter passed is the address of the NCB:

```
extern unsigned NETBIOS(char far *);
```

5. NetBIOS returns the control to the calling thread differently depending on whether the command is issued in *wait* or *no-wait* modes:

wait The requesting thread is blocked until the command completes.

no-wait Control is returned to the calling thread at the earliest time possible, usually before the command completes. Note that each active no-wait command costs you an OS/2 thread. So if you have too many outstanding commands, you may eventually run out of system resources.

In either case, when the command completes, OS/2 places the appropriate return code in the NCB. In addition, OS/2 can invoke a post-routine when the command completes if the NCB specifies it. The NCB is owned by OS/2 until the command completes. The calling thread can reuse the NCB only after the command completes.

The Network Control Block (NCB)

NetBIOS is operated through the NCB. The nice thing about NetBIOS is that it only has one control block structure. Once you've understood its structure, all that remains for us to explain is which NCB fields get used for a particular command. We present the NCB structure and a definition of its fields in this reference section. Figure 19-3 shows the C-language data structure that defines the NCB.

```
struct      network_control_block
  {
  BYTE          command;              /* Netbios command code          */
  BYTE          retcode;              /* Return code                   */
  BYTE          lsn;                  /* Local session number          */
  BYTE          num;                  /* Number of application name    */
  PBYTE         _Seg16 buffer_address; /* Address of message buffer     */
  USHORT        length;               /* length of message buffer      */
  BYTE          callname[16];         /* Destination name              */
  BYTE          name[16];             /* Source name                   */
  BYTE          rto;                  /* Receive timeout               */
  BYTE          sto;                  /* Send timeout                  */
  PBYTE         _Seg16 post_address;  /* Address of post routine       */
  BYTE          lana_num;             /* Adapter number                */
  BYTE          cmd_cplt;             /* Command status                */
  BYTE          reserve[14];          /* Reserved (except RESET)       */
  };
```

Figure 19-3. NetBIOS Network Control Block (NCB) Type Definitions.

The following is a field-by-field description of the NCB:

command   This field contains the NetBIOS command number. When the high-order bit of the command field is set to 1, the command executes in the no-wait mode. NetBIOS will queue a no-wait command and allow several commands to be pending at one time.

retcode   This field contains the immediate return code from NetBIOS for both wait and no-wait commands. A zero return code indicates the command completed successfully. In the no-wait mode, NetBIOS first sets this field to X'FF' which means "don't touch the control block or data associated with this command; I'm still working on the command." Eventually, the return_code changes from X'FF' indicating that the command completed. If the value returned is zero, the command is successful.

lsn   This field contains a handle that identifies the local session number. It is assigned by NetBIOS after a successful session is established. NetBIOS assigns session numbers between 1 and 254. This field is not used for datagram support.

num   This field contains a handle that identifies a network name. It is returned by NetBIOS after an **ADD_NAME** or **ADD_GROUP_NAME** command is executed. This handle and not the name must be used with *all* the datagram commands and for the **RECEIVE_ANY** command. NetBIOS assigns name numbers between 2 and 254. Name number 1 is permanently assigned to NETBIOS_NAME_NUMBER_1 (which is 10 bytes of zeroes followed by the six byte burned-in adapter address).

buffer_address This field contains a pointer to the data buffer. The data buffers are supplied by the application program. (Note that the Reset command uses this field differently.)

length   This field indicates the length in bytes of the data buffer. For receive type commands, the field is updated by NetBIOS to indicate the number of bytes actually received. (Note that the Reset command uses this field differently.)

callname   This field contains the 16-byte network name of the remote application the program wants to communicate with. NetBIOS also allows you to send messages to names on your own adapter (this may be useful for testing software). The **CHAIN_SEND** command uses the first six bytes of the callname field to specify the second buffer in the chain. The first two bytes are the length of the buffer and the remaining four bytes point to the second data buffer's location in memory. (Note that the Reset command uses this field differently.)

name This field contains the 16-byte network name of the local application. The NETBIOS_NAME_NUMBER_1 (which is 10 bytes of zeroes followed by the six byte node burned-in adapter address) may be used as a name. Any 16-byte combination can be used for the name with the following exceptions:

- The first character cannot be a binary zero or an asterisk "*".
- IBM reserves the values X'00' through X'1F' for the 16th character.
- IBM reserves the characters "IBM" as the first three characters of any name.

(Note that the Reset command uses this field differently.)

rto This field is used by the **CALL** and **LISTEN** commands to specify the timeout period (in half-seconds) for all the **RECEIVE** commands associated with that session. The timeout specifies how long to wait for the command to complete before returning an error. The timeout value may be different for each session, but is fixed when the session is first established. The timeout period on the partner's side of the session may also be different. You can use the value X'00' to specify no timeout. (Note that the Reset command uses this field differently.)

sto This field is used by the **CALL** and **LISTEN** commands to specify the timeout period (in half-seconds) for all the **SEND** commands associated with that session. The timeout specifies how long to wait for the command to complete before returning an error. The timeout value may be different for each session, but is fixed when the session is first established. The timeout period on the partner's side of the session may also be different. Send timeouts should be used with caution because they will end the session if they expire. You can use the value X'00' to specify no time-out. (Note that the Reset command uses this field differently.)

post_address This field contains a pointer to a *post routine* that gets executed when the command completes. For OS/2, this is an ordinary procedure that returns control by issuing an ordinary C-language return. NetBIOS will only look at this field for no-wait commands, otherwise it gets ignored. If this field contains all zeros, the post routine will not be called by NetBIOS, and the application program must check the retcode field for a change from X'FF' for no-wait commands. (Note that the Reset command uses this field differently.)

lana_num This field defines which LAN adapter should handle the command. In the case of IBM adapters, X'00' defines the primary adapter and X'01' defines the secondary adapter. (Note that the adapter must have the corresponding primary/alternate switch set correctly.)

cmd_cplt This field is the same as the retcode field.

reserve This field contains 14 bytes reserved as a work area by NetBIOS.

FXNETB.C: THE NETBIOS FX DLL

The code we present in this section *does not* contain a main() procedure. The FX DLLs are simply functions that get linked to a (.EXE) file at run time. The main() procedure is provided by the program that calls the DLL functions. This means **FXNETB.C** is not a separate program; it contains a list of functions that get packaged in a DLL.

FXNETB.C: General Stuff

The listing (see Figure 19-4) contains all the miscellaneous programming "stuff" that will be used by the FX procedures. This includes the usual declarations of constants, global variables, and forward declarations of functions. Notice that we've included, with the header material, all the OS/2 NetBIOS structures. The NCB was declared as C-language union to take care of all the deviations introduced by the **RESET** command.

The functions that are provided in this module fall into two categories: **FX** functions and *helper* functions. The helper functions, as usual, are used to provide common services for that module. In addition to the ubiquitous **print_error**(), we introduce seven general-purpose NetBIOS helper functions. These functions are general enough so that they can be reused "as is" in future programs. We will introduce the helper functions at the point where they first get used.

```
/******************************************************************************/
/*  MODULE NAME: FXNETB  - NETBIOS communication.                         */
/*                                                                        */
/*  PROGRAM DESCRIPTION:  This module is a part of the FX file transfer   */
/*    programs.  Refer to the FXREQ.C program module for a program overview. */
/*    This module implements the fx_* file transfer procedures using OS/2 */
/*    NETBIOS.                                                             */
/*                                                                        */
/******************************************************************************/
#include <stdio.h>                    /* For printf() & NULL               */
#include <stdlib.h>                   /* For conversion routines           */
#include <string.h>                   /* For string functions              */

#include <os2.h>
#include "fxfer.h"                    /* For FX functions                  */
/*----------------------------------------------------------------------------*/
/* defines                                                                  */
/*----------------------------------------------------------------------------*/
                         /*--------------------------------------*/
                         /* NCB command code defines             */
                         /*--------------------------------------*/
#define    NB_CALL_WAIT                          0x0010
#define    NB_LISTEN_WAIT                        0x0011
#define    NB_HANG_UP_WAIT                       0x0012
#define    NB_SEND_WAIT                          0x0014
#define    NB_RECEIVE_WAIT                       0x0015
#define    NB_ADD_NAME_WAIT                      0x0030
#define    NB_RESET_WAIT                         0x0032
```

Figure 19-4 (Part 1 of 4).   FXNETB.C: General Header Stuff and print_error().

```
                      /*————————————————————————*/
                      /* Netbios session resource  defines   */
                      /*————————————————————————*/
#define LANA              0          /* lan adapter number              */
#define NET_LSN           2          /* number of sessions              */
#define NET_NCB           4          /* number of outstanding NCBs      */
#define NET_NAMES         2          /* number of names                 */
#define REQUEST_RESOURCES 0          /* request new resources           */
#define RELEASE_RESOURCES 1          /* release all resources           */

                      /*————————————————————————*/
                      /* Netbios timeout defines             */
                      /*————————————————————————*/
#define RECV_TIMEOUT     20          /* receive timeout in seconds      */
#define SEND_TIMEOUT     20          /* send timeout in seconds         */

/*————————————————————————————————————————————————*/
/* typedefs for NCB structures                                          */
/*————————————————————————————————————————————————*/
                      /*————————————————————————*/
                      /* general structure for NCB commands  */
                      /*————————————————————————*/
typedef struct
    { BYTE    command;              /* Netbios command code            */
      BYTE    retcode;              /* Return code                     */
      BYTE    lsn;                  /* Local session number            */
      BYTE    num;                  /* Number of application name      */
      PBYTE   _Seg16 buffer_address; /* Address of message buffer      */
      USHORT  length;              /* length of message buffer         */
      BYTE    callname[16];        /* Destination name                 */
      BYTE    name[16];            /* Source name                      */
      BYTE    rto;                 /* Receive timeout                  */
      BYTE    sto;                 /* Send timeout                     */
      PBYTE   _Seg16 post_address; /* Address of post routine          */
      BYTE    lana_num;            /* Adapter number                   */
      BYTE    cmd_cplt;            /* Command status                   */
      BYTE    reserve[14];         /* Reserved (except RESET)          */
    } CMD_NCB;

                      /*————————————————————————*/
                      /* reset NCB structure as used in DLL  */
                      /*————————————————————————*/
typedef struct
    { BYTE    command;              /* Netbios command code            */
      BYTE    retcode;              /* Return code                     */
      BYTE    lsn;                  /* 0 = request 1= free resources   */
      BYTE    num;                  /* Not Used                        */
      PBYTE   _Seg16 dd_name_address; /* Not Used                      */
      USHORT  length;              /* Not used                         */
      BYTE    req_sessions;        /* # of sessions requested          */
      BYTE    req_commands;        /* # of commands requested          */
      BYTE    req_names;           /* # of names requested             */
      BYTE    req_name_one;        /* Name number one request          */
      BYTE    not_used2[12];       /* Not used                         */
      BYTE    act_sessions;        /* # of sessions obtained from DLL  */

      BYTE    act_commands;        /* # of commands obtained from DLL  */
      BYTE    act_names;           /* # of names obtained from DLL     */
      BYTE    act_name_one;        /* Name number one response from DLL */
      BYTE    not_used3[4];        /* Not used                         */
      BYTE    load_session;        /* Number of sessions at load from DLL*/
```

Figure 19-4 (Part 2 of 4).   FXNETB.C: General Header Stuff and print_error().

```
      BYTE    load_commands;              /* Number of commands at load from DLL*/
      BYTE    load_names;                 /* Number of names at load from DLL   */
      BYTE    load_stations;              /* Number of stations at load from DLL*/
      BYTE    not_used4[2];               /* Not used                           */
      BYTE    load_remote_names;          /* Number of remote names from DLL    */
      BYTE    not_used5[5];               /* Not used                           */
      USHORT dd_id;                       /* Not used                           */
      BYTE    lana_num;                   /* Adapter number                     */
      BYTE    not_used6;                  /* Not used                           */
      BYTE    reserve[14];                /* NCB error information              */
    } RESET_NCB;

typedef union
    { CMD_NCB    cmd_ncb;
      RESET_NCB reset_ncb;
    } NCB;

/*—————————————————————————————————————————————————*/
/* forward declaration for functions in this module                          */
/*—————————————————————————————————————————————————*/
                    /*—————————————————————————————*/
                    /* netbios helper functions        */
                    /*—————————————————————————————*/
BYTE netbios_reset(BYTE);
BYTE netbios_reset(BYTE);
BYTE netbios_add_name(PCHAR);
BYTE netbios_call(PCHAR, PCHAR, PBYTE);
BYTE netbios_listen(PCHAR, PCHAR, PBYTE);
BYTE netbios_hang_up(BYTE);
BYTE netbios_send(PVOID, USHORT, BYTE);
BYTE netbios_recv(PVOID, USHORT, BYTE, PUSHORT);

                    /*—————————————————————————————*/
                    /* error display function          */
                    /*—————————————————————————————*/
VOID print_error(USHORT, PCHAR, PCHAR, USHORT);

                    /*—————————————————————————————*/
                    /* netbios dynamic link function   */
                    /*—————————————————————————————*/
extern unsigned NETBIOS (NCB *);
#pragma linkage(NETBIOS, far16 pascal)            /* needed for 16 bit call    */

/*—————————————————————————————————————————————————*/
/* Configuration variables, initialized after fx_Initialize()                */
/* function call.                                                            */
/*—————————————————————————————————————————————————*/
CHAR    PipeName[128];
USHORT FileBufferSize;

/*—————————————————————————————————————————————————*/
/* global variables for this module.                                         */
/*—————————————————————————————————————————————————*/
BYTE    lsn;                             /* NetBIOS local session number       */
USHORT rc;                               /* return code                        */
CHAR    server_name[17];                 /* server name for ncb name field     */
CHAR    requester_name[17];              /* requester name for ncb name field  */
USHORT server;                           /* client/server indicator            */
NCB     ncb;                             /* network control block              */
```

Figure 19-4 (Part 3 of 4).   FXNETB.C: General Header Stuff and print_error().

```
/*————————————————————————————————————————————————————*/
/* Error Display Routine                                 */
/*————————————————————————————————————————————————————*/
VOID print_error(USHORT Error, PCHAR msg, PCHAR file, USHORT line)
{
 printf("NETBIOS Error %u (0x%x) detected while %s at line %u in file %s.\n",
          Error, Error, msg, line, file);
} /* end print_error */
```

Figure 19-4 (Part 4 of 4). FXNETB.C: General Header Stuff and print_error().

FXNETB.C: fx_Initialize()

The **fx_Initialize()** function (see Figure 19-5) reads a protocol-specific configuration file to obtain the parameters required to initialize the system. The name of the user specified configuration file for NetBIOS is: **fxnetb.cfg**. Here is an example of a such a file:

```
PIPE_NAME         = NETSVR
FILE_BUFFER_SIZE  = 512
```

Here's what these two parameters do:

- **PIPE_NAME**   This parameter is used to derive the network name of the client and server. The configuration file given above will result with a client machine called NETSVR.REQ and a server machine called NETSVR.SVR.

- **FILE_BUFFER_SIZE**   This parameter defines the size (in bytes) of the message buffer. This is the buffer we will use for reading and writing data to the disk and for exchanging messages across the LAN or the IPC. The memory space for this parameter will be dynamically allocated. The **fx_Initialize()** function returns a pointer to this buffer and its size to the application. One of the factors we will measure in our benchmarks is the effect of the message buffer size on performance.

```
/*———————————————————————————————————————————*/
/* This function reads communication specific parameters and allocates a   */
/* buffer for communication.  A pointer to the buffer and the buffer size is */
/* returned.                                                               */
/*———————————————————————————————————————————*/
ULONG fx_Initialize(PPACKET *buffer_p , PUSHORT size)
{
  FILE    *config_file;                /* Input file control block       */
  CHAR    line[80];                    /* one line of config file        */
  PPACKET _Seg16 bufferp;

  printf("Reading configuration parameters.\n");
  /*———————————————————————————————————*/
  /* open the configuration file         */
  /*———————————————————————————————————*/
  if (NULL == (config_file = fopen("fxnetb.cfg","r")))
      {print_error(rc,"opening configuration file",__FILE__,__LINE__);
       return(FAILED);
      }
  else
      /*———————————————————————————————————*/
      /* read the configuration parameters.  */
      /* The parameters are expected to be:  */
      /*    - in the form <name = value>     */
      /*    - if value is a string enclose   */
      /*        in double quotes             */
      /*    - in the order read below        */
      /*———————————————————————————————————*/
      {
        fgets(line, sizeof(line), config_file);
        if (sscanf(line,"PIPE_NAME = %s ", PipeName) != 1)
            {print_error(rc,"reading PipeName from configuration",
                  __FILE__,__LINE__);
             return(FAILED);
            }
        printf("PIPE_NAME = %s \n", PipeName);

        fgets(line, sizeof(line), config_file);
        if (sscanf(line,"FILE_BUFFER_SIZE = %u ", &FileBufferSize) != 1)
            {print_error(rc,"reading FileBufferSize from configuration",
                  __FILE__,__LINE__);
             return(FAILED);
            }
        printf("FILE_BUFFER_SIZE = %u \n", FileBufferSize);
      } /* end if */

  fclose(config_file);
  /*———————————————————————————————————*/
  /* initialize server_name and          */
  /*    requester_name variable for use  */
  /*    in ncb commands.                 */
  /*———————————————————————————————————*/
  strcat(PipeName,"                 "); /* make pipe name >=16 char long    */

  strncpy(server_name, PipeName, 16);
  strncpy(&server_name[12], ".SVR", 4);

  strncpy(requester_name, PipeName, 16);
  strncpy(&requester_name[12], ".REQ", 4);
```

Figure 19-5 (Part 1 of 2).   FXNETB.C: fx_Initialize().

```
/*_____*/
/* allocate buffer, return pointer    */
/* and size                           */
/*_____*/
bufferp = (malloc)(FileBufferSize);
if (bufferp == NULL)
    {print_error(rc,"allocating file buffer",__FILE__,__LINE__);
     return(FAILED);
    }
*buffer_p = bufferp;
*size = FileBufferSize;
return(GOOD);
} /* end fx_Initialize */
```

Figure 19-5 (Part 2 of 2). FXNETB.C: fx_Initialize().

FXNETB.C: fx_MakePipe()

The **fx_MakePipe()** function (see Figure 19-6) is used by the server side of an FX pipe to establish the pipe. Using NetBIOS we provide the function as follows:

1. Issue a NetBIOS **RESET** command to allocate network resources to the process. The NetBIOS **RESET** command is executed by the **netbios_reset()** helper function listed in Figure 19-7.
2. Issue a NetBIOS **ADD NAME** to place the server's name on the network. The NetBIOS **ADD NAME** command is executed by the **netbios_add_name()** helper function listed in Figure 19-8.

```
/*_____*/
/* This function establishes the server end of the communication pipe.    */
/*_____*/
ULONG fx_MakePipe(VOID)
{
    /*_____*/
    /* remember that this is a server    */
    /*_____*/
    server = TRUE;

    /*_____*/
    /* perform netbios reset             */
    /*_____*/
    rc = netbios_reset(REQUEST_RESOURCES);
    if (rc)
        {print_error(rc,"resetting netbios",__FILE__,__LINE__);
         return(FAILED);
        }
```

Figure 19-6 (Part 1 of 2). FXNETB.C: MakePipe().

```
/*——————————————————————————*/
/* perform netbios add name           */
/*——————————————————————————*/
rc = netbios_add_name(server_name);
if (rc)
   {print_error(rc,"adding netbios name",__FILE__,__LINE__);
    return(FAILED);
   }

return(GOOD);

} /* end fx_MakePipe */
```

Figure 19-6 (Part 2 of 2). FXNETB.C: MakePipe().

FXNETB.C: netbios_reset()

The NetBIOS **RESET** command can be used in one of two ways:

- To request resources from the NetBIOS pool
- To release resources to the NetBIOS pool

The **netbios_reset()** helper routine (see Figure 19-7) performs either reset, depending on the value of the *request_release* parameter that gets passed to it. Here is what **netbios_reset()** does:

1. It clears the NCB.
2. It fills in the NCB request fields for this command. The **RESET** command uses the **ncb.reset_ncb** type (whose typedef is given in Figure 19-4). This is a special type of NCB used only by **RESET**, which requires a redefinition of the fields so that it can specify the resources obtained from, or released to, the NetBIOS pool.
3. It issues a NetBIOS API call in wait mode.
4. It returns the *retcode* field contents.

```
/*————————————————————————————————————————————*/
/* netbios reset helper routine                                   */
/*————————————————————————————————————————————*/
BYTE netbios_reset(BYTE request_release)
{
   memset(&ncb.reset_ncb, 0, sizeof(ncb.reset_ncb));/* set ncb to all zeros  */
   ncb.reset_ncb.command  = NB_RESET_WAIT;         /* command = reset       */
   ncb.reset_ncb.lana_num = LANA;                  /* lan adapter number    */
   ncb.reset_ncb.lsn = request_release;            /* 0=request, 1=release  */
   ncb.reset_ncb.req_sessions = NET_LSN;           /* number of sessions    */
   ncb.reset_ncb.req_commands = NET_NCB;           /* number of outstanding NCB*/
   ncb.reset_ncb.req_names    = NET_NAMES;         /* number of names       */

   NETBIOS(&ncb);                                  /* netbios call          */

   return(ncb.reset_ncb.retcode);
}
```

Figure 19-7. FXNETB.C: netbios_reset().

FXNETB.C: netbios_add_name()

The **netbios_add_name()** helper routine (see Figure 19-8) adds a specified name to the network. It does this by first clearing the NCB. Then it fills the NCB request fields for this command using a regular **ncb.cmd_ncb** type. Next, a NetBIOS API call is issued in wait mode. Finally, the *retcode* field content is returned to the caller.

```
/*————————————————————————————————————————————————*/
/* netbios add name helper routine                 */
/*————————————————————————————————————————————————*/
BYTE netbios_add_name(PCHAR name)
{
  memset(&ncb.cmd_ncb, 0, sizeof(ncb.cmd_ncb));   /* set ncb to all zeros     */
  ncb.cmd_ncb.command  = NB_ADD_NAME_WAIT;        /* command = add name       */
  ncb.cmd_ncb.lana_num = LANA;                    /* lan adapter number       */
  strncpy(ncb.cmd_ncb.name, name, 16 );           /* copy 16 char name to ncb */

  NETBIOS(&ncb);                                  /* netbios call             */

  return(ncb.cmd_ncb.retcode);
}
```

Figure 19-8. FXNETB.C: netbios_add_name().

FXNETB.C: fx_ConnectPipe()

The **fx_ConnectPipe()** function (see Figure 19-9) is used to establish a connection on the server side of an FX pipe. Using NetBIOS we provide this function by issuing a **LISTEN** command. This is done by calling **netbios_listen()**, the NetBIOS helper routine listed in Figure 19-10.

```
/*————————————————————————————————————————————————————————————*/
/* function to enable the server end of the communication pipe. */
/*————————————————————————————————————————————————————————————*/
ULONG fx_ConnectPipe(VOID)
{
  /*————————————————————————————*/
  /* perform netbios listen     */
  /*————————————————————————————*/
  rc = netbios_listen(requester_name,  /* caller's name              */
                      server_name,      /* this station's name        */
                      &lsn);            /* local session number returned */
  if (rc)
    {print_error(rc,"performing a netbios listen",__FILE__,__LINE__);
     return(FAILED);
    }

  return(GOOD);
} /* end fx_ConnectPipe */
```

Figure 19-9. FXNETB.C: fx_ConnectPipe().

FXNETB.C: netbios_listen()

The **netbios_listen()** helper routine (see Figure 19-10) waits for a remote *caller_name* to call a local *station_name*. It does this by first clearing the NCB. Then it fills the NCB request fields for this command using a regular **ncb.cmd_ncb** type. Next a NetBIOS API call is issued in wait mode. The call completes when a call is received from the remote station. The session is then established. Finally, the *retcode* field content is returned to the caller as well as a pointer to the local session number field (*lsn*) returned by NetBIOS. The *lsn* contains a number that uniquely identifies the session.

```
/*-------------------------------------------------------------------*/
/* netbios listen name helper routine                                */
/*-------------------------------------------------------------------*/
BYTE netbios_listen(PCHAR caller_name, PCHAR station_name, PBYTE lsn)
{
   memset(&ncb.cmd_ncb, 0, sizeof(ncb.cmd_ncb));  /* set ncb to all zeros    */
   ncb.cmd_ncb.command  = NB_LISTEN_WAIT;         /* command = listen_wait   */
   ncb.cmd_ncb.lana_num = LANA;                   /* lan adapter number      */
   ncb.cmd_ncb.rto      = RECV_TIMEOUT<<1;        /* times 2 since in         */
   ncb.cmd_ncb.sto      = SEND_TIMEOUT<<1;        /* steps of 500 msecs      */
   strncpy(ncb.cmd_ncb.name, station_name, 16 );  /* local station name      */
   strncpy(ncb.cmd_ncb.callname, caller_name, 16);/* caller's name           */

   NETBIOS(&ncb);                                 /* netbios call            */

   *lsn = ncb.cmd_ncb.lsn;
   return(ncb.cmd_ncb.retcode);
}
```

Figure 19-10.   FXNETB.C: netbios_listen().

FXNETB.C: fx_DisconnectPipe()

The **fx_DisconnectPipe()** function (see Figure 19-11) is used to disconnect the server side of an FX pipe. Using NetBIOS we provide this function by issuing a **HANG UP** command. This is done by calling **netbios_hang_up()**, the NetBIOS helper routine listed in Figure 19-12.

```
/*————————————————————————————————————————————*/
/* function to disable the server end of the communication pipe.        */
/*————————————————————————————————————————————*/
ULONG fx_DisconnectPipe(VOID)
{
    /*——————————————————————————————*/
    /* perform netbios hangup            */
    /*——————————————————————————————*/
    rc = netbios_hang_up(lsn);
    if (rc)
        {print_error(rc,"performing a netbios hang up",__FILE__,__LINE__);
         return(FAILED);
        }

    return(GOOD);
} /* end fx_DisconnectPipe */
```

Figure 19-11. FXNETB.C: fx_DisconnectPipe().

FXNETB.C: netbios_hang_up()

The **netbios_hang_up**() helper routine (see Figure 19-12) disconnects from a session identified by a *lsn* handle. It does this by first clearing the NCB. It then fills the NCB request fields for this command using a regular **ncb.cmd_ncb** type. Following that, a NetBIOS API call is issued in wait mode. Finally, the *retcode* field content is returned to the caller.

```
/*————————————————————————————————————————————*/
/* netbios hang up helper routine                                       */
/*————————————————————————————————————————————*/
BYTE netbios_hang_up(BYTE lsn)
{
    memset(&ncb.cmd_ncb, 0, sizeof(ncb.cmd_ncb));  /* set ncb to all zeros    */
    ncb.cmd_ncb.command  = NB_HANG_UP_WAIT;        /* command = hang_up_wait  */
    ncb.cmd_ncb.lana_num = LANA;                   /* lan adapter number      */
    ncb.cmd_ncb.lsn      = lsn;                    /* local session number    */

    NETBIOS(&ncb);                                 /* netbios call            */

    return(ncb.cmd_ncb.retcode);
}
```

Figure 19-12. FXNETB.C: netbios_hang_up().

FXNETB.C: fx_Open()

The **fx_Open**() function (see Figure 19-13) is used to establish the client side of an FX pipe. Using NetBIOS we provide the function as follows:

1.   We first issue a **RESET** command to obtain resources from the NetBIOS pool. This is done by invoking the **netbios_reset**() helper function listed in Figure 19-7.

2. We then issue an **ADD NAME** command to add the client's name to the network. This is done by invoking the **netbios_add_name()** helper function listed in Figure 19-8.

3. We then issue a **CALL** command to establish a session with the server. This is done by invoking the **netbios_call()** helper function listed in Figure 19-14. (Note that the requester_name and server_name are both derived from the user-specified name in **fxnetb.cfg**.)

```
/*------------------------------------------------------------*/
/* function a requester uses to prepare a pipe for communication. */
/*------------------------------------------------------------*/
ULONG fx_Open(VOID)
{
    /*--------------------------------------*/
    /* remember that this is not a server   */
    /*--------------------------------------*/
    server = FALSE;

    /*--------------------------------------*/
    /* perform netbios reset                */
    /*--------------------------------------*/
    rc = netbios_reset(REQUEST_RESOURCES);
    if (rc)
        {print_error(rc,"resetting netbios",__FILE__,__LINE__);
         return(FAILED);
        }

    /*--------------------------------------*/
    /* perform netbios add name             */
    /*--------------------------------------*/
    rc = netbios_add_name(requester_name);
    if (rc)
        {print_error(rc,"adding a netbios name",__FILE__,__LINE__);
         return(FAILED);
        }

    /*--------------------------------------*/
    /* perform netbios call                 */
    /*--------------------------------------*/
    rc = netbios_call(server_name,       /* name being called            */
                      requester_name,    /* station name                 */
                      &lsn);             /* local station number returned */
    if (rc)
        {print_error(rc,"performing a netbios call",__FILE__,__LINE__);
         return(FAILED);
        }

    return(GOOD);
} /* end fx_Open */
```

Figure 19-13.   FXNETB.C: fx_Open().

FXNETB.C: netbios_call()

The **netbios_call()** helper routine (see Figure 19-14) issues a **CALL** command. The purpose is to establish a session between remote *callname* (which has an outstanding **LISTEN**) and a local *station_name*. This is done by first clearing the NCB. The NCB request fields for this command are then entered using a regular **ncb.cmd_ncb** type. Next, a NetBIOS API call is issued in wait mode. The function then completes when a session is established with the remote name. Finally, the *retcode* field content is returned to the caller, as well as a pointer to the local session number field (*lsn*) returned by NetBIOS. The *lsn* contains a number that uniquely identifies the session.

```
/*_____*/
/* netbios call name helper routine                              */
/*_____*/
BYTE netbios_call(PCHAR callname, PCHAR station_name, PBYTE lsn)
{
  memset(&ncb.cmd_ncb, 0, sizeof(ncb.cmd_ncb));  /* set ncb to all zeros    */
  ncb.cmd_ncb.command  = NB_CALL_WAIT;           /* command = call wait     */
  ncb.cmd_ncb.lana_num = LANA;                   /* lan adapter number      */
  ncb.cmd_ncb.rto      = RECV_TIMEOUT<<1;        /* times 2 since in        */
  ncb.cmd_ncb.sto      = SEND_TIMEOUT<<1;        /* steps of 500 msecs      */
  strncpy(ncb.cmd_ncb.name, station_name, 16 ); /* local station name      */
  strncpy(ncb.cmd_ncb.callname, callname, 16);  /* call name               */

  NETBIOS(&ncb);                                 /* netbios call            */

  *lsn = ncb.cmd_ncb.lsn;
  return(ncb.cmd_ncb.retcode);
}
```

Figure 19-14.   FXNETB.C: netbios_call().

FXNETB.C: fx_Write()

The **fx_Write()** function (see Figure 19-15) is used to send information over an FX pipe. Using NetBIOS we provide this function by invoking **netbios_send()**, helper function listed in Figure 19-16.

```
/*_____*/
/* function both requester and server use to write to a pipe.   */
/*_____*/
ULONG fx_Write(PVOID BufferArea, USHORT BufferLength, PUSHORT BytesWritten)
{
  /*_____*/
  /* perform netbios send           */
  /*_____*/
  rc = netbios_send(BufferArea,          /* buffer to send      */
                    BufferLength,        /* length of buffer    */
                    lsn);                /* session number      */
  if (rc)
     {print_error(rc,"performing a netbios send",__FILE__,__LINE__);
      return(FAILED);
     }

  *BytesWritten = BufferLength;          /* success, all bytes sent   */
  return(GOOD);
} /* end fx_Write */
```

Figure 19-15.   FXNETB.C: fx_Write().

FXNETB.C: netbios_send()

The **netbios_send()** helper routine (see Figure 19-16) issues a **SEND** command. This is done by first clearing the NCB. The NCB request fields for this command are then entered using a regular **ncb.cmd_ncb** type. Next, a NetBIOS API call is issued in wait mode. The function completes when the message is sent successfully. The *retcode* field content is returned to the caller.

```
/*------------------------------------------------------------------*/
/* netbios send helper routine                                      */
/*------------------------------------------------------------------*/
BYTE netbios_send(PVOID buffer, USHORT length, BYTE lsn)
{
   memset(&ncb.cmd_ncb, 0, sizeof(ncb.cmd_ncb));  /* set ncb to all zeros    */
   ncb.cmd_ncb.command  = NB_SEND_WAIT;           /* command = send_wait     */
   ncb.cmd_ncb.lana_num = LANA;                   /* lan adapter number      */
   ncb.cmd_ncb.lsn      = lsn;                     /* local session number    */
   ncb.cmd_ncb.buffer_address = buffer;           /* address of buffer to send*/
   ncb.cmd_ncb.length   = length;                 /* length of send buffer   */

   NETBIOS(&ncb);                                  /* netbios call            */

   return(ncb.cmd_ncb.retcode);
}
```

Figure 19-16.   FXNETB.C: netbios_send().

FXNETB.C: fx_Read()

The **fx_Read()** function (see Figure 19-17) is used to read information over an FX pipe. Using NetBIOS we provide this function by invoking the **netbios_recv()** helper function listed in Figure 19-18.

```
/*------------------------------------------------------------------*/
/* function both requester and server use to read from a pipe.      */
/*------------------------------------------------------------------*/
ULONG fx_Read(PVOID BufferArea, USHORT BufferLength, PUSHORT BytesRead)
{
   /*----------------------------------*/
   /* perform netbios receive          */
   /*----------------------------------*/
   rc = netbios_recv(BufferArea,        /* buffer to send               */
                     BufferLength,      /* length of buffer             */
                     lsn,               /* session number               */
                     BytesRead);        /* number of bytes read returned */

   if (rc)
      {print_error(rc,"performing a netbios receive",__FILE__,__LINE__);
       return(FAILED);
      }

   return(GOOD);
} /* end fx_Read */
```

Figure 19-17.   FXNETB.C: fx_Read().

FXNETB.C: netbios_recv()

The **netbios_recv()** helper routine (see Figure 19-18) issues a **RECEIVE** command. This is done by first clearing the NCB. The NCB request fields for this command are then entered using a regular **ncb.cmd_ncb** type. Next, a NetBIOS API call is issued in wait mode. The function completes when a message is successfully received. The *retcode* field content is returned to the caller.

```
/*───────────────────────────────────────────────────*/
/* netbios receive helper routine                     */
/*───────────────────────────────────────────────────*/
BYTE netbios_recv(PVOID buffer, USHORT length, BYTE lsn, PUSHORT bytes_received)
{
  memset(&ncb.cmd_ncb, 0, sizeof(ncb.cmd_ncb));  /* set ncb to all zeros     */
  ncb.cmd_ncb.command   = NB_RECEIVE_WAIT;       /* command = receive        */
  ncb.cmd_ncb.lana_num = LANA;                   /* lan adapter number       */
  ncb.cmd_ncb.lsn       = lsn;                    /* local session number     */
  ncb.cmd_ncb.buffer_address = buffer;           /* address of receive buffer*/
  ncb.cmd_ncb.length    = length;                /* length of receive buffer */

  NETBIOS(&ncb);                                  /* netbios call             */

  *bytes_received = ncb.cmd_ncb.length;           /* length of data received  */
  return(ncb.cmd_ncb.retcode);
}
```

Figure 19-18.   FXNETB.C: netbios_recv().

FXNETB.C: fx_Transact()

The **fx_Transact()** function (see Figure 19-19) sends a message and receives a reply over an FX pipe. This function is provided in NetBIOS by issuing a **SEND** command followed by a **RECEIVE** command. This is done by invoking **fx_write()** (see Figure 19-15), followed by **fx_read()** (see Figure 19-17).

```
/*_____*/
/* function requester uses to request a service.                  */
/*_____*/
ULONG fx_Transact(PVOID InBufferArea,  USHORT InBufferLength,
                  PVOID OutBufferArea, USHORT OutBufferLength,
                  PUSHORT BytesRead)
{
  USHORT BytesWritten;

  rc = fx_Write(InBufferArea, InBufferLength, &BytesWritten);
  if (rc)
     {print_error(rc,"writing during a transaction",__FILE__,__LINE__);
      return(FAILED);
      }

  rc = fx_Read(OutBufferArea, OutBufferLength, BytesRead);
  if (rc)
     {print_error(rc,"reading during a transaction",__FILE__,__LINE__);
      return(FAILED);
      }

  return(GOOD);
} /* end fx_Transact */
```

Figure 19-19.   FXNETB.C: fx_Transact.

FXNETB.C: fx_Close()

The **fx_Close()** function (see Figure 19-20) closes an FX pipe. In terms of NetBIOS, this means issuing a **RESET** command with the directive to RELEASE_RESOURCES. This function is only performed on the client side. On the Server side, the process is terminated by a Control-Break. OS/2 automatically issues a NetBIOS **RESET** on behalf of a terminating process, which means that no action is required from our program.

```
/*_____*/
/* function requester uses to end communication with a server.    */
/*_____*/
ULONG fx_Close(VOID)
{
  if (!server)
     {
       /*_____*/
       /* perform netbios reset          */
       /*_____*/
       rc = netbios_reset(RELEASE_RESOURCES);
       if (rc)
          {print_error(rc,"resetting netbios",__FILE__,__LINE__);
           return(FAILED);
           }
     }

  return(GOOD);
} /* end fx_Close */
```

Figure 19-20.   FXNETB.C: fx_Close().

Chapter 20

A Tutorial on TCP/IP Sockets

This chapter presents a tutorial on Berkeley Sockets, a *peer-to-peer* LAN protocol, for TCP/IP networks. In this tutorial, we answer the following questions: Where do TCP/IP Sockets fit in the scheme of things? What services are provided by TCP/IP Sockets? How are sockets used? The intimate details on how to program sockets will appear in a later chapter.

SOCKETS: A PEER-TO-PEER LAN PROTOCOL

This section describes the C socket API provided with TCP/IP for OS/2. The OS/2 socket API provides a standard call-based interface to the transport and internet layers of TCP/IP. Sockets allow a program to communicate across the TCP/IP internet with other programs using file-like semantics. Before diving into the gory details of sockets, you should review the TCP/IP for OS/2 overview in Part I.

Situating Sockets

As you may recall from Part I, TCP/IP is the Unix world's premier network protocol, and *sockets* are TCP/IP's premier peer-to-peer API. Sockets were introduced in 1981 as the Unix BSD 4.2 generic interface that would provide UNIX-to-UNIX communications over networks. In 1985, SunOS introduced NFS and RPC over sockets. In 1986, AT&T introduced the *Transport Independent Interface (TLI)* that provides functionality similar to sockets but in a more network-independent fashion. Unix SVR4 incorporates both sockets and TLI, but AT&T encourages programmers to develop new applications using TLI rather than sockets. As it stands, sockets are, by far, more prevalent than TLI in the Unix world. The good news is that sockets and TLI are very similar from a programmer's perspective. TLI is just a cleaner version of sockets. Most of this tutorial on sockets also applies to TLI.

Support for sockets exists on a multiplicity of operating system environments, including MS-DOS, OS/2, UNIX, Mac OS, and most mainframe environments. In the BSD Unix system, sockets are part of the kernel and provide both a stand-alone and networked IPC service. Non-BSD Unix systems, MS-DOS, Mac OS, and OS/2 provide sockets in the form of libraries. In Unix SVR4, sockets are implemented in terms of streams. Streams in SVR4 provide the mechanism for hooking external drivers to the kernel. It is safe to say that sockets provide the current de facto portable standard for network application providers on TCP/IP networks.

What Is a Socket?

A socket is a peer-to-peer communication *endpoint* (it has a name and a network address). From a programmer's perspective, a socket hides the details of the network. It is represented by a "magic cookie" called the *socket descriptor*. Sockets are differentiated by the domain (or protocol family) in which they operate and by the type of socket.

The OS/2 product supports a single socket family, **AF_INET** (for the TCP/IP internet). Other socket families are **AF_UNIX** (for Unix-to-Unix IPC), **AF_PUP** (for the Xerox XNS internet), and **AF_APPLETALK** (for the Appletalk network). Family affiliations, among other things, define a style of addressing. For example, all networked machines in the **AF_INET** domain subscribe to the same TCP/IP internet addressing scheme on their socket endpoints.

Within the TCP/IP family, the OS/2 product supports three socket types: *stream*, *datagram*, and *raw*. Stream and datagram sockets interface to the transport layer protocols, and raw sockets interface to the network layer protocols. The programmer must specify the type of socket desired at creation time. You must, of course, use the same socket type as your peer at the other end of a socket. In the OS/2 implementation of sockets, stream sockets interface to TCP, datagram sockets interface to UDP, and raw sockets interface to ICMP and IP. In theory, the socket interface can be extended, and you can define new socket types to provide additional services.

How Do You Like Your Socket?

The following describes the characteristics of the three socket types:

- **Datagram Sockets** provide an interface to the UDP datagram service. UDP handles network transmissions as independent packets and provides no guarantees. UDP does include a checksum, but it makes no attempt to detect duplicate packets or to maintain any form of sequencing on multipacket transmissions. You're on your own: data can be lost, duplicated, or received in the wrong order. You're in charge of retransmissions when an error occurs (UDP does not save your message either). No acknowledgement of receipt is built into the protocol. The size of a datagram is limited to the size that can be sent in a single message (the maximum length is 32,768 bytes). On the plus side datagrams are fast and require little overhead. On the minus side datagrams impose a limit on the amount of data transferred, and require that you provide all the reliability mechanisms.

- **Stream Sockets** provide an interface to the reliable TCP transport protocol. TCP provides a session-based service and takes care of flow control, packet reassembly, and connection maintenance. The stream socket guarantees that packets are sent without errors or duplication, and that they are received in the same order as they are sent. No boundaries are imposed on the data; it is considered to be a stream of bytes. On the plus side TCP provides a reliable peer-to-peer mechanism. On the negative side TCP is slower than UDP and requires more programming overhead. Be warned: *TCP knows nothing about the preservation of message boundaries*. This is to be expected because the Unix file system, whose semantics TCP models, knows nothing about record boundaries. We'll show you how to work around this minor irritant when we get to the programming sections.

- **Raw Sockets** provide an interface to the lower layer protocols such as IP and Internet Control Message Protocol (ICMP). This interface does not provide traditional peer-to-peer services. It is used to test new protocols or to gain access to some of the more advanced facilities of an existing protocol.

Socket Addressing on the TCP/IP Internet

A socket address on the TCP/IP internet consists of two parts: an internet address (IP_address) and a port address (see Figure 20-1). So what's an internet address? And what's a port?

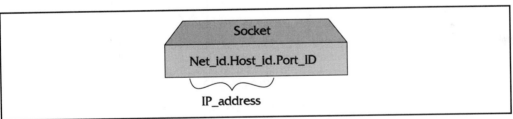

Figure 20-1.   SOCKET = Internet Address (IP) + Port Address.

An *internet address* is a 32-bit number, usually represented by four decimal numbers separated by dots, that must be unique for each TCP/IP network interface card within an administered AF_INET domain. A TCP/IP *host* (i.e., networked machine) may have as many internet addresses as it has network interfaces.

A *port* is an entry point to an application that resides on a host. It is represented by a 16-bit integer. Ports are commonly used to define the entry points for services provided by server applications. The TCPIP\ETC\SERVICES file contains a list of *well-known ports* that are reserved for specific services. You should only use these reserved port numbers as a client or provider of one of the "well-known" services.

Providing Services the Sockets Way

Sockets have a reputation for being programmer friendly. Yet the OS/2 TCP/IP socket API consists of a grand total of 58 calls. So how should we go about explaining this friendly service that comes with such an exorbitant number of APIs? The answer is to *divide and conquer*. So, we will first divide the socket library into 21 *core* socket commands, and 37 socket *utility* commands.

The *socket core* commands (see Table 20-1) provide the traditional peer-to-peer communication services. These are the original socket API calls included with all the major implementations of sockets (usually at the kernel level). These calls allow you to create sockets, manage sessions, transfer data using datagram or session-based exchanges, and provide miscellaneous functions that help you with socket dynamics. The core socket calls use familiar file-like semantics and are easily understood.

Table 20-1. Main Socket Calls.

Socket Endpoint Setup	Connection Management	Connected Data Exchanges	Unconnected Data Exchanges	Miscellaneous Socket Functions
sock_init() socket() bind() soclose()	connect() listen() accept() shutdown()	send() recv() writev() readv()	sendto() recvfrom()	gethostid() getpeername() getsockname() getsockopt() setsockopt() select() ioctl()

The *socket utility* commands (see Table 20-2) provide many helpful support functions. These functions are used in so many programs that they are now an integral part of the socket interface. The functions on the top row, the so-called *get* routines, are used to read and fetch entries from the TCP/IP configuration files (and sometimes from a network name server). These configuration files are found in the \ETC directory (in conformance with the Unix TCP/IP practice). The utility functions in the bottom row provide services such as, "big endian/little endian" translations, reorganizing and converting network addresses, determining one's own address, and resolving domain names.

Table 20-2. Socket Network Utilities.

Host Names Information	Network Names Information	Protocol Names Information	Service Names Information
gethostbyaddr()	getnetbyaddr()	getprotobynumber()	getservbyname()
gethostbyname()	getnetbyname()	getprotobyname()	getservbyport()
sethostent()	setnetent()	setprotoent()	setservent()
gethostent()	getnetent()	getprotoent()	getservent()
endhostent()	endnetent()	endprotoent()	endservent()
Byte Order Translation	**Internet Address Manipulation**	**Domain Name Resolution**	
htonl()	inet_addr()	res_mkquery()	
htons()	inet_network()	res_send()	
ntohl()	inet_ntoa()	res_init()	
ntohs()	inet_netof()	dn_comp()	
bswap()	inet_lnaof()	dn_expand()	
lswap()	inet_makeaddr()		

The Socket Core Commands

As part of our divide and conquer strategy, we placed the socket core commands (see Table 20-1) into the following five categories:

- Endpoint management and setup
- Connection services
- Connected data exchanges
- Unconnected data exchanges
- Miscellaneous socket management functions

Socket Core: EndPoint Management and Setup Commands

The endpoint management commands are used to create sockets, bind the new socket to a name/address structure, and to release the socket when it is no longer needed. Table 20-3 presents a quick summary of the function each socket endpoint command provides.

Table 20-3. **Socket Endpoint Setup.**

Command	Description
sock_init()	This call initializes the socket data structures and checks whether TCP/IP is running. It should be issued at the start of each program that uses sockets.
socket()	This call creates a socket and returns a socket descriptor. You must specify the protocol family to be used with the socket. The OS/2 product supports the AF_INET family, which stands for the TCP/IP internet. Other socket families not supported by OS/2 are AF_UNIX (for Unix-to-Unix IPC), AF_PUP (for the Xerox XNS internet), and AF_APPLETALK (for the Appletalk network). In addition to the socket family, you must specify the type of socket desired. OS/2 supports three socket types: SOCK_STREAM, SOCK_DGRAM, and SOCK_RAW.
bind()	This call binds a unique local address (the port number) to a socket. This is important for server processes that need to specify a "well-known port" for their service (otherwise, you can let the system assign a port for you automatically).
soclose()	This call shuts down a socket, frees its resources, and closes a TCP connection (if one is open).

Socket Core: Connection Services

The socket connection services are used in connection oriented communications. These services have different semantics depending on whether they're used on stream or datagram sockets. With stream sockets, they are used to establish a TCP session between two partners (socket peers). Once a TCP session is in place, applications can exchange data reliably using sequenced packet exchanges. When the session is no longer needed, a command is provided to release that resource and break the connection. With a datagram socket, the connection services are, optionally, used to retain the name of the communication partner so that it does not have to be specified with each command. Datagram sockets build on top of UDP, which does not support the notion of a session. Table 20-4 presents a quick summary of the functions provided by the socket connection services.

Table 20-4. **Socket Connection Management Services.**

Command	Description
connect()	This call establishes a connection (or session) on a reliable stream socket. It is used with datagrams to specify the destination, making it possible to transfer data without explicitly specifying the destination each time (but no session is established).
listen()	This call listens for connections on a socket. It says: "There is some process at this socket ready to accept a connection." The call establishes a queue on a stream socket to accept incoming connection requests. Once the queue fills, additional connection requests are ignored. The call indicates a readiness to accept client connection requests and transforms an active socket into a passive socket. Once called, the socket cannot be used as an active socket that initiates connection requests. This queue is useful for networked applications that need to capture incoming requests from clients while the server is busy servicing a request.
accept()	This call is used by a server to accept a connection request from a client. The call accepts the first connection on its queue of pending connections. The accept call creates a new socket descriptor and returns it to the caller. The original socket still remains open and can accept new connections. If the queue has no pending connection requests, accept blocks the caller, unless it is in nonblocking mode.
shutdown()	This call ends all or part of a duplex connection. You can end the communication from the socket, to the socket, or both to and from the socket.

Socket Core: Connected Data Exchanges

Once a connection is established, applications can use the connected data exchange services. You can send/recv or writev/readv, depending on your needs. Use the writev/readv if you need to create messages from data that is in noncontiguous blocks of memory. It will save you a copy. Table 20-5 presents a quick summary of the commands used for connected data exchanges.

Table 20-5. **Connected Data Exchange Services.**

Command	Description
send()	This call sends packets on a connected socket.
recv()	This call receives data on a connected socket and stores it in a buffer. The call returns the length of the incoming message. If a datagram packet is too long to fit in the supplied buffer, datagram sockets discard excess bytes. If data is not available at the socket, the call blocks waiting for a message to arrive, unless the socket is in nonblocking mode.
writev()	This call writes data on a connected socket. The data may be gathered from the buffers specified by iovec structure. This makes it possible to send a message without copying it into contiguous bytes of memory. This facility is called "scatter write."
readv()	This call reads data on a socket and can be used to store the incoming data in noncontiguous memory buffers. This is called "scatter read." The buffers are specified by a set of pointers in the iovec structure. If data is not available at the socket, the call blocks waiting for data to arrive, unless the socket is in nonblocking mode.

Socket Core: Unconnected Data Exchanges

These commands are generally used for datagram exchanges. Table 20-6 presents a quick summary of the commands used for unconnected data exchanges.

Table 20-6.   **Unconnected Data Exchange Services.**

Command	Description
sendto()	This call sends packets to a specified destination. It is generally used to send datagrams on an unconnected socket. It can also be used on connected sockets.
recvfrom()	This call is typically used to receive datagrams on an unconnected socket. The call can be issued on any datagram socket, whether connected or unconnected. The call returns the length of the incoming message or data. If a datagram packet is too long to fit in the supplied buffer, datagram sockets discard excess bytes. If datagram packets are not available at the socket the call blocks waiting for a message to arrive, unless the socket is in nonblocking mode. You can specify with the call a variable in which the sender's address will be recorded.

Socket Core: Miscellaneous Socket Management Functions

These commands perform miscellaneous socket management functions. We've included in this category a command that is used in any program to determine the name/address of one's own computer. Another command provides the network address of your conversation partner. Two of the commands are used to query and modify the socket options. The **select()** command is useful in situations where you have multiple sockets waiting on events. Finally, the **ioctl()** command can be used to create nonblocking mode sockets. Table 20-7 provides a summary explanation of what these commands can do for you.

Table 20-7.   **(Part 1 of 2)**   **Miscellaneous Socket Functions.**

Command	Description
gethostid()	The gethostid() call gets the unique 32-bit identifier for the current host. This id should be unique across all hosts.
getpeername()	The getpeername() call returns the address of the peer with which this socket is connected. The call only works with connected sockets.
getsockname()	This call returns the address to which the current socket is bound. If the socket is not bound to an address, the call returns with the family type of the socket (such as AF_INET for TCP/IP). Sockets assign an address after a successful call to either bind(), connect(), or accept(). This call is often used to discover the port assigned to a socket after the socket has been implicitly bound to a port.
getsockopt()	This call returns information (called options) about a socket. These options can exist at multiple protocol levels; socket is the highest level (the SOL_SOCKET level). The SOL_SOCKET level is the only level supported with the OS/2 product. This call can be used to determine if the socket supports broadcast transmissions, buffer sizes, timeout parameters, and the type of socket.

Table 20-7. (Part 2 of 2) **Miscellaneous Socket Functions.**

Command	Description
setsockopt()	This call allows an application to program the options associated with a socket (see getsockopt call).
select()	This call monitors activity on a group of sockets to see if any sockets are ready for reading or writing, or if any exceptional conditions are pending. The call can poll all indicated sockets at the same time without becoming blocked. It can also block waiting on a ready socket or a timeout to expire. There are two versions of this call: an OS/2 version and a BSD version. The OS/2 version monitors the sockets by specifying the numbers of the sockets. The BSD version does it by setting a mask of socket numbers. The select call is useful in server situations where you work with multiple sockets. It can be used for load balancing.
ioctl()	This call is used to control the operating characteristics of a socket. The operations to be controlled are determined by cmd. The data parameter is a pointer to data associated with the particular command, and its format depends on the command that is requested. Two of the more important ioctl commands are FIONBIO which controls the blocking/nonblocking mode for that socket, and FIONREAD, which gets the number of immediately readable bytes for the socket. *Caution:* Use the ioctl calls only when absolutely necessary because it can easily place a socket into an unworkable state.

The Socket Network Utility Commands

As part of our divide and conquer strategy we placed the socket network utility commands (see Table 20-2) into the following seven categories:

- Host names information commands
- Network names information commands
- Protocol names information commands
- Service names information commands
- Byte order translation commands
- Internet address manipulation commands
- Domain name resolution commands

Socket Utility: Host Names Information Commands

TCP/IP, like other networks, provides a symbolic name service for network addresses. TCP/IP calls it the *domain name service.* The socket library provides five calls for obtaining name services. You can use these calls to obtain information about a host given either its symbolic name or its internet address. The database for these calls is provided by a network name server. The library calls transform the calling process into a client. If a name server is not present on the network or is unable to resolve the host name, the calls interact with a local TCPIP\ETC\HOSTS file. This file contains the symbolic name of internet hosts, alias names, the host address family, and the host address. Table 20-8 presents a quick summary of the name information commands.

Table 20-8. Host Names Information.

Command	Description
gethostbyaddr()	This call returns the symbolic name of a host address. The call will obtain that information from a network name server, if one is present. If a name server is not present, or unable to resolve the host name, the calls search the local TCPIP\ETC\HOSTS file until a matching host address is found or an EOF marker is reached. The call places the requested information in a **hostent** structure.
gethostbyname()	This call returns the address of a symbolic host name. The call will obtain that information from a network name server, if one is present. If a name server is not present, or unable to resolve the host name, the call searches the TCPIP\ETC\HOSTS file until a matching host name is found or an EOF marker is reached. The call places the requested information in a **hostent** structure.
gethostent()	This call reads the next line of the TCPIP\ETC\HOSTS file.
sethostent()	This call opens and rewinds the TCPIP\ETC\HOSTS file.
endhostent()	This call closes the TCPIP\ETC\HOSTS file.

Socket Utility: Network Names Information Commands

TCP/IP allows network administrators to maintain their own database of network information in addition to the domain name system. The sockets library provides five calls for accessing the network information database. The information is kept in a local TCPIP\ETC\NETWORKS file. The network administrators may enter their own network addresses and numbers in that file. An entry consists of the name of the network, aliases, the network address family, and the network number. Table 20-9 presents a quick summary of the network names information commands.

Table 20-9. Network Names Information.

Command	Description
getnetbyaddr()	This call searches the TCPIP\ETC\NETWORKS file for the specified network address.
getnetbyname()	This call searches the TCPIP\ETC\NETWORKS file for the specified network name.
getnetent()	This call reads the next entry of the TCPIP\ETC\NETWORKS file.
setnetent()	This call opens and rewinds the TCPIP\ETC\NETWORKS file.
endnetent()	This call closes the TCPIP\ETC\NETWORKS file.

Socket Utility: Protocol Names Information Commands

The TCP/IP socket library provides five calls to access information about protocols. The database for this information is kept on a local TCPIP\ETC\PROTOCOL file. It contains entries on names of protocols, aliases, and protocol numbers. You can obtain information about protocols either by name or by number. Table 20-10 provides a quick summary of the protocol names information commands.

Table 20-10.   Protocol Names Information.

Command	Description
getprotobyname()	This call searches the TCPIP\ETC\PROTOCOL file for the specified protocol name. It returns the information in a **protoent** structure.
getprotobynumber()	This call searches the TCPIP\ETC\PROTOCOL file for the specified protocol number. It returns the information in a **protoent** structure.
getprotoent()	This call returns a pointer to the next entry in the TCPIP\ETC\PROTOCOL file.
setprotoent()	This call opens and rewinds the TCPIP\ETC\PROTOCOL file.
endprotoent()	This call closes the TCPIP\ETC\PROTOCOL file.

Socket Utility: Service Names Information Commands

In TCP/IP networks some of the ports are reserved for *well-known services*. The socket library provides five calls for obtaining well-known socket information. The information on well-known services is kept in the TCPIP\ETC\SERVICES file. The information maintained in this file includes entries for the name of each service, optional aliases, port number, and protocol. This file is read by programs at start-up. Table 20-11 provides a quick summary of the service names information commands.

Table 20-11.   Service Names Information Calls.

Command	Description
getservbyname()	This call searches the TCPIP\ETC\SERVICES file for the specified service name and protocol (if specified). The call returns a pointer to a **servent** structure for the network service specified on the call. This structure contains fields for the name of the service, an array of aliases, the port number of the service, and the protocol used to communicate with the service.
getservbyport()	This call sequentially searches the TCPIP\ETC\SERVICES file for the specified port number and protocol (if specified). The call returns a pointer to a **servent** structure for the port number specified on the call.
getservent()	This call searches for the next line in the TCPIP\ETC\SERVICES file.
setservent()	This call opens and rewinds the TCPIP\ETC\SERVICES file.
endservent()	This call closes the TCPIP\ETC\SERVICES file.

Socket Utility: Byte Order Translation Commands

Machines on a network may have different ways of storing integers ("little endian" Intel versus "big endian" Motorola and SPARC). TCP/IP sockets require that both incoming and outgoing data be converted to *Network Order*, defined as the most significant byte first (i.e., "big endian"). Ports and addresses are usually specified to calls using the network byte ordering convention. This means that the byte order on Intel machines must be swapped. It is your job to handle byte order differences across dissimilar machines on the network. The sockets library provides four functions that convert between local machine byte order and the TCP/IP standard byte order. You should get in the habit of using these functions every time you copy an integer into a network packet, even when you know the networked machines are compatible. This will make your programs more portable. Table 20-12 provides a quick summary of the byte order conversion commands.

Table 20-12. Network Byte Order Translation.

Command	Description
htonl()	This call converts a long integer from host byte order to network byte order.
htons()	This call converts a short integer from host byte order to network byte order.
ntohl()	This call converts a long integer from network byte order to host byte order.
ntohs()	This call converts a short integer from network byte order to host byte order.
bswap()	This call swaps bytes in a short integer.
lswap()	This call swaps bytes in a long integer.

Socket Utility: Internet Address Manipulation Commands

The TCP/IP socket library provides a set of six commands that help you convert 32-bit internet addresses (IP addresses) into the corresponding dotted decimal notation and vice versa. These commands allow you to manipulate the network number and local network address portions of an internet address. Table 20-13 provides a quick summary of the internet address manipulation commands.

Socket Utility: Domain Name Resolution Commands

A domain name service provides symbolic names that humans can relate to for cryptic internet addresses. TCP/IP provides five *resolver* calls for resolving the symbolic host name into an internet address and for extracting more information about the host from a name server database (network yellow pages) if one is present on the network. The resolver calls determine whether the name server is present by referencing the TCPIP\ETC\RESOLV file. If no name server is present, the resolver calls check the local TCPIP\ETC\HOSTS file for an entry that maps the name to an address. You can use the resolver calls to make, send, and interpret packets for name servers on the internet. Table 20-14 provides a quick summary of the domain name resolution commands.

Table 20-13. Internet Address Manipulation Calls.

Command	Description
inet_addr()	This call maps a dotted decimal notation ASCII string into a 32-bit internet address (in network byte order). If you specify a four-part address, each part is interpreted as a byte of data and assigned, from left to right, to one of the four bytes of an internet address. If you specify a three-part address, the last part is interpreted as a 16-bit quantity and placed in the two rightmost bytes of the network address. This makes the three-part address format convenient for specifying Class B networks addresses as 128.net.host. If you specify a two-part address, the last part is interpreted as a 24-bit quantity and placed in the three rightmost bytes of the network address. This makes the two-part address format convenient for specifying Class A network addresses as net.host. When a one-part address is specified, the value is stored directly in the network address space without any rearrangement of its bytes.
inet_network()	This call maps a dotted decimal notation to a network number (host byte order).
inet_ntoa()	This call maps a 32-bit internet address (network byte order) to dotted decimal notation.
inet_netof()	This call extracts the network number (host byte order) from 32-bit internet address (network byte order).
inet_lnaof()	This call extracts the local network address (host byte order) from 32-bit internet address (network byte order).
inet_makeaddr()	This call constructs an internet address (network byte order) from a network number and a local network address.

Table 20-14. Domain Name Resolution Commands.

Command	Description
res_init()	This call reads the TCPIP\ETC\RESOLV file for the default domain name and the internet address of the initial hosts running the name server. If the TCPIP\ETC\RESOLV file does not exist, the call attempts name resolution using the TCPIP\ETC\HOSTS file. The domain information is returned and stored in the **_res** global structure. This call must be issued before any other resolver calls.
res_mkquery()	This call creates a query message that is then sent by res_send() to a name server. Queries can obtain all sorts of useful internet information including mailbox addresses, mail routings, user info, group IDs, etc.
res_send()	The res_send() call sends a query message to the local name server based on information in the global **_res** structure. The call handles time-outs and retries if the server is on the network.
dn_comp()	This call translates an ASCII domain name into the compressed domain name used in queries. It returns the size of the compressed name.
dn_expand()	This call expands a compressed domain name to a full ASCII domain name. The expanded name is returned in uppercase letters.

The Anatomy of a Sockets Program

The following describes the anatomy of a typical client/server interaction using stream sockets:

1. *Create the socket endpoints*. Every process that uses sockets must first initialize the sockets runtime using the **sockinit()** call. Next, each process must create a socket using the **socket()** call.

2. *Establish a well-known service port*. Server processes must **bind()** their sockets to a unique port name to become known on the network. The **getservbyname()** command is used to find a local address with a well-known port number for a specific service from the TCPIP\ETC\SERVICES file.

3. *Listen for connection requests to arrive*. Server processes using stream sockets must issue a **listen()** call to indicate their readiness to accept connections from clients. The server is now open for business on this socket. The call defines the size of the queue for incoming requests. Additional requests are ignored by the server.

4. *Connect to server*. The client issues a **connect()** call on a stream socket to initiate a connection to the port with the well-known service. The client process could have called **gethostbyname()** to locate the internet address of the server from either a name server or the TCPIP\ETC\HOSTS file. The client may optionally block until the connection is accepted by the server. On a successful return, the client socket is associated with the connection to the server.

5. *Accept the connection*. The server side accepts a connection request on a stream socket with the **accept()** call. The call will optionally block if no connections are pending. If many requests are pending, it will pop the first one off the queue. When the call returns, it will have created a *new* socket that has its destination connected to the requesting client. This is the socket that will be used for all subsequent communication with the connected client. This leaves the original well-known server socket free to receive requests from new clients. The server process can choose to handle the communication with the connected client on the current thread, or it can start a new thread and hand it the new socket. The original thread will continue looking for new clients on the well-known socket.

6. *Conduct network business*. Clients and servers have many calls from which to choose for their data exchanges. The **readv()**, **writev()**, **send()** and **recv()** calls can be used only on sockets that are in the connected state. The **sendto()** and **recvfrom()** calls can be used at any time, but they require additional address information.

7. *Close the socket*. The client and server must both issue **soclose()** to terminate their end of the TCP session. The well-known socket on the server side is still open and ready for new business. If the server was executing on a separate service thread, it terminates the thread.

8. ***Accept new business or close for the day***. The server can accept new connections from clients or issue **soclose**() to close the original well-known socket.

The client/server interaction described here was conducted on a stream socket. We will show you in the scenarios that follow how to conduct this type of interaction using datagram as well as stream sockets.

SOCKET SCENARIOS

The scenarios that follow will help demonstrate the use of sockets in typical peer-to-peer exchanges.

Scenario 1: A Simple Transaction Involving Two Processes

Scenario 1 is the socket version of the simple transaction:

```
What is Bob's Balance?  ──────────────────▶

                        ◀──────────────  $300
```

We show two implementations of this simple transaction (or Remote Procedure Call):

1. Using a stream socket (see Figure 20-2).
2. Using a datagram socket (see Figure 20-3).

So which implementation is better? It's a tossup. The stream may be overkill for a two-message exchange. It does, however, provide all the built-in sequencing and error recovery. The datagram requires a lower setup overhead, but you have to include information with the data that uniquely identifies each message.

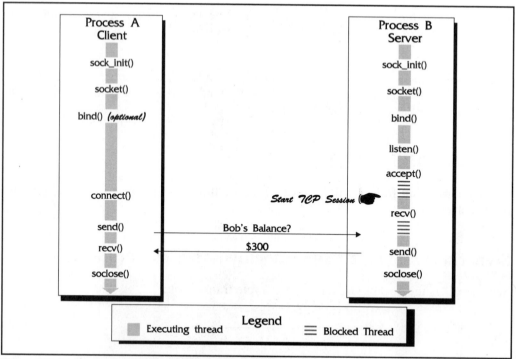

Figure 20-2.   Scenario 1a: Simple Transaction Using a Stream Socket.

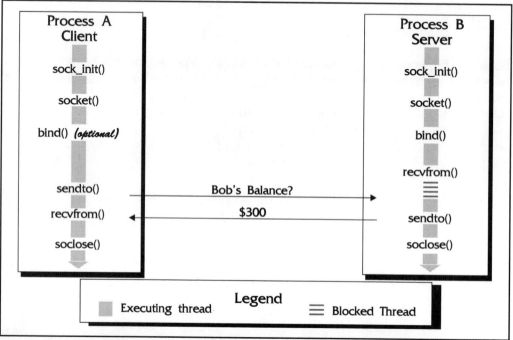

Figure 20-3.   Scenario 1b: Simple Transaction Using a Datagram Socket.

Scenario 2: One Server with a Serially Reusable Session

Scenario 2 shows how a single socket session is used to serially service two clients (see Figure 20-4). The scenario can easily be expanded to "n" clients. After the serving a client the server closes the connection and reissues an **accept()** call to handle a new client request. We assume that all the clients will be executing simple transactions such as the one described in Scenario 1.

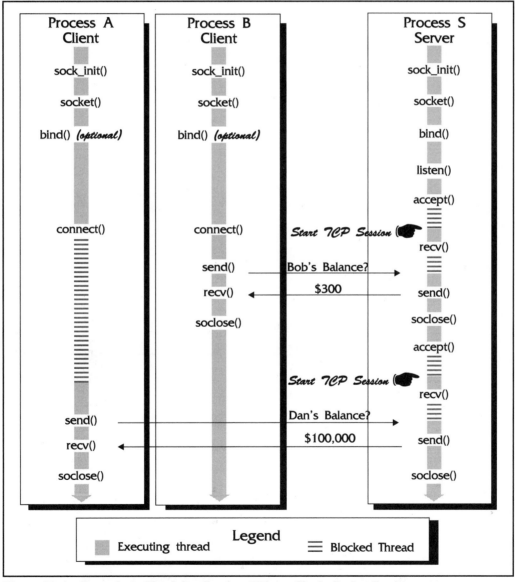

Figure 20-4. Scenario 2: Obtaining Services Using a Single Socket Session.

Scenario 3: A Multithreaded Socket Server

Scenario 3 shows how we can take advantage of OS/2's multitasking to create a server that does not serialize responses to client requests. The original thread will continue looking for new clients while a server thread takes care of the connected client. The **accept()** call is reissued to wait on a new client connection (see Figure 20-5). The scenario can easily be expanded to "n" server threads.

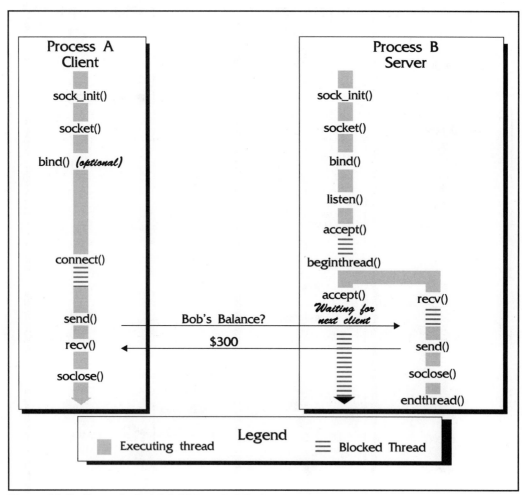

Figure 20-5.   Scenario 3: A Multithreaded Socket Server.

Scenario 4: Sending Bulk Data Over a Stream Socket.

Scenario 4 shows how moving bulk data, such as a file transfer, may get implemented over a sockets session (see Figure 20-6). Initially, the server is blocked waiting for the client. The client starts the file transfer by telling the server that it is about to receive a file, and gives it the name of the file and its size. The server says "OK" and issues a **recv()**; it then blocks waiting on the first file segment to arrive. The file copy is done through a series of exchanges. *Warning*: TCP does not guarantee message boundaries. It may take many consecutive **recv()** invocations to consume one message (we do not show this randomness in the scenario). Eventually, the server finishes consuming the file and sends a message to the client saying the file got there OK after which both sides break their end of the session.

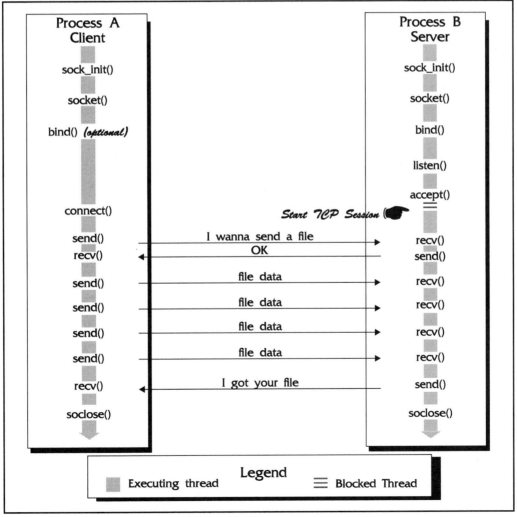

Figure 20-6. Scenario 4: Moving Bulk Data Over a Stream Socket.

Chapter 21

FX Using TCP/IP Sockets

This chapter presents an implementation of the communication layer of the FX protocol using OS/2's **TCP/IP Sockets** LAN protocol. The interface will be packaged as a Dynamic Link Library (FXTCPIP.DLL). The DLL will be created from **FXTCPIP.C** using the FX make file introduced in Chapter 16.

The sockets communication DLL makes it possible to transfer files using FXREQ and FXSVR, the client/server programs developed in Chapter 16. Figure 21-1 shows how this all comes together. We will use this setup to collect benchmark numbers on the performance of TCP/IP by measuring the time it takes to exchange files between the client and the server.

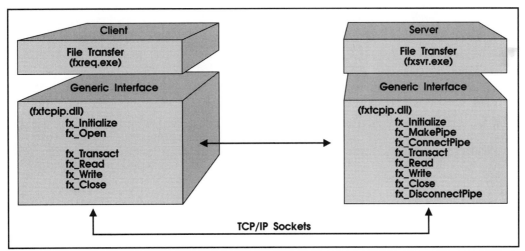

Figure 21-1. Implementing the FX Interface Using the TCP/IP Sockets DLL.

The plan for this chapter is to make use of whatever mechanisms are provided by OS/2's TCP/IP sockets LAN protocol to implement the nine **FX** interface calls shown in Figure 21-1. Figure 21-2 demonstrates how each of the FX calls is implemented by the FXTCPIP.DLL using the socket LAN services. It also shows the effect each call has on the partner transaction.

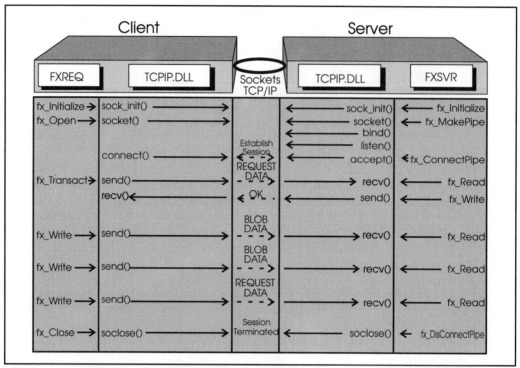

Figure 21-2. Sending a File Using the FXTCPIP.DLL.

PROGRAMMING TCP/IP SOCKETS

C programmers will find sockets easy to program. Sockets use a call-based interface that has the "look and feel" of the standard I/O functions that you find in C libraries. However, there are three areas where some minor surprises lurk:

1. The OS/2 sockets implementation handles certain calls differently from BSD sockets. These are minor differences, but they may catch veteran BSD programmers by surprise.
2. Some thunking is needed to call the 16-bit TCP/IP socket functions from a 32-bit OS/2 program. TCP/IP for OS/2 does not provide 32-bit headers, so we will create our own. This will provide us an opportunity to explain how to create headers using C Set/2's 32-to-16 calling facilities.
3. The stream model used by sockets may confuse programmers used to message based exchanges. Sending or receiving data on a socket may result in the transfer of fewer bytes than requested. Programmers may have to issue more than one send and receive to transfer the remaining bytes in a message.

We will first cover the differences between the OS/2 and BSD socket implementations. We will explain the 32-to-16 headers and the message streams when we encounter them in the code.

From Berkeley to OS/2 With Love

The OS/2 socket implementation differs from the Berkeley sockets in the following areas:

1. In the Unix environments where Berkeley sockets first appeared, sockets are directly related to file or device handles. The OS/2 socket numbers, on the other hand, have no relationship to OS/2 file handles. The BSD **read()**, **write()**, and **close()** do not work on OS/2 sockets. Instead, you must use the **recv()**, **send()**, and **soclose()** functions. Interestingly, the OS/2 Named Pipes work more like the BSD sockets in that respect.
2. With OS/2, you must first issue **sock_init()** before invoking other socket calls.
3. You must issue **tcperrno()** rather than **errno()** to access TCP/IP system and network return values.
4. The **select()** call under OS/2 cannot be used to wait for activity on devices other than sockets.

As you can see, these are minor differences that can easily be worked around when porting code from BSD to OS/2 or vice versa. For all practical purposes, sockets are still sockets whether they're on OS/2 or Unix.

FXTCPIP.C: THE TCP/IP SOCKETS FX DLL

The code we present in this section *does not* contain a main() procedure. The FX DLLs are simply functions that get linked to a (.EXE) file at run time. The main() procedure is provided by the program that calls the DLL functions. This means **FXTCPIP.C** is not a separate program; it contains a list of functions that get packaged in a DLL. The functions that are provided in this module fall into two categories: **FX** functions and *helper* functions. The helper functions, as usual, are used to provide common services for that module. The only helper function we provide is the ubiquitous **print_error()**. This should tell you that it will be easy to map the **FX** calls to sockets.

FXTCPIP.C: General Stuff

The following listing (see Figure 21-3) contains all the miscellaneous programming "stuff" that will be used by the FX procedures. This includes the usual declarations of constants, global variables, and forward declarations of functions. You will notice that we're providing our own version of the sockets data structures and not depending on those that come with the TCP/IP product. We're also providing forward declarations of the socket library calls. Why? Because we're going to call the 16-bit TCP/IP calls from within a 32-bit program. So we have to do certain things that tell C Set/2 to do some 32-to-16 bit thunking for us. Elsewhere in this book, the products that we use provide header files that have already done this kind of work for us. TCP/IP for OS/2 is not one of those products. So let's go through the steps involved in creating your own 32-to-16 bit linkages:

1. *Fix the pointers.* Pointers cannot be shared directly between 16-bit programs and 32-bit programs. Use the C Set/2 provided **_Seg16** type qualifier to declare 16-bit pointers in a 32-bit program so that they are usable directly by a 16-bit application. The parameter types in the forward declarations (see Figure 21-3) use this type qualifier. It is a good programming practice to include prototype declarations for 16-bit functions.
2. *Specify a 16-bit linkage type for each 16-bit function.* You can specify the linkage type for a function using either linkage keywords or the **#pragma linkage** directive. **In the listing we use pragmas. The far16** argument tells the compiler to use the a 16-bit C calling convention with the specified function. This is equivalent to the **cdecl** convention used in Microsoft C Version 6.0. What this means is that parameters will be pushed on the stack in a right-to-left order and that the caller will clean up the parameters on the stack. If, instead, you were to specify **far16 pascal**, a Pascal calling convention would be used. In Pascal, the parameters are pushed on the stack in left-to-right order, and the function being called is responsible for cleaning up the stack. The TCP/IP sockets library uses the C calling convention.
3. *Specify the stack size for the 16-bit code.* The default stack size is 4 KBytes. You can change the stack size using the **pragma stack16** directive. The stack size you specify will be used for all 16-bit functions called after the directive. We specify 8192 bytes of stack in our program.

```
/*********************************************************************/
/*   MODULE NAME: FXTCPIP - TCP/IP Communication.                  */
/*                                                                  */
/*   PROGRAM DESCRIPTION:  This module is a part of the FX file transfer */
/*      programs.  Refer to the FXR.C program module for a program overview. */
/*      This module implements the fx_* file transfer procedures using OS/2 */
/*      TCP/IP 1.2.                                                 */
/*                                                                  */
/*   PROCEDURES IN THIS MODULE:                                    */
/*                                                                  */
/*      fx_Initialize(buffer_p, size);                             */
/*      fx_MakePipe();                                             */
/*      fx_ConnectPipe();                                          */
/*      fx_DisconnectPipe();                                       */
/*      fx_Open();                                                 */
/*      fx_Write(BufferArea, BufferLength, BytesWritten);          */
/*      fx_Read(BufferArea, BufferLength, BytesRead);              */
/*      fx_Transact(InBufferArea, InBufferLength,                  */
/*                  OutBufferArea, OutBufferLength, BytesRead);     */
/*      fx_Close();                                                */
/*                                                                  */
/*********************************************************************/
#include <stdio.h>                 /* For printf() & NULL          */
#include <malloc.h>                /* For memory allocation        */
#include <string.h>                /* For string functions         */

#include <os2.h>
#include "fxfer.h"                 /* For FX functions             */
```

Figure 21-3 (Part 1 of 3).   FXTCPIP.C: General Header Stuff and print_error().

```
/*----------------------------------------------------------------*/
/* TCP/IP Structures                                              */
/*----------------------------------------------------------------*/
typedef struct IN_ADDR
        { ULONG s_addr; } IN_ADDR;

typedef struct
        { SHORT   sin_family;
          USHORT  sin_port;
          IN_ADDR sin_addr;
          CHAR    sin_zero[8];
        } SOCKADDR_IN;

typedef struct
        { CHAR *  _Seg16 h_name;        /* official name of host           */
          CHAR ** _Seg16 h_aliases;     /* alias list                      */
          SHORT          h_addrtype;    /* host address type               */
          SHORT          h_length;      /* length of address               */
          CHAR ** _Seg16 h_addr_list;   /* list of addresses from name server */
#define    h_addr  h_addr_list[0]       /* address, for backward compatiblity */
        } HOSTENT;

/*----------------------------------------------------------------*/
/* forward declarations                                           */
/*----------------------------------------------------------------*/
SHORT accept(SHORT socket, SOCKADDR_IN * _Seg16 name, SHORT * _Seg16 namelen );
SHORT bind(SHORT socket, SOCKADDR_IN * _Seg16 name, SHORT namelen);
SHORT connect(SHORT socket, SOCKADDR_IN * _Seg16 name, SHORT namelen);
SHORT listen(SHORT socket, SHORT backlog);
SHORT recv(SHORT socket, CHAR * _Seg16 buffer, SHORT length, SHORT flags);
SHORT send(SHORT socket, CHAR * _Seg16 message, SHORT length, SHORT flags);
SHORT sock_init(VOID);
SHORT socket(SHORT domain, SHORT type, SHORT protocol);
SHORT soclose(SHORT socket);
USHORT bswap(USHORT addr );
ULONG inet_addr(CHAR * _Seg16 addr);
SHORT tcperrno(VOID);

#pragma linkage(accept, far16)
#pragma linkage(bind, far16)
#pragma linkage(connect, far16)
#pragma linkage(listen, far16)
#pragma linkage(recv, far16)
#pragma linkage(send, far16)
#pragma linkage(sock_init, far16)
#pragma linkage(socket, far16)
#pragma linkage(soclose, far16)
#pragma linkage(gethostbyname, far16)
#pragma linkage(bswap, far16)
#pragma linkage(inet_addr, far16)
#pragma linkage(tcperrno, far16)

#pragma stack16(8192)

VOID print_error(SHORT, PCHAR, PCHAR, USHORT);

/*----------------------------------------------------------------*/
/* Configuration variables, initialized after fx_Initialize()     */
/* function call.                                                 */
/*----------------------------------------------------------------*/
CHAR    HostAddressStr[128];            /* Server TCP/IP Host Address string */
SHORT   ServerPort;                     /* Server port number              */
USHORT  FileBufferSize;                 /* file and message buffer         */
```

Figure 21-3 (Part 2 of 3).   FXTCPIP.C: General Header Stuff and print_error().

```
/*————————————————————————————————————————————————*/
/* global variables for this module.                                    */
/*————————————————————————————————————————————————*/
SHORT     server_socket;              /* Server socket number            */
SHORT     connection_socket;          /* Socket number for connection    */
SOCKADDR_IN server_addr;              /* server address information       */
SOCKADDR_IN client_addr;              /* client address information       */

SHORT     namelen;                    /* address structure length        */
SHORT     rc;                         /* return code                     */
BOOL      server;                     /* client/server indicator         */

typedef struct TCPIP_PACKET
    { ULONG  length;                  /* length of TCP/IP message data   */
      PACKET fxpacket;                /* FX packet data                  */
    } TCPIP_PACKET, *PTCPIP_PACKET;

PTCPIP_PACKET bufferp;                /* pointer to a TCPIP packet buffer */

/*————————————————————————————————————————————————*/
/* Error Display Routine                                                 */
/*————————————————————————————————————————————————*/
VOID print_error(SHORT  Error, PCHAR msg, PCHAR file, USHORT line)
{
 printf("TCPIP Error %hd (0x%hx) detected while %s at line %lu in file %s.\n",
        Error, Error, msg, line, file);
 rc = tcperrno();
 printf("errno = %hd (0x%hx).\n", rc, rc);
} /* end print_error */
```

Figure 21-3 (Part 3 of 3). FXTCPIP.C: General Header Stuff and print_error().

FXTCPIP.C: fx_Initialize()

The **fx_Initialize()** function (see Figure 21-4) reads a protocol-specific configuration file to obtain the parameters required to initialize the system. The name of the user specified configuration file for sockets is: **fxtcpip.cfg**. Here is an example of a such a file:

```
SERVER_PORT       = 1027
HOST_ADDRESS      = 2.0.0.1
FILE_BUFFER_SIZE  = 4096
```

Here's what these parameters do:

- **SERVER_PORT** specifies the port number on the server.
- **HOST_ADDRESS** specifies the internet address of the server.
- **FILE_BUFFER_SIZE** specifies the size (in bytes) of the message buffer. This is the buffer we will use for reading and writing data to the disk and for exchanging messages across the LAN or the IPC. The memory space for this parameter will be dynamically allocated. The **fx_Initialize()** function returns a pointer to this buffer and its size to the application. One of the factors we will measure in our benchmarks is the effect of the message buffer size on performance.

Notice that we allocated (see Figure 21-4) a message buffer that is four bytes larger than specified. Why? It has something to do with creating a message boundary on top of stream sockets. We added a four-byte length field to explicitly specify the length of each packet sent. You'll see how it works when we send and receive packets. Other than that, the only new and exciting this function introduces is the socket call **sock_init()**. The description of this call follows.

sock_init()

The **sock_init()** API call initializes the socket data structures and checks whether TCP/IP is running. It should be issued at the start of each program that uses sockets. The prototype for this call is:

```
sock_init(VOID);
```

There are no parameters associated with this call. A return value 0 indicates success; 1 indicates an error.

```
/*_____*/
/* function to read communication specific parameters and allocate a buffer  */
/* for communication.  A pointer to the buffer and the buffer size is         */
/* returned.                                                                   */
/*_____*/
ULONG fx_Initialize(PPACKET *buffer_p , PUSHORT size)
{
  FILE     *config_file;              /* Input file control block        */
  CHAR     line[80];                  /* one line of config file         */
  INT      scancount;

  printf("Reading configuration parameters.\n");
  /*_____*/
  /* open the configuration file             */
  /*_____*/
  if (NULL == (config_file = fopen("fxtcpip.cfg","r")))
     {print_error(rc,"opening configuration file",__FILE__,__LINE__);
      return(FAILED);
      }
  else
     /*_____*/
     /* read the configuration parameters.      */
     /* The parameters are expected to be:      */
     /*    - in the form <name = value>         */
     /*    - in the order read below            */
     /*_____*/
     {
     fgets(line, sizeof(line), config_file);
     if (sscanf(line,"SERVER_PORT = %d ", &ServerPort) != 1)
        {print_error(rc,"reading ServerPort from configuration",
                     __FILE__,__LINE__);
         return(FAILED);
         }
     printf("SERVER_PORT = %d \n", ServerPort);
```

Figure 21-4 (Part 1 of 2). FXTCPIP.C: fx_Initialize().

```
        fgets(line, sizeof(line), config_file);
        if (sscanf(line, "HOST_ADDRESS = %s ", HostAddressStr) != 1)
            {print_error(rc,"reading Host Address from configuration",
                        __FILE__,__LINE__);
             return(FAILED);
            }
        printf("HOST_ADDRESS = %s \n", HostAddressStr);

        fgets(line, sizeof(line), config_file);
        if (sscanf(line,"FILE_BUFFER_SIZE = %u ", &FileBufferSize) != 1)
            {print_error(rc,"reading FileBufferSize from configuration",
                        __FILE__,__LINE__);
             return(FAILED);
            }
        printf("FILE_BUFFER_SIZE = %u \n", FileBufferSize);
    } /* end if */

    fclose(config_file);

    /*_____*/
    /* allocate buffer, return pointer    */
    /* and size                      */
    /*_____*/
    bufferp = malloc(FileBufferSize+4);
    if (bufferp == NULL)
        {print_error(rc,"allocating file buffer",__FILE__,__LINE__);
         return(FAILED);
        }
    *buffer_p = &bufferp->fxpacket;
    *size = FileBufferSize;

    /*_____*/
    /* initialize TCP/IP sockets          */
    /*_____*/
    rc = sock_init();
    if (rc != 0)
        {print_error(rc,"initializing socket",__FILE__,__LINE__);
         return(FAILED);
        }

    return(GOOD);
} /* end fx_Initialize */
```

Figure 21-4 (Part 2 of 2).   FXTCPIP.C: fx_Initialize().

FXTCPIP.C: fx_MakePipe()

The **fx_MakePipe()** function (see Figure 21-5) is used by the server side of an FX pipe
to establish the pipe. We provide the function using sockets as follows:

1. Create a socket using the **socket()** command. The call returns a socket descriptor.
    Notice that we've created a stream socket for the TCP/IP internet family.
2. Convert the port number to "big endian" 16-bit integer notation using **bswap()**. Set
    the fields in the **SOCKADDR_IN** name/address structure.
3. Bind the socket to the server internet address and port using **bind()**. Allow
    connections from all clients by specifying the wild-card value, **INADDR_ANY**.

Any message sent to that host (on any of the host's network adapters) will be delivered to the server socket.

4. Issue a **listen()** command on the server socket to set up a queue of up to five connection requests.

The **fx_MakePipe()** function (see Figure 21-5) introduces four socket commands: **socket()**, **bswap()**, **bind()**, and **listen()**. These functions are described below.

socket()

The **socket()** API call creates a socket and returns a socket descriptor. You must specify the protocol family to be used with the socket. The OS/2 product supports the AF_INET family, which stands for the TCP/IP internet. The prototype for this call is:

```
socket(SHORT    domain,    /* Address domain must be AF_INET  */
       SHORT    type,      /* Type of socket created          */
       ULONG    protocol);/* Transport protocol               */
```

A description of the parameters follows:

- The *domain* parameter specifies the communication domain. The choice of domain will determine the format of the internet address structure. The only family supported by the OS/2 product is **AF_INET**, which stands for the TCP/IP internet.
- The *type* parameter specifies the type of socket created. The OS/2 product supports three socket types: **SOCK_STREAM**, **SOCK_DGRAM**, and **SOCK_RAW**.
- The *protocol* parameter specifies the transport protocol to be used on that socket. If this field is set to 0, the system selects the default protocol number for the domain and socket type requested. The defaults are TCP for stream sockets and UDP for datagram sockets. There is no default for raw socket. Protocol numbers are found in the TCPIP\ETC\PROTOCOL file.

bswap()

The **bswap()** API call swaps bytes in an unsigned short integer. It is used for conversions between Intel "little endian" and "big endian" TCP/IP network byte ordering. The prototype for this call is:

```
bswap(USHORT    number); /* Number whose bytes will be swapped*/
```

A description of the parameters follows:

- The *number* parameter is the short integer whose bytes are to be swapped. The call returns the translated short integer.

bind()

The **bind()** API call associates a unique local address (the port number) to a socket. This is important for server processes that need to specify a "well-known port" for their service (otherwise, you can let the system assign a port for you automatically). The prototype for this call is:

```
bind(SHORT                   socket,      /* Socket descriptor            */
     SOCKADDR_IN * _Seg16     name,        /* Points to socket name/addr   */
     SHORT                    namelen);    /* Size of name struct in bytes */
```

A description of the parameters follows:

- The *socket* parameter specifies the socket descriptor to be bound. Think of it as a handle or "magic cookie" for that socket.
- The *name* parameter is a pointer to a structure that contains the port number and network address to be bound to the socket. If you set the *sin_port* field to 0, the system will assign an available port. You must explicitly assign a port when you need a well-known port for a service. You can bind the socket to a specific network interface card (NIC) address or to all the NICs on a machine. If you want the packets from all the NICs routed to your socket, assign the **INADDR_ANY** wild-card constant to the *sin_addr* field. This allows a server to service clients on multiple networks. The following is a description of the **SOCKADDR_IN** structure:

```
typedef struct
        { SHORT   sin_family;   /* Socket family: AF_INET for TCP/IP   */
          USHORT  sin_port;     /* Port number in network byte order   */
          IN_ADDR sin_addr;     /* Internet address in network byte order*/
                                /* INADDR_ANY binds to all NICs on host */
          CHAR    sin_zero[8];  /* Not used must be set to zeroes       */
        } SOCKADDR_IN;


typedef struct IN_ADDR
        { ULONG s_addr;         /* This is a single-field structure     */
        } IN_ADDR;
```

- The *namelen* parameter contains the size (in bytes) of the name structure.

listen()

The **listen()** API call listens for connections on a socket. It says: "There is some process at this socket ready to accept a connection." The call establishes a queue on a stream socket to accept incoming connection requests. The prototype for this call is:

```
listen(SHORT                  socket,      /* Socket descriptor            */
       SHORT                  backlog);    /* Defines max length of queue  */
```

A description of the parameters follows:

- The *socket* parameter specifies the socket descriptor (or handle).
- The *backlog* parameter defines the maximum length for the queue of pending connections. Once the queue fills, additional connection requests are ignored. This queue is useful for networked applications that need to capture incoming requests from clients while the server is busy servicing another client.

```
/*_____*/
/* function to establish the server end of the communication pipe.  */
/*_____*/
ULONG fx_MakePipe(VOID)
{
  #define SOCK_STREAM      1              /* stream socket */
  #define SOCK_DGRAM       2              /* datagram socket */
  #define AF_INET          2              /* internetwork: UDP, TCP, etc. */
  #define INADDR_ANY       0              /* internetwork: UDP, TCP, etc. */

  /*_____*/
  /* remember that this is a server      */
  /*_____*/
  server = TRUE;

  server_socket = socket(AF_INET, SOCK_STREAM, 0);
  if (server_socket < 0)
     {print_error(server_socket,"creating server socket",__FILE__,__LINE__);
      return(FAILED);
     }

  server_addr.sin_family      = AF_INET;
  server_addr.sin_port        = bswap(ServerPort);
  server_addr.sin_addr.s_addr = INADDR_ANY;

  rc = bind(server_socket, &server_addr, sizeof(server_addr));
  if (rc < 0)
     {print_error(rc,"binding",__FILE__,__LINE__);
      return(FAILED);
     }

  rc = listen(server_socket, 5);
  if (rc < 0)
     {print_error(rc,"listening",__FILE__,__LINE__);
      return(FAILED);
     }

  return(GOOD);

} /* end fx_MakePipe */
```

Figure 21-5. FXTCPIP.C: MakePipe().

FXTCPIP.C: fx_ConnectPipe()

The **fx_ConnectPipe()** function (see Figure 21-6) is used to establish a connection on the server side of an FX pipe. We provide the function with sockets using the **accept()** call described below:

accept()

The **accept()** API call is used by a server to accept a connection request from a client. The call accepts the first connection on its queue of pending connections. The accept call creates a new socket descriptor and returns it to the caller as the return value. The original socket still remains open and can accept new connections. The prototype for this call is:

```
accept(SHORT                   socket,  /* Socket descriptor            */
       SOCKADDR_IN * _Seg16    name,    /* Points to socket name/addr   */
       SHORT                   namelen);/* Size of name struct in bytes */
```

A description of the parameters follows:

- The *socket* parameter specifies the socket descriptor.
- The *name* parameter is a pointer to a structure that contains the socket address of the connecting client. This information is returned by the system. Set this parameter to NULL if you don't want that information returned. The **SOCKADDR_IN** structure is the same as the one used by the **bind()** command.
- The *namelen* parameter must be set to the size (in bytes) of the name structure. On return, it will contain the size of the data (in bytes) returned in the name structure. If the *name* field is NULL, this field can be ignored. Just set it to NULL.

```
/*_____*/
/* function to enable the server end of the communication pipe.   */
/*_____*/
ULONG fx_ConnectPipe(VOID)
{
  namelen = sizeof(client_addr);
  connection_socket = accept(server_socket, &client_addr, &namelen);
  if (connection_socket < 0)
     {print_error(connection_socket,"accepting a connection",
              __FILE__,__LINE__);
      return(FAILED);
     }

  return(GOOD);
} /* end fx_ConnectPipe */
```

Figure 21-6. FXTCPIP.C: fx_ConnectPipe().

FXTCPIP.C: fx_DisconnectPipe()

The **fx_DisconnectPipe()** function (see Figure 21-7) is used to disconnect the server side of an FX pipe. We provide the function using the socket **soclose()** command described below.

soclose()

The **soclose()** API call shuts down a socket, frees its resources, and closes a TCP connection (if one is open). The prototype for this call is:

```
soclose(SHORT          socket);    /* Socket descriptor           */
```

A description of the parameters follows:

- The *socket* parameter specifies the socket descriptor.

```
/*_____*/
/* function to disable the server end of the communiation pipe.    */
/*_____*/
ULONG fx_DisconnectPipe(VOID)
{
  rc = soclose(connection_socket);
  if (rc < 0)
     {print_error(rc,"closing a socket",__FILE__,__LINE__);
      return(FAILED);
     }
  return(GOOD);
} /* end fx_DisconnectPipe */
```

Figure 21-7. FXTCPIP.C: fx_DisconnectPipe().

FXTCPIP.C: fx_Open()

The **fx_Open()** function (see Figure 21-8) is used to establish the client side of an FX pipe. We provide the function using two socket calls: **socket()** and **connect()**. We've already encountered the **socket()** call on the server side; it is used in the same manner on the client side. The **connect()** call is new; it is used to associate the client socket with the *server's* socket address. Notice how the address is specified in network byte ordering. The **connect()** call is described below.

connect()

The **connect()** API call establishes a connection (or session) on a reliable stream socket. It can be used with datagrams to specify the destination, making it possible to transfer data without explicitly specifying the destination each time (however, no session is established). The prototype for this call is:

```
connect(SHORT              socket,  /* Socket descriptor           */
        SOCKADDR_IN * _Seg16  name,    /* Points to socket name/addr  */
        SHORT              namelen);/* Size of name struct in bytes */
```

A description of the parameters follows:

- The *socket* parameter specifies the socket descriptor.
- The *name* parameter is a pointer to a structure in which you provide the socket address of the server to which you want to connect. The **SOCKADDR_IN** structure is the same as the one used by the **bind()** command.
- The *namelen* parameter must be set to the size (in bytes) of the name structure.

```
/*_____*/
/* function a requester uses to prepare a pipe for communication.    */
/*_____*/
ULONG fx_Open(VOID)
{
    /*_____*/
    /* remember that this is a client    */
    /*_____*/
    server = FALSE;

    /*_____*/
    /* establish a connection using server */
    /*    name and port                  */
    /*_____*/
    connection_socket = socket(AF_INET, SOCK_STREAM, 0);
    if (connection_socket < 0)
        {print_error(connection_socket,"creating socket",__FILE__,__LINE__);
         return(FAILED);
        }

    /*_____*/
    /* Set up the server address structure.*/
    /*_____*/
    server_addr.sin_family      = AF_INET;
    server_addr.sin_port        = bswap(ServerPort);
    server_addr.sin_addr.s_addr = inet_addr(HostAddressStr);

    rc = connect(connection_socket, &server_addr, sizeof(server_addr));
    if (rc < 0)
        {print_error(rc,"connecting",__FILE__,__LINE__);
         return(FAILED);
        }

    return(GOOD);
} /* end fx_Open */
```

Figure 21-8.   FXTCPIP.C: fx_Open().

FXTCPIP.C: fx_Write()

The **fx_Write()** function (see Figure 21-9) is used to send information over an FX pipe. The only strange thing here is a 4-byte length field we appended to the packet so that we could specify the length of the message sent. We did that to create a message boundary on top of stream sockets (you'll see how it works when we receive the message). Other than that, the function is rather straightforward. We use a single new socket call, **send()**, which is explained below.

send()

The send() API call sends packets on a connected socket. The prototype for this call is:

```
send(SHORT          socket,   /* Socket descriptor           */
       CHAR * _Seg16  message,  /* Points to socket name/addr  */
       SHORT          length,   /* Size of name struct in bytes */
       SHORT          flags);   /* Diagnostic and routing flags */
```

A description of the parameters follows:

- The *socket* parameter specifies the socket descriptor.
- The *message* parameter points to a buffer containing the message to transmit.
- The *length* parameter contains the size of the message buffer in bytes.
- The *flags* parameter is usually set to 0. The flags are used by diagnostic or routing programs.

```
/*_____*/
/* function both requester and server use to write to a pipe.    */
/*_____*/
ULONG fx_Write(PVOID BufferArea, USHORT BufferLength, PUSHORT BytesWritten)
{
  bufferp->length = BufferLength;
  rc = send(connection_socket, (CHAR * _Seg16)bufferp, BufferLength+4, 0);
  if (rc < 0)
      {print_error(rc,"sending",__FILE__,__LINE__);
       return(FAILED);
      }

  *BytesWritten = BufferLength;
  return(GOOD);
} /* end fx_Write */
```

Figure 21-9. FXTCPIP.C: fx_Write().

FXTCPIP.C: fx_Read()

The **fx_Read()** function (see Figure 21-10) is used to read information over an FX pipe. We did some strange things to make this function work with stream sockets. Since TCP does not guarantee message boundaries we have to issue consecutive receives until we get the entire FX message. In the code, we first loop on **recv()** until we read the 4-byte FX length header. Now that we know how much data is going to be sent, we can specify a receive buffer size and then loop again on **recv()** to read the message contents. Remember, with streams TCP may decide to send a message a single byte-at-a-time or, most likely, it may decide to send the whole message in a single transfer. Your code must deal with either extreme. Other than the strange loops, we're only introducing a single new socket call: **recv()**. This call is explained below.

recv()

The **recv()** API call receives data on a connected socket and stores it in a buffer. The call returns the length of the incoming message. If data is not available at the socket, the call blocks waiting for a message to arrive, unless the socket is in nonblocking mode. The prototype for this call is:

```
recv(SHORT              socket,  /* Socket descriptor           */
     CHAR * _Seg16      message, /* Points to socket name/addr  */
     SHORT              length,  /* Size of name struct in bytes */
     SHORT              flags);  /* MSG_PEEK for peeking at buffer */
```

A description of the parameters follows:

- The *socket* parameter specifies the socket descriptor.
- The *message* parameter points to a buffer that receives the data.
- The *length* parameter contains the size of the data buffer in bytes.
- The *flags* parameter allows you to peek at the data present on the socket without consuming the message. This allows a subsequent recv() operation to see the same data. You can do that by specifying the **MSG_PEEK** flag.

```
/*_____*/
/* function both requester and server use to read from a pipe.     */
/*_____*/
ULONG fx_Read(PVOID BufferArea, USHORT BufferLength, PUSHORT BytesRead)
{
  ULONG bytes;
  ULONG total_bytes_rcvd;
  CHAR * _Seg16 buffer;

  /*_____*/
  /* get the length of the message. */
  /*_____*/
  total_bytes_rcvd = 0;
  do
  { buffer = (CHAR *)bufferp + total_bytes_rcvd;
    bytes = recv(connection_socket, buffer,
                 sizeof(bufferp->length) - total_bytes_rcvd, 0);
    if (bytes <= 0)
       {print_error(bytes,"receiving",__FILE__,__LINE__);
        return(FAILED);
       }
    total_bytes_rcvd = total_bytes_rcvd + bytes;
  } while (total_bytes_rcvd < sizeof(bufferp->length));

  /*_____*/
  /* get the message data.          */
  /*_____*/
  total_bytes_rcvd = 0;
  do
  { buffer = (CHAR *)bufferp + sizeof(bufferp->length) + total_bytes_rcvd;
    bytes = recv(connection_socket, buffer,
                 bufferp->length - total_bytes_rcvd, 0);
    if (bytes <= 0)
       {print_error(bytes,"receiving",__FILE__,__LINE__);
        return(FAILED);
       }
    total_bytes_rcvd = total_bytes_rcvd + bytes;
  } while (total_bytes_rcvd < bufferp->length);

  *BytesRead = total_bytes_rcvd;
  return(GOOD);
} /* end fx_Read */
```

Figure 21-10. FXTCPIP.C: fx_Read().

FXTCPIP.C: fx_Transact()

The **fx_Transact**() function (see Figure 21-11) sends a message and receives a reply over an FX pipe. This function is provided using sockets by invoking **fx_write**() (see Figure 21-9) followed by **fx_read**() (see Figure 21-10). No new socket calls are introduced.

```
/*_____*/
/* function requester uses to request a service.                  */
/*_____*/
ULONG fx_Transact(PVOID InBufferArea,  USHORT InBufferLength,
                  PVOID OutBufferArea, USHORT OutBufferLength,
                  PUSHORT BytesRead)
{
  USHORT BytesWritten;

  rc = fx_Write(InBufferArea, InBufferLength, &BytesWritten);
  if (rc)
     {print_error(rc,"writing during a transaction",__FILE__,__LINE__);
      return(FAILED);
     }

  rc = fx_Read(OutBufferArea, OutBufferLength, BytesRead);
  if (rc)
     {print_error(rc,"reading during a transaction",__FILE__,__LINE__);
      return(FAILED);
     }

  return(GOOD);
} /* end fx_Transact */
```

Figure 21-11. FXTCPIP.C: fx_Transact().

FXTCPIP.C: fx_Close()

The **fx_Close()** function (see Figure 21-12) closes an FX pipe. In terms of sockets, this means issuing a **soclose()** command. This is the same call we used earlier in **fx_Disconnect**. The client and server sockets are very symmetrical when it comes to disconnecting.

```
/*_____*/
/* function reqester uses to end communication with a server.     */
/*_____*/
ULONG fx_Close(VOID)
{
  soclose(connection_socket);        /* close connection socket, ignore errors */

  if (server)
     { rc = soclose(server_socket);
       if (rc < 0)
          {print_error(rc,"closing the server socket",__FILE__,__LINE__);
           return(FAILED);
          }
     } /* endif */

  return(GOOD);
} /* end fx_Close */
```

Figure 21-12. FXTCPIP.C: fx_Close().

Chapter 22

A Tutorial on CPI-C and APPC

This chapter presents a tutorial on APPC and CPI-C. Our focus is on APPC and CPI-C as *peer-to-peer* communication protocols. When necessary, the prerequisite SNA background information is provided. The aim of this tutorial is to demystify the SNA jargon and make APPC and CPI-C perfectly understandable to the professional programmer.

SITUATING CPI-C AND APPC

Using APPC, an OS/2 program can converse through one of SNA's 50,000 installed networks with peers located anywhere in the world. These peers can run on PCs, RS/6000s, AS/400s, S/38s, and S/370s, as well as on many non-IBM host platforms. Unlike NetBIOS or Named Pipes, APPC allows you to hook into an SNA APPC/APPN backbone that interconnects many networks. Data and session protocol transparency is handled by APPC/APPN across the SNA internet. The APPC stack also provides advanced services such as network security. IBM's SAA architecture for distributed transaction processing and remote database access is currently built entirely on an APPC communication base.

From a programmer's perspective, APPC provides a *verb with control-block* API for peer-to-peer communications within an SNA network (see Figure 22-1). APPC suc-

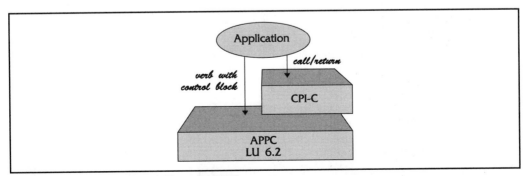

Figure 22-1. CPI-C Sits on Top of APPC.

471

ceeded in providing interoperability between platforms, but its implementation was not consistent across platforms. Each platform implemented the verb-based API differently. Even when implementations were similar, often the parameters would be in a different order. To correct this deficiency, IBM introduced the **Common Programming Interface-Communications (CPI-C)** and anointed it the official SAA interface for communications.

CPI-C provides a consistent *call-based* API on top of APPC. The CPI-C API is common across different operating systems and programming languages. CPI-C on an APPC stack is currently available on all the IBM operating system platforms (see Figure 22-2). **Networking Services/DOS**, available from IBM 3Q 1992, will provide CPI-C and APPN for the DOS/Windows platform. The X/Open consortium has licensed the CPI-C interface from IBM, so have several companies (including Novell and Apple). CPI-C is becoming an important "de facto" (and possibly "de jure") API standard for peer-to-peer communications.

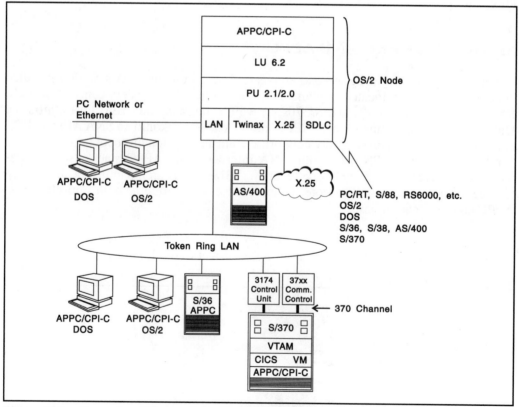

Figure 22-2. Examples of Connectivity Support Provided by the APPC/CPI-C Stack.

What all this means is that the APPC stack, the APPN SNA backbone, and the CPI-C API will most likely be your peer-to-peer protocol of choice if you are writing distributed applications across a network that includes mainframes from IBM or most other host vendors. In the future, when IBM delivers its multiprotocol blueprint, your CPI-C applications will be able to run, unchanged, on a broad selection of transport stacks, including TCP/IP, OSI, IPX/SPX, SNA, and NetBIOS (see Figure 22-3). Applications written to CPI-C will, in the meantime, run on an APPC foundation which in turn is built on SNA. So you will need to know something about SNA and APPC to fully appreciate what CPI-C can do for you today. This is precisely the plan we will follow in this tutorial.

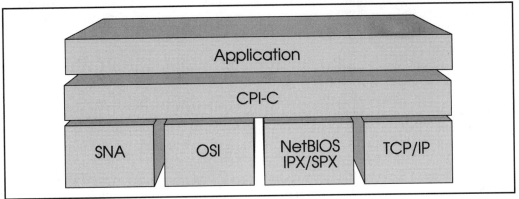

Figure 22-3. CPI-C: A Stack-Independent API (Source: IBM Blueprint for Networking, March 1992).

DO YOU SPEAK SNA?

One of the barriers to understanding APPC is the nearly unintelligible SNA jargon that surrounds it. Programmers need to understand this jargon to configure an APPC node and understand the mechanics of starting an SNA session. If you want to take advantage of the "intergalactic" connectivity that APPC offers, you'll have to learn how to configure an SNA node. In practice, what this means is figuring out how to answer a score of arcane questions about your application and all of its partners. These questions ask you to specify things like the SNA base profile, the PU name, the LU profiles, session limits, the TP profiles, the conversation type, security, and the synchronization level. Worse yet, you will almost inevitably need to interface to system programmers from the host MIS group, and you will need to tell them what you need from VTAM and CICS on the host side of the interface. So, welcome to the new partnership! In the next sections, we will provide you with the information you need in order to play in this league.

Demystifying the SNA Jargon

The purpose of this section is to introduce you to the SNA, APPC, and CPI-C terminology so that we can make that jargon "perfectly clear."

What Is a Transaction Program (TP)?

This is the logical network name that an application uses to communicate over the network. An application can define itself to APPC as multiple transaction programs (TPs). A single OS/2 process can contain many TPs. The primary goal of APPC is to provide the ability for transaction programs to communicate via conversations across the SNA network. A TP issues a request to APPC, in the form of a verb, to perform some action for your application program. APPC supplies verbs for starting and stopping a TP within an OS/2 program and for a TP to converse with other TPs. A TP has a 64-byte name and an 8-byte identifier (the TP ID).

What Is a Logical Unit (LU)?

This is the "socket" used by a Transaction Program to obtain access to an SNA network. The LU is the SNA software that accepts and executes the verbs from your programs. An LU manages the network on behalf of TPs and is responsible for the routing of data packets. A TP gains access to SNA via an LU. Multiple TPs can use the services provided by one LU. The LU to which the transaction program issues APPC API calls is the *local* LU. The local LU communicates with *partner* LUs on other nodes. When Communications Manager is configured, your local and partner LUs are defined once for each machine. APPC uses a particular type of LU known as **LU 6.2**. This is SNA's strategic LU service for program-to-program communications. The older SNA LU types are built with the assumption that one LU represents an application program and its partner LUs represent dumb terminals or printers. With these older LUs, the application program is always the *primary* LU and has responsibility for error recovery. With LU 6.2, either partner can act as the primary, and that role is negotiated as part of the session initiation process. The APPC stack is an implementation of the LU 6.2 architecture.

What Is an SNA Session?

This is an SNA logical connection between two LUs across the network. Before TPs can talk to each other, their LUs must be connected through a session. Sessions can be seen as providing the LU-to-LU links over which conversations can flow. In network protocol terms, sessions provide a reliable sequenced packet protocol service. The number of active sessions a local LU can have with a partner LU is configurable through the *session limits* parameter. *Parallel sessions* denote situations where more than one session is active between an LU pair. These sessions are used to allow multiple conversations to take place concurrently between the same LU pair. Typically, sessions remain active even when there are no active conversations. This ensures that a session is available when a conversation requests it.

What Is an APPC Conversation?

The actual exchange of information between two TPs is done over a conversation. Conversations are TP-to-TP links that are carried out over a session. Preferably, a conversation lasts only a short time, typically the time it takes to process a simple transaction. The idea is to have a series of conversations use the same session, one after the other. You can look at conversations as the mechanism to serially share sessions. However, only one conversation can be carried over a session at any one time. Conversations provide a way to avoid the overhead of establishing an SNA session for each network transaction (for our readers who are SNA experts, it's the cost of an SNA bracket versus that of an SNA Bind). Two TPs involved in a conversation are referred to as partners.

What Is a Physical Unit (PU)?

This is a program on an SNA node that manages certain network resources on behalf of all the LUs on that node. A PU, for example, manages the connections of the node to adjacent nodes. The PU manages the physical data links on behalf of LUs that manage the sessions or *logical* needs between nodes. There needs to be one PU on each SNA node. PUs have types which distinguish a node's connection and routing capabilities. Your PU needs to be defined only once for each machine. Communications Manager provides **PU type 2.1** support for communications among peripheral nodes without any host involvement. PU 2.1 was designed to serve as the platform for LU 6.2's symmetrical form of peer-to-peer communications. It provides support for multiple links, multiple sessions, and parallel sessions between directly attached nodes (for example, nodes on the same LAN). The more restrictive **PU type 2.0** may also be used for communication with host subarea nodes. A PU 2 node can only support a single active session, and it's partner can only be a host LU (i.e., a subarea node).

What Is APPN?

As we explained in Part I, *APPN* is IBM's strategic internet platform. It allows an application (a TP/LU) to find its peer across several LANs and WANs using the optimal communication path for a desired class-of-service. APPN **Network Nodes (NNs)** act as gateway machines on an SNA internet; these nodes are constantly keeping track of the network's changing topologies and conditions. The NN is automatically informed of nodes joining or leaving the network and of new links coming up or going down. It knows how to locate machines and calculate the time to traverse routes. It also knows how to detect and avoid congested paths and "rush-hour" network bottle-necks. With APPN, no definition of the partner addresses or network routes is required. Each NN keeps a copy of the NN topology (all the NNs in the internet) that it automatically discovers. And each NN is responsible for maintaining a directory of local network nodes. The NNs are part of a distributed network directory (see Figure 22-4).

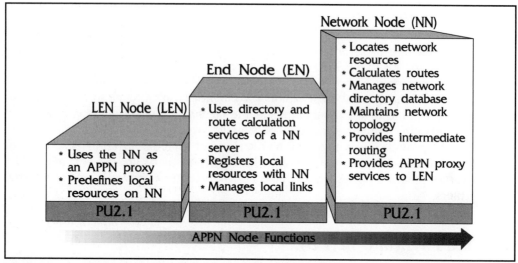

Figure 22-4.   APPN Provides a Hierarchy of Network Services on Top of PU 2.1.

APPN **Low Entry Nodes (LENs)** and **End Nodes (ENs)** are clients that use the NN's services to locate partners on the network. An EN is a well-endowed client node that can exchange control messages with an NN. An EN issues a control message to register itself with the NN when it first comes up. It also issues control messages to the NN asking it to locate a remote node. The NN uses those messages to create and maintain a directory of ENs. ENs also maintain a limited directory of local LUs and adjacent LUs. OS/2's Communications Manager provides both EN and NN services.

LENs are minimalist clients not endowed with the smarts to dynamically participate in the network by automatically exchanging control messages with NNs. Instead, LENs are manually configured in the NN's database. A LEN is also manually configured with the address of the NN that acts as its proxy on the network. This offloading of function (to the NN) helps the LEN stay skinny, but it creates more work for the network administrator. A LEN node cannot communicate with another node without the presence of an NN on the network. Network Services/DOS is an example of a LEN only product.

LENs, ENs, and NNs all build on top of PU 2.1's services. They provide the invisible glue that lets an LU discover its partner across an internet when an LU-to-LU session is created. Mercifully, all this dynamic network activity does not involve us programmers. We simply issue the verbs that create a session between two named LUs and let the network do all the behind-the-scenes work.

What Is an APPC Verb?

Like NetBIOS, APPC uses a control block type of API. An APPC verb is equivalent to a NetBIOS command. Your program obtains APPC services by passing a verb record to the APPC API. Verb sequences are used to communicate with remote partner programs.

What Is the Attach Manager?

The Attach Manager is a powerful service Communications Manager provides for starting APPC Transaction Programs in response to remote conversation requests. This gives your programs the ability to load and execute programs on other network nodes. If the Attach Manager is not started, a node cannot accept any incoming APPC conversation requests. Through the Attach Manager's configuration services, you can specify which OS/2 process is to be started when a remote conversation request is received for a particular TP name. In addition, the Attach Manager can be configured on a per TP name basis to provide the following start-up services:

- It will pass remote arguments to your OS/2 process as if they were command line arguments.
- It will check the incoming user ID and password required to start the OS/2 process.
- It will handle conversation requests on behalf of busy processes. If you specify the *Queued Mode* at configuration time, Attach Manager will queue the requests for the busy process in the order at which they arrive. If you specify *Non Queued Mode*, Attach Manager will start another instance of the process in response to a busy request.
- It can display a message window that informs an operator that a request has arrived to start a particular application. The operator can then choose to manually start the application. Applications configured in this mode are referred to as *Operator Started*.

How the Pieces Play Together

Now that we understand the terminology, let's see how the pieces play together.

Sessions, Conversations, and LUs

The relationship between TPs, LUs, PUs, conversations, and sessions is depicted in Figure 22-5. The example shows a local workstation where TP C is involved in active conversations with the remote TPs: A and D. Remote TP B is also waiting for TP A to finish so that it can start its own conversation with TP C. Notice that the LU in the local workstation can handle more than one session; it is in active session with its partner LUs on workstations X and Y, simultaneously. Notice also that the session with the partner LU (in workstation X) is used to support multiple conversations in serial fashion.

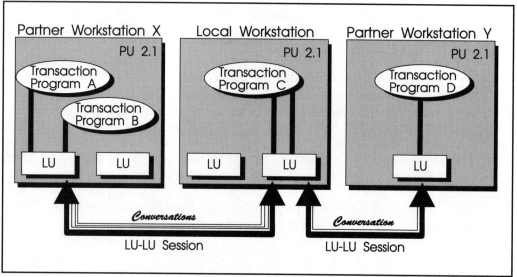

Figure 22-5.   Example of a Local LU Communicating With Two Remote Partner LUs.

Parallel Sessions and Parallel Conversations

Figure 22-6 demonstrates how *parallel sessions* between LUs can be used to provide concurrent conversations over the same LU pair. In this example, three conversations are being held concurrently over three parallel sessions between the local LU X and its partner LU Y.

Parallel sessions are an LU 6.2 feature that offers improved performance over single sessions. Work can now be queued against a pool of active sessions rather than waiting for a single session to free up. Parallel sessions are used to provide full-duplex communication channels (more on that later), high priority channels, and for balancing transmission loads. By using parallel sessions, you don't have to provide separate LUs for each session. This cuts down on your LU management overhead.

In Summary

An APPC network is made up of SNA nodes and links. A node has a PU, one or more LUs, and one or more TPs. LUs communicate through sessions, and TPs communicate through conversations over those sessions. Finally, your user program will consist of a series of verbs that are organized into conversations. The conversations are carried out with partner TPs over the network in accordance to the rules of the APPC protocol.

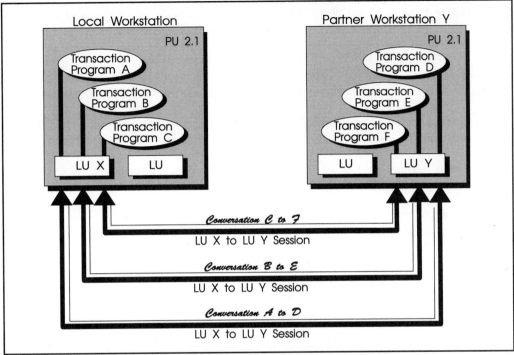

Figure 22-6. Example of a Parallel LU Sessions and Concurrent Conversations.

THE APPC API

The APPC verb categories are shown in Table 22-1. These verbs fall into the following six categories:

1. *Control Verbs*. These verbs start or end a transaction program.

2. *Conversation Verbs*. These verbs are used to exchange information between transaction programs. An APPC conversation may either be Basic or Mapped:

   - *Basic Conversations* require that you provide a two-byte length prefix at the start of all your exchange records. The benefit they provide is some amount of flexibility in terms of error-handling. The cost is that they are more complicated than Mapped conversations and frequently require more parameters and data formatting. The error recovery, although more flexible, is less automatic than with Mapped conversations. Basic conversations are meant to be used by service TPs.

   - *Mapped Conversations* are intended for use by end-user programs written in high-level languages. With Mapped conversations, APPC handles all the details of the underlying data stream used by LU 6.2, and provides a data mapping service that makes your programs more data independent.

3. *Operator Verbs*. These verbs are used to manage sessions, links, and the APPC Attach Manager through API calls. These are the same functions that can manually be performed using an operator panel.

4. *Configuration Verbs*. These verbs are used to manage the SNA/APPN subsystem parameters associated with the node. These include the LU, PU, and password.

5. *Network Management Verbs*. These verbs are used to communicate alerts to Netview or to a local collection point.

6. *Common Services Verbs*. These verbs provide some common utilities to all the network applications that run on top of Communications Manager.

We will now cover in some detail each of APPC's verb categories.

Table 22-1. The APPC Verb Categories.

TP Control Verbs	Conversation Verbs (Mapped or Basic)	Operator Verbs
RECEIVE_ALLOCATE TP_STARTED TP_ENDED GET_TYPE GET_TP_PROPERTIES	ALLOCATE CONFIRM CONFIRMED DEALLOCATE FLUSH GET_ATTRIBUTES PREPARE_TO_RECEIVE RECEIVE_AND_POST RECEIVE_AND_WAIT RECEIVE_IMMEDIATE REQUEST_TO_SEND SEND_CONVERSATION SEND_DATA SEND_ERROR TEST_RTS	ACTIVATE_DLC ACTIVATE_LOGICAL_LINKS CNOS DEACTIVATE_CONVERSATION_- GROUP DEACTIVATE_DLC DEACTIVATE_LOGICAL_LINK DEACTIVATE_SESSION DISPLAY DISPLAY_APPN START_AM STOP_AM
Configuration Verbs		**Common Services Verbs**

DEFINE_COS
DEFINE_LOCAL_LU
DEFINE_LOGICAL_LINK
DEFINE_LU_LU_-
    PASSWORD
DEFINE_MODE
DEFINE_PARTNER_LU
DEFINE_PARTNER_LU_-
    LOCATION
DEFINE_TP
DEFINE_USER_ID_-
    PASSWORD
	DELETE_COS
	DELETE_LOCAL_LU
	DELETE_LOGICAL_LINK
	DELETE_LU_LU_PASSWORD
	DELETE_MODE
	DELETE_PARTNER_LU
	DELETE_PARTNER_LU_-
	    LOCATION
	DELETE_TP
	DELETE_USER_ID_PASSWORD
		CONVERT
		COPY_TRACE_TO_FILE
		DEFINE_DUMP
		DEFINE_TRACE
		GET_CP_CONVERT_TABLE
		LOG_MESSAGE
		SET_USER_LOG_QUEUE
		
		Network Management Verbs
		
		SEND_MDS_MU
		REGISTER_MS_APPLICATION
		TRANSFER_MS_DATA
		UNREGISTER_MS_APPLICATION

APPC's Control Verbs

These verbs are used to start or end a TP. For an application to start a conversation with a remote application, it must first create a TP. This is done by issuing a **TP_STARTED** command which returns a handle called the TP ID. An application can start multiple TPs; each is identified by a respective TP ID handle. TPs created in this manner are referred to as locally initiated TPs. To establish a conversation, a partner TP needs to be remotely initiated through the Attach Manager. This kind of TP is called a remotely initiated TP. This is done by having the remote application issue **RECEIVE_ALLO-CATE**, an APPC verb that combines the following functions:

1. It handles remote TP initiation (for APPC/PC old timers, this function is equivalent to a TP_INITIATE remote). The Attach Manager starts the application after it gets a remote invocation or displays a window that informs the operator to start the application.
2. It accepts (or rejects) the request to carry out a conversation. This means that when the command completes successfully, the TPs on both ends are linked in a conversation (for APPC/PC old timers, this is equivalent to a GET_ALLOCATE).

The **RECEIVE_ALLOCATE** verb executes when it receives an **ALLOCATE** request from a remote TP and returns two handles: a TP ID and a Conversation ID. Thus, to start a TP and initiate a conversation, one side issues **TP_STARTED** followed by **ALLOCATE**; the partner then issues a **RECEIVE_ALLOCATE**. The partner side should have previously started the Attach Manager. The **TP_ENDED** verb is issued to return the TP resources to APPC. Table 22-2 provides a quick summary of APPC's Control Verbs.

Table 22-2. The APPC TP Control Verbs.

Verb Name	Function Description
RECEIVE_ALLOCATE	This command establishes a new TP and conversation in response to an ALLOCATE issued by a partner TP. If no incoming ALLOCATE is present, the command waits for the amount of time configured in the TP Receive Timeout configuration panel field. You must configure a Remotely Attachable TP profile for each unique TP to be started by RECEIVE_ALLOCATE. APPC returns a TP ID and a Conversation ID.
TP_STARTED	This command tells APPC to reserve resources for a new TP initiated locally (meaning not from an incoming ALLOCATE). You do not have to configure a profile for this TP name. APPC returns a TP ID.
TP_ENDED	This command ends a TP and frees up its resources. APPC will then free all the conversations associated with this TP. You can tell APPC to terminate gracefully and wait for all active verbs to complete (this is called the "soft" option).
GET_TYPE	This command returns the conversation type: Basic or Mapped.
GET_TP_PROPERTIES	This command returns the properties associated with the specified TP.

APPC's Conversation Verbs

In this section, we cover the verbs that allocate the conversation and actually do the talking. Table 22-3 provides a quick summary of APPC's Conversation Verbs. The explanations apply to both the Basic and Mapped conversation modes. There is a one-to-one relationship between the set of Mapped and Basic conversation verbs. The two sets of verbs are distinguished by the **MC_** prefix, which stands for Mapped Conversation. We did not show the **MC_** verbs in the table to save on space. For the sake of clarity, we will drop the use of the **MC_** prefix for Mapped in the remainder of this chapter. Our interest, of course, is in Mapped conversations. So unless otherwise stated, the discussion of verbs always assumes the Mapped conversation. Remember that the conversation mode is specified when it is first allocated, and from then on both sides must issue either Basic or Mapped verbs; no "mix and match" is allowed by APPC.

Table 22-3 (Part 1 of 3). The APPC Conversation Verbs.

Verb Name	Function Description
ALLOCATE	This command establishes a conversation between two TPs and creates an LU-to-LU session if one does not already exist. You must supply to this verb your local TP ID, the local name of your partner LU, and the TP name of your partner. You can also specify a password, the level of synchronization you need, and point to Program Initialization Parameters (PIP) you want passed to your partner. Finally, you can specify if you want the verb to return control to your program immediately or after a session is allocated or freed. APPC returns a conversation ID.
CONFIRM	This command sends a confirmation request to a partner and awaits a reply. This is done to allow the two programs to synchronize their actions. This verb can only be used over conversations that are allocated with a synchronization level of CONFIRM.
CONFIRMED	This command sends a confirmation reply to the partner TP. The local program can only issue this verb in response to a confirmation request. This verb can only be used over conversations that are allocated with a synchronization level of CONFIRM.
DEALLOCATE	This command deallocates the specified conversation. The send buffer of the LU is flushed with this command. If your conversation is using the synchronization level CONFIRM, then APPC will also send a CONFIRM as part of the deallocation (unless you specify otherwise).
FLUSH	This command flushes the send buffer of the local LU and sends all buffered information to the partner LU. This verb is very useful in speeding up the sending of local data. It circumvents APPC's normal buffering of send data (from send verbs) until it reaches a transmission threshold. You can also issue this verb immediately after an ALLOCATE to make sure the partner gets the connection request immediately.

Table 22-3 (Part 2 of 3). The APPC Conversation Verbs.

Verb Name	Function Description
GET_ATTRIBUTES	This command returns information such as the attributes of the specified conversation, the local and partner LU names, the level of processing synchronization, and any user ID provided for security. It also returns the network name and the mode name. Many of the parameters returned are in EBCDIC. You can use the common CONVERT utility to translate them into ASCII.
PREPARE_TO_RECEIVE	This command changes a conversation from the Send to the Receive state in preparation for receiving data; it also causes the send buffer to be flushed. If the synchronization level is CONFIRM, APPC will send a CONFIRM directive to the partner requesting confirmation for this change of direction.
RECEIVE_AND_POST	This command causes APPC to return immediate control to the local program and post a semaphore when a sufficient amount of information is received for the specified conversation. APPC will place the received data in the specified buffer. You cannot use this conversation until the command completes. But your program can wait on several semaphores to clear on different conversations. The information received can be data, status, a request for confirmation, or a combination. APPC indicates the type of information received and the length of the data. It also tells you if there is more data coming, whether a confirmation is required, and when it's your turn to send. The maximum number of bytes that can be received is 65,535.
RECEIVE_AND_WAIT	This command waits for information to arrive for the specified conversation. Otherwise, it is similar to RECEIVE_AND_POST.
RECEIVE_IMMEDIATE	This command receives any currently available information for the specified conversation. Otherwise, it is similar to RECEIVE_AND_WAIT.
REQUEST_TO_SEND	This command requests from the partner TP permission to enter the Send state. APPC places the conversation in the Send state when the SEND permission is received from the partner. This is obtained in the what_receive parameter through any of the receive verbs.
SEND_CONVERSATION	This new command is used for sending one-way data. It combines the function of ALLOCATE, SEND_DATA, and DEALLOCATE in one operation.
SEND_DATA	This command sends the contents of a data buffer to the partner TP. The type parameter allows the program to combine sending data with certain other functions such as: FLUSH, CONFIRM, PREPARE_TO_RECEIVE, and DEALLOCATE. If you specify type = NONE, APPC will store data in the send buffer until it accumulates a sufficient amount of data for transmission. What constitutes a "sufficient" amount is a characteristic of the session allocated for that conversation. The number of bytes a local TP can send with this command is between 0 and 65,535.

Table 22-3 (Part 3 of 3).   **The APPC Conversation Verbs.**

Verb Name	Function Description
SEND_ERROR	This command tells the partner TP that an error was detected. You can specify whether the error is in the data you just received or in the data you were about to send. For example, if an error gets encountered while doing a database transaction, then there may be no data to send to the partner. This command can also be used to reject a confirmation request.
TEST_RTS	This command tests whether the a REQUEST_TO_SEND was received from the partner TP.

APPC's Operator Verbs

The Communications Manager version of APPC provides a visual interface for controlling the network environment. These operator functions can also be issued through API calls. With the exception of the **START_AM** command, you will probably not be issuing any of the Operator verbs from within your program. You should be aware of the existence of these verbs just in case you have some exceptional needs, such as writing an application that controls the network environment. Table 22-4 provides a very brief summary of APPC's Operator Verbs.

Table 22-4. (Part 1 of 2) **The APPC Operator Verbs.**

Verb Name	Function Description
ACTIVATE_DLC	This command allows you to activate a data link.
ACTIVATE_LOGICAL_LINKS	This command allows you to activate a specific logical link or all the logical links that are configured as automatically activated.
CNOS	This command allows you to change the limits on the number of sessions that can exist between two LUs. You can also do this through the session limit panel when configuring APPC.
DEACTIVATE_CONVERSATION_GROUP	This command allows you to deactivate a session identified by a conversation group ID.
DEACTIVATE_DLC	This command allows you to deactivate a specified DLC adapter.
DEACTIVATE_LOGICAL_LINK	This command allows you to deactivate the specified SNA link. You can do this gracefully, and the command will wait for all sessions on that link to end. A possible use of this function is to end a deadlocked TP.

Table 22-4 (Part 2 of 2). The APPC Operator Verbs.

Verb Name	Function Description
DEACTIVATE_SESSION	This command allows you to deactivate an SNA LU 6.2 session identified by an internal session ID or to deactivate all the sessions for a given LU pair and a given transmission service mode name. This command may be used to end a deadlocked TP.
DISPLAY	This command returns a wealth of SNA information and can be very useful if you are writing a network monitor program. You can obtain the following types of SNA information: global info (including version and release numbers, network name, node-ID, machine type, PU name etc.) LU 6.2 specific info, Attach Manager info, session info, TP info, link types info, and information about the SNA gateways on the network.
DISPLAY_APPN	This command returns a wealth of APPN-related information and can be very useful if you are writing a network monitor program. You can obtain the current operating values for your node.
START_AM	This command starts the Attach Manager. Your node is now enabled to accept incoming allocation requests that can be matched with pending RECEIVE_ALLOCATEs.
STOP_AM	This command stops the Attach Manager. All incoming and queued allocates are rejected.

APPC's Configuration Verbs

The Communications Manager version of APPC provides a set of verbs that allow your programs to control the network configuration of your node. This is the information contained in the APPC configuration files. Unless you're doing some very strange things, you will probably never be issuing any of the configuration verbs from your programs. You should, however, be aware of the existence of these verbs just in case you have some of those exceptional needs. Table 22-5 provides a very brief summary of APPC's Configuration Verbs.

Table 22-5. The APPC Configuration Verbs.

Verb Name	Function Description
DEFINE_COS	This command allows you to update or modify the class of service (COS) definition.
DEFINE_LOCAL_LU	This command allows you to define or update the definition of a local LU.
DEFINE_LOGICAL_LINK	This command allows you to define or update the characteristics of a link to an adjacent node.
DEFINE_LU_LU_PASSWORD	This command allows you to define or replace the password to be used for LU-LU sessions between the specified local LU (including the local Control Point or CP) and the remote LU (including an adjacent CP). The CP is the agent used by APPN nodes to exchange network information.
DEFINE_MODE	This command allows you to define or replace the characteristics of a particular SNA session transmission mode.
DEFINE_PARTNER_LU	This command allows you to define or replace the parameters of a partner LU for LU-LU sessions between a specified local LU (including the local CP) and the partner LU (including an adjacent CP).
DEFINE_PARTNER_LU_LOCATION	This command allows you to define or replace directory information for a partner LU.
DEFINE_TP	This command allows you to define the TP information that the APPC attach manager uses when processing incoming Attaches from LUs.
DEFINE_USER_ID_PASSWORD	This command allows you to define a user ID and password used for conversation-level security. Incoming Attaches containing access security information must contain a user ID and, if present in the Attach, a password.
DELETE_COS	This command allows you to delete a class-of-service definition.
DELETE_LOCAL_LU	This command allows you to remove a local LU from your node.
DELETE_LOGICAL_LINK	This command allows you to drop a link to an adjacent node.
DELETE_LU_LU_PASSWORD	This command allows you to delete a password used between sessions.
DELETE_MODE	This command allows you to delete a mode definition.
DELETE_PARTNER_LU	This command allows you to delete a partner LU definition.
DELETE_PARTNER_LU_LOCATION	This command allows you to delete a partner LU entry from the directory data base.
DELETE_TP	This command allows you to delete an APPC TP definition.
DELETE_USER_ID_PASSWORD	This command allows you to delete a user ID and password used for conversation-level security.

APPC's Network Management Verbs

The Communications Manager version of APPC provides a set of verbs that allow your programs to communicate with NetView or a similar type of network management focal point. Table 22-6 provides a very brief summary of APPC's Network Management Verbs.

Table 22-6. The APPC Network Management Verbs.

Verb Name	Function Description
REGISTER_MS_APPLICATION	This command allows you to registers your program with the Communications Manager management services application routing list so that your node will route requested management services data to your program.
SEND_MDS_MU	This command sends management services data to another management services application.
TRANSFER_MS_DATA	This command will build and send a network alert to Netview (or whatever you've defined as your system manager focal point). The data is also logged in the Communications Manager error log.
UNREGISTER_MS_APPLICATION	This command removes your program from the Communications Manager management services application routing list so that management services data can no longer be routed to it.

Common Services API

The Communications Manager Common Services provide some useful protocol-independent services. They can be issued with any of the Communications Manager protocols to obtain common services. Traditionally, these services are associated with SNA; this is why we include them in this APPC tutorial. Their control block structure, and method for calling the API, is very much like APPC's. APPC programs make heavy use of the **CONVERT** verb which translates character strings from ASCII to EBCDIC, and vice versa. This is because all the LU 6.2 control information that flows to a partner when a conversation is started must be in EBCDIC. This includes passwords, TP names, user IDs, and the mode name. The **TRANSFER_MS_DATA** command for sending alerts to NetView (described in the previous section) is also part of the common services. Table 22-7 provides a brief summary of those services.

Table 22-7. The Communications Manager's Common Services API.

Verb Name	Function Description
CONVERT	This command allows you to convert an ASCII character string to EBCDIC and vice versa. To use this verb you specify the direction of the conversion and the conversion table: Table A converts uppercase strings. Table AE converts both character cases. Table C lets you create your own string conversion table.
COPY_TRACE_TO_FILE	This command formats the data in a trace storage buffer and writes it to a specified file.
DEFINE_DUMP	This command specifies the components for which dumping is to be performed and the file to which the dump data is to be written.
DEFINE_TRACE	This command allows you to specify the API verbs or events you want to trace.
GET_CP_CONVERT_TABLE	This command allows you to perform country code conversions on character strings. It builds a conversion table to be used by the CONVERT verb to convert character strings from one supported code page to another. This is useful if the recipient of your data is using a different code page.
LOG_MESSAGE	This command allows you to write a message into the message log. You may also specify that the message gets displayed as a popup.
SV_TRANSFER_MS_DATA	This command will build and send a network alert to Netview. The data is also logged in the Communications Manager error log. We also included this command under Network Management verbs. It is a common service available to all network protocols (not just APPC).
SET_USER_LOG_QUEUE	This command allows you to specify an OS/2 user-created queue that can be notified of system and error messages. You can also select using filters the message types and number ranges you have an interest in. Communications Manager will forward selected message or error logs (or both) to the queue.

Security and PIP Parameters

When a TP establishes a conversation with another TP located somewhere on an SNA network, it issues the **ALLOCATE** verb giving all the information needed to establish the connection. This includes the conversation type (Mapped or Basic), the synchronization level required (see next section), the security parameters required to access the remote TP, and the *Program Initialization Parameters* or **PIP data**. In this section, we discuss the security and PIP elements.

APPC Conversation Security

The **ALLOCATE** verb supports a security parameter that can be issued with the following options:

None   Meaning that no conversation-level security is needed.

Same   Meaning that the local program has already verified the User ID and password. The User ID information is still sent to the partner LU. This *already verified* capability is useful when multiple sites are participating in a distributed transaction and the remote LUs may be willing to accept the already verified status from another LU.

Pgm   Meaning that the partner LU must validate the security parameters which include the User ID and password, both of which can be up to 10 EBCDIC characters long. You should right-pad both with EBCDIC blanks, if they are less than 10 characters. The security parameters are checked by the Attach Manager on the partner's machine and they have to match what was specified on the partner's Conversation Security menu. If the partner LU's profile specifies the password at the *session level*, then each conversation on that session uses the same password, which gets verified with each incoming conversation request.

APPC PIP Data

Program Initialization Parameters, or PIP data, provide a mechanism for passing initialization parameters or environment setup information to a partner TP or operating system. For example, PIP data is used by APPC on the IBM S/36 for establishing the environment of the TPs it starts. The Communications Manager version of APPC can send PIP data, but currently *does not* support the receipt of incoming PIP data.

APPC's Synchronization Services

Client/server transactions may require the update of resources that reside on multiple nodes. Synchronization capabilities are very important for such occasions. The APPC architecture specifies three levels of synchronization services:

None   With this level, APPC provides no synchronization. You specify this level by allocating a conversation with **sync_level** = NONE.

Confirm   This level allows application programs to agree that processing has been completed without errors. You specify this level by allocating a conversation with **sync_level** = CONFIRM. APPC will enforce confirmation exchanges and error reporting. An application can explicitly request that the partner TP confirm that the data sent so far was received and processed successfully. Applications can then issue a **CONFIRM** verb to request a confirmation from the partner. The partner can either respond with a **CONFIRMED**, indicating everything is OK, or with a **SEND_ERROR,** which reports an error condition. You can also request a confirmation from a partner before a TP ends successfully by issuing a **DEALLOCATE** with **type** = SYNC_LEVEL.

Syncpoint   This is an even more stringent level of synchronization, which allows certain resources to be defined as LU protected. The LU is then responsible for *committing* the changes after a successful transaction, or *backing out* the changes if an error occurs during the processing of the transaction. Syncpoint protection addresses the problem of maintaining the integrity of the network transaction. Its full implementation requires a two-phase commit protocol with rollback and resynchronization capabilities.

The Communications Manager APPC supports the first two levels of synchronization. Future releases will support the Syncpoint option. This is required to make distributed database updates work across multiple databases on a network. When it is fully implemented, it may become one of APPC's strongest selling points.

Peer-to-Peer Exchanges the APPC Way

We now cover some of the APPC "features," which may confuse programmers more accustomed to a *free form* peer-to-peer protocol such as NetBIOS. The confusion clears up when you realize that APPC is designed to accommodate some of the needs of *transaction processing* at a communications level. The extra service APPC provides deals with issues like "whose turn is it to send?" and "what to do in case of errors." Future releases of APPC will introduce more such features to be used primarily in distributed database management.

Taking Turns

The APPC protocol imposes a set of stringent rules for communications between partners at the session level. APPC has rules for how the permission to talk is granted. Even though the APPC communication links are full-duplex (i.e., bi-directional), the APPC protocol imposes and enforces a *logical half-duplex* protocol on both partners. This means that the partners take turns at sending and receiving. APPC does not support "anarchistic network behavior" such as broadcasts or datagrams. All exchanges are session-based and very much under the strict control of the protocol. In all fairness, the designers of APPC felt that the protocol should help the transaction partners maintain some kind of "law and order." All network applications, they reasoned, have to deal with issues like, "who gets to send data next?" and "who gets to do what in case of an error?" and "how race conditions can be avoided." Their conclusion was that if these rules were not built into the protocol, they would have to be reinvented for every application. Here is a list of session level rules APPC imposes:

- The partner that initiates the conversation goes first.
- Only one command can be outstanding at any one time.
- Partners take turns sending and receiving. Two APPC verbs are specifically designed to effect changes in the conversation direction: **REQUEST_TO_SEND**, which requests permission to send, and **PREPARE_TO_RECEIVE**, which grants the partner permission to receive.
- The verbs that an APPC transaction can issue depend on the state of the conversation (more on that later).

Blocking and Flushing

APPC attempts to optimize performance by blocking a series of commands and then sending them as one communication message. This, in a sense, is a mixed blessing because things may not be where you may think they ought to be. To get around that, your application will have to explicitly issue commands that "flush" the buffer and cause the message to be delivered at the other end. You can use the **FLUSH** verb to force APPC to send the data in its buffers. If you want to ensure that the partner LU has received the information, issue a **CONFIRM** verb. The following receive verbs will cause a change of state which will implicitly cause data to flow to the partner LU: **PREPARE_TO_RECEIVE**, **RECEIVE_AND_WAIT**, and **RECEIVE_AND-_POST**. The issuing of a **DEALLOCATE** verb at the end of a conversation will also flush the buffers.

APPC Conversation States

The verbs that an APPC transaction can issue at any one time (and for a particular conversation) depend on the state of the conversation. States are used to determine the next set of actions that can take place in a conversation. The state of a conversation can change as a result of the program (or its partner) issuing verbs. The detection of network errors may also cause changes in state. APPC will manage the state of a conversation and enforce that your program only issue the verbs that are correct for a particular conversation state. The state of the conversation is always defined from the local program's perspective. A conversation can be in one of the following states:

Reset   This is the state of a conversation before a TP allocates it.

Send   While in this state, the program can send data, report errors, and request confirmations. An application also needs to be in the Send state before it can issue a **DEALLOCATE** to terminate a conversation because APPC notifies the partner TP that the conversation is terminated. If the application wants to exit and is not in the Send state, it can terminate the process. This causes APPC to deallocate the conversation automatically.

Receive   While in this state, the program can receive data and respond to a request for confirmation.

Sending_Pending   APPC recently split the Send state into Send and Send_Pending. Send_Pending is entered if a **RECEIVE_AND_WAIT** verb is issued and APPC returns both data and a status indicator of send.

Pending_Post   This is the state entered after issuing a **RECEIVE_AND_POST**. In this state the program waits to receive data. Verbs can be issued to *other* conversations while waiting.

Confirm   APPC recently split the Confirm state into three states: Confirm, Confirm_Send, and Confirm_Deallocate. The particular state to be entered depends on what appears in the *status_received* parameter of the message received from the partner TP. If the partner TP sets this parameter to CONFIRM (or sends an explicit CONFIRM request call), it causes the confirm state to be entered. The verbs that may be issued in this state are **CONFIRMED, SEND_ERROR, DEALLOCATE**, and **TP_ENDED**.

Confirm_Send   This is the state entered after a **RECEIVE_AND_WAIT** or **RECEIVE_IMMEDIATE** returns a CONFIRM_SEND in the *status_received* field. This means that both a confirmation request and send control have been received from the remote partner. The verbs that may be issued in this state are **CONFIRMED, SEND_ERROR, DEALLOCATE**, and **TP_ENDED**. Normally, the program responds with CONFIRMED, and the local partner enters the send state.

Confirm_Deallocate   This is the state entered after a **RECEIVE_AND_WAIT** or **RECEIVE_IMMEDIATE** returns a CONFIRM_DEALLOCATE in the *status_received* field. This means that both a confirmation request and a deallocation notification have been received from the remote partner. The verbs that may be issued in this state are **CONFIRMED, SEND_ERROR, DEALLOCATE**, and **TP_ENDED**. Normally the program responds with CONFIRMED, and the conversation is deallocated.

An OS/2 process can manage multiple conversations concurrently. This means that one TP may be in the Send state while another TP may be in the Receive state, etc.

The Anatomy of an APPC Program

A typical APPC program goes through the following sequence of operations:

1. *Creates the local TP*. This is done by issuing a TP_STARTED command which returns a TP ID. An application can start multiple TPs, each of which is identified by a respective handle. TPs created in this manner are referred to as locally initiated TPs.

2. *Creates the remotely initiated TP*. To establish a conversation, a partner TP needs to be remotely initiated through the Attach Manager. This kind of TP is called a remotely initiated TP. The remote application does that by issuing a RECEIVE_AL-LOCATE verb. The Attach Manager should have been previously configured and started.

3. *Allocate the conversation*. An ALLOCATE is issued to request a conversation with the remote application. A conversation ID is returned. This is followed by issuing a CONFIRM to force the conversation request to flow to the partner, and to wait for a verification that the remote TP has accepted the conversation request. The incoming request causes the partner's Attach Manager to start the application directly or to display a window that instructs the operator to start the application. Once the application is started, the partner's previously issued RECEIVE_ALLO-CATE verb executes and returns two handles: a TP ID and a Conversation ID. The two sides are now in conversation, but the initiating TP is still blocked waiting for a confirmation.

4. *Confirms the conversation*. The partner's application issues a RE-CEIVE_AND_WAIT as its first conversation verb (remember, it starts out in the Receive state). The RECEIVE command waits for either data or for status indicators. In this case, the command returns immediately with a *receive confirm* indicator, which tells the partner that a confirm must be issued. The partner then issues what the local TP was awaiting: the CONFIRMED verb. Now the two applications are in active conversation mode, the requesting TP is still in the Send state, and the partner TP is in the Receive state.

5. *Conducts network business*. This business will be conducted in an orderly logical half-duplex fashion. After the start of a conversation, the partner application is still in the Receive state and will typically issue another RECEIVE_AND_WAIT to obtain more data or status information. The initiating TP can then use SEND_DATA to send a buffer's worth of data. Every so often, a FLUSH should be issued to force the data to be sent to the partner. A CONFIRM can be issued to flush the data and wait for the receipt of a CONFIRMED or SEND_ERROR indicator from the partner. A TP can implicitly relinquish the right to send, by issuing a RECEIVE verb, or it can do that explicitly by issuing a PREPARE_TO_RECEIVE. Either partner can request permission to send by issuing a REQUEST_TO_SEND verb.

6. *Deallocates the conversation*. A conversation can be deallocated from the Send state by issuing a DEALLOCATE verb. The partner receives a Deallocate indicator and may be asked to confirm the deallocation, or (in the case of deallocate ABEND) simply terminate.

7. **Terminates the TPs**. The two sides terminate their TPs by issuing TP_ENDED. If your process terminates at the same time as it stops using the network, then it can exit and let APPC issue a DEALLOCATE followed by a TP_ENDED on its behalf..

THE CPI-C API

The CPI-C API resides on top of APPC and provides the same set of services. The difference is that a CPI-C TP uses a call-based interface to invoke each APPC function and pass it the appropriate parameters. Most CPI-C calls correspond to APPC verbs. The exceptions are the *set* calls that initialize a conversation prior to allocating it, and the *extract* calls that obtain individual conversation characteristics.

We will divide the Communications Manager CPI-C API set into calls that are common to all SAA environments and OS/2 specific CPI-C extensions. These calls are explained in the sections that follow.

Standard CPI-C Calls

The standard CPI-C calls are common across all SAA platforms. The Communications Manager provides a set of standard CPI-C calls that correspond to the underlying APPC verbs. The OS/2 CPI-C implementation provides both starter and advanced functions. It is a very complete CPI-C implementation that supports all the CPI-C calls except for the *Resource Recovery* services. This is not surprising, since the OS/2 APPC implementation does not currently support the *LU 6.2 Syncpoint recovery option* (i.e., a two-phase commit protocol). The four "unofficial" CPI-C calls that OS/2 does not currently support are: **Prepare**, **Request_Commit**, **Committed**, and **Backout**.[1]

Table 22-8 provides a very brief summary of the standard CPI-C call provided by Communications Manager. There should be no surprises. It's only APPC with a new face.

---

[1] The OS/2 product supports all the CPI-C calls as defined in the **SAA CPI-C Reference**, #SC26-4399 (March, 1991). The recovery verbs are not part of the "official" CPI-C standard yet. They are part of the LU 6.2 architecture.

Table 22-8 (Part 1 of 3). The OS/2 Communications Manager's Standard CPI-C Calls.

CPI-C call	Pseudonym	Description
CMACCP	Accept_Conversation	Accepts a conversation with a partner. This is the first call issued on the receiving side of a conversation. It returns the conversation ID that is used by subsequent verbs.
CMALLC	Allocate	Requests a conversation with partner TP.
CMCFM	Confirm	Requests a confirmation from partner TP.
CMCFMD	Confirmed	Replies to a confirm request.
CMDEAL	Deallocate	Terminates a conversation. The deallocation can either be completed as part of this call or deferred until it confirms with the partner. The partner program receives the deallocate notification by means of a return_code or status_received indication.
CMECS	Extract_Conversation_State	Returns the current state of a conversation.
CMECT	Extract_Conversation_Type	Returns a value that indicates whether the conversation is mapped or basic.
CMEMN	Extract_Mode_Name	Returns the transmission service mode name of the session.
CMEPLN	Extract_Partner_LU_Name	Returns the name of the LU servicing the partner TP.
CMESL	Extract_Sync_Level	Returns a value indicating which synchronization level is being used.
CMFLUS	Flush	Forces the LU to transmit its send buffer.
CMINIT	Initialize_Conversation	Initializes the conversation characteristics before the conversation is allocated. This is the first call issued on the initiating side of a conversation. It returns the conversation ID that is used by subsequent verbs. A program can override the values initialized by this call by using the *set* verbs.
CMPTR	Prepare_To_Receive	Grants the partner TP permission to send in preparation to receiving data.
CMRCV	Receive	Receives information on a particular conversation. The information received includes data, conversation status, or a request for confirmation. The default receive is receive and wait. A set call may be issued before this call to receive immediately (i.e., no wait).
CMRTS	Request_To_Send	Requests permission to send from partner TP.
CMSCT	Set_Conversation_Type	Specifies conversation type as basic or mapped. *The CPI-C default is mapped.*

Table 22-8 (Part 2 of 3). The OS/2 Communications Manager's Standard CPI-C Calls.

CPI-C call	Pseudonym	Description
CMSDT	Set_Deallocate_Type	Specifies what to do if a deallocate should abnormally terminate the conversation. Choices are CONFIRM or NONE. *The CPI-C default is CONFIRM.*
CMSED	Set_Error_Direction	Specifies whether an error was detected while sending or receiving data. *The CPI-C default is receive error.*
CMSEND	Send_Data	Sends data.
CMSERR	Send_Error	Informs partner that your TP has detected an error.
CMSF	Set_Fill	Specifies whether the TP's buffer is to be filled with a single record or with multiple records on subsequent Receive calls. This call is not used with mapped conversations.
CMSLD	Set_Log_Data	Specifies a log-data message to be used if an error is reported or if the conversation terminates abnormally. *The CPI-C default is NULL.*
CMSMN	Set_Mode_Name	Specifies the transmission service mode name to be used when the conversation is allocated.
CMSPLN	Set_Partner_LU_Name	Specifies the LU name of the partner TP's to be used when conversation is allocated.
CMSPTR	Set_Prepare_To_Receive_Type	Specifies whether Prepare_To_Receive calls are to request some form of synchronization (CONFIRM) or simply to force the LU to flush its send buffer (NONE or FLUSH). *The CPI-C default is CONFIRM.*
CMSRC	Set_Return_Control	Specifies whether Allocate should return immediately if a free session cannot be found or wait until a free session is available. *The CPI-C default is to wait until a session is available.*
CMSRT	Set_Receive_Type	Specifies whether a Receive call should return immediately with only the data that has arrived so far or wait for enough data to satisfy the request. *The CPI-C default is RECEIVE_AND_WAIT.*
CMSSL	Set_Sync_Level	Specifies the synchronization level for a given conversation. The specification takes effect when the conversation is allocated. Only the program that initiates the conversation can issue this call, and it cannot be issued after a conversation is allocated. OS/2 currently supports two levels of synchronization: CONFIRM and NONE. *The CPI-C default is NONE.*

Table 22-8 (Part 3 of 3). **The OS/2 Communications Manager's Standard CPI-C Calls.**

CPI-C call	Pseudonym	Description
CMSST	Set_Send_Type	Specifies whether a Send_Data call should send control information to the partner TP along with the data, whether the buffer is to be sent immediately, and whether the data is to be sent along with a the send control (Equivalent to Prepare_To_Receive). *The CPI-C default is not to send the data until a buffer's worth is accumulated.*
CMSTPN	Set_TP_Name	Specifies the partner TP's name to be used with Allocate.
CMTRTS	Test_Request_to_Send_Received	Returns a value indicating whether the partner TP has requested permission to send.

Non-Standard CPI-C Calls

The non-standard CPI-C calls are specific to the OS/2 platform. They provide functions that help your programs manage side information and conversation security. So what is *side information*? Side information is used to assign initial characteristic values on the **Initialize_Conversation (CMINIT)** call. The set of parameters associated with a symbolic destination name is called a *side information entry*. CPI-C requires a certain amount of initialization information, such as the name of the partner program, the name of the partner's LU Node, and the *mode name* that specifies the properties of the session (for example the class of service). This information can be provided through a Communications Manager user interface that creates entries in a configuration file, or it can be done through the extended CPI-C API calls. CPI-C programs can reference this information through a *sym_dest_name* parameter.[2] On the partner side, CPI-C receives all the side information from the LU at the time when the conversation starts (i.e., it is dynamic).

Table 22-9 provides a very brief summary of the OS/2 product-specific CPI-C calls. Keep in mind that using these calls may cause you to modify your programs to run on other CPI-C platforms. These calls may be implemented differently and sometimes not at all.

---

[2] Side information will be useful in the future for mapping symbolic destination names to OSI TPs and perhaps even to TCP/IP sockets. Remember, CPI-C is destined to become a transport-layer independent protocol.

Table 22-9. The OS/2 Communications Manager's Non-Standard CPI-C Calls.

CPI-C call	Pseudonym	Description
XCMSSI	Set_CPIC_Side_Information	Sets the side information for a symbolic destination name, creating an entry if one does not exist.
XCMDSI	Delete_CPIC_Side_Information	Deletes the side information for a given symbolic destination name.
XCMESI	Extract_CPIC_Side_Information	Returns the side information values for a given symbolic destination name.
XCECST	Extract_Conversation_Security_Type	Returns a value that indicates whether conversation security is being used and how the security parameters are obtained.
XCECSU	Extract_Conversation_Security_User_ID	Returns the user ID associated with the given conversation.
XCSCSP	Set_Conversation_Security_Password	Specifies the password associated with the conversation when it is allocated.
XCSCST	Set_Conversation_Security_Type	Specifies if conversation security is to be used when the conversation is allocated and whether the security parameters should be obtained from the system or provided explicitly.
XCSCSU	Set_Conversation_Security_User_ID	Specifies the userID to be used when the conversation is allocated.

CPI-C OR APPC?

From what we've said, so far, CPI-C appears to be the natural choice for writing SNA peer-to-peer programs. Unfortunately, there are some hidden gotchas with the current CPI-C implementation. We will provide a brief comparison of CPI-C and APPC, point out the "gotchas," and let you decide which programming platform is best for you.

Programming APPC and CPI-C

APPC, like NetBIOS, uses the *command with a control block* style of programming that is popular in the communications world. APPC calls its control blocks **verb control blocks**. Unlike NetBIOS, APPC has a multiplicity of these verb control blocks. A program can request the various APPC commands by issuing the *verbs* described in this tutorial through their appropriate control blocks. The first two bytes of every control block identify the APPC verb. Verb control block fields can contain pointers to associated data buffers. The APPC service is provided by a single API call-return function.

For each APPC call, you have to: 1) allocate the verb control block, 2) initialize its fields to zeroes, 3) fill in the required fields, 4) if required, use the *common services* to convert strings from ASCII to EBCDIC, 5) issue the APPC API call, and 6) wait for APPC to return. When it completes processing the verb, APPC places the return parameters in the control block. Every verb contains a pair of fields where APPC returns the *return_code*.

CPI-C uses a call/return model with an API call defined for each verb. CPI-C provides a single entry-point for each verb: the API call. APPC requires two steps for each verb: filling the control block and issuing the generic APPC API call.

The CPI-C verbs are functionally equivalent to their APPC counterparts (see Table 22-10). CPI-C does not support sending or receiving PIP data or the **RECEIVE_POST** verb. The CPI-C *set* and *extract* calls that have no APPC equivalents. These verbs nicely encapsulate the many APPC control block structures (you never have to see them). With CPI-C, you set a parameter once and the setting will remain in effect for all subsequent calls. APPC requires that you stuff the control blocks with all the appropriate parameters for every call. The set calls have the added benefit of preventing you from creating "illegal" state changes or changing parameters in a way that conflicts with the characteristics of the conversation in process.

Table 22-10. A Comparison of CPI-C Calls and APPC Conversational Verbs.

CPI-C Call	Pseudonym	Corresponding APPC Calls
CMACCP	Accept_Conversation	CONVERT followed by RECEIVE_ALLOCATE
CMALLC	Allocate	ALLOCATE
CMCFM	Confirm	CONFIRM
CMCFMD	Confirmed	CONFIRMED
CMDEAL	Deallocate	DEALLOCATE followed by TP_ENDED
CMFLUS	Flush	FLUSH
CMINIT	Initialize_Conversation	CONVERT followed by TP_STARTED
CMPTR	Prepare_To_Receive	PREPARE_TO_RECEIVE
----	----	RECEIVE_AND_POST
CMRCV	Receive	RECEIVE_AND_WAIT RECEIVE_IMMEDIATE
CMRTS	Request_To_Send	REQUEST_TO_SEND
CMSEND	Send_Data	SEND_DATA
CMSERR	Send_Error	SEND_ERROR
CMTRTS	Test_Request_to_Send_Received	TEST_RTS

APPC and CPI-C States

The CPI-C and APPC states (and state changes) are roughly equivalent (see Table 22-11). CPI-C provides an additional state, *Initialize*, that helps remove ambiguities after a TP is started (APPC assumes a TP is still in the reset state after it is started). APPC provides a *Pending_Post* state that has no CPI-C equivalent. This is to be expected because CPI-C does not support the **RECEIVE_AND_POST** verb.

Table 22-11 (Part 1 of 2). A Comparison of CPI-C and APPC States.

CPI-C State	APPC State	CPI-C Calls That May be Used From State
Reset	Reset	Initialize_Conversation(CMINIT) Accept_Conversation(CMACCP) Allocate(CMALLC) Deallocate(CMDEAL)
Initialize	----	Allocate(CMALLC) Deallocate(CMDEAL)
Send	Send	Confirm(CMCFM) Deallocate(CMDEAL) Flush(CMFLUS) Prepare_To_Receive(CMPTR) Receive(CMRCV) Request_To_Send(CMRTS) Send_Data(CMSEND) Send_Error(CMSERR) Test_Request_to_Send_Received(CMTRTS)
Receive	Receive	Deallocate(CMDEAL) Receive(CMRCV) Test_Request_to_Send_Received(CMTRTS) Send_Error(CMSERR) Test_Request_to_Send_Received(CMTRTS)
Send_Pending	Send_Pending	Confirm(CMCFM) Deallocate(CMDEAL) Flush(CMFLUS) Prepare_To_Receive(CMPTR) Receive(CMRCV) Request_To_Send(CMRTS) Send_Data(CMSEND) Send_Error(CMSERR) Test_Request_to_Send_Received(CMTRTS)
---	Pending_Post	---
Confirm	Confirm	Confirmed(CMCFMD) Request_To_Send(CMRTS) Send_Error(CMSERR)

Table 22-11 (Part 2 of 2). A Comparison of CPI-C and APPC States.

CPI-C State	APPC State	CPI-C Calls That May be Used From State
Confirm_Send	Confirm_Send	Confirmed(CMCFMD) Request_To_Send(CMRTS) Send_Error(CMSERR)
Confirm_Deallocate	Confirm_Deallocate	Confirmed(CMCFMD) Request_To_Send(CMRTS) Send_Error(CMSERR)

APPC, CPI-C, and Multithreaded Servers

The current implementation of CPI-C supports a single TP per OS/2 process. The OS/2 process starts the TP implicitly when it initializes its first outbound conversation or accepts an inbound conversation and ends the TP when the process itself ends (see Figure 22-7). This limitation means that CPI-C cannot be used with multithreaded servers where multiple conversations are accepted by the same process. CPI-C is not very good with reusable TPs. You cannot deallocate a conversation and start a new one within a single process. You must end both the TP and the process. CPI-C does not allow more than one process to use the same TP or conversation. CPI-C restricts a TP (and therefore, a conversation) to a single process.

These limitations do not apply to APPC TPs (see Figure 22-7). The APPC API allows you to develop applications that start multiple TPs in the same OS/2 process and allow multiple processes to use the same TP. APPC was designed to fully exploit OS/2's

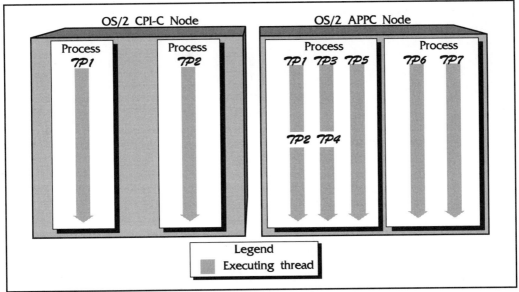

Figure 22-7. APPC's Multiple TP per Process versus CPI-C's Single TP.

multithread capabilities while CPI-C was designed to be portable and provide a common implementation across multiple OSs (most OSs do not support threads).

The CPI-C limitations mean that you must use APPC, today, to create multithreaded servers that accept multiple conversations per process. You can use CPI-C with servers that accept a single persistent communication session per process. This means you'll create one process (and TP) for each client you serve. This is how most (non-OS/2) servers conduct their business today. OS/2 has spoiled us with its advanced thread capabilities. In either case, you'll want to use CPI-C on the clients since CPI-C and APPC nodes interoperate and CPI-C provides more portable programs.[3]

CPI-C SCENARIOS

The scenarios that follow will help demonstrate the use of CPI-C in typical peer-to-peer exchanges.

Scenario 1: A Simple Transaction Involving Two Processes

Scenario 1 presents the CPI-C version of the simple transaction:

```
What is Bob's Balance?   ----------------------->
                         <----------------------
                                                    $300
```

We show two implementations of this simple transaction (or remote procedure call):

- *Without* the CPI-C confirmation services (see Figure 22-8)
- *With* the CPI-C confirmation services (see Figure 22-9).

In both scenarios, we show the CPI-C conversation state before each verb is issued. In both scenarios, the client is the local TP and the server is the partner TP that is remotely invoked by an incoming conversation request.

Simple Transaction: Without Confirmation Services

This is how scenario 1 (see Figure 22-8) plays *without* confirmation services:

---

[3] The CPI-C people at IBM are very much aware of the multithreaded limitations. They will provide some kind of solution by the next release. We recommend that you program to CPI-C for portability. We will program FX using CPI-C in the next chapter.

1. The client issues an **Initialize_Conversation** verb to start a Transaction Program (TP). CPI-C will return a TP ID, which all subsequent verbs must use with this TP. Note that the program that initializes conversation (the client) gets its name, partner's name, mode name, from the side information referenced by *sym_dest_name*. This is not shown in the figure.

2. The client then requests a conversation by issuing an **Allocate** verb. Note that the sync_level parameter is set to NONE (the CPI-C default), meaning that no confirmation services are required. CPI-C returns a conversation ID and starts an LU-to-LU session if none is available. The actual request for a conversation is not yet sent because CPI-C blocks records into a logical record. This means that, so far, no information was passed between the client and server TPs.

3. The client issues a **Flush** verb to force the conversation request to flow to the partner. Otherwise the control data may not be sent until CPI-C has a full buffer.

4. The arrival of the conversation request causes the Attach Manager to start the server program.

5. The server issues a **Accept_Conversation** verb, which returns both a TP ID and Conversation ID. Now both sides have established their end of the conversation.

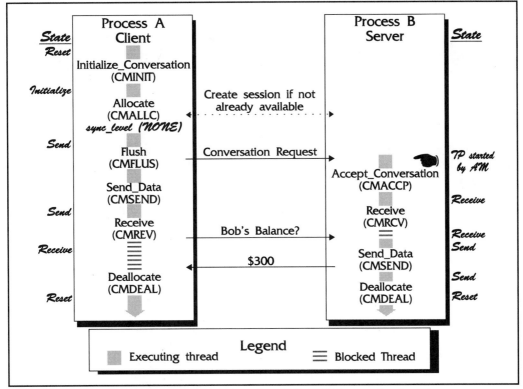

Figure 22-8. Scenario 1a: A Simple Transaction CPI-C With sync_level = None.

Note that the server is immediately placed in the **Receive** state after a conversation is created.

6. The server issues a **Receive** call (the CPI-C default is RECEIVE_AND_WAIT) to find out what the client wants.

7. The client in the meantime has issued a **Send_Data** requesting Bob's balance, followed by **Receive,** which flushes the message and changes the state to **Receive.** The client is now blocked waiting for the reply to arrive. The server has received the right to transmit.

8. The server sends back the reply, and because it is still in the Send state, it issues a **Deallocate** to close the conversation and release the TP.

9. The client receives the reply and issues a **Deallocate** to release its TP.

Simple Transaction: With Confirmation Services

We now demonstrate how scenario 1 plays *with* confirmation services (see Figure 22-9). Note how CPI-C's confirmation services can be used to enhance the integrity of the implementation. Here are the differences:

1. The confirmation services are activated with sync_level parameter set to CON-FIRM. Note that this is done using a **Set_Sync_Level** verb prior to **Allocate.** If you attempt to change the sync-level after the conversation is allocated, you will get an error.

2. The client can now issue a **Confirm** verb to flush the buffer and cause the conversation request to flow to the server TP.

3. When the server TP issues a **Receive** verb, it gets an indication that a confirmation is required.

4. The server issues a **Confirmed** command, which lets the client know that the conversation has succeeded. Notice that the server is still in the **Receive** state; consequently it issues a second **Receive** to find out what the client wants.

5. The client proceeds with the simple bank transaction just like it did in the previous implementation.

6. The **Deallocate** verb makes use of the confirmation services. By setting the type parameter to SYNC_LEVEL (the CPI-C default), the server requests that the client confirm the receipt of the **Deallocate** before ending the TP.

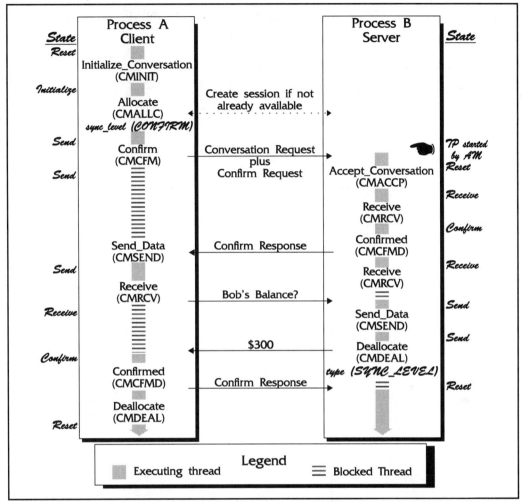

Figure 22-9. Scenario 1b: A Simple Transaction CPI-C With sync_level = CONFIRM.

Scenario 2: Sending Bulk Data Over an CPI-C Conversation

Scenario 2 shows how moving bulk data, such as a file transfer, may get implemented over an CPI-C conversation (see Figure 22-10). This is an area where CPI-C's blocking capabilities should favorably come into play. The client just sends logical records and CPI-C takes care of deciding when to send the accumulated records based on the network's buffering and transmission capabilities. Initially, the server is blocked waiting for the client.

The client starts the file transfer by telling the server that it is about to receive a file and gives it the name of the file and its size. The server says "OK" and issues a receive waiting on the first file segment to arrive. The file copy gets done through a series of message sends. Eventually, the server finishes consuming the file and sends a message to the client saying the file got there OK, after which both sides deallocate their end of the conversation.

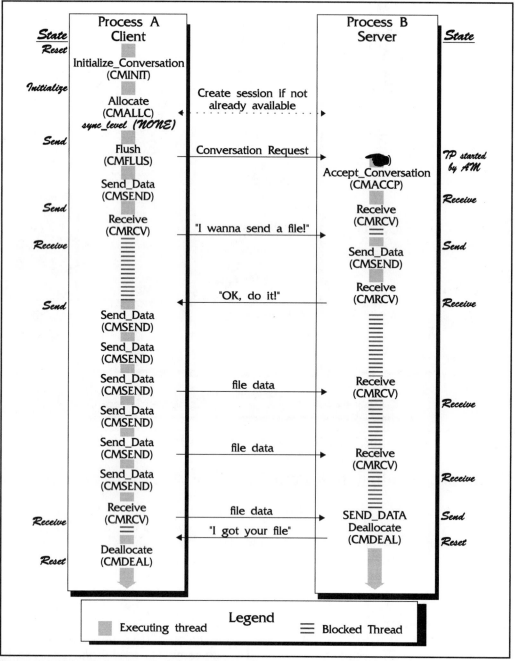

Figure 22-10. Scenario 2: Moving Bulk Data Over an CPI-C Conversation.

Chapter 23

FX with CPI-C

This chapter presents an implementation of the communication layer of the FX protocol using the OS/2 Communications Manager's **CPI-C** LAN protocol on top of APPC. The interface will be packaged as a Dynamic Link Library (FXAPPC.DLL). The DLL will be created from **FXAPPC.C** using the FX make file introduced in Chapter 16.

The CPI-C communication DLL enables you to transfer files using FXREQ and FXSVR, the client/server programs developed in Chapter 16. Figure 23-1 shows how this all comes together. We will use this setup to collect benchmark numbers on the performance of CPI-C on top of the APPC communication stack by measuring the time it takes to exchange files between the client and the server.

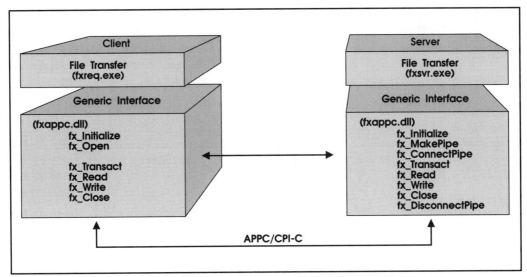

Figure 23-1. Implementing the FX Interface Using the FXAPPC.DLL (CPI-C).

The plan for this chapter is to make use of whatever mechanisms are provided by the CPI-C protocol to implement the nine **FX** interface calls shown in Figure 23-1. Figure 23-2 demonstrates how the FXAPPC.DLL is used to transfer a file and shows the effect each call has on the CPI-C partner transaction. Note that the server program in the scenario is not started by the Attach Manager. We start from the command line like any other program. The figure also demonstrates CPI-C's blocking feature. As was explained in the tutorials, blocking is used to lump together the data from many commands and send it over the network in one chunk.

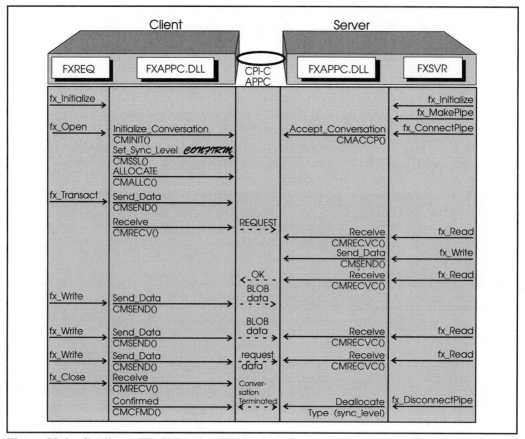

Figure 23-2. Sending a File Using the FXAPPC.DLL.

PROGRAMMING CPI-C

Programming to the CPI-C interface is a "piece of cake", after you understand the behavior and logic of the APPC protocol. The tutorial covers all you need to know (and perhaps more) to get you there. Then all you have to do is issue the right API calls. The CPI-C API is one of the cleanest you'll find in the communications world.

As explained in the tutorial, a CPI-C program is executed as a single TP instance on a single LU. In contrast, an APPC program can execute as multiple TP instances on one or more LUs. When CPI-C starts the program, it registers an exit list function that lets CPI-C release resources, deallocate dangling conversations, and cleanup after the program.

Thunked Header Files for CPI-C

The **CMC.H** file which the Communications Manager provides, contains all the CPI-C constant and type declarations and function prototypes that allow you to issue the 16-bit CPI-C calls from a 32-bit OS/2 program. This means that we do not have to create the "thunk" definitions, as was the case with TCP/IP sockets. All the pointers that are passed to the CPI-C API have the **_Seg16** attribute. The compiler takes care of all the conversions automatically. Consequently you do not have to worry about any of that stuff.

Converting ASCII to EBCDIC

APPC, or rather LU 6.2, requires that transmitted control parameters use the EBCDIC character representation. This representation includes TP names, LU names, mode names, user IDs, and passwords. The data itself, however, can be in any format that two partner programs agree on. CPI-C will automatically convert the control parameters to EBCDIC. You can use ASCII strings with all the CPI-C call parameters, including the *Set* calls and the *Extract* calls.

Obviously, if you're moving data between a PC and an IBM host, somebody's going to have to do some translation. CPI-C does *not* get involved with the contents of your message buffers. You should use the **CONVERT** verb to provide two-way conversions between ASCII and EBCDIC.

CPI-C Defaults

CPI-C maintains a set of conversation characteristics. The initial values provided by CPI-C may be changed using *Set* calls. Table 23-1 provides a very brief summary of the standard defaults CPI-C provides for some of the most common conversation characteristics.

Table 23-1. CPI-C: The Default Conversation Parameters.

Conversation Characteristic	CPI-C Default
Conversation Type	Mapped
Receive Type	RECEIVE_AND_WAIT
Sync Level	NONE
Error Direction	Error in the receive direction
Log Data	Null
Send Type	Buffered data

FXAPPC.C: THE CPI-C FX DLL

The code we present in this section *does not* contain a main() procedure. The FX DLLs are simply functions that get linked to a (.EXE) file at run time. The main() procedure is provided by the program that calls the DLLs. This means **FXAPPC.C** is not a separate program; it contains a list of functions that get packaged as DLLs.

FXAPPC.C: General Stuff

The listing (see Figure 23-3) contains all the miscellaneous programming "stuff" that will be used by the FX procedures. This includes the usual declarations of constants, global variables, and forward declarations of functions. Note that the functions provided in this module fall into two categories: **FX** functions and *helper* functions. The helper functions, as usual, are used to provide common services for that module. In addition to the ubiquitous **print_error()**, we only introduce one new helper function: **request_send_state**. This should tell you that creating the FX functions using CPI-C will not be too difficult. You'll breeze through this chapter in record time.

```
/***************************************************************************/
/*   MODULE NAME: FXAPPC  - APPC communication using CPI-C.              */
/*                                                                        */
/*   PROGRAM DESCRIPTION:  This module is a part of the FX file transfer  */
/*     programs.  Refer to the FXR.C program module for a program overview.*/
/*     This module implements the fx_* file transfer procedures using     */
/*     the SAA Common Programming Interface for Communications (CPIC).    */
/*                                                                        */
/*   PROCEDURES IN THIS MODULE:                                           */
/*                                                                        */
/*     Communication Functions                                            */
/*     ----------------------                                             */
/*       fx_Initialize(buffer_p, size);                                   */
/*       fx_MakePipe();                                                   */
/*       fx_ConnectPipe();                                                */
/*       fx_DisconnectPipe();                                             */
/*       fx_Open();                                                       */
/*       fx_Write(BufferArea, BufferLength, BytesWritten);               */
/*       fx_Read(BufferArea, BufferLength, BytesRead);                    */
/*       fx_Transact(InBufferArea, InBufferLength,                        */
/*                 OutBufferArea, OutBufferLength, BytesRead);            */
/*       fx_Close();                                                     */
/*                                                                        */
/***************************************************************************/
#include <stdio.h>                    /* For printf() & NULL            */
#include <stdlib.h>                   /* For conversion routines        */
#include <string.h>                   /* For string functions           */

#include <os2.h>
#include "fxfer.h"                    /* For FX functions               */
#include <cmc.h>                      /* include for CPI-C functions and */
                                      /* constants                      */
```

Figure 23-3 (Part 1 of 2). FXAPPC.C: General Header Stuff and print_error().

```
/*'''''''''''''''''''''''''''''''''''''''''''''''''''''''''''''''''''''''''''*/
/* defines                                                                   */
/*'''''''''''''''''''''''''''''''''''''''''''''''''''''''''''''''''''''''''''*/
                 /*'''''''''''''''''''''''''''''''''''''''*/
                 /* APPC conversation states              */
                 /*'''''''''''''''''''''''''''''''''''''''*/
#define CPIC_RESET                 1
#define CPIC_SEND                  2
#define CPIC_RECEIVE               3
#define CPIC_PENDING_POST          4
#define CPIC_CONFIRM               5
#define CPIC_CONFIRM_SEND          6
#define CPIC_CONFIRM_DEALLOCATE    7

/*'''''''''''''''''''''''''''''''''''''''''''''''''''''''''''''''''''''''''''*/
/* forward declaration for functions in this module                         */
/*'''''''''''''''''''''''''''''''''''''''''''''''''''''''''''''''''''''''''''*/
                 /*'''''''''''''''''''''''''''''''''''''''*/
                 /* miscellaneous functions               */
                 /*'''''''''''''''''''''''''''''''''''''''*/
USHORT request_send_state(VOID);
VOID print_error(LONG, PCHAR, PCHAR, USHORT);

/*'''''''''''''''''''''''''''''''''''''''''''''''''''''''''''''''''''''''''''*/
/* Configuration variables, initialized after fx_Initialize()               */
/* function call.                                                           */
/*'''''''''''''''''''''''''''''''''''''''''''''''''''''''''''''''''''''''''''*/
UCHAR   sym_dest_name[9];              /* CPIC symbolic destination name     */
USHORT FileBufferSize;

/*'''''''''''''''''''''''''''''''''''''''''''''''''''''''''''''''''''''''''''*/
/* global variables for this module.                                        */
/*'''''''''''''''''''''''''''''''''''''''''''''''''''''''''''''''''''''''''''*/
USHORT        rc;                      /* return code                        */
UCHAR         conv_id[8];              /* CPIC conversation id               */
SHORT         server;                  /* client/server indicator            */
SHORT         cpic_state;              /* state of APPC conversation         */
USHORT        bytes_read;              /* how many bytes received            */
USHORT        bytes_written;           /* how many bytes written             */
CM_INT32      received_len;            /* number of bytes read               */
CM_INT32      what_rcvd;               /* what received verb field           */
CM_SYNC_LEVEL sync_level = CM_CONFIRM; /* sync level to use                  */
CM_INT32      rts_rcvd;                /* request to send indicator          */
CM_INT32      status_rcvd;             /* status indicator                   */
CM_RETURN_CODE conv_rc;                /* status indicator                   */

/*'''''''''''''''''''''''''''''''''''''''''''''''''''''''''''''''''''''''''''*/
/* Error Display Routine                                                     */
/*'''''''''''''''''''''''''''''''''''''''''''''''''''''''''''''''''''''''''''*/
VOID print_error(LONG Error, PCHAR msg, PCHAR file, USHORT line)
{
 printf("CPIC Error %ld (0x%lx) detected while %s at line %u in file %s.\n",

        Error, Error, msg, line, file);
} /* end print_error */
```

Figure 23-3 (Part 2 of 2).   FXAPPC.C: General Header Stuff and print_error().

FXAPPC.C: fx_Initialize()

The **fx_Initialize**() function (see Figure 23-4) reads a protocol-specific configuration file to obtain the parameters required to initialize the system. The name of the user-specified configuration file for CPI-C is **fxappc.cfg**. Here is an example of such a file:

```
SYM_DEST_NAME     = CPICSVR
FILE_BUFFER_SIZE  = 4096
```

Here's what these parameters do:

- **SYM_DEST_NAME** This parameter points to an entry in the *side information table*. This entry is used by the client at **Initialize_Conversation** to locate the server's LU name, TP name, and the mode name of the conversation. The server will determine that information from the session and conversation information provided by the LU in the conversation start-up request.

- **FILE_BUFFER_SIZE** This parameter defines the size (in bytes) of the message buffer, which we will use for reading and writing data to the disk and for exchanging messages across the LAN or the IPC. The memory space for this parameter will be dynamically allocated. The fx_Initialize function returns a pointer to this buffer and its size to the application. One of the factors we will measure in our benchmarks is the effect of the message buffer size on performance.

The **fx_Initialize**() function acts as a FX protocol "catch-all" for performing protocol-specific start-up actions. There are no new CPI-C calls in this function.

```
/*''''''''''''''''''''''''''''''''''''''''''''''''''''''''''''''''''''''''''''*/
/* function to read communication specific parameters and allocate a buffer  */
/* for communication.  A pointer to the buffer and the buffer size is        */
/* returned.                                                                 */
/*''''''''''''''''''''''''''''''''''''''''''''''''''''''''''''''''''''''''''''*/
ULONG fx_Initialize(PPACKET *buffer_p , PUSHORT size)
{
  FILE     *config_file;                  /* Input file control block        */
  CHAR     line[80];                      /* one line of config file         */
  PPACKET  _Seg16 bufferp;

  printf("Reading configuration parameters.\n");
  /*''''''''''''''''''''''''''''''''''''''''*/
  /* open the configuration file           */
  /*''''''''''''''''''''''''''''''''''''''''*/
  if (NULL == (config_file = fopen("fxappc.cfg","r")))
     {print_error(0L,"opening configuration file",__FILE__,__LINE__);
      return(FAILED);
     }
  else
```

Figure 23-4 (Part 1 of 2).   FXAPPC.C: fx_Initialize().

```
            /*'''''''''''''''''''''''''''''''''''''''*/
            /* read the configuration parameters.  */
            /* The parameters are expected to be:  */
            /*    - in the form <name = value>     */
            /*    - if value is a string enclose   */
            /*       in double quotes              */
            /*    - in the order read below        */
            /*'''''''''''''''''''''''''''''''''''''''*/
            {
              fgets(line, sizeof(line), config_file);
              memset(sym_dest_name,' ',sizeof(sym_dest_name));
              if (sscanf(line,"SYM_DEST_NAME = %s ", sym_dest_name) != 1)
                  {print_error(0L,"reading SYM_DEST_NAME from configuration",
                              __FILE__,__LINE__);
                   return(FAILED);
                  }
              sym_dest_name[strlen(sym_dest_name)] = ' ';
              printf("SYM_DEST_NAME = %s \n", sym_dest_name);

              fgets(line, sizeof(line), config_file);
              if (sscanf(line,"FILE_BUFFER_SIZE = %u ", &FileBufferSize) != 1)
                  {print_error(0L,"reading FileBufferSize from configuration",
                              __FILE__,__LINE__);
                   return(FAILED);
                  }
              printf("FILE_BUFFER_SIZE = %u \n", FileBufferSize);
            } /* end if */

        fclose(config_file);

        /*'''''''''''''''''''''''''''''''''''''''''*/
        /* allocate buffer, return pointer       */
        /* and size                              */
        /*'''''''''''''''''''''''''''''''''''''''''*/
        bufferp = (malloc)(FileBufferSize);
        if (bufferp == NULL)
            {print_error(rc,"allocating file buffer",__FILE__,__LINE__);
             return(FAILED);
            }
        *buffer_p = bufferp;
        *size = FileBufferSize;                    /* return buffer size        */

        return(GOOD);
} /* end fx_Initialize */
```

Figure 23-4 (Part 2 of 2). FXAPPC.C: fx_Initialize().

FXAPPC.C: fx_MakePipe()

The **fx_MakePipe()** function (see Figure 23-5) is used by the server side of an FX pipe to establish its side of the pipe. With CPI-C, there is not much to do because most of the initialization is established through configuration files and the Attach Manager. All this function does is initialize its state variable to Reset.

```
/*_____*/
/* function to establish the server end of the communication pipe.    */
/*_____*/
ULONG fx_MakePipe(VOID)
{
    /*_____*/
    /* set APPC state                  */
    /*_____*/
    cpic_state = CPIC_RESET;

    /*_____*/
    /* remember that this is a server  */
    /*_____*/
    server = TRUE;

    return(GOOD);
} /* end fx_MakePipe */
```

Figure 23-5. FXAPPC.C: MakePipe().

FXAPPC.C: fx_ConnectPipe()

The **fx_ConnectPipe()** function (see Figure 23-6) is used to establish a connection on the server side of an FX pipe. This function is provided using CPI-C by issuing an **Accept_Conversation** call (described below). The state variable is now changed to Receive. The server is now waiting to hear from the outside world.

Accept_Conversation - cmaccp()

The **cmaccp()** API call accepts a conversation with a partner TP. This is the first call issued on the receiving side of a conversation. It returns the conversation ID that is used by subsequent verbs. The prototype for this call is:

```
cmaccp(PUCHAR   _Seg16     conv_id,  /* Conversation ID          */
         PLONG   _Seg16     conv_rc); /* Conversation return code */
```

A description of the parameters follows:

- The *conv_id* parameter is an 8-character string buffer that accepts the value returned by CPI-C to represent a conversation identifier. The TP verbs that follow will use this id as the "magic cookie" that identifies the conversation.
- The *conv_rc* parameter returns the results of the call execution. CM_OK denotes success.

```
/*''''''''''''''''''''''''''''''''''''''''''''''''''''''''''''''''''''''''*/
/* function to enable the server end of the communication pipe.            */
/*''''''''''''''''''''''''''''''''''''''''''''''''''''''''''''''''''''''''*/
ULONG fx_ConnectPipe(VOID)
{
   /*''''''''''''''''''''''''''''''''''''*/
   /* perform Accept_Conversation        */
   /*''''''''''''''''''''''''''''''''''''*/
   memset(conv_id, 0, sizeof(conv_id));
   cmaccp(conv_id,                                /* Accept Conversation    */
          &conv_rc);                              /* Return Code            */

   if (conv_rc != CM_OK)
      {print_error(conv_rc,"performing Accept_Conversation", __FILE__,__LINE__);
       exit(FAILED);
      }

   /*''''''''''''''''''''''''''''''''''''*/
   /* set APPC state                     */
   /*''''''''''''''''''''''''''''''''''''*/
   cpic_state = CPIC_RECEIVE;

   return(GOOD);
} /* end fx_ConnectPipe */
```

Figure 23-6. FXAPPC.C: fx_ConnectPipe().

FXAPPC.C: fx_DisconnectPipe()

The **fx_DisconnectPipe()** function (see Figure 23-7) is used to disconnect the server side of an FX pipe. A "graceful" implementation of this function is provided using CPI-C as follows:

- If we're not in the Receive state, we disconnect by simply issuing a CPI-C **Deallocate** call (see explanation below).
- If we're in the Receive state, we politely ask for permission to send by invoking the helper function **request_send_state()** (see listing in Figure 23-8). If we don't obtain the permission to send, we return with an error. Otherwise, we issue a CPI-C **Deallocate** call.

Deallocate - cmdeal()

The **cmdeal()** API call terminates a conversation. The deallocation can either be completed as part of this call or deferred until it confirms with the partner. The partner program receives the deallocate notification by means of a return_code or status_received indication. The prototype for this call is:

```
cmdeal(PUCHAR   _Seg16    conv_id,    /* Conversation ID           */
       PLONG    _Seg16    conv_rc);   /* Conversation return code  */
```

A description of the parameters follows:

- The ***conv_id*** parameter specifies the identifier of an initialized conversation.
- The ***conv_rc*** parameter returns the results of the call execution. CM_OK denotes success.

```
/*'''''''''''''''''''''''''''''''''''''''''''''''''''''''''''''''''''''''*/
/* function to disable the server end of the communication pipe.         */
/*'''''''''''''''''''''''''''''''''''''''''''''''''''''''''''''''''''''''*/
ULONG fx_DisconnectPipe(VOID)
{
    /*'''''''''''''''''''''''''''''''''''''*/
    /* test state, change state if         */
    /*    necessary                        */
    /*'''''''''''''''''''''''''''''''''''''*/
    if (cpic_state == CPIC_RECEIVE)
        {
            if (request_send_state() != GOOD)
                return(FAILED);
        }

    /*'''''''''''''''''''''''''''''''''''''*/
    /* Perform Deallocate                  */
    /*'''''''''''''''''''''''''''''''''''''*/
    cmdeal(conv_id,                             /* conversation ID      */
           &conv_rc);                           /* return code          */

    if (conv_rc != CM_OK)
        {print_error(conv_rc,"performing Deallocate",
                             __FILE__,__LINE__);
         return(FAILED);
        }

    /*'''''''''''''''''''''''''''''''''''''*/
    /* set APPC state                      */
    /*'''''''''''''''''''''''''''''''''''''*/
    cpic_state = CPIC_RESET;

    return(GOOD);
} /* end fx_DisconnectPipe */
```

Figure 23-7.   FXAPPC.C: fx_DisconnectPipe().

FXAPPC.C: request_send_state()

The **request_send_state()** helper routine (see Figure 23-8) notifies the partner TP that the local TP is requesting to enter the Send state. It does that by performing the following:

- It issues a CPI-C **Request_To_Send** call.
- It issues a CPI-C **Receive** call to hear from the partner. The permission to send is returned in the *status_rcvd* parameter. (For APPC "hackers," this is a mapping of the *what_received* parameter).
- If the partner is friendly and it all works out, the state is changed to send and the function returns with the good news.

The **request_send_state()** introduces two new CPI-C calls: **Request_To_Send** and **Receive**. These calls are explained below.

Request_To_Send - cmrts()

The **cmrts()** API call is used to notify the partner that the local TP wants permission to send. This notification is normally returned to the partner as a parameter in the send or receive calls (see Send_Data and Receive API descriptions). CPI-C retains the request until it gets a chance to pass it in one of the exchanged messages (as a parameter). The remote partner complies with this request by issuing a Receive or Prepare_To_Receive call. The prototype for this call is:

```
cmrts(PUCHAR   _Seg16    conv_id,    /* Conversation ID           */
      PLONG    _Seg16    conv_rc);   /* Conversation return code  */
```

A description of the parameters follows:

- The *conv_id* parameter specifies the identifier of an initialized conversation.
- The *conv_rc* parameter returns the results of the call execution. CM_OK denotes success.

Receive - cmrcv()

The **cmrcv()** API call is used to receive information on a particular conversation. The information received includes data, conversation status, or a request for confirmation. The default receive is receive and wait. A set call may be issued prior to this call to receive immediately (i.e., no wait). The prototype for this call is:

```
cmrcv(PUCHAR  _Seg16   conv_id,       /* Conversation ID            */
      PUCHAR  _Seg16   buffer_area,   /* Pointer to Data Buffer     */
      PLONG   _Seg16   buffer_length, /* Size of Data Buffer        */
      PLONG   _Seg16   what_rcvd,     /* what was received          */
      PLONG   _Seg16   bytes_read,    /* length of data received    */
      PLONG   _Seg16   status_rcvd,   /* conversation status        */
      PLONG   _Seg16   rts_rcvd,      /* request_to_send_received   */
      PLONG   _Seg16   conv_rc);      /* conversation return code   */
```

A description of the parameters follows:

- The *conv_id* parameter specifies the identifier of an initialized conversation.
- The *buffer_area* parameter points to the buffer where CPI-C returns the information received.
- The *buffer_length* points to a variable in which you specify the maximum amount of data the program is to receive. Valid values range from 0 to 32,767.
- The *what_rcvd* points to a variable that returns whether or not data was returned. If data is returned, is it complete or there is more to come. You must issue another

receive to obtain the rest of the message. The values returned are one of the following:

```
Value  Meaning
  0    (CM_NO_DATA_RECEIVED); No data was received.
  2    (CM_COMPLETE_DATA_RECEIVED); The complete message arrived.
  3    (CM_INCOMPLETE_DATA_RECEIVED); More to come.  Issue another receive.
```

- The *bytes_read* points to a variable that returns the number of bytes received. If the program receives information other than data, the value returned is meaningless.
- The *status_rcvd* points to a variable that returns the status of the conversation. For APPC programmers, this variable contains the return value of APPC's famous *what_received* field. The following values may be returned based on the actions taken by the conversation partner:

```
Value  Meaning
  0    (CM_NO_STATUS_RECEIVED); No conversation status received.
  1    (CM_SEND_RECEIVED); You can send now.  The partner will receive.
  2    (CM_CONFIRM_RECEIVED); Your partner requests a CONFIRMED.
  3    (CM_CONFIRM_SEND_RECEIVED); Issue a CONFIRMED then you can SEND.
  4    (CM_CONFIRM_DEALLOC_RECEIVED); Issue a CONFIRMED then DEALLOCATE.
```

- The *rts_rcvd* parameter returns an indication of whether or not the remote program issued a **Request_To_Send** call. The following values are returned:

```
Value  Meaning
  0    (CM_REQ_TO_SEND_NOT_RECEIVED); No, it was not received.
  1    (CM_REQ_TO_SEND_RECEIVED); Yes, it was received.  Do something.
```

- The *conv_rc* parameter returns the results of the call execution. CM_OK denotes success.

```
/*''''''''''''''''''''''''''''''''''''''''''''''''''''''''''''''''''''''''''''*/
/* Request Send State                                                         */
/*''''''''''''''''''''''''''''''''''''''''''''''''''''''''''''''''''''''''''''*/
USHORT request_send_state(VOID)
{
  static CM_INT32 length = 0;

  /*''''''''''''''''''''''''''''''''''''''*/
  /* request to send                      */
  /*''''''''''''''''''''''''''''''''''''''*/
  cmrts(conv_id,                                  /* conversation ID       */
       &conv_rc);                                 /* return code           */

  if (conv_rc != CM_OK)
     {print_error(conv_rc,"performing Request_to_Send",
                        __FILE__,__LINE__);
      return(FAILED);
     }


  /*''''''''''''''''''''''''''''''''''''''*/
  /* perform CPIC Receive to see if       */
  /*   Request_to_Send was received by    */
  /*   partner                            */
  /*''''''''''''''''''''''''''''''''''''''*/
```

Figure 23-8 (Part 1 of 2). FXAPPC.C: request_send_state() Helper Routine.

```
  cmrcv(conv_id,                         /* conversation ID          */
        NULL,                            /* Data Pointer             */
        &length,                         /* Size of Data Buffer      */
        &what_rcvd,                      /* what was received        */
        &received_len,                   /* length of data received  */
        &status_rcvd,                    /* conversation status      */
        &rts_rcvd,                       /* remote program issued cmrts? */
        &conv_rc);                       /* return code              */

  if (conv_rc != CM_OK)
     {print_error(conv_rc,"performing Receive",
                          __FILE__,__LINE__);
      return(FAILED);
     }

  if (status_rcvd != CM_SEND_RECEIVED)
     {print_error(0L,"requesting SEND state", __FILE__,__LINE__);
      return(FAILED);
     }

  cpic_state = CPIC_SEND;
  return(GOOD);
} /* end request_send_state */
```

Figure 23-8 (Part 2 of 2). FXAPPC.C: request_send_state() Helper Routine.

FXAPPC.C: fx_Open()

The **fx_Open()** function (see Figure 23-9) is used to establish the client side of an FX pipe. We provide the function using CPI-C by:

1. Issuing an **Initialize_Conversation** CPI-C call. This will notify CPI-C that the program is requesting resources for initiating a TP.
2. Issuing a **Set_Sync_Level** CPI-C call. We set the conversation synchronization level to CONFIRM.
3. Issuing an **Allocate** CPI-C call to establish the connection with the server TP. CPI-C will start a mapped conversation with the partner TP.

```
/*''''''''''''''''''''''''''''''''''''''''''''''''''''''''''''''''''''''''''*/
/* function a requester uses to prepare a pipe for communication.           */
/*''''''''''''''''''''''''''''''''''''''''''''''''''''''''''''''''''''''''''*/
ULONG fx_Open(VOID)
{
  /*''''''''''''''''''''''''''''''''''''''*/
  /* set APPC state                       */
  /*''''''''''''''''''''''''''''''''''''''*/
  cpic_state = CPIC_RESET;

  /*''''''''''''''''''''''''''''''''''''''*/
  /* remember that this is not a server   */
  /*''''''''''''''''''''''''''''''''''''''*/
  server = FALSE;
```

Figure 23-9 (Part 1 of 2). FXAPPC.C: fx_Open().

```
/*''''''''''''''''''''''''''''''''''''*/
/* Initialize conversation            */
/*''''''''''''''''''''''''''''''''''''*/
cminit(conv_id,                          /* conversation ID (returned)  */
       sym_dest_name,                    /* symbolic destination name   */
       &conv_rc);                        /* return code                 */

if (conv_rc != CM_OK)
    {print_error(conv_rc,"performing Initialize_Conversation",
                     __FILE__,__LINE__);
     return(FAILED);
    }

/*''''''''''''''''''''''''''''''''''''*/
/* Set Sync Level to confirm          */
/*''''''''''''''''''''''''''''''''''''*/
cmssl(conv_id,                           /* conversation ID             */
      &sync_level,                       /* sync level                  */
      &conv_rc);                         /* return code                 */

if (conv_rc != CM_OK)
    {print_error(conv_rc,"performing Set_Sync_Level",
                     __FILE__,__LINE__);
     return(FAILED);
    }

/*''''''''''''''''''''''''''''''''''''*/
/* Allocate the conversation          */
/*''''''''''''''''''''''''''''''''''''*/
cmallc(conv_id,                          /* conversation ID             */
       &conv_rc);                        /* return code                 */

if (conv_rc != CM_OK)
    {print_error(conv_rc,"performing Allocate",
                     __FILE__,__LINE__);
     return(FAILED);
    }

/*''''''''''''''''''''''''''''''''''''*/
/* set APPC state                     */
/*''''''''''''''''''''''''''''''''''''*/
cpic_state = CPIC_SEND;

return(GOOD);
} /* end fx_Open */
```

Figure 23-9 (Part 2 of 2). FXAPPC.C: fx_Open().

If everything succeeds, the client and server TPs are now in session. The client is in
the send state, and the server TP is in the receive state waiting to hear from the client.
This function introduces three new CPI-C calls: **Initialize_Conversation**,
Set_Sync_Level, and **Allocate**. These calls are described below.

Initialize_Conversation - cminit()

The **cminit()** API call initializes the conversation characteristics before the conversation is allocated. A program can override the values initialized by this call using the *set* verbs. The prototype for this call is:

```
cminit(PUCHAR  _Seg16  conv_id,       /* Conversation ID          */
        PUCHAR  _Seg16  sym_dest_name, /* Symbolic destination name */
        PLONG   _Seg16  conv_rc);      /* Conversation return code  */
```

A description of the parameters follows:

- The *conv_id* parameter is an 8-character string buffer that accepts the value returned by CPI-C to represent a conversation identifier. The TP verbs that follow will use this id as the "magic cookie" that identifies the conversation.
- The *sym_dest_name* parameter is an 8-character name you provide to point to an entry in a side-information table. The entry table specifies the name of the destination LU, the partner TP, and the mode name of the session on which this conversation is to be carried. If you choose to specify the destination information using set calls, instead of using a side information table, set this parameter to all blanks.
- The *conv_rc* parameter returns the results of the call execution. CM_OK denotes success.

Set_Sync_Level - cmssl()

The **cmssl()** API call sets the synchronization level for a given conversation. The specification takes effect when the conversation is allocated. OS/2 currently supports two levels of synchronization: CONFIRM and NONE (default). Only the program that initiates the conversation can issue this call, and it cannot be issued after a conversation is allocated. The prototype for this call is:

```
cmssl(PUCHAR  _Seg16  conv_id,     /* Conversation ID          */
       PLONG   _Seg16  sync_level,  /* sync_level               */
       PLONG   _Seg16  conv_rc);    /* Conversation return code  */
```

A description of the parameters follows:

- The *conv_id* parameter specifies the identifier of an initialized conversation.
- The *sync_level* parameter specifies the level of synchronization required on this conversation. The current choices are:

```
Value   Meaning
  0     (CM_NONE); The TPs will not issue synchronization calls.
  1     (CM_CONFIRM); The TPs can issue synchronization calls.
```

- The *conv_rc* parameter returns the results of the call execution. CM_OK denotes success.

Allocate - cmallc()

The **cmallc()** API call requests a conversation with partner TP. CPI-C will establish a session with the partner LU if one does not exist. The prototype for this call is:

```
cmallc(PUCHAR   _Seg16    conv_id,    /* Conversation ID            */
       PLONG    _Seg16    conv_rc);   /* Conversation return code   */
```

A description of the parameters follows:

- The *conv_id* parameter specifies the identifier of an initialized conversation.
- The *conv_rc* parameter returns the results of the call execution. CM_OK denotes success.

FXAPPC.C: fx_Write()

The **fx_Write()** function (see Figure 23-10) is used to send information over an FX pipe. We provide this function using CPI-C as follows:

- If we're in the Receive state, we politely ask for permission to send by invoking the **request_send_state()** helper routine (see listing in Figure 23-8). If that request is granted, we proceed with the **Send_Data**; otherwise we return an error.
- If we're *not* in the Receive state, we simply call **Send_Data**.

This function introduces one new CPI-C call: **Send_Data**. This call is explained below.

Send_Data - cmsend()

The **cmsend()** API call sends one data record (or message) to the remote TP. The actual data is not sent until enough data is accumulated to fill the LU's transmit buffer or until a call is issued to flush the buffer's contents. This call is often preceded by set calls that set the conversation status parameters. The prototype for this call is:

```
cmsend(PUCHAR   _Seg16    conv_id,        /* Conversation ID              */
       PUCHAR   _Seg16    buffer_area,    /* Pointer to Data Buffer       */
       PLONG    _Seg16    bytes_written,  /* Send length                  */
       PLONG    _Seg16    rts_rcvd,       /* request_to_send_received     */
       PLONG    _Seg16    conv_rc);       /* conversation return code     */
```

A description of the parameters follows:

- The *conv_id* parameter specifies the identifier of an initialized conversation.
- The *buffer_area* parameter points to the buffer that contains the data record (i.e., message) to be sent. The length of the record is given by the *bytes_written* parameter (see below).

- The *bytes_written* points to a variable in which you specify the length of the send record (or message). Valid values range from 0 to 32,767.
- The *rts_rcvd* parameter returns an indication of whether or not the remote program issued a **Request_To_Send** call. The following values are returned:

```
Value    Meaning
  0      (CM_REQ_TO_SEND_NOT_RECEIVED); No, it was not received.
  1      (CM_REQ_TO_SEND_RECEIVED); Yes, it was received.  Do something.
```

- The *conv_rc* parameter returns the results of the call execution. CM_OK denotes success.

```
/*''''''''''''''''''''''''''''''''''''''''''''''''''''''''''''''''''''*/
/* function both requester and server use to write to a pipe.         */
/*''''''''''''''''''''''''''''''''''''''''''''''''''''''''''''''''''''*/
ULONG fx_Write(PVOID BufferArea, USHORT BufferLength, PUSHORT BytesWritten)
{
  CM_INT32 bytes_written;

  /*'''''''''''''''''''''''''''''''''''''''*/
  /* test state, change state if           */
  /*    necessary                          */
  /*'''''''''''''''''''''''''''''''''''''''*/
  if (cpic_state == CPIC_RECEIVE)
     {
       if (request_send_state() != GOOD)
          return(FAILED);
     }

  /*'''''''''''''''''''''''''''''''''''''''*/
  /* send data                             */
  /*'''''''''''''''''''''''''''''''''''''''*/
  bytes_written = BufferLength;
  cmsend(conv_id,                             /* Send Data               */
         BufferArea,                          /* data pointer            */
         &bytes_written,                      /* length of data sent     */
         &rts_rcvd,                           /* request to send indicator */
         &conv_rc);                           /* return code             */

  if (conv_rc != CM_OK)
     {print_error(conv_rc,"performing Receive",
                         __FILE__,__LINE__);
      return(FAILED);
     }

   *BytesWritten = (USHORT)bytes_written;
   return(GOOD);
} /* end fx_Write */
```

Figure 23-10. FXAPPC.C: fx_Write().

FXAPPC.C: fx_Read()

The **fx_Read()** function (see Figure 23-11) is used to read information over an FX pipe. We provide this function using CPI-C issuing a **Receive** call. If the call returns status instead of data, we reissue the call to get the data. The status of interest is a request-to-send permission from the partner. Note how simply this information is obtained.

The CPI-C **Receive** call was already introduced in this chapter. Please review the explanation to acquaint yourself with all the subtleties associated with receiving status and data.

```
/*''''''''''''''''''''''''''''''''''''''''''''''''''''''''''''''''''''''''*/
/* function both requester and server use to read from a pipe.            */
/*''''''''''''''''''''''''''''''''''''''''''''''''''''''''''''''''''''''''*/
ULONG fx_Read(PVOID BufferArea, USHORT BufferLength, PUSHORT BytesRead)
{
  CM_INT32 buffer_length;
  CM_INT32 bytes_read;

  /*'''''''''''''''''''''''''''''''''''''''''*/
  /* receive data                           */
  /*'''''''''''''''''''''''''''''''''''''''''*/
  buffer_length = BufferLength;
  cmrcv(conv_id,                          /* conversation ID               */
        BufferArea,                       /* Data Pointer                  */
        &buffer_length,                   /* Size of Data Buffer           */
        &what_rcvd,                       /* what was received             */
        &bytes_read,                      /* length of data received       */
        &status_rcvd,                     /* conversation status           */
        &rts_rcvd,                        /* remote program issued cmrts?  */
        &conv_rc);                        /* return code                   */

  if (conv_rc != CM_OK)
     {print_error(conv_rc,"performing Receive",
                      __FILE__,__LINE__);
      return(FAILED);
     }

  /*'''''''''''''''''''''''''''''''''''''''''*/
  /* if request to send received,           */
  /* reissue the receive.                   */
  /*'''''''''''''''''''''''''''''''''''''''''*/
  if (rts_rcvd == CM_REQ_TO_SEND_RECEIVED)
     {buffer_length = BufferLength;
      cmrcv(conv_id,                      /* conversation ID               */
            BufferArea,                   /* Data Pointer                  */
            &buffer_length,               /* Size of Data Buffer           */
            &what_rcvd,                   /* what was received             */
            &bytes_read,                  /* length of data received       */
            &status_rcvd,                 /* conversation status           */
            &rts_rcvd,                    /* remote program issued cmrts?  */
            &conv_rc);                    /* return code                   */

      if (conv_rc != CM_OK)
         {print_error(conv_rc,"performing Receive",
                          __FILE__,__LINE__);
          return(FAILED);
         }
     } /* endif */

  if (what_rcvd != CM_COMPLETE_DATA_RECEIVED)
     {print_error(what_rcvd,"receiving data", __FILE__,__LINE__);
      return(FAILED);
     }
```

Figure 23-11 (Part 1 of 2). FXAPPC.C: fx_Read().

```
/*,,,,,,,,,,,,,,,,,,,,,,,,,,,,,,,,,,,,,,*/
/* set APPC state                       */
/*,,,,,,,,,,,,,,,,,,,,,,,,,,,,,,,,,,,,,,*/
*BytesRead = (USHORT)bytes_read;
cpic_state = CPIC_RECEIVE;

return(GOOD);
} /* end fx_Read */
```

Figure 23-11 (Part 2 of 2). FXAPPC.C: fx_Read().

FXAPPC.C: fx_Transact()

The **fx_Transact()** function (see Figure 23-12) sends a message and receives a reply over an FX pipe. This function is provided by invoking the **fx_write()** function (see Figure 23-10) followed by the **fx_read()** function (see Figure 23-11). No new CPI-C calls here.

```
/*,,,,,,,,,,,,,,,,,,,,,,,,,,,,,,,,,,,,,,,,,,,,,,,,,,,,,,,,,,,,,,,,,,,,,,,,,,,*/
/* function requester uses to request a service.                           */
/*,,,,,,,,,,,,,,,,,,,,,,,,,,,,,,,,,,,,,,,,,,,,,,,,,,,,,,,,,,,,,,,,,,,,,,,,,,,*/
ULONG fx_Transact(PVOID InBufferArea,   USHORT InBufferLength,
                  PVOID OutBufferArea,  USHORT OutBufferLength,
                  PUSHORT BytesRead)
{
  USHORT BytesWritten;

  rc = fx_Write(InBufferArea, InBufferLength, &BytesWritten);
  if (rc)
     {print_error((LONG)rc,"writing during a transaction",__FILE__,__LINE__);
      return(FAILED);
     }

  rc = fx_Read(OutBufferArea, OutBufferLength, BytesRead);
  if (rc)
     {print_error((LONG)rc,"reading during a transaction",__FILE__,__LINE__);
      return(FAILED);
     }

  return(GOOD);
} /* end fx_Transact */
```

Figure 23-12. FXAPPC.C: fx_Transact().

FXAPPC.C: fx_Close()

The **fx_Close()** function (see Figure 23-13) closes an FX pipe. This function will be performed differently depending on whether we're dealing with a client or a server. By design, the server does the **Deallocate**, and the client **Confirms** it. Also by design, the client's TP ends after the transaction while the server's TP will persist.

Follow these steps to close a *server*:

1. If we're in the Send state, we disconnect by simply issuing a CPI-C **Deallocate** call.

2. Else, if we're in the Receive state, we politely ask our partner TP for permission to send by invoking the **request_send_state()** helper routine (see listing in Figure 23-8). If we don't obtain the permission to send, we return with an error; otherwise, we issue a CPI-C **Deallocate** call.

Follow these steps to close a *client*:

1. Issue a CPI-C **Receive** and wait for the deallocate confirmation request to arrive from the server. Reissue **Receive** if request_to_send is returned instead.
2. Issue a **Confirmed** CPI-C call, meaning that the client confirms the deallocate request that was issued by the server. Everybody is being real careful.

When all this successfully takes place, the conversation between the client and server comes to a graceful end. We've already encountered the CPI-C **Deallocate** and **Receive** calls earlier in the chapter. The only new CPI-C call, **Confirmed**, is explained below.

Confirmed - cmcfmd()

The **cmcfmd()** API call is used as a reply to a confirm request. It says to the nervous partner: "I'm in sync with you." This call can only be used in reply to a confirmation request. The prototype for this call is:

```
cmcfmd(PUCHAR    _Seg16    conv_id,    /* Conversation ID            */
       PLONG     _Seg16    conv_rc);   /* Conversation return code   */
```

A description of the parameters follows:

- The *conv_id* parameter specifies the identifier of an initialized conversation.
- The *conv_rc* parameter returns the results of the call execution. CM_OK denotes success.

```
/*'''''''''''''''''''''''''''''''''''''''''''''''''''''''''''''''''''''''*/
/* function reqester uses to end communication with a server. '''''''''''*/
/*'''''''''''''''''''''''''''''''''''''''''''''''''''''''''''''''''''''''*/
ULONG fx_Close(VOID)
{
          CM_INT32 bytes_read;
  static CM_INT32 length = 0;

  if (server)
      {
      /*'''''''''''''''''''''''''''''''''''''''*/
      /* test state, change state if           */
      /*    necessary                          */
      /*'''''''''''''''''''''''''''''''''''''''*/
      if (cpic_state == CPIC_RECEIVE)
          {
            if (request_send_state() != GOOD)
               return(FAILED);
          }

      /*'''''''''''''''''''''''''''''''''''''''*/
      /* deallocate                            */
      /*'''''''''''''''''''''''''''''''''''''''*/
      cmdeal(conv_id,                        /* conversation ID           */
             &conv_rc);                      /* return code               */

      if (conv_rc != CM_OK)
          {print_error(conv_rc,"performing Deallocate",
                          __FILE__,__LINE__);

           return(FAILED);
          }

      /*'''''''''''''''''''''''''''''''''''''''*/
      /* set APPC state                        */
      /*'''''''''''''''''''''''''''''''''''''''*/
      cpic_state = CPIC_RESET;

      }
   else
      {
      /*'''''''''''''''''''''''''''''''''''''''*/
      /* receive deallocate confirmation       */
      /*'''''''''''''''''''''''''''''''''''''''*/
      cmrcv(conv_id,                         /* conversation ID           */
            NULL,                            /* Data Pointer              */
            &length,                         /* Size of Data Buffer       */
            &what_rcvd,                      /* what was received         */
            &bytes_read,                     /* length of data received   */
            &status_rcvd,                    /* conversation status       */
            &rts_rcvd,                       /* remote program issued cmrts?*/
            &conv_rc);                       /* return code               */

      if (conv_rc != CM_OK)
          {print_error(conv_rc,"performing Receive",
                          __FILE__,__LINE__);

           return(FAILED);
          }
```

Figure 23-13 (Part 1 of 2). FXAPPC.C: fx_Close().

```
        /*''''''''''''''''''''''''''''''''''''''*/
        /* if request to send received,         */
        /* reissue the receive.                 */
        /*''''''''''''''''''''''''''''''''''''''*/
        if (rts_rcvd == CM_REQ_TO_SEND_RECEIVED)
           {cmrcv(conv_id,                       /* conversation ID            */
                  NULL,                           /* Data Pointer               */
                  &length,                        /* Size of Data Buffer        */
                  &what_rcvd,                     /* what was received          */
                  &bytes_read,                    /* length of data received    */
                  &status_rcvd,                   /* conversation status        */
                  &rts_rcvd,                      /* remote program issued cmrts?*/
                  &conv_rc);                      /* return code                */

            if (conv_rc != CM_OK)
               {print_error(conv_rc,"performing Receive",
                                  __FILE__,__LINE__);
                return(FAILED);
               }
           } /* endif */

        if (status_rcvd  == CM_CONFIRM_DEALLOC_RECEIVED)
           cpic_state = CPIC_RESET;
        else
           {print_error(status_rcvd,"deallocating partner LU",__FILE__,__LINE__);
            return(FAILED);
           }

        /*''''''''''''''''''''''''''''''''''''''*/
        /* issue confirmed                      */
        /*''''''''''''''''''''''''''''''''''''''*/
        cmcfmd(conv_id,                           /* conversation ID            */
               &conv_rc);                         /* return code                */

        if (conv_rc != CM_OK)
           {print_error(conv_rc,"performing Confirmed",
                              __FILE__,__LINE__);
            return(FAILED);
           }
      }

  return(GOOD);
} /* end fx_Close */
```

Figure 23-13 (Part 2 of 2).   FXAPPC.C: fx_Close().

Chapter 24

FX Using LAN Server, NetWare, and Remote Named Pipes

This chapter adds three more powerful network protocols to our repertoire of FX file transfer comparisons: Remote Named Pipes over NetWare, Remote Named Pipes over LAN Server, and the LAN Server file redirector (see Figure 24-1). The NetWare implementation runs on top of Novell's **NetWare Requester for OS/2,** which runs on top of the IPX/SPX protocol stack. Both LAN Server implementations build on top of the **IBM LAN Requester/Server,** which in turn, runs on top of the NetBIOS stack. The LAN Server protocols require that you install a copy of IBM's OS/2 LAN Server program on the server machine. In theory, the LAN Server programs should also work with Microsoft's LAN Manager.

The purpose of this chapter is to make you aware that OS/2 can be extended into a full-fledged network operating system with programs like IBM's LAN Server, Microsoft's LAN Manager, and the NetWare Requester for OS/2. You will also discover that the network operating system allows your standalone programs to work over the network without requiring any changes to your code. In other words, the network operating system makes the network transparent.

ABOUT NETWORK OPERATING SYSTEMS

The transparency feature that a network operating system provides makes it easy for you to develop network software. A typical network operating system also provides scores of network utilities which can make life on a network very enjoyable. Chapter 9 contains a list of the benefits provided by IBM's LAN Server, Microsoft's LAN Manager, and the NetWare Requester For OS/2. These three products form the de facto standard for extending OS/2 and MS-DOS services to the network. But, there are no free lunches in life or operating systems, as we will see.

In discussing the costs and benefits of network operating systems, we will use the IBM LAN Server as a case study. Very similar arguments can be made for the Microsoft LAN Manager and Novell's NetWare 3.X. We are trying to compare network operating systems with peer-to-peer network APIs.

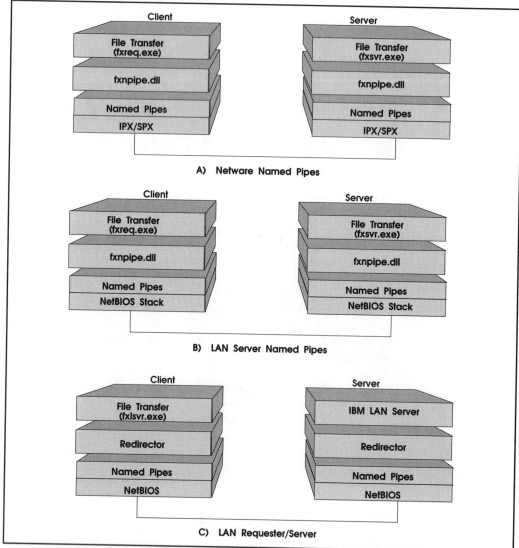

Figure 24-1. FX Named Pipes (Over IPX/SPX and NetBIOS) and FX LAN Requester/Server.

What Are the Costs?

Here's what a network operating system ends up costing you:

- The dollar price of a new program. You need to purchase at least one copy of LAN Server for your server (in addition to the client requesters). On the other hand, peer-to-peer protocols like NetBIOS, Sockets, and CPI-C do not require a server to be present.
- More memory on the server. LAN server adds two MBytes to the server.

- The loss of peer-to-peer symmetry. LAN Server is an asymmetrical protocol. You can only create a Named Pipe on a server machine. You can only offer to share subdirectories and printers on your server. If you want to make your protocols fully symmetrical, you need to install a full LAN Server on every machine. This is obviously an expensive solution. On the other hand, APPC and NetBIOS are fully symmetrical protocols.[1]
- Some performance degradation (perhaps). We're introducing an extra layer on top of the NetBIOS or IPX/SPX stacks. We'll provide you the exact cost (if any) in performance when we present the comparative benchmark figures for FX in the next chapter.
- The logistics of installing and managing an additional program on the server. This always adds a certain level of complexity.

The bottom line is that a LAN Server is *not* the right protocol for you if each one of your clients can also be a server. In this case, you are better off with a plain peer-to-peer protocol like NetBIOS, CPI-C, NetWare Named Pipes, or TCP/IP sockets; on top of protocols like these you can create your custom network services.

What Are the Benefits?

On the other hand, the LAN Server is good for the following situations:

- If your networks consist of many clients and few servers. This is the case where the services are centralized on a few high-powered superserver machines.
- If you have mixed networks of DOS and OS/2 clients. The LAN Server requester works with either DOS or OS/2. It extends the concept of Named Pipes to DOS and Windows requesters. In all fairness, NetBIOS, Sockets, and APPC/CPI-C also work well in mixed environments. APPC/DOS used to take up too much memory on DOS machines, but the new Network Services/DOS is reputedly much slimmer.
- If your networks require other LAN services such as shared files, a print server, or network management services. The LAN Server offers a myriad of network services, including network management, shared files, shared printers, network configuration, network installation of software, remote boot, resource management, security, audit trails, etc. Please review Chapter 9 for the full list of functions offered by the LAN Server.
- For networks that require an *open standard*. The Microsoft LAN Manager, IBM LAN Server, and NetWare are de facto industry standards. The publication of their internal APIs makes them an *open* standard. Such a standard will make it easier to

---

[1] The **NetWare Requester for OS/2** provides a very economical solution. NetWare provides both the client and server Named Pipes without requiring a NetWare server. The price is an unbelievable $200 one-time charge per network installation.

share distributed resources across operating systems (DOS, OS/2, and UNIX) and network platforms.

How Does It Work?

The key concept in a network operating system is *redirection*. The idea is that the call to any device controlled by the operating system can be *redirected* to the network. This simple idea makes it easy to create a virtual service space that extends over the network. The *binding* of the service with the server machine is performed by the operating system.

What Is a Redirector?

A *redirector* is a software component that intercepts system calls for remote resources, packages them, and sends them over the network for execution. It then unpackages the reply and returns the results to the caller. All this is done transparently at the API level. Figure 24-2 shows it all.

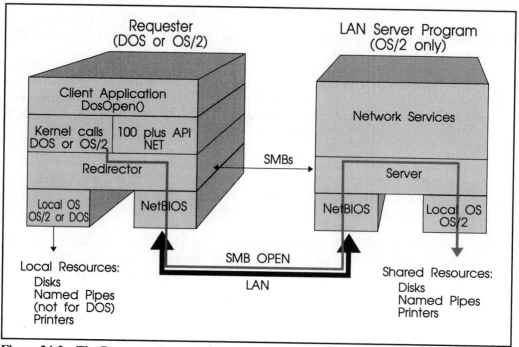

Figure 24-2. The Requester/Server Protocol Used by LAN Server and LAN Manager.

The client workstation on the left of the figure is either running DOS or OS/2. On the right, we show a server workstation that runs the OS/2 LAN Server Program on top of OS/2. The LAN Server program is a client/server application. In addition to the full server element, it requires a redirector on each of its clients.

So How Does a Redirector Work?

The redirector routes or *redirects* DOS or OS/2 system calls. For example, when you issue a call to open a file, named pipe, printer, or some other resource, the redirector determines if the resource is local or remote. If the resource is local, it hands over the call to the local OS. If the resource is remote, it packages the request in an envelope called a **Server Message Block (SMB)** and ships it over the LAN using NetBIOS to the destination server. The SMB protocol consists of message exchanges conducted between servers and requesters to perform network operating system functions. In the example in Figure 24-2, the **DosOpen()** call is for a remote resource. So, it gets shipped over the network to the server, which accepts the call and reissues it to a local resource. When the server completes the open, it returns the results to the client redirector via an **SMB** reply message.

Local or Remote: It's All in the Name

How does the redirector know if the resource is local or remote? It infers it from the resource name. A fully qualified resource pathname includes the optional name of the machine on which it resides. The machine name is preceded by two backslashes (\\) in the pathname. Consequently all you have to do in your programs to access remote resources is call them using their fully qualified network name, and then let the network operating system handle everything else.

Explicit Network API Calls

Figure 24-2 also shows a category of **NET** API services that are available to your application. An application that makes NET calls as opposed to relying on simple redirection is "network aware." The network API services are extensive. They allow you to explicitly control, through programming interfaces, many of the Network Operating System functions. The API calls support alerts, network, and resource management services, security, and access control. For more details, please review the descriptions in Chapter 9.

FX USING REMOTE NAMED PIPES ON NETWARE AND LAN SERVER

This section is short and sweet. Our design objective is to create the FX DLLs that use *remote* Named Pipes on both NetWare and LAN Server. Well, the job couldn't be easier; it's just a question of changing the name of the pipe and running the program developed in Chapter 17. The code remains unchanged. This is a good example of a *network transparent program.*

FX Named Pipes On LAN Server

OS/2 applications call Named Pipes by issuing regular Named Pipe calls to the OS/2 kernel which redirects the calls to the LAN Server. To make the program run on a LAN Server network, just follow these steps:

1. Install a copy of LAN Requester on your client machine and LAN Server on your server machine.

2. Change the name of the Named Pipe in the (.CFG) file for Named Pipes (in Chapter 17) to include a server name as part of the pipe name. This is done by specifying the COMPUTER_NAME parameter as a server name preceded by "\\".

3. The program will now run "as is" remotely; there is no need to even recompile it.

Now we have a version of FX that can run in the great network derby (see Chapter 25) as a remote Named Pipes DLL on a LAN Server network. Named Pipes, of course, build their network services on top of the *redirector*. Wouldn't it be nice if all our software projects were that simple?

FX Named Pipes On NetWare

Figure 24-3 shows the client and server implementations of named pipes provided by the NetWare Requester for OS/2 2.0. Note that an OS/2 application calls named pipes by issuing normal OS/2 kernel calls. These calls get redirected to the NetWare Requester as shown in the figure.

To make the FX Named Pipes DLL run on the NetWare Requester for OS/2 2.0, just follow these steps:

1. Install the NetWare requester Named Pipe client drivers on your client machine and the NetWare requester Named Pipe server drivers on your server machine.

2. Change the name of the Named Pipe in the (.CFG) file for Named Pipes (in Chapter 17) to include a server name as part of the pipe name. This is done by specifying the COMPUTER_NAME parameter as a server name preceded by "\\".

3. The program will now run "as is" remotely; there is no need to even recompile it.

Now we have a version of FX that can run NetWare in the great network derby (see Chapter 25). This is another simple software project thanks to the ubiquity of Named Pipes.

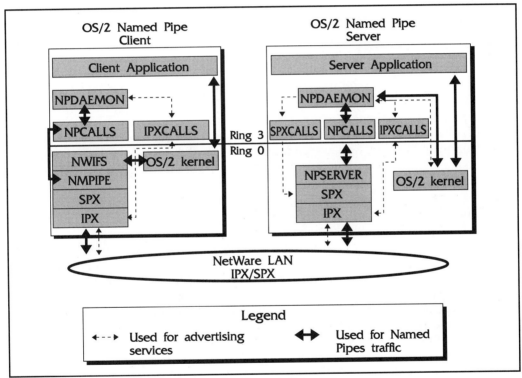

Figure 24-3. The NetWare Requester Implementation of Named Pipes.

FX USING THE LAN REQUESTER-SERVER

In this section, we demonstrate once more the power of *redirected* LAN services with a program that makes direct use of the network operating system. Our design objective is to measure the file transfer performance of the LAN Server. We'll meet this objective by introducing a single program that replaces the FXREQ and FXSVR programs as well as the FX DLLs. This program performs the file transfer using a single OS/2 command: **DosCopy**. Requester magic working in tandem with the LAN Server will take care of all the details involved in the intercomputer file transfer. So what's left for us to do? We still have to issue the **DosCopy** and create (or mostly borrow) the code that measures the file transfer performance. Our program must be able to participate in the great network derby (in the next chapter) as the LAN Requester/Server champion. This means that it needs to be equipped with all the FX performance-measuring paraphernalia.

The FXLSCR.C Program

Figure 24-4 includes the listing of **FXLSVR.C**, the program that implements the file transfer using the LAN Server. The file is copied using the **DosCopy** from a local drive to a drive on the LAN Server machine. Unlike the other FX file transfer programs in this book, this one does not have a server peer component (actually it's built-in). Since it takes two parties to implement a protocol, and we can only control one of them, the requester, here's what we ended up doing:

1. We created a shared subdirectory on the server machine.
2. We wrote **FXLSVR.C** to implement the equivalent of a file COPY.
3. We ported all our timers and stopwatch procedures from the FX programs into **FXLSVR.C**. This program has been made an honest contender to run in the great FX derby as the LAN Server champion. We put all the hooks in the right places to measure and report the file transfer time. These are the same timing tools we used in all the other FX programs.

Except for the **DosCopy** feature, the **FXLSVR.C** program (see listing in Figure 24-4) is nothing more than the repackaging of FX timing and reporting functions. The listing contains the entire program. We don't even need a communication-specific DLL function. As a matter of fact, the code does not contain a single network API call. So how does the file get moved over the network? Where is the equivalent of the NetBIOS, CPI-C, Sockets, or Named Pipes calls of the previous chapters? They've all been replaced by a simple *redirected* OS/2 call, **DosCopy**. One invocation of this call will cause the file to "automagically" get copied from one machine to the next. A description of this call follows.

DosCopy

This API call copies a file or subdirectory. The prototype for this call is:

```
DosCopy(PSZ     sourcefile,   /*Pointer to name of source file*/
        PSZ     targetfile,   /*Pointer to name of target     */
        ULONG   options);     /*Copy over or append to target */
```

The following is a description of the parameters:

- The *sourcefile* parameter points to the null terminated name of the file or directory to copy. No wild cards are permitted.

- The *targetfile* parameter points to the null terminated name of the file or directory that specifies the name of the destination. The path of the destination must be specified; you cannot just specify a drive.
- The *options* parameter specifies how the copy should be handled if a file already exists at the destination. Set this parameter to DCPY_EXISTING if you want to overwrite the destination file contents. Or set it to DCPY_APPEND if you want the data appended to the end of the destination file. If the destination file does not exist, a new file is created. You can also *OR* the DCPY_FAILEAS constant with either option to make the copy fail when the destination file system does not support Extended Attributes.

Now that we've explained the one OS/2 call, the **FXLSVR.C** code that follows is readable "as is." So we've left it all in one piece. If you get lost, you can always go back to main() to understand what the program does.

```
/***********************************************************************/
/*   PROGRAM NAME: FXLSVR - File Transfer example using LAN SERVER and  */
/*                          LAN REQUESTER                               */
/*                                                                      */
/*   PROGRAM DESCRIPTION:  This module uses the LAN Server program to    */
/*      implement a file transfer program.  The file transfer is accomplished */
/*      by using DosCopy to copy a file from a local drive to a redirected */
/*      on the LAN Server machine.                                      */
/*                                                                      */
/*      A summary report is displayed showing how long it took to transfer */
/*      the file.                                                       */
/*                                                                      */
/*   PROGRAM INVOCATION:                                                */
/*                                                                      */
/*      FXLSVR direction file-name                                      */
/*                                                                      */
/*      where:                                                          */
/*           direction is either SEND or RECV.                          */
/*                                                                      */
/*           file-name is the name of the file to transfer.  If a path is */
/*                     specified the path must exist on the requester and */
/*                     server machines.                                 */
/*                                                                      */
/*                                                             .        */
/*      EXAMPLE INVOCATIONS:                                            */
/*                                                                      */
/*      FXLSVR  SEND MYFILE.TMP                                         */
/*      FXLSVR  RECV MYFILE.TMP                                         */
/*                                                                      */
/***********************************************************************/
#include <process.h>           /* For exit()          */
#include <stdio.h>             /* For printf() & NULL */
#include <stdlib.h>            /* For printf          */
#include <string.h>            /* For printf          */
#include <sys\types.h>         /* For time()          */
#include <sys\timeb.h>         /* For time()          */
```

Figure 24-4 (Part 1 of 5). FXLSVR.C: File Transfer with LAN Server.

```
#include <sys\stat.h>          /* For stat()        */
#include <io.h>                /* For file I/O      */
#include <fcntl.h>             /* For file I/O      */
#include <sys\types.h>         /* For file I/O      */

#include <os2.h>               /* for types only    */

#include "fxfer.h"
#include "fxreq.h"

/*_____*/
/* Global variables, declares for this module              */
/*_____*/
CHAR rdr_drive[3];
CHAR rdr_file_name[128];

VOID read_config(VOID);

/*_____*/
/* Main routine. Performs a file transfer and calculates statistics.  */
/*_____*/
VOID main(SHORT argc, PCHAR argv[], PCHAR envp[])
{
    /*_____*/
    /* get command line arguments      */
    /*_____*/
    if (get_args(argc, argv))
        { print_help();
          exit(FAILED);
        }

    /*_____*/
    /* initialize                      */
    /*_____*/
    read_config();

    /*_____*/
    /* perform the file transfer       */
    /*_____*/
    open_bgn_time = save_time();
    xfer_bgn_time = save_time();

    switch (service)
      {
        case FILE_SEND_TO_SERVER:      send_file();
                                       break;

        case FILE_RECEIVE_FROM_SERVER: receive_file();
                                       break;
      } /* end switch */

    close_bgn_time = save_time();
    end_time = save_time();

    /*_____*/
    /* print the statistics            */
    /*_____*/
    printf("File transfer completed.\n");
    file_size = get_file_size(file_name);
    print_statistics();
```

Figure 24-4 (Part 2 of 5). FXLSVR.C: File Transfer with LAN Server.

```
    exit(GOOD);

} /* end main */


/*_____*/
/* Initialize program variables from command line.                */
/*_____*/
USHORT get_args(SHORT argc, PCHAR argv[])
{
   /*_____*/
   /* are there the right number of args? */
   /*_____*/
   if (argc != 3)

     return(FAILED);

   /*_____*/
   /* send or receive?                    */
   /*_____*/
   if (strcmp("SEND", strupr(argv[1])) == 0)
     service = FILE_SEND_TO_SERVER;
   else
     if (strcmp("RECV", strupr(argv[1])) == 0)
       service = FILE_RECEIVE_FROM_SERVER;
     else return(FAILED);

   /*_____*/
   /* get the file name                   */
   /*_____*/
   strcpy(file_name, argv[2]);

   /*_____*/
   /* everything is OK!                   */
   /*_____*/
   return(GOOD);
} /* end eget_args */

/*_____*/
/* Read configuration data                                        *
/*_____*/
VOID read_config(VOID)
{
   FILE    *config_file;              /* Input file control block    */
   CHAR    line[80];                  /* one line of config file     */

   printf("Reading configuration parameters.\n");
   /*_____*/
   /* open the configuration file         */
   /*_____*/
   if (NULL == (config_file = fopen("fxlsvr.cfg","r")))
     {printf("\nError opening configuration file\n",__FILE__,__LINE__);
      exit(FAILED);
     }
   else
     /*_____*/
     /* read the configuration parameters.  */
     /* The parameters are expected to be:  */
     /*    - in the form <name = value>     */
     /*    - in the order read below        */
     /*_____*/
```

Figure 24-4 (Part 3 of 5).   FXLSVR.C: File Transfer with LAN Server.

```
      {
       fgets(line, sizeof(line), config_file);
       if (sscanf(line,"REDIRECTED_DRIVE = %2s ", rdr_drive) != 1)
          {printf("\nError reading REDIRECTED_DRIVE from configuration file\n");
           exit(FAILED);
          }
      }
   fclose(config_file);
} /* end read_config */

/*_____*/
/* Function to receive a file from the server.           *
/*_____*/
VOID receive_file(VOID)
{ CHAR rdr_file_name[128];

   sprintf(rdr_file_name,"%s%s",rdr_drive,file_name);
   if (DosCopy(rdr_file_name, file_name, DCPY_EXISTING))
      {printf("\nError copying file from LAN Server\n");
       exit(FAILED);
      }
} /* end receive_file */

/*_____*/
/* Function to send a file to the server.                */
/*_____*/
VOID send_file(VOID)
{
   sprintf(rdr_file_name,"%s%s",rdr_drive,file_name);
   if (DosCopy(file_name, rdr_file_name, DCPY_EXISTING))
      {printf("\nError copying file to LAN Server\n");
       exit(FAILED);
      }
} /* end send_file */

/*_____*/
/* Start timing an event.                                */
/*_____*/
double save_time(VOID)
{
   ftime(&timebuff);
   return((double)timebuff.time+((double)timebuff.millitm)/(double)1000);
} /* end save_time */

/*_____*/
/* Get File Size                                         */
/*_____*/
ULONG get_file_size(PCHAR name)
{
   int fhandle;
   unsigned long size;

   if (-1 == (fhandle = open(name, O_BINARY | O_RDONLY )))
      {printf("\nError opening file.\n");
       return(FAILED);
      }
   size = filelength(fhandle);
   close(fhandle);

   return(size);
} /* end get_file_size */
```

Figure 24-4 (Part 4 of 5). FXLSVR.C: File Transfer with LAN Server.

```
/*————————————————————————————————————————————————*/
/* Print Statistics.                                               */
/*————————————————————————————————————————————————*/
VOID print_statistics(VOID)
{
  if (service == FILE_SEND_TO_SERVER)
    printf("\n%s sent to the server.\n", file_name);
  else
    printf("\n%s received from the server.\n",file_name);

  printf("Communication link open time was %f seconds.\n",
         xfer_bgn_time-open_bgn_time);
  printf("%ld bytes transferred in %f seconds.\n",
         file_size, close_bgn_time-xfer_bgn_time);
  printf("The average transfer rate was %.2f kilobytes/second.\n",
         file_size/((close_bgn_time-xfer_bgn_time)*1000));
  printf("Communication link close time was %f seconds.\n",
         end_time-close_bgn_time);
} /* end print_statistics */


/*————————————————————————————————————————————————*/
/* Print Help.                                                     */
/*————————————————————————————————————————————————*/
VOID print_help(VOID)
{
  printf("\nIncorrect command invocation.  Enter as follows:\n");
  printf("\n");
  printf("FXLSVR direction file-name                              \n");
  printf("                                                        \n");
  printf(" where:                                                 \n");

  printf("        direction is either SEND or RECV.               \n");
  printf("                                                        \n");
  printf("        file-name is the name of the file to transfer.  If a  \n");
  printf("                  path is specified the path must exist on the \n");
  printf("                  requester and server machines.        \n");
  printf("                                                        \n");
  printf("\n\n");
} /* end print_help */
```

Figure 24-4 (Part 5 of 5). FXLSVR.C: File Transfer with LAN Server.

Chapter 25

The Great FX LAN Derby

In this chapter, we will run the races between the different protocol implementations of the FX file transfer. The first race compares the performance of local versus remote Named Pipes. This comparison will give us a feel for the network overhead in interprocess communication. Next, we present a multiprotocol race that compares the network performance of NetBIOS, Sockets over TCP/IP, CPI-C over APPC, Named Pipes over LAN Server and NetWare, and the LAN Server redirector. This race is run varying the file sizes and message buffers. Finally, we present some *Sniffer* traces of the network exchanges. This is done to validate our benchmark numbers and to give you some idea of what network protocol analyzers can do for you. Before declaring a winner, please take note of the disclaimer section. There are some interesting results in this race. This edition's winner, which was "edged out by a nose" in our first edition, has undergone new "training" and pulls through for the win. But we're getting ahead of our story.

THE BLOBS ARE COMING

Images, video, voice, graphics, intelligent documents, and database snapshots are about to test the capabilities of our LANs for moving large data objects quickly. These large objects are affectionately called **BLOBs,** which stands for Binary Large Objects. Client/server applications, as they increasingly become multimedia, will be called upon to move these BLOBs over LANs. The clients will capture and display BLOBs then send them to the servers for storage. As a result, clients will expect to retrieve BLOBs from servers as part of ordinary transactions.

Client/Server Future: BLOBS Everywhere

Client *and* server technologies for capturing and storing BLOBs are improving rapidly. On the client side, scanners are getting faster and more reliable. Compression technology for video and images is keeping up the pace. On the server side, optical jukeboxes are doubling in density and are allowing volumes of images, voice (and other sounds), and video to be stored and distributed efficiently.

The rapid improvement of these technologies is making multimedia applications a reality in corporations. For many applications, it is now more cost effective to automate access to multimedia information than to handle it manually (it costs 17 cents per megabyte to store information on a 12-inch optical store). Little wonder that a recent survey found that 40% of corporations are planning to install imaging applications within the next two years. And, many corporations are ready to roll pilot tests into production uses.[1]

All of this is going to put the squeeze on our LAN protocols. The throughput requirements of multimedia applications goes way beyond that seen by even the most heavily used file servers in operation. Office use of imaging works well over today's LANs. But, today's 75 KByte images, which a user might access once every five minutes or so, will turn into tomorrow's 300 KByte/second video stream.

Are current peer-to-peer LAN protocols up to this new challenge? Which of our leading LAN protocols is best at moving BLOBs? And, is that good enough? We'll try to answer these questions.

BLOB Olympics

To get the answers, we first built a carefully layered server to provide a common "BLOB transport" interface that can work on top of various LAN protocols. The server has built-in timers that measure different BLOB transfer events. This serves as the level playing field for running BLOB Transfer Olympics. Running in these Olympics were six popular peer-to-peer protocols: NetBIOS, CPI-C over APPC, NetWare Named Pipes over IPX/SPX, Named Pipes over LAN Server, Sockets over TCP/IP, and the LAN Server redirector. We used the protocol stacks provided by a single vendor (IBM) to ensure that the race was between protocols, not vendors. Is this beginning to sound familiar?

In this chapter, you will relive the BLOB Olympics. Get your tickets ready. We'll first show you how we set the level playing field by describing the benchmark environment. Then, we'll show you the results of different races. Finally, we'll use network "sniffs" to show you in slow replay motion how each protocol performed.

---

[1] Source: Jeri Edwards, "Images and OLTP: Manifest Destiny," **Database Programming and Design** (July, 1991). This is the definitive article on how BLOBs are impacting client/server OLTP.

The BLOB Server Benchmark Kit

The field for the race is set using a specially designed BLOB client/server benchmark kit. The client/server program consists of three layers: application, file transfer, and communication. This section describes these layers.

The Application Layer

A BLOB Server provides a network repository for BLOBs. Clients on the LAN can request a BLOB from the server. This results in a BLOB getting copied to the client's disk drive. Clients can also ask the server to store a BLOB.

BLOB servers manage BLOBs. In a production application, this may involve sophisticated workflow tracking systems where servers maintain complex indexing and inter-BLOB relationships (such as folders, bill of materials, and version control), BLOB routes, and work queues.

Of course, our benchmark-oriented server doesn't include all this functionality, but it does provide timers that calculate and display the performance of the BLOB transfer. The timers calculate and display the overhead for establishing a connection between the client and server, the total number of bytes transferred, the average transfer rate in KBytes/sec, and the overhead for closing a connection. The application layer is provided jointly by two programs: **FXREQ.C** on the client side, and **FXSVR.C** on the server side.

The File Transfer Layer

This layer provides a logical file transfer protocol for moving the BLOB from a client to the server and vice versa. The protocol includes a method for requesting a remote service as well as an implementation of the requested service. The BLOB transfer protocol specifies how a service is requested, the handshaking for transferring the file, and the message structures used. The BLOB transfer layer only provides the logical protocols. It "delegates" the actual moving of the data to the layers below it. The data movement is done through the, by now infamous, FX nine API-call interface. FX can be used for transaction processing as well as for the bulk movement of data required by BLOB transfer protocols.

The Communication Layer

This layer performs the actual movement of data between processes. The communication layer implements the generic interface calls using the FX DLL version of either NetBIOS, CPI-C over APPC, Named Pipes over IPX/SPX, Named Pipes over LAN Server, Sockets over TCP/IP, or the LAN Server redirector.

Yes, there was some method behind all the FX madness in Part III. We were busy creating the playing field to run our BLOB Olympics.

"Lies, Damned Lies, and Benchmarks"

Benchmarking is a tricky business where many factors can affect the overall network performance. When dealing with benchmarks, you should really make sure that you're comparing "apples to apples." Always make it a point to understand what factors are being measured. The numbers presented in this chapter should only be used to evaluate *relative* design trade-offs. All the measurements are of interest only in terms of the comparative information they convey. So, please don't get hung up on any absolute numbers.

What the FX Benchmarks Measure

The benchmark numbers we present measure the data transfer times after a link is established. We do not include the time to initialize, open, and close a link; these are the areas where comparisons may be subject to controversy. On the left side of Figure 25-1 we show where the test starts and where it ends. The results are reported by FXREQ. The FX benchmarks measure:

- Code complexity versus gains in performance.
- The effect of BLOB size on performance.
- The effect of message size on performance.
- The performance degradation that can be expected when a peer process is run on a remote machine versus a local one.

- How well do each of Named Pipes (over Novell and LAN Server), NetBIOS, CPI-C over APPC, Sockets over TCP/IP, and the LAN Server perform when it comes to moving BLOBs on the network.

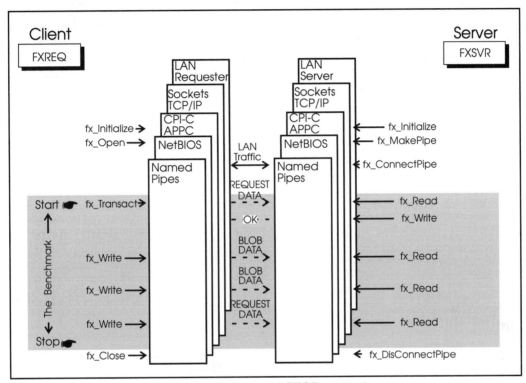

Figure 25-1. Benchmark is Between START and STOP.

What the FX Benchmarks Do Not Measure

Here's what the FX benchmarks do **not** measure or quantify:

- The performance of simple request/reply transactions used in Remote Procedure Calls. FX gives you the hooks to try that yourself.
- Protocol features such as broadcast, datagrams, security, etc.
- The overhead required to establish sessions. FX is equipped to do that, but we didn't record the results. You can try that yourself.
- Ease of installation and configuration.
- Network management.
- Connectivity to other networks and operating systems.

What Makes Our Benchmarks "Honest"

Now that we've recorded the disclaimer, let us tell you what's good about the FX benchmark:

- The code is *available*. It's all in this book. This means that you can see for yourself where we placed the measurement probes and how the results were derived. If you don't like something we did, just enter a change and see what the effects are.
- The protocols, with the exception of LAN Server, are all driven by a *common driver*. This is as close as it ever comes to creating a common test bed.
- The relative results of the tests are easy to reproduce and duplicate. You should be looking at the test ratios independent of the hardware. Don't look at the absolute numbers. These can vary wildly with machine power, network bandwidth, network utilization and LAN adapters.
- The test results were validated with network Sniffer traces.
- The tests are representative of network *bulk transfer* situations. They test the buffering capabilities of the various protocols and how they chunk network transmissions.
- All the protocols that were measured are provided by the same vendor. This means we don't have an axe to grind.

BENCHMARK 1: COMPARING LOCAL AND REMOTE NAMED PIPES

This benchmark first runs FXREQ and FXSVR on the same machine and then on separate machines attached by a 4 Mb/sec Token Ring LAN. What we're looking for is a measure of the overhead which the network introduces over local interprocess communications. Table 25-1 presents the results of moving a 100 KByte file using various buffer sizes. *The file exchanges always use RAM disk to remove the effects of the disk access from the measurements.*

Table 25-1. **100 KByte File Transfer: Local Named Pipes vs. Remote Named Pipes.**

Protocol	Message Buffer Sizes			
	4 KByte Buffer	**16 KByte Buffer**	**32 Kbyte Buffer**	**64 KByte Buffer**
Named Pipes (Local)	400.0 KByte/sec	625.0 KByte/sec	801.1 KByte/sec	1111.1 KByte/sec
Named Pipes (Remote)	138.9 KByte/sec	111.1 KByte/sec	138.9 KByte/sec	158.7 KByte/sec

Commentary
- Yes, the network does slow things down. If you're going to move a peer process to a remote machine, prepare yourself for a substantial performance degradation in the IPC.
- Yes, transfer buffer sizes matter when it comes to moving bulk data. The larger the buffer, the better off you are.

BENCHMARK 2: COMPARING LAN PROTOCOLS

The second benchmark runs FXREQ and FXSVR on separate machines attached by a 4 Mb/sec Token Ring LAN. We'll be driving the different protocols by dynamically linking to their FX DLLs one protocol set at a time. This is done by copying the appropriate FX DLL (from the previous chapters) into the working subdirectory and running the tests. The exception is the LAN Server protocol, which is totally self-contained in FXLSVR.EXE and doesn't have a DLL. The benchmark consists of sending a file from FXREQ to FXSVR. *Here again, the file exchanges always use RAM disk to remove the effects of the disk access from the measurements.* We will conduct two variations of this benchmark:

- The first measures varying *message buffer* sizes.
- The second measures varying files sizes.

Varying the Message Buffer Sizes

We run the benchmark using four message buffer sizes: 4 KByte, 16 KByte, 32 KByte, and 64 KByte. The message size is varied by changing a parameter in the FX (.CFG) file. The file sent is 100 KBytes in size. The idea of this test is to measure how the different protocols perform when this message buffer factor is varied. Table 25-2 presents the averaged results of the runs.

Table 25-2. 100 KByte File Transfer Using the Olympic Protocols.

Protocol	Message Buffer Sizes			
	4 KByte Buffer	**16 KByte Buffer**	**32 Kbyte Buffer**	**64 KByte Buffer**
APPC (CPI-C)	144.9 KByte/sec	178.6 KByte/sec	185.2 KByte/sec	(see Note 1)
NetBIOS	138.9 KByte/sec	200.0 KByte/sec	212.8 KByte/sec	212.8 KByte/sec
TCP/IP	128.2 KByte/sec	153.8 KByte/sec	158.7 KByte/sec	(see Note 1)
Named Pipes (LAN Server)	138.9 KByte/sec	111.1 KByte/sec	138.9 KByte/sec	158.7 KByte/sec
Named Pipes (NetWare)	84.0 KByte/sec	109.9 KByte/sec	114.9 KByte/sec	114.9 KByte/sec
LAN Server	(see Note 2)	(see Note 2)	(see Note 2)	200.0 KByte/sec

Note 1: The maximum transfer size is limited to 32 KBytes so we excluded the 64 KByte buffer test for this protocol.

Note 2: In the case of the LAN Server program, the minimum allocation unit for the message buffer is 64 KBytes. This means we couldn't measure anything smaller.

Commentary
- It appears that when it comes to raw transfer speeds NetBIOS is the winner. The work by IBM to improve NetBIOS's performance clearly shows.
- Yes, transfer buffer sizes matter when it comes to moving bulk data. Each of the protocols shows improved performance as buffer size increases.

Varying File Sizes

We run the benchmark and transfer files of three different sizes: 1 KByte, 10 KByte, and 100 KByte. The idea is to measure how the different protocols perform when the file size factor is varied (also remember that all transfers are from RAM disk).

The message size is 4 KByte, except for LAN Server, which is 64 KByte.

Table 25-3. **Varying File Sizes Using the Olympic Protocols.**

Protocol	File Sizes		
	1 KByte File Size	**10 KByte File Size**	**100 KByte File Size**
APPC (CPI-C)	8.3 KByte/sec	55.5 KByte/sec	144.9 KByte/sec
NetBIOS	8.3 KByte/sec	79.2 KByte/sec	138.9 KByte/sec
TCP/IP	14.3 KByte/sec	62.5 KByte/sec	128.2 KByte/sec
Named Pipes (LAN Server)	14.3 KByte/sec	69.5 KByte/sec	138.9 KByte/sec
Named Pipes (NetWare)	7.7 KByte/sec	45.5 KByte/sec	84.0 KByte/sec
LAN Server	11.1 KByte/sec	52.6 KByte/sec	200.0 KByte/sec

Commentary
- Note that each of the protocols suffer at the smaller file sizes but some more than others.
- In general, the larger the file to be moved, the better the effective transfer rates for all the protocols. They get to send more for the same amount of fixed overhead.

VALIDATING THE BENCHMARK WITH A SNIFFER

What's a Sniffer? It's a *Network Analyzer* made by Network General. A network analyzer is an indispensable tool for anyone doing serious LAN work (its our profession's microscope). It works by capturing all the frames it sees on the network in a buffer (you can filter the capture to what you're interested in seeing). Once a set of frames are in its buffer, this marvelous tool can display the information in hundreds of interesting ways. It can show you all the details at the byte stream level, or it can interpret the protocol for you. It can also show you conversational exchanges between two workstations and the elapsed time between packets. The purpose here is not to tell you all about the wonderful things Sniffers can do, we're just using the Sniffer to *validate* our benchmark results. Remember the old saying about *lies and benchmarks*.

What the Sniffer Sees?

We captured the Sniffer Traces for the 10 KByte file transfers of the previous section. We've included them here for your consideration. The traces displayed in this section are the summary reports of the network frames captured during a time interval. The summary corresponds to the topmost layer of protocol the Sniffer was able to decipher on a particular frame. Here is your guide to reading the summary Sniffer traces:

M   This is a marker that indicates the base time for all subsequent time measurements. The time on all the frames which follow is measured relative to the frame with the "M" marker.

number   The numbers in the first column identify the frame's position in the Sniffer's capture buffer. The numbers shown are not contiguous because we filtered out of the summary frames which did not contain protocol relevant information. We're only interested in APPC (SNA), NetBIOS (NET), TCP/IP (TCP), NetWare Named Pipes (XNS), and the SMB protocol (SMB) used by LAN Server Named Pipes and the LAN Server.

Rel Time   This is the time elapsed in seconds measured relative to the frame marked with "M".

Size   This is the size in bytes of the frame. The size includes user data and all the communication headers which encapsulate it.

From Client This packet was sent by the requester (i.e., client). The Sniffer displays the results of the trace as a two-way communication handshake between the "Requester" and the "Server" machines.

From Server This packet was sent by the "Server." This is the server end of the two-way exchange.

For more information on the Sniffer, refer to Network General's documentation.

APPC Sniff

```
SUMMARY Rel Time  Size    From Client                From Server

M   1    0.000    216   SNA C FMD ATTACH FileServer
    3    0.024     34                               SNA C SIG
    5    0.028     28   SNA R SIG
    7    0.030     34                               SNA C LUSTAT
    9    0.038     32   SNA C LUSTAT
   11    0.040     32                               SNA R FMD
   13    0.045     37                               SNA C FMD user data
   15    0.058     32   SNA C SIG
   17    0.060     30                               SNA R SIG
   19    0.065     32   SNA C LUSTAT
   21    0.069     34                               SNA C LUSTAT
   23    0.090   1947   SNA C FMD user data
   25    0.096   1947   SNA C FMD user data
   27    0.108   1947   SNA C FMD user data
   29    0.115   1947   SNA C FMD user data
   31    0.124   1947   SNA C FMD user data
   33    0.167    619   SNA C FMD user data
   35    0.184     32                               SNA R FMD
```

Figure 25-2. APPC Sniff: 10 KByte File; Elapsed Time = 0.184 Secs.

Commentary
- According to the APPC Sniffer trace, it takes 0.184 seconds to transfer a 10 KByte file. This translates into a 54.3 KByte/s transfer rate.
- The equivalent result using FX timers is 55.5 KByte/s (see Table 25-3). We're validated.

NetBIOS Sniff

```
SUMMARY Rel Time  Size    From Client                 From Server

        1  -0.109     32   NETB D=0C S=16 Session initialize
        3  -0.108     32                               NETB D=16 S=0C Session confirm
M       5   0.000    164   NETB D=0C S=16 Data, 132 bytes
        6   0.000     32                               NETB D=16 S=0C Data ACK
        8   0.007     36                               NETB D=16 S=0C Data, 4 bytes
        9   0.008     32   NETB D=0C S=16 Data ACK
       11   0.033   4128   NETB D=0C S=16 Data, 4096 bytes
       12   0.033     32                               NETB D=16 S=0C Data ACK
       14   0.058   4128   NETB D=0C S=16 Data, 4096 bytes
       15   0.058     32                               NETB D=16 S=0C Data ACK
       17   0.072   1870   NETB D=0C S=16 Data, 1838 bytes
       18   0.073     32                               NETB D=16 S=0C Data ACK
       20   0.078     42   NETB D=0C S=16 Data, 10 bytes
       21   0.079     32                               NETB D=16 S=0C Data ACK
       23   0.118    164   NETB D=0C S=16 Data, 132 bytes
       24   0.119     32                               NETB D=16 S=0C Data ACK
       26   0.120     32                               NETB D=16 S=0C Session end
```

Figure 25-3. NetBIOS Sniff: 10 KByte File; Elapsed Time = 0.12 Secs.

Commentary

- According to the NetBIOS Sniffer trace, it takes 0.12 seconds to transfer a 10 KByte file. This translates into a 83.3 KByte/s transfer rate.
- The equivalent result using FX timers is 79.2 KByte/s (see Table 25-3). We're validated.

TCP/IP Sniff

```
SUMMARY Rel Time Size  From Client  From Server

     2   -0.089   68  TCP D=1027 S=1032 SYN SEQ=4277758465 LEN=0 WIN=28672
     3   -0.087   68               TCP D=1032 S=1027 SYN ACK=4277758466 SEQ=4277041153 LEN=0 WIN=28672
     4   -0.081   64  TCP D=1027 S=1032    ACK=4277041154 WIN=28672
M    5   0.000   200  TCP D=1027 S=1032    ACK=4277041154 SEQ=4277758466 LEN=136 WIN=28672
     6   0.012    72               TCP D=1032 S=1027    ACK=4277758602 SEQ=4277041154 LEN=8 WIN=28672
     7   0.053    64  TCP D=1027 S=1032    ACK=4277041162 WIN=28672
     8   0.070  1524  TCP D=1027 S=1032    ACK=4277041162 SEQ=4277758602 LEN=1460 WIN=28672
     9   0.074  1524  TCP D=1027 S=1032    ACK=4277041162 SEQ=4277760062 LEN=1460 WIN=28672
    10   0.077  1244  TCP D=1027 S=1032    ACK=4277041162 SEQ=4277761522 LEN=1180 WIN=28672
    11   0.078    64              TCP D=1032 S=1027    ACK=4277760062 WIN=27216
    12   0.081    64              TCP D=1032 S=1027    ACK=4277762702 WIN=28672
    13   0.096  1524  TCP D=1027 S=1032    ACK=4277041162 SEQ=4277762702 LEN=1460 WIN=28672
    14   0.100  1524  TCP D=1027 S=1032    ACK=4277041162 SEQ=4277764162 LEN=1460 WIN=28672
    15   0.104  1244  TCP D=1027 S=1032    ACK=4277041162 SEQ=4277765622 LEN=1180 WIN=28672
    16   0.105    64              TCP D=1032 S=1027    ACK=4277765622 WIN=28672
    17   0.107    64              TCP D=1032 S=1027    ACK=4277766802 WIN=28672
    18   0.119  1524  TCP D=1027 S=1032    ACK=4277041162 SEQ=4277766802 LEN=1460 WIN=28672
    19   0.120   446  TCP D=1027 S=1032    ACK=4277041162 SEQ=4277768262 LEN=382 WIN=28672
    20   0.124    64              TCP D=1032 S=1027    ACK=4277768644 WIN=28672
    21   0.154    78  TCP D=1027 S=1032    ACK=4277041162 SEQ=4277768644 LEN=14 WIN=28672
    22   0.162   200  TCP D=1027 S=1032 FIN ACK=4277041162 SEQ=4277768658 LEN=136 WIN=28672
    23   0.164    64              TCP D=1032 S=1027    ACK=4277768795 WIN=28536
    24   0.167    64              TCP D=1032 S=1027 FIN ACK=4277768795 SEQ=4277041162 LEN=0 WIN=28672
```

Figure 25-4. TCP/IP Sniff: 10 KByte File; Elapsed Time = 0.167 Secs.

Commentary

- According to the TCP/IP Sniffer trace, it takes 0.167 seconds to transfer a 10 KByte file. This translates into a 59.9 KByte/s transfer rate.
- The equivalent result using FX timers is 62.5 KByte/s (see Table 25-3). We're validated.

LAN Server Named Pipe Sniff

```
SUMMARY Rel Time   Size    From Client              From Server

     7   -0.096    111   SMB C Open \PIPE\FILESVR
     9   -0.092     97                              SMB R Opened F=4180
    11   -0.084    110   SMB C Transaction Set Attributes\PIPE\
    13   -0.082     88                              SMB R Transaction
    15   -0.026     32   NETB D=17 S=25 Data ACK
M   17    0.000    240   SMB C Transaction Write/Read \PIPE\
    19    0.010     92                              SMB R Transaction
    21    0.041   4188   SMB C F=4180 Write 4096 at 0
    23    0.042     79                              SMB R OK
    25    0.066   4188   SMB C F=4180 Write 4096 at 0
    27    0.067     79                              SMB R OK
    29    0.082   1930   SMB C F=4180 Write 1838 at 0
    31    0.083     79                              SMB R OK
    33    0.088    102   SMB C F=4180 Write 10 at 0
    35    0.090     79                              SMB R OK
    37    0.127    224   SMB C F=4180 Write 132 at 0
    38    0.129     79                              SMB R OK
    39    0.133     73   SMB C F=4180 Close
    40    0.136     67                              SMB R Closed
```

Figure 25-5. LAN Server Named Pipe Sniff: 10 KByte File; Elapsed time = 0.136 Secs.

Commentary

- According to the LAN Server Named Pipes Sniffer trace, it takes 0.136 seconds to transfer a 10 KByte file. This translates into a 73.5 KByte/s transfer rate.
- The equivalent result using FX timers is 69.5 KByte/s (see Table 25-3). We're validated.
- Note how Named Pipes use the SMB protocol on top of NetBIOS.

NetWare Named Pipe Sniff

```
SUMMARY Rel Time  Size   From Client          From Server

M  24   0.000    215   XNS SPP    D=EC91 S=AB09 NR=2 NS=2
   25   0.000     59                           XNS SPP A D=AB09 S=EC91 NR=3
   26   0.002     59                           XNS SPP A D=AB09 S=EC91 NR=3
   27   0.012     87                           XNS SPP   D=AB09 S=EC91 NR=3 NS=2
   28   0.014     59   XNS SPP A D=EC91 S=AB09 NR=3
   29   0.023     59   XNS SPP A D=EC91 S=AB09 NR=3
   30   0.034   2168   XNS SPP   D=EC91 S=AB09 NR=3 NS=3
   31   0.035     59                           XNS SPP A D=AB09 S=EC91 NR=4
   32   0.038     59                           XNS SPP A D=AB09 S=EC91 NR=4
   33   0.050   2094   XNS SPP   D=EC91 S=AB09 NR=3 NS=4
   34   0.051     59                           XNS SPP A D=AB09 S=EC91 NR=5
   35   0.053     59                           XNS SPP A D=AB09 S=EC91 NR=5
   36   0.059     83                           XNS SPP   D=AB09 S=EC91 NR=5 NS=3
   37   0.060     59   XNS SPP A D=EC91 S=AB09 NR=4
   38   0.068     59   XNS SPP A D=EC91 S=AB09 NR=4
   39   0.080   2168   XNS SPP   D=EC91 S=AB09 NR=4 NS=5
   40   0.080     59                           XNS SPP A D=AB09 S=EC91 NR=6
   41   0.084     59                           XNS SPP A D=AB09 S=EC91 NR=6
   42   0.095   2094   XNS SPP   D=EC91 S=AB09 NR=4 NS=6
   43   0.095     59                           XNS SPP A D=AB09 S=EC91 NR=7
   44   0.098     59                           XNS SPP A D=AB09 S=EC91 NR=7
   45   0.106     83                           XNS SPP   D=AB09 S=EC91 NR=7 NS=4
   46   0.108     59   XNS SPP A D=EC91 S=AB09 NR=5
   47   0.114     59   XNS SPP A D=EC91 S=AB09 NR=5
   48   0.124   1921   XNS SPP   D=EC91 S=AB09 NR=5 NS=7
   49   0.124     59                           XNS SPP A D=AB09 S=EC91 NR=8
   50   0.126     59                           XNS SPP A D=AB09 S=EC91 NR=8
   51   0.129     83                           XNS SPP   D=AB09 S=EC91 NR=8 NS=5
   52   0.131     59   XNS SPP A D=EC91 S=AB09 NR=6
   53   0.136     59   XNS SPP A D=EC91 S=AB09 NR=6
   54   0.137     93   XNS SPP   D=EC91 S=AB09 NR=6 NS=8
   55   0.138     59                           XNS SPP A D=AB09 S=EC91 NR=9
   56   0.139     59                           XNS SPP A D=AB09 S=EC91 NR=9
   57   0.143     83                           XNS SPP   D=AB09 S=EC91 NR=9 NS=6
   58   0.144     59   XNS SPP A D=EC91 S=AB09 NR=7
   59   0.184     59   XNS SPP A D=EC91 S=AB09 NR=7
   60   0.186    215   XNS SPP   D=EC91 S=AB09 NR=7 NS=9
   61   0.186     59                           XNS SPP A D=AB09 S=EC91 NR=10
   62   0.188     59                           XNS SPP A D=AB09 S=EC91 NR=10
   63   0.206     83                           XNS SPP   D=AB09 S=EC91 NR=10 NS=7
```

Figure 25-6. NetWare Named Pipes Sniff: 10 KByte File; Elapsed Time = 0.206 Secs.

Commentary

- According to the NetWare Named Pipes Sniffer trace, it takes 0.206 seconds to transfer a 10 KByte file. This translates into a 48.5 KByte/s transfer rate.
- The equivalent result using FX timers is 45.5 KByte/s (see Table 25-3). We're validated.
- Note how NetWare Named Pipes use the XNS protocol.
- The NetWare Named Pipes protocol didn't perform as well as some of the other protocols in our test runs. But then, don't take our word for it; run your own tests and perform your own validations before coming to a final conclusion!

LAN Server Sniff

```
SUMMARY Rel Time  Size    From Server     From Client

       2  -1.006    32  NETB Session alive
       4  -0.036    77                   SMB C Get File Attributes
       5  -0.031    87  SMB R OK
       7  -0.024    77                   SMB C Get File Attributes
       8  -0.019    87  SMB R OK
M     10   0.000   106                   SMB C Open \10k.fil
      11   0.009    97  SMB R Opened F=0000
      13   0.080    32                     NETB D=17 S=25 Data ACK
      14   0.097  4188                   SMB C F=0000 Write Block Raw 10000 at 0
      15   0.097    69  SMB R OK
      17   0.117  4192                     NETB D=17 S=25 Data, 4160 bytes
      18   0.119  1776                     NETB D=17 S=25 Data, 1744 bytes
      19   0.120    32  NETB D=25 S=17 Data ACK
      21   0.123    95                   SMB C Set File Attributes
      22   0.128    67  SMB R OK
      24   0.133   130                   SMB C Transact2 SetFileInfo
      25   0.135    90  SMB R Transact2 (Interim Response)
      27   0.139    73                   SMB C F=0000 Close
      28   0.143    67  SMB R Closed
      33   0.184    32                     NETB D=17 S=25 Data ACK
```

Figure 25-7. LAN Server Sniff: 10 KByte File; Elapsed time = 0.184 Secs.

Commentary

- According to the LAN Server Sniffer trace, it takes 0.184 seconds to transfer a 10 KByte file. This translates into a 54.3 KByte/s transfer rate.
- The equivalent result using FX timers is 52.6 KByte/s (see Table 25-3). We're validated.
- Note how the LAN Server uses the SMB protocol on top of NetBIOS.

CONCLUSION

The FX benchmarks demonstrate that existing peer-to-peer protocols can meet current BLOB transfer requirements (a typical business document is 75-100 KBytes). Our test results show that these typical BLOBs can be moved in subseconds. And, we could have done twice as well using 16 Mbit/sec Token Ring and faster PCs.

However, we foresee an enormous surge of bandwidth demand with the introduction of new multimedia PC clients (the standards are now coming into place). The current protocols and hardware will be very hard pressed to keep up with the new BLOB transfer requirements. Full motion video, for example, requires 300 KBytes/sec (30 frames/sec, each compressed frame holding 10 KBytes or more). So keep an eye on BLOB traffic; it can easily gridlock your LANs!

Part IV

The Database Manager

The chapters in Part IV teach you how to program the OS/2 Extended Services Database Manager that provides the SQL Server component of the client/server platform. An SQL network server provides the *heart* of both the Database and Transaction Server platforms. The effort you spend understanding what an SQL server can do for you is well worth it. There is no better productivity "enabler" available for writing robust distributed applications that involve shared data. What are the software structures that best take advantage of that power? To answer this question, we go beyond the normal textbook expositions of SQL as a query tool or a decision-support language. Instead, we look at SQL as a key ingredient for building client/server, industrial-strength applications that run over networks. This means that Part IV will focus on issues such as:

- Transaction processing
- Referential Integrity
- Remote Procedure Calls
- Fine-tuning a production database
- The administration of a production database

We assume no prior knowledge on your part, so we kick-off Part IV with a complete three-chapter tutorial on the Database Manager's programming interfaces. As usual, we focus on the material that is of interest to C-language programmers. Following the tutorial, we run a set of command *scripts* that demonstrate the power of SQL and the special Database Administration Services that supplement it. These scripts are created and executed using **RSQL**, an "all-in-one" utility program that we develop in subsequent chapters of Part IV. To put it modestly, RSQL is a world-class hacker's tool for probing into the OS/2 Database Manager. You can use RSQL to run SQL command scripts, fine-tune the database, look at the system configuration parameters, run reports, and measure performance. There is nothing in the Database Manager that you can't get at with a simple RSQL script. In addition, the RSQL program itself serves as a template for production-quality SQL code. We will dissect the RSQL program and use it as an exhaustive example of how to write code for the OS/2 Database Manager.

Here is the roadmap we will follow in Part IV:

- In Chapter 26, "OS/2 Database Manager API Tutorial," we provide a tutorial on the Database Manager's SQL services. We introduce embedded SQL and cover all the static and dynamic SQL constructs.
- In Chapter 27, "Tutorial on the Database Administration Services," we provide a tutorial on the Database Administration Services and DDCS/2. These are the services used to automate the maintenance, performance-tuning, and control of a database engine.
- In Chapter 28, "RSQL: The "All-In-One" Database Manager Utility," we introduce RSQL and use it to run various scripts that demonstrate the concepts covered in the tutorials.
- In Chapter 29, "RSQL: Programming Dynamic SQL," we use the RSQL program as an example of how to write Dynamic SQL code.
- In Chapter 30, "RSQL: Programming the Database Administration API," we use the RSQL program as an example of how to program SQL extensions provided by the Database Administration Services.

Chapter 26

OS/2 Database Manager API Tutorial

This chapter starts out by presenting a taxonomy of the Database Manager's services. This will serve as your navigation map for the Database Manager's API services. Following the taxonomy, we present an in-depth tutorial on the Database Manager's SQL services. These are the key services provided by an SQL engine. The tutorial introduces embedded SQL and covers all the static and dynamic SQL constructs.

A TAXONOMY OF THE DATABASE MANAGER API SERVICES

The Database Manager API services (see Table 26-1) fall into two broad categories: the SQL API and the Database Administration API. The Database Manager also provides an API to the Query Manager, which we will not be covering because it falls in the domain of tools.[1] Here's a brief overview of the main API categories and their respective subcategories.

1. **The SQL API:** The Database Manager is primarily a SQL language processor. It implements the SQL command set as defined by the ANSI standard and with some SAA superset extensions. The SQL command statements are either precompiled or dynamically created at run time. SQL commands are not issued through the traditional API calls. Instead, they are treated like a separate language whose statements are *embedded* within a C-language program. You can think of it as a "language within a language." Before the program is submitted to a C-language compiler, the SQL language statements are precompiled during the program preparation process. The precompiler replaces the SQL statements with calls that are recognized by the C-language compiler. We will present the trade-offs of precompilation later in this chapter. In accordance with tradition, the taxonomy scheme employed in Table 26-1 further subdivides the SQL commands into four subcategories:

---

[1] Many tool vendors support the OS/2 Database Manager. Some, like Enfin/3, provide very graphical query pickers, report writers, screen painters, business graphics, and decision support capabilities.

Table 26-1. A Taxonomy of the Database Manager's API Services.

SQL API	Database Administration API	
Data Definition Language	**Environment Services**	**Application Services**
CREATE	START DATABASE MGR	BIND with options
DROP	STOP DATABASE MGR	RETRIEVE MESSAGE
ALTER TABLE	CREATE DATABASE	
COMMENT ON	START USING DATABASE	**General Utilities**
	STOP USING DATABASE	BACKUP DATABASE
Data Manipulation Language	RESTART DATABASE	RESTORE DATABASE
	DROP DATABASE	ROLL FORWARD DATABASE
DELETE	CHANGE DATABASE COMMENT	EXPORT TABLE
INSERT	MIGRATE DATABASE	IMPORT TABLE
SELECT	CATALOG DATABASE	RUNSTATS TABLE
UPDATE	UNCATALOG DATABASE	REORG TABLE
	CATALOG NODE	GET ADMIN AUTHORIZATION
	UNCATALOG NODE	
Data Control Language	CATALOG DCS DATABASE	**Configuration Services**
COMMIT	UNCATALOG DCS DATABASE	RESET DATABASE
ROLLBACK	OPEN DATABASE	CONFIGURATION FILE
GRANT	DIRECTORY SCAN	UPDATE DATABASE
REVOKE	GET NEXT DATABASE	CONFIGURATION FILE
LOCK TABLE	DIRECTORY ENTRY	GET COPY OF DATABASE
	CLOSE DATABASE	CONFIGURATION FILE
	DIRECTORY SCAN	RESET DATABASE MANAGER
Program Language Constructs	OPEN NODE DIRECTORY SCAN	CONFIGURATION FILE
	GET NEXT NODE ENTRY	UPDATE DATABASE MANAGER
BEGIN DECLARE	CLOSE NODE DIRECTORY SCAN	CONFIGURATION FILE
SECTION	OPEN DCS DIRECTORY SCAN	GET COPY OF DATABASE MANAGER
END DECLARE	GET DCS DIRECTORY	CONFIGURATION FILE
SECTION	ENTRY FOR DATABASE	
DECLARE CURSOR	GET DCS DIRECTORY ENTRIES	**Generic Services**
OPEN	CLOSE DCS DIRECTORY SCAN	LOG ON
CLOSE	INSTALL SIGNAL HANDLER	LOG OFF
FETCH	INTERRUPT	
PREPARE	DATABASE APPLICATION	
EXECUTE	REMOTE INTERFACE	
EXECUTE	COLLECT DATABASE STATUS	
IMMEDIATE	GET NEXT DATABASE	
DESCRIBE	STATUS BLOCK	
INCLUDE	GET USER STATUS	
WHENEVER	FREE DATABASE	
SELECT INTO	STATUS RESOURCES	

- *Data Definition Language (DDL)* consists of SQL commands that define database objects such as tables, views, and indexes. The DDL is also used to define the integrity constraints on the objects created. This allows the Database Manager to ensure that the things users do to those objects are correct.
- *Data Manipulation Language (DML)* consists of SQL commands through which users can select, update, insert, or delete rows of information. These data access and manipulation functions are, of course, the principal reason for using the Database Manager.
- *Data Control Language (DCL)* consists of SQL commands that control the execution of other SQL commands. Controls must be provided to protect the

database against a variety of possible internal and external threats. The controls manage the recovery, concurrency, security, and consistency aspects of a database. This includes controlling the execution of a transaction and undoing its effects if it fails. This also includes obtaining and releasing locks during the course of executing a transaction. Finally, the DCL provides commands for authorizing the access to tables, views, and database objects.

- *Program Language Constructs* consist of the SQL commands that cannot be issued in interactive SQL mode. These SQL commands can only be issued from a programming language. Their purpose is to facilitate the interfacing of SQL to procedural languages such as C. They allow C-language applications to share variables with the SQL sublanguage and to mediate between SQL's set-orientation and the C-language's row-at-a-time limitation. The program language constructs also provide the mechanisms for a C program to prepare and execute SQL statements dynamically.

2. **The Database Administration API:** The Database Manager makes a rich set of database administration services available to your application through standard API calls. These services complement the SQL language and make it possible for your programs to automate, view, and control almost every aspect of the database engine. Our taxonomy (see Table 26-1) further subdivides the database administration API into five subcategories of commands:

- The *Environment Services* are used to manage the environment of a database. They include the commands through which you can create and delete a database. Once a database is created, you can start or stop using it. Using environment commands, you can also catalog databases and maintain database directories.
- The *General Utilities* enable you to write programs that automate and control the maintenance operations on individual databases. As an example, you can program an application to perform a daily database backup or to periodically reorganize tables to enhance performance.
- The *Application Services* are useful in developing your programs.
- The *Generic Services* are used to log on and log off.
- The *Configuration Services* allow you to view or change the configuration parameters that affect database performance, the degree of concurrency, and resource utilization.

In the rest of this chapter, we explain the Database Manager's SQL services. We introduce embedded SQL and cover all the static and dynamic SQL constructs. In the next chapter, we will explain the Database Administration Services.

THE SQL API

Programming the SQL API is very different from the OS/2 call-based API model we've encountered so far in this book. Understanding what makes the SQL API different will prepare you for the anticipated "culture shock" of programming in SQL. We start out this section by first giving you a brief history of SQL and the benefits it provides. Then we explain the SQL sublanguage model and tell you about the changes in "style" it requires from C programmers. We end the section with a brief description of the SQL verbs and what they each do.

The Origins of SQL

The Relational model of database management was developed at IBM's San Jose Research Lab in the early 1970s by E.F Codd. SQL was developed, also in San Jose, in the mid-1970s to serve as an "English-like" front-end query language to the System R Relational database prototype. Even though the SQL language is "English-like," it is firmly rooted in the solid mathematical foundation of set theory and predicate calculus. What this really means is that SQL consists of a short list of powerful, yet highly flexible, *verbs* that can be used to manipulate information collected in tables. Through SQL, you manipulate and control *sets* of records at a time. You tell the SQL Database Manager what data you need; then it figures out how to get to the data. The Relational model frees you from having to concern yourself with the details of how the data is stored and makes the access to data purely logical. Using SQL statements, you only need to specify the tables, columns, and row qualifiers to get to any data item.

Oracle Corporation was the first company to offer a commercial version of SQL with its Oracle database in 1979. In the early 1980s, IBM came out with its own SQL products: SQL/DS and DB2. Today, over 200 vendors offer SQL products on PCs, superminis, and mainframes. Most of these products are based on the SQL standard that the X3H2 Database Committee of ANSI started developing in 1982. The ANSI standard, which was ratified in 1986, is very similar to IBM's DB2 dialect of SQL. The ANSI X3H2 committee is currently working on a specification of SQL extensions. The OS/2 Database Manager's SQL conforms to ANSI SQL and is nearly identical to its IBM mainframe brethren. This is not surprising considering that SQL is SAA's Database Access language and OS/2 has been designed from the ground up with SAA compatibility in mind.

The Benefits of SQL

SQL provides a number of advantages to system builders:

- SQL enforces the separation of data from code.
- SQL relies on the Relational model, which is modular and versatile.
- SQL enforces a good methodology for data definition. Conveniently, the same language that is used to define the database is also used to manipulate it.
- SQL provides a high-level data manipulation language, thus enhancing productivity and cutting down on errors.
- SQL provides security.

- SQL provides good reliability features such as data validation, referential integrity, rollback (undo transaction), automatic locking, and deadlock detection and resolution in a multiuser LAN environment.
- SQL provides utilities for the import of files into and the export of files from database tables. Utilities are also provided for maintaining and fine-tuning the database.
- SQL provides an active data dictionary. The structure and organization of an SQL database is stored in the database itself.
- SQL brings to the PC world a database administration methodology and allows better communication between PC programmers and Database Administrators. Data is now better defined and documented in a PC environment.
- SQL can be embedded as a sublanguage within the C language.
- SQL provides a consistent language for programming with data. This raises programmer productivity and helps produce a more maintainable and easy to change system.
- SQL provides an excellent vehicle to specify product requirements in an unambiguous manner. This helps communications between customers, developers, and Database Administrators.
- SQL is supported as an SAA and ANSI standard.

By combining the SQL transaction discipline with the C language, we can now create an OS/2 Server platform for the development of LAN-based transaction processing.

"Them" versus "Us"

When you first start using SQL in your programs, you are likely to experience acute "culture shock." Don't worry, it's only natural. Like "our C programming subculture," SQL has its own strong subculture with folk heroes, gurus, and "set ways for doing things." These people have created some de facto standards for how SQL is to be used from within a programming language such as C. The bottom line is that they want us to use their SQL sublanguage "as is" within the C language. Incidentally, they view this process as extending SQL with procedural capabilities. Here is the price a C programmer pays for this intercultural marriage:

- We have to use the (.SQC) extension for any source code file that contains embedded SQL statements.
- We have to run the (.SQC) source file through their precompiler, **SQLPREP**, to generate the (.C) source code file that our compiler understands.
- We have to locate the errors our compiler reports against the statement line numbers from the (.C) file. Then we need to locate and change the corresponding statement in the (.SQC) file.
- We have to have a running database with fully defined tables as part of the code preparation process. This means that you have to define and create your data tables before you can compile any code.

- We have to store the SQL packages (also known as plans) prepared by the precompiler into a database.
- We have to look at the funny code their precompiler generates while debugging our code.
- We have to match their data types to our C-language types. In many cases, they don't exactly match.
- We have to learn a whole new vocabulary from the world of Database Administrators (DBAs) and SQL transaction processing.

Fortunately, there are benefits to be obtained from doing things their way:

- The SQL sublanguage is almost independent of the programming language, compiler, and operating system used. This means that you can embed the same sublanguage statements in C, Cobol, or Pascal with only a few minor changes. With some additional minor changes, the same sublanguage program can easily be ported to SAA and other SQL engine platforms.
- We've retained the use of the C-language for writing procedural code. The alternative could have been letting "them" design a new procedural language for SQL, as some database vendors have done (wrongly in our opinion).
- The precompiler separates SQL processing from the C-language statements, which means that new SQL features can easily be introduced with minimum impact.
- We've gained the full power of SQL and the non-procedural discipline it entails.
- It is remarkably easy and productive to program in the SQL sublanguage.

In the coming sections we help you overcome the SQL culture shock so that you can take full advantage of this powerful sublanguage. And who knows, perhaps once you've gotten over the minor irritations, you may turn into an SQL true-believer and overcome the "us" vs "them" barrier.

Embedded SQL: The Precompile and Bind Process

A SQL precompiler is a tool the Database Manager provides for extending the C language with the power of the SQL data management language. The result is a powerful combination of SQL's non-procedural *set-at-a-time* constructs with the C-language's flexible procedural constructs. A precompiler processes your source code replacing SQL statements with C-language statements, and the result is "modified source" code that can be processed by the C Set/2 compiler.

A precompiler provides four functions:

- It manages the C-language variables that can be used directly inside SQL statements. These common variables are called *host-variables*.

- It checks the validity of SQL statements including the user's authority to issue such statements. This includes verifying that the table names and columns referenced in your SQL statements actually exist and that their types are compatible with the host-variables declared in your programs.

- It generates a *modified source* C-language file. It does that by generating a (.C) file that can be compiled by a C-language compiler. The embedded SQL statements are changed into comments and the appropriate API calls are generated in their place. The precompiler takes as its input a (.SQC) file (see Figure 26-1) containing your C-language source and embedded SQL statements.

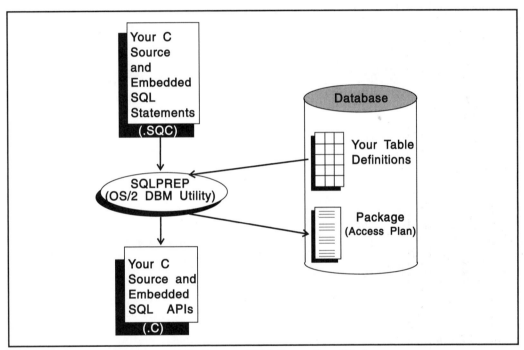

Figure 26-1. The SQL Precompile Process With Immediate Bind.

- It builds *packages* that contain access plans that tell the database engine how each SQL statement should be executed.[2] These access plans use sophisticated heuristics that optimize the data access strategy based on the current state of the database. The access plans are stored as objects in the database. The process of storing the access plans is called *binding*. The access plans are part of a package. You can bind the packages to the database during precompilation (see Figure 26-1) or do it later through a separate bind utility (see Figure 26-2). If you want to defer the binding, the precompiler will store the packages it creates in *bind files* with (.BND) extensions. You can bind the (.BND) files at a later time with the production database of

---

[2] The term package was introduced in the current release of Database Manager. DRDA uses the term package to refer to plans.

your choice (see Figure 26-2) through either the **SQLBIND** utility or by issuing an API call. The DRDA architecture allows you to bind these packages to other SAA databases including DB2, SQL/DS, and the AS/400 Database Manager. The packages become portable interchange units of SQL code. The bind attaches the packages to the database environment of choice.

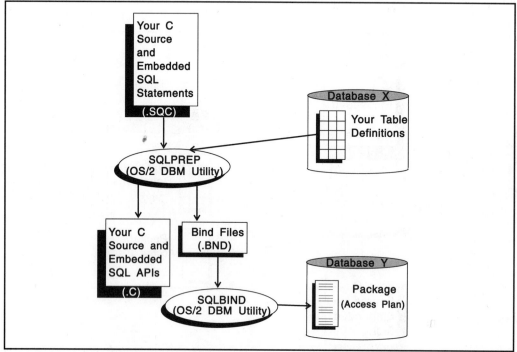

Figure 26-2.   The SQL Precompile Process With Deferred Bind.

Embedded SQL: The Command Syntax

An embedded SQL statement or precompiler directive must start with the **EXEC SQL** key-word pair and end with a semi-colon "**;**". These bracketed statements will be processed by the precompiler and anything else in your source code will be passed through unchanged. An embedded SQL statement can span across multiple lines, as shown in the following example:

```
EXEC SQL CREATE TABLE JUNK (NAME       VARCHAR(16) NOT NULL, -- SQL comment
                      PROFESSION VARCHAR(20),            /* C   comment */
                      AGE        SMALLINT,               -- SQL comment
                      SALARY     DECIMAL(7,2));          /* C   comment */
```

Embedded SQL: Static versus Dynamic SQL Commands

- **Static SQL** statements are defined in your code and converted into an access plan by the precompiler at program preparation time. The SQL statement is known before your program is run. The database objects need to exist when precompiling static SQL statements. You can think of static SQL as being a compiled form of the SQL language. Static SQL is a performance enhancement feature.

- **Dynamic SQL** statements are created and issued at run time. They offer maximum flexibility at the expense of execution speed. You can think of dynamic SQL as an interpretive form of the SQL language. The database objects need not exist when precompiling dynamic SQL statements. The compilation of dynamic SQL statements is done at run time and must be repeated every time the same statement gets executed again.

In this book, we will be using static SQL for writing highly optimized transaction programs, and dynamic SQL for writing general database programming utilities.

Embedded SQL: Error Handling

You may be wondering how error information gets passed from the embedded sublanguage to C. This information passing is done through a fixed-size global data structure called the **SQL Communications Area,** or **SQLCA**. This is an SQL defined data structure that returns error return codes and warnings after the execution of each SQL statement or Database Manager API call. We will develop some techniques for database error handling in later sections.

Embedded SQL: Host Variables

The *host variable* is the primary mechanism the SQL sublanguage provides for the exchange of data between a C-language application and embedded SQL statements. The idea is to get data from your program into the database and from the database into your program, where you can provide additional manipulation. Host variables are nothing more than C-language variables that are preceded by a colon ":" whenever they are placed inside an SQL statement. Here are some rules for using host variables from within C-language programs:

- Declare the host variables to the precompiler before referencing them in an SQL statement.
- You can have multiple precompiler host variable declaration sections within one source file.
- From the C-language perspective, host variables can be local or global, and their storage class can be *extern*, *static*, or *auto*.

- From the precompiler perspective, host variables are global to a source file. This means a host variable must have a unique name within a source file, even if it is declared as a local C variable.
- Almost any C-language data type can be used as a host variable. Here are some of the features:

    - C pointers are supported.
    - C arrays are supported, provided that the array-size is explicitly declared.
    - C-language structures are acceptable host variables, but the embedded fields are not. For example, **structure_name.field_name** is not allowed; but **structure_name** is allowed.
    - C-language data type macros are not supported.

- You can initialize host variables; however, the SQL precompiler will not validate initialized data values.
- Your host variables must be of a data-type compatible with the SQL table column types to which they correspond. Table 26-2 provides a list of the main Database Manager SQL column types and their C-language host variable equivalents.

Embedded SQL: The SQL Descriptor Area (SQLDA)

In addition to host variables, the SQL sublanguage provides a predefined C-language structure called the **SQLDA** through which a C-language program can exchange data with embedded SQL statements. The **SQLDA** is used mainly by Dynamic SQL programs that have no previous knowledge of the data types that are used in a SQL statement. Here are the three main uses of the **SQLDA**:

1. To return a description of the SQL command to an application program. This includes the name, length, and type of variables used by the Dynamic SQL statement. SQL provides two verbs for this purpose: **PREPARE** and **DESCRIBE**.
2. To pass data and to receive data from the SQL statements. You can use the **SQLDA** instead of host variables where the C language does not have a corresponding column type, or for Dynamic SQL row fetches where the column data type is not known previously.
3. As a general-purpose self-describing data buffer used with the **Application Remote Interface** database services. This is the Database Manager service that allows clients to execute stored SQL procedures on remote servers. The **in_sqlda** structure is used to pass inbound parameters to the stored procedure, and the **out_sqlda** structure is used to return the results.

Embedded SQL: SQL Types and C-Language Data Types

Table 26-2. The Correspondence Between SQL Column-Types and C-Language Data Types.

Table Column SQL Data Type	SQL Type Number	SQL Type Description	You Can Use This C Data Structure
SMALLINT	500	16-bit, signed integer	short or short int
INTEGER	496	32-bit, signed integer	long or long int
FLOAT	480	8-byte floating point	double
DECIMAL(p,s)	484	Packed decimal	Not supported in C. Use double instead with some loss of precision.
CHAR(1)	452	1 char fixed-length	char or unsigned char
CHAR(n)	452	n-byte char string	char[n] 1 <= n <= 254
VARCHAR(n)	460	Variable length string (null terminated by SQL).	char[n] 1 <= n <= 4000

VARCHAR(n)	448	Variable length string (not null terminated by SQL length indicator field used). Is used to store binary data. Declare column for BIT DATA.	struct {short length;
			        char data[n];
			      }var_name;
			where 1 <= n <= 4000

LONG VARCHAR(n)	456	Variable length string (not null terminated by SQL length indicator field used). Is used to store bulk data such as text, code, or images.	struct { short length;
			        char data[n];
			      } var_name;
			where 1 <= n <= 32700

DATE	384	10-byte char string	char[10]
TIME	388	8-byte char string	char[8]
TIMESTAMP	392	26-byte char string	char[26]
NULL	..	NULL indicator flag used to indicate NULL data in column.	short

The SQL Data Definition Language (DDL) Commands

The SQL Data Definition Language is used to define and maintain the user created database objects: tables, views, indexes, and packages (access plans). The DDL is also used to define the *referential integrity* relationships between table objects.

Objects in General

Objects here, are things about which Database Manager retains information. Loosely speaking, a database is an administrative entity that provides the context for a collection of related named objects such as tables, views, and indexes (see Figure 26-3). The Database context includes such things as: system catalogs, recovery logs, passwords, disk directories, and memory. User objects are always accessed from within the context of a database. What follows is a description of the user objects that are managed through the DDL.

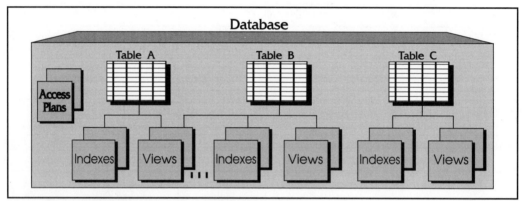

Figure 26-3.   User Objects Within a Database Context.

The Table Object

A table object, also known as the *base* table, is the most basic database object. Like all major objects, a table has a name and an optional comment. Tables are defined as a series of *columns* each of which is identified by a name, a data type, and an optional comment. Each table is an unordered collection of rows; each has a fixed number of columns. Unlike the rows, columns in a table are ordered from left to right just as they appear in the **CREATE TABLE** command. Each column has a SQL data type (see Table 26-2) used by the Database Manager to ensure that only data of the correct type gets put in the tables. In addition, you can specify the following optional *column constraints*:

- A column may be specified as NOT NULL, which causes the Database Manager to enforce that a value gets supplied for that column with every insert or update.
- A character column can be specified FOR BIT DATA to indicate that it contains binary non-textual information. In the default mode, the Database Manager assumes character columns to contain valid ASCII characters. The effect of FOR BIT DATA is not to translate the data when going to a machine with a different code page.
- A column may be identified as being part of a *primary key* or *foreign key* as part of the table definition. More on that when we discuss referential constraints.

The View Object

Views provide "logical tables." These are tables that do not exist in physical storage but consist of data obtained through a query against one or more tables. Views do not contain data; instead, they refer to data stored in base tables. A view is defined as a query against other base tables and/or other views. When a view is created, the Database Manager stores the query under a named view object. The query itself is not issued. A view is a way of creating "windows" through which data in base tables can be viewed. These windows can be used to simplify the view of data, to reorder columns, or to rename a table.

Views can also be used to enforce data security. For example, by creating a view, you can restrict data access to certain rows and columns in the base tables. Views, like base tables, can be used to retrieve, update, or delete data. There are some exceptions; for example, data from a view that is created by joining two tables cannot be inserted, updated, or deleted. A **join** is a query that combines information from two or more tables. A view may be created with the WITH CHECK OPTION constraint. This constraint is a data integrity check that causes all data inserts and updates through that view to be checked for compatibility with the search condition of the view definition.

The Index Object

An index object consists of a set of pointers that are logically ordered by the values of a key. A *key* consists of one or more columns that identify one or more rows within a table. An index object provides a way for defining keys outside of the table definition. It also stores a pointer to the key values of each row in an indexed table. The pointers are stored in B-Tree format, which speeds up row access and updates. You typically create indexes on frequently accessed columns to improve performance. One or more indexes may be defined on a table. Each index key consists of one or more columns, and, optionally, an attribute that specifies the order in which to access the rows (either ascending or descending). Typically, index keys are used in the following situations:

- To speed up the retrieval of data. If an index is present, the Database Manager may use an *index scan* instead of the usual *table scan*. What this means is that an index B-Tree is searched for matches instead of sequentially searching through every table row. The performance improvements in reading data have to be weighed against the costs of maintaining the index B-Tree during updates and inserts.
- To uniquely identify a table row. A *unique index* key defines exactly one row in a table and is used by the Database Manager to enforce that each row in a table is unique (i.e., no two rows will have the same values in their unique index columns). This helps maintain the integrity of the information in a table. If you specify a unique index, then the database will make sure you do not create duplicate rows. This may help reflect real world situations where, for example, duplicate departments make no sense.

- To speed up the joining of tables by indexing the join columns.
- To speed up referential integrity checks.

You're only involvement with indexes is to define them. After that, the Database Manager retains full control of when to use an index for retrieval. The Database Manager is also fully in charge of maintaining the indexes and keeping them synchronized with the underlying base tables.

Object Naming Conventions

User object names normally follow a two-level naming convention. A qualified name consists of an authorization-id qualifier, followed by a period, followed by the name you assign to the object. The *authorization-id* identifies a database user; it can be up to 8 characters long and cannot contain lowercase letters, the underscore character, or begin with numerals or the reserved words: IBM, SQL, and SYS. The *object name* is the name you assign to the object. The object name does not have special character restrictions. Typically, you refer to an object through its unqualified name. The authorization-id is implied by the context. However, in multiuser situations you should use fully qualified names to keep track of which user owns which objects. An object gets assigned the authorization-id of the user that created it. Here's a "trivial pursuit" guide to the length of object names:

- The names of columns, correlations, cursors, indexes, tables, and views can be from 1 to 18 characters long.
- A fully qualified column name uses a three-level naming convention consisting of: the authorization-id, a period, then the name of a table or view followed by a period, and finally the name of the column.
- The names of packages, constraints, and databases can only be up to eight characters long.
- A password consists of 4-8 characters.

Referential Relationships

The Database Manager provides, through *referential constraints*, a mechanism which ensures that cross-references between tables are always valid. What this means is that, if there is a reference to something, then that something should exist; otherwise, the reference is invalid. The rules for referential integrity are specified as part of the **CREATE TABLE** statement through two sets of keys:

1. **Primary Key.** This is a key that uniquely identifies a single row within a table. The primary key consists of one or more columns; none of which can be null. Each table can have only one primary key. A Unique Index is automatically created by the Database Manager for the primary key, which means you do not have to issue a separate CREATE UNIQUE INDEX command.

2. **Foreign Key**. This is a key that points to (or references) a primary key. The foreign key columns must match those of the primary key one for one. A foreign key establishes a referential link to a primary key. Each table (including the one with the primary key) can have one or more optional foreign keys.

A foreign key link to a primary key establishes a *referential constraint* between information stored in one or more tables. Through these referential constraints, the Database Manager will enforce, on your behalf, the integrity of dependent data (foreign key data) on parent data (primary key data). Referential constraints may be created between columns on the same table or in different tables. A table is *self-referencing* when it contains both the primary key and the foreign key.

The example in Figure 26-4 will help clarify these relationships. It shows these three referential constraint links:

- The link between the dept_num foreign key on the EMPLOYEE table and the dept_num primary key on the DEPARTMENT table. In this link, the EMPLOYEE is the *dependent* table and DEPARTMENT is the *parent* table.
- The link between the mgr_id foreign key and the empl_id primary key; both are on the same EMPLOYEE table. This is an example of a *self-referencing* table.
- The link between the empl_id foreign key on the HOME_PHONE table and the empl_id primary key on the EMPLOYEE table. In this link, the EMPLOYEE is the *parent* table and HOME_PHONE is the *dependent* table.

As you can see from the figure, a table can be a parent, a dependent, or both, in an arbitrary number of referential constraints. The figure also shows that a particular table can have multiple foreign keys, but only a single primary key is allowed.

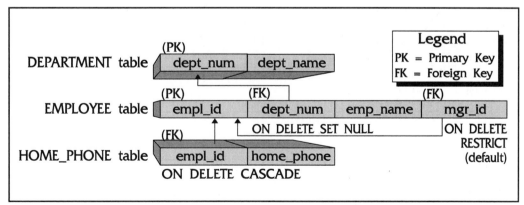

Figure 26-4. Referential Constraint Elements: Primary Keys and Foreign Keys.

Enforcing Referential Integrity

Once you've defined the relational constraints, here is what the Database Manager can do for you in terms of integrity checks:

- It will check for the existence of the primary keys when a table with foreign keys is first created.
- It will check for the existence of a primary key value that matches the non-null value of the foreign key for every row that is inserted or updated in a dependent table.
- It will prevent the update of primary key data in the parent table if any dependent rows are found through matching foreign key values.
- It will enforce a user-specified rule on dependent rows when a row is deleted from the parent table. The action taken on dependent rows is specified in the *Delete Rule* for the foreign key and can be one of the following:

   RESTRICT   means don't let the parent row get deleted if it has dependents. This is the default action.

   CASCADE   means if the row gets deleted from the parent table, then delete the dependent rows too.

   SET NULL   means if the row gets deleted from the parent table, then set to null the foreign key fields in the dependent rows.

An Example of Referential Integrity Rules Enforcement

The rules defined on the foreign keys in Figure 26-4 have the following effects:

- If a row is dropped from the DEPARTMENT table, then dept_num column is set to NULL for all the rows in the EMPLOYEE table that have employees belonging to the dept_num being dropped. This is consistent with the ON DELETE SET NULL *delete rule,* which in effect says: "If the department is dropped, then set the dept_num value to an unknown for all the employees that belong to that department." Note that if we had chosen instead to impose the ON DELETE CASCADE rule, then all the employees in the dropped department would have gotten immediately "terminated" (by getting dropped from the EMPLOYEE table). So, setting the dept_num to NULL is a nice way of keeping the employees on the payroll until they get reassigned to a new department!

- An attempt to drop a row from the EMPLOYEE table will cause the following to happen:

  1. First, a check is made to see if the empl_id in the row to be dropped is a manager; this is true for any row in the EMPLOYEE table that has a mgr_id value equal to the empl_id being dropped. If a match occurs, then the drop will fail because of the RESTRICT rule that has been placed on the foreign key. What the referential constraint rule is in effect saying is: "Anybody is free to leave except managers" (perhaps they've been given tenure...).

2. The delete succeeds if the employee is not a manager. In this case, the Database Manager will automatically delete the employee's home phone row from the HOME_PHONE table. This is consistent with the CASCADE rule which says: "If an employee is no longer there, then there is no need for that employee's home phone number either."

The DDL and the User Objects

Table 26-3 provides a quick summary of the function each SQL DDL command provides. If you think of the SQL command as the "verb" that operates on an object, then ideally you should be able to apply each DDL verb to every object. Unfortunately, this is not the case. Here is a guide to the different verb/object combinations:

CREATE   This verb breaks down into three SQL verbs: **CREATE TABLE**, **CREATE VIEW**, and **CREATE INDEX**. Each SQL verb has its own distinct syntax structure.

DROP   This verb breaks down into five SQL verbs: **DROP TABLE**, **DROP VIEW**, **DROP INDEX**, **DROP PACKAGE**, and **DROP PROGRAM**. The five verbs have an identical structure. It consists of the verb followed by the name of the object to be dropped. The **PROGRAM** object is another name for a package (or access plan). You can delete a package through the SQL API, but a package can only be created through the Precompile and Bind process described earlier.

ALTER   This verb can be used only on **TABLE** objects. Other objects that need to be altered should be dropped and then recreated.

COMMENT ON   This verb can be used on **TABLE** and **VIEW** objects as well as on the individual columns in a table or view object.

Table 26-3 (Part 1 of 3).   The SQL Data Definition Language (DDL).

SQL Command	Description
| **CREATE TABLE** | This command is used to define a base table.  You need to provide a table name and define all table columns up to a maximum of 255 columns.  Note that the maximum length of a row (not including LONG VARCHAR) is 4005 characters.  Each column must have a unique name and a SQL data type.  You can define a column as NOT NULL if you want the Database Manager to enforce that a value is supplied for that column with every INSERT or UPDATE.  A character column is to be specified FOR BIT DATA if it will contain binary data.  You may specify referential constraints through the PRIMARY and FOREIGN key clauses.  The REFERENCES keyword is used to identify the table on which the PRIMARY KEY resides.  The Database Manager will check for the existence of the referenced PRIMARY KEY when creating the table.  You can optionally include an ON DELETE rule with the FOREIGN KEY.  Note that PRIMARY KEY or FOREIGN KEYs that consist of single columns may be specified as part of the column definition instead of via a separate key clause.  The statements that follow will create the set of tables you previously encountered in the Referential Integrity example.<br><br>```
EXEC SQL CREATE TABLE department      /* primary KEY on column */
         (dept_num    SMALLINT NOT NULL PRIMARY KEY,
          dept_name   VARCHAR(20));
EXEC SQL CREATE TABLE employee         /* separate KEY clauses  */
         (empl_id     INT NOT NULL,
          dept_num    SMALLINT REFERENCES department,
          emp_name    VARCHAR(40) NOT NULL,
          mgr_id      INT,
          PRIMARY KEY (empl_id),
          FOREIGN KEY mgr(mgr_id) REFERENCES employee);
EXEC SQL CREATE TABLE home_phone          /* separate KEY clause*/
         (empl_id     INT NOT NULL,       /* with rule          */
          home_phone  CHAR(10),
          FOREIGN KEY homenum(empl_id) REFERENCES employee
                      ON DELETE CASCADE);
``` |
| **CREATE VIEW** | This command defines a view.  You provide the view name, the optional names of the columns in the view, and the SELECT query that defines the scope of the view.  A view may be created from one or more base tables or views.  You may specify an integrity check on the view with the optional WITH CHECK OPTION, which indicates that any updates or inserts to the view must be checked against the view definition.  These updates or inserts are rejected if they do not satisfy the view defining conditions.<br><br>```
Example: EXEC SQL CREATE VIEW managers (manager_name,department)
              AS SELECT emp_name,dept_num
                 FROM employee WHERE empl_id = mgr_id
                 WITH CHECK OPTION;
``` |

Table 26-3 (Part 2 of 3).   The SQL Data Definition Language (DDL).

SQL Command	Description

CREATE INDEX	This command creates an index on a table. You provide an index name and specify the name of the table and the columns that constitute the index. You can optionally specify the index as being UNIQUE. The index is created by default in ascending order; you can change that to a descending order index by including the DESC keyword.
	
	`Example:  EXEC SQL CREATE UNIQUE INDEX xhome_phone1`
	`                     ON home_phone (empl_id DESC);`

DROP TABLE	This command is used to delete a table and all its dependent objects. You specify the name of the table you want dropped, and it will be deleted from the catalog along with all its dependent indexes, views, primary keys, and foreign keys. Access plans that reference the table or its dependent objects are invalidated. `Example:  EXEC SQL DROP TABLE home_phone;`
DROP VIEW	This command is used to delete a view and all its dependent objects. You specify the name of the view you want dropped, and it will be deleted from the catalog along with any dependent views. Any access plans that reference the view or dependent views are invalidated. `Example:  EXEC SQL DROP VIEW managers;`
DROP INDEX	This command is used to delete an index. You specify the name of the of the index you want dropped, and it will be deleted from the catalog. Any access plans that reference that index are invalidated. `Example:  EXEC SQL DROP INDEX xhome_phone1;`
DROP PROGRAM	This command is used to delete an access plan. You specify the name of the access plan you want dropped, and it will be deleted from the catalog. `Example:  EXEC SQL DROP PROGRAM xyz;`
DROP PACKAGE	This command is synonymous with DROP PROGRAM (used in the previous version of the product). This command was introduced for SAA-compliance. `Example:  EXEC SQL DROP PACKAGE xyz;`

Table 26-3 (Part 3 of 3). **The SQL Data Definition Language (DDL).**

SQL Command	Description

ALTER TABLE	This command allows you to add new columns or referential constraints to an existing table. New columns are added after the last column to the right of the table to preserve the order of the original columns. Consequently, access plans created before the table is altered will remain valid. The format for the column attributes and referential constraints is similar to that of CREATE TABLE. You must specify the keyword ADD when adding new columns and the keyword DROP to delete PRIMARY or FOREIGN keys. You do not need to include the ADD keyword when adding a new referential constraint.
	
	`Examples:`
	`EXEC SQL ALTER TABLE home_phone    /* Add an address column    */`
	`            ADD address VARCHAR(100);`
	
	`EXEC SQL ALTER TABLE home_phone    /* Drop homenum foreign key */`
	`            DROP FOREIGN KEY homenum;`
	
	`EXEC SQL ALTER TABLE home_phone    /* Add homenum foreign key  */`
	`            FOREIGN KEY homenum(empl_id) REFERENCES employee`
	`                        ON DELETE RESTRICT;`

COMMENT ON TABLE	This command adds or replaces comments in the catalog description of tables or views. The IS keyword is used to introduce a comment string that can be up to 254 characters long.
	
	`Example:   EXEC SQL COMMENT ON TABLE home_phone`
	`                       IS 'This table employee home phone numbers';`

COMMENT ON COLUMN	This command adds or replaces comments in the catalog description of columns. The IS keyword is used to introduce a comment string that can be up to 254 characters long.
	
	`Example:   EXEC SQL COMMENT ON COLUMN home_phone.empl_id`
	`                       IS 'This column serves as a foreign key';`

The SQL Data Manipulation Language (DML) Commands

The SQL Data Manipulation Language provides the verbs used for entering and manipulating data (after you've defined the database and created its tables, indexes, and views). The **SELECT** verb is the heart of the SQL DML language and is used for retrieving information. The power of SELECT lies in its ability to construct complex queries with an infinite number of variations using a finite set of rules. The SELECT verb is recursive, meaning that the input of a SQL statement can be the output of a successive number of nested SELECTs. For example, nested SELECT subqueries can be embedded within the **INSERT**, **UPDATE**, **DELETE**, and **CREATE VIEW** SQL commands.

To do anything useful with SQL, you will need to fully master the SELECT command and understand its various subtleties. In the following sections, we start you off with the most rudimentary form of SELECT, and then use it as a base from which we introduce progressively more sophisticated (and perhaps less used) features.

The "Minimal" SELECT

The SELECT verb in its most basic form consists of the **SELECT-FROM-WHERE** statement whose structure is shown below:

```
EXEC SQL
    DECLARE cursorname CURSOR FOR
      SELECT <selection_list>
      FROM   <table_list>
      WHERE  <search_condition> ;
```

- The **selection_list** is the comma-separated list of columns that you want to retrieve. An asterisk "*" can be used to obtain all the columns in a table without listing each column name. SELECT by default returns all the rows that match the query conditions including duplicate rows. The DISTINCT qualifier can be used to retrieve only the unique rows that match the query. The selection_list can also be used to perform arithmetic operations on data you select and to compute values for a group of rows based on column functions such as average or sum.

- The **table_list** is the comma-separated list of tables or views that are used in the query. The table_list also defines *correlated names*. These are shorthand alternate names for tables or views, which are used when joining a table to itself or with subqueries that uses the same table name.

- The **search_condition** describes the rows in which you are interested and consists of one or more predicates. A *predicate* specifies a test that you want Database Manager to apply to each row of a table and evaluates to "true," "false," or "unknown." One or more predicates in a search can be combined by using parentheses or Boolean operators such as AND, OR, and NOT. When the predicates result in "true," it means that the SQL statement is to be applied to that row; "false" means no operation is required for that row. Predicates compare a column with a value or a column with another column from the same table or from different tables. A *basic predicate* compares two values; a *quantified predicate* compares a value with a collection of values. All values specified in predicates must be of compatible types:

  - Numbers can only be compared with numbers. The Database Manager performs temporary conversions to match number types when necessary.
  - Strings can only be compared with strings.
  - Date and Time can only be compared with Date and Time types or string representations of Date and Time.

Predicates use the familiar relational operators as well as a variety of special operators to specify the condition to be evaluated in the search. SELECT statements can also be embedded within certain predicates; they are called *subqueries* when used in this mode. The following is a list of the comparison operators that can be used in predicates:

Logic Operators   These are the familiar relational operators: =, <>, <, >, <=, >=, NOT. These operators can be used to compare two expressions, or an expression with the result of a subquery. The NOT operator can be used to form the negative of any of the other operators.

IS NULL   Is used in a predicate to test for NULL expressions.

BETWEEN...AND   Is used in a predicate to compare a value with a range of values. The search condition is satisfied by any value that falls between the two specified values.

IN   Is used in a predicate to test group membership. The group can be specified through a subquery or through lists of values in a statement.

LIKE   Is used in a predicate to search for strings that match certain patterns. The special matching character "%" may be used for an unknown string of zero or more characters. The underscore character "_" may be used as a pattern match for any single character.

EXISTS   Is used in a predicate to test for the existence of certain rows. The predicate is true if the subquery returns one or more rows.

ALL   Is used in predicates that involve subqueries. A predicate is true when the specified relationship is true for *all* rows returned by a subquery. It is also true if no rows are returned.

SOME or ANY   Are used in predicates that involve subqueries. The predicate is true when the specified relationship is true for *at least one* row returned by a subquery.

The Ordering of Output Rows

A relational database has no explicit order. However, the output of a query can be sorted by applying the ORDER BY clause on the columns you want to order by. The output will follow the ascending order by default. You can override the default by specifying the DESC keyword on descending order columns. You can name the columns to order by, or you can use a number. For example, ORDER BY 2 specifies that you want the results ordered by the second column as specified in the query.

Column Functions

Built-in functions and expressions are supported as part of the SELECT column-list statement. These functions operate on the aggregate values of a single column and produce a single result (nulls are not part of the calculation):

- SUM returns the sum of all the values in a column.
- AVG returns the average of all the values in a column.
- MAX returns the largest value in a column.
- MIN returns the smallest value in a column.
- COUNT returns the number of values in a column.

The special function COUNT(*) is provided to count all rows in a table without the elimination of duplicates.

Arithmetic Operations

You can use the SELECT column-list statement to perform arithmetic operations on the data you select before the data is presented to your program. This may be useful if you want to evaluate the effects of certain changes before updating the database. The following arithmetic operators are supported: +, -, *, and /.

Groups and Summaries

Summary rows can be obtained with GROUP BY and HAVING clauses, which allow you to find out the characteristics of groups of rows as opposed to those of individual rows. The GROUP BY operator groups all rows that have the same value for a given column into a single row. The Database Manager then processes each group to produce a single-row result for the group. The SELECT clause, when applied to groups, is used with functions that return a single value for a given column within a group. HAVING can be thought of a "WHERE clause for groups," and is used as a search condition for eliminating groups just as WHERE is used as a search condition for eliminating rows. This means HAVING can only be used with GROUP BY.

JOIN

Join is a powerful feature of relational databases that allows you to retrieve data from two or more tables by means of a single SELECT statement. The SELECT retrieves the requested information based on matching column values in the tables involved. The Database Manager supports joins that include up to 15 tables.

Subqueries

A subquery is a query within a query. These nested queries appear within the search condition of a WHERE or HAVING clause. A subquery may be used within a search condition for the INSERT, DELETE, and UPDATE SQL commands. A subquery may include search conditions of its own, and these search conditions may in turn include subqueries. The Database Manager first performs the innermost query and uses the results to execute the next outer SQL statement, and so on. The subquery can either return a single value or a set of values. The set of values requires the use of the keywords IN, ALL, ANY, SOME, EXIST, and NOT EXIST.

Correlated Subqueries

Correlated Subqueries are special cases of subqueries where the inner SELECT executes once for each result row in the outer SELECT. You use a correlated subquery to search for some value that can be different for each row.

UNION, EXCEPT, and INTERSECT

These are set operations that can be applied on the result sets from different SELECT statements. The SELECT statements must have the same number of columns. The columns must have equivalent types; none of which can be a LONG VARCHAR.

UNION   Combines or "merges" the result tables of two SELECTs and eliminates duplicate rows.

EXCEPT   Generates a result table consisting of all unique rows from the first SELECT statement that are not generated by the second SELECT statement.

INTERSECT   Generates a result table consisting of unique rows that are common in the results of two SELECT statements.

The "Full-Featured" SELECT

The SELECT verb in its full-featured form consists of six clauses; except for SELECT-FROM, all clauses are optional:

```
EXEC SQL
   DECLARE cursorname CURSOR FOR
      SELECT   <ALL or DISTINCT > <selection_list>
      FROM     <table_list>
      WHERE    <search_condition>
      GROUP BY <column_names>
      HAVING   <search_condition>
      ORDER BY <column_names> ;
```

The SELECT Statement and the SQL API

Here are the different ways the SELECT statement can appear in your code:

- Through a DECLARE CURSOR if the SELECT statement returns multiple rows
- Through a SELECT INTO statement to retrieve one row of data
- Through the PREPARE statement for a Dynamic SQL command (this also includes the processing of a cursor)
- Through a subquery that is part of the search condition of another SQL command such as INSERT, DELETE, or UPDATE

What this means in terms of our code taxonomy scheme is that even though the multirow SELECT statement is the most important DML command, it can only be invoked through the DECLARE CURSOR, which falls under Program Language Constructs SQL API category. The more constrained SELECT INTO call is also included under the Program Language Constructs because it can only be issued through a programming language and has no interactive SQL equivalent. The taxonomy shown in Table 26-4 is therefore in line with the "purist" SQL division. It also shows the kinks introduced when bridging between the set-based tradition of SQL and our row-at-a-time procedural orientation.

Table 26-4. **The SQL Data Manipulation Language (DML).**

SQL Command	Description
SELECT	This command is used to retrieve rows from tables. The general format of the SELECT command was introduced earlier in this section. The SELECT can be embedded in SQL subqueries issued by INSERT, UPDATE, and DELETE. The direct execution of a multirow SELECT requires the DECLARE CURSOR construct. A single-row SELECT can be directly executed with the SELECT INTO verb (also see SQL Program Language Constructs).
INSERT	This command is used to add new rows to a table or a view. You can specify VALUES for a single column to be inserted, or you can include a SELECT statement in the INSERT statement that tells the Database Manager that the data for the new rows is contained in another table or view. In either case, you must supply a value for each non-null column. ```Examples: EXEC SQL` ` INSERT INTO home_phone (empl_id, home_phone)` ` VALUES (905,'4082223333');` ` EXEC SQL` ` INSERT INTO home_phone` ` VALUES (906,'4152224444');` ` EXEC SQL` ` INSERT INTO home_phone (empl_id)` ` SELECT empl_id FROM employee` ` WHERE dept_num = 40 ;``
UPDATE	This command allows you to change data in a table. This is a set operation, which in this case means one command will change the value of one or more columns in all the rows that satisfy the search condition of a WHERE clause. ```Example: EXEC SQL /* shows the use of host variables */` ` UPDATE employee` ` SET dept_num = 333,` ` mgr_id = :pgm_mgrid` ` WHERE dept_num = :pgm_dept;``
DELETE	This command allows you to remove entire rows from tables. This is a set operation, which in this case means that one command will delete all the rows that satisfy the search condition of a WHERE clause. If you omit a WHERE clause, all rows from that table will be deleted. ```Examples: EXEC SQL` ` DELETE FROM employee` ` WHERE dept_num = 333;` ` EXEC SQL /* all rows are deleted from the table */` ` DELETE FROM employee;``

The SQL Data Control Language (DCL) Commands

The SQL Data Control Language (DCL) consists of verbs that perform transaction management, locking, and data access control. The DCL verbs control the execution of other SQL verbs in order to ensure the consistency and security of the database in multiuser environments. In this section, we discuss how the Database Manager provides data consistency, crash recovery, data integrity, and security in a multiuser network environment. At the end of this lengthy introduction, we present the DCL verbs that are used with those services.

Data Consistency

Data Consistency refers to the capabilities of Database Manager for maintaining the quality and integrity of data in a multiuser environment. In a network environment requests for database services may be concurrently generated by remote clients. How does Database Manager protect your data from the inconsistencies that can be introduced in a multiuser environment? There are three kinds of inconsistencies that can happen during the concurrent execution of requests for database services: lost updates, dirty reads, and non-repeatable reads.

- A *lost update* is caused by two users who read the same record at about the same time and then each perform an update. Without the proper database consistency protection, one of the updates is lost.
- *Dirty reads* occur when one user submits a transaction that updates a database but subsequently gets undone or "rolled back." If in the meantime a second user had read the same data before the rollback, that user would be working with "dirty" data (i.e., it does not exist anymore). Obviously, this is an integrity violation.
- *Non-repeatable reads* occur when one user reads data that subsequently gets altered by another user. If the first user rereads the data, the value read will be different from what was obtained the first time. The implication is that two or more read operations on the same data may yield different results (i.e., non-repeatable reads).

The Database Manager solves the problems of data consistency through two techniques: *transaction control* and *locking*.

Transaction Control

A *transaction* is the fundamental unit of recovery, consistency, and concurrency in the Database Manager. A "database" transaction consists of one or more related SQL commands that are treated as a single *unit of work*. Either all the commands within the unit of work complete fully, or the effects of every command get "undone" fully. A transaction terminates with either a **COMMIT** verb, which makes all the database changes permanent, or a **ROLLBACK** verb, which cancels the changes and returns the database to its previous commit point state. Figure 26-5 shows the effects of a successful transaction and one that fails. The successful transaction transforms the system from an initial consistent state to a final consistent state. The unsuccessful transaction undoes its work and leaves the system in the previous consistent state (all the intermediate work gets rolled back). A transaction may be aborted by a user program that detects an error and then issues a rollback (suicide); or it may be aborted by external events like a power failure or a deadlock tiebreaker, in which case the system issues the rollback (murder).

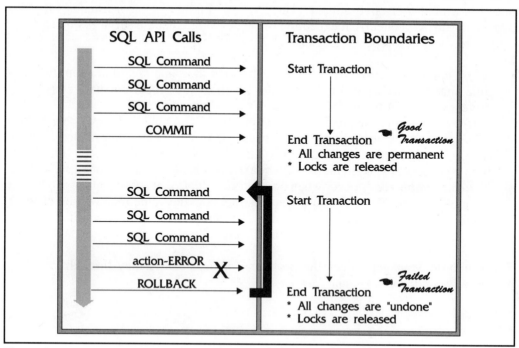

Figure 26-5. A Transaction Groups a Sequence of SQL Commands as an Atomic Unit.

Transaction Logs and Crash Recovery

Crash recovery requires a clean termination of a program. We've seen how transactions provide "all or nothing" protection and ensure that either all of the requested services are performed or none are. Thus, a program terminates and produces either the intended results or none at all. The Database Manager uses a write-ahead log technique in which before and after images of the transaction are kept on a log file. If the system crashes or the transaction gets aborted, the system can rollback the unsuccessful updates using the before and after image files.

Another technique called *roll forward* is used to recover a damaged database. This technique requires that all database updates be recorded on a log file that resides in a separate device. In case of a database disk crash, the logged updates are applied against the last backed-up copy of the database to provide a recovered database. The current release of the Database Manager includes the "roll forward" capability.

Transactions and Concurrency

In addition to being a *unit of recovery*, a transaction is also a *unit of consistency*. At the end of each transaction, the system releases all locks, cursors, and dynamically pre-pared SQL statements created or acquired during a transaction. An SQL application should always be divided into a number of sequential transactions. In environments where many active transactions are accessing the database at the same time, the number and type of SQL commands that make up a transaction can dramatically affect the concurrency of a system. Consequently, transactions that execute in concurrent environments should be written at a much finer level of granularity while not compromising the consistency of the data. It is your responsibility to define, through transactions, the acceptable units of recovery and consistency for your application. It is the Database Manager's responsibility to automatically provide the right amount of locking to keep the database consistent (at the isolation level you specify) on transaction boundaries. Note that only one transaction at a time can be active on each process or remote application.

Locking

The Database Manager provides data consistency by introducing various locking techniques down to the row level. The effect of the various locks is to serialize, in one way or another, multiaccess to shared resources. Locking techniques have to provide a sufficient degree of *isolation* for users to maintain control over the data they are working on; without locking out other users for prolonged durations. This is a delicate balancing act.

The good news is that once you've structured your SQL application into transactions, the Database Manager will then automatically handle locks on your behalf. The Database Manager obtains the required locks at the start of a transaction and releases all locks when a transaction ends. It is never necessary for your programs to explicitly request locks. However, the **LOCK TABLE** verb gives you a way to override the Database Manager's rules for acquiring locks; but use it sparingly because it will negatively effect concurrency. Note that no corresponding verb is provided for explicitly locking individual table rows; only the Database Manager can do that. The only way you can effect row locking is by following the transaction discipline. Also, where possible, let your intentions be known so that you can help the Database Manager act smarter on behalf of your application. There are at least three ways you can communicate your intentions to the Database Manager:

- You can specify FOR UPDATE OF in a SELECT clause. This states your intention to update a certain column at a later time.
- You can delay issuing the statements that acquire locks until the time when you actually need them. For example, you can delay issuing an OPEN CURSOR command that contains a FOR UPDATE clause and increase the concurrency of your application.
- You can specify the required *isolation level* when precompiling or binding your application. The isolation level tells the Database Manager how much isolation from other processes your data requires.

Isolation Levels

Besides the exclusive lock required during an update, there are various levels of locking associated with database reads. This is an area where you're given the latitude to specify lesser levels of locking in exchange for higher levels of performance. The Database Manager allows you to specify one of three **isolation levels** or "degrees of isolation" required during database *reads*:

- **Read Repeatability** is the level that provides the most isolation for your reads. In fact, you obtain the same amount of locking that is provided for updates. This level of locking may be required for non-browsing applications such as a financial report generator. With this level of isolation, any rows acquired by your transaction (for SELECT or UPDATE) cannot be altered (but they can be read) by another transaction. Your transaction will hold locks on any row it touches until it completes. This stringent level of isolation provides maximum protection and guarantees that you will get the same result from a SELECT statement throughout the duration of a transaction. The trade-off for this higher level of isolation is less overall concurrency.

- **Cursor Stability** is the default level of isolation. It provides an intermediate level of locking where only the current row pointed to by a SQL cursor is locked instead of all the rows involved in a query. This means other transactions can read or update rows that your transaction previously read. However, you retain exclusive locks for rows on which the cursor is currently positioned. As a result of this more relaxed level of isolation, you can reissue the same SELECT statement at a later point in a transaction, and get a different set of result rows each time. On the positive side, cursor stability enhances the overall level of concurrency in the system.

- **Uncommitted Read** provides the least amount of isolation. This is essentially an option to run without "read" locks, which therefore has little effect on transaction processing rates. Any application can read uncommitted data that may subsequently be rolled back. There are two situations where some protection is provided: (1) When the read cursor is for UPDATE; and (2) when an application is about to drop the table.

This highly relaxed level of isolation may introduce some mysterious bugs into your programs and should be used only in "safe" situations, such as applications that browse only.

In summary, the Database Manager uses its *under-the-cover* locking schemes to guarantee that no program will have access to data that has been changed by another program but not yet committed, unless it is using the Uncommitted Read isolation level.

Deadlocks

Wherever there are locks, the danger of *deadlocks* looms. This "side effect" is caused when two transactions go after the same set of resources and each holds the resource the other needs to complete the job. The result is that both transactions get locked out and wait indefinitely. The Database Manager overcomes this problem by providing a deadlock detection and resolution mechanism. This is a background task that comes to life at a user-specified wakeup interval and then looks for deadlocked transactions. If a deadlock is detected, the deadlock detector breaks it by declaring one transaction the "winner" and the other the "victim." The deadlock detector kills the victim's transaction (a -911 error code is returned); consequently, all its locks are released. The "winner" transaction resumes work where it left off. The "victim" transaction will need to be restarted by the application.

Authorization and Privileges

These are the mechanisms the Database Manager provides to ensure that multiple users can share a database and retain control over their objects. Security of the database is handled at two levels:

- At the workstation level, where OS/2 provides a *User Profile Management (UPM)* facility for handling the common security needs of all of its services. This includes the Communications Manager, the Database Manager, and the LAN Server program. For example, it does not make sense for you to define a user ID, password, and authentication process for each service you want to use; instead, the UPM provides a single authentication system for the entire workstation.
- At the Database Manager level, where SQL provides its own authorization subsystem that extends security to individual database objects. SQL provides a very granular level of security that defines the authority (or privilege) of a user to perform certain actions on certain objects.

User Profile Management (UPM) Services

When the Database Manager is first installed, part of the installation procedure involves the automatic creation of the UPM facility for the workstation. The UPM provides a default *superuser* (defined as USERID) with a predefined password (defined as PASS-WORD). The *superuser* or system administrator can do anything that involves security on any of the Database Manager components on that machine. For example, the *superuser* is automatically given a SYSADM authority that allows the user to perform every database operation the system supports. If you are interested in securing your database, we suggest you follow these steps:

1. Log on to the UPM from the OS/2 Desktop as the *superuser*.
2. Add the user ID and password of your *administrator*.
3. Delete the *superuser* entry from the UPM. This will prevent anyone who has read this section of the book from taking full control of your machine.
4. Add to the UPM the authorization IDs and passwords of all the users of your database, including remote requesters.
5. Give the users a UPM authority of *user*. Only the UPM administrator can define a user to UPM.

Now your system is secure at the UPM level. Users and administrators will have to identify themselves through the LOGON command, which requires a valid UPM password and authorization ID.

The SQL Authorization Facility

The Database Manager's authorization subsystem provides the next level of defense after the UPM. It controls which objects and resources you can access or create, based on your authorization ID. Granting rights is done using the SQL **GRANT** command; revoking rights is done through the SQL **REVOKE** command. The authorization subsystem maintains a system of privilege hierarchies (see Figure 26-6) that closely parallel the object hierarchies you've already encountered. To perform any SQL operation, the user must have the appropriate authority for that operation. More specifically, the Database Manager provides three broad levels of control:

- Control at the system level specifies the authority needed to create the system itself, including the database.
- Control at the database level specifies the authority needed to create objects within an existing database. It also specifies the authority required just to connect to a database.
- Control at the individual object level specifies the authority to manipulate specific objects that exist within a database.

Protection Level	Protection Services	Authority or "Privilege"
Workstation	Authority to log on to database "services" privided by the OS/2 User Profile Manager (UPM)	User ID and password
Database Manager	Authority to create a database and control any Database Manager resource	SYSADM
Individual Database	Authority to control a database	DBADM
	Authority to connect to a database	CONNECT
	Authority to create tables	CREATETAB
	Authority to create packages (aka plans)	BINDADD
Individual Object	Authority on a table, view, plan or index	CONTROL
	Limited privileges on tables and views	ALL ALTER (table only) DELETE INDEX (table only) INSERT REFERENCES (table only) SELECT UPDATE
	Limited privileges on plans	BIND EXECUTE

Figure 26-6. Authorization and Privilege Hierarchies.

Authorization at the System Level

SYSADM   This is the highest level of authority the Database Manager provides; It is needed to create a new database. In addition, only a user with this authority level can perform the following tasks:

- Create or drop a database.
- Catalog or uncatalog remote workstations and databases.
- Migrate a database or reinstall the Database Manager.
- Change the database configuration file.
- Restore a database from backup.
- Grant or revoke the next highest level of authority: DBADM.

When the database is created, the creator is automatically given unlimited privileges to any database object; this is the DBADM level of authority. CONNECT, CREATETAB, and BINDADD privileges are automatically granted to the PUBLIC for the new database.

Authorization at the Database Level

DBADM   This is the second highest level of authority. A user with this level of authority has unlimited privileges on any object within a specific database. Only users with DBADM (or SYSADM) authority can:

- Backup the database.
- Grant and revoke lower level privileges, including CREATETAB, BINDADD, CONNECT, and CONTROL.

CREATETAB   This level of authority enables a user to create tables in the database.

BINDADD   This level of authority enables a user to create new packages (access plans) in the database.

CONNECT   This level of authority enables a user to connect to the database.

Authorization at the Object Level

CONTROL This level of authority provides a user full control over a specific database object, such as a table, package, or index. The creator of an object obtains automatic CONTROL privilege for that object. The creator of a view does not automatically receive CONTROL privileges, and can only have privileges on that view equal to those held for each of the tables referenced by the view. SYSADM and DBADM users have automatic CONTROL privileges on any database object.

Here is what each of the CONTROL privileges lets you do at the individual object level:

- With **table objects**, the CONTROL privilege allows you to reorganize the table and run statistics against it. In addition, it provides a full set of privileges on any of the table operations. These privileges can, in turn, be granted to other users of the table. Here is a breakdown of the more limited table privileges:

ALTER	Allows you to alter the base table and primary key definition.
INSERT	Allows you to insert rows into the table.
UPDATE	Allows you to change rows in the table.
DELETE	Allows you to delete rows from that table.
SELECT	Allows you to run selects against the table.

INDEX Allows you to create indexes on that table. The creator of the index automatically gets CONTROL privileges on that index.

REFERENCE Allows you to specify referential constraints which specify the table as the parent in a foreign key.

ALL is a short-hand keyword for all of the privileges on tables listed above.

- With **index objects**, the CONTROL privilege allows you to drop a specific index on a specific table.

- With **package objects**, the CONTROL privilege allows you to rebind a specific plan, execute it, and drop it. In addition, you can grant to others the more limited privilege to:

BIND is the authority to rebind the package.

EXECUTE is the authority to execute an existing package.

- With **view objects**, the CONTROL privilege works differently depending on whether the view is:

  - **updatable**, where a user with CONTROL authority can drop the view or perform a full set of view operations; the user can in turn grant authority to other users. These operations are SELECT, INSERT, UPDATE, or DELETE.
  - **not-updatable**, where a user with CONTROL authority can drop the view, but they can only perform or grant the SELECT operation.

The DCL SQL Commands

After this lengthy introduction to the SQL transaction management, locking, and authorization services, we are now positioned to introduce the verbs that participate in those functions. The DCL commands consist of a surprisingly small number of verbs, as shown in Table 26-5. **COMMIT** and **ROLLBACK** provide transaction management. **LOCK TABLE** is used for explicit locking. The **GRANT** and **REVOKE** commands are used to interface to the SQL authorization services.

Table 26-5 (Part 1 of 2).   **The SQL Data Control Language (DCL).**

SQL Command	Description

COMMIT	This command is used to terminate a transaction and make the changes to the database permanent. All the locks acquired by the transaction are released, except table locks for open cursors that are declared WITH HOLD. All open cursors not declared WITH HOLD are closed. All dynamically prepared SQL statements not associated with a WITH HOLD cursor are destroyed; likewise, prepared statements that reference open cursors defined WITH HOLD are retained. Database changes are automatically committed when an application terminates normally or when it issues a stop using the database.
	
	`Example:   EXEC SQL`
	`           COMMIT WORK;    /* The keyword WORK is optional */`

ROLLBACK	This command is used to terminate a transaction and "undo" any database changes that were made. All the locks acquired by the transaction are released, all open cursors are closed, and all dynamically prepared statements are destroyed. If a program terminates abnormally, the Database Manager issues an automatic rollback.
	
	`Example:   EXEC SQL`
	`           ROLLBACK WORK;  /* The keyword WORK is optional */`

LOCK TABLE	This command allows you to acquire a shared or exclusive lock on the named table. A shared mode lock acquires the lock for the transaction that executes the command and only lets other transactions access the table for read-only operations. The exclusive mode lock prevents concurrent transactions from executing any operations on the identified table unless they are using the Uncommitted Read isolation level.
	
	`Examples: EXEC SQL               /* Other programs are not     */`
	`          LOCK TABLE employee /* allowed to read/update table*/`
	`          IN EXCLUSIVE MODE;`
	`          EXEC SQL              /* Other programs can read    */`
	`          LOCK TABLE employee /* from table but not update   */`
	`          IN SHARE MODE;`

Table 26-5 (Part 2 of 2). The SQL Data Control Language (DCL).

SQL Command	Description

GRANT	This command grants authorization privileges to other users. Privileges are granted ON objects, TO specific authorization IDs, or PUBLIC (meaning everybody). The privileges or authorizations are the ones we presented earlier in this chapter. The objects are DATABASE, TABLE name, PROGRAM name, and INDEX name. The keyword TABLE is optional; if a name immediately follows the ON keyword, it is assumed to be a table or view.
	
	`Examples: EXEC SQL         /* Granting a privilege to many   */`
	`          GRANT CONNECT    /* users, sales is a group name  */`
	`          ON DATABASE TO Bob, Jeri, Sales;`
	`          EXEC SQL                       /* Granting many          */`
	`          GRANT CREATETAB, BINDADD /* privileges to one user*/`
	`          ON DATABASE TO Sandy;`
	`          EXEC SQL         /* Granting a privilege          */`
	`          GRANT EXECUTE  /* to all users                  */`
	`          ON PROGRAM plan1 TO PUBLIC;`
	`          EXEC SQL         /* Granting control privileges   */`
	`          GRANT CONTROL  /* on a table to all users       */`
	`          ON TABLE employee TO PUBLIC;`
	`          EXEC SQL         /* Granting all privileges on a  */`
	`          GRANT ALL      /* table to a group of users     */`
	`          ON TABLE salary TO managers;`

REVOKE	This command revokes authorization privileges from users. Privileges are revoked ON objects, FROM specific authorization IDs, or PUBLIC (meaning everybody). The privileges or authorizations are the ones we presented earlier in this chapter. The objects are DATABASE, TABLE name, PROGRAM name, and INDEX name. The keyword TABLE is optional; if a name immediately follows the ON keyword, it is assumed to be a table or view.
	
	`Examples: EXEC SQL              /* Increase security after   */`
	`          REVOKE CONNECT /* creating a database        */`
	`          ON DATABASE FROM PUBLIC;`
	`          EXEC SQL                       /* Revoking many          */`
	`          REVOKE CREATETAB, BINDADD  /* privileges to    */`
	`          ON DATABASE FROM Sandy;  /* a single user    */`
	`          EXEC SQL         /* Revoking a table privilege */`
	`          REVOKE SELECT`
	`          ON TABLE salary FROM Sales;`
	`          EXEC SQL         /* Revoking most privileges on*/`
	`          REVOKE ALL     /* a table from a group name  */`
	`          ON TABLE salary FROM managers;`

The SQL Program Language Constructs (PLC) Commands

The Program Language Constructs (PLC) consist of commands and constructs that facilitate the use of SQL with programming languages, such as C. The PLC commands provide the following:

- Precompiler directives for declaring host variables
- A precompiler directive for processing error codes
- Cursor manipulation
- The SELECT... INTO command for retrieving a single row
- Dynamic SQL processing

Precompiler Declarations

These directives tell the precompiler where to find host variables and "common" data structures to include. The **BEGIN DECLARE SECTION** and **END DECLARE SECTION** tell the precompiler where to find host variables. The **INCLUDE** command is used to declare the SQLCA and SQLDA data structures. As was previously described, the SQLCA conveys error information from the embedded SQL sublanguage to the C program; the SQLDA is used for the passing self-describing data.

The Precompiler Directive for Processing Error Codes

The Database Manager provides a **WHENEVER** directive that instructs the precompiler to generate source code that checks the SQLCA return codes and directs an application to a specified label. Essentially, you can instruct the precompiler to generate code for three types of conditions:

- **Errors**, which return a negative sqlcode.
- **Warnings**, which return a positive sqlcode.
- **Row not found**, which is an sqlcode of 100.

You can also tell the precompiler not to generate code by using the CONTINUE keyword.

Cursor Manipulation

A database *cursor*, like its famous cousin the familiar blip on the screen, is a pointing mechanism. The database cursor points to rows and enables procedural languages, such as C, to handle SQL queries that extract multiple rows called a *result set*. Using the cursor as a pointer, you can navigate from a C program through a set of rows, one row at a time, and pick out the information you need. Here is how a cursor works:

1. Issue a **DECLARE CURSOR** command to associate a cursor name with a particular SELECT statement. The cursor name is used by your program as a handle for that cursor-based SELECT.

2. Issue an **OPEN** command on that cursor, which conceptually causes the SELECT to execute and produce a result set. The cursor will be positioned before the first row.

3. Issue a **FETCH** command repeatedly on the opened cursor. Each fetch execution positions that cursor to the next row in the result set and then retrieves that row.

4. Issue an UPDATE or DELETE command with the keyword **CURRENT** to update or delete a row on which the cursor is currently positioned.

5. Issue a **CLOSE** command, to close the cursor after you're done with processing the rows in the result set.

The SELECT... INTO for Retrieving a Single Row

The Database Manager provides a "non-cursored" version of the **SELECT** command, which allows you to place the row contents directly **INTO** the specified host variables. You can only use this command to retrieve a single row of data. If more than one row is returned, it will result in an error condition. You'll find this command to be of limited use, because most queries generally produce "result sets" that consist of multiple rows of data. In addition, you cannot use this command with dynamic SQL which only supports the cursor-based SELECT.

Dynamic SQL Commands

Dynamic SQL commands provide maximum flexibility by piecing together SQL statements for execution at run time. This flexibility comes at a price. Your programs must now handle dynamically prepared SQL statements whose fields and data types may vary with each call. You may also have to handle data types, tables, and table structures that are totally unknown at the time you write the program. The dynamic SQL statement is built up as a null-terminated ASCII string variable (up to 32765 characters). Your choice of method for dynamically preparing and executing the statement will depend on the nature of the command and how much information is available about host variables in the statement to be executed. The following four methods, presented in order of increasing complexity (and increased flexibility), illustrate how the dynamic SQL verbs are used:

- The simplest form of dynamic SQL execution is the **EXECUTE IMMEDIATE** command, which prepares and executes an SQL statement in a single operation. The statement to be executed cannot be a SELECT or contain any program variables or parameter markers.

- The second form of dynamic SQL execution separates the preparation of the command from its execution by using a two separate verbs: **PREPARE** and

EXECUTE. With this method, you can place in your dynamic SQL statements a fixed number of placeholders for variables whose data types are fixed. These placeholders, also called *parameter markers*, are represented in an SQL statement by a question mark "?" for each program variable. A statement is prepared once and assigned a name. The name can then be executed multiple times using different parameter values each time. The separation of **PREPARE** from **EXECUTE** means that the access plan does not have to be recreated for each execution. This improves the performance in situations where the same statement gets repeatedly re-executed. This two-step execution also allows you to prepare multiple statements before any are executed. However, all statements must be prepared again once a transaction ends.

• The third form of dynamic SQL execution combines the **PREPARE** verb with a cursor mechanism. This method is used for the dynamic execution of SELECT statements whose columns are fixed and known at precompile time. Here's how you do it:

1. Issue a **DECLARE CURSOR** on a string variable. Contrast this with static SQL, where the full text of the select is declared as a cursor.
2. Issue a **PREPARE** to assign the dynamically prepared select statement to the cursor that was previously declared on the string variable.
3. Retrieve rows using these cursor verbs: **OPEN, FETCH** and **CLOSE**.
4. You can reuse the cursor serially by issuing an **OPEN USING** with different parameters each time. This is done without "re-preparing" the select statement.

The only limitation of this method is that you are required to know ahead of time the number of columns being fetched and their type. This is because the INTO clause expects a fixed number of host variables, whose types are declared at precompile time.

• This fourth method of dynamic SQL execution provides the greatest amount of flexibility. This is because it makes no assumptions about the types of SQL statements used or on the number of host variables and their data types. All of this is discovered at run time by issuing a **PREPARE** with a **SQLDA**. The Database Manager parses the statement to be prepared and places its description into the **SQLDA**. This includes a description of the data type, length, and name of each column in the statement. A **DESCRIBE** command is provided, which places a description of a dynamic SQL statement into the **SQLDA** without precompiling it or creating an access plan. This provides a way of obtaining the type and description of a dynamic SQL statement before executing it. Using either of those verbs you have all the necessary information in the **SQLDA** to process the statement dynamically. Be warned, however, that a substantial amount of code is required to decipher all the SELECT parameters and their column names and types using the **SQLDA** as a descriptor.

The Program Language Constructs (PLC) SQL Commands

Now that you know all about cursors and dynamic SQL, we can describe the verbs that provide those functions. The PLC verbs and precompiler directives are briefly described in Table 26-6.

Table 26-6 (Part 1 of 5). The SQL Program Language Constructs (PLC).

SQL Command	Description
BEGIN DECLARE SECTION	This precompiler directive marks the beginning of a host variable declaration. This statement may appear in the application program wherever C-language variable declarations can. This statement must be paired with a END DECLARE SECTION statement and may not be nested. SQL statements cannot be included within the declare section. Variables referenced in SQL statements must first be declared in a declare section. Variable names must be unique both inside and outside the declare section. ``` Example: EXEC SQL BEGIN DECLARE SECTION; double emplid; /* these host variable */ short vdeptnum; /* descriptions represent*/ char empname[41]=""; /* the columns of the */ double mgrid; /* EMPLOYEE table */ EXEC SQL END DECLARE SECTION; ```
END DECLARE SECTION	This precompiler directive marks the end of a host variable declare section (see BEGIN DECLARE SECTION above).
INCLUDE	This precompiler directive inserts declarations for a SQLCA or SQLDA into a source program. When your program is precompiled, the INCLUDE statement is replaced by source statements. Space is allocated for a sqlca variable; however, you must allocate space for the sqlda variable yourself. You can do this allocation with the Database Manager provided macro, SQLDASIZE, which returns the SQLDA size in bytes. ``` Examples: EXEC SQL INCLUDE SQLCA; /* declares a variable */ /* sqlca of type SQLCA */ EXEC SQL INCLUDE SQLDA; /* declares a definition */ /* for a SQLDA struct */ struct sqlda *sqlda = NULL;/* declare a pointer */ /* to a sqlda */ slqda = malloc(/* obtain dynamic memory for SQLDA */ SQLDASIZE(10)); /* size macro for 10-element SQLDA */ ```

Table 26-6 (Part 2 of 5). The SQL Program Language Constructs (PLC).

SQL Command	Description

WHENEVER	This precompiler directive specifies the action to take when a specified exception condition occurs. The exception can be NOT FOUND, SQLERROR or SQLWARNING. The action can be GOTO a specified address, or CONTINUE.
	
	 ```Example: EXEC SQL WHENEVER SQLERROR GOTO error_handler;```
	 ```error_handler: /* this is a C-language label */```
	 ``` printf("SQL error code = %ld \n",SQLCODE);```

DECLARE CURSOR	This command associates a cursor name with the results of a SELECT statement. If the SELECT statement is not known at precompile time, the cursor can be declared against a statement name and the SELECT gets prepared dynamically at run time through PREPARE. Use the keyword HOLD if you do not want to "re-declare" the cursor at the end of a transaction.
	
	 ```Example 1: /* a cursor with a static SQL SELECT */```
	 ``` EXEC SQL DECLARE cur1 CURSOR WITH HOLD FOR```
	 ``` SELECT dept_num, dept_name /* example of a static */```
	 ``` FROM department; /* SQL cursor with HOLD */```
	 ``` EXEC SQL OPEN CURSOR cur1;```
	 ```Example 2: /* a cursor with a dynamic fixed SELECT list */```
	 ``` EXEC SQL BEGIN DECLARE SECTION;```
	 ``` char select_string[1000]; /* declare host var. */```
	 ``` EXEC SQL END DECLARE SECTION;```
	 ``` EXEC SQL DECLARE cur1```
	 ``` CURSOR FOR name1; /* declare a cursor for name1 */```
	 ``` . . .```
	 ``` /* later... build SELECT into select_string */```
	 ``` EXEC SQL PREPARE name1```
	 ``` FROM :select_string;/* assign SELECT to name1 */```
	 ``` EXEC SQL OPEN cur1; /* now you can go to work */```

OPEN	This command opens a cursor and causes the SELECT statement to be evaluated. The cursor is placed in the open state and positioned before the first row of its result set. The keyword USING can be used to introduce a list of host variables for the parameter markers of a prepared dynamic SQL statement. The keywords USING DESCRIPTOR may also be used to supply the values of the parameter markers to a dynamic SQL statement through the SQLDA. The SQLDA must contain a description and value for each parameter. ```Example: EXEC SQL OPEN cur1; /* no parameter markers */```

Table 26-6 (Part 3 of 5). The SQL Program Language Constructs (PLC).

SQL Command	Description

FETCH	This command positions a cursor on the next row of its result table and fetches the row. If the INTO keyword is used, the row contents are placed into a list of host variables. If USING DESCRIPTOR is used, the row contents are placed inside the SQLDA.
	
	``
	Examples: EXEC SQL FETCH cur1 /* fetch a single row */
	               INTO :vdeptnum, :vdeptname;/* using host vars. */
	          EXEC SQL FETCH cur1 /* fetch a single row */
	               USING DESCRIPTOR :sqlda1; /* using a SQLDA */
	``

CLOSE	This command closes a cursor. The Database Manager will automatically close any open cursors when a program terminates. ``` Example: EXEC SQL CLOSE cur1; ```

PREPARE	This command dynamically creates an access plan for a SQL statement. The prepared statement is a named object that persists only for the duration of the transaction where it gets created, unless it is associated with an open cursor defined WITH HOLD. To execute this command, you need to provide a name for the statement and the SQL string FROM which it gets prepared. You may optionally specify an INTO keyword followed by a SQLDA in which the Database Manager will return information about the prepared statement's structure. The dynamic SQL statement that gets prepared cannot contain host variables; however, it can contain parameter markers. The parameter markers have to be substituted one for one with host variables when an OPEN (for selects) or EXECUTE (for non-selects) gets issued.
	
	``
	Example: /* non-select dynamic SQL command (build then prepare)*/
	         strcpy(stm, "INSERT INTO department VALUES(?,?)");
	         EXEC SQL PREPARE dept_insert FROM :stm;
	Example: /*This is the select example that was used in DECLARE */
	         /*CURSOR. It is assigned to CURSOR name1 */
	         EXEC SQL PREPARE name1 FROM :select_string;
	``

EXECUTE	This command executes a dynamically prepared non-SELECT SQL command. The keyword USING can be used to introduce a list of host variables for the parameter markers of a prepared dynamic SQL statement. The keywords USING DESCRIPTOR may also be used to supply the values of the parameter markers to a dynamic SQL statement through the SQLDA. The SQLDA must contain for each parameter a description and a value.
	
	``
	Example: EXEC SQL
	         EXECUTE dept_insert /* execute the previously */
	         USING :var1, :var2; /* PREPAREd dept_insert SQL */
	                             /* command and substitutes */
	                             /* markers with host variables */
	``

Table 26-6 (Part 4 of 5). The SQL Program Language Constructs (PLC).

SQL Command	Description

EXECUTE IMMEDIATE	This command prepares and executes a dynamically prepared non-SELECT SQL command. No parameter markers may be introduced. If the same SQL statement is to be executed multiple times, it is more efficient to use PREPARE and EXECUTE.
	
	`Example: strcpy(stm,"DELETE FROM department");/*build statement*/`
	`         EXEC SQL EXECUTE IMMEDIATE :stm;    /*execute command */`

DESCRIBE	This command returns information about a dynamically prepared SQL statement. You need to specify the name of the prepared SQL statement and the SQLDA where you want the information returned to. `Example:  EXEC SQL DESCRIBE dept_insert INTO :sqlda1;`

SELECT INTO	This static SQL command produces a result set consisting of at most one row, and assigns the values INTO a list of host variables. If no rows are returned, the command returns a +100 sqlcode and does not assign values to the host variables. If more than one row is returned, an error occurs.
	
	`Example:  EXEC SQL`
	`             SELECT dept_num, dept_name`
	`             INTO :var1, :var2;`
	`             FROM department`
	`             WHERE dept_num = 2500;`

Chapter 27

Tutorial on the Database
Administration Services and DDCS/2

This chapter provides the second part of the tutorial on the OS/2 Extended Services Database Manager. This part of the tutorial covers the Database Administration API services and DDCS/2.

THE DATABASE ADMINISTRATION API

These are the services used to automate the maintenance, performance tuning, and control of a database engine. The Database Administration API uses the call/return convention and is not part of the standard SQL sublanguage. This is where you'll find all the database services that are particular to the OS/2 Database Manager environment. Wherever possible, the Database Manager designers tried to maintain compatibility with the DB2 model for database administration services. In the sections that follow we provide a description of the functions for the Database Administration API services broken down according to the subdivisions shown in the figure below:

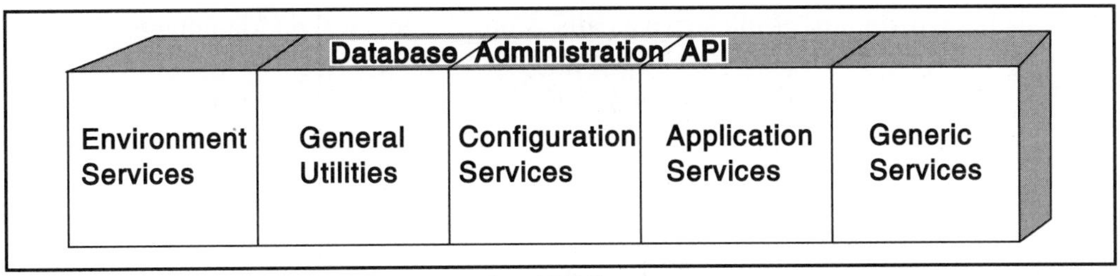

Database Administration API

| Environment Services | General Utilities | Configuration Services | Application Services | Generic Services |

Figure 27-1. The Database Administration API Services.

Before plunging into the description of the services, we need to clarify two areas that are common to all of those services:

1. What is the naming convention used by the Database Administration API services?

2. What are the client/server implications of the Database Administration API services? Which services are available to DOS, Windows, and OS/2 database client machines? Which services are server only?

API Naming Convention

The OS/2 API services we've encountered so far, were endowed with luxuriously long and expressive names. Unfortunately, the Database Administration API does not sustain this legacy. Instead, each function name is creatively packed with as much information as eight characters can provide. What follows is an explanation of the naming convention that may help you decipher, and perhaps even remember, some of these cryptic API names:

*   Each API name has a maximum of eight characters.

*   Each API name starts with **sql**.

*   The fourth character in every name denotes the functional area to which the API call belongs; here are the conventions:

    e   is used for C-language specific Environment Services.
    u   is used for C-language specific General Utilities.
    f   is used for C-language specific Configuration Services.
    a   is used for C-language specific Application Services.
    g   is used for a Generic (language independent) version of the above services.

*   The last four characters describe the function. This "four letter" limitation results in some strange sounding acronyms.

The C-language version of the service calls is optimized for the C-language. There is a C-language substitute call for almost every language-independent generic call. We recommend that you use the C-language specific version of the calls because they are better suited for C programs. However, two commands, **LOG ON** and **LOG OFF,** have no C-language specific counterparts and can only be used in their generic form. There is one more catch. Both of these commands start with **upm** instead of **sql**. If you are planning on making your programs language independent, you should, of course, consider using the generic commands instead of their C-language optimized counterparts.

Remote Execution of the API Services

With the SQL API calls that were presented in the previous chapter, any command that can be executed locally can also be executed on a remote database with no changes to your code. This property makes the SQL API *transparent* to the database location. This means that SQL applications can be moved on a network without requiring any changes to your code; only the workstation directory and configuration files need to be modified. Unfortunately, this advanced level of network transparency does not carry over to the Database Administration Services API. An asymmetry exists between what clients can do and what servers can do, which means that not all Database Administration Services can be executed on client machines.

To complicate matters further, OS/2 and DOS/Windows database clients were not "created equal." The DOS and Windows clients have a slightly more limited repertoire of Database Administration services than their OS/2 counterparts. To help you differentiate between the various remote capabilities, we added two columns to the description of the Database Administration API services. The entries in these columns indicate whether the service can execute from a DOS or Windows database client.

When we say a service is *not remotely executable*, it can mean one of two things:

1. The API is not available to a remote client.
2. The function is not applicable in a remote context.

Warning: In some cases, the function is supported but it can only operate on resources that reside in the client machine. We count these functions as being supported and give you a warning about this "side effect" in the text. So make sure you read all the fine print in the explanation.

DATABASE ADMINISTRATION API: ENVIRONMENT SERVICES

These are the API functions through which you can manipulate the Database Manager environment. The environment services fall into the following subcategories:

- Start or stop the Database Manager
- Database creation services
- Database connection services
- Database directory services
- DDCS/2 directory services
- Interrupt handling
- Database or user status collection
- Remote Procedure Calls

Table 27-1 classifies the Environment Services API commands according to the subcategory of service. Most of these API services are straightforward and do not require an introduction. However, there are two areas which are not exactly "intuitive," and may benefit from a short introduction: directory services (for the Database Manager and DDCS/2), and remote procedures.

Table 27-1. The Environment Services API Commands, Divided by Function.

Environment Service Type	API Commands
Start or stop Database Manager	START DATABASE MANAGER and STOP DATABASE MANAGER
Database creation services	CREATE DATABASE, DROP DATABASE, MIGRATE DATABASE, and CHANGE DATABASE COMMENT
Database connection services	START USING DATABASE, STOP USING DATABASE, and RESTART DATABASE
Database directory services	CATALOG DATABASE, UNCATALOG DATABASE, OPEN DATABASE DIRECTORY SCAN, GET NEXT DATABASE DIRECTORY ENTRY, CLOSE DATABASE DIRECTORY SCAN, CATALOG NODE, UNCATALOG NODE, OPEN NODE DIRECTORY SCAN, GET NEXT NODE ENTRY, and CLOSE NODE DIRECTORY SCAN
DDCS/2 directory services	CATALOG DCS DATABASE, UNCATALOG DCS DATABASE, OPEN DCS DIRECTORY SCAN, GET DCS DIRECTORY ENTRY FOR DATABASE, GET DCS DIRECTORY ENTRIES, CLOSE DCS DIRECTORY SCAN
Interrupt handling	INSTALL SIGNAL HANDLER and INTERRUPT
Database or user status collection	COLLECT DATABASE STATUS, GET NEXT DATABASE STATUS BLOCK, GET USER STATUS, and FREE DATABASE STATUS RESOURCES
Remote procedure calls	DATABASE APPLICATION REMOTE INTERFACE

Database and DDCS/2 Directory Services

If your application will only run in standalone mode, meaning that it will only access a local database, the Database Manager will automatically maintain the database directories on your behalf, and you can skip over the rest of this section. On the other hand, if your application runs in either database client or server mode, or if you will create databases on other machines and port them to a local machine through floppies, then read on.

Remote Data Services (RDS)

This is the component of the Database Manager that turns the OS/2 database engine into a networked database server. RDS uses the client/server model with SQL messages passed between clients and servers over a network. In other words, RDS follows the database server model. With RDS, a workstation can be configured to be either:

- A standalone database workstation (OS/2 only)
- A database client (DOS, Windows, or OS/2)

- A database server (OS/2 only)
- A database client and server (OS/2 only)

DDCS/2, as we explained in Part I, further extends RDS's reach to IBM's other SAA DBMSs: DB2, SQL/DS, and the OS/400 SQL/400. DDCS/2 serves as a gateway that allows the OS/2 Database Manager to operate in heterogeneous server environments where the data is spread across PCs, AS/400s, and mainframes. With DDCS/2, a workstation can be configured to be either:

- A standalone DDCS/2 client workstation (OS/2 only)
- A DDCS/2 server workstation (OS/2 with ES Server only)
- A database client that obtains DDCS/2 services using a DDCS/2 server (DOS, Windows, or OS/2)

For the most part, the operation of RDS and DDCS/2 is transparent to your programs. This transparency, however, comes at a price; you need to understand how to use and configure database directories. Part of the database directory services are executed automatically by the Database Manager, and the other part requires your explicit involvement. You can manipulate the directories that require your intervention through either a program that uses the directory services API or through the **Database Directory Tool**.

The purpose of the database directory services is to make the application as independent from the database location as possible. To achieve this independence, the Database Manager provides three types of database directories: *System*, *Volume*, and *Workstation* (also known as "node"). DDCS/2 introduces a fourth directory type: the *Database Connection Services Directory* (see Figure 27-2).

Here is what each RDS configuration needs in terms of database directories:

- *A client* workstation must contain a System directory and a Workstation directory.

- *A database server* workstation must contain a System directory and at least one Volume directory; an additional Volume directory is required for each logical drive on which a database is installed.

- *A DDCS/2 Server* workstation must contain a System directory, a Workstation directory, and a Database Connection Services directory.

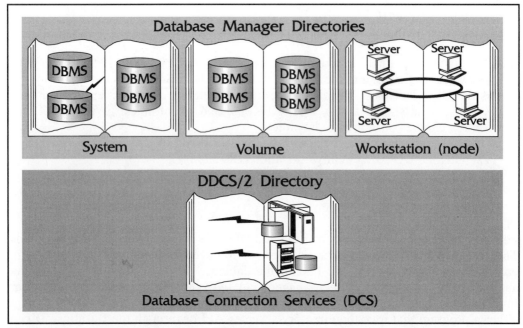

Figure 27-2.   Database Manager and DDCS/2 Directories.

The System Directory

This directory can be thought of as the master directory for a workstation. It contains an entry for each cataloged local or remote database that can be accessed from that workstation. The System directory resides on the drive where the Database Manager client or server software is installed. Each entry maintained in this directory consists of the following fields:

- The **database name** (up to 8 characters).
- An optional database **alias** (up to 8 characters), which can be used if the workstation needs to access more than one database with the same database name.
- The **disk drive** on which the database resides.
- The **product name and release number** for this database (up to 20 characters).
- An optional **comment** (up to 30 characters) associated with the database and the **code page** of the comment (for National Language Support).
- The database **entry type**, which denotes whether the database is *indirect,* meaning it resides on this node or *remote*.
- The **node name** (up to 8 characters) on which the remote database resides; this item is required if the entry type specifies the database as being *remote*.

The Volume Directory

This directory contains an entry for every database on a logical disk drive. This type of directory is maintained implicitly by the Database Manager each time a database is created or deleted on an OS/2 logical disk drive. An instance of this directory must exist on every OS/2 drive that contains one or more databases. Each entry maintained in this directory consists of the following fields:

- The **database name** (up to 8 characters).
- The **internal name** (up to 8 characters), which identifies the subdirectory off the root where the Database Manager stores the database objects.
- An optional **database alias** (up to 8 characters), which can be used if the workstation needs to access more than one database with the same database name.
- The **product name and release number** for this database (up to 20 characters).
- An optional **comment** (up to 30 characters) associated with the database and the **code page** of the comment (for National Language Support).
- The database **entry type**, which is always *Home* for Volume directories, since the Volume directory keeps track of where the database is physically located.

The Workstation (or Node) Directory

Each database client maintains one Workstation (also known as Node) directory. The Workstation directory contains an entry for each remote server that can be accessed. Each entry contains information on how to reach that server over the network. This information includes the server's address and the network protocol it speaks. The Database Manager supports three network protocols: NetBIOS (the default), APPC, and APPC/APPN. The system will create or update the workstation directory every time a remote server is cataloged on the client machine. The following protocol information must be provided: for NetBIOS, the adapter number and the server name; for APPC, the Local LU, partner LU, and mode; for APPN, all the APPC information plus a network ID. An entry in the Workstation directory is a superset of all that information; it contains the following fields:

- The **node name** (up to 8 characters) of a server workstation where a remote database resides. This name must match the database alias used in the System directory. This field is used by all the protocols.
- The **local LU** name (up to 8 characters), which identifies the local LU alias. This alias contains SNA information such as the LU session limit and the maximum number of TPs. This field is used by APPC and APPN only.
- The **partner LU name** (up to 8 characters), which identifies the partner LU alias. This alias contains SNA information such as conversation security, partner LU session limits, and the Data Link Controller type. This field is used by APPC and APPN only.
- The **mode name** (up to 8 characters), which identifies the SNA transmission service profile. This profile contains SNA information such as the RU size, the session

limits, and the pacing limit. The Database Manager provides over 20 sets of transmission modes from which your application can choose. You can also create your own SNA transmission profile using the configuration services. This field is used by APPC and APPN only.

- The **network ID** (up to 8 characters), which identifies the APPN network. This field is used by APPN only.
- The **server name** (up to 8 characters), the NetBIOS network name of the server where the database resides. This field is used by NetBIOS only.
- The **adapter number** (0 or 1) used for the NetBIOS session. This field is used by NetBIOS only.
- An optional **comment** (up to 30 characters) associated with the database and the code page of the comment for National Language Support. This field is used by all the protocols.
- The **network protocol,** a single character used to identify the network protocol used in the entry. This field is used by all the protocols.

The field information is returned in a data structure. Only the fields that are specific to a protocol are valid; the others are ignored. For example, if the *network protocol* field specifies NetBIOS, only the returned NetBIOS-relevant fields are valid; the APPC and APPN fields are ignored.

The Database Connection Services Directory

This directory is only used if the DDCS/2 program is installed on your system. It is created by the system on the same drive where DDCS/2 is installed. The directory contains an entry for each SAA database that your system can access using the DDCS/2 DRDA gateway services. Each entry maintained in this directory consists of the following fields:

- The **local database name** (up to 8 characters) matching the database alias maintained in the System Directory.
- The **target database name** (up to 18 characters) containing the actual name of the SAA database.
- The **application requester** (up to 8 characters) containing the name of the DLL file that executes the protocol used to communicate with the SAA database (the default is SQLJDRD1.DLL—for the DRDA-1 protocol).
- The **parameter field** (up to 512 characters) containing the TP prefix (the default is the DB2 prefix, "07"), the TP name (the default is the DB2 TP name, "6DB"), a mapping file name for translating error codes (the default is the DB2-to-ES mapping file, DCS1DSN.MAP in the \SQLLIB directory), and the disconnect options that specify how -300XX SQLCODES form the host must be handled (the default is do not disconnect). The parameters in the string are separated by commas. You can substitute any parameter with a comma and obtain its default.
- An optional **comment** (up to 30 characters) associated with the database and the **code page** of the comment (for National Language Support).

A Tool for Maintaining Directories

Figure 27-3 shows a screen capture of the *Directory Tool* that comes with the Database Manager. This tool provides a graphical interface that lets you:

- Create, drop, catalog, and uncatalog a database.
- Catalog or uncatalog a workstation.
- View the contents of the System database directory which includes a list of all the local and remote databases that were cataloged on the workstation.
- View the contents of all the Volume database directories which includes a list of all the databases created on the workstation (in all the disk drives and disk partitions).
- View the contents of the Database Connection Services Directory which includes a list of all the SAA databases that can be accessed from that workstation using DDCS/2.
- View the contents of the Workstation Directory which includes a list of all the servers that can be accessed from that workstation using RDS or DDCS/2.
- Update the comment in any directory entry.

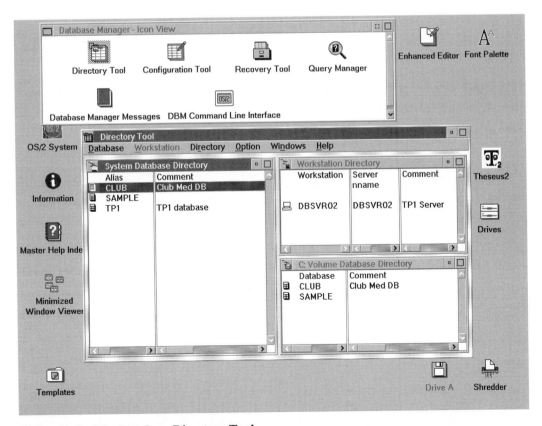

Figure 27-3. The Database Directory Tool.

Example 1: An RDS Client/Server

Figure 27-4 shows a network configuration that consists of an OS/2 database client on node WS1, and an OS/2 database server on node WS2. The client and server communicate using the default NetBIOS protocol. We first walk you through the configuration of the directories—on both the database client and server workstations— and then show how directories are used to establish the client/server connection.

Configuring the Database Server in Example 1

The System and Volume directory entries on the database server (see Figure 27-4) are automatically created and initialized by the Database Manager when you create a new database. Let's walk through the process:

1. Use the **CREATE DATABASE** command to create databases DB1 and DB2 on disk drive C, and databases DB3 and DB4 on disk drive D.

2. The Database Manager automatically creates an OS/2 subdirectory (off the root) for each database. The directory names are supplied by the Database Manager using a naming convention starting with SQL00001. The suffix in the name is incremented for each new database on a particular drive. Each table in a database is stored within the database subdirectory in its own (.DAT) file; the indexes for a table are stored in a (.INX) file. The Database Manager also creates a log subdirectory for each database (SQLOGDIR).

3. The Database Manager automatically creates a Volume database directory for each of drives C and D. The Volume directory is initialized with a row for each database on that drive. Notice that the entry type for those databases is **home** because this is the directory to which those databases belong. Also notice the correspondence between the logical database name you provide and the internal subdirectory name controlled by the Database Manager.

4. The Database Manager automatically creates a System Database directory for your machine and creates entries for all your newly created databases. Each database entry has an **indirect** type, meaning that the database resides on the WS2 machine.

Note that the server in the example is self-sufficient when it comes to databases; therefore it does not need a Workstation (Node) directory.

Configuring the Database Client in Example 1

The Workstation and System directory entries on the database client (see Figure 27-4) must be provided by you. You can do this manually with the Directory Tool (see Figure

27-3). You can also write a program that uses the API services. In any case, the database directories have to exist and be properly initialized before your remote application can start using the database server. Let's walk through the process and introduce the information that needs to be provided:

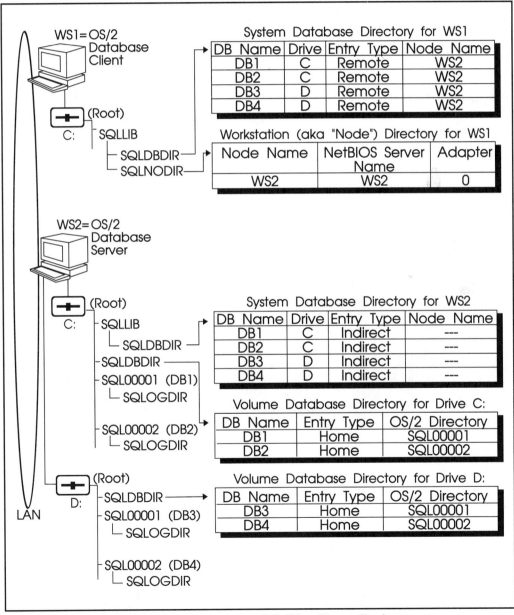

Figure 27-4. The Database Directories in an RDS Client/Server Environment.

1. Use the **CATALOG NODE** command to catalog the remote server node, WS2. In our example, there is only one entry, WS2, because all the remote databases reside on the same server.

2. Use the **CATALOG DATABASE** command to catalog the remote databases DB1 through DB4 in the client's System database directory. In this example, all the databases are cataloged as being of type **remote** and residing on node WS2.

Bringing the Client and Server Together in Example 1

Let's assume the client workstation, WS1, needs to access data stored in DB3 on server WS2 (see Figure 27-4). Here is a scenario that conceptually explains what takes place in this example:

1. The client issues a **START USING DATABASE** specifying DB3 as the name of the database.

2. The RDS service on the client searches for a DB3 entry in its **System Directory**. In our "ideal" example, a match is found. The directory entry identifies DB3 as being a remote database located on node WS2. The RDS then searches the **Workstation Directory** for a WS2 node which, of course, it finds! The entry contains the information required to establish a NetBIOS session.

3. The RDS then uses the Communications Manager to establish the connection between the client and server.

4. At the other end of the NetBIOS session, when the remote connection request arrives, the RDS service on the server searches for a DB3 entry in its **System Directory** and it, of course, finds one. The entry type "indirect" indicates that the database is local. The drive field identifies the database as being on the drive D.

5. The RDS on the server then searches the D drive **Volume Directory** for a DB3 entry. Once again, an entry is found and the client/server database connection can now be established.

6. The session remains active as long as the application does not issue a **STOP USING DATABASE** command.

7. The good news is that once you've got a connection, RDS will maintain *database consistency* across the communication link. Consequently if a remote workstation or the communications link fails during a database connection, NetBIOS notifies RDS. RDS will then roll back the application's database transaction.

8. You can use your remote connection to execute the full complement of SQL commands, remote procedures, and quite a few of the APIs that will be introduced in this chapter.

Example 2: A DDCS/2 Client/Server

Figure 27-5 shows a network configuration that consists of an OS/2 DDCS/2 database gateway server on node WS1 that talks to a S/370 mainframe running SNA/VTAM and MVS. The mainframe contains a DB2 database called HOSTDB. WS1 communicates with the mainframe using APPC/APPN. To make this connection the WS1 DDCS/2 machine must be setup with three directories: a System directory that catalogs the remote HOSTDB, a Workstation directory that contains the network information, and the Data Connection Service (DCS) directory that contains the gateway information.

The information in all three directories must be provided by you. You can do this manually with the Directory Tool (see Figure 27-3), or you can write a program that uses the API services. In either case, the database directories have to exist and be properly initialized before your application can start using the mainframe (or any other SAA database) as if it were a local database server.

Let's walk through the process of creating these three directories and introduce the information that you need to provide:

1. Use the **CATALOG DATABASE** API call to catalog the database BigDB in the System database directory. BigDB is the local name for the BigDB_Is_Here database on DB2. The type is, of course, **remote**, since BigDB resides on the mainframe. We will give the BigDB a node name of HQ.

2. Use the **CATALOG NODE** API call to catalog the remote mainframe server node, HQ. We must provide APPC/APPN info for HQ. We'll put the mainframe on the HQNET APPN network, and use an SNA mode name called IBMRDB. We must also specify the APPC Partner LU, and Local LU information.

3. Use the **CATALOG DCS DATABASE** API call to catalog BigDB with DDCS/2. We must tell DDCS/2 that BigDB is the local name for the DB2 system containing the BigDB_Is_Here database. We also show in Figure 27-5 the contents of the PARM and Application Requester fields that are specific to DB2.

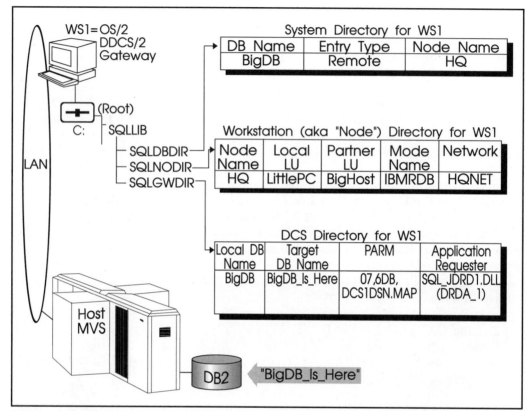

Figure 27-5. The Database Directories in a DDCS/2 Gateway Server Environment.

The worst is behind us. Now that the DDCS/2 gateway server is set up, any DOS, Windows, or OS/2 database client on the network can issue a **START USING DATA-BASE** command and execute SQL programs on any SAA database (see Figure 27-6). The directory linkages make these connections transparent to your programs. While not perfect, DDCS/2 has gone a long way toward making the mainframe database connection almost seamless to your programs. There are some caveats, however, that will be explained later in this chapter.

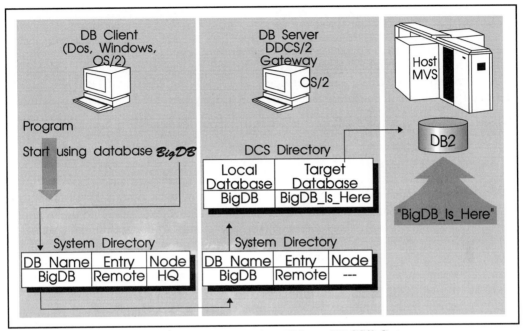

Figure 27-6. Client/Server Database Connections Using a DDCS/2 Gateway.

The Power of Remote Procedures

Database Server Remote Procedure Calls

Many database vendors are now offering an RPC-like mechanism for database. This mechanism is sometimes referred to as "OLTP lite" or "stored procedures."[1] Its purpose is to improve the performance of SQL on networks. This advanced database feature uses a message service to trigger the execution of a remote procedure. The remote procedure typically executes a collection of precompiled SQL statements. The SQL statements can also accept parameters so that a single procedure can be used over the network by multiple clients using different input data. The primary use of remote procedures (in all of its variations) is to support a class of performance-critical applications known as Online Transaction Processing or **OLTP**. These applications typically:

1. Receive a fixed set of inputs from remote clients.
2. Perform multiple precompiled SQL commands against a **local** database.
3. Commit the work.

---

[1] The concept of "stored procedures" was pioneered by Sybase in 1986.

4.   Return a fixed set of results.

The Remote Procedure Call serves as the foundation on which *Transaction Servers* are built. It reduces communications traffic, improves response times, and provides an object-oriented flavor of database service that is well suited for OLTP applications. The main drawback of remote procedures is that they provide less ad hoc flexibility than remote SQL.

A Client/Server for OLTP

The remote procedure call is an extension of the client/server model for transaction processing environments. You may recall that the client/server model splits an application into two parts: a client and a server. The client and server communicate requests and responses through messages. This simple construct allows intelligence to be easily distributed across a network and provides a framework for the design of loosely coupled network-based applications. Here is how this model has evolved to fit the needs of various distributed environments, including the more demanding needs of **OLTP** types of applications:

*   With a *File Server*, the client passes requests for file data over a network. This is a very primitive form of service interface that typically necessitates many message exchanges over the network to find the required data.

*   With a *Database Server*, the client passes SQL requests for information. This higher-level service interface allows the server to use its own processing power to find the required data. Only the final results of the search are returned over the network. The code that processes the SQL request and the data reside on the same machine. This results in a much more efficient use of distributed processing power than that provided by file servers.

*   With a *Transaction Server*, the client invokes a remote procedure and passes it the parameters required to do a job. A single remote message triggers the execution of a collection of stored SQL statements. The result is an even greater reduction of network traffic and better performance. This approach also provides better *site autonomy*, because the remote modification of tables can only occur through locally executing programs. If the tables change, you don't need to recompile all your remote applications. In general, this implementation of client/server provides better distribution of intelligence, but there is some loss of remote flexibility.

Benefits of Database Manager Remote Procedures

As you may have surmised from your readings in this book, there are many ways to provide a Remote Procedure Call. The OS/2 Database Manager's **DATABASE AP-PLICATION REMOTE INTERFACE** API provides an advanced implementation of

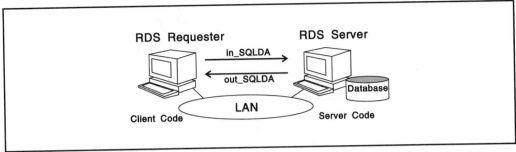

Figure 27-7. The Database Manager's Remote Procedure Call.

a Remote Procedure Call for databases. The OS/2 Database Manager implementation of remote calls contains many advanced features. Here are some of the highlights (also see Figure 27-7):

- The Remote Procedure Call is transparent to the location of the procedure. The stored procedure can reside in either a local or remote site.
- The Remote Procedure Call is optimized for the execution of a collection of SQL statements.
- The C language is used to create the remote procedures as opposed to inventing a new transaction language.
- The remote procedures are implemented as DLLs, which provide an almost ideal package for such constructs.
- The remote parameters are passed over the network using self-describing data structures of type **SQLDA**. This choice of a container for passing data is consistent with the SQL programming paradigm.
- The reconstruction of the SQLDA at the remote location after it is sent over the network is an attractive feature in its own right. It is also an effective way of providing location transparency. It can provide this transparency because RDS handles the situation where the call may be local; in this case, the SQLDA is shared through common memory and does not need to be reconstructed.
- The remote procedures can terminate after execution or remain active in memory. This choice of termination method allows remote procedures to provide both non-persistent simple transactions and persistent conversational programs.

Warning: Remote procedures are currently not supported on the other SAA database platforms. In the DB2 world, *Transaction Monitors*, like CICS, are used to provide OLTP capabilities. There is no concept of "stored procedures."[2]

---

[2] A Transaction Monitor provides an OS-like environment for scheduling and managing transactions. The services a Transaction Monitor provides may include message queuing, load balancing, routing, nesting, and two-phase commit synchronization. Examples of Transaction Monitors are IBM's CICS, Tandem's Pathway, AT&T's Tuxedo, NCR's Top End, and Transarc's Encina.

How the Database Manager's Remote Procedure Call Works

Figure 27-8 presents a more detailed description of how the OS/2 Database Manager Remote Procedure Call works.

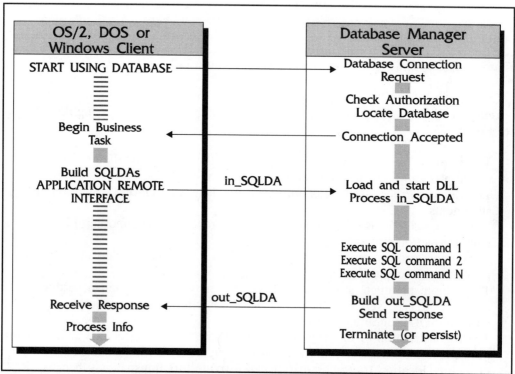

Figure 27-8. The Application Remote Interface's Remote Procedure Call.

The following sections explain what's going on in Figure 27-8:

The Client Side of the Call

The client must first issue a **START USING DATABASE** API call to connect to the remote database. Once this is done, the client sets up two SQLDA structures. The information to be sent to the server is placed inside an in_SQLDA structure. The information returned from the server will be placed in the assigned out_SQLDA structure. The client then issues a **DATABASE APPLICATION REMOTE INTERFACE** command to call a remote program on the server.

The SQLDA Exchange

The RDS on the client side automatically extracts the necessary information from the SQLDAs and transmits it to its RDS counterpart on the server. The RDS on the server side loads the server program requested by the remote call, and then places the reconstructed SQLDA structures in its local memory. The server program must exist as an OS/2 Dynamic Link Library (DLL) procedure. The remote call interface can also be used if the database is local. In this case, the RDS loads the DLL, locally calls the procedure, and makes the SQLDAs available to it through shared memory. This feature makes the remote call interface transparent to the location of the server application.

Invoking the Remote Procedure

The client can specify the name of the procedure to be run on the server in one of two ways:

1. By a single **funcname**, which causes a **funcname.dll** file to be loaded in memory. It is assumed that this file contains a function by the same name.

2. By the back-slash delimitation **dllname.dll\funcname**. In this case, the **dllname** is the name of the file to be loaded, and **funcname** is the name of the function to be executed. A single (.DLL) file can contain multiple, remotely executable functions. Note that in this naming convention, backslash does not indicate a subdirectory.

Executing the Remote Procedure

The remote procedure obtains its input data from the in_SQLDA. Each data item in the in_SQLDA has a SQL type, a length, and a pointer to the data in local memory. The remote procedure updates the database and places any results to be returned in the out_SQLDA. The RDS on the server returns the information to the RDS on the client.

Terminating the Remote Procedure

Depending on the return code from the server application, the RDS will either:

*   Retain the server application DLL function in memory. This mode is used for *persistent conversational programs* that require many calls and returns via the interface. The return code from the server program code in such instances is SQL_HOLD_PROC.
*   Terminate the server application DLL function from memory and free all resources. This is used for simple transactions consisting of one call and one return after which the remote application terminates. The return code from the server program code in such instances is SQLZ_DISCONNECT_PROC.

The Environment Services Commands

We are finally ready to present the individual API calls that constitute the Environment Services. These calls (see Table 27-2) are quite numerous. They provide the bulk of the Database Administration API services. Notice that we've added two columns to our normal description of the API functions to denote whether the function can be executed on DOS and Windows clients.

Table 27-2 (Part 1 of 6). **The Database Administration API: Environment Services.**

Function Call Name	Descriptive Name	Client		Description
		DOS	**WIN**	
sqlestar()	**START DATABASE MANAGER**	Yes	Yes	This command starts the Database Manager as a background process and allocates resources to it. This command must be issued before any application running on that workstation can access the Database Manager. The communications must be started on a client workstation before this command can be issued.
sqlestdm()	**STOP DATABASE MANAGER**	Yes	Yes	This command terminates the Database Manager background process and releases its resources. Unless explicitly stopped, the Database Manager will continue to be active even if all the processes that were using it terminate. DOS and Windows clients must issue this call before they terminate (an automatic disconnect on their behalf is not performed by the Database Manager).
sqlecred()	**CREATE DATABASE**	No	No	This command creates a new database. You must specify the name of the database, the drive on which it will reside, an optional comment, and the code page for that comment. The Database Manager will create a subdirectory, off the root, for the new database and initialize the system tables and the recovery log. It will also automatically catalog the new database on the Volume and System database directories. The code page and country code of the creating application is stored on the configuration file for this database.
sqledrpd()	**DROP DATABASE**	No	No	This command deletes all the tables in a database and removes the entry for this database from both the Volume and System database directories. In addition, the disk subdirectory on which the database resides is deleted.
sqledchg()	**CHANGE DATABASE COMMENT**	Yes	Yes	This command substitutes a new comment for an existing one for that database. It can only be executed on local directory entries.
sqlemigd()	**MIGRATE DATABASE**	Yes	Yes	This command converts older database versions into the current format. You must provide the password and name of the database to be migrated. The Database Manager will grant the initial user authorities.

Table 27-2 (Part 2 of 6). The Database Administration API: Environment Services.

Function Call Name	Descriptive Name	Client		Description
		DOS	WIN	
sqlestrd()	START USING DATABASE	Yes	Yes	This command connects an application to a database. You must execute this command prior to performing any operations on a specific database. A process can be connected to only one database at a time. Subsequent database accesses can be made by any thread within that process. If you are the first user connecting to the database, you can request exclusive use and prevent any subsequent users from accessing the database.
sqlestpd()	STOP USING DATABASE	Yes	Yes	This command disconnects an application from the database. A COMMIT is issued on behalf of any uncommitted transactions.
sqlerest()	RESTART DATABASE	Yes	Yes	This command recovers a database left in an inconsistent state during a previous session. This could happen, for example, as the result of a power failure or any other form of abnormal termination. You will typically issue this call after a START USING DATABASE fails and the sqlcode indicates that the database must be restarted. A second START USING DATABASE must be issued to connect to the database after this command executes.
sqlecatd()	CATALOG DATABASE	Yes	Yes	This command creates an entry for a new database in the System database directory. The parameters you supply include the name of the database, an optional alias name, an optional comment, whether the database resides on this machine (indirect) or whether it is remote, the node name of the remote database, and, finally, the drive on which this database resides. The new database can be located on the default drive, on other drives, on diskettes, or on a remote node. The DOS and Windows clients use the drive parameter to indicate the LAN adapter (0 = primary; 1 = alternate).
sqleuncd()	UNCATALOG DATABASE	Yes	Yes	This command deletes a database entry from the System database directory. Home entries in the Volume database directory must be deleted by using the DROP DATABASE command.
sqlegdad()	CATALOG DCS DATABASE	No	No	This command creates an entry for a database in the Data Connection Services (DCS) directory. The parameters you supply include the local_name of the database, the target_database name, an optional comment, and the application requester DLL name. You must also provide a PARM string that contains the host transaction program name, the SQLCODE return codes mapping file name, and the disconnect option.
sqlegdel()	UNCATALOG DCS DATABASE	No	No	This command deletes a database entry from the Database Connection Services directory.

Table 27-2 (Part 3 of 6).   The Database Administration API: Environment Services.

Function Call Name	Descriptive Name	Client		Description
		DOS	**WIN**	
sqlecatn()	CATALOG NODE	No	No	This command creates an entry in the Workstation (aka Node) database directory for the workstation (or node) on which a remote database resides. The entry contains the information required to establish a connection with the remote workstation. This information includes the name of the remote node, a comment, and protocol-specific information. Three protocols are supported: NetBIOS (the default), APPC, and APPC/APPN. When using NetBIOS, you must specify the adapter number and server name. When using APPC, you must specify the Local LU, Partner LU, and the mode profile of the SNA session. You may create and name your own APPC transmission service mode profile through configuration services, or you may use one of the 20 profiles supported by Database Manager. When using APPC/APPN, you specify all the APPC parameters and, additionally, the APPN Network ID where the server resides. This command is supported on OS/2 clients. Windows and DOS clients do not use a Workstation directory. The network information is contained in the System Directory (they only use NetBIOS and provide the adapter number in the drive parameter).
sqleuncn()	UNCATALOG NODE	No	No	This command deletes an entry for a node name from the Workstation (aka Node) database directory.
sqledops()	OPEN DATABASE DIRECTORY SCAN	Yes	Yes	This command retrieves all the entries of a database directory and places them in memory. You specify a Volume database directory by providing a drive name. The ASCII zero drive name returns the contents of the System database directory. The command returns the contents of the directory you specify, the number of entries, and a handle to be used with subsequent scan commands.
sqledgne()	GET NEXT DATABASE DIRECTORY ENTRY	Yes	Yes	This command returns an entry from the database directory and points to the next entry after it. Most of the fields returned are common to both the System and Volume directories. However, a few of the fields are only valid for one or the other directory types.
sqledcls()	CLOSE DATABASE DIRECTORY SCAN	Yes	Yes	This command frees the memory resource allocated by the OPEN DIRECTORY SCAN command.
sqlegdsc()	OPEN DCS DIRECTORY SCAN	No	No	This command retrieves all the entries of a Database Connection Services directory, places them in memory, and returns the number of entries.

Table 27-2 (Part 4 of 6). The Database Administration API: Environment Services.

Function Call Name	Descriptive Name	Client		Description
		DOS	WIN	
sqlegdge()	GET DCS DIRECTORY ENTRY FOR DATABASE	No	No	This command returns a specific entry from the Database Connection Services directory. The information returned includes the local_name of the database, the target_name on the host, the comment, the name of the application client, and the parameter contents.
sqlegdgt()	GET DCS DIRECTORY ENTRIES	No	No	This command transfers a copy of the Database Connection Services directory to a buffer you supply. If all the entries are copied, the DCS scan is automatically closed and all resources are released.
sqlegdcl()	CLOSE DCS DIRECTORY SCAN	No	No	This command frees the memory resource allocated by the OPEN DCS DIRECTORY SCAN command.
sqlenops()	OPEN NODE DIRECTORY SCAN	No	No	This command retrieves all the entries of a Workstation (or node) database directory, places them in memory, returns the number of entries in the directory, and returns a handle to be used with subsequent scan commands.
sqlengne()	GET NEXT NODE DIRECTORY ENTRY	No	No	This command returns an entry from the node database directory and points to the next entry after it.
sqlencls()	CLOSE NODE DIRECTORY SCAN	No	No	This command frees the memory resource allocated by the OPEN NODE DIRECTORY SCAN command.
sqleisig()	INSTALL SIGNAL HANDLER	No	No	This command installs a simple interrupt handling routine for servicing the control interrupts that are generated when a user presses either the Ctrl + Break or the Ctrl + C key combinations. The interrupt handler resets the interrupt signal and then issues an INTERRUPT command that rolls back any active SQL transactions or commands. Language specific library signal functions can be used if you need a more elaborate signal handler.

Table 27-2 (Part 5 of 6).   The Database Administration API: Environment Services.

Function Call Name	Descriptive Name	Client		Description
		DOS	**WIN**	
sqleintr()	**INTERRUPT**	Yes	No	This command allows an SQL request-in-progress to be halted and causes its effects to be rolled back. You cannot interrupt a transaction after a COMMIT or ROLLBACK command is issued. When this command is issued from a DOS or OS/2 client, it rolls back any in-progress transaction and disconnects the application from the database. A Windows client uses the **INTERRUPT2** command, which allows a Windows client to terminate a database request made by another Windows client and disconnect it from the database (with rollback).
sqleproc()	**DATABASE APPLICA-TION REMOTE INTERFACE**	Yes	Yes	This command allows an application to execute a procedure stored at the location of a database. The remote procedure processes the results and returns the data to the application. This command reduces network traffic and improves the performance of network-based transactions. Your program will run in two parts. One part runs on the database client; the other runs on the database server. The stored procedure on the server side runs within the same transaction as the procedure on the client side. The program can be designed as a simple transaction (one call and one return) or as a conversational transaction (a set of calls and returns). The parameters you pass to this command are the name of the remote program, an in_sqlda that contains the name and memory addresses of variables you want sent to the server program, and an out_sqlda where variables will be returned to your program. For remote calls, the Database Manager transmits and reconstructs the sqlda(s), including their data fields. This means you can refer to host variables by name on both sides of the program. The server program must be written as a DLL function.
sqlestat()	**COLLECT DATABASE STATUS**	No	No	This command is used to collect a snapshot of the database activity at the time of the request. Status can be obtained at the system, database, or user level (for both local or remote users and databases). The command returns as system status the product ID, the release level, and the corrective level. For each database, it returns the last backup time, the number of current connects, the location of the database (local or remote), the drive where the database resides, the node name, and the type of database ("OS2 DBM" is the OS/2 Database Manager reserved type). For each user, it returns the number of transactions since connect, the number of SQL calls made, the elapsed time since connect, the elapsed time of the current transaction, the authorization ID and authority level of the user, the transaction state, the lock state, and the node name.

Table 27-2 (Part 6 of 6).   The Database Administration API: Environment Services.

Function Call Name	Descriptive Name	Client		Description
		DOS	WIN	
sqlenext()	GET NEXT DATABASE STATUS BLOCK	No	No	This command returns the next database entry from the results of a previous COLLECT DATABASE STATUS.
sqleuser()	GET USER STATUS	No	No	This command returns the status of all users connected to a specific database from the results of a previous COLLECT DATABASE STATUS command.
sqlefree()	FREE DATABASE STATUS RESOURCES	No	No	This command frees the resources held by a previously issued COLLECT DATABASE STATUS command.

DATABASE ADMINISTRATION API: GENERAL UTILITIES

These are the API calls through which you can automate the management of database chores. Like a fancy sports car, a database needs to be maintained and serviced at regular intervals. A database needs to be backed up periodically. Its tables need to be physically reorganized on disk when the access performance becomes sluggish. The statistics maintained on the tables have to be refreshed after certain amounts of cumulative changes, to keep the plan heuristics in working order. Like car owners, database users tend to procrastinate when it comes to preventive maintenance. Many users of PC databases who do not have full-time DBAs on their staffs may not even be aware of the need to perform those maintenance chores. This is where the General Utilities APIs presented in this section will prove to be handy. They allow you to write programs that routinely perform the maintenance chores, and thereby help to offset the cost of ownership of a database system. The Utility commands fall into the following subcategories:

- Backup, Restore and Roll-Forward database
- Bulk Data Exchange
- Performance Tuning
- Authorization Status

Table 27-3 classifies the General Utilities API commands according to the subcategory of service. There are no surprises there except, possibly, in the area of roll forward.

Table 27-3. The General Utilities API Commands, Divided by Function.

Utility Service Type	API Commands
Backup and Restore Database	BACKUP DATABASE, RESTORE DATABASE, and ROLL FORWARD DATABASE
Bulk Data Exchange	EXPORT TABLE and IMPORT TABLE
Performance Tuning	RUNSTATS TABLE and REORGANIZE TABLE
Authorization Status	GET ADMIN AUTHORIZATION

Forward Recovery: The Roll-Forward Service

The roll-forward service is used to restore a damaged database. This is done by applying transactions recorded in the online archive log files against a backup of the database. You can rebuild the database up to a point in time or to the end of the database logs (i.e., to the last transaction). If you specify a point in time, all the transactions in the logs after the time specified will *not* be reapplied to the database. Here's your quick hitchhiker's guide to roll forward:

1. Create the database.
2. Use the Configuration Tool (or an API call) to enable the database for roll-forward recovery (*log_retain* option).
3. Use the Configuration Tool to optionally change the path of the log files (*newlog-path* option) to a drive that is different from the one where the database resides. The Database Manager, by default, places the database logs in \SQLOGDIR, a subdirectory of the database directory. This introduces a single point of failure: the drive. You'll want to change that.
4. Use the Configuration Tool, to optionally increase the number of primary log files (the *logprimary* option) and their size (the *logfilsiz* option). Making these two parameters larger will improve performance, but will cost you more disk space.
5. Run your database in roll-forward mode. The Database Manager will create two types of logs. *Active* log files contain information for transactions whose changes have not yet been committed to the database; this information is used to roll-back a failed transaction; *Online archive* log files contain information used to roll forward the database, these log files reside in the database log path directory.
6. Backup the database at regular intervals. This will shorten the repair cycle after a catastrophic failure occurs.[3] Frequent backups result in the execution of fewer transactions at recovery time; roll-forward is incremental from the last backup. The backup can be performed using the Recovery Tool (see Figure 27-9) or through API calls.

---

[3] Remember, there are two types of disk drives: those that have crashed and those that will crash.

7. Provide an optional *user exit* program that is triggered by the Database Manager when the log files are filled or needed for recovery. Your program can transfer log files from the *online* archive log to an *offline* archive log and vice versa. The offline archive log is defined as being "anywhere but in the database log directory." It can be on another drive, tape, optical disk, or a mainframe. Writing such a program can be useful if you need to retain old logs or old backup copies of the database for version control or disaster recovery.

8. Perform the recovery after a catastrophic failure. In a worst case scenario, the disk on which the database resides crashes; you will then replace the disk, reinstall the Database Manager, restore the database from the last backup, and roll forward the database until the last transaction (i.e., to the end of journal log). You can do all of this using the Recovery Tool. This tool recreates an up-to-date database. Figure 27-10 shows the steps involved.

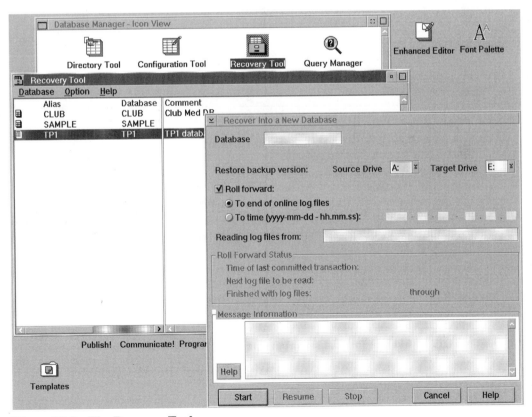

Figure 27-9. The Recovery Tool.

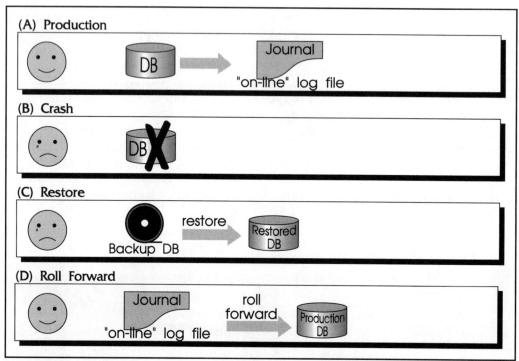

Figure 27-10.   The Roll-Forward Process: Resuscitating a Dead Database.

The Utility Services Commands

We are now ready to present the individual API calls that constitute the Utility Services. These calls are described in Table 27-4. Notice that we've added two columns to our normal description of the API functions to denote whether the function can be executed on Windows and DOS clients. Here are some rules that apply to the Utility API commands:

- With the exception of RUNSTATS and GET ADMIN AUTHORIZATION, you don't have to be connected to the database to use Utility commands. All the other Utility commands connect to the database through a separate OS/2 process.

- The BACKUP and RESTORE command use the standard OS/2 backup and restore services. The OS/2 services create their own Session and interact directly with the user if multiple diskette swaps are required. The space on the diskettes is automatically managed by OS/2.

- For Utility commands other than BACKUP, RESTORE, and ROLL FORWARD, an error sqlcode is returned when diskette swapping is needed. Your application must provide the code to prompt the user for the next diskette. After the user places the next diskette in the drive, you will need to re-issue the Utility command with the **callerac** parameter set to 1 to continue the command. The first time the command is invoked, the **callerac** parameter set to zero. If you want to abort the command, set **callerac** to 2.

Table 27-4 (Part 1 of 6). **The Database Administration API: General Utilities Commands.**

Function Call Name	Descriptive Name	Client		Description
		DOS	WIN	
slquback()	BACKUP DATABASE	No	No	This command creates a backup copy of a database. You can specify through the API whether you want the entire database copied or just the incremental changes made since the last backup. You can apply incremental backups only after a full database copy is initially issued. You must provide the name of the database to back up and the drive on which the backup files are to be placed; the backup drive must be different from the drive on which the database resides. This command will fail if other applications are connected to the database. This command uses the standard OS/2 backup facility and starts its own OS/2 session and screen group. If multiple diskettes are required, the interaction with the user is done directly by the OS/2 utility.
sqludres()	RESTORE DATABASE	No	No	This command restores the contents of a previously backed up database. You must provide the name of the database to restore, the drive to which it is to be restored, and the drive on which the backup copy resides. This command will drop the database first and will fail if other applications are connected to the database. This command uses the standard OS/2 restore facility and starts its own OS/2 session and screen group. When a user interaction is required, control returns to your application. Your appplication should look at the return code and determine whether to continue or terminate. You do this by issuing another RESTORE DATABASE command, with the callerac flag set to either continue or terminate. The initial call must be issued with the callerac flag set to 0. If multiple diskettes are required, the interaction with the user is done directly by the OS/2 utility and not through the callerac flag. This command is sometimes used to copy a database to another file system or workstation. This command is also used to rebuild a damaged database by following it with a ROLL FORWARD DATABASE command. The database is placed in a roll-forward pending state after this command is executed (provided the database was previously backed up with roll-forward enabled).

Table 27-4 (Part 2 of 6). **The Database Administration API: General Utilities Commands.**

Function Call Name	Descriptive Name	Client		Description
		DOS	**WIN**	
sqlufrol()	ROLL FORWARD DATABASE	No	No	This command restores a damaged database by applying transactions recorded and retained in the archive online log files against the restored backup of the database. You must restore the database using the RESTORE DATABASE call before issuing this command. The database logs, both active and archived, are used to reapply the changes to the database that were made since the time the last backup was made. You can rebuild the database up to a point in time or to the end of the database logs. If you roll forward a database to a specified point in time, all transactions in the logs after the time specified will not be reapplied to the database. You must provide the name of the database to roll forward, and an optional *stoptime* if you want to stop the recovery before the last transaction in the log (the default is to apply all the log files beginning with the log file that is matched with the backup image and until no more log files are found). The API call can also be used to return useful information that helps you manage your log files and feed them to the roll-forward process on demand. The information is obtained by invoking the API with the following *callerac* values: *(Continued...)*

Table 27-4 (Part 3 of 6). The Database Administration API: General Utilities Commands.

Function Call Name	Descriptive Name	Client		Description
		DOS	**WIN**	
sqlufrol() (Cont.)	ROLL FORWARD DATABASE (Cont.)			<pre>Callerac Value Action 1 SQLUM_ROLLFWD: Roll forward until the point in time specified by stoptime or until the next archive log file is not found. 2 SQLUM_STOP: Stop roll forward. Any uncommitted transactions are rolled back and the database is ready for use. 3 SQLUM_ROLLFWD_STOP: This action is equivalent to a SQLUM_ROLLFWD followed by a SQLUM_STOP. 4 SQLUM_QUERY: This action is used to query log file info. It returns the name of the first archive log file no longer needed for recovery, the name of the next required log file, and the name of the last archived log file that can be removed from the log directory. With this information, you can dynamically copy into the online log directory the next log file when it's needed from an offline archive. You can also copy into an offline archive log information that is no longer needed.</pre> The Database Manager starts its log files at S0000000.LOG and goes to S9999999.LOG (more than 10,000,000) log files. It will go to zero when roll forward is enabled or disabled and when the log files wrap. You have plenty of warning for doing clean-up work. If you are rolling forward changes in a database and the Database Manager cannot find the next log file, it will return the next file name in the SQLCA. At this time, if there are no log files available (for example on an offline archive log), stop the roll forward and you're done. If there are more files, copy them from the offline to the online log, then continue the rolling forward.

Table 27-4 (Part 4 of 6).   The Database Administration API: General Utilities Commands.

Function Call Name	Descriptive Name	Client		Description
		DOS	**WIN**	
sqluexp()	**EXPORT TABLE**	Yes	Yes	This command copies data from a database table into an OS/2 file using one of several external file formats. You specify the data to be extracted by supplying an SQL SELECT statement. You must also supply the name of the file where you want the exported data to be copied to. The callerac flag repeat call facility can be used to prompt the user for additional diskettes. You should supply the name of a message file where error, warning, and informational messages can be placed by OS/2. The following exchange file formats are supported:
				IXF The internal Integrated eXchange Format (this format also exports the table DDL).
				WSF Lotus Worksheet formats.
				DEL ASCII Delimited, for exchanges with dBase.
				You should complete all database operations and release all locks before calling this API. This is best done by issuing STOP USING DATABASE.
				Note: The DOS and Windows clients do not support the export of LONG VARCHAR columns or support data export to multiple diskettes.
sqluimp()	**IMPORT TABLE**	Yes	Yes	This command copies data from an OS/2 file, using one of several file formats, to a database table. An INSERT, REPLACE, CREATE, or REPLACE_CREATE statement controls what to do with existing data in the specified table and column list. The data types in the file columns are converted into the data type of the corresponding SQL type, if possible. Minor incompatibilities are tolerated; for example, numeric data can be imported with a different numeric SQL type. You must also supply the name of the file that contains the data to be imported. The callerac flag repeat call facility can be used to prompt the user for additional diskettes. You should supply the name of a message file where error, warning, and informational messages can be placed by OS/2. The following exchange file formats are supported:
				(Continued...)

Table 27-4 (Part 5 of 6). The Database Administration API: General Utilities Commands.

Function Call Name	Descriptive Name	Client		Description
		DOS	**WIN**	
sqluimp() (Cont.)	IMPORT TABLE (Cont.)	Yes	Yes	**IXF** The internal Integrated eXchange Format (this format also exports the table DDL). **WSF** Lotus Worksheet formats. **DEL** ASCII Delimited, for exchanges with dBase. **ASC** ASCII non-delimited. Since the data for ASC files is non-delimited, you must specify through the dcoldata column structure positions of the input data. You must complete all database operations and release all locks before calling this command. The best way to do that is to issue a STOP USING DATABASE command first.
sqlureor()	REORGANIZE TABLE	Yes	Yes	This command reorganizes the physical storage for a base table. You typically issue this command when a table has become too fragmented due to many updates or deletes. You will know a table is fragmented and needs to be reorganized if the performance deteriorates. You can specify with this command how you want your tables physically ordered based on an index. To obtain the best results, reorganize the table using an index that is often used in queries. This command is fairly time-consuming (in the order of minutes). You must complete all database operations and release all locks before calling this command. The best way to do that is to issue a STOP USING DATABASE command first. Immediately after a table is reorganized, RUN STATISTICS should be run on it to generate current statistics for the reorganized table. You must then rebind all the packages that use this table.
sqlustat()	RUNSTATS TABLE	Yes	Yes	This command updates statistics about the physical characteristics of a base table and/or its indexes. This command should be called when a table has had: • massive updates, inserts, or deletes. • after a table REORGANIZE command. • after creating a table index. The statistics tracked are the number of records and average record length. The optimizer uses this statistical information to determine optimal path lengths to tables when building the access plans. You must rebind any static SQL applications (packages) that use this table so that it can take full advantage of the updated statistics. You should be connected to the database and not have any outstanding locks before issuing this command.

Table 27-4 (Part 6 of 6). The Database Administration API: General Utilities Commands.

Function Call Name	Descriptive Name	Client		Description
		DOS	**WIN**	

sqluadau()	GET ADMIN- ISTRATIVE AUTHOR- IZATION	Yes	Yes	This command returns the current user's database authority and privileges. The authorization list is returned in an array. A value of 1 indicates the user has the authority or privilege. This is a partial list of array elements:
				
				    Element **Authority**
				      0 SYSADM authority
				      1 DBADM authority
				      2 CREATETAB privilege
				      3 BINDADD privilege
				      4 CONNECT privilege
				
				You should be connected to the database to use this command.

DATABASE ADMINISTRATION API: CONFIGURATION SERVICES

These services are the API calls through which your applications can manipulate and view the configuration parameters that affect database performance.

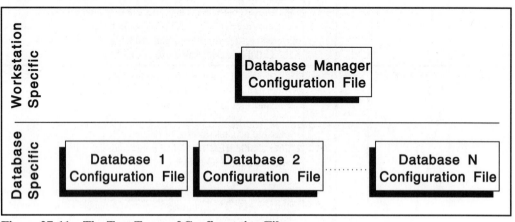

Figure 27-11.   The Two Types of Configuration Files.

The Database Manager has two types of configuration files (see Figure 27-11):

- **The Database Manager Configuration File** contains configuration parameters that affect the overall performance of the Database Manager and its global resource requirements. This file also contains the database information specific to a workstation. The configuration parameters in this file can be grouped as follows:

- Memory management
- Concurrent databases
- Workstation information

There are a total of 10 configuration parameters, 8 can be changed through the API services on server machines.

- **The Database Configuration File** which contains configuration parameters that affect the performance of an individual database and its resource requirements. Each database has its own configuration file that gets created when a **CREATE DATABASE** command is executed. The entries in this file can be changed to produce optimum performance depending on the type and activity of a database. The configuration parameters in this file can be grouped as follows:

- Memory management
- Lock management
- File handle limits
- Deadlock detection time
- Log file management and roll-forward services
- Database information

There are a total of 32 configuration parameters; 21 can be changed through the API services on server machines.

The Configuration Services Subcategories

The Configuration Services API provide the commands to manipulate configuration information. These commands fall into the following subcategories:

- Reset the configurations files to their system defaults.
- Update configuration file entries.
- Retrieve the values of configuration parameters from configuration files.

Table 27-5 classifies the Configuration services API commands according to the subcategory of service.

The Configuration services API will rarely be used in general programs. Only programs that provide generalized database utilities will need to use this API service. Most users will use the *Configuration Tool* to manually manipulate the configuration file parameters (see Figure 27-12). Serious database users need to fully understand how to use the configuration parameters to get the best performance out of their databases. We will use the Configuration Services API to introduce you to the configuration file parameters and to prepare you for one of those rare programs that uses the Configuration Services API.

Table 27-5.   The Configuration Services API Commands, Divided by Function.

Configuration Service Type	API Commands
Reset Configuration	RESET DATABASE MANAGER CONFIGURATION FILE and RESET DATABASE CONFIGURATION FILE
Update Configuration	UPDATE DATABASE MANAGER CONFIGURATION FILE and UPDATE DATABASE CONFIGURATION FILE
Retrieve Configuration	GET COPY OF DATABASE MANAGER CONFIGURATION FILE and GET COPY OF DATABASE CONFIGURATION FILE

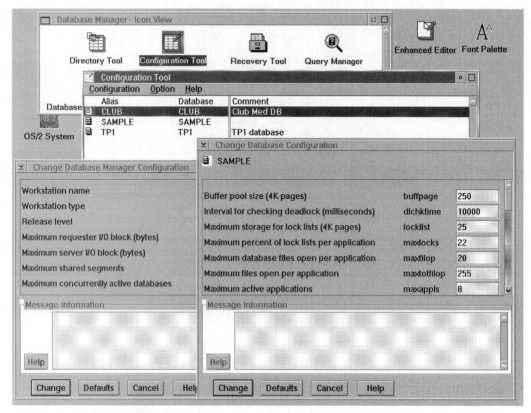

Figure 27-12.   The Configuration Tool.

The Database Manager Configuration File Parameters

Table 27-6 (Part 1 of 2). The Database Manager Configuration Parameters.

Configuration Parameter	Description
Memory Management Parameters	
sqlenseg	This parameter specifies the total number of 64 KByte **shared segments** available to the database manager. The defaults are 25 segments for standalone workstations, 80 segments for database server workstations, and 1 segment for database client workstations. At a minimum, you will need 6 segments for each additional activated database. The maximum number of shared segments is 802. *Recommendation: Use the default.*
rqioblk	This parameter specifies the maximum **I/O block size** in KBytes for client workstations. This value can vary between 4 (default) and 64 KBytes. The I/O block is used to store a group of rows that have been transmitted from the server. *Recommendation: Use the default.*
srvioblk	This parameter specifies the maximum **I/O block size** in KBytes for Database Server workstations. This value can vary between 4 (default) and 64 KBytes. The server I/O block is used to store a group of rows that have been read from the database for transmission to a client. *Recommendation: Use the default.*
comheapsz	This parameter specifies the total number of 64 KByte segments available for the **communication heap**. This is the dynamic memory used to allocate communication blocks. This value is always 0 for standalone workstations. This value can range from 1 to 255 segments for database client (default is 3) or server (default is 4) workstations. *Recommendation: Increase this number if you use many concurrent cursors.*
rsheapsz	This parameter specifies the total number of 64 KByte segments available for the **Remote Data Services heap**. This is the dynamic memory used by RDS. This value is always 0 for standalone workstations. This value can range from 1 to 255 segments for database client (default is 2) or server (default is 3) workstations. *Recommendation: Use the default.*
numrc	This parameter indicates the maximum number of **remote connections** to or from this workstation. This value is 0 for Database standalone workstations. The defaults are 10 connections for database server workstations and 3 connections for database client workstations. The maximum is 255 connections.

Table 27-6 (Part 1 of 2). **The Database Manager Configuration Parameters.**

Configuration Parameter	Description
Concurrent Database Parameters	
numdb	This parameter specifies the maximum number of **concurrently active databases** allowed. This value must be 0 for database clients. The defaults are 3 databases for standalone workstations and 8 databases for database server workstations. The maximum number of concurrently active databases is 8. *Recommendation: Don't use more than needed.*
Workstation Information Parameters	
nodetype	This parameter returns the **workstation configuration**. It indicates whether the workstation was configured as a standalone node (0), a database server (1), a client (2), or a client with a local database (3).
release	This parameter contains the **release number** of the Database Manager software. You can only change this parameter by reinstalling the system.
nodename	This parameter **names the workstation**. The name can be 1 to 8 characters long and must be null terminated. This parameter is not used by standalone workstations.

The Database Configuration File Parameters

Table 27-7 (Part 1 of 4). **The Database Configuration Parameters.**

Configuration Parameter	Description
Memory Management Parameters	
maxappls	This parameter specifies the maximum **number of active** applications (or processes) that can concurrently connect to the database. The default is 8 applications. The maximum is 256 applications. Remember that utilities require 1 connection.
buffpage	This parameter specifies the number of 4 KByte pages used for a **buffer pool** for that database. A buffer pool is a memory cache where database records are read and changed. The data can be accessed much faster from RAM than from disk. The client default is 25 pages; the server default is 250 pages. The maximum is 1500 pages. This is the *single most important parameter* through which you can improve database performance (at the cost of buying more memory).
sortheap	This parameter specifies the maximum **number of private segments for sort buffers** per application. This is the dynamic buffer heap used for sort lists. The default is 2 segments. The allowable range is from 1 to 20 segments. *Recommendation: Use indexes to minimize the sort heap.*
stmtheap	This parameter specifies the maximum **storage heap used for compiling dynamic SQL statements**. The default for this value is 64 segments. The allowable range is from 8 to 255 segments.

Table 27-7 (Part 2 of 4). The Database Configuration Parameters.

Configuration Parameter	Description
Lock Management Parameters	
locklist	This parameter specifies the number of 4 KByte pages used for the **storage of locklists**. The size of this parameter affects the maximum number of locks available for all applications that are concurrently using a database. The default for this value is 2 pages. The allowable range is from 4 to 250 pages. *Recommendation: Use 6 pages.*
maxlocks	This parameter specifies the maximum **percent of locklists** allowed per application. The range is from 1 to 100 percent. The default is 22 percent.
File Handle Limit Parameters	
maxfilop	This parameter specifies the maximum **number of open database files** per application. The default is 20 files. The allowable range is from 2 to 235 files. The greater the value specified, the less frequently Database Manager must open and close files.
maxtotfilop	This parameter specifies the maximum **number of open OS/2 files** per process. This includes all database and user files. The default is 255 files. The allowable range is from 25 to 32,700 files.
Deadlock Detection Time Parameters	
dlchktime	This parameter specifies the **time interval for checking deadlocks** in units of milliseconds. Increasing this parameter improves run-time performance but at the risk of freezing your applications for longer durations while a deadlock remains undetected. The default for this value is 10,000 msecs. The allowable range is from 1,000 to 600,000 msecs.
Log File Management Parameters	
logfilsiz	This parameter specifies the number of 4 KByte pages on disk used for the **log files**. The size of this parameter affects the amount of changes to the database that can be done by active transactions. The changes a transaction makes to a database are written to the log files where the records are kept until the transaction terminates. If there are many changes or many concurrent transactions, the log file can become full. When the primary log files becomes full, the overflow records are stored on secondary log files. The secondary log files are created empty but are extended by the size specified by this parameter when space is needed. They are truncated back to empty when space is no longer needed. The default for this value is 50 pages (on servers). The allowable range is from 4 to 65,535 pages. *Recommendation: Use lots of COMMIT statements in your code, and make the size larger if you're using roll forward.*
logprimary	This parameter specifies the number of **primary log files** that will be created. These are the preallocated files that require the same amount of disk space whether they are empty or full. The default for this value is 3 files. The allowable range is from 2 to 63 files. *Recommendation: Make this parameter larger for databases that are enabled for roll-forward recovery. A roll forward enabled database uses primary log files only. When a log full warning is issued it is based on the number of configured primary log files.*

Table 27-7 (Part 3 of 4). The Database Configuration Parameters.

Configuration Parameter	Description
Log File Management Parameters (Continued)	
logsecond	This parameter specifies the number of **secondary log files**. These are empty log files that can be extended as needed when the primary log files run out of space. The default for this value is 2 files. The allowable range is from 0 to 61 files.
softmax	This parameter specifies the maximum number of log records that can be written before a **soft checkpoint** is applied. A soft checkpoint establishes a pointer in the log at which recovery of a database is to begin. The recovery process will skip over old records (pre-checkpoint) and only process new records for recovery purposes. Making this number large extends the duration of a database restart in the event of failure, especially if the log file is very large. A smaller value for this parameter slows your transactions at run time. The default value is 100 records. The allowable range is from 0 to 65,535 records. The value 0 indicates no soft checkpoints.
newlogpath	This parameter specifies the **path of the current location of log files** on disk. The recovery log file is first created in the same directory as the database and this parameter is set to null. A null setting indicates the default path. *Recommendation: Place the log on a different disk from the database to avoid a single point of failure.*
Database Information Parameters	
copyprotect	This parameter is used to enable or disable **copy protection**. When copy protection is enabled (the default), a database cannot be used on a workstation other than the one on which it was created. *Reccommendation: Remove the copy protection from all databases before reinstalling. After installation you can re-enable copy protection.*
release	This parameter contains the **release number** of the Database Manager system software. You can only change this parameter by reinstalling the system.
country	This parameter contains the **country code** of the database. The country code affects, among other things, database TIME and DATA formats. You can only change this parameter by reinstalling the database.
codepage	This parameter contains the **codepage** of the database. The codepage of a database affects the presentation of text. You can only change this parameter by reinstalling the database.
backup_pending	This status parameter indicates that a backup of the database must be performed before anybody can connect to the databases. This situation occurs after roll forward is enabled.
database_consistent	This status parameter indicates that the database is in a consistent state. It may be useful during roll forward.
logpath	This status parameter indicates the current path to the log files.
autorestart	This status parameter indicates the current path to the log files.

Table 27-7 (Part 4 of 4). The Database Configuration Parameters.

Configuration Parameter	Description
Forward Recovery Parameters	
log_retain	This parameter is used to enable or disable roll forward. The log files will be retained the next time the database is started. The default is disable roll forward.
log_retain_status	This status parameter indicates whether roll forward is enabled or disabled.
userexit	This parameter is used to enable or disable a user log exit the next time the database is started. The user log exit is a form of trigger that calls a program you provide (IBM calls these programs user exits or SQLUEXIT) when the log files are filled or needed for recovery. You can use this trigger to copy archived log files *offline*, which in this case means a location other than the database log path directory, and to bring them back *online* when needed. This trigger can be useful for disaster recovery, for moving log file data on tape or optical disk, and for alerting your programs when the log files are full. The default condition is disable user exit.
user_exit_status	This status parameter indicates whether your trigger program will be called when the log files are filled or needed for recovery.
rollfwd_pending	This status parameter indicates that roll-forward recovery of the database must be performed before connecting to the database. This is the state the database is in after a RESTORE.
loghead	This status parameter returns the name of the log file at the head of the active log. Log files created prior to this file are no longer *active* log files needed for normal processing. The files that are no longer active can be moved from the database log path directory using a "user exit."

The Configuration Service Commands

We are now ready to present the individual API calls that constitute the Configuration Services. These calls are described in Table 27-8. Notice that we've added two columns to our normal description of the API functions to denote whether the function can be executed on Windows and DOS clients. Here are some rules that apply to the Configuration Services API commands:

- The updates or resets to the Database Manager configuration files are not effective until all applications have completed and a **STOP DATABASE MANAGER** command has been performed. The changes are activated by the next **START DATABASE MANAGER** command.

- The updates or resets to the database configuration files are not effective until all applications have completed and a **STOP USING DATABASE** command has been performed. The changes are activated by the next **START USING DATABASE** command.

- If two applications modify the configuration files before the updates are made effective, the later update overrides the earlier one.

- The configuration parameters are updated or retrieved by passing an **array of items** to the API. Each item contains a number (the token) that identifies a parameter in the configuration file, and a pointer to a memory location for the parameter value to be returned or updated.

Table 27-8 (Part 1 of 3).   The Database Administration API: Configuration Services.

Function Call Name	Descriptive Name	Client		Description
		DOS	WIN	
sqlfrsys()	RESET DATABASE MANAGER CONFIGURA-TION FILE	No	No	This command resets the Database Manager config file to the shipped parameter defaults. The default values will be based on the current node type.

sqlfxsys()	GET COPY OF DATABASE MANAGER CONFIGURA-TION FILE	No	No	This command retrieves individual entries in the Database Manager configuration file. You must provide a count parameter that indicates the number of entries you want retrieved. You must also provide an array of elements for the returned entries. Each element in the array consists of a token and an address. The token is a number that identifies the parameter field. The address points to a variable which will receive the returned parameter. The following shows the token to Database Manager config file parameter correspondence:
				
				 `Token Field Nm.   Data Type Description`
				 `  1   rqrioblk  SMALLINT  max requester block`
				 `  3   svrioblk  SMALLINT  max server block`
				 `  5   sqlenseg  SMALLINT  max shared segs.`
				 `  6   numdb     SMALLINT  max active DBs`
				 `  7   nodename  CHAR[9]   workstation name`
				 `  8   comheapsz SMALLINT  max comm heap size`
				 `  9   rsheapsz  SMALLINT  max RDS heap size`
				 ` 10   numrc     SMALLINT  max connections`
				 `100   nodetype  SMALLINT  node type (read)`
				 `101   release   SMALLINT  DB release (read)`

sqlfusys()	UPDATE DATABASE MANAGER CONFIGURA-TION FILE	No	No	This command allows individual entries in the Database Manager config files to be modified. You must provide a count of the number of parameters you want modified and an array of elements. Each element in the array contains a token number that identifies the field to be modified and an address that points to the new field value (see token description above).
sqlfrdb()	RESET DATABASE CONFIGURA-TION FILE	No	No	This command resets the Database config file to the shipped parameter defaults.

Table 27-8 (Part 2 of 3). The Database Administration API: Configuration Services.

Function Call Name	Descriptive Name	Client		Description
		DOS	WIN	
sqlfxdbc()	RETURN COPY OF DATABASE CONFIGURA-TION FILE	No	No	This command retrieves individual entries in the Database config file. You must provide a count parameter that indicates the number of entries you want retrieved. You must also provide an array of elements for the returned entries. Each element in the array consists of a token and an address. The token is a number that identifies the parameter field. The address points to a variable that will receive the returned parameter. The following shows the token to the DB config file parameter correspondence:

```
Token Field Nm.    Data Type Description
    1  locklist     SMALLINT  max locklist sz.
    2  buffpage     SMALLINT  max buffer pool
    3  maxfilop     SMALLINT  max DB files
    5  softmax      SMALLINT  max soft checkpt
    6  maxappls     SMALLINT  max active users
    7  applheapsz   SMALLINT  application heap
    8  dbheap       SMALLINT  database heap
    9  dlchktime    INTEGER   deadlock chk ms
   10  maxtotfilop  SMALLINT  max appl files
   11  sortheap     SMALLINT  sort heap size
   14  agentheap    SMALLINT  appl agent heap
   15  maxlocks     SMALLINT  % of locklist
   16  logprimary   SMALLINT  prim log files
   17  logsecond    SMALLINT  sec log files
   18  logfilsiz    SMALLINT  prim file size
   19  stmtheap     SMALLINT  SQL stmt heap
   20  newlogpath   CHAR[248] changed log path
   21  attributes   SMALLINT  see below
   22  copyprotect  SMALLINT  enable copy protect
   23  logretain    SMALLINT  enable roll forward
   24  user exit    SMALLINT  enable user-exit
   25  autorestart  SMALLINT  enable auto restart
  100  country      SMALLINT  country (read)
  101  codepage     SMALLINT  DB codepage(rd.)
  102  release      SMALLINT  DB release(read)
  103  logpath      CHAR[248] log path (read)
  105  loghead      CHAR[14]  log head (read)
  107  nextactive   CHAR[14]  next log file (read)
  104  status       SMALLINT  status see below (read)
  111  db_consist   SMALLINT  DB consistent status
  112  backup_pend  SMALLINT  backup pending status
  113  rollf_pend   SMALLINT  roll-forward pending status
  114  retain_stat  SMALLINT  roll-forward status
  115  exit_status  SMALLINT  user exit status
```

Table 27-8 (Part 3 of 3). The Database Administration API: Configuration Services.

Function Call Name	Descriptive Name	Client		Description
		DOS	WIN	
sqlfeudb()	UPDATE DATABASE CONFIGURA- TION FILE	No	No	This command allows individual entries in the Database config files to be modified. You must provide a count of the number of parameters you want modified and an array of elements. Each element in the array contains a token number which identifies the field to be modified and an address that points to the new field value (see token description above).

DATABASE ADMINISTRATION API: APPLICATION SERVICES

There are two API calls that fall into the Application Services category: **BIND** and **GET ERROR MESSAGE**. Neither of these two calls requires any new background information. We can go on to the description in Table 27-9 where, as previously noted, we added two columns to our normal description of the API functions to denote whether the function can be executed on Windows and DOS clients.

Table 27-9. The Database Administration API: Application Services Commands.

Function Call Name	Descriptive Name	Remote		Description
		DOS	WIN	
sqlabndr()	BIND WITH OPTIONS	No	No	This command calls the BIND utility from within an application program. This is the version of the BIND that supports isolation levels and other options. This command binds a precompiled application program to the database, and creates access plans that get stored in the database (packages). You must provide the name of the (.BND) bind file or a file containing a list of bind file names. You can specify a path for these files. You should supply the name of a message file where error, warning, and informational messages can be placed by OS/2. You can also specify through a SQLOPT structure an array of bind options: **Option Token**　　　　　　　　　　**Description** **SQL_FORMAT_OPT** This option determines the format 　　　of the date and time fields: 　　　　**SQL_FMT_0**　　　　　Machine Default 　　　　**SQL_FMT_1**　　　　　USA 　　　　**SQL_FMT_2**　　　　　EUROPE 　　　　**SQL_FMT_3**　　　　　ISO 　　　　**SQL_FMT_4**　　　　　JIS (Japan) 　　　　**SQL_FMT_5**　　　　　LOCAL **SQL_ISO_OPT**　　This option indicates the isolation level: 　　　　**SQL_REP_READ**　　　Repeatable Read (RR) 　　　　**SQL_CUR_STAB**　　　Cursor Stability (CS) 　　　　**SQL_UNCOM_READ**　Uncommitted Read (UR) **SQL_BLOCK_OPT**　　This option indicates the type 　　　of record blocking and the manner in which ambiguous 　　　cursorsare treated: 　　　　**SQL_BL_ALL**　　　　all cursors 　　　　**SQL_BL_UNAMBIG**　fetch-only cursors 　　　　**SQL_NO_BL**　　　　no blocking **Note:** Record blocking can be used to decrease network traffic for applications that access a remote database.
sqlaintp()	GET ERROR MESSAGE	Yes	Yes	This command returns the error message that corresponds to an error code in the SQLCODE field of the SQLCA. This is a very useful function for error handling. You provide a message buffer and specify the maximum line width of the message. The message will be broken down into a series of lines separated by CR/LF. A null is placed at the end of the message.

DATABASE ADMINISTRATION API: GENERIC SERVICES

We will make use of two API calls that fall into the Generic Services category: **LOG ON** and **LOG OFF**. These are the commands you need to interface with the User Profile Manager (UPM) that we introduced in the previous chapter. Neither of these two calls requires any new background information, and we can go on to the description of the commands in Table 27-10. Again, notice that we've added two columns to our normal description of the API functions to denote whether the function can be executed on Windows and DOS clients.

Table 27-10. The Database Administration API: Generic Services Commands.

Function Call Name	Descriptive Name	Client		Description
		DOS	**WIN**	
upmglgn()	**LOG ON**	Yes	Yes	This command logs on the user to a specified node. You must supply a user ID, the password and the remote node name or domain. A remote type parameter specifies the type of remote node, as follows:
				UPM_LOCAL Identifies the node as the local workstation. In this case, the remote name parameter is ignored.
				PM_DNODE Identifies the remote node as an APPC node.
				PM_DOMAIN Identifies the remote node as the name of a LAN domain.
				The program issuing the logon must have been started by an authorized user. Valid indicators of the authority required to issue the logon are:
				PM_CONFIG The calling process must have been started by config.sys or from a process that was so started.
				PM_ADMIN The logged on local user for the calling session must have administrative authority.
				PM_USER The calling process does not require any additional authority.
				When logging on to a remote workstation, no logon actually occurs. The user ID and password are stored to be used for the next connection with the remote workstation.
upmglgff()	**LOG OFF**	Yes	Yes	This command disconnects the user from a session. A log on session remains active until you either issue this command or you turn off your workstation. To use this command, you must supply a user ID and the remote node name or domain, and the remote type parameter that was described in LOG ON.

DRDA: OPPORTUNITY AND CAVEATS

DDCS/2 supports connections to DB2 V2.3, SQL/DS V3.3, and SQL/400 V2.11. How easy will it be to port OS/2 SQL applications to these platforms? Will they really run unchanged? Where are the pitfalls? What is the development process? What tools are provided? We will attempt to answer all these questions in the remainder of this chapter.

The DRDA Development Environment

The good news is that your friendly OS/2 Database Manager gives you everything you need to develop portable applications across SAA platforms. To create your development environment, follow these steps:

1. Install DDCS/2 on a server machine. The installation takes a few minutes. There are no surprises here.
2. Configure the DDCS/2 environment. You must configure Communications Manager and the directory services. This is what we did earlier in this chapter.
3. Develop your programs on the local OS/2 Database Manager. Start with the (.SQC) files and run them through SQLPREP with the deferred bind option. This will create (.BND) files that you can later bind to the host database of choice. Compile and link your programs using C Set/2. This process was explained earlier in the chapter.
4. Issue a **START USING DATABASE** command to connect to the host SAA database of choice. The directories are all setup to make the connection transparent to your programs, as was shown earlier.
5. Use the DDCS/2 supplied **SQLJBIND** program to bind all the SQL utilities to the host. These include SQLBIND, the Command Line Interface (CLI), REXX (if needed), IMPORT, and EXPORT. We're assuming that you're dealing with a virgin host with nothing installed on it. You must bind the SQLBIND utility to bind your programs to the host; the rest of the utilities are optional.
6. Issue the **BIND** command to bind your (.BND) files to the host database.

DDCS/2 Development Tools

The DDCS/2 product provides a set of tools that help you develop and debug DRDA applications:

SQLJSETP sets environment variables to provide more explicit error messages when you BIND your programs on different host environments. The additional information returned in messages includes the server type, the package type, and the complete SQLCA contents. It tells you in clear terms what error occurred (for example, which column does not exist) and what to do about it.

SQLJTRC   traces the DRDA message flows. The trace information is entered in the default SQLJTRC.DMP file. The trace tool is useful for debugging, but should not be used in production environments. It introduces too much overhead.

SQLJBIND binds OS/2 SQL utilities to the host.

The DRDA Runtime Environment

The DRDA runtime environment is totally transparent to the client/server programs. Here's how it works:

1. Log on to your workstation and provide the UPM password and security information. This information will be used to identify you to the host security subsystems like RACF.
2. Issue a **START USING DATABASE** command to connect to the host SAA database of choice. The directories are all set up to make the connection transparent to your programs as was shown earlier.
3. Run your programs. You're connected in client/server mode with the host. You can run static SQL packages, dynamic SQL, and multiple cursors.
4. Issue a **STOP USING DATABASE** when you're done. You can then start using any other SAA host by repeating the process. It couldn't be easier.

Programming for DRDA

DRDA introduces the first heterogeneous DBMS platform in the industry that supports both static and dynamic SQL across dissimilar operating systems, networks, and hardware platforms. As you can imagine, this complex environment will have some impact on our SQL programming practices. There are also some caveats. This section examines some of those issues.

SQL Is not Always SQL

Different DBMS platforms have introduced their own extensions of SQL. The SQL-PREP precompiler was relaxed to accept "unknown dialects." This new level of tolerance means that you can use SQL dialects for other SAA target machines in your programs. The compiling process leaves it up to the BIND program to check for allowable commands on a target DBMS. Of course, the four SAA DBMSs have some different tastes and will get different bind results (see Figure 27-13). Notice that only OS/2 supports the DATABASE APPLICATION REMOTE INTERFACE; only DB2 supports TABLESPACES. These differences are detected at bind time.

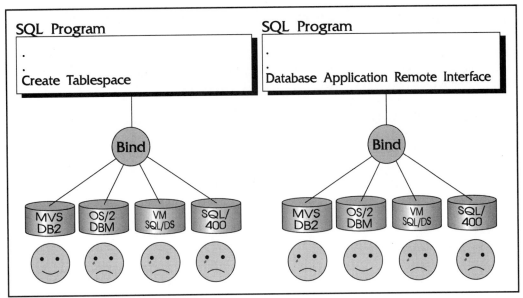

Figure 27-13. Platform-Specific SQL Extensions.

You must avoid target-specific SQL extensions if you want your programs to be portable across SAA platforms. So what is a portable SQL? For DRDA DBMSs, it is the SAA SQL dialect.[4] There are, in general, two areas where SQL deviates from the standard: the DDL and the advanced SQL extensions. The OS/2 DDL is SAA compliant. However, OS/2 does offer advanced constructs that go above and beyond SAA, like the DATABASE APPLICATION REMOTE INTERFACE. Should you use them? It depends on whether you need performance or portability. There are always trade-offs in this business.

How to Handle Sorts

ASCII and EBCDIC sort differently. In ASCII numeric values come first. In EBCDIC, it's the inverse. Your programs may see different ordering results depending on which platform they execute on. This will be true for any ORDER BY, GROUP BY, or DISTINCT clause. To get around this limitation, DRDA provides collating sequences. These are tables that allow you to explicitly specify how sorting will occur. You can make "z" come before "a" if you so choose. DDCS/2 provides an ASCII/EBCDIC collating table.

---

[4] See **CPI Database Level 2 Reference**, IBM Order Number SC26-4798 (April, 1991). This publication marks in green the DBMS platform deviations from SAA SQL. The current implementation of Database Manager removes most of the green from OS/2.

How to Handle "Common" Errors

The different SAA platforms have, over time, created their own error return codes. In OS/2, these are the codes returned in the SQLCODE field of the SQLCA structure. DDCS/2 provides two ways to write portable return codes:

1. Using the SQLSTATE field in the SQLCA. This field will return standardized SAA error codes that are consistent across SAA platforms. This standard complies with the ISO/ANSI SQL draft.
2. Using the DDCS/2 error mapping tables. These tables, specified in the DCS directory, map error codes between SAA platforms. You can continue to use the SQLCODE field for error returns, and it's business as usual.

System Catalogs Variations

SQL Database Managers use system catalogs to maintain information about themselves. These catalogs are ordinary SQL tables that your programs can query to obtain all sorts of useful information at run time. For example, a report builder may query the catalog to obtain the column names and types for a particular table. Unfortunately, the SAA DBMSs have some differences in their catalogs (see Table 27-11). You can get around this limitation by creating VIEWs that mask the differences between the tables. The DBMSs also use different qualifiers for their system tables. The OS/2 Database Manager and DB2 use *SYSIBM*; SQL/DS uses *SYSTEM*.

Table 27-11. Differences in System Catalogs Across SAA DBMSs.

OS/2 DBM	MVS DB2	VM SQL/DS	OS/400 SQL/400
Sysindexes	Sysindexes	Sysindexes	Sysindexes
Sysplan	Sysplan	Sysplan	Sysaccess
Systables	Systables	Syscatalog	Systables
Sysviews	Sysviews	Sysviews	Sysviews

Beware of Locks and Isolation Levels

The different SAA DBMS platforms support different locking and isolation levels. Locking is transparent to your code. So, there is not too much you can do to protect yourself from these different locking strategies other than to be aware of their existence. Table 27-12 shows the different isolation levels supported by SAA DBMSs. These isolation levels are specified at BIND time. Table 27-13 shows the different levels of locking support.

Table 27-12. Differences in Isolation Level Support Across SAA DBMSs.

Isolation Level	OS/2 DBM	MVS DB2	VM SQL/DS	OS/400 SQL/400
Read Repeatability (RR)	Yes	Yes	Yes	No
Cursor Stability (CS)	Yes	Yes	Yes	No
Uncommitted Read (UR)	Yes	No	No	No
LCKLVL (ALL)	No	No	No	Yes
LCKLVL (CHG)	No	No	No	Yes

Table 27-13. Differences in Locking Support Across SAA DBMSs.

Lock Support	OS/2 DBM	MVS DB2	VM SQL/DS	OS/400 SQL/400
Row Level Locking	Yes	No	Yes	Yes
Page Locking	No	Yes	Yes	No
Table Locking	Yes	Yes	Yes	Yes
Lock Escalation	Yes	Yes	Yes	No

Which Server Type?

DRDA makes the server type and location transparent to your code. So, how do you know which type of server you're connected to? You may need this information to allow your programs to modify their behavior at run time, to accommodate for the variations between SAA DBMSs. For example, a query picker may modify its SELECT statement against a System Catalog Table.

DDCS/2 provides a mechanism that allows you to discover which system type you're working with. This information is returned when you first issue a **START USING DATABASE** command. The command returns (in the SQLCA.SQLERRP field) a 3-character code that identifies the database type. The codes used are: "DSN" for DB2, "ARI" for SQL/DS, "QSQ" for AS/400, and "SQL" for OS/2.

Not All Utilities Are Supported

DDCS/2 only supports the IMPORT and EXPORT utility for exchanging table contents from OS/2 to other SAA DBMSs; and only the PC/IXF interchange format is supported. DDCS/2 does not allow you to issue REORGs, RUNSTATs, or ROLL FORWARDs against other SAA DBMSs. It also does not support the GET ADMIN or AUTHORIZATION commands. You must perform these tasks from within the host environment using SPUFI, QMF, or CICS tools.

Other Miscellaneous Differences

This is a "catch-all" list for the differences that remain between the SAA platforms. The list is not exhaustive:

- OS/2 does not support the CONNECT command; instead it uses START USING DATABASE.
- OS/2 does not support INCLUDE files in its precompiler.
- OS/2 uses the application's Date/Time and code page as BIND defaults. DB2 uses ISO. *Use explicit BIND options to avoid discrepancies.*
- Long fields (greater than 254 characters) are treated differently by each SAA DBMS.

DRDA Summary

Yes, DRDA is not perfect, but it's a quantum leap toward realizing the SQL dream of seamless access to data across dissimilar platforms. The mainframes contain huge amounts of data. The PCs provide cheap MIPs and ease-of-use. DRDA makes them work together almost painlessly. The DDCS/2 product allows you to get to the mainframe data without writing a line of mainframe code. Your entire development environment is on a PC running OS/2. We've certainly come a long way.

Chapter 28

RSQL: The "All-In-One" Database Manager Utility

This chapter introduces **RSQL**, the "all-in-one" utility we will create for the OS/2 Database Manager. Think of **RSQL** as a Swiss Army Knife for the OS/2 Database Manager. You can use it to run SQL command scripts, fine-tune the database, look at the system configuration parameters, and measure performance. You'll find it to be the ultimate learning tool for familiarizing yourself with the Database Manager and observing its performance trade-offs. You may also discover, as we did, that playing with **RSQL** is a lot of fun. It's a great hacker's tool for the OS/2 Database Manager. There is nothing in the Database Manager that you can't get at with a simple **RSQL** script. This chapter teaches you how to use **RSQL** through scripts that demonstrate:

- The power of the SQL language
- How to use the Database Manager's Administration Utilities

These scripts mirror the material presented in the database tutorial chapters. Live examples will make those concepts more real and help demonstrate the power that is packed into the OS/2 Database Engine. Going through the scripts will also help you with the programming chapters that follow. These are the chapters where we dissect the **RSQL** program and use it as an exhaustive example of how to write code for the OS/2 Database Manager. So happy hacking and welcome to the world of scripts.

THE PLAN FOR THIS CHAPTER

We'll assume you've read the database tutorial chapters and absorbed every word of wisdom they contain. It's important that you start there because we won't be providing elaborate explanations in this chapter. Instead, we'll be running back-to-back **RSQL** scripts that demonstrate the concepts introduced in the tutorials. We'll try to present the scripts in the same order as the tutorial material. Here's the three-course menu of what we will be covering in this chapter:

- How to write an **RSQL** script.

- How to use **SQL**. We demonstrate with simple RSQL scripts the following SQL features:

  1. Simple Queries, Subqueries, and Multitable Queries (Joins).
  2. Database Inserts, Updates, and Deletes.
  3. Creating Tables, Indexes, and Views.
  4. Enforcing transactional units of recovery through COMMIT and ROLLBACK.
  5. Providing data integrity using Unique Indexes, Views, and Referential Integrity.
  6. Using Indexes to maximize performance.
  7. SQL security.
  8. The system catalogs.

- How to use the **Database Administration** services. We demonstrate with simple RSQL scripts the following features:

  1. How to Export and Import "external" files.
  2. How to Create and Catalog a database.
  3. How to fine-tune database performance with Table Reorganizations and Run-stats.
  4. How to Bind programs to the database.
  5. How to view and update the database and system configuration parameters.
  6. How to view the node and database directories.
  7. How to Backup, Restore, and Roll Forward a database.

CREATING AN RSQL SCRIPT

Creating an **RSQL** script is easy. Use an ASCII editor to create a script file of the commands you want to run. We'll call this file a *run* file. The following example demonstrates a simple script in a *run* file called **club.run**.

```
--        /*''''''''''''''''''''''''''''''''''''''''''''''''''''''''''''''''''''''''*/
--      /*           A simple example of an RSQL Script                          */
--        /*''''''''''''''''''''''''''''''''''''''''''''''''''''''''''''''''''''''''*/
--                  /*** connect to the database in shared mode ***/
EXEC DBA:    STARTUSE club S;

--                        /*** display table data ***/
EXEC SQL:    SELECT village, country
             FROM vacations
             WHERE country = Mexico;

--                        /*** disconnect from the database ***/
EXEC DBA:    STOPUSE club;
```

Figure 28-1. A Simple RSQL Script File: CLUB.RUN.

The RSQL RUN File Format

As you can see from this simple example, writing an **RSQL** *script* isn't too difficult. Here's what you should know about writing a script file:

1. Comment lines starts with "--" in the first column, the ANSII standard for SQL comments. Comments cannot be placed inside commands.
2. Commands start with a two-word header that identifies the command type. The command types adhere to the classification scheme we introduced in the tutorial chapters:

   EXEC SQL: is the header for SQL commands. The command that follows is the text for any valid dynamic SQL statement.

   EXEC DBA: is the header for Database Administration commands. The command that follows can be almost any of the Database Administration commands described in the tutorial.

   EXEC DOS: is the header for executing an OS/2 program from within an **RSQL** script. The header is followed by the name of an OS/2 program and its parameters.

3. The railroad diagrams in the programming chapters describe how you can place these commands in your scripts.
4. Commands are separated from their parameters by at least 1 blank space or CR/LF (i.e., new-line).
5. A script is automatically committed to the database at the end of a successful run (that is, when the **RSQL** program terminates). You can, of course, place your explicit commits anywhere within a script. Likewise, rollbacks may also be issued anywhere in the script.
6. You can specify through explicit directives whether **RSQL** should continue to execute the program after an error is encountered or whether it should terminate.
7. You can tell **RSQL** to pause execution through explicit pause directives. The execution is resumed by hitting any key.

RUN THE SCRIPT

The next step after creating the script is to run it. You do this by invoking **RSQL** at the OS/2 prompt as follows:

```
RSQL club.run answers.rsp
```

The syntax for invoking the program is:

```
RSQL    run    response
```

where *run* is file that contains the commands and *response* is the file where you want
RSQL to put the results of a run.

VIEW THE RESPONSE FILE

The final step is to view the contents of the *response* file, **answers.rsp**, using any ASCII
editor. For each command in the *run* file, **RSQL** will write the following to the *result*
file:

* The input command text, including comments (from the *run* file)
* The results of running the command
* The value of the SQLCA completion code
* The time it took to execute the command

This is what **answers.rsp** will contain after a successful run:

```
--      /*''''''''''''''''''''''''''''''''''''''''''''''''''''''''''''''''''''''*/
--      /*            A simple example of an RSQL Script                       */
--      /*''''''''''''''''''''''''''''''''''''''''''''''''''''''''''''''''''''''*/
--              /*** connect to the database in shared mode ***/
EXEC DBA:    STARTUSE club S;

 OK, sql_rcd = 0,        Execution time =     2.2200 secs

--                      /*** display table data ***/
EXEC SQL:    SELECT village, country
             FROM vacations
             WHERE country = Mexico;

 VILLAGE              COUNTRY
 ----------------     ------------
 CANCUN               MEXICO
 IXTAPA               MEXICO
 PLAYA BLANCA         MEXICO
 HUATULCO             MEXICO

 Total Number of Rows SELECTED = 4
 OK, sql_rcd = 0,        Execution time =     0.3600 secs

--                      /*** disconnect from the database ***/
EXEC DBA:    STOPUSE club;

 OK, sql_rcd = 0,        Execution time =     0.3700 secs
```

Figure 28-2. The Response File ANSWERS.RSP.

EXPLORING THE POWER OF SQL WITH SCRIPTS

The scripts that follow use the SAMPLE database supplied with the OS/2 Database
Manager. SAMPLE is a database for a hypothetical marketing firm consisting of two
tables:

- **ORG** contains information about the firm's structure. This includes department names, managers, and the divisions and locations of departments.
- **STAFF** contains information about the employees of this firm. This includes the number of years they've been employed, the department to which they belong, their salaries, etc.

Simple Queries: SELECT FROM

Our first script does the following:

1. Installs the SAMPLE database and fills it with data by executing the Database Manager supplied **sqlsampl.exe** program. It is placed in **\SQLLIB** at installation time.
2. Binds the **RSQL.BND** file to the newly created database.
3. Connects to the SAMPLE database.
4. Issues a SELECT with the wild card "*" for all columns. This will display all the rows and columns in the table.

```
--      /*'''''''''''''''''''''''''''''''''''''''''''''''''''''''''''''''''''''*/
--      /*              A simple SQL Query Demonstration                       */
--      /*'''''''''''''''''''''''''''''''''''''''''''''''''''''''''''''''''''''*/
--      /***************** Install the Sample Database ********************/
EXEC DOS:      sqlsampl.exe;

Program completed with a return code of 0.
 OK,                      Execution time =    48.3100 secs


--      /************* BIND the rsql program to database  ******************/
EXEC DBA: BIND SAMPLE RSQL.BND ISO UNCOMMITTED_READ BLOCK_ALL PUBLIC;

No messages in msgfile.msg

 OK, sql_rcd = 0,        Execution time =    1.5600 secs


--      /************* connect to the database in shared mode **************/
EXEC DBA:      STARTUSE sample S;

 OK, sql_rcd = 0,        Execution time =    0.6300 secs


--      /********* Display all rows and columns in  the ORG table ***********/
EXEC SQL:      SELECT * FROM org;

DEPTNUMB  DEPTNAME        MANAGER  DIVISION   LOCATION
--------  --------------  -------  ---------  -------------
   10     Head Office     160      Corporate  New York
   15     New England     50       Eastern    Boston
   20     Mid Atlantic    10       Eastern    Washington
   38     South Atlantic  30       Eastern    Atlanta
   42     Great Lakes     100      Midwest    Chicago
   51     Plains          140      Midwest    Dallas
```

Figure 28-3 (Part 1 of 2). Script 1: Demonstrating Simple SQL Queries.

```
66          Pacific          270     Western     San Francisco
84          Mountain         290     Western     Denver

Total Number of Rows SELECTED = 8

OK, sql_rcd = 0,          Execution time =        0.1500 secs


--      /*********** display all rows and columns in the STAFF table ********/
EXEC SQL:        SELECT *
                 FROM staff;

ID      NAME        DEPT    JOB     YEARS   SALARY      COMM
------  ---------   ------  -----   ------  --------    --------
10      Sanders     20      Mgr     7       18357.50    NULL
20      Pernal      20      Sales   8       18171.25     612.45
30      Marenghi    38      Mgr     5       17506.75    NULL
40      O'Brien     38      Sales   6       18006.00     846.55
50      Hanes       15      Mgr     10      20659.80    NULL
60      Quigley     38      Sales   NULL    16808.30     650.25
70      Rothman     15      Sales   7       16502.83    1152.00
80      James       20      Clerk   NULL    13504.60     128.20
90      Koonitz     42      Sales   6       18001.75    1386.70
100     Plotz       42      Mgr     7       18352.80    NULL
110     Ngan        15      Clerk   5       12508.20     206.60
120     Naughton    38      Clerk   NULL    12954.75     180.00
130     Yamaguchi   42      Clerk   6       10505.90      75.60
140     Fraye       51      Mgr     6       21150.00    NULL
150     Williams    51      Sales   6       19456.50     637.65
160     Molinare    10      Mgr     7       22959.20    NULL
170     Kermisch    15      Clerk   4       12258.50     110.10
180     Abrahams    38      Clerk   3       12009.75     236.50
190     Sneider     20      Clerk   8       14252.75     126.50
200     Scoutten    42      Clerk   NULL    11508.60      84.20
210     Lu          10      Mgr     10      20010.00    NULL
220     Smith       51      Sales   7       17654.50     992.80
230     Lundquist   51      Clerk   3       13369.80     189.65
240     Daniels     10      Mgr     5       19260.25    NULL
250     Wheeler     51      Clerk   6       14460.00     513.30
260     Jones       10      Mgr     12      21234.00    NULL
270     Lea         66      Mgr     9       18555.50    NULL
280     Wilson      66      Sales   9       18674.50     811.50
290     Quill       84      Mgr     10      19818.00    NULL
300     Davis       84      Sales   5       15454.50     806.10
310     Graham      66      Sales   13      21000.00     200.30
320     Gonzales    66      Sales   4       16858.20     844.00
330     Burke       66      Clerk   1       10988.00      55.50
340     Edwards     84      Sales   7       17844.00    1285.00
350     Gafney      84      Clerk   5       13030.50     188.00

Total Number of Rows SELECTED = 35

OK, sql_rcd = 0,          Execution time =        0.1200 secs
```

Figure 28-3 (Part 2 of 2).   Script 1: Demonstrating Simple SQL Queries.

Narrowing the Query: The WHERE Clause

The following script shows how "search conditions" are used in a WHERE clause to help narrow down the SELECT (i.e., query) so that you can find exactly what you want. The search clauses use **predicate** logic which makes these clauses very powerful and flexible. Predicates can either compare two values or compare a value with a collection of values. The result of these comparisons is a condition of "true", "false", or "unknown" about a given row or a set of rows.

```
 --        /*'''''''''''''''''''''''''''''''''''''''''''''''''''''''''''''''''''''''*/
 --        /*            A Demonstration of the WHERE search clause               */
 --        /*'''''''''''''''''''''''''''''''''''''''''''''''''''''''''''''''''''''''*/
 --        /***** A simple relational predicate with no duplicate rows ********/
EXEC SQL:      SELECT DISTINCT *
               FROM org
               WHERE division = 'Eastern';

 DEPTNUMB  DEPTNAME          MANAGER  DIVISION    LOCATION
 --------  --------------    -------  ----------  -------------
 15        New England       50       Eastern     Boston
 20        Mid Atlantic      10       Eastern     Washington
 38        South Atlantic    30       Eastern     Atlanta

 Total Number of Rows SELECTED = 3

 OK, sql_rcd = 0,        Execution time =      0.4200 secs


 --        /******* Using AND to connect relational predicates    **************/
EXEC SQL:      SELECT *
               FROM staff
               WHERE (job = 'Sales' AND years > 8)
               OR (job = 'Sales' AND comm >= 1200);

 ID     NAME       DEPT    JOB    YEARS  SALARY     COMM
 ------ ---------  ------  -----  ------ --------   --------
 90     Koonitz    42      Sales  6      18001.75   1386.70
 280    Wilson     66      Sales  9      18674.50    811.50
 310    Graham     66      Sales  13     21000.00    200.30
 340    Edwards    84      Sales  7      17844.00   1285.00

 Total Number of Rows SELECTED = 4

 OK, sql_rcd = 0,        Execution time =      0.1200 secs


 --        /**** Wild-card pattern-matching with the LIKE predicate    *********/
EXEC SQL:      SELECT id, name
               FROM staff
               WHERE name LIKE 'Lu%';

 ID     NAME
 ------ ---------
 210    Lu
 230    Lundquist

 Total Number of Rows SELECTED = 2

 OK, sql_rcd = 0,        Execution time =      0.0300 secs


 --        /****** The BETWEEN predicate for comparing ranges of values  ******/
EXEC SQL:      SELECT id, name, salary
               FROM staff
               WHERE salary BETWEEN 20000 and 21000;
```

Figure 28-4 (Part 1 of 2).   Script 2: Demonstrating Search Conditions With WHERE.

```
ID        NAME       SALARY
------    ---------  --------
50        Hanes      20659.80
210       Lu         20010.00
310       Graham     21000.00

Total Number of Rows SELECTED = 3

OK, sql_rcd = 0,          Execution time =      0.0400 secs


--        /******* The IN predicate for testing group membership    **********/
EXEC SQL:         SELECT id, name, dept
                  FROM staff
                  WHERE dept IN (66,84);

ID        NAME       DEPT
------    ---------  ------
270       Lea        66
280       Wilson     66
290       Quill      84
300       Davis      84
310       Graham     66
320       Gonzales   66
330       Burke      66
340       Edwards    84
350       Gafney     84

Total Number of Rows SELECTED = 9

OK, sql_rcd = 0,          Execution time =      0.0300 secs


--        /******* The NULL predicate testing for NULL values    ********/
EXEC SQL:         SELECT id, name, dept
                  FROM staff
                  WHERE years IS NULL;

ID        NAME       DEPT
------    ---------  ------
60        Quigley    38
80        James      20
120       Naughton   38
200       Scoutten   42

Total Number of Rows SELECTED = 4

OK, sql_rcd = 0,          Execution time =      0.0300 secs
```

Figure 28-4 (Part 2 of 2). Script 2: Demonstrating Search Conditions With WHERE.

Sorting the Query: The ORDER BY Clause

So far, the query results were not returned in any order. The script below shows how the **ORDER BY** clause is used to sort the query in some specified order.

```
--        /*'''''''''''''''''''''''''''''''''''''''''''''''''''''''''''''''''''''*/
--        /*              A Demonstration of the ORDER BY clause                 */
--        /*'''''''''''''''''''''''''''''''''''''''''''''''''''''''''''''''''''''*/
--        /**********    The default sorting order is ascending (ASC)   ********/
EXEC SQL:        SELECT dept, name, id
                 FROM staff
                 WHERE (dept = 10 or dept = 20)
                 ORDER BY dept, name;

DEPT    NAME        ID
------  ---------   ------
10      Daniels     240
10      Jones       260
10      Lu          210
10      Molinare    160
20      James       80
20      Pernal      20
20      Sanders     10
20      Sneider     190

Total Number of Rows SELECTED = 8

OK, sql_rcd = 0,        Execution time =      0.0600 secs


--        /**********  You can over-ride the default by specifying (DESC)   ****/
EXEC SQL:        SELECT *
                 FROM org
                 ORDER BY division DESC, deptnumb DESC;

DEPTNUMB  DEPTNAME        MANAGER  DIVISION    LOCATION
--------  --------------  -------  ----------  -------------
84        Mountain        290      Western     Denver
66        Pacific         270      Western     San Francisco
51        Plains          140      Midwest     Dallas
42        Great Lakes     100      Midwest     Chicago
38        South Atlantic  30       Eastern     Atlanta
20        Mid Atlantic    10       Eastern     Washington
15        New England     50       Eastern     Boston
10        Head Office     160      Corporate   New York

Total Number of Rows SELECTED = 8

OK, sql_rcd = 0,        Execution time =      0.1200 secs
```

Figure 28-5. Script 3: Demonstrating the Ordering of Query Results With ORDER BY.

Simple Nested Queries

The following script shows how SELECT statements can be nested within one another. The **subquery** is an inner SELECT statement nested in the WHERE or HAVING clause of the outer SELECT statement. The results of the subquery are fed to the outer SELECT. If the subquery returns more than one value, you must use the keywords, IN, ALL, ANY, SOME, or EXISTS in the WHERE clause. The subquery table does not have to be the same as the outer query table.

```
--      /*''''''''''''''''''''''''''''''''''''''''''''''''''''''''''*/
--      /*           A Demonstration of Simple Nested Queries         */
--      /*''''''''''''''''''''''''''''''''''''''''''''''''''''''''''*/
--      /********    The inner SELECT returns a single value   *************/
EXEC SQL:   SELECT name, job, years, salary, comm
            FROM staff
            WHERE job='Sales'
            AND   salary > (SELECT AVG(salary) FROM staff where job='Mgr');

 NAME        JOB    YEARS   SALARY     COMM
 ---------   -----  ------  --------   --------
 Graham      Sales  13      21000.00   200.30

 Total Number of Rows SELECTED = 1

 OK, sql_rcd = 0,        Execution time =     0.0900 secs


--      /********    The inner SELECT returns multiple values   *************/
EXEC SQL:   SELECT name, job, years, salary, comm
            FROM staff
            WHERE job='Sales'
            AND   years  > ALL
            (SELECT years FROM staff where job='Mgr');

 NAME        JOB    YEARS   SALARY     COMM
 ---------   -----  ------  --------   --------
 Graham      Sales  13      21000.00   200.30

 Total Number of Rows SELECTED = 1

 OK, sql_rcd = 0,        Execution time =     0.0700 secs


--      /********  Different tables involved in inner and outer query   *****/
EXEC SQL:   SELECT name, job, years, salary, comm
            FROM staff
            WHERE job='Sales'
            AND dept IN
            (SELECT deptnumb FROM org WHERE division = 'Eastern')
            ORDER BY years;

 NAME        JOB    YEARS   SALARY     COMM
 ---------   -----  ------  --------   --------
 O'Brien     Sales  6       18006.00   846.55
 Rothman     Sales  7       16502.83   1152.00
 Pernal      Sales  8       18171.25   612.45
 Quigley     Sales  NULL    16808.30   650.25

 Total Number of Rows SELECTED = 4

 OK, sql_rcd = 0,        Execution time =     0.5300 secs
```

Figure 28-6. Script 4: Demonstrating Nested Queries.

Compound Nested Queries

The following script demonstrates queries that contain multiple subqueries. The subqueries can be at the same level (and tied together by AND or OR), or they can be nested into other subqueries. SELECT statements with multiple subqueries are known as **Compound Queries**.

```
--        /*''''''''''''''''''''''''''''''''''''''''''''''''''''''''''''''''''''''*/
--        /*          A Demonstration of Compound Nested Queries               */
--        /*''''''''''''''''''''''''''''''''''''''''''''''''''''''''''''''''''''''*/
--        /***********   Two subqueries at the same level    *****************/
EXEC SQL:    SELECT name, job, years, salary, comm
             FROM staff
             WHERE job='Sales'
             AND (salary + comm) >
                 (SELECT MIN(salary) FROM staff where job='Mgr')
             AND dept IN
                 (SELECT deptnumb FROM org WHERE division = 'Eastern')
             ORDER BY job, salary;

NAME        JOB    YEARS    SALARY    COMM
---------   -----  ------   --------  --------
Rothman     Sales  7        16502.83  1152.00
O'Brien     Sales  6        18006.00   846.55
Pernal      Sales  8        18171.25   612.45

Total Number of Rows SELECTED = 3

OK, sql_rcd = 0,        Execution time =     0.2800 secs


--        /********   A subquery inside another subquery        *************/
EXEC SQL:    SELECT name, job, years, salary, comm
             FROM staff
             WHERE job='Sales'
             AND    years  > ALL
             (SELECT years FROM staff where job='Mgr'
             AND dept IN
                 (SELECT deptnumb FROM org WHERE division = 'Eastern'))
             ORDER BY years;

NAME        JOB    YEARS    SALARY    COMM
---------   -----  ------   --------  --------
Graham      Sales  13       21000.00   200.30

Total Number of Rows SELECTED = 1

OK, sql_rcd = 0,        Execution time =     0.1900 secs
```

Figure 28-7.   Script 5: Demonstrating Compound Nested Queries.

Correlated Subqueries

The following script demonstrates a special kind of nested query, where the subquery is run once for each row in the outer query. These two queries are **correlated** in the sense that the inner query requires information from the outer query. Here's how to find the highest paid employee per job category: for each job category a subquery identifies the maximum salary and an outer query identifies the employee that earns it.

```
--        /*''''''''''''''''''''''''''''''''''''''''''''''''''''''''''''''''''''*/
--        /*            A Demonstration of Correlated Subqueries              */
--        /*''''''''''''''''''''''''''''''''''''''''''''''''''''''''''''''''''''*/
--        /*********** Inner query runs once for each job category  ***********/
EXEC SQL:   SELECT name, job, years, salary, comm
            FROM staff s
            WHERE salary =
                   (SELECT MAX(SALARY) FROM staff WHERE job= s.job)
            ORDER BY job, salary;

NAME         JOB     YEARS   SALARY     COMM
---------    -----   ------  --------   --------
Wheeler      Clerk   6       14460.00    513.30
Molinare     Mgr     7       22959.20   NULL
Graham       Sales   13      21000.00    200.30

Total Number of Rows SELECTED = 3

OK, sql_rcd = 0,        Execution time =     0.4400 secs
```

Figure 28-8. Script 6: A Demonstration of Correlated Subqueries.

Merging Query Results With Set Operators

The following script demonstrates how the results from two or more autonomous SELECT statements can be merged using the following set operators:

UNION	Combines the results of two queries
EXCEPT	Picks out all the rows from the first query that do not appear in the second query.
INTERSECT	Picks out all the rows in the first query that also appear in the second query.

The corresponding columns in the SELECT statements need not have the same name but they must have equivalent data types. Do not use a column name after ORDER BY, instead use a column number.

```
--        /*''''''''''''''''''''''''''''''''''''''''''''''''''''''''''''''''''''*/
--        /*            A Demonstration of set operators                       */
--        /*''''''''''''''''''''''''''''''''''''''''''''''''''''''''''''''''''''*/
--        /********* Merging two Queries with the INTERSECT set operator *****/
EXEC SQL:   SELECT name, job
            FROM staff WHERE job = 'Sales'
            INTERSECT
            SELECT name, job
            FROM staff WHERE years > 10;

1            2
---------    -----
Graham       Sales

Total Number of Rows SELECTED = 1

OK, sql_rcd = 0,        Execution time =     0.2200 secs
```

Figure 28-9 (Part 1 of 2). Script 7: Merging Result Tables Using Set Operators.

```
--      /********  Merging two Queries with the EXCEPT  set operator *****/
EXEC SQL:   SELECT name, job
            FROM staff WHERE job = 'Sales'
            EXCEPT
            SELECT name, job
            FROM staff WHERE years > 10
            ORDER by 1;

1          2
---------  -----
Davis      Sales
Edwards    Sales
Gonzales   Sales
Koonitz    Sales
O'Brien    Sales
Pernal     Sales
Quigley    Sales
Rothman    Sales
Smith      Sales
Williams   Sales
Wilson     Sales

Total Number of Rows SELECTED = 11

OK, sql_rcd = 0,        Execution time =     0.2100 secs


--      /********  Merging two Queries with the UNION set operator   *******/
EXEC SQL:   SELECT name, job
            FROM staff WHERE job = 'Sales'
            UNION
            SELECT name, job
            FROM staff WHERE years > 10
            ORDER by 1;

1          2
---------  -----
Davis      Sales
Edwards    Sales
Gonzales   Sales
Graham     Sales
Jones      Mgr
Koonitz    Sales
O'Brien    Sales
Pernal     Sales
Quigley    Sales
Rothman    Sales
Smith      Sales
Williams   Sales
Wilson     Sales

Total Number of Rows SELECTED = 13

OK, sql_rcd = 0,        Execution time =     0.1000 secs
```

Figure 28-9 (Part 2 of 2). Script 7: Merging Result Tables Using Set Operators.

Multitable Queries (Joins)

The previous scripts have demonstrated the retrieval of data from one table. Many times, the data you want will not always be in one table. A single SELECT can be used to retrieve data from more than one table through a process called **join**. To join two or more tables, you specify the table names in the FROM clause and the connection between them in the WHERE clause (this is called the **join predicate**). A join predicate based on the equality relationship is called an **equijoin**. If you use columns from different tables that have the same name, you must qualify the name of the columns to show which table they come from. We will qualify all column names involved in joins to better document the query. Theoretically, up to 15 tables can participate in a very slow **multijoin**.

```
--      /*'''''''''''''''''''''''''''''''''''''''''''''''''''''''''''''''''*/
--      /*                   A Demonstration of Joins                      */
--      /*'''''''''''''''''''''''''''''''''''''''''''''''''''''''''''''''''*/
--      /********   Two-table equijoin using fully qualified names   *******/
EXEC SQL:   SELECT org.deptname, org.location, staff.name, staff.salary
            FROM staff, org
            WHERE org.manager = staff.id
            ORDER BY org.deptname;

DEPTNAME        LOCATION        NAME        SALARY
-------------   -------------   ---------   --------
Great Lakes     Chicago         Plotz       18352.80
Head Office     New York        Molinare    22959.20
Mid Atlantic    Washington      Sanders     18357.50
Mountain        Denver          Quill       19818.00
New England     Boston          Hanes       20659.80
Pacific         San Francisco   Lea         18555.50
Plains          Dallas          Fraye       21150.00
South Atlantic  Atlanta         Marenghi    17506.75

Total Number of Rows SELECTED = 8

OK, sql_rcd = 0,         Execution time =      0.3100 secs

--      /********   Two-table equijoin using correlation names   *********/
EXEC SQL:   SELECT o.deptname, o.location, s.name, s.salary
            FROM staff s, org o
            WHERE o.manager = s.id
            ORDER BY o.deptname;

DEPTNAME        LOCATION        NAME        SALARY
-------------   -------------   ---------   --------
Great Lakes     Chicago         Plotz       18352.80
Head Office     New York        Molinare    22959.20
Mid Atlantic    Washington      Sanders     18357.50
Mountain        Denver          Quill       19818.00
New England     Boston          Hanes       20659.80
Pacific         San Francisco   Lea         18555.50
Plains          Dallas          Fraye       21150.00
South Atlantic  Atlanta         Marenghi    17506.75

Total Number of Rows SELECTED = 8

OK, sql_rcd = 0,         Execution time =      0.3100 secs
```

Figure 28-10.   Script 8: Demonstrating Joins.

Creating Tables, Inserts, Updates, and Deletes

The following script gets into "the meat and potatoes" of SQL. It shows how to create a table, put some data in it, update the data, and delete some of the data. These are all your basic every day SQL operations. The table we'll be creating, NEWSTAFF, is a carbon copy of the STAFF table. We'll be inserting data one row at a time and through a subquery.

```
--        /*'''''''''''''''''''''''''''''''''''''''''''''''''''''''''''''''''''''''*/
--        /*              Creating Tables, Inserts, Updates and Deletes            */
--        /*'''''''''''''''''''''''''''''''''''''''''''''''''''''''''''''''''''''''*/
--        /*************      Create the staff table's twin         **************/
EXEC SQL:   CREATE TABLE newstaff
                        (id            SMALLINT NOT NULL,
                         name          VARCHAR(9),
                         dept          SMALLINT,
                         job           CHAR(5),
                         years         SMALLINT,
                         salary        DECIMAL(7,2),
                         comm          DECIMAL(7,2));

 OK, sql_rcd = 0,          Execution time =      0.4100 secs


--       /*************      Insert into newstaff two rows      **************/
EXEC SQL:   INSERT INTO newstaff
            VALUES (500, 'Bob' , 99, 'Nerds', 5, 45000.00, 0 );

 OK, sql_rcd = 0,          Execution time =      0.0600 secs


EXEC SQL:   INSERT INTO newstaff
            VALUES (501, 'Dan', 99, 'Nerds', 4, 42000.00, 0 );

 OK, sql_rcd = 0,          Execution time =      0.0300 secs


--       /*************      Use a subquery to insert rows from staff *********/
EXEC SQL:   INSERT INTO newstaff
            SELECT * from staff where job= 'Sales' and salary > 18000;

 OK, sql_rcd = 0,          Execution time =      0.0600 secs


--       /*************      commit the work done so far         *********/
EXEC SQL:   COMMIT;

 OK, sql_rcd = 0,          Execution time =      0.0700 secs
```

Figure 28-11 (Part 1 of 2). Script 9: Creating Tables, Inserts, Updates, and Deletes.

```
--      /*************       Let's see what we've got so far        **********/
EXEC SQL:    SELECT * from newstaff
             ORDER BY salary DESC;

  ID       NAME        DEPT     JOB     YEARS    SALARY     COMM
------   ---------   ------   -----   ------   --------   --------
 500      Bob          99      Nerds    5       45000.00     00.00
 501      Dan          99      Nerds    4       42000.00     00.00
 310      Graham       66      Sales   13       21000.00    200.30
 150      Williams     51      Sales    6       19456.50    637.65
 280      Wilson       66      Sales    9       18674.50    811.50
  20      Pernal       20      Sales    8       18171.25    612.45
  40      O'Brien      38      Sales    6       18006.00    846.55
  90      Koonitz      42      Sales    6       18001.75   1386.70

Total Number of Rows SELECTED = 8

OK, sql_rcd = 0,        Execution time =      0.0600 secs


--      /*************       Let's give ourselves a good raise...    **********/
EXEC SQL:    UPDATE newstaff
             SET salary = salary * 1.8
             WHERE job = 'Nerds';

OK, sql_rcd = 0,        Execution time =      0.0300 secs


--      /*************       Things look better now...       **********/
EXEC SQL:    SELECT * from newstaff
             WHERE salary + comm > 21000
             ORDER BY salary DESC;

  ID       NAME        DEPT     JOB     YEARS    SALARY     COMM
------   ---------   ------   -----   ------   --------   --------
 500      Bob          99      Nerds    5       81000.00     00.00
 501      Dan          99      Nerds    4       75600.00     00.00
 310      Graham       66      Sales   13       21000.00    200.30

Total Number of Rows SELECTED = 3

OK, sql_rcd = 0,        Execution time =      0.1000 secs


--      /*************       Here's How delete works        **********/
EXEC SQL:    DELETE  from newstaff
             WHERE job = 'Sales';

OK, sql_rcd = 0,        Execution time =      0.0600 secs


--      /*************       Let's see what happened        **********/
EXEC SQL:    SELECT * from newstaff
             ORDER BY salary DESC;

  ID       NAME        DEPT     JOB     YEARS    SALARY     COMM
------   ---------   ------   -----   ------   --------   --------
 500      Bob          99      Nerds    5       81000.00     00.00
 501      Dan          99      Nerds    4       75600.00     00.00

Total Number of Rows SELECTED = 2

OK, sql_rcd = 0,        Execution time =      0.0600 secs
```

Figure 28-11 (Part 2 of 2). Script 9: Creating Tables, Inserts, Updates, and Deletes.

Data Integrity Scripts

Data integrity is concerned with the correctness and consistency of data in a database. The scripts that follow demonstrate some of the mechanisms provided by the OS/2 Database Manager to help enforce the validity of the data entrusted to it. The following data integrity mechanisms will be demonstrated through scripts: Transaction Recovery, the NOT NULL constraint, Entity Integrity, Views with check option, and Referential Integrity.

Transactional Units of Recovery: COMMIT and ROLLBACK

A transaction is a sequence of one or more SQL statements that get treated as an atomic unit of work. Either all the statements execute successfully, or none of the statements execute. The following script demonstrates the use of the SQL transaction processing.

```
--        /*''''''''''''''''''''''''''''''''''''''''''''''''''''''''''''''''''*/
--        /*           A Demonstration of SQL Transactions                    */
--        /*''''''''''''''''''''''''''''''''''''''''''''''''''''''''''''''''''*/
--        /*************      Start a Unit of Recovery      *************/
EXEC SQL:   COMMIT;

 OK, sql_rcd = 0,        Execution time =     0.0000 secs


--        /*************      Let's see what we've got to start  *************/
EXEC SQL:   SELECT * from newstaff;

  ID      NAME        DEPT    JOB    YEARS    SALARY    COMM
 ------  ---------   ------  -----  ------   --------  --------
  500     Bob         99      Nerds  5        81000.00   00.00
  501     Dan         99      Nerds  4        75600.00   00.00

 Total Number of Rows SELECTED = 2

 OK, sql_rcd = 0,        Execution time =     0.0900 secs


--        /*************      Delete all rows in table        *************/
EXEC SQL:   DELETE  from newstaff;

 OK, sql_rcd = 0,        Execution time =     0.0000 secs


--        /*************      Undo the transaction            *************/
EXEC SQL:   ROLLBACK;

 OK, sql_rcd = 0,        Execution time =     0.0400 secs
```

Figure 28-12 (Part 1 of 2). Script 10: Transactions: COMMIT and ROLLBACK.

```
--       /*************      Magic we're back where we started    **************/
EXEC SQL:   SELECT * from newstaff;

   ID      NAME        DEPT    JOB    YEARS   SALARY    COMM
  ------   ---------   ------  -----  ------  --------  --------
   500     Bob         99      Nerds  5       81000.00  00.00
   501     Dan         99      Nerds  4       75600.00  00.00

   Total Number of Rows SELECTED = 2

   OK, sql_rcd = 0,        Execution time =     0.0300 secs
```

Figure 28-12 (Part 2 of 2). Script 10: Transactions: COMMIT and ROLLBACK.

The No Nulls Constraint

This is the simplest data integrity constraint. You can require that a column should always contain a value by specifying it as **NOT NULL**. The Database Manager will automatically enforce that constraint on your behalf. This simple concept is demonstrated in the following script:

```
--       /*''''''''''''''''''''''''''''''''''''''''''''''''''''''''''''''''''''*/
--       /*                 Data Integrity with NO NULLS                       */
--       /*''''''''''''''''''''''''''''''''''''''''''''''''''''''''''''''''''''*/
--       /**** Here's one way to insert missing values in regular columns *****/
EXEC SQL:   INSERT INTO newstaff (id, name, dept, job)
            VALUES (506, 'Ray', 99, 'Nerds');

   OK, sql_rcd = 0,        Execution time =     0.0300 secs


--       /**** Here's another way to insert missing values in regular columns */
EXEC SQL:   INSERT INTO newstaff
            VALUES (507, 'Dan', 99, 'Nerds',NULL, NULL, NULL);

   OK, sql_rcd = 0,        Execution time =     0.0300 secs


--       /*************      Let's see what we got        *********/
EXEC SQL:   SELECT * from newstaff
            ORDER BY salary DESC;

   ID      NAME        DEPT    JOB    YEARS   SALARY    COMM
  ------   ---------   ------  -----  ------  --------  --------
   506     Ray         99      Nerds  NULL    NULL      NULL
   507     Dan         99      Nerds  NULL    NULL      NULL
   500     Bob         99      Nerds  5       81000.00  00.00
   501     Dan         99      Nerds  4       75600.00  00.00

   Total Number of Rows SELECTED = 4

   OK, sql_rcd = 0,        Execution time =     0.0600 secs
```

Figure 28-13 (Part 1 of 2). Script 11: Data Integrity With NO NULLS.

```
--        /**** Watch what happens if we insert into a NOT NULL column    *******/
EXEC SQL:    INSERT INTO newstaff
                VALUES (NULL, 'Joe', 99, 'Nerds',1, 30000.00, 0.0);

 ERROR, sql_code = -407

 SQL0407N  Assignment of a null value to a NOT NULL column "ID" was attempted on
 UPDATE or INSERT.


--        /*************         Let's get rid of the garbage data      **********/
EXEC SQL:    ROLLBACK;

 OK, sql_rcd = 0,          Execution time =       0.0400 secs
```

Figure 28-13 (Part 2 of 2). Script 11: Data Integrity With NO NULLS.

Entity Integrity

The Entity Integrity constraint ensures that each row in a table is unique. This is done
to reflect "real-world" situations where we deal with unique entities. You can specify,
through **primary keys** or **unique indexes**, that each row in a table uniquely identify the
entity represented by that row. The Database Manager will prevent rows with duplicate
primary keys from being entered accidentally. The script shown below demonstrates
this concept.

```
--        /*''''''''''''''''''''''''''''''''''''''''''''''''''''''''''''''''''''''''''*/
--        /*              Data Integrity with  Unique keys                  */
--        /*''''''''''''''''''''''''''''''''''''''''''''''''''''''''''''''''''''''''''*/
--        /**** Let's try inserting a duplicate record into NEWSTAFF  **********/
EXEC SQL:    INSERT INTO newstaff
                VALUES (501, 'Dan', 99, 'Nerds', 4, 75600.00, 0 );

 OK, sql_rcd = 0,          Execution time =       0.0300 secs


--        /**** As you can see we're not protected against duplicates   ********/
EXEC SQL:    SELECT * from newstaff
                ORDER BY id;

 ID     NAME        DEPT   JOB    YEARS   SALARY    COMM
 ------  ---------   ------ -----  ------  --------  --------
 500     Bob         99     Nerds  5       81000.00   00.00
 501     Dan         99     Nerds  4       75600.00   00.00
 501     Dan         99     Nerds  4       75600.00   00.00

 Total Number of Rows SELECTED = 3

 OK, sql_rcd = 0,          Execution time =       0.1200 secs


--        /*************         Let's get rid of this entry           **********/
EXEC SQL:    ROLLBACK;

 OK, sql_rcd = 0,          Execution time =       0.0000 secs
```

Figure 28-14 (Part 1 of 2). Script 12: Data Integrity With Unique Keys.

```
--      /****** Let's protect ourselves: add a unique index on id    **********/
EXEC SQL:   CREATE UNIQUE INDEX xid ON newstaff (id);

 OK, sql_rcd = 0,          Execution time =     1.4400 secs


--      /******* Let's see if "entity integrity" really works?      **********/
EXEC SQL:   INSERT INTO newstaff
            VALUES (501, 'Dan', 99, 'Nerds', 4, 42000.00, 0 );

 ERROR, sql_code = -803

 SQL0803N  One or more values in the INSERT or UPDATE statement are not valid
 because they would produce duplicate rows for a table with a unique index.


--      /*************    commit the work done so far    **********/
EXEC SQL:   COMMIT;

 OK, sql_rcd = 0,          Execution time =     0.0600 secs
```

Figure 28-14 (Part 2 of 2).   Script 12: Data Integrity With Unique Keys.

Using Views With Check Option and Validity Checks

The **Validity Check Constraint** restricts the values that can appear in a column. When
a table is created, each column is assigned a SQL data type and the Database Manager
automatically ensures that only data of the specified type is introduced in a column.
But what about restricting the set of legal values of the same column type? The
Database Manager provides a **check** option with views, which automatically enforces
that each INSERT and UPDATE meets the search criteria (domain restrictions) in the
view definition. This search criteria can be used to further restrict the set of values that
can appear in a column. The script that follows demonstrates this concept.

```
--      /*'''''''''''''''''''''''''''''''''''''''''''''''''''''''''''''''''''''''*/
--      /*          Data Integrity using Views with Check Option              */
--      /*'''''''''''''''''''''''''''''''''''''''''''''''''''''''''''''''''''''''*/
--      /****** Create a View PROTECT_STAFF with CHECK option      **********/
EXEC SQL:   CREATE VIEW  protect_staff
                      AS SELECT * FROM newstaff
                      WHERE job = 'Nerds' OR job= 'Sales'
                      WITH CHECK OPTION;

 OK, sql_rcd = 0,          Execution time =     0.5300 secs
```

Figure 28-15 (Part 1 of 2).   Script 13: Data Integrity Using Views With Check Option.

```
--       /****** Let's see what's in this view so far          **********/
EXEC SQL:    SELECT * FROM protect_staff;

 ID      NAME       DEPT    JOB     YEARS    SALARY     COMM
 ------  ---------  ------  -----   ------   --------   --------
 500     Bob        99      Nerds   5        81000.00   00.00
 501     Dan        99      Nerds   4        75600.00   00.00

 Total Number of Rows SELECTED = 2

 OK, sql_rcd = 0,         Execution time =      0.1000 secs


--       /****** Let's put some more data in PROTECT_STAFF       **********/
EXEC SQL:    INSERT INTO protect_staff
             SELECT * from staff where job= 'Sales' and salary > 20000;

 OK, sql_rcd = 0,         Execution time =      0.0600 secs


--       /**** Now let's insert another well paid nerd          **********/
EXEC SQL:    INSERT INTO protect_staff
             VALUES (508, 'Joe', 99, 'Nerds',4, 99000.00, 0.0);

 OK, sql_rcd = 0,         Execution time =      0.0600 secs


--       /**** Watch what happens if we violate the CHECK and insert a Mgr ****/
EXEC SQL:    INSERT INTO protect_staff
             VALUES (603, 'Sam', 99, 'Mgr',4, 89000.00, 0.0);

 ERROR, sql_code = -161

 SQL0161N  The resulting row of the INSERT or UPDATE does not conform to the
 view definition.


--       /*************     commit the work done so far          **********/
EXEC SQL:    COMMIT;

 OK, sql_rcd = 0,         Execution time =      0.0700 secs
```

Figure 28-15 (Part 2 of 2). Script 13: Data Integrity Using Views With Check Option.

Referential Integrity

Referential Integrity is a powerful data integrity feature that ensures cross-references *between* tables are always valid. This is done by enforcing that **foreign key** values match existing values in **primary keys**. For example, the Database Manager can automatically enforce a relation such as "no employee gets assigned to a department that does not exist." As we explained in the tutorial, see "Referential Relationships" on page 574, this is done through the magic of the parent/child relationships between **primary keys** and **foreign keys**. Support for foreign keys takes the form of clauses in the CREATE TABLE or ALTER TABLE SQL commands. In the script that follows, we create such a parent/child dependency.

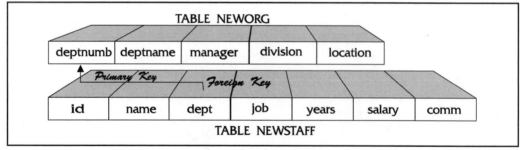

Figure 28-16.   The Foreign Key/Primary Key Reference Used in Script.

We then show you what happens when this dependency is violated. The violation we demonstrate is an insert in table NEWSTAFF for a department that is not in table NEWORG. You will get to watch first-hand the wrath of the Database Manager when it detects such violations.

```
--      /*''''''''''''''''''''''''''''''''''''''''''''''''''''''''''''''''''''*/
--      /*          Enforcing Data Integrity with Referential Integrity       */
--      /*''''''''''''''''''''''''''''''''''''''''''''''''''''''''''''''''''''*/
--      /************        Create the org table's cousin      ************/
EXEC SQL:    CREATE TABLE neworg
                        (deptnumb    SMALLINT NOT NULL PRIMARY KEY,
                        deptname    VARCHAR(14),
                        manager     SMALLINT,
                        division    VARCHAR(10),
                        location    VARCHAR(13));

 OK, sql_rcd = 0,       Execution time =      1.0900 secs


--      /************      Let's put some data in it       ************/
EXEC SQL:    INSERT INTO neworg
            VALUES (99, 'Software', NULL, 'Oceanview','Hawaii');

 OK, sql_rcd = 0,       Execution time =      0.0000 secs


EXEC SQL:    INSERT INTO neworg
            VALUES (90, 'Multimedia', NULL, 'Oceanview','Tahiti');

 OK, sql_rcd = 0,       Execution time =      0.0300 secs


--      /************    Let's start with nerds only in the table    *********/
EXEC SQL:    DELETE FROM newstaff
            WHERE job <> 'Nerds';

 OK, sql_rcd = 0,       Execution time =      0.0300 secs
```

Figure 28-17 (Part 1 of 2).   Script 14: Data Integrity With Referential Integrity.

```
--       /************    Let's see what we've got so far    **************/
EXEC SQL:    SELECT * from neworg;

DEPTNUMB  DEPTNAME          MANAGER  DIVISION     LOCATION
--------  --------------    -------  ----------   -------------
99        Software          NULL     Oceanview    Hawaii
90        Multimedia        NULL     Oceanview    Tahiti

Total Number of Rows SELECTED = 2

OK, sql_rcd = 0,        Execution time =      0.0400 secs


EXEC SQL:   SELECT * from newstaff;

ID      NAME        DEPT    JOB     YEARS   SALARY      COMM
------  ---------   ------  -----   ------  --------    --------
500     Bob         99      Nerds   5       81000.00    00.00
501     Dan         99      Nerds   4       75600.00    00.00
508     Joe         99      Nerds   4       99000.00    00.00

Total Number of Rows SELECTED = 3

OK, sql_rcd = 0,        Execution time =      0.0300 secs


--      /**** Make the dept column a foreign key to primary key in neworg  ***/
EXEC SQL:    ALTER TABLE newstaff
             FOREIGN KEY keyname1(dept) REFERENCES neworg
             ON DELETE RESTRICT;

OK, sql_rcd = 0,        Execution time =      0.5600 secs


--      /**** Insert  data for a valid department           *************/
EXEC SQL:    INSERT INTO newstaff
             VALUES (605, 'Newhire', 99, 'Nerds',0, 29000.00, 0.0);

OK, sql_rcd = 0,        Execution time =      0.0300 secs


--      /**** Insert  data for a valid department           *************/
EXEC SQL:    INSERT INTO newstaff
             VALUES (607, 'Newhire', 90, 'Nerds',0, 29000.00, 0.0);

OK, sql_rcd = 0,        Execution time =      0.0300 secs


--      /**** Watch what happens with a non-valid department (not in NEWORG) */
EXEC SQL:    INSERT INTO newstaff
             VALUES (609, 'Newhire', 20, 'Sales',0, 29000.00, 0.0);

ERROR, sql_code = -530

SQL0530N The insert or update value of FOREIGN KEY "KEYNAME1" is not equal to
some value of the primary key of the parent table.

--      /*************    commit the work done so far       **********/
EXEC SQL:   COMMIT;

OK, sql_rcd = 0,        Execution time =      0.0600 secs
```

Figure 28-17 (Part 2 of 2). Script 14: Data Integrity With Referential Integrity.

Enforcing DELETE Rules Using Referential Integrity

The Referential Integrity clauses can specify how to treat rows in dependent tables if a parent row is deleted. The question is what to do with the orphan rows? For each foreign key, you can specify one of three "delete rules":

1. **The RESTRICT rule** tells the Database Manager to prevent the deletion of the parent row if that row has any children (this is the default rule).
2. **The SET NULL rule** tells the Database Manager to automatically set the foreign key values to Nulls in all the child rows when the parent row gets deleted.
3. **The CASCADE rule** tells the Database Manager to automatically delete all orphan rows when the parent row gets deleted.

The script below demonstrates how to specify those rules and shows their effects when a delete is attempted for a parent row with dependents.

```
--      /*''''''''''''''''''''''''''''''''''''''''''''''''''''''''''''''''''''''''*/
--      /*         Enforcing Delete Rules with Referential Integrity          */
--      /*''''''''''''''''''''''''''''''''''''''''''''''''''''''''''''''''''''''''*/
--      /****** Observe how the default RESTRICT rule protects dependents ****/
EXEC SQL:    DELETE FROM neworg
             WHERE location = 'Tahiti';

 ERROR, sql_code = -532

 SQL0532N  A parent row cannot be deleted because the relationship "KEYNAME1"
 restricts the deletion.


--      /*************     commit the work done so far          *********/
EXEC SQL:    COMMIT;

 OK, sql_rcd = 0,        Execution time =     0.0300 secs


--      /*************     Let's see what data is in our tables   *********/
EXEC SQL:    SELECT * from neworg;

 DEPTNUMB  DEPTNAME        MANAGER  DIVISION    LOCATION
 --------  --------------  -------  ----------  -------------
 99        Software        NULL     Oceanview   Hawaii
 90        Multimedia      NULL     Oceanview   Tahiti

 Total Number of Rows SELECTED = 2

 OK, sql_rcd = 0,        Execution time =     0.0300 secs


EXEC SQL:    SELECT * from newstaff;

 ID      NAME       DEPT    JOB     YEARS    SALARY     COMM
 ------  ---------  ------  -----   ------   --------   --------
 500     Bob        99      Nerds   5        81000.00   00.00
 501     Dan        99      Nerds   4        75600.00   00.00
 605     Newhire    99      Nerds   0        29000.00   00.00
```

Figure 28-18 (Part 1 of 3). Script 15: The Delete Rules Using Referential Integrity.

```
508     Joe         99      Nerds  4       99000.00     00.00
607     Newhire     90      Nerds  0       29000.00     00.00

Total Number of Rows SELECTED = 5

OK, sql_rcd = 0,          Execution time =       0.1600 secs


--        /**** DROP the referential constraint              ***************/
EXEC SQL:   ALTER TABLE newstaff
            DROP FOREIGN KEY keyname1;

OK, sql_rcd = 0,          Execution time =       0.1500 secs


--        /**** Let's change the referential constraint to SET NULLs **********/
EXEC SQL:   ALTER TABLE newstaff
            FOREIGN KEY keyname1(dept) REFERENCES neworg
            ON DELETE SET NULL;

OK, sql_rcd = 0,          Execution time =       0.2200 secs


--        /***** Commit the change                             *********/
EXEC SQL:   COMMIT;

OK, sql_rcd = 0,          Execution time =       0.0300 secs


--        /**** Let's see what  referential integrity does for us now    ******/
EXEC SQL:   DELETE FROM neworg
            WHERE location = 'Tahiti';

OK, sql_rcd = 0,          Execution time =       0.0300 secs


--        /****  The Tahiti department is dropped (this is the parent row) ****/
EXEC SQL:   SELECT * from neworg;

DEPTNUMB  DEPTNAME        MANAGER  DIVISION    LOCATION
--------  --------------  -------  ----------  -------------
99        Software        NULL     Oceanview   Hawaii

Total Number of Rows SELECTED = 1

OK, sql_rcd = 0,          Execution time =       0.0300 secs


--        /****  The Tahiti department in child rows is set to NULL      ****/
EXEC SQL:   SELECT * from newstaff;

ID      NAME        DEPT    JOB    YEARS   SALARY    COMM
-----   ----------  ------  -----  ------  --------  --------
500     Bob         99      Nerds  5       81000.00     00.00
501     Dan         99      Nerds  4       75600.00     00.00
605     Newhire     99      Nerds  0       29000.00     00.00
508     Joe         99      Nerds  4       99000.00     00.00
607     Newhire     NULL    Nerds  0       29000.00     00.00

Total Number of Rows SELECTED = 5

OK, sql_rcd = 0,          Execution time =       0.0300 secs
```

Figure 28-18 (Part 2 of 3).   Script 15: The Delete Rules Using Referential Integrity.

```
--       /*************        Let's get back our data               **************/
EXEC SQL:    ROLLBACK;

 OK, sql_rcd = 0,           Execution time =       0.0300 secs


--       /**** DROP the referential constraint                       **************/
EXEC SQL:    ALTER TABLE newstaff
             DROP FOREIGN KEY keyname1;

 OK, sql_rcd = 0,           Execution time =       0.1900 secs


--       /**** Let's change the referential rule to CASCADE          *************/
EXEC SQL:    ALTER TABLE newstaff
             FOREIGN KEY keyname1(dept) REFERENCES neworg
             ON DELETE CASCADE;

 OK, sql_rcd = 0,           Execution time =       0.2500 secs


--       /***** Commit the change                                    *********/
EXEC SQL:    COMMIT;

 OK, sql_rcd = 0,           Execution time =       0.0600 secs


--       /**** Let's see what  referential integrity will do for us now  ******/
EXEC SQL:    DELETE FROM neworg
             WHERE location = 'Hawaii';

 OK, sql_rcd = 0,           Execution time =       0.0600 secs


--       /***** The parent department for Hawaii is gone...          *************/
EXEC SQL:    SELECT * from neworg;

DEPTNUMB  DEPTNAME        MANAGER  DIVISION     LOCATION
--------  --------------  -------  ----------   -------------
90        Multimedia      NULL     Oceanview    Tahiti

Total Number of Rows SELECTED = 1

 OK, sql_rcd = 0,           Execution time =       0.0300 secs


--       /***** All the Hawaii employees (the child rows) are gone also  ******/
EXEC SQL:    SELECT * from newstaff;

ID      NAME       DEPT    JOB    YEARS   SALARY    COMM
------  ---------  ------  -----  ------  --------  --------
607     Newhire    90      Nerds  0       29000.00  00.00

Total Number of Rows SELECTED = 1

 OK, sql_rcd = 0,           Execution time =       0.0000 secs

--       /*************        Let's bring back our data, we made the point  *******/
EXEC SQL:    ROLLBACK;
 OK, sql_rcd = 0,           Execution time =       0.0000 secs
```

Figure 28-18 (Part 3 of 3).   Script 15: The Delete Rules Using Referential Integrity.

Enforcing Cascaded DELETEs Using Referential Integrity

The RESTRICT rule is a *"single-level"* rule that only affects the parent row in a referential relationship. The SET NULL rule is a two-level rule whose impact stops with the child table. The CASCADE rule, however, is a *"multilevel"* rule whose effects ripple throughout all the descendant tables. The database tables illustrated in Figure 28-19 will be used to demonstrate these concepts.

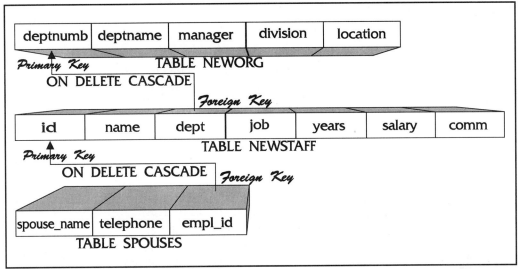

Figure 28-19. The "Delete Rules" Used in the Script.

In the sadistic script that follows, we first create the relationships between the tables shown above. We then close down a department in one of our paradise islands and watch its unfortunate effects on the workers and their spouses.

```
 --      /*_____*/
 --      /*           Cascaded  Delete  Rules with Referential Integrity      */
 --      /*_____*/
 --      /************       Create the spouses table                 ***************/
EXEC SQL:    CREATE TABLE spouses
                        (spouse_name   VARCHAR(20),
                         telephone     VARCHAR(10),
                         empl_id       SMALLINT,
                         FOREIGN KEY  homenum(empl_id) REFERENCES newstaff
                         ON DELETE CASCADE);

  OK, sql_rcd = 0,        Execution time =       0.6600 secs
```

Figure 28-20 (Part 1 of 3).   Script 16: Cascaded Deletes Using Referential Integrity.

```
--      /*************     Insert some data in spouses      **************/
EXEC SQL:   INSERT INTO spouses
            VALUES ('Michiko','4152223333',501);

 OK, sql_rcd = 0,        Execution time =     0.0300 secs


EXEC SQL:   INSERT INTO spouses
            VALUES ('Jeri','4154445555',500);

 OK, sql_rcd = 0,        Execution time =     0.0300 secs


--      /*************     Let's take stock of what we've got **************/
EXEC SQL:   SELECT * FROM neworg;

 DEPTNUMB  DEPTNAME         MANAGER  DIVISION    LOCATION
 --------  -------------    -------  ----------  -------------
 99        Software         NULL     Oceanview   Hawaii
 90        Multimedia       NULL     Oceanview   Tahiti

 Total Number of Rows SELECTED = 2

 OK, sql_rcd = 0,        Execution time =     0.0300 secs


EXEC SQL:   SELECT * FROM newstaff;

 ID      NAME       DEPT    JOB    YEARS   SALARY    COMM
 ------  ---------  ------  -----  ------  --------  --------
 500     Bob        99      Nerds  5       81000.00  00.00
 501     Dan        99      Nerds  4       75600.00  00.00
 605     Newhire    99      Nerds  0       29000.00  00.00
 508     Joe        99      Nerds  4       99000.00  00.00
 607     Newhire    90      Nerds  0       29000.00  00.00

 Total Number of Rows SELECTED = 5

 OK, sql_rcd = 0,        Execution time =     0.0400 secs


EXEC SQL:   SELECT * FROM spouses;

 SPOUSE_NAME          TELEPHONE   EMPL_ID
 --------------------  ----------  -------
 Michiko              4152223333  501
 Jeri                 4154445555  500

 Total Number of Rows SELECTED = 2

 OK, sql_rcd = 0,        Execution time =     0.0300 secs
```

Figure 28-20 (Part 2 of 3).   Script 16: Cascaded Deletes Using Referential Integrity.

```
--      /****** Watch this cruel and unusual punishment: No more Hawaii ******/
EXEC SQL:    DELETE  FROM neworg
             WHERE location='Hawaii';

OK, sql_rcd = 0,         Execution time =     0.0900 secs


--      /*************   Let's see the damage this has created  ***********/
EXEC SQL:   SELECT * FROM neworg;

DEPTNUMB  DEPTNAME        MANAGER  DIVISION   LOCATION
--------  ---------------  -------  ---------- -------------
90        Multimedia       NULL     Oceanview  Tahiti

Total Number of Rows SELECTED = 1

OK, sql_rcd = 0,         Execution time =     0.0300 secs


EXEC SQL:   SELECT * FROM newstaff;

ID      NAME       DEPT    JOB    YEARS   SALARY    COMM
------  ---------  ------  -----  ------  --------  --------
607     Newhire    90      Nerds  0       29000.00  00.00

Total Number of Rows SELECTED = 1

OK, sql_rcd = 0,         Execution time =     0.0000 secs


EXEC SQL:   SELECT * FROM spouses;

SPOUSE_NAME           TELEPHONE   EMPL_ID
--------------------  ----------  -------

Total Number of Rows SELECTED = 0

OK, sql_rcd = 0,         Execution time =     0.0000 secs


--      /*************   Let's bring back our data, we made the point   ******/
EXEC SQL:   ROLLBACK;

OK, sql_rcd = 0,         Execution time =     0.2500 secs
```

Figure 28-20 (Part 3 of 3). Script 16: Cascaded Deletes Using Referential Integrity.

Using Indexes to Maximize Performance

An index is an SQL structure that provides rapid access to table data. The purpose of this script is to give you a feel for the performance improvements you can obtain by using indexes. To get some meaningful numbers, we'll create a table that contains 10,000 rows, and then measure the effects of a SELECT with and without an index. We're going to borrow the table definitions and data for this script from the TP1 chapters that come later in this book. The script below demonstrates *dramatic* improvements in performance when we introduce the query with the index.

```
--        /*_____*/
--        /*                                                       */
--        /*        A demonstration of how indexes affect performance    */
--        /*_____*/
--        /*************    Create a bank accounts table called ACCT *********/
EXEC SQL: CREATE TABLE ACCT  (ACCT_NUM    INT       NOT NULL,
                              NAME        CHAR(20)  NOT NULL,
                              BRANCH_ID   SMALLINT  NOT NULL,
                              BALANCE     INT       NOT NULL,
                              ADDRESS     CHAR(30)  NOT NULL,
                              TEMP        CHAR(40)  NOT NULL);

OK, sql_rcd = 0,        Execution time =      0.3200 secs


--        /*************    Commit the work done so far          *********/
EXEC SQL:        COMMIT;

OK, sql_rcd = 0,        Execution time =      0.0600 secs


--        /*************  Let's fill the ACCT table with 10,000 records ********/
EXEC DBA: IMPORT sample  c:\acct.del    REPLACE DEL ACCT;
SQL3109N  The Import utility is beginning to import data from file
"c:\acct.del".
SQL3110N  The Import utility has completed processing.  "10000" rows were read
from the input file.
SQL3149N  "10000" rows were processed from the input file.  "10000" rows were
successfully inserted into the table.  "0" rows were rejected.

OK, sql_rcd = 0,        Execution time =      95.6200 secs


--        /*************    Commit the work done so far          *********/
EXEC SQL:        COMMIT;

OK, sql_rcd = 0,        Execution time =      0.1300 secs


--        /*************  Let's make sure the ACCT table has 10,000 rows *******/
EXEC SQL:        SELECT COUNT(*) FROM ACCT;

1
-----------
10000

Total Number of Rows SELECTED = 1

OK, sql_rcd = 0,        Execution time =      3.4700 secs
```

Figure 28-21 (Part 1 of 2). Script 17: Using Indexes to Maximize Performance.

```
--       /************* Perform a Query On that table with no Indexes    *******/
EXEC SQL:        SELECT acct_num, name, branch_id, balance
                 FROM ACCT
                 WHERE ACCT_NUM
                 BETWEEN 7000 and 7001
                 ORDER BY ACCT_NUM;

ACCT_NUM     NAME                      BRANCH_ID  BALANCE
- - - - - - - - -    - - - - - - - - - - - - - - - - - -   - - - - - - - - -   - - - - - - - - - - -
7000         <--20 BYTE STRING-->  20         1000
7001         <--20 BYTE STRING-->  4          1200

Total Number of Rows SELECTED = 2

OK, sql_rcd = 0,        Execution time =      3.0000 secs


--        /*************       Create an Index on that table       ************/
EXEC SQL: CREATE INDEX ACCTINDX ON ACCT(ACCT_NUM);

OK, sql_rcd = 0,        Execution time =     13.5600 secs


--        /*************       Commit the work done so far          ************/
EXEC SQL:        COMMIT;

OK, sql_rcd = 0,        Execution time =      0.0700 secs


--        /************* disconnect from to free all buffers        ************/
EXEC DBA:        STOPUSE sample;

OK, sql_rcd = 0,        Execution time =      1.7500 secs


--        /************* Reconnect  with a clean slate              ************/
EXEC DBA:        STARTUSE sample S;

OK, sql_rcd = 0,        Execution time =      1.1800 secs


--        /************* Perform the same query with an index.  Is it faster? **/
EXEC SQL:        SELECT acct_num, name, branch_id, balance
                 FROM ACCT
                 WHERE ACCT_NUM
                 BETWEEN 7000  and 7001
                 ORDER BY ACCT_NUM;

ACCT_NUM     NAME                      BRANCH_ID  BALANCE
- - - - - - - - -    - - - - - - - - - - - - - - - - - -   - - - - - - - - -   - - - - - - - - - - -
7000         <--20 BYTE STRING-->  20         1000
7001         <--20 BYTE STRING-->  4          1200

Total Number of Rows SELECTED = 2

OK, sql_rcd = 0,        Execution time =      0.3800 secs
```

Figure 28-21 (Part 2 of 2). Script 17: Using Indexes to Maximize Performance.

SQL Security

With SQL making access to the data so easy, it becomes important for a Database Manager to provide access protection. You can define the overall framework for securing your data using the SQL language. The enforcement of the security then becomes the responsibility of the Database Manager. As we explained in the tutorial, database security is based on the interplay of three concepts: *users*, *database objects*, and *access* privileges. The **privileges** define the actions that a *user* can perform on a given *database object*. The script assumes you've read the UPM and SQL security tutorial (see "Authorization and Privileges" on page 591). The UPM for our machine is setup with an *administrator* called "Jeri" and two *users*: "Dan" and "Bob." The following script shows some of the things "Jeri" can do for "Dan," a trusted knowledge worker, and "Bob," an occasional consumer of information.

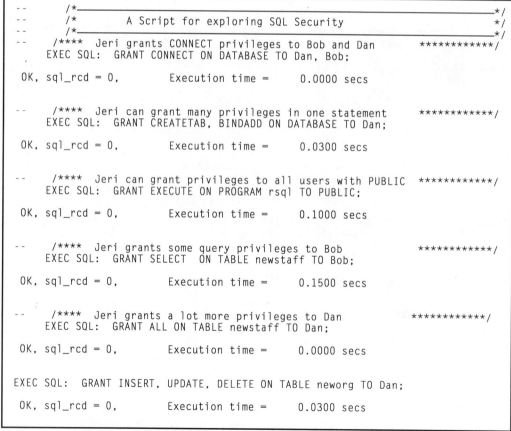

```
--        /*_____*/
--        /*          A Script for exploring SQL Security                   */
--        /*_____*/
--    /**** Jeri grants CONNECT privileges to Bob and Dan      ************/
      EXEC SQL:  GRANT CONNECT ON DATABASE TO Dan, Bob;

  OK, sql_rcd = 0,          Execution time =      0.0000 secs


--    /**** Jeri can grant many privileges in one statement    ************/
      EXEC SQL:  GRANT CREATETAB, BINDADD ON DATABASE TO Dan;

  OK, sql_rcd = 0,          Execution time =      0.0300 secs


--    /**** Jeri can grant privileges to all users with PUBLIC ************/
      EXEC SQL:  GRANT EXECUTE ON PROGRAM rsql TO PUBLIC;

  OK, sql_rcd = 0,          Execution time =      0.1000 secs


--    /**** Jeri grants some query privileges to Bob           ************/
      EXEC SQL:  GRANT SELECT  ON TABLE newstaff TO Bob;

  OK, sql_rcd = 0,          Execution time =      0.1500 secs


--    /**** Jeri grants a lot more privileges to Dan           ************/
      EXEC SQL:  GRANT ALL ON TABLE newstaff TO Dan;

  OK, sql_rcd = 0,          Execution time =      0.0000 secs


EXEC SQL:  GRANT INSERT, UPDATE, DELETE ON TABLE neworg TO Dan;

  OK, sql_rcd = 0,          Execution time =      0.0300 secs
```

Figure 28-22 (Part 1 of 2). Script 18: A "Brief" Introduction to SQL Security.

```
--      /****           Commit the work done so far          ***********/
     EXEC SQL:       COMMIT;

  OK, sql_rcd = 0,        Execution time =       0.0700 secs


--      /****    What Jeri "gives" she can take back          ***********/
     EXEC SQL:  REVOKE CONNECT ON DATABASE FROM PUBLIC;

  OK, sql_rcd = 0,        Execution time =       0.0300 secs


EXEC SQL:  REVOKE INSERT  ON TABLE neworg FROM Dan;

  OK, sql_rcd = 0,        Execution time =       0.2500 secs


--      /***************  Commit the work done so far          *********/
EXEC SQL:       COMMIT;

  OK, sql_rcd = 0,        Execution time =       0.0300 secs
```

Figure 28-22 (Part 2 of 2).   Script 18: A "Brief" Introduction to SQL Security.

The System Catalogs

The Database Manager, like most relational databases, is self-describing. It automatically maintains information about its own structure in the database. These self-describing tables, collectively known as the **catalog tables**, can be accessed (but not modified) through standard queries. This means you can ask the Database Manager to describe its own tables where it maintains its structures for views, columns, privileges, plans, ownership, user comments, and all sorts of useful systemic information. Database tools can use this information very advantageously. All the catalog tables have the same user ID, **SYSIBM**. We introduce the catalog tables in the script below.

```
--      /*_____*/
--      /*        A Script for exploring the System Catalog Tables    */
--      /*_____*/
--      /************* List name and time-stamp of all system tables ********/
EXEC SQL:       SELECT creator, name, type, colcount, ctime
                FROM SYSIBM.SYSTABLES
                WHERE CREATOR = 'SYSIBM'  ORDER BY ctime;

CREATOR    NAME            TYPE  COLCOUNT  CTIME
--------   -------------   ----  --------  -----------------------
SYSIBM     SYSTABLES       T     20        1992-04-30-11.51.50.900000
SYSIBM     SYSCOLUMNS      T     16        1992-04-30-11.51.51.280000
SYSIBM     SYSINDEXES      T     13        1992-04-30-11.51.51.400000
SYSIBM     SYSVIEWS        T     5         1992-04-30-11.51.51.530000
SYSIBM     SYSVIEWDEP      T     6         1992-04-30-11.51.51.650000
SYSIBM     SYSPLAN         T     12        1992-04-30-11.51.51.780000
SYSIBM     SYSPLANDEP      T     7         1992-04-30-11.51.52.000000
SYSIBM     SYSSECTION      T     5         1992-04-30-11.51.52.210000
```

Figure 28-23 (Part 1 of 3).   Script 19: An Introduction to the Catalog Tables.

```
SYSIBM     SYSSTMT          T    6        1992-04-30-11.51.52.280000
SYSIBM     SYSDBAUTH        T    6        1992-04-30-11.51.52.400000
SYSIBM     SYSPLANAUTH      T    7        1992-04-30-11.51.52.500000
SYSIBM     SYSTABAUTH       T    13       1992-04-30-11.51.53.060000
SYSIBM     SYSINDEXAUTH     T    5        1992-04-30-11.51.53.210000
SYSIBM     SYSRELS          T    11       1992-04-30-11.51.53.430000

Total Number of Rows SELECTED = 14

OK, sql_rcd = 0,         Execution time =      0.4000 secs


--       /************* List all the tables we created in this chapter ********/
EXEC SQL:      SELECT creator, name, type, colcount, ctime
               FROM SYSIBM.SYSTABLES
               WHERE CREATOR = USER
               AND type = 'T'  ORDER BY ctime;

CREATOR    NAME             TYPE  COLCOUNT  CTIME
--------   ---------------  ----  --------  ----------------------------
JERI       ORG              T     5         1992-04-30-11.52.08.620000
JERI       STAFF            T     7         1992-04-30-11.52.09.530000
JERI       NEWSTAFF         T     7         1992-04-30-11.52.17.870000
JERI       NEWORG           T     5         1992-04-30-11.52.21.810000
JERI       ACCT             T     6         1992-04-30-11.52.26.710000

Total Number of Rows SELECTED = 5

OK, sql_rcd = 0,         Execution time =      0.1600 secs


--       /************* List all the views  we created in this chapter ********/
EXEC SQL:      SELECT creator, name, type, colcount, ctime
               FROM SYSIBM.SYSTABLES
               WHERE CREATOR = USER
               AND type = 'V';

CREATOR    NAME             TYPE  COLCOUNT  CTIME
--------   ---------------  ----  --------  ----------------------------
JERI       PROTECT_STAFF    V     7         1992-04-30-11.52.21.150000

Total Number of Rows SELECTED = 1

OK, sql_rcd = 0,         Execution time =      0.0900 secs


--       /************* List all the users and their authorizations    ********/
EXEC SQL:      SELECT *
               FROM SYSIBM.SYSDBAUTH;

GRANTOR    GRANTEE   DBADMAUTH   CREATETABAUTH  BINDADDAUTH   CONNECTAUTH
--------   -------   ---------   -------------  -----------   -----------
SYSIBM     JERI      Y           Y              Y             Y
SYSIBM     PUBLIC    N           Y              Y             N
JERI       DAN       N           Y              Y             Y
JERI       BOB       N           N              N             Y

Total Number of Rows SELECTED = 4

OK, sql_rcd = 0,         Execution time =      0.0300 secs
```

Figure 28-23 (Part 2 of 3). Script 19: An Introduction to the Catalog Tables.

```
--         /************* List all the access plans that have been compiled *****/
EXEC SQL:       SELECT name, creator, valid, isolation, block
                FROM SYSIBM.SYSPLAN
                WHERE CREATOR = USER;

NAME      CREATOR   VALID  ISOLATION  BLOCK
--------  --------  -----  ---------  -----
RSQL      JERI      Y      U          B

Total Number of Rows SELECTED = 1

OK, sql_rcd = 0,        Execution time =      0.0600 secs


--         /************* List all the referential relationships we created *****/
EXEC SQL:       SELECT  tbname, relname, reftbname, deleterule, updaterule
                FROM SYSIBM.SYSRELS
                WHERE CREATOR = USER;

TBNAME                RELNAME    REFTBNAME              DELETERULE  UPDATERULE
------------------    --------   -------------------    ----------  ----------
NEWSTAFF              KEYNAME1   NEWORG                 C           R

Total Number of Rows SELECTED = 1

OK, sql_rcd = 0,        Execution time =      0.1600 secs
```

Figure 28-23 (Part 3 of 3).   Script 19: An Introduction to the Catalog Tables.

EXPLORING THE DATABASE ADMINISTRATION COMMANDS WITH SCRIPTS

The scripts that follow demonstrate the versatility of RSQL as a system administrator's tool.

How to Fine-Tune a Database Using RUNSTATs and REORGs

The following script shows how to fine-tune the performance of your database using **RUNSTATs** and **REORGs**. A great deal of the credit for the improved performance of relational databases goes to the *optimizer*. As we explained in the tutorial, the optimizer is an expert at determining the minimum number of disk accesses for getting to the requested data. The information at the optimizer's disposal for making such decisions consists of statistics stored in the system catalog. Based on those statistics, the optimizer will decide whether to use an index or to sequentially scan an entire table. The OS/2 Database Manager gives you control of when these table statistics are generated. You should refresh those statistics after significant changes have occurred to the database, including the import of a large number of data records, the restructuring of tables, threshold points in the steady growth of a database, and after an index is added or deleted. You should rebind your static SQL programs after a refresh of statistics so that the applications can take the new statistics into account.

The **REORG** command reorganizes the physical storage of a base table. You typically issue this command when a table has become too fragmented due to many updates or deletes. You will know a table is fragmented and needs to be reorganized if the performance deteriorates. This command is fairly time-consuming (in the order of minutes). You should complete all database operations and release all locks before executing this command. Our script will apply a REORG and RUNSTATs on the ACCT table. We will then re-run the query in "Using Indexes to Maximize Performance" on page 686 to see if the performance improved any.

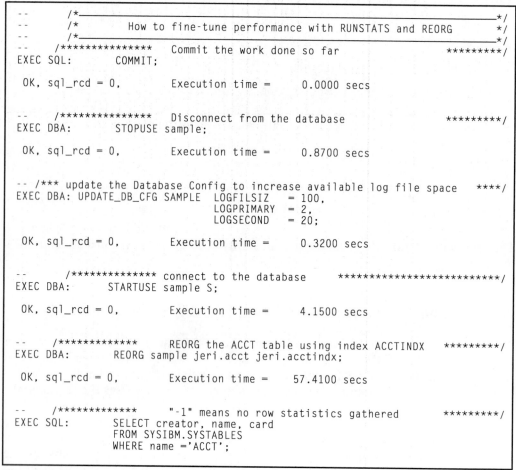

```
--        /*_____*/
--        /*          How to fine-tune performance with RUNSTATS and REORG      */
--        /*_____*/
--        /************** Commit the work done so far              *********/
EXEC SQL:       COMMIT;

  OK, sql_rcd = 0,        Execution time =      0.0000 secs


--        /************** Disconnect from the database            *********/
EXEC DBA:       STOPUSE sample;

  OK, sql_rcd = 0,        Execution time =      0.8700 secs


-- /*** update the Database Config to increase available log file space   ****/
EXEC DBA: UPDATE_DB_CFG SAMPLE   LOGFILSIZ   = 100,
                                 LOGPRIMARY  = 2,
                                 LOGSECOND   = 20;

  OK, sql_rcd = 0,        Execution time =      0.3200 secs


--        /************** connect to the database    ***********************/
EXEC DBA:       STARTUSE sample S;

  OK, sql_rcd = 0,        Execution time =      4.1500 secs


--        /************        REORG the ACCT table using index ACCTINDX  *********/
EXEC DBA:       REORG sample jeri.acct jeri.acctindx;

  OK, sql_rcd = 0,        Execution time =     57.4100 secs


--        /************        "-1" means no row statistics gathered      *********/
EXEC SQL:       SELECT creator, name, card
                FROM SYSIBM.SYSTABLES
                WHERE name ='ACCT';
```

Figure 28-24 (Part 1 of 2). Script 20: Fine-Tuning Performance With RUNSTATS and REORG.

```
CREATOR   NAME                    CARD
--------  -------------------    -----------
JERI      ACCT                    -1

Total Number of Rows SELECTED = 1

OK, sql_rcd = 0,        Execution time =     0.3100 secs


  --    /************     RUNSTAT refreshes the statistics on table ACCT  *****/
EXEC DBA:      RUNSTATS jeri.acct;

OK, sql_rcd = 0,        Execution time =     26.6600 secs


  --    /************     View the row statistics after RUNSTATs      *********/
EXEC SQL:      SELECT creator, name, card
               FROM SYSIBM.SYSTABLES
               WHERE name ='ACCT';

CREATOR   NAME                    CARD
--------  -------------------    -----------
JERI      ACCT                    10000

Total Number of Rows SELECTED = 1

OK, sql_rcd = 0,        Execution time =     0.0600 secs


  --      /*** Perform the same query as in script 17.  Is it faster?     *****/
EXEC SQL:      SELECT acct_num, name, branch_id, balance
               FROM ACCT
               WHERE ACCT_NUM
               BETWEEN 7000 and 7001
               ORDER BY ACCT_NUM;

ACCT_NUM    NAME                   BRANCH_ID  BALANCE
----------- -------------------    ---------  -----------
7000        <--20 BYTE STRING-->   20         1000
7001        <--20 BYTE STRING-->   4          1200

Total Number of Rows SELECTED = 2

OK, sql_rcd = 0,        Execution time =     0.0900 secs
```

Figure 28-24 (Part 2 of 2).   Script 20: Fine-Tuning Performance With RUNSTATS and REORG.

The Database and Database Manager Configuration Files

The OS/2 Database Manager maintains system configuration information about the Database Manager and the individual databases in configuration files. The information contained in those files was explained in the tutorials ("Database Administration API: Configuration Service" on page 638). The following script demonstrates the database environment for our scripts. We also display the user and database status information maintained by the OS/2 Database Manager. Finally, we display the authority information kept by the Database Manager for the current user. There is a lot of information out there! Perhaps you'll find some of it useful.

```
--       /*_____*/
--       /*          Viewing and Updating the System Configuration Files  */
--       /*_____*/
--       /***************   Commit the work done so far        *********/
EXEC SQL:      COMMIT;

 OK, sql_rcd = 0,        Execution time =      0.0900 secs


--       /***************   Show SAMPLE's database configuration  *********/
EXEC DBA:      SHOW_DB_CFG sample;

Database Configuration for Database sample
==================================================

Configuration Parameter             Current  Parm.      Parm.      Parm.
Description                         Value    Units      Range      Default
----------------------------------  -------- ---------- ---------- -------
Max. Active Applications                  8  Appl.      1-256            8
Max. DB Files Open/Application           20  files      2-235           20
Max. Files Open/Application             255  files      25-32700       255
Buffer Pool Size                        250  4K pages   2-1500         (1)
Time Interval for Deadlocks           10000  millisecs. 1-600 sec.      10
Max. Storage for Locklists               25  4K pages   4-250            8
Max. percent locklist/appl.              22  percent    1-100           22
Default Application Heap                  3  segments   2-20             3
Application Agent Heap                    2  segments   2-85             2
Sort List Heap                           2  segments   1-20             2
Database Heap                            3  segments   1-45            (2)
SQL Statement Heap                      64  segments   8-255           64
Log File Size                          100  4K pages   4-65535        (3)
Primary Log Files                        2  files      2-63             3
Secondary Log Files                     20  files      0-61             2
Log Records/soft checkpoint            100  records    0-65535        100

Current Log Location = E:\SQL00001\SQLOGDIR\
New Log Location     =
First Log File       =
Current Log File     =
Copy Protection      =      1 (1 = Protected, Default = 1)
Log Retain           =      0 (1 = Retain Log Files, Default = 0)
User Exit            =      0 (1 = Enable User Exit, Default = 0)
Auto Restart         =      1 (1 = Enable Auto Restart, Default = 1)
Country              =      1
Code Page            =    437
Release              =    768
DB Consistency       =      0 (1 = Consistent)
Backup Pending       =      0 (1 = Backup Pending)
Roll Forward Pending =      0 (1 = Roll Forward Pending)
User Exit Status     =      0 (1 = User exit Enabled)
Log Retain Status    =      0 (1 = log files retained)

(1) - client or standalone 25, server 250
(2) - client or standalone  2, server   3
(3) - client or standalone 32, server 200
OK, sql_rcd = 0,        Execution time =      0.1900 secs
```

Figure 28-25 (Part 1 of 3).   Script 21: Looking Inside the Configuration Files.

```
  --    /**************  Show the Database Manager's configuration  ********/
EXEC DBA:      SHOW_DM_CFG;

Database Manager Configuration
================================

Configuration Parameter          Current  Parm.     Parm.       Parm.
Description                       Value    Units     Range       Default
--------------------------------- -------- --------- ----------- -------
Max. Shared Segments                  80   Segments  1-255       0,3,2,2 (1)
Max. Concurrently Active apps.         8   Number    1-8    (3)  3,8,0,3 (1)
Max. Reqestor I/O Block Size        4096   bytes     4k-64k(2)   0,4,4,4 (1)
Max. Server   I/O Block Size        4096   bytes     4k-64k(2)   0,4,0,0 (1)
Communication Heap Size                4   Segments  1-255 (2)   0,4,3,3 (1)
Remote Data Services Heap size         3   Segments  1-255 (2)   0,3,2,2 (1)
Max. Remote Connections               10   Number    1-255 (2)   0,10,3,3 (1)

Node Type       =       1
Node Name       =  DBSVR02
Release Level = 768

(1) - Standalone, Server, Client, Client w/Local DB
(2) - Standalone range = 0
(3) - Client range      = 0
OK, sql_rcd = 0,       Execution time =      0.1300 secs


  --    /**************  Up the number of allowable databases    ********/
EXEC DBA:      UPDATE_DM_CFG  NUMDB    = 8 ;

OK, sql_rcd = 0,       Execution time =      0.3400 secs


  --    /**************  Collect system, database, and user status  ********/
EXEC DBA:      COLLECT_STATUS sample;

System Status
-------------
  Current Normalized time        = 704634958 seconds elapsed from 1-1-1970
  Time Zone Displacement         = -1 seconds different from UTC
  Product name                   = IBM Extended Services Database
  Component Identification       = 562121302
  Release Level                  = 1.00
  Correct Service Level          = WR06000_

Database Status
---------------
  Normalized time of last backup = 0 seconds elapsed from 1-1-1970
  Time Zone Displacement         = 0 seconds different from UTC
  Number of connects             = 1
  Database alias                 = SAMPLE
  Database Name                  = SAMPLE
  Location                       = L
  Database drive                 = E:
  Node Name                      =
  Database Type                  = OS2 DBM
```

Figure 28-25 (Part 2 of 3).   Script 21: Looking Inside the Configuration Files.

```
User Status
-----------
  Transactions since connect        = 6
  Requests since connect            = 25
  Requests current transaction      = 0
  Elapsed time since connect        = 90 seconds
  Elapsed time, current transaction = 1 seconds

  Authorization ID          = JERI
  Node Name                 =  DBSVR02
  Authority Level           = 7967
  Transaction State         = S
  Lock State                = N

OK, sql_rcd = 0,          Execution time =       0.3400 secs


--      /*************** What is the current ID authorized to do?     *********/
EXEC DBA:      GET_ADMIN;

  Authorization type               Authorized? (0=NO, 1=YES)
  ------------------               -------------------------
  System Adminstrator                     1
  Database Administrator                  1
  Create Tables                           1
  Bind new Programs                       1
  Access current database                 1
  Group System Adminstrator               1
  Group Database Administrator            1
  Group Create Tables                     1
  Group Bind new Programs                 1
  Group Access current database           1

OK, sql_rcd = 0,          Execution time =       0.0700 secs
```

Figure 28-25 (Part 3 of 3). Script 21: Looking Inside the Configuration Files.

Creating a Database and Viewing the Directories

In the script that follows we look at the contents of the **System**, **Volume** and **Node** (aka Workstation) directories. You may recall from the tutorial (see "Database Directory Services" on page 608) that the Database Manager uses a distributed directory strategy which involves keeping on every RDS machine information about local database objects as well as information about how to get to remote databases. Here is a refresher on database directories:

System   This is the master directory for a workstation. It contains an entry for each local or remote database that can be accessed from that workstation.

Volume   This is a directory which contains an entry for every database on a logical disk drive. This directory gets updated automatically by the Database Manager each time a database is created or deleted on an OS/2 logical disk drive. This directory must exist on every OS/2 drive that contains one or more databases.

Node   This directory, also known as the Workstation directory, contains an entry for each remote database server site that can be accessed. The information in this directory is used by RDS to connect with the remote workstations.

```
--      /*─────────────────────────────────────────────────────────────*/
--      /*          Viewing the Node, System, and Volume Directories     */
--      /*─────────────────────────────────────────────────────────────*/
--      /**************  Show the contents of the SYSTEM directory  *********/
EXEC DBA:      SHOW_DB_DIR 0;

Database Directory for Drive 0:
================================

Alias    Name     Drive Directory Node    Comment                          Type
-------- -------- ----- --------- -------- ------------------------------ ----
TP1      TP1      F:                       TP1 database                     0
CLUB     CLUB     C:                       TEST_DATABASE                    0
SAMPLE   SAMPLE   E:                                                        0

OK, sql_rcd = 0,       Execution time =     0.0300 secs


--      /**************  Show the VOLUME directory for drive C:    *********/
EXEC DBA:      SHOW_DB_DIR C;

Database Directory for Drive C:
================================

Alias    Name     Drive Directory Node    Comment                          Type
-------- -------- ----- --------- -------- ------------------------------ ----
CLUB     CLUB     C:    SQL00003           TEST_DATABASE                    2

OK, sql_rcd = 0,       Execution time =     0.0600 secs


--      /**************  Show the NODE directory for this machine  *********/
EXEC DBA:      SHOW_NODE_DIR;

Node Directory
===============

Node      Local LU  Partner LU  Mode      Comment
--------- --------- ----------- --------- -----------------------------------
DBSVR02             DBSVR02                NODE_02_COMMENT

OK, sql_rcd = 0,       Execution time =     0.2800 secs


--      /**************  Disconnect from the sample database    *********/
EXEC DBA:      STOPUSE sample;

OK, sql_rcd = 0,       Execution time =     1.2500 secs


--      /**************  Create a database called NEW_DB1 on drive C: *********/
EXEC DBA:      CREATE_DB new_db1 C This_is_a_test;

OK, sql_rcd = 0,       Execution time =     40.7800 secs
```

Figure 28-26 (Part 1 of 2).   Script 22: Creating a DB and Viewing the Directories.

```
--      /**************   Show the contents of the SYSTEM directory   *********/
EXEC DBA:       SHOW_DB_DIR 0;

Database Directory for Drive 0:
===============================

Alias     Name      Drive Directory Node     Comment                       Type
--------  --------  ----- --------- --------  ----------------------------  ----
NEW_DB1   NEW_DB1   C:                        This_is_a_test                0
TP1       TP1       F:                        TP1 database                  0
CLUB      CLUB      C:                        TEST_DATABASE                 0
SAMPLE    SAMPLE    E:                                                      0

OK, sql_rcd = 0,        Execution time =    0.1000 secs


--      /*************   Let's get rid of the junk databases   *********/
EXEC DBA:       DROP_DB new_db1;

OK, sql_rcd = 0,        Execution time =    5.2800 secs
```

Figure 28-26 (Part 2 of 2). Script 22: Creating a DB and Viewing the Directories.

How to Backup and Restore a Database

The script below shows how RSQL can be used to perform routine maintenance tasks on a database.

```
--      /*_____*/
--      /*       A Script for how to Backup and Restore a database */
--      /*_____*/
--      /************** connect to the database      ************************/
EXEC DBA:       STARTUSE sample S;

OK, sql_rcd = 0,        Execution time =    0.7200 secs


--      /**************   To make things go faster...           *********/
EXEC SQL:       DROP TABLE ACCT;

OK, sql_rcd = 0,        Execution time =    1.3700 secs


--      /**************   Disconnect from the sample database   *********/
EXEC DBA:       STOPUSE sample;

OK, sql_rcd = 0,        Execution time =    1.2500 secs


--      /**************   Backup "ALL" the database to the A:  drive *********/
EXEC DBA:       BACKUP sample ALL A;

OK, sql_rcd = 0,        Execution time =  167.9100 secs
```

Figure 28-27 (Part 1 of 2). Script 23: How to Backup and Restore a Database.

```
--      /**************    Delete the sample database from the system  *********/
EXEC DBA:        DROP_DB   sample;

 OK, sql_rcd = 0,        Execution time =     3.2500 secs


--      /**************    Let's restore it from the backup A: to  C:  *********/
EXEC DBA:        RESTORE sample C  A;

 OK, sql_rcd = 0,        Execution time =   115.9400 secs


--      /**************    BIND the RSQL   program                     *********/
EXEC DBA: BIND sample rsql.bnd ISO UNCOMMITTED_READ BLOCK_ALL USERID;

 No messages in msgfile.msg

 OK, sql_rcd = 0,        Execution time =     1.6800 secs


--      /************* Reconnect  to database sample                   *********/
EXEC DBA:        STARTUSE sample S;

 OK, sql_rcd = 0,        Execution time =     0.6600 secs


--      /************* Let's see if it still works                     *********/
EXEC SQL:        SELECT * FROM neworg;

 DEPTNUMB  DEPTNAME         MANAGER  DIVISION    LOCATION
 --------  ---------------  -------  ----------  --------------
 99        Software         NULL     Oceanview   Hawaii
 90        Multimedia       NULL     Oceanview   Tahiti

 Total Number of Rows SELECTED = 2

 OK, sql_rcd = 0,        Execution time =     0.0900 secs
```

Figure 28-27 (Part 2 of 2). Script 23: How to Backup and Restore a Database.

Forward Recovery Using Roll Forward

The following script shows how RSQL can be used to restore a damaged database using forward recovery. Here's an explanation of what the script does:

1. Drops the old SAMPLE database and creates a new one.
2. Enables the roll-forward mode by updating the *log_retain* parameter in the Database Configuration file.
3. Backs up the SAMPLE database.
4. Creates a table and inserts two rows in it.
5. Simulates a disk crash by dropping the SAMPLE database. Unfortunately DROP DATABASE also deletes the log files, regardless of the drive on which they reside. So, we protect our log files by copying them to an archive disk using XCOPY.
6. Performs the forward recovery by: 1) restoring the database, 2) XCOPYing the log files into the log directory, and 3) issuing a roll forward. Our two rows are still there!

Trick Question: Why is "9999-12-31-23.59.59.999999" passed to Roll Forward? This number is the the OS/2 version of an *infinite date/time*. It will cause transactions to be rolled forward until the end of the log files is reached.

```
--      /*_____*/
--      /*              Roll-Forward Recovery Script                     */
--      /*_____*/
--      /******** drop any existing database named SAMPLE  ******************/
EXEC DBA: DROP_DB   SAMPLE;

 OK, sql_rcd = 0,        Execution time =    3.2800 secs

--   ****************************************************************************
--   ** Create a new  SAMPLE Database Using the SQLSAMPL.EXE Utility       **
--   ****************************************************************************

EXEC DOS: SQLSAMPL.EXE;

 Program completed with a return code of 0.
 OK,                     Execution time =    46.1900 secs

-- bind the rsql program
EXEC DBA: BIND SAMPLE RSQL.BND ISO REPEATABLE_READ BLOCK_ALL PUBLIC;

 No messages in msgfile.msg

 OK, sql_rcd = 0,        Execution time =    1.7500 secs

--   ****************************************************************************
--   ** Enable Roll-Forward Mode (LOG RETAIN) then BACKUP the database     **
--   ****************************************************************************

--   /***** update the Database Configuration for database: SAMPLE **********/
EXEC DBA: UPDATE_DB_CFG sample  LOG_RETAIN   = 1;

 OK, sql_rcd = 0,        Execution time =    0.2800 secs

--   /************* backup the database ******************************/
EXEC DBA: BACKUP SAMPLE ALL C;

 OK, sql_rcd = 0,        Execution time =    226.9100 secs


--   ****************************************************************************
--   ** Create NEWSTAFF TABLE, ADD some people                            **
--   ****************************************************************************

--   /************* connect to the database     *********************/
EXEC DBA: STARTUSE sample S;

 OK, sql_rcd = 0,        Execution time =    0.6800 secs


--   /*************    Create a NEWSTAFF table        **************/
EXEC SQL:   CREATE TABLE newstaff
                  (id         SMALLINT NOT NULL,
                   name       VARCHAR(9),
                   dept       SMALLINT,
                   job        CHAR(5),
```

Figure 28-28 (Part 1 of 3). Script 24: Recovering a Damaged Database Using Roll Forward.

```
                                   years        SMALLINT,
                                   salary       DECIMAL(7,2),
                                   comm         DECIMAL(7,2));

 OK, sql_rcd = 0,         Execution time =      3.4400 secs


 --      /************       Insert into newstaff two rows       ***************/
 EXEC SQL:   INSERT INTO newstaff
             VALUES (500, 'Bob' , 99, 'Nerds', 5, 45000.00, 0 );

 OK, sql_rcd = 0,         Execution time =      0.0300 secs


 EXEC SQL:   INSERT INTO newstaff
             VALUES (501, 'Dan', 99, 'Nerds', 4, 42000.00, 0 );

 OK, sql_rcd = 0,         Execution time =      0.0300 secs


 --      /************       commit the work done so far       *********/
 EXEC SQL:   COMMIT;

 OK, sql_rcd = 0,         Execution time =      0.0600 secs


 --      /************       See what we've got in the table       *********/
 EXEC SQL:   SELECT * FROM newstaff;
 ID      NAME       DEPT    JOB    YEARS   SALARY     COMM
 ------  ---------  ------  -----  ------  ---------  --------
 500     Bob        99      Nerds  5       45000.00   00.00
 501     Dan        99      Nerds  4       42000.00   00.00

 Total Number of Rows SELECTED = 2

 OK, sql_rcd = 0,         Execution time =      0.0000 secs


 --      /***************       disconnect from SAMPLE       ******************/
 EXEC DBA:    STOPUSE sample;

 OK, sql_rcd = 0,         Execution time =      0.9100 secs


 --   *****************************************************************************
 --   **   Save log files to an archive disk using XCOPY                        **
 --   *****************************************************************************

 EXEC DOS: cmd.exe /c xcopy e:\sql00001\sqlogdir e:\archive ;

 Program completed with a return code of 0.
 OK,                      Execution time =      6.9700 secs

 --      /************       disconnect from the database       *************/
 EXEC DBA:    STOPUSE;

 OK, sql_rcd = 0,         Execution time =      0.6600 secs
```

Figure 28-28 (Part 2 of 3). Script 24: Recovering a Damaged Database Using Roll Forward.

```
--   *****************************************************************************
--   **  Simulate a disk crash by dropping the SAMPLE database...              **
--   *****************************************************************************
EXEC DBA: DROP_DB SAMPLE;

 OK, sql_rcd = 0,          Execution time =    3.4100 secs


--   *****************************************************************************
--   ** RESTORE SAMPLE from backup,  XCOPY log files, ROLLFORWARD              **
--   *****************************************************************************

--       /*********** restore SAMPLE database ****************************/
EXEC DBA: RESTORE SAMPLE E C;

 OK, sql_rcd = 0,          Execution time =    50.3800 secs


--       /******** XCOPY log files back into the directory ******************/
EXEC DOS: cmd.exe /c xcopy e:\archive e:\sql00001\sqlogdir  ;

 Program completed with a return code of 0.
 OK,                       Execution time =    7.0600 secs


--       /******** Apply Roll Forward          ****************************/
EXEC DBA: ROLL_FORWARD SAMPLE SQLUM_ROLLFWD_STOP 9999-12-31-23.59.59.999999;

 Next Log File          =

 First Archive Log File =  S0000001.LOG
 Last  Archive Log File =  S0000003.LOG
 Last Commit Time       =  1992-04-28-15.51.39.000000
 OK, sql_rcd = 0,          Execution time =    7.2500 secs


--       /************* connect to the database     ***********************/
EXEC DBA:   STARTUSE sample S;

 OK, sql_rcd = 0,          Execution time =    0.7800 secs


--       /************* show rows in newstaff Table          **********/
EXEC SQL:   SELECT * FROM newstaff;

 ID     NAME       DEPT   JOB    YEARS   SALARY    COMM
 ----   --------   ----   ----   -----   -------   --------
 500    Bob        99     Nerds  5       45000.00  00.00
 501    Dan        99     Nerds  4       42000.00  00.00

 Total Number of Rows SELECTED = 2

 OK, sql_rcd = 0,          Execution time =    0.4100 secs
```

Figure 28-28 (Part 3 of 3). Script 24: Recovering a Damaged Database Using Roll Forward.

Chapter 29

RSQL: Programming Dynamic SQL

This is the first of a two-chapter series that examines the inner workings of the **RSQL.SQC** program. You've already seen in the last chapter how **RSQL**, the "all-in-one" database utility, was used to explore almost every aspect of the OS/2 Database Manager. As expected, this "all-in-one" capability comes at a price: a long journey into the **RSQL** code lies ahead. This is the bad news! The good news is that by the time you finish this long journey, which spans across two chapters, you will have accomplished the following:

- You will learn how to precompile and build a Database Manager program.
- You will learn how to program dynamic SQL.
- You will learn how to program the Database Administration commands.
- You will have completed 80% of the journey towards your accreditation as an OS/2 Database Manager "programming guru."
- You will experience absolute ecstasy once you've gone through the whole thing and come out alive!

With this cheerful preview of wonderful things to come, let us now tell you how this two-chapter series is organized:

- The first chapter in the series introduces the main outline of the RSQL code, and covers the following areas:

    1. **RSQL.MAK**, the *make* file for the RSQL program
    2. **RSQL.H**, the common header file for the RSQL program
    3. The **main()** procedure of the RSQL program
    4. The command handlers for the execution of **dynamic SQL** statements
    5. The command handler for the execution of OS/2 programs from RSQL
    6. The internals of the **SQLDA** and **SQLCA** data structures
    7. The *common* procedures used by RSQL to read input commands, decode the parameters, measure performance, and perform error handling.

- The second chapter in the series examines the RSQL code that executes the **Database Administration Services**.

The RSQL code breaks nicely into two distinct functional areas: **Dynamic SQL** and the **Database Administration Services**. The first chapter contains common procedures that you may occasionally need to reference from the other chapter. This minor inconvenience is incurred to keep RSQL whole so that at the end of the exercise you will have a single general purpose "all-in-one" utility.

THE RSQL.MAK MAKE FILE

The **RSQL.MAK** make file (see Figure 29-1) demonstrates the process used to build a Database Manager program. Here are the points of interest:

- The database services requires a new library, **sql_dyn** for dynamic sql services. In addition, the **upm** library is needed for the User Profile Management (UPM).
- The precompiler and binder require the name of an existing database on the machine where you are compiling the program.
- The **.sqc** inference rule was introduced to precompile and bind your (.SQC) source code. If you're not clear on what this means, please review "Embedded SQL: The Precompile and Bind Process" on page 566.
- The precompiler, **SQLPREP**, is run with the following options:

    /B   This option is used to defer the binding. We do that to create (.BND) files. We provide an explicit BIND by running **sqlbind** separately.

    /FISO   This option specifies the use of the International Standards Organization (ISO) format for date (yyyy-mm-dd) and time (hh.mm.ss) in the access plans.

    /ICS   This option specifies the locking isolation level as being **Cursor Stability**; for a review of what this means, refer to "Locking and Isolation Levels" on page 590.

- The modified (.C) file generated by the precompiler and binder is run through the C compiler and linker to produce executable code.

RSQL.SQC main() Listing

RSQL is fairly straightforward; the program reads a command from a *run* file, executes it, and returns the output in a *response* file. RSQL executes the entire repertoire of OS/2 Database Manager commands, with two exceptions: static SQL commands and stored procedure calls, which are both fully covered in **Part V**. We start the journey into the RSQL code with the **main()** function (see listing in Figure 29-2), which of course serves as the outline for the **RSQL.SQC** program. The first few statements are the usual *includes* for the various C library header files. Like any good OS/2 program, RSQL includes header material from **OS2.H,** which serves as the "master file" for a set

```
#***********************************************************************
# Make File for RSQL programs
#***********************************************************************

#********************    MACROS   ********************************
cflags= /C /Ti+ /Q+ /Sp1 /Sm /Gs+ /Gm+ /Ge+ /Gd+ /DES32TO16 /DINCL_32
lflags= /ST:64000/CO/NOLOGO/NOI/LI/MAP:FULL/PM:VIO
exe_libs= sql_dyn upm
database= SAMPLE

#********************    INFERENCE RULES ************************
.SUFFIXES: .sqc

.obj.exe:
        echo LINKING   $** to create $*.exe
        link386  $(lflags) $**,,, $(exe_libs), $*.def;

.c.obj:
        echo COMPILING $*.c
        icc $(cflags) $*.c

.sqc.c:
        echo PREPARING $*.sqc
        sqlprep $*.sqc $(database) /B /FISO /ICS
        echo BINDING   $*.bnd
        sqlbind $*.bnd $(database)

#********************    BUILD STATEMENTS   ********************
all: rsql.exe

rsql.exe                  : rsql.obj           # SQL executable module
rsql.c      rsql.obj      : rsql.sqc rsql.h    # SQL source module
```

Figure 29-1. The RSQL.MAK MAKE File.

of IBM-provided include files that contain definitions for specific groups of OS/2 functions. The following conditional include flags are enabled:

```
#define INCL_DOSMEMMGR
#define INCL_DOSPROCESS
```

These flags indicate that RSQL will be using OS/2's memory management and tasking services.

Following the OS/2 header file are header files specific to the Database Manager. We're including the header files for the SQL services, Database Administration services, the User Profile Management, and the header files for SQL data structures and return codes. The final header file to be included is **RSQL.H**, listed in Figure 29-14. This file contains RSQL's forward function declarations, the definitions of constants and data types, and the program's global variables.

The **main()** function's code follows. It serves as RSQL's executive. Here is how **main()** controls the execution of the RSQL application:

- It first invokes **initialize_rsql()**, listed in Figure 29-3. This procedure registers **exit_proc()**, also listed in Figure 29-3, as the Exit List function for RSQL. The sole purpose of this exit function is to close the *response* file in case of program failure. (This will save the results of the RSQL commands that executed before disaster struck.)

- It then invokes **check_args_and_prepare_files()**, also listed in Figure 29-3. This function accepts two user supplied program input parameters:

  - The name of the *run* file, which contains the script of RSQL commands you want executed.
  - The name of the *response* file, which is the file where you want RSQL to place the results of an execution run.

  These two files are opened and RSQL is now initialized and ready to perform its run.

- The RSQL *run* file is executed as a do loop that terminates when all the commands in *run* have been executed. Here is how the loop goes about doing its thing:

  1. A command is read from the *run* file. The command type and number is decoded by **get_command()**, listed in Figure 29-4.
  2. The timer is started. The timer code is listed in Figure 29-6.
  3. Each command is executed by the appropriate command handler. Here is a guide to where you can find these command handlers:

     - The command handler for immediate dynamic SQL commands is **sql_immediate()**, listed in Figure 29-7.
     - The command handler for varying-list dynamic SQL SELECTs is **sql_select()**, listed in Figure 29-9.
     - The command handler which executes OS/2 programs from within RSQL is **dos_exec()**, listed in Figure 29-11.
     - The top-level command handler for the Database Administration Commands is **dba_exec()**. The code for that handler and its numerous assistants is provided in Chapter 30.

  4. The timer is stopped. The elapsed time for the execution of the command is saved (the timer procedures are listed in Figure 29-6).
  5. The results of the execution of the command, including the elapsed time, are recorded in the *response* file by our results handler. The name of the results handler is **record_command_results()**, and its code listing can be found in Figure 29-13.

- When there are no commands left to process in the *run* file, the program exits the loop and the function **terminate_program()**, listed in Figure 29-3, is invoked to close all open files.

```
/**************************************************************************/
/*   PROGRAM NAME:  RSQL.SQC    -- Run SQL program                       */
/*                                                                        */
/*   DESCRIPTION:  This program allows a user to run a batch file consisting */
/*     of SQL and Database Administrator commands against an OS2 database. */
/*     The script is submitted to RSQL in a command file and the results  */
/*     appear in a response file.  RSQL runs as an OS2 task and does not   */
/*     require the services of Query Manager.                             */
/*                                                                        */
/*   PROGRAM INVOCATION:                                                  */
/*                                                                        */
/*     rsql cmd_file resp_file                                            */
/*                                                                        */
/*          cmd_file  = run file that contains the user script           */
/*          resp_file = response file that contains the output           */
/*                                                                        */
/**************************************************************************/
#include <process.h>                    /* For exit()                     */
#include <stdio.h>                      /* For printf() & NULL            */
#include <stdlib.h>                     /* For printf                     */
#include <string.h>                     /* For printf                     */
#include <sys\types.h>                  /* For time()                     */
#include <sys\timeb.h>                  /* For time()                     */
#include <sys\stat.h>                   /* For stat()                     */
#include <io.h>                         /* For file I/O                   */
#include <conio.h>                      /* For getch and kbhit            */
#include <fcntl.h>                      /* For file I/O                   */

#define INCL_DOSMEMMGR
#define INCL_DOSPROCESS
#include <os2.h>

#include <sqlca.h>                      /* For sqlca                      */
#include <sql.h>                        /* For error msg retrieval        */
#include <sqlcodes.h>                   /* For SQL return code constants  */
#include <sqlenv.h>                     /* For environment functions      */
#include <sqlutil.h>                    /* For utility functions          */
#include <upm.h>                        /* For logon/logoff functions     */
struct   sqlca sqlca;                   /* For DB mgr return codes        */

#include "rsql.h"
#pragma stack16(8192)
/*_____*/
/* Main function.                                                        */
/*_____*/
int main(int argc, char **argv)
{
  SHORT cmd_type;
  SHORT ch;

  initialize_rsql();

  check_args_and_prepare_files(argc, argv);

  /*_____*/
  /* Process commands one at a time              */
  /*_____*/
  while (!feof(cmd_stream))
    {
    /*_____*/
    /* get next command                            */
    /*_____*/
```

Figure 29-2 (Part 1 of 2).   RSQL.SQC main().

```
        cmd_type = get_command(parm_buf);

        /*————————————————————————————*/
        /* Initialize Timer                        */
        /*————————————————————————————*/
        reset_timer();
        start_timer();

        /*————————————————————————————*/
        /* Execute the command.                    */
        /*————————————————————————————*/
        switch (cmd_type)
        {
                    /*————————————————————————————*/
                    /*     Dynamic SQL commands         */
                    /*————————————————————————————*/
          case CMD_SQL_IMMEDIATE       : rcd = sql_immediate(parm_buf);   break;
          case CMD_SQL_SELECT          : rcd = sql_select(parm_buf);      break;

                    /*————————————————————————————*/
                    /*     Execute an OS/2 program      */
                    /*————————————————————————————*/
          case CMD_DOS                 : rcd = dos_exec(parm_buf);        break;

                    /*————————————————————————————*/
                    /* Database Administration Commands */
                    /*————————————————————————————*/

          case CMD_DBA                 : rcd = dba_exec(parm_buf);        break;

                    /*————————————————————————————*/
                    /*   RSQL execution controls        */
                    /*————————————————————————————*/
          case CMD_DBA_CONTINUE_ON_ERROR : rcd = RECORD_NOTHING;
                                         continue_on_error = TRUE;        break;
          case CMD_DBA_STOP_ON_ERROR   : rcd = RECORD_NOTHING;
                                         continue_on_error = FALSE;       break;
          case CMD_DBA_PAUSE           : rcd = RECORD_NOTHING;
                                         printf("\nPausing! Press any key "
                                                "to continue...");
                                         while (!kbhit());

                                         ch = getch();
                                         break;
          case CMD_SYNTAX_ERROR        : rcd = RECORD_ERR_MSG;            break;
          case CMD_NO_CMD              : rcd = RECORD_NOTHING;            break;

          default: break;
        } /* endswitch */
        /*————————————————————————————*/
        /* Stop the timer, record the results,     */
        /* terminate command processing if error   */
        /*————————————————————————————*/
        stop_timer();
        if (record_command_results(rcd)  == TERMINATE)
          break;

      }/* endwhile not eof */

    terminate_program();

} /* end main */
```

Figure 29-2 (Part 2 of 2).   RSQL.SQC main().

RSQL.SQC: Listing of Top-Level Functions

The functions listed in this section are the non-command handler functions called by RSQL's **main()** procedure. The listing for those functions is provided in Figure 29-3. Collectively, these top-level functions initialize RSQL, open its *run* and *response* files, and then close those files when the program either terminates normally or abnormally. This ensures that you will always know what last happened by looking at the contents of the *response* file, even if the RSQL program terminates abnormally. Notice that we're using **malloc** to allocate dynamic memory to a sqlda variable. The SQLDASIZE macro, supplied by Database Manager, returns the size (in bytes) of the sqlda based on the number of columns you specify. We specified the maximum number of columns: 255. We have a lot more to say about sqlda later in this chapter.

```
/*_____*/
/* perform required program initialization                        */
/*_____*/
VOID initialize_rsql(VOID)
{
    /*_____*/
    /* allocate a sqlda                       */
    /*_____*/
    sqlda = (struct sqlda *)malloc(SQLDASIZE(255));

    /*_____*/
    /* Enable the exit list procedure         */
    /*_____*/
    DosExitList(1,                          /* 1 = Add to exit list    */
               (PFNEXITLIST) exit_proc);    /* pointer to procedure    */

} /* end initialize_rsql */

/*_____*/
/* Check for the right number of program arguments and open files. */
/*_____*/
VOID check_args_and_prepare_files(USHORT argc, PCHAR argv[])
{
    /*_____*/
    /* Are the required parameters there?     */
    /*_____*/
    if (argc < 3)
    { fprintf(stderr,"\nCalling syntax is: rsql run_file resp_file");
      exit(1);
    } /* endif */
    /*_____*/
    /* Open the RUN and RESPONSE files.       */
    /*_____*/
    if (NULL == (cmd_stream = fopen(argv[1], "r")))
    { printf("\nError opening the RUN file :  %s", argv[1]);
      exit(1);
    } /* endif */

    if (NULL == (out_stream = fopen(argv[2], "w")))
    { printf("\nError opening the RESPONSE file :  %s", argv[2]);
      exit(1);
    } /* endif */

} /* end check_args_and_prepare_files */
```

Figure 29-3 (Part 1 of 2). RSQL.SQC Listing of Top Level Functions.

```
/*————————————————————————————————————————————————————*/
/* Clean up and terminate the program.                 */
/*————————————————————————————————————————————————————*/
VOID terminate_program(VOID)
{
  free(sqlda);
  fclose(cmd_stream);
  fclose(out_stream);
} /* end terminate_program */


/*————————————————————————————————————————————————————*/
/*  This procedure displays how the program terminated and performs cleanup */
/*  if abnormal termination.                           */
/*————————————————————————————————————————————————————*/
VOID APIENTRY exit_proc(ULONG term_code)
{
                    /*————————————————————*/
                    /*Determine cause      */
                    /*————————————————————*/
   switch (term_code)
    { case  0 :
            printf("\n**program terminated normally**\n");
            break;
      case  1 :
            printf("\n**program terminated by hard error**\n");
            break;
      case  2 :
            fclose(cmd_stream);
            fclose(out_stream);
            printf("\n**program terminated by a trap**\n ");
            break;
      case  3 :
            fclose(cmd_stream);
            fclose(out_stream);
            printf("\n**program terminated by a DosKillProcess**\n");
            break;

     default :
                printf("\n**unknown program termination**\n");
    } /* end switch */


                    /*————————————————————*/
                    /* Allow next exit list*/
                    /*————————————————————*/
   DosExitList(3,                              /* 3 allows next exit to run */
            (void far *) 0);                   /* null pointer              */
} /* end exit_proc */
```

Figure 29-3 (Part 2 of 2). RSQL.SQC Listing of Top Level Functions.

The get_command() Function

The **get_command**() procedure (see Figure 29-4) retrieves a command from the *run* file and provides a first-level parsing of the command and its parameters. This information is used by **main**() to dispatch the appropriate command handler. The **get_command**() procedure will format the commands so that they can be directly executed. The extracted parameters are placed in a global **parm_str** variable. Most of the parameters will need further parsing, but this will be done by the individual command handlers.

The following is a step-by-step summary of what **get_command()** does:

1. Reads a command from the *run* file. The C-language **fscanf()** is used to read in a string of characters from the *run* file until a ";" terminator is found. The string of characters may span across multiple lines in the *run* file, especially in the case of multiline commands.

2. Writes the command line in the *response* file. As a result you'll be able to see command/response pairs when viewing the results of a run.

3. Removes comment lines from the command.

4. Parses the first four tokens of a command to determine the type of the command.

5. Performs the following command and parameter preparation based on the type of command that is parsed:

   • For *SQL commands*, the "EXEC SQL:" header and the Carriage-Return and Line-Feed characters are stripped off the command string. In addition, the third token in the header is decoded to determine whether this is an SQL SELECT command. Based on the decode, the procedure either returns a CMD_SQL_SE-LECT or a CMD_SQL_IMMEDIATE. The **parm_str** variable will contain the SQL command to be executed.

   • For *DOS commands*, the "EXEC DOS:" header is stripped off the command string. The **parm_str** variable will contain the name of the OS/2 program to be executed, followed by a NULL, and then any parameters to be passed to the **DosExecPgm** API call.

   • For *DBA commands*, the "EXEC DBA:" header is stripped off the command string. A **cmds** array is searched for a Database Administration command name that matches this command. If a match is found, a command number and the maximum number of parameters for this command is retrieved from the array. The **parm_str** variable will contain the command parameters in their input string format. In addition, the entries from the **cmds** array for this command are placed in the **parms** data structure. As you will see later, **parms** serves as a *global blackboard* that maintains context for the Database Administration command currently being executed. The definition of **parms** is given in RSQL.H (see Figure 29-14).

The **get_command()** procedure does not introduce any new OS/2 programming constructs. It's just straight C code that is part of the overhead required for making RSQL end-user friendly.

```
/*──────────────────────────────────────────────────────────────*/
/*  This procedure determines the command type                    */
/*──────────────────────────────────────────────────────────────*/
SHORT get_command(PCHAR parm_str)
{
  char   cmd[MAX_CMD_SIZE];               /* temp buffer for cmd processing  */
  char   token1[5];                       /* token to receive EXEC           */
  char   token2[5];                       /* token to receive DBA: or SQL:   */
  char   token3[25];                      /* token to receive cmd name       */
  char   token4[MAX_CMD_SIZE];            /* token to receive parms          */
  char   comment_line[MAX_CMD_SIZE];      /* comment line temporary variable */
  char   delim1,delim2;                   /* variables for sscanf            */

    /*──────────────────────────────────────*/
    /* Initialize cmds table                */
    /*──────────────────────────────────────*/
    typedef struct
    {
      CHAR      cmd_name[40];             /* cmd name                         */
      CHAR      cmd_num;                  /* numerical representation of cmd  */
      USHORT    num_parms;               /* number of parms for this command */
    }  CMD_TYPE;

    static CMD_TYPE cmds[] =
    {/*<--- cmd_name --><-- cmd_num ------------------><-- num_parms -->*/
      {"BACKUP",            CMD_DBA_BACKUP                , 3         },
      {"BIND",              CMD_DBA_BIND                  , 6         },
      {"CATALOG_DB",        CMD_DBA_CATALOG_DB            , 6         },
      {"CATALOG_NODE",      CMD_DBA_CATALOG_NODE          , 4         },
      {"COLLECT_STATUS",    CMD_DBA_COLLECT_STATUS        , 1         },
      {"CONTINUE_ON_ERROR", CMD_DBA_CONTINUE_ON_ERROR     , 0         },
      {"CREATE_DB",         CMD_DBA_CREATE_DB             , 3         },
      {"DROP_DB",           CMD_DBA_DROP_DB               , 1         },
      {"EXPORT",            CMD_DBA_EXPORT                , 4         },
      {"GET_ADMIN",         CMD_DBA_GET_ADMIN             , 0         },
      {"IMPORT",            CMD_DBA_IMPORT                , 5         },
      {"LOGOFF",            CMD_DBA_LOGOFF                , 3         },
      {"LOGON",             CMD_DBA_LOGON                 , 5         },
      {"PAUSE",             CMD_DBA_PAUSE                 , 0         },
      {"REORG",             CMD_DBA_REORG                 , 3         },
      {"RESET_DM_CFG",      CMD_DBA_RESET_DM_CFG          , 0         },
      {"RESET_DB_CFG",      CMD_DBA_RESET_DB_CFG          , 1         },
      {"RESTORE",           CMD_DBA_RESTORE               , 3         },
      {"ROLL_FORWARD",      CMD_DBA_ROLL_FORWARD          , 3         },
      {"RUNSTATS",          CMD_DBA_RUNSTATS              , 1         },
      {"SHOW_DB_CFG",       CMD_DBA_SHOW_DB_CFG           , 1         },
      {"SHOW_DB_DIR",       CMD_DBA_SHOW_DB_DIR           , 1         },
      {"SHOW_DM_CFG",       CMD_DBA_SHOW_DM_CFG           , 0         },
      {"SHOW_NODE_DIR",     CMD_DBA_SHOW_NODE_DIR         , 0         },
      {"STARTDM",           CMD_DBA_STARTDM               , 0         },
      {"STARTUSE",          CMD_DBA_STARTUSE              , 2         },
      {"STOPDM",            CMD_DBA_STOPDM                , 0         },
      {"STOP_ON_ERROR",     CMD_DBA_STOP_ON_ERROR         , 0         },
      {"STOPUSE",           CMD_DBA_STOPUSE               , 0         },
      {"UNCATALOG_DB",      CMD_DBA_UNCATALOG_DB          , 1         },
      {"UNCATALOG_NODE",    CMD_DBA_UNCATALOG_NODE        , 1         },
      {"UPDATE_DB_CFG",     CMD_DBA_UPDATE_DB_CFG         , 2         },
      {"UPDATE_DM_CFG",     CMD_DBA_UPDATE_DM_CFG         , 0         }
    };

    SHORT      cmd_not_found;             /* True if a match is found         */
    USHORT     i;                         /* loop index variable              */
    PCHAR      char_ptr;                  /* used to remove CRLF from SQL stmts*/
```

Figure 29-4 (Part 1 of 3). RSQL.SQC Listing of the get_command() Function.

```
/*————————————————————*/
/* Read a command from the RUN file          */
/*————————————————————*/
num_parms = fscanf(cmd_stream," %[^;]%*c ", cmd);
if (num_parms == EOF)
   return(CMD_NO_CMD);                        /* empty file         */
strcat(cmd,";");                              /* maintain cmd delim. */

/*————————————————————*/
/* Echo command to the response file         */
/*————————————————————*/
fprintf(out_stream,"%s\n", cmd);

/*————————————————————*/
/* Remove any comment lines                  */
/*————————————————————*/
while ((cmd[0] == '-') && (cmd[1] == '-'))
   {
   num_parms = sscanf(cmd,"%[^\n;]%*c %[^;]%*c ",
                  comment_line, &delim1, cmd, &delim2);/* remove comment line */
   if (delim1 == ';')
      return (CMD_NO_CMD);                    /* ";" within a comment*/
   strcat(cmd,";");                           /* maintain cmd delim. */
   }

/*————————————————————*/
/* parse the command, make some validity     */
/* checks                                    */
/*————————————————————*/
num_parms = sscanf(cmd, " %4s %4s %24s %[^;]",
                      token1, token2, token3, token4);

if (num_parms == 3)                           /* no parms, parse accordingly */
   {
   num_parms = sscanf(cmd, " %4s %4s %24[^;]",

                        token1, token2, token3);
   strcpy(token4,"");
   }

if ( (num_parms < 3)  ||
     (strcmp(token1,"EXEC") != 0)  ||
     ((strcmp(token2,"DBA:" ) != 0) &&
      (strcmp(token2,"DOS:" ) != 0) &&
      (strcmp(token2,"SQL:" ) != 0)) )
   {
   sprintf(err_msg,
   "\nSYNTAX ERROR: Expected EXEC SQL: or EXEC DBA: etc... to begin a command.");
   return(CMD_SYNTAX_ERROR);
   }

/*————————————————————*/
/* SQL CMD, return command type,             */
/* remove EXEC SQL:                          */
/*————————————————————*/
if (strcmp(token2,"SQL:" ) == 0)
   {
   char_ptr = strpbrk(token4,"\n\r");         /* remove CRLF chars   */
   while (char_ptr != NULL)
      {
```

Figure 29-4 (Part 2 of 3). RSQL.SQC Listing of the get_command() Function.

```
            char_ptr[0] = ' ';
            char_ptr = strpbrk(char_ptr,"\n\r");
          }

       sprintf(parm_str, "%s %s", token3, token4);    /* return the cmd for  */
       if (strcmp(strupr(token3),"SELECT" ) == 0)     /*     processing      */
           return(CMD_SQL_SELECT);
       else
           return(CMD_SQL_IMMEDIATE);
     } /* end if */

  /*_____*/
  /* DOS CMD, return command type,     */
  /* remove EXEC DOS:                  */
  /*_____*/
  if (strcmp(token2,"DOS:" ) == 0)
     {

       sprintf(parm_str, "%s%c%s", token3, 0, token4);  /* return the cmd for  */
                                                        /* in the form for     */
                                                        /*    DosExecPgm       */
       return(CMD_DOS);
     } /* end if */

  /*_____*/
  /* DBA CMD, return command type,     */
  /* remove "EXEC DBA: cmd_name"       */
  /*_____*/
  i = 0 ;
  cmd_not_found = TRUE ;

  while ( cmd_not_found && (i < CMD_LAST_CMD))
    {
      cmd_not_found = strcmp(cmds[i].cmd_name,token3);
      if (!cmd_not_found)
         break;
      else
         i++;
    }

  if (cmd_not_found )
    {
      sprintf(err_msg,
      "\nSYNTAX ERROR: Unknown Command. ");
      return(CMD_SYNTAX_ERROR);
    }

  if ((cmds[i].cmd_num ==CMD_DBA_CONTINUE_ON_ERROR) ||
      (cmds[i].cmd_num ==CMD_DBA_STOP_ON_ERROR) ||
      (cmds[i].cmd_num ==CMD_DBA_PAUSE))
    {
      return(cmds[i].cmd_num);
    } /* endif */

  sprintf(parm_str, "%s", token4);
  strcpy(parms.cmd_name,cmds[i].cmd_name);
  parms.cmd_num = cmds[i].cmd_num;
  parms.num_parms = cmds[i].num_parms;
  return(CMD_DBA);
} /* end get_command */
```

Figure 29-4 (Part 3 of 3).   RSQL.SQC Listing of the get_command() Function.

The Timer Functions

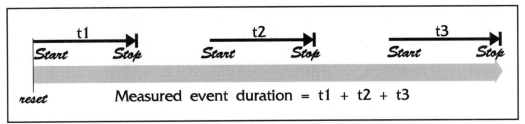

Figure 29-5. Playing with the RSQL Timer Functions.

This section contains the listing for three very straightforward procedures that are used to measure the execution time of an RSQL command. The **reset_timer()** function initializes the timer variables. You can then use **start_timer()** and **stop_timer()** calls to start and stop time measurements (see Figure 29-5 and Figure 29-6). This allows us to refine our command performance measurements by pausing the timers during processing intervals that are not part of the command performance.

```
/*_____*/
/*   This procedure initializes the time variables.        */
/*_____*/
VOID    reset_timer(VOID)
{
   event_time = 0.0 ;
   start_time = 0.0 ;
   end_time   = 0.0 ;
} /* end reset_time */

/*_____*/
/*   This procedure records the time at the start of an interval */
/*_____*/
VOID    start_timer(VOID)
{
   ftime(&timebuff);
   start_time = (double)timebuff.time+((double)timebuff.millitm)/(double)1000;
} /* end start_time */

/*_____*/
/*   This procedure records the time at the end of an interval */
/*   and calculates the elapsed time for an event.         */
/*_____*/
VOID    stop_timer(VOID)
{
   ftime(&timebuff);
   end_time = (double)timebuff.time+((double)timebuff.millitm)/(double)1000;
   event_time = event_time  + (end_time - start_time);
} /* end stop_time */
```

Figure 29-6. RSQL.SQC Listing of the Timer Functions.

The Dynamic SQL Command Handler: sql_immediate()

The **sql_immediate()** function (see Figure 29-7) presents a gentle introduction to SQL programming. The function itself packs a lot of power. It can directly execute any SQL command with the exception of the SELECT command. Before you go on, please make sure you understand the dynamic SQL material in the tutorial "Dynamic SQL Commands" on page 599.

The dynamic SQL statement to be executed is loaded into a character-string host variable. This is done by declaring the **cmd** pointer to be a host variable using:

- **BEGIN DECLARE SECTION**

- **END DECLARE SECTION**

The host variable is then assigned to point at the **cmd_sql** input parameter, which in turn points to **parm_str**, which contains the SQL command obtained from the *run* file by **get_command()**. The **EXECUTE IMMEDIATE** command is then used to prepare and execute the SQL statement in a single operation.

The SQL command's return code is contained in **sqlca**, a global variable of type SQLCA declared at the start of the program. The constant, RECORD_SQLCA, is returned by the procedure to indicate that the sqlca results should be processed. The processing of **sqlca** is performed by **record_command_results()**, listed in Figure 29-13.

```
/*_____*/
/* This procedure executes an sql command dynamically.        */
/*_____*/
SHORT sql_immediate(PCHAR cmd_sql)
{
    /*_____*/
    /* Declare cmd to DBM                   */
    /*_____*/
    EXEC SQL BEGIN DECLARE SECTION;
        char        * cmd;                        /* command buffer    */
    EXEC SQL END DECLARE SECTION;
    cmd = cmd_sql;

    /*_____*/
    /* Execute cmd                          */
    /*_____*/
    EXEC SQL EXECUTE IMMEDIATE   :cmd;

    return (RECORD_SQLCA);
}/* end sql_immediate */
```

Figure 29-7.   RSQL.SQC Listing of the Dynamic SQL sql_immediate() Function.

The Dynamic SQL Command Handler: sql_select()

If the last section was the "gentle" introduction to SQL programming, then this section is its "brutal" counterpart. The varying-list SELECT is definitely the most difficult form of SQL programming. When you're done with this command handler, everything else will seem easy.

The **sql_select()** procedure gets invoked when **main()** discovers that it has a SELECT command to execute. The SELECT statement in an RSQL *run* file is of the **varying-list** variety. So, you can't make any assumptions about the number of columns in the SELECT statements or their data types. All of this is to be discovered at run time by using a **PREPARE** with a variable of type **SQLDA**. If you haven't yet done so, please make sure you go through the tutorial on the dynamic SQL commands, which starts with "Dynamic SQL Commands" on page 599.

The **sql_select()** procedure, listed in Figure 29-9, processes a SQL SELECT statement dynamically. The helper procedure **print_format_row()** (see Figure 29-10) formats the output of the result file. This two-level hierarchy will help you better navigate through the code.

The SQLDA Structure

The varying-list SELECT is one of the few SQL commands that require an intimate knowledge of the SQLDA. The definition of a SQLDA type is provided in Figure 29-8 for quick reference.

```
struct SQLDA
{
   BYTE           sqldaid[8];          /* Eye catcher = 'SQLDA   '         */
   LONG           sqldabc;             /* SQLDA size in bytes = 16+44*sqln */
   SHORT          sqln;                /* Number of SQLVAR elements        */
   SHORT          sqld;                /* # of used SQLVAR elements        */
   struct sqlvar
   {
      SHORT          sqltype;          /* Variable data type               */
      SHORT          sqllen;           /* Variable data length             */
      BYTE         * _Seg16 sqldata;   /* Pointer to variable data value   */
      SHORT        * _Seg16 sqlind;    /* Pointer to Null indicator        */
      struct sqlname                   /* Variable Name                    */
      {
         SHORT          length;        /* Name length [1..30]              */
         BYTE           data[30];      /* Variable or Column name          */
      } sqlname;
   } sqlvar[SQLVAR_NUM];
};
```

Figure 29-8. The SQLDA Structure.

Executing Varying-list SELECT: A Step-by-Step Overview

The following is a step-by-step recipe of how **sql_select()** executes a varying-list SELECT:

1. A static **sqlca** variable is declared in the include file RSQL.H (see Figure 29-14).

2. A **sqlda** pointer is also declared in the RSQL.H. We used malloc to allocate the maximum size.

3. The SQL SELECT statement to be executed is loaded into a character-string host variable. This is done by declaring the **cmd** pointer to be a host variable through the SQL **BEGIN DECLARE SECTION** and **END DECLARE SECTION** statements. The host variable is then assigned to point at the **cmd_sql** input parameter. This parameter in turn points to **parm_str**, which contains the SQL command obtained from the *run* file by **get_command()**.

4. The **sqlda** header fields are initialized. The SQLVAR_NUM constant is 255; the maximum number of columns in a SELECT.

5. The SELECT statement is PREPARED by issuing the following command:

   ```
   EXEC SQL PREPARE st INTO :*sqlda FROM :cmd_sql;
   ```

   where **st** is the name assigned to the statement in **cmd_sql**. Later, this statement name will be associated with a cursor.

6. The Database Manager parses the contents of **cmd_sql** and returns the description in the **sqlda**. The number of column elements in the SELECT is returned in the **sqld** field. Each column is represented by an array element of **sqlvar**. The Database Manager fills a description of the column **sqltype** and **sqllen**. In addition, it returns the name of the column and the length of the name.

7. The information returned in the **sqlda** is used to allocate the storage needed to hold a row of retrieved data and the null indicators. Because this is the first time **sql_select()** finds out about the data types, it will allocate the storage dynamically for each item in the select list and store the pointers to data areas in the **sqlda**. Notice how the **sqlda** is being used as a global black-board where all the relevant information is stored as the execution of the statement progresses.

8. At this point, there is enough information in the **sqlda** to format the names of the column headings of the result file. This is done by issuing two calls to the **print_format_row()** helper function:

   - The first invocation of **print_format_row()** passes the SET_TABS_WIDTH parameter, which tells **print_format_row()** to calculate start position in a line, of each table column that is part of the SELECT query. This information is calculated once for each query and stored in a data structure.

- The second invocation of **print_format_row()** passes PRINT_COLUMNS parameter, which tells **print_format_row()** to write a line to the *response* file containing the name of each table column that is part of the SELECT query.

9. A cursor named **cur** is then declared for the **st** statement name by invoking the command:

```
EXEC SQL DECLARE cur CURSOR FOR st;
```

At this point, the SELECT statement is associated with a cursor.

10. The cursor is then opened by invoking:

```
EXEC SQL OPEN cur;
```

11. We are now ready to retrieve all the rows of data that meet the SELECT conditions. This is done by repeatedly executing the fetch command until all the rows in the result-set have been retrieved.

12. The repeated fetches are done in a loop by issuing:

```
EXEC SQL FETCH cur USING DESCRIPTOR :*sqlda;
```

The results of the fetch are placed in the **sqlda**. The **print_format_row()** helper function is called with the PRINT_SELECTED_ROW option, which extracts the data out of the **sqlda** and writes it to the *response* file. The code in the loop also keeps track of the number of rows read. A column heading is written to the *response* file after a specified number of rows have been read to make the final report more readable.

13. After all the rows have been read, the cursor is closed by issuing the command:

```
EXEC SQL CLOSE cur;
```

14. At this point, the number of rows read is written to the *response* file.

15. The command processor terminates normally by returning the RECORD_SQLCA parameter. Abnormal terminations return RECORD_ERR_MSG. In all cases, the return codes from running the SQL command is contained in the **sqlca**, a global variable. The **record_command_results()** processes the **sqlca** results (see Figure 29-13).

This concludes the main logic of the code that processes the **varying-list** SELECT. We still have to look at the **print_format_row()** code in the next section to understand the intricacies of information passing using the **sqlda**.

Note: The **start_timer()** and **stop_timer()** functions are used repeatedly by **sql_se-lect()** to bracket time measurements. In order to provide a fair measure of the command execution time, we disable the counter during a write to the *response* file, or while allocating dynamic memory.

```
/*_____*/
/*  This procedure executes an sql command dynamically.       */
/*_____*/
SHORT sql_select(PCHAR cmd)
{
  SHORT   index, i ;                      /* for counting                   */
  SHORT   num_of_rows;                    /* number of rows selected        */
  SHORT   num_brk;                        /* number of rows since break     */
  SHORT   byte_count;                     /* number of bytes to allocate    */

  /*_____*/
  /* Declare cmd to DBM   */
  /*_____*/
  EXEC SQL BEGIN DECLARE SECTION ;
   char        * cmd_sql;                 /* command buffer                 */
  EXEC SQL END DECLARE SECTION ;

  cmd_sql     = cmd;
  num_of_rows = 0;
  num_brk     = 0;

  /*_____*/
  /* Initialize the sqlda           */
  /*_____*/
  strncpy( sqlda->sqldaid, "SQLDA   ", 8) ;
  sqlda->sqldabc =  (long ) SQLDASIZE(255);
  sqlda->sqln = SQLVAR_NUM;
  sqlda->sqld = 0 ;

  /*_____*/
  /* Prepare cmd                    */
  /*_____*/
  EXEC SQL PREPARE st INTO :*sqlda FROM :cmd_sql;
  if (SQLCODE != 0)
     return(RECORD_SQLCA);

  /*_____*/
  /* Stop  timer                    */
  /*_____*/
  stop_timer();

  /*_____*/
  /*Allocate space for select variables   */
  /*_____*/
  for (index=0; index< sqlda->sqld; index++)
    {
     if ((sqlda->sqlvar[index].sqltype ==SQL_TYP_DECIMAL) ||
         (sqlda->sqlvar[index].sqltype ==SQL_TYP_NDECIMAL)    )
      byte_count = ( LOBYTE(sqlda->sqlvar[index].sqllen) + 2 ) / 2;
     else
      byte_count = sqlda->sqlvar[index].sqllen;

     sqlda->sqlvar[index].sqldata = (unsigned char *)malloc(byte_count);
```

Figure 29-9 (Part 1 of 3).   RSQL.SQC Listing of the Dynamic SQL sql_select().

```
    if ( sqlda->sqlvar[index].sqldata == NULL )
    {
      fprintf(out_stream,
      "\nOut of dynamic memory while space for select column %d",index + 1);
      return(RECORD_ERR_MSG);
    }

    /*_____*/
    /*Allocate space for null indicators    */
    /*_____*/
    if ( sqlda->sqlvar[index].sqltype & 1 )                    /*  odd    */
    {
      sqlda->sqlvar[index].sqlind =  (short *)malloc(2) ;
      if ( sqlda->sqlvar[index].sqldata == NULL )
      {
        fprintf(out_stream,
        "\nOut of dynamic memory while space for NULL  column %d",index +1);
        return(RECORD_ERR_MSG);
      }/* end if NULL */
    } /* end if odd */
  } /* end for */
rcd = print_format_row(SET_TABS_WIDTH);
if (rcd != 0 )
    return(RECORD_ERR_MSG);

rcd = print_format_row(PRINT_COLUMNS);
if (rcd != 0 )
    return(RECORD_ERR_MSG);

/*_____*/
/* Start timer                          */
/*_____*/
start_timer();

EXEC SQL DECLARE cur CURSOR FOR st ;
if (SQLCODE != 0)
   return(RECORD_SQLCA);

EXEC SQL OPEN cur ;
if (SQLCODE != 0)
   return(RECORD_SQLCA);

/*_____*/
/*Handle data one row at a time         */
/*_____*/
EXEC SQL FETCH cur USING DESCRIPTOR :*sqlda ;
if ((SQLCODE != 0) && (SQLCODE != SQL_RC_W100))
    return(RECORD_SQLCA);

while ( SQLCODE == 01 )
{
  stop_timer();
  num_of_rows++;
  if (num_brk++ > BREAK_SEP)
  {

    for (i=0; i < BREAK_ROWS ; i++)
      fputs("\n",out_stream);

    print_format_row(PRINT_COLUMNS);
    num_brk = 0;
  }
```

Figure 29-9 (Part 2 of 3). RSQL.SQC Listing of the Dynamic SQL sql_select().

```
     rcd =    print_format_row(PRINT_SELECTED_ROW);
     if (rcd != 0 )
        return(RECORD_ERR_MSG);
     else
     {
        start_timer();
        EXEC SQL FETCH cur USING DESCRIPTOR :*sqlda ;
        if ((SQLCODE != 0) && (SQLCODE != SQL_RC_W100))
           return(RECORD_SQLCA);
     }/* end else*/
   }/*end while */

   EXEC SQL CLOSE cur ;
   if (SQLCODE != 0)
      return(RECORD_SQLCA);

   /*_____*/
   /* Stop timer                      */
   /*_____*/
   stop_timer();
   fprintf(out_stream,"\n\n Total Number of Rows SELECTED = %d\n",num_of_rows);

   /*_____*/
   /* Free space for select variables */
   /*_____*/
   for (index=0; index< sqlda->sqld; index++)
     {
       free(sqlda->sqlvar[index].sqldata);

       /*_____*/
       /*Free space for null indicators   */
       /*_____*/
       if ( sqlda->sqlvar[index].sqltype & 1 )              /*  odd   */
       {
         free(sqlda->sqlvar[index].sqlind);
       } /* end if odd */
     } /* end for */

   return(RECORD_SQLCA);
 }/* end sql_select */
```

Figure 29-9 (Part 3 of 3).   RSQL.SQC Listing of the Dynamic SQL sql_select().

The Helper Function for Dynamic SELECT: print_format_row()

The **print_format_row()** function, listed in Figure 29-10, is used to format the results of a dynamic SELECT query and write them to the *response* file. Essentially, we are creating a pretty output format of the query results (at a minimum, this is something a human being could comfortably read). The function is told through an invocation parameter to perform one of three actions:

- **SET_TABS_WIDTH** causes the width of each SELECT field to be calculated. The displacement or **tab** of each field within an output line is calculated and stored.

- **PRINT_COLUMNS** causes the underscored column headings to be written to the *response* file.

- **PRINT_SELECTED_ROW** causes one row of SELECT data to be formatted and written to the *response* file.

The **print_format_row()** obtains its information from the **sqlda**. It writes the formatted output it generates directly to the *response* file. The function maintains its internal data in a static structure of type **FLD_TYPE**, which contains the tab location and maximum width for each column that is part of a SELECT statement. A call requesting the SET_TABS_WIDTH action must be issued first for each execution of a SELECT query. A call requesting PRINT_ROW must be issued for each row fetched. The PRINT_COLUMNS request is issued at whatever row interval you feel is most visually pleasing to see the column headings for the report.

What the SET_TABS_WIDTH Action Does

For each field in the SELECT statement (as stored in the sqlda), do the following:

1. Record the length of the column's name and the length of the data field from the **sqlda**, and assign them to the variables **col_name_width** and **col_fld_width**.
2. If the field is a non-string SQL type, then over-write the **col_fld_width** variable with the string-representation width of that type. This is what the switch is all about.
3. Store the larger of **col_name_width** or **col_fld_width** in the width field of the array **FLD_TYPE**.
4. Calculate the tab position by adding the field width just calculated to the tab displacement of the previous field and the length of the column separator. Store the calculated tab value in tab position field of the array of **FLD_TYPE**.

What the PRINT COLUMNS Action Does

This is a simple function to perform:

1. The column names are concatenated in a buffer using the information in the array of **FLD_TYPE**.
2. The buffer is then written to the *response* file.
3. The buffer is then cleared.
4. A row of underscores for the column names is assembled in the buffer also using the information in the array of **FLD_TYPE**.
5. The buffer is then written to the *response* file.

What the PRINT_SELECTED_ROW Action Does

For each field in the SELECT statement (i.e., sqlda), do the following:

1. Test if the field is null; if so, write the string "NULL" in the **temp** character string variable.
2. If the field is not NULL, format the string-representation of the output value of the field and write it to the **temp** variable. As you can see, there are three types of formatting conversions:

    *   The SQL character types do not require any formatting and are simply copied "as is" using the strncpy() call.

    *   The SQL data types that have C-language equivalents are formatted using sprintf().

    *   The SQL data types for which there are no C-language equivalents are formatted through "brute force" code. We do whatever it takes to convert the data into a string-format representation, and it may not be pretty.

3. The contents of **temp** are copied into the output buffer using the positional information in the array of **FLD_TYPE**.

When all the fields have been processed, the buffer is then written to the *response* file.

```
/*------------------------------------------------------------------*/
/*  This procedure performs requested format actions:               */
/*                                                                  */
/*  SET_TABS_WIDTH calculates the tab position for each field in a Query */
/*  PRINT_COLUMNS  formats one row of columns using the tabs and sqlda  */
/*  PRINT_SELECTED_ROW                                              */
/*                 formats one SELECT row using the tabs and sqlda   */
/*------------------------------------------------------------------*/
SHORT print_format_row(USHORT action)
{
    #define     MAX_FLDS      50           /* for this exercise          */
    SHORT       index, i, y;               /* for counting               */
    CHAR        row[MAX_LINE_SIZE+1];      /* row to be printed          */
    CHAR        temp[MAX_LINE_SIZE+10];    /* temp buffer                */
    CHAR        temp1[100];                /* second temp buffer         */
    typedef struct
    {
      SHORT       tab_pos;                 /* column position            */
      SHORT     max_width;                 /* max_width str width of type */
    } FLD_TYPE;
    static FLD_TYPE    field[MAX_FLDS];    /* contains the field descriptors*/

    SHORT       col_name_width;            /* width of col name          */
    SHORT       col_fld_width;             /* width of col fld           */
```

Figure 29-10 (Part 1 of 6). RSQL.SQC Listing of the Dynamic SQL Helper Functions.

```
static SHORT   max_num_flds;              /* number of printable columns */
SHORT          null_not_found;            /* a flag                      */
USHORT         top, precision, scale ;    /* for decimal flds            */
SHORT          bottom, point;             /* for decimal flds            */
SHORT          len;                       /* for decimal flds            */
UCHAR          *ptr ;                      /* for decimal flds            */
BOOL           output_blank;              /* for decimal flds            */

/*_____*/
/* Initialize                     */
/*_____*/
memset(row,' ',sizeof(row));
row[sizeof(row) - 1] = '\0';
i = 0 ;
rcd = GOOD;

/*_____*/
/* Do action                      */
/*_____*/
switch (action)
{ case SET_TABS_WIDTH :
        field[0].tab_pos = 1;             /* Start    with column 1      */
        for (index=0; index< sqlda->sqld; index++)
          {
            col_name_width = sqlda->sqlvar[index].sqlname.length;
            col_fld_width  = sqlda->sqlvar[index].sqllen;

            switch (sqlda->sqlvar[index].sqltype)
            {
              case SQL_TYP_INTEGER:
              case SQL_TYP_NINTEGER:
              case SQL_TYP_FLOAT:
              case SQL_TYP_NFLOAT:
                            col_fld_width = 11;
                            break ;
              case SQL_TYP_SMALL:
              case SQL_TYP_NSMALL:
                            col_fld_width = 6;
                            break ;
              case SQL_TYP_DECIMAL:
              case SQL_TYP_NDECIMAL:
                            col_fld_width =
                              LOBYTE(sqlda->sqlvar[index].sqllen) + 1;
                                       /* precision + decimal point */
                            break ;
              case SQL_TYP_DATE:
              case SQL_TYP_NDATE:
                            col_fld_width = 10;
                            break ;
              case SQL_TYP_TIME:
              case SQL_TYP_NTIME:
                            col_fld_width = 8;
                            break ;
              case SQL_TYP_STAMP:
              case SQL_TYP_NSTAMP:
                            col_fld_width = 26;
                            break ;

              default :                       /* string type            */
                            break;
            } /* endswitch */
```

Figure 29-10 (Part 2 of 6).   RSQL.SQC Listing of the Dynamic SQL Helper Functions.

```
                    /*_____*/
                    /* Use the larger of col_name or col_fld   */
                    /*_____*/
                    if (col_name_width > col_fld_width)
                            field[index].max_width =  col_name_width;
                    else
                            field[index].max_width =  col_fld_width;

                    /*_____*/
                    /* Update tab field 1 space between columns*/
                    /*_____*/
                    field[index + 1].tab_pos = field[index].tab_pos +
                                               field[index].max_width +
                                               COL_SEP ;

                    /*_____*/
                    /*Check limits                        */
                    /*_____*/
                    if (field[index + 1].tab_pos >  MAX_LINE_SIZE)
                    { max_num_flds =  index;
                      break;                            /* out of for loop      */
                    }
                    else
                      max_num_flds = index + 1;

                    if ( max_num_flds > MAX_FLDS)
                      break;                            /* out of for loop      */

                } /* end for */


            break; /* end of action SET_TABS_WIDTH */

        case PRINT_COLUMNS :
                    /*_____*/
                    /* Print column names                 */
                    /*_____*/
                    for (index=0; index< max_num_flds; index++ )
                        memcpy(&row[field[index].tab_pos],
                               sqlda->sqlvar[index].sqlname.data,
                               sqlda->sqlvar[index].sqlname.length);
                    fprintf(out_stream,"\n%s",row);

                    /*_____*/
                    /* Clear row buffer                   */
                    /*_____*/
                    memset(row,' ',sizeof(row));
                    row[sizeof(row) + 1] = '\0';

                    /*_____*/
                    /* Underline  names                   */
                    /*_____*/
                    row[sizeof(row) - 1] = '\0';
                    for (index=0; index< max_num_flds; index++)
                    {
                      memset(temp,'-',field[index].max_width);
                      memcpy(&row[field[index].tab_pos],
                             temp,field[index].max_width);
                    } /* end for */
                    fprintf(out_stream,"\n%s",row);
                    break;
```

Figure 29-10 (Part 3 of 6).   RSQL.SQC Listing of the Dynamic SQL Helper Functions.

```
case PRINT_SELECTED_ROW:
    for (index=0; index< max_num_flds ; index++)
      {
        /*_____*/
        /* Initialize                                 */
        /*_____*/
        null_not_found = TRUE;

        /*_____*/
        /* Is it null?                                */
        /*_____*/
        if (sqlda->sqlvar[index].sqltype & 1)
          {
            if (* (sqlda->sqlvar[index].sqlind) ==  -1  )
              {
               sprintf(temp,"NULL");
               null_not_found = FALSE;
              }
            else
              {
                if (* (sqlda->sqlvar[index].sqlind) !=  0   )
                   {
                     sprintf(err_msg,
                     "\n Truncated field  col = %d ",
                     index + 1);
                     rcd = FAILED;
                     break;
                   }
              } /* end if */
          } /* end if */

        /*_____*/
        /* Is not NULL field                          */
        /*_____*/
        if (null_not_found)
          {
            switch (sqlda->sqlvar[index].sqltype)
              {
                case SQL_TYP_INTEGER:
                case SQL_TYP_NINTEGER:
                    sprintf(temp,"%ld", *(PLONG)sqlda->sqlvar[index].sqldata);
                    break ;
                case SQL_TYP_SMALL:
                case SQL_TYP_NSMALL:
                    sprintf(temp,"%d", *(PSHORT)sqlda->sqlvar[index].sqldata);
                    break ;
                case SQL_TYP_DECIMAL:
                case SQL_TYP_NDECIMAL:
                    len = sqlda->sqlvar[index].sqllen ;
                    ptr = sqlda->sqlvar[index].sqldata;
                    sprintf(temp,"");
                    scale    = HIBYTE(len);
                    precision = LOBYTE(len);
                    y    = ( precision + 2 ) / 2 ;    /* total number bytes */
                    point = precision - scale ;
                    bottom = *(ptr + y  -   1) & 0x000F ;           /* sign */
                    if ( (bottom == 0x000D) || (bottom == 0x000B) )
                            strcat(temp,"-") ;
                    output_blank = TRUE;
                    for (i = 0; i < y ; i++  )
                      {
                        top = *(ptr + i ) & 0x00F0 ;
                        top = (top >> 4 ) ;
```

Figure 29-10　(Part 4 of 6).　RSQL.SQC Listing of the Dynamic SQL Helper Functions.

```
                        bottom = *(ptr + i) & 0x000F ;
                        if ( point-- == 0 )
                           strcat(temp,".") ;

                        if ( ((output_blank) && (top != 0)) || (point <= 1) )
                           output_blank = FALSE;
                        if (output_blank)
                           strcat(temp," ") ;
                        else
                           {
                            sprintf(temp1,"%d", top ) ;
                            strcat(temp,temp1) ;
                           }
                     /*_____*/
                     /* Ignore bottom of last         */
                     /* half byte because its the sign */
                     /*_____*/
                     if ( i < (y - 1) )
                     { /* sign half byte ? */
                           if ( point-- == 0 )
                              strcat(temp,".") ;

                           if ( ((output_blank) && (bottom != 0))
                              || (point <= 1) )
                              output_blank = FALSE;
                           if (output_blank)
                              strcat(temp," ") ;
                           else
                              {
                               sprintf(temp1,"%d", bottom ) ;
                               strcat(temp,temp1) ;
                              }
                     }/* end if */

                  } /* end for */
                if ( scale == 0 )
                    strcat(temp,".") ;
                break ;
         case SQL_TYP_FLOAT:                                /* double */
         case SQL_TYP_NFLOAT:
                sprintf(temp,"%e",*(float *)sqlda->sqlvar[index].sqldata);
                break ;
         case SQL_TYP_CHAR:           /* fixed length character string */
         case SQL_TYP_NCHAR:
                strncpy(temp,
                        sqlda->sqlvar[index].sqldata,
                        sqlda->sqlvar[index].sqllen);
                temp[sqlda->sqlvar[index].sqllen] = '\0';   /*terminate */
                break ;
         case SQL_TYP_VARCHAR:     /* varying length character string */
         case SQL_TYP_NVARCHAR:
         case SQL_TYP_LONG:   /* long varying length character string */
         case SQL_TYP_NLONG:
                strncpy(temp,
                        sqlda->sqlvar[index].sqldata + 2,
                        (SHORT)*sqlda->sqlvar[index].sqldata);
                temp[(SHORT)*sqlda->sqlvar[index].sqldata]
                        = '\0';                             /*terminate */
                break ;
         case SQL_TYP_DATE:                                /* date */
         case SQL_TYP_NDATE:
                strncpy(temp,
                        sqlda->sqlvar[index].sqldata,
```

Figure 29-10 (Part 5 of 6).   RSQL.SQC Listing of the Dynamic SQL Helper Functions.

```
                                    10);
                      temp[10] = '\0';                          /*terminate */
                      break ;
              case SQL_TYP_TIME:                                /* time */
              case SQL_TYP_NTIME:
                      strncpy(temp,
                              sqlda->sqlvar[index].sqldata,
                              8);
                      temp[8] = '\0';                           /*terminate */
                      break ;
              case SQL_TYP_STAMP:                               /* timestamp */
              case SQL_TYP_NSTAMP:
                      strncpy(temp,
                              sqlda->sqlvar[index].sqldata,
                              26);
                      temp[26] = '\0';                          /*terminate */
                      break ;
              case SQL_TYP_LSTR:  /* varying length string, 1-byte length */
              case SQL_TYP_NLSTR:
                      strncpy(temp,
                              sqlda->sqlvar[index].sqldata + 1,
                              sqlda->sqlvar[index].sqllen);
                      temp[sqlda->sqlvar[index].sqllen] = '\0';   /*terminate */
                      break ;
              case SQL_TYP_CSTR: /* null terminated varying length string */
              case SQL_TYP_NCSTR:
                      sprintf(temp,"%s",sqlda->sqlvar[index].sqldata + 2);
                      break ;
              default:
                      sprintf(err_msg,
                      "\n Unknown type col = %d type = %d",
                      index + 1,sqlda->sqlvar[index].sqltype);
                      rcd = FAILED;
                      break;
          }   /* endswitch type*/
      } /* if null_not_found */

      if (rcd == FAILED)
         break;                                      /* break out of for loop */
      if (strlen(temp) <= field[index].max_width)
        memcpy(&row[field[index].tab_pos],
               temp,
               strlen(temp) );
      else
      { sprintf(err_msg,
         "\n Field too long col = %d value  = %s",
         (index + 1) ,temp);
        rcd = FAILED;
        break;                                       /* break out of for loop */
      }
     } /* end for */

     /*————————————————————*/
     /*Print selected row                           */
     /*————————————————————*/
     fputs("\n",out_stream);
     fputs(row,out_stream);
     break;
  } /* endswitch  action */

  return (rcd);

} /* end print_format_row */
```

Figure 29-10 (Part 6 of 6). RSQL.SQC Listing of the Dynamic SQL Helper Functions.

The dos_exec() Command Handler

The **dos_exec()** command handler (see listing in Figure 29-11) executes an external program from the within an RSQL program. This is a very uncomplicated command handler since all it does is turn around and issue an OS/2 **DosExecPgm** API call (this was previously covered in "DosExecPgm" in Chapter 14).

The parameters required by **DosExecPgm** are passed to **dos_exec()** in the correct format. The input parameter, **cmd_dos,** contains the name of the child program to be executed and its parameters. This is the string **get_command()** prepared in the **parm_str** variable from reading an EXEC DOS command in the *run* file. The string is already in the format required by **DosExecPgm**. It contains the program name, a NULL, the program arguments (separated by spaces), and finally by a double NULL termination. A command line string may look like this:

```
"program.exe\0arg1 arg2 arg3 ...argN\0\0"
```

The child program is run synchronously to the RSQL parent process, which means RSQL waits for the child process to terminate and then obtains the child's result code. Since this is a synchronous call, the **RESULTCODES** structure **codeTerminate** field contains the Terminate code for the child process, and the **codeResult** field contains the Exit code.

```
/*_____*/
/*  This procedure performs invokes an OS/2 Program and passes it         */
/*  parameters.                                                           */
/*_____*/
SHORT dos_exec(PCHAR cmd_dos)
{
        /*_____*/
        /* Execute the program                    */
        /*_____*/
    api_rcd = DosExecPgm(object_name,      /* failing object if progam fails*/
                sizeof(object_name), /* the object size           */
                0,                   /* sync. program execution   */
                cmd_dos,             /* program name and parameters */
                NULL,                /* inherit environment       */
                &ExecResult,         /* termination reason code   */
                cmd_dos);            /* program name              */
    if (api_rcd)
        {sprintf(err_msg,
                 "\n ERROR: DosExecProgram API call failed with a %d return code",
                 api_rcd);
         return(RECORD_DOS_EXEC_RESULTS);
        }
        /*_____*/
        /* Format the return codes                */
        /*_____*/

    switch (ExecResult.codeTerminate)
      { case  0 :
```

Figure 29-11 (Part 1 of 2). RSQL.SQC Listing of the dos_exec() Function.

```
                    sprintf(err_msg,"\n Program completed with a return code of %d.",
                            ExecResult.codeResult);
                    api_rcd = ExecResult.codeResult;
                    break;

        case  1 :
                    sprintf(err_msg,"\n Program terminated by hard error.");
                    api_rcd = ExecResult.codeTerminate;
                    break;

        case  2 :
                    sprintf(err_msg,"\n Program terminated by a TRAP.");
                    api_rcd = ExecResult.codeTerminate;
                    break;

        case  3 :
                    sprintf(err_msg,"\n Program terminated by a DosKill Process.");
                    api_rcd = ExecResult.codeTerminate;
                    break;

        default :
                    sprintf(err_msg,"\n Unknown Program termination code.");
                    api_rcd = ExecResult.codeTerminate;
      } /* end switch */
      return(RECORD_DOS_EXEC_RESULTS);

} /* end exec_dos */
```

Figure 29-11 (Part 2 of 2).   RSQL.SQC Listing of the dos_exec() Function.

The Results Processor: record_command_results()

RSQL introduces an all-purpose return-code processor to handle the diversity and variety in Database Manager API styles. The **record_command_results()** procedure (see listing in Figure 29-13) records the command return codes in the *response* file along with the elapsed time for the execution of a command. Commands can fail because of a syntax error, a bad error code from an api call, or a non-zero return code in the **SQLCA**. Depending on the action required, an error message, API return code, or all of the SQLCA information is respectively written to the *response* file along with a "user-friendly" error message that describes what happened. The following is the list of actions and their effects:

- **RECORD_NOTHING** causes two blank lines to be entered in the *response* file.

- **RECORD_DOS_EXEC_RESULTS** causes return codes of an OS/2 program that executed under RSQL, to be recorded. The execution time of the program is also recorded.

- **RECORD_SQLCA** causes the results of the execution of a SQL command to be recorded. The return codes and the execution time are written to the *response* file. If a failure is detected in the **sqlcode**, the error or warning message is recorded along with the contents of the **sqlca** (more on that below).

- **RECORD_API_RCD** causes the results of the execution of a Database Administration API call to be recorded. The return codes and the execution time are written to the *response* file.

- **RECORD_ERR_MSG** causes a general error message to be recorded in the *response* file.

In addition, the error handlers also decide, based on the return codes and the state of the **continue_on_error** directive, whether to CONTINUE or TERMINATE the program.

SQL Error Handling: The SQLCA and the sqlaintp()

This is what the **SQLCA** structure looks like:

```
/* SQL Communication Area - SQLCA */
struct sqlca
{
    unsigned char   sqlcaid[8];      /* Eyecatcher = 'SQLCA     '        */
    long            sqlcabc;         /* SQLCA size in bytes = 136        */
    long            sqlcode;         /* SQL return code                  */
    short           sqlerrml;        /* Length for SQLERRMC              */
    unsigned char   sqlerrmc[70];    /* Error message tokens             */
    unsigned char   sqlerrp[8];      /* Diagnostic information           */
    long            sqlerrd[6];      /* Diagnostic information           */
    unsigned char   sqlwarn[11];     /* Warning flags                    */
    unsigned char   sqlstate[5];     /* State corresponding to SQLCODE   */
};
```

Figure 29-12. SQLCA Structure.

You will notice in the listing (on Figure 29-13) that the **RECORD_SQLCA** action results in a flurry of code. What we're trying to do is provide you with a dump of the **sqlca** contents when an error occurs. Perhaps this information may mean something to you, so we've included it in the *response* file output. There are three gems in that piece of code that deserve your attention:

- The **sqlcode** field, which contains the command return code. A zero return code is OK. A positive return code indicates a warning. A negative return code indicates a serious error. To make your code easier to read, use the Database Manager's SQLCODE (#define SQLCODE sqlca.sclcode).
- The **sqlstate** field, which contains the "official" DRDA return codes (also the ISO/ANSI SQL standard). Zero indicates no error.
- The **sqlaintp()** call. This is the famous **GET ERROR MESSAGE** API provided by the Database Manager. This command returns the error message text that corresponds to the error code in the **sqlcode** field of the SQLCA. You must provide a message buffer and specify the maximum line width of the message. The returned message will be broken down into a series of lines separated by CR/LF, with a null indicating the end of message.

```
/*————————————————————————————————————————————————*/
/*  This procedure records the command results along with the elapsed time  */
/*  of execution of a command.                                              */
/*————————————————————————————————————————————————*/
SHORT record_command_results(SHORT rcd)
{
  CHAR              display_msg[1000];       /* temporary buffer      */
  CHAR              msgbuf[512];             /* rcd explanation       */
  SHORT             index;                   /* for counting          */
  CHAR              temp[20];                /* char buffer           */
  CHAR              *err_line;               /* a line of error info. */

  switch (rcd)
     {
       case RECORD_NOTHING :
            fprintf(out_stream, "\n\n");
            return(CONTINUE); break;

       case RECORD_DOS_EXEC_RESULTS :
            if (api_rcd == 0)
              /*————————————————————————————————*/
              /* If success...                           */
              /*————————————————————————————————*/
              {
               fprintf(out_stream, " %s", err_msg);
               fprintf(out_stream,
               "\n OK,                         "
               "Execution time = %10.4lf secs\n\n\n",
               (double)event_time) ;
               return(CONTINUE);
              }
            else
              {
               /*————————————————————————————————*/
               /* Otherwise ...                          */
               /*————————————————————————————————*/
               fprintf(out_stream, " %s", err_msg);
               fprintf(out_stream,
               "\n ERROR,                      "
               "Execution time = %10.4lf secs\n\n\n",
               (double)event_time) ;
               if (continue_on_error)
                  return(CONTINUE);
               else
                  return(TERMINATE);
              }
            break;
       case RECORD_SQLCA    :
            if (SQLCODE == 0)
              /*————————————————————————————————*/
              /* If success...                           */
              /*————————————————————————————————*/
              {
               fprintf(out_stream,
               "\n OK, sql_rcd = %ld,          "
               "Execution time = %10.4lf secs\n\n\n",
               SQLCODE,(double)event_time) ;
               return(CONTINUE);
              }
            else
              {
```

Figure 29-13 (Part 1 of 3).   RSQL.SQC Listing of record_command_results()

```
/*_____*/
/* Otherwise ...                                   */
/*_____*/
if (SQLCODE >  0)
    sprintf(display_msg,
    "\n WARNING, sql_code = %ld,      Execution time = %10.4lf secs",
    SQLCODE,(double)event_time) ;
else
    sprintf(display_msg,
    "\n ERROR, sql_code = %ld\n",
    SQLCODE) ;
/*_____*/
/* RETRIEVE ERROR MESSAGE                          */
/*_____*/
rcd = sqlaintp(msgbuf,                    /* buffer for msg text */
               512,                       /* buffer size         */
               79,                        /* line width          */
               &sqlca);                   /* SQLCA               */

if (rcd < 0)                              /* message retrieve err*/
  sprintf(msgbuf,"\n SQLAINTP ERROR. Return code = %d \n",rcd);

err_line = strtok(msgbuf,"\n");
while (err_line != NULL)
    {
    sprintf(display_msg,"%s\n %s", display_msg, err_line);
    err_line = strtok(NULL,"\n");
    }
strcat(display_msg,"\n\n ------ ADDITIONAL SQLCA info --------");
fputs(display_msg,out_stream);

/*_____*/
/* Display SQLCA  sqlerrmc                         */
/*_____*/
if(sqlca.sqlerrml)
{
 sqlca.sqlerrmc[sqlca.sqlerrml] = '\0';          /* NULL terminate */
 while ( sqlca.sqlerrml-- )
 {
    if (sqlca.sqlerrmc[sqlca.sqlerrml] == 0xFF)     /* remove FFs */
      sqlca.sqlerrmc[sqlca.sqlerrml] = ' ';
 }
 fprintf(out_stream,"\n SQLERRMC's:  %s",sqlca.sqlerrmc);
}

/*_____*/
/* Display SQLCA sqlerrp                           */
/*_____*/
sprintf(display_msg,"\n SQLERRP: ") ;
for(index=0;index<8;index++)
{
 sprintf(temp,"%c", sqlca.sqlerrp[index]) ;
 strcat(display_msg,temp);
}
fputs(display_msg,out_stream);

/*_____*/
/* Display SQLCA sqlerrd                           */
/*_____*/
sprintf(display_msg,"\n SQLERRD: ") ;
for(index=0;index<6;index++)
{
 sprintf(temp,"%10ld",sqlca.sqlerrd[index]) ;
```

Figure 29-13 (Part 2 of 3). RSQL.SQC Listing of record_command_results()

```
            strcat(display_msg,temp);
         }
         fputs(display_msg,out_stream);

         /*———————————————————*/
         /* Display SQLCA Warnings                 */

         /*———————————————————*/
         sprintf(display_msg,"\n Warning Indicators: ") ;
         for(index=0;index<5;index++)
         {
          sprintf(temp,"%c",sqlca.sqlwarn[index]) ;
          strcat(display_msg,temp);
         }
         fprintf(out_stream,"%s\n\n\n",temp);

         if (continue_on_error)
             return(CONTINUE);
         else
             return(TERMINATE);

      } /*else otherwise*/

   case RECORD_API_RCD :
      if (api_rcd == 0)
         /*———————————————————*/
         /* If success...                          */
         /*———————————————————*/
         {
          fprintf(out_stream,
          "\n OK, api_rcd = %ld,          "
          " Execution time = %10.4lf secs\n\n\n",
          api_rcd,(double)event_time) ;
          return(CONTINUE);
         }
      else
         {
          /*———————————————————*/
          /* Otherwise ...                         */
          /*———————————————————*/
          fprintf(out_stream,
                  "\n API for command %s failed with "
                  "a return code of %d.\n\n\n",
                  parms.cmd_name, api_rcd);
          if (continue_on_error)
             return(CONTINUE);
          else
             return(TERMINATE);

         }
         break;

   case RECORD_ERR_MSG  :
         fprintf(out_stream, " %s\n\n\n", err_msg);
         return(TERMINATE);
   }
} /* end record_command_results */
```

Figure 29-13 (Part 3 of 3).   RSQL.SQC Listing of record_command_results()

RSQL.H Include File

```
/*-------------------------------------------------------------------------*/
/*  INCLUDE FILE NAME: RSQL.H - declarations for RSQL program              */
/*-------------------------------------------------------------------------*/

/*-------------------------------------------------------------------------*/
/* defines                                                                 */
/*-------------------------------------------------------------------------*/

                        /*-------------------------------------------------*/
                        /* Constants used as command values    */
                        /*-------------------------------------------------*/
#define CMD_SYNTAX_ERROR          (-1)
#define CMD_NO_CMD                  0
#define CMD_SQL_IMMEDIATE           1
#define CMD_SQL_SELECT              2
#define CMD_DOS                     3
#define CMD_DBA                     4
#define CMD_DBA_BACKUP              5
#define CMD_DBA_BIND                6
#define CMD_DBA_CATALOG_DB          7
#define CMD_DBA_CATALOG_NODE        8
#define CMD_DBA_COLLECT_STATUS      9
#define CMD_DBA_CONTINUE_ON_ERROR  10
#define CMD_DBA_CREATE_DB          11
#define CMD_DBA_DROP_DB            12
#define CMD_DBA_EXPORT             13
#define CMD_DBA_GET_ADMIN          14
#define CMD_DBA_IMPORT             15
#define CMD_DBA_LOGOFF             16
#define CMD_DBA_LOGON              17
#define CMD_DBA_PAUSE              18
#define CMD_DBA_REORG              19
#define CMD_DBA_RESET_DM_CFG       20
#define CMD_DBA_RESET_DB_CFG       21
#define CMD_DBA_RESTORE            22
#define CMD_DBA_ROLL_FORWARD       23
#define CMD_DBA_RUNSTATS           24
#define CMD_DBA_SHOW_DB_CFG        25
#define CMD_DBA_SHOW_DB_DIR        26
#define CMD_DBA_SHOW_DM_CFG        27
#define CMD_DBA_SHOW_NODE_DIR      28
#define CMD_DBA_STARTDM            29
#define CMD_DBA_STARTUSE           30
#define CMD_DBA_STOPDM             31
#define CMD_DBA_STOP_ON_ERROR      32
#define CMD_DBA_STOPUSE            33
#define CMD_DBA_UNCATALOG_DB       34
#define CMD_DBA_UNCATALOG_NODE     35
#define CMD_DBA_UPDATE_DB_CFG      36
#define CMD_DBA_UPDATE_DM_CFG      37
#define CMD_LAST_CMD               38

                        /*-------------------------------------------------*/
                        /* Constants used as return codes      */
                        /*-------------------------------------------------*/
#define TRUE                        1
#define FALSE                       0
#define YES                         1
```

Figure 29-14 (Part 1 of 5).   RSQL.H Include File.

```
#define NO                       0
#define GOOD                     0
#define FAILED                   (-1)
#define CONTINUE                 0
#define TERMINATE                (-1)
#define RECORD_NOTHING           0
#define RECORD_SQLCA             1
#define RECORD_API_RCD           2
#define RECORD_ERR_MSG           3
#define RECORD_DOS_EXEC_RESULTS  4

#define          RESTART    -1015          /* database needs restart      */
                 /*─────────────────────────────*/
                 /* Parsing delimiter            */
                 /*─────────────────────────────*/
#define DLM                 " \n"

                 /*─────────────────────────────*/
                 /* Row Formatting Parameters    */
                 /*─────────────────────────────*/
#define       SET_TABS_WIDTH       1
#define       PRINT_COLUMNS        2
#define       PRINT_SELECTED_ROW   3

                 /*─────────────────────────────*/
                 /* Other Constants              */
                 /*─────────────────────────────*/
#define MAX_CMD_SIZE             1500
#define MAX_LINE_SIZE            220
#define COL_SEP                  2
#define BREAK_SEP                40
#define BREAK_ROWS               1

                 /*─────────────────────────────*/
                 /* SQLDA/SQLCA                  */
                 /*─────────────────────────────*/
#define SQLVAR_NUM              255          /* max number of columns in SELECT */
struct sqlda      *sqlda;                    /* declare a pointer to a sqlda    */
struct sqlca      sqlca;                     /* declare a static sqlca variable */

                 /*─────────────────────────────*/
                 /* DBM/Database configuration   */
                 /*─────────────────────────────*/
typedef struct
   {
   SHORT       locklist;                     /* Max. Storage for Locklists  */
   SHORT       buffpage;                     /* Buffer Pool Size            */
   SHORT       maxfilop;                     /* Max. DB Files Open/Appl,    */
   SHORT       softmax;                      /* Log Records/soft checkpoint */
   SHORT       maxappls;                     /* Max. Active Applications    */
   SHORT       applheapsz;                   /* Default Application Heap    */
   SHORT       dbheap;                       /* Database Heap               */
   LONG        dlchktime;                    /* Time Interval for Deadlocks */
   SHORT       maxtotfilop;                  /* Max. Files Open/Application  */
   SHORT       sortheap;                     /* Sort List Heap              */
   SHORT       agentheap;                    /* Application Agent Heap      */
   SHORT       maxlocks;                     /* Max. percent locklist/appl. */
   SHORT       logprimary;                   /* Primary Log Files           */
   SHORT       logsecond;                    /* Secondary Log Files         */
   SHORT       logfilsiz;                    /* Log File Size               */
   SHORT       stmtheap;                     /* SQL Statement Heap          */
```

Figure 29-14 (Part 2 of 5). RSQL.H Include File.

```
        CHAR        newlogpath[248];        /* New Log Location          */
        SHORT       copy_prot;              /* Copy Protection flag       */
        SHORT       log_retain;             /* Log Retain flag            */
        SHORT       user_exit;              /* User Exit flag             */
        SHORT       auto_rest;              /* Auto Restart flag          */
        SHORT       country;                /* Country                    */
        SHORT       codepage;               /* Code Page                  */
        SHORT       release;                /* Release                    */
        CHAR        logpath[248];           /* Current Log Location       */
        SHORT       consistent;             /* Consistency Flag           */
        SHORT       backup_pending;         /* Backup Pending Flag        */
        SHORT       rollfwd_pending;        /* Roll Forward Pending Flag  */
        SHORT       log_retain_status;      /* Log Retain Flag            */
        SHORT       user_exit_status;       /* User Exit Status Flag      */
        CHAR        loghead[14];            /* Log File with Log Head     */
        CHAR        nextactive[14];         /* Current Log File           */
   } DBCFG;
DBCFG dbcfg;                        /* variable for database configuration   */

   typedef struct
        {
        SHORT       nodetype;               /* node type (remote/indirect) */
        SHORT       rqrioblk;               /* requester I/O block size     */
        SHORT       svrioblk;               /* Server I/O block size        */
        SHORT       sqlenseg;               /* Database segments            */
        SHORT       numdb;                  /* number of active databases   */
        CHAR        nname[9];               /* node name                    */
        SHORT       comheapsz;              /* communication heap size      */
        SHORT       rsheapsz;               /* Remote Data Services heap    */
        SHORT       numrc;                  /* number of remote connections */
        SHORT       release;                /* release number               */
   } DMCFG;
DMCFG dmcfg;                        /* variable for database manager config. */

                      /*——————————————————*/
                      /* command parameters structure      */
                      /*——————————————————*/
   typedef struct
        {
        CHAR        cmd_name[40];       /* Cmd name                         */
        CHAR        cmd_num;            /* Numerical representation of cmd  */
        USHORT      num_parms;          /* Number of parms for this command */
        } parms_type;
parms_type          parms;          /* Variable that contains parameters*/

   typedef struct
   {
    USHORT          token;              /* which field to return       */
    CHAR  * _Seg16 ptrvalue;           /* where to put field info      */
   } CONFG_ENTRY_TYPE;

/*——————————————————————————————————————*/
/* Global variables                                                  */
/*——————————————————————————————————————*/
                      /*——————————————————*/
                      /* timing                            */
                      /*——————————————————*/
struct   timeb  timebuff;            /* Timer buffer              */
double          start_time = 0.0;    /* Start of command time     */
double          end_time   = 0.0;    /* End of command time       */
double          event_time = 0.0;    /* Elapsed time              */
```

Figure 29-14 (Part 3 of 5).   RSQL.H Include File.

```
                        /*———————————————————*/
                        /* buffers and misc. variables      */
                        /*———————————————————*/
CHAR          err_msg[512];                 /* for errors                       */
CHAR          parm_buf[MAX_CMD_SIZE];       /* buffer for processing cmds       */
SHORT         rcd;                          /* general return code variable     */
SHORT         api_rcd;                      /* api return code variable         */
BOOL          continue_on_error;            /* error stop/continue indicator    */
                                            /*   FALSE = stop on error,         */
                                            /*   TRUE  = continue on error      */

                        /*———————————————————*/
                        /* file variables                   */
                        /*———————————————————*/
USHORT        num_parms;                    /* # parms returned from fscanf     */
FILE          *cmd_stream;                  /* CMD file handle                  */
FILE          *out_stream;                  /* RESPONSE  file handle            */
static CHAR   msgfile[]="msgfile.msg";      /* msgfile name                     */

                        /*———————————————————*/
                        /* variables for DosExecPgm         */
                        /*———————————————————*/
CHAR object_name[13];                 /* buffer for failure name          */
RESULTCODES ExecResult;               /* structure for child proc. results */

/*———————————————————————————————————————*/
/* Forward declarations of procedures                                            */

/*———————————————————————————————————————*/

                        /*———————————————————*/
                        /* file variables                   */
                        /*———————————————————*/
VOID initialize_rsql(VOID);
VOID check_args_and_prepare_files(USHORT argc, PCHAR argv[]);
VOID terminate_program(VOID);

                        /*———————————————————*/
                        /* command/parm parsing functions   */
                        /*———————————————————*/
SHORT get_command(PCHAR cmd);
SHORT decode_parm_string(PCHAR parm, PUSHORT parm_num);
SHORT decode_dmcfg_string(PCHAR parm, PUSHORT parm_num,
                      PCHAR *parm_val_ptr, PUSHORT parm_val_type);
SHORT decode_dbcfg_string(PCHAR parm, PUSHORT parm_num,
                      PCHAR *parm_val_ptr, PUSHORT parm_val_type);

                        /*———————————————————*/
                        /* EXEC SQL functions               */
                        /*———————————————————*/
SHORT sql_immediate(PCHAR cmd_sql);
SHORT sql_select(PCHAR cmd);

                        /*———————————————————*/
                        /* EXEC DBA functions               */
                        /*———————————————————*/

SHORT dba_exec(PCHAR parms);
SHORT dba_backup(PCHAR parms);
SHORT dba_bind(PCHAR parms);
```

Figure 29-14 (Part 4 of 5).   RSQL.H Include File.

```
SHORT  dba_catalog_db(PCHAR parms);
SHORT  dba_catalog_node(PCHAR parms);
SHORT  dba_collect_status(PCHAR parms);
SHORT  dba_create_db(PCHAR parms);
SHORT  dba_drop_db(PCHAR parms);
SHORT  dba_export(PCHAR parms);
SHORT  dba_get_admin(VOID);
SHORT  dba_import(PCHAR parms);
SHORT  dba_logoff(PCHAR parms);
SHORT  dba_logon(PCHAR parms);
SHORT  dba_reorg(PCHAR parms);
SHORT  dba_reset_dm_cfg(VOID);
SHORT  dba_reset_db_cfg(PCHAR parms);
SHORT  dba_restore(PCHAR parms);
SHORT  dba_roll_forward(PCHAR parms);
SHORT  dba_runstats(PCHAR parms);
SHORT  dba_show_db_cfg(PCHAR parms);
SHORT  dba_show_db_dir(PCHAR parms);
SHORT  dba_show_dm_cfg(VOID);
SHORT  dba_show_node_dir(VOID);
SHORT  dba_startdm(VOID);
SHORT  dba_startuse(PCHAR parms);
SHORT  dba_stopdm(VOID);
SHORT  dba_stopuse(VOID);
SHORT  dba_uncatalog_db(PCHAR parms);
SHORT  dba_uncatalog_node(PCHAR parms);
SHORT  dba_update_db_cfg(PCHAR parms);
SHORT  dba_update_dm_cfg(PCHAR parms);

                      /*————————————————————————————*/
                      /* EXEC DOS function          */
                      /*————————————————————————————*/

SHORT  dos_exec(PCHAR cmd_dos);

                      /*————————————————————————————*/
                      /* helper functions           */
                      /*————————————————————————————*/

SHORT  merge_file(FILE *dest_stream, char  * merge_file_name);
SHORT  record_command_results(SHORT rcd);
VOID   reset_timer(VOID);
VOID   start_timer(VOID);
VOID   stop_timer(VOID);
SHORT  print_format_row(USHORT action);
VOID   APIENTRY exit_proc(ULONG term_code);
```

Figure 29-14 (Part 5 of 5).   RSQL.H Include File.

Chapter 30

RSQL: Programming the Database Administration API

This is the second part of a two-chapter series that examines the inner workings of the **RSQL.SQC** program. In this chapter, we walk through the command handlers that execute the Database Administration services. This chapter has two hard-prerequisites:

- Chapter 27, "Tutorial on the Database Administration Services"
- Chapter 29, "RSQL: Programming Dynamic SQL"

The presentation of the Database Administration services closely mirrors the exposition in the tutorial chapter. The command handlers follow to the letter the taxonomy scheme that was presented in the tutorial. This means that for almost every command described in the tutorial, there is a command handler in this chapter that serves as its coding template. Of course, the command handlers are not isolated programming examples. They provide powerful database administration tools that are a core component of RSQL's "all-in-one" database services.

HOW TO READ THE CODE IN THIS CHAPTER

This chapter looks at what happens after the **RSQL.SQC**'s **main**() procedure invokes **dba_exec**(), the dispatcher for Database Administration command handlers. The **dba_exec**() function will serve as the "jumping off" point for the code in this chapter. But before jumping off into new code, let's quickly review what **main**()'s already done for us in terms of command parsing. You may recall from Chapter 29 that **main**() invokes the **get_command**() function when it needs to fetch and decode a command from the *run* file. Here's what **get_command**() does when it finds a Database Administration command:

1. Looks up a command number which corresponds to the command name, and inserts the value in the **parms**'s structure **num** field.
2. Obtains the minimum number of parameters from the look-up table that the command expects, and then inserts that number in the **parms**'s structure **num_parms** field.

3. Strips off the command string, the **"EXEC DBA:"** header, and the command name that follows it.
4. Returns control to **main()**.

The **main()** procedure then turns around and invokes the Database Administration's command router, **dba_exec()**, and passes it the command string. Now the ball is in the court of the Database Administration command handlers that make up the bulk of this chapter. Here is how these handlers go about conducting their business:

- The **dba_exec()** function's sole purpose in life is to route the commands it receives from **main()** to the appropriate command handler and pass it a command parameter string where necessary (see listing in Figure 30-1).
- The command handlers are the real workers. They sometimes have helpers, which are mainly used for decoding parameters.
- The command handlers will do their own parameter parsing using the C function, **sscanf()**.
- The command handlers are functionally organized along the same categories that were introduced in the Database Administration Tutorial chapter. However, a command handler may, in some cases, perform more than one related Database Administration API call.
- The code for the command handlers was designed to be intuitive and self-contained. Each parameter used by an API call is defined inside the command handler code or in the text that surrounds it. This includes the type definitions of the relevant structures. The benefit of this approach is that we do not have to provide API prototype descriptions in an already very long chapter. You should also consult the command descriptions in the Database Administration Tutorial chapter whenever something is not "perfectly clear."
- When the command handler is done "doing its thing", it returns control to **dba_exec()** and passes it a return code that is either RECORD_SQLCA, RE-CORD_API_RCD, CMD_SYNTAX_ERROR, or RECORD_ERR_MSG. This return code is in turn passed to **main()**, which in turn passes it to the common return code handler, (previously described on page 731), which analyzes the **sqlca** and writes the results to *response* file.
- There are many command handlers and this accounts for the bulk of the material in this chapter. However, if you do not feel like doing a lot of reading you can always selectively go to the command handler you're interested in without having to read the rest of the code in the chapter.

THE DATABASE ADMINISTRATION COMMAND ROUTER: DBA_EXEC()

The **dba_exec()** (see listing in Figure 30-1) acts as the central dispatcher for calls to the Database Administration command handlers. The function knows which handler to call by switching on the **cmd_num** field of the **parms** variable. This is the field in which **get_command()** places the command number to be executed. The parameter in

parm_buf is passed as required. When the command handler has completed its job, it passes back a return code which in turn gets passed back to **main()**.

```
/*''''''''''''''''''''''''''''''''''''''''''''''''''''''''''''''''''''''*/
/*  Dispatch Database Administration Command Handler                    */
/*''''''''''''''''''''''''''''''''''''''''''''''''''''''''''''''''''''''*/
SHORT dba_exec(PCHAR parm_buf)
{
    /*'''''''''''''''''''''''''''''''''''''''''*/
    /*  Execute the command.                   */
    /*'''''''''''''''''''''''''''''''''''''''''*/
    switch (parms.cmd_num)
    {       /*'''''''''''''''''''''''''''''''*/
            /* Environment Services        */
            /*'''''''''''''''''''''''''''''''*/
        case CMD_DBA_STARTDM         : rcd = dba_startdm();               break;
        case CMD_DBA_STOPDM          : rcd = dba_stopdm();                break;
        case CMD_DBA_CREATE_DB       : rcd = dba_create_db(parm_buf);     break;
        case CMD_DBA_STARTUSE        : rcd = dba_startuse(parm_buf);      break;
        case CMD_DBA_STOPUSE         : rcd = dba_stopuse();               break;
        case CMD_DBA_DROP_DB         : rcd = dba_drop_db(parm_buf);       break;
        case CMD_DBA_CATALOG_DB      : rcd = dba_catalog_db(parm_buf);    break;
        case CMD_DBA_UNCATALOG_DB    : rcd = dba_uncatalog_db(parm_buf);  break;
        case CMD_DBA_CATALOG_NODE    : rcd = dba_catalog_node(parm_buf);  break;
        case CMD_DBA_UNCATALOG_NODE  : rcd = dba_uncatalog_node(parm_buf);break;
        case CMD_DBA_SHOW_DB_DIR     : rcd = dba_show_db_dir(parm_buf);   break;
        case CMD_DBA_SHOW_NODE_DIR   : rcd = dba_show_node_dir();         break;
        case CMD_DBA_COLLECT_STATUS  : rcd = dba_collect_status(parm_buf);break;

            /*'''''''''''''''''''''''''''''''*/
            /* General Utilities           */
            /*'''''''''''''''''''''''''''''''*/

        case CMD_DBA_BACKUP          : rcd = dba_backup(parm_buf);        break;
        case CMD_DBA_RESTORE         : rcd = dba_restore(parm_buf);       break;
        case CMD_DBA_ROLL_FORWARD    : rcd = dba_roll_forward(parm_buf);  break;
        case CMD_DBA_EXPORT          : rcd = dba_export(parm_buf);        break;
        case CMD_DBA_IMPORT          : rcd = dba_import(parm_buf);        break;
        case CMD_DBA_RUNSTATS        : rcd = dba_runstats(parm_buf);      break;
        case CMD_DBA_REORG           : rcd = dba_reorg(parm_buf);         break;
        case CMD_DBA_GET_ADMIN       : rcd = dba_get_admin();             break;

            /*'''''''''''''''''''''''''''''''*/
            /* Configuration Services      */
            /*'''''''''''''''''''''''''''''''*/

        case CMD_DBA_RESET_DB_CFG    : rcd = dba_reset_db_cfg(parm_buf);  break;
        case CMD_DBA_UPDATE_DB_CFG   : rcd = dba_update_db_cfg(parm_buf); break;
        case CMD_DBA_SHOW_DB_CFG     : rcd = dba_show_db_cfg(parm_buf);   break;
        case CMD_DBA_RESET_DM_CFG    : rcd = dba_reset_dm_cfg();          break;
        case CMD_DBA_UPDATE_DM_CFG   : rcd = dba_update_dm_cfg(parm_buf); break;
        case CMD_DBA_SHOW_DM_CFG     : rcd = dba_show_dm_cfg();           break;

            /*'''''''''''''''''''''''''''''''*/
            /* Application Services        */
            /*'''''''''''''''''''''''''''''''*/

        case CMD_DBA_BIND            : rcd = dba_bind(parm_buf);          break;
```

Figure 30-1 (Part 1 of 2). RSQL.SQC's DB Administration Command Router: dba_exec().

```
          /*'''''''''''''''''''''''''''''*/
          /* Generic Services             */
          /*'''''''''''''''''''''''''''''*/

     case CMD_DBA_LOGON            : rcd = dba_logon(parm_buf);        break;
     case CMD_DBA_LOGOFF           : rcd = dba_logoff(parm_buf);       break;

     default: RECORD_NOTHING;              break;

  } /* endswitch */

  return(rcd);
} /* end dba_exec */
```

Figure 30-1 (Part 2 of 2).   RSQL.SQC's DB Administration Command Router: dba_exec().

RSQL.SQC: ENVIRONMENT SERVICES COMMAND HANDLERS

Start Database Manager: dba_startdm()

The **dba_startdm()** command handler, whose code is listed in Figure 30-2, executes the RSQL command:

▶▶— EXEC DBA: STARTDM ——————————————————————————————◀◀

This command handler simply executes a **sqlestar()** API call.

```
/*'''''''''''''''''''''''''''''''''''''''''''''''''''''''''''''''''''''''''''''*/
/*   execute the STARTDM DBA function                                          */
/*'''''''''''''''''''''''''''''''''''''''''''''''''''''''''''''''''''''''''''''*/
SHORT dba_startdm(VOID)
{
  /*'''''''''''''''''''''''''''''''''''''''''''''*/
  /* call the START DBM API                      */
  /*'''''''''''''''''''''''''''''''''''''''''''''*/
  api_rcd = sqlestar();                               /* no SQLCA            */

  return(RECORD_API_RCD);
} /* end dba_start_dm */
```

Figure 30-2.   Start Database Manager Command Handler: dba_startdm()

Stop Database Manager: dba_stopdm()

The **dba_stopdm()** command handler, whose code is listed in Figure 30-3, executes the RSQL command:

```
▶▶─ EXEC DBA: STOPDM ─────────────────────────────────────────────────▶◀
```

This command handler simply executes a **sqlestop()** API call.

```
/*''''''''''''''''''''''''''''''''''''''''''''''''''''''''''''''''''''*/
/*  execute the STOPDM DBA function                                   */
/*''''''''''''''''''''''''''''''''''''''''''''''''''''''''''''''''''''*/
SHORT dba_stopdm(VOID)
{
   /*'''''''''''''''''''''''''''''''''''''''*/
   /* call the STOP DBM API                 */
   /*'''''''''''''''''''''''''''''''''''''''*/
   sqlestop(&sqlca);                                  /* SQLCA          */

   return(RECORD_SQLCA);
} /* end dba_stopdm */
```

Figure 30-3. Stop Database Manager Command Handler: dba_stopdm().

Create Database: dba_create_db()

The **dba_create_db()** command handler, whose code is listed in Figure 30-4, executes the RSQL command:

```
▶▶─ EXEC DBA: CREATE_DB ──── database_name ──── drive ── comment ──────▶◀
```

This command handler decodes its parameters and then executes a **sqlecred()** API call.

```
/*''''''''''''''''''''''''''''''''''''''''''''''''''''''''''''''''''''*/
/*  execute the CREATE_DATABASE DBA function                          */
/*''''''''''''''''''''''''''''''''''''''''''''''''''''''''''''''''''''*/
SHORT dba_create_db(PCHAR parm_str)
{
   BYTE    database_name[9];        /* Database name, null terminated   */
   UCHAR   db_drive;                /* Drive on which DB resides e.g. C */
   CHAR    comment[31];             /* Comment on DB, null terminated   */
   struct
   { CHAR  sqldbid[8];              /* structure descriptor             */
     LONG  sqldbccp;                /* database code page               */
     LONG  sqldbcss;                /* collating sequence type          */
     CHAR  sqldbudc[256];           /* collating sequence weights       */
     CHAR  sqldbcmt[31];            /* database comment                 */
   } dbdesc;


   /*'''''''''''''''''''''''''''''''''''''''''''''*/
   /* get the parm strings                        */
   /*'''''''''''''''''''''''''''''''''''''''''''''*/
   if (sscanf(parm_str, " %8s %c %30s ", database_name, &db_drive,
                                         dbdesc.sqldbcmt)
             != parms.num_parms)
     {
       sprintf(err_msg, "\nSYNTAX ERROR: invalid parameters");
```

Figure 30-4 (Part 1 of 2). Create Database Command Handler: dba_create_db().

```
       return(RECORD_ERR_MSG);
     }

  /*''''''''''''''''''''''''''''''''''''''''''''*/
  /* call the CREATE_DATABASE API              */
  /*''''''''''''''''''''''''''''''''''''''''''''*/
  strncpy(dbdesc.sqldbid,"SQLDBDB0",8);          /* initialize eyecatcher   */
  dbdesc.sqldbccp = 0L;                          /* default code page       */
  dbdesc.sqldbcss = SQL_CS_SYSTEM;               /* system collating sequence*/
  sqlecrdb(database_name,                        /* database                */
           db_drive,                             /* database drive          */
           (struct sqledbdesc *)&dbdesc,         /* database descriptor     */
           &sqlca);                              /* SQLCA                   */
  return(RECORD_SQLCA);
} /* end dba_create_database */
```

Figure 30-4 (Part 2 of 2). Create Database Command Handler: dba_create_db().

Start Use Database: dba_startuse()

The **dba_startuse()** command handler, whose code is listed in Figure 30-5, executes the RSQL command:

where "S" designates the shared use of the database, and "X" designates exclusive use.

The only strange thing in the command handler code is what happens if the **sqlestrd()** call fails and returns a RESTART code in the **sqlca**. As you may remember from the tutorial, this is the Database Manager's way of telling you that the last time the database was used, it was left in an inconsistent state by an abnormal termination or a power outage. When that happens, don't worry. Just issue a **sqlerest()** restart command. This command will rollback any unfinished work and return the database to its last consistent state. Once that's done, reissue the start command, and off you go. This command handler also installs a signal handler for trapping Ctrl+Break. This is done once at start-up time so that you can safely interrupt an RSQL program at any time by hitting Ctrl + Break.

```
/*'''''''''''''''''''''''''''''''''''''''''''''''''''''''''''''''''''''''''''*/
/*   execute the STARTUSE DBA function                                      */
/*'''''''''''''''''''''''''''''''''''''''''''''''''''''''''''''''''''''''''''*/
SHORT dba_startuse(PCHAR parm_str)
{
  BYTE       database_name[9];          /* Database name, null terminated  */
  CHAR       share_mode;                /* Share mode for STARTUSE         */
```

Figure 30-5 (Part 1 of 2). Start Use Database Command Handler: dba_startuse().

```
/*'''''''''''''''''''''''''''''''''''''''''''*/
/* get the parm strings                      */
/*'''''''''''''''''''''''''''''''''''''''''''*/
if (sscanf(parm_str, " %8s %c ", database_name, &share_mode
          ) != parms.num_parms)
   {
    sprintf(err_msg, "\nSYNTAX ERROR: invalid parameters.");
    return(RECORD_ERR_MSG);
   }

/*'''''''''''''''''''''''''''''''''''''''''''*/
/* call the START USING DB API               */
/*'''''''''''''''''''''''''''''''''''''''''''*/
sqlestrd(database_name,                          /* database           */
         share_mode,                             /* share mode         */
         &sqlca);                                /* SQLCA              */

if (SQLCODE == RESTART)                           /* if start db func   */
{                                                /* fails, call restart */
   /*'''''''''''''''''''''''''''''''''''''''''''*/
   /* call the RESTART DB API                   */
   /*'''''''''''''''''''''''''''''''''''''''''''*/
   sqlerest(database_name,                       /* database           */
            &sqlca);                             /* SQLCA              */

   if (SQLCODE != 0)                             /* restart failed, exit*/
       return(RECORD_SQLCA);
   else
   /*'''''''''''''''''''''''''''''''''''''''''''*/
   /* call the START USING DB API (again)       */
   /*'''''''''''''''''''''''''''''''''''''''''''*/
   sqlestrd(database_name,                       /* database           */
            share_mode,                          /* share mode         */
            &sqlca);                             /* SQLCA              */
}

if (SQLCODE != 0)                                /* second start use   */
    return(RECORD_SQLCA);                        /* failed, record SQLCA*/


sqleisig(&sqlca);                                /* handle Ctrl + Break */
                                                 /* signal handler     */

return(RECORD_SQLCA);
} /* end dba_startuse */
```

Figure 30-5 (Part 2 of 2). Start Use Database Command Handler: dba_startuse().

Stop Use Database: dba_stopuse()

The **dba_stopuse()** command handler, whose code is listed in Figure 30-6, executes the RSQL command:

▶▶── EXEC DBA: STOPUSE ──────────────────────────────────────◀◀

This command handler simply executes a **sqlestpd()** API call.

```
/*''''''''''''''''''''''''''''''''''''''''''''''''''''''''''''''''''''''*/
/*   execute the STOPUSE DBA function                                    */
/*''''''''''''''''''''''''''''''''''''''''''''''''''''''''''''''''''''''*/
SHORT dba_stopuse(VOID)
{
   /*''''''''''''''''''''''''''''''''''''''''''''*/
   /* call the STOP USING DB API              */
   /*''''''''''''''''''''''''''''''''''''''''''''*/
   sqlestpd(&sqlca);                                      /* SQLCA            */

   return(RECORD_SQLCA);
} /* end dba_stopuse */
```

Figure 30-6. Stop Use Database Command Handler: dba_stopuse().

Drop Database: dba_drop_db()

The **dba_drop_db**() command handler, whose code is listed in Figure 30-7, executes
the RSQL command:

▶▶─ EXEC DBA: DROP_DB ─────── database_name ──────────────────────────────▶◀

This command handler decodes its parameters and then executes a **sqledrpd**() API call.

```
/*''''''''''''''''''''''''''''''''''''''''''''''''''''''''''''''''''''''*/
/*   execute the DROP_DB  DBA function                                   */
/*''''''''''''''''''''''''''''''''''''''''''''''''''''''''''''''''''''''*/
SHORT dba_drop_db(PCHAR parm_str)
{
  BYTE        database_name[9];              /* Database name, null terminated   */

   /*''''''''''''''''''''''''''''''''''''''''''''*/
   /* get the parm strings                    */
   /*''''''''''''''''''''''''''''''''''''''''''''*/
   if (sscanf(parm_str, " %8s ", database_name) != parms.num_parms)
      {
       sprintf(err_msg, "\nSYNTAX ERROR: invalid parameters");
       return(RECORD_ERR_MSG);
      }

   /*''''''''''''''''''''''''''''''''''''''''''''*/
   /* call the DROP_DATABASE API              */
   /*''''''''''''''''''''''''''''''''''''''''''''*/
   sqledrpd(database_name,                              /* database         */
            &sqlca);                                    /* SQLCA            */
   return(RECORD_SQLCA);
} /* end dba_drop_db */
```

Figure 30-7. Drop Database Command Handler: dba_drop_db().

Catalog Database: dba_catalog_db()

The **dba_catalog_db**() command handler, whose code is listed in Figure 30-8, executes
the RSQL command:

```
▶▶─ EXEC DBA: CATALOG_DB── database_name ── alias ┬ LOCAL ┬──────▶
                                                  └ REMOTE ┘

▶──── node_name ──────────── drive ──── comment ──────────────▶◀
```

This is the first time we use the helper function, **decode_parm_str**(), whose code is listed in Figure 30-9. We pass a string to the helper and it returns the database number representation of that string. For example, "LOCAL" translates to 0, and "REMOTE" translates to 1. The handler then uses the decoded parameters to issue a **sqlecatd**() API call.

```
/*'''''''''''''''''''''''''''''''''''''''''''''''''''''''''''''''''''''''*/
/*  execute the CATALOG_DB DBA function                                  */
/*'''''''''''''''''''''''''''''''''''''''''''''''''''''''''''''''''''''''*/
SHORT dba_catalog_db(PCHAR parm_str)
{
  BYTE      database_name[9];        /* Database name, null terminated  */
  CHAR      database_alias[9];       /* alias id for a database         */
  UCHAR     db_drive;                /* Drive on which DB resides e.g. C */
  CHAR      node_name[9];            /* node name for a database        */
  CHAR      comment[31];             /* Comment on DB, null terminated  */
  USHORT    database_location;       /* db location 0=local, 1=remote   */
  CHAR      database_location_parm[9]; /* local/remote database string  */

  /*'''''''''''''''''''''''''''''''''''''''''''''*/
  /* get the parm strings                        */
  /*'''''''''''''''''''''''''''''''''''''''''''''*/
  if (sscanf(parm_str, " %8s %8s %8s %c %8s %31s ",
                   database_name, database_alias, database_location_parm,
                   &db_drive, node_name, comment)
                != parms.num_parms)
     {sprintf(err_msg, "\nSYNTAX ERROR: invalid parameters.");
      return(RECORD_ERR_MSG);
      }

  /*'''''''''''''''''''''''''''''''''''''''''''''*/
  /* decode the parms                          . */
  /*'''''''''''''''''''''''''''''''''''''''''''''*/
  if ( decode_parm_string(database_location_parm, &database_location) )
     {sprintf(err_msg, "\nSYNTAX ERROR: invalid parameter.");
      return(RECORD_ERR_MSG);
      }

  /*'''''''''''''''''''''''''''''''''''''''''''''*/
  /* call the CATALOG API                        */
  /*'''''''''''''''''''''''''''''''''''''''''''''*/
  sqlecatd(database_name,                      /* database          */
           database_alias,                     /* database alias    */
           database_location,                  /* database location */
           node_name,                          /* node name         */
           db_drive,                           /* database drive    */
           comment,                            /* comment           */
           0,                                  /* current code page */
           &sqlca);                            /* SQLCA             */
  return(RECORD_SQLCA);
} /* end dba_catalog_db */
```

Figure 30-8. Catalog Database Command Handler: dba_catalog_db().

The Helper Function: decode_parm_string()

The **decode_parm_string**() helper function takes a character string as an input and returns the Database Manager's numeric value for that string. This is done through a look-up table created as a static C structure, which gets initialized with strings and their corresponding numeric values. You may find this structure to be a useful reference of non-string parameters used by the Database Manager.

```
/*''''''''''''''''''''''''''''''''''''''''''''''''''''''''''''''''''''''''*/
/*  This procedure converts a parameter string into a value.              */
/*''''''''''''''''''''''''''''''''''''''''''''''''''''''''''''''''''''''''*/
SHORT decode_parm_string(PCHAR parm, PUSHORT parm_num)
{
  SHORT      parm_not_found;          /* True if a match is found          */
  USHORT     i;                       /* loop index variable               */

  /*''''''''''''''''''''''''''''''''''''''''''''''''''''*/
  /* Initialize cmds table                              */
  /*''''''''''''''''''''''''''''''''''''''''''''''''''''*/
  typedef struct
  {
    CHAR       parm_str[40];          /* cmd name                          */
    SHORT      parm_num;              /* numerical representation of cmd   */
  }   PARM_TYPE;

  #define PARM_COUNT    31
  static PARM_TYPE parms[PARM_COUNT] =
  {/*<--- parm_str --------><-- parm_num------------------->*/
    {"ALL",                 0                                 },
    {"INCREMENTAL",         1                                 },
    {"LOCAL",               '0'                               },
    {"REMOTE",              '1'                               },
    {"REPEATABLE_READ",     SQL_REP_READ                      },
    {"CURSOR_STABILITY",    SQL_CURSOR_STAB                   },
    {"UNCOMMITTED_READ",    SQL_UNCOM_READ                    },
    {"BLOCK_UNAMBIG",       SQL_BL_UNAMBIG                    },
    {"BLOCK_ALL",           SQL_BL_ALL                        },
    {"NO_BLOCKING",         SQL_NO_BL                         },
    {"DEF",                 SQL_FMT_0                         },
    {"USA",                 SQL_FMT_1                         },
    {"EUR",                 SQL_FMT_2                         },
    {"ISO",                 SQL_FMT_3                         },
    {"JIS",                 SQL_FMT_4                         },
    {"LOC",                 SQL_FMT_5                         },
    {"UPM_LOCAL",           UPM_LOCAL                         },
    {"UPM_DNODE",           UPM_DNODE                         },
    {"UPM_DOMAIN",          UPM_DOMAIN                        },
    {"UPM_CONFIG",          UPM_CONFIG                        },
    {"UPM_ADMIN",           UPM_ADMIN                         },
    {"UPM_USER",            UPM_USER                          },
    {"SQLUM_ROLLFWD",       SQLUM_ROLLFWD                     },
    {"SQLUM_STOP",          SQLUM_STOP                        },
    {"SQLUM_ROLLFWD_STOP",  SQLUM_ROLLFWD_STOP                },
    {"SQLUM_QUERY",         SQLUM_QUERY                       },
    {"SQL_PROTOCOL_APPC",   SQL_PROTOCOL_APPC                 },
    {"SQL_PROTOCOL_NETB",   SQL_PROTOCOL_NETB                 },
    {"SQL_PROTOCOL_APPN",   SQL_PROTOCOL_APPN                 },
```

Figure 30-9 (Part 1 of 2). The Helper Procedure: decode_parm_string().

```
   {"SQL_ADAPTER_0",          SQL_ADAPTER_0                    },
   {"SQL_ADAPTER_1",          SQL_ADAPTER_1                    }
 };


 /*'''''''''''''''''''''''''''''''''''''''''''*/
 /* decode the parm string                    */
 /*'''''''''''''''''''''''''''''''''''''''''''*/
 i = 0 ;
 parm_not_found = TRUE ;

 while ( parm_not_found && (i < PARM_COUNT))
 {
   parm_not_found = strcmp(parms[i].parm_str,parm);
   if (!parm_not_found)
     break;
   else
     i++;
 }

 if (parm_not_found )
    {
     sprintf(err_msg,
       "\nSYNTAX ERROR: Unknown parameter string. ");
     return(CMD_SYNTAX_ERROR);
    }
 else
    {
     *parm_num = parms[i].parm_num;
     return(GOOD);
    }
} /* end decode_parm_string */
```

Figure 30-9 (Part 2 of 2).   The Helper Procedure: decode_parm_string().

Uncatalog Database : dba_uncatalog_db()

The **dba_uncatalog_db()** command handler, whose code is listed in Figure 30-10, executes the RSQL command:

▶▶— EXEC DBA: UNCATALOG_DB— database_name ─────────────────────────◀◀

This command handler decodes its parameters and then executes a **sqleuncd()** API call.

```
/*'''''''''''''''''''''''''''''''''''''''''''''''''''''''''''''''''''''''''''''*/
/*  execute the UNCATALOG_DB DBA function                                       */
/*'''''''''''''''''''''''''''''''''''''''''''''''''''''''''''''''''''''''''''''*/
SHORT dba_uncatalog_db(PCHAR parm_str)
{
  BYTE        database_name[9];              /* Database name, null terminated   */

   /*'''''''''''''''''''''''''''''''''''''''''*/
   /* get the parm strings                    */
   /*'''''''''''''''''''''''''''''''''''''''''*/
   if (sscanf(parm_str, " %8s ", database_name
            ) != parms.num_parms)
      {
```

Figure 30-10 (Part 1 of 2).   Uncatalog Database Command Handler: dba_uncatalog_db().

```
        sprintf(err_msg, "\nSYNTAX ERROR: invalid parameters.");
        return(RECORD_ERR_MSG);
      }

  /*''''''''''''''''''''''''''''''''''''''''''*/
  /* call the START USING DB API             */
  /*''''''''''''''''''''''''''''''''''''''''''*/
  sqleuncd(database_name,                              /* database         */
           &sqlca);                                    /* SQLCA            */
  return(RECORD_SQLCA);
} /* end dba_uncatalog_db */
```

Figure 30-10 (Part 2 of 2).   Uncatalog Database Command Handler: dba_uncatalog_db().

Catalog Node: dba_catalog_node()

The **dba_catalog_node**() command handler, whose code is listed in Figure 30-11,
executes the RSQL command:

```
▶▶─ EXEC DBA: CATALOG_NODE──node_name ───────── comment ─────────────────▶

 ▶┬─SQL_PROTOCOL_APPC ───────────────local_lu ────── remote_lu ── mode ─┬▶◀
  ├─SQL_PROTOCOL_APPN ─ netid ──────local_lu ────── remote_lu ── mode ─┤
  └─SQL_PROTOCOL_NETB ───────────────remote_nname ─ adapter_no ────────┘
```

This command handler decodes its parameters, fills up its protocol structure (for either
NetBIOS, APPC, or APPN), and then executes a **sqlecatn**() API call.

```
/*''''''''''''''''''''''''''''''''''''''''''''''''''''''''''''''''''''''''''''''*/
/*   execute the CATALOG_NODE DBA function                                      */
/*''''''''''''''''''''''''''''''''''''''''''''''''''''''''''''''''''''''''''''''*/
SHORT dba_catalog_node(PCHAR parm_str)
{
  CHAR       protocol_parm[18];          /* Protocol (NETBIOS, APPN, APPC)  */

  struct
  { USHORT   struct_id;                  /* structure identifier            */
    USHORT   code_page;                  /* comment code page               */
    CHAR     comment[31];                /* Comment on DB, null terminated   */
    CHAR     node_name[9];               /* Name of database node           */
    USHORT   protocol;                   /* Protocol value                  */
  } node;

  union
  { struct
    { USHORT    adapter;                 /* Adapter number for NetBIOS      */
      CHAR      remote_nname[9];         /* Remote Node Name for NetBIOS    */
    } netb;
    struct
    { CHAR      network_id[9];           /* Network ID for APPN             */
      CHAR      remote_lu[9];            /* Remote LU alias for APPC/APPN    */
      CHAR      local_lu[9];             /* Local LU alias for APPC/APPN     */
      CHAR      mode[9];                 /* Mode for APPC/APPN              */
```

Figure 30-11 (Part 1 of 3).   Catalog Node Command Handler: dba_catalog_node().

```
     } appn;
     struct
     { CHAR        remote_lu[9];              /* Remote LU alias for APPC/APPN  */
       CHAR        local_lu[9];               /* Local LU alias for APPC/APPN   */
       CHAR        mode[9];                   /* Mode for APPC/APPN             */
     } appc;
   } protocol;

   /*''''''''''''''''''''''''''''''''''''''''''*/
   /* get the parm strings                     */
   /*''''''''''''''''''''''''''''''''''''''''''*/
   if (sscanf(parm_str, " %8s %31s %17s %[^;] ",
                        node.node_name, node.comment, protocol_parm, parm_str)
                   != parms.num_parms)
     {
       sprintf(err_msg, "\nSYNTAX ERROR: invalid parameters.");
       return(RECORD_ERR_MSG);
     }

   node.struct_id = SQL_NODE_STR_ID;        /* structure identifier           */
   node.code_page = 0;                      /* accept default code page       */
   if (decode_parm_string(protocol_parm, &node.protocol))
     {
       sprintf(err_msg, "\nSYNTAX ERROR: invalid parameter.");
       return(RECORD_ERR_MSG);
     }

   /*''''''''''''''''''''''''''''''''''''''''''''''*/
   /* get the protocol specific parms and       */
   /*   setup protocol specific structure       */
   /*''''''''''''''''''''''''''''''''''''''''''''''*/
   switch (node.protocol)
   {
     case SQL_PROTOCOL_APPC:
        if (sscanf(parm_str, " %8s %8s %8s ", protocol.appc.local_lu,
                             protocol.appc.remote_lu, protocol.appc.mode)
                      != 3)
          {
            sprintf(err_msg, "\nSYNTAX ERROR: invalid parameters.");
            return(RECORD_ERR_MSG);
          }
        break;

     case SQL_PROTOCOL_NETB:
        if (sscanf(parm_str, " %8s %hd ", protocol.netb.remote_nname,
                                    &protocol.netb.adapter) != 2)
          {
            sprintf(err_msg, "\nSYNTAX ERROR: invalid parameters.");
            return(RECORD_ERR_MSG);
          }
        break;

     case SQL_PROTOCOL_APPN:
        if (sscanf(parm_str, " %8s %8s %8s %8s ", protocol.appn.network_id,
                             protocol.appn.local_lu, protocol.appn.remote_lu,
                             protocol.appn.mode) != 4)
          {
            sprintf(err_msg, "\nSYNTAX ERROR: invalid parameters.");
            return(RECORD_ERR_MSG);
          }
        break;

   } /* endswitch */
```

Figure 30-11 (Part 2 of 3). Catalog Node Command Handler: dba_catalog_node().

```
/*''''''''''''''''''''''''''''''''''''''''*/
/* call the CATALOG API                   */
/*''''''''''''''''''''''''''''''''''''''''*/
sqlectnd((struct sqle_node_struct *)&node,
                                 /* pointer to node structure    */
         (PVOID)&protocol,       /* pointer to protocol structure */
         &sqlca);                /* SQLCA                        */
return(RECORD_SQLCA);
} /* end dba_catalog_node */
```

Figure 30-11 (Part 3 of 3). Catalog Node Command Handler: dba_catalog_node().

Uncatalog Node: dba_uncatalog_node()

The **dba_uncatalog_node()** command handler, whose code is listed in Figure 30-12, executes the RSQL command:

▶▶─ EXEC DBA: UNCATALOG_NODE ── nodename ─────────────────────◀◀

This command handler decodes its parameters and then executes a **sqleuncn()** API call.

```
/*''''''''''''''''''''''''''''''''''''''''''''''''''''''''''''''''''''''''''*/
/*  execute the UNCATALOG_NODE DBA function                                 */
/*''''''''''''''''''''''''''''''''''''''''''''''''''''''''''''''''''''''''''*/
SHORT dba_uncatalog_node(PCHAR parm_str)
{
  CHAR      node_name[9];                /* node name for a database      */

  /*''''''''''''''''''''''''''''''''''''''''*/
  /* get the parm strings                   */
  /*''''''''''''''''''''''''''''''''''''''''*/
  if (sscanf(parm_str, " %8s ", node_name
          ) != parms.num_parms)
    {
      sprintf(err_msg, "\nSYNTAX ERROR: invalid parameters.");
      return(RECORD_ERR_MSG);
    }

  /*''''''''''''''''''''''''''''''''''''''''*/
  /* call the START USING DB API            */
  /*''''''''''''''''''''''''''''''''''''''''*/
  sqleuncn(node_name,                             /* node name    */
          &sqlca);                                /* SQLCA        */
  return(RECORD_SQLCA);
} /* end dba_uncatalog_node */
```

Figure 30-12. Uncatalog Node Command Handler: dba_uncatalog_node().

Show Database Directory: dba_show_db_dir()

The **dba_show_db_dir()** command handler, whose code is listed in Figure 30-13, executes the RSQL command:

▶▶─ EXEC DBA: SHOW_DB_DIR ── db_drive ─────────────────────────◀◀

The command handler does the following:

1. Obtains the number of database directory entries by issuing the open directory call **sqledops()**.
2. Goes into a loop fetching one directory entry at a time by issuing, repeatedly, the **sqledgne()** get next entry API call.
3. Finally, the command handler issues a **sqledcls()** API call to close the session with the database directory.

```
/*'''''''''''''''''''''''''''''''''''''''''''''''''''''''''''''''''''''''*/
/*                                                                       */
/*   execute the SHOW_DB_DIR DBA function                                */
/*'''''''''''''''''''''''''''''''''''''''''''''''''''''''''''''''''''''''*/
SHORT dba_show_db_dir(PCHAR parm_str)
{
  USHORT          dir_handle;                  /* db directory handle    */
  USHORT          dir_count;                   /* num of directory items */

  typedef struct
  {
    CHAR          alias[8];                    /* Alias name             */
    CHAR          dbname[8];                   /* Database name          */
    CHAR          drive[2];                    /* Drive 'd:'             */
    CHAR          intname[8];                  /* Database subdirectory   */
    CHAR          nodename[8];                 /* Node name              */
    CHAR          dbtype[20];                  /* Release information     */
    CHAR          comment[30];                 /* Comment                */
    SHORT         com_codepage;                /* Code page of comment    */
    CHAR          type;                        /* Entry type defines above*/
  } DIR_ENTRY_TYPE;
  DIR_ENTRY_TYPE * _Seg16 dir_entry;           /* directory entry returned*/

  UCHAR           db_drive;                    /* drive dir, "0" =home dir*/

  /*'''''''''''''''''''''''''''''''''''''''''*/
  /* get the parm strings                    */
  /*'''''''''''''''''''''''''''''''''''''''''*/
  if (sscanf(parm_str, " %c ", &db_drive
          ) != parms.num_parms)
    {
      sprintf(err_msg, "\nSYNTAX ERROR: invalid parameters.");
      return(RECORD_ERR_MSG);
    }

  /*'''''''''''''''''''''''''''''''''''''''''*/
  /* call the OPEN DB DIRECTORY API          */
  /*'''''''''''''''''''''''''''''''''''''''''*/
  sqledops(db_drive,                           /* database drive         */
           &dir_handle,                        /* directory handle       */
           &dir_count,                         /* number of entries      */
           &sqlca);                            /* SQLCA                  */

  if (SQLCODE != 0)
      return(RECORD_SQLCA);                    /* open failed            */

  /*'''''''''''''''''''''''''''''''''''''''''*/
  /* print a header                          */
  /*'''''''''''''''''''''''''''''''''''''''''*/
  fprintf(out_stream,
```

Figure 30-13 (Part 1 of 2). Show DB Directory Handler: dba_show_db_dir().

```
"\n Database Directory for Drive %c:"
"\n ================================="
"\n\n Alias     Name      Drive Directory Node     "
"Comment                         Type"
"\n -------- -------- ----- --------- -------- "
"--------------------------- ----", db_drive);

while( dir_count-- )
{
/*'''''''''''''''''''''''''''''''''''''''''*/
/* call the GET NEXT DIRECTORY ENTRY API   */
/*'''''''''''''''''''''''''''''''''''''''''*/
sqledgne(dir_handle,                              /* directory handle   */
         (struct sqledinfo ** _Seg16)&dir_entry, /* directory item     */
         &sqlca);                                 /* SQLCA              */
if (SQLCODE != 0)
    break;                                        /* read failed        */

fprintf(out_stream, "\n %8.8s %8.8s %2.2s    %8.8s  %8.8s %30.30s %c",
        dir_entry->alias, dir_entry->dbname, dir_entry->drive,
        dir_entry->intname, dir_entry->nodename,
        dir_entry->comment, dir_entry->type);

} /* end while */
fprintf(out_stream,"\n");

/*'''''''''''''''''''''''''''''''''''''''''*/
/* call the CLOSE DB DIRECTORY API         */
/*'''''''''''''''''''''''''''''''''''''''''*/
sqledcls(dir_handle,                              /* directory handle   */
         &sqlca);                                 /* SQLCA              */
return(RECORD_SQLCA);
} /* end dba_show_db_dir */
```

Figure 30-13 (Part 2 of 2).   Show DB Directory Handler: dba_show_db_dir().

Show Node Directory: dba_show_node_dir()

The **dba_show_node_dir()** command handler, whose code is listed in Figure 30-14, executes the RSQL command:

▶▶— EXEC DBA: SHOW_NODE_DIR ───◀◀

The command handler does the following:

1. Obtains the number of node directory entries by issuing the open directory call **sqlenops()**.
2. Goes into a loop fetching one directory entry at a time by issuing, repeatedly, the **sqlengne()** get next entry API call.
3. Issues a **sqlencls()** API call to close the session with the node directory.

```
/*''''''''''''''''''''''''''''''''''''''''''''''''''''''''''''''''''''''*/
/*  execute the SHOW_NODE_DIR DBA function                              */
/*''''''''''''''''''''''''''''''''''''''''''''''''''''''''''''''''''''''*/
SHORT dba_show_node_dir(VOID)
{
  USHORT node_dir_handle;
  USHORT node_dir_count;
  struct sqleninfo * _Seg16 node_dir_entry;

  /*'''''''''''''''''''''''''''''''''''''''''''*/
  /* call the OPEN NODE DIRECTORY API         */
  /*'''''''''''''''''''''''''''''''''''''''''''*/
  sqlenops(&node_dir_handle,                          /* node dir  handle   */
           &node_dir_count,                           /* node dir  entries  */
           &sqlca);                                   /* SQLCA              */

  if (SQLCODE != 0)
      return(RECORD_SQLCA);                           /* open failed        */

  /*'''''''''''''''''''''''''''''''''''''''''''*/
  /* print a header                           */
  /*'''''''''''''''''''''''''''''''''''''''''''*/
  fprintf(out_stream,
          "\n Node Directory"
          "\n =============="
          "\n\n Node      Local LU  Partner LU  Mode      Comment"
          "\n --------  --------  ----------  --------"
          " ----------------------------");

  while( node_dir_count-- )
  {
  /*'''''''''''''''''''''''''''''''''''''''''''*/
  /* call the OPEN DB DIRECTORY ENTRY API     */
  /*'''''''''''''''''''''''''''''''''''''''''''*/
  sqlengne(node_dir_handle,                           /* directory handle   */
           (struct sqleninfo ** _Seg16)&node_dir_entry, /* directory item  */
           &sqlca);                                   /* SQLCA              */
  if (SQLCODE != 0)
      break;                                          /* read failed        */

  fprintf(out_stream,
          "\n %8.8s  %8.8s  %8.8s    %8.8s  %30.30s",
          node_dir_entry->nodename, node_dir_entry->local_lu,
          node_dir_entry->partner_lu, node_dir_entry->mode,
          node_dir_entry->comment);
  } /* end while */
  fprintf(out_stream,"\n");

  /*'''''''''''''''''''''''''''''''''''''''''''*/
  /* call the CLOSE DB DIRECTORY API          */
  /*'''''''''''''''''''''''''''''''''''''''''''*/
  sqlencls(node_dir_handle,                           /* directory handle   */
           &sqlca);                                   /* SQLCA              */
  return(RECORD_SQLCA);
} /* end dba_show_node_dir */
```

Figure 30-14. Show Node Directory Handler: dba_show_node_dir().

Collect Database Status: dba_collect_status()

The **dba_collect_status()** command handler, whose code is listed in Figure 30-15, executes the RSQL command:

▶▶— EXEC DBA: COLLECT_STATUS — database_name ——————————————————▶◀

Here's what this command handler does:

1. It first obtains the system and database status (for the named database) by issuing the **sqlestat()** API call. The system status information is obtained using the data structure:

```
typedef struct      /* System Status data structure */
{   ULONG  current_time;          /* Current time               */
    LONG   time_zone_disp;        /* Time zone of current time  */
    UCHAR  product_name[30];      /* Product name               */
    UCHAR  component_id[9];       /* Component Id               */
    UCHAR  reserved;              /* Reserved byte              */
    UCHAR  release_lvl[4];        /* Release level              */
    UCHAR  corr_serv_lvl[8];      /* Corrective service level   */
} sqlesystat;
```

2. It also obtains the database status information through the same call, using the data structure:

```
typedef struct      /* Database Status data structure */
{   ULONG  backup_time;           /* Last backup time           */
    LONG   time_zone_disp;        /* Time zone of backup time   */
    USHORT connects;              /* Number of current users    */
    UCHAR  db_alias[16];          /* Alias name                 */
    UCHAR  db_name[16];           /* Database name              */
    UCHAR  location;              /* 'L' = Local, 'R' = Remote  */
    UCHAR  reserved;              /* Reserved byte              */
    UCHAR  drive[2];              /* Drive containing database  */
    UCHAR  node[8];               /* Node containing database   */
    UCHAR  db_type[20];           /* Type of database ="OS2 DBM" */
} sqledbstat;
```

3. If users are connected to the database, then the command handler does the following:

    a. It allocates dynamic memory that is large enough to hold the status entries for all the users that are connected to the database.
    b. It issues the API call **sqleuser()** to read into memory the status entries of all the connected users.
    c. It goes through a loop which reads from memory one user status entry at a time, formats it, and writes the output to the *response* file.
    d. It frees the dynamic memory which was previously allocated.

4. The user information is obtained through the following data structure:

```
typedef struct sqleusrstat   /* User Status data structure */
   {   ULONG  con_trans;                 /* Transactions since connect  */
       ULONG  con_reqs;                  /* Requests since connect      */
       ULONG  cur_reqs;                  /* Requests current transact   */
       ULONG  connect_time;              /* Time since connect          */
       ULONG  trans_time;                /* Time since current transact */
       UCHAR  authid[8];                 /* User's Id                   */
       UCHAR  node[8];                   /* Nodename of connected user  */
       USHORT authority_lvl;             /* User's authority level      */
       UCHAR  trans_state;               /* Transaction state           */
       UCHAR  lock_state;                /* Transaction lock state      */
   } sqleusrstat;
```

5. All three data structures are defined in the Database Manager's **sqlenv.h** include file.

6. It frees resources by issuing the **sqlefree()** API call.

```
/**************************************************************************/
/*  execute the COLLECT_STATUS DBA function                               */
/**************************************************************************/
SHORT dba_collect_status(PCHAR parm_str)
{
  typedef struct
      {
        struct sqlesystat   system_status;    /* system status variable    */
        struct sqledbstat   database_status;  /* db   status variable      */
      } status;
  status              stat;                   /* system/db status          */
  typedef struct
      {
        struct sqleusrstat  user_status[1];   /* user status variable      */
      } user_stat;

  user_stat  *user_stat_ptr;                  /* user status variable      */

  USHORT status_blocks_remaining;
  USHORT index;
  SEL    selector;
  BYTE   database_name[9];                     /* Database name, null term.  */

  /******************************************/
  /* get the parm strings                  */
  /******************************************/
  if (sscanf(parm_str, " %8s ", database_name)
                  != parms.num_parms)
      {
        sprintf(err_msg, "\nSYNTAX ERROR: invalid parameters.");
        return(RECORD_ERR_MSG);
      }

  /******************************************/
  /* call the COLLECT STATUS API           */
  /******************************************/
  sqlestat(SQL_OPSTAT_ALL,                     /* Collect System and DB status */
           SQL_OBJECT_DATABASE,                /* The DB status is for specific DB*/
           strlen(database_name) + 1,          /* Length of the DB name        */
           database_name,                      /* DB name                      */
           &status_blocks_remaining,           /* We're only getting one DB entry */
```

Figure 30-15 (Part 1 of 3). Collect Database Status Handler: dba_collect_status().

```
                (UCHAR *)&stat,                 /* buffer pointer to status struct */
                &sqlca);                        /* SQLCA                            */
      if (SQLCODE != 0 )
         return(RECORD_SQLCA);

      /*''''''''''''''''''''''''''''''''''''''''''*/
      /* record system status                     */
      /*''''''''''''''''''''''''''''''''''''''''''*/

      fprintf(out_stream,
      "\n System Status "
      "\n ------------- "
      "\n  Current Normalized time        = %lu seconds elapsed from 1-1-1970"
      "\n  Time Zone Displacement         = %ld seconds different from UTC"
      "\n  Product name                   = %30.30s"
      "\n  Component Identification       = %9.9s"
      "\n  Release Level                  = %4.4s"
      "\n  Correct Service Level          = %8.8s\n",
      stat.system_status.current_time, stat.system_status.time_zone_disp,
      stat.system_status.product_name, stat.system_status.component_id,
      stat.system_status.release_lvl,  stat.system_status.corr_serv_lvl);

      /*''''''''''''''''''''''''''''''''''''''''''*/
      /* record database status                   */
      /*''''''''''''''''''''''''''''''''''''''''''*/
      fprintf(out_stream,
      "\n Database Status "
      "\n --------------- "
      "\n  Normalized time of last backup = %lu seconds elapsed from 1-1-1970"
      "\n  Time Zone Displacement         = %ld seconds different from UTC"
      "\n  Number of connects             = %u"
      "\n  Database alias                 = %8.8s"
      "\n  Database Name                  = %8.8s"
      "\n  Location                       = %c"
      "\n  Database drive                 = %2.2s"
      "\n  Node Name                      = %8.8s"
      "\n  Database Type                  = %20.20s\n",
      stat.database_status.backup_time, stat.database_status.time_zone_disp,
      stat.database_status.connects,    stat.database_status.db_alias,
      stat.database_status.db_name,     stat.database_status.location,
      stat.database_status.drive,       stat.database_status.node,
      stat.database_status.db_type);

      /*''''''''''''''''''''''''''''''''''''''''''*/
      /* get user status                          */
      /*''''''''''''''''''''''''''''''''''''''''''*/

      if (stat.database_status.connects == 0)
         fprintf(out_stream,
         "\n Database Status "
         "\n --------------- "
         "\n No users connected to the database \n");
      else
         {
         user_stat_ptr = malloc(sizeof(struct sqleusrstat));
         sqleuser(strlen(database_name) + 1,           /* length of DB name */
                  database_name,                        /* database name     */
                  (UCHAR *)user_stat_ptr,               /* buffer pointer    */
                  &sqlca);                              /* SQLCA             */
         if (SQLCODE != 0 )
            return(RECORD_SQLCA);
```

Figure 30-15 (Part 2 of 3).   Collect Database Status Handler: dba_collect_status().

```
/*'''''''''''''''''''''''''''''''''''''''''''*/
/* record user status                        */
/*'''''''''''''''''''''''''''''''''''''''''''*/
for (index=0; index < stat.database_status.connects; index++)
    {
    fprintf(out_stream,
    "\n User Status "
    "\n ----------- "
    "\n  Transactions since connect        = %lu"
    "\n  Requests since connect            = %lu"
    "\n  Requests current transaction      = %lu"
    "\n  Elapsed time since connect        = %lu seconds"
    "\n  Elapsed time, current transaction = %lu seconds"
    "\n  Authorization ID                  = %8.8s"
    "\n  Node Name                         = %8.8s"
    "\n  Authority Level                   = %u"
    "\n  Transaction State                 = %c"
    "\n  Lock State                        = %c\n",

    user_stat_ptr->user_status[index].con_trans,
    user_stat_ptr->user_status[index].con_reqs,
    user_stat_ptr->user_status[index].cur_reqs,
    user_stat_ptr->user_status[index].connect_time,
    user_stat_ptr->user_status[index].trans_time,
    user_stat_ptr->user_status[index].authid,
    user_stat_ptr->user_status[index].node,
    user_stat_ptr->user_status[index].authority_lvl,
    user_stat_ptr->user_status[index].trans_state,
    user_stat_ptr->user_status[index].lock_state);
    } /* end while */
    free(user_stat_ptr);
 } /* end else */

 /*'''''''''''''''''''''''''''''''''''''''''''*/
 /* call the FREE DB STATUS RESOURCES         */
 /*'''''''''''''''''''''''''''''''''''''''''''*/
 sqlefree(&sqlca);
 if (SQLCODE != 0 )
    return(RECORD_SQLCA);


return(RECORD_SQLCA);

} /* end dba_collect_status */
```

Figure 30-15 (Part 3 of 3).   Collect Database Status Handler: dba_collect_status().

RSQL.SQC: GENERAL UTILITIES COMMAND HANDLERS

Backup Database: dba_backup()

The **dba_backup()** command handler, whose code is listed in Figure 30-16, executes the RSQL command:

```
▶▶─ EXEC DBA: BACKUP ─ database_name ──┬─INCREMENTAL─┬─ drive ─────────▶◀
                                       └─ALL ────────┘
```

The "ALL" option is used to backup an entire database. The "INCREMENTAL" option is used to back up the changes made since the last backup, and is therefore much faster. Before an "INCREMENTAL" backup can be issued, the database must be backed up once with the "ALL" option. The handler issues a **sqluback()** API call to backup the database.

```
/*''''''''''''''''''''''''''''''''''''''''''''''''''''''''''''''''''''''''*/
/*  execute the BACKUP DBA function                                       */
/*''''''''''''''''''''''''''''''''''''''''''''''''''''''''''''''''''''''''*/
SHORT dba_backup(PCHAR parm_str)
{
  BYTE      database_name[9];          /* Database name, null terminated  */
  USHORT    type_of_backup;            /* A = 0, I = 1                    */
  UCHAR     bk_drive;                  /* Drive where backup resides e.g D */
  CHAR      type_of_backup_parm[12];   /* from user command               */

  /*'''''''''''''''''''''''''''''''''''''''''''*/
  /* get the parm strings                      */
  /*'''''''''''''''''''''''''''''''''''''''''''*/
  if (sscanf(parm_str, " %8s %11s %c ",
                  database_name, type_of_backup_parm, &bk_drive)
                  != parms.num_parms)
    {
     sprintf(err_msg, "\nSYNTAX ERROR: invalid parameters.");
     return(RECORD_ERR_MSG);
    }

  if (decode_parm_string(type_of_backup_parm, &type_of_backup))
    {
     sprintf(err_msg, "\nSYNTAX ERROR: invalid parameter.");
     return(RECORD_ERR_MSG);
    }

  /*'''''''''''''''''''''''''''''''''''''''''''*/
  /* call the BACKUP API                       */
  /*'''''''''''''''''''''''''''''''''''''''''''*/
  sqluback(database_name,                              /* database        */
          type_of_backup,                             /* type, Changes or all*/
          bk_drive,                                   /* backup drive    */
          &sqlca);                                    /* SQLCA           */
  return(RECORD_SQLCA);
} /* end dba_backup */
```

Figure 30-16. Backup Database Command Handler: dba_backup().

Restore Database: dba_restore()

The **dba_restore()** command handler, whose code is listed in Figure 30-17, executes the RSQL command:

▶▶─EXEC DBA: RESTORE─── database_name─── db_drive─── bk_drive ───◀◀

This command handler decodes its parameters and then executes a **sqludres()** API call.

```
/*,,,,,,,,,,,,,,,,,,,,,,,,,,,,,,,,,,,,,,,,,,,,,,,,,,,,,,,,,,,,,,,,,,,,,,,,*/
/*   execute the RESTORE DBA function                                     */
/*,,,,,,,,,,,,,,,,,,,,,,,,,,,,,,,,,,,,,,,,,,,,,,,,,,,,,,,,,,,,,,,,,,,,,,,,*/
SHORT dba_restore(PCHAR parm_str)
{
  BYTE      database_name[9];            /* Database name, null terminated  */
  UCHAR     db_drive;                    /* Drive on which DB resides e.g. C */
  UCHAR     bk_drive;                    /* Drive where backup resides e.g D */
  /*,,,,,,,,,,,,,,,,,,,,,,,,,,,,,,,,,,,,,,,,,,,,,*/
  /* get the parm strings                       */
  /*,,,,,,,,,,,,,,,,,,,,,,,,,,,,,,,,,,,,,,,,,,,,,*/
  if (sscanf(parm_str, " %8s %c %c ",
             database_name, &db_drive, &bk_drive
           ) != parms.num_parms)
    {
      sprintf(err_msg, "\nSYNTAX ERROR: invalid parameters.");
      return(RECORD_ERR_MSG);
    }

  /*,,,,,,,,,,,,,,,,,,,,,,,,,,,,,,,,,,,,,,,,,,,,,*/
  /* call the RESET DATABASE CONFIG API      */
  /*,,,,,,,,,,,,,,,,,,,,,,,,,,,,,,,,,,,,,,,,,,,,,*/
  sqludres(database_name,                           /* database          */
           db_drive,                                /* database drive    */
           bk_drive,                                /* backup drive      */
           0,                                       /* caller action     */
           &sqlca);                                 /* SQLCA             */
  return(RECORD_SQLCA);
} /* end dba_restore */
```

Figure 30-17. Restore Database Command Handler: dba_restore().

Roll Forward Database: dba_roll_forward()

The **dba_roll_forward**() command handler, whose code is listed in Figure 30-18, executes the RSQL command:

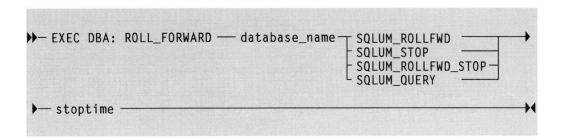

This command handler decodes its parameters and then executes a **sqlufrol()** API call.

```
/*''''''''''''''''''''''''''''''''''''''''''''''''''''''''''''''''''''''''*/
/*  execute the ROLL FORWARD DATABASE function                            */
/*''''''''''''''''''''''''''''''''''''''''''''''''''''''''''''''''''''''''*/
SHORT dba_roll_forward(PCHAR parm_str)
{
  BYTE      database_name[9];         /* Database name, null terminated  */
  UCHAR     action_parm[19];          /* roll forward action string      */
  USHORT    action;                   /* roll forward action             */
  UCHAR     stop_time[27];            /* ISO stop time                   */
  UCHAR     next_arc_file[13];        /* next required archive file      */
  UCHAR     first_del_arc[13];        /* first archive file for deletion */
  UCHAR     last_del_arc[13];         /* last arcive file for deletion   */
  UCHAR     last_commit[27];          /* last commit time                */

  /*'''''''''''''''''''''''''''''''''''''''''''*/
  /* get the parm strings                      */
  /*'''''''''''''''''''''''''''''''''''''''''''*/
  if (sscanf(parm_str, " %8s %18s %26s ",
            database_name, action_parm, &stop_time
            ) != parms.num_parms)
    {
     sprintf(err_msg, "\nSYNTAX ERROR: invalid parameters.");
     return(RECORD_ERR_MSG);
    }

  if (decode_parm_string(action_parm, &action))
    {
     sprintf(err_msg, "\nSYNTAX ERROR: invalid parameter.");
     return(RECORD_ERR_MSG);
    }

  /*'''''''''''''''''''''''''''''''''''''''''''*/
  /* call the ROLL FORWARD DATABASE API        */
  /*'''''''''''''''''''''''''''''''''''''''''''*/
  sqlufrol(database_name,             /* database                        */
          action,                     /* roll forward action             */
          stop_time,                  /* ISO stop time                   */
          next_arc_file,              /* next required archive file      */
          first_del_arc,              /* first archive file for deletion */
          last_del_arc,               /* last archive file for deletion  */
          last_commit,                /* last commit time                */
          &sqlca);                    /* SQLCA                           */
  if (SQLCODE != 0 )
     return(RECORD_SQLCA);

  fprintf(out_stream,
  "\n Next Log File         = %s"
  "\n First Archive Log File = %s"
  "\n Last  Archive Log File = %s"
  "\n Last Commit Time       = %s",
  next_arc_file, first_del_arc, last_del_arc, last_commit);
  return(RECORD_SQLCA);
} /* end dba_restore */
```

Figure 30-18.   Roll Forward Database Command Handler: dba_roll_forward().

Export Table: dba_export()

The **dba_export()** command handler, whose code is listed in Figure 30-19, executes the RSQL command:

where **datafile** is the name of the OS/2 file which will receive the exported data, and **tname** is the fully qualified name of a table or view from which the data is extracted.

Here is what this command handler does:

1. Parses the parameters in the usual manner.
2. Sets the **dcoldata** parameter to NULL. This tells Database Manager to use the same names for the output columns as those in the database table columns.
3. Uses the table name to format a SELECT statement, which it places in the *data* field of the **tcolstrg** parameter.
4. Specifies a **msgfile** parameter which points to the name and path of an OS/2 file where additional error messages will be written to by the Database Manager.
5. Issues the **sqluexp()** API call.
6. Calls the **merge_file()** helper function (see Figure 30-20) to append the contents of the **msgfile** returned by the Database Manager to the *response* file.

```
/*''''''''''''''''''''''''''''''''''''''''''''''''''''''''''''''''''''''''''''*/
/*   execute the EXPORT DBA function                                          */
/*''''''''''''''''''''''''''''''''''''''''''''''''''''''''''''''''''''''''''''*/
SHORT dba_export(PCHAR parm_str)
{
   static struct   sqldcol  *dcoldata = NULL;       /* dcoldata               */
   typedef struct
   {
    SHORT           length;                          /* string length         */
    CHAR            data[100];                       /* string of data        */
   } NUM_STR_TYPE;
   NUM_STR_TYPE    tcolstrg;                         /* tcolstrg              */
   BYTE            database_name[9];     /* Database name, null terminated    */
   CHAR            datafile[80];         /* Path name of file, null terminat. */
   CHAR            exchange_format[4];   /* ASC, DEL etc., null terminated    */
   CHAR            table_name[29];       /* fully qualif., null terminated    */

   /*''''''''''''''''''''''''''''''''''''''''''*/
   /* get the parm strings                     */
   /*''''''''''''''''''''''''''''''''''''''''''*/
   if (sscanf(parm_str, " %8s %80s %3s %28s ",
                   database_name,datafile, exchange_format, table_name)
              != parms.num_parms)
   {
```

Figure 30-19 (Part 1 of 2). Export Table Command Handler: dba_export().

```
        sprintf(err_msg, "\nSYNTAX ERROR: invalid parameters.");
        return(RECORD_ERR_MSG);
    }

   sprintf(tcolstrg.data,"SELECT * FROM %s", table_name);
   tcolstrg.length = strlen(tcolstrg.data);

   /*'''''''''''''''''''''''''''''''''''''''*/
   /* call the EXPORT API                   */
   /*'''''''''''''''''''''''''''''''''''''''*/
   sqluexp(database_name,                              /* database      */
           datafile,                                   /* datafile      */
           dcoldata,                                   /* dcoldata      */
           (struct sqlchar *)&tcolstrg,                /* tcolstrg      */
           exchange_format,                            /* filetype      */
           NULL,                                       /* filetmod      */
           msgfile,                                    /* message file  */
           0,                                          /* caller action */
           &sqlca);                                    /* SQLCA         */
   merge_file(out_stream,msgfile);
   return(RECORD_SQLCA);
} /* end dba_export */
```

Figure 30-19 (Part 2 of 2). Export Table Command Handler: dba_export().

The Helper Procedure: merge file()

```
/*''''''''''''''''''''''''''''''''''''''''''''''''''''''''''''''''''''''''''''''*/
/*   This procedure copies the contents of a file into another.                */
/*   The file to be copied must exist.  It will be merged and then erased.      */
/*   The destination file must be already open and will be left that way.      */
/*''''''''''''''''''''''''''''''''''''''''''''''''''''''''''''''''''''''''''''''*/
SHORT merge_file(FILE *dest_stream, char  * merge_file_name)
{
  FILE           *merge_stream;                 /* merge file handle   */
  CHAR           in_line[256];                  /* store a line        */

  /*'''''''''''''''''''''''''''''''''''''''''*/
  /* Open to_be_merged file                  */
  /*'''''''''''''''''''''''''''''''''''''''''*/
  if (NULL == (merge_stream = fopen(merge_file_name, "r")))
    { fprintf(dest_stream,"\n No messages in %s\n",merge_file_name);
      return(GOOD);
    }
  else
    {
      /*'''''''''''''''''''''''''''''''''''''''''''*/
      /* Copy contents...                          */
      /*'''''''''''''''''''''''''''''''''''''''''''*/
      while (!feof(merge_stream))
      {
        if (NULL == fgets(in_line,sizeof(in_line), merge_stream))
          break;
        else
          fputs(in_line,dest_stream);
      }  /* endwhile */
} /* end if */
```

Figure 30-20 (Part 1 of 2). The Helper Procedure: merge file().

```
/*,,,,,,,,,,,,,,,,,,,,,,,,,,,,,,,,,,,,,,,,,,,*/
/* Close file and erase contents...        */
/*,,,,,,,,,,,,,,,,,,,,,,,,,,,,,,,,,,,,,,,,,,,*/
fclose(merge_stream);
merge_stream = fopen(merge_file_name, "w+");  /* this opens the file and  */
fclose(merge_stream);                          /* destroys its contents    */

return(GOOD);
} /* end merge_file */
```

Figure 30-20 (Part 2 of 2).   The Helper Procedure: merge file().

Import Table: dba_import()

The **dba_import()** command handler, whose code is listed in Figure 30-21, executes the RSQL command:

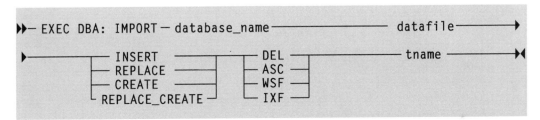

where **datafile** is the name of the OS/2 file that contains the data to be imported, and **tname** is the fully qualified name of a table or a view that can be updated and will be the recipient of the data.

Here is what this command handler does:

1. Parses the parameters in the usual manner.
2. Sets the **dcoldata** parameter to NULL. This will let the Database Manager choose the columns in the same order as they appear in the datafile.
3. Formats a string that specifies how the data is to be imported. The choices are INSERT, REPLACE, CREATE, and REPLACE_CREATE. This string is placed in the **data** field of the **tcolstrg** parameter.
4. Specifies a **msgfile** parameter that points to the name and path of an OS/2 file where additional error messages will be written to by the API handler.
5. Issues the **sqluimp()** API call.
6. Calls the **merge_file** helper function (see Figure 30-20) to append the contents of the returned **msgfile** to the *response* file.

```
/*''''''''''''''''''''''''''''''''''''''''''''''''''''''''''''''''''''*/
/*  execute the IMPORT DBA function                                   */
/*''''''''''''''''''''''''''''''''''''''''''''''''''''''''''''''''''''*/
SHORT dba_import(PCHAR parm_str)
{
  static struct     sqldcol  *dcoldata = NULL;      /* dcoldata            */
  typedef struct
  {
   SHORT             length;                         /* string length      */
   CHAR              data[100];                      /* string of data     */
  } NUM_STR_TYPE;
  NUM_STR_TYPE      tcolstrg;                        /* tcolstrg           */
  BYTE              database_name[9];                /* Database name, null term*/
  CHAR              import_verb[9];                  /* REPLACE etc, null term. */
  CHAR              table_name[29];                  /* Qualified and null term.*/
  CHAR              datafile[80];                    /* Path name, null term.   */
  CHAR              exchange_format[4];              /* ASC, DEL etc., null term*/


  /*''''''''''''''''''''''''''''''''''''''''*/
  /* get the parm strings                   */
  /*''''''''''''''''''''''''''''''''''''''''*/
  if (sscanf(parm_str, " %8s %80s %8s %3s %28s ",
                    database_name, datafile, import_verb, exchange_format,
                    table_name)
                 != parms.num_parms)
    {
      sprintf(err_msg, "\nSYNTAX ERROR: invalid parameters.");
      return(RECORD_ERR_MSG);
    }
  sprintf(tcolstrg.data,"%s INTO %s", import_verb, table_name);
  tcolstrg.length = strlen(tcolstrg.data);

  /*''''''''''''''''''''''''''''''''''''''''*/
  /* call the IMPORT API                    */
  /*''''''''''''''''''''''''''''''''''''''''*/
  sqluimp(database_name,
          datafile,                                 /* database       */
          dcoldata,                                 /* datafile       */
          (struct sqlchar *)&tcolstrg,              /* dcoldata       */
          exchange_format,                          /* tcolstrg       */
          NULL,                                     /* filetype       */
          msgfile,                                  /* filetmod       */
          0,                                        /* message file   */
          &sqlca);                                  /* caller action  */
  merge_file(out_stream,msgfile);                   /* SQLCA          */
  return(RECORD_SQLCA);
} /* end dba_import */
```

Figure 30-21. Import Table Command Handler: dba_import().

RUNSTATS: dba_runstats()

The **dba_runstats()** command handler, whose code is listed in Figure 30-22, executes
the RSQL command:

```
▶▶─ EXEC DBA: RUNSTATS──────────── tname ──────────────────────◀◀
```

This command handler decodes its parameters and then executes a **sqlustat()** API call. The handler, through its parameters, specifies that statistics are to be generated on the table as well as all of its indexes. Make sure to read the comments that are associated with the API parameters in the following code.

```
/*''''''''''''''''''''''''''''''''''''''''''''''''''''''''''''''''''''''''''''*/
/*  execute the RUNSTATS DBA function                                         */
/*''''''''''''''''''''''''''''''''''''''''''''''''''''''''''''''''''''''''''''*/
SHORT dba_runstats(PCHAR parm_str)
{
  CHAR           table_name[29];              /* fully qualif., null terminated    */

  /*''''''''''''''''''''''''''''''''''''''''''*/
  /* get the parm strings                     */
  /*''''''''''''''''''''''''''''''''''''''''''*/
  if (sscanf(parm_str, " %28s ", table_name
          ) != parms.num_parms)
    {
     sprintf(err_msg, "\nSYNTAX ERROR: invalid parameters.");
     return(RECORD_ERR_MSG);
    }

  /*''''''''''''''''''''''''''''''''''''''''''*/
  /* call the RUNSTATS API                    */
  /*''''''''''''''''''''''''''''''''''''''''''*/
  sqlustat(table_name,               /* name of the table                 */
           0,                        /* run statistics on all indexes     */
           NULL,                     /* empty index list because all is chosen*/
           'B',                      /* run stats on both table and indexes   */
           'R',                      /* read-only access to others during cmd.*/
           &sqlca);                  /* SQLCA                             */
  return(RECORD_SQLCA);
} /* end dba_runstats */
```

Figure 30-22. RUNSTATS Command Handler: dba_runstats().

REORG Table: dba_reorg()

The **dba_rerog()** command handler, whose code is listed in Figure 30-23, executes the RSQL command:

▶▶— EXEC DBA: REORG —— database_name —— tname —— tindex ——————◀◀

where **tindex** is the fully qualified index name to be used in the reorganization. Rows will be physically ordered according to this index. A NULL may be entered if no index is to be used for the reorganization. The command handler decodes its parameters and then executes a **sqlureor()** API call.

```
/*''''''''''''''''''''''''''''''''''''''''''''''''''''''''''''''''''''''*/
/*  execute the REORG DBA function                                      */
/*''''''''''''''''''''''''''''''''''''''''''''''''''''''''''''''''''''''*/
SHORT dba_reorg(PCHAR parm_str)
{
  BYTE            database_name[9];          /* Database name, null term*/
  CHAR            table_name[29];            /* Qualified and null term.*/
  CHAR            index_name[29];            /* Qualified and null term.*/

  /*''''''''''''''''''''''''''''''''''''''''*/
  /* get the parm strings                   */
  /*''''''''''''''''''''''''''''''''''''''''*/
  if (sscanf(parm_str, " %8s %28s %28s ",
                    database_name, table_name, index_name)
                 != parms.num_parms)
    {
      sprintf(err_msg, "\nSYNTAX ERROR: invalid parameters.");
      return(RECORD_ERR_MSG);
    }

  /*''''''''''''''''''''''''''''''''''''''''*/
  /* call the REORG  API                    */
  /*''''''''''''''''''''''''''''''''''''''''*/
  sqlureor(database_name,
          table_name,                              /* database          */
          index_name,                              /* table_name        */
          NULL,                                    /* index_name        */
          &sqlca);                                 /* temp file path    */
  return(RECORD_SQLCA);                            /* SQLCA             */
} /* dba_reorg */
```

Figure 30-23.   REORG Table Command Handler: dba_reorg().

Get Admin Authorization: dba_get_admin()

The **dba_get_admin()** command handler, whose code is listed in Figure 30-24, executes the RSQL command:

▶▶─ EXEC DBA: GET_ADMIN ──◀◀

The handler issues the **sqluadau()** API call and the authorization list is returned in a Database Manager defined structure that is included in **sqlutil.h** and reproduced below:

```
typedef struct       /* System Status data structure */
{ USHORT sql_authorizations_len; /* User provided length of struct  */
  USHORT sql_sysadm_auth;          /* System Administrator? 0=No 1=Yes*/
  USHORT sql_dbadm_auth;           /* DB Administrator auth?0=No 1=Yes*/
  USHORT sql_createtab_auth;       /* Create table auth?    0=No 1=Yes*/
  USHORT sql_bindadd_auth;         /* BindAdd auth?         0=No 1=Yes*/
  USHORT sql_connect_auth;         /* Connect auth?         0=No 1=Yes*/
  USHORT sql_sysadm_grp_auth;      /* Group Sysadm auth?    0=No 1=Yes*/
  USHORT sql_dbadm_grp_auth;       /* Group DB admin  auth? 0=No 1=Yes*/
  USHORT sql_createtab_grp_auth;   /* Group Create table?   0=No 1=Yes*/
  USHORT sql_bindadd_grp_auth;     /* Group BindAdd?        0=No 1=Yes*/
  USHORT sql_connect_grp_auth;     /* Group Connect?        0=No 1=Yes*/
} sql_authorizations;
```

```
/*''''''''''''''''''''''''''''''''''''''''''''''''''''''''''''''''''''''''*/
/*  execute the GET_ADMIN DBA function                                    */
/*''''''''''''''''''''''''''''''''''''''''''''''''''''''''''''''''''''''''*/
SHORT dba_get_admin(VOID)
{
  struct sql_authorizations  author_list;

  /*''''''''''''''''''''''''''''''''''''''''''*/
  /* call the GET_ADMIN API                   */
  /*''''''''''''''''''''''''''''''''''''''''''*/
  author_list.sql_authorizations_len = sizeof(author_list);
  sqluadau(&author_list,                            /* authorization list */
           &sqlca);                                 /* SQLCA              */
  if (SQLCODE != 0 )
     return(RECORD_SQLCA);

  /*''''''''''''''''''''''''''''''''''''''''''*/
  /* record authorizations                    */
  /*''''''''''''''''''''''''''''''''''''''''''*/
  fprintf(out_stream,
  "\n Authorization type             Authorized? (0=NO, 1=YES)"
  "\n -----------------              -------------------------"
  "\n System Adminstrator                        %d"
  "\n Database Administrator                     %d"
  "\n Create Tables                              %d"
  "\n Bind new Programs                          %d",
  author_list.sql_sysadm_auth,        author_list.sql_dbadm_auth,
  author_list.sql_createtab_auth,     author_list.sql_bindadd_auth);
  fprintf(out_stream,
  "\n Access current database                    %d"
  "\n Group System Adminstrator                  %d"
  "\n Group Database Administrator               %d"
  "\n Group Create Tables                        %d"
  "\n Group Bind new Programs                    %d"
  "\n Group Access current database              %d\n",
  author_list.sql_connect_auth,        author_list.sql_sysadm_grp_auth,
  author_list.sql_dbadm_grp_auth,      author_list.sql_createtab_grp_auth,
  author_list.sql_bindadd_grp_auth, author_list.sql_connect_grp_auth);

  return(RECORD_SQLCA);
} /* end dba_get_admin */
```

Figure 30-24.   Get Admin Authorization Handler: dba_get_admin().

RSQL.SQC: CONFIGURATION SERVICES COMMAND HANDLERS

Reset Database Configuration: dba_reset_db_cfg()

The **reset_db_cfg()** command handler, whose code is listed in Figure 30-25, executes the RSQL command:

▶▶── EXEC DBA: RESET_DB_CFG──── database_name─────────────────────◀│

This command handler decodes its parameters and then executes a **sqlfrdb()** API call.

```
/*''''''''''''''''''''''''''''''''''''''''''''''''''''''''''''''''''''''''*/
/*  execute the RESET_DB_CFG DBA function                                 */
/*''''''''''''''''''''''''''''''''''''''''''''''''''''''''''''''''''''''''*/
SHORT dba_reset_db_cfg(PCHAR parm_str)
{
  BYTE              database_name[9];                /* Database name, null term*/

  /*'''''''''''''''''''''''''''''''''''''''''*/
  /* get the parm strings                    */
  /*'''''''''''''''''''''''''''''''''''''''''*/
  if (sscanf(parm_str, " %8s ", database_name) != parms.num_parms)
    {
      sprintf(err_msg, "\nSYNTAX ERROR: invalid parameters.");
      return(RECORD_ERR_MSG);
    }

  /*'''''''''''''''''''''''''''''''''''''''''*/
  /* call the RESET DATABASE CONFIG API      */
  /*'''''''''''''''''''''''''''''''''''''''''*/
  sqlfrdb(database_name,                                 /* database          */
          &sqlca);                                       /* SQLCA             */
  return(RECORD_SQLCA);
} /* end dba_reset_db_cfg */
```

Figure 30-25.   Reset Database Configuration Command Handler: dba_reset_db_cfg().

Update Database Configuration: dba_update_db_cfg()

The **dba_update_db_cfg()** command handler, whose code is listed in Figure 30-26, executes the RSQL command:

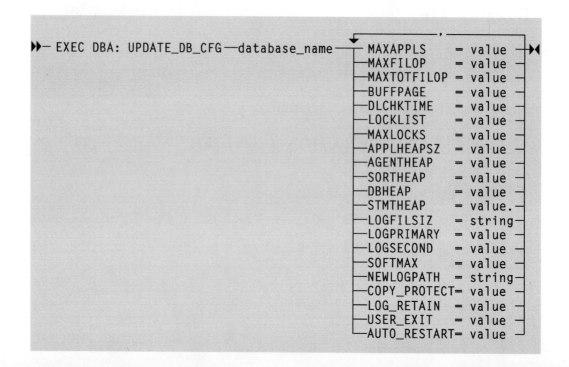

These parameters are all explained in "Database Administration API: Configuration Service" on page 638. The command handler first parses the database name. After that, its job is to create an entry for each of the configuration parameters specified in the RSQL command in a **db_cfg_array** of type **CONFG_ENTRY_TYPE**. This type is defined in RSQL.H and reproduced below for your convenience:

```
typedef struct
{
  USHORT        token;          /* which field to return    */
  CHAR          *ptrvalue;      /* where to put field info   */
} CONFG_ENTRY_TYPE;
```

The command handler parses the configuration parameters by iterating through a loop once for each parameter that is passed to it. This is what happens during each loop iteration:

1. The parameter name is parsed into the **parm_name** variable.
2. The helper routine **decode_dbcfg_string()** (see listing in Figure 30-27) is invoked and passed the parameter name. This routine takes the parameter name and looks up a Database Manager defined token constant for it. These tokens are defined in **sqlutil.h**. The routine then returns the token number, a pointer to a global variable, and the data type of that variable.
3. The command handler uses the returned type to parse the value on the right of the equal sign and convert it to the appropriate type. It does this by creating "on the fly" a type-specific **format_string**, which it then uses in conjunction with **sscanf()** to extract the parameter value and assign it to the global variable that the **ptrvalue** field in the array points to.

At the end of the loop, the command handler knows how many configuration items need to be updated and, for each item, it has created an entry in the **db_cfg_array**. The handler is now ready to issue the update database configuration API call **sqlfudb()**.

```
/*''''''''''''''''''''''''''''''''''''''''''''''''''''''''''''''''''''''''*/
/*   execute the UPDATE_DB_CFG DBA function                               */
/*''''''''''''''''''''''''''''''''''''''''''''''''''''''''''''''''''''''''*/
SHORT dba_update_db_cfg(PCHAR parm_str)
{
  CHAR    parm_name[15];             /* config token name        */
  SHORT   rcd;                       /* return code temp var     */
  USHORT  index;                     /* array index              */
  USHORT  parm_val_type;             /* config parm type         */
  CONFG_ENTRY_TYPE db_cfg_array[21]; /* array of token and item  */
                                     /*     parameters           */

  PCHAR   ptrvalue;                  /* var for 0:32 pointer     */
  CHAR    delimiter;                 /* config parm delimiter    */
  BYTE    database_name[9];          /* Database name, null term */
```

Figure 30-26 (Part 1 of 3). Update DB Config Handler: dba_update_db_cfg().

```
/*''''''''''''''''''''''''''''''''''''''''''*/
/* get the database name                     */
/*''''''''''''''''''''''''''''''''''''''''''*/
strcat(parm_str,";");                                      /* add a delimiter   */
if (sscanf(parm_str, " %8s %[^;] ", database_name, parm_str
        ) != parms.num_parms)
  {
    sprintf(err_msg, "\nSYNTAX ERROR: invalid parameters.");
    return(RECORD_ERR_MSG);
  }

/*''''''''''''''''''''''''''''''''''''''''''*/
/* get the parm strings and their values   */
/*    to form the configuration array       */
/*''''''''''''''''''''''''''''''''''''''''''*/
index=0;
do
 {
    /*''''''''''''''''''''''''''''''''''''''''''*/
    /* get a parm name                          */
    /*''''''''''''''''''''''''''''''''''''''''''*/
    strcat(parm_str,";");                                  /* add a delimiter   */
    if (sscanf(parm_str, " %14s = %[^;] ", parm_name, parm_str) != 2)
      {sprintf(err_msg, "\nSYNTAX ERROR: invalid parameters.");
        return(RECORD_ERR_MSG);
      }
    strcat(parm_str,";");                                  /* add a delimiter   */

    /*''''''''''''''''''''''''''''''''''''''''''*/
    /* convert to a parm number, value_ptr,    */
    /*    and value_type                        */
    /*''''''''''''''''''''''''''''''''''''''''''*/
    if (decode_dbcfg_string(parm_name, &db_cfg_array[index].token,
                         &ptrvalue, &parm_val_type))
       {sprintf(err_msg,
             "\nSYNTAX ERROR: Invalid configuration parameter %s.",
              parm_name);
        return(RECORD_ERR_MSG);
       }
    db_cfg_array[index].ptrvalue = ptrvalue;   /* assignment here causes  */
                                               /* 0:32 -> 16:16 pointer   */
                                               /* conversion              */
    /*''''''''''''''''''''''''''''''''''''''''''*/
    /* read the value                           */
    /*''''''''''''''''''''''''''''''''''''''''''*/
    switch (parm_val_type)
      {
        case SQL_TYP_SMALL:                              /* small integer(SHORT)*/
            rcd = sscanf(parm_str, " %hd %c %[^;]",
                         (PSHORT)ptrvalue, &delimiter, parm_str);
            break;
        case SQL_TYP_INTEGER:                            /* integer (LONG)     */
            rcd = sscanf(parm_str, " %d %c %[^;]",
                         (PLONG)ptrvalue, &delimiter, parm_str);
            break;
        case SQL_TYP_CSTR:                               /* c string           */
            rcd = sscanf(parm_str, " %[^ ,;] %c %[^;]",
                         ptrvalue, &delimiter, parm_str);
            break;
      } /* endswitch */
```

Figure 30-26 (Part 2 of 3).   Update DB Config Handler: dba_update_db_cfg().

```
      if ( ((delimiter == ';') && (rcd != 2)) ||
           ((delimiter == ',') && (rcd != 3)) ||
           ((delimiter != ',') && (delimiter != ';')) )
         {sprintf(err_msg,
                 "\nSYNTAX ERROR: Invalid configuration parameter %s.",
                 parm_name);
          return(RECORD_ERR_MSG);
         }

      ++index;                                          /* increment array index*/

   } while (delimiter != ';'); /* enddo */

   /*'''''''''''''''''''''''''''''''''''''''''*/
   /* call the UPDATE DB CONFIG API           */
   /*'''''''''''''''''''''''''''''''''''''''''*/
   sqlfudb(database_name,                           /* database name     */
           index,                                   /* number of items   */
           (struct sqlfupd *)db_cfg_array,          /* list of items     */
           &sqlca);                                 /* SQLCA             */

   return(RECORD_SQLCA);
} /* end dba_update_db_cfg */
```

Figure 30-26 (Part 3 of 3). Update DB Config Handler: dba_update_db_cfg().

The Helper Procedure: decode_dbcfg_string()

```
/*''''''''''''''''''''''''''''''''''''''''''''''''''''''''''''''''''''''''''''*/
/*  This procedure converts a parameter string into a value and a pointer     */
/*  to a variable and a type for update database manager configuration.       */
/*''''''''''''''''''''''''''''''''''''''''''''''''''''''''''''''''''''''''''''*/
SHORT decode_dbcfg_string(PCHAR    parm,
                          PUSHORT  parm_num,
                          PCHAR    *parm_val_ptr,
                          PUSHORT  parm_val_type)
{
   /*''''''''''''''''''''''''''''''''''''''''''''*/
   /* Initialize cmds table                      */
   /*''''''''''''''''''''''''''''''''''''''''''''*/
   typedef struct
   {
     CHAR      parm_str[40];              /* cmd name                          */
     SHORT     parm_num;                  /* numerical representation of cmd   */
     PCHAR     parm_val_ptr;              /* parameter value pointer           */
     SHORT     parm_val_type;             /* parameter value pointer           */
   }   PARM_TYPE;

   #define DBCFG_COUNT    21
   static PARM_TYPE parms[DBCFG_COUNT] =
     {/*<-parm_str><- parm_num--------><-- parm_val_ptr--------><-parm_val_type>*/
   {"LOCKLIST",    SQLF_DBTN_LOCKLIST,   (CHAR *)&dbcfg.locklist,   SQL_TYP_SMALL},
   {"BUFFPAGE",    SQLF_DBTN_BUFFPAGE,   (CHAR *)&dbcfg.buffpage,   SQL_TYP_SMALL},
   {"MAXFILOP",    SQLF_DBTN_MAXFILOP,   (CHAR *)&dbcfg.maxfilop,   SQL_TYP_SMALL},
   {"SOFTMAX",     SQLF_DBTN_SOFTMAX,    (CHAR *)&dbcfg.softmax,    SQL_TYP_SMALL},
   {"MAXAPPLS",    SQLF_DBTN_MAXAPPLS,   (CHAR *)&dbcfg.maxappls,   SQL_TYP_SMALL},
   {"APPLHEAPSZ" ,SQLF_DBTN_APPLHEAPSZ, (CHAR *)&dbcfg.applheapsz, SQL_TYP_SMALL},
```

Figure 30-27 (Part 1 of 2). The Helper Procedure: decode_dbcfg_string().

```
{"DBHEAP",       SQLF_DBTN_DBHEAP,       (CHAR *)&dbcfg.dbheap,     SQL_TYP_SMALL},
{"DLCHKTIME",    SQLF_DBTN_DLCHKTIME,    (CHAR *)&dbcfg.dlchktime,SQL_TYP_INTEGER},
{"MAXTOTFILOP",  SQLF_DBTN_MAXTOTFILOP,  (CHAR *)&dbcfg.maxtotfilop,SQL_TYP_SMALL},
{"SORTHEAP",     SQLF_DBTN_SORTHEAP,     (CHAR *)&dbcfg.sortheap,   SQL_TYP_SMALL},
{"AGENTHEAP",    SQLF_DBTN_AGENTHEAP,    (CHAR *)&dbcfg.agentheap,  SQL_TYP_SMALL},
{"MAXLOCKS",     SQLF_DBTN_MAXLOCKS,     (CHAR *)&dbcfg.maxlocks,   SQL_TYP_SMALL},
{"LOGPRIMARY",   SQLF_DBTN_LOGPRIMARY,   (CHAR *)&dbcfg.logprimary, SQL_TYP_SMALL},
{"LOGSECOND",    SQLF_DBTN_LOGSECOND,    (CHAR *)&dbcfg.logsecond,  SQL_TYP_SMALL},
{"LOGFILSIZ",    SQLF_DBTN_LOGFILSIZ,    (CHAR *)&dbcfg.logfilsiz,  SQL_TYP_SMALL},
{"STMTHEAP",     SQLF_DBTN_STMTHEAP,     (CHAR *)&dbcfg.stmtheap,   SQL_TYP_SMALL},
{"NEWLOGPATH",   SQLF_DBTN_NEWLOGPATH,   (CHAR *) dbcfg.newlogpath, SQL_TYP_CSTR },
{"COPY_PROTECT", SQLF_DBTN_COPY_PROTECT, (CHAR *)&dbcfg.copy_prot,  SQL_TYP_SMALL},
{"LOG_RETAIN",   SQLF_DBTN_LOG_RETAIN,   (CHAR *)&dbcfg.log_retain, SQL_TYP_SMALL},
{"USER_EXIT",    SQLF_DBTN_USER_EXIT,    (CHAR *)&dbcfg.user_exit,  SQL_TYP_SMALL},
{"AUTO_RESTART", SQLF_DBTN_AUTO_RESTART, (CHAR *)&dbcfg.auto_rest,  SQL_TYP_SMALL}
};

   SHORT      parm_not_found;           /* True if a match is found    */
   USHORT     i;                        /* loop index variable         */

   /*''''''''''''''''''''''''''''''''''''''''''*/
   /* decode the parm string                   */
   /*''''''''''''''''''''''''''''''''''''''''''*/
   i = 0 ;
   parm_not_found = TRUE ;

   while ( parm_not_found && (i < DBCFG_COUNT))
   {
     parm_not_found = strcmp(parms[i].parm_str,parm);
     if (!parm_not_found)
        break;
     else
        i++;
   }

   if (parm_not_found )
      {
       sprintf(err_msg,
         "\nSYNTAX ERROR: Unknown Configuration parameter string. ");
       return(FAILED);
      }
   else
      {
       *parm_num      = parms[i].parm_num;
       *parm_val_ptr  = parms[i].parm_val_ptr;
       *parm_val_type = parms[i].parm_val_type;
       return(GOOD);
      }
} /* end decode_dbcfg_string */
```

Figure 30-27 (Part 2 of 2).   The Helper Procedure: decode_dbcfg_string().

Show Database Configuration: dba_show_db_cfg()

The **dba_show_db_cfg()** command handler, whose code is listed in Figure 30-28, executes the RSQL command:

```
▶▶─EXEC DBA: SHOW_DB_CFG── database_name──────────────────────◀◀
```

This command handler will format and write all the configuration parameters to the *response* file for the specified database. This is how it does that:

1. A static C array of type CONFG_ENTRY_TYPE is initialized with an entry for each database parameter. You've already encountered this type in the previous section:

```
typedef struct
{
  USHORT        token;              /* which field to return   */
  CHAR          *ptrvalue;          /* where to put field info */
} CONFG_ENTRY_TYPE;
```

2. Each array entry is initialized to contain a token number (remember, these are defined by the Database Manager in **sqlutil.h**) and a pointer to a variable that will receive the value of the parameter. These variables are all part of a structure defined in RSQL.H.
3. The **sqlfxdbc()** API is called and told to go and fetch all 32 database parameters and put the results in the variables the **db_cfg_array** points to.
4. Finally, the results are formatted and inserted in the *response* file. If you are not clear on what those parameters do, please make sure to refer to the tutorial (see "Database Administration API: Configuration Service" on page 638).

```
/*-----------------------------------------------------------------*/
/*  execute the SHOW_DB_CFG DBA function                           */
/*-----------------------------------------------------------------*/
SHORT dba_show_db_cfg(PCHAR parm_str)
{
  static CONFG_ENTRY_TYPE db_cfg_array[] =        /* array of token and items*/
    {/*<--- token ------------------><-- pointer -------------------->*/
      {SQLF_DBTN_LOCKLIST         ,  (CHAR *)&dbcfg.locklist      },
      {SQLF_DBTN_BUFFPAGE         ,  (CHAR *)&dbcfg.buffpage      },
      {SQLF_DBTN_MAXFILOP         ,  (CHAR *)&dbcfg.maxfilop      },
      {SQLF_DBTN_SOFTMAX          ,  (CHAR *)&dbcfg.softmax       },
      {SQLF_DBTN_MAXAPPLS         ,  (CHAR *)&dbcfg.maxappls      },
      {SQLF_DBTN_APPLHEAPSZ       ,  (CHAR *)&dbcfg.applheapsz    },
      {SQLF_DBTN_DBHEAP           ,  (CHAR *)&dbcfg.dbheap        },
      {SQLF_DBTN_DLCHKTIME        ,  (CHAR *)&dbcfg.dlchktime     },
      {SQLF_DBTN_MAXTOTFILOP      ,  (CHAR *)&dbcfg.maxtotfilop   },
      {SQLF_DBTN_SORTHEAP         ,  (CHAR *)&dbcfg.sortheap      },
      {SQLF_DBTN_AGENTHEAP        ,  (CHAR *)&dbcfg.agentheap     },
      {SQLF_DBTN_MAXLOCKS         ,  (CHAR *)&dbcfg.maxlocks      },
      {SQLF_DBTN_LOGPRIMARY       ,  (CHAR *)&dbcfg.logprimary    },
      {SQLF_DBTN_LOGSECOND        ,  (CHAR *)&dbcfg.logsecond     },
      {SQLF_DBTN_LOGFILSIZ        ,  (CHAR *)&dbcfg.logfilsiz     },
      {SQLF_DBTN_STMTHEAP         ,  (CHAR *)&dbcfg.stmtheap      },
      {SQLF_DBTN_NEWLOGPATH       ,  (CHAR *) dbcfg.newlogpath    },
      {SQLF_DBTN_COPY_PROTECT     ,  (CHAR *)&dbcfg.copy_prot     },
      {SQLF_DBTN_LOG_RETAIN       ,  (CHAR *)&dbcfg.log_retain    },
      {SQLF_DBTN_USER_EXIT        ,  (CHAR *)&dbcfg.user_exit     },
      {SQLF_DBTN_AUTO_RESTART     ,  (CHAR *)&dbcfg.auto_rest     },
      {SQLF_DBTN_COUNTRY          ,  (CHAR *)&dbcfg.country       },
      {SQLF_DBTN_CODEPAGE         ,  (CHAR *)&dbcfg.codepage      },
      {SQLF_DBTN_RELEASE          ,  (CHAR *)&dbcfg.release       },
```

Figure 30-28 (Part 1 of 3). Show DB Config Command Handler: dba_show_db_cfg().

```
    {SQLF_DBTN_LOGPATH              ,  (CHAR *) dbcfg.logpath           },
    {SQLF_DBTN_CONSISTENT          ,  (CHAR *)&dbcfg.consistent        },
    {SQLF_DBTN_BACKUP_PENDING      ,  (CHAR *)&dbcfg.backup_pending    },
    {SQLF_DBTN_ROLLFWD_PENDING     ,  (CHAR *)&dbcfg.rollfwd_pending   },
    {SQLF_DBTN_LOG_RETAIN_STATUS   ,  (CHAR *)&dbcfg.log_retain_status },
    {SQLF_DBTN_USER_EXIT_STATUS    ,  (CHAR *)&dbcfg.user_exit_status  },
    {SQLF_DBTN_LOGHEAD             ,  (CHAR *) dbcfg.loghead           },
    {SQLF_DBTN_NEXTACTIVE         ,  (CHAR *) dbcfg.nextactive        }
  };

BYTE    database_name[9];                          /* Database name, null term*/

/*'''''''''''''''''''''''''''''''''''''''''''''''*/
/* get the parm strings                          */
/*'''''''''''''''''''''''''''''''''''''''''''''''*/
if (sscanf(parm_str, " %8s ", database_name
          ) != parms.num_parms)
    {
      sprintf(err_msg, "\nSYNTAX ERROR: invalid parameters.");
      return(RECORD_ERR_MSG);
    }

/*'''''''''''''''''''''''''''''''''''''''''''''''*/
/* call the GET DB CONFIG API                    */
/*'''''''''''''''''''''''''''''''''''''''''''''''*/
sqlfxdb(database_name,                             /* database            */
        32,                                        /* num of fields reqd  */
        (struct sqlfupd   *)db_cfg_array,          /* array of cfg items  */
        &sqlca);                                   /* SQLCA               */

if (SQLCODE != 0)
  return(RECORD_SQLCA);                            /* command failed      */

/*'''''''''''''''''''''''''''''''''''''''''''''''*/
/* record the results                            */
/*'''''''''''''''''''''''''''''''''''''''''''''''*/
fprintf(out_stream,
"\n Database Configuration for Database %s"
"\n ==========================================="
"\n\n Configuration Parameter          Current  Parm.      Parm.      Parm."
"\n Description                        Value    Units      Range      Default"
"\n ------------------------------ -------- ---------- ---------- -------",
database_name);
fprintf(out_stream,
"\n Max. Active Applications         %5d    Appl.      1-256         8"
"\n Max. DB Files Open/Application   %5d    files      2-235        20"
"\n Max. Files Open/Application      %5d    files      25-32700    255"
"\n Buffer Pool Size                 %5d    4K pages   2-1500       (1)"
"\n Time Interval for Deadlocks      %9ld   millisecs. 1-600 sec.   10",
dbcfg.maxappls, dbcfg.maxfilop, dbcfg.maxtotfilop,
dbcfg.buffpage, dbcfg.dlchktime);
fprintf(out_stream,
"\n Max. Storage for Locklists       %5d    4K pages   4-250         8"
"\n Max. percent locklist/appl.      %5d    percent    1-100        22"
"\n Default Application Heap         %5d    segments   2-20          3"
"\n Application Agent Heap           %5d    segments   2-85          2"
"\n Sort List Heap                   %5d    segments   1-20          2"
"\n Database Heap                    %5d    segments   1-45         (2)"
"\n SQL Statement Heap               %5d    segments   8-255        64",
dbcfg.locklist, dbcfg.maxlocks, dbcfg.applheapsz, dbcfg.agentheap,
dbcfg.sortheap, dbcfg.dbheap, dbcfg.stmtheap);
fprintf(out_stream,
```

Figure 30-28 (Part 2 of 3).   Show DB Config Command Handler: dba_show_db_cfg().

```
 "\n Log File Size                      %5d   4K pages   4-65535      (3)"

 "\n Primary Log Files                  %5d   files      2-63          3"
 "\n Secondary Log Files                %5d   files      0-61          2"
 "\n Log Records/soft checkpoint        %5d   records    0-65535     100",
 dbcfg.logfilsiz, dbcfg.logprimary, dbcfg.logsecond, dbcfg.softmax);
 fprintf(out_stream,
 "\n\n Current Log Location = %-80.80s"
 "\n New Log Location      = %-80.80s"
 "\n First Log File        = %-80.80s"
 "\n Current Log File      = %-80.80s",
 dbcfg.logpath, dbcfg.newlogpath, dbcfg.loghead, dbcfg.nextactive);
 fprintf(out_stream,
 "\n Copy Protection       = %5d (1 = Protected, Default = 1)"
 "\n Log Retain            = %5d (1 = Retain Log Files, Default = 0)"
 "\n User Exit             = %5d (1 = Enable User Exit, Default = 0)"
 "\n Auto Restart          = %5d (1 = Enable Auto Restart, Default = 1)"
 "\n Country               = %5d"
 "\n Code Page             = %5d"
 "\n Release               = %5d",
 dbcfg.copy_prot, dbcfg.log_retain, dbcfg.user_exit, dbcfg.auto_rest,
 dbcfg.country, dbcfg.codepage, dbcfg.release);
 fprintf(out_stream,
 "\n DB Consistency        = %5d (1 = Consistent)"
 "\n Backup Pending        = %5d (1 = Backup Pending)"
 "\n Roll Forward Pending  = %5d (1 = Roll Forward Pending)"
 "\n User Exit Status      = %5d (1 = User exit Enabled)"
 "\n Log Retain Status     = %5d (1 = log files retained)"
 "\n\n (1) - client or standalone 25, server 250"
 "\n (2) - client or standalone  2, server   3"
 "\n (3) - client or standalone 32, server 200",
 dbcfg.consistent, dbcfg.backup_pending, dbcfg.rollfwd_pending,
 dbcfg.user_exit_status, dbcfg.log_retain_status);

 return(RECORD_SQLCA);
} /* end dba_show_db_cfg */
```

Figure 30-28 (Part 3 of 3).   Show DB Config Command Handler: dba_show_db_cfg().

Reset Database Mgr Configuration: dba_reset_dm_cfg()

The **dba_reset_dm_cfg**() command handler, whose code is listed in Figure 30-29, executes the RSQL command:

▶▶── EXEC DBA: RESET_DM_CFG───▶◀

This command handler simply issues an **sqlfrsys**() API call.

```
/*············································································*/
/*   execute the RESET_DM_CFG DBA function                                  */
/*············································································*/
SHORT dba_reset_dm_cfg(VOID)
{
  sqlfrsys(&sqlca);                                         /* SQLCA         */
  return(RECORD_SQLCA);
} /* end dba_reset_dm_cfg */
```

Figure 30-29.   Reset Database Mgr Config Handler: dba_reset_dm_cfg().

Update Database Mgr Configuration: dba_update_dm_cfg()

The **dba_update_dm_cfg**() command handler, whose code is listed in Figure 30-30, executes the RSQL command:

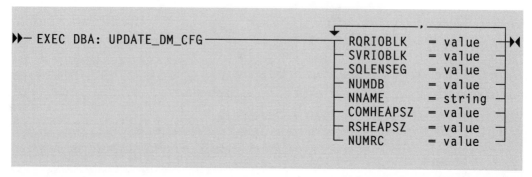

This command handler is like "Update Database Configuration: dba_update_db_cfg()" on page 772. The API uses the same "array of tokens and pointers" mechanism to pass the values of the parameters to be updated. The different tokens are obtained by calling the helper routine **decode_dmcfg_string**() (see listing in Figure 30-31). This helper routine works just like **decode_dbcfg_string**(), but uses a different internal look-up table for its tokens. The API call **sqlfisys**() is issued instead of **sqlfudb**().

```
/*''''''''''''''''''''''''''''''''''''''''''''''''''''''''''''''''''''''''*/
/*  execute the UPDATE_DM_CFG DBA function                                */
/*''''''''''''''''''''''''''''''''''''''''''''''''''''''''''''''''''''''''*/
SHORT dba_update_dm_cfg(PCHAR parm_str)
{
  CHAR    parm_name[12];                        /* config token name      */
  SHORT   rcd;                                  /* return code temp var   */
  USHORT  index;                                /* array index            */
  USHORT  parm_val_type;                        /* config parm type       */
  PCHAR   ptrvalue;                             /* var for 0:32 pointer    */
  CONFG_ENTRY_TYPE dm_cfg_array[8];             /* configuration array    */
  CHAR    delimiter;                            /* config parm delimiter  */

  /*'''''''''''''''''''''''''''''''''''''''''''''*/
  /* get the parm strings and their values      */
  /*    to form the configuration array         */
  /*'''''''''''''''''''''''''''''''''''''''''''''*/
  index=0;
  do
    {
    /*'''''''''''''''''''''''''''''''''''''''''''''*/
    /* get a parm name                            */
    /*'''''''''''''''''''''''''''''''''''''''''''''*/
    strcat(parm_str,";");                               /* add a delimiter    */
    if (sscanf(parm_str, " %11s = %[^;] ", parm_name, parm_str) != 2)
      {sprintf(err_msg, "\nSYNTAX ERROR: invalid parameters.");
       return(RECORD_ERR_MSG);
      }
    strcat(parm_str,";");                               /* add a delimiter    */
```

Figure 30-30 (Part 1 of 2). Update DB Mgr Config Handler: dba_update_dm_cfg().

```
/*''''''''''''''''''''''''''''''''''''''''''*/
/* convert to a parm number, value_ptr,    */
/*    and value_type                       */
/*''''''''''''''''''''''''''''''''''''''''''*/
if (decode_dmcfg_string(parm_name, &dm_cfg_array[index].token,
                        &ptrvalue, &parm_val_type))
   {sprintf(err_msg,
            "\nSYNTAX ERROR: Invalid configuration parameter %s.",
            parm_name);
    return(RECORD_ERR_MSG);
   }
dm_cfg_array[index].ptrvalue = ptrvalue;   /* assignment here causes  */
                                           /* 0:32 -> 16:16 pointer   */
                                           /* conversion              */


/*''''''''''''''''''''''''''''''''''''''''''*/
/* read the value                          */
/*''''''''''''''''''''''''''''''''''''''''''*/
switch (parm_val_type)
   {
   case SQL_TYP_SMALL:                              /* small integer(SHORT)*/
        rcd = sscanf(parm_str, " %hd %c %[^;]",
                     (PSHORT)ptrvalue, &delimiter, parm_str);

        break;
   case SQL_TYP_INTEGER:                            /* integer (LONG)     */
        rcd = sscanf(parm_str, " %d %c %[^;]",
                     (PLONG)ptrvalue, &delimiter, parm_str);

        break;
   case SQL_TYP_CSTR:                               /* c string          */
        rcd = sscanf(parm_str, " %[^ ,;] %c %[^;]",
                     ptrvalue, &delimiter, parm_str);

        break;
   } /* endswitch */

if ( ((delimiter == ';') && (rcd != 2)) ||
     ((delimiter == ',') && (rcd != 3)) ||
     ((delimiter != ',') && (delimiter != ';')) )
   {sprintf(err_msg,
            "\nSYNTAX ERROR: Invalid configuration parameter %s.",
            parm_name);
    return(RECORD_ERR_MSG);
   }

++index;                                          /* increment array index*/

} while (delimiter != ';'); /* enddo */

/*''''''''''''''''''''''''''''''''''''''''''*/
/* call the UPDATE DM CONFIG API           */
/*''''''''''''''''''''''''''''''''''''''''''*/
sqlfusys(index,                                   /* number of items   */
         (struct sqlfupd   *)dm_cfg_array,        /* list of items     */
         &sqlca);                                 /* SQLCA             */

return(RECORD_SQLCA);
} /* end dba_update_dm_cfg */
```

Figure 30-30 (Part 2 of 2). Update DB Mgr Config Handler: dba_update_dm_cfg().

The Helper Procedure: decode_dmcfg_string()

```
/*''''''''''''''''''''''''''''''''''''''''''''''''''''''''''''''''''''''''''*/
/*  This procedure converts a parameter string into a value and a pointer   */
/*  to a variable and a type for update database manager configuration.     */
/*''''''''''''''''''''''''''''''''''''''''''''''''''''''''''''''''''''''''''*/
SHORT decode_dmcfg_string(PCHAR    parm,
                          PUSHORT parm_num,
                          PCHAR   *parm_val_ptr,
                          PUSHORT parm_val_type)
{
  /*'''''''''''''''''''''''''''''''''''''''''*/
  /* Initialize cmds table                   */
  /*'''''''''''''''''''''''''''''''''''''''''*/
  typedef struct
  {
    CHAR       parm_str[40];             /* cmd name                        */
    SHORT      parm_num;                 /* numerical representation of cmd */
    PCHAR      parm_val_ptr;             /* parameter value pointer         */
    SHORT      parm_val_type;            /* parameter value pointer         */
  }  PARM_TYPE;

  #define DMCFG_COUNT      8
  static PARM_TYPE parms[DMCFG_COUNT] =
  {/*<-parm_str><- parm_num-------><-- parm_val_ptr--------><-parm_val_type>*/
    {"RQRIOBLK", SQLF_KTN_RQRIOBLK, (CHAR *)&dmcfg.rqrioblk,  SQL_TYP_SMALL},
    {"SVRIOBLK", SQLF_KTN_SVRIOBLK, (CHAR *)&dmcfg.svrioblk,  SQL_TYP_SMALL},
    {"SQLENSEG", SQLF_KTN_SQLENSEG, (CHAR *)&dmcfg.sqlenseg,  SQL_TYP_SMALL},
    {"NUMDB",    SQLF_KTN_NUMDB,    (CHAR *)&dmcfg.numdb,     SQL_TYP_SMALL},
    {"NNAME",    SQLF_KTN_NNAME,    (CHAR *) dmcfg.nname,     SQL_TYP_CSTR },
    {"COMHEAPSZ",SQLF_KTN_COMHEAPSZ,(CHAR *)&dmcfg.comheapsz, SQL_TYP_SMALL},
    {"RSHEAPSZ", SQLF_KTN_RSHEAPSZ, (CHAR *)&dmcfg.rsheapsz,  SQL_TYP_SMALL},
    {"NUMRC",    SQLF_KTN_NUMRC,    (CHAR *)&dmcfg.numrc,     SQL_TYP_SMALL}
  };

  SHORT       parm_not_found;           /* True if a match is found         */
  USHORT      i;                        /* loop index variable              */

  /*'''''''''''''''''''''''''''''''''''''''''*/
  /* decode the parm string                  */
  /*'''''''''''''''''''''''''''''''''''''''''*/
  i = 0 ;
  parm_not_found = TRUE ;

  while ( parm_not_found && (i < DMCFG_COUNT))
  {
    parm_not_found = strcmp(parms[i].parm_str,parm);
    if (!parm_not_found)
       break;
    else
       i++;
  }

  if (parm_not_found )
    {
      sprintf(err_msg,
        "\nSYNTAX ERROR: Unknown Configuration parameter string. ");
      return(FAILED);
    }
  else
```

Figure 30-31 (Part 1 of 2). The Helper Procedure: decode_dmcfg_string().

```
      {
       *parm_num      = parms[i].parm_num;
       *parm_val_ptr  = parms[i].parm_val_ptr;
       *parm_val_type = parms[i].parm_val_type;
       return(GOOD);
      }
} /* end decode_dmcfg_string */
```

Figure 30-31 (Part 2 of 2). The Helper Procedure: decode_dmcfg_string().

Show Database Mgr Configuration: dba_show_dm_cfg()

The **dba_show_dm_cfg()** command handler, whose code is listed in Figure 30-32, executes the RSQL command:

```
▶▶— EXEC DBA: SHOW_DM_CFG ——————————————————————◀◀
```

This command handler works just like the one in "Show Database Configuration: dba_show_db_cfg()" on page 776, with the following exceptions:

- The **sqlfxsys()** API call is issued instead of **sqlfxdbc()**.
- The results are formatted differently, which is to be expected because we're displaying Database Manager-related parameters instead of Database-related parameters.

```
/*'''''''''''''''''''''''''''''''''''''''''''''''''''''''''''''''''''''''''''''*/
/*  execute the SHOW_DM_CFG DBA function                                       */
/*'''''''''''''''''''''''''''''''''''''''''''''''''''''''''''''''''''''''''''''*/
SHORT dba_show_dm_cfg(VOID)
{
 static CONFIG_ENTRY_TYPE dm_cfg_array[] =         /* array of token and items*/
    {/*<--- token ------------><-- pointer -------------------->*/
     {SQLF_KTN_NODETYPE      ,  (CHAR *)&dmcfg.nodetype    },
     {SQLF_KTN_RQRIOBLK      ,  (CHAR *)&dmcfg.rqrioblk    },
     {SQLF_KTN_SVRIOBLK      ,  (CHAR *)&dmcfg.svrioblk    },
     {SQLF_KTN_SQLENSEG      ,  (CHAR *)&dmcfg.sqlenseg    },
     {SQLF_KTN_NUMDB         ,  (CHAR *)&dmcfg.numdb       },
     {SQLF_KTN_NNAME         ,  (CHAR *) dmcfg.nname       },
     {SQLF_KTN_COMHEAPSZ     ,  (CHAR *)&dmcfg.comheapsz   },
     {SQLF_KTN_RSHEAPSZ      ,  (CHAR *)&dmcfg.rsheapsz    },
     {SQLF_KTN_NUMRC         ,  (CHAR *)&dmcfg.numrc       },
     {SQLF_KTN_RELEASE       ,  (CHAR *)&dmcfg.release     },
    };

    /*'''''''''''''''''''''''''''''''''''''''''''''*/
    /* call the GET DM CONFIG API                  */
    /*'''''''''''''''''''''''''''''''''''''''''''''*/
    sqlfxsys(10,                                        /* num of fields reqd. */
             (struct sqlfupd   *)dm_cfg_array,          /* array of cfg items  */
             &sqlca);                                   /* SQLCA               */

    if (SQLCODE != 0)
      return(RECORD_SQLCA);                             /* command failed      */
```

Figure 30-32 (Part 1 of 2). Show DB Mgr Config Handler: dba_show_dm_cfg().

```
/*''''''''''''''''''''''''''''''''''''''''''*/
/* record the results                       */
/*''''''''''''''''''''''''''''''''''''''''''*/
fprintf(out_stream,
"\n Database Manager Configuration"
"\n =============================="
"\n\n Configuration Parameter         Current  Parm.      Parm.      Parm."
"\n Description                       Value   Units      Range      Default"
"\n ------------------------------- -------- ---------- ---------- -------"
);
fprintf(out_stream,
"\n Max. Shared Segments              %5d   Segments   1-255      0,3,2,2 (1)"
"\n Max. Concurrently Active apps.    %5d   Number     1-8   (3)  3,8,0,3 (1)"
"\n Max. Reqestor I/O Block Size      %5d   bytes      4k-64k(2)  0,4,4,4 (1)"
"\n Max. Server  I/O Block Size       %5d   bytes      4k-64k(2)  0,4,0,0 (1)"
"\n Communication Heap Size           %5d   Segments   1-255 (2)  0,4,3,3 (1)",
dmcfg.sqlenseg, dmcfg.numdb, dmcfg.rqrioblk, dmcfg.svrioblk, dmcfg.comheapsz);
fprintf(out_stream,
"\n Remote Data Services Heap size    %5d   Segments   1-255 (2)  0,3,2,2 (1)"
"\n Max. Remote Connections           %5d   Number     1-255 (2) 0,10,3,3 (1)"
"\n\n Node Type     = %8d"
"\n Node Name     = %8.8s"
"\n Release Level = %5d"
"\n\n (1) - Standalone, Server, Client, Client w/Local DB"
"\n (2) - Standalone range = 0"
"\n (3) - Client range     = 0",
dmcfg.rsheapsz, dmcfg.numrc, dmcfg.nodetype, dmcfg.nname, dmcfg.release);

return(RECORD_SQLCA);
} /* end dba_show_dm_cfg */
```

Figure 30-32 (Part 2 of 2). Show DB Mgr Config Handler: dba_show_dm_cfg().

RSQL.SQC: APPLICATION SERVICES COMMAND HANDLERS

BIND: dba_bind()

The **dba_bind()** command handler, whose code is listed in Figure 30-33, executes the RSQL command:

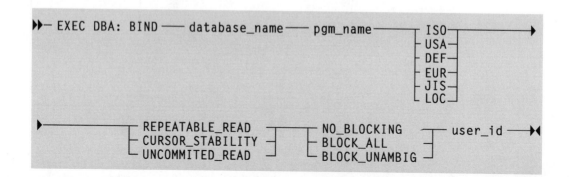

These parameters are all explained in the tutorial in Chapter 27. We're only interested here in how the command handler conveys that information using the **sqlabndr()** API call. This is done as follows:

1. The parameters are parsed in the usual manner.

2. The parameters that need to be converted from strings to numbers are passed to **decode_parm_string()**, which does its usual magic.

3. The next step is to fill in the contents of **bind_options**, a structure of type SQLOPT. This structure has a fixed header portion and a variable array of elements. The BIND API has four options, so we set the header's *allocated* field to four. We allocate an array of four option elements, and place in each element the option type and a pointer to the option value. The four option types are:

    - **SQL_FRMT_OPT** defines the date-time format, such as ISO or USA.
    - **SQL_ISO_OPT** defines the isolation level of the program, such as Read Repeatability or Cursor Stability.
    - **SQL_BLOCK_OPT** defines the blocking, such as BLOCK_ALL.
    - **SQL_GRANT_OPT** defines the grant ID.

4. The **sqlabndr()** call is then issued to do the BIND.

5. The **merge_file()** helper function is called (see Figure 30-20) to append the contents of the **msgfile** to the *response* file.

```
/************************************************************************/
/*   execute the BIND DBA function                                      */
/************************************************************************/
SHORT dba_bind(PCHAR parm_str)
{
  typedef struct
  {
    SHORT length;
    BYTE  data[9];
  } GRANTID;
  GRANTID  grant_id;                   /* grant id for bind               */

  typedef struct                       /* options structure for binder    */
  {
    struct sqloptheader                /* Header for sqlopt structur       */
    {
      ULONG allocated;                 /* Number of options allocated      */
      ULONG used;                      /* Number of options used           */
    } header;
    struct sqlbindopt                  /* Array of bind options            */
    {
      ULONG type;                      /* Type of bind option              */
      ULONG val;                       /* Value of bind option             */
    } option[3];
    struct                             /* Array of bind options            */
    {
```

Figure 30-33 (Part 1 of 2). Bind Command Handler: dba_bind().

```
         ULONG type;                          /* Type of bind option        */
         GRANTID * _Seg16 val;                /* Value of bind option       */
    } grantopt[1];
 } SQLOPT;

 SQLOPT bind_options;                         /* variable for binder options  */
 USHORT date_time_option;                     /* temp variable for option value */
 USHORT isolation_level_option;               /* temp variable for option value */
 USHORT blocking_option;                      /* temp variable for option value */
 BYTE   database_name[9];                     /* Database name, null terminated */
 CHAR   pgm_name[80];                         /* Path name bind file, null term. */
 CHAR   date_time_format[4];                  /* ISO, DEF, USA etc. null term. */
 CHAR   isolation_level[17];                  /* isolation level for bind     */
 CHAR   blocking_type[14];                    /* type of blocking for bind    */

 /*''''''''''''''''''''''''''''''''''''''''*/
 /* get the parm strings                   */
 /*''''''''''''''''''''''''''''''''''''''''*/
 if (sscanf(parm_str, " %8s %80s %4s %17s %14s %8s ",
                   database_name, pgm_name, date_time_format,
                   isolation_level, blocking_type, grant_id.data)
              != parms.num_parms)
   {
     sprintf(err_msg, "\nSYNTAX ERROR: invalid parameters.");
     return(RECORD_ERR_MSG);
   }

 grant_id.length = strlen(grant_id.data);     /* calculate grant id length */

 /*''''''''''''''''''''''''''''''''''''''''*/
 /* decode the parms, set up options struc. */
 /*''''''''''''''''''''''''''''''''''''''''*/
 if ( decode_parm_string(date_time_format, &date_time_option) ||
      decode_parm_string(isolation_level,  &isolation_level_option) ||
      decode_parm_string(blocking_type,    &blocking_option) )
   {
     sprintf(err_msg, "\nSYNTAX ERROR: invalid parameter.");
     return(RECORD_ERR_MSG);
   }

 bind_options.header.allocated = 4;
 bind_options.header.used      = 4;
 bind_options.option[0].type   = SQL_FRMT_OPT;
 bind_options.option[0].val    = (ULONG)date_time_option;
 bind_options.option[1].type   = SQL_ISO_OPT;
 bind_options.option[1].val    = (ULONG)isolation_level_option;
 bind_options.option[2].type   = SQL_BLOCK_OPT;
 bind_options.option[2].val    = (ULONG)blocking_option;
 bind_options.grantopt[0].type = SQL_GRANT_OPT;
 bind_options.grantopt[0].val  = &grant_id;

 /*''''''''''''''''''''''''''''''''''''''''*/
 /* call the bind API                      */
 /*''''''''''''''''''''''''''''''''''''''''*/
 sqlabndr(pgm_name,                           /* name of program to BIND  */
          database_name,                      /* database name            */
          msgfile,                            /* message file name        */
          (struct sqlopt *)&bind_options,     /* options structure        */
          &sqlca);                            /* SQLCA                    */
 merge_file(out_stream,msgfile);
 return(RECORD_SQLCA);
} /* end dba_bind */
```

Figure 30-33 (Part 2 of 2).   Bind Command Handler: dba_bind().

RSQL.SQC: GENERIC SERVICES COMMAND HANDLERS

LOG ON: dba_logon()

The **dba_logon()** command handler, whose code is listed in Figure 30-34, executes the RSQL command:

This command handler parses its parameters and issues a **upmelgn()** API call.

```
/**********************************************************************/
/*   execute the LOGON DBA function                                   */
/**********************************************************************/
SHORT dba_logon(PCHAR parm_str)
{
  CHAR   password[9];                    /* Current password, null terminat. */
  CHAR   userid[9];                      /* logon ID                         */
  CHAR   remote_name[9];                 /* name of a remote node            */
  USHORT remote_type;                    /* logon type                       */
  USHORT authority_check;                /* authority required for logon     */
  CHAR   remote_type_parm[11];           /* logon type                       */
  CHAR   authority_check_parm[11];       /* authority required for logon     */

  /*****************************************/
  /* get the parm strings                  */
  /*****************************************/
  if (sscanf(parm_str, " %8s %8s %8s %10s %10s ",
                      userid, password, remote_name, remote_type_parm,
                      authority_check_parm)
                  != parms.num_parms)
    {
     sprintf(err_msg, "\nSYNTAX ERROR: invalid parameters.");
     return(RECORD_ERR_MSG);
    }

  if ( decode_parm_string(remote_type_parm,     &remote_type) ||
     decode_parm_string(authority_check_parm, &authority_check) )
    {
     sprintf(err_msg, "\nSYNTAX ERROR: invalid parameter.");
     return(RECORD_ERR_MSG);
    }

  /*********************************************/
  /* call the LOGON  API                       */
  /*********************************************/
```

Figure 30-34 (Part 1 of 2). LOG ON Command Handler: dba_logon().

```
   api_rcd = upmelgn (userid,                           /* userid          */
                      password,                          /* password        */
                      remote_name,                       /* remotename      */
                      remote_type,                       /* remote type     */
                      authority_check);                  /* authority_check */

   return(RECORD_API_RCD);
} /* end dba_logon */
```

Figure 30-34 (Part 2 of 2). LOG ON Command Handler: dba_logon().

LOG OFF: dba_logoff()

The **dba_logoff**() command handler, whose code is listed in Figure 30-35, executes the
RSQL command:

```
▶▶─ EXEC DBA: LOGOFF ─ user_id ── remotename ─┬─ UPM_LOCAL ─┬──────────────▶◀
                                              ├─ UPM_DNODE ─┤
                                              └─ UPM_DOMAIN ┘
```

This command handler parses its parameters and issues a **upmelgff**() API call.

```
/*''''''''''''''''''''''''''''''''''''''''''''''''''''''''''''''''''''''*/
/*  execute the LOGOFF DBA function                                     */
/*''''''''''''''''''''''''''''''''''''''''''''''''''''''''''''''''''''''*/
SHORT dba_logoff(PCHAR parm_str)
{
  CHAR   userid[9];                     /* logon ID                     */
  CHAR   remote_name[9];                /* name of a remote node        */
  USHORT remote_type;                   /* logon type                   */
  CHAR   remote_type_parm[11];          /* logon type                   */

  /*''''''''''''''''''''''''''''''''''''''''''''''''*/
  /* get the parm strings                           */
  /*''''''''''''''''''''''''''''''''''''''''''''''''*/
  if (sscanf(parm_str, " %8s %8s %10s ",
                       userid, remote_name, remote_type_parm)
                  != parms.num_parms)
     {
     sprintf(err_msg, "\nSYNTAX ERROR: invalid parameters.");
     return(RECORD_ERR_MSG);
     }
  if (decode_parm_string(remote_type_parm, &remote_type))
     {
     sprintf(err_msg, "\nSYNTAX ERROR: invalid parameter.");
     return(RECORD_ERR_MSG);
     }

  /*''''''''''''''''''''''''''''''''''''''''''''''''*/
  /* call the LOGOFF API                            */
  /*''''''''''''''''''''''''''''''''''''''''''''''''*/
  api_rcd = upmelgff(userid,                            /* userid          */
                     remote_name,                       /* remotename      */
                     remote_type);                      /* remote type     */
  return(RECORD_API_RCD);
} /* end dba_logoff */
```

Figure 30-35. LOG OFF Command Handler: dba_logoff().

Part V

Why Transaction Servers
Are Best for OLTP

The chapters in Part V introduce you to the issues of Online Transaction Processing (*OLTP*) client/server computing by developing and running the famous TP1 benchmark for OLTP. The recent TP1 Database Benchmark Wars, conducted as if they were major Olympic Game events, captured a great deal of attention in the industry and a large number of column-inches in the press. But benchmarking can contribute more than just comparing the maximum performances of various vendors' database engines. In Part V, we will introduce a new TP1 Olympic event. We will conduct TP1 races that measure the performance of different client/server architectures. Instead of telling you which is the world's fastest database server, we will show *what really matters in client/server design* using the TP1 benchmark:

- How slow is Dynamic SQL?
- Which is faster, a Transaction Server or a Database Server?
- What is the effect of CPU speed?
- What is the effect of the database cache?
- What is the effect of the *network* on transaction performance?
- How well does the Database Manager's *Application Remote Interface* perform. Can you do better with a native Named Pipes do-it-yourself TP monitor?

The answers to these questions will help you make the right design trade-offs in the client/server applications you create. To avoid refueling the benchmark wars (and, of course, to create a common testbed for our evaluation), we limited our tests to a single database product, the OS/2 Database Manager. These tests allow us to study architectural issues that affect performance, while maintaining other things equal. Our tests differ radically from the previous TP1 benchmarks in that we focus on *relative* performance measurements of client/server architectures instead of on maximum raw performance. This difference leads us, for example, to purposely run our tests on commonly available 80486 type machines and on a 4 MBit/s Token Ring. We chose not to run the tests on top-of-the-line "superservers" (from IBM, Compaq, Netframe or Parallan), because we are deliberately not trying to test the Database Manager's maximum performance or how it compares with other vendor products.

The major programming effort in Part V is to develop a *Transaction Benchmark Kit* for the Database Manager using **TP1**, the industry's best-known OLTP benchmark. Our toolkit will include the old favorites: MULTI, RSQL, and Named Pipes. It will also include a multiuser Transaction Server kernel and a set of specially designed TP1 database programs that demonstrate the techniques and performance trade-offs in networked client/server software. We will provide four flavors of the TP1 benchmark:

1. A *Database Server* flavor that uses Static SQL and Database Manager's Remote Data Services(RDS).
2. A *Database Server* flavor that uses Dynamic SQL and the Database Manager's Remote Data Services.
3. A *Transaction Server* flavor that uses the Database Manager's standard stored procedures: the **Database Application Remote Interface**. The TP1 transaction is coded in Static SQL.
4. A *Transaction Server* flavor that uses Named Pipes and a "do-it-yourself" version of "stored procedures." The TP1 transaction is coded in Static SQL.

The toolkit is an excellent learning aid, which you can use to compare the performance of the various client/server alternatives. It is especially good at measuring the perform-ance of remote services on a network server.

Here is the roadmap we will follow in Part V:

- In Chapter 31, "A Transaction Benchmark Kit for the Database Manager," we introduce the *Transaction Benchmark Kit* for the Database Manager. This chapter covers OLTP benchmark considerations and provides toolkit components for creat-ing and loading a TP1 database.
- In Chapter 32, "The Static SQL Database Server TP1," we develop a *Database Server* version of TP1 that uses static SQL and can be run either on the same machine as the server or on a remote machine using **Remote Data Services** (RDS).
- In Chapter 33, "The Application Remote Interface Transaction Server TP1," we develop a *Transaction Server* version of TP1, where the communications is provided by the **Application Remote Interface** services.
- In Chapter 34, "The Named Pipes Transaction Server TP1," we develop a *Transac-tion Server* version of TP1 including a "do-it-yourself" remote Named Pipes server.
- In Chapter 35, "The Dynamic SQL Database Server TP1," we develop a *Database Server* version of TP1 that uses Dynamic SQL. We expect this version to be the poorest performer of the bunch. We've included it in the series so that we can gather some empirical measurements on performance trade-offs between static SQL and the more flexible but much slower Dynamic SQL.
- In Chapter 36, "Transaction Servers Are Best for OLTP," we present a summary of the TP1 benchmark results and some observations on the design of OLTP applica-tions using the client/server model.

Chapter 31

A Transaction Benchmark Kit
for the Database Manager

This chapter starts us on a new journey, which takes us into the world of benchmarks designed to measure the power of transaction servers. With SQL database servers becoming commodity items, benchmarks have become a powerful marketing tool for differentiating the SQL Ferraris from the Volkswagens. This is called "benchmarketing." We will introduce you to **TP1**, the industry's best-known benchmark for Online Transaction Processing (or **OLTP**). This is the benchmark that can make or break a company in the lucrative OLTP market. TP1 has become the universal test of SQL engine "machismo." It defines a contest in which all can participate, from the largest mainframe database engines to Database Manager running on a PC. The unit of measure in this race is the dollar price of a transaction per second (or **tps**). The server that provides the lowest-priced **tps** wins!

THE TP1 BENCHMARK MARATHON SERIES

Our journey spans over six chapters and will take us straight into the heart of TP1. We will do this by writing our *own* version of a TP1 toolkit for the OS/2 Database Manager. This toolkit includes the old favorites: MULTI, RSQL, and Named Pipes. It will also include a set of specially designed TP1 database programs that demonstrate the techniques and performance trade-offs in networked client/server software. Here's how this six-chapter marathon is organized:

- The first chapter in the series introduces the benchmark kit and covers the following areas:

  1. OLTP benchmark considerations and the definition of the TP1 benchmark
  2. The constituents of our TP1 benchmark kit and how it departs from the standard
  3. The toolkit components for creating and loading the TP1 database
  4. The *make* files for our benchmark programs

- The second chapter in the series provides a *Database Server* version of the TP1 transaction that uses static SQL. This version can be run either on the same machine

791

as the server or on a remote machine using **Remote Data Services** (RDS). The TP1 transaction performance will be measured using the following configurations:

1. On a local versus remote database server
2. On a slower server versus a faster server
3. On the same server but using different buffer pool sizes

- The third chapter in the series provides a *Transaction Server* version of the TP1 transaction, where the communications is provided by the **Application Remote Interface** services. This is the Database Manager's implementation of remote procedures.

- The fourth chapter in the series provides a *Transaction Server* version of the TP1 transaction, which is invoked through a do-it-yourself remote Named Pipe communication mechanism.

- The fifth chapter in the series provides a *Database Server* version of the TP1 transaction, which is implemented using Dynamic SQL. We expect this transaction to be the worst performer of the bunch. We've included it in the series so that we can gather some empirical measurements on performance trade-offs between static SQL and the more flexible, but supposedly much slower, Dynamic SQL.

- The sixth chapter in the series presents a summary of the test results.

Note: The performance numbers we produce should only be used to compare different transaction coding techniques or hardware configurations, with all other things being equal. They are not meant to serve as absolute performance benchmark numbers to be quoted.

WHAT YOU WILL LEARN FROM THIS MARATHON

At the end of this TP1 benchmarking exercise, you will have acquired the following new database skills:

- How to design and develop working models of Database Servers and Transaction Servers
- How to write a static SQL program
- How to write remote SQL procedures and transactions
- How to create complete database systems from the ground up
- How to fine-tune a database
- An understanding of the performance trade-offs of the various transaction processing techniques
- An understanding of the basic design of OLTP applications

OLTP BENCHMARK CONSIDERATIONS

OLTP applications are designed to support multiple users submitting their transactions against a large database. A typical OLTP application is characterized by the repeated execution of a set of predefined transactions by a number of simultaneous users. Transaction atomicity and record-level locking are mandatory requirements. The important issues for designers of OLTP applications are throughput, response time, and number of concurrent users. OLTP tests exercise virtually every system facility including the database hardware and software, the server's operating system and CPU, the data communications network, and the client/server message exchanges. A well-designed OLTP test that takes all these factors into account may very well be *the ultimate system benchmark*. The following is a list of what should be measured and reported in an OLTP benchmark:

- **Throughput:** This is the rate at which the OLTP system can process transactions. The unit of measure is stated in terms of transactions per second (**tps**). As users are added, the system reaches a maximum throughput which then starts to drop as more users are added. A target in the design of a good OLTP system is to maintain a stable throughput as more users are added.
- **Response Time:** This is the elapsed time a user experiences from the time a transaction is submitted until a response is returned. Response time should grow linearly (as opposed to exponentially) as users are added to the system.
- **Concurrent Users:** The number of users concurrently using the system is an important consideration in OLTP systems. Throughput and response times are meaningful when measured as a function of number of users. The performance of the system at peak times should be of considerable interest to OLTP developers.
- **The exact definition of a transaction:** For a **tps** measure to be meaningful it is important to agree on what exactly we mean by a transaction. What constitutes a *transaction*, of course, varies from application to application. A transaction that reserves an airline seat is obviously different from a manufacturing shop floor transaction. A benchmark needs to specify at an exact level a "generic" transaction which performs a representative set of SQL commands. The specification must include the actual SQL commands and how the commit, logging, and locking are to be applied.
- **System Steady State Verification:** A system reaches "steady state" when its performance remains constant from that point on. The system performance may vary by 20% or more before it reaches a steady state. This variance may be attributed to many factors, including buffers that fill up and the swapping of pages from memory to disk as the system load increases. Benchmark results must be reported at the steady state conditions.
- **Cost per transaction:** The system cost is used to normalize **tps** test results across widely differing systems. It requires reporting cost per **tps**. This is necessary so that if an abnormally large system is used to obtain a high **tps** rating, it will be reflected in a poor cost-per-tps figure. As you may expect, it will not be easy to come up with an objective measure of system cost.

- **The Test Environment:** A benchmark must specify the system's hardware and software configuration. The hardware configuration must include the speed of the processor, the amount of memory, the size of the buffer pool, the speed of the disks, and the type of disk controller. It is also important to specify the communications environment (LANs or TP lines including bandwidth and loading factors) and the type of front-end client (a terminal or workstation).
- **Full Disclosure:** There is a substantial agreement within the benchmark community that some form of "full disclosure" should be made part of the standard. This will provide an added check on the work of an auditor and will allow an end user to replicate a vendor's test results.

A HISTORY OF TP1

TP1 was first specified in *Datamation* in an article submitted by 24 computer professionals active in transaction processing.[1] The purpose of the article was *"to record the folklore we use to measure system performance."* Traditional measures of computer performance such as MIPS, MFLOPS, and Whetstones focus on CPU speed and don't capture the features that make one transaction processing system faster or cheaper than another. The TP1 Datamation benchmark was published to fill this void. The Datamation benchmark, also known as **DebitCredit** and **ET1** in some circles, was further refined and clarified over the years. The following are some of the key milestones in this refinement process:

1. In February 1987, Tandem Computers published the results of an extensive series of tests using DebitCredit to measure the performance of NonStop SQL.[2] These tests were audited by Codd and Date, and they became the new basis for the industry's de facto standard.

2. In late 1988, a Transaction Processing Council (TPC) was formed to develop a formal OLTP benchmark based on the DebitCredit de facto standard. The council consists of over 30 members representing the major database vendors. As of this writing, the council split DebitCredit into two separate standards:

   TPC-A Also known as ET1, TPC-A is based on the original DebitCredit transaction definition. A TPC-A server is front-ended with block-mode terminals, which submit their transactions to the server via X.25 lines, a WAN, or a LAN. The results of the test must be qualified as *tpsA-wide* (for WANs and X.25) or *tpsA-local* (for LANs). The management of the terminal network is part of the server's overhead. The TPC-A standard was approved by the consortium in

---

[1] Anon et al., "A Measure of Transaction Processing Power," **Datamation** (April 1, 1985).

[2] Jim Gray, **NonStop SQL Benchmark White Paper** (February, 1987).

October 1989. It is the recommended benchmark for DBMS hardware vendors.

TPC-B   Also known as TP1, TPC-B is also based on the original DebitCredit transaction definition. However, the TPC-B does not use a terminal network. Instead, TPC-B replaces the front-end clients with one or more "transaction generators" that produce back-to-back transactions. The transaction generators may run on the same system as the server and deliver their transactions directly through shared memory. They may also reside on separate client machines and deliver their transactions to the server via a LAN. TPC-B is generally considered to be the less demanding version of DebitCredit. The TPC-B standard was approved by the consortium in August 1990. It is the recommended benchmark for DBMS software vendors.

3. In June 1989, Ashton-Tate/Microsoft published an extensive benchmark study of their OS/2 SQL Server using the TP1 definition of DebitCredit.[3] The publication of their benchmark kit further helped refine the TP1 definition. The audit of the Microsoft TP1 benchmark was carried out by Richard Finkelstein and Colin White; both are independent industry experts specializing in SQL performance.

4. In June 1991, Jim Gray published the "Benchmark Handbook for Database and Transaction Systems," which describes the TPC benchmarks and provides a Benchmark Software package.[4]

5. In February 1992, the Transaction Processing Council introduced the TPC-C benchmark draft for public review and comment. The TPC-C transaction is modeled after an order-entry application. It uses several transactions that simulate more diverse forms of business activity. The TPC-C workload is a mixture of read-only and update-intensive transactions. The performance metric reported, *tpm-C*, measures the number of orders processed per minute (i.e., the orders entered, paid for, delivered, and checked for status). The TPC-C benchmark will become the recommended benchmark for very large enterprise DBMSs.

WHAT IS TP1?

The TP1 transaction models a hypothetical debit/credit banking application. It defines a standard transaction called the *DebitCredit* transaction, a standard database, a scaling method for larger systems, and a measure of throughput and price performance of the resulting system.

---

[3] "SQL Server Benchmarking Kit," Microsoft part number 098-11955 (June, 1989).

[4] Jim Gray et al., **The Benchmark Handbook For Database and Transaction Processing Systems**, Morgan Kaufmann (1991).

The TP1 Database

The TP1 database consists of four tables and a set of rules that define their contents and sizes. The four tables are:

- A table of bank accounts
- A table of tellers
- A table of bank branches
- A history table containing a record of all the transactions

The benchmark specifies an automatic scaling of the three key tables: account, tellers, and branches. A **1-tps** system supports a database with 100,000 accounts, 100 tellers, and 10 branches. A system that runs at a higher **tps** rate is required to scale its database linearly. For example, a **100-tps** system has a database which is 100 times larger than that of a **1-tps** system. For such a system, the accounts table should use 10 million account records, which translates into at least 1 GByte of disk space. The history table should be able to hold 90 days of transaction history. This innocent looking provision may turn out to be a tough requirement to meet.

The Definition of the TP1 Transaction

The TP1 transaction is deceptively simple and quite general. The transaction simulates an online teller who enters a debit/credit transaction. This is how the transaction executes:

1. A screen message containing a teller-generated deposit/withdrawal transaction is received from a teller terminal (or workstation).
2. An account record is randomly retrieved, updated, and rewritten to reflect the transaction.
3. The teller record is retrieved and updated to reflect the transaction.
4. A branch totals record is retrieved and updated to reflect the transaction.
5. A record is written to the history table to record the transaction.
6. A screen message is formatted and sent to the teller terminal (or workstation).

Each terminal generates a transaction every 100 seconds which implies 100 terminals for each reported **tps**. The more popular alternative is to have the transaction driver simulate the terminal message load.

How the TP1 Response-Time Is Measured

The transaction response time (as shown in Figure 31-1) is measured as the wall-clock time between the send and the completion of the receive in the Transaction Generator system.

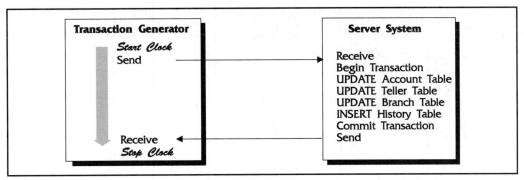

Figure 31-1. Measuring the Response-Time of a TP1 Transaction.

The TP1 Constraints

Here is a list of the constraints that must be met by the system:

- Each TP1 transaction must **randomly** generate the account branch and teller numbers, and at least 15% of the transactions must be inter-branch. The random generation of numbers is usually sufficient to meet this requirement (especially with a large database).
- All the tables must be protected by a fine granularity of **locking** and **logging**.
- The OLTP system under test should be observed over ten-minute windows.
- 95% of the transactions must provide a response time of less than 1 second. A system that can run 1 transaction per second giving less than one second response times to 95% of all transactions, is classified as a **1-tps** system.

Price/Performance of TP1

The price/performance of a TP1 server is measured in **dollars per tps**. A **1-tps** system is defined as a system which can run 1 TP1 transaction per second with less than one second response times for 95% of all transactions. As was mentioned earlier, the "cost" of a transaction can be quite tricky to measure. The cost formula TP1 prescribes is the *"five-year cost of ownership of the computing facility."* This is further defined as the five-year capital cost of vendor supplied hardware and software in the computer room. It does not include expenditures for terminals (or client PCs), communications, application development, or operations. It does, however, include installation and maintenance charges without specifying what type of maintenance support should be included. Should support be full on-site or just remote? Should price discounts be disallowed? By the admission of the original TP1 authors, the cost measure they specified is *"typically a fifth of the total cost of ownership of a system."*

PCs benefit from the disclosure of the full cost of ownership in TP1 tests as opposed to the simplified cost version. The cost of ownership of PC-based systems tends to be very small compared to conventional host-based systems.

The TP1 benchmark does not explicitly report an average response time. Instead, it measures throughput and normalizes it by the cost-of-ownership. TP1 rates a system using two simple numbers: tps and $/tps.

THE TP1 BENCHMARK KIT FOR DATABASE MANAGER

TP1 is a difficult and demanding benchmark to install and run. Depending on the available tools, it can take anywhere from a day to several months to install, configure, and build a TP1 test system. The good news is that the TP1 toolkit we will develop in Part V is a world-class "hacker's" tool. It is powerful, flexible, and a pleasure to experiment with.

Build Your TP1 Test System in One Afternoon

You should be able to build a custom TP1 test system in less than half a day. Once you've got a system up and running, you'll find yourself mesmerized by its user interface and the interactive control knobs it provides. After all, the user interface is provided by none other than **MULTI**, our old friend that puts you at the controls! But, we're getting ahead of our story. Let's first describe our benchmarking toolkit.

What Does the TP1 Kit Provide?

We've put together a very flexible toolkit that allows you to mix and match pieces to your heart's content. And if that's not enough, you can always modify and recompile the source code to create any variation you may fancy. The benchmark toolkit brings together many of the programs that were previously developed in this book, and then integrates them with the new TP1 programs that we develop in this six-chapter series. The essence of good architecture is to build on top of existing foundations. We will now tell you how we do it.

RSQL

RSQL, our old friend, is used to create the TP1 tables, load the tables with data, bind the transaction programs to the database, add indexes to the tables, run statistics against the tables, log on to the database, and change the database configuration parameters. We provide samples of RSQL run files that perform these tasks. You can, of course, modify any of these run files to run the benchmarks with the system environment of your choice.

TP1MKEXE.MAK and TP1MKDLL.MAK

These are the *make* files with which we build the different flavors of TP1 transaction programs that we will develop in this series.

TP1LOAD.SQC

This is a new program we will create to load TP1 tables with the data as specified in the standard. This includes generating the random numbers and representative data. This program will also scale the database to the size you specify through a **tps** scaling parameter. This program will also serve as a gentle introduction to static SQL programming.

Four TP1 Transaction Flavors

The toolkit provides four flavors of TP1 transactions. We will develop these programs in Part V:

1. The **SQLTP1.SQC** program provides a static SQL transaction. Instances of this transaction can be executed against either a local or remote database engine.
2. The **SQLTP1RI.SQC** program provides a client application that submits its TP1 transactions using the *Application Remote Interface*. The Transaction Server code is provided by **SQLTP1DL.SQC**. It is packaged as a **DLL**.
3. The **SQLTP1RQ.C** program provides a client application that submits its TP1 transactions using Named Pipes. The Transaction Server code is provided by **SQLTP1SV.SQC**.
4. The **SQLTP1DY.SQC** program provides a Dynamic SQL flavor of a TP1 transaction.

The MULTI Process Driver Program

MULTI is another dear old friend that we use to execute multiple instances (or processes) of the TP1 programs. Through MULTI, you can start and stop the benchmark runs, you can start or stop the transaction processes, you can specify the process priorities, and you can literally watch the TP1s execute, each in their little MULTI window. MULTI displays the total number of transactions executed per process, as well as the number of transactions that ran under the response time threshold, which you specify through the MULTI configuration file.

Figure 31-2 shows a MULTI screen for a four-process TP1 run. You can read the following information off this screen:

- Four **SQLTP1** processes were run concurrently for 600 seconds (10 minutes).

- During this period, a total of 3192 TP1 transactions ran successfully.
- A total of 3184 (add the TXNS in the four windows) TP1 transactions ran below the user-specified response time threshold.

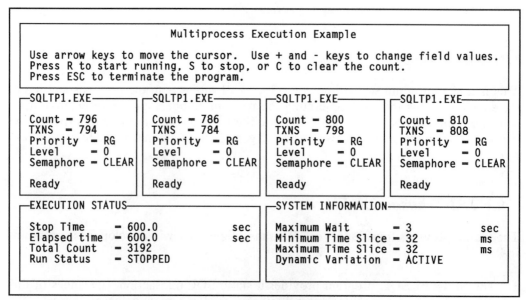

Figure 31-2.   A MULTI Screen of a Four-Process TP1 Run.

This machine may be classified as being in the 5.3 TP1 range (3184 divided by 600). To add more TP1 drivers, simply run the MULTI program on more networked client machines. MULTI becomes an incremental TP1 driver with some very powerful control knobs and displays.

TP1: To Cheat or Not to Cheat?

To produce correct results, the TP1 benchmark specification must be strictly followed. The TP1 toolkit lets you control the benchmark environment at a very granular level. It lets you decide what level of adherence you're going to abide by when running the benchmark. The benchmark runs that you will see in this book follow a very lax interpretation of the benchmark rules. This is another way of saying *we will do a little bit of cheating.* Why?

Remember, our focus is on the relative performance measurements of client/server architectures. We are *purposely not measuring maximum raw performance* so as not to get embroiled in the controversial benchmark wars. This difference leads us to purposely run our tests on an ordinary Mod-95 (80486/33 MHz) server and 4 MBit/s Token Ring (the newer Mod-95 models from IBM, with 50 MHz double-clock frequency, are reportedly three times faster than the model we used). We also chose to run a lax interpretation of TP1 (as you will soon see) that gives us a consistent set of performance numbers. We purposely chose not to run the tests on "superservers" since we are not trying to test Database Manager's maximum performance or how it compares with other vendor products. So, please don't quote absolute numbers!

Having made this disclaimer, we are quick to point out that the toolkit provides a very credible set of tools for doing some very serious benchmark work, if you can afford the right hardware platform. By that we mean lots of memory, many client machines on a network, a heavy-duty OS/2 "superserver" machine with disk arrays, and lots of disk space for the 60-day history table. For your information, we've included a list of "common shortcuts" (this is another polite word for cheating). This is what people in the business warn you to look for when evaluating *other* people's benchmark results (see Table 31-1).

Table 31-1. TP1: To Cheat or Not to Cheat.

TP1 Requirements	Common "Shortcuts"	What You Can Do With the Toolkit
Database Scaling	None	Yes. Specify the required tps level.
Some user interface	None	Yes. We have MULTI screens.
Open Benchmark Code	Not Available	Source and executable code is available and fully documented in this book.
Network Support	None	3 versions of networked TP1s: - Remote SQL (static and dynamic) using RDS - Remote Procedures using RDS - Remote Procedures using Named Pipes
Single History table	Multiple tables	Single table.
1-second response time	Not Measured	Yes. We provide two numbers: 1) total transactions; 2) total transactions under a user-specified response time.
95 percent of transactions under 1 second	Not Measured	100 percent of transactions which are under toolkit-specified response time.
Random Account Numbers	Not Provided	Yes.
90-day History	No provisions	Yes, if you provide enough disk space.
Error-checking	None	SQL return codes. Will check if account is non-existent.
Frequent checkpoints	Not activated	Under user control using RSQL.
Granular locks	None	Under user control using RSQL's Bind options. (i.e., toolkit).
Steady State Response	Not measured	Under user control using MULTI.

CREATING THE TP1 DATABASE

Creating a database is the first step in the development of a database program. Without a database you can't even compile the program. RSQL makes the process of database creation easy. You can see that for yourself by looking at Figure 31-3, which contains the results of a simple RSQL run that creates a **TP1** database consisting of four tables:

ACCT   This table contains an entry for each customer account record.
BRANCH   This table contains an entry for each branch office of that bank.
TELLER   This table contains an entry for each teller in all of the branch offices.
HISTORY   This table contains an entry for each TP1 transaction executed against the database.

```
--                    Create TP1 Database
-- ==============================================================================
-- logon
EXEC DBA: LOGON USERID PASSWORD DBSVR03 UPM_LOCAL UPM_USER;

 OK, api_rcd = 0,          Execution time =     0.2800 secs

-- create a database called TP1
EXEC DBA: CREATE_DB TP1 G TP1_TEST_DATABASE;

 OK, sql_rcd = 0,          Execution time =    35.3100 secs

-- bind the rsql program
EXEC DBA: BIND TP1 RSQL.BND ISO REPEATABLE_READ BLOCK_ALL PUBLIC;

 No messages in msgfile.msg

 OK, sql_rcd = 0,          Execution time =    15.3200 secs


-- connect to the database
EXEC DBA: STARTUSE TP1 S;

 OK, sql_rcd = 0,          Execution time =     0.5600 secs


-- create tables
EXEC SQL: CREATE TABLE ACCT(ACCT_NUM       INT       NOT NULL,
                            NAME           CHAR(20) NOT NULL,
                            BRANCH_ID      SMALLINT NOT NULL,
                            BALANCE        INT       NOT NULL,
                            ADDRESS        CHAR(30) NOT NULL,
                            TEMP           CHAR(40) NOT NULL);

 OK, sql_rcd = 0,          Execution time =     0.7800 secs


EXEC SQL: CREATE TABLE BRANCH(BRANCH_ID    SMALLINT NOT NULL,
                            BRANCH_NAME CHAR(20) NOT NULL,
                            BALANCE        INT       NOT NULL,
                            AREA_CODE   CHAR(4)  NOT NULL,
                            ADDRESS        CHAR(30) NOT NULL,
                            TEMP           CHAR(40) NOT NULL);
```

Figure 31-3 (Part 1 of 2). Creating a TP1 Database Using RSQL.

```
OK, sql_rcd = 0,         Execution time =      0.3800 secs


EXEC SQL: CREATE TABLE TELLER(TELLER_ID    SMALLINT NOT NULL,
                              TELLER_NAME CHAR(20) NOT NULL,
                              BRANCH_ID    SMALLINT NOT NULL,
                              BALANCE      INTEGER  NOT NULL,
                              TELLER_CODE CHAR(2)  NOT NULL,
                              ADDRESS      CHAR(30) NOT NULL,
                              TEMP         CHAR(40) NOT NULL);

OK, sql_rcd = 0,         Execution time =      0.4000 secs


EXEC SQL: CREATE TABLE HISTORY(ACCT_NUM    INTEGER  NOT NULL,
                               TELLER_ID   SMALLINT NOT NULL,
                               BRANCH_ID   SMALLINT NOT NULL,
                               BALANCE     INTEGER  NOT NULL,
                               DELTA       INTEGER  NOT NULL,
                               PID         INTEGER  NOT NULL,
                               TRANSID     INTEGER  NOT NULL,
                               ACCTNAME    CHAR(20) NOT NULL,
                               TEMP        CHAR(6)  NOT NULL);

OK, sql_rcd = 0,         Execution time =      0.3800 secs

-- commit the tables
EXEC SQL: COMMIT;

OK, sql_rcd = 0,         Execution time =      0.0100 secs

-- disconnect from the database
EXEC DBA: STOPUSE TP1;

OK, sql_rcd = 0,         Execution time =      0.8400 secs

-- logoff
EXEC DBA: LOGOFF USERID DBSVR03 UPM_LOCAL;

OK, api_rcd = 0,            Execution time =      0.0300 secs
```

Figure 31-3 (Part 2 of 2). Creating a TP1 Database Using RSQL.

THE TP1 MAKE FILES

Now that we have a database, we can use it to precompile SQL programs against it. The **TP1MKEXE.MAK** and **TP1MKDLL.MAK** *make* files (see Figure 31-4 and Figure 31-5) will be used to create seven new database programs which will be offered as part of the TP1 benchmark kit. These programs will be explained in great detail in this chapter and in the TP1 chapters that follow.

The TP1 make files does not introduce any new constructs. However, notice that the **.def.lib** and **.obj.dll** inference rules are used in Figure 31-5 to create a dynamic link library (.DLL). This is for **sqltp1dl.sqc**, the server part of the Remote Application Interface version of the TP1 program. You may remember from the tutorial (see "The Power of Remote Procedures" in Chapter 28) that a Remote Application Server must exist as an OS/2 Dynamic Link Library (.DLL). The process for the creation of DLLs was explained in Chapter 16.

```
#********************************************************************************
# Make File for TP1 program .EXEs
#********************************************************************************

#** MACROS *********************************************************************
cflags= /C /Ti+ /Q+ /Sp1 /Sm /Gs- /Gm+ /Ge+ /Gd+ /DES32TO16
lflags= /ST:15000/CO/NOLOGO/NOI/L/M:FULL/PM:VIO
exe_libs=sql_dyn
DATABASE=TP1

#** INFERENCE RULES ************************************************************
.SUFFIXES: .sqc

.obj.exe:
        echo LINKING      $** to create $*.exe
        link386 $(lflags) $**,,, $(exe_libs),;

.c.obj:
        echo COMPILING    $*.c
        icc $(cflags) $*.c

.sqc.c:
        echo PRECOMPILING $*.sqc for database $(DATABASE)
        sqlprep  $*.sqc $(DATABASE) /b
        echo BINDING      $*.bnd to  database $(DATABASE)
        sqlbind  $*.bnd $(DATABASE)

#** BUILD STATEMENTS ***********************************************************

all: tp1load.exe sqltp1.exe sqltp1ri.exe \
     sqltp1rq.exe sqltp1sv.exe sqltp1dy.exe launcher.exe

tp1load.exe:            tp1load.obj              # Load TP1 tables
tp1load.c tp1load.obj: tp1load.sqc

sqltp1.exe:            sqltp1.obj               # TP1 transaction using
sqltp1.c sqltp1.obj:  sqltp1.sqc               # embedded SQL

sqltp1ri.exe:         sqltp1ri.obj             # TP1 transaction using
sqltp1ri.obj:         sqltp1ri.c               # remote interface req

sqltp1sv.exe:            sqltp1sv.obj          # TP1 transaction using
sqltp1sv.c sqltp1sv.obj: sqltp1sv.sqc          # named pipe server

launcher.exe:            launcher.obj          # Named Pipe server
launcher.obj:            launcher.c            # launcher

sqltp1rq.exe:         sqltp1rq.obj             # TP1 transaction using
sqltp1rq.obj:         sqltp1rq.c               # named pipe requester

sqltp1dy.exe:            sqltp1dy.obj          # TP1 transaction using
sqltp1dy.c sqltp1dy.obj: sqltp1dy.sqc          # dynamic sql
```

Figure 31-4. The TP1MKEXE.MAK MAKE File.

```
#***********************************************************************
# Make File for TP1 program .DLL
#***********************************************************************

#** MACROS ************************************************************
cflags= /C /Ti+ /Q+ /Sp1 /Sm /Gs- /Gm+ /Ge- /Gd+ /DES32TO16
lflags= /ST:15000/SE:1024/CO/NOLOGO/NOI/L/M:FULL/PM:VIO
dll_libs=sql_dyn
DATABASE=TP1

#** INFERENCE RULES ***************************************************
.SUFFIXES: .sqc

.obj.dll:
      echo LINKING      $* to create $*.dll
      LINK386 $(lflags) $*,$*.dll,, $(dll_libs), $*.def;

.c.obj:
      echo COMPILING    $*.c
      icc $(cflags) $*.c

.sqc.c:
      echo PRECOMPILING $*.sqc for database $(DATABASE)
      sqlprep  $*.sqc $(DATABASE) /b
      echo BINDING      $*.bnd to  database $(DATABASE)
      sqlbind  $*.bnd $(DATABASE)

#** BUILD STATEMENTS **************************************************

all: sqltp1dl.dll

sqltp1dl.dll:             sqltp1dl.obj sqltp1dl.def # TP1 transaction DLL for
sqltp1dl.c sqltp1dl.obj: sqltp1dl.sqc               # interface server
```

Figure 31-5.   The TP1MKDLL.MAK MAKE File.

TP1LOAD.SQC: A PROGRAM FOR LOADING TP1 DATABASE TABLES

In this section, we introduce **TP1LOAD.SQC**, a program whose sole function is to load data into the three newly created TP1 database tables. This program shows how to write code using static SQL. As you will soon appreciate, static SQL is both powerful and simple. The following is a step-by-step description of what the **TP1LOAD.SQC** program (see listing in Figure 31-6) does:

1. The program starts by including the C-language, OS/2 and Database Manager header files that are needed for system services. Notice that the **sqlenv.h** file is included to obtain the Database Administration's Environment services.

2. A structure of type **SQLCA** is created by issuing the directive:

   ```
   EXEC SQL INCLUDE SQLCA;
   ```

3. The host variables that will be used to exchange data between SQL and the C program are declared. As you can see, it's OK to initialize host variables.

4. The **main**() program obtains the tps argument that defines the size of the database to be built. The database of a 1-tps system is defined as:

```
100,000 Accounts
    100 Tellers
     10 Branches
```

The program will create a database whose size is a multiple of the 1-tps numbers shown above. The scaling factor is provided by the tps parameter that gets passed to the program. If no argument is passed, the default is to create a 1-tps database. Make sure you have enough disk space to accommodate the tps number you provide.

5. The **sqlestrd**() API call is issued to connect to the TP1 database in shared mode.

6. The **ACCT** table data is generated one row at a time and placed into host variables. The information is passed directly to the database through an embedded SQL INSERT statement with host variables containing the data to be placed into the named table columns. Notice the following:

   - The **ACCT** table contains (tps*100,000) rows.
   - Each row is 100 bytes long and represents a customer's bank account. It contains the account number, the account balance, the customer's name and address, and the branch_id. The account records have account numbers from 1 to (tps*100,000).
   - The branch_id is a random number from 1 to (tps*10). The TP1 benchmark requires that the selection of the accounts used for a given transaction be truly random to test the non-cached performance of the database. To accomplish this effect, we generate the branch_id field as a pseudo random number based on an input seed.
   - We commit to the database after every 10,000 inserts to prevent our logs from overflowing.

7. The **TELLER** table data is generated one row at a time and the SQL INSERT command is used to write the contents of the host variables to the database. Notice the following:

   - The **TELLER** table contains (tps*100) rows.
   - Each row is 100 bytes long and represents a bank teller in a branch office. It contains the teller_id, the teller name, the branch_id, the teller balance, a teller code of "ab" and the address strings.
   - The branch_id is a random number from 1 to (tps*10).
   - The teller_id's are generated sequentially and range from 1 to (tps*100).

8. The **BRANCH** table data is generated one row at-a-time and the SQL INSERT command is used to write the contents of the host variables to the database. Notice the following:

    - The **BRANCH** table contains (tps*10) rows.
    - Each row is 100 bytes long and represents a bank branch office. It contains the branch_id, the branch name and address strings, and the branch balance.
    - The branch numbers are generated sequentially and range from 1 to (tps*10).

9. The program issues a **sqlestpd()** API call to disconnect from the TP1 database. We're done!

```
/***************************************************************************/
/*   PROGRAM NAME:  TP1LOAD.SQC -- LOAD TP1 table data                     */
/*                                                                         */
/*   DESCRIPTION:  This program inserts data into the ACCOUNT,             */
/*      TELLER, and BRANCH tables to prepare the database for running the  */
/*      TP1 benchmark.                                                     */
/*                                                                         */
/*   PROGRAM INVOCATION:    tp1load                                        */
/*                                                                         */
/***************************************************************************/
#include <stdio.h>                        /* For printf() & NULL           */
#include <stdlib.h>                        /* For printf                    */
#include <sqlenv.h>                        /* For environment functions     */
#include <os2.h>                           /* for OS/2 types                */

EXEC SQL INCLUDE SQLCA;

                       /*_____*/
                       /* Host variables for SQL calls    */
                       /*_____*/
EXEC SQL BEGIN DECLARE SECTION;
    char   name[21]    = "<--20 BYTE STRING-->";
    char   address[31] = "<------ 30 BYTE STRING ------>";
    char   temp[41]    = "<----------- 40 BYTE STRING ----------->";
    long   acct_num;
    short  branch_id;
    short  teller_id;
EXEC SQL END DECLARE SECTION;

/*_____*/
/* Main function.                                              */
/*_____*/
INT main(USHORT argc, PCHAR argv[])
{
 USHORT    tps;                                  /* number of tps        */

    /*_____*/
    /* Get number of tps from arguments    */
    /*_____*/

 if (argc != 2)
    printf ("\nThe default 1-tps database will be built...");
 else
    tps  = atoi(argv[2]);                         /* get tps value        */
```

Figure 31-6 (Part 1 of 3). The TP1LOAD.SQC program.

```
      /*───────────────────────────────────────*/
      /* Initialize random number generator      */
      /*───────────────────────────────────────*/
      srand(37);                                  /* seed = 37 for random numbers  */

      /*───────────────────────────────────────*/
      /* Connect to the TP1 database             */
      /*───────────────────────────────────────*/
      printf("\nConnecting to TP1 database");
      sqlestrd( "TP1", SQL_USE_SHR, &sqlca);
      if (SQLCODE)
          { printf("\nERROR during connect, sqlcode= %d\n",SQLCODE);
            exit(1);
          }
      /*───────────────────────────────────────────*/
      /* Load ACCOUNT table data                     */
      /*───────────────────────────────────────────*/
      printf ("\nInserting Data into ACCT Table....");

      for (acct_num=1; acct_num <= tps*100000; acct_num++)
          {
          branch_id = rand();
          branch_id = branch_id % tps*10;

              /*───────────────────────────────────────*/
              /* Insert one row into table               */
              /*───────────────────────────────────────*/
              EXEC SQL
              INSERT INTO ACCT (ACCT_NUM, NAME, BRANCH_ID, BALANCE, ADDRESS, TEMP)
              VALUES ( :acct_num, :name, :branch_id, 1000, :address, :temp );

              if (SQLCODE)
                 { printf("\nError on Insert number %ld, sqlcode= %ld\n",
                           acct_num, SQLCODE);
                   exit(1);
                 }

              /*───────────────────────────────────────*/
              /* Commit after every 10,000 rows inserted */
              /*───────────────────────────────────────*/
              if ((acct_num % 10000)==0)
              {
                EXEC SQL COMMIT;
                if (SQLCODE)
                   { printf("\nError on Commit, sqlcode= %ld\n", SQLCODE);
                     exit(1);
                   }
                printf("\n %8ld accounts created",acct_num);
          } /* end if */
      } /* end for */
      /*───────────────────────────────────────────*/
      /* Load TELLER  table data                     */
      /*───────────────────────────────────────────*/
      printf ("\nInserting Data into TELLER Table....");

      for (teller_id = 1; teller_id <= tps*100; teller_id++)
          {
          branch_id = rand();
          branch_id = branch_id % tps*10 ;
              /*───────────────────────────────────────*/
              /* Insert one row into table               */
              /*───────────────────────────────────────*/
```

Figure 31-6 (Part 2 of 3). The TP1LOAD.SQC program.

```
      EXEC SQL
      INSERT INTO TELLER (TELLER_ID, TELLER_NAME, BRANCH_ID, BALANCE,
                          TELLER_CODE, ADDRESS, TEMP)
      VALUES ( :teller_id, :name, :branch_id, 1000, 'ab', :address, :temp );

      if (SQLCODE)
         { printf("\nError on Insert number %d, sqlcode= %ld\n",
                  teller_id, SQLCODE);
           exit(1);
         }
      } /* end for */
EXEC SQL COMMIT;
if (SQLCODE)
   { printf("\nError on Commit, sqlcode= %ld\n", SQLCODE);
     exit(1);
   }
printf("\n %8d teller entries created", teller_id-1);

 /*———————————————————————————————*/
 /* Load BRANCH  table data                                    */
 /*———————————————————————————————*/
printf ("\nInserting Data into BRANCH Table....");


for (branch_id = 1; branch_id <= tps*10; branch_id++)
    {
        /*———————————————————————————————*/
        /* Insert one row into table                          */
        /*———————————————————————————————*/
        EXEC SQL
        INSERT INTO BRANCH (BRANCH_ID, BRANCH_NAME, BALANCE,
                            AREA_CODE, ADDRESS, TEMP)
        VALUES ( :branch_id, :name, 1000, 'abcd', :address, :temp );
        if (SQLCODE)
            { printf("\nError on Insert number %d, sqlcode= %ld\n",
                     branch_id, SQLCODE);
              exit(1);
            }
    }/* end for */
EXEC SQL COMMIT;
if (SQLCODE)
    { printf("\nError on Commit, sqlcode= %ld\n", SQLCODE);
      exit(1);
    }
printf("\n %8d branch entries created", branch_id-1);

 /*———————————————————————————————*/
 /* Disconnect from the database                               */
 /*———————————————————————————————*/
printf ("\nDisconnecting from TP1 database");
sqlestpd(&sqlca);
if (SQLCODE)
    { printf("\nError on Disconnect from database, sqlcode= %ld\n",
             SQLCODE);
      exit(1);
    }
printf("\nTP1 database created successfully.\n");

 return(0);
} /* end main */
```

Figure 31-6 (Part 3 of 3).   The TP1LOAD.SQC program.

LOADING THE TP1 DATABASE

Now that we've got a program that can generate TP1 data, let's run it. We'll run the program using RSQL because there are some additional tasks that need to be taken care of when loading such large amounts of data. Figure 31-7 shows what some of those additional tasks are. It contains the results of an RSQL run that is used to load the database tables with TP1 data. Let's go through this run step-by-step to get some idea what typically needs to be done with loading large amounts of data in tables:

1. Log on to the database.

2. BIND **TP1LOAD** program to the database.

3. Execute the **TP1LOAD** program using the RSQL "DOS EXEC:" command. This is the C program we developed in the previous section to load the TP1 tables.

4. Create the indexes on the TP1 tables. Why is this done here instead of at table create time? The answer is that it is much faster to do inserts without an index. The **TP1LOAD** program already takes 839 (about 14 minutes) to run. If the TP1 tables had indexes, that program would have literally taken hours to run. So what we do instead is create the indexes after the bulk data is loaded.

5. Run statistics against the tables so that the Database Manager optimizer has the right information for the execution of its plans.

```
 --                     Load TP1 Table Data
 --  ============================================================================
 -- logon
EXEC DBA: LOGON USERID PASSWORD DBSVRO3 UPM_LOCAL UPM_USER;

 OK, api_rcd = 0,          Execution time =      1.3100 secs

 -- bind the tp1 load tables program
EXEC DBA: BIND TP1 TP1LOAD.BND ISO REPEATABLE_READ BLOCK_ALL PUBLIC;

 No messages in msgfile.msg

 OK, sql_rcd = 0,          Execution time =      3.2200 secs

 -- use a program to load table data
EXEC DOS: TP1LOAD.EXE;

 Program completed with a return code of 0.
 OK,                       Execution time =    839.2500 secs

 -- connect to the database
EXEC DBA: STARTUSE TP1 S;

 OK, sql_rcd = 0,          Execution time =      0.5900 secs
```

Figure 31-7 (Part 1 of 2). Loading a TP1 Database with Data Using RSQL.

```
-- create table indices
EXEC SQL: CREATE INDEX ACCTINDX ON ACCT(ACCT_NUM);

 OK, sql_rcd = 0,         Execution time =    122.4700 secs

EXEC SQL: CREATE INDEX BRANINDX ON BRANCH(BRANCH_ID);

 OK, sql_rcd = 0,         Execution time =      0.9000 secs

EXEC SQL: CREATE INDEX TELLINDX ON TELLER(TELLER_ID);

 OK, sql_rcd = 0,         Execution time =      1.9100 secs

EXEC SQL: COMMIT;

 OK, sql_rcd = 0,         Execution time =      0.0900 secs

-- perform runstats on the tables
EXEC DBA: RUNSTATS USERID.ACCT;

 OK, sql_rcd = 0,         Execution time =    257.6000 secs

EXEC DBA: RUNSTATS USERID.BRANCH;

 OK, sql_rcd = 0,         Execution time =      0.4700 secs

EXEC DBA: RUNSTATS USERID.TELLER;

 OK, sql_rcd = 0,         Execution time =      2.9000 secs

-- disconnect from the database
EXEC DBA: STOPUSE TP1;

 OK, sql_rcd = 0,         Execution time =      1.1900 secs

-- logoff
EXEC DBA: LOGOFF USERID DBSVRO3 UPM_LOCAL;

 OK, api_rcd = 0,          Execution time =      0.0000 secs
```

Figure 31-7 (Part 2 of 2).   Loading a TP1 Database with Data Using RSQL.

WHERE DO WE GO FROM HERE?

This concludes our presentation of the common tools that the **SQLTP1** benchmarking toolkit offers. To summarize, these tools include:

- **RSQL** run files

- **TP1MKEXE.MAK**, the common *make* file for building TP1 transactions

- **TP1LOAD.SQC**, the static SQL-based program for loading the TP1 tables

- **MULTI**, which can run TP1 transactions as processes and display their results

So, where do we go from here? The next step is to create our four flavors of TP1 transactions and measure their performance. We will be developing one transaction flavor per chapter. The first transaction will be the longest because this is where all the common procedures are described. In subsequent chapters, we will be using some of those common procedures. Instead of repeating their code, we will refer you to the chapter where the code was first described. This way, the remaining chapters will become progressively shorter, and we will maintain our focus on the new concepts being introduced.

Chapter 32

The Static SQL Database Server TP1

This is the second of a six-chapter series, in which we develop a TP1 Benchmark toolkit for the OS/2 Database Manager. This chapter provides a static SQL *Database Server* version of the TP1 transaction. The code that implements this transaction is provided in the **SQLTP1.SQC** program. Instances of this transaction can be executed against either a local or remote database engine. The TP1 transaction performance will be measured using the following configurations:

1. On a local versus remote Database Server
2. On a slower server versus a faster Database Server machine
3. On the same Database Server but using different buffer pool sizes

This chapter has two hard prerequisites:

- The SQL tutorial (see Chapter 26)
- The first chapter in the Benchmark Series (see Chapter 31)

In addition, you should review the **MULTI** chapter in Part II, and you should be familiar with **RSQL** at the user level.

THE STATIC SQL VERSION OF TP1

We have a database, we have the data, so let's create the program that does the TP1. The **SQLTP1.SQC** program is designed to run as a **MULTI** process. This means **MULTI** will create the process, pass it the parameters, and tell it when to start or stop executing TP1 transactions. When the process is told to start executing TP1s, it will go into a continuous loop submitting TP1 transactions against the database, and displaying the running count of the results. Two counts are displayed in each of the four process windows:

- The total number of transactions executed
- The total number of transactions executed with a response time that is equal to or less than the specified threshold

The user specifies the transaction threshold as a parameter to be passed to the process at start-up time. Another parameter that is specified is the seed for the random number generator that the process will use to generate its TP1 requests. The **tps** scaling factor for the database is also passed and it will also be used to generate the random number.

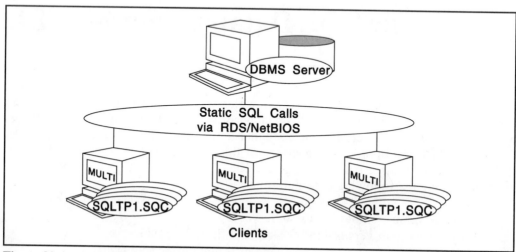

Figure 32-1.   A 12-Client Static SQL TP1 Database Server.

LOCAL AND REMOTE TP1 CONFIGURATIONS

The TP1 transactions execute as static SQL statements against a database. This database may be either local or remote. The location of the database is totally transparent to the code. If the database is remote, then the **Remote Data Services (RDS)** client component of the Database Manager will pass the SQL statement to the remote database using NetBIOS.

Each instance of **MULTI** can run four **SQLTP1.SQC** processes. If you need more TP1 generators, simply add more **MULTI** client workstations. Figure 32-1 shows you how to create a 12-client TP1 system. You can scale this configuration in any direction depending on your budget considerations. We will be scaling our experiments downward to a four-client TP1 system and we'll throw in a network! We'll then run benchmarks against the local and remote database configurations to understand the overhead that **RDS** introduces.

WALKING THROUGH THE SQLTP1.SQC CODE

SQLTP1.SQC: The main() Procedure

In this section, we present the **main()** procedure of the **SQLTP1** program whose code listing is shown in Figure 32-2. The following is a step-by-step description of what this code does:

1. The program starts by including the C-language, OS/2, and Database Manager header files that are needed for system services. Our current interest is on the Database Manager header files for the Database Services:

sqlca.h	This include file provides the type definition of a **SQLCA** structure. We have to create a variable of that type in the program, which the Database Manager uses to return error information.
sql.h	This include file contains the text of SQL error messages.
sqlcodes.h	This include file contains SQL constant definitions.
sqlenv.h	This include file contains the function prototypes and type definitions for the Database Administration's Environment API services.

2. We then include two of our program header files:

const.h	You've already encountered this include file when we developed **MULTI**. It contains **MULTI**-related constants and structures. The listing for this file is provided in Figure 14-11 in Part II.
sqltp1.h	This include file contains the forward declarations, type definitions, and global variables for all the TP1 transaction programs. The listing for this file is provided in Figure 32-10.

3. The **EXEC SQL WHENEVER** statements that follow indicate that we will do our own error detection in-line.

4. We then declare our host variables.

5. The **main()** program follows, and you can see that it's not going to be a monster. Here's what **main()** does:

   - Invokes **get_args()**, listed in Figure 32-4, to obtain the arguments **MULTI** passes when it invokes the program. **MULTI** gets these arguments from reading the **MULTI.CFG** file.

- Invokes **initialize_multi_ipc()**, listed in Figure 32-5, to perform all the inter-process communication chores required from a process that runs under **MULTI**'s control.

- Invokes **initialize_task()**, listed in Figure 32-6, to connect to the database, install a signal handler, and do all kinds of one-time housekeeping in preparation for the *big TP1 loop*.

- Invokes **execute_task()**, listed in Figure 32-7. This is the home of the *big TP1 loop*, which forever executes TP1 transactions. **MULTI** can at any time pause and resume the execution of TP1 transactions through semaphores. The TP1 transaction is executed by the helper routine, **tp1_transaction()**, whose code is listed in Figure 32-8.

```
/***********************************************************************/
/*   PROGRAM NAME: SQLTP1 - A process program that MULTI starts       */
/*                                                                     */
/*   PROGRAM DESCRIPTION:  This program is run as a child task of MULTI. */
/*       It executes static SQL TP1 Transactions as part of a DB benchmark. */
/***********************************************************************/
#include <process.h>               /* For exit()                      */
#include <string.h>                /* For printf                      */
#include <sys\types.h>             /* For time()                      */
#include <sys\timeb.h>             /* For time()                      */
#include <sys\stat.h>              /* For stat()                      */
#include <stdlib.h>                /* For atoi                        */
#include <stdio.h>                 /* For sprintf, printf             */
#define INCL_VIO                   /* include VIO calls               */
#define INCL_DOSPROCESS            /* include process   api calls     */
#define INCL_DOSSEMAPHORES         /* include semaphore api calls     */
#define INCL_DOSMEMMGR             /* include segment   api calls     */
#define INCL_ERRORS                /* include error definitions       */
#include <os2.h>

#include <sqlca.h>                 /* sqlca                           */
#include <sql.h>                   /* error msg. retrieval            */
#include <sqlcodes.h>              /* SQL return code constants       */
#include <sqlenv.h>                /* environment functions and       */

#include "const.h"                 /* constants for multi             */
#include "sqltp1.h"                /* tp1 program vars, declares,etc.  */

/*'''''''''''''''''''''''''''''''''''''''''''''''''''''''''''''''''''''*/
/* database includes, defines, etc. for task function                 */
/*'''''''''''''''''''''''''''''''''''''''''''''''''''''''''''''''''''''*/
struct sqlca sqlca;

EXEC SQL WHENEVER SQLERROR CONTINUE;
EXEC SQL WHENEVER SQLWARNING CONTINUE;
EXEC SQL WHENEVER NOT FOUND CONTINUE;

EXEC SQL BEGIN DECLARE SECTION;
 long  acct_num;
 short branch_id;
 short teller_id;
```

Figure 32-2 (Part 1 of 2). SQLTP1.SQC: The main() Procedure.

```
  long  balance;
  long  delta        = 100;
  char  acct_name[20] = "<--20 BYTE STRING-->";
EXEC SQL END   DECLARE SECTION;

/*'''''''''''''''''''''''''''''''''''''''''''''''''''''''''''''''''''''*/
/* Main routine.                                                       */
/*'''''''''''''''''''''''''''''''''''''''''''''''''''''''''''''''''''''*/
VOID main(USHORT argc, PCHAR argv[])
{
  get_args(argc, argv);              /* get program arguments          */

  initialize_multi_ipc();           /* Init MULTI semaphores/shared memory */

  initialize_task();                /* perform one time intializations */

  execute_task();                   /* Issue TP1s in a loop            */

} /* end main */
```

Figure 32-2 (Part 2 of 2). SQLTP1.SQC: The main() Procedure.

SQLTP1.SQC: The get_args() Function

In this section, we present the **get_args()** function, whose code listing is shown in Figure 32-4. This function obtains the arguments that **MULTI** passes to the program when it invokes it. **MULTI** gets those arguments from reading the **MULTI.CFG** file; here is an example:

```
PROGRAM_TYPE     = PROCESS
STOP_TIME_MS     = 600000
TASK_NAME        = SQLTP1.EXE 0 17 2.0 1;
TASK_NAME        = SQLTP1.EXE 1 23 2.0 1;
TASK_NAME        = SQLTP1.EXE 2 29 2.0 1;
TASK_NAME        = SQLTP1.EXE 3 57 2.0 1;
```

Figure 32-3. A MULTI.CFG File for Running Four TP1 Processes.

The arguments appear right after the program's name. The **get_args()** function expects four parameters:

- A process number, which determines which **MULTI** window this process will use to display its output.
- A seed value for the random number generator.
- A threshold value which indicates the required TP1 response time. All transactions whose response time is less or equal to this threshold will be counted in the window's **TXNS** field.
- A *tps scale value* which indicates the scaling factor used for building the TP1 database was built. This number will be used in conjunction with the random number generated to calculate a random account number.

```
/*''''''''''''''''''''''''''''''''''''''''''''''''''''''''''''''''''''''''*/
/* Get program arguments.  Arguments are 1) process_number, 2) seed_value,  */
/* 3) threshold 4) tps                                                      */
/*''''''''''''''''''''''''''''''''''''''''''''''''''''''''''''''''''''''''*/
VOID get_args(USHORT argc, PCHAR argv[])
{
  /*''''''''''''''''''''''''''''''''''''''''''*/
  /* validate and get arguments            */
  /*''''''''''''''''''''''''''''''''''''''''''*/
  if (argc != 5)
    { print_error(0, "reading command arguments",
                  __FILE__,__LINE__);
      exit(FAILED);
    }

  process_number = atoi(argv[1]);              /* get process number         */
  if ((process_number < 0) || (process_number > 3))
    { print_error(0, "reading process number", __FILE__,__LINE__);
      exit(FAILED);
    }

  seed_value = atoi(argv[2]);                  /* get seed value             */
  threshold  = atof(argv[3]);                  /* get threshold value        */
  tps        = atoi(argv[4]);                  /* get tps scale factor       */

} /* end get_args */
```

Figure 32-4. SQLTP1.SQC: The get_args() Function.

SQLTP1.SQC: The initialize_multi_ipc() Function

In this section, we present the **initialize_multi_ipc()** function, whose code listing is shown in Figure 32-5. This function does all the interprocess communication chores required from a process that runs under **MULTI**'s control. If the code looks unfamiliar, then please review the chapter in Part II on **MULTI** and its child processes. Briefly, a **MULTI** child process execution is controlled by two semaphores:

• The **RUNx** Mutex semaphore which controls when this individual task can run.
• The **RUNALL** Event semaphore which controls when all the child tasks under MULTI can run. When this semaphore posts all processes that are enabled can start participating in a TP1 benchmark run.

This function also obtains a pointer to the shared memory array in which it will write its count results.

```
/*''''''''''''''''''''''''''''''''''''''''''''''''''''''''''''''''''''''''*/
/* initialize semaphores and shared memory for communication between this  */
/* process and the MULTI process.                                          */
/*''''''''''''''''''''''''''''''''''''''''''''''''''''''''''''''''''''''''*/
VOID initialize_multi_ipc(VOID)
{
  CHAR sem_name[30];
```

Figure 32-5 (Part 1 of 2). SQLTP1.SQC: The initialize_multi_ipc() Function.

Figure 32-6 (Part 1 of 2). SQLTP1.SQC: The initialize_task() Function.

```
/*'''''''''''''''''''''''''''''''''''''''*/
/* open and initialize the semaphores  */
/*'''''''''''''''''''''''''''''''''''''''*/
sprintf(sem_name,"\\SEM32\\RUN%d", process_number);
if (rc = DosOpenMutexSem(sem_name,       /* handle to semaphore returned*/
                         &sem_handle))  /* ASCIIZ name of semaphore    */
   { print_error(rc,"during DosOpenMutexSem", __FILE__,__LINE__);
     exit(FAILED);
   }

sprintf(sem_name,"\\SEM32\\RUNALL");
if (rc = DosOpenEventSem(sem_name,                /* handle to semaphore returned*/
                         &control_sem_handle))/* ASCIIZ name of semaphore    */
   { print_error(rc,"during DosOpenEventSem", __FILE__,__LINE__);
     exit(FAILED);
   }

/*'''''''''''''''''''''''''''''''''''''''*/
/* get a shared segment for the count   */
/*    values                             */
/*'''''''''''''''''''''''''''''''''''''''*/
sprintf(name,"\\SHAREMEM\\TASK");
rc = DosGetNamedSharedMem((PVOID)&count_ptr, name, PAG_READ | PAG_WRITE);
if (rc)
    {print_error(rc,"allocating count buffer",__FILE__,__LINE__);
     exit(FAILED);
    }
} /* end initialize_multi_ipc */
```

Figure 32-5 (Part 2 of 2). SQLTP1.SQC: The initialize_multi_ipc() Function.

SQLTP1.SQC: The initialize_task() Function

In this section, we present the **initialize_task()** function, whose code listing is shown
in Figure 32-6. This function does the following task-specific one-time chores:

1. Connects to the TP1 database.
2. Installs a signal handler that intercepts CTRL + Break and gracefully terminates the
   program.
3. Adds a TXNS field to the task's window. This is where the count is displayed for
   TP1 transactions which meet the response time threshold.
4. Seeds the random number generator.

```
/*''''''''''''''''''''''''''''''''''''''''''''''''''''''''''''''''''''''''''*/
/* Perform onetime initializations for the task such as database connects.  */
/*''''''''''''''''''''''''''''''''''''''''''''''''''''''''''''''''''''''''''*/
VOID  initialize_task(VOID)
{
  /*'''''''''''''''''''''''''''''''''''''''''''''''''''''*/
  /* connect to the database, restart if necessary   */
  /*'''''''''''''''''''''''''''''''''''''''''''''''''''''*/
  sqlestrd("TP1", 'S', &sqlca);
```

Figure 32-6 (Part 1 of 2). SQLTP1.SQC: The initialize_task() Function.

```
    if (SQLCODE == SQLE_RC_DB_RESTART)
        sqlerest("TP1", &sqlca);

    if (SQLCODE)
        { sprintf(error_string,"connnecting to the database, SQLCODE = %ld",
                SQLCODE);
          print_error(0, error_string, __FILE__,__LINE__);
          exit(FAILED);
        }

    /*''''''''''''''''''''''''''''''''''''''*/
    /* install database signal handler      */
    /*''''''''''''''''''''''''''''''''''''''*/
    sqleisig(&sqlca);
    if (SQLCODE)
        { sprintf(error_string,"installing signal handler, SQLCODE = %ld",
                SQLCODE);
          print_error(0, error_string, __FILE__,__LINE__);
          exit(FAILED);
        }

    /*''''''''''''''''''''''''''''''''''''''*/
    /* add transaction count field          */
    /*''''''''''''''''''''''''''''''''''''''*/
    write_str("TXNS  = ", FIELD_TEXT_ATTR,
            (process_number * 20) + 2, 10); /* calculate display location */
                                            /*  based on process number   */

    /*''''''''''''''''''''''''''''''''''''''*/
    /* initialize random number generator   */
    /*''''''''''''''''''''''''''''''''''''''*/
    srand(seed_value);
} /* end initialize_task */
```

Figure 32-6 (Part 2 of 2). SQLTP1.SQC: The initialize_task() Function.

SQLTP1.SQC: The execute_task() Function

In this section, we present the **execute_task()** function, whose code listing is shown in Figure 32-7. This function provides the control loop for executing TP1 transactions. Here is how it works:

1. It waits on the **RUNx** Mutex sempaphore through which **MULTI** controls the execution of a particular task. When this semaphore resets, the task can move to the next step.
2. It waits on the **RUNALL** Event semaphore through which **MULTI** synchronizes the execution of all its child tasks. When this semaphore posts, all the enabled processes can start participating in a TP1 benchmark run.
3. It starts the timer and obtains two random numbers.
4. It invokes the helper procedure **tp1_transaction()** to execute a TP1 transaction (see Figure 32-8).
5. It calculates the elapsed time.
6. It increments the result counters and displays the new results in the **MULTI** process window. Note that the display is a critical resource protected by a semaphore. The

task waits on the semaphore to clear. When that happens it sets the semaphore, writes the counts to the process display window, and then clears the semaphore.

As you can see, this control procedure does the typical stuff expected from a program executing under **MULTI**. There is no new material here.

```
/*'''''''''''''''''''''''''''''''''''''''''''''''''''''''''''''''''''''''*/
/* Task routine. This routine continuously 1) requests a semaphore,      */
/*   2) increments and displays a count, 3) clears the semaphore.  The user */
/*   can disable counting by setting the semaphore from the display panel. */
/*'''''''''''''''''''''''''''''''''''''''''''''''''''''''''''''''''''''''*/
VOID execute_task(VOID)
{
  CHAR   count_str[10];
  USHORT rc;

  count_ptr->count[process_number] = 0;

  /*'''''''''''''''''''''''''''''''''''''''*/
  /* display process status                */
  /*'''''''''''''''''''''''''''''''''''''''*/
  write_str("Ready        ", PANEL_STATUS_ATTR,
            (process_number * 20) + 2, 15); /* calculate display location  */
                                            /*  based on thread number     */

  /*'''''''''''''''''''''''''''''''''''''''*/
  /* continuous count loop                 */
  /*'''''''''''''''''''''''''''''''''''''''*/
  while (TRUE)
    {
      /*'''''''''''''''''''''''''''''''''''''''''*/
      /* wait for control sem to clear           */
      /*'''''''''''''''''''''''''''''''''''''''''*/
      if (rc = DosWaitEventSem(control_sem_handle,       /* semaphore handle */
                               -1L))                     /* infinite timeout */
         { print_error(rc,"executing DosSemWait",
                       __FILE__,__LINE__);
           exit(FAILED);
         }

      /*'''''''''''''''''''''''''''''''''''''''''*/
      /* request the semaphore                   */
      /*'''''''''''''''''''''''''''''''''''''''''*/
      if (rc = DosRequestMutexSem(sem_handle,            /* semaphore handle */
                                  -1L))                  /* infinite timeout */
         { print_error(rc,"executing DosRequestMutexSem",
                       __FILE__,__LINE__);
           exit(FAILED);
         }

      /*'''''''''''''''''''''''''''''''''''''''''*/
      /* execute a TP1 transaction               */
      /*'''''''''''''''''''''''''''''''''''''''''*/
      reset_timer();
      start_timer();

      random1 =  rand();
      random2 =  rand();
```

Figure 32-7 (Part 1 of 2). SQLTP1.SQC: The execute_task() Function.

```
        if ( tp1_transaction( ) )
           exit(FAILED);

        stop_timer();

        /*'''''''''''''''''''''''''''''''''''''*/
        /* increment the count                 */
        /*'''''''''''''''''''''''''''''''''''''*/
        rc = DosWaitEventSem(control_sem_handle, 0L); /* Don't count if test  */
        if (rc == 0)                                  /*      is done.         */
           {
              ++(count_ptr->count[process_number]);

              if (event_time <= threshold)
                 ++(count_ptr->count[process_number + 4]);
           }

        /*'''''''''''''''''''''''''''''''''''''*/
        /* display the count value             */
        /*'''''''''''''''''''''''''''''''''''''*/
        sprintf(count_str, "%-7lu", count_ptr->count[process_number]);
        write_str(count_str, OUTPUT_FIELD_ATTR,   /* calculate display location*/
                 (process_number * 20) + 10,  9);/*  based on thread number   */

        sprintf(count_str, "%-7lu", count_ptr->count[process_number + 4]);
        write_str(count_str, OUTPUT_FIELD_ATTR,   /* calculate display location*/
                 (process_number * 20) + 10, 10);/*  based on thread number   */

        /*'''''''''''''''''''''''''''''''''''''*/
        /* clear the semaphore                 */
        /*'''''''''''''''''''''''''''''''''''''*/
        if (rc = DosReleaseMutexSem(sem_handle))
           { print_error(rc,"executing DosReleaseMutexSem", __FILE__,__LINE__);
             exit(FAILED);
           }
     }/* end while */
} /* end execute_task */
```

Figure 32-7 (Part 2 of 2).   SQLTP1.SQC: The execute_task() Function.

SQLTP1.SQC: The tp1_transaction() Function

In this section, we present the **tp1_transaction()** function, whose code listing is shown in Figure 32-8. This is the function that does the "real TP1 work." So, let's take a close look at what it does:

1. It generates a set of random numbers, for the account number, the teller ID, and the branch ID. This simulates a real-world, random event as required by the TP1 specification.

2. It retrieves the balance for that random account from the ACCT table and adds some money to it. We're going to be generous with everybody! This operation demonstrates the use of the cursor in a static SQL context. Let's see how it works:

- The **DECLARE CURSOR** command associates CURSOR1 with the **SELECT** statement. From now on, CURSOR1 can be used as a handle for that **SELECT** statement.

- The **OPEN** command on CURSOR1 causes the **SELECT** to execute and produces a "result set"; there should only be one account returned. The cursor will be positioned before the first row.

- The **FETCH** command positions that cursor to the first row in the "result set," and then retrieves that row and puts the result **INTO** the host variable, **balance**.

- The **UPDATE** with the keyword **CURRENT** updates the row on which the cursor is currently positioned. We credit this account with the contents of the host variable, **delta**.

- The **CLOSE** command is issued to close the cursor. We've done our first TP1 update, to the ACCT table. Only three more to go.

3. It updates the balance for a random teller in the TELLER table. This is a "simple" non-cursored SQL **UPDATE**.

4. It updates the balance for a random branch in the BRANCH table. This is also a "simple" non-cursored SQL **UPDATE**.

5. It inserts a record for that transaction into the HISTORY table using a SQL **INSERT**. Again, this is straightforward; we just have to be sure that the host variables and literals in the list of **VALUES** map to the list of named columns.

6. It issues a **COMMIT**, so that the TP1 is recorded for posterity in the database, making all parties slightly richer. It's a bit like printing money, isn't it?

7. Congratulations, we've just completed the first of our TP1 flavors!

```
/*''''''''''''''''''''''''''''''''''''''''''''''''''''''''''''''''''''''''*/
/* function for TP1 transaction                                           */
/*''''''''''''''''''''''''''''''''''''''''''''''''''''''''''''''''''''''''*/
SHORT APIENTRY tp1_transaction(VOID)
{
  CHAR    msgbuf[512];

       /*''''''''''''''''''''''''''''''''''''''*/
       /* generate some random data            */
       /*''''''''''''''''''''''''''''''''''''''*/
  acct_num = (random1 * random2) % (tps*1000001) + 1;/* generate account num */
  teller_id= (short)(random1 % (tps*100)) + 1;       /* generate teller id   */
  branch_id= (short)(random2 % (tps*10)) + 1;        /* generate branch id   */
```

Figure 32-8 (Part 1 of 3). SQLTP1.SQC: The tp1_transaction() Function.

```
      /*''''''''''''''''''''''''''''''''''''''*/
      /* get the current balance from ACCT    */
      /*''''''''''''''''''''''''''''''''''''''*/
EXEC SQL DECLARE CURSOR1 CURSOR FOR
         SELECT BALANCE FROM ACCT WHERE ACCT_NUM = :acct_num
         FOR UPDATE OF BALANCE;

EXEC SQL OPEN CURSOR1;
if (SQLCODE != 0)
   { sqlaintp(msgbuf, sizeof(msgbuf), 80, &sqlca);
     printf("%s\n",msgbuf);
     print_error((SHORT)SQLCODE, "during SQL OPEN",
                 __FILE__, __LINE__);
     return(FAILED);
   }

EXEC SQL FETCH CURSOR1 INTO :balance;
if (SQLCODE != 0)
   { sqlaintp(msgbuf, sizeof(msgbuf), 80, &sqlca);
     printf("%s\n",msgbuf);
     print_error((SHORT)SQLCODE, "during SQL FETCH",
                 __FILE__, __LINE__);
     return(FAILED);
   }


      /*''''''''''''''''''''''''''''''''''''''*/
      /* Credit the balance in the ACCT table */
      /*''''''''''''''''''''''''''''''''''''''*/
EXEC SQL UPDATE ACCT
         SET BALANCE = BALANCE + :delta
         WHERE CURRENT OF CURSOR1;
if (SQLCODE != 0)
   { sqlaintp(msgbuf, sizeof(msgbuf), 80, &sqlca);
     printf("%s\n",msgbuf);
     print_error((SHORT)SQLCODE, "during SQL UPDATE",
                 __FILE__,__LINE__);
     return(FAILED);
   }

EXEC SQL CLOSE CURSOR1;
if (SQLCODE != 0)
   { sqlaintp(msgbuf, sizeof(msgbuf), 80, &sqlca);
     printf("%s\n",msgbuf);
     print_error((SHORT)SQLCODE, "during SQL CLOSE",
                 __FILE__,__LINE__);
     return(FAILED);
   }


      /*''''''''''''''''''''''''''''''''''''''*/
      /* Update the TELLER table's balance    */
      /*''''''''''''''''''''''''''''''''''''''*/
EXEC SQL UPDATE TELLER
         SET BALANCE = BALANCE + :delta
         WHERE TELLER_ID = :teller_id;
if (SQLCODE != 0)
   { sqlaintp(msgbuf, sizeof(msgbuf), 80, &sqlca);
     printf("%s\n",msgbuf);
     print_error((SHORT)SQLCODE, "during SQL UPDATE",
                 __FILE__,__LINE__);
     return(FAILED);
   }
```

Figure 32-8 (Part 2 of 3).   SQLTP1.SQC: The tp1_transaction() Function.

```
        /*'''''''''''''''''''''''''''''''''''''*/
        /* Update the BRANCH table's balance   */
        /*'''''''''''''''''''''''''''''''''''''*/
EXEC SQL UPDATE BRANCH
        SET BALANCE = BALANCE + :delta
        WHERE BRANCH_ID = :branch_id;
if (SQLCODE != 0)
    { sqlaintp(msgbuf, sizeof(msgbuf), 80, &sqlca);
      printf("%s\n",msgbuf);
      print_error((SHORT)SQLCODE, "during SQL UPDATE",
                  __FILE__,__LINE__);
      return(FAILED);
    }


        /*'''''''''''''''''''''''''''''''''''''*/
        /* Insert transaction in HISTORY table */
        /*'''''''''''''''''''''''''''''''''''''*/
EXEC SQL INSERT
        INTO HISTORY(ACCT_NUM, TELLER_ID, BRANCH_ID, BALANCE,
                     DELTA, PID, TRANSID, ACCTNAME, TEMP)
        VALUES(:acct_num, :teller_id, :branch_id, :balance,
               :delta, 1, 3, :acct_name, 'hist ');
if (SQLCODE != 0)
    { sqlaintp(msgbuf, sizeof(msgbuf), 80, &sqlca);
      printf("%s\n",msgbuf);
      print_error((SHORT)SQLCODE, "during SQL INSERT",
                  __FILE__,__LINE__);
      return(FAILED);
    }

        /*'''''''''''''''''''''''''''''''''''''*/
        /* Commit the transaction to database  */
        /*'''''''''''''''''''''''''''''''''''''*/
EXEC SQL COMMIT;
if (SQLCODE != 0)
    { sqlaintp(msgbuf, sizeof(msgbuf), 80, &sqlca);
      printf("%s\n",msgbuf);
      print_error((SHORT)SQLCODE, "during SQL COMMIT",
                  __FILE__, __LINE__);
      return(FAILED);
    }

  return(GOOD);

} /* end tp1_transaction */
```

Figure 32-8 (Part 3 of 3). SQLTP1.SQC: The tp1_transaction() Function.

Helper Functions

In this section, we present the helper functions whose code is listed in Figure 32-9. These are just our standard timer and print error functions that you've already seen throughout this book.

```
/*''''''''''''''''''''''''''''''''''''''''''''''''''''''''''''''''''''''''*/
/*  This procedure initializes the time variables.                       */
/*''''''''''''''''''''''''''''''''''''''''''''''''''''''''''''''''''''''''*/
VOID   reset_timer(VOID)
{ event_time = 0.0 ;
  start_time = 0.0 ;
  end_time   = 0.0 ;
} /* end reset_time */


/*''''''''''''''''''''''''''''''''''''''''''''''''''''''''''''''''''''''''*/
/*  This procedure records the time at the start of an interval          */
/*''''''''''''''''''''''''''''''''''''''''''''''''''''''''''''''''''''''''*/
VOID   start_timer(VOID)
{ ftime(&timebuff);
  start_time = (double)timebuff.time+((double)timebuff.millitm)/(double)1000;
} /* end start_time */


/*''''''''''''''''''''''''''''''''''''''''''''''''''''''''''''''''''''''''*/
/*  This procedure records the time at the end of an interval            */
/*  and calculates the elapsed time for an event.                        */
/*''''''''''''''''''''''''''''''''''''''''''''''''''''''''''''''''''''''''*/
VOID   stop_timer(VOID)
{ ftime(&timebuff);
  end_time = (double)timebuff.time+((double)timebuff.millitm)/(double)1000;
  event_time = event_time  + (end_time - start_time);
} /* end stop_time */


/*''''''''''''''''''''''''''''''''''''''''''''''''''''''''''''''''''''''''*/
/* write a character string to the screen.                               */
/*''''''''''''''''''''''''''''''''''''''''''''''''''''''''''''''''''''''''*/
VOID write_str(PCHAR charstr, CHAR attribute, USHORT x, USHORT y)
{ if (rc = VioWrtCharStrAtt(charstr,    /* character string          */
                       strlen(charstr),/* number of times           */
                       y, x,            /* screen position           */
                       &attribute,      /* attribute                 */
                       0))              /* reserved                  */
     print_error(rc,"during VioWrtCharStrAtt",__FILE__,__LINE__);
} /* end write_str */


/*''''''''''''''''''''''''''''''''''''''''''''''''''''''''''''''''''''''''*/
/* Error Display Routine                                                 */
/*''''''''''''''''''''''''''''''''''''''''''''''''''''''''''''''''''''''''*/
VOID print_error(USHORT Error, PCHAR msg, PCHAR file, USHORT line)
{
 if (Error == 0)
    printf("Error detected while %s at line %d in file %s.\n",
           msg, line, file);
 else
    printf("Error %d detected while %s at line %d in file %s.\n",
           Error, msg, line, file);
} /* end print_error */
```

Figure 32-9. SQLTP1.SQC: Helper Functions.

SQLTP1.H Include File

In this section, we present the **sqltp1.h** include file, whose code is listed in Figure 32-10. Again, this is just your "garden variety" C include file, with all the forward function declarations, type definitions, and global variables.

```
/***************************************************************************/
/*   INCLUDE NAME: SQLTP1 - declarations for TP1 task programs          */
/***************************************************************************/

/*'''''''''''''''''''''''''''''''''''''''''''''''''''''''''''''''''''''''''*/
/* Forward declarations of procedures in this module                     */
/*'''''''''''''''''''''''''''''''''''''''''''''''''''''''''''''''''''''''''*/
                 /*'''''''''''''''''''''''''''''''''''''''*/
                 /* top level routines                  */
                 /*'''''''''''''''''''''''''''''''''''''''*/
VOID get_args(USHORT argc, PCHAR argv[]);
VOID initialize_multi_ipc(VOID);
VOID initialize_task(VOID);
VOID execute_task(VOID);
SHORT APIENTRY tp1_transaction(VOID);

                 /*'''''''''''''''''''''''''''''''''''''''*/
                 /* VIO call helper functions           */
                 /*'''''''''''''''''''''''''''''''''''''''*/
VOID write_str(PCHAR, CHAR, USHORT, USHORT);

                 /*'''''''''''''''''''''''''''''''''''''''*/
                 /* timer routines                      */
                 /*'''''''''''''''''''''''''''''''''''''''*/
VOID   reset_timer(VOID);
VOID   start_timer(VOID);
VOID   stop_timer(VOID);

                 /*'''''''''''''''''''''''''''''''''''''''*/
                 /* Error display routine               */
                 /*'''''''''''''''''''''''''''''''''''''''*/
VOID print_error(USHORT, PCHAR, PCHAR, USHORT);


/*'''''''''''''''''''''''''''''''''''''''''''''''''''''''''''''''''''''''''*/
/* Global variables/type definitions for this module                     */
/*'''''''''''''''''''''''''''''''''''''''''''''''''''''''''''''''''''''''''*/
                 /*'''''''''''''''''''''''''''''''''''''''*/
                 /* for program parameters              */
                 /*'''''''''''''''''''''''''''''''''''''''*/
USHORT process_number;                   /* number of this process       */
USHORT seed_value;                       /* initial seed for random number gen*/
double threshold;                        /* time thresholds for TP1 txns  */
USHORT tps;                              /* the tps database scaling factor  */

                 /*'''''''''''''''''''''''''''''''''''''''*/
                 /* for multi IPC                       */
                 /*'''''''''''''''''''''''''''''''''''''''*/
HMTX    sem_handle;                      /* handle for task semaphore     */
HEV     control_sem_handle;              /* handle for global control sem. */
typedef struct
        { ULONG count[8];
        } COUNT;
COUNT   *count_ptr;                      /* structure for count variables  */

                 /*'''''''''''''''''''''''''''''''''''''''*/
                 /* for task execution                  */
                 /*'''''''''''''''''''''''''''''''''''''''*/
USHORT random1, random2;
```

Figure 32-10 (Part 1 of 2). SQLTP1.H Include File.

```
                    /*_____*/
                    /* global variables for timing       */
                    /*_____*/
struct   timeb   timebuff;                    /* Timer buffer              */
double           start_time = 0.0;            /* Start of command time     */
double           end_time   = 0.0;            /* End of command time       */
double           event_time = 0.0;            /* Elapsed time              */

                    /*_____*/
                    /* misc variables                     */
                    /*_____*/
CHAR     name[80];                    /* variable for building ascii names */
USHORT   selector;                    /* variable for selector values      */
USHORT rc;                            /* return code variable              */
CHAR     error_string[80];
```

Figure 32-10 (Part 2 of 2). SQLTP1.H Include File.

RUNNING FOUR TP1 BENCHMARK TESTS USING SQLTP1.SQC

Now that we've got some code, let's run some benchmarks to see how well this TP1 flavor performs. We will run three local TP1 benchmark tests and one remote one:

- The **local** benchmark tests measure performance as a function of improved server hardware (see Figure 32-12).

  1. A PS/2 Mod-80 with a 20-MHz clock and a 500 KByte RAM buffer.
  2. A PS/2 Mod-95 with a 33-MHz clock and a 500 KByte RAM buffer.
  3. A PS/2 Mod-95 with a 33-MHz clock and a 1000-KByte RAM buffer.

- The remote benchmark uses for its server, a PS/2 Mod-95 with a 33-MHz clock and a 1000-KByte memory buffer. The clients run on a PS/2 Mod 80 with a 20-MHz clock (see Figure 32-13).

All four benchmarks use the same software configuration; a four-process **MULTI** whose configuration file is shown below:

```
PROGRAM_TYPE     = PROCESS
STOP_TIME_MS     = 600000
TASK_NAME        = SQLTP1.EXE 0 17 2.0 1;
TASK_NAME        = SQLTP1.EXE 1 23 2.0 1;
TASK_NAME        = SQLTP1.EXE 2 29 2.0 1;
TASK_NAME        = SQLTP1.EXE 3 57 2.0 1;
```

Figure 32-11. A MULTI.CFG File for Running Four TP1 Processes.

As you can see from the configuration file, the benchmarks are set up to run for 10-minute tests (i.e., 600,000 milliseconds). The response time threshold is set to 2.0 seconds, and a 1-tps database size is specified.

Note: Our liberal interpretation of TP1 uses a 2-second response threshold and a 1-tps database. However, on the plus side we're measuring 100% transaction completions as opposed to the 95% threshold required by the benchmark.

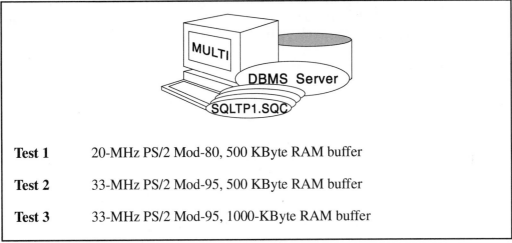

Test 1	20-MHz PS/2 Mod-80, 500 KByte RAM buffer
Test 2	33-MHz PS/2 Mod-95, 500 KByte RAM buffer
Test 3	33-MHz PS/2 Mod-95, 1000-KByte RAM buffer

Figure 32-12. Local Static SQL TP1 Benchmark Configurations.

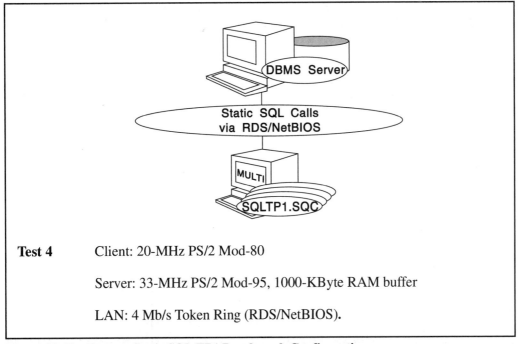

Test 4	Client: 20-MHz PS/2 Mod-80
	Server: 33-MHz PS/2 Mod-95, 1000-KByte RAM buffer
	LAN: 4 Mb/s Token Ring (RDS/NetBIOS).

Figure 32-13. Remote Static SQL TP1 Benchmark Configurations.

Running SQLTP1 Against a Local Database (Benchmark1)

The configuration for this benchmark is a four-client MULTI running against a local database. The test is run on a PS/2 Mod-80 with a 20-MHz clock and a 500 KByte RAM buffer (*BufPage parameter*). The database is already loaded for a 1-tps database scale. The following RSQL run is used to set up the 500 KByte buffer (we're allocating 128 4k-pages) and prepare the database for Benchmark1.

```
--                    Change TP1 Database Configuration
-- ==============================================================================
-- update the Database Configuration for database for a 500k buffer
EXEC DBA: UPDATE_DB_CFG TP1      MAXAPPLS    = 8,
                                 DLCHKTIME   = 10000,
                                 BUFFPAGE    = 128,
                                 LOGFILSIZ   = 50,
                                 LOGPRIMARY  = 2,
                                 LOGSECOND   = 20;


  OK, sql_rcd = 0,         Execution time =     0.3400 secs

  -- Show the database configuration for database TP1
  EXEC DBA: SHOW_DB_CFG TP1;

  Database Configuration for Database TP1
  ===============================================

  Configuration Parameter          Current  Parm.      Parm.        Parm.
  Description                       Value    Units      Range        Default
  -------------------------------- -------- ---------- ------------ -------
  Max. Active Applications               8   Appl.      1-256           8
  Max. DB Files Open/Application        20   files      2-235          20
  Max. Files Open/Application          255   files      25-32700      255
  Buffer Pool Size                     128   4K pages    2-1500        (1)
  Time Interval for Deadlocks        10000   millisecs. 1-600 sec.     10
  Max. Storage for Locklists            25   4K pages   4-250           8
  Max. percent locklist/appl.           22   percent    1-100          22
  Default Application Heap               3   segments   2-20            3
  Application Agent Heap                 2   segments   2-85            2
  Sort List Heap                         2   segments   1-20            2
  Database Heap                          3   segments   1-45           (2)
  SQL Statement Heap                    64   segments   8-255          64
  Log File Size                         50   4K pages   4-65535        (3)
  Primary Log Files                      2   files      2-63            3
  Secondary Log Files                   20   files      0-61            2
  Log Records/soft checkpoint          100   records    0-65535       100

  Current Log Location = F:\SQL00001\SQLOGDIR\
  New Log Location    =
  First Log File      =
  Current Log File    =
  Copy Protection     =     1 (1 = Protected, Default = 1)
  Log Retain          =     0 (1 = Retain Log Files, Default = 0)
  User Exit           =     0 (1 = Enable User Exit, Default = 0)
  Auto Restart        =     1 (1 = Enable Auto Restart, Default = 1)
  Country             =     1
  Code Page           =   437
```

Figure 32-14 (Part 1 of 2). Preparing the Database for Benchmark1.

```
Release                 =     768
DB Consistency          =       1 (1 = Consistent)
Backup Pending          =       0 (1 = Backup Pending)
Roll Forward Pending    =       0 (1 = Roll Forward Pending)
User Exit Status        =       0 (1 = User exit Enabled)
Log Retain Status       =       0 (1 = log files retained)

(1) - client or standalone 25, server 250
(2) - client or standalone  2, server   3
(3) - client or standalone 32, server 200
OK, sql_rcd = 0,          Execution time =       0.1300 secs

-- bind the tp1 program
EXEC DBA: BIND TP1 SQLTP1.BND ISO REPEATABLE_READ BLOCK_ALL PUBLIC;

 No messages in msgfile.msg

 OK, sql_rcd = 0,          Execution time =       2.7800 secs

-- Connect to the TP1 database
EXEC DBA: STARTUSE TP1 S;

 OK, sql_rcd = 0,          Execution time =       0.6900 secs

-- delete all of the history data
EXEC SQL: DELETE FROM HISTORY;

 WARNING, sql_code = 100,    Execution time =       2.3700 secs
 SQL0100W  No row was found for FETCH, UPDATE or DELETE; or the result of a

 query is an empty table.
```

Figure 32-14 (Part 2 of 2).   Preparing the Database for Benchmark1.

```
                        Multiprocess Execution Example

 Use arrow keys to move the cursor.  Use + and - keys to change field values.
 Press R to start running, S to stop, or C to clear the count.
 Press ESC to terminate the program.
┌SQLTP1.EXE─────────┐ ┌SQLTP1.EXE─────────┐ ┌SQLTP1.EXE─────────┐ ┌SQLTP1.EXE─────────┐
│                   │ │                   │ │                   │ │                   │
│ Count = 796       │ │ Count = 786       │ │ Count = 800       │ │ Count = 810       │
│ TXNS  = 794       │ │ TXNS  = 784       │ │ TXNS  = 798       │ │ TXNS  = 808       │
│ Priority  = RG    │ │ Priority  = RG    │ │ Priority  = RG    │ │ Priority  = RG    │
│ Level     = 0     │ │ Level     = 0     │ │ Level     = 0     │ │ Level     = 0     │
│ Semaphore = CLEAR │ │ Semaphore = CLEAR │ │ Semaphore = CLEAR │ │ Semaphore = CLEAR │
│                   │ │                   │ │                   │ │                   │
│ Ready             │ │ Ready             │ │ Ready             │ │ Ready             │
└───────────────────┘ └───────────────────┘ └───────────────────┘ └───────────────────┘
┌EXECUTION STATUS───────────────────────┐ ┌SYSTEM INFORMATION───────────────────────┐
│                                       │ │                                         │
│ Stop Time    = 600.0        sec       │ │ Maximum Wait        = 3         sec      │
│ Elapsed time = 600.0        sec       │ │ Minimum Time Slice = 32         ms       │
│ Total Count  = 3192                   │ │ Maximum Time Slice = 32         ms       │
│ Run Status   = STOPPED                │ │ Dynamic Variation  = ACTIVE             │
│                                       │ │                                         │
└───────────────────────────────────────┘ └─────────────────────────────────────────┘
```

Figure 32-15.   Benchmark1: 4-Client TP1 on Local DB (20 MHz Mod-80, 0.5MB bufPage).

Benchmark1 Results: The MULTI screen capture in Figure 32-15 shows the results of a 10-minute test. During this period a total of 3192 TP1 transactions ran successfully. However, only (794 + 784 + 798 + 808 = 3184) transactions had a response time under the 2-second threshold. Using the liberal interpretation of TP1 introduced earlier, this machine is in the *5.3 TP1* range.

Running SQLTP1 Against a Local Database (Benchmark2)

The configuration for this benchmark is a four-client MULTI running against a local database. The test is run on a PS/2 Mod-95 with a 33-MHz clock and a 500 KByte buffer. What we've done is upgraded the server machine to a PS/2 Mod-95, and left everything else the same. We assume the database is already loaded for a 1-tps database scale. The 500 KByte buffer configuration is the same as in the previous benchmark.

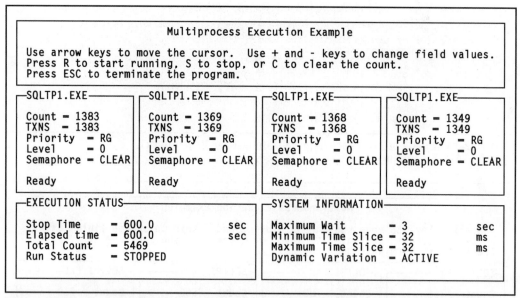

```
                    Multiprocess Execution Example

  Use arrow keys to move the cursor.  Use + and - keys to change field values.
  Press R to start running, S to stop, or C to clear the count.
  Press ESC to terminate the program.

 ┌SQLTP1.EXE──────┐ ┌SQLTP1.EXE──────┐ ┌SQLTP1.EXE──────┐ ┌SQLTP1.EXE──────┐

  Count  = 1383      Count  = 1369      Count  = 1368      Count  = 1349
  TXNS   = 1383      TXNS   = 1369      TXNS   = 1368      TXNS   = 1349
  Priority  = RG     Priority  = RG     Priority  = RG     Priority  = RG
  Level    = 0       Level    = 0       Level    = 0       Level    = 0
  Semaphore = CLEAR  Semaphore = CLEAR  Semaphore = CLEAR  Semaphore = CLEAR

  Ready              Ready              Ready              Ready

 ┌EXECUTION STATUS──────────────────┐ ┌SYSTEM INFORMATION──────────────────┐

  Stop Time     = 600.0      sec       Maximum Wait       = 3        sec
  Elapsed time  = 600.0      sec       Minimum Time Slice = 32       ms
  Total Count   = 5469                 Maximum Time Slice = 32       ms
  Run Status    = STOPPED              Dynamic Variation  = ACTIVE
```

Figure 32-16.   Benchmark2: 4-Client TP1 on Local DB (33 MHz Mod-95, 0.5MB bufPage).

Benchmark2 Results: The MULTI screen capture in Figure 32-16 shows the results of a 10-minute test. During this period, a total of 5469 TP1 transactions ran successfully. All transactions had a response time under the 2-second threshold. Using the liberal interpretation of TP1 introduced earlier, this machine is therefore in the *9.1 TP1* range.

Running SQLTP1 Against a Local Database (Benchmark3)

The configuration for this benchmark is a four-client MULTI running against a local database. The test is run on a PS/2 Mod-95 with a 33-MHz clock and a 1000-KByte buffer. What we've done is upgraded the buffer on the server machine to 1000 KBytes and left everything else the same. We assume the database is already loaded for a 1-tps database scale.

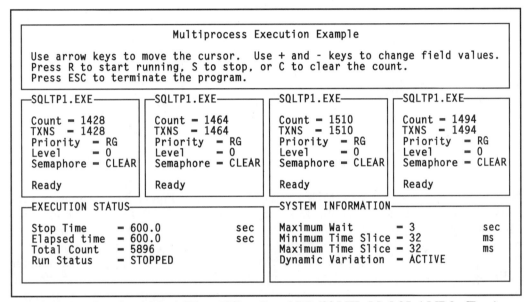

```
                    Multiprocess Execution Example
 Use arrow keys to move the cursor.  Use + and - keys to change field values.
 Press R to start running, S to stop, or C to clear the count.
 Press ESC to terminate the program.
┌SQLTP1.EXE────────┐ ┌SQLTP1.EXE────────┐ ┌SQLTP1.EXE────────┐ ┌SQLTP1.EXE────────┐
│                  │ │                  │ │                  │ │                  │
│ Count   = 1428   │ │ Count   = 1464   │ │ Count   = 1510   │ │ Count   = 1494   │
│ TXNS    = 1428   │ │ TXNS    = 1464   │ │ TXNS    = 1510   │ │ TXNS    = 1494   │
│ Priority   = RG  │ │ Priority   = RG  │ │ Priority   = RG  │ │ Priority   = RG  │
│ Level      = 0   │ │ Level      = 0   │ │ Level      = 0   │ │ Level      = 0   │
│ Semaphore = CLEAR│ │ Semaphore = CLEAR│ │ Semaphore = CLEAR│ │ Semaphore = CLEAR│
│                  │ │                  │ │                  │ │                  │
│ Ready            │ │ Ready            │ │ Ready            │ │ Ready            │
└──────────────────┘ └──────────────────┘ └──────────────────┘ └──────────────────┘
┌EXECUTION STATUS──────────────────────┐ ┌SYSTEM INFORMATION────────────────────┐
│                                       │ │                                       │
│ Stop Time    = 600.0        sec       │ │ Maximum Wait       = 3         sec     │
│ Elapsed time = 600.0        sec       │ │ Minimum Time Slice = 32        ms      │
│ Total Count  = 5896                   │ │ Maximum Time Slice = 32        ms      │
│ Run Status   = STOPPED                │ │ Dynamic Variation  = ACTIVE            │
│                                       │ │                                       │
└───────────────────────────────────────┘ └───────────────────────────────────────┘
```

Figure 32-17.   Benchmark3: 4-Client TP1 on Local DB (33 MHz Mod-95, 1 MB bufPage).

Benchmark3 Results: This MULTI screen in Figure 32-17 shows the results of a 10-minute test. During this period, a total of 5896 TP1 transactions ran successfully. All transactions had a response time under the 2-second threshold. Using the liberal interpretation of TP1 we introduced earlier, this machine is therefore in the *9.8 TP1* range. The results show a very slight improvement in performance with the 500 KByte buffer increase.

Running SQLTP1 Against a Remote Database (Benchmark4)

The configuration for this benchmark is a four-client MULTI running against a remote database. The test is run on a PS/2 Mod-95 database server with a 33-MHz clock and a 1000-KByte buffer. The client machine is a PS/2 Mod-80 with a 20-MHz clock. We're effectively working with the same database set up as in Benchmark3, but we've offloaded the clients to a separate machine. As a result, we introduced the *network* factor. RDS uses NetBIOS (the default protocol). We assume the database is already loaded for a 1-tps database scale.

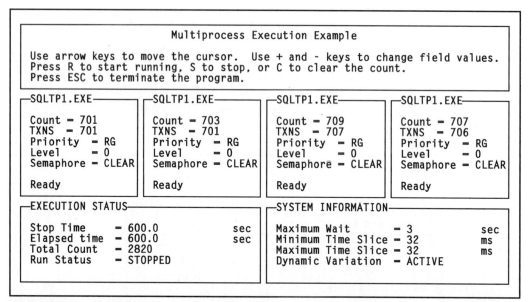

Figure 32-18. Benchmark4: 4-Client TP1 on Remote DB (33 MHz Mod 95, 1 MB bufPage).

Benchmark4 Results: The MULTI screen capture in Figure 32-18 shows the results of a 10-minute test. During this period, a total of 2820 TP1 transactions ran successfully. However, only (701 + 701 + 707 + 706 = 2815) transactions had a response time under the 2-second threshold. Using the liberal interpretation of TP1 we introduced earlier, this machine is therefore in the *4.7 TP1* range. This number indicates that the Remote Data Service component introduces a significant performance overhead. In this implementation, each SQL statement is sent over the network using NetBIOS.

WHAT DO THESE BENCHMARKS TELL US?

Here are some general observations about the benchmarks we ran:

- *Database servers are CPU-intensive, right?* Yes, absolutely. The results of the tests strongly suggest that SQL servers are very CPU-intensive. We were able to improve the performance by about 71% (from *5.32 TP1* to *9.1 TP1*) by just going from a 20 MHz 80386 machine (Benchmark1) to a 33 MHz 80486 machine (Benchmark2). Just imagine the gains you could achieve by going to a 80586 "superserver."

- *More RAM buffer is always better, right?* Yes, more or less! The 500 KByte increment in buffer space introduced in Benchmark3, had a minor effect on performance (from *9.1 TP1* to *9.8 TP1*). It's not earth shattering, but every improvement counts. You can run your own tests to find out where the curve hits the knee (when more RAM is not necessarily better). It is important to find this knee before you go out and buy an extra 10 MBytes of RAM for your database.

- *Surely a faster disk will help?* No! We tried a much faster disk drive. After all, the data must be stored either in RAM or on disk. The result was surprising: **no** performance improvement was registered.

- *Networks take their toll?* Yes, very much so with SQL database servers. Running the client/server application across the network was more than twice as slow. It went from *9.8 TP1* (Benchmark3) down to *4.7 TP1* (Benchmark4). This dramatic slowdown is the Achilles heel of database servers. The benchmarks that were run in this chapter use the "vintage" static SQL *Database Server* implementation of TP1. In later chapters, we demonstrate how Remote Procedure Calls on *Transaction Servers* can significantly improve the TP1 numbers for network servers.

OTHER QUESTIONS YOU CAN ANSWER

The code for the benchmark is available and you can use it to measure other factors that may be of interest.[1]

- What is the effect of roll-forward logging?

- What is the effect of upwardly scaling the TP1 database?

- What is the effect of running APPC (or APPN) instead of NetBIOS?

---

[1] See coupon at the end of the book.

- What is the effect of running static SQL (using DDCS/2) on DB2, SQL/400, or SQL/DS?

- What is the effect of using the DDCS/2 server gateway versus standalone DDCS/2?

- What is the effect of running on a 16 Mbit/s Token Ring instead of a 4 Mbit/s?

- What is the effect of SDLC on a TP line instead of a LAN?

- What is the effect of a multihop APPN network?

- etc.

When we ran the BLOB Olympics in Part III, we brought to your attention the lament from the computer industry that: *"There are lies, damned lies, and benchmarks."* On the other hand, the numbers we're uncovering in this chapter, and the chapters that follow, show that benchmarks are a great *investigative reporting* tool. We've put all those tools in your hands, which means that you can keep us honest, and in the process you can also go about making your own discoveries. And, yes, there are a lot more investigations to be made. You will see some interesting cases in the chapters that follow.

Chapter 33

The Application Remote Interface Transaction Server TP1

This is the third of a six chapter series, in which we develop a TP1 Benchmark toolkit for the OS/2 Database Manager. This chapter provides the **Database Application Remote Interface** *Transaction Server* version of TP1. This is the Database Manager's implementation of remote procedures using RDS on an APPC/APPN or NetBIOS LAN.

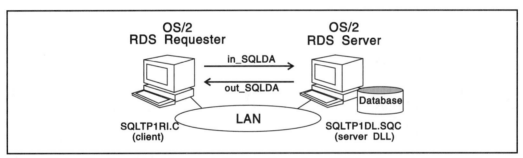

Figure 33-1. The Database Manager's Remote Procedure Call Implementation of TP1.

The plan for this chapter is to split the **SQLTP1.SQC** program that you saw in the last chapter into two programs:

1. The **SQLTP1RI.C** client program drives the TP1s and interacts with **MULTI**.

2. The **SQLTP1DL.SQC** server program executes the TP1 transaction against the database; this program's code is packaged as a **DLL**.

The client and server programs communicate through the Remote Procedure Call mechanism provided by the **Database Application Remote Interface**. The client and server programs can execute in the same machine or on separate machines connected by a LAN (see Figure 33-1). The TP1 transaction performance will be measured using both configurations.

WHAT YOU WILL LEARN

This chapter serves as an elaborate example of how to use the mechanics of the **Database Application Remote Interface**. On the client side of the code, you will learn how to set up the **SQLDAs** and issue the Remote Procedure Call. On the server side, you will learn how to write a remote procedure DLL, and you will see how this DLL obtains its parameters and sends back its response. This chapter has the following prerequisites:

- An understanding of the SQL tutorial in Chapter 26.
- The Database Administration Tutorial in Chapter 27, with special emphasis on the section "The Power of Remote Procedures" in Chapter 28.
- The first two chapters in the TP1 Benchmark Series (Chapters 31 and 32). Much of the code in this chapter is identical to code you've already seen in **SQLTP1.SQC**. This common code will not be repeated. Instead, we will refer you to the appropriate **SQLTP1.SQC** listings where the common code is first introduced.

In addition, you should review the **MULTI** chapter in Part II, and you should be familiar with **RSQL** at the user level.

THE APPLICATION REMOTE INTERFACE TP1

The **Database Application Remote Interface** provides a Remote Procedure Call extension of the client/server model for *Transaction Server* environments. You may recall that the client/server model splits an application into two parts: a client and a server. The client and server communicate requests and responses through messages. This simple construct allows intelligence to be easily distributed across a network and provides a framework for the design of loosely coupled networked based applications. A client uses the **Database Application Remote Interface** API to trigger the execution of a TP1 remote procedure on a server machine and passes it the parameters required to do a job. The server procedure is a DLL that executes the TP1 as a collection of static SQL statements. The Remote Procedure Call is transparent to the location of the stored procedure, which can reside in either a local or remote site.

Transaction Servers are designed to reduce network traffic, improve response times, and provide a more object-oriented database service that is well suited for **OLTP** applications. They export procedures instead of data. Transaction Servers also provide improved *site autonomy*. For example, if your tables change, you don't need to recompile all your client applications. Your changes are localized to the server's procedures. Here is how we divide the TP1 task between the client and the server:

- The **SQLTP1RI.C** client program runs as a **MULTI** process. This means **MULTI** will create the process, pass it the parameters, and tell it when to start or stop executing. The client goes into an endless loop, which repeatedly issues requests for the execution of a TP1 transaction on the server side. The loop, of course, runs under the control of **MULTI**. The request to execute the TP1 is done by invoking the **Database Application Remote Interface** API. The information to be sent to the server is placed inside an **in_SQLDA** structure. It consists of three variables: **random1**, **random2**, and **tps**. When a failure occurs, the server will return a message in the **out_SQLDA** structure. Success consists of a SQLCA return code of zero (the remote SQLCA gets returned). The client will display running counts of transaction execution results in its process window.

- The server **SQLTP1DL.SQC** program is packaged as a **DLL**. When a remote request is received, the RDS on the server side loads the **SQLTP1DL.DLL** server program, then places the SQLDA structures in its local memory. The server program then simply executes a TP1 using static SQL code. The random numbers for the account, teller, and branch are generated from the three parameters received in the SQLDA. The RDS on the server returns the information to the RDS on the requester. The return code from the server program is SQL_HOLD_PROC, which tells RDS to keep this instance of the server program active in memory.

TP1 CONFIGURATIONS

The location of the TP1 server procedure is transparent to the client code. If the server is remote, then the **Remote Data Services** (RDS) component of the Database Manager client will invoke the remote procedure on the server using NetBIOS (the RDS default) or APPC/APPN. Each instance of **MULTI** can run up to four **SQLTP1RI.C** client processes. If you need more TP1 generators, simply add more workstations that run **MULTI**. Figure 33-2 shows an example of a 12-client remote driver system.

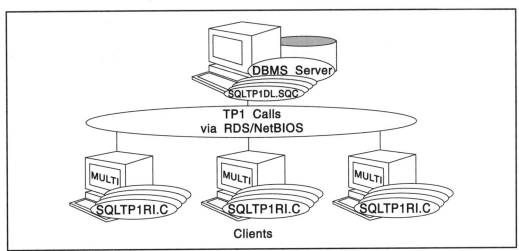

Figure 33-2. 12-Client TP1 Driver Using the Application Remote Interface Over a LAN.

You can scale this configuration in either direction depending on your budget considerations. As usual, we will be scaling our experiments to a four-client TP1 system and a network. We'll then run a benchmark using a remote client/server configuration. We can also run TP1 transactions against a local machine. This is done mainly for calibration purposes so that you can get a feel for the network overhead.

WALKING THROUGH THE SQLTP1RI.C REQUESTER

SQLTP1RI.C: The main() Procedure

In this section, we present the **main()** procedure of the **SQLTP1RI.C** requester program, whose code listing is shown in Figure 33-3. You will find that much of the code is identical to the **SQLTP1.SQC** code from the previous chapter. This similarity is not surprising since both programs have a front-end that interacts with **MULTI**. The difference is that the code presented here does *not* execute the TP1 transaction directly. Instead, it issues a remote procedure call to the server through the **Database Application Remote Interface**. What you will learn that's new and exciting is how to issue this call. We will not repeat the code and explanations that deal with the interaction with **MULTI**. Instead, we will point you to the appropriate sections in the previous chapter. We only introduce code listings that do something new. The following is a step-by-step description of what **main()** does:

1. The program starts by including the C-language, OS/2, and Database Manager header files that are needed for system services. These files are identical to the header files that were discussed in the previous chapter, because much of what we do is interact with **MULTI**.

2. The following program header files are included:

    const.h This is the same header file that was used in **SQLTP1.SQC** in the previous chapter. It contains **MULTI**-related constants and structures. The listing for this file is provided in Figure 14-11.

    sqltp1.h This is the same header file that was used in **SQLTP1.SQC** in the previous chapter. Its listing can be found in Figure 32-10.

3. A structure of type **SQLCA** is declared.

4. Two pointers to **SQLDA** structures are declared. These structures are used to exchange parameters between the client and server.

5. The **main()** program follows and, as you can see, it's almost a carbon copy of **SQLTP1.SQC**'s **main()**. However, there are also some key differences which will be the focus of our presentation. Here's what **main()** does:

    •   Invokes the previously encountered **get_args()** function, whose listing can be found in the previous chapter in Figure 32-4. This function obtains the arguments **MULTI** passes to the program. **MULTI**, of course, gets these arguments from reading the **MULTI.CFG** file.

- Invokes the previously encountered **initialize_multi_ipc()** function, whose listing can be found in the previous chapter in Figure 32-5. This function performs all the interprocess communication chores required from a process that runs under **MULTI**'s control.

- Invokes the previously encountered **initialize_task()** function, whose listing can be found in the previous chapter in Figure 32-6. This function connects to the database, installs a signal handler, and does all kinds of one-time housekeeping chores in preparation for the **big loop**.

- Invokes **initialize_sqldas()**, a new function (see listing in Figure 33-5). This function initializes the **SQLDA** structures that the **Database Application Remote Interface** uses as carriers for remote parameters. We will be explaining what this all means when we get to that section.

- Invokes the previously encountered **execute_task()** function, listed in Figure 32-7. This is the home of the **big loop**, which forever executes TP1 transactions. **MULTI** can pause and resume (at any time) the execution of TP1 transactions through semaphores. This is where we part company in a major way with the code in the previous chapter. The TP1 transaction is *not* directly executed by the helper routine, **tp1_transaction()**. Instead, this function (see listing in Figure 33-6) merely issues a remote call to a server procedure through the **Database Application Remote Interface**. The server procedure executes the TP1. This is one of the key differences between *Transaction Servers* and *Database Servers*.

```
/***************************************************************************/
/*   PROGRAM NAME: SQLTP1RI.C - A process program that MULTI starts        */
/*                                                                         */
/*   PROGRAM DESCRIPTION:  This program is run as a child task of MULTI.   */
/*   This code provides the requester for an Application Remote Interface TP1 */
/***************************************************************************/
#include <process.h>                    /* For exit()                      */
#include <string.h>                     /* For printf                      */
#include <sys\types.h>                  /* For time()                      */
#include <sys\timeb.h>                  /* For time()                      */
#include <sys\stat.h>                   /* For stat()                      */
#include <stdlib.h>                     /* For atoi                        */
#include <stdio.h>                      /* For sprintf, printf             */
#define INCL_VIO                        /* include VIO calls               */
#define INCL_DOSSEMAPHORES              /* include semaphore api calls     */
#define INCL_DOSMEMMGR                  /* include segment   api calls     */
#define INCL_ERRORS                     /* include error definitions       */
#include <os2.h>
```

Figure 33-3 (Part 1 of 2). SQLTP1RI.C: The main() Procedure.

```
#include <sqlca.h>              /* sqlca                          */
#include <sqlda.h>              /* sqlda                          */
#include <sql.h>                /* error msg. retrieval           */
#include <sqlcodes.h>           /* SQL return code constants      */
#include <sqlenv.h>             /* environment functions and      */

#include "const.h"              /* constants for multi            */
#include "sqltp1.h"             /* tp1 program vars, declares,etc. */

#pragma stack16(8192)

struct sqlca sqlca;
struct sqlda *sqlda_in;                 /* input sqlda for sqleproc    */
struct sqlda *sqlda_out;                /* output sqlda for sqleproc   */
CHAR    msgbuf[512];                    /* msg buffer for sqleintp     */
CHAR    ri_msgbuf[512];                 /* msg buffer for remote ifc   */
VOID initialize_sqldas(VOID);

/*''''''''''''''''''''''''''''''''''''''''''''''''''''''''''''''''''''''*/
/* Main routine.                                                        */
/*''''''''''''''''''''''''''''''''''''''''''''''''''''''''''''''''''''''*/
VOID main(USHORT argc, PCHAR argv[])
{
  get_args(argc, argv);             /*  get program arguments         */

  initialize_multi_ipc();           /*  Init MULTI semaphores/shared memory*/

  initialize_task();                /*  perform one time intializations */

  initialize_sqldas();              /*  prepare for APPLICATION REMOTE IFC */

  execute_task();                   /*  Remote Procedure Call  loop   */

} /* end main */
```

Figure 33-3 (Part 2 of 2). SQLTP1RI.C: The main() Procedure.

SQLTP1RI.C: The initialize_sqldas() Procedure

In this section, we present the **initialize_sqldas()** procedure, whose code listing is shown in Figure 33-5. The remote parameters are passed over the network using self-describing data structures of type **SQLDA**. This choice of a container for passing data is consistent with the SQL programming paradigm. The Database Manager's Remote Data Services (RDS) takes care of reconstructing of the SQLDA at the remote location after it is sent over the network. The RDS also takes care of situations where the call is local. In such cases, the SQLDAs are exchanged through shared memory. The code in this section takes care of all this SQLDA handling. For your quick reference, we repeat the SQLDA type definition in Figure 33-4.

```
struct SQLDA
{
    BYTE            sqldaid[8];          /* Eye catcher = 'SQLDA    '     */
    LONG            sqldabc;             /* SQLDA size in bytes = 16+44*sqln */
    SHORT           sqln;                /* Number of SQLVAR elements     */
    SHORT           sqld;                /* # of used SQLVAR elements     */
    struct sqlvar
    {
        SHORT           sqltype;         /* Variable data type            */
        SHORT           sqllen;          /* Variable data length          */
        BYTE          * _Seg16 sqldata;  /* Pointer to variable data value */
        SHORT         * _Seg16 sqlind;   /* Pointer to Null indicator     */
        struct sqlname                   /* Variable Name                 */
        {
            SHORT           length;      /* Name length [1..30]           */
            BYTE            data[30];     /* Variable or Column name       */
        } sqlname;
    } sqlvar[SQLVAR_NUM];
};
```

Figure 33-4. The SQLDA Structure.

Here is what the **initialize_sqldas()** function does:

1. It allocates memory for two SQLDA structures:

    sqlda_in   This structure is sized to contain the three parameters to be sent to the
                     server.

    sqlda_out   This structure is sized to contain the single parameter the server returns.

    The size of the SQLDAs is automatically calculated using the Database Manager
    supplied macro, SQLDASIZE.

2. It places the three parameters to be sent to the server inside the **sqlda_in**: **random1**,
    random2, and **tps**. Each of these parameters is described in a SQLDA field of type
    sqlvar. From Figure 33-4, you can see that **sqlvar** requires the following informa-
    tion for each parameter passed:

    *   The parameter's SQL data type
    *   The parameter's length in bytes
    *   A pointer to the variable which contains the parameter
    *   A pointer to Null indicator which is applicable for this type of SQLDA usage
    *   The name and name length of the parameter

3. It specifies, to the **sqlda_out**, the name of the variable where the response from the
    server is to be placed. The variable **ri_msgbuf** is used to receive messages from
    the server (mostly error messages). This buffer will only be checked when the
    SQLCA returns an error. Again, all the information describing **ri_msgbuf** has to
    be provided in a **sqlvar** element of the **sqlda_out** variable.

4. In summary, we're sending three variables of type *short* to the server, and then getting back from the server a single variable of type *array of characters*. The code in this section shows how to prepare the SQLDAs that will be used for the Remote Procedure Call.

```
/*''''''''''''''''''''''''''''''''''''''''''''''''''''''''''''''''''''*/
/* Perform onetime initializations for the sqldas                     */
/*''''''''''''''''''''''''''''''''''''''''''''''''''''''''''''''''''''*/
VOID  initialize_sqldas(VOID)
{
  /*''''''''''''''''''''''''''''''''''''*/
  /* Allocate sqldas and fill headers   */
  /*''''''''''''''''''''''''''''''''''''*/
  sqlda_in = (struct sqlda *)malloc(SQLDASIZE(3));
  sqlda_in->sqldabc = 148;
  sqlda_in->sqln    = 3;
  sqlda_in->sqld    = 3;

  sqlda_out = (struct sqlda *)malloc(SQLDASIZE(1));
  sqlda_out->sqldabc = 60;
  sqlda_out->sqln    = 1;
  sqlda_out->sqld    = 1;

  /*''''''''''''''''''''''''''''''''''''*/
  /* initialize 3 parameters in sqlda_in */
  /*''''''''''''''''''''''''''''''''''''*/
                  /*'''''''''''''''''''''*/
                  /* random1 parm        */
                  /*'''''''''''''''''''''*/
  sqlda_in->sqlvar[0].sqltype        = SQL_TYP_SMALL;
  sqlda_in->sqlvar[0].sqllen         = SQL_SMALL_LENGTH;
  sqlda_in->sqlvar[0].sqldata        = (UCHAR *)&random1;
  sqlda_in->sqlvar[0].sqlind         = NULL;
  sqlda_in->sqlvar[0].sqlname.length = strlen("RANDOM1");
  strcpy(sqlda_in->sqlvar[0].sqlname.data,"RANDOM1");

                  /*'''''''''''''''''''''*/
                  /* random2 parm        */
                  /*'''''''''''''''''''''*/
  sqlda_in->sqlvar[1].sqltype        = SQL_TYP_SMALL;
  sqlda_in->sqlvar[1].sqllen         = SQL_SMALL_LENGTH;
  sqlda_in->sqlvar[1].sqldata        = (UCHAR *)&random2;
  sqlda_in->sqlvar[1].sqlind         = NULL;
  sqlda_in->sqlvar[1].sqlname.length = strlen("RANDOM2");
  strcpy(sqlda_in->sqlvar[1].sqlname.data,"RANDOM2");

                  /*'''''''''''''''''''''*/
                  /* tps parm            */
                  /*'''''''''''''''''''''*/
  sqlda_in->sqlvar[2].sqltype        = SQL_TYP_SMALL;
  sqlda_in->sqlvar[2].sqllen         = SQL_SMALL_LENGTH;
  sqlda_in->sqlvar[2].sqldata        = (UCHAR *)&tps;
  sqlda_in->sqlvar[2].sqlind         = NULL;
  sqlda_in->sqlvar[2].sqlname.length = strlen("TPS");
  strcpy(sqlda_in->sqlvar[2].sqlname.data,"TPS");
```

Figure 33-5 (Part 1 of 2). SQLTP1RI.C: The initialize_sqldas() Procedure.

```
/*''''''''''''''''''''''''''''''''''''''*/
/* initialize 1 parameter in sqlda_out */
/*''''''''''''''''''''''''''''''''''''''*/
              /*''''''''''''''''''''''''*/
              /* ri_msgbuf parm        */
              /*''''''''''''''''''''''''*/
sqlda_out->sqlvar[0].sqltype        = SQL_TYP_CSTR;
sqlda_out->sqlvar[0].sqllen         = sizeof(ri_msgbuf);
sqlda_out->sqlvar[0].sqldata        = ri_msgbuf;
sqlda_out->sqlvar[0].sqlind         = NULL;
sqlda_out->sqlvar[0].sqlname.length = strlen("RI_MSGBUF");
strcpy(sqlda_out->sqlvar[0].sqlname.data,"RI_MSGBUF");

} /* end initialize_sqldas */
```

Figure 33-5 (Part 2 of 2). SQLTP1RI.C: The initialize_sqldas() Procedure.

SQLTP1RI.C: The tp1_transaction() Procedure

In this section, we present the **tp1_transaction**() procedure, whose code listing is shown in Figure 33-6. This procedure, unlike its counterpart in the previous chapter, does not perform the actual TP1 transaction. Instead, it invokes a procedure on the server (that executes the TP1) through the **Database Application Remote Interface**.

The remote call is performed by the Database Manager **sqleproc**() API, which is described below. The **sqlca.sqlcode** is non-zero if the call fails. Failure in this case also includes any SQL failure detected in the remote procedure. When the code detects such a failure, it issues a **sqlaintp**() to print the message text of the SQL return code. In addition, the contents of **ri_msgbuf** will be printed. This variable contains the text of an error message created at the server. Notice how conveniently it got mapped into the local address space through the remote SQLDA magic!

sqleproc()

This Database Environment Service API call is known as the **Database Application Remote Interface**. It allows a DOS, Windows, or OS/2 database client application to execute a DLL procedure stored at the location of a database. This command reduces network traffic and improves the performance of network-based transactions. The stored procedure can be designed as a simple transaction (one call and return) or as a conversational transaction (a set of calls and returns). The prototype for this call is:

```
sqleproc(CHAR   * _Seg16 funcname,    /* The remote procedure name  */
          CHAR   * _Seg16 data_area,   /* Variable length data area  */
          SQLDA  * _Seg16 in_SQLDA,    /* Pointer to input SQLDA     */
          SQLDA  * _Seg16 out_SQLDA,   /* Pointer to output SQLDA    */
          SQLCA  * _Seg16 sqlca);      /* Pointer to SQLCA           */
```

A description of the parameters follows:

- The *funcname* parameter points to the name of the procedure to be run on the server. This can be specified in one of two ways:

  1. By a **funcname** with no extensions. This causes a **funcname.dll** file to be loaded into memory. It is assumed that this file contains a function by the same name.
  2. By the back-slash delimitation **dllname.dll\funcname**. In this case, the **dllname** is the name of the file to be loaded, and **funcname** is the name of the function to be executed. A single (.DLL) file can contain multiple remotely executable functions. In this naming convention backslash does *not* indicate a subdirectory. For example: "**sqltp1dl.dll\tp1_transaction**" is read as the function **tp1_transaction** which is found in the **sqltp1dl.dll** (.DLL) file.

- The *data_area* parameter points to a variable length data area. This data area is used to pass information to the server routine. The first two bytes contain the length of the next **n** bytes. Set this parameter to NULL if you're not going to use it.

- The *in_SQLDA* parameter points to the input SQLDA, which is used to pass data to the remote procedure. This structure is defined in Figure 33-4.

- The *out_SQLDA* parameter points to the output SQLDA, where variables will be returned to your program. This structure is defined in Figure 33-4. If the call is remote, the Database Manager transmits the sqldas over the network and reconstructs them in the server's memory, including the data fields they point to. This means that you can refer to host variables by name on both sides of the program.

- The *sqlca* parameter points to the SQLCA.

```
/*'''''''''''''''''''''''''''''''''''''''''''''''''''''''''''''''''''''''''*/
/* function for TP1 transaction                                            */
/*'''''''''''''''''''''''''''''''''''''''''''''''''''''''''''''''''''''''''*/
SHORT APIENTRY tp1_transaction(VOID)
{
    /*'''''''''''''''''''''''''''''''''''''''''*/
    /* call remote transaction                 */
    /*'''''''''''''''''''''''''''''''''''''''''*/
    sqleproc("sqltp1dl.dll\\tp1_transaction", NULL,
             sqlda_in, sqlda_out, &sqlca);

    if (SQLCODE != 0)
        {
            sqlaintp(msgbuf, sizeof(msgbuf), 80, &sqlca);
            printf("%s\n",msgbuf);
            printf("%s\n",ri_msgbuf);
            return(FAILED);
        }

    return(GOOD);
} /* end tp1_transaction */
```

Figure 33-6. SQLTP1RI.C: The tp1_transaction() Procedure.

WALKING THROUGH THE SQLTP1DL.SQC SERVER

SQLTP1DL.SQC: The tp1_transaction() Remote Procedure

In this section, we present the **tp1_transaction()** procedure, whose code listing is shown in Figure 33-8. This procedure is part of the **SQLTP1DL.DLL**. This is what the RDS does when an **Database Application Remote Interface** call is received on the *server* side for a **tp1_transaction()** function which, is part of the **SQLTP1DL.DLL**:

* It constructs a copy in local memory of the SQLDA structures that were sent.
* It loads the DLL, **SQLTP1DL.DLL**, from disk.
* It calls the function **tp1_transaction()**, and passes it the reconstructed SQLDA parameters.
* When the function completes, it returns the information to the requester.

So, what does a DLL for remote procedures look like? Let's take a look at what's in Figure 33-8:

1. Notice that there is no **main()** function in this code.

2. The familiar include files, WHENEVER directives, and host variable declarations are all present.

3. The forward declarations of the functions in the DLL follows. Only the first of these two functions, **tp1_transaction()** is "exported" to the outside world. This also happens to be a function that can be invoked through the **DATABASE APPLICATION REMOTE INTERFACE**. Here is how this function is declared:

```
SHORT APIENTRY16 tp1_transaction(struct sqlchar * _Seg16 parms,
                                 struct sqlda   * _Seg16 sqlda_in,
                                 struct sqlda   * _Seg16 sqlda_out,
                                 struct sqlca   * _Seg16 sqlca_in);
```

Notice the correspondence between this function's parameters and those of "sqleproc()" on page 845.

4. The **tp1_transaction()** is exported—that is, made known to the outside world—through the (.DEF) file **SQLTP1DL.DEF** show below.

```
LIBRARY SQLTP1DL INITINSTANCE
DESCRIPTION 'TP1 transaction routine'
PROTMODE
EXPORTS TP1_TRANSACTION
DATA MULTIPLE NONSHARED
```

Figure 33-7. The Definition File: SQLTP1DL.DEF.

5. The code for the TP1 transaction, with a few minor exceptions, is identical to the static SQL implementation of TP1 which was described in the last chapter (see Figure 32-8). Here are the exceptions:

    a. The random numbers are obtained through **sqlda_in**. These are the parameters the client sends to the server through the RDS mechanism.

    b. When an error occurs, the sqlca is copied over to **sqlca_in**. The contents of **sqlca_in** are shipped over the network by RDS and placed into the client's **sqlca**.

    c. When an error occurs, the **format_error()** function (see Figure 33-9) is passed the name of the file and line number where the error occurred, a pointer to a parameter in **sqlda_out**, and the sqlca's **sqlcode** value. The **format_error()** function takes all this information and formats an error message. The **sqlda_out**, including its message parameter, is then copied by RDS over the network and into the client's **sqlda_out**, where it magically updates the value of the client's **ri_msgbuf** variable. (see Figure 33-5).

    d. The sqlca is copied over to **sqlca_in**. The contents of **sqlca_in** are shipped over the network by RDS and placed into the client's **sqlca**.

    e. The constant code **SQLZ_HOLD_PROC** is returned, which tells RDS not to terminate the DLL.

6. Congratulations, we've just completed the second of our TP1 flavors!

```
/*******************************************************************************/
/*    PROGRAM NAME: TP1DLL - A DLL for the TP1 transaction                     */
/*                                                                             */
/*    PROGRAM DESCRIPTION:  This program is invoked as a result of a           */
/*       sqleproc database manager API.                                        */
/*                                                                             */
/*******************************************************************************/
#include <process.h>                   /* For exit()                          */
#include <string.h>                    /* For printf                          */
#include <sys\types.h>                 /* For time()                          */
#include <sys\timeb.h>                 /* For time()                          */
#include <sys\stat.h>                  /* For stat()                          */
#include <stdlib.h>                    /* For atoi                            */
#include <stdio.h>                     /* For sprintf, printf                 */

#define INCL_VIO                       /* include VIO calls                   */
#define INCL_DOSSEMAPHORES             /* include semaphore api calls         */
#define INCL_DOSMEMMGR                 /* include segment   api calls         */
#include <os2.h>

#include <sqlca.h>                     /* sqlca                               */
#include <sqlda.h>                     /* sqlda                               */
#include <sql.h>                       /* error msg. retrieval                */
#include <sqlcodes.h>                  /* SQL return code constants           */
#include <sqlenv.h>                    /* environment functions and           */
#include <sqlutil.h>                   /* for sqlchar structure               */

/*'''''''''''''''''''''''''''''''''''''''''''''''''''''''''''''''''''''''''''''*/
/* database includes, defines, etc.                                           */
/*'''''''''''''''''''''''''''''''''''''''''''''''''''''''''''''''''''''''''''''*/
#pragma stack16(8192)
```

Figure 33-8 (Part 1 of 4).   SQLTP1DL.SQC: The tp1_transaction() Remote Procedure.

```
struct sqlca sqlca;

EXEC SQL WHENEVER SQLERROR CONTINUE;
EXEC SQL WHENEVER SQLWARNING CONTINUE;
EXEC SQL WHENEVER NOT FOUND CONTINUE;

EXEC SQL BEGIN DECLARE SECTION;
 long   acct_num;
 short branch_id;
 short teller_id;
 long   balance;
 long   delta       = 100;
 char   acct_name[20] = "<--20 BYTE STRING-->";
EXEC SQL END  DECLARE SECTION;

/*''''''''''''''''''''''''''''''''''''''''''''''''''''''''''''''''''''''''''''*/
/* function forward declarations                                              */
/*''''''''''''''''''''''''''''''''''''''''''''''''''''''''''''''''''''''''''''*/
SHORT APIENTRY16 tp1_transaction(struct sqlchar * _Seg16 parms,
                                 struct sqlda    * _Seg16 sqlda_in,
                                 struct sqlda    * _Seg16 sqlda_out,
                                 struct sqlca    * _Seg16 sqlca_in);

#pragma handler(tp1_transaction)

VOID format_error(PCHAR msgbuf, LONG Error, PCHAR msg,
                  PCHAR file, USHORT line);

/*''''''''''''''''''''''''''''''''''''''''''''''''''''''''''''''''''''''''''''*/
/* function for TP1 transaction                                               */
/*''''''''''''''''''''''''''''''''''''''''''''''''''''''''''''''''''''''''''''*/
SHORT APIENTRY16 tp1_transaction(struct sqlchar * _Seg16 parms,
                                 struct sqlda    * _Seg16 sqlda_in,
                                 struct sqlda    * _Seg16 sqlda_out,
                                 struct sqlca    * _Seg16 sqlca_in)

{
  USHORT   random1, random2, tps ;              /* local variables          */

      /*'''''''''''''''''''''''''''''''''''''''*/
      /* Extract parms from SQLDA            */
      /*'''''''''''''''''''''''''''''''''''''''*/
  random1 =   *((USHORT *)sqlda_in->sqlvar[0].sqldata);
  random2 =   *((USHORT *)sqlda_in->sqlvar[1].sqldata);
  tps     =   *((USHORT *)sqlda_in->sqlvar[2].sqldata);

      /*'''''''''''''''''''''''''''''''''''''''*/
      /* generate some random data           */
      /*'''''''''''''''''''''''''''''''''''''''*/
  acct_num = (random1 * random2) % (tps*1000001) + 1;/* generate account num */
  teller_id= (short)(random1 % (tps*100)) + 1;       /* generate teller id   */
  branch_id= (short)(random2 % (tps*10)) + 1;        /* generate branch id   */

      /*'''''''''''''''''''''''''''''''''''''''*/
      /* get the current balance from ACCT   */
      /*'''''''''''''''''''''''''''''''''''''''*/
  EXEC SQL DECLARE CURSOR1 CURSOR FOR
          SELECT BALANCE FROM ACCT WHERE ACCT_NUM = :acct_num
          FOR UPDATE OF BALANCE;

  EXEC SQL OPEN CURSOR1;
  if (SQLCODE != 0)
     { format_error(sqlda_out->sqlvar[0].sqldata, SQLCODE,
```

Figure 33-8 (Part 2 of 4). SQLTP1DL.SQC: The tp1_transaction() Remote Procedure.

```
                            "during SQL OPEN", __FILE__, __LINE__);
        memcpy(sqlca_in, &sqlca, sizeof(struct sqlca)); /* return the sqlca   */
        return(SQLZ_HOLD_PROC);
     }

  EXEC SQL FETCH CURSOR1 INTO :balance;
  if (SQLCODE != 0)
     { format_error(sqlda_out->sqlvar[0].sqldata, SQLCODE,
                        "during SQL FETCH", __FILE__, __LINE__);
        memcpy(sqlca_in, &sqlca, sizeof(struct sqlca)); /* return the sqlca   */
        return(SQLZ_HOLD_PROC);
     }

     /*′′′′′′′′′′′′′′′′′′′′′′′′′′′′′′′′′′′′′′*/
     /* Credit the balance in the ACCT table */
     /*′′′′′′′′′′′′′′′′′′′′′′′′′′′′′′′′′′′′′′*/

  EXEC SQL UPDATE ACCT
           SET BALANCE = BALANCE + :delta
           WHERE CURRENT OF CURSOR1;

  if (SQLCODE != 0)
     { format_error(sqlda_out->sqlvar[0].sqldata, SQLCODE,
                     "during SQL UPDATE", __FILE__,__LINE__);
        memcpy(sqlca_in, &sqlca, sizeof(struct sqlca)); /* return the sqlca   */
        return(SQLZ_HOLD_PROC);
     }

  EXEC SQL CLOSE CURSOR1;
  if (SQLCODE != 0)
     { format_error(sqlda_out->sqlvar[0].sqldata, SQLCODE,
                     "during SQL CLOSE", __FILE__,__LINE__);
        memcpy(sqlca_in, &sqlca, sizeof(struct sqlca)); /* return the sqlca   */
        return(SQLZ_HOLD_PROC);
     }

     /*′′′′′′′′′′′′′′′′′′′′′′′′′′′′′′′′′′′′′′′′*/
     /* Update the TELLER table's balance    */
     /*′′′′′′′′′′′′′′′′′′′′′′′′′′′′′′′′′′′′′′′′*/
  EXEC SQL UPDATE TELLER
           SET BALANCE = BALANCE + :delta
           WHERE TELLER_ID = :teller_id;
  if (SQLCODE != 0)
     { format_error(sqlda_out->sqlvar[0].sqldata, SQLCODE,
                     "during SQL UPDATE", __FILE__,__LINE__);
        memcpy(sqlca_in, &sqlca, sizeof(struct sqlca)); /* return the sqlca   */
        return(SQLZ_HOLD_PROC);
     }

     /*′′′′′′′′′′′′′′′′′′′′′′′′′′′′′′′′′′′′′′′′*/
     /* Update the BRANCH table's balance    */
     /*′′′′′′′′′′′′′′′′′′′′′′′′′′′′′′′′′′′′′′′′*/
  EXEC SQL UPDATE BRANCH
           SET BALANCE = BALANCE + :delta
           WHERE BRANCH_ID = :branch_id;
  if (SQLCODE != 0)
     { format_error(sqlda_out->sqlvar[0].sqldata, SQLCODE,
                     "during SQL UPDATE", __FILE__,__LINE__);
        memcpy(sqlca_in, &sqlca, sizeof(struct sqlca)); /* return the sqlca   */
        return(SQLZ_HOLD_PROC);
     }
```

Figure 33-8 (Part 3 of 4). SQLTP1DL.SQC: The tp1_transaction() Remote Procedure.

```
        /*''''''''''''''''''''''''''''''''''*/
        /* Insert transaction in HISTORY table */
        /*''''''''''''''''''''''''''''''''''*/
EXEC SQL INSERT
        INTO HISTORY(ACCT_NUM, TELLER_ID, BRANCH_ID, BALANCE,
                     DELTA, PID, TRANSID, ACCTNAME, TEMP)
        VALUES(:acct_num, :teller_id, :branch_id, :balance,
               :delta, 1, 3, :acct_name, 'hist  ');
if (SQLCODE != 0)
    { format_error(sqlda_out->sqlvar[0].sqldata, SQLCODE,
                "during SQL INSERT", __FILE__,__LINE__);
      memcpy(sqlca_in, &sqlca, sizeof(struct sqlca)); /* return the sqlca    */
      return(SQLZ_HOLD_PROC);
    }

        /*''''''''''''''''''''''''''''''''''''*/
        /* Commit the transaction to database  */
        /*''''''''''''''''''''''''''''''''''''*/
EXEC SQL COMMIT;
if (SQLCODE != 0)
    { format_error(sqlda_out->sqlvar[0].sqldata, SQLCODE,
                "during SQL COMMIT", __FILE__, __LINE__);
      memcpy(sqlca_in, &sqlca, sizeof(struct sqlca)); /* return the sqlca    */
      return(SQLZ_HOLD_PROC);
    }

  memcpy(sqlca_in, &sqlca, sizeof(struct sqlca));      /* return the sqlca    */
  return(SQLZ_HOLD_PROC);

} /* end tp1_transaction */
```

Figure 33-8 (Part 4 of 4). SQLTP1DL.SQC: The tp1_transaction() Remote Procedure.

SQLTP1DL.SQC: The format_error() Helper Procedure

This section contains the code for the **format_error()** helper procedure, which essentially formats an error message from the parameters that are passed to it. This is the error message that will magically end up in the client's **ri_msgbuf**.

```
/*'''''''''''''''''''''''''''''''''''''''''''''''''''''''''''''''''''*/
/*                                                                   */
/* Error Routine                                                     */
/*'''''''''''''''''''''''''''''''''''''''''''''''''''''''''''''''''''*/
VOID format_error(PCHAR msgbuf, LONG Error, PCHAR msg,
                  PCHAR file, USHORT line)
{
    sprintf(msgbuf,"Error %d detected while %s at line %d in file %s.\n",
          Error, msg, line, file);
} /* end format_error */
```

Figure 33-9. SQLTP1DL.SQC: The format_error() Helper Procedure.

RUNNING TWO TP1 BENCHMARK TESTS USING THE APPLICATION REMOTE INTERFACE

Now that we've got some code, let's run some benchmarks to see how well this TP1 flavor performs. We will run two TP1 benchmark tests:

1. A **local** benchmark test, where the client and servers are on the same machine. The machine is a PS/2 Mod-95 with a 33-MHz clock and a 1000-KByte buffer pool (see Figure 33-11).
2. A **remote** benchmark test, where the clients and servers are on different machines. The client machine is a PS/2 Mod 80 with a 20-MHz clock. The server machine is a PS/2 Mod-95 with a 33-MHz clock and a 1000-KByte buffer pool (see Figure 33-12).

The two benchmarks use the same software configuration: a four-process **MULTI** whose configuration file is shown below:

```
PROGRAM_TYPE        = PROCESS
STOP_TIME_MS        = 600000
TASK_NAME           = SQLTP1RI.EXE 0 17 2.0 1;
TASK_NAME           = SQLTP1RI.EXE 1 23 2.0 1;
TASK_NAME           = SQLTP1RI.EXE 2 29 2.0 1;
TASK_NAME           = SQLTP1RI.EXE 3 57 2.0 1;
```

Figure 33-10. A MULTI.CFG File for Running Four TP1 Processes.

The benchmarks are set up to run for 10-minute tests (i.e., 600,000 milliseconds). The response time threshold is set to 2.0 seconds, and a 1-tps database size is specified.

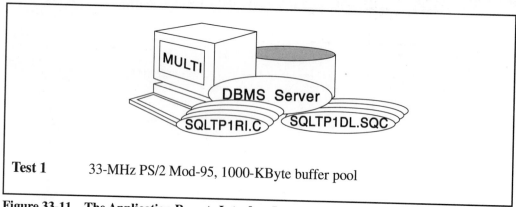

Test 1   33-MHz PS/2 Mod-95, 1000-KByte buffer pool

Figure 33-11. The Application Remote Interface Local Benchmark Configuration.

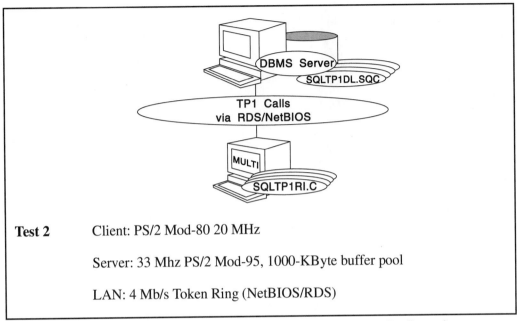

Test 2   Client: PS/2 Mod-80 20 MHz

Server: 33 Mhz PS/2 Mod-95, 1000-KByte buffer pool

LAN: 4 Mb/s Token Ring (NetBIOS/RDS)

Figure 33-12. The Application Remote Interface Local Benchmark Configuration.

Running the Application Remote TP1 Locally (Benchmark1)

The configuration for this benchmark is a four-client MULTI running against a local database. The test is run on a PS/2 Mod-95 with a 33-MHz clock and a 1000-KByte buffer pool. We assume the database is already loaded for a 1-tps database scale. The following RSQL run is used to set up the 1000-KByte buffer configuration and prepare the database for the benchmark1 run.

```
--                    Change TP1 Database Configuration
-- ===============================================================================
-- update the Database Configuration for database for a 1000k buffer
EXEC DBA: UPDATE_DB_CFG TP1      MAXAPPLS    = 8,
                                 DLCHKTIME   = 10000,
                                 BUFFPAGE    = 256,
                                 LOGFILSIZ   = 50,
                                 LOGPRIMARY  = 2,
                                 LOGSECOND   = 20;

 OK, sql_rcd = 0,        Execution time =      0.3100 secs

-- Show the database configuration for database TP1
EXEC DBA: SHOW_DB_CFG TP1;

 Database Configuration for Database TP1
 ==============================================
```

Figure 33-13 (Part 1 of 2). Preparing the Database for Benchmark1.

```
Configuration Parameter                Current  Parm.      Parm.         Parm.
Description                            Value    Units      Range         Default
-------------------------------------  -------  ---------  -----------   -------
Max. Active Applications                   8    Appl.      1-256             8
Max. DB Files Open/Application             20   files      2-235            20
Max. Files Open/Application               255   files      25-32700        255
Buffer Pool Size                          256   4K pages   2-1500          (1)
Time Interval for Deadlocks             10000   millisecs. 1-600 sec.       10
Max. Storage for Locklists                 25   4K pages   4-250             8
Max. percent locklist/appl.                22   percent    1-100            22
Default Application Heap                    3   segments   2-20              3
Application Agent Heap                      2   segments   2-85              2
Sort List Heap                             2    segments   1-20              2
Database Heap                              3    segments   1-45            (2)
SQL Statement Heap                        64    segments   8-255            64
Log File Size                             50    4K pages   4-65535         (3)
Primary Log Files                          2    files      2-63              3
Secondary Log Files                       20    files      0-61              2
Log Records/soft checkpoint              100    records    0-65535         100

Current Log Location = F:\SQL00001\SQLOGDIR\
New Log Location     =
First Log File       =
Current Log File     =
Copy Protection      =     1 (1 = Protected, Default = 1)
Log Retain           =     0 (1 = Retain Log Files, Default = 0)
User Exit            =     0 (1 = Enable User Exit, Default = 0)
Auto Restart         =     1 (1 = Enable Auto Restart, Default = 1)
Country              =     1
Code Page            =   437
Release              =   768
DB Consistency       =     1 (1 = Consistent)
Backup Pending       =     0 (1 = Backup Pending)
Roll Forward Pending =     0 (1 = Roll Forward Pending)
User Exit Status     =     0 (1 = User exit Enabled)
Log Retain Status    =     0 (1 = log files retained)

(1) - client or standalone 25, server 250
(2) - client or standalone  2, server   3
(3) - client or standalone 32, server 200
OK, sql_rcd = 0,         Execution time =      0.1000 secs

-- bind the tp1 program
EXEC DBA: BIND TP1 SQLTP1DL.BND ISO REPEATABLE_READ BLOCK_ALL PUBLIC;

No messages in msgfile.msg

OK, sql_rcd = 0,         Execution time =      3.1200 secs

- Connect to the TP1 database
EXEC DBA: STARTUSE TP1 S;

OK, sql_rcd = 0,         Execution time =      0.6900 secs

delete all of the history data
EXEC SQL: DELETE FROM HISTORY;

WARNING, sql_code = 100,    Execution time =      2.3700 secs
SQL0100W  No row was found for FETCH, UPDATE or DELETE; or the result of a
query is an empty table.
```

Figure 33-13 (Part 2 of 2). Preparing the Database for Benchmark1.

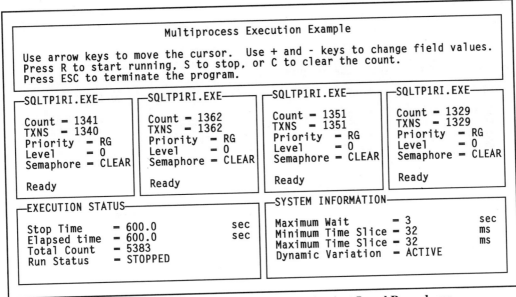

Figure 33-14.   The Results of a Four-Process TP1 Run Against Local Procedures.

Benchmark1 Result: The MULTI screen capture in Figure 33-14 shows the results of a 10-minute test. During this period, a total of 5383 TP1 transactions ran successfully. However, only (1340 + 1362 + 1351 + 1329 = 5382) transactions had a response time that was under the 2-second threshold. Using the liberal interpretation of TP1 introduced in the previous chapter, this machine is therefore in the *9.0 TP1* range.

Commentary: This number demonstrates that using remote procedures locally does not improve performance over the straight SQL implementation of the previous chapter. In fact, the performance is worse (9.1 TP1s versus 9.8 TP1s).

Running the Application Remote TP1 Remotely (Benchmark2)

The configuration for this benchmark is a four-client MULTI running against a remote database. The database runs on a PS/2 Mod-95 with a 33-MHz clock and a 1000-KByte buffer pool.

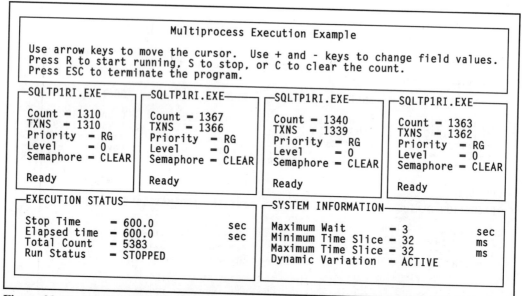

Figure 33-15. The Results of a Four-Process TP1 Run Against Remote Procedures.

Benchmark2 Result: The MULTI screen capture in Figure 33-15 shows the results of a 10-minute test. During this period, a total of 5380 TP1 transactions ran successfully. However, only (1310 + 1366 + 1339 + 1362 = 5377) transactions had a response time that was under the 2-second threshold. Using the liberal interpretation of TP1 introduced in the previous chapters, this machine is therefore in the *9.0 TP1* range.

Commentary: This result demonstrates *a very significant performance gain* over the remote SQL as used in the previous chapter (9.0 TP1 versus 4.7 TP1). This improvement is directly attributed to the reduced network utilization of stored procedures. A single message exchange takes place, as opposed to an exchange for each SQL statement in the transaction.

Chapter 34

The Named Pipes
Transaction Server TP1

This is the fourth of a six-chapter series, in which we develop a TP1 Benchmark toolkit for the OS/2 Database Manager. This chapter provides a "do-it-yourself" *Transaction Server* version of TP1 using Named Pipes. The TP1 client drivers run under **MULTI** and issue requests to the server via Named Pipes (see Figure 34-1). The server receives the request from a client, executes a TP1, and returns the results to the client via a Named Pipe. The TP1 server maintains a pool of TP1 server processes. All the TP1 processes on a machine are known by the same pipe "name." However, each server process controls its own instance of that Named Pipe. So, what we've essentially put together is a multiuser server machine on a Named Pipes platform.

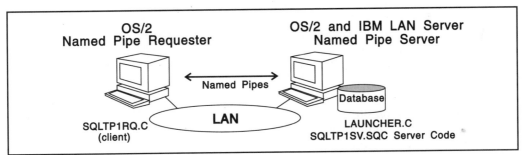

Figure 34-1. The Named Pipes Remote Program Execution Implementation of TP1.

The Named Pipes TP1 *Transaction Server* is similar to the **Database Application Remote Interface** from the previous chapter. However, the two approaches differ significantly in the following areas:

- In the Named Pipes approach, clients and servers communicate using Named Pipes over NetBIOS. In the **Database Application Remote Interface** approach, clients and servers communicate using NetBIOS/RDS. They could also use APPC/APPN if you change the default RDS configuration.

857

- The server element in the Named Pipes approach is a remote process at the end of a Named Pipe. In the **Database Application Remote Interface** approach, the server element is a "well-known" procedure loaded as a DLL.

- The Named Pipes approach requires a running copy of the IBM **LAN Server program** on the server. With the **LAN Server Program**, you also get a file server, print server, and a general purpose Network Operating System. The **Application Remote Interface** approach requires the Database Manager client component (RDS) on every client machine.

- The Named Pipes approach can be used in any client/server situation. The **Application Remote Interface** approach is optimized for SQL-based remote procedures.

This chapter splits the original **SQLTP1.SQC** program (see Chapter 32) into three programs:

1. The **SQLTP1RQ.C** client program drives TP1s and runs under **MULTI** control.
2. The **SQLTP1SV.SQC** server program executes the TP1 transactions against the database.
3. The **LAUNCHER.C** program starts "n" process instances of the **SQLTP1SV.SQC** program on the server machine.

WHAT YOU WILL LEARN

This chapter serves as an elaborate example of how "custom" servers can be put together using the building blocks provided in this book. The TP1 example developed here applies to any client/server program that uses Named Pipes. This chapter has the following prerequisites:

- The Tutorial chapter on Named Pipes in Part II.
- The Named Pipes implementation of **FX** in Parts II and III.
- The SQL Tutorial chapter.
- The first two chapters in the TP1 Benchmark Series. Much of the code in this chapter is identical to code you've already seen in **SQLTP1.SQC**. This common code will not be repeated. Instead, we will refer you to the appropriate **SQLTP1.SQC** listings where the common code is first introduced.
- You should review the **MULTI** chapters in Part II, and you should be familiar with **RSQL** at the user level.

THE NAMED PIPES VERSION OF TP1

This application serves as another example of how the client/server model extends to transaction processing environments. The client and server processes in this application communicate requests and responses through messages via the Named Pipes

Interprocess Communication (IPC). Named Pipes makes the location of the server program transparent to the code. A server program can be moved from a local machine to a remote machine by simply preceding the pipe name with the name of a server machine. The arrival of a message at the *Transaction Server* triggers the execution of a TP1 transaction. A server process executes the TP1 as a collection of static SQL statements.

Why are we using processes instead of threads? The Database Manager allows only one open database connection per process. This keeps the user applications in isolated address spaces. We want the TP1 transactions to execute concurrently, so we will start a separate process for each concurrent database connection. The number of server processes to be started is a parameter which gets passed to the **LAUNCHER** program. Here is how we divide the TP1 task between the clients and servers:

- The **SQLTP1RQ.C** client program runs as a **MULTI** process. This means **MULTI** will create the process, pass it the parameters, and tell it when to start or stop executing. The client goes into an endless loop that repeatedly issues requests for the execution of a TP1 transaction on the server side. The loop, of course, runs under the control of **MULTI**. The request to execute the TP1 is done by invoking a **DosCallNPipe**. This API call is ideal for non-persistent sessions that consist of a single request-reply message exchange. Here is what happens during such an exchange:

    1. A session is opened with the server pipe.
    2. A message is sent to the server consisting of three variables: **random1**, **random2**, and **tps**.
    3. A reply is received from the server indicating success or failure of the TP1 execution.
    4. The pipe is closed.

- The **SQLTP1SV.SQC** server program creates a Named Pipe, and then blocks waiting for a request to arrive. When a request arrives, the server reads the two random numbers and tps count that were sent by the client, and generates random numbers for the account, teller, and branch. The server program then executes a TP1 transaction using static SQL and returns an error message over the pipe in case of failure. Otherwise, an empty message is returned. The server process then disconnects the pipe instance with that particular client and reissues a **DosConnectNPipe**, which blocks the server process until the next request for work arrives.

TP1 CONFIGURATIONS

The location of the TP1 server process is transparent to the client code. The MULTI configuration file contains an optional server name field for remote configurations. The Named Pipes IPC determines whether the server is local or remote from its name, and handles all the transport mechanics accordingly. Each instance of **MULTI** can run up to four **SQLTP1RI.C** client processes. If you need more TP1 generators, simply add more workstations that run **MULTI**. Figure 34-2 shows an example of a 12-client remote driver system. You can scale this configuration in either direction depending on your budget considerations. We will be scaling our experiments downward, of course, to a four-client TP1 system. We'll then run a benchmark using a remote client/server configuration. We will also run TP1 transactions against a local machine, mainly to get a feel for the network overhead. We are especially interested in how the Named Pipes remote TP1 measures up to its **Application Remote Interface** counterpart.

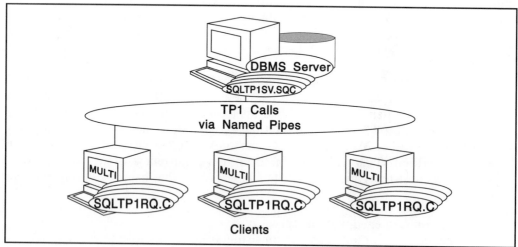

Figure 34-2. 12-client TP1 Driver Using Remote Named Pipes Over a LAN.

WALKING THROUGH THE SQLTP1RQ.C CLIENT

SQLTP1RQ.C: The main() Procedure

In this section, we present the **main()** procedure of the **SQLTP1RQ.C** client program, whose code listing is shown in Figure 34-3. You will find that much of the code is identical to the original **SQLTP1.SQC** code from Chapter 32. This is not surprising because both programs have a front-end which interacts with **MULTI**. The difference is that the code presented here does *not* execute the TP1 transaction directly. Instead, it issues a request to a TP1 server process via a Named Pipe. What you will learn that's "new and exciting," is how to issue this call using the **DosCallNPipe** API call. We will not repeat the code and explanations that deal with the interaction with **MULTI**. Instead, we will point you to the appropriate sections in the previous chapters. We only introduce code listings that do something new. The following is a step-by-step description of what **main()** does:

1. The program starts by including the C-language, OS/2, and Database Manager header files that are needed for system services. These are identical to the header

files that were discussed in the previous chapters, because much of what we do is interact with **MULTI**.

2. The following program header files are included:

const.h   This is the same header file that was used in the previous chapters. Its listing can be found in Figure 14-11.

sqltp1.h   This is the same header file that was used in the previous chapters. Its listing can be found in Figure 32-10.

3. The **main()** program follows and, as you can see, it's almost a carbon copy of **SQLTP1.SQC**'s **main()**. However, there are also some key differences on which we will focus our presentation. Here's what **main()** does:

- Invokes the **get_args()** function, which is listed in Figure 34-5. This function obtains the arguments **MULTI** passes to the program. It is similar to the **get_args()** function we encountered in the previous chapters, with the exception that the name of a remote server can be specified as an input parameter to the program. This name is then concatenated to the pipe name when the client and server execute on different machines. **MULTI**, of course, gets these arguments from reading the **MULTI.CFG** file.

- Invokes the previously encountered **initialize_multi_ipc()** function, whose listing can be found on page 813 in Figure 32-5. This function performs all the interprocess communication chores required from a process that runs under **MULTI**'s control.

- Invokes the **initialize_task()** function, whose listing can be found in Figure 34-6. This function does one-time housekeeping chores in preparation for the *big loop*. It is similar to the previously encountered **initialize_task** functions, with the exception that it does *not* connect to the database or install a signal handler.

- Invokes the previously encountered **execute_task()** function listed in Figure 32-7. This is the home of the *big loop*, which forever requests TP1 transactions. **MULTI** can pause at any time and resume the execution of TP1 transactions through semaphores.

  Note: This is where we part company in a major way with the code in Chapter 32. The TP1 transaction is *not* directly executed by the helper routine, **tp1_transaction()**. Instead, this function (see listing in Figure 34-7) merely sends a request to execute a TP1 to a server process through the **DosCallNPipe** API call. The server process executes the TP1.

```
/**********************************************************************/
/*   PROGRAM NAME: SQLTP1RQ - A process program that MULTI starts     */
/*                                                                    */
/*   PROGRAM DESCRIPTION:  This program is run as a child task of MULTI */
/*     This code provides the driver side of a Named Pipe TP1 application. */
/*                                                                    */
/**********************************************************************/
#include <process.h>              /* For exit()                      */
#include <string.h>               /* For printf                      */
#include <sys\types.h>            /* For time()                      */
#include <sys\timeb.h>            /* For time()                      */
#include <sys\stat.h>             /* For stat()                      */
#include <stdlib.h>               /* For atoi                        */
#include <stdio.h>                /* For sprintf, printf             */

#define INCL_VIO                  /* include VIO calls               */
#define INCL_DOSSEMAPHORES        /* include semaphore api calls     */
#define INCL_DOSMEMMGR            /* include segment   api calls     */
#define INCL_DOSNMPIPES           /* include named pipe api calls    */
#define INCL_ERRORS               /* include error definitions       */
#include <os2.h>

#include "const.h"                /* constants for multi             */
#include "sqltp1.h"               /* tp1 program vars, declares,etc. */

/*_____*/
/* includes, defines, etc. for task function                          */
/*_____*/
CHAR    input_msgbuf[512];                 /* msg buffer for receiving txn  */
CHAR    output_msgbuf[512];                /* msg buffer for sending resp.  */

USHORT  pipe_handle;
CHAR    pipe_name[] = "\\PIPE\\TP1";
CHAR    server_pipe_name[25];
ULONG   bytes_read;

/*_____*/
/* Main routine.                                                      */
/*_____*/
VOID main(USHORT argc, PCHAR argv[])
{
  get_args(argc, argv);            /*  get program arguments          */

  initialize_multi_ipc();          /*  Init MULTI semaphores/shared memory*/

  initialize_task();               /*  perform one time intializations */

  execute_task();                  /*  Remote Procedure Call  loop    */

} /* end main */
```

Figure 34-3. SQLTP1RQ.C: The main() Procedure.

SQLTP1RQ.C: The get_args() Procedure

In this section, we present the **get_args()** function, whose code listing is shown in Figure 34-5. This function obtains the arguments **MULTI** passes to the program when MULTI invokes it. **MULTI** itself gets these arguments from reading the **MULTI.CFG** file, an example of which is shown below:

```
PROGRAM_TYPE      = PROCESS
STOP_TIME_MS      = 600000
TASK_NAME         = SQLTP1RQ.EXE 0 17 2.0 1 \\RemoteServerName;
TASK_NAME         = SQLTP1RQ.EXE 1 23 2.0 1 \\RemoteServerName;
TASK_NAME         = SQLTP1RQ.EXE 2 29 2.0 1 \\RemoteServerName;
TASK_NAME         = SQLTP1RQ.EXE 3 57 2.0 1 \\RemoteServerName;
```

Figure 34-4. A MULTI.CFG File for Running Four TP1 Processes.

The arguments appear right after the program's name. The **get_args()** function requires the first four parameters, which are identical to the parameters from the previous
chapters. The fifth parameter is *optional*. It indicates the **network name** of a remote
server machine. Don't forget to enter the double backslash (\\) in front of the name.

```
/*_____*/
/* Get program arguments.  Argument are 1) process_number, 2) seed_value,  */
/* 3) threshold, 4) tps count, 5) server_name (optional)                   */
/*_____*/
VOID get_args(USHORT argc, PCHAR argv[])
{
   /*_____*/
   /* validate and get arguments     */
   /*_____*/
   if (argc < 5)
      { print_error(0, "reading command arguments",
                    __FILE__,__LINE__);
        exit(FAILED);
      }

   process_number = atoi(argv[1]);            /* get process number         */
   if ((process_number < 0) || (process_number > 3))
      { print_error(0, "reading process number", __FILE__,__LINE__);
        exit(FAILED);
      }

   seed_value = atoi(argv[2]);            /* get seed value      */
   threshold  = atof(argv[3]);            /* get threshold value */
   tps        = atoi(argv[4]);            /* get tps scale       */
   if (argc > 5)
       sprintf(server_pipe_name,"%s%s",      /* remote pipe with server name */
          argv[5],pipe_name);
   else
       sprintf(server_pipe_name,"%s",        /* local pipe          */
          pipe_name);

} /* end get_args */
```

Figure 34-5. SQLTP1RQ.C: The get_args() Procedure.

SQLTP1RQ.C: The initialize_task() Function

In this section, we present the **initialize_task()** function, whose code listing is shown
in Figure 34-6. This function does the following task-specific, one-time chores:

1. Adds a TXNS field to the task's window, which is where the count is displayed for TP1 transactions that meet the response time threshold.

2. Seeds the random number generator.

```
/*_____*/
/* Perform onetime initializations for the task such as database connects.  */
/*_____*/
VOID  initialize_task(VOID)
{
   /*_____*/
   /* add transaction count field           */
   /*_____*/
   write_str("TXNS  = ", FIELD_TEXT_ATTR,
            (process_number * 20) + 2, 10); /* calculate display location  */
                                            /*  based on thread number     */

   /*_____*/
   /* initialize random number generator    */
   /*_____*/
   srand(seed_value);

} /* end initialize_task */
```

Figure 34-6. SQLTP1RQ.C: The initialize_task() Function.

SQLTP1RQ.C: The tp1_transaction() Function

In this section, we present the **tp1_transaction()** function, whose code listing is shown in Figure 34-7. This procedure, unlike its counterpart in Chapter 32, does not perform the actual TP1 transaction. Instead, it calls a process on the server through the **DosCallNPipe** API, which executes the TP1. This is the first time we encounter this Named Pipe API call, so it will be described in the following section. The **DosCallNPipe** is used to connect to the server process, send a request, receive a reply and disconnect. The message sent is placed in the **input_msgbuf**. It consists of three parameters: **random1**, **random2**, and **tps**. When the server process receives this message, it executes a TP1; and if all goes well, it returns in the **output_msgbuf** an empty string. Otherwise, it returns a message describing what failed.

DosCallNPipe

The **DosCallNPipe** API call opens a Named Pipe, writes to it, reads from it, and closes it, all in one operation. This call combines in a single operation **DosOpen, DosSetN-PHState, DosTransactNPipe**, and a **DosClose**, for a duplex message pipe. This aggregate call is the preferred way to code "non-persistent" connections that get established and terminated just to issue a single request/reply. The aggregate call is simpler to read and also generates less network traffic. This is because the acknowledgements are "piggybacked" with returned data, resulting in increased efficiency. The prototype for this call is:

```
DosCallNPipe(PSZ      Name,          /* Name of pipe \\serv\pipe\name */
             PVOID    InBuf,         /* Read buffer address           */
             ULONG    InLen,         /* Read buffer length            */
             PVOID    OutBuf,        /* Write buffer address          */
             ULONG    OutLength,     /* Write buffer length           */
             PULONG   BytesRead,     /* Actual number of Bytes read   */
             ULONG    TimeOut);      /* In milliseconds               */
```

A description of the parameters follows:

- The *Name* parameter points to a null-terminated string that contains the name of the Named Pipe to be opened. Named Pipes are named **\PIPE\PipeName**, where **\PIPE** is the name of a virtual subdirectory in memory.
- The *InBuf* parameter points to the input buffer (where the message is received).
- The *InLen* parameter specifies the size in bytes of the input buffer.
- The *OutBuf* parameter points to the buffer containing the data to be written to the pipe.
- The *OutLength* parameter specifies the size in bytes of the output buffer.
- The *BytesRead* parameter points to a variable that receives the actual number of bytes read into the input buffer.
- The *TimeOut* parameter specifies in milliseconds the amount of time OS/2 should wait for the pipe to become available.

```
/*_____*/
/* function for TP1 transaction                                   */
/*_____*/
SHORT APIENTRY tp1_transaction(VOID)
{
    sprintf(input_msgbuf,"\\RANDOM1=%u \\RANDOM2=%u \\TPS=%u",
                    random1, random2, tps);

    do { rc = DosCallNPipe(server_pipe_name,       /* name of the pipe       */
                    input_msgbuf,                  /* input  msg             */
                    strlen(input_msgbuf) + 1,      /* input  msg size        */
                    output_msgbuf,                 /* output msg             */
                    sizeof(output_msgbuf),         /* output msg max size    */
                    &bytes_read,                   /* output msg actual size */
                    NP_INDEFINITE_WAIT);           /* timeout (wait forever) */
    } while ( rc == ERROR_PIPE_BUSY || rc == ERROR_PIPE_NOT_CONNECTED );
    if (rc)
       { print_error(rc,"during DosCallNPipe", __FILE__,__LINE__);
         exit(FAILED);
       }

    if (strcmp(output_msgbuf,"") != 0)
       {
         printf("%s\n",output_msgbuf);
         return(FAILED);
       }

    return(GOOD);
} /* end tp1_transaction */
```

Figure 34-7. SQLTP1RQ.SQC: The tp1_transaction() Procedure.

WALKING THROUGH THE SQLTP1SV.SQC SERVER

SQLTP1SV.SQC: The main() Procedure

In this section, we present the **main()** procedure of the TP1 server for the Named Pipes benchmark. Here's an overview of what this server code does:

1. Accepts client requests to perform a TP1 transaction.
2. Obtains the input parameters to perform the TP1.
3. Executes the TP1.
4. Returns the results.
5. Disconnects from the client and waits for the next request to come in.

The following is a step-by-step description of what **main()** does:

1. The program starts by including the C-language, OS/2, and Database Manager header files that are needed for system services. These files are identical to the header files that were discussed in the previous chapters.

2. A structure of type SQLCA is declared.

3. The SQL WHENEVER directions are issued.

4. The SQL host variables are declared.

5. The **main()** program follows and, as you can see, it's very similar to the TP1 back-end part of the programs we've already encountered. We will focus our presentation on what's new and different. As you will soon find out, there is nothing in this program that you did not previously encounter elsewhere in this book. This may be a sign of progress. Here's what **main()** does:

   • Invokes a "slimmed-down" version of the previously encountered **initialize_task()** function. We provide the listing of this slim version in Figure 34-9. This function connects to the database and installs a signal handler.

   • Invokes **initialize_pipe()**, a new function listed in Figure 34-10. This function creates a Named Pipe for this process. All the server processes use the **same** pipe name. This means that when a pipe is created, the process obtains a handle for a pipe instance with that common name. We will explain what this all means when we get to that section.

   • Invokes a "slimmed-down" version of the previously encountered **execute_task()** function. The code for this slim version is in Figure 34-11. This function is the home of the *big loop*, which forever executes TP1 transactions.

The difference is that it is not under **MULTI** control. The loop ends when the process gets killed by its parent, the **LAUNCHER** program.

- The TP1 transaction is executed by the helper routine, **tp1_transaction()**. This is a straight implementation of a TP1 using static SQL. We've listed this helper procedure (see listing in Figure 34-12) because it handles errors slightly differently from the TP1 code in the previous chapters.

```
/***********************************************************************/
/*  PROGRAM NAME: SQLTP1SV.SQC                                       */
/*                                                                  */
/*  PROGRAM DESCRIPTION:  This program is run as a child task of the LAUNCHER*/
/*    program and executes the TP1 transaction using Named Pipes to     */
/*    communicate with a client.                                    */
/*    This code provides the server side of a Name Pipe TP1           */
/*                                                                  */
/***********************************************************************/
#include <process.h>                    /* For exit()                */
#include <string.h>                     /* For printf                */
#include <sys\types.h>                  /* For time()                */
#include <sys\timeb.h>                  /* For time()                */
#include <sys\stat.h>                   /* For stat()                */
#include <stdlib.h>                     /* For atoi                  */
#include <stdio.h>                      /* For sprintf, printf       */

#define INCL_VIO                        /* include VIO calls         */
#define INCL_DOSSEMAPHORES              /* include semaphore api calls */
#define INCL_DOSMEMMGR                  /* include segment  api calls */
#define INCL_DOSNMPIPES                 /* include named pipe api calls */
#define INCL_ERRORS                     /* include error definitions */
#include <os2.h>

#include <sqlca.h>                      /* sqlca                     */
#include <sql.h>                        /* error msg. retrieval      */
#include <sqlcodes.h>                   /* SQL return code constants */
#include <sqlenv.h>                     /* environment functions and */

                    /*_____*/
                    /* forward declarations of functions    */
                    /*_____*/

VOID initialize_task(VOID);
VOID initialize_pipe(VOID);
VOID execute_task(VOID);
SHORT APIENTRY tp1_transaction(VOID);
VOID print_error(USHORT, PCHAR, PCHAR, USHORT);
VOID format_error(PCHAR msgbuf, USHORT Error, PCHAR msg,
                  PCHAR file, USHORT line);

                    /*_____*/
                    /* constant definitions                */
                    /*_____*/

#define GOOD                   0
#define FAILED                -1
```

Figure 34-8. (Part 1 of 2). SQLTP1SV.SQC: The main() Procedure.

```
                         /*————————————————————*/
                         /* variables                            */
                         /*————————————————————*/

USHORT seed_value;                    /* initial seed for random number gen*/
double threshold;                     /* time thresholds for TP1 txns      */
USHORT tps;                           /* the tps scale, input from client  */
USHORT random1, random2;              /* inputs from client                */
CHAR   input_msgbuf[512];             /* msg buffer for receiving txn      */
CHAR   output_msgbuf[512];            /* msg buffer for sending resp.      */
USHORT rc;                            /* return code variable              */
CHAR   error_string[80];              /* error string container            */

HPIPE  pipe_handle;
CHAR   pipe_name[] = "\\PIPE\\TP1";
ULONG  bytes_read;
ULONG  bytes_written;

struct sqlca sqlca;

EXEC SQL WHENEVER SQLERROR CONTINUE;
EXEC SQL WHENEVER SQLWARNING CONTINUE;
EXEC SQL WHENEVER NOT FOUND CONTINUE;

EXEC SQL BEGIN DECLARE SECTION;
 long  acct_num;
 short branch_id;
 short teller_id;
 long  balance;
 long  delta         = 100;
 char  acct_name[20] = "<--20 BYTE STRING-->";
EXEC SQL END   DECLARE SECTION;

/*————————————————————————————————————*/
/* Main routine.                                                  */
/*————————————————————————————————————*/
VOID main(USHORT argc, PCHAR argv[])
{

   initialize_task();                        /* perform database connect etc. */

   initialize_pipe();                        /* create Named Pipe             */

   execute_task();                           /* Loop executing TP1s           */

} /* end main */
```

Figure 34-8. (Part 2 of 2). SQLTP1SV.SQC: The main() Procedure.

SQLTP1SV.SQC: The initialize_task() Procedure

In this section, we present the **initialize_task**() procedure whose code is listed in Figure 34-9. This function does the following task-specific, one-time chores:

1. Connects to the TP1 database.
2. Installs a signal handler that intercepts CTRL + Break, and then gracefully termi-nates the program.

```
/*_____*/
/* Perform onetime initializations for the task such as database connects. */
/*_____*/
VOID  initialize_task(VOID)
{
   /*_____*/
   /* connect to the database, restart if */
   /*      necessary                      */
   /*_____*/
   sqlestrd("TP1", 'S', &sqlca);

   if (SQLCODE == SQLE_RC_DB_RESTART)
      sqlerest("TP1", &sqlca);

   if (SQLCODE)
      { sprintf(error_string,"connnecting to the database, SQLCODE = %ld",
              SQLCODE);
       print_error(0, error_string, __FILE__,__LINE__);
       exit(FAILED);
      }

   /*_____*/
   /* install database signal handler    */
   /*_____*/
   sqleisig(&sqlca);
   if (SQLCODE)
      { sprintf(error_string,"installing signal handler, SQLCODE = %ld",
              SQLCODE);
       print_error(0, error_string, __FILE__,__LINE__);
       exit(FAILED);
      }

} /* end initialize_task */
```

Figure 34-9. SQLTP1SV.SQC: The initialize_task() Procedure.

SQLTP1SV.SQC: The initialize_pipe() Procedure

In this section, we present the **initialize_pipe()** procedure whose code is listed in Figure 34-10. This function simply issues a **DosCreateNPipe** API call. This API is fully described in "DosCreateNPipe" in Chapter 17. Here are some points worth noting:

- The **PIPE_OPENMODE** parameter is specified for the following pipe attributes:

  1. Data is sent over LAN after each write (no blocking).
  2. Either the server or the client can send data (duplex).

- The **PIPEMODE** parameter is specified for the following pipe attributes:

  1. The pipe will operate in message stream mode.
  2. An instance count of 128 is specified. The maximum is 254 instances. Any attempts to make a pipe will fail if the maximum number of allowed instances already exists. This parameter is looked at only when the first instance of a pipe is created (OS/2 ignores it after that). When multiple instances are allowed,

multiple clients can simultaneously issue DosOpen to the same pipe name and get handles to distinct pipe instances.

```
/*─────────────────────────────────────────────────────────────*/
/* Perform onetime initializations for the Named Pipe           */
/*─────────────────────────────────────────────────────────────*/
VOID  initialize_pipe(VOID)
{

  #define PIPE_OPENMODE    0x4002    /* no write-behind allowed, duplex */
  #define PIPEMODE         0x0580    /* message pipe, 128  instances    */
  #define TIMEOUT          0L        /* wait forever timeout value      */

  rc = DosCreateNPipe(pipe_name,       /* PipeName                      */
                      &pipe_handle,     /* pipe handle returned          */
                      PIPE_OPENMODE,
                      PIPEMODE,
                      512,              /* Output buffer size in bytes   */
                      512,              /* Input  buffer size in bytes   */
                      TIMEOUT);
  if (rc)
     {print_error(rc,"Creating a named pipe",__FILE__,__LINE__);
      exit(FAILED);
     }
} /* end initialize_pipes */
```

Figure 34-10.   SQLTP1SV.SQC: The initialize_pipe() Procedure.

SQLTP1SV.SQC: The execute_task() Procedure

In this section, we present the **execute_task()** procedure, whose code is listed in Figure 34-11. This code executes as a loop that ends only when the task is killed by its parent, the **LAUNCHER** program. Here is what this loop does:

1. Issues the **DosConnectNPipe** API call and waits for a client to open this pipe instance. The process is blocked waiting for that to happen. This API call is described in "DosConnectNPipe" in Chapter 17.
2. Issues a **DosRead** API call to receive a message from the client on this Named Pipe instance. This API call is described in "DosRead" in Chapter 17.
3. Receives and decodes three parameters from the client **random1**, **random2**, and **tps**.
4. Executes a TP1 transaction by invoking the **tp1_transaction()** helper function.
5. Issues a **DosWrite** API call to send a reply message to the client on this Named Pipe instance. This API call is described in "DosWrite" in Chapter 17.
6. Issues a **DosDisConnectNPipe** API call to disconnect from the client. This API call is described in "DosDisConnectNPipe" in Chapter 17.

```
/*_____*/
/* Task routine. This routine continuously 1) waits for a remote request  */
/*   2) reads the incoming parameters,   3) invokes the TP1 helper procedure */
/*   4) sends back response  5) disconnects from client            */
/*_____*/
VOID execute_task(VOID)
{

    /*_____*/
    /* continuous TP1 loop                     */
    /*_____*/
    while (TRUE)
      {
        /*_____*/
        /* execute a TP1 transaction               */
        /*_____*/
        rc = DosConnectNPipe(pipe_handle);
        if (rc)
           {print_error(rc,"Connecting to pipe",__FILE__,__LINE__);
            exit(FAILED);
           }

        rc = DosRead(pipe_handle,
                      input_msgbuf,
                      sizeof(input_msgbuf),
                      &bytes_read);
        if (rc)
           {print_error(rc,"Reading from pipe",__FILE__,__LINE__);
            exit(FAILED);
           }

        if (sscanf(input_msgbuf,"\\RANDOM1=%hu \\RANDOM2=%hu \\TPS=%hu",
                &random1, &random2, &tps) != 3)
           {print_error(rc,"Reading TP1 Parameters",__FILE__,__LINE__);
            exit(FAILED);
           }

        if ( tp1_transaction( ) )
           exit(FAILED);

        rc = DosWrite(pipe_handle,
                      output_msgbuf,
                      strlen(output_msgbuf) + 1,
                      &bytes_written);
        if (rc)
           {print_error(rc,"Writing to pipe",__FILE__,__LINE__);
            exit(FAILED);
           }

        rc = DosDisConnectNPipe(pipe_handle);
        if (rc)
           {print_error(rc,"Disconnecting from Pipe",__FILE__,__LINE__);
            exit(FAILED);
           }

      }/* end while */
} /* end execute_task */
```

Figure 34-11. SQLTP1SV.SQC: The execute_task() Procedure.

SQLTP1SV.SQC: The tp1_transaction() Procedure

In this section, we present the **tp1_transaction()** procedure, whose code is listed in Figure 34-12. There is nothing new in this code; it is the standard static SQL implementation of a TP1 which was described in the previous two chapters.

```
/*_____*/
/* function for TP1 transaction                                  */
/*_____*/
SHORT APIENTRY tp1_transaction(VOID)
{

        /*_____*/
        /* generate some random data               */
        /*_____*/

    acct_num = (random1 * random2) % (tps*1000001) + 1;/* generate acct number */
    teller_id= (short)(random1 % (tps*100)) + 1;       /* generate teller id    */
    branch_id= (short)(random2 % (tps*10)) + 1;        /* generate branch id    */

        /*_____*/
        /* get the current balance from ACCT       */
        /*_____*/
    EXEC SQL DECLARE CURSOR1 CURSOR FOR
            SELECT BALANCE FROM ACCT WHERE ACCT_NUM = :acct_num
            FOR UPDATE OF BALANCE;

    EXEC SQL OPEN CURSOR1;
    if (SQLCODE != 0)
        { format_error(output_msgbuf, (SHORT)SQLCODE,
                    "during SQL OPEN", __FILE__, __LINE__);
          return(GOOD);
        }

    EXEC SQL FETCH CURSOR1 INTO :balance;
    if (SQLCODE != 0)
        { format_error(output_msgbuf, (SHORT)SQLCODE,
                    "during SQL FETCH", __FILE__, __LINE__);
          return(GOOD);
        }

        /*_____*/
        /* Credit the balance in the ACCT table */
        /*_____*/
    EXEC SQL UPDATE ACCT
            SET BALANCE = BALANCE + :delta
            WHERE CURRENT OF CURSOR1;
    if (SQLCODE != 0)
        { format_error(output_msgbuf, (SHORT)SQLCODE,
                    "during SQL UPDATE", __FILE__,__LINE__);
          return(GOOD);
        }

    EXEC SQL CLOSE CURSOR1;
    if (SQLCODE != 0)
        { format_error(output_msgbuf, (SHORT)SQLCODE,
                    "during SQL CLOSE", __FILE__,__LINE__);
          return(GOOD);
        }
```

Figure 34-12 (Part 1 of 2). SQLTP1SV.SQC: The tp1_transaction() Procedure.

```
        /*_____*/
        /* Update the TELLER table's balance   */
        /*_____*/

EXEC SQL UPDATE TELLER
        SET BALANCE = BALANCE + :delta
        WHERE TELLER_ID = :teller_id;
if (SQLCODE != 0)
   { format_error(output_msgbuf, (SHORT)SQLCODE,
                "during SQL UPDATE", __FILE__,__LINE__);
     return(GOOD);
   }


        /*_____*/
        /* Update the BRANCH table's balance   */
        /*_____*/

EXEC SQL UPDATE BRANCH
        SET BALANCE = BALANCE + :delta
        WHERE BRANCH_ID = :branch_id;
if (SQLCODE != 0)
   { format_error(output_msgbuf, (SHORT)SQLCODE,
                "during SQL UPDATE", __FILE__,__LINE__);
     return(GOOD);
   }


        /*_____*/
        /* Insert transaction in HISTORY table */
        /*_____*/

EXEC SQL INSERT
        INTO HISTORY(ACCT_NUM, TELLER_ID, BRANCH_ID, BALANCE,
                   DELTA, PID, TRANSID, ACCTNAME, TEMP)
        VALUES(:acct_num, :teller_id, :branch_id, :balance,
               :delta, 1, 3, :acct_name, 'hist   ');
if (SQLCODE != 0)
   { format_error(output_msgbuf, (SHORT)SQLCODE,
                "during SQL INSERT", __FILE__,__LINE__);
     return(GOOD);
   }

        /*_____*/
        /* Commit the transaction to database  */
        /*_____*/

EXEC SQL COMMIT;
if (SQLCODE != 0)
   { format_error(output_msgbuf, (SHORT)SQLCODE,
                "during SQL COMMIT", __FILE__, __LINE__);
     return(GOOD);
   }

output_msgbuf[0] = '\0';                    /* no errors        */
return(GOOD);

} /* end tp1_transaction */
```

Figure 34-12 (Part 2 of 2). SQLTP1SV.SQC: The tp1_transaction() Procedure.

SQLTP1SV.SQC: format_error() and print_error()

In this section, we present the **format_error()** and the **print_error()** helper functions. There are, of course, no surprises in this code.

```
/*————————————————————————————————————*/
/* Error Format Routine                                    */
/*————————————————————————————————————*/
VOID format_error(PCHAR msgbuf, USHORT Error, PCHAR msg,
                  PCHAR file, USHORT line)
{
    sprintf(msgbuf,"Error %d detected while %s at line %d in file %s.\n",
            Error, msg, line, file);
} /* end format_error */
```

Figure 34-13. SQLTP1SV.SQC: The format_error() Helper Function.

```
/*————————————————————————————————————*/
/* Error Display Routine                                   */
/*————————————————————————————————————*/
VOID print_error(USHORT Error, PCHAR msg, PCHAR file, USHORT line)
{
 if (Error == 0)
    printf("Error detected while %s at line %d in file %s.\n",
           msg, line, file);
 else
    printf("Error %d detected while %s at line %d in file %s.\n",
           Error, msg, line, file);
} /* end print_error */
```

Figure 34-14. SQLTP1SV.SQC: The print_error() Helper Function.

WALKING THROUGH THE LAUNCHER.C CODE

In this section, we present the code for a standalone program, **LAUNCHER.C**, whose sole function in life is to start child processes. We will be using this program to "launch" several TP1 server processes. If you want to be extra generous, you can start one server process for each concurrent client. For example, if you have six concurrent clients, you could issue:

```
LAUNCHER  sqltp1sv 6
```

This creates a six-server process pool. The TP1 benchmark will run moderately well with a pool consisting of a single server process, but you won't be getting the maximum throughput from such a benchmark. Here is what the **LAUNCHER.C** program does:

1. It reads two input arguments:

    *   The name of the program you want to "launch"
    *   The number of instances of that program you want to start

2. Issues a **DosExecPgm** API call once for each instance of that program requested.
    The instances created are child processes of the **LAUNCHER** program.
3. Blocks waiting for any key to be hit.
4. Kills all the child processes it created so you don't have to reboot your machine.

Congratulations, we've just completed the final piece of code that makes up the third
flavor of our TP1 benchmark!

```
/**************************************************************************/
/*   PROGRAM NAME: LAUNCHER                                             */
/*                                                                     */
/*   PROGRAM DESCRIPTION:  This simple program is used to launch        */
/*     multiple instances of a child process.  The user specifies the  */
/*     name of the program to launch and the number of instances.      */
/*     This program is used as part of the TP1 toolkit to start multiple*/
/*     instances of a named pipe server program.  One server process   */
/*     instance is needed for each concurrent client                   */
/*                                                                     */
/**************************************************************************/
#include <process.h>              /* For exit()                        */
#include <stdio.h>                /* For printf() & NULL               */
#include <conio.h>                /* For getch()                       */
#include <stdlib.h>               /* For printf                        */
#include <string.h>               /* For printf                        */
#define  INCL_BASE
#include <os2.h>

#define GOOD                0
#define FAILED             -1

/*_____*/
/* Main routine.                                                       */
/*_____*/
VOID main(USHORT argc, PCHAR argv[], PCHAR envp[])
{ UCHAR       program_name[128];            /* includes path          */
  UCHAR       object_name[128];             /* buffer for fail object */
  RESULTCODES ExecResult;                   /* defined by OS/2        */
  UCHAR       rc;                           /* return code            */
  UINT        i;                            /* counter                */
  UINT        instances;                    /* number of child processes*/
  USHORT      processid[100];               /* process ids to terminate */

  /*_____*/
  /* Get input parameters                */
  /*_____*/
  if (argc != 3)
  { printf("Enter command as follows: LAUNCHER program-name instances \n");
    exit(FAILED);
  }
  sprintf(program_name,"%s.exe", argv[1]);
  instances      = atoi(argv[2]);
```

Figure 34-15 (Part 1 of 2). The LAUNCHER.C Code.

```
/*_____*/
/* start the processes           */
/*_____*/
for (i=0; i<instances; ++i)
{
    rc = DosExecPgm(object_name,          /* failing object if program fails*/
                    sizeof(object_name),/* the object size              */
                    2,                    /* async. program execution     */
                    OL,                   /* no program parameters        */
                    OL,                   /* no inherit environment       */
                    &ExecResult,          /* child process id             */
                    program_name);        /* program name                 */
    if (rc)
    { printf("Error rc = %u, while creating  process instance = %u \n",
              rc, instances);
      exit(FAILED);
    }
    printf("process instance %u started successfully \n", i + 1);
    processid[i] = ExecResult.codeTerminate;    /* save process id        */

} /* end for */

/*_____*/
/* Wait for user request         */
/*_____*/
printf("Hit any key to kill all server processes \n");
getch();

/*_____*/
/* Kill all the processes        */
/*_____*/
for (i=0; i<instances; ++i)
{
    rc = DosKillProcess(1,                      /* only kill one process */
                    processid[i]);              /* process handle        */
    if (rc)
    { printf("Error killing process instance = %u \n",  instances);
      exit(FAILED);
    }
}
exit(GOOD);

} /* end main */
```

Figure 34-15 (Part 2 of 2). The LAUNCHER.C Code.

RUNNING TWO TP1 BENCHMARK TESTS USING NAMED PIPES

Now that we've got some code, let's run some benchmarks to see how well this TP1 flavor performs. We will run two TP1 benchmark tests:

1. A **local** benchmark test where the client and servers are on the same machine. The machine is a PS/2 Mod-95 with a 33-MHz clock and a 1000-KByte buffer pool (see Figure 34-18).

2. A **remote** benchmark test where the clients and servers are on different machines. The client machine is a PS/2 Mod 80 with a 20-MHz clock. The server machine is a PS/2 Mod-95 with a 33-MHz clock and a 1000-KByte buffer pool (see Figure 34-19).

The two benchmarks use identical four-process software configurations. The **MULTI** configuration file used for the local test is:

```
PROGRAM_TYPE      = PROCESS
STOP_TIME_MS      = 600000
TASK_NAME         = SQLTP1RQ.EXE 0 17 2.0  1;
TASK_NAME         = SQLTP1RQ.EXE 1 23 2.0  1;
TASK_NAME         = SQLTP1RQ.EXE 2 29 2.0  1;
TASK_NAME         = SQLTP1RQ.EXE 3 57 2.0  1;
```

Figure 34-16. A MULTI.CFG file for Running Four TP1 Processes Locally.

The **MULTI** configuration file used for the remote test is:

```
PROGRAM_TYPE      = PROCESS
STOP_TIME_MS      = 600000
TASK_NAME         = SQLTP1RQ.EXE 0 17 2.0  1 \\LSVRO3;
TASK_NAME         = SQLTP1RQ.EXE 1 23 2.0  1 \\LSVRO3;
TASK_NAME         = SQLTP1RQ.EXE 2 29 2.0  1 \\LSVRO3;
TASK_NAME         = SQLTP1RQ.EXE 3 57 2.0  1 \\LSVRO3;
```

Figure 34-17. A MULTI.CFG File for Running Four TP1 Processes Remotely.

The benchmarks are set up to run for 10-minute tests (i.e., 600,000 milliseconds). The response time threshold is set to 2.0 seconds, and a 1-tps database size is specified.

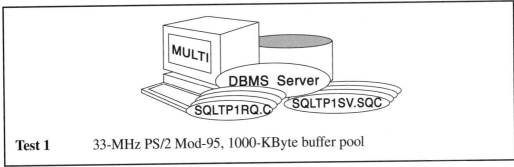

Test 1   33-MHz PS/2 Mod-95, 1000-KByte buffer pool

Figure 34-18. The Named Pipes Local Benchmark Configuration.

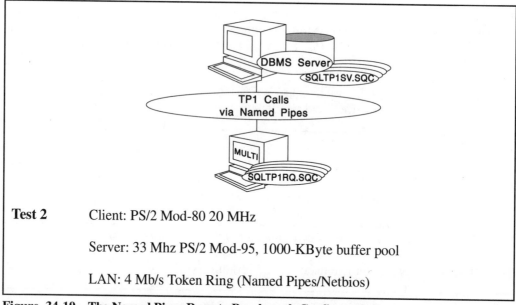

Test 2   Client: PS/2 Mod-80 20 MHz

Server: 33 Mhz PS/2 Mod-95, 1000-KByte buffer pool

LAN: 4 Mb/s Token Ring (Named Pipes/Netbios)

Figure 34-19.   The Named Pipes Remote Benchmark Configuration.

Running the Named Pipes Remote TP1 Locally (Benchmark1)

The configuration for this benchmark is a four-client MULTI running against a local database. The test is run on a PS/2 Mod-95 with a 33-MHz clock and a 1000-KByte buffer pool. We assume the database is already loaded for a 1-tps database scale. The following RSQL run is used to set up the 1000-KByte buffer configuration and prepare the database for the benchmark1 run.

```
--                     Change TP1 Database Configuration
-- ===============================================================================
-- update the Database Configuration for database for a 1000k buffer
EXEC DBA: UPDATE_DB_CFG TP1     MAXAPPLS    = 8,
                                DLCHKTIME   = 10000,
                                BUFFPAGE    = 256,
                                LOGFILSIZ   = 50,
                                LOGPRIMARY  = 2,
                                LOGSECOND   = 20;


 OK, sql_rcd = 0,          Execution time =      0.3100 secs


-- Show the database configuration for database TP1
EXEC DBA: SHOW_DB_CFG TP1;

Database Configuration for Database TP1
=================================================

Configuration Parameter             Current  Parm.     Parm.      Parm.
Description                          Value    Units     Range      Default
-----------------------------       -------- --------- ---------- -------
```

Figure 34-20 (Part 1 of 2).   Preparing the Database for Benchmark1.

```
Max. Active Applications           8    Appl.        1-256          8
Max. DB Files Open/Application     20    files        2-235         20
Max. Files Open/Application       255    files        25-32700     255
Buffer Pool Size                  256    4K pages      2-1500       (1)
Time Interval for Deadlocks     10000    millisecs.   1-600 sec.    10
Max. Storage for Locklists         25    4K pages     4-250          8
Max. percent locklist/appl.        22    percent      1-100         22
Default Application Heap            3    segments      2-20          3
Application Agent Heap              2    segments      2-85          2
Sort List Heap                     2    segments      1-20          2
Database Heap                      3    segments      1-45         (2)
SQL Statement Heap                64    segments      8-255         64
Log File Size                     50    4K pages     4-65535       (3)
Primary Log Files                  2    files         2-63          3
Secondary Log Files               20    files         0-61          2
Log Records/soft checkpoint       100    records      0-65535      100

Current Log Location = F:\SQL00001\SQLOGDIR\
New Log Location      =
First Log File        =
Current Log File      =
Copy Protection       =    1 (1 = Protected, Default = 1)
Log Retain            =    0 (1 = Retain Log Files, Default = 0)
User Exit             =    0 (1 = Enable User Exit, Default = 0)
Auto Restart          =    1 (1 = Enable Auto Restart, Default = 1)
Country               =    1
Code Page             =  437
Release               =  768
DB Consistency        =    1 (1 = Consistent)
Backup Pending        =    0 (1 = Backup Pending)
Roll Forward Pending  =    0 (1 = Roll Forward Pending)
User Exit Status      =    0 (1 = User exit Enabled)
Log Retain Status     =    0 (1 = log files retained)

(1) - client or standalone 25, server 250
(2) - client or standalone  2, server   3
(3) - client or standalone 32, server 200
OK, sql_rcd = 0,        Execution time =      0.1200 secs


-- bind the tp1 program
EXEC DBA: BIND TP1 SQLTP1SV.BND ISO REPEATABLE_READ BLOCK_ALL PUBLIC;

No messages in msgfile.msg

OK, sql_rcd = 0,        Execution time =      2.7900 secs


-- Connect to the TP1 database
EXEC DBA: STARTUSE TP1 S;

OK, sql_rcd = 0,        Execution time =      0.6500 secs


-- delete all of the history data
EXEC SQL: DELETE FROM HISTORY;

WARNING, sql_code = 100,    Execution time =     2.4100 secs
SQL0100W  No row was found for FETCH, UPDATE or DELETE; or the result of a
query is an empty table.
```

Figure 34-20 (Part 2 of 2). Preparing the Database for Benchmark1.

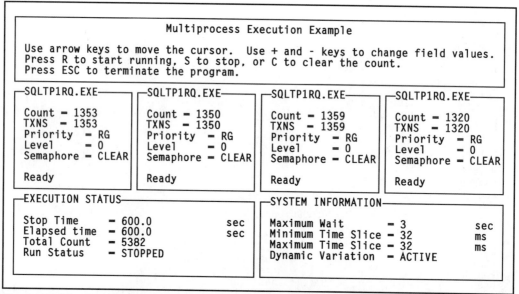

```
                        Multiprocess Execution Example

    Use arrow keys to move the cursor.  Use + and - keys to change field values.
    Press R to start running, S to stop, or C to clear the count.
    Press ESC to terminate the program.

  ┌─SQLTP1RQ.EXE──────┐ ┌─SQLTP1RQ.EXE──────┐ ┌─SQLTP1RQ.EXE──────┐ ┌─SQLTP1RQ.EXE──────┐

    Count    = 1353      Count    = 1350      Count    = 1359      Count    = 1320
    TXNS    = 1353       TXNS    = 1350       TXNS    = 1359       TXNS    = 1320
    Priority  = RG       Priority  = RG       Priority  = RG       Priority   = RG
    Level    = 0         Level    = 0         Level     = 0        Level     = 0
    Semaphore = CLEAR    Semaphore = CLEAR    Semaphore = CLEAR    Semaphore = CLEAR

    Ready                Ready                Ready                Ready

  ┌─EXECUTION STATUS──────────────────────┐ ┌─SYSTEM INFORMATION────────────────────┐

    Stop Time    = 600.0         sec         Maximum Wait       = 3          sec
    Elapsed time = 600.0         sec         Minimum Time Slice = 32         ms
    Total Count  = 5382                      Maximum Time Slice = 32         ms
    Run Status   = STOPPED                   Dynamic Variation  = ACTIVE
```

Figure 34-21.   The Results of a 4-Process TP1 Run Against a Local Named Pipes Server.

Benchmark1 results: The MULTI screen in Figure 34-21 shows the results of a 10-minute test. During this period, a total of 5382 TP1 transactions ran successfully. All transactions had a response time under the 2-second threshold. Using the liberal interpretation of TP1 introduced in the previous chapters, this machine is therefore in the *9.0 TP1* range.

Commentary: This result shows a slight degradation in performance compared to both the local SQL version of TP1 and the local Application Remote Interface version of TP1. Why? Perhaps we could attribute this degradation to the interprocess communication overhead introduced by Named Pipes.

Running the Named Pipes Remote TP1 Remotely (Benchmark2)

The configuration for this benchmark is a four-client MULTI running against a remote database. The database is on a PS/2 Mod-95 with a 33-MHz clock and a 1000-KByte buffer.

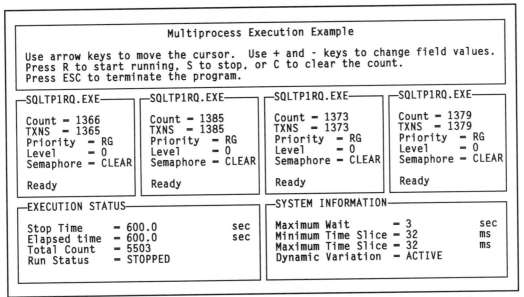

Figure 34-22. The Results of a 4-Process TP1 Run Against a Remote Named Pipes Server.

Benchmark2 Results: The MULTI screen in Figure 34-22 shows the results of a 10-minute test. During this period, a total of 5503 TP1 transactions ran successfully. All but one transaction had a response time that was under the 2-second threshold. Using the liberal interpretation of TP1 introduced in the previous chapters, this machine is in the *9.2 TP1* range.

Commentary: Like the Application Remote Interface version of TP1, this result shows a substantial improvement in performance over the remote SQL version of TP1. *In fact, this is the best remote performance we've seen in all of the remote benchmarks.* This improvement is attributed to the better network utilization inherent in the stored procedures approach. A single message exchange takes place as opposed to an exchange for each SQL statement in the transaction. The results also show that Named Pipes' **DosCallNPipe** utilizes the network very effectively.

Why does the remote version of the Named Pipes TP1 outperform its local version (*9.2 TP1s* versus *9.0 TP1s*)? What happened to the network overhead? A possible explanation is that the overhead introduced by the network is offset by the offloading of the four client processes from the server machine.

Chapter 35

The Dynamic SQL
Database Server TP1

This is the fifth chapter of the TP1 Benchmark Series. In this chapter, we develop a Dynamic SQL version of a TP1 transaction. Why would anybody want to run a TP1 benchmark on a *Database Server* using the notoriously slow Dynamic SQL? We do this to obtain a precise measure of *"just how slow is slow?"* Dynamic SQL commands provide maximum flexibility by preparing SQL statements for execution at run time. You can think of dynamic SQL as an interpretive form of the SQL language. The database objects need not exist when precompiling dynamic SQL statements. The compilation of dynamic SQL statements is done at run time and must be repeated every time the same statement is executed. This flexibility comes at the expense of execution speed. However, there are many situations where the flexibility of Dynamic SQL outweighs its poor performance. The Dynamic SQL TP1 benchmark will give you information you can use for making *trade-offs between performance and flexibility*.

WHAT YOU WILL LEARN

The **SQLTP1DY.SQC** program we develop in this chapter is the Dynamic SQL version of the original **SQLTP1.SQC** program in Chapter 32. All we need to do in this chapter is code the Dynamic SQL version of the **tp1_transaction**() procedure and we'll have our final TP1 flavor. This chapter has the following prerequisites:

- The SQL Tutorial chapter.
- The **RSQL** chapter on Programming Dynamic SQL. We'll assume you're an old hand at this kind of programming.
- The first two chapters in the TP1 Benchmark Series. Much of the code in this chapter is identical to code you've already seen in **SQLTP1.SQC**. This common code will not be repeated. Instead, we will refer you to the appropriate **SQLTP1.SQC** listings where the common code is first introduced.
- You should review the **MULTI** chapters in Part II, and you should be familiar with **RSQL** at the user level.

THE DYNAMIC SQL VERSION OF TP1

The **SQLTP1DY.SQC** program is designed to run as a **MULTI** process. This means **MULTI** will create the process, pass it the parameters, and tell it when to start or stop executing TP1 transactions. When the process is told to start executing TP1s, it will go into a continuous loop submitting TP1 transactions against the database, and displaying the running count of the results.

LOCAL AND REMOTE TP1 CONFIGURATIONS

The TP1 transactions execute as Dynamic SQL statements against a database. This database may be either local or remote. The location of the database is totally transparent to the code. If the database is remote, then the **Remote Data Services** (RDS) component of the Database Manager will pass the SQL statement to the remote database using NetBIOS/RDS.

Each instance of **MULTI** can run four **SQLTP1DY.SQC** processes. If you need more TP1 generators, simply add more **MULTI** client workstations. Figure 35-1 shows you how to create a 12-client TP1 system. You can scale this configuration in any direction depending on your budget considerations. As usual, we will be scaling our experiments downward to a four-client TP1 system. We'll then run benchmarks against the local and remote database configurations to understand the overhead **RDS** introduces. The idea behind this dynamic benchmark is not to obtain numbers you can "write home about." Instead, the idea is to get a feel for how slow Dynamic SQL really is so that we can make intelligent design decisions on when to use it in our programs.

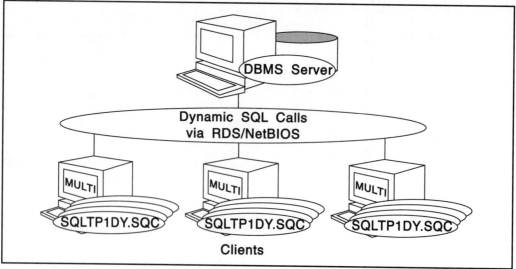

Figure 35-1. A 12-Client Dynamic SQL TP1 Database Server System.

WALKING THROUGH THE SQLTP1DY.SQC CODE

SQLTP1DY.SQC: The main() Procedure

In this section, we present the **main()** procedure of the **SQLTP1DY.SQC** Dynamic SQL TP1 program, whose code listing is shown in Figure 35-2. You will find that much of the code is identical to the original **SQLTP1.SQC** code from Chapter 32. This is not surprising since both programs are structurally identical. They both consist of a front-end that interacts with **MULTI** and of a back-end that uses the Database Manager's SQL API services.

The difference is that the code presented in this chapter performs the TP1 transactions using *Dynamic* SQL instead of *Static* SQL. What you will learn that's "new and exciting" is how to issue the TP1 SQL calls using Dynamic SQL statements. We will not repeat the code and explanations that you've already encountered **SQLTP1.SQC** program. Instead, we will refer you to the appropriate sections in Chapter 32. We only introduce code listings that do something new. The following is a step-by-step description of what **main()** does:

1. The program starts by including the C-language, OS/2, and the Database Manager header files that are needed for system services. These are identical to the header files that were discussed in the previous chapters because much of what we do is interact with **MULTI**.

2. The following program header files are included:

    const.h   This is the same header file that was used in the previous chapters. Its listing can be found in Figure 14-11.

    sqltp1.h   This is the same header file that was used in the previous chapters. Its listing can be found in Figure 32-10.

3. A structure of type SQLCA is declared.

4. The SQL WHENEVER directions are issued.

5. The SQL host variables are declared. This is where the fun starts. You will notice that most of the SQL statements used for the TP1 are declared as host variable strings. Here is an example:

```
char ins_hist[240] =   "INSERT INTO HISTORY(ACCT_NUM, TELLER_ID,
                        BRANCH_ID, BALANCE, \
                        DELTA, PID, TRANSID, ACCTNAME, TEMP) \
                        VALUES(?, ?, ?, ?, ?, 1, 3, ?, 'hist    ')";
```

What are the question marks **"?"** in the middle of the SQL statement? These are *parameter markers*, or placeholders for variables whose data types are fixed but whose values are unknown at the time the code is created. A Dynamic SQL statement is prepared once with these placeholders and assigned a name. The name can then be executed multiple times using different parameter values each time.

6. The **main()** program follows and, as you can see, it's a carbon copy of **SQLTP1.SQC**'s **main()**. The key difference is in the helper function that executes the Dynamic SQL TP1. Here's what **main()** does:

    -   Invokes the previously encountered **get_args()** function from Chapter 32. The listing for this function can be found in Figure 32-4. This function obtains the arguments **MULTI** passes to the program. **MULTI**, of course, gets these arguments from reading the **MULTI.CFG** file.
    -   Invokes the previously encountered **initialize_multi_ipc()** function, whose listing can be found in Chapter 32 in Figure 32-5. This function performs all the interprocess communication chores required from a process that runs under **MULTI**'s control.
    -   Invokes the previously encountered **initialize_task()** function, whose listing can be found in Chapter 32. on page 813. This function connects to the database, installs a signal handler, and does all kinds of one-time housekeeping chores in preparation for the *big loop*.
    -   Invokes the previously encountered **execute_task()** function listed in Figure 32-7. This is the home of the *big loop*, which forever requests TP1 transactions. **MULTI** can at any time pause and resume the execution of TP1 transactions through semaphores. The TP1 transaction is executed by the helper routine, **tp1_transaction()**.

Note: This is where we part company in a major way with the code in Chapter 32. The **tp1_transaction()** presented in this chapter (see listing in Figure 35-3) uses Dynamic SQL instead of static SQL. So, all we need to do now is see how this is done and we'll be finished with the SQL benchmark code, at least as far as this book is concerned.

```
/*****************************************************************************/
/*   PROGRAM NAME: SQLTP1DY - A process program that MULTI starts           */
/*                                                                          */
/*   PROGRAM DESCRIPTION: This program is run as a child task of the MULTI  */
/*      program.  It executes the TP1 Benchmark program using Dynamic SQL   */
/*                                                                          */
/*****************************************************************************/
#include <process.h>              /* For exit()                            */
#include <string.h>               /* For printf                            */
#include <sys\types.h>            /* For time()                            */
#include <sys\timeb.h>            /* For time()                            */
#include <sys\stat.h>             /* For stat()                            */
#include <stdlib.h>               /* For atoi                              */
#include <stdio.h>                /* For sprintf, printf                   */
```

Figure 35-2 (Part 1 of 3). SQLTP1DY.SQC: The main() Procedure.

```
#define INCL_VIO                    /* include VIO calls               */
#define INCL_DOSSEMAPHORES          /* include semaphore api calls     */
#define INCL_DOSMEMMGR              /* include segment   api calls     */
#define INCL_ERRORS                 /* include error definitions       */
#include <os2.h>

#include <sqlca.h>                  /* sqlca                           */
#include <sql.h>                    /* error msg. retrieval            */
#include <sqlcodes.h>               /* SQL return code constants       */
#include <sqlenv.h>                 /* environment functions and       */

#include "const.h"                  /* constants for multi             */
#include "sqltp1.h"                 /* tp1 program vars, declares,etc. */

/*────────────────────────────────────────────────────────────────────*/
/* database includes, defines, etc. for task function                 */
/*────────────────────────────────────────────────────────────────────*/
struct sqlca sqlca;

EXEC SQL WHENEVER SQLERROR CONTINUE;
EXEC SQL WHENEVER SQLWARNING CONTINUE;
EXEC SQL WHENEVER NOT FOUND CONTINUE;

EXEC SQL BEGIN DECLARE SECTION;
 long  acct_num;
 short branch_id;
 short teller_id;
 long  balance;
 long  delta      = 100;
 char  acct_name[20] = "<--20 BYTE STRING-->";

                   /*─────────────────────────────────────────*/
                   /* SQL statements for dynamic SQL          */
                   /*─────────────────────────────────────────*/
 char  sel_bal[120]   = "SELECT BALANCE FROM ACCT WHERE ACCT_NUM = ? \
                         FOR UPDATE OF BALANCE";

 char  upd_acct[120]  = "UPDATE ACCT \
                         SET BALANCE = BALANCE + ? \
                         WHERE CURRENT OF CURSOR1";

 char  upd_teller[120]= "UPDATE TELLER \
                         SET BALANCE = BALANCE + ? \
                         WHERE TELLER_ID = ?";

 char  upd_branch[120]= "UPDATE BRANCH \
                         SET BALANCE = BALANCE + ? \
                         WHERE BRANCH_ID = ?";

 char  ins_hist[240] = "INSERT \
                        INTO HISTORY(ACCT_NUM, TELLER_ID, BRANCH_ID, BALANCE, \
                                     DELTA, PID, TRANSID, ACCTNAME, TEMP) \
                        VALUES(?, ?, ?, ?, ?, 1, 3, ?, 'hist  ')";

 char  sql_commit[8]  = "COMMIT";

EXEC SQL END   DECLARE SECTION;

/*────────────────────────────────────────────────────────────────────*/
/* Main routine.                                                       */
/*────────────────────────────────────────────────────────────────────*/
VOID main(USHORT argc, PCHAR argv[])
{
```

Figure 35-2 (Part 2 of 3). SQLTP1DY.SQC: The main() Procedure.

```
    get_args(argc, argv);            /*  get program arguments        */

    initialize_multi_ipc();          /*  Init MULTI semaphores/shared memory*/

    initialize_task();               /*  perform one time intializations  */

    execute_task();                  /*  Remote Procedure Call  loop     */

} /* end main */
```

Figure 35-2 (Part 3 of 3). SQLTP1DY.SQC: The main() Procedure.

SQLTP1DY.SQC: The tp1_transaction() Procedure

In this section, we present the Dynamic SQL **tp1_transaction**() procedure, whose code is listed in Figure 35-3. This procedure executes the Dynamic SQL command strings, which were previously declared and intialized as the host variables. As you should know by now, the SQL statements that constitute up a TP1 transaction are known ahead of time. We also know, ahead of time, the SQL types of the data that is used in a TP1 transaction. The only thing we don't know is the actual run-time values for that data. What all this means is that we're much better off in terms of what we know in this chapter than was the case in the **RSQL** Dynamic SQL chapter. None of the statements we'll be executing here are as difficult as the varying-list SELECT we encountered in **RSQL**. We're *not* even going to be using a **SQLDA**. Here's how Dynamic SQL handles situations where much of the SQL statement is known at compile time:

- The part of the SQL statement we know is placed in a null-terminated string and declared as a host variable.
- The things we don't know at compile time are represented by "?" placeholders.
- We will provide the values that go into the placeholders when the statement is prepared and executed at run time.
- All of our SQL command strings contain *parameter markers*, so we have to separate the preparation of the SQL command from its execution. This is done using two verbs: **PREPARE** and **EXECUTE**.
- When a statement is prepared, it is assigned a name. We assign the names, **S1** through **S5**, for our five SQL statements when we **PREPARE** them. For example:

```
    EXEC SQL PREPARE S1 FROM :sel_bal;
```

The statement above assigns the prepared **sel_bal** command to **S1**, which can then be executed multiple times using different parameter values each time.

- The **sel_bal** host variable was previously declared and initialized with the SQL statement:

```
    char sel_bal[120] = "SELECT BALANCE FROM ACCT WHERE ACCT_NUM = ? \
                    FOR UPDATE OF BALANCE";
```

Our first Dynamic SQL command is a SELECT. This command requires, in addition to a **PREPARE** and **EXECUTE**, the declaration and use of a cursor. This is similar to what we did for static SQL. Here's how we read and update the TP1 ACCT table using Dynamic SQL:

1. The **DECLARE CURSOR** command is issued to make CURSOR1 a cursor for S1. Contrast this with static SQL where the full text of the select is declared as a cursor.
2. The SELECT is used to retrieve a row using the cursor verbs: **OPEN** and **FETCH**.

    *   The **OPEN** verb with the **USING** clause substitutes the value in the host variable **acct_num** for the placeholder in the SELECT statement.
    *   The **FETCH** verb with the **INTO** clause places the row in the host variable string **balance**.

3. To update the balance in the ACCT table, we **PREPARE S2** from the contents of **upd_acct** command string:

```
char  upd_acct[120]  = "UPDATE ACCT \
                        SET BALANCE = BALANCE + ? \
                        WHERE CURRENT OF CURSOR1";
```

4. We **EXECUTE** S2 to perform the actual update using the still open CURSOR1 and the appropriate run-time variables that are provided through the **USING** clause.
5. We **CLOSE** the cursor because the balance in the ACCT table has been updated.

The remaining two TP1 updates to the TELLER and BRANCH tables and the insert into HISTORY table are handled by simple **PREPARE** and **EXECUTE** commands. No cursor is needed. The simplest and last TP1 Dynamic SQL command to execute is COMMIT. This command has no placeholders, so it can be executed with a single **EXECUTE IMMEDIATE** command as opposed to the two-step **PREPARE** and **EXECUTE**.

Congratulations, we have just completed the code for our fourth and final flavor of the TP1 transaction. Now let's run the benchmark on this flavor and see how it performs compared to its peers.

```
/*-------------------------------------------------------------*/
/* function for TP1 transaction                                */
/*-------------------------------------------------------------*/
SHORT APIENTRY tp1_transaction(VOID)
{
  CHAR   msgbuf[512];

        /*----------------------------------------*/
        /* generate some random data              */
        /*----------------------------------------*/
    acct_num = (random1 * random2) % (tps*1000001) + 1;/* generate acct number */
    teller_id= (short)(random1 % (tps*100)) + 1;      /* generate teller id    */
    branch_id= (short)(random2 % (tps*10)) + 1;       /* generate branch id    */
```

Figure 35-3 (Part 1 of 4). SQLTP1DY.SQC: The tp1_transaction() Procedure.

```
        /*_____*/
        /* get the current balance from ACCT   */
        /*_____*/
EXEC SQL PREPARE S1 FROM :sel_bal;
if (SQLCODE != 0)
    {
        sqlaintp(msgbuf, sizeof(msgbuf), 80, &sqlca);
        printf("%s\n",msgbuf);
        print_error((SHORT)SQLCODE, "preparing SQL statement S1",
                    __FILE__, __LINE__);
        return(FAILED);
    }

EXEC SQL DECLARE CURSOR1 CURSOR FOR S1;
EXEC SQL OPEN CURSOR1 USING :acct_num;
if (SQLCODE != 0)
    {
        sqlaintp(msgbuf, sizeof(msgbuf), 80, &sqlca);
        printf("%s\n",msgbuf);
        print_error((SHORT)SQLCODE, "during SQL OPEN",
                    __FILE__, __LINE__);
        return(FAILED);
    }

EXEC SQL FETCH CURSOR1 INTO :balance;
if (SQLCODE != 0)
    {
        sqlaintp(msgbuf, sizeof(msgbuf), 80, &sqlca);
        printf("%s\n",msgbuf);
        print_error((SHORT)SQLCODE, "during SQL FETCH",
                    __FILE__, __LINE__);
        return(FAILED);
    }
        /*_____*/
        /* Credit the balance in the ACCT table */
        /*_____*/
EXEC SQL PREPARE S2 FROM :upd_acct;
if (SQLCODE != 0)
    {
        sqlaintp(msgbuf, sizeof(msgbuf), 80, &sqlca);
        printf("%s\n",msgbuf);
        print_error((SHORT)SQLCODE, "preparing SQL statement S2",
                    __FILE__, __LINE__);
        return(FAILED);
    }

EXEC SQL EXECUTE S2 USING :delta;
if (SQLCODE != 0)
    {
        sqlaintp(msgbuf, sizeof(msgbuf), 80, &sqlca);
        printf("%s\n",msgbuf);
        print_error((SHORT)SQLCODE, "during SQL UPDATE",
                    __FILE__,__LINE__);
        return(FAILED);
    }

EXEC SQL CLOSE CURSOR1;
if (SQLCODE != 0)
    {
        sqlaintp(msgbuf, sizeof(msgbuf), 80, &sqlca);
```

Figure 35-3 (Part 2 of 4). SQLTP1DY.SQC: The tp1_transaction() Procedure.

```
        printf("%s\n",msgbuf);
        print_error((SHORT)SQLCODE, "during SQL CLOSE",
                    __FILE__,__LINE__);
        return(FAILED);
    }
    /*_____*/
    /* Update the TELLER table's balance    */
    /*_____*/
EXEC SQL PREPARE S3 FROM :upd_teller;
if (SQLCODE != 0)
    {
        sqlaintp(msgbuf, sizeof(msgbuf), 80, &sqlca);
        printf("%s\n",msgbuf);
        print_error((SHORT)SQLCODE, "preparing SQL statement S3",
                    __FILE__, __LINE__);
        return(FAILED);
    }

EXEC SQL EXECUTE S3 USING :delta, :teller_id;
if (SQLCODE != 0)
    {
        sqlaintp(msgbuf, sizeof(msgbuf), 80, &sqlca);
        printf("%s\n",msgbuf);
        print_error((SHORT)SQLCODE, "during SQL UPDATE",
                    __FILE__,__LINE__);
        return(FAILED);
    }

    /*_____*/
    /* Update the BRANCH table's balance    */
    /*_____*/
EXEC SQL PREPARE S4 FROM :upd_branch;
if (SQLCODE != 0)
    {
        sqlaintp(msgbuf, sizeof(msgbuf), 80, &sqlca);
        printf("%s\n",msgbuf);
        print_error((SHORT)SQLCODE, "preparing SQL statement S4",
                    __FILE__, __LINE__);
        return(FAILED);
    }

EXEC SQL EXECUTE S4 USING :delta, :branch_id;
if (SQLCODE != 0)
    {
        sqlaintp(msgbuf, sizeof(msgbuf), 80, &sqlca);
        printf("%s\n",msgbuf);
        print_error((SHORT)SQLCODE, "during SQL UPDATE",
                    __FILE__,__LINE__);
        return(FAILED);
    }
    /*_____*/
    /* Insert transaction in HISTORY table */
    /*_____*/
EXEC SQL PREPARE S5 FROM  :ins_hist;
if (SQLCODE != 0)
    {
        sqlaintp(msgbuf, sizeof(msgbuf), 80, &sqlca);
        printf("%s\n",msgbuf);
        print_error((SHORT)SQLCODE, "preparing SQL statement S5",
                    __FILE__, __LINE__);
        return(FAILED);
    }
EXEC SQL EXECUTE S5 USING :acct_num, :teller_id, :branch_id, :balance,
```

Figure 35-3 (Part 3 of 4). SQLTP1DY.SQC: The tp1_transaction() Procedure.

```
                                :delta, :acct_name;
    if (SQLCODE != 0)
       {
          sqlaintp(msgbuf, sizeof(msgbuf), 80, &sqlca);
          printf("%s\n",msgbuf);
          print_error((SHORT)SQLCODE, "during SQL INSERT",
                     __FILE__,__LINE__);
          return(FAILED);
       }
       /*_____*/
       /* Commit the transaction to database  */
       /*_____*/
    EXEC SQL EXECUTE IMMEDIATE :sql_commit;
    if (SQLCODE != 0)
       { sqlaintp(msgbuf, sizeof(msgbuf), 80, &sqlca);
          printf("%s\n",msgbuf);
          print_error((SHORT)SQLCODE, "during SQL COMMIT",
                     __FILE__, __LINE__);
          return(FAILED);
       }

    return(GOOD);
} /* end tp1_transaction */
```

Figure 35-3 (Part 4 of 4).   SQLTP1DY.SQC: The tp1_transaction() Procedure.

RUNNING TWO TP1 BENCHMARK TESTS USING DYNAMIC SQL

Now that we've got some code, let's run some benchmarks to see how well this TP1 flavor performs. We will run two TP1 benchmark tests:

1. A **local** benchmark test, where the client and servers are on the same machine. The machine is a PS/2 Mod-95 with a 33-MHz clock and a 1000-KByte buffer pool (see Figure 35-5).

2. A **remote** benchmark test, where the clients and servers are on different machines. The client machine is a PS/2 Mod 80 with a 20-MHz clock. The server machine is a PS/2 Mod-95 with a 33-MHz clock and a 1000-KByte buffer pool (see Figure 35-6).

The two benchmarks use identical four-process software configurations. The **MULTI** configuration file used for both tests is:

```
PROGRAM_TYPE     = PROCESS
STOP_TIME_MS     = 600000
TASK_NAME        = SQLTP1DY.EXE 0 17 2.0  1;
TASK_NAME        = SQLTP1DY.EXE 1 23 2.0  1;
TASK_NAME        = SQLTP1DY.EXE 2 29 2.0  1;
TASK_NAME        = SQLTP1DY.EXE 3 57 2.0  1;
```

Figure 35-4. A MULTI.CFG File for Running Four TP1 Processes Using Dynamic SQL.

The benchmarks are set up to run for 10-minute tests (i.e., 600,000 milliseconds). The response time threshold is set to 2.0 seconds, and a 1-tps database size is specified.

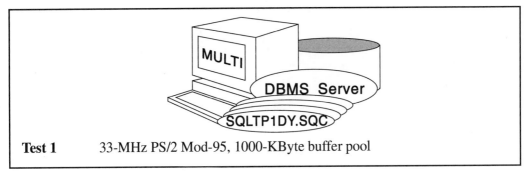

Test 1   33-MHz PS/2 Mod-95, 1000-KByte buffer pool

Figure 35-5. The The Dynamic SQL TP1: Local Benchmark Configuration.

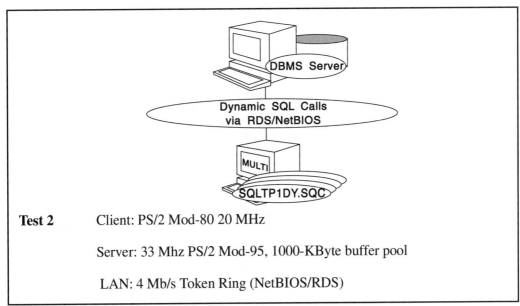

Test 2   Client: PS/2 Mod-80 20 MHz

Server: 33 Mhz PS/2 Mod-95, 1000-KByte buffer pool

LAN: 4 Mb/s Token Ring (NetBIOS/RDS)

Figure 35-6. The Dynamic SQL TP1: Remote Benchmark Configuration.

Running the Dynamic SQL TP1 Locally (Benchmark1)

The configuration for this benchmark is a four-client MULTI running against a local database. The test is run on a PS/2 Mod-95 with a 33-MHz clock and a 1000-KByte buffer pool. We assume the database is already loaded for a 1-tps database scale. The following RSQL run is used to set up the 1000-KByte buffer configuration and prepare the database for the benchmark1 run.

```
--              Change TP1 Database Configuration
-- ================================================================
-- update the Database Configuration for database for a 1000k buffer
EXEC DBA: UPDATE_DB_CFG TP1      MAXAPPLS    = 8,
                                 DLCHKTIME   = 10000,
                                 BUFFPAGE    = 256,
                                 LOGFILSIZ   = 50,
                                 LOGPRIMARY  = 2,
                                 LOGSECOND   = 20;

  OK, sql_rcd = 0,        Execution time =     0.3100 secs

-- Show the database configuration for database TP1
EXEC DBA: SHOW_DB_CFG TP1;

Database Configuration for Database TP1
================================================

Configuration Parameter          Current  Parm.      Parm.        Parm.
Description                       Value    Units      Range        Default
--------------------------------  -------  ---------  ----------   -------
Max. Active Applications              8    Appl.      1-256            8
Max. DB Files Open/Application       20    files      2-235           20
Max. Files Open/Application         255    files      25-32700       255
Buffer Pool Size                    256    4K pages   2-1500         (1)
Time Interval for Deadlocks       10000    millisecs. 1-600 sec.     10
Max. Storage for Locklists           25    4K pages   4-250            8
Max. percent locklist/appl.          22    percent    1-100           22
Default Application Heap              3    segments   2-20             3
Application Agent Heap               2    segments   2-85             2
Sort List Heap                       2    segments   1-20             2
Database Heap                        3    segments   1-45            (2)
SQL Statement Heap                  64    segments   8-255           64
Log File Size                       50    4K pages   4-65535        (3)
Primary Log Files                    2    files      2-63             3
Secondary Log Files                 20    files      0-61             2
Log Records/soft checkpoint        100    records    0-65535        100

Current Log Location = F:\SQL00001\SQLOGDIR\
New Log Location     =
First Log File       =
Current Log File     =
Copy Protection      =      1 (1 = Protected, Default = 1)
Log Retain           =      0 (1 = Retain Log Files, Default = 0)
User Exit            =      0 (1 = Enable User Exit, Default = 0)
Auto Restart         =      1 (1 = Enable Auto Restart, Default = 1)
Country              =      1
Code Page            =    437
Release              =    768
DB Consistency       =      1 (1 = Consistent)
Backup Pending       =      0 (1 = Backup Pending)
Roll Forward Pending =      0 (1 = Roll Forward Pending)
User Exit Status     =      0 (1 = User exit Enabled)
Log Retain Status    =      0 (1 = log files retained)

(1) - client or standalone 25, server 250
(2) - client or standalone  2, server   3
(3) - client or standalone 32, server 200
  OK, sql_rcd = 0,        Execution time =     0.1000 secs

-- bind the tp1 program
EXEC DBA: BIND TP1 SQLTP1DL.BND ISO REPEATABLE_READ BLOCK_ALL PUBLIC;
```

Figure 35-7 (Part 1 of 2). Preparing the Database for Benchmark1.

```
No messages in msgfile.msg

OK, sql_rcd = 0,          Execution time =     3.1200 secs

- Connect to the TP1 database
EXEC DBA: STARTUSE TP1 S;

OK, sql_rcd = 0,          Execution time =     0.6900 secs

delete all of the history data
EXEC SQL: DELETE FROM HISTORY;

WARNING, sql_code = 100,    Execution time =     2.3700 secs
SQL0100W  No row was found for FETCH, UPDATE or DELETE; or the result of a
query is an empty table.
```

Figure 35-7 (Part 2 of 2). Preparing the Database for Benchmark1.

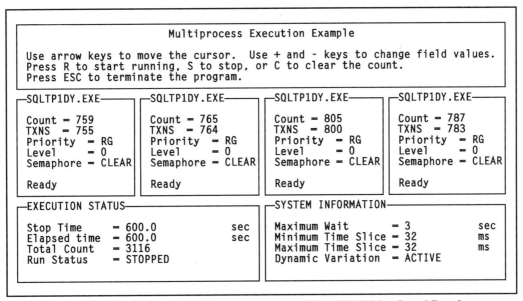

Figure 35-8. The Results of a Four-Process Dynamic SQL TP1 With a Local Database.

Benchmark1 Results

The MULTI screen capture in Figure 35-8 shows the results of a 10-minute test. During this period, a total of 3116 TP1 transactions ran successfully. However, only (755 + 764 + 800 + 783 = 3102) transactions had a response time that was under the 2-second threshold. Using the liberal interpretation of TP1 from the previous chapters, this machine is in the *5.2 TP1* range.

Commentary: How often is it that you can put an exact price tag on flexibility? We have it: Dynamic SQL is roughly 2 times slower than Static SQL. This is the high price you pay for flexibility. Do you need it?

Running the Dynamic SQL TP1 Remotely (Benchmark2)

The configuration for this benchmark is a four-client MULTI running against a remote database. The database will be run on a PS/2 Mod-95 with a 33-MHz clock and a 1000-KByte buffer pool.

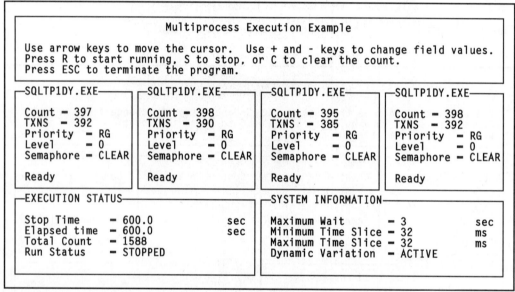

Figure 35-9.   The Results of a 4-Process Dynamic SQL TP1 Run Against a Remote Database.

Benchmark2 Results

The MULTI screen capture in Figure 35-9 shows the results of a 10-minute test. During this period a total of 1588 TP1 transactions ran successfully. However, only (392 + 390 + 385 + 392 = 1569) transactions had a response time that was under the 2-second threshold. This machine is therefore in the *2.6 TP1* range.

Commentary: This is another illustration of *"how slow is slow"* when it comes to Dynamic SQL. You will need to think at least twice before submitting dynamic SQL statements over the network.

Chapter 36

Transaction Servers Are Best for OLTP

This is the final chapter of our OLTP benchmark series. We will present a summary of the TP1 Benchmark results so that you can have it all in one place for easy reference. We will also inject some further commentary on how both the *network* and the *message-passing mechanism* affect the performance of client/server systems.

Fat Clients or Fat Servers?

Slim and fat are relative terms. It's all in the eyes of the beholder. The same is true with fat clients and fat servers. Compared to file server clients, the database clients are really *slim*; database servers do a lot more work for their clients than lazy file servers. On the other hand compared to transaction servers, database server clients are *fat*; database servers do a lot less work for their clients than their superactive transaction server counterparts.

Since we're only comparing database and transaction servers, we will consider the database clients to be our fat clients and the transaction servers to be our fat servers. Our benchmarks show that the fatness of the client or the server does matter. One of them needs to go on a serious diet. As you can see from Figure 36-1 this is all a question

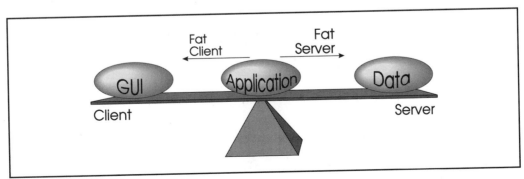

Figure 36-1. Fat Clients vs. Fat Servers.

of how much function to place on the client versus the server. The database servers export data while the transaction servers export procedures. The benchmarks results should help us make some informed decisions on what this all means.

Fat Clients and Thin Database Servers

With a database server, the client passes SQL requests as messages to a database server. Only the final results of the data search are returned over the network. The code that processes the SQL request and the data reside on the same machine. This allows the server to use its own processing power to find the requested data, instead of passing all the records back to a client and let it find its own data. With this approach, the server code is shrinkwrapped by the vendor, but you need to write the client application. The requests a client sends over the network can be *Dynamic* SQL, *Static* SQL, or both.

Table 36-1. Database Server Benchmark Results.

Benchmark	Description	TP1 Rating
Chapter 32/Benchmark1 (see page 830)	Standalone Static SQL Server PS/2 Mod-80, 20-MHz 500 KByte RAM buffer	5.3
Chapter 32/Benchmark2 (see page 832)	Standalone Static SQL Server PS/2 Mod-95, 33-MHz 500 KByte RAM buffer	9.1
Chapter 32/Benchmark3 (see page 833)	Standalone Static SQL Server PS/2 Mod-95, 33-MHz 1000-KByte RAM buffer	9.8
Chapter 32/Benchmark4 (see page 833)	Network Static SQL Server with RDS/NetBIOS over a 4 Mb/s Token Ring (Server same as Benchmark3)	4.7
Chapter 35/Benchmark1 (see page 893)	Standalone Dynamic SQL Server (Server same as Benchmark3)	5.2
Chapter 35/Benchmark2 (see page 896)	Network Dynamic SQL Server with RDS/NetBIOS over 4 Mb/s Token Ring (Server same as above)	2.6

So what can we say about Database Servers? The results of the benchmarks from the previous chapters (see Table 36-1) lead to some interesting general observations about *Database Servers*:

• The network slows them down significantly.

- Dynamic SQL is slow over the network. You should use static SQL if you do not need all the flexibility dynamic SQL provides.
- Invest in a "superserver" machine if you can afford one.

Thin Clients and Fat Transaction Servers

With a transaction server, the client invokes remote procedures that reside on a server that also contains an SQL database engine. Remote procedures execute a group of SQL statements (i.e., transactions). The SQL statements either all succeed or fail as a unit. You create your client/server applications by writing the code for both the server transactions and the client component, which usually includes a graphical user interface. These OLTP type of applications tend to be mission-critical, with 1-3 second response-time requirements (100% of the time). OLTP applications also require tight controls over the security and integrity of the database. The communication overhead in this approach is kept to a minimum. The exchange consists of a single request/reply (as opposed to multiple SQL statements). In the previous chapters, we benchmarked two types of *Transaction Servers* using both Named Pipes and the Application Remote Interface.

Table 36-2. Transaction Server Benchmark Results.

Benchmark	Description	TP1 Rating
Chapter 33/Benchmark1 (see page 853)	Standalone Transaction Server RPC= Application Remote Interface PS/2 Mod-95, 33-MHz 1000-KByte RAM buffer	9.0
Chapter 34/Benchmark1 (see page 877)	Standalone Transaction Server RPC= Named Pipes (Server same as above)	9.0
Chapter 33/Benchmark2 (see page 855)	Network Transaction Server RPC= Application Remote Interface with RDS/NetBIOS 4 Mb/s Token Ring (Server same as above)	9.0
Chapter 34/Benchmark2 (see page 881)	Network Transaction Server RPC= Named Pipes Named Pipes over NetBIOS 4 Mb/s Token Ring (Server same as above)	9.2

So what can we say about Transaction Servers? The results (see Table 36-2) lead to some interesting observations about *Transaction Servers*:

- They are incredibly fast on the network. In one case, it appears they executed faster on the network than on the same machine.
- Invest in a "superserver" machine if you can afford one.

Conclusion: Fat Servers Win!

The network performance comparison chart (see Table 36-3) shows that Transaction servers are super fast on the network, much faster than database servers (9.2 TP1s and 9.0 TP1s versus 4.7 TP1s for the Static SQL Database Server). These results demonstrate that Transaction Servers are the way to go for OLTP systems, where the transactions can be precoded. The significant performance gain is directly attributed to the reduced network utilization of stored procedures. A single message exchange takes place as opposed to an exchange for each SQL statement in the transaction. The Named Pipes Transaction Server (9.2 TP1s) provides the best remote performance on the network. The Application Remote Interface also provides a respectable network performance (9.0 TP1s). Transaction Servers allow you to centrally manage (on the server) your transaction code. This provides an object-oriented flavor to network services. Security is also enhanced.

Table 36-3. Server Network Performance Comparison.

LAN Database Servers		LAN Transaction Servers	
Dynamic SQL (RDS/NetBIOS)	Static SQL (RDS/NetBIOS)	Application Remote Interface (RDS/NetBIOS)	Roll-Your-Own Named Pipes (NetBIOS)
2.6 TP1s	4.7 TP1s	9.0 TP1s	9.2 TP1s

However, before you run out and convert all your applications to Transaction Servers, *beware of the following:*

• Transaction Servers are not as *flexible* as Database Servers (they are not suitable for running ad hoc queries),

• Transaction Servers are not as portable across platforms. The remote procedure calls are non-standard database extensions; the code is not portable across SQL platforms (for example, DB2, SQL/DS, and SQL/400 do not support stored procedures).

As a closing observation, life and client/server architectures are full of interesting trade-offs where the maxim *there is no free lunch* always seems to be with us. Our TP1 benchmarks served to make that observation painfully obvious!

Part VI

Presentation Services for Clients

This part of the book focuses on the design of visual client applications. The design of human computer dialogs is one of the most time-consuming and least understood elements of client/server application development. It is relatively easy for an intelligent robot to generate a simple transaction. On the other hand, human-driven dialogs that generate transactions are more intricate, ad hoc, and complex. This makes them much more difficult to design, build, and test. Ironically, this is a subject which receives minimal attention in proportion to all the headaches it creates. These headaches only get worse in distributed client/server environments and in the graphical world of Object-Oriented User Interfaces (OOUIs) and Graphical User Interfaces (GUIs).

- **GUI clients** interact with a server using a graphical user interface like the Windows desktop. The user typically starts an application by clicking on an icon and is then led through a series of dialog windows sometimes disguised as visual business forms. The user has some degree of control over the client/server application through the menu bar (and the big red switch). But, by and large, the application retains much of the control over the flow of the dialogs. These type of client/server applications are structurally similar to the predominant OLTP, forms-based, terminal applications. The difference is that the green uglies got a facelift; they've gone *WIMP*, which stands for Windows, Icons, Menus, and Pointers.

- **OOUI clients** interact with the a server using the Workplace Shell. The OOUIs don't have the notion of servers, or applications; they just present visual objects on the desktop whose persistent data happens to be on a server. OOUI objects can seamlessly interact with any other Workplace Shell object. The user is totally in control of the desktop and uses the familiar icons, views, notebooks, folders and shredders to get work done. OOUIs, when combined with networks of servers, broaden the semantics of the electronic business transaction. They allow client/server applications to incorporate new data types (such as image and voice) to seamlessly interact with desktop devices (such as fax, printers, and scanners), and to incorporate mail, electronic distribution, and workflow semantics. In short, desktop transactions start to look more like real-world transactions. OOUIs combined with client/server technology are revolutionary, not evolutionary.

Part VI is about creating highly graphic front-ends to transaction servers. We will explain the principles of GUI and OOUI design using IBM's Common User Access model. We will then introduce the tools that should allow us to develop GUIs and OOUIs in record time. Tools also help make your code more maintainable, thereby reducing the cost of software ownership. The best tool, at the time of writing, for creating Workplace Shell OOUIs is the OO-based **System Object Model (SOM)** and the Workplace Shell Class Library. Both are part of the OS/2 2.0 Toolkit. SOM will serve as an introduction into object-oriented programming and class libraries.

Since we assume no prior knowledge on your part, we kick off Part VI with tutorials on CUA 91, GUI tools, Presentation Manager, SOM, and the Workplace Shell. We then introduce two small Hello Programs. The first uses PM, and the second uses SOM and the Workplace Shell class libraries. The goal is to make you PM and SOM literate. But, we're not going to cover all of PM's 900 plus API calls or the Workplace Shell's hundreds of class methods. Instead, we'll focus on how to read a PM or SOM/WPS program. Our programs will create SOM/WPS class wrappers around the Presentation Manager. This is like writing in C and dropping into assembler when you need special things done.

Here is the road map we will follow in Part VI:

- In Chapter 37, "The CUA Standard for Graphical User Interfaces," we start our discussion of graphical user interfaces by introducing the CUA'91 standard. CUA'91 provides some extensive insights on the principles of human computer dialogs. We will cover some of the CUA'91 principles for human computer dialogs.
- In Chapter 38, "A Taxonomy of GUI and OOUI Tools," we explain what to look for in the area of GUI/OOUI tools. Picking the right GUI tool is essential for doing serious client/server development work.
- In Chapter 39, "The Presentation Manager," we provide a crash course in Presentation Manager "literacy." We focus on the structure of a PM program and on understanding the PM programming paradigm. At the end of this chapter, you should be able to read a PM program and follow its logic.
- In Chapter 40, "SOM, OOP, and WPS Classes," we provide another crash course. This time the topic is SOM and the Workplace Shell Class library. Again, the focus is on SOM and Workplace Shell class literacy.
- In Chapter 41, "Hello World From SOM/WPS," we develop our first Workplace Shell User object, a smiling guy that says hello. To make this guy smile and say hello, we created a new object class using SOM/WPS parent classes.

Chapter 37

The CUA Standard for Graphical User Interfaces

The real revolution in client/server architecture is in the graphic front-end. Ninety-nine percent of the multiuser database applications in the world today consist of dumb terminals attached to a host DBMS. These applications do not exploit the intuitive power of graphics. Moving the client code to PCs using the client/server technology makes it possible to front-end databases with the full power of a **GUI** or **OOUI**. This chapter starts off our investigation of graphical user interfaces for client/server by introducing the CUA'91 model.

CUA PRINCIPLES FOR HUMAN COMPUTER DIALOG

Until recently, the design of dialogs between humans and machines was pure art and intuition. There were probably as many theories of *human computer* dialog as the number of computer users. There were also, unfortunately, many variants of sadistic command-driven user interfaces that were very successful at turning off large numbers of potential computer users. To those users who persisted, the name of the game was how to beat the computer by memorizing endless sets of commands and all the "kinky" ways in which they could be used.

The friendly *look and feel* of the Xerox Star and Apple Macintosh GUIs demonstrated that it was possible to introduce some method and kindness in the design of user interfaces. IBM's **Common User Access (CUA)** architecture, as described in the **CUA Advanced Interface Design Guide**, is probably the most complete attempt to codify the principles of interface design and common presentation techniques.[1]

---

[1] See **CUA Guide To User Interface Design**, IBM publication SC34-4289 (October, 1991). Also see the OS/2 2.0 Multimedia Specifications.

CUA Credo: The User Is at the Controls

CUA is built on the following design concepts:

- The interface should be consistent. The goal of CUA is to provide users with a familiar *look and feel* across applications. This consistency is especially needed in a multitasking desktop where the user can, at any time, switch back and forth between different applications.
- The user controls the dialog, not the computer. Users should be able to perform tasks in any sequence they choose. The computer should never ignore the user. Your client applications should always keep the user informed and provide immediate feedback. During operations of uncertain durations, be sure to display progress messages or status indicators.
- The dialog should incorporate familiar metaphors and represent them visually wherever possible. Metaphors help the user create a conceptual image of the subject and associate the interface with previous world knowledge. Examples of metaphors are business objects, work folders, or desktops. An entire application can be designed around a single metaphor.
- The interface should be intuitive. Users want to concentrate on solutions, not on how the computer operates.
- The interface should *conform in a reasonable manner* to the user's expectations. The more natural that the interface seems to the user, the more it recedes from the user's consciousness and lets the user focus on the task itself.
- The interface should not rely on the user's memory. Controls should be visible and concrete. The user should be asked to *point-and-select* rather than recall commands. Point-and-select implies recognition rather than memorization.
- The interface should be forgiving of user errors. Users should feel comfortable *learning by exploring*. User actions that are potentially destructive should require confirmation. A cancel action should always take a user one logical step backwards in a dialog.

CUA and Object-Action Design

In a typical dialog, the first major hurdle for the user is getting started. CUA simplifies this hurdle by defining an object-action processing sequence for all applications. Users select certain objects, and then select the actions to be performed on these objects. This approach gives the users a feeling of freedom. They can select objects in any order, and they can then browse through an application's action choices to identify the action they want to apply. The object-action approach follows a *Noun-Verb* model. The user says: "Here's an object (the noun) and apply this action (the verb) on it."

Why object-action as opposed to action-object? Objects are *things* that need to be manipulated; they are metaphors for real things in life. There are typically more things in life than actions on things. When an object is selected, your interface code can easily tailor the list of allowable actions and display them to the user.

You can reinforce the parallel between objects on the screen and real-life concepts through the use of icons (i.e., small pictures). CUA prescribes a consistent approach to option selections and entry fields. This is done through the use of metaphors such as notebooks, containers, check box controls, radio buttons, list boxes, combo boxes, and multiple-line entry fields. Actions are selected through the use of an action bar, pull-down menus, action buttons, or by direct manipulation.

CUA'91: USER OBJECTS EVERYWHERE

In a multitasking environment, many applications can share the screen. How? By having applications interact with objects on the screen, instead of with the entire screen. The user can then control the size and placement of these objects on the screen. CUA'91 introduces an *Object-Oriented User Interface (OOUI)* paradigm to create visual consistency in the way people interact with their various computer applications.

The OOUI Desktop

Prior to 1991, the CUA guidelines defined what can be termed an *application-centered* user interface. This is the familiar Windows 3.X and OS/2 1.X GUI paradigm in which a user interacts with a computer by starting an application from a list of programs (or icons representing them) displayed in a window. CUA '91, on the other hand, introduces the concept of an OOUI, where the user interacts with the computer by manipulating visual business objects.

In an OOUI, the concept of applications is transparent to the user. The desktop is a collection of objects (icons) and windows associated with those objects, as opposed to GUIs, where the desktop is a collection of windows or icons representing windows associated with applications. In OOUI environments, the user interacts with objects rather than with the operating system or with separate programs. The interaction has the same look and feel across all tasks.

Visual Object Types

An object is a visual component with which a user can work, independently of other items, to perform a task. An object can be represented by one or more graphic images, called icons. The user can interact with an object (or its icon) just as the user can interact with objects in the real world. CUA defines three types of visual objects:

- **Container Objects** are used to organize the objects you're working with. A container can store any other object including containers. The Workplace Shell provides a standard container called the *folder* whose icon looks like a manila folder. Folders are used as desktop organizers. The folder is "passive" in nature; it simply stores objects and allows them to be opened (or started) from within it. The

Workplace Shell also makes available an "active" folder called the *work area*. You can turn a folder into a work area by checking the file page option in the settings notebook. A work area remembers the objects that were opened from within it. When a work area is minimized, it automatically minimizes all dependent views that were created from within it. When a work area is restored, all the objects within it have their views restored. When a work area is closed, it closes all the objects within it.

- **Data Objects** contain text, graphics, audio, video, or tabular information. Data objects can contain other objects. For example, a folder can contain database objects.

- **Device Objects** often represent a physical device in the real world such as telephones, mailboxes, and printers. Some devices represent logical objects. For example, a shredder object can represent a logical object that disposes of other objects. Device objects can also contain other objects. For example, a printer object can contain a queue of objects to be printed.

Views of Objects

A view is simply a way of looking at what's inside an object (i.e., its information). The user opens the object, usually by double-clicking on the icon, to get to the different views that lurk beneath its iconic surface. An object can have more than one view type. The CUA guidelines describe four basic types of views:

- **Composed Views** arrange the object's data in a structure that conveys the data's meaning. Examples include a directory tree structure, or a city map with blinking red squares that denote the five star restaurants.

- **Contents Views** display the components of an object in lists, or tabular formats. CUA describes two kinds of contents views: 1) **Icon Views**, which display each object as an icon that can be directly manipulated by the user, and 2) **Details Views**, which combine small icons with text to provide additional information about objects.

- **Settings Views** display information about the characteristics, attributes, or properties of an object, and provide a way for the user to change the settings of some characteristics or properties. A settings view is typically provided for each type of object in the form of a notebook.

- **Help Views** display information that can assist the user in working with an object. Users can get contextual help at any time in CUA by pressing the F1 key. CUA also defines an extensive help subsystem with a Help Index and Extended Help to guide users through an application. The indexed help is organized in topics. *Hypertext* links may be used to provide further information about highlighted words or phrases.

Templates: The Object Cookie Cutter Factory

In the OOUI environment, the users do not load programs. In fact, they're not even supposed to know what a program is. So how does anybody get any work done without programs running on a desktop? You work with objects, of course. OK, but how are these objects created? Where do they come from? The Workplace Shell provides some predefined system objects like clocks, games, shredders, and so on. The user supplements these objects with "user objects" that they create by cloning a template of an existing object. A *template* is the OO terminology for a cookie cutter. Instead of creating cookies, it creates identical objects.

Where does the user get these templates from? The Workplace Shell provides a special folder called the *templates folder*. This folder is your "object factory." Users "tear off" templates out of the templates folder and drag them to the folder or desktop area where they want to work (see Figure 37-1). The next question that begs for an answer is: *Who creates these object templates?* Us programmers, of course! You probably saw it coming.

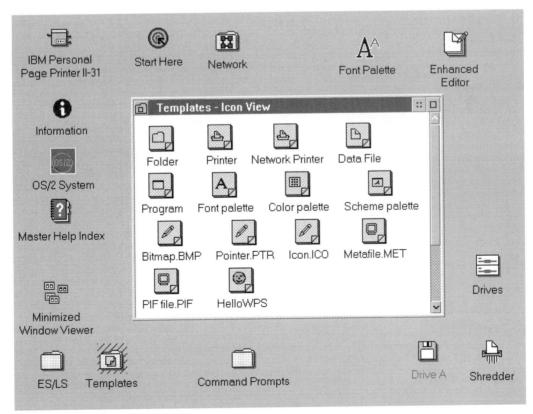

Figure 37-1. The Template Folder: An Object Factory.

So how do we programmers do this magical work? We must supply to our users a new object class in the form of a DLL (we'll be showing you how in the next few chapters). The DLL must then be placed in a subdirectory that is included in the LIBPATH statement in CONFIG.SYS. After that is done, the next time the user opens the *templates folder*, the new object class will automagically appear in it. For the users, it's all fun and games from then on: *cookie cutting and cloning object clones*.

Interacting With Objects

Different objects have different actions that can be performed on them. Action choices for an object are displayed in pop-up menus, called *context menus*, that appear next to an object when the user presses the appropriate mouse button (see Figure 37-2). The choices in the pop-up menu show, at any given time, the set of actions that can be performed on it. The interaction with an object through choice menus is called *indirect manipulation*.

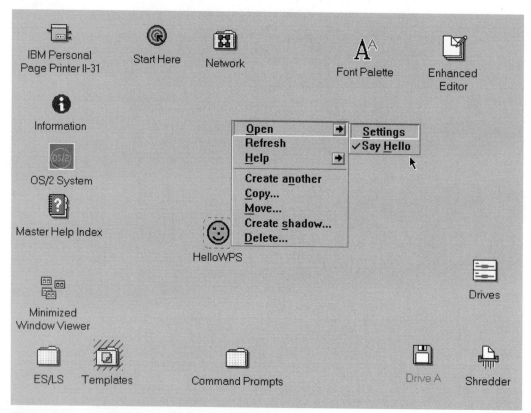

Figure 37-2. An Object and Its Context Menu Pop-Up.

The other way to interact with objects is by *direct object manipulation*, a technique that allows objects to have actions directly performed on them. This technique gives the user the freedom to carry out some functions without a menu. A mouse is used to *drag* an object and *drop* it on its target. For example, the user can pick up an object and put it into a folder or FAX it to the next continent. This computer simulation of the way users interact with real world objects is known as "drag and drop." Direct manipulation frees the user from language and makes applications more graphic. It provides a good fit with object-orientation and the OOUI paradigm.

Currently, some of the pitfalls associated with direct manipulation are:

- Some actions are impossible to specify with any precision.
- Actions with more than two objects are difficult.
- Some of the graphic metaphors are *overly stretched* and may end up confusing the user.
- Icons drawn by amateurs may not be recognizable to the user.
- Highly iconic interfaces make inflexible database front-ends. The current Relational paradigm for database is centered around alphanumeric data tables. The most flexible front-end to such a database is a tabular view of rows and columns of alphanumeric information. Custom graphics, however, can be hand-tailored to create very visual database front-ends that are application-specific.

Windows

CUA'91 recognizes only two types of Windows: Primary and Pop-Ups. Windows are just a way to look inside objects; they provide views. Here's what the two window types do:

- **Primary Windows** present the user with object choices, a menu bar, and pull-down menus. In CUA'89 (or GUIs), every application must have a primary window that serves as the main focal point of the user's activity. Primary windows in CUA'89 applications persist throughout the life of an application. CUA'91 treats primary windows as mere windows into objects. The heart of the application is the collection of user objects.
- **Pop-Up Windows** present the user with choices that are supportive of the primary window or the object. In CUA'89, secondary windows were used to conduct parallel dialogs with users. This is not needed in CUA'91 because the dialog is conducted with the object and parallel dialogs are simply dialogs that involve more than one object.

GUIs and OOUIs

In this section, we explore the differences between GUIs and OOUIs from the viewpoint of an application designer. We faced the "OOUI versus GUI" dilemma ourselves when writing this book. Had we stayed with a GUI Club Med, we could have brought the book to market much earlier. Instead, we felt there were some significant architectural and functional benefits to OOUI. There was also a good SOM/Workplace Shell "bleeding-edge" story to tell.

Club Med: GUIs and OOUI

The best way to compare GUIs and OOUIs is to put the two side-by-side and contrast some of their features. In Figure 37-3 and Figure 37-4 we present two vintages of a Club Med application: CUA'89 and CUA'91. The GUI Club Med was developed in the previous edition of our book; the OOUI Club Med will be developed in Part VII. By just looking at these two pictures, can you tell what the OOUI fuss is all about?

- The OOUI Club Med is an extension of the Workplace Shell. You can't tell where the application starts and OS/2 ends. They appear to be seamlessly integrated. The clubs on the Workplace look like any other object.
- The OOUI Club Med invites the user to manipulate the visual Club Med objects through drag-and-drop. For example, a transaction may be triggered by dragging a guest object to the shredder to delete it. Or, if we want to be kind, we'll drop it on the FAX machine icon to send a confirmation of the reservation. [2]
- The OOUI Club Med icon can be opened at any time to reveal a notebook view of the information inside it. The notebook is a CUA'91 control that makes it possible to visually staple together hundreds of dialog windows and let the user find the information needed. This is a giant step forward for OLTP-type of applications.
- The OOUI Club Med set-up will reappear the way the user left it when the machine is turned on again. The desktop configuration is persistent.
- The OOUI Club Med is very familiar especially to kids. It feels like a video game. Kids feel quite at home with drag and drop, icons, and direct manipulation. The OOUI is a simulation of reality that they can easily recognize. Can we say the same about adults?
- The OOUI Club Med can be extended to seamlessly work with any other OOUI object with very little new code. We could easily think of mail-enabling it or allowing scanned pages to be dragged into the notebook view. The OLTP transaction is starting to look more like its real-world counterpart.
- The GUI Club Med, on the other hand, is your typical WIMP interface. The icon is just there to represent the application to the desktop. You're not invited to play with it. You start the application by clicking on the icon. From then on, you're in menu land. The user is quite aware that there is a running Club Med application.

---

[2] The FAX function is not supported yet, so don't raise your expectations.

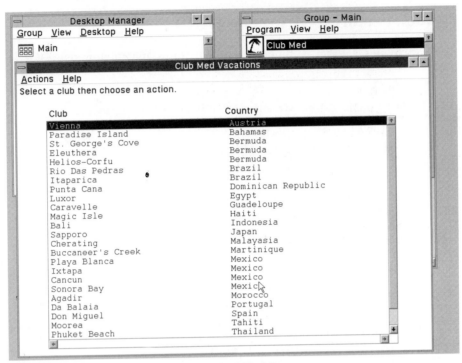

Figure 37-3.   GUI Application "Look and Feel."

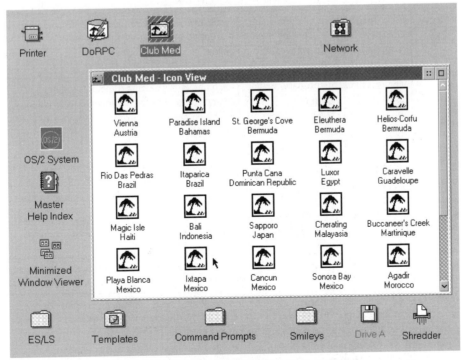

Figure 37-4.   A Club Med OOUI Application "Look and Feel."

Application Features: GUI versus OOUI

Table 37-1 provides a quick summary of the features that distinguish OOUIs from GUIs.

Table 37-1 (Part 1 of 2). A Comparison of CUA'89 and CUA'91 Models.

Feature	CUA'89 Graphical Model (GUI)	CUA'91 Workplace Model (OOUI)
Application structure	A graphic application consists of an icon, a primary window with a menu bar, and one or more secondary windows. The focus is on the main task. Ancillary tasks are supported by secondary windows and pop-ups. Users must follow the rigid task structure (and may get trapped in a task). An application represents a task.	A graphic application consists of a collection of cooperating user objects. Everything that you see is an object. Each object is represented by an icon and has at least one view. Objects can be reused in many tasks. The application's boundaries are fuzzy. The user defines what's an application by assembling a collection of objects. These objects may come from one or more programs and are integrated with the desktop objects the system provides (like printers and shredders). The users can innovate and create their own leggo-like object collections.
Icons	Icons represent a running application.	Icons represent objects that can be directly manipulated.
Starting an application	Users start application before selecting an object to work with.	Users open the object on the desktop, which causes a window view of the object to be displayed.
Windows	Users open a primary window and then specify the objects they want to interact with. The same window can be used to display other objects.	A window is a view of what's inside an object. There is a one-to-one relationship between a window and an object.
Menus	Menus provide the primary method for navigating within an application.	Each object has a context menu. You navigate within an application or across applications by directly manipulating objects. The desktop functions as one big menu; icons represent the objects that you can manipulate.
Dialogs	The application leads the user through a series of dialog windows.	In addition to dialog windows, new CUA'91 controls like the notebook may contain a collection of dialogs. The user controls the dialog by flipping pages.
Active application visual	Icons represent minimized windows of active applications.	Icons are augmented with the *in-use* emphasis to represent an active object.
Direct manipulation	An application may provide direct manipulation on an ad hoc basis.	Objects are created, communicated with, moved, and manipulated through drag-and-drop manipulation.
Creating new objects	Objects are created in an application-specific manner, usually through some form of copy mechanism or using the menu choices: new or open.	A templates folder contains a template for every object type. To create a new instance of an object, drag its template to where you want the new object to reside.

Table 37-1 (Part 2 of 2). A Comparison of CUA'89 and CUA'91 Models.

Feature	CUA'89 Graphical Model (GUI)	CUA'91 Workplace Model (OOUI)
Actions	Choose object; then choose action from menu bar.	In addition to choosing actions from menus, a user can drag objects to icons to perform operations. Example: drag a file to a printer icon.
Containers	Text-based list boxes provides the primary form of containment.	In addition to list boxes, CUA'91 defines new container objects including folders and notebooks. These in turn can contain other objects. Actions performed on container objects impact all the objects inside them.
Closing an application	No desktop information is retained.	The visual state and settings of an application are saved, the application will restart where you left off.
Who is in Control?	Control alternates between the user and the application.	All the applications behave the same and the user acts as the conductor. Think of the user as the visual programmer of the desktop.
Product Examples	Windows, Motif, and OS/2 1.3	OS/2 2.0 Workplace Shell and Macintosh.

GUI or OOUI

CUA'89's window-based GUI paradigm adequately supports a way of doing business on computers with a limited amount of visual bandwidth and resources; the success of Windows 3.X attests to that. CUA'91's OOUI paradigm extends the graphical model with direct object manipulation, object containers, and interobject communications. OOUIs address the needs of a new generation of computer users who grew up on MTV and in the video game arcades.

Commercial software designers must make some hard decisions: Should they to be at the "bleeding edge" of display technology and invest a fortune in "groundbreaking" new user interface code and tools? Or, should they use the current interface paradigm which, today, is CUA '89 (that is, Windows 3.X). Consider, when making your choice, that the user interface code has never been known to be a trivial development effort. It can easily chew up 70% of an application's development budget. Staying within the current paradigm provides the following benefits:

- A well-supported graphical user interface technology.
- A common "look and feel" with Microsoft Windows.
- A wide selection of GUI tools.
- A level of stability that protects developers from being at the continual mercy of shifting Graphical User Interface *fashions*.
- A low development cost.

Developing OOUI applications that fully take advantage of the OS/2 2.0 Workplace Shell provides the following benefits:

- A well-supported graphical user interface, the Workplace Shell.
- A competitive edge. Your OOUI applications will have superior functionality, including OO, CUA'91 controls, GPI graphics, IPF/Help, 32-bit graphic engine, true multitasking, and crash protection.
- A better positioning for the future. Macintosh and Motif are both going OOUI; the predominant visual paradigm will be OOUI. The users will demand it.
- A better acceptance with neophyte computer users. As a result, new markets will appear.
- A better platform for exploiting new technology. OOUI is made for the age of multimedia.

Go OOUI

We were very conservative in our last book; we chose to stay deep within the GUI boundaries. In this edition of the book, we feel that OOUI is a technology whose time has come. Even conservative mainstream business areas (like the huge OLTP market) will find that OOUIs make great mission-critical application front-ends (and they're fun). We will show you how to get a jump start with OOUI technology as it stands today.

Chapter 38

A Taxonomy of GUI and OOUI Tools

A good client/server platform should be able to support the greatest number of graphic front-end clients. We feel the easiest way to achieve this goal is to build your client applications using a GUI/OOUI tool and let the tool vendor worry about porting the code to multiple GUI platforms such as PM, Windows 3.X, Motif, OPEN LOOK, and Macintosh. GUI/OOUI tools also create more maintainable code and shorten the development cycle. There are dozens of excellent tools on the market, and it will be worth your while to do some comparison shopping. To help you with your evaluation of graphic tools, we will first point out some of the pitfalls to avoid in a tool. We then introduce a classification scheme that will help you sort through the paradigms on which the different tools are based. We feel that it is very important to use the right tool for the job, and that it pays to research the matter.

WHAT TO LOOK FOR IN A TOOL

We looked at tools from the point of view of what would be best for a C (or 32-bit C++ when it is available) programmer. The discussion refers to PM, since this book uses OS/2, but the concepts apply to other platforms. Here's a list of requirements we compiled when we did our comparison shopping:

- *The tool should let you "Call Out" outside code; and let the outside code "Call In" the tool*. The tool should include a message-passing mechanism that invokes external RPCs, DLLs, and class methods. The non-presentation aspects of the client code (i.e., the "model" in Smalltalk terminology) should be done outside the tool's environment. We prefer to code the client initialization, LAN communications, and Remote Procedure Calls using C (or C++), as opposed to using a vendor-specific script language.
- *The tool should let you drop into PM from within it*. This is an important requirement because PM will always contain new graphic constructs, which a tool does not "yet" provide.
- *The tool should be able to access pointers in shared memory*. If not, we'll have to create protocols to copy everything back and forth. It's a headache.
- *The tool should generate separate visual objects, not in-line code*. It is important to be able to maintain visual objects separately from the code. This makes the

objects more reusable and maintainable. It makes it easier to support other *national* languages. Tools that generate tons of in-line PM code should be shunned. You have to read, maintain, and manage that code. It is not a flexible environment and the code that is produced is hard to maintain and change.

- *The tool should be fast*. Some of the tools on the market are general purpose but interpretive. That's slow.
- *The tool's runtime should be small*. Some of the tools on the market require runtimes in excess of 1.5 MBytes, in addition to OS/2 and whatever code you write. Be careful; this added memory goes into client workstations that we would prefer to keep "skinny."
- *No run-time license charges, please*. Some of the best tools on the market require a runtime charge of over $150 per workstation on which they run. This adds to the cost of the client, to say nothing of how difficult it is to administer those charges on a LAN workstation basis. Remember, the competition to LAN workstations using client/server architectures is the $500 dumb terminal attached to a time-sharing minicomputer.
- *Low-cost development package*. Some of those tools cost over $7000 per developer software package. If you have a large team of programmers, this can quickly eat into your profits. However, if the tool *really* improves productivity, paying $7000 is a steal.
- *Enforcement of CUA'91*. The last thing you want to worry about is keeping up with the hundreds of little rules your application needs to adhere to in order to be CUA compatible. Let the tool do it for you.
- *Multiple-GUI platform support*. Pick a tool that allows your code to run on multiple GUI platforms if this is a requirement.
- *Other value-added benefits*. A long list comes to mind: a WYSIWYG screen painter, multimedia support, audio/image capture and playback, libraries of screen objects, clip-art, and so on.

WHY ARE GUI TOOLS TAKING OFF?

Graphical tools are an exciting growth area whose time has come. Here's why:

- The graphic capability of PCs is improving in quantum leaps, and it is now in the affordable price range. We're seeing more color and sharper screen resolutions at lower costs. PCs can attach to all kinds of image frame grabbers and scanners. Mass data storage for graphic objects is economically available with CD-ROMs and optical disks. What this all means is that the hardware for supporting multimedia is becoming available at the right prices.

- The base software platform to support GUIs and OOUIs is in place (see Figure 38-1). Graphic engines, such as Windows 3.X and OS/2 PM, are now available on a large installed base of PCs. Graphic engines provide rich graphic primitives, a desktop manager, icons, and data exchange facilities.

- The technology for GUI software to coexist on desktops is coming together. Standard desktops (such as the Workplace Shell) are defining how to start applications and how these applications should communicate using DDE, the clipboard, and drag-and-drop direct manipulation techniques. A visual object model is enforced so that the applications appear to work together naturally, even when they are provided by different vendors.

- The multi-GUI desktop, such as the Workplace Shell, provides a new level of GUI independence and choice to end users. For example, users may buy OS/2 to run Windows.

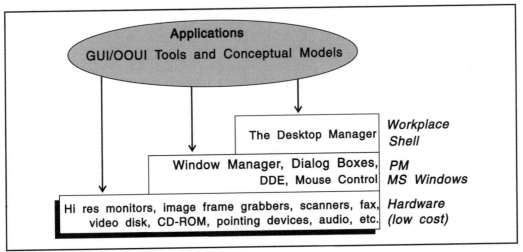

Figure 38-1. The Graphic Layers.

A new generation of tools is focused on facilitating the design of visual objects that represent the user's activities. The emphasis is now on the relationship between objects and how they react to manipulation from the user and from other objects. Vendors are beginning to provide libraries of objects that an application designer can use to "plug and play." Another hot area of vendor activity is in the WYSIWYG screen layout editors to create graphic applications. Finally, we believe that all the pieces are here for tool providers to focus on making it easy to create graphic multimedia applications.

A TAXONOMY OF GUI/OOUI TOOLS

There is a choice of GUI tool offerings for PM and Windows on the market (OOUI tools are another story). Many of the GUI tools are the embodiment of many years of research in programming paradigms for graphic front-ends. They all promise to make you more productive in generating PM applications. Instead of reviewing all the tools on the market, we present in this section a classification scheme for tools based on the software paradigm they build on. As shown in Figure 38-2, we divide the GUI tools into five categories: inline code generator tools, C language-based tools, event-driven tools, object-oriented tools, and OOUI tools. These categories are explained in the sections which follow.

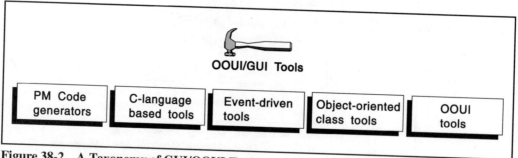

OOUI/GUI Tools

| PM Code generators | C-language based tools | Event-driven tools | Object-oriented class tools | OOUI tools |

Figure 38-2. A Taxonomy of GUI/OOUI Tools.

Tools That Generate PM Code Outlines

The tools in this category generate PM code that you can include in your C language programs. These tools usually provide a WYSIWYG editor with which you can lay out screens consisting of regular PM window classes. The tool then produces PM code, including (.C) files, (.H) files, (.RC) files, (.DEF) files, and the *make* file (see Figure 38-3). The code creates the PM main() loop and provides skeleton window and dialog procedures. You can then edit the source code files created by the tool to add whatever code is required by your application. In addition, you must write the code that services many of the low-level PM constructs. For example, you have to provide the code that services scroll-bars, action selections, information in list boxes, variables, help, display messages, etc. These are all low-level constructs that you would normally expect a tool to handle on your behalf.

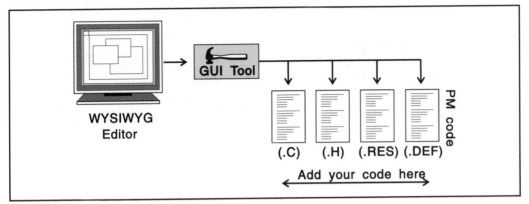

Figure 38-3.   Tools That Generate PM Code Outlines.

Benefits: These tools are great for learning PM. They can be very useful if you plan to stay within the PM environment and your applications are kept small. These tools usually handle a lot of the CUA layout rules on behalf of your application. A final advantage is that tools of this kind are not too expensive (under $1000) and do not require a run-time license for the code they produce.

Costs: These tools provide a "jump start" into PM, but eventually leave you inside the PM environment. You have to deal with all the low-level PM constructs instead of focusing on the logic of your application. You will essentially be maintaining and debugging a PM program. You cannot use this kind of tool for the direct manipulation of objects using drag-and-drop techniques, DDE is not supported, and you are mostly limited to creating PM dialog forms.

C Language-Based Tools

Tools in this category allow you to manipulate *external* display objects directly from within your C or C++ programs. It is business as usual for C programmers. You specify in your C programs which objects to display and when. Your interface to screen objects is through the familiar API method. You display objects and wait for events to happen. There are no control loops or event handlers or PM calls. The tool takes care of all these details. So, how do you specify your screen objects and their behavior? This is done outside your code. The tool usually allows you to specify display objects and their layout through WYSIWYG editors (see Figure 38-4). One of the key areas that differentiate these tools is how data is exchanged with the screen objects and how the user selections (and actions) are returned to the C program.

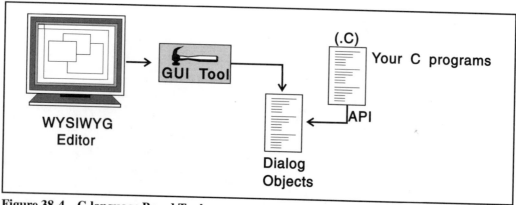

Figure 38-4. C-language Based Tools.

Benefits: It is business as usual for C or C++ programmers with the benefit that there is a clean separation of the code from the screen objects. Screen objects are created and managed outside of the code. This helps program maintenance and allows the developer to focus on the logic of the visual elements independently of the code. You can impose by choice an event-driven methodology on your code.

Costs: You're limited by the constructs, which can be described using the WYSIWYG editor. These constructs tend to be PM dialog-type forms. To fully exploit the power of PM, you must write PM code.

Event-Driven Tools

These tools build on the event-driven programming paradigm. They provide a full-fledged, event-driven environment where you can create your events and code the event-handlers that respond to them. They require that you plan your application event by event. For each event, you must supply the appropriate event-handler. A WYSIWYG editor is usually provided by the tool vendor to define the windows and dialog boxes in your application. Some vendors call these event-driven tools "programming with forms."

The WYSIWYG editor allows you to associate event names with various window components. An event can be a push-button selection, a keyboard input, a mouse click in graphic areas that are made "mouse-sensitive" (i.e., *hot-spots*), and so on. The editor will generate a core script (or outline) of object definitions and the stimulus events they produce (usually in an English-like proprietary tool language).

You can then add to the core script the action statements that describe your responses to the various events (see Figure 38-5). Most of the action statements will be coded in the language supplied by the tool vendor. You need to do that in order to take advantage of the libraries of "canned" event-handlers that are typically supplied with the tool. However, most vendors will allow you to call out C language functions (packaged in

DLLs) from within your action statements. The source code for the script is eventually compiled into run-time files. The event-driven code executes when the end user performs actions like pushing buttons.

Two factors differentiate vendors in the "event-driven" tool market:

1. *The scripting environment*. The script is really an outliner for the program. A whole environment can be built around this outliner. Here are some examples of what the best of breed tools provide:

   - The text outline is used to navigate through the program. The WYSIWYG screen objects are displayed side-by-side with the outline code. A very complete browsing environment is provided. Different conceptual views of the outline are provided.
   - A debugging environment based on the outline. You should be able to run the program, set break-points and view the output from within the outline.
   - A code library and versioning system.

2. *The scope of the event-triggers*. What is the level of granularity of the event-triggers? What information do they convey? How are event-triggers managed?

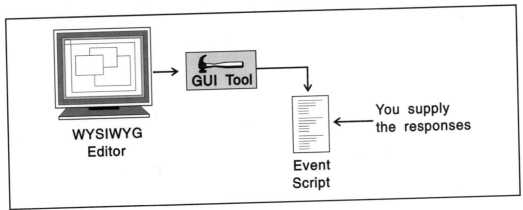

Figure 38-5. Event-Driven Tools.

Benefits: An event-driven program is a collection of event-handlers that respond to various kinds of inputs and stimuli. This is an elegant paradigm for organizing reactive user interface programs. Once a core script is put together, you can reuse parts of it with minor modifications for new applications. The control of events is organized via forms (or panels), which preserve the logic of the application.

Costs: You need to learn a new language and environment, which is typically proprietary. Most of your front-end programming will be done using a proprietary tool language instead of the C language. All the screens required for an application get compiled into a single file, which could become unmanageable for major applications.

The constructs provided by the vendor will typically lag behind what PM provides. This means you'll still have to program in PM and C whenever you need to create user interfaces that go beyond the PM dialog style. The development environment for such tools is expensive (in the vicinity of $5000 for the better tools). These tools typically require a run-time license (of $150 or more per workstation). The runtime can also be a memory hog (1 MByte or more in some cases).

Object-Oriented (OO) Tools

These tools provide the most complete environment to build and maintain complex *direct manipulation* style user interfaces. Object-oriented tools use object-oriented language features to provide powerful libraries of reusable code and the "glue" that makes it all work together. You can then use this code "as is" or customize it to provide your own display constructs. The power of this code is that it describes not only the object's structure but also its behavior and its interface to other objects. The notion of independent interacting objects seems to naturally represent objects that can be directly manipulated on a screen.

Like the other tools, object-oriented tools also come with WYSIWYG layout editors. These editors typically allow you to create screens from a library of predefined display classes. A *class* encapsulates (or brings together) data structures and the procedures (also called *methods*) that manipulate these structures. The bottom line is that when you create an object of a particular class, you automatically *inherit* all its methods and attributes. You can create your own composite subclasses from multiple parent classes and inherit their combined behaviors.

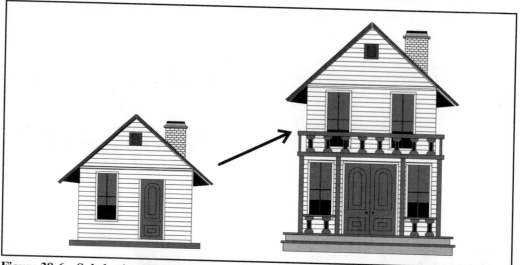

Figure 38-6.   Subclassing With Single-Inheritance: Start with a House and Create a Mansion.

Figure 38-6 demonstrates *single-inheritance* subclassing. You take an existing class, such as house, and by adding your own methods create a "mansion" class. Figure 38-7 demonstrates *multiple-inheritance*. This process allows you to create new classes by mix and matching the attributes of several parent classes. The figure shows how a motorcycle class can be created from the parent classes: car and bicycle.

Figure 38-7.   Multiple-Inheritance: Start with a Car and Bicycle and Create a Motorcycle.

Typically, you will use existing vendor classes and customize your own subclasses using the following object-oriented techniques:

- By inheriting *all* the class methods of a parent and augmenting them by adding some of your own
- By inheriting *some* of the methods of a parent and overriding some of the methods with your own
- By *combining* class attributes and methods of more than one parent class through multiple-inheritance

The result is that you can "mix and match" classes to your heart's content using libraries of vendor-provided visual classes. The vendor is happy because even though you get all the effects of the classes, you never get to see a line of the vendor's code. It's all encapsulated in the classes. This is a classic "win-win" situation.

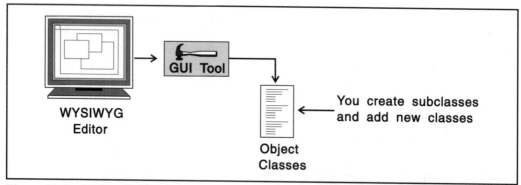

Figure 38-8. Object-Oriented Tools.

Benefits: You will be using the vendor's extensive libraries of debugged code. This gives you a lot of power for very little additional code. Typically, an object-based debugging environment is provided to allow you to place breakpoints on messages and look at the object's state. The environment typically supplies class-browsing tools that display class family trees. Objects can send messages directly to other objects instead of indirectly through an event loop. The object discipline makes you write your programs as a collection of reusable objects. Inheritance and method "overriding" capabilities encourage you to flexibly reuse existing code. This means that your programs will be highly maintainable and reusable. Because objects are self-contained, you can add features by adding new classes with a minimal change to existing code.

Costs: An object environment *really* requires an object-oriented language like C++ or Smalltalk. Most vendors today provide their own homemade object language on top of PM (they're all waiting for C++). If you can afford to wait, you may be better off starting with C++ rather than with a proprietary object language and environment. SOM solves the problem of creating language-independent reusable class libraries. We will have more to say in the SOM chapters.

The major obstacle to most programmers in adopting object programming is the *steep learning curve*. It may take you up to six months to become proficient with an object-based environment and the vendor's class library. Much of this time will be invested in trying to understand what may appear to be a frighteningly large collection of vendor-supplied classes. Most beginners feel overwhelmed by hundreds of new classes, each with its own name, purpose, and messages. However, the consolation is that you can start out with a few classes and build your class knowledge base gradually (understanding how an individual class works is usually not difficult).

Another problem is that you may still have to drop into C and PM occasionally to create graphic classes that cannot be subclassed from vendor libraries. Lastly, today's object-based tools are expensive. The best of the breed sell their development environment for $7000 (as we mentioned earlier, this money is well spent if the tool is good). A run-time license (of over $150 per workstation) may also be required. The runtime can also be a memory hog (1 MByte, or more in some cases). We expect to see sharp drops in the price of OO tools when Borland comes out with its C++ product. In the meantime, SOM and the Workplace Shell Class libraries are available with the OS/2 Toolkit, and they require no run-time license (we know a bargain when we see one).

OOUI Tools

What's an OOUI tool? It's a tool that creates applications consisting of collections of business objects (see Figure 38-9). These are end-user objects as opposed to class libraries and programming objects. In the OS/2 2.0 Workplace Shell environment, an OOUI tool creates new types of business objects that can be registered in the templates folder. The OOUI tool builds two types of business objects: *base* objects and *container* objects. With container objects, the tool lets you specify population rules, persistence storage, and other such attributes. However, the OOUI tool's primary role in life is to build base objects. These are you're everyday visual objects like fax machines, employees, customers, parts, Club Meds, cars, and so on. The OOUI tool lets you build these base objects by specifying their structural and behavioral components.

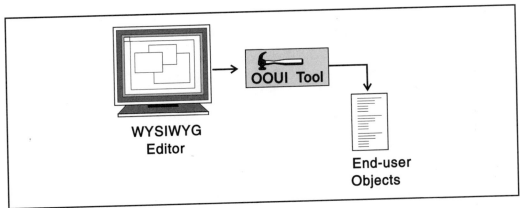

Figure 38-9. OOUI Tools.

The *structural OOUI components* are the CUA'91 representations of a visual object. These include the object's icon, its views, the and its context menu. The *behavioral OOUI components* define the active logic associated with the object. What to do when another object is dropped on it? How to respond to user actions? How to validate entry fields? How to pass the information to other objects? How to respond to messages from other objects? How to communicate with the external world (i.e., your DLLs, RPCs, DDE, or class methods)?

Like the other tools, OOUI tools also come with WYSIWYG layout editors. These editors allow you to define the object, paint its views, and specify the behavior of the different visual elements in response to outside events (see Figure 38-10). One of the main source of events are messages generated by other objects within the application.

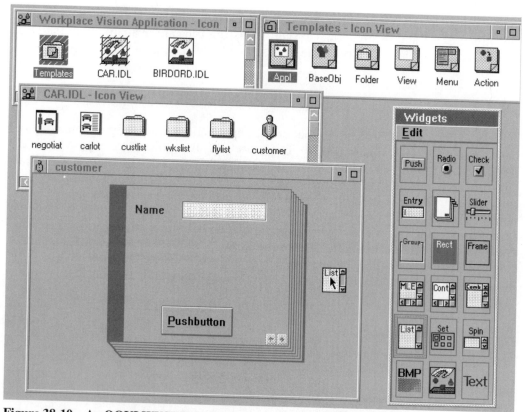

Figure 38-10. An OOUI WYSIWYG Tool (Courtesy of Arcadia Technologies, Inc.).

Before talking about the benefits and costs of OOUI tools, it is important to note that no such tool is on the market as this book goes to press. OOUI environments, in the form of the Workplace Shell, have just become available and it will take some time for tool vendors to catch up.[1]

Benefits: If we had such a tool, we could have trimmed the size of this book by 50 pages or so. You create using a WYSIWYG tool business objects that snap into SOM and the Workplace Shell and coexist with other business objects and Workplace Shell objects. You get all the benefits of SOM and the Workplace Shell without having to write OOUI code (other than your application's model). The library of business objects is reusable. The installation is simple and incremental; *you just add new objects to the Workplace Shell.*

---

[1] A vendor planning to create a SOM/Workplace Shell based OOUI tool, was "sighted" demonstrating an early prototype at the "OS/2 Tools Conference" in San Francisco (May 5, 1992). So we know somebody is working on such a tool.

Costs: The lack of portability to other GUI environments, such as Windows. OOUIs are a "cutting-edge" technology. You get to "wow" the Jones, but because of that you can't be like everybody else. An OOUI tool removes you from PM and contact with the "bits and bytes." The vendor must provide a way for programmers to extend the visual widgets that come with the WYSIWYG. Since, there is no such tool on the market, it is too early to assess the negatives.

WHICH TOOL SHOULD I USE?

Use whatever tool does the job for you. The tool we'll use in this book is SOM and the Workplace Shell Class libraries. This puts us into the object-oriented tool category. Is this the right choice? We found it to be the "tool of the day" that did the best job for us. Remember, we decided to go "bleeding edge" and exploit the power of OOUI and the Workplace Shell; this was the only tool that could do that in our time frame. We're a beta for many other tools that will be coming out by year-end 1992. So, we can tell you with some certainty that there will be more choices soon.

The good news is that we grew very fond of SOM and the Workplace Shell class library after we helped them find their *last* bug. There is a lot of power in that package. The Workplace Class library allows us to subclass anything you see on the OS/2 2.0 desktop. This is really a lot of "bang for the buck!" The beauty of the Workplace Shell class libraries is that they went through a beta test that involved 30,000 early OS/2 2.0 users; they're being used daily by more than a million users; and they're continuously being refined, improved, and expanded. All this power is yours for the price of the OS/2 Toolkit (less than $300 as we write). You can develop your value-added product starting where they left off, and then resell it without paying any run-time license fees. The only catch, of course, is learning how to use SOM and Workplace Shell classes. We will provide a jump start to help you do just that in the remaining parts of this book. The effort you spend is well worth it.

SOM is another interesting product in its own right. It's a cutting-edge OO tool that allows you to write class libraries using ordinary C code. Why would you ever want to do that? In our case there was no choice: C Set/2 was the only 32-bit compiler available to write the code for this book. Luckily, it turned out to be a great compiler. However, SOM will allow you to work with C++ or Smalltalk, and to create truly exportable and importable class libraries. In other words, SOM does for classes what DLLs do for procedural languages: *it makes them portable*. This means that you can export your SOM classes into Borland's 32-bit C++ for OS/2 when it becomes available and go from there. In general, writing language independent portable classes is not a bad idea for developers of commercial software. SOM is a good choice to provide this independence because it will comply with the Object Management Group's CORBA specification for an open object broker (more on that later).

In summary, SOM/WPS allows us to create OOUI objects, it gives us the capability to use any Workplace Shell object as our base, it allows us to use production strength classes, and it guarantees us object portability and future CORBA compliance. All this for a mere $300. What else could we want? Perhaps, we could use an OOUI tool that creates SOM and Workplace Shell objects, and cuts down on the amount of PM programming and program maintenance we have to do. It is probably in the nature of human beings to always want more, especially in the area of tools.

Chapter 39

The Presentation Manager

This chapter provides a crash course in Presentation Manager "literacy." We will not be covering PM's 900 plus API calls. Instead, we will focus on the structure of a PM program and on understanding the PM (and Windows 3.X) programming paradigm. At the end of this chapter, you should be able to read a PM or Windows 3.X program and follow its logic. This is a very important prerequisite for the chapters that follow, where we will be introducing some of PM's more advanced functions. To give you a feel for what it takes to program in PM, we will present the PM version of "Hello World."

WHAT MAKES PM PROGRAMS SO DIFFERENT?

The Reactive Event-Driven Paradigm

PM programs are mostly reactive (see Figure 39-1). They spend most of their time in an "idle" state waiting for events to happen. When an event such as a keypress or a mouse click occurs, PM routes the input to the appropriate procedure in your code in the form of messages. The procedure can then choose to either react to the event or just return it to PM and let it handle it. If the procedure needs to display information in a window, it calls PM to do so. After making the appropriate response, the procedure returns to its idle state waiting for the next event. So, the first thing we can say about a PM program is that it is made up of a collection of lazy, event-driven procedures that wait for work to find them. No self-respecting PM procedure ever goes out of its way to look for work.

The Heart of PM: "Everything Is a Window"

How does PM associate procedures with events? It does that through the magic of windows. Windows in PM are more than just the familiar overlapping rectangles that appear on a screen. A window is an "object." It becomes "an object that knows what to do" when it teams up with an event-handler procedure (more on that later). A PM program is conceptually a number of windows and the stuff that makes them know what

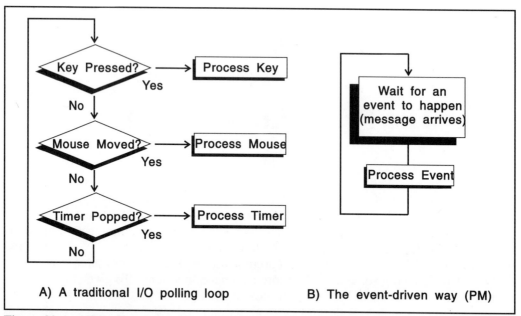

Figure 39-1. I/O Polling Loops Versus PM's Event-Driven Processing.

to do. Some windows look like the traditional rectangular areas, typically called windows. On the other hand, structures that are not "window-like"— such as scroll bars, buttons, and menus—are also considered to be windows in PM. A window may or may not be visible on the screen. PM even provides a window type, called the *object window*, that has nothing to do with visual components; it is there to tap into the PM message loop and exchange messages with PM applications. Most traditional PM applications, however, create at least one "traditional" window called the main window, which is typically visible and represents the application to the outside world. Here is a quick guide to PM's window terminology:

- A **frame window** provides a border and serves as a base for constructing composite windows, such as the main window or a dialog window. Think of the frame window as a "border" which contains an assembly of child windows that act as an ensemble. Frames provide the visual unity that gives the window its "look and feel" to end users.
- A **main window,** or "standard window," is a frame window which contains control windows such as a title bar, an action bar, and a scroll bar. Every main window includes a client window area. This is the area where an application does all its work. Figure 39-2 shows four "standard" windows.
- A **dialog window** is a frame window that contains one or more control windows that are used primarily to prompt the user for input.
- A **message window** is a frame window that an application uses to display a message.
- A **client window** is the area in the window where the application displays its information. The insides of the four windows in Figure 39-2 are client areas. Every main window typically has a client window. What is displayed in the client window

is entirely application specific. The frame window receives events from the control windows that surround the client window and passes them to the client window. The application program provides the event-handler procedures that service these events.

- A **control window** is used in conjunction with another window to provide control structures. PM provides several pre-defined control windows such as: push buttons, spin buttons, entry fields, list boxes, check boxes, menus, scroll bars, combo boxes, and multiple line editors (MLEs). A number of new control window classes are provided under OS/2 2.0 to aid in the implementation of the Workplace Shell and CUA/91. These new controls include a container, a notebook, a slider, a value set and a progress indicator.

An application may consist of several main windows, dialog windows, and all the child windows associated with them.

Window Lineage

Every window has a parent window. A window is positioned relative to the coordinates of its parent. When a parent window is hidden, so are its children. When the parent moves, its children move with it. Children are always drawn on top of the parent, and they get "clipped" if they go past the parent's borders. Windows that have the same parent are called siblings. In PM, just like in real life, a parent can have several children, each of which has its own children, and so on. This parent/child relationship is useful in situations where a window and its children need to be manipulated as a single unit.

Figure 39-2 visually demonstrates the window hierarchy depicted in Figure 39-3. WIN1 and WIN2 are sibling "standard windows" that have a common parent: the PM desktop. WIN1a is the child of WIN1, and WIN2a is the child of WIN2; both children are "standard windows." While this four-window hierarchy is "visually" quite obvious, what is not as obvious is that each "standard window" has its own set of child windows. Figure 39-4 shows the standard window's offspring. It's quite a prolific tribe, isn't it?

The concept of *parenting* should not be confused with PM's concept of *ownership*. In PM, a window can "own" other windows. An owner window is the recipient of all messages for the windows that it owns. Note that parents do not necessarily "own" their children. The parenting relationship is mainly concerned with display, while the ownership relationship is mainly concerned with function. An owner is interested in the events that take place within the windows it owns.

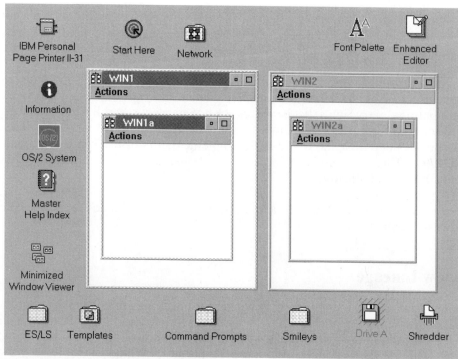

Figure 39-2.   Four "Standard Windows:" Two Main Siblings with One Child Each.

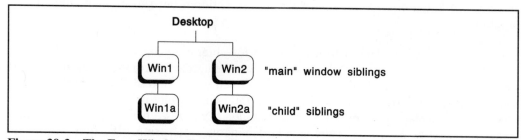

Figure 39-3.   The Four-Window Family Tree.

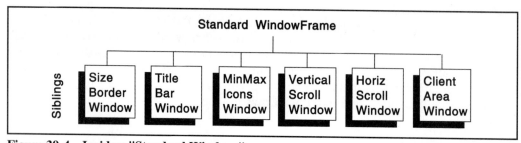

Figure 39-4.   Inside a "Standard Window."

The Brains of the Window: Classes and Procedures

The "smart" element that defines a window's behavior is the **window class**. This is the element that knows "what to do." Every window is an instance of a window class, which determines the style of the window and specifies the event-driven procedure that will handle the messages for the window. In PM terminology, these event-driven procedures are called **window procedures**. The window procedures are at the heart of programming in PM. Each window class has one window procedure that is responsible for all the processing aspects of a window's class including:

- How the window appears
- How the window behaves and responds to state changes
- How the window handles user input

All user interaction with the window is passed as messages to its window procedure. When an application creates a window, it must specify a window class. The "class" tells PM which window procedure gets to process the messages generated by some window activity. Multiple windows can belong to the same class. This means that the window procedure can handle events from more than one window. A good programming practice is to make the window procedure code reentrant, because it may be called from several sources simultaneously. In object-oriented terms, the window procedure contains *all* the "methods" that control a window. The window procedure decides which method to invoke based on the message it receives. In the next chapter, you will see how SOM/WPS elevates this interface and routes the event to the appropriate method.

PM supplies a number of preregistered *public window classes* that are available to all the applications in the system. You should use these public classes to give your applications a "common look" which, by no coincidence, is very CUA-like. Examples of the built-in public classes are scrollbar, menu, button, frame, entry field, list box, combo box, MLE, notebook, slider, and container. In addition to PM's public window classes, you can create your own application-specific *private window classes* and register them with PM when your application is initialized.

PM's Message-Based Nervous System

If windows are the heart of PM and window procedures its brain, then *messages are its nervous system*. Typically, dozens of messages will be circulating around the PM system. A message can contain information, the request for information, or a request for an action. In PM, messages are generated when a user interacts with a window on the screen, when one window needs to communicate with another window, or when the system detects an event such as a window being moved or resized. Applications can also use PM's message system to communicate with each other; it's a very handy way of creating general-purpose, event-driven applications.

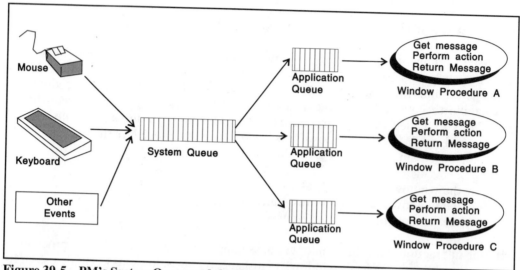

Figure 39-5. PM's System Queue and the Window Procedure Queues.

Even though OS/2 is a true multitasking operating system, PM applications must share the computer's keyboard, mouse, and screen. OS/2 places input events into PM's single system queue (see Figure 39-5), which has a capacity for handling in the vicinity of 60 keystrokes or mouse clicks. Messages are read off the system queue by the PM message router on a first-in, first-out basis. The PM input router converts the system input information into a message for the application that controls the window where the event was generated. The router can communicate the message to the application in one of two ways:

- By **posting** the message to the application's PM message queue using **WinPostMsg()**. Control is returned to the caller immediately after the message is placed on the queue. This call is used for messages that do not require immediate action. Every PM application needs at least one message queue to receive input. An application can create one message queue per thread. A window is associated with the message queue of the thread which creates it. A single queue can, of course, handle more than one window. An application thread can retrieve and process the message from its queue at the appropriate time.

- By **sending** the message directly to the application's window procedure using **WinSendMsg()**. Control is not returned to the caller until the processing at the other end is completed. This mechanism is similar to a call/return procedure call, but it is done from within PM's messaging structure (this helps preserve the consistency of the event-driven model). An application sends instead of posts when the caller requires immediate action from the recipient. The window procedure can carry out the request or pass the unprocessed messages to a default window procedure provided by PM.

A word of caution: Use send only if you really need it. The message is sent directly to the window procedure, which disturbs PM's normal serialization of events. For example, when multiple windows are sending messages to a single window, the PM queue preserves the order in which messages are received. Sending, in this situation, is "cutting in line" ahead of somebody else.

The window procedure handles both queued and non-queued messages in the same manner. It doesn't care how the message got to it.

The PM Message Etiquette

A message will not be presented to an application until the previous message has been processed. Since the majority of an application's time is spent waiting for a message to arrive, PM will allow during the interim other applications to process their respective messages. This is a form of cooperative multitasking using message processing to schedule applications. An ill-behaved application can slow down or even stop PM if it starts a time-consuming task while processing a PM message. There is a rule of thumb that says *messages must be processed within 0.1 seconds.* More on that later.

The PM Message Structure

PM can generate about 100 general-purpose messages and 150 special-purpose messages which serve special control windows. You can also create your own application-specific messages for communicating between windows. A PM message is always addressed to a particular window and each message contains the following information:

- **A window handle:** This parameter identifies the window for which a message is destined. This parameter is useful because most message queues and window procedures handle more than one window. Your code can use the handle to determine the window for which this is addressed.
- **A message ID:** This is an integer value that uniquely identifies the message class to which this message belongs. The symbolic names for all the system-defined message classes are defined by PM (see Table 39-1 for a sampling).
- **Two message parameters:** Each message parameter is a 32-bit value that specifies either the data or the data's address for that message. An application will process the message parameters based on the message ID. These parameters usually contain a variety of message-specific information. When large data structures are required to be passed as parameters, the convention is to allocate a shared memory object and to pass a pointer to that memory object using one of the parameter fields.

Table 39-1 provides a brief sampling of some of the more common PM system messages.

Table 39-1. Examples of some commonly used PM Messages.

PM Message	Description
WM_CREATE	This message notifies a window procedure that its window is about to be made visible on the screen (this is creation time). This gives the window procedure a chance to do some processing before the window is displayed on the screen for the first time.
WM_PAINT	This message tells a window procedure that its window needs repainting.
WM_ERASEBACKGROUND	This message gives a window procedure an opportunity to paint the window background in some preferred color. Returning TRUE causes PM to paint the background itself, using the default color: CLR_BACKGROUND.
WM_SIZE	This message tells a window procedure that the window is being resized. Both the old and new dimensions are passed in the message parameters.
WM_CHAR	This message tells a window procedure that a key was pressed or released.
WM_MOUSEMOVE	This message tells a window procedure (or a mouse capture handler) that the mouse pointer has moved. It supplies the new mouse coordinates relative to the receiving window.
WM_BUTTON1DOWN	This message tells a window procedure (or a mouse capture handler) that the mouse button has been depressed. It supplies the mouse coordinates where that happened.
WM_COMMAND	This message tells a window procedure that one of the control windows in its frame has a significant action to report. These messages are typically originated by push buttons and pull-down menu selections.
WM_CONTROL	This message tells a window procedure that one of the control windows in its frame has a significant control event to report. These messages are typically originated by radio buttons, check boxes, MLEs and entry fields.
WM_HELP	This message tells a window procedure that a help button (or the F1 key) was entered. We can make use of this message to consolidate help related processing.
WM_DESTROY	This message tells a window procedure that its window is about to be destroyed.
WM_CLOSE	This message tells a window procedure that the window is about to be closed.
WM_QUIT	This message marks the end of message processing for a window queue. It does not get dispatched to the window procedure.

So What Does a PM Programmer Do?

A PM application will, at the very minimum, define one new window and one new window procedure. Commercial PM programs will typically consist of hundreds of "custom" window procedures that are developed to meet an application's requirements. For each window the PM programmer will:

- Define the window attributes.
- Identify the window input messages that the procedure will process. The rest of the messages are passed on to PM's default message handlers.
- Write the window procedure that handles the responses to the input messages that are of interest.
- Document the output messages created by the window procedure.

In a nutshell, a PM program consists of a main procedure that initializes the PM environment (more on that later) and of one or more window procedures that act on anything they're interested in and leave the rest for OS/2 to handle.

Putting It All Together

Here's how the concepts we've introduced so far come together:

- The combination of the window and the window procedure is the PM version of an object-like architecture. The window procedure defines the class to which the window belongs.
- The window procedure receives messages on behalf of its window and responds appropriately.
- The PM windows have a genealogy. Each window must have a parent, and the parent-child relationships determine how windows are positioned and moved on the screen.
- Messages are used in PM for conveying information and events between windows. Transmitting a message to a window is in effect making a call to its window procedure.
- Messages may be sent directly to a window procedure or they may be posted on a message queue. The receiver of the message can't tell the difference.
- PM makes available a number of predefined windows and their message procedures (public classes) in DLLs. These windows help create the CUA "common look."
- Programming in PM consists mostly of defining windows and then coding their window procedures.

RESOURCES AND TOOLS

Resources are "things" that are created separately from your programs using specialized tools. Here are some reasons for using resources in PM:

1. Changes may be made to the resources without recompiling your source code. An example is National language-specific data.
2. PM tools that create resources are available in the OS/2 Toolkit. Without tools, these resources would be very difficult to create.
3. Multiple instances of your application can share resources without reloading them into memory.

A PM resource starts out as a file that is managed independently from your program. It contains data, bitmaps, or other independently created resources that your program will use. These resources get added to your program's (.EXE) or are placed in DLLs. They usually end up in the read-only segments of your programs. The items in resource files are loaded in memory using specialized PM API calls.

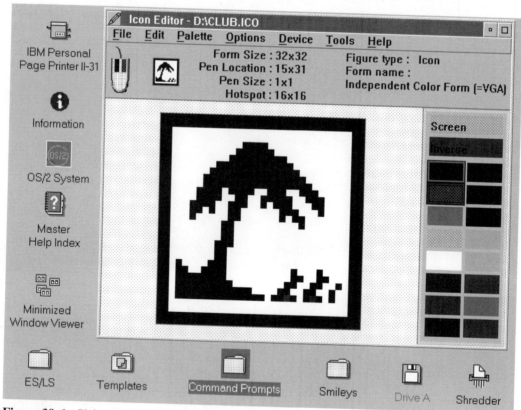

Figure 39-6. Using the Icon Editor to Create the Club Med Icon.

Here are some of the tools PM makes available for the creation of specialized resources:

*   **ICONEDIT.EXE** is an icon editor used to create the following resource files: bitmaps (.BMP), icons (.ICO), and pointers (.PNT). Figure 39-6 shows the icon editor screen capture.

- **FONTEDIT.EXE** is a font editor used to create your own font files (.FNT). Note that PM comes with a number of built-in fonts that can be used with your applications.

- **DIALOG.EXE** is a WYSIWYG editor used to create dialog boxes that use PM's built-in control windows.

- **RC.EXE** is a resource compiler. After you create the resource, you declare them in a resource definition file (.DEF) and then compile them using the RC utility. The resources then get added to your executable file. In other words, RC binds the resources to the (.EXE) file created by LINK.

USING IPF TO CREATE ONLINE HELP

Online help is an absolute requirement in any visual application. You can't let the user get lost in the system. Context-based help information must always be provided consistently and on demand. CUA '91 defines what it means to provide consistent help. The Workplace Shell faithfully follows these rules. PM makes it very easy for you to enable your applications with consistent "help" facilities that will appear natural. Remember, we're trying to create a totally seamless desktop for the user.

The Presentation Manager's powerful **Information Presentation Facility (IPF)** provides extensive tools for creating and managing online help resources. You can use IPF's authoring tools to create the *help panels* that are displayed in help windows at run time when a user presses the F1 (help) key, selects Help from the menu bar, or presses a Help button. In addition to providing online help for Presentation Manager applications, IPF can also be used in a standalone mode to provide online documentation, tutorials, or as a general-purpose hypertext authoring facility.

Creating Help

Help information is created in ASCII source files using a tag language that embeds formatting information directly into the text (it uses the GML markup language). Once the source files are created, they are run through the IPF compiler that translates them into an IPF library format. The IPF compiler can generate a table of contents and an index for help information. IPF allows you to embed pictures (bitmaps) inside the help panels (using the artwork tag). Help panels can be nested using "hypertext-like" links (the link tag). Bitmaps may also be "hot-spotted" with hypertext links into other panels.

Information within help windows is displayed in *viewports*. The default viewport occupies the entire help window. Multiple viewports may be defined within the same help window, and handled separately. For example, two viewports may be defined in a help window; the first may be used to display a picture, while the second contains text that explains the picture. The user may scroll the text in the window, but the picture won't move because it occupies a separate viewport. In addition, application-controlled viewports allow an application to take direct control of a viewport at run time, and to display in it any kind of information (for example, a film clip).

Compiling Help Files

The help source files (.IPF) are compiled to produce a help library. The IPF compiler is invoked using the **IPFC** command. Support for languages other than English is provided by specifying the /COUNTRY, /CODEPAGE, and /LANGUAGE parameters in the IPFC command. These parameters affect the collating sequence used when creating a table of contents or index.

Invoking Help From a PM Application

Before a PM application can display help panels, it must go through the following preparation steps:

1. *Create a Help Table as a PM Resource.* A help table is a PM resource that is defined in a resource script file using the HELPTABLE keyword. The entries inside the help table define each application window for which help is provided and point to a HELPSUBTABLE resource that contain a list of help HELPSUBITEM resources. The HELPSUBITEM resources identify each item within the window for which help is to be provided, and the panel identifier of the help panel.
2. *Create a Help Instance.* The application must pass the help table to IPF and create a help instance, using the **WinCreateHelpInstance()** function. This function is normally called from the main() program immediately after creating the application's main window, but before entering the PM message processing loop. The call creates the application's main help window (initially invisible) and passes it the name of the help library to be loaded.
3. *Associate the Help Instance.* The help instance is associated with an application.
4. *Display the Help Panel.* Help panels are displayed in help windows by IPF as a result of user hitting the F1 key, selecting help from the menu, or pressing a Help pushbutton. Each of these actions generate a **WM_HELP** message that is trapped by IPF. The IPF runtime then determines the active application window and uses the current help table to identify the help panel for that window. The displayed help panel appears as a child window of the main help window.
5. *Ending Help.* Before an application terminates, it should terminate its help instance by issuing a **WinDestroyHelpInstance()** call. This function is called before destroying the application's main window.

THE ANATOMY OF A PM PROGRAM

A PM program consists of a main() procedure and a set of window procedures. The main() procedure allocates global data, does initialization, and creates the PM objects. It then goes into a loop waiting for messages to be placed on its queue. When it finds a message, it dispatches it to the appropriate window procedure. When a special WM_QUIT message is received, main() cleans up after itself and terminates the program.

All PM programs use more or less the same main() template which consists of about 40 lines of code. PM programmers usually paste this setup code into a source file when writing a new program. The heart of a PM application is its window procedures. This is the code that controls the attributes of a window and responds to the messages it generates. Figure 39-7 presents the structure of a PM program. Here's a step-by-step description:

1. **Connect to PM**. Issue a WinInitialize call to obtain an anchor block handle from PM. This handle is used with subsequent commands.

2. **Load the resources**. This is a good place to load the separate resources you created using the PM tools. These separate resources can be text strings, text files, binary files containing graphics, help, or other separate pieces of information. PM provides several specialized API calls for loading resources such as WinLoadString, WinLoadPtr, WinLoadDlg, WinLoadMenu, and so on. Help-enabled applications require that you issue a WinCreateHelpInstance followed by WinAssociateHelpInstance.

3. **Create the message queue**. Issue the WinCreateMsgQueue call to create your application's message queue and obtain a handle for it. You can specify the queue size through a parameter. The default size is 10 messages. The queue is the primary mechanism by which your application communicates with PM.

4. **Register the window classes**. You must issue a WinRegisterClass call for every window class before creating one or more instances of a window. This call registers the window class and its associated window procedure with PM.

5. **Create and display the main windows**. First, create all the windows that are direct children of the PM desktop. These are the most "senior" windows in your application. Issue a WinCreateStdWindow call to create a "standard" window. This call returns two handles, one that identifies the frame of the standard window, and one that identifies its client area.

6. **Create and display the child windows**. Now that you've obtained the handles of the parent windows, you can create child windows using WinCreateStdWindow or WinCreateWindow. Continue this process until you've created all the descendant windows for your application. You may also want to issue WinSetWindowPos calls to position the windows on your desktop. Remember, the child windows always

get displayed on top of their parent window. Child windows are positioned relative to the lower-left corner of the parent window.

7. ***Enter the message dispatch loop.*** At this point, your PM program is ready to receive messages and do some work. The main program enters a "while" loop issuing WinGetMsg calls to obtain messages from PM and then turns around and issues WinDispatchMsg calls to call the appropriate window procedure via PM. The program will remain in this loop until the WinGetMsg call receives a WM_QUIT message. An application can terminate its own loop by posting a WM_QUIT message to its queue.

8. ***Get a message.*** A WinGetMsg call retrieves a message from the application queue. If there are no messages in the queue the WinGetMsg call blocks until a message arrives.

9. ***Dispatch a message.*** A WinDispatchMsg will call the appropriate window procedure via PM and pass it the message to be processed. Notice in the figure that control is now passed to a window procedure. The window procedure's code is straightforward. It consists of a switch statement with a case for each message type the procedure intends to process. The real work of a PM application is done within the case statements. The messages that are not of interest to the window procedure, end up in the default section of the switch statement. Notice that the default consists of handing the message over to WinDefWindowProc. This is a PM-supplied window procedure that handles all the messages your window procedure is not interested in processing.

10. ***Destroy all windows.*** A well-behaved PM application cleans up after itself when it drops out of the loop. The WinDestroyWindow call releases the window's resources.

11. ***Destroy the message queue.*** The WinDestroyMsgQueue is issued to release the queue.

12. ***Disconnect from PM.*** The WinTerminate call disconnects the application from PM.

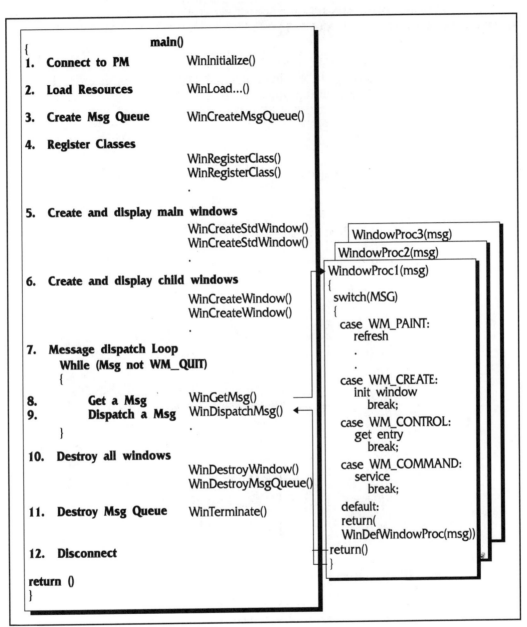

Figure 39-7. The Anatomy of a PM Program.

"HELLO WORLD FROM PM"

This section shows you the steps necessary to develop a simple PM application. We're going to code the PM version of the world famous "Hello World" application. The code will display "Hello from Presentation Manager" on the screen.

The Display

Figure 39-8 is a screen capture of the output produced by this program.

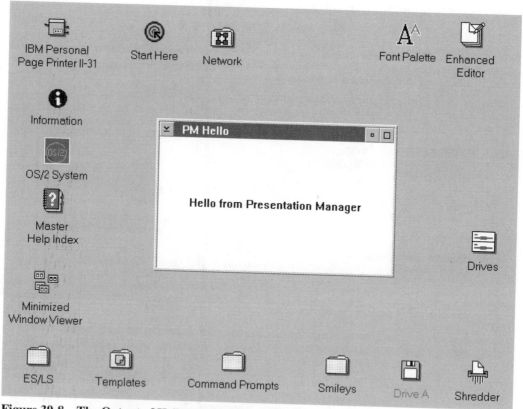

Figure 39-8. The Output of Hello World Using PM.

The HELLOPM.C Program

Figure 39-9 shows the listing for the program that created "Hello from PM." Like all PM programs, this program consists of a **main()** procedure that provides the initialization and setup and the window procedures. The code for the **main()** procedure is straightforward. Here is what it does:

1. Declares the global variables.

2. Connects to PM and creates the application queue.

3. Registers a window class called "HelloWindow" and associates it with the window procedure: **HelloWindowProc()**. It tells PM that the window is resizable.

4. Sets the flags for all the child control windows and options that will appear in the window's frame.

5. Issues the call to create a standard window with the control options that are specified.

6. Positions the window on the desktop.

7. Executes the message loop until WM_QUIT is issued.

8. Terminates PM and releases resources.

The code for the window procedure **HelloWindowProc()** is also straightforward. It consists of a switch statement which processes only three messages: WM_ERASE-BACKGROUND, WM_PAINT, and WM_CLOSE. The rest of the message types are of no interest and get returned to PM's default handler window procedure. The bulk of the code is used to process the WM_PAINT message. Here's how this message gets processed:

1. A WinBeginPaint call is issued to obtain a presentation space handle from PM.

2. A WinDrawText call is issued to display the text. Notice how the different attribute options are specified.

3. A WinEndPaint call is issued to release the presentation space.

This may seem like a lot of work just to issue a simple "Hello World." In fairness to PM, a lot of this code consists of the standard **main()** template. PM also provides many window features that are not included in your standard "Hello World" programs. Of course, the purpose of this exercise was to get you acquainted with the structure of a PM program. "Hello World" does that well.

```
/******************************************************************************/
/*    PROGRAM NAME: HELLOPM - a Presentaion Manager hello example             */
/*                                                                            */
/*    PROGRAM DESCRIPTION:  This program demonstrates a simple PM program     */
/*                          which only displays hello.                        */
/*                                                                            */
/*    PROGRAM INVOCATION:    HELLOPM                                          */
/******************************************************************************/
#include <string.h>
#define INCL_WIN
#define INCL_GPI                              /* include Win calls            */
#include <os2.h>                              /* include Gpi calls            */
                                              /* PM header file               */
/*_____
/* global variables and declares                                           __*/
/*_____
HAB   hab;                                  /* PM anchor block handle        */
CHAR  szHello[] = "Hello from Presentation Manager";

MRESULT EXPENTRY HelloWindowProc(HWND hwnd, ULONG msg, MPARAM mp1, MPARAM mp2);

/*_____
/* Main routine.                                                           __*/
/*_____
void cdecl main(  )
{
  HMQ    hmq;
  HWND   hwndClient;                         /* Message queue handle          */
  HWND   hwndFrame;                          /* Client area window handle     */
  QMSG   qmsg;                               /* Frame window handle           */
  ULONG  flCreate;                           /* Message from message queue    */
                                             /* Window creation control flags */

  hab = WinInitialize( NULL );               /* Initialize PM                 */
  hmq = WinCreateMsgQueue( hab, 0 );         /* Create a message queue        */

  WinRegisterClass(
    hab,                                     /* Register window class         */
    "HelloWindow",                           /* Anchor block handle           */
    HelloWindowProc,                         /* Window class name             */
    CS_SIZEREDRAW,                           /* Address of window procedure   */
    0);                                      /* Class style                   */
                                             /* No extra window words         */

  flCreate = FCF_TITLEBAR | FCF_SYSMENU |    /* Set frame control flags       */
             FCF_SIZEBORDER | FCF_MINMAX |
             FCF_SHELLPOSITION | FCF_TASKLIST;

  hwndFrame = WinCreateStdWindow(
             HWND_DESKTOP,                    /* Desktop window is parent      */
             0L,                              /* No frame styles               */
             &flCreate,                       /* Frame control flag            */
             "HelloWindow",                   /* Client window class name      */
             "Hello PM",                      /* No window text                */
             0L,                              /* No special class style        */
             NULL,                            /* Resource is in .EXE file      */
             255,                             /* Frame window identifier       */
             &hwndClient);                    /* Client window handle          */

  WinSetWindowPos(hwndFrame, HWND_TOP, 230, 150, 300, 185,
             SWP_SIZE | SWP_MOVE | SWP_ACTIVATE | SWP_SHOW);
```

Figure 39-9 (Part 1 of 2).   The HELLOPM.C Listing.

```
/*_____*/
/* Get and dispatch messages    */
/*_____*/
while( WinGetMsg( hab, &qmsg, NULL, 0, 0 ) )
   WinDispatchMsg( hab, &qmsg );

WinDestroyWindow( hwndFrame );      /* Destroy the window  */
WinDestroyMsgQueue( hmq );          /* Destroy the queue   */
WinTerminate( hab );                /* terminate           */
}
/*_____*/
/* Window Procedure for Hello.                           */
/*_____*/
MRESULT EXPENTRY HelloWindowProc( HWND hwnd, ULONG msg,
                                  MPARAM mp1, MPARAM mp2 )
{
   HPS    hps;                       /* Presentation Space handle */
   RECTL  rc;                        /* Rectangle coordinates     */

   switch( msg )
   {
     case WM_ERASEBACKGROUND:
       /*_____*/
       /* cause window background to be */
       /* painted in SYSCLR_WINDOW      */
       /*_____*/
       return (MRESULT)( TRUE );

     case WM_PAINT:
       /*_____*/
       /* paint the window             */
       /*_____*/
       hps = WinBeginPaint( hwnd, NULL, &rc ); /* Create a presentation space */
       WinDrawText(hps,                        /* presentation space          */
                   -1,szHello,                 /* string, calculate strlen    */
                   &rc,                         /* rectangle from WinBeginPaint*/
                   CLR_DARKBLUE,SYSCLR_WINDOW,  /* Fore/Background colors      */
                   DT_VCENTER | DT_CENTER);     /* string placement in rect.   */

       WinEndPaint( hps );
       break;

     case WM_CLOSE:
       /*_____*/
       /* cause the application to end */
       /*_____*/
       WinPostMsg( hwnd, WM_QUIT, OL, OL );
       break;

     default:
       /*_____*/
       /* unknown messages to default  */
       /*_____*/
       return WinDefWindowProc( hwnd, msg, mp1, mp2 );
   }
   return FALSE;
}
```

Figure 39-9 (Part 2 of 2). The HELLOPM.C Listing.

Chapter 40

SOM, OOP, and WPS Classes

"If you want to shrink something, you must first allow it to expand.
If you want to take something, you must first allow it to be given.
This is called the subtle perception of the way things are."

Lao-tzu

This chapter provides a crash course that covers the System Object Model (SOM), Object-Oriented programming (OOP), and the Workplace Shell (WPS) class libraries. The WPS class libraries contain the gold, SOM is the key to the vault, and OOP is something you must know about to understand SOM terminology. We're really after tools to write these sizzling OOUI applications we've been raving about. In this crash course, we start by clarifying the SOM and OOP terminology, and we then provide you a shopper's view of the SOM/WPS classes. What are they? What do they do? How do I use them in my programs? In the next chapter we will show you how to develop a SOM/WPS application. This chapter and the next will prepare you for Part VII, where we develop an elaborate OOUI Club Med client using SOM/WPS classes.

SOM AND OBJECT-ORIENTED PROGRAMMING

Why are we introducing OOP near the end of a nice C book? In Chapter 38, "A Taxonomy of GUI and OOUI Tools," we explained that we were in the market for a good OOUI tool that could help us generate the Club Med client. We concluded that the best choice in our time frame was SOM and the OS/2 2.0 Workplace Shell classes. SOM thrusts us right into the world of objects, class libraries, and OOP. The task ahead of us is to master "the subtle perception of the way things are" in the world of objects. We will start by explaining the concepts and terminology that capture the essence of SOM objects.

What Is SOM?

The System Object Model (SOM) provides a language-neutral environment for defining, manipulating, and releasing class libraries. SOM objects are language-neutral in the sense that they can be defined in one programming language and used by applications or objects written in another programming language (see Figure 40-1). SOM makes it possible for objects and classes to be shared and ported across OO languages. It does not compete with C++, Smalltalk, C, or any programming language; it just complements them. SOM provides a solution to this very real and pressing problem: *How do you develop class libraries that have properties similar to our current procedure libraries?*

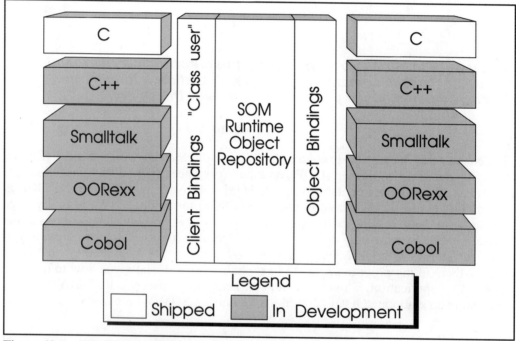

Figure 40-1. The SOM Architecture *(adapted with permission from Roger Sessions).*

Today, SOM allows a developer to define classes and methods using C. This means that C programmers should be able to use SOM quickly to develop object-oriented programs without having to learn a new language syntax. SOM, however, is specifically designed to work with both procedural (non-object-oriented) languages and object-oriented languages such as C++. SOM will support both the Borland and IBM C++ products in late 1992. Once 32-bit C++ is available, it will become the language of choice for many programmers wishing to build system class libraries. However, C++ without the SOM runtime is not usable for building binary class libraries, because:

1. The binaries of one C++ compiler are not acceptable to another.
2. An application that binds to a C++ DLL will need to be recompiled if the DLL is replaced with a new release, unless the developers make almost no changes to their implementation.
3. The use of the libraries from any other language (even C) would be almost impossible.

When C or C++ is combined with SOM, these problems are removed. This is what made it practical to build the Workplace Shell using SOM as an OO platform. SOM class libraries (present and future) are designed to be part of the operating system (OS/2 today and AIX tomorrow). The promise of SOM is to make *OO technology part of the operating system, not part of a programming language.* SOM allows the integration between operating-system objects and user-supplied objects to be as efficient as possible without requiring users to recompile their programs when the next version of the operating system appears.

SOM is packaged as part of the OS/2 2.0 Toolkit. It comes with a run-time library and a set of utilities for building, externalizing, and manipulating software objects.

SOM and CORBA

The next release of SOM will comply with the Object Management Group's (OMG) **Common Object Request Broker (CORBA)**. So what does this mean? The OMG consortium, which includes more than 160 corporate and associate members, was founded to specifically advance the use of object technology in distributed environments. The OMG's charter is to create nothing less than a platform-independent communication highway for distributed objects. The Object Request Broker (ORB) will ultimately allow objects to transparently make requests and receive responses (see Figure 40-2). The ORB "will provide interoperability between applications on different machines in heterogeneous distributed environments and seamlessly interconnect multiple object systems."[1]

OMG will achieve this ambitious goal by following two steps: 1) "It will turn everything into nails," and 2) "It will give everyone a hammer."

- The "nail" is the CORBA Interface Definition Language (IDL). The IDL allows object providers to specify in a standard definition language the interface and structure of the objects they provide. An IDL-defined *contract* binds the providers of distributed object services to their clients. It also provides a standard mechanism for interfacing to the object highway.
- The "hammer" includes the set of distributed services OMG providers will supply. These services will determine which objects are on the network, which methods are provided, and which *object interface adapters* are supported. The location of the object should be transparent to the client and object implementation. It should not matter whether the object is in the same process or across the world.

Does this all sound familiar? It should be. We're describing the "object wave" of client/server computing; this time it's between cooperating objects as opposed to

---

[1] From **Object Management Architecture Guide**, "Revision 1.0" (OMG TC Document 90.9.1).

cooperating processes. The goal of this new wave is to create multivendor, multiOS, multilanguage "legoware" using objects. Vendors such as Sun, HP, IBM, and NCR will all be using CORBA as their standard IDL-defined interface into the object highway. The IDL is the *contract* that brings it all together. The CORBA compliant SOM is the packaging foundation on which IBM is building most of its OO plans (including some of the Taligent work).

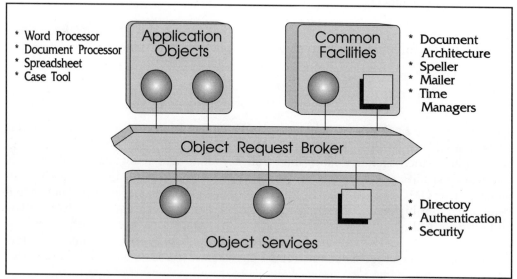

Figure 40-2. OMG's Reference Model. (Source: Object Management Group).

SOM: Objects

The basic unit of organization of SOM programs is the object. A SOM *object* consists of instance data and the *methods—that is, actions to be performed on the data. An object has a public* interface that defines how other objects or applications can interact with it. An object also has a *private* component that implements the methods. The object's implementation is *encapsulated*—that is, hidden from the public view. *Instance data*—that is, object variables—can be declared private (the default) or public. Private instance data can only be accessed by methods of the class. Public instance data, on the other hand, is part of the published external interface.

The public methods and instance data are the permanent interface between the object and the outside world. Old methods must continue to be supported when an object changes. The public interface is a *binding contract* between the class providers and their clients.

SOM allows you to change the object's internal implementation—including adding new methods, changing unpublished instance variables, relocating methods upward in the class hierarchy, and inserting new classes above your class in the hierarchy—without affecting the applications that use your objects. In fact, the client applications don't even need to be recompiled. This is one of SOM's great strengths.

SOM: Classes, Inheritance, and Polymorphism

SOM *classes* define the behavior of sets of like objects. You can think of the class as a description of an object. The class defines the object's instance data and methods (see Figure 40-3).

Polymorphism is a high-browed way of saying that the same method can do different things depending on the class that implements it. Polymorphism is the mechanism that allows subclasses to override an inherited method (and "do their own thing") without affecting the ancestor's methods. Looking at Figure 40-4, you can see polymorphism in action (hit the "accelerator" on a Maserati and on a Volvo, and then compare notes).

Inheritance is the mechanism that allows you to create new child classes, also known as *subclasses*, from existing parent classes. The child classes inherit their parent's methods and data structures. You can add new methods to a child's class or *override*—that is, modify—inherited methods to define new class behaviors. The parent's method is not affected by this modification. Figure 40-5 shows a typical class family tree.

Encapsulation, inheritance, and polymorphism are the three pillars of object-oriented programming. They allow you to create reusable objects without distributing the source code. They form the essence of the "subtle perception of the way things are."

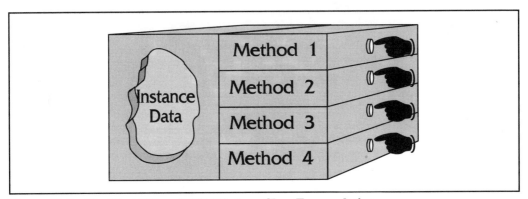

Figure 40-3. The First Pillar of OO Wisdom: Class Encapsulation.

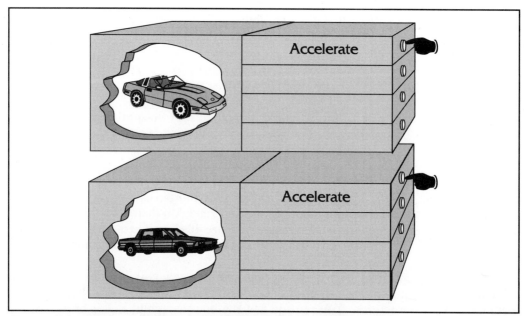

Figure 40-4.   The Second Pillar of OO Wisdom: Polymorphism.

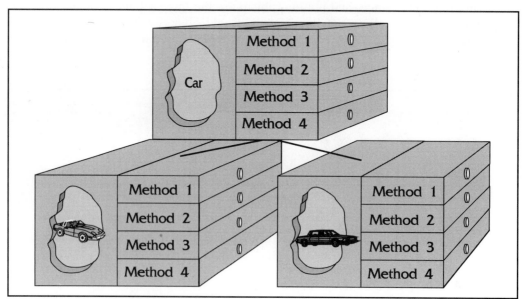

Figure 40-5.   The Third Pillar of OO Wisdom: Inheritance and Subclassing.

SOM's Object Factory: The Metaclass

The *metaclass* is a class description of an object that creates other objects. This very useful SOM feature is not as intuitive as the rest of OO programming. As a result it may take some time to grow on you. The trick is to understand that every SOM class is itself a real object. Because SOM classes are real objects, and all objects are instances of some class, it follows that a SOM class object must also be an instance of some other class. SOM calls this special class a *metaclass*. Let's further explore this concept.

A SOM class is defined at compile time. A SOM *class object* is a run-time implementation of a SOM class. Objects that are instances of the class are also created dynamically at run time by the application. The methods that an object responds to are called *instance methods* because any object instance can perform them. But before instance methods can be used, an object instance must exist. Who creates the object instances?

The answer is the *class methods* (also called factory methods or constructors). These are methods that an object's class responds to. But all object instances must belong to a class; so what is the class of an object class? It belongs to its *metaclass*. What is a metaclass? It's a SOM class that defines factory methods for classes. Metaclasses are classes of classes. The class methods for an object are listed in the description of its metaclass (just like an object's instance methods are given in its class description). The relationship between objects, classes, and metaclasses is shown in Figure 40-6.

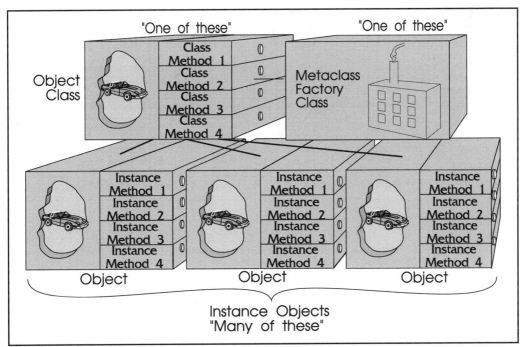

Figure 40-6. The relationship between objects, a class object, and metaclasses.

Metaclasses and Class Hierarchies

Don't confuse the notion of a "parent class" with a "metaclass." The parent of a class is another class from which instance methods are inherited. The "metaclass," on the other hand, provides the factory methods for a class, not instance methods. The parent class and the metaclass of a class will always will be different. In addition, a metaclass has its own inheritance hierarchy.

The example shown in Figure 40-7 should help clarify these relationships. The left-hand side of the figure shows the parent-child relationships between user-written classes (**vehicles** and its descendants) and the built-in SOM classes. The right-hand side shows the class (and metaclass) relationships. This elaborate class hierarchy (ours and SOM's) is used to create two type of object instances: sports car objects and family car objects. The instances of these objects belong to the **sports car** class and **family car** class. Both these classes are descendants of the **automobile** class, which in turn is a descendant of **vehicles**. And **vehicles** is a descendant of **SOMObject**. The buck stops there.

Looking at the top right of Figure 40-7, you'll notice that **SOMClass** is the root class for all SOM metaclasses. It defines the essential behavior common to all SOM class objects.[2] If a metaclass is not explicitly specified, it automatically defaults to the one associated with its parent's class. Notice that we've created our own hierarchy of user-written metaclasses (**vehicle-factory** and its descendants). Why?

Typically, you create your own metaclasses to define new class methods for your objects, or to override the behavior of the generic class methods supplied in SOMClass. Here's some reasons why you would want to supply your own metaclasses:

- To create metaclass instance data (by overriding the methods somInit, somUninit, and somDumpSelfInt).
- To intercept the constructor methods (somNew, somRenew, and somClassReady) and add your own hooks at creation time. For example, you may want to log information about new objects in a database for persistent object storage.
- To track object instances and provide object management information that is global to a set of object instances. For example, you can create your own object broker and have it communicate with other brokers to provide distributed object directory services. However, if you can wait SOM/CORBA will provide these services in future releases.
- To allocate and deallocate memory and provide your own automatic garbage collection services.

---

[2] **SOMClass** is also a subclass of **SOMObject**. This causes all classes to inherit the same set of basic instance methods common to all SOM objects, and allows SOM classes to be real objects in the SOM run-time environment. **SOMClass** also has the unique distinction of being its own metaclass.

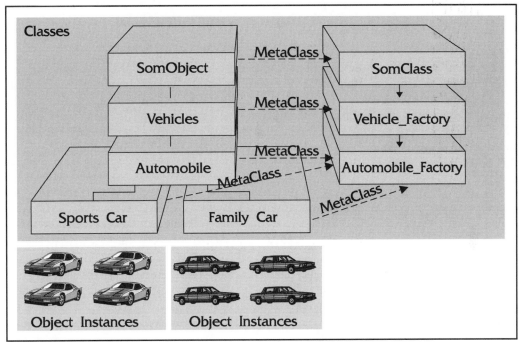

Figure 40-7. Hierarchies of Classes, Metaclasses, and Objects.

SOM's Object Management Services

The classes that make up the SOM run-time environment—**SOMObject**, **SOMClass**, and **SOMClassMgr**—are packaged in a DLL named SOM.DLL. This library also contains a collection of related functions for initializing and customizing the SOM run-time environment. A single instance of a special **SOMClassMgr** class is created during SOM initialization, and is referred to as the **SOMClassMgrObject**. Its job is to maintain a *registry*—that is, a run-time directory—of all SOM classes that exist within the current process, and to assist in the dynamic loading and unloading of class libraries packaged as OS/2 DLLs. When a class is referenced for the first time, the **SOMClassMgrObject** will load the appropriate OS/2 DLL and construct a run-time instance of the class.

As we explained in the previous section, one of the key features of SOM is that SOM classes are real objects that play an active role in the run-time environment. **SOMClass** provides the methods for manufacturing object instances (somNew and somRenew), which you may want to override to create your own metaclasses. These metaclasses can be used by your applications to dynamically obtain (and provide) information about a class and its methods at run time.

SOM's: Object Interface Definition Language (OIDL)

SOM, like CORBA, provides an Object Interface Definition Language (OIDL) for defining classes in a language-independent manner. This is SOM's way of turning everything into "nails" so that it can provide everybody with a "hammer." The OIDL completely describes a class. This includes its methods, instance data, relationship to other classes, and its metaclasses. The OIDL is a *contract* between SOM class implementers and the programs that use their classes. It is also the entry point for creating SOM applications. We will be seeing a lot more of the OIDL in the remaining part of this book.

SOM and the Workplace Shell Classes

Yes, SOM is marvelous and is destined for a great future, but how does it help us create OOUI front-ends for client/server today? Remember, this is what got us into the world of OO in the first place. The answer, of course, is that the OS/2 2.0 is implemented as a set of class libraries that use SOM for their object model. So let's move on to the next section and discover what the Workplace Shell classes can do for us.

THE WORKPLACE SHELL CLASSES

So how do I know a class library when I see one? Where do I start? What do I look for? In this section, we will walk you step by step through the Workplace Shell class library and answer some questions as we walk along.

Which Class Library?

This can be a difficult question to answer if you're faced with dozens of competing class libraries. Here's the thought process we went through:

1. *What problem am I trying to solve?* The problem at hand is finding a class library that will allow us to create WPS objects. Remember, we're in the market for a class library for creating OOUI front-ends that are totally integrated into the WPS. This requirement at the time of writing leaves us with one choice: the SOM/WPS class libraries using the 32-bit C Set/2 compiler.

2. *Who else is using this class library?* Check references. You don't want to build your code using "fly-by-night" class libraries that are no longer supported. The WPS class libraries run the OS/2 desktop. They are used by millions of end users, they have gone through a long product test cycle, and they appear to work. When bugs are found, we expect a million people to call IBM support and get them fixed (bad bugs will make the headlines in PC Week). We're already working on an OS/2 platform, so it looks like we haven't increased our risks.

3. *So what does this class library do?* That's an easy one to answer. Go to any OS/2 machine and look at the Workplace Shell (see Figure 40-8). Every object that you see on that desktop was created using WPS classes. This includes the folders, the shredder, the clock, the desktop, the system folder, the printer object, the file object, and everything else.

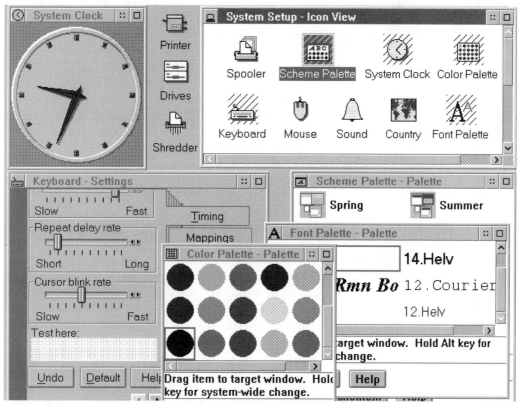

Figure 40-8.   These Objects Can All be in Your Programs Using WPS Classes.

First Encounters: The WPS Class Hierarchy

But, what does a programmer see? The first thing a class provider typically shows you is a family tree of classes, also known as the "class hierarchy." By looking at one, you can see at a glance all the classes in the system and their ancestral origins. The class hierarchy for the WPS classes is shown in Figure 40-9. We've put a three-dimensional frame around the "classes of interest." These are the classes you'll want to get to know very intimately. Why? Because it takes intimate knowledge to know what goodies you can inherit from a class when you create yours.

Looking at Figure 40-9, we've already talked quite a bit about the SOM ancestral classes. The WPS classes were created using SOM, so it is not surprising that the three SOM classes are at the very top of the hierarchy. **SOMObject** is the great ancestor of all the WPS classes. **SOMClass** is the root of all WPS class objects; it is the original *metaclass*. **SOMClassMgr** maintains the *registry* of all the WPS classes at run time.

Moving down the class pecking order, we meet **WPObject**, the "Grandpa" of all the WPS classes. This is the class that contains all the WPS family jewels. At the next level, we encounter a trio of siblings, known as the "storage classes." They add persistent storage to the WPS class services. The first sibling, **WPAbstract**, uses the (.INI) system file as a storage medium; it maintains pointers to objects that appear on the Workplace but are not part of the file system, such as running programs. The second sibling, **WPFileSystem**, uses files as its persistent store; its objects, such as bitmaps and folders, live permanently in the file system. The third sibling, **WPTransient**, has no persistent store; it is used to subclass short-lived objects such as print jobs. Your application should subclass the WPS storage class (or one of its descendants) that best models the persistent behavior of your object.

Going further down the hierarchy, you will encounter the familiar Workplace Shell Objects in the form of classes. They are all yours to subclass. If you see anything you like on the desktop and you want it in your program, just "subclass" it. In the Club Med application, we will also be subclassing **WPFolder**, a child of **WpFileSystem** that knows how to create folders. We will be using lots of folders, which explains why **WpFolder** also got the 3-D look.

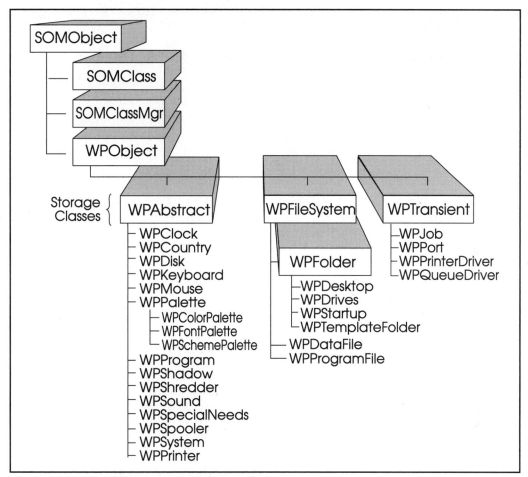

Figure 40-9. The SOM/WPS Class Hierarchy.

Second Encounters: WPS Classes and Methods

So now that you know how these objects are organized, where do you go for more information? You must obtain the object's "spec sheet." Like spec sheets everywhere, an object spec sheet gives you the features, functions, and benefits of the product they describe: in this case, the object. An object spec sheet will describe the object and the methods it provides. The methods provide the object's contractual interfaces to the outside world. Methods can be categorized by the type of service they provide, whether they are instance methods or class methods (review SOM section for explanation), and whether they are new methods or overrides of old ones.

Table 40-1 provides the spec sheets for eight WPS/SOM Classes. We've included the three SOM venerable ancestor classes, the supercharged **WPObject** root WPS class, the WPS storage class trio, and finally the **WPFolder** class. These are the classes we put in 3-D boxes on the class hierarchy to mark their importance. Each class spec sheet includes a class description and the enumeration of the methods they support by category. Please take a few minutes to quickly read the spec sheets as part of our "let's get acquainted with the WPS classes" process. You should get some idea of what these classes really do, how complicated they are, and the functions they provide. If, after looking at the specs, you're still interested, than read on.

Table 40-1 (Part 1 of 4). SOM/WPS Class Descriptions.

SOMObject Class Description			
This is the root class for all SOM classes. It defines the essential behavior common to all SOM objects. As SOMObject has no instance data, so it contributes nothing to the size of derived classes.			
Initialization/ Termination Methods	**Get Info Methods**	**Testing Methods**	**Debug Methods**
somFree somInit somUninit	somGetClass somGetClassName somGetSize	somIsA somIsInstance somRespondsTo	somDumpSelf somDumpSelfInt somPrintSelf
Dispatch Methods			
somDispatchA	somDispatchD	somDispatchL	somDispatchV
SOMClass Class Description			
This is the root class for all SOM metaclasses. It defines the essential behavior common to all SOM classes. It has two generic methods for manufacturing object instances (somNew and somRenew), and a suite of methods for constructing classes. It also has methods that can be used to dynamically obtain or modify information about a class and its methods at run time. SOMClass is the only class with itself as a metaclass (life has to start somewhere). All the derived SOM classes are expected to have SOMClass or a class derived from SOMClass as their metaclass.			
Get Info Methods	**Initialization/ Termination Methods**	**Update Info Methods**	**Find Methods**
somGetApplyStub somGetClassData somGetClassMtab somGetInstanceOffset somGetInstancePartSize somGetInstanceSize somGetMethodOffset somGetName somGetNumMethods somGetNumStaticMethods somGetParent somGetPClsMtab	somAddStaticMethod somClassReady somInitClass somOverrideSMethod	somSetClassData	somFindMethod somFindMethodOk
	Instance Creation (Factory) Methods	**Testing Methods**	**Overridden Methods**
	somNew somRenew	somCheckVersion somDescendedFrom somSupportsMethod	somDumpSelfInt somInit somUninit
SOMClassMgr Class Description			
One instance of SOMClassMgr is created during SOM initialization. It acts as a run-time registry for all SOM class objects that have been created or dynamically loaded by the current process. Each SOM class automatically registers itself with the SOMClassMgr instance (pointed to by the global variable, SOMClassMgrObject) during the final stage of its initialization. You can subclass SOMClassMgr to augment the functionality of its registry (for example, to make it persistent).			
Registration Methods	**Get Info Methods**	**Find Methods**	**Overridden methods**
somLoadClassFile somLocateClassFile somRegisterClass somUnloadClassFile somUnregisterClass	somGetInitFunction **Misc. Methods** somMergeInto	somFindClass somFindClsInFile somClassFromId	somDumpSelfInt somInit somUninit

Table 40-1 (Part 2 of 4). SOM/WPS Class Descriptions.

WPObject Class Description				
This is the root Workplace object class. This is the fundamental class from which all workplace objects are derived, irrespective of where they are actually stored. Immediate descendant classes of WPObject are called storage classes, since they take responsibility for storing the object information, typically in a persistent form. Predefined workplace object storage classes are listed here.				

Settings Notebook Methods	Error Handling Methods	Object Usage Methods	Memory Management Methods

wpAddObjectGeneral-
  Page
wpAddSettingsPages
wpInsertSettingsPage
	wpQueryError
	wpSetError
		wpAddToObjUseList
		wpDeleteFromObj-
		  UseList
		wpFindUseItem
		wpUnlockObject
			wpAllocMem
			wpFreeMem

Save/Restore Methods	Object Info Methods	Popup Menu Methods	Overridden Methods

wpRestoreData
wpRestoreLong
wpRestoreState
wpRestoreString
wpSaveData
wpSaveImmediate
wpSaveLong
wpSaveState
wpSaveString
	wpQueryConfirmations
	wpQueryDefaultHelp
	wpQueryDefaultView
	wpQueryDetailsData
	wpQueryIcon
	wpQueryIconData
	wpQueryStyle
	wpQueryTitle
	wpSetDefaultHelp
	wpSetDefaultView
	wpSetIcon
	wpSetIconData
	wpSetStyle
	wpSetTitle
		wpClose
		wpCopyObject
		wpCreateFromTemplate
		wpCreateShadowObject
		wpDelete
		wpDisplayHelp
		wpFilterPopupMenu
		wpHide
		wpInsertPopup-
		  MenuItems
		wpMenuItemHelp-
		  Selected
		wpMenuItemSelected
		wpModifyPopupMenu
		wpMoveObject
		wpOpen
		wpPrintObject
		wpRestore
			somFree
			somInit
			somUninit
			wpclsCreateDefault-
			  Templates
			wpclsFindObjectEnd
			wpclsFindObjectFirst
			wpclsFindObjectNext
			wpclsInitData
			wpclsMakeAwake
			wpclsNew
			wpclsQueryDefaultHelp
			wpclsQueryDefaultView
			wpclsQueryDetails
			wpclsQueryDetailsInfo
			wpclsQueryError
			wpclsQueryFolder
			wpclsQueryIcon
			wpclsQueryIconData
			wpclsQueryObject
			wpclsSetError

Miscellaneous Methods	Direct Manipulation Methods	Setup/Methods Methods	
wpCnrInsertObject wpCnrRemoveObject wpCnrSetEmphasis wpConfirmDelete wpCopiedFromTemplate wpDoesObjectMatch wpRegisterView wpSwitchTo	wpDragOver wpDraggedOverObject wpDrop wpDroppedOnObject wpEndConversation wpFormatDragItem wpRender wpRenderComplete	wpFree wpInitData wpScanSetupString wpSetup wpUnInitData	wpclsQuerySettings- PageSize wpclsQueryStyle wpclsQueryTitle wpclsUnInitData somUnInit somInitClass somNew somRenew

Table 40-1 (Part 3 of 4). SOM/WPS Class Descriptions.

WPTransient Class Description
This is the non-persistent object storage class. The WPTransient class is a storage class with no storage medium. That means that instances of object classes derived from WPTransient do not persist across reboots. This class is available for applications that need to utilize a large amount of workplace functionality (such as context menus and settings notebooks) in their object class without having to be a file, directory, or a record in the INI file. An instance of this class can be created as a Workplace object. There are no instances of this class initially created by the system.

Overridden Methods			
wpCopyObject	wpclsQueryIconData	wpclsQueryStyle	wpclsQueryTitle

WPAbstract Class Description
This is the abstract object storage class. The storage medium for objects that are descendants of the WPAbstract class is the INI file. In other words, any object class derived from WPAbstract will have persistent storage for its instance variables in the INI file. Note that an abstract object does not have a file name, just a numeric handle that can be used to identify it. An instance of this class can be created as a Workplace object. There are no instances of this class initially created by the system.

Overridden Methods			
wpCopyObject	wpCreateFromTemplate	wpSaveImmediate	wpSaveState
wpRestoreState	wpMoveObject	wpQueryIconData	wpSetIconData
wpSetTitle	wpclsQueryTitle		

WPFileSystem Class Description
This is the file system object storage class. WPFileSystem is the storage class that represents all file system objects including directory (folder), data file, executable file, and root directory (drive) objects. This class also provides persistent storage of instance variables for all classes derived from it. A Workplace object of this class cannot be created.

New Methods	Overridden Methods		
wpAddFileMenuPage	wpAddSettings	wpCopyObject	wpCreateFromTemplate
wpAddFile1Page	wpDoesObjectMatch	wpDraggedOverObject	wpDroppedOnObject
wpAddFile2Page	wpFilterPopupMenu	wpFormatDragItem	wpMenuItemSelected
wpAddFile3Page	wpModifyPopupMenu	wpMoveObject	wpOpen
wpQueryHandle	wpQueryDetailsData	wpQueryIconData	wpRestoreState
wpQueryRealName	wpSaveImmediate	wpSaveState	wpSetIconData
wpQueryType	wpSetTitle	wpUnInitData	wpclsQueryInstanceFilter
wpSetRealName	wpclsQueryInstanceType	wpclsInitData	wpclsQueryDetailsInfo
wpSetType	wpclsQueryIconData	wpclsQueryTitle	

Table 40-1 (Part 4 of 4).   SOM/WPS Class Descriptions.

WPFolder Class Description

This is the folder object class. An instance of this class can be created as a Workplace object. An instance of this class is created initially by the system in its template form. It has the title "Folder" and resides in the "Templates" folder.

Object Position Methods	Folder Attributes Methods	Overridden Methods	
wpQueryNextIconPos	wpQueryFldrAttr	wpAddFile2Page	wpAddFile3Page
wpSetNextIconPos	wpQueryFldrDetailsClass	wpAddSettingsPages	wpConfirmDelete
Folder State Methods	wpQueryFldrFlags	wpDelete	wpDragOver
	wpQueryFldrFont	wpDrop	wpFilterPopupMenu
wpHideFldrRunObjs	wpSetFldrAttr	wpFormatDragItem	wpFree
	wpSetFldrDetailsClass	wpInitData	wpMenuItemHelpSelected
	wpSetFldrFlags	wpMenuItemSelected	wpModifyPopupMenu
	wpSetFldrFont	wpMoveObject	wpOpen
Folder Content Methods	**Settings Notebook Methods**	wpRender	wpRestoreState
		wpSaveState	wpSetup
wpDeleteContents	wpAddFolderBack-	wpUnInitData	wpclsQueryOpenFolders
wpPopulate	groundPage	wpclsQueryDefaultHelp	wpclsQueryDefaultView
wpQueryContent	wpAddFolderIncludePage	wpclsQueryIconData	wpclsQueryStyle
wpRefresh	wpAddFolderSortPage	wpclsQueryTitle	
	wpAddFolderView1Page		
	wpAddFolderView2Page		
	wpAddFolderView3Page		

Third Encounters: Know Your Classes Intimately

You've read the spec sheets, and you're back. This means that you've probably found your dream WPS class and are now ready to absorb it into your code. Let us congratulate you for your smart move! You'll be appropriating, in record time, tens of thousands of lines of production strength debugged code. So what's next Doc? More class exploration (of the "touchy feely" type) and a deeper level of class appreciation. In master Lao-tzu's words: "if you want to take something, you must first allow it to be given."

If we were writing normal C code (they call it procedural programming), this is about the time when you would see some APIs and jump into a program that shows how to use them. With OOP, it's not that simple. Reading the description of 2000 methods will bore you to tears, leave you with a terrible headache, and still not give you a "feel" for how to take advantage of the object class. Yes, you have to develop a feel for the object before you do anything else with it. There's no way around it.

So how do we get that object feel? You do that by *playing object*. What this means is that you'll have to think through scenarios of how the object behaves from the time it is created to the time it dies. The scenarios will have to anticipate sequences of method invocations. In other words, you can't just think of individual methods. You'll have to get used to methods getting invoked in related clusters as the result of some event or client request. Subclassing is about overriding existing methods with yours (as well as adding new ones). You'll have to first know how to ride the wave with the existing method before you can override it. In addition, old methods never go away. They're there as part of the parent's class. You may override a parent method, add your code, and then reinvoke the parent method to also let it "do its thing."

To take advantage of a class, you have to reverse engineer the thought process that originally went into the design of it's interfaces, but not the inner details of how it gets done. What were the original designer's goals for that class? What's the logic of the interface? No, you don't get to see the code that goes inside the class. You're normally dealing with a black box. The trick is to reuse the original code and not have to redesign it from scratch. This the hardest part of OOP. We programmers, of course, know that we could have always done it better. Instead, we're now confronted with the "80/20 iron rule" of classes: reuse at least 80% of the original code, and add (or remove) the other 20%.

As master Lao-tzu puts it: "if you want to shrink something, you must first allow it to expand." With that in mind we've created for your enjoyment Table 40-1. The idea was not to come up with the world's longest table, but to give you an all-in-one reference for **WPObject**. The technical manuals don't show it all in one place, which makes it hard to follow the class's logic. This table should help you design at the conceptual level (you get the forest and the trees), but you'll still have to go to the manuals for the bits and bytes. We only did the exercise for **WPObject** because this is the one class you'll have to really understand inside out to take advantage of the WPS class system. We recommend at this stage that you take a quick look at the table—don't spend more than 10 minutes on it since we'll be seeing it again. Then meet us at the end of the chapter for more instructions on the search for "inner class truth."

Table 40-2 (Part 1 of 9).   WPObject Class Methods.

Settings Notebook Methods

Overview: Workplace objects inherit the Settings notebook view. They can modify this very visual construct by adding and removing pages to suit their needs. The notebook can be used as a general container of dialogs. WPObject defines a "General" page. You can add new pages by overriding **wpAddSettingsPages** method with a new method that inserts new pages.   The new method calls the **wpInsertSettingsPage** method to insert the new page into the notebook. New pages can be placed at the top or at the bottom of pages inherited from the object's ancestor classes. You add a new page at the top by calling the parent method before calling your new method. Reverse the calling order to add the page at the bottom of the notebook. You can remove a page by overriding the ancestor's method that inserts it.

Method	Description
wpAddObjectGeneralPage **wpAddSettingsPages** **wpInsertSettingsPage**	Add the General page to the object's settings notebook. Add pages to the object's settings notebook. Insert a page into the object's settings notebook.

Save/Restore State Methods

| Overview: The Save/Restore State methods are used to support persistent objects. When an object is awakened, **wpRestoreState** is called by the Shell. The **wpSaveImmediate** method calls **wpSaveState**. When an object is closed or made dormant, or when the system shuts down the Shell calls **wpSaveImmediate** and **wpSaveState**. The **wpSaveImmediate** method can also be called by an object's methods when a critical instance variable is changed.

To save or restore data relevant to an object, override the **wpSaveState** and **wpRestoreState** methods. The override for **wpSaveState** calls **wpSaveData**, **wpSaveLong**, and **wpSaveString**, depending on the type of instance data associated with your object. The override for **wpRestoreState** calls **wpRestoreData**, **wpRestoreLong**, and **wpRestoreString**. |
|---|

Method	Description
wpRestoreData **wpRestoreLong** **wpRestoreState** **wpRestoreString** **wpSaveData** **wpSaveImmediate** **wpSaveLong** **wpSaveState** **wpSaveString**	Restore blocks of instance data. Restore a 32-bit instance data value. Restore the object's state. Restore an ASCII instance data string. Save blocks of instance data. Save the object's state. Save a 32-bit instance data value. Save the object's state. Save an ASCII instance data string.

Table 40-2 (Part 2 of 9). WPObject Class Methods.

Object Usage Methods

Overview: Each Workplace object in the system has an *in-use list* that provides the object with information, including the number of container windows into which the object has been inserted, the number of open views (contents and settings) of the object that already exist, and how much memory the object has allocated. The in-use list is a linked list of USEITEM data structures.

The **wpAddToObjUseList** method adds items to the object's in-use list when memory is allocated for an object by its **wpAllocMem** method, when a view of an object is opened by the object's **wpOpen** method, and when an object is inserted into a container window.

The **wpDeleteFromObjUseList** method is called when memory is freed by the object's **wpFreeMem** method, when views are closed by the object's **wpClose** method, and when objects are removed from a container window by the object's **wpCnrRemoveObject** method.

The **wpFindUseItem** method is used to determine how an object is currently being used. It searches an object's in-use list for items of a specified type and returns a pointer to the USEITEM structure that matches the specified type.

Method	Description
wpAddToObjUseList	Add an item to the object's in-use list.
wpDeleteFromObjUseList	Remove an item from the object's in-use list.
wpFindUseItem	Retrieve an item from the object's in-use list.
wpUnlockObject	Allow the object to go into a dormant state.

Error Handling Methods

Overview: The error handling service consists of two methods that record and retrieve the last error to occur in the system. By overriding these methods you can tap into object error calls and create your own error management system.

Method	Description
wpQueryError	Retrieve error id set by last **wpSetError** call.
wpSetError	Record the error on an object before exiting method.

Memory Management Methods

Overview: The memory management service consists of two methods that allocate and deallocate memory for objects. By overriding these methods, you can provide your own storage management system. For example, you could create a persistent storage system for objects.

Method	Description
wpAllocMem	Allocate memory to be used by this object only.
wpFreeMem	Free memory allocated.

Table 40-2 (Part 3 of 9). WPObject Class Methods.

Popup Menu Methods

Overview: Pop-up menu methods support the actions that the user can perform on an object. These actions appear in a context, or pop-up menu, when the user presses the pointing button (mouse button 2). A pop-up menu contains action choices for an object in its current context, or state. The contents of a pop-up menu depend on the state of the object.

The Pop-up Methods allow you to add new menu items to or remove menu items from the pop-up menu inherited from the ancestor classes. When a pop-up is activated the WPS calls **wpFilterPopupMenu** and **wpModifyPopupMenu**. The **parent_wpFilterPopupMenu** method returns the flags that represent the pop-up menu items for the object's parent. The override to **wpFilterPopupMenu** can mask the flags that correspond to the item being removed from the standard pop-up menu items inherited from the object's parent.

The **wpModifyPopupMenu** method can be overridden to add new options using **wpInsertPopupMenuItems**. The new menu items must be defined in a PM resource file. The method requires a handle to the DLL module where the menu resource is defined, the id for the menu resource, and the ID for the menu where the item is being inserted.

Views are displayed when the user selects the Open action on the pop-up menu. The Workplace supplies a set of predefined views that have meaning only to certain Workplace classes: OPEN_RUNNING is meaningful to a program; OPEN_TREE is meaningful to file system objects such as folders, drives, and directories. The more general views are OPEN_CONTENTS, OPEN_DEFAULT, OPEN_DETAILS, OPEN_HELP, and OPEN_SETTINGS. You may also create class-specific open views by using values greater than OPEN_USER.

Here's what you must do to define a new Open View for an object: 1) Add the new view menu item to the pop-up (as described above), 2) Override the **wpMenuItemSelected** method to support the user selection of the new menu item, 3) Override the **wpOpen** method to open the new view, 4) Create and open a PM standard window for the new view by calling the PM function WinCreateStdWindow, 5) Add a USAGE_VIEW item to the object's in-use list by calling the **wpAddToObjUseList** method, and 6) Register the view by calling the **wpRegisterView** method.

The preferred method for displaying application views of an object is for the object to start a separate process (using DosExecPgm) for the application. This approach moves the larger part of the application code out of the Shell's process, thus conserving the Shell's resources. It also helps prevent a misbehaved application from potentially interfering with the execution of the Shell.

Help for Workplace objects is provided in the same manner as for PM applications using the IPF facility. Help instances are created for, and associated with, objects by the Shell. The IPF creates help libraries that must reside in any directory in the LIBPATH. The library's help panels are associated with windows and window controls by help tables defined in the object's resource file (see PM tutorial). Help for Workplace objects is supported by the object's: **wpDisplayHelp**, **wpQueryDefaultHelp** and **wpMenuItemHelpSelected** methods. You can override **wpQueryDefaultHelp** and **wpMenuItemHelpSelected** to provide class-specific help views and menu items.

Table 40-2 (Part 4 of 9). WPObject Class Methods.

Method	Description
wpClose	Close all open views of an object.
wpCopyObject	Create a new copy of the object.
wpCreateFromTemplate	Create an object from a template.
wpCreateShadowObject	Create a shadow of an object.
wpDelete	Delete an object and prompt for confirmation if necessary.
wpDisplayHelp	Display a help panel.
wpFilterPopupMenu	Filter out options from object's pop-up menu that don't apply.
wpHide	Hide or minimize open views of an object.
wpInsertPopupMenuItems	Insert items into object's pop-up menu.
wpMenuItemHelpSelected	Display the help associated with class-specific pop-up menu item.
wpMenuItemSelected	Process class-specific pop-up menu item.
wpModifyPopupMenu	Add new options to the object's pop-up menu.
wpMoveObject	Move the object to a different location.
wpOpen	Open a view of the object.
wpPrintObject	Print a view of the object.
wpRestore	Restore hidden or minimized views of an object.
Object Information Methods	

Overview: Object Information Methods allow you to set and query information (default help, default view, details, icon, style, and title) associated with an object. Workplace objects have object (instance) styles that define the object behavior. They can be changed after an object has been created by calling the **wpSetStyle** method. Object styles include OBJSTYLE_NOCOPY (object cannot be copied), OBJSTYLE_NODELETE (object cannot be deleted), OBJSTYLE_NODRAG (object cannot be dragged), OBJSTYLE_NOSHADOW (object cannot have shadow created), OBJSTYLE_NOMOVE (object cannot move), OBJSTYLE_NOPRINT (object cannot be printed), OBJSTYLE_NOTDEFAULTICON (destroy icon when object goes dormant), OBJSTYLE_TEMPLATE (object is a template), OBJSTYLE_NOTVISIBLE (object is hidden), and OBJSTYLE_NORENAME (object cannot be renamed).

A template is the primary user mechanism for creating new instances of objects. A template is created automatically when a class is registered, unless the **wpclsQueryStyle** class method returns CLSSTYLE_NEVERTEMPLATE. When the operating system is first installed, template objects reside in the templates folder on the Desktop. The templates folder always contains a template object for each class of object installed on the system that supports the Create Another action. Any new object registered by the WinRegisterObjectClass function that supports the "Create Another" action automatically appears in this folder. A template for each object class registered using this function cannot be removed from the templates folder.

Some Workplace classes define a set of information that a user can display in a details view of all instances of objects belonging to the class. A details view is a container control window; it consists of a window with data arranged in columns which have headings. A row of data (a record) provides information for a specific instance of an object belonging to the class. Each element in the details view can either be text, an icon, a bitmap, or a custom OWNERDRAW element. The column headings for a details view are specified by overriding the **wpclsQueryDetailsInfo** class method. A record that contains information for an object instance of the class is constructed by overriding the **wpQueryDetailsData** instance method.

Table 40-2 (Part 5 of 9).   **WPObject Class Methods.**

Method	Description
wpQueryConfirmations	Query which confirmations are set in object.
wpQueryDefaultHelp	Query default help panel for object.
wpQueryDefaultView	Query default view for object.
wpQueryDetailsData	Query current details data for object.
wpQueryIcon	Query current icon for an object.
wpQueryIconData	Query current icon and icon data for an object.
wpQueryStyle	Query current style of an object.
wpQueryTitle	Query current title of an object.
wpSetDefaultHelp	Set default help panel for object.
wpSetDefaultView	Set default view for object.
wpSetIcon	Set current icon for an object.
wpSetIconData	Set current icon and icon data for an object.
wpSetStyle	Set current style of an object.
wpSetTitle	Set current title of an object.

Setup/Cleanup Methods

Overview: The Setup/Cleanup methods support object creation and cleanup services. You can define the behavior of the object using a setup string of attribute/value pairs separated by semicolons (;). Example:

    pszSetupString="TITLE=Club;ICONFILE=CLUB.ICO;OBJECTID=;"

The values take effect when the object is created using WinCreateObject or when a change in the behavior of an existing object is initiated using WinSetObjectData. The attributes also have default values and do not have to be explicitly specified in the string. Every class defines its own set of attributes and values. These attributes can also be changed by direct method invocations but the setup string is really more convenient. The set up string attributes, also called KEYNAMEs, are defined below:

KEYNAME (attribute)	Value	Description
TITLE	Title	Sets the object's title.
ICONFILE	filename	Sets the object's icon.
HELPPANEL	id	Sets the object's default help panel.
TEMPLATE	YES/NO	User can/cannot create object template.
NODELETE	YES/NO	User cannot/can delete object.
NOCOPY	YES/NO	User cannot/can copy object.
NOMOVE	YES/NO	User cannot/can move object.
NOSHADOW	YES/NO	User cannot/can create shadow.
NOTVISIBLE	YES/NO	Object is not or is visible.
NOPRINT	YES/NO	User cannot/can print object.
ICONRESOURCE	id,module	Sets the object's icon. The id is icon's resource ID in the DLL module.

Table 40-2 (Part 6 of 9). WPObject Class Methods.

ICONPOS	x,y	Sets the object's initial icon position in a folder. The x and y values represent the position in the folder in percentage coordinates.
OBJECTID	name	Sets a persistent ID for the object. The OBJECTID can be used to obtain a pointer or handle to the object by calling the **wpclsQueryObject** method or WinQueryObject function. An OBJECTID is any unique string preceded and terminated by double-quotes.
NORENAME	YES/NO	User cannot/can rename object.
NODRAG	YES/NO	User cannot/can drag object.
VIEWBUTTON	HIDE/MINIMIZE	Views of object have a hide button or a minimize button.
MINWIN	HIDE/VIEWER/ DESKTOP	Views of object are hidden, when the minimize button is selected. **OR** Views of object are minimized in the minimized window viewer, when the minimize button is selected. **OR** Views of object are minimized on the Desktop, when the minimize button is selected.
CONCURRENTVIEW	YES/NO	New view of object is created every time user selects open. **OR** Open view of object resurfaces when user selects open.
OPEN	SETTINGS/ DEFAULT	Open the settings view, when the object is created or when WinSetObjectData is called. **OR** Open the default view, when the object is created or when WinSetObjectData is called.

Attributes are processed by an object's **wpSetup** method, which is called when WinCreateObject and WinSetObjectData are called by an application. Classes that define their own KEYNAMES, override the **wpSetup** method. The override for wpSetup scans the setup string for its KEYNAMES and processes them. Applications can also cause changes to objects that already exist on the on the WPS. For example, to effect changes to the icons for objects that already exist, an application calls: 1) WinQueryObject to get a handle to the object using the object's OBJECTID and 2) WinSetObjectData with ICONDATA KEYNAME value specified in the setup string.

Method	Description
wpFree	Destroy the object and deallocate its associated resources.
wpInitData	Allocate and Initialize the object's instance data.
wpScanSetupString	Parse the setup string that is specified when the object is created.
wpSetup	Change the object characteristics and behavior as specified in setup string.
wpUnInitData	Deallocate the object's instance data.

Table 40-2 (Part 7 of 9).   WPObject Class Methods.

Direct Manipulation Methods

Overview: Direct Manipulation methods support "drag and drop" of one object on another. The object being dragged is the *source* object, and the object on which the source object is dropped is the *target* object. The Workplace Shell tracks a source object that the user drags. It then notifies target objects and windows when the source object is being dragged over them, and when it is dropped on them. For target objects in the Workplace, the Shell calls the target object's Direct Manipulation methods to process the source object being dragged and dropped. For PM applications, the Shell sends DM messages to PM windows using the standard drag and drop protocol.

The Shell will drag source objects rendered as OBJECT or as OS2FILE, and will accept source objects rendered in the same way. The Shell also sends a DM_PRINTOBJECT message to items dropped on the printer object. Users can drag source objects over windows that an object creates. When this occurs, the Shell sends DM_ messages to these windows. The window procedures associated with the windows that the object creates must be able to process the DM_ messages.

Target objects are not necessarily able to process every type of source object that is dropped on them. They are, however, capable of processing more than one type of dropped source object. Printer objects, for example, cannot print binary files, but they can print both text files and graphics files. Because of these differing capabilities, each target object should determine if it can process the source object being dropped on it.

Method	Description
wpDragOver	Inform an object that other objects are being dragged over it (returns PM DM_DRAGOVER message info).
wpDraggedOverObject	Inform the dragged object of the target object id that it is currently on top of. This gives the dragged object a chance to accept or reject the drop based on the id of the target object.
wpDrop	Inform target object that another object was dropped on it (returns the PM DM_DROP message info).
wpDroppedOnObject	Inform the source object that the target object it was dropped on does not know what to do with it. This gives the source object a chance to figure out what to do next.
wpEndConversation	Notify target object that the drag/drop is complete. It gives a chance to the target to perform post drop actions (returns PM DM_ENDCONVERSATION message info).
wpFormatDragItem	Notify source object that user started to drag it. This gives the object a chance to format its drag information.
wpRender	Request a drag/drop rendering format from object (returns PM DM_RENDER message info).
wpRenderComplete	Notify the object that the drag/drop render request is complete (returns PM DM_RENDERCOMPLETE message info).

Table 40-2 (Part 8 of 9). WPObject Class Methods.

Overridden Methods
Overview: All Workplace objects have implied metaclasses which define all the class methods for a class. Class methods act on class data common to all object instances of the class. Metaclasses define class properties that include default attributes for all instances of the class. Examples include: the default object title, the default help panel, the default icon, and so forth. Workplace class methods are prefixed by "wpcls." Default class characteristics are inherited by instances of the class unless the class overrides the methods that operate on those characteristics. For example, to define a default object style for instances of ClubObject, ClubObject overrides the **wpclsQueryStyle** method and returns the appropriate default class style. The class methods **wpclsFindObjectFirst**, **wpclsFindObjectNext**, and **wpclsFindObjectEnd** are used to search for objects. They are typically overridden with user methods that initiate searches for an object.

Method	Description
wpclsCreateDefault- **Templates**	Called by system when class is registered. It allows you to create a default template for class.
wpclsFindObjectEnd	End a search for an object belonging to the class.
wpclsFindObjectFirst	Begin a search for an object belonging the class.
wpclsFindObjectNext	Find another object belonging to the class.
wpclsInitData	Called by system when object is awakened. Allows the object to initialize its instance data.
wpclsMakeAwake	Called to allow class to awaken an object.
wpclsNew	Create a new instance of this object.
wpclsQueryDefaultHelp	Get the default help panel for instances of the class.
wpclsQueryDefaultView	Get the default open view for instances of the class.
wpclsQueryDetails	Get the default details view items for instances of the class.
wpclsQueryDetailsInfo	Get details information for instances of the class.
wpclsQueryError	Get error information for instances of the class.
wpclsQueryFolder	Get a pointer to a folder object.
wpclsQueryIcon	Get the default icon for instances of the class
wpclsQueryIconData	Get default icon data for instances of the class
wpclsQueryObject	Get pointer or handle to persistent object.
wpclsSetError	Set error for instances of the class.
wpclsQuerySettingsPageSize	Get settings page size for instances of the class
wpclsQueryStyle	Get the default object style for instances of the class.
wpclsQueryTitle	Get the default title for instances of the class.
wpclsUnInitData	Called by system when class object is made dormant (i.e., when last instance of class is made dormant). Used to free resources.

Table 40-2 (Part 9 of 9). WPObject Class Methods.

Miscellaneous Methods	
Overview: This is a miscellaneous group of methods that extend your control of the Workplace Shell environment. The miscellaneous methods include support for populating a container, deleting an object, creating an object, and opening a view.	

Method	Description
wpCnrInsertObject	Insert a record into a container.
wpCnrRemoveObject	Remove a record from a container.
wpCnrSetEmphasis	Change visual emphasis of object inserted in a container.
wpConfirmDelete	Called during processing of **wpDelete** if the "confirm delete flag" is on. Allows you to prompt the user before deleting the object.
wpCopiedFromTemplate	Called when a new object is created from template.
wpDoesObjectMatch	Called to ask object if it can match the extended search attributes passed in a buffer.
wpRegisterView	Called during **wpOpen** to register a new view with PM.
wpSwitchTo	Called to allow an object to give focus to a specified view.

Overridden SOM Methods	
Overview: All Workplace objects are descendants of SOM classes. You can override SOM methods to perform class-specific functions. You are better off overriding Workplace Shell methods that provide much higher levels of abstraction than SOM.	

Method	Description
somFree	Release object's storage; use **somUninit** instead.
somInit	Initialize instance data of newly created object.
somUninit	Release object's resources.
somInitClass	Initialize a newly created class object.
somNew	Create a new object instance.
somRenew	Create a new object instance with a pointer to storage used to create object.

Fourth Encounters: Do It in Small Steps

Now that we've developed the "subtle perception of the way things are," we're ready for some hands on work with SOM/WPS classes. We'll start you in the next chapter with a gentle program that says "Hello from the Workplace Shell." This program will be used to demonstrate the SOM class development environment, and how to use the WPS class library. We will then be ready for the Club Med OOUI Client in Part VII.

Chapter 41

Hello World From SOM/WPS

This is second chapter of our tutorial on creating objects using the System Object Model (SOM) and Workplace Shell (WPS) Classes. In this chapter, we conclude the tutorial by showing you how to develop a complete SOM/WPS application. We will do that by developing a SOM/WPS class that says "Hello World From SOM/WPS." This program will serve as a gentle introduction to SOM/WPS programming. After this introduction, you will be ready for Part VII, where we develop an elaborate OOUI Club Med client using SOM/WPS classes.

DEVELOPING SOM/WPS Objects

As you may have guessed, SOM/WPS object classes introduce new steps in the application development process. These steps are in addition to what you need to create ordinary Presentation Manager programs. In a SOM/WPS environment, the world starts with objects and ends with objects. But tucked away in these objects, you'll typically find rather large patches of PM and C code. Whether you are developing code that you will implement in the form of one or more SOM classes, or writing code that makes use of existing WPS classes, the development process always starts with a class definition and involves the following steps:

1. *Define the classes using the OIDL*. The Object Interface Definition Language (OIDL) is used to define a class and its relationship to other classes. The OIDL class definition files are ASCII files with an extension of (.CSC).

2. *Run the OIDL file through the SOM Precompiler*. The Precompiler (they call it a compiler) processes the OIDL (.CSC) file and produces a set of language-specific bind files, which include a template for the C-language source program (.C) that does the class implementation. This program template contains stub procedures for all new and override methods specified in the class definition file.

3. *Add the object code to the class stubs*. You must supply the C and PM code that implements the methods for which the SOM Precompiler created stubs in the (.C) file.

4. ***Create the PM Resources***. You do that using the OS/2 Toolkit tools such as the Dialog and Icon editors. Put all the resources that will need to be translated (National Language Support) into resource files that are separate from your program. This is a standard PM programming practice.

5. ***Compile and link the code and resources to produce the new class DLL***. The class DLL is produced using your garden variety C Set/2 compile/link process. The PM resource files (.RC) must be run through a separate Resource Compiler prior to linking. There's nothing new here.

6. ***Copy the class DLL to the machine where it will be used***. The DLL must be copied into a subdirectory referenced by the LIBPATH statement in CONFIG.SYS. This is typically the C:\OS2\DLL directory.

7. ***Register the class with the Workplace Shell***. You use a standard WPS API call **WinRegisterObjectClass** that registers and loads the new DLL. You can also use a REXX utility.

8. ***Create an object***. You create an object instance of the new class by issuing **WinCreateObject**. You can also use a REXX utility.

We will go through each of these steps in some detail as part of developing the "Hello World From SOM/WPS" application.

HELLO WORLD FROM SOM/WPS

In this section, we develop a complete SOM/WPS program by creating a new class: **HelloWPS** (see Figure 41-1). This class produces the smiling face object that says "hello" when you open it. We will create this new class by going through each of the steps outlined in the previous section.

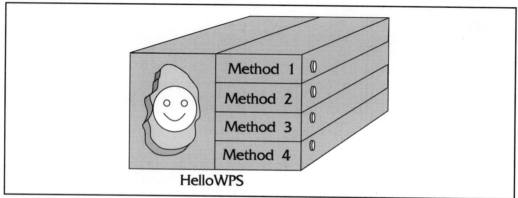

Figure 41-1. Hello World Using HelloWPS.

Defining Classes Using OIDL

You must create a SOM OIDL file (.CSC) for each class of SOM/WPS objects you create. Each (.CSC) file defines a class, including its interfaces and relationships to other classes, using the OIDL's specification language. Figure 41-2 shows the listing for the (.CSC) definitions that we created to define the **HelloWPS** class. We'll go over this file in some depth to explain the OIDL syntax. We'll even explain the optional sections that are left blank in the listing.

The OIDL class definition file for the C language is divided into eight sections as shown in Figure 41-2. Discardable (.CSC) comments start with "#" and can be placed anywhere (they are discarded by the SOM Precompiler). Non-discardable comments start with "--" and can also be placed anywhere. The sections in Figure 41-2 are in an order that worked for us (we couldn't get the SOM-recommended order to work):

1. *The Include section (required)* tells the SOM Precompiler where to find the class's parent class, metaclass, and any ancestor class for which this class overrides one or more of its methods. We're only including one entry: **wpabs.sc**, which tells the Precompiler that **HelloWPS** is subclassed from the **WPSAbsract** class. You might have guessed, that we liked the smiling face so much that we decided to make the **HelloWPS** persistent at the desktop level.

2. *The Class section (required)* provides basic information about the new class, specifying its name, attributes, and directions that tell the SOM compiler how to name and build the binding files it generates. All classes must have a *name*, ours is **HelloWPS**. The *external stem* specifies the file name to be used by the SOM Precompiler for the generated files. The *local* parameter causes local include files to be referenced first. The *external prefix* is used by the SOM Precompiler to qualify the function names (it precedes the function name with the prefix followed by an underscore; for example, HelloWPS_Foo).[1] The *class prefix* is similar to the external prefix, except that it is used to qualify the methods in the class. The *major version* and *minor version* are used to ensure that the bindings are at the right level for the class implementation code.

3. *The Parent Class section (required)* specifies the parent of the new class. All classes must have this section. The parent class in our case is the **WPAbstract** class (one of the storage class trio supplied by WPS).

4. *The Metaclass section (optional)* is used to specify the name of a class's metaclass. You only need to do that if the class's metaclass is not the same as its parent's. If

---

[1] The SOM Precompiler also generates a macro for all methods defined by the class, that allows the method to be called in the source code by its defined name, preceded by an underscore character (for example, _Foo). This helps make the source code more readable.

this is the case, the location for the metaclass definition must be added to the Include section. We left this section blank, so **HelloWPS**'s metaclass is the same as its parent's metaclass. When a class has the same metaclass as its parent, new methods can be added to the existing class methods, or existing class methods can be overridden by specifying the CLASS attribute in the Data and Methods sections. SOM will then create an *implied metaclass*, which is a subclass of the parent class's metaclass. This eliminates the overhead of creating a separate (.CSC) file required by an explicit metafile.

5. *The Release Order section (optional))* contains a list of all the methods and public instance variables that you create for that class. The list of names directs the SOM Precompiler to process the data declarations and method definitions in the order specified, not as they occur in the source. Adding a new method name to the end of the Release Order list allows you to insert the method's body anywhere in the source and still maintain backward compatibility with client applications. The ordered list ensures that other programs using this class will not have to be recompiled every time something new is added. This powerful feature is SOM's answer to maintaining interface compatibility between changing class definitions. Notice that we did not take advantage of this feature, because we do not anticipate that **HelloWPS** will make it big commercially.

6. *The Passthru section (optional)* allows you to pass blocks of C source code to any of the files generated by the SOM Precompiler. You must tell the SOM Precompiler in the passthru statement the name of the language and the extension of the file where you want the block to be inserted: *passthru: Language.extension*; for example, "C.ih" tells the SOM Precompiler to insert the passthru header declarations in the HelloWPS.ih class header file. Why use passthru? You use passthru because the (.ih) file gets regenerated every time we run the Precompiler and SOM puts a lot of junk in the header file around your stuff. By using passthru we do not have to look at the (.IH) file.

7. *The Data section (optional)* contains the instance variables for the objects belonging to this class. Instance data can be declared private (the default) or public. Public instance data is part of the published external interface and can be accessed by client applications. Hello does not require instance data.

8. *The Methods section (optional)* contains new and override methods defined for this class. You must specify the C-language function prototypes that define the calling sequence for each new method you create. For overrides, you only need to specify the names of inherited methods. Methods can be made private or public (the default). From the listing (see Figure 41-2), you can tell that **HelloWPS** does not introduce any new methods. However, we do override six of **WPAbstract**'s methods (three class methods and three instance methods).

HELLOWPS.CSC

```
/*********************************************************************/
/* Module Name: HELLOWPS - A Hello World Object                      */
/*********************************************************************/

#*******************************************************************
#   Include Section
#*******************************************************************
include <wpabs.sc>

#*******************************************************************
#   Class Section
#*******************************************************************
class: HelloWPS,
        external stem   = hellowps,
        local,
        external prefix = hellowps_,
        classprefix     = hellowpsM_,
        major version   = 1,
        minor version   = 2;

#*******************************************************************
#   Parent Class
#*******************************************************************
parent: WPAbstract;

#*******************************************************************
#   Metaclass Section
#*******************************************************************

#*******************************************************************
#   Release Order Section
#*******************************************************************

#*******************************************************************
#   Passthru Section
#*******************************************************************
passthru: C.ih;

#define INCL_WIN
/*      #define INCL_DOS            */
/*      #define INCL_GPIBITMAPS     */
#include <os2.h>

#define INCL_WPCLASS
#include <pmwp.h>

/*_____*/
/* Defines                                                      */
/*_____*/
/*_____*/
/* ICON identifiers                    */
/*_____*/
#define ID_ICON           100
```

Figure 41-2 (Part 1 of 2). HELLOWPS.CSC: The OIDL File That Creates HelloWPS.

```
/*——————————————————————*/
/* MENU and MENUITEM identifiers */
/*——————————————————————*/
#define ID_OPENMENU      0x6501           /* ID for selection added to open */
#define OPEN_HELLOWPS    OPEN_USER + 1     /* ID for View Say Hello          */


/*——————————————————————*/
/* Hello Window ID             */
/*——————————————————————*/
#define ID_FRAME         255              /* client window id               */


/*——————————————————————*/
/* DEBUG helper macro          */
/*——————————————————————*/
#define ShowMsg(title, text) \
        WinMessageBox(HWND_DESKTOP, HWND_DESKTOP, (PSZ) text, (PSZ) title, \
                      20, MB_OK | MB_INFORMATION | MB_MOVEABLE)

endpassthru;    /* .ih */


#**********************************************************************************
#    Data Section
#**********************************************************************************


#**********************************************************************************
#    Methods Section
#**********************************************************************************
methods:


#————————————————————————————————————————————————
#   Specify class methods being overridden
#————————————————————————————————————————————————
override wpclsQueryStyle, class;
override wpclsQueryTitle, class;
override wpclsQueryDefaultView, class;


#————————————————————————————————————————————————
#   Specify Instance Methods being overridden
#————————————————————————————————————————————————
override wpModifyPopupMenu;
override wpMenuItemSelected;
override wpOpen;
```

Figure 41-2 (Part 2 of 2). HELLOWPS.CSC: The OIDL File That Creates HelloWPS.

Precompile The OIDL (.CSC) File

The next step is to run the (.CSC) file we just created through the SOM Precompiler to
create the object stubs. Later, we will add our C and PM code to these stubs. We show
the entire development process for creating WPS classes in Figure 41-3. Notice that
any Presentation Manager resources must be compiled using the resource compiler
(RC), and then incorporated into the application's executable code or in a DLL module.
The (.RC) file contains resource script definitions for Presentation Manager resources,
as well as statements that include resources from other files. If an application creates
dialog boxes using Dialog Editor, a dialog file (.DLG) is generated with the definitions
of the dialog box and its control windows. This file is normally included in the resource
script file using an appropriate statement.

Notice in Figure 41-3 that when the SOM Precompiler is run successfully against a (.CSC) class definition file, it creates (or "emits") the seven files described in Table 41-1. The most important of these files from a programmer's perspective is the (.C) file that contains definitions and function stubs for all the methods defined by the class. This is the file that you must edit to add the actual code that performs each method. We will be discussing this process in the next section.

The make file that creates the **HelloWPS** class is listed in Figure 41-4. The SOM Precompiler is invoked as a consequence of the (.csc.ih) inference rule. At this point in the development process, we're only interested in the (.C) file that creates the stubs. Later, when we're done writing our code, we'll reinvoke the NMAKE utility to create the final class DLLs (this is process shown in the bottom of Figure 41-3).

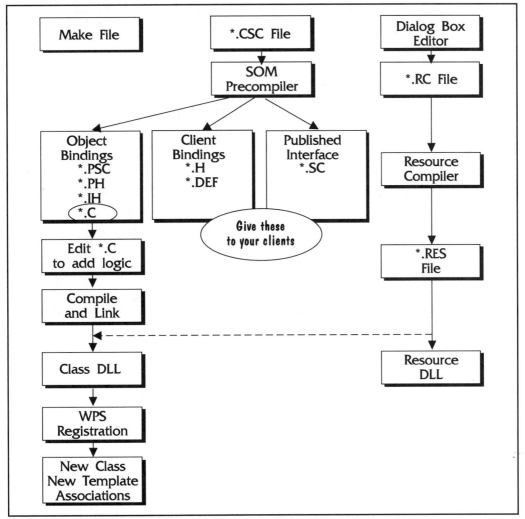

Figure 41-3. The Development Process for Creating New WPS Classes.

Table 41-1. SOM Precompiler Emitter File Descriptions.

Emitter File Extension	File Description
.C	A template C file where you add your code to implement the class.
.H	A public include file for all C-language programs that need to access the SOM class.
.IH	An implementation header file containing most of the automatically generated implementation details for the class. It also provides support for the implementation of the class.
.PH	A private header file, which provides usage bindings and macros that can be used by any of the private methods defined in the class.
.DEF	A file containing instructions to the linker on how to build a class library. This is a regular OS/2 module definition with EXPORT declarations needed to implement the class.
.SC	A language-neutral class definition that is a subset of the SOM class definition file with the private implementation details removed. This file should be published and made available to users of the class. It defines the contract (or interface) for using the class.
.PSC	A supplement to .SC file that contains information about private methods of a class.

HELLOWPS.MAK

```
#*****************************************************************************
# Make File for HelloWPS CLASS
#*****************************************************************************
#** MACROS *******************************************************************
cflags = /c /Q /Ge- /Gd- /Se /Re /ss /Ms /Gm+
lflags = /NOI /NOL /ALIGN:16 /M /PACKCODE /PACKDATA /EXEPACK /MAP
dll_libs = os2386.lib som.lib

#** INFERENCE RULES **********************************************************
.SUFFIXES:
.SUFFIXES: .c .obj .dll .csc .sc .h .ih .ph .psc .rc .res .def

.csc.ih:
      echo SOM COMPILING          $*.CSC
      sc -r $*.csc

.c.obj:
      echo COMPILING              $*.C
      icc $(cflags) $*.c

.obj.dll:
      echo LINKING.               $* to create $*.DLL
      LINK386 $(lflags) $*, $*.dll, $*.map, $(dll_libs), $*.def;
      rc $*.res $*.dll
```

Figure 41-4 (Part 1 of 2). HELLOWPS.MAK: The Make File.

```
          copy $*.dll F:\toolkt20\dll

.rc.res:
          echo RESOURCE COMPILING  $*.RC
          rc -r $*.rc $*.res

#** BUILD STATEMENTS *****************************************************

all:          HelloWPS.dll

HelloWPS.ih:  HelloWPS.csc
HelloWPS.obj: HelloWPS.c   HelloWPS.ih  HelloWPS.h   HelloWPS.sc
HelloWPS.res: HelloWPS.rc  HelloWPS.ih  HelloWPS.ico
HelloWPS.dll: HelloWPS.obj HelloWPS.def HelloWPS.res
```

Figure 41-4 (Part 2 of 2). HELLOWPS.MAK: The Make File.

Writing the Methods Behind the Class Stubs

The (.C) file generated by the SOM Precompiler contains the stub procedures for all the new and override methods specified in the (.CSC) class definition file (see Figure 41-5). This file is rather messy looking (we didn't write it; SOM did), but it contains the object constructs you will need to create your classes. So, it's important that you understand what you're reading.

How Do You Read the Class Stubs?

The first thing to notice in the (.C) program template is that SOM includes the HELLOWPS.IH header file. This SOM-generated file contains a wealth of data structures, macros, and functions that you can use to access the data and methods for object instances of the **HelloWPS** class. It gives C some OO-like features (not as elegant as C++, but they're here today).

In fact, SOM places these macros within the stubs it created in the (.C) file. This is how you read a method stub generated by SOM:

```
SOM_Scope void SOMLINK  <methodname>(<classname> *somSelf)
   {
       <classname>Data *somThis = <classname>GetData(somSelf);
       <classname>MethodDebug("<classname>", "<methodname>");
                             .
                             .
       return (parent_classname(somself, parm1, parm2,.. parmN));
   }
```

Here's what this all means:

- *SOM_Scope* and *SOMLINK* are C macros used internally by SOM. Just ignore them.

- *somSelf* is a pointer to the object instance (i.e., the object whose method is getting invoked). In OO, every object has a unique ID. For C-language methods, SOM always passes the object ID as the first parameter in any method. This allows the same method to be invoked on different objects but implemented differently (polymorphism).
- *somThis* is a pointer to data for that object instance.
- *GetData* is a SOM class macro that initializes somThis. After somThis is initialized you can access your instance data using SOM compiler generated macros formed by prefixing an underscore (_) to your instance data name. If your class does not have instance data, this line will be commented out.
- *MethodDebug* is a SOM class macro that is used for method-tracing. When SOM_TraceLevel is set to either 1 or 2, a message is produced each time a method is entered. Setting SOM_TraceLevel to 2 also traces the methods supplied as part of the SOM run time. You can control and suppress the method tracing by placing the following after the #include statement for <classname>.ih:

```
_#define <classname>MethodDebug(c,m) SOMNoTrace(c,m)
```

- *return* invokes the parent class for an override method. The SOM Precompiler assumes you'll want to add value to a method, and then let the parent do what it usually does.

HELLOWPS.CSC: The Output of the SOM Precompiler

```
/*
 * This file was generated by the SOM Compiler.
 * FileName: D:\OS220BK\HELLOWPS\HELLOWPS.c.
 * Generated using:
 *      SOM Precompiler spc: 1.22
 *      SOM Emitter emitc: 1.24
 */

/*
 *
 *    Module Name: HELLOWPS - A Hello World Object
 *
 */


#define HelloWPS_Class_Source
#include "HELLOWPS.ih"

#undef SOM_CurrentClass
#define SOM_CurrentClass SOMMeta
SOM_Scope ULONG   SOMLINK hellowpsM_wpclsQueryStyle(M_HelloWPS *somSelf)
{
    /* M_HelloWPSData *somThis = M_HelloWPSGetData(somSelf); */
    M_HelloWPSMethodDebug("M_HelloWPS","hellowpsM_wpclsQueryStyle");

    return (parent_wpclsQueryStyle(somSelf));
}
```

Figure 41-5 (Part 1 of 2). HELLOWPS.CSC: What The SOM Precompiler Returns.

```
SOM_Scope PSZ    SOMLINK hellowpsM_wpclsQueryTitle(M_HelloWPS *somSelf)
{
    /* M_HelloWPSData *somThis = M_HelloWPSGetData(somSelf); */
    M_HelloWPSMethodDebug("M_HelloWPS","hellowpsM_wpclsQueryTitle");

    return (parent_wpclsQueryTitle(somSelf));
}

SOM_Scope ULONG   SOMLINK hellowpsM_wpclsQueryDefaultView(M_HelloWPS *somSelf)
{
    /* M_HelloWPSData *somThis = M_HelloWPSGetData(somSelf); */
    M_HelloWPSMethodDebug("M_HelloWPS","hellowpsM_wpclsQueryDefaultView");

    return (parent_wpclsQueryDefaultView(somSelf));
}

#undef SOM_CurrentClass
#define SOM_CurrentClass SOMInstance
SOM_Scope BOOL    SOMLINK hellowps_wpModifyPopupMenu(HelloWPS *somSelf,
HWND hwndMenu,
HWND hwndCnr,
ULONG iPosition)
{
    /* HelloWPSData *somThis = HelloWPSGetData(somSelf); */
    HelloWPSMethodDebug("HelloWPS","hellowps_wpModifyPopupMenu");

    return (parent_wpModifyPopupMenu(somSelf,hwndMenu,hwndCnr,iPosition));
}

SOM_Scope BOOL    SOMLINK hellowps_wpMenuItemSelected(HelloWPS *somSelf,
HWND hwndFrame,
ULONG ulMenuId)
{
    /* HelloWPSData *somThis = HelloWPSGetData(somSelf); */
    HelloWPSMethodDebug("HelloWPS","hellowps_wpMenuItemSelected");

    return (parent_wpMenuItemSelected(somSelf,hwndFrame,ulMenuId));
}

SOM_Scope HWND    SOMLINK hellowps_wpOpen(HelloWPS *somSelf,
HWND hwndCnr,
ULONG ulView,
ULONG param)
{
    /* HelloWPSData *somThis = HelloWPSGetData(somSelf); */
    HelloWPSMethodDebug("HelloWPS","hellowps_wpOpen");

    return (parent_wpOpen(somSelf,hwndCnr,ulView,param));
}
```

Figure 41-5 (Part 2 of 2). HELLOWPS.CSC: What The SOM Precompiler Returns.

Writing the Method Code

To complete the class-implementation process, you must modify the stubs and supply the code for each of the stubbed method procedures. The light areas in the listing (see Figure 41-6) show the code we created; the dark areas are the stubs generated by the SOM Precompiler.

First, lets walk through the three class method overrides and explain what they each do. These methods will be invoked at the time when the object is created. By overriding them, we are able to give the **HelloWPS** object its special look. Here's what these class overrides do:

- *hellowpsM_wpclsQueryStyle* this method specifies that the object not allow creation from a template. We then return control to the parent method. Why? Actually, this item that should only be of interest to "irate" developers.[2]

- *hellowpsM_wpclsQueryTitle* this method simply returns the class title "HelloWPS." Notice that we do not return control to the parent method; it would defeat what we just did. The title will appear with the object icon and is given to any instances of the class that are instantiated without a title. Since the default title applies to all instances of the class, it is implemented in a class method rather than an instance method.

- *hellowpsM_wpclsQueryDefaultView* this method returns the default view menu item for the object. This is the view that we created. The menu item ID will be explained in the next few methods.

Now, let's lets walk through the three instance method overrides and explain what they each do:

- *hellowps_wpModifyPopupMenu* is called when an object's context menu pop-up is activated (see SOM/WPS tutorial). The method adds a menu item "Say Hello" to the set of menu choices (this is the same choice that we said was going to be the default open view). However, menu items are Presentation Manager resources in the class DLL. This means that we will need to obtain the module handle for that class DLL, which is required when loading Presentation Manager resources such as strings, pointers, or dialogs (see Figure 41-7). To do that, we first call the _somLocateClassFile, which returns the class DLL's file name and path (this is part of SOM's resource location run-time services). Then we issue the PM DosQueryModuleHandle API call to obtain the module handle. Now that we have a module handle, we can invoke the method _wpInsertPopupMenuItems (see tutorial) and tell it to insert the ID_OPEN-MENU item, which was defined in Figure 41-7.

- *hellowps_wpMenuItemSelected* gets invoked when any pop-up item is selected. The method consists of a case statement that determines the item selected from the context menu. Our method override is only interested in the OPEN_HELLOWPS

---

[2] It turns out that you can't replace a class DLL until you've eliminated all instances of that class in the WPS. So why not just drag every object to the shredder and get a clean slate? Yes, but you can't drag a template to the shredder. So being irate developers we just suppressed the creation of the default template for this object, by ORing a CLSSTYLE_NEVERTEMPLATE.

menu item. If it is selected, we invoke the **_wpOpen** method on our own object; otherwise, we return control to the parent method and let it do the work.

• *hellowps_wpOpen* gets invoked when a user opens a view of the object. If the view selected is OPEN_HELLOWPS, the method issues a **_wpQueryIcon** to obtain the icon that appears on the main menu bar and then calls **CreateHelloWPS_View**. If it's not OPEN_HELLOWPS that is selected, control is returned to the parent method. The **CreateHelloWPS_View** and **HelloWindowProc** are similar to the PM procedures that were described in Chapter 39, "The Presentation Manager."

HELLOWPS.CSC: After We Add the Class Logic.

```
/**********************************************************************/
/*  OBJECT NAME:  HELLOWPS -- Hello Workplace Shell object          */
/*                                                                   */
/*  DESCRIPTION:  This object displays a Hello window from a workplace */
/*    shell object.                                                  */
/*                                                                   */
/**********************************************************************/
#define HelloWPS_Class_Source
#define M_HelloWPS_Class_Source

#include "hellowps.ih"     /* implementation header emitted from CSC file */
#include "hellowps.ph"     /* private header emitted from CSC file        */

/*_____*/
/* global variables and function declarations for this module        */
/*_____*/
CHAR       ClassTitle[] = "HelloWPS";              /* Title of this class */
HPOINTER   ptrIcon;

HWND CreateHelloWPS_View(HelloWPS* somSelf);
MRESULT EXPENTRY HelloWindowProc(HWND hwnd, ULONG msg, MPARAM mp1, MPARAM mp2);

/**********************************************************************/
/* Class Method Overrides                                           */
/**********************************************************************/
#undef SOM_CurrentClass
#define SOM_CurrentClass SOMMeta

/*_____*/
/* OVERRIDE: _wpclsQueryStyle                                         */
/*_____*/
SOM_Scope ULONG    SOMLINK hellowpsM_wpclsQueryStyle(M_HelloWPS *somSelf)
{
    /* M_HelloWPSData *somThis = M_HelloWPSGetData(somSelf); */
    M_HelloWPSMethodDebug("M_HelloWPS","hellowpsM_wpclsQueryStyle");

    return (parent_wpclsQueryStyle(somSelf) | CLSSTYLE_NEVERTEMPLATE);
}

/*_____*/
/* OVERRIDE: _wpclsQueryTitle                                         */
/*_____*/
SOM_Scope PSZ    SOMLINK hellowpsM_wpclsQueryTitle(M_HelloWPS *somSelf)
```

Figure 41-6 (Part 1 of 5). HELLOWPS.CSC: The Completed Program.

```
{
    /* M_HelloWPSData *somThis = M_HelloWPSGetData(somSelf); */
    M_HelloWPSMethodDebug("M_HelloWPS","hellowpsM_wpclsQueryTitle");

    return (ClassTitle);
}

/*_____*/
/* OVERRIDE: _wpclsQueryDefaultView                            */
/*_____*/
SOM_Scope ULONG   SOMLINK hellowpsM_wpclsQueryDefaultView(M_HelloWPS *somSelf)
{
    /* M_HelloWPSData *somThis = M_HelloWPSGetData(somSelf); */
    M_HelloWPSMethodDebug("M_HelloWPS","hellowpsM_wpclsQueryDefaultView");

    return(OPEN_HELLOWPS);
}

/****************************************************************************/
/* Instance Method overrides                                              */
/****************************************************************************/
#undef SOM_CurrentClass
#define SOM_CurrentClass SOMInstance

/*_____*/
/* OVERRIDE: _wpModifyPopupMenu                                */
/*_____*/
SOM_Scope BOOL    SOMLINK hellowps_wpModifyPopupMenu(HelloWPS *somSelf,
                HWND hwndMenu,
                HWND hwndCnr,
                ULONG iPosition)
{
    zString     ModulePathName;              /* DLL Module path and name*/
    HMODULE     hmod;                        /* DLL MODULE handle       */

    /* HelloWPSData *somThis = HelloWPSGetData(somSelf); */
    HelloWPSMethodDebug("HelloWPS","hellowps_wpModifyPopupMenu");

    /*_____*/
    /* Get Module Name and Handle */
    /*_____*/
    ModulePathName = _somLocateClassFile(SOMClassMgrObject,
                    SOM_IdFromString(ClassTitle),
                    HelloWPS_MajorVersion, HelloWPS_MinorVersion);
    DosQueryModuleHandle( ModulePathName, &hmod);

    /*_____*/
    /* Insert "Say Hello" into Open */
    /* Menu                      */
    /*_____*/
    if (!_wpInsertPopupMenuItems( somSelf, hwndMenu, 0,
                        hmod, ID_OPENMENU, WPMENUID_OPEN))
      { ShowMsg(" HelloWPS ", "ERROR: _wpInsertPopupMenuItems");
      }
    return (TRUE);
}

/*_____*/
/* OVERRIDE: _wpMenuItemSelected                               */
/*_____*/
SOM_Scope BOOL    SOMLINK hellowps_wpMenuItemSelected(HelloWPS *somSelf,
```

Figure 41-6 (Part 2 of 5). HELLOWPS.CSC: The Completed Program.

```
                    HWND hwndFrame,
                    ULONG ulMenuId)
{
    /* HelloWPSData *somThis = HelloWPSGetData(somSelf); */
    HelloWPSMethodDebug("HelloWPS","hellowps_wpMenuItemSelected");

    switch( ulMenuId )
    {
        case OPEN_HELLOWPS:
            _wpOpen(somSelf, NULLHANDLE, OPEN_HELLOWPS, 0);
            break;

        default:
            return parent_wpMenuItemSelected(somSelf, hwndFrame, ulMenuId);

            break;
    }
    return TRUE;
}

/*_____*/
/* OVERRIDE: _wpopen                                                  */
/*_____*/
SOM_Scope HWND    SOMLINK hellowps_wpOpen(HelloWPS *somSelf,
                    HWND hwndCnr,
                    ULONG ulView,
                    ULONG param)
{
    /* HelloWPSData *somThis = HelloWPSGetData(somSelf); */
    HelloWPSMethodDebug("HelloWPS","hellowps_wpOpen");

    switch (ulView)
    {
      case OPEN_HELLOWPS:
            ptrIcon = _wpQueryIcon(somSelf);
            return CreateHelloWPS_View(somSelf);
            break;

        default:
            return parent_wpOpen(somSelf,hwndCnr,ulView,param);
            break;

    }   /* end switch (ulView) */

    return (parent_wpOpen(somSelf,hwndCnr,ulView,param));
}

/***********************************************************************/
/* Non-Method Functions                                               */
/***********************************************************************/
/*_____*/
/* Routine to Create Hello Object View.                               */
/*_____*/
HWND CreateHelloWPS_View (HelloWPS* somSelf)
{
  HAB   hab;                            /* PM anchor block handle     */
  HWND  hwndClient;                     /* Client area window handle  */
  HWND  hwndFrame;                      /* Frame window handle        */
  ULONG flCreate;                       /* Window creation control flags*/

  hab = WinQueryAnchorBlock(HWND_DESKTOP);
```

Figure 41-6 (Part 3 of 5).   HELLOWPS.CSC: The Completed Program.

```
    WinRegisterClass(                          /* Register window class      */
        hab,                                   /* Anchor block handle        */
        "HelloWindow",                         /* Window class name          */
        HelloWindowProc,                       /* Address of window procedure */
        CS_SIZEREDRAW,                         /* Class style                */
        0);                                    /* No extra window words      */

    flCreate = FCF_TITLEBAR | FCF_SYSMENU |    /* Set frame control flags    */
               FCF_SIZEBORDER | FCF_MINMAX |
               FCF_SHELLPOSITION | FCF_TASKLIST;


    hwndFrame = WinCreateStdWindow(
                HWND_DESKTOP,                  /* Desktop window is parent   */
                0L,                            /* No frame styles            */
                &flCreate,                     /* Frame control flag         */
                "HelloWindow",                 /* Client window class name    */
                "Hello WPS",                   /* Window Title               */
                0L,                            /* No special class style     */
                NULLHANDLE,                    /* Resource is in .EXE file   */
                ID_FRAME,                      /* Frame window identifier    */
                &hwndClient);                  /* Client window handle       */

    WinSendMsg(hwndFrame, WM_SETICON, (MPARAM)ptrIcon, (MPARAM)0);

    WinSetWindowPos(hwndFrame, HWND_TOP, 230, 150, 300, 185,
                    SWP_SIZE | SWP_MOVE | SWP_ACTIVATE | SWP_SHOW | SWP_ZORDER);

    return hwndFrame;                          /* success */
}

/*_____*/
/* Window Procedure for Say Hello View                            */
/*_____*/
MRESULT EXPENTRY HelloWindowProc( HWND hwnd, ULONG msg,
                                  MPARAM mp1, MPARAM mp2 )
{
  HPS    hps;                                  /* Presentation Space handle  */
  RECTL  rc;                                   /* Rectangle coordinates      */
  CHAR   szHello[] = "Hello from the Workplace Shell";
  HWND   hwndFrame;

  hwndFrame = WinQueryWindow(hwnd, QW_PARENT);

  switch( msg )
  {
    case WM_ERASEBACKGROUND:
      /*_____*/
      /* cause window background to be */
      /* painted in SYSCLR_WINDOW      */
      /*_____*/
      return (MRESULT)( TRUE );

    case WM_PAINT:
      /*_____*/
      /* paint the window              */
      /*_____*/
      hps = WinBeginPaint(hwnd,
                    (HPS)NULLHANDLE,
                    &rc );                      /* Create a presentation space */
```

Figure 41-6 (Part 4 of 5). HELLOWPS.CSC: The Completed Program.

```
      WinDrawText(hps,                              /* presentation space        */
                  -1,szHello,                       /* string, calculate strlen  */
                  &rc,                              /* rectangle from WinBeginPaint*/
                  CLR_DARKBLUE,SYSCLR_WINDOW,       /* Fore/Background colors     */
                  DT_VCENTER | DT_CENTER);          /* string placement in rect.  */
      WinEndPaint( hps );
      break;

    case WM_CLOSE:
      /*———————————————————————*/
      /* cause the application to end       */
      /*———————————————————————*/
      WinPostMsg( hwnd, WM_QUIT, OL, OL );
      WinDestroyWindow ( hwndFrame ) ;
      break;

    default:
      /*———————————————————————*/
      /* unknown messages to default       */

      /*———————————————————————*/
      return WinDefWindowProc( hwnd, msg, mp1, mp2 );
  }
  return FALSE;
}
```

Figure 41-6　(Part 5 of 5).　HELLOWPS.CSC: The Completed Program.

HELLOWPS.RC:　Creating the PM Resource

The (.RC) file contains resource script definitions for Presentation Manager resources, as well as statements that include resources from other files. Figure 41-7 points to the icon resource hellpwps.ico and contains the definition for the additional menu item, "Say Hello."

```
#include "hellowps.ih"

POINTER ID_ICON LOADONCALL MOVEABLE DISCARDABLE hellowps.ico

MENU ID_OPENMENU LOADONCALL MOVEABLE DISCARDABLE
BEGIN
    MENUITEM "Say ~Hello", OPEN_HELLOWPS, OL, MIA_CHECKED
END
```

Figure 41-7.　HELLOWPS.RC: The Menu (.RC) File.

Compiling and Linking the Object DLL

We've defined the C code that executes the object's methods, and we created the PM resources. We're ready to create the object's DLL. This step is easy. We just complete the build process shown in the bottom of Figure 41-3. This means that we reinvoke the NMAKE utility using the same make file shown in Figure 41-4.

How smart is the SOM Precompiler? What happens if you've written tons of (.C) code for your methods, and then need to modify the (.CSC) file to create an additional method? Will the Precompiler replace your existing code with empty stubs and destroy your work?

The answer is that the SOM Precompiler is smart enough to know not to touch existing code. This Precompiler will add the stub for the new method at the bottom of the (.C) file; it will not mess with your code. However, if you were to change the prototype declaration in the (.CSC) file for one of your existing methods, the Precompiler would not recognize it. So it's smart, but not that smart. You can still confuse it if you want.

Registering the Class With the Workplace Shell

Now that you have a DLL for that class and have copied it to the machine's "\OS2\DLL" subdirectory, you must register the class with the WPS. This is normally done using the **WinRegisterObjectClass** call. Or if you're lazy, like we are, you can use the system-supplied REXX utility to do the call for you. The REXX code you need is shown in Figure 41-8.

```
/* Register the a WPS class */

/* load the REXX utility */
call RxFuncAdd 'SysLoadFuncs', 'RexxUtil', 'SysLoadFuncs'
call SysLoadFuncs

/* Register Class with WPS shell */
if SysRegisterObjectClass('HelloWPS',,              /* Class Name        */
                          'HELLOWPS')               /* DLL Name          */
    then say 'HelloWPS class registered sucessfully.'
    else say 'Error registering HelloWPS class.'
```

Figure 41-8.   REGISTER.CMD: The REXX Calls to Register a New WPS Class.

Creating An Object Instance

Now that WPS knows about your class, you can create an object that's an instance of the new class by issuing **WinCreateObject**. Or, you can also do that using the REXX utility (see Figure 41-9). Notice that we can specify the name of the WPS folder where we want that object to appear. We placed it on the desktop, and then what you see is a smiling little guy (see Figure 41-10).

```
/* Make an instance of a HelloWPS object */

/* load the REXX utility */
call RxFuncAdd 'SysLoadFuncs', 'RexxUtil', 'SysLoadFuncs'
call SysLoadFuncs

/* make the object instance */
if SysCreateObject('HelloWPS',          ,        /* Class name        */
                   'Hello',             ,        /* Instance name     */
                   '<WP_DESKTOP>',      ,        /* Folder for object */
                   'ICONRESOURCE=100,HELLOWPS')  /* Object ID */
   then say 'HelloWPS instance created sucessfully.'
   else say 'Error creating HelloWPS instance.'
```

Figure 41-9. INSTANCE.CMD: The REXX Calls to Create an Object Instance.

Saying Hello From WPS

It was a long journey to say Hello, but we have a little guy that can do it. Was it worth it? There was certainly a lot of code just to say "Hello." But look at the universe that you've unlocked. This object is totally Workplace Shell aware. Building OOUIs is that easy once you've got the hang of it. The screen captures (Figure 41-10 through Figure 41-15) show what you can do with this Hello object. How much code does a traditional PM program require to do that?

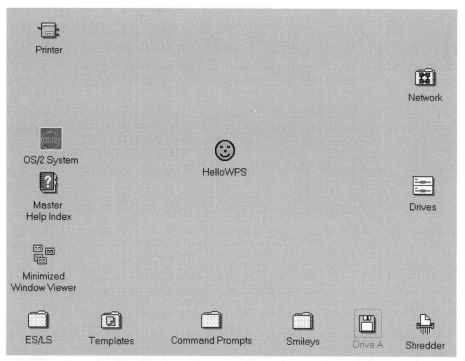

Figure 41-10. A "HelloWPS" Object After It Is First Created on the Desktop.

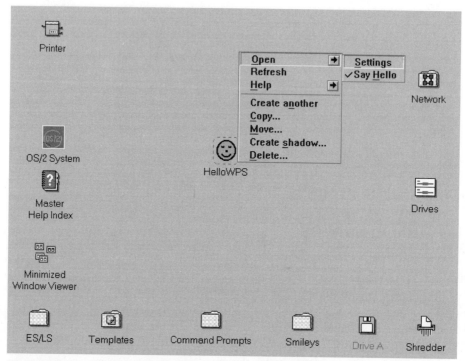

Figure 41-11.   The Context Pop-Up Menu for "HelloWPS."

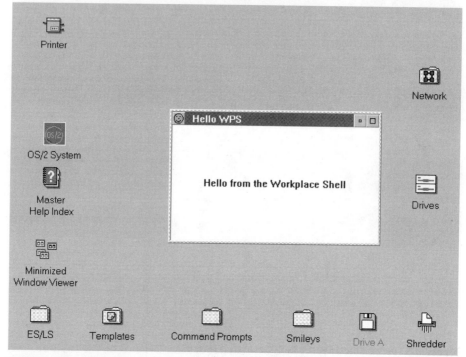

Figure 41-12.   The Default View of the "HelloWPS" Object.

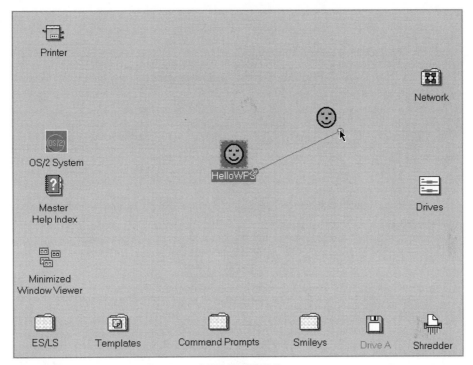

Figure 41-13. Create a Shadow of "HelloWPS."

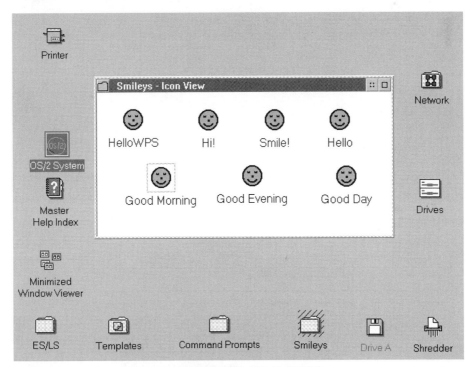

Figure 41-14. Populating the World With "HelloWPS."

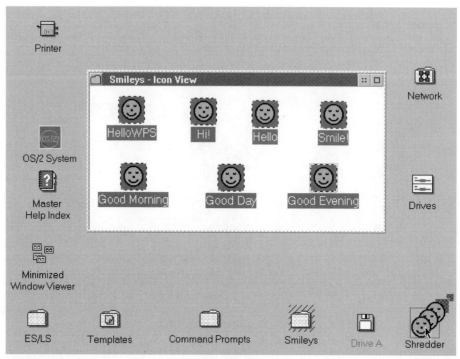

Figure 41-15.   Taking "HelloWPS" to the Shredder.

Part VII

The Grand Finale, Club Med Client/Server Application

We will end the book with a fun program that connects an OOUI front-end client with a back-end *Transaction Server*. This is the adventurous grand finale that brings together all the elements developed in this book. The project of Part VII is to take you through the complete design and implementation of a client/server application. To pick on a fun topic, we will develop an Online Transaction Program (OLTP) that provides a fictitious reservation system for Club Med. Here are some highlights of what Part VII provides:

- A conceptual model that helps you design, rapidly prototype, develop, and document client/server applications.

- A multithreaded, event-driven OOUI client that was created using WPS/SOM classes.

- A multiuser transaction server. The server is based on Named Pipes and it supports the movement of Binary Large Objects (BLOBs) between the clients and the server.

- An object "helper" that encapsulates advanced PM graphic constructs for the display of Bitmaps, Metafiles, and text files.

- A WPS/SOM object that encapsulates the mechanics of a Named Pipes based RPC.

- A WPS/SOM container object that uses the server for persistent storage.

- A working client/server application.

Here is the road map we will follow in Part VII:

- In Chapter 42, "Which Comes First: The Client or The Server," we present a short diatribe on the design of client/server applications that will serve as an appetizer for the Club Med program.
- In Chapter 43, "Designing the Club Med Application," we start the three-chapter Grand Finale, which consists of writing a complete Club Med client/server program. This chapter introduces the Club Med application and database, and walks you through the user interface.
- Chapter 44, "The Club Med Client," develops the client side of the Club Med application. The code consists of six new WPS/SOM classes that provide the OOUI object look, PM views, and thread-based interaction with the transaction server using RPCs. This chapter provides an architectural foundation for the creation of OOUI front-ends for OLTP.
- Chapter 45, "The Club Med Server," provides the code that implements the *back-end* of the Club Med application. This is essentially a transaction server engine that receives requests for work from networked clients using Named Pipes. We created our own "slim RPC" implementation on top of Named Pipes (no bells and whistles, but very fast).

Chapter 42

Which Comes First:
The Client or The Server?

Database application designers and programmers have had it easy. In the past, user interfaces were simple constructs driven by simple terminals. The primary focus was on the database and transaction code, leaving the human to simply respond, like an extension of the application. But with client/server applications, the tables have turned. The ultimate goal of client/server solutions is to provide mission-critical applications that have the ease-of-use and responsiveness of standalone PCs.

Client/Server is primarily a relationship between programs running on separate machines. As such, it requires an infrastructure to do things standalone PCs never had to worry about. For example, robust interprocess communications over LANs must be included in the design. Graphical interfaces using GUIs and OOUIs must be exploited to make applications look and feel more like real-world objects instead of programming processes. User interfaces are becoming complex, responsive, ad hoc environments that put the emphasis on the work of the human. OOUI clients bring humans into the distributed loop, which inevitably adds a host of complications. Humans make lots of errors, do unexpected things, and typically require lots of information from diverse sources. The more advanced OOUIs will introduce a new breed of *superclients* that turn the client workstation into multimedia "workplaces" where many parallel dialogs are conducted with the server.[1]

OOUIs also give the user much more freedom than GUIs or terminal-based systems. Users are free to organize their visual objects (and desktop) in any way they please. They are not tied to the rigid logic of task-oriented applications. OOUIs have no main

---

[1] The term "superclient" was introduced by **Forrester Research** (May, 1992) to describe client workstations that are connected to multiple servers, provide a highly visual desktop with intertwined applications, and require preemptive multitasking. Forrester predicts that US shipments for such workstations will grow from 829k in 1992 to 2.7 M in 1994 (23% of these clients are expected to run OS/2 2.0).

panels and navigation screens. In fact, with the Workplace Shell, it is hard to tell where one application starts and another ends (or what is an application object versus a system object). There are just visual objects everywhere.

This begs two important questions: does client/server require a new approach to system development? Where design used to predominantly start at the database, which comes first now: the client or the server?

This chapter examines these questions. To answer them we will discuss the anatomy of database centered client/server applications, taking into account the three components of client/server applications: the client, the server, and the network transactions. Based on this discussion, we will propose a system development strategy for client/server applications.

COMPARING OLTP AND DECISION SUPPORT CLIENT/SERVERS

Database centered client/server applications fall into two categories: Decision Support Systems (DSS), and Online Transaction Processing (OLTP). These two client/server categories provide dramatically different types of business solutions. These differences will have to be understood before answering, which comes first: the client or the server?

The Anatomy of Client/Server Systems for Decision Support

Decision support systems are used to analyze data and create reports. They provide the business professional with the means to obtain exactly the information they need for making better business decisions. A successful decision support system must provide the user with flexible access to data and the tools to manipulate and present that data in all kinds of report formats. Users should be able to construct elaborate queries, answer "what if" questions, search for correlations in the data, plot the data, and move it into other applications such as spreadsheets and word processor documents. Decision support systems are not generally time-critical and can tolerate slower response times. Client/Server decision support systems are typically not suitable for mission-critical production environments. They have poor integrity controls and limited multi-table access capabilities. The operations invoked in finding the information may involve large quantities of data which means that the level of concurrency control is not very granular; for example, a user may want to view and update an entire table.

Decision Support systems are built using dynamic SQL on database servers. This type of server was demonstrated to be very slow in Part V. The client side of the application is typically built using a new generation of screen-layout tools that allow non-programmers to build GUI front-ends and reports by painting, pointing, and clicking (see Chapter 38, "A Taxonomy of GUI and OOUI Tools").

These database-aware tools visually let you combine graphical objects like radio buttons, check boxes, menus, and scroll-bars to create sophisticated display panels that integrate directly with the database. Most of these GUI tools have built-in capabilities to automatically generate forms that can be used to add, update, and delete database records. They provide the ability to create multi-table queries (joins) and display the results in one record-per-form format or multiple-record columnar forms with pick lists. The tools make use of the database dictionary to map table columns to fields on a screen. SQL statements can be built "on-the-fly" and associated with a particular push button or menu item. Point and click query builders take the work out of formulating the question. The tools provide visual facilities for creating base tables and defining relations between tables. All this is done with "canned" event-handlers provided by the tool vendor.

The more sophisticated tools allow the user to create links with other applications on the desktop using the clipboard or Dynamic Data Exchange (DDE). Cut and paste through the clipboard is used to transfer information into other applications under user control. DDE is used to automatically update documents and spreadsheets with the results of a query. It lets you automate scripts such as "Place the output of this query into this spreadsheet, then run it through a graphics package, print the report, and send the results to a distribution list through electronic mail."

The Anatomy of Client/Server Systems for OLTP

OLTP client/server systems are used to create applications in all walks of business. These include reservation systems, point-of-sale, tracking systems, inventory control, stockbroker workstations, and manufacturing shop floor control. These are, typically, mission-critical applications that require a 1-3 second response time one hundred percent of the time. The number of clients supported by an OLTP system may vary dramatically, but the response time must be maintained. OLTP applications also require tight controls over the security and integrity of the database. The reliability and availability of the overall system must be very high. Data must be kept consistent and correct.

In OLTP systems, the client interacts with a Transaction Server instead of a Database Server. This interaction is necessary to provide the high performance these applications require (see TP1 Benchmarks in Part V). With a transaction server, the client invokes *remote procedures* that reside on a server. These remote procedures execute as transactions against the server's database (see Part V). OLTP client/server applications require code to be written for both the client component and for the server transactions. The communication overhead in OLTP applications is kept to a minimum. The client interaction with the transaction server is typically limited to short, structured exchanges. The exchange consists of a single request/reply (as opposed to multiple SQL statements). A peer-to-peer protocol is needed to issue the call to the remote procedure and obtain the results.

So, as you can see, developing OLTP in a client/server setting still requires intensive programmer involvement. Programmers are needed to write the transaction code on the server, work out the semantics of the network exchanges, and develop the client application. Non-GUI OLTP clients such as robots, testers, ATMs may require less coding on the client side. But, GUIs and OOUIs are becoming the predominant face of OLTP business computing. Rather than typing at the keyboard, users of GUI clients can interact with the OLTP server via their mouse and graphical icons, menus, and forms.

Tools are becoming available to help developers create GUI clients (but not yet OOUIs) for OLTP systems. GUI generator tools allow developers (typically programmers) to associate predefined graphical objects—such as forms, fields, menus, list boxes, and push buttons—with programs. These associations are event-driven, so event-handlers must then be coded to provide the logic of the application. This is different from decision support tools, which provide canned event-handlers. GUI tools, as we explained in Part VI, are categorized by the event-handler programming facilities and metaphors they provide.

The Development Effort for OLTP and Decision Support

As we show in Table 42-1, decision support applications can be created directly by end users. Network administrators are still needed to help set up the client/server system, and DBAs may help assemble collections of tables, views, and columns that are relevant to the user (the user should then be able to create decision support applications without further DBA involvement). Because the design of client/server systems for OLTP is a lot more involved, consequently it requires a large amount of custom programming effort. To develop these systems successfully, we will need creative new approaches to systems development. These new approaches will emphasize the importance of rapid-prototyping, as we will explain in the next sections.

Table 42-1. Comparing the Programming Effort for Decision Support and OLTP.

Client/Server Application	Client	Server	Messages
Decision Support	Off-the-shelf decision support tool with end-user programming. Canned event-handlers and communications with the server.	Off-the-shelf database server. Tables usually defined for OLTP application. DBA creates flexible views to make user autonomous.	SQL messages that are being standardized for multivendor interoperability.
OLTP	Custom application. GUI tool lays out screen, but the event-handlers and remote procedure calls require programming at the C level.	Custom application. Transaction code must be programmed at the C level. The database is off-the-shelf.	Custom messages are optimized for performance and secure access.

Which Comes First: Decision Support or OLTP?

There is another interesting question lurking in our examination of client/server application design: *Which comes first: decision support or OLTP?* We need to answer this question because both systems usually go after the same data, and we need to know where to start the system development process. An OLTP application is a production system that represents the state of a business unit. OLTP client/server applications usually replace (or automate) a manual system or a terminal-based system that runs on mainframes or superminis. So, typically the design of an application and its database starts at the OLTP level. The decision support system is used to query the state of the business as collected by the OLTP application. Very few multiuser databases are specified for decision support only. In other words, it takes an OLTP system to collect the data that will be analyzed by the decision support system. This means that the OLTP application should be the primary focus of the client/server system design (at least until a production system is in place).

THE CLIENT/SERVER DEVELOPMENT PROCESS

Traditional (terminal-based) OLTP system design has started with the data. The screens were developed primarily to drive the process of filling in the database, so they are designed after the transactions and tables are defined. Client/Server OLTP applications, on the other hand, require a far more complex design approach:

- The interface is more flexible than terminals, and the user is allowed more latitude.
- The object-based front-end designs place a lot more intelligence on the client side of the application.
- The messages between the client and the server are custom-built and application-specific.
- The design must be optimized to take advantage of the parallelism inherent in the distributed application.

This leads us to a design approach unique to OLTP client/server applications: you must start your design with both the client and the server. So, you have two starting points in a client/server application: the GUI/OUUI and the data (unless the data for a business process is already in place). The GUI/OOUI and data designs come together at the transaction level. The transaction maps the screen to the database and vice versa. Sounds complex? The rest of this chapter will explain how this is done. We will also focus solely on OOUI clients to prepare you for the Club Med application.

Rapid Prototyping Is Essential

One way to avoid a "chicken and egg" situation, like the one in Figure 42-1, from developing between OOUI-centric clients and DBMS-centric servers is to use a rapid prototyping methodology. Rapid prototyping allows you to develop your system incrementally. You start with the client and work your way iteratively towards the server. You always move in small steps, constantly refining the design as you go along. Make sure to involve your end user during all the stages of the interface design. In this form of delta development, the system is incrementally refined until you develop a working prototype that is mature enough to be placed into production. This approach may place a larger burden on the programmer than the traditional approaches, which rely on up-front analysis and design. And, with rapid-prototyping, you also run the risk that a cost-cutting management decision may place a non-optimized "working" proto-type prematurely into production. At the other extreme, you may encounter another risk: the perpetual prototyping syndrome.

Figure 42-1. Parallel Development Process of OLTP Client/Server Applications.

These risks are easily outweighed by the benefits that "rapid-prototyping" provides in developing a OOUI client/server OLTP system. In client/server environments, it is difficult to determine a priori how the system is supposed to work (the OOUI design, the network performance, and multi-user loading). It has been our experience that user specs cannot anticipate all the needs of the users. Specs cannot adequately convey the potential OOUI technology offers. If you ask the users for guidance, the chances are that they'll give you the wrong answers based on existing solutions (manual or termi-nal-based solutions). Instead, you should show them what the technology can do for them and the new visual dimensions OOUIs offer; then work with them on developing the application.

Invariably, OOUIs can capture more of the business process than either GUIs or terminal-based front-ends. A rapid-prototype will help in the discovery of the applica-tion objects (or business objects). Users will find it easier to discuss visual business objects, and the visual prototype will help develop the design specifications.

Build a prototype; try it out. The trick is to be able to build the application many times. It is easier to talk about something that can be demonstrated live and used. Moreover, it is important that the prototype be developed in an environment where the issues of client/server performance, network overheads, system management, and transaction server design can be tested live. OLTP systems require a lot of monitoring, fine-tuning, and administration. It is better for you to get acquainted with these issues early in the game.

From Prototype to Working System

The OOUI and the objects which make it up permeate the entire application and determine its shape. An application can be seen as a collection of visual business objects. The design of the application starts from the objects (and views) the user sees on the screen, and then works its way towards the server and the database structure. Prototypes are used to identify, with your customer's participation, the user model: What business objects are needed and what do they do? Prototyping is an iterative activity with many false starts. Here is how the typical prototype evolves:

1. *Understand the business process*. It is a prerequisite that you understand what the application is all about at the business level. So gather the requirements and study the tasks: What does the customer really want?

2. *Define your business objects*. What the user sees in an OLTP application are objects containing views that react to user input and actions. The objects are manipulated according to the requirements of the business process. You should create user objects that correspond to real-life entities, for example, a seat on an airplane. What are the main object types in the application? What other objects do they contain? What are the attributes of the objects? What functions do they have? How do they behave? What are the relationships between objects? What are the "composed of" relationships (is-part-of)? What are the dependency and collaboration relationships (is-analogous-to, is-kind-of, depends-upon)?

3. *Work on the detailed object views*. What context menu actions apply to each object? What views are required? Are business forms views required? Can the views be grouped in Notebook pages? What widgets controls including—input/output fields, list boxes, pushbuttons, menus, sliders, value-sets, and so on—will appear in the views? What level of help is needed? What data validation at the field level is required? What level of triggers are required (on error, on message etc.)? How are external procedures and RPC invoked?

4. *Develop dry run scenarios*. You can create your screen objects and animate the application (OOUI tools should provide this capability). Use the scenarios to validate the object model of the user interface. The scenarios should also help you identify the major event-driven interactions.

5. *Walk through a system scenario*. Such a scenario should follow a transaction from its source through its execution. Identify the protocols that link the different elements. Blow up this scenario in areas that require more detail. Run an application scenario for each business object. Identify redundant behaviors. Which objects can be reused?

6. *Identify transaction sources*. A client/server system can be thought of as a client-driven event system. The server is, in a sense, passively waiting on requests from clients. The client in turn is driven by the user who is at the "controls" within the confines of the business process. The drag and drop of visual objects is typically the source of transactions. Information required upon opening a container or view may also be the source of a transaction. Object/action intersections almost always lead to the generation of a transaction. There is also a high probability that events such as data entry, menu selections, pushing a button, and action dialogs will generate transactions. The visual client interface will eventually be "brought to life" by writing the transactions that are triggered by the user interaction. OO purists can think of transactions as methods that manipulate persistent data.[2]

7. *Define your database tables*. You are now in a position to take a first stab at defining the database objects that correspond to the visual business objects you just created. Iterate on this step until you get it right. Many trade-offs are involved. The object/action orientation of the client design can help transform the visual objects into an entity-relationship model for database objects. The actions translate into transactions on database entities. A database entity, in turn, consists of a structure of relationships and constraints between database tables. Publish the resulting CREATE TABLE statements, and then use them to document the data types and the relationships between tables (such as referential integrity constraints).

8. *Publish the client/server messages*. Messages are the methods by which the clients execute transactions on servers. Define the major transactions and the request/reply messages associated with them, including any required file transfers. The messages provide the only coupling between the clients and the server. The publication of the messages advertises to the world what a server does. It is a *binding contract* between the server and its clients. A message typically has a command field and a data field, which contains the command parameters. In our scheme of things, we divide transactions (or commands) into two broad categories based on the type of responses they produce:

---

[2]In strict OO terms, a raw transaction server is a single object that encapsulates the entire database (as its private instance data). A back-end application could be written as a set of objects that exports methods (the transactions). You will eventually hit a design point where SQL's shared data tables and OO's encapsulation discipline don't mix very well.

1. *Request/reply transactions* are transactions that generate short replies. These transactions are usually updates, inserts, deletes, or single-row queries against database objects.
2. *Bulk response transactions* are transactions that generate one or more result files. Think of a result file as a BLOB, which may result from a multirow SELECT or from the request for a metafile or bitmap.

9. ***Develop your code one object at a time***. Write the SQL code for each transaction. Do that one object at a time. There are typically many transactions per business object. Validate the user interface and the performance of the system with your customer.

10. ***From prototype to working system***. A working system is the sum of all the business objects it contains. Since you are developing your system incrementally, you will have a full working system when you've coded your last business object.

What About Decision Support?

We're not done yet. Where does decision support come into play? After a suitable prototype is developed, you can involve the user with writing the reports and the decision support forms, and then try them out against the prototype. This may lead to some changes in the design of the system. In the final production system, it may be wise to provide a separate server for decision support. The decision support server can then be fed snapshots of the production data at predetermined intervals.

WALKING ON TWO FEET

Client/Server technology offers developers the potential to create revolutionary new visual applications. Creating these kind of applications requires the seamless integration of OOUI technology, operating systems, network architectures, and DBMSs. To succeed, we will need new approaches to systems development that emphasize rapid-prototyping and the end-user involvement. Doing that will allow us to exploit the synergy between database objects and OOUI objects. We will also be in a better position to understand early in a project the opportunities (for example, parallelism) and pitfalls (for example, performance and error recovery) introduced by splitting an application across a network.

This prototype-based approach to design eliminates the need for lengthy specifications. More importantly, this approach allows the customer to participate in the specification of the product and its stepwise refinement. The approach also lends itself well to the design of distributed applications, since you can refine and fine tune the distribution of function as you learn more about your system's real-life behavior.

So, the successful design starts in parallel with both the client and the server. The two starting points are the OOUI objects and the data objects. The "glue" that ties them together are the transactions using network RPCs. Start with the client and move towards the server, or vice versa. In either case, move in small steps and iterate. The visual prototype brings the design to life early. So, which comes first: the client or the server? They both come first!

Chapter 43

Designing the
Club Med Application

This is the first of a three-chapter "grand finale" that brings together all the building blocks developed in this book into a single client/server application: Club Med. We will develop an Online Transaction Program (OLTP) that provides a fictitious reservation system for Club Med.

Club Med is a classical client/server application (see Figure 43-1). The OOUI client provides the front-end using five new WPS/SOM classes. The server executes the back-end transactions provided by the CLUB.SQC program and a CLUB database. The client and the server communicate using Named Pipes and the LAN Server's file services. Transactions are submitted over Named Pipes and large files (BLOBs) are moved over the network using the LAN Server's redirector.

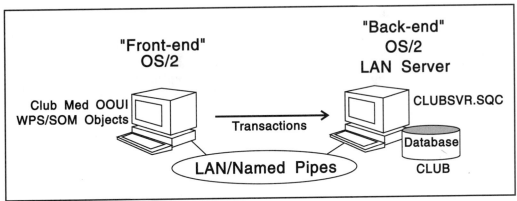

Figure 43-1. Club Med Client and Server.

You can see that this application provides "the whole works." It ties the OOUIs to the transaction server. Here's the plan for presenting all this information:

* The current chapter, the first of the three-chapter series, presents an overview of the Club Med application. We start with the OOUI objects the user sees. We then go

over the transactions that are triggered by users interacting with OOUI objects. We conclude with RSQL statements that create the database. At the end of this chapter, you should have a good feeling for what the Club Med application does and how the pieces come together. In general, OOUI scenarios, the published list of transactions, and the database description are the best place to start understanding any client/server application.

- The second chapter in the series, Chapter 44, "The Club Med Client," presents the front-end client. This is an important chapter which demonstrates how to create OOUI clients using WPS/SOM classes.

- The third and last chapter in the series, Chapter 45, "The Club Med Server," shows you how to create a multiuser transaction server. We develop the code for database transactions which use SQL. The code also includes a primitive transaction monitor built on top of Named Pipes and LAN server.

CLUB MED OOUI: WHAT THE USER SEES

A client/server application is by its very nature *client-driven*. OOUIs go one step further and place the controls of the client in the hands of a user manipulating visual objects. Whatever the user does to these visual objects become the sources of client/server transactions. The server, meanwhile, passively waits on requests from clients that trigger the execution of its transactions.

In this section, we will go over what the user sees and does with the Club Med OOUI front-end. As we walk through the scenario, take note of the new OOUI objects we introduce on the Workplace Shell. We will also point out the OOUI events that trigger transactions on the server. You'll find that this scenario does more to explain the Club Med application than hundreds of pages of non-visual specifications. We're only sorry that you can't see the application live on the pages of your book. But we'll substitute a live demo of Club Med with "not so live" screen captures (starting with Figure 43-2). We will also annotate the scenario with some juicy tidbits on what goes on "behind the scenes" or, to be more exact, "behind the glass" of the screen.

Here's a snapshot of ten minutes in the life of a Club Med OOUI:

1. **Seeing Club Med for the first time.** When Club Med is first installed, you will see a container object on the desktop for clubs (see screen capture Figure 43-2). **Behind the scenes:** What is this strange object that also appeared on the desktop? It is an icon for a new *DoRPC* object that submits transactions to the server. We put it on the desktop to allow administrators to kill the object and its multiple threads

(by moving it to the shredder). For now, you may want to move the icon into a folder where no one but you can see it.[1]

2. **Opening the club folder object**. You can do that several ways. The most direct way is to double-click on the icon with the select button. The other way is to bring up the pop-up menu and click on open. *Behind the scenes:* the client workstation first obtains the list of clubs from the server. The result is returned in a file, which is used by the club folder object to populate itself by creating instances of club objects on the fly. The client/server transaction that returns the list of clubs is *get_club_names*. All the transaction handlers on the client side are spawned as threads by our DoRPC object. Screen capture Figure 43-3 shows the club folder after it is populated with club objects.

3. **Selecting a club object and its pop-up menu**. The context pop up menu shows that a club object has four views: Settings (Club Prices), Club Visual (the default), Club Description, and Club Reservation. Screen capture Figure 43-4 shows the pop-up menu for the club object.

4. **Where is Ixtapa?** Opening the Club Visual view allows you to find out all about the Club Med's village in Ixtapa. Where is Ixtapa? What sports are offered? This view graphically shows it. *Behind the scenes:* the opening of this view triggers the transaction *get_club_graphics* for the Ixtapa club object. The transaction returns a metafile that draws the club's location on a map of the world. It also returns several bitmaps, which display icons of the sports offered in the Ixtapa club. The graphics you see are the work of our *Clubview* object helper program. This program is started by our Club object as a separate process when the Club Visual view is selected. The Clubview process displays each sport icon and plays the metafile worldmap. You can see that Ixtapa is located on the West Coast of Mexico. Screen capture Figure 43-5 shows what we're talking about here.

5. **Obtaining a text description of Ixtapa**. Club Description, another view of the club object, displays a text file of information on Ixtapa. *Behind the scenes:* opening this view triggers a *get_club_description* transaction to the server. The server returns a text file. This file is then displayed using a Multiline Entry (MLE) PM control. Screen capture Figure 43-6 shows a simple text panel displayed in a PM window.

---

[1] We had some wild ideas for this RPC object that didn't make it into the code. However, since you too have the code, let's entice you with a couple of "fun" projects. The first project is to allow users to visually submit transactions by dropping objects on the RPC icon. The mechanics to do that are mostly there, but you will need to override and augment the object's drag-and-drop methods. Your override method can invoke the object's RPC method when a drop occurs. Do you want another fun project? Add a view to the RPC object that allows users to connect to different transaction servers; each server can be made into a separate object. Don't forget to include authentication.

6. **Obtaining Club Prices**. This is another view that shows up as a Notebook page that contains information on the club prices. The prices for Ixtapa vary by the week, and they are displayed in a scrollable listbox. *Behind the scenes:* opening this view triggers a *get_club_prices* transaction on the server. The server returns a file containing a list of prices for this particular club. This view shows how a CUA'91 Notebook control can be used as a container of dialog windows. This technique will be inherited by the reservation object that will be introduced shortly. Screen capture Figure 43-7 shows the Club Prices Notebook page.

7. **The Club Reservation View**. This view opens up another folder containing the reservation objects (we're really talking about Club Med guests) for the Ixtapa club. Objects, as you can see, can contain other objects, and so on. *Behind the scenes:* the opening of this view leads to the creation of a reservation folder object (another one of our classes). The opening of this folder object triggers a *find_all_reserv* transaction that returns a list of reservation objects. The folder object populates itself by creating a new reservation object for each record returned from the server. This is an object's version of a three ring circus. Screen capture Figure 43-8 shows a reservation folder object populated with reservation objects.

8. **Opening a guest folder**. This is the default view for a club reservation object. We opened the object called Meryl Street (we're still talking about guests), which displays a Notebook view with many dialogs, organized in pages. You may browse backward or forward through pages of dialogs on the Meryl Street party, or click on the Notebook tabs to get to a particular dialog. Our reservation system consists of four dialog pages: reservation, party members, confirmation, and pricing. The screen captures Figure 43-9 and Figure 43-10 show the two dialog pages used to obtain information on the lucky vacationers, "Bob and Meryl."

9. **Getting the prices for the week**. Notice that we've turned the page to a dialog that looks very similar to the one you saw in the clubs object. We're asking Meryl to choose the week of her vacation. *Behind the scenes:* the reservation class inherits this dialog from its club parent class. With class inheritance, it doesn't cost us anything to repeat dialogs. The code and the transaction submitted is identical to the one for club prices. The screen capture for the get prices dialog is shown in Figure 43-11.

10. **Submit the reservation**. Click on the button "Confirm Reservation." Notice that we're in the confirmation page. *Behind the scenes:* the *add_reservation* transaction is submitted to the server. The confirmation dialog is shown in screen capture Figure 43-12.

11. **Cancel Bob and Meryl's reservation**. It was a mistake, of course. The reservation object gets dragged to the shredder. *Behind the scenes:* the shredder informs its objects when they're about to be obliterated; thank you, shredder. This notification triggers a *cancel_reservation* transaction; no more "Bob and Meryl" after that. The reservation object is also destroyed. Figure 43-13 captures the homicidal shredding of the Meryl Street party.

12. **Context Help**. Help is available everywhere. Hit F1 for context help; or select help from the menus or pushbuttons. The appropriate Club Med help panel is displayed. ***Behind the scenes:*** local IPF help panels get invoked. The CUA'91 help model is used. Help is shown in screen capture Figure 43-14.

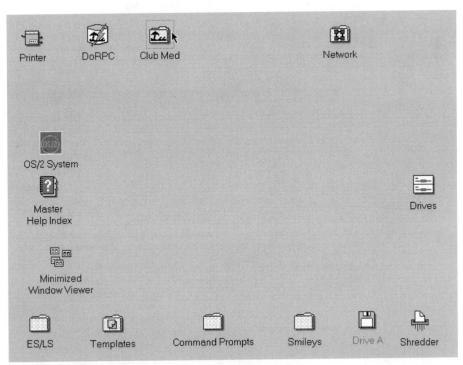

Figure 43-2. Double Click on Club Med Folder Object.

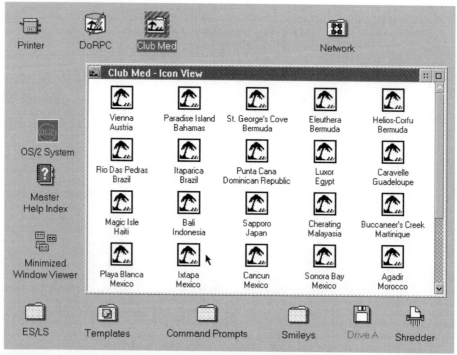

Figure 43-3.   An Iconic View of a Populated Club Med Folder.

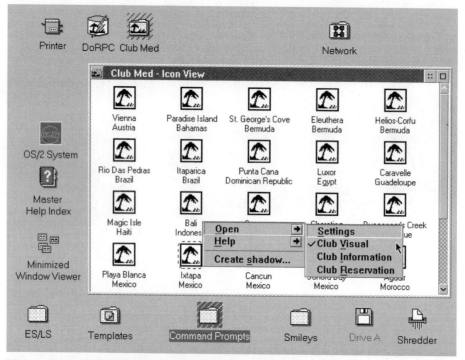

Figure 43-4.   The Club Object Context Pop-Up Menu.

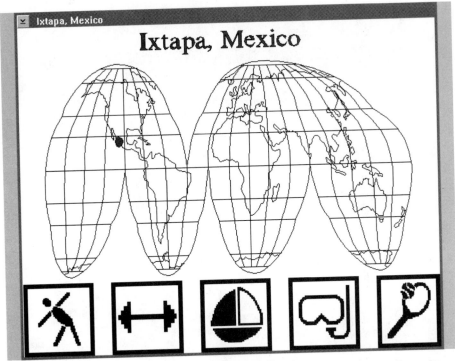

Figure 43-5. A View of Ixtapa's Location and Sports.

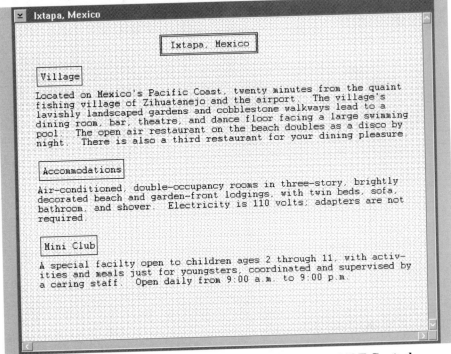

Figure 43-6. A View of Text Information on Ixtapa Using a MLE Control.

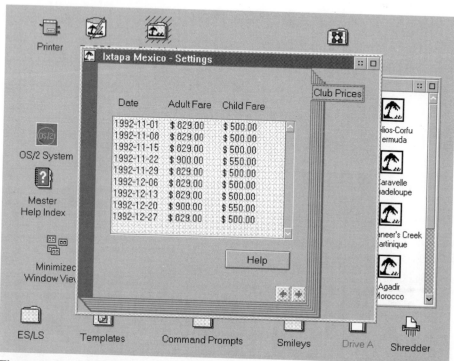

Figure 43-7. A View of Price Information on Ixtapa Using a CUA'91 Notebook.

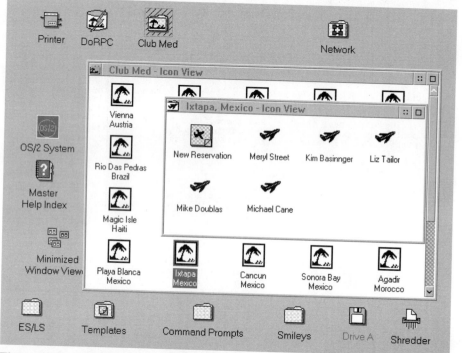

Figure 43-8. A Folder Containing Ixtapa Reservation Objects (aka guests).

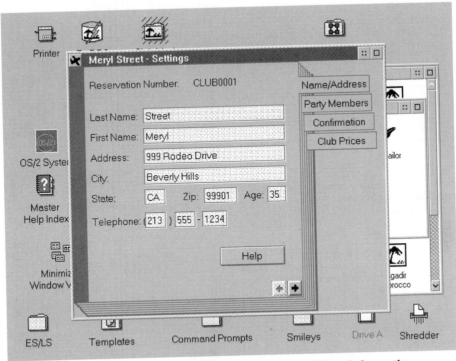

Figure 43-9. A Reservation Dialog Page Containing Address Information.

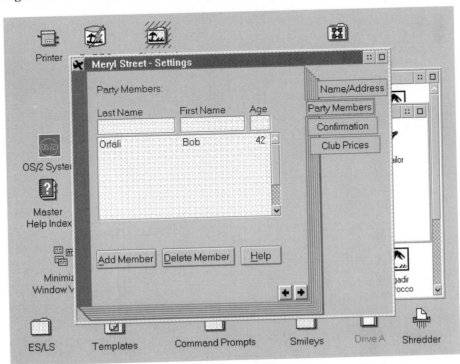

Figure 43-10. A Reservation Dialog Page of Additional Party Members.

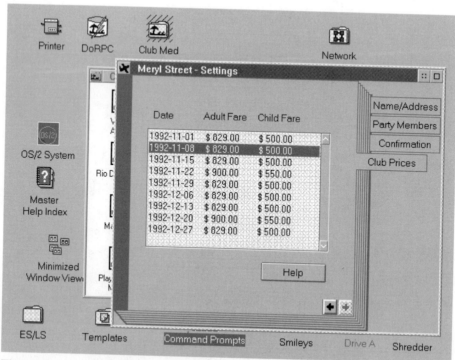

Figure 43-11. A Reservation Dialog Page That Lists Ixtapa's Prices.

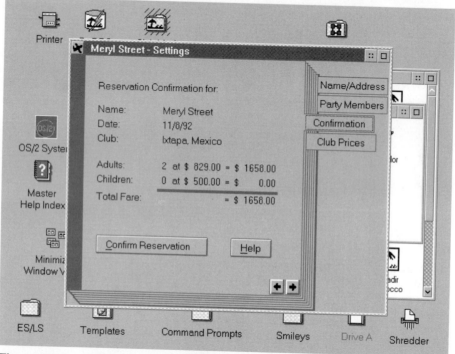

Figure 43-12. A Reservation Dialog Page for Confirming the Reservation.

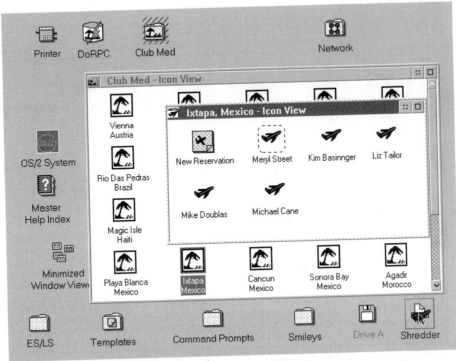

Figure 43-13.   The Homicidal Shredding of the Street Party.

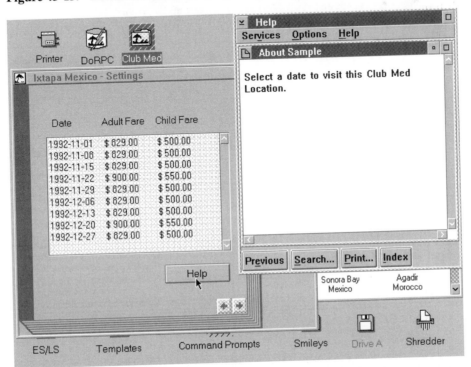

Figure 43-14.   Help Is Everywhere.

THE CLUB MED TRANSACTIONS

The Club Med client generates eight simple transactions. These transactions, as we never tire of saying, are a binding contract between a server and its clients. They represent the set of remote procedure calls exported by the server. The transaction message interface is the next piece of crucial information you will need to understand the Club Med Client/Server application. So here it is:

Table 43-1 (Part 1 of 3). **The Club Med Transactions.**

Transaction 1: GET_CLUB_NAMES

Description: This transaction obtains the list of club names.

Input Msg: ——— "TRANSACTION_ID= 1" ———————→ |

Process: SELECT from CLUBS
                                                generate response file
                                                COMMIT
                                                    |
Response Msg ——— "TXN_COMPLETION = SUCCESS RESPONSE_FILE = file_name"

Transaction 2: GET_CLUB_GRAPHICS

Description: This transaction obtains the name of a metafile and the name
             of all the sport bitmaps associated with a club. This info
             is displayed in the panel that has the map and sport icons.

Input Msg: ——— "TRANSACTION_ID= 2 CLUB=name" ——→ |
                                                SELECT from CLUBS
Process: SELECT from ACTIVITIES
                                                generate response file
                                                COMMIT
                                                    |
Response Msg ——— "TXN_COMPLETION = SUCCESS RESPONSE_FILE = file_name"

Transaction 3: GET_CLUB_DESCRIPTION

Description: This transaction obtains the name of a file
             containing a textual description of the specified Club Med.
             This is the information file which gets displayed in the
             MLE.

Input Msg: ——— "TRANSACTION_ID= 3 CLUB=name" ——→ |
                                                SELECT from CLUBS
Process: generate response file
                                                COMMIT
                                                    |
Response Msg ——— "TXN_COMPLETION = SUCCESS RESPONSE_FILE = file_name"

Table 43-1 (Part 2 of 3). The Club Med Transactions.

Transaction 4: GET_CLUB_PRICES
Description: This transaction obtains a price list for a club. The list contains the week number, The price for adults, and the price for children.

Input Msg: ——— "TRANSACTION_ID= 4 CLUB=name" ——→ |
                                             SELECT from PRICES
Process: generate response file
                                       COMMIT

Response Msg ——— "TXN_COMPLETION = SUCCESS RESPONSE_FILE = file_name" |

Transaction 5: FIND_ALL_RESERV
Description: This transaction obtains a list of the names of people who have confirmed reservations for this club.

Input Msg: ——— "TRANSACTION_ID= 5 CLUB=name" ——→ |
                                           SELECT from RESERVATIONS
Process: generate response file
                                       COMMIT

Response Msg ——— "TXN_COMPLETION = SUCCESS RESPONSE_FILE = file_name" |

Transaction 6: FIND_RESERVATION
Description: This transaction obtains all the reservation information associated with a particular reservation number.

Input Msg ——— "TRANSACTION_ID= 6 RESERV_NO=number" ——→
                                         SELECT from RESERVATIONS
Process: generate response file
                                       COMMIT

Response Msg ——— "TXN_COMPLETION = SUCCESS RESPONSE_FILE = file_name" |

Table 43-1 (Part 3 of 3). The Club Med Transactions.

Transaction 7: ADD_RESERVATION

Description: This transaction creates a reservation. The club
and weekdate are identified in the message. The file
contains all the information on accompanying party
members, telephone number, method of payment, address, etc.

Input Msg ———— "TRANSACTION_ID= 7 CLUB=club WEEKDATE=date FILENAME=name ——→

Process: INSERT into RESERVATIONS
                                                            COMMIT

Response Msg ←"TXN_COMPLETION = SUCCESS
                        RESPONSE_FILE = NONE RESERV_NO=number"

Transaction 8: CANCEL_RESERVATION

Description: This transaction cancels a reservation identified
by a reservation number.

Input Msg ——————— "TRANSACTION_ID= 8 CLUB=club RESERV_NO=number ————→

                                                        DELETE from RESERVATIONS
Process: COMMIT

Response Msg ——— "TXN_COMPLETION = SUCCESS RESPONSE_FILE = NONE"

The CLUB Database

Figure 43-15 presents the RSQL *run* script that is used to create the Club Med database. The database consists of four tables. These tables are loaded with data from import files. The tables provide another important piece of the client/server jigsaw puzzle.

```
-- create a database called club
EXEC DBA: CREATE_DB CLUB D TEST_DATABASE;

-- bind the rsql program
EXEC DBA: BIND CLUB \ZBK\RSQL\RSQL.BND ISO REPEATABLE_READ BLOCK_ALL PUBLIC;

EXEC DBA: STARTUSE CLUB S;

EXEC SQL: CREATE TABLE CLUBS(          CLUB          CHAR(32) NOT NULL,
                                       COUNTRY       CHAR(32) NOT NULL,
                                       PICTURE       CHAR(20) NOT NULL,
                                       DESCRIPTION   CHAR(20) NOT NULL );
EXEC SQL: CREATE UNIQUE INDEX CLUBSX1 ON CLUBS(CLUB);

EXEC SQL: CREATE TABLE ACTIVITIES(     CLUB      CHAR(32) NOT NULL,
                                       ACTIVITY  CHAR(20) NOT NULL);

EXEC SQL: CREATE TABLE PRICES(         CLUB          CHAR(32) NOT NULL,
                                       WEEK_DATE     DATE     NOT NULL,
                                       ADULT_PRICE   CHAR(8)  NOT NULL,
                                       CHILD_PRICE   CHAR(8)  NOT NULL );
EXEC SQL: CREATE UNIQUE INDEX PRICESX1 ON PRICES(CLUB, WEEK_DATE);

EXEC SQL: CREATE TABLE RESERVATIONS( CLUB            CHAR(32) NOT NULL,
                                     WEEK_DATE       DATE     NOT NULL,
                                     LAST_NAME       CHAR(32) NOT NULL,
                                     FIRST_NAME      CHAR(32) NOT NULL,
                                     AGE             CHAR(3)  NOT NULL,
                                     PARTY_MEMBER    CHAR(1)  NOT NULL,
                                     RESERV_NO       CHAR(9)  NOT NULL,
                                     PAYMENT_METHOD  CHAR(9),
                                     PHONE_NO        CHAR(20),
                                     ADDRESS         CHAR(32),
                                     CITY            CHAR(32),
                                     STATE           CHAR(2),
                                     ZIP             CHAR(10));
EXEC SQL: CREATE INDEX RESERVX1 ON RESERVATIONS(CLUB, WEEK_DATE);

EXEC SQL: COMMIT;

-- disconnect from the database for export
   EXEC DBA: STOPUSE CLUB;

-- import table data
EXEC DBA: IMPORT CLUB D:\ZBK\CLUB\CLUBS.DEL    REPLACE DEL CLUBS;
EXEC DBA: IMPORT CLUB D:\ZBK\CLUB\ACTIVITY.DEL REPLACE DEL ACTIVITIES;
EXEC DBA: IMPORT CLUB D:\ZBK\CLUB\PRICES.DEL   REPLACE DEL PRICES;
```

Figure 43-15. Create a 4-Table DB Called CLUB and Import Data.

Chapter 44

The Club Med Client

This is the second of a three-chapter series on the Club Med client/server application. In this chapter, we demonstrate how to create OOUIs for Online Transaction Processing (OLTP) using SOM/WPS classes. Here are the highlights for this chapter:

- A class design that is optimized for an OOUI client/server environment. We introduce five SOM/WPS-derived classes that demonstrate how to populate folders from Transaction Servers, how to put class wrappers around Remote Procedure Calls (RPCs) to the server, how to create elaborate dialogs using Notebook views, how to add help to your applications, and how to integrate the client application into the Workplace Shell.
- A mulithreaded design that allows the client to respond to the user in the foreground while one or more lengthy transactions are executing in the background.
- A client/server exchange protocol that uses Named Pipes and the LAN Server. This protocol is RPC-like, and it supports the movement of BLOBs.
- A "class helper", implemented as a separate program, that handles a variety of complex PM tasks including displaying bitmaps, metafiles, and text using PM's Multiline Entry (MLE) field.

In short, this chapter provides the core technology you'll need to create elaborate client applications that are fully integrated into the Workplace Shell. This core technology builds on top of the SOM/WPS classes and extends them to client/server environments. It solves problems like how to populate folders with database objects, how to communicate with processes that are outside the address space of the WPS (in this case, on other machines), and how to structure a complex SOM/WPS client using inheritance and class encapsulation.

THE NEW CLUB MED SOM/WPS CLASSES

The Club Med Client Objects

The Club Med client is very simple to grasp at the conceptual level. It consists of five classes derived from the SOM/WPS class library. Why did we choose these five classes? How did we choose them? Where are they derived from? These are all valid architectural questions, and we answer them in this section.

How Did We Choose Our Classes?

There are no hard rules on how to pick classes. You must take into account the logic of your objects, the level of coupling required, the functions that can easily be reused through subclassing, crash protection, performance, memory requirements, and the list goes on. In this section, we share with you how we picked our five classes mostly using Voodoo and some common sense.

The Base Object Classes: Club and Resv

You may have noticed in last chapter's scenario that the Club Med OOUI has two business objects that really stand out: clubs and customer reservations. So naturally, we created the two classes: **Club** and **Resv** (Figure 44-1). You also saw from the scenario that these two objects were very similar. For example, they both had Notebook views with a Club Med price page. "Similar" in OOP translates into subclassing and inheritance. So, we will make **Resv** a child class of **Club**.

So, who's the Daddy of **Club**? We picked the **WPTransient** class because it makes a good Daddy for classes that don't require the object persistence provided by WPS (we're getting our persistence from the server). It also introduces less overhead than the other WPS classes.

Remember, too, that there is a supporting member in our cast of objects: the **Clubview** program. This program presents the Club Visual and Club Description views when selected from the Club object pop-up menu. We chose to implement these views as a program (which runs as an independent process) to illustrate a point and a technique. The Workplace Shell is implemented as a single process and your WPS classes execute within the Workplace Shell process. Consequently, your class resource limitations, such as window handles and device contexts are based on the limitations of the Workplace Shell process. The technique for getting around this problem is to implement function in separate processes where possible. But there is a downside to this technique: *WPS methods can only be called from within the Workplace Shell process.*

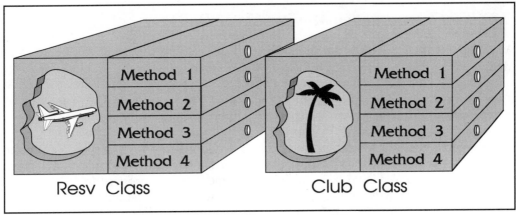

Figure 44-1. The Club Med Base Object Classes: Clubs and Resv.

The "Special" Folder Classes: Clubfldr and Resvfldr

The scenarios also show that the clubs and reservations each had their own folder container. Yes, folders are objects. So, we introduce two new objects: **Clubfldr** and **Resvfldr**. Why not just use the standard **WPFolder** class? Or, better yet, why not just let Club Med users create their own folders by tearing off a standard template?

The answer is that we want a "special folder." It has to look like the ordinary folders on the Workplace Shell, yet be able to do a few strange things for us. For example, we want persistent storage on the Club Med Transaction Server—not the local file system. This special folder must automatically populate itself with objects (or records that represent objects) kept on a Transaction Server. This is why we created our own two "special" folder-like classes (see Figure 44-2). As you may have guessed, their Mommy is none other than the **WPFolder** class.

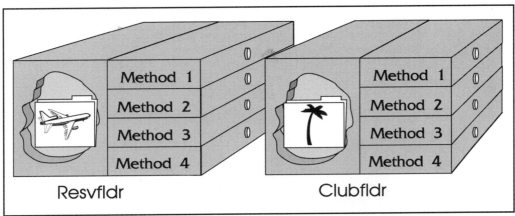

Figure 44-2. The Club Med "Special" Folder Classes: Clubfldr and Resvfldr.

The Client's Transaction Monitor Class: DoRPC

What about **DoRPC**? This is the strange class that showed up on the desktop with Club Med; it's the one we told you to hide and use for "special" projects. Actually, **DoRPC** is the class in charge of interacting with the server (see Figure 44-3). You can think of it as a "Transaction Monitor" on the client's workstation. Why do we need one of these? Why doesn't each class issue the RPC directly?

The answer is that the system must not block while waiting for a response from the server. This would make the OOUI very unresponsive to users. Remember, OOUIs are supposed to do many visual tasks at the same time. So, we propose to create a new thread every time an RPC is issued. These threads will handle the interactions with the server while the other classes keep interacting with the user. Everybody will be happy. So, **DoRPC** is the "well-known" class object that accepts RPC requests and spawns off threads. What does the thread do with the response from the server? We defined a protocol that tells the thread which object/method to call when it gets back the response. The thread calls the method and then dies.

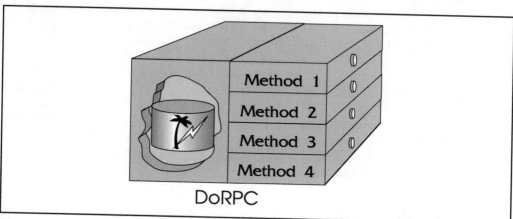

Figure 44-3. The Club Med DoRPC Class: A Transaction Monitor for Clients.

The Club Med Class Hierarchy

Figure 44-4 shows all of our Club Med classes and their relationship to the SOM/WPS classes.

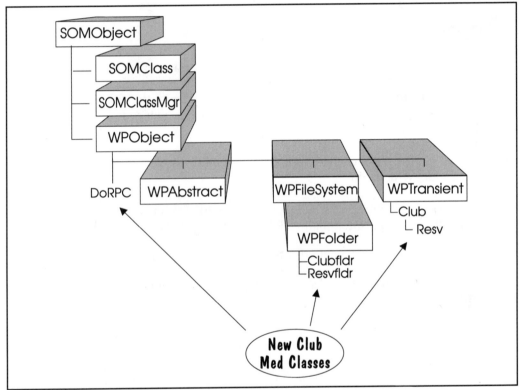

Figure 44-4.   The Club Med Class Family Tree.

WALKING THROUGH THE CLUB CLASSES

In this section, we present the code for three of the five Club Med SOM/WPS classes: **Club, Clubfldr,** and **DoRPC.** These three classes demonstrate the principles of client design. The remaining two classes, **Resv** and **Resvfldr,** use the same programming concepts as **Club** and **Clubfldr** and are not included.[1] We will also take a brief look at the **Clubview** program.

---

[1] Our publisher informed us that if we made the book any thicker it would have to be split into two volumes. The code for **Resv** and **Resvfldr** classes is included in the program diskette (see coupon in the back of the book).

We will explain the classes by first looking at their OIDLs. As we explained in Part VI, the OIDL is the contract between the class provider and the rest of the world. You can understand what a class is all about by reviewing the contract before you plunge into the C code that implements it. Also, don't forget to use the reference material in Part VI to fill in the details for the SOM/WPS classes and methods we use.

The Clubfldr Class

The OIDL for the **Clubflder** class (see Figure 44-5) shows we are overriding three of the SOM/WPS **WPFolder** methods and introducing one new method. This is a good time to review the tutorial in Part VI to get reacquainted with the **WPFolder** class and what it can do for you. We will, of course, be building our own code on top of the class to introduce some new function.

The code that implements the methods is listed in Figure 44-6. Here's a quick overview of what the four methods do:

- *wpclsQueryStyle* returns a default style for the **Clubfldr** class. In our case, we have disabled the creation of templates. Refer to Part VI for other available styles.

- *wpclsQueryTitle* returns a default title for the **Clubfldr** class.

- *populateFolder* and *wpPopulate* work as a pair to implement the population of the **Clubfldr** folder with **Club** objects. Here is the sequence of events:

  1. **wpPopulate**, as an override of the **WPFolder** class, is invoked when the folder is opened. Folder population can be a multistep process; we test the folder flags to populate the folder only as it is first opened.
  2. We then find the **DoRPC** instance, prepare the GET_CLUB_NAMES transaction, and begin the transaction by invoking the **DoRPC** method, **Execute_Transaction**. The parameters of **Execute_Transaction** indicate that **populateFolder** for the **Clubfldr** instance should be invoked after the transaction completes.
  3. When **populateFolder** executes, it finds the Folder ID for the **Clubfldr** instance, finds the **Club** class, and then populates the folder with **Club** objects using the **wpclsNew** SOM/WPS method. Note that we have passed a setup string to each instance of the **Club** class to tailor its folder position and to pass the club name and country to the instance. Each Club object uses the setup string to initialize its instance data.

The Clubfldr Class OIDL

```
/***************************************************************************/
/*  Class Name: Clubfldr - Folder class for Club Med Club objects         */
/***************************************************************************/

#*************************************************************************
#    Include the class definition file for the parent class
#*************************************************************************
include <wpfolder.sc>

#*************************************************************************
#    Define the new class
#*************************************************************************
class: Clubfldr,
        external stem   = clubfldr,
        local,
        external prefix = clubfldr_,
        classprefix     = clubfldrM_,
        major version   = 1,
        minor version   = 2;

#*************************************************************************
#    Parent Class
#*************************************************************************
parent: WPFolder;

#*************************************************************************
#    Release Order
#*************************************************************************
release order: populateFolder;

#*************************************************************************
#    Passthru IMPLEMENTATION definitions to the .ih file
#*************************************************************************
passthru: C.ih;

#define INCL_WIN
#define INCL_DOS
#define INCL_GPIBITMAPS
#include <os2.h>

#define INCL_WPCLASS
#define INCL_WPFOLDER
#include <pmwp.h>

#define ID_ICON          100

#define ShowMsg(title, text) \
        WinMessageBox(HWND_DESKTOP, HWND_DESKTOP, (PSZ) text, (PSZ) title, \
                    20, MB_OK | MB_INFORMATION | MB_MOVEABLE)

endpassthru;    /* .ih */
```

Figure 44-5 (Part 1 of 2).   CLUBFLDR.CSC: The Clubfldr Class OIDL.

```
#*******************************************************************************
#    Define methods
#*******************************************************************************
methods:
#*******************************************************************************
#    Specify class methods being overridden
#*******************************************************************************
override wpclsQueryStyle, class;
override wpclsQueryTitle, class;


#*******************************************************************************
#    Specify new Methods
#*******************************************************************************
BOOL populateFolder(PSZ  txn_rsp_file, PSZ  datafile_drive_path,
                    PSZ  txn_response);
#*******************************************************************************
#    Specify methods being overridden
#*******************************************************************************
override wpPopulate;
```

Figure 44-5 (Part 2 of 2).   CLUBFLDR.CSC: The Clubfldr Class OIDL.

The Clubfldr Class C Implementation

```
/******************************************************************************/
/*    OBJECT NAME:  CLUBFLDR -- A Folder Class for Clubs                      */
/*                                                                            */
/*    DESCRIPTION:  This object provides a folder for Club Med clubs.         */
/*                                                                            */
/******************************************************************************/
#define Clubfldr_Class_Source
#define M_Clubfldr_Class_Source
#include <string.h>
#include <stdio.h>
#include <memory.h>
#include <stdlib.h>
#include "clubfldr.ih"                              /* implementation header  */
#include "clubfldr.ph"                              /* private header emitted */
#include "club.h"                                   /* Club class header      */
#include "dorpc.h"                                  /* doRPC class header     */
#include "clubtxns.h"                               /* Transaction defines    */

/*_____*/
/* global variables and function declarations for this module               */
/*_____*/
HMODULE     hmod = NULLHANDLE;
CHAR        ClassTitle[] = "Clubfldr";              /* Title of this class    */

/******************************************************************************/
/* Class Method Overrides                                                     */
/******************************************************************************/
#undef SOM_CurrentClass
#define SOM_CurrentClass SOMMeta
```

Figure 44-6 (Part 1 of 5).   CLUBFLDR.C: The Clubfldr Class C Implementation.

```
/*-----------------------------------------------------------------------*/
/* OVERRIDE: _wpclsQueryStyle                                            */
/*-----------------------------------------------------------------------*/
SOM_Scope ULONG   SOMLINK clubfldrM_wpclsQueryStyle(M_Clubfldr *somSelf)
{
    /* M_ClubfldrData *somThis = M_ClubfldrGetData(somSelf); */
    M_ClubfldrMethodDebug("M_Clubfldr","clubfldrM_wpclsQueryStyle");

    return (parent_wpclsQueryStyle(somSelf) | CLSSTYLE_NEVERTEMPLATE);
}

/*-----------------------------------------------------------------------*/
/* OVERRIDE: _wpclsQueryTitle                                            */
/*-----------------------------------------------------------------------*/
SOM_Scope PSZ   SOMLINK clubfldrM_wpclsQueryTitle(M_Clubfldr *somSelf)
{
    /* M_ClubfldrData *somThis = M_ClubfldrGetData(somSelf); */
    M_ClubfldrMethodDebug("M_Clubfldr","clubfldrM_wpclsQueryTitle");

    return (ClassTitle);
}

/*************************************************************************/
/* New Methods                                                           */
/*************************************************************************/
#undef SOM_CurrentClass
#define SOM_CurrentClass SOMInstance

/*-----------------------------------------------------------------------*/
/* New Method: populateFolder                                            */
/*-----------------------------------------------------------------------*/
SOM_Scope BOOL   SOMLINK clubfldr_populateFolder(Clubfldr *somSelf,
                                                 PSZ   txn_rsp_file,
                                                 PSZ   datafile_drive_path,
                                                 PSZ   txn_response)

{
    WPObject *Folder;
    SOMAny   *NewObj;
    SOMAny   *ClubClass;
    CHAR      clubname[33];
    CHAR      clubcountry[33];
    CHAR      title[160];
    ULONG     i;
    CHAR      RealName[CCHMAXPATH];
    ULONG     RealNameLen;
    CHAR      SetupString[256];
    CHAR      filename[CCHMAXPATH];
    FILE     *rsp_file;
    HAB       hab;                            /* PM anchor block handle   */
    HMQ       hmq;                            /* Message queue handle     */
    QMSG      qmsg;                           /* Message from message queue */

    /* ClubfldrData *somThis = ClubfldrGetData(somSelf); */
    ClubfldrMethodDebug("Clubfldr","clubfldr_populateFolder");
```

Figure 44-6 (Part 2 of 5).   CLUBFLDR.C: The Clubfldr Class C Implementation.

```
/*_____*/
/* find the pointer to our folder object */
/*_____*/
RealNameLen = sizeof(RealName);
_wpQueryRealName(somSelf,
                 RealName,
                 &RealNameLen,
                 TRUE);
Folder = _wpclsQueryFolder(_somGetClass(somSelf),
                           RealName,
                           TRUE);
if (Folder == NULL)
    ShowMsg(" Clubfldr ", "Error: _wpclsQueryFolder");

/*_____*/
/* find Club Object                    */
/*_____*/
ClubClass = _somFindClass(SOMClassMgrObject, SOM_IdFromString("Club"), 1,2);
if (ClubClass == NULL)
    { ShowMsg(" Clubfldr ", "Error: _somFindClass: Club");
      return(FALSE);
    }

/*_____*/
/* read file from transaction and create */
/* Club objects in the Clubfldr folder   */
/*_____*/
sprintf(filename,"%s\\%s", datafile_drive_path, txn_rsp_file);
rsp_file = fopen(filename,"r");
if (rsp_file == NULL)
    { ShowMsg(" Clubfldr ", "Error: Opening response file.");
      return(FALSE);
    }

i=0;
do
 {

    memset(clubname,'\0', sizeof(clubname));
    memset(clubcountry,'\0', sizeof(clubcountry));
    if ( fscanf(rsp_file,"%32c  %32c\n",
         clubname, clubcountry) != 2)
         break;

    /*_____*/
    /* strip trailing blanks                 */
    /*_____*/
    while (clubcountry[strlen(clubcountry)-1]==' ')
    { clubcountry[strlen(clubcountry)-1] = 0;
    } /* endwhile */
    while (clubname[strlen(clubname)-1]==' ')
    { clubname[strlen(clubname)-1] = 0;
    } /* endwhile */

    /*_____*/
    /* create club object in folder         */
    /*_____*/
    sprintf(title,"%s\n%s", clubname, clubcountry);
    sprintf(SetupString,"CLUB=%s;COUNTRY=%s;ICONPOS=%d,%d;",
            clubname, clubcountry, (i*15)%75 + 5, 100 - ((i/5)*15));
    NewObj = _wpclsNew(ClubClass, title, SetupString, Folder, FALSE);
```

Figure 44-6 (Part 3 of 5). CLUBFLDR.C: The Clubfldr Class C Implementation.

```
        if (NewObj == NULL)
          { ShowMsg(" Clubfldr ", "Error Creating Club Instance");
            return(FALSE);
          }
        i++;
      } while (TRUE);

   fclose(rsp_file);
   remove(filename);
   return(TRUE);
}

/*********************************************************************************/
/* Method overrides                                                              */
/*********************************************************************************/
/*_____*/
/* OVERRIDE: _wpPopulate                                                        */
/*_____*/
SOM_Scope BOOL    SOMLINK clubfldr_wpPopulate(Clubfldr *somSelf,
                 ULONG ulReserved,
                 PSZ   pszPath,
                 BOOL  fFoldersOnly)
{
    WPObject *Folder;
    ULONG     FldrFlags;
    SOMAny   *DoRPCClass;
    SOMAny   *DoRPCObject;
    SOMAny   *NewObj;
    BOOL      rc;
    CHAR      txn_string[80];

    /* ClubfldrData *somThis = ClubfldrGetData(somSelf); */
    ClubfldrMethodDebug("Clubfldr","clubfldr_wpPopulate");

    FldrFlags = _wpQueryFldrFlags(somSelf);

    if (FldrFlags == 0)
    {
      /*_____*/
      /* Find the DoRPC class                        */
      /*_____*/
      DoRPCClass = _somFindClass(SOMClassMgrObject,
                               SOM_IdFromString("DoRPC"), 1,2);
      if (DoRPCClass == NULL)
        { ShowMsg(" Clubfldr ", "Error: _somFindClass DoRPC");
          return(FALSE);
        }

      /*_____*/
      /* Find DoRPC Object instance                  */
      /*_____*/
      DoRPCObject = _wpclsQueryObject(DoRPCClass,
                                    WinQueryObject("<DoRPC>"));
      if (DoRPCObject == NULL)
        {
          ShowMsg(" Clubfldr ", "Error: _wpclsQueryObject DoRPC");
          return(FALSE);
        }
```

Figure 44-6 (Part 4 of 5).   CLUBFLDR.C: The Clubfldr Class C Implementation.

```
    /*————————————————————*/
    /* Create Transaction String        */
    /*————————————————————*/
    sprintf(txn_string, "TRANSACTION_ID=%d", GET_CLUB_NAMES);
    rc = _Execute_Transaction(DoRPCObject,
                              txn_string,
                              somSelf,
                              "populateFolder");
    if (!rc)
        ShowMsg(" Clubfldr ", "Error: _Execute_Transaction");
    }

    return (parent_wpPopulate(somSelf,ulReserved,pszPath,fFoldersOnly));
}
```

Figure 44-6 (Part 5 of 5). CLUBFLDR.C: The Clubfldr Class C Implementation.

The Club Class

The OIDL for the **Club** class (see Figure 44-7) shows we are overriding ten of the SOM/WPS **WPTransient** methods and introducing five new methods.

The code that implements the methods is listed in Figure 44-8. Here's a quick overview of what the methods do:

- *wpclsQueryModuleHandle* returns the module handle for a specified class. A module handle is needed when we access resources bound to our object's DLL. Icon and dialog page resources are bound to the **Club** object's DLL. You will see how we use this method when we specify the class icon and add pages to the settings notebook. The **Resv** class also needs the function this method provides, but doesn't need to implement the method because **Resv** inherits the method from the **Club** class.

- *wpclsQueryStyle* returns a default style for the **Clubfldr** class. In our case, we have disabled the creation of templates and disabled copying, moving, renaming, and deleting of our **Club** objects. We have done this so the **Club** objects will always represent those objects stored in our database.

- *wpclsQueryTitle* returns a default title for the **Club** class.

- *wpclsQueryIconData* returns a default icon for the **Club** class. In this case, the icon is bound to the object's DLL, and we use **wpclsQueryModuleHandle** to find the DLL's module handle. **Resv** also makes use of this method by inheritance.

- *wpclsQueryDefaultView* specifies the view that is invoked when a user double clicks on our Club icon. We specify the Club Visual view as our default view.

- *wpAddSettingsPages* is overridden to add our Club Prices page to the object's settings notebook. Our instance method, *AddClubPricesPage*, does all the work. However, in this case, it is a simple task, requiring only the initialization of a

PAGEINFO structure. Note that the PAGEINFO structure is initialized with style information, the dialog procedure for this page, a resource module handle and ID, a title, and a help filename and resource ID. Also note that the instance pointer, **somSelf**, is passed as the pCreateParms value. This pointer provides a link from the relative isolation of a PM dialog procedure to its associated object. This link is used to access the object's instance data.

- *wpModifyPopupMenu, wpMenuItemSelected,* and **wpOpen** are overridden to add the Club Visual, Club Description, and Club Reservation views and their associated function to the **Club** object's popup menu. Note that **wpModifyPopupMenu** calls **wpInsertMenuItems** to add the menu items to the Open selection on the popup menu. The selection of a menu item by a user causes the **wpMenuItemSelected** method to be invoked. If the method is one of our new views, the **wpOpen** method is called. Our override of this method initiates transactions for the Club Visual and Club Description views. If the Club Reservation view is selected, a **Resvfldr** folder is created. In case you are wondering about the Settings view, no intervention is required. It is displayed by our parent class **WPTransient,** including our Club Prices settings notebook page. As you will see later in this chapter, we have a PM dialog procedure that implements the function of our Club Prices settings notebook page. This dialog procedure is also where the transaction for retrieving the Club price data is initiated.

- The *showClubVisual*, *showClubDescription,* and *showClubPrices* methods are invoked at the completion of the GET_CLUB_GRAPHICS, GET_CLUB_DE-SCRIPTION, and GET_CLUB_PRICES transactions, respectively. The **show-ClubVisual** and **showClubDescription** methods start the Clubview program and pass to it the results of the transaction. The transaction results for **showClubPrices** must ultimately be displayed by the Club Prices settings notebook page. This is done by posting a message to the dialog procedure for the Club Prices view notifying it of the transaction completion.

- *wpSetup* is last on our list of methods implemented by our **Club** class. This method updates the instance variables *clubname* and *clubcountry* from the setup string values passed at the time the object instance was created. **wpScanSetupString** is used to retrieve the keyword values.

Also listed in Figure 44-8 is the dialog procedure, **ClubPricesDlgProc.** This procedure implements the function of the Club Prices dialog page. The Club Prices notebook page implements its function by intercepting three PM messages, as described here:

- **WM_INITDLG** is received at the time the notebook page is initialized. We initiate the GET_CLUB_PRICES transaction from this point. Note that the instance pointer *somSelf* is retrieved from the PM message parameter mp2. This is where the create parameter, initialized in the PAGEINFO structure of **AddClubPricesPage**, ended up in this strange world of PM. With the *somSelf* parameter, we can access the object's instance data by initializing the local variable *somThis* and then accessing the instance variable by its name preceded by an underscore character (_). As an example, we initialize the *pricesDlgWindow* instance variable with the statement:

```
_pricesDlgWindow = hwndDlg;
```

This instance variable is used to notify the dialog procedure of the GET_CLUB_PRICES transaction completion, our next topic of discussion.

- **WM_READ_CLUB_PRICES** is a PM message we defined for the notification of the GET_CLUB_PRICES transaction completion. When this message is received, the Club Prices list box is updated with information from the transaction.

- The **WM_CONTROL** is intercepted to implement the interactions of the user with the list box containing the club prices. When a user selects an item in the list box, which represents a reservation date and the price for that date, the information is saved in an instance variable. This pricing information is used for completing the reservation.

The Club Class OIDL

```
/***********************************************************************/
/*  Class Name: Club - Class for Club Med clubs                        */
/***********************************************************************/
#*********************************************************************
#    Include the class definition file for the parent class
#*********************************************************************
include <wptrans.sc>

#*********************************************************************
#    Define the new class
#*********************************************************************
class: Club,
       external stem   = club,
       local,
       external prefix = club_,
       classprefix     = clubM_,
       major version   = 1,
       minor version   = 2;


#*********************************************************************
#    Parent Class
#*********************************************************************
parent: WPTransient;
#*********************************************************************
#    Release Order
#*********************************************************************
release order:
AddClubPricesPage,
showClubPrices,
showClubVisual,
showClubDescription,
clsQueryModuleHandle;
```

Figure 44-7 (Part 1 of 3). CLUB.CSC: The Club Class OIDL.

```
#/******************************************************************************
#   Passthru IMPLEMENTATION definitions to the .ih file
#/******************************************************************************
passthru: C.ih;

#define INCL_WIN
#define INCL_DOS
#define INCL_GPIBITMAPS
#include <os2.h>

#define INCL_WPCLASS
#include <pmwp.h>

/*---------------------------------------------------------------------------*/
/* Defines                                                                   */
/*---------------------------------------------------------------------------*/
/*---------------------------------------------*/
/* Title and ICON identifiers     */
/*---------------------------------------------*/
#define ID_ICON           100                    /* ICON identifier          */

/*---------------------------------------------*/
/* Help Identifiers               */
/*---------------------------------------------*/
#define ID_CLUBHELP          1000
#define ID_PRICESHELP        2000
#define ID_CLUBDESCRIPTION   1000


/*---------------------------------------------*/
/* MENU and MENUITEM identifiers */
/*---------------------------------------------*/
#define ID_OPENMENU              0x6501      /* OPEN cascade menu identifier  */
#define OPEN_CLUBVISUAL          OPEN_USER + 1 /* ID for Club Visual View     */
#define OPEN_CLUBDESCRIPTION     OPEN_USER + 2 /* ID for View Info   View     */
#define OPEN_CLUBRESERVATION     OPEN_USER + 3 /* ID for View Reservation View*/
#define OPEN_CLUBPRICES          OPEN_USER + 4 /* ID for Club Visual View     */

/*---------------------------------------------*/
/* defines for Club data          */
/*---------------------------------------------*/
#define   NAMEWIDTH          33
#define   PRICEDATALEN       73
#define   FILENAMEWIDTH      32
#define   MAXBITMAPS          5

/*---------------------------------------------*/
/* defines for User Messages      */
/*---------------------------------------------*/
#define WM_READ_CLUB_PRICES  WM_USER+1

/*---------------------------------------------*/
/* Club Graphics/Text View IDs    */
/*---------------------------------------------*/
#define   CLUB_GRAPHICS_VIEW     1
#define   CLUB_TEXT_VIEW         2

/*---------------------------------------------*/
/* DEBUG helper                   */
/*---------------------------------------------*/
#define ShowMsg(title, text) \
        WinMessageBox(HWND_DESKTOP, HWND_DESKTOP, (PSZ) text, (PSZ) title, \
                  20, MB_OK | MB_INFORMATION | MB_MOVEABLE)
endpassthru;    /* .ih */
```

Figure 44-7 (Part 2 of 3). CLUB.CSC: The Club Class OIDL.

```
#****************************************************************************
#    Define Instance data
#****************************************************************************
data:
HWND         pricesDlgWindow;                     /* window handle for prices page */
CHAR         clubname[NAMEWIDTH];                 /* name of the Club Med club     */
CHAR         clubcountry[NAMEWIDTH];              /* country where club is located */
CHAR         selected_price_data[PRICEDATALEN];   /* array for prices data      */
CHAR         rsp_filename[FILENAMEWIDTH];          /* transaction response file*/
CHAR         datafile_drive_path[FILENAMEWIDTH];  /* response file path        */

#****************************************************************************
#    Define methods
#****************************************************************************
methods:

#----------------------------------------------------------------------------
#    Specify New Class Methods
#----------------------------------------------------------------------------
HMODULE   clsQueryModuleHandle (PSZ        ClassName,
                                integer4   ClassMajorVersion,
                                integer4   ClassMinorVersion), class;

#----------------------------------------------------------------------------
#    Specify Class methods being overridden
#----------------------------------------------------------------------------
override wpclsQueryStyle, class;
override wpclsQueryTitle, class;
override wpclsQueryIconData, class;
override wpclsQueryDefaultView, class;

#----------------------------------------------------------------------------
#    Specify New Instance Methods
#----------------------------------------------------------------------------
ULONG AddClubPricesPage    (HWND hwndNotebook);
ULONG showClubPrices       (PSZ  txn_rsp_file, PSZ  datafile_drive_path,
                            PSZ  txn_response);
ULONG showClubVisual       (PSZ  txn_rsp_file, PSZ  datafile_drive_path,
                            PSZ  txn_response);
ULONG showClubDescription  (PSZ  txn_rsp_file, PSZ  datafile_drive_path,
                            PSZ  txn_response);

#----------------------------------------------------------------------------
#    Specify Instance Methods Being Overridden
#----------------------------------------------------------------------------
override wpAddSettingsPages;
override wpModifyPopupMenu;
override wpMenuItemSelected;
override wpOpen;
override wpSetup;
```

Figure 44-7 (Part 3 of 3). CLUB.CSC: The Club Class OIDL.

The Club Class C Implementation

```
/******************************************************************/
/*  OBJECT NAME:  CLUB -- A Class for Club                        */
/*                                                                */
/*  DESCRIPTION:  Club Med club object.                           */
/*                                                                */
/******************************************************************/
#define Club_Class_Source
#define M_Club_Class_Source
#include <string.h>
#include <stdio.h>
#include <memory.h>
#include <stdlib.h>
#include "club.ih"                          /* implementation header  */
#include "club.ph"                          /* private header         */
#include "dorpc.h"                          /* DoRPC class header      */
#include "clubtxns.h"                       /* Transaction defines    */
#include "clubdlg.h"                        /* Header for Dialogs      */

/*_____*/
/* global variables and function declarations for this module      */
/*_____*/
HMODULE      hmod = NULLHANDLE;
CHAR         ClassTitle[] = "Club";          /* Title of this class   */
CHAR         szHelpLibrary[] = "club.hlp";
CHAR         pszMsg[120];

MRESULT EXPENTRY ClubPricesDlgProc(HWND hwndDlg, ULONG msg,
                          MPARAM mp1, MPARAM mp2);

/******************************************************************/
/*                                                                */
/* Class Method Overrides                                         */
/******************************************************************/
#undef SOM_CurrentClass
#define SOM_CurrentClass SOMMeta

/*_____*/
/* New CLass Method: clsQueryModuleHandle                          */
/*_____*/
SOM_Scope HMODULE   SOMLINK clubM_clsQueryModuleHandle(M_Club *somSelf,
              PSZ ClassName,
              integer4 ClassMajorVersion,
              integer4 ClassMinorVersion)
{
    HMODULE      hmod = NULLHANDLE;             /* DLL MODULE handle      */
    zString      ModulePathName;                /* DLL Module path and name*/
    APIRET       rc;

    /* M_ClubData *somThis = M_ClubGetData(somSelf); */
    M_ClubMethodDebug("M_Club","clubM_clsQueryModuleHandle");

    /*_____*/
    /* Get Module Name             */
    /*_____*/
    ModulePathName =
    _somLocateClassFile(SOMClassMgrObject,
                        SOM_IdFromString(ClassName),
                        ClassMajorVersion,
                        ClassMinorVersion);
```

Figure 44-8 (Part 1 of 10). CLUB.C: The Club Class C Implementation.

```
    rc = DosQueryModuleHandle( ModulePathName, &hmod);
    if (rc)
    { ShowMsg(" Club ", "Failed to find module");
      return;
    }

    return (hmod);
}

/*————————————————————————————————————————————————————*/
/* OVERRIDE: _wpclsQueryStyle                          */
/*————————————————————————————————————————————————————*/
SOM_Scope ULONG    SOMLINK clubM_wpclsQueryStyle(M_Club *somSelf)
{
    /* M_ClubData *somThis = M_ClubGetData(somSelf); */
    M_ClubMethodDebug("M_Club","clubM_wpclsQueryStyle");

    return (parent_wpclsQueryStyle(somSelf) | CLSSTYLE_NEVERTEMPLATE |
            CLSSTYLE_NEVERMOVE | CLSSTYLE_NEVERCOPY | CLSSTYLE_NEVERRENAME |
            CLSSTYLE_NEVERDELETE);
}

/*————————————————————————————————————————————————————*/
/* OVERRIDE: _wpclsQueryTitle                          */
/*————————————————————————————————————————————————————*/
SOM_Scope PSZ    SOMLINK clubM_wpclsQueryTitle(M_Club *somSelf)
{
    /* M_ClubData *somThis = M_ClubGetData(somSelf); */
    M_ClubMethodDebug("M_Club","clubM_wpclsQueryTitle");

    return (ClassTitle);
}

/*————————————————————————————————————————————————————*/
/* OVERRIDE: _wpclsQueryIconData                       */
/*————————————————————————————————————————————————————*/
SOM_Scope ULONG    SOMLINK clubM_wpclsQueryIconData(M_Club *somSelf,
                PICONINFO pIconInfo)
{
    /* M_ClubData *somThis = M_ClubGetData(somSelf); */
    M_ClubMethodDebug("M_Club","clubM_wpclsQueryIconData");

    /*————————————————————————*/
    /* Get Module handle       */
    /*————————————————————————*/
    hmod = _clsQueryModuleHandle(somSelf, ClassTitle, 1, 2);

    /*————————————————————————*/
    /* Fill in ICONINFO structure */
    /*————————————————————————*/
    if (pIconInfo)
    {
        pIconInfo->fFormat = ICON_RESOURCE;
        pIconInfo->hmod    = hmod;
        pIconInfo->resid   = ID_ICON;
    }
    return (sizeof(ICONINFO));
}
```

Figure 44-8 (Part 2 of 10).   CLUB.C: The Club Class C Implementation.

```
/*_____*/
/* OVERRIDE: _wpclsQueryDefaultView                                */
/*_____*/
SOM_Scope ULONG   SOMLINK clubM_wpclsQueryDefaultView(M_Club *somSelf)
{
    /* M_ClubData *somThis = M_ClubGetData(somSelf); */
    M_ClubMethodDebug("M_Club","clubM_wpclsQueryDefaultView");


    return (OPEN_CLUBVISUAL);
}

/******************************************************************/
/*                                                                */
/* New Instance Methods                                           */
/******************************************************************/
#undef SOM_CurrentClass
#define SOM_CurrentClass SOMInstance

/*_____*/
/*                                                                */
/* New Method: _AddClubPricesPage                                 */
/*_____*/
SOM_Scope ULONG SOMLINK club_AddClubPricesPage(Club *somSelf,
             HWND hwndNotebook)
{
    PAGEINFO pageinfo;

    /* ClubData *somThis = ClubGetData(somSelf); */
    ClubMethodDebug("Club","club_AddClubPricesPage");

    memset((PCH)&pageinfo,0,sizeof(PAGEINFO));
    pageinfo.cb                  = sizeof(PAGEINFO);
    pageinfo.hwndPage            = NULLHANDLE;
    pageinfo.usPageStyleFlags    = BKA_MAJOR;
    pageinfo.usPageInsertFlags   = BKA_FIRST;
    pageinfo.pfnwp               = ClubPricesDlgProc;
    pageinfo.resid               = hmod;
    pageinfo.dlgid               = IDD_CLUBDLG;
    pageinfo.pszName             = "Club Prices";
    pageinfo.pCreateParams       = somSelf;
    pageinfo.idDefaultHelpPanel  = 2000;
    pageinfo.pszHelpLibraryName  = szHelpLibrary;

    return _wpInsertSettingsPage( somSelf, hwndNotebook, &pageinfo );
}

/*_____*/
/*                                                                */
/* New Method: showClubPrices                                     */
/*_____*/
SOM_Scope BOOL    SOMLINK club_showClubPrices(Club *somSelf,
                                      PSZ    txn_rsp_file,
                                      PSZ    datafile_drive_path,
                                      PSZ    txn_response)
{
    ClubData *somThis = ClubGetData(somSelf);
    ClubMethodDebug("Club","club_showClubPrices");

    /*_____*/
    /* Interpret TXN reponse, update instance */
    /* variables, post message to dialog.     */
    /*_____*/
    strcpy(_rsp_filename, txn_rsp_file);
```

Figure 44-8 (Part 3 of 10). CLUB.C: The Club Class C Implementation.

```
        strcpy(_datafile_drive_path, datafile_drive_path);
        WinPostMsg(_pricesDlgWindow, WM_READ_CLUB_PRICES,
                (MPARAM)0, (MPARAM)0);

        return(TRUE);
}

/*_____*/
/* New Method: showClubVisual                                 */
/*_____*/
SOM_Scope BOOL    SOMLINK club_showClubVisual(Club *somSelf,
                                        PSZ    txn_rsp_file,
                                        PSZ    datafile_drive_path,
                                        PSZ    txn_response)
{
    CHAR       msg[120];              /* error message buffer        */
    CHAR       object_name[13];       /* buffer for failure name     */
    RESULTCODES ExecResult;           /* child process results       */
    CHAR       program[160];          /* program/parms for DosExecPgm */
    ULONG      rc;                    /* DosExecPgm return code       */

    ClubData *somThis = ClubGetData(somSelf);
    ClubMethodDebug("Club","club_showClubVisual");

    sprintf(program,"%s%c %d %s %s %s %s%c",
            "clubview.exe" , 0, CLUB_GRAPHICS_VIEW,
            _clubname, _clubcountry, datafile_drive_path, txn_rsp_file, 0);
    rc = DosExecPgm(object_name,          /* failing object if program fails */
                sizeof(object_name),      /* the object size             */
                EXEC_ASYNC,               /* sync. program execution     */
                program,                  /* program name and parameters */
                NULL,                     /* inherit environment         */
                &ExecResult,              /* termination reason code     */
                program);                 /* program name                */

    if (rc)
    { sprintf(msg, "DosExecPgm RC=%d\n<%s>", rc, program);
      ShowMsg(" Club ", msg);
    } /* endif */

    return(TRUE);
}

/*_____*/
/* New Method: showClubDescription                            */
/*_____*/
SOM_Scope BOOL    SOMLINK club_showClubDescription(Club *somSelf,
                                        PSZ    txn_rsp_file,
                                        PSZ    datafile_drive_path,
                                        PSZ    txn_response)
{
    CHAR       msg[120];              /* error message buffer        */
    CHAR       object_name[13];       /* buffer for failure name     */
    RESULTCODES ExecResult;           /* child process results       */
    CHAR       program[160];          /* program/parms for DosExecPgm */
    ULONG      rc;                    /* DosExecPgm return code       */

    ClubData *somThis = ClubGetData(somSelf);
    ClubMethodDebug("Club","club_showClubDescription");
```

Figure 44-8 (Part 4 of 10).   CLUB.C: The Club Class C Implementation.

```
    sprintf(program,"%s%c %d %s %s %s %s%c",
            "clubview.exe" , 0, CLUB_TEXT_VIEW,
            _clubname, _clubcountry, datafile_drive_path, txn_rsp_file, 0);

    rc = DosExecPgm(object_name,             /* failing object if program fails */
                    sizeof(object_name),     /* the object size                 */
                    EXEC_ASYNC,              /* sync.  program execution        */
                    program,                 /* program name and parameters     */
                    NULL,                    /* inherit environment             */
                    &ExecResult,             /* termination reason code         */
                    program);                /* program name                    */

    if (rc)
    { sprintf(msg, "DosExecPgm RC=%d\n<%s>", rc, program);
      ShowMsg(" Club ", msg);
    } /* endif */

    return(TRUE);
}

/***********************************************************************************/
/*                                                                                 */
/* Instance Method Overrides                                                       */
/***********************************************************************************/
/*-------------------------------------------------------------------------------*/
/*                                                                                 */
/* New Method: _AddResvConfirmPage                                                 */
/*-------------------------------------------------------------------------------*/
SOM_Scope BOOL    SOMLINK club_wpAddSettingsPages(Club *somSelf,
               HWND hwndNotebook)

{
    /* ClubData *somThis = ClubGetData(somSelf); */
    ClubMethodDebug("Club","club_wpAddSettingsPages");

    if (_AddClubPricesPage(somSelf, hwndNotebook))
       return(TRUE);
    else
    {
       ShowMsg("Club_wpAddSettingsPages", " Failed to add a settings page.");
       return( FALSE );
    }
}

/*-------------------------------------------------------------------------------*/
/*                                                                                 */
/* OVERRIDE: _wpModifyPopupMenu                                                    */
/*-------------------------------------------------------------------------------*/
SOM_Scope BOOL    SOMLINK club_wpModifyPopupMenu(Club *somSelf,
               HWND hwndMenu,
               HWND hwndCnr,
               ULONG iPosition)

{
    /* ClubData *somThis = ClubGetData(somSelf); */
    ClubMethodDebug("Club","club_wpModifyPopupMenu");

    if (!_wpInsertPopupMenuItems(somSelf, hwndMenu, 1,
                         hmod, ID_OPENMENU, WPMENUID_OPEN))
       { ShowMsg(" ClubWPS ", "ERROR: _wpInsertPopupMenuItems");
         return(FALSE);
       }
    return (parent_wpModifyPopupMenu(somSelf,hwndMenu,hwndCnr,iPosition));
}
```

Figure 44-8 (Part 5 of 10). CLUB.C: The Club Class C Implementation.

```
/*_____
/* OVERRIDE: _wpMenuItemSelected                                          */
/*_____ */
SOM_Scope BOOL    SOMLINK club_wpMenuItemSelected(Club *somSelf,
                 HWND hwndFrame,
                 ULONG ulMenuId)
{
    /* ClubData *somThis = ClubGetData(somSelf); */
    ClubMethodDebug("Club","club_wpMenuItemSelected");

    switch( ulMenuId )
    {

       case OPEN_CLUBVISUAL:
       case OPEN_CLUBDESCRIPTION:
       case OPEN_CLUBRESERVATION:
         _wpOpen(somSelf, NULLHANDLE, ulMenuId, 0);
         break;

       default:
         return parent_wpMenuItemSelected(somSelf, hwndFrame, ulMenuId);
         break;
    }
}


/*_____
/* OVERRIDE: _wpopen                                                       */
/*_____ */
SOM_Scope HWND    SOMLINK club_wpOpen(Club *somSelf,
                 HWND hwndCnr,
                 ULONG ulView,
                 ULONG param)
{
    WPObject  *Folder;
    SOMANY    *DoRPCClass;
    SOMANY    *DoRPCObject;
    SOMAny    *ResvfldrClass;
    SOMANY    *NewObj;
    CHAR       ClientMethod[32];
    CHAR       txn_string[80];
    BOOL       rc;
    CHAR       SetupString[256];

    ClubData *somThis = ClubGetData(somSelf);
    ClubMethodDebug("Club","club_wpOpen");

    /*_____*/
    /* Prepare for RPC call                 */
    /*_____*/
    DoRPCClass = _somFindClass(SOMClassMgrObject,
                          SOM_IdFromString("DoRPC"), 1,2);
    if (DoRPCClass == NULL)
       { ShowMsg(" Clubfldr ", "Error: _somFindClass DoRPC");
         return(NULLHANDLE);
       }
    DoRPCObject = _wpclsQueryObject(DoRPCClass,
                          WinQueryObject("<DoRPC>"));
    if (DoRPCObject == NULL)
       { ShowMsg(" Clubfldr ", "Error: _wpclsQueryObject DoRPC");
         return(NULLHANDLE);
       }
```

Figure 44-8 (Part 6 of 10).   CLUB.C: The Club Class C Implementation.

```
/*—————————————————————————*/
/* Prepare the Transaction based on the   */
/* view selected.                         */
/*—————————————————————————*/
switch (ulView)
{
  case OPEN_CLUBVISUAL:
          sprintf(txn_string, "TRANSACTION_ID=%d CLUB=%s",
                              GET_CLUB_GRAPHICS, _clubname);
          strcpy(ClientMethod, "ShowClubVisual");
          rc = _Execute_Transaction(DoRPCObject,
                                    txn_string,
                                    somSelf,
                                    "ShowClubVisual");
          return(NULLHANDLE);
          break;

  case OPEN_CLUBDESCRIPTION:
          sprintf(txn_string, "TRANSACTION_ID=%d CLUB=%s",
                              GET_CLUB_DESCRIPTION, _clubname);
          rc = _Execute_Transaction(DoRPCObject,
                                    txn_string,
                                    somSelf,

                                    "ShowClubDescription");
          return(NULLHANDLE);
          break;

  case OPEN_CLUBRESERVATION:
          ShowMsg(" Club ", "OPEN_CLUBRESERVATION");
          Folder = _wpclsQueryFolder(_somGetClass(somSelf),
                                     "<WP_DESKTOP>",
                                     TRUE);
          if (Folder == NULL)
             { ShowMsg(" Club ", "Error finding desktop folder ID");
               return(FALSE);
             }

          ShowMsg(" Club ", "Find Resvfldr Class");
          ResvfldrClass = _somFindClass(SOMClassMgrObject,
                                     SOM_IdFromString("Resvfldr"), 1,2);
          if (ResvfldrClass == NULL)
             { ShowMsg(" Clubfldr ", "Error: _somFindClass: Resvfldr");
               return(FALSE);
             }
          sprintf(SetupString,
                  "TITLE=%s, %s;OPEN=DEFAULT;ICONRESOURCE=100,"
                  "RESVFLDR;CLUB=%s;COUNTRY=%s;",
                  _clubname, _clubcountry, _clubname, _clubcountry);

          ShowMsg(" Club : Create Resvfldr Folder", SetupString);
          NewObj = _wpclsNew(ResvfldrClass, "Resvfldr",
                          SetupString, Folder, FALSE);
          ShowMsg(" Club ", "after Create Resvfldr");
          if (NewObj == NULL)
             { ShowMsg(" Club ", "Error Creating Reservation Folder");
               return(FALSE);
             }
          break;
```

Figure 44-8 (Part 7 of 10). CLUB.C: The Club Class C Implementation.

```
            default:
                return(parent_wpOpen(somSelf,hwndCnr,ulView,param));
        }
}

/*————————————————————————————————————————————*/
/* OVERRIDE: _wpSetup                                            */
/*————————————————————————————————————————————*/
SOM_Scope BOOL   SOMLINK club_wpSetup(Club *somSelf,
                  PSZ pszSetupString)
{
    ULONG stringlen;

    ClubData *somThis = ClubGetData(somSelf);
    ClubMethodDebug("Club","club_wpSetup");

    _wpScanSetupString(somSelf, pszSetupString, "CLUB",
                    _clubname, &stringlen);
    _wpScanSetupString(somSelf, pszSetupString, "COUNTRY",
                    _clubcountry, &stringlen);

    return (parent_wpSetup(somSelf,pszSetupString));
}


/********************************************************************/
/* Dialog Procedures                                               */
/********************************************************************/
MRESULT EXPENTRY ClubPricesDlgProc(HWND hwndDlg, ULONG msg,
                    MPARAM mp1, MPARAM mp2)
{
  Club      *somSelf;                  /* Instance pointer          */
  ClubData *somThis;                   /* Instance data pointer     */

  SOMAny    *DoRPCClass;               /* DoRPC Class pointer        */
  SOMANY    *DoRPCObject;
  CHAR      txn_string[80];            /* use to build Txn message  */
  BOOL      rc;                        /* return code               */
  FILE      *stream;                   /* txn response file handle  */
  ULONG     i;                         /* loop index variable       */
  CHAR      clubprice[PRICEDATALEN];   /* used to read file data    */
  SHORT     LboxSelection;             /* list box selection index  */
  CHAR      filename[CCHMAXPATH];

  switch (msg)
  {
     case WM_INITDLG:
        /*————————————————————————————*/
        /* Use Window words to save instance       */
        /* pointer.                                */
        /*————————————————————————————*/
        WinSetWindowPtr(hwndDlg, QWL_USER, (PVOID)mp2);
        somSelf = (Club *)mp2;
        somThis = ClubGetData(somSelf);

        DoRPCClass = _somFindClass(SOMClassMgrObject,
                          SOM_IdFromString("DoRPC"), 1,2);
        if (DoRPCClass == NULL)
           { ShowMsg(" Clubfldr ", "Error: _somFindClass DoRPC");
             return(FALSE);
           }
```

Figure 44-8 (Part 8 of 10). CLUB.C: The Club Class C Implementation.

```
        DoRPCObject = _wpclsQueryObject(DoRPCClass,
                                  WinQueryObject("<DoRPC>"));
      if (DoRPCObject == NULL)
         { ShowMsg(" Clubfldr ", "Error: _wpclsQueryObject DoRPC");
           return(FALSE);
         }

      _pricesDlgWindow = hwndDlg;
      sprintf(txn_string, "TRANSACTION_ID=%d CLUB=%s",
                        GET_CLUB_PRICES, _clubname);
      rc = _Execute_Transaction(DoRPCObject,
                              txn_string,
                              somSelf,
                              "ShowClubPrices");
      if (!rc)
         { ShowMsg("Club","Error: Executing GET_CLUB_PRICES Transaction.");
           return(FALSE);
         }
      return (MRESULT) TRUE;
      break;

   case WM_READ_CLUB_PRICES:
      /*_____*/
      /* Get access to instance data          */
      /*_____*/
      somSelf = WinQueryWindowPtr(hwndDlg, QWL_USER);
      if (somSelf == NULL)
      { ShowMsg("ClubPricesDlgProc", "Couldn't get window words");
        break;
      }
      somThis = ClubGetData(somSelf);

      /*_____*/
      /* Fill the list box with Txn Data      */
      /*_____*/
      sprintf(filename,"%s\\%s",_datafile_drive_path,_rsp_filename);
      stream = fopen(filename,"r");
      if (stream == NULL)
         { ShowMsg(" Clubfldr Error: Opening Club Prices File", filename);
           return(FALSE);

         }

      do
        { if (fgets(clubprice,PRICEDATALEN,stream) == 0) break;
           clubprice[strlen(clubprice)-1] = 0;
           WinInsertLboxItem(WinWindowFromID(hwndDlg,ID_PRICELIST),
                           LIT_END,
                           clubprice);
        } while (TRUE); /* enddo */
      fclose(stream);
      remove(filename);
      break;

   case WM_CONTROL:
      /*_____*/
      /* Get access to instance data          */
      /*_____*/
      somSelf = WinQueryWindowPtr(hwndDlg, QWL_USER);
      if (somSelf == NULL)
      { ShowMsg("ClubPricesDlgProc", "Couldn't get window words");
        break;
      }
```

Figure 44-8 (Part 9 of 10). CLUB.C: The Club Class C Implementation.

```
        somThis = ClubGetData(somSelf);

        /*_____*/
        /* Handle list box selection messages    */
        /*_____*/
        switch (SHORT2FROMMP(mp1))
        {
          /*_____*/
          /* Update price data when list box item  */
          /* is selected.                          */
          /*_____*/
          case LN_SELECT:
              LboxSelection =
                 (USHORT)WinSendDlgItemMsg( hwndDlg,
                          ID_PRICELIST,
                          LM_QUERYSELECTION,
                          (MPARAM)0,
                          (MPARAM)0);
              WinSendDlgItemMsg( hwndDlg,
                          ID_PRICELIST,
                          LM_QUERYITEMTEXT,
                          MPFROM2SHORT(LboxSelection, PRICEDATALEN),
                          (MPARAM)_selected_price_data);
              break;
        }   /* end switch (SHORT2FROMMP(mp1)) */

     return (MRESULT) TRUE;
     break;

  }   /* end switch(msg) */

  return (WinDefDlgProc(hwndDlg, msg, mp1, mp2) );

}   /* end ClubDlgProc() */
```

Figure 44-8 (Part 10 of 10). CLUB.C: The Club Class C Implementation.

The DoRPC Class

The OIDL for the **DoRPC** class (see Figure 44-9) shows we are overriding three of the SOM/WPS **WPAbstract** methods and introducing one new method.

The code that implements the methods is listed in Figure 44-10. Here's a quick overview of what the methods do:

- *Execute_Transaction* is a method that, along with the **send_txn_thread** function, executes the client end of a transaction. Between these two functions, the following steps are performed:

  1. A transaction parameter structure is initialized to pass to the transaction thread. This includes an ASCIIZ string to method address conversion. The method address is the address of the method to be invoked when the transaction completes.
  2. A transaction thread is started using the **_beginthread** C runtime library routine.
  3. The thread then uses **DosCallNPipe** to pass the transaction to the Club Server and retrieve the results of the transaction.
  4. The successful completion of the transaction is verified. If the transaction completed successfully, the method, whose address we determined in step 1, is invoked; otherwise, an error message is displayed. Note that a message queue was established for this thread after the **DosCallNPipe** execution. Without this message queue, our error messages and any messages displayed in the class methods invoked from this thread would not be seen.

- The *wpSetup, wpSaveState,* and *wpRestoreState* are **WPAbstract** methods that are overridden to implement persistent configuration data for the **DoRPC** class. This data includes the name of the Club Server Pipe, the name of the computer where the server is located, and the path where the transaction response files can be found. The values for this configuration data are initially passed in a setup string when the **DoRPC** object is created. The method **wpScanSetupString** is used in **wpSetup** to scan the setup string and initialize instance variables. The values are retained in the instance variables as long as the computer is active, but after the next system boot, the values will be lost.

Instance data is made permanently available by storing the data in persistent storage (in the **OS2.INI** file) using the **wpSaveString** method. You can call this method when your override of **wpSaveState** is called by the Workplace Shell as the object is made dormant or the system is shutdown. During **wpRestoreState**, which is called when the object is activated again, you can call **wpRestoreString** to restore the values of your instance data from persistent storage values saved earlier.

The DoRPC Class OIDL

```
/****************************************************************************/
/*  Class Name: do_RPC - Class for accessing the Club Med database server   */
/****************************************************************************/
#***************************************************************************
#    Include Section
#***************************************************************************
include <wpabs.sc>

#***************************************************************************
#    Class Section
#***************************************************************************
class: DoRPC,
        external stem   = doRPC,
        local,
        external prefix = doRPC_,
        classprefix     = doRPCM_,
        major version   = 1,
        minor version   = 2;

#***************************************************************************
#    Parent Class Section
#***************************************************************************
parent: WPAbstract;

#***************************************************************************
#    Release Order Section
#***************************************************************************
release order:
Execute_Transaction;

#***************************************************************************
#    Passthru Section
#***************************************************************************
passthru: C.ih;

#define INCL_WIN
#define INCL_DOS
#define INCL_ERRORS
#include <os2.h>

#define INCL_WPCLASS
#include <pmwp.h>


#define COMPUTER_NAME_SIZE          11
#define PIPE_NAME_SIZE              260
#define DATAFILE_DRIVE_PATH_SIZE    260

#define DORPC_COMPUTER_NAME          1
#define DORPC_PIPE_NAME              2
#define DORPC_DATAFILE_DRIVE_PATH    3

#define ShowMsg(title, text) \
        WinMessageBox(HWND_DESKTOP, HWND_DESKTOP, (PSZ) text, (PSZ) title, \
                   20, MB_OK | MB_INFORMATION | MB_MOVEABLE)

endpassthru;    /* .ih */
```

Figure 44-9 (Part 1 of 2). DORPC.CSC: The DoRPC Class OIDL.

```
#****************************************************************************
#    Data Section
#****************************************************************************
data:
CHAR   computer_name[COMPUTER_NAME_SIZE];
CHAR   pipe_name[PIPE_NAME_SIZE];
CHAR   datafile_drive_path[DATAFILE_DRIVE_PATH_SIZE];

#****************************************************************************
#    Methods Section
#****************************************************************************
methods:

#---------------------------------------------------------------------------
#    Specify Class Methods being overridden
#---------------------------------------------------------------------------
/*-------------------------------------------------------------------------*/
/* OVERRIDE: _wpclsQueryStyle                                              */
/*-------------------------------------------------------------------------*/
override wpclsQueryStyle, class;

#---------------------------------------------------------------------------
#    Specify New Methods
#---------------------------------------------------------------------------
BOOL Execute_Transaction (PSZ      ClientTransaction,
                          SOMAny *ClientInstance,
                          PSZ      ClientMethod);

#---------------------------------------------------------------------------
#    Specify Instance Methods being overridden
#---------------------------------------------------------------------------
override wpSetup;
override wpSaveState;
override wpRestoreState;
```

Figure 44-9 (Part 2 of 2). DORPC.CSC: The DoRPC Class OIDL.

The DoRPC Class C Implementation

```
/***********************************************************************/
/*   OBJECT NAME: DoRPC - A Class for accessing the Club Med Database Server   */
/*                                                                     */
/*   DESCRIPTION:  This object spawns a thread for accessing the server.   */
/*                                                                     */
/***********************************************************************/
#define DoRPC_Class_Source
#define M_DoRPC_Class_Source
#include <string.h>
#include <stdio.h>
#include <memory.h>
#include <stdlib.h>
#include "DORPC.ih"

/*-------------------------------------------------------------------*/
/* global variables and function declarations for this module        */
/*-------------------------------------------------------------------*/
typedef struct _TXN_PARMS
        { CHAR     txn_string[1024];
          CHAR     rsp_string[1024];
          CHAR     datafile_drive_path[CCHMAXPATH];
          integer4 SOMLINK (* ClientMethod)(SOMAny *ClientInstance,
                                            PSZ     txn_resp_file,
                                            PSZ     datafile_drive_path,
                                            PSZ     txn_response);

          SOMAny *ClientInstance;
        } TXN_PARMS;
typedef TXN_PARMS *PTXN_PARMS;

CHAR ClassTitle[] = "DoRPC";                    /* Title of this class        */
CHAR RemotePipeName[260];                       /* pipe name for DosCallNPipe */

VOID _Optlink send_txn_thread(PVOID parms);

/***********************************************************************/
/* Class Method Overrides                                              */
/***********************************************************************/
#undef SOM_CurrentClass
#define SOM_CurrentClass SOMMeta
SOM_Scope ULONG   SOMLINK doRPCM_wpclsQueryStyle(M_DoRPC *somSelf)
{
    /* M_DoRPCData *somThis = M_DoRPCGetData(somSelf); */
    M_DoRPCMethodDebug("M_DoRPC","doRPCM_wpclsQueryStyle");

    return (parent_wpclsQueryStyle(somSelf) | CLSSTYLE_NEVERTEMPLATE |
            CLSSTYLE_NEVERMOVE | CLSSTYLE_NEVERCOPY |
            CLSSTYLE_NEVERRENAME);
}


/***********************************************************************/
/* New Methods                                                         */
/***********************************************************************/
#undef SOM_CurrentClass
#define SOM_CurrentClass SOMInstance
```

Figure 44-10 (Part 1 of 5).   DORPC.C: The DoRPC Class C Implementation.

```
/*————————————————————————————————————*/
/* New Method: Execute_Transaction                                      */
/*————————————————————————————————————*/
SOM_Scope BOOL  SOMLINK doRPC_Execute_Transaction(DoRPC *somSelf,
                PSZ ClientTransaction,
                SOMAny *ClientInstance,
                PSZ ClientMethod)
{
    CHAR msg[80];
    somId ClientMethodID;
    PTXN_PARMS  txn_parms;

    DoRPCData *somThis = DoRPCGetData(somSelf);
    DoRPCMethodDebug("DoRPC","doRPC_Execute_Transaction");

    /*———————————————————————————*/
    /* allocate memory for transaction   */
    /* thread parameters                 */
    /*———————————————————————————*/
    txn_parms = malloc(sizeof(TXN_PARMS));
    strcpy(txn_parms->txn_string, ClientTransaction);
    strcpy(txn_parms->datafile_drive_path, _datafile_drive_path);

    /*———————————————————————————*/
    /* get client method pointer         */
    /*———————————————————————————*/
    if (ClientInstance != NULL)
    {
     txn_parms->ClientInstance = ClientInstance;
     ClientMethodID = SOM_IdFromString(ClientMethod);
     _somFindMethod(_somGetClass(ClientInstance),
                    ClientMethodID,
                    &txn_parms->ClientMethod);
     if (ClientInstance == NULL)
        return(FALSE);
    }
    else
    {
     txn_parms->ClientMethod == NULL;
    } /* endif */

    /*———————————————————————————*/
    /* start the transaction thread      */
    /*———————————————————————————*/
    _beginthread(send_txn_thread,           /* name of function      */
                NULL,                        /* stack ptr (not used)  */
                12288,                       /* size of stack         */
                txn_parms);                  /* no parms              */

    return(TRUE);
}
```

Figure 44-10 (Part 2 of 5). DORPC.C: The DoRPC Class C Implementation.

```
/***************************************************************************/
/* Instance Method Overrides                                               */
/***************************************************************************/
/*-----------------------------------------------------------------------*/
/* Override: wpSetup                                                       */
/*-----------------------------------------------------------------------*/
SOM_Scope BOOL    SOMLINK doRPC_wpSetup(DoRPC *somSelf,
                  PSZ pszSetupString)
{
    ULONG size;

    DoRPCData *somThis = DoRPCGetData(somSelf);
    DoRPCMethodDebug("DoRPC","doRPC_wpSetup");

        /*----------------------------------------*/
        /* Initialize instance data from the      */
        /* setup string.                          */
        /*----------------------------------------*/
    size = COMPUTER_NAME_SIZE;
    _wpScanSetupString(somSelf, pszSetupString,

                        "COMPUTER_NAME", _computer_name, &size);
    size = PIPE_NAME_SIZE;
    _wpScanSetupString(somSelf, pszSetupString,
                        "PIPE_NAME", _pipe_name, &size);
    size = DATAFILE_DRIVE_PATH_SIZE;
    _wpScanSetupString(somSelf, pszSetupString,
                        "DATAFILE_DRIVE_PATH", _datafile_drive_path, &size);

    sprintf(RemotePipeName,"%s%s", _computer_name, _pipe_name);

    return (parent_wpSetup(somSelf,pszSetupString));
}


/*-----------------------------------------------------------------------*/
/* Override: wpSaveState                                                   */
/*-----------------------------------------------------------------------*/
SOM_Scope BOOL    SOMLINK doRPC_wpSaveState(DoRPC *somSelf)
{
    DoRPCData *somThis = DoRPCGetData(somSelf);
    DoRPCMethodDebug("DoRPC","doRPC_wpSaveState");

    _wpSaveString(somSelf, ClassTitle, DORPC_COMPUTER_NAME, _computer_name);
    _wpSaveString(somSelf, ClassTitle, DORPC_PIPE_NAME     , _pipe_name);
    _wpSaveString(somSelf, ClassTitle, DORPC_DATAFILE_DRIVE_PATH,
                                        _datafile_drive_path);

    return (parent_wpSaveState(somSelf));
}


/*-----------------------------------------------------------------------*/
/* Override: wpRestoreState                                                */
/*-----------------------------------------------------------------------*/
SOM_Scope BOOL    SOMLINK doRPC_wpRestoreState(DoRPC *somSelf,
                  ULONG ulReserved)
{
    ULONG size;

    DoRPCData *somThis = DoRPCGetData(somSelf);
    DoRPCMethodDebug("DoRPC","doRPC_wpRestoreState");
```

Figure 44-10 (Part 3 of 5). DORPC.C: The DoRPC Class C Implementation.

```
        size = COMPUTER_NAME_SIZE;
        _wpRestoreString(somSelf, ClassTitle, DORPC_COMPUTER_NAME,
                         _computer_name, &size);
        size = PIPE_NAME_SIZE;
        _wpRestoreString(somSelf, ClassTitle, DORPC_PIPE_NAME,
                         _pipe_name, &size);
        size = DATAFILE_DRIVE_PATH_SIZE;
        _wpRestoreString(somSelf, ClassTitle, DORPC_DATAFILE_DRIVE_PATH,
                         _datafile_drive_path, &size);

        sprintf(RemotePipeName,"%s%s", _computer_name, _pipe_name);

        return (parent_wpRestoreState(somSelf,ulReserved));
}
/*****************************************************************************/
/* Thread functions                                                         */
/*****************************************************************************/
/*-------------------------------------------------------------------------*/
/* thread to execute a transaction                                          */
/*-------------------------------------------------------------------------*/
#pragma handler(send_txn_thread)
VOID _Optlink send_txn_thread(PVOID parms)
{
 #define PIPE_TIMEOUT    10000

 PTXN_PARMS    txn_parms;                    /* pointer to thread parm block */
 CHAR          completion[10];               /* TXN success indicator       */
 CHAR          rsp_file_name[13];            /* Response file if any        */
 CHAR          rsp_parms[1024];              /* any other response data     */
 CHAR          error_string[1024];           /* error message buffer        */
 ULONG         PipeBytesRead;                /* number of pipe bytes read   */
 HAB           hab;                          /* PM anchor block handle      */
 HMQ           hmq;                          /* Message queue handle        */
 ULONG         rc;

 txn_parms = parms;

 completion[0]     = '\0';
 rsp_file_name[0] = '\0';
 rsp_parms[0]      = '\0';
 txn_parms->rsp_string[0] = '\0';

 do { rc = DosCallNPipe(
         RemotePipeName,                        /* name of CLUBSVR pipe     */
         txn_parms->txn_string,                 /* input buffer             */
         strlen(txn_parms->txn_string)+1,       /* input buffer size        */
         txn_parms->rsp_string,                 /* output buffer            */
         sizeof(txn_parms->rsp_string),         /* output buffer size       */
         &PipeBytesRead,                        /* number of response bytes */
         PIPE_TIMEOUT);                         /* timout fir this call     */
 } while ( rc == ERROR_PIPE_BUSY || rc == ERROR_PIPE_NOT_CONNECTED );

 hab = WinInitialize( 0 );
 hmq = WinCreateMsgQueue( hab, 0 );
 if (rc != 0)
 { sprintf(error_string, "DosCallNPipe Error: RC = %u", rc);
   ShowMsg(" DoRPC : DosCallNPipe RC ", error_string);
 } /* endif */

 if (txn_parms->ClientMethod != NULL)
 {
```

Figure 44-10 (Part 4 of 5). DORPC.C: The DoRPC Class C Implementation.

```
    strcat(txn_parms->rsp_string,";");
    sscanf(txn_parms->rsp_string,
          "TXN_COMPLETION = %s RESPONSE_FILE = %[^ ;] %[^;]",
          completion, rsp_file_name, rsp_parms);
    if (strcmp(completion,"SUCCESS") == 0)
        {
        /*_____*/
        /* call client method                      */
        /*_____*/
        txn_parms->ClientMethod(txn_parms->ClientInstance,
                                rsp_file_name,
                                txn_parms->datafile_drive_path,
                                rsp_parms);
        }
    else
        { /*_____*/
        /* display error message                   */
        /*_____*/
        sprintf(error_string,"TRANSACTION FAILURE: \nMESSAGE: %s \nRESPONSE: %s",
                          txn_parms->txn_string, txn_parms->rsp_string);
        ShowMsg(" DoRPC Transaction Failure", error_string);
        } /* endif */
    free(txn_parms);

    }


  WinDestroyMsgQueue( hmq );                    /* Destroy the queue          */
  WinTerminate( hab );                          /* terminate                  */
  _endthread();
  } /* elapsed_time_thread */
```

Figure 44-10 (Part 5 of 5). DORPC.C: The DoRPC Class C Implementation.

The Clubview Program

We now present the Clubview Program. The program is shown in Figure 44-11; it has these parts:

- A *main* procedure interprets parameters and displays views based on the parameters provided. The name of a transaction response file is passed as a parameter and the bitmap, metafile, and text file names are retrieved from this file. This procedure also establishes the PM basics (such as a message queue) for this process.
- The *DisplayViewWindow* and *ViewWindowProc* procedures create a frame window. The client area of this window is the "canvas" where our bitmaps, metafiles, and text files will be "painted."
- The *DisplayMetafile, MetafileProc, DisplayBitmap, BitmapProc,* and *DisplayText* procedures implement the PM function of painting metafiles, bitmaps, and text files.

CLUBVIEW.C: the Clubview Program

```
/************************************************************************/
/*  PROGRAM NAME: CLUBVIEW - Display a graphical view of a Club Med Location.*/
/*                                                                      */
/*  PROGRAM INVOCATION:                                                 */
/*      CLUBVIEW view club country datafile_drive_path rsp_file         */
/************************************************************************/
#include <string.h>
#include <stdio.h>
#include <malloc.h>
#include <sys\types.h>
#include <sys\stat.h>
#define   INCL_WIN                           /* include Win calls       */
#define   INCL_GPI                           /* include Gpi calls       */
#include <os2.h>                             /* PM header file          */
#include "club.ih"


/*----------------------------------------------------------------------*/
/* global variables and declares                                        */
/*----------------------------------------------------------------------*/
#define ID_META      250
#define ID_BITMAP    251
#define ID_MLE       252
#define ID_FRAME     255
#define MAXBITMAPS     5

HAB      hab;                          /* PM anchor block handle      */
HDC      hdc;                          /* device context handle         */
HPS      hps;                          /* Presentation space handle     */
HMF      hmf;                          /* Metafile handle               */
LONG     SegCount;
BOOL     Success;
SIZEL    Size = {0,0};
LONG     alOptions[] = {0L,             /* PMF_SEGBASE                   */
                    LT_ORIGINALVIEW, /* PMF_LOADTYPE                  */
                    RS_DEFAULT,      /* PMF_RESOLVE                   */
                    LC_LOADDISC,     /* PMF_LCIDS                     */
                    RES_DEFAULT,     /* PMF_RESET                     */
                    SUP_DEFAULT,     /* PMF_SUPPRESS                  */
                    CTAB_REPLACE,    /* PMF_COLORTABLES               */
                    CREA_DEFAULT,    /* PMF_COLORREALIZABLE           */
                    };
CHAR         metafile_desc[256];

MATRIXLF matlfXform   =
     {MAKEFIXED(1, 0x4000), MAKEFIXED(0, 0      ),  0L,
      MAKEFIXED(0, 0      ), MAKEFIXED(1, 0x8000),  0L,
      0L,              0L,                   1L
     };

                     /*------------------------------------*/
                     /* variables for drawing bit maps     */
                     /*------------------------------------*/
HDC      hdcMem;                            /* Memory device context handle   */
HPS      hpsMem;                            /* Presentation space handle      */
HBITMAP  hbmMem;                            /* Bit maps held in a resource file */
```

Figure 44-11 (Part 1 of 12). CLUBVIEW.C: The Clubview Program.

```
POINTL   bmarray [5];                         /* bit map src, dst pointers        */

PBITMAPFILEHEADER bm_header_ptr;              /* pointer to bitmap header in memory */
PBITMAPINFOHEADER bm_info_ptr;                /* pointer to bitmap info   in memory */
PBYTE           bm_data_ptr;                  /* pointer to bitmap pels   in memory */

PSZ           dcdatablk[9] = {(PSZ)0 ,(PSZ)"DISPLAY"    /* for device context    */
                             ,(PSZ)0 ,(PSZ)0 ,(PSZ)0
                             ,(PSZ)0 ,(PSZ)0 ,(PSZ)0
                             ,(PSZ)0 };

                    /*———————————————————————————*/
                    /* variables for MLEs                        */
                    /*———————————————————————————*/
CHAR szFontName[] = "8.Courier";

/*———————————————————————*/
/* Error Message Helper        */
/*———————————————————————*/
#define ShowMsg(title, text) \
        WinMessageBox(HWND_DESKTOP, HWND_DESKTOP, (PSZ) text, (PSZ) title, \
                  20, MB_OK | MB_INFORMATION | MB_MOVEABLE)

/*—————————————————————————————————————————————*/
/* foward declaration of functions                                      */
/*—————————————————————————————————————————————*/
HWND DisplayViewWindow(PSZ Title, ULONG x, ULONG y, ULONG cx, ULONG cy);
HWND DisplayMetafile(HWND  hwndFrame, ULONG x, ULONG y, ULONG cx, ULONG cy,
                  PSZ filename);
HWND DisplayBitmap(HWND  hwndFrame, ULONG x, ULONG y, ULONG cx, ULONG cy,
                  PSZ filename);
HWND DisplayText(HWND  hwndFrame, ULONG x, ULONG y, ULONG cx, ULONG cy,
               PSZ   filename, PSZ FontName);
MRESULT EXPENTRY ViewWindowProc( HWND hwnd, ULONG msg, MPARAM mp1, MPARAM mp2);
MRESULT EXPENTRY MetafileProc(HWND hwnd, ULONG msg, MPARAM mp1, MPARAM mp2);
MRESULT EXPENTRY BitmapProc(HWND hwnd, ULONG msg, MPARAM mp1, MPARAM mp2);

/*—————————————————————————————————————————————*/
/* main.                                                                */
/*—————————————————————————————————————————————*/
void cdecl main(int argc, char **argv)
{
  HMQ    hmq;                                 /* Message queue handle        */
  QMSG   qmsg;                                /* Message from message queue  */
  HWND   hwndView;
  HWND   hwndViewClient;
  HWND   hwndMeta;
  HWND   hwndBitmap;
  HWND   hwndMLE;
  CHAR   title[80];
  CHAR   filename[13];
  CHAR   rsp_file_path_name[CCHMAXPATH];
  ULONG  i;
  FILE *rsp_file;
  CHAR   meta_filename[CCHMAXPATH];
  CHAR   bmap_filename[CCHMAXPATH];

  CHAR   text_filename[CCHMAXPATH];
```

Figure 44-11 (Part 2 of 12).   CLUBVIEW.C: The Clubview Program.

```
hab = WinInitialize( NULL );              /* Initialize PM              */
hmq = WinCreateMsgQueue( hab, 0 );        /* Create a message queue     */

sprintf(title,"%s, %s", argv[2], argv[3]);
sprintf(rsp_file_path_name, "%s\\%s", argv[4], argv[5]);
if ((rsp_file = fopen(rsp_file_path_name,"r")) == NULL)
    { ShowMsg("Clubview", "Error Opening Response File");
      exit(TRUE);
    }
fscanf(rsp_file," %20s ", filename);

switch (atoi(argv[1]))
{
 case CLUB_GRAPHICS_VIEW:
    hwndViewClient  = DisplayViewWindow(title, 20, 0, 600, 480);

    sprintf(meta_filename, "%s\\%s", argv[4], filename);
    hwndMeta = DisplayMetaFile(hwndViewClient, 30, 100, 600, 400,
                               meta_filename);

    for (i=0;i< MAXBITMAPS ; i++)
    { if (fscanf(rsp_file," %20s ", filename) == EOF)
        break;
      else
        { sprintf(bmap_filename,"%s\\%s", argv[4], filename);
          hwndBitmap = DisplayBitmap(hwndViewClient, 1+(i*125),
                                     0, 100, 100, bmap_filename);
        }
    } /* end for */
    break;
 case CLUB_TEXT_VIEW:
    hwndViewClient  = DisplayViewWindow(title, 20, 0, 600, 480);
    sprintf(text_filename, "%s\\%s", argv[4], filename);
    hwndMeta = DisplayText(hwndViewClient, 0, 100, 600, 400,
                           text_filename, szFontName);
    break;
} /* endswitch */
remove(rsp_file_path_name);

/*───────────────────────────────────────*/
/* Get and dispatch messages             */
/*───────────────────────────────────────*/
while( WinGetMsg( hab, &qmsg, NULL, 0, 0 ) )
  WinDispatchMsg( hab, &qmsg );

hwndView = WinQueryWindow(hwndViewClient, QW_PARENT);
WinDestroyWindow( hwndView );             /* Destroy the window         */
WinDestroyMsgQueue( hmq );                /* Destroy the queue          */
WinTerminate( hab );                      /* terminate                  */
}

/*───────────────────────────────────────────────────────────────────*/
/* Create Frame window for an object view.                            */
/*───────────────────────────────────────────────────────────────────*/
HWND DisplayViewWindow(PSZ Title, ULONG x, ULONG y, ULONG cx, ULONG cy)
{
  HWND   hwndFrame;                       /* Frame window handle        */
  HWND   hwndClient;                      /* Client window handle       */
  ULONG  flCreate;                        /* Window creation control flags*/
  FRAMECDATA flFrameCtlData;              /* Frame Control Data         */
```

Figure 44-11 (Part 3 of 12). CLUBVIEW.C: The Clubview Program.

```
    WinRegisterClass(                          /* Register window class       */
        hab,                                   /* Anchor block handle         */
        "ViewWindowClass",                     /* Window class name           */
        ViewWindowProc,                        /* Address of window procedure */
        CS_SIZEREDRAW,                         /* Class style                 */
        4);                                    /* 4 window words for pointer  */

    flFrameCtlData.cb          = sizeof( flFrameCtlData );
    flFrameCtlData.flCreateFlags = FCF_TITLEBAR | FCF_SYSMENU | FCF_DLGBORDER;

    hwndFrame =                                          /* create frame window */
    WinCreateWindow(
        HWND_DESKTOP,              /* parent-window handle                      */
        WC_FRAME,                  /* pointer to registered class name          */
        Title,                     /* pointer to window text                    */
        0,                         /* window style                              */
        0, 0, 0, 0,                /* position of window                        */
        NULLHANDLE,                /* owner-window handle                       */
        HWND_TOP,                  /* handle to sibling window                  */
        (USHORT) ID_FRAME,         /* window identifier                         */
        (PVOID) &flFrameCtlData,   /* pointer to buffer                         */
        NULL);                     /* pointer to structure with pres. params.   */

    hwndClient =               /* use WinCreateWindow so we can pass pres params */
    WinCreateWindow(
        hwndFrame,                 /* parent-window handle                      */
        "ViewWindowClass",         /* pointer to registered class name          */
        NULL,                      /* pointer to window text                    */
        0,                         /* window style                              */
        0, 0, 0, 0,                /* position of window                        */
        hwndFrame,                 /* owner-window handle                       */
        HWND_TOP,                  /* handle to sibling window                  */
        FID_CLIENT,                /* window identifier                         */
        NULL,                      /* pointer to buffer                         */
        NULL);                     /* pointer to structure with pres. params.   */


    WinSetWindowPos(hwndFrame, HWND_TOP, x, y, cx, cy,
                    SWP_SIZE | SWP_MOVE | SWP_ACTIVATE | SWP_SHOW);

    return(hwndClient);
}

/*------------------------------------------------------------------------------*/
/* Window Procedure for View Frame Window                                       */
/*------------------------------------------------------------------------------*/
MRESULT EXPENTRY ViewWindowProc( HWND hwnd, ULONG msg,
                                 MPARAM mp1, MPARAM mp2 )
{
  HPS    hps;                                   /* Presentation Space handle    */

  RECTL  rc;                                    /* Rectangle coordinates        */
  HWND   hwndFrame;
```

Figure 44-11 (Part 4 of 12). CLUBVIEW.C: The Clubview Program.

```
    hwndFrame = WinQueryWindow(hwnd, QW_PARENT);

    switch( msg )
    {
      case WM_ERASEBACKGROUND:
        /*_____*/
        /* cause window background to be   */
        /* painted in SYSCLR_WINDOW        */
        /*_____*/
        return (MRESULT)( TRUE );

      case WM_CLOSE:
        /*_____*/
        /* cause the application to end    */
        /*_____*/
        WinPostMsg( hwnd, WM_QUIT, OL, OL );
        break;

      default:
        /*_____*/
        /* unknown messages to default     */
        /*_____*/
        return WinDefWindowProc( hwnd, msg, mp1, mp2 );
    }
    return FALSE;
}


/*_____*/
/* Method for Displaying a Metafile.                                      */
/*_____*/
HWND DisplayMetafile(HWND  hwndClient, ULONG x, ULONG y, ULONG cx, ULONG cy,
                     PSZ filename)
{ HWND hwndMetafile;
  HWND hwndFrame;

  hwndFrame = WinQueryWindow(hwndClient, QW_PARENT);

  WinRegisterClass(                        /* Register window class         */
      hab,                                 /* Anchor block handle           */
      "MetafileClass",                     /* Window class name             */
      MetafileProc,                        /* Address of window procedure   */
      CS_SIZEREDRAW,                       /* Class style                   */
      0);                                  /* No extra window words         */

  hwndMetafile =
  WinCreateWindow(
      hwndClient,              /* parent-window handle                 */
      "MetafileClass",         /* pointer to registered class name     */
      NULL,                    /* pointer to window text               */
      0,                       /* window style                         */
      0, 0, 0, 0,              /* position of window                   */
      hwndFrame,               /* owner-window handle                  */
      HWND_TOP,                /* handle to sibling window             */
      ID_BITMAP,               /* window identifier                    */
      filename,                /* pointer to buffer                    */
      NULL);                   /* pointer to structure with pres. params. */

  WinSetWindowPos(hwndMetafile, HWND_TOP, x, y, cx, cy,
                  SWP_SIZE | SWP_MOVE | SWP_ACTIVATE | SWP_SHOW);
  return(hwndMetafile);
}
```

Figure 44-11 (Part 5 of 12). CLUBVIEW.C: The Clubview Program.

```
/*—————————————————————————————————————————————————————*/
/* Window Procedure for Displaying a Metafile.                         */
/*—————————————————————————————————————————————————————*/
MRESULT EXPENTRY MetafileProc( HWND hwnd, ULONG msg,
                               MPARAM mp1, MPARAM mp2 )
{
  RECTL  rc;                                   /* Rectangle coordinates      */
  CHAR filename[CCHMAXPATH];

  switch( msg )
  {
    case WM_CREATE:
      /*—————————————————————————————*/
      /* load Metafile                                */
      /*—————————————————————————————*/
      if (hdc==NULL)
          hdc = WinOpenWindowDC(hwnd);
      hps = GpiCreatePS( (HAB)NULL, hdc, &Size,
                         (LONG) PU_LOENGLISH | GPIT_NORMAL | GPIA_ASSOC);
      strcpy(filename, PVOIDFROMMP(mp1));
      hmf = GpiLoadMetaFile( (HAB)NULL, filename);
      break;

    case WM_PAINT:
      /*———————————————————————————————————*/
      /* set pointer to hourglass                            */
      /*———————————————————————————————————*/
      WinSetPointer(HWND_DESKTOP,
                    WinQuerySysPointer(HWND_DESKTOP, SPTR_WAIT, FALSE));

      Success = GpiSetDefaultViewMatrix(hps, 9L, &matlfXform,
                                        TRANSFORM_REPLACE);
      hps = WinBeginPaint( hwnd, hps, NULL );
      GpiPlayMetaFile(hps, hmf, 8L, alOptions, &SegCount,
                      (LONG)sizeof(metafile_desc), metafile_desc);
      WinEndPaint( hps );

      /*———————————————————————————————————*/
      /* return pointer to normal                            */
      /*———————————————————————————————————*/
      WinSetPointer(HWND_DESKTOP, WinQuerySysPointer(HWND_DESKTOP,
                                  SPTR_ARROW, FALSE));
    break;

    case WM_CLOSE:
      /*————————————————————————————————*/
      /* cause the application to end                      */
      /*————————————————————————————————*/
      GpiDeleteMetaFile(hmf);
      GpiAssociate( hps, (HDC)NULL );
      GpiDestroyPS( hps );
      hdc = (HDC)NULL;
      WinPostMsg( hwnd, WM_QUIT, OL, OL );
      break;
```

Figure 44-11 (Part 6 of 12).   CLUBVIEW.C: The Clubview Program.

```
    default:
        /*_____*/
        /* unknown messages to default        */
        /*_____*/
        return WinDefWindowProc( hwnd, msg, mp1, mp2 );
  }
  return FALSE;
}

/*_____*/
/* Method for Displaying a bitmap.                                */
/*_____*/
HWND DisplayBitmap(HWND  hwndClient, ULONG x, ULONG y, ULONG cx, ULONG cy,
                   PSZ filename)
{ HWND hwndBitmap;
  HWND hwndFrame;

  hwndFrame = WinQueryWindow(hwndClient, QW_PARENT);

  WinRegisterClass(                          /* Register window class       */
      hab,                                   /* Anchor block handle         */
      "BitmapClass",                         /* Window class name           */
      BitmapProc,                            /* Address of window procedure  */
      CS_SIZEREDRAW,                         /* Class style                 */
      4);                                    /* 4 bytes for pointer         */

  hwndBitmap =
  WinCreateWindow(
      hwndClient,               /* parent-window handle                   */
      "BitmapClass",            /* pointer to registered class name        */
      NULL,                     /* pointer to window text                  */
      0,                        /* window style                            */
      0, 0, 0, 0,               /* position of window                      */
      hwndFrame,                /* owner-window handle                     */
      HWND_TOP,                 /* handle to sibling window                */
      (USHORT)ID_BITMAP,        /* window identifier                       */
      filename,                 /* pointer to buffer                       */
      NULL);                    /* pointer to structure with pres. params. */

  WinSetWindowPos(hwndBitmap, HWND_TOP, x, y, cx, cy,
                  SWP_SIZE | SWP_MOVE | SWP_ACTIVATE | SWP_SHOW);
  return(hwndBitmap);
}

/*_____*/
/* Window Procedure for Bitmap display.                           */
/*_____*/
MRESULT EXPENTRY BitmapProc( HWND hwnd, ULONG msg, MPARAM mp1, MPARAM mp2 )
{
  RECTL       rc;                            /* Rectangle coordinates       */
  int         return_code;
  FILE        *file;
  struct stat StatBuff;
  SIZEL       bmSize;
  HPS         hps;
  RECTL       PaintArea;
  PSZ         pszFilename;
  CHAR        filename[CCHMAXPATH];
```

Figure 44-11 (Part 7 of 12). CLUBVIEW.C: The Clubview Program.

```
                        /*─────────────────────────────────*/
                        /* variables for drawing metafiles    */
                        /*─────────────────────────────────*/
switch( msg )
{
  case WM_CREATE:
    pszFilename = (PSZ)malloc(32);
    strcpy(pszFilename, PVOIDFROMMP(mp1));
    Success = WinSetWindowPtr(hwnd, QWL_USER, (PVOID)pszFilename);
    if (!Success)
    { WinMessageBox( HWND_DESKTOP, HWND_DESKTOP,
                     "Error setting Window Pointer", "BITMAP",
                     1, MB_OK );
    } /* endif */
    break;

  case WM_PAINT:
    /*─────────────────────────────────*/
    /* Open file and read entire bitmap into   */
    /* a buffer                                 */
    /*─────────────────────────────────*/
    pszFilename = (PSZ)WinQueryWindowPtr(hwnd, QWL_USER);
    strcpy(filename,pszFilename);

    file = fopen(filename, "rb" );
    if ( file != NULL )
    {
        /*─────────────────────────────────*/
        /* set pointer to hourglass            */
        /*─────────────────────────────────*/
        WinSetPointer(HWND_DESKTOP,
                      WinQuerySysPointer(HWND_DESKTOP, SPTR_WAIT, FALSE));

        return_code = stat( filename, &StatBuff );
        bm_header_ptr = (PBITMAPFILEHEADER)malloc( (size_t)StatBuff.st_size );
        if ( bm_header_ptr == NULL )
           WinMessageBox( HWND_DESKTOP, HWND_DESKTOP,
                          "Can't allocate storage", "BITMAP",
                          1, MB_OK );

        fread( (PVOID)bm_header_ptr, sizeof(CHAR),
               (size_t)StatBuff.st_size, file );
        fclose( file );

        /*─────────────────────────────────*/
        /* make pointers to bitmap info header     */
        /* and pel data portions of the buffer     */
        /*─────────────────────────────────*/
        bm_info_ptr = (PBITMAPINFOHEADER)((ULONG)bm_header_ptr
                        + sizeof(BITMAPFILEHEADER)
                        - sizeof(BITMAPINFOHEADER));
        bm_data_ptr = (PBYTE)((ULONG)bm_header_ptr + bm_header_ptr->offBits);

        bmSize.cx = bm_header_ptr->bmp.cx;
        bmSize.cy = bm_header_ptr->bmp.cy;
```

Figure 44-11 (Part 8 of 12). CLUBVIEW.C: The Clubview Program.

```
/*————————————————————————*/
/* remove any old bitmaps                    */
/*————————————————————————*/
if (hbmMem)
   {
     GpiSetBitmap (hpsMem, (HBITMAP)NULL);
     GpiDeleteBitmap(hbmMem);
     GpiAssociate( hpsMem, (HDC)NULL );
     GpiDestroyPS( hpsMem );
     DevCloseDC( hdcMem );
     hbmMem = (HBITMAP)NULL;
   }

/*————————————————————————*/
/* load bit map and create a memory bit map*/
/*————————————————————————*/
hdcMem   = DevOpenDC((HAB)NULL, OD_MEMORY, "*", 8L,
                        (PDEVOPENDATA)dcdatablk, (HDC)NULL);

hpsMem   = GpiCreatePS((HAB)NULL, hdcMem, &bmSize,
                        (LONG) PU_PELS | GPIT_NORMAL | GPIA_ASSOC);

hbmMem   = GpiCreateBitmap(hpsMem, (PBITMAPINFOHEADER2)bm_info_ptr,
                        (ULONG)0,
                        (PBYTE)NULL, (PBITMAPINFO2)NULL);

GpiSetBitmap(hpsMem, hbmMem);


GpiSetBitmapBits(hpsMem,                        /* memory presentation space */
                 0L,                            /* starting row              */
                 (LONG)bm_info_ptr->cy, /* ending row                */
                 bm_data_ptr,                   /* pointer to bit map data   */
                 (PBITMAPINFO2)bm_info_ptr); /* pointer to bit info   */
free((PVOID)bm_header_ptr);

hps = WinBeginPaint( hwnd, (HPS)NULL, &PaintArea );

/*————————————————————————*/
/* set bitmap sizes (source and target)     */
/*————————————————————————*/
bmarray[2].x = 0;
bmarray[2].y = 0;
bmarray[3].x = bmSize.cx;
bmarray[3].y = bmSize.cy;

bmarray[0].x = PaintArea.xLeft;
bmarray[0].y = PaintArea.yBottom;
bmarray[1].x = PaintArea.xRight;
bmarray[1].y = PaintArea.yTop;

/*————————————————————————*/
/* bitblt  between bitmap load from a file */
/*     and user control area               */
/*————————————————————————*/
GpiBitBlt(hps, hpsMem, 4L, (PPOINTL)bmarray,
          (LONG) ROP_SRCCOPY, (LONG) BBO_IGNORE);

WinEndPaint( hps );
```

Figure 44-11 (Part 9 of 12). CLUBVIEW.C: The Clubview Program.

```
          /*_____*/
          /* return pointer to normal               */
          /*_____*/
          WinSetPointer(HWND_DESKTOP, WinQuerySysPointer(HWND_DESKTOP,
                                          SPTR_ARROW, FALSE));

      } /* endif */

      break;

   case WM_CLOSE:
          /*_____*/
          /* cause the application to end           */
          /*_____*/
          pszFilename = (PSZ)WinQueryWindowPtr(hwnd, QWL_USER);
          free(pszFilename);
          GpiSetBitmap (hpsMem, (HBITMAP)NULL);
          GpiDeleteBitmap(hbmMem);
          GpiAssociate( hpsMem, (HDC)NULL );
          GpiDestroyPS( hpsMem );
          DevCloseDC( hdcMem );
          hbmMem = (HBITMAP)NULL;
          WinPostMsg( hwnd, WM_QUIT, 0L, 0L );
          break;

   default:
          /*_____*/
          /* unknown messages to default            */
          /*_____*/
          return WinDefWindowProc( hwnd, msg, mp1, mp2 );
   }
   return FALSE;
}

/*_____*/
/* Method for Displaying a textfile in a MLE.                     */
/*_____*/
HWND DisplayText(HWND  hwndClient, ULONG x, ULONG y, ULONG cx, ULONG cy,
                 PSZ   filename, PSZ FontName)
{ HWND hwndMLE;
  HWND hwndFrame;
  MRESULT     WinRC;
  int         return_code;
  CHAR        *Buffer;
  IPT         ipt;
  FILE        *Stream;
  CHAR        szMsg[256];
  struct stat StatBuff;
  RECTL       rcl;

  hwndFrame = WinQueryWindow(hwndClient, QW_PARENT);

  hwndMLE =
  WinCreateWindow(
     hwndClient,            /* parent-window handle                */
     WC_MLE,                /* pointer to registered class name    */
     NULL,                  /* pointer to window text              */
     WS_VISIBLE
     MLS_READONLY
     MLS_HSCROLL
     MLS_VSCROLL
```

Figure 44-11 (Part 10 of 12). CLUBVIEW.C: The Clubview Program.

```
        MLS_BORDER,                 /* window style                           */
        x, x, cx, cy,               /* position of window                     */
        hwndFrame,                  /* owner-window handle                    */
        HWND_TOP,                   /* handle to sibling window               */
        (USHORT)ID_MLE,             /* window identifier                      */
        NULL,                       /* pointer to buffer                      */
        NULL);                      /* pointer to structure with pres. params. */

    WinQueryWindowRect(hwndClient, &rcl);

    WinSetWindowPos(hwndMLE, HWND_TOP, 0, 0,
                    rcl.xRight - rcl.xLeft, rcl.yTop - rcl.yBottom,
                    SWP_SIZE | SWP_MOVE | SWP_ACTIVATE | SWP_SHOW);

    /*————————————————————————————————*/
    /* set font for the MLE                                */
    /*————————————————————————————————*/
    WinSetPresParam( hwndMLE,
                     PP_FONTNAMESIZE,
                     (LONG)strlen( FontName ) + 11,
                     (PVOID)FontName );

    /*————————————————————————————————*/
    /* Open file and read data into a buffer               */
    /*————————————————————————————————*/
    Stream = fopen( filename, "rb" );
    if ( Stream == NULL )
        {
         sprintf( szMsg, "Can't open the file < %s >", filename);
         WinMessageBox( HWND_DESKTOP,
                        HWND_DESKTOP,
                        szMsg,
                        "MLE",
                        1,
                        MB_OK );
        } /* endif */

    return_code = stat( filename, &StatBuff);
    Buffer = (CHAR *)malloc( (size_t)StatBuff.st_size );
    if ( Buffer == NULL )
        WinMessageBox( HWND_DESKTOP,
                       HWND_DESKTOP,
                       "Can't allocate storage",
                       "MLE",
                       1,
                       MB_OK );

    fread( (void *)Buffer,
           sizeof(CHAR),
           (size_t)StatBuff.st_size,
           Stream );
    fclose( Stream );
```

Figure 44-11 (Part 11 of 12).   CLUBVIEW.C: The Clubview Program.

```
    /*————————————————————————————*/
    /* import buffer data into the MLE Control */
    /*   - clear the buffer                     */

    /*   - import from location 0 (beginning)  */
    /*   - import the data                      */
    /*   - make the MLE read only               */
    /*————————————————————————————*/
    ipt = 0;   /* delete buffer data */
    WinRC = WinSendMsg(hwndMLE,MLM_DELETE,(MPARAM)ipt, MPFROMLONG((ULONG)100000));
    ipt = 0;   /* Import from the beginning  */
    WinRC = WinSendMsg(hwndMLE, MLM_SETIMPORTEXPORT, (MPARAM)Buffer,
                       MPFROMLONG( (LONG)StatBuff.st_size-1 ) );
    WinRC= WinSendMsg(hwndMLE, MLM_IMPORT, (MPARAM)&ipt,
                       MPFROMLONG( (ULONG)StatBuff.st_size-1 ) );
    return(hwndMLE);
    }
```

Figure 44-11 (Part 12 of 12).   CLUBVIEW.C: The Clubview Program.

Chapter 45

The Club Med Server

This is the third and last of a three-chapter series on the Club Med client/server application. This chapter walks you through the transaction server code. We show you how to create a multiuser transaction server that uses Named Pipes, the IBM LAN Server, and the OS/2 Database Manager. This program demonstrates how a transaction is processed using the CLUB database, and how the results are returned to the OOUI client. We start this chapter with a short discussion on the design of transaction servers.

WHAT'S A CLUB MED TRANSACTION SERVER?

The Club Med transaction server is simply a dedicated computer on the network; this server provides code that executes transactions on a database. The transaction code and the database reside on the same machine. The multiuser capabilities are provided by creating multiple instances of the transaction server process. The client invokes the execution of transactions on the server through request messages sent over the network using Named Pipes. For each request, a reply message is returned using the same Named Pipe instance. Large result files (BLOBs) are returned via the IBM Lan Server.

Does this all sound like "deja vu"? It should. The program we will be walking through in this chapter is just a revisit of the TP1 implementation described in Chapter 34. The only difference is that we replaced the TP1 transaction with Club Med-specific transactions. We're also introducing the concept of returning a BLOB as part of the execution of a transaction. The simple TP1 DebitCredit transaction consists of a single request-reply message exchange; it does not contain the notion of a large response file.

The good news, then, is that because you've already seen it all, we expect the walk through the server end of the Club Med application to be fairly brisk. To keep the code well-focused and reasonable in size, we're only presenting one transaction: *get_club_names*. The other eight server transactions are available on the program diskette with their client counterparts.

THE CLUB TRANSACTION SERVER ELEMENTS

The purpose of this section is to get you acquainted with the different components of the Club Med Transaction Server, and then show you how they play together. You should first review Chapter 45, "The Club Med Server," to get the big picture of how the client and server interact at the system level.

Why Is a Multiuser Server Needed?

You clearly don't want your clients to depend on a single server process. If you do so, you run the risk of having a client hog all the system's resources and starve out its fellow clients. A server should be designed to provide the best overall performance for all of its clients. Consequently, your server processes must provide a certain level of multitasking and support more than one client at the same time.

What Does a Multiuser Server Need?

Now that we've introduced the notion of a multitasking server instead of a serially reusable server, we open up a flood gate of new requirements. All of these requirements are to sharing the server's resources. Let's go down the list of what is needed:

1. *Multisession Peer-to-Peer Communications:* We obviously can't have a single communication session, because it will quickly become the serially reusable bottle-neck. So, we need a protocol that supports multiple concurrent sessions. How many? It depends on whether your sessions are persistent or non-persistent. If they're persistent, you will need one session per client. If they're non-persistent, you can create a pool of reusable sessions. We will take the non-persistent design approach, which allows us to provide service on demand and play the law of statistical averages. This means we'll be providing fewer sessions than the number of clients. So, a client may occasionally wait on a reusable session to free up. Of course, we do not place an upper limit on the number of clients that our server pool will support. The concept of dynamic allocation of connections when needed makes the network easier to manage than with static session allocations. The Named Pipes protocol allows us to create a single Named Pipe with multiple instances. The Named Pipe transaction services, such as **DosCallNPipe,** make it easy to create non-persistent service calls.

2. *Multitasking Transaction Server Processes:* The transaction server process inter-faces with the client and executes the SQL transactions. *Why is it a process and not a thread?* Because the OS/2 Database Manager allows only a single database connection per process. *How many processes are needed?* As many as the number of concurrent sessions you have chosen to support. In our design, each transaction server process will own one Named Pipe instance and one connection to the Database Manager.

3. ***Shared Access to Data:*** Our server needs to protect the integrity of shared data while allowing concurrent access to the data. No problem! Our transaction server is built on top of the OS/2 Database Manager, which is a multiuser SQL server engine.

4. ***Shared File Access:*** Our server needs to support the return of large result files to its clients. These result files may contain multiple table rows or large objects (BLOBs) such as bitmaps, metafiles, text files, or image frames. How are these objects passed to the client? The servers produce the large file objects and return their name and location to the clients as part of the reply message. The clients can then either directly manipulate the files or copy them over. A file server, such as the IBM LAN Server program, is needed to provide multiple client and server processes network access to a shared file system.

How Are the Transaction Processes Started and Killed?

This is an area that can get really wild. There are many schemes for starting processes dynamically to match incoming client requests. Each scheme introduces its own set of interesting heuristics. However, remember that it takes time to create a process. Do you want that to happen when a request comes in? You may be better off priming a static number of processes. If the processes take up too much space in memory, share some of the functions using DLLs. Occasionally, you may have to fine-tune your server by adding or removing some transaction processes.

Our aim in this chapter is to provide you with a "bare bones" process launcher program that provides the basic function. You can then take that code and modify it to suit your requirements. The good news is that we already have such a program: the one for the TP1 transaction server LAUNCHER developed in Chapter 34. We will use this program to start "n" process instances of the Club Med transaction server program (see Figure 45-1). The launcher program takes, as input parameters, the name of the process

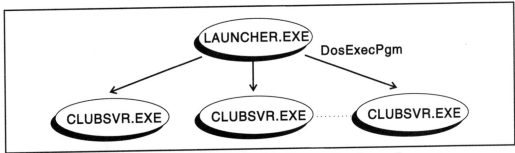

Figure 45-1. Launcher Starts "n" Instances of the Transaction Server Program.

to be launched and the number of times to "clone" it. For example, to start three concurrent Club Med transaction server processes issue:

```
LAUNCHER  clubsvr 3
```

where *clubsvr* is the name of Club Med transaction server program we will be developing in this chapter. After it creates the three processes, the launcher blocks itself and waits for any key to be hit on the server machine. A key hit wakes up the launcher and causes it to kill all the processes it created and then terminate the server application.

The Transaction Server and the Database Server

Figure 45-2 shows the elements of the Club Med transaction server. The server machine contains both the transaction server processes and the OS/2 Database Manager. The transaction server processes are instances of the CLUBSVR program, whose code we will shortly be walking through. Each CLUBSVR process creates an instance of a Named Pipe and connects to the CLUB database. Clients submit their transactions by issuing **DosCallNPipe** calls. This call will be handed automatically to the first available server process. If no server process is available, the clients will queue their requests until one frees up. All this queuing is provided by Named Pipes automatically. Remember, all the clients use instances of the *same* Named Pipe.

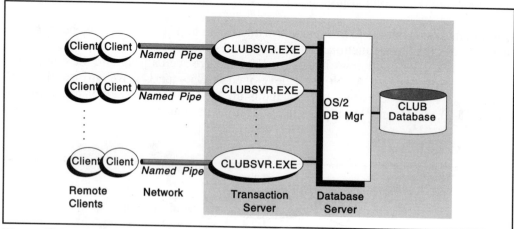

Figure 45-2. The Transaction Server Processes and the Database Server.

The Transaction Server and the File Server

Figure 45-3 shows another element of our Club Med server: the file server. The file server is the IBM LAN Server program, which is also installed on the server machine. The server processes create response files (or BLOBs) on the file servers; clients can then directly access these files over the network using the OS/2 LAN Requester.

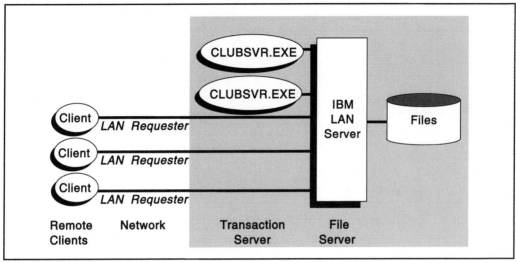

Figure 45-3.　Using a File Server to Make BLOBs Available to Clients.

CLUBSVR.SQC: THE TRANSACTION SERVER

Now that we know how the pieces play together, we are ready to introduce the element that customizes the Club Med transaction server: the CLUBSVR.SQC program (see listing in Figure 45-4). This is a program designed to run Club Med-specific transactions. The transactions operate on data stored in the CLUB database. Transactions are triggered by messages sent by remote clients using Named Pipes.

The core of the CLUBSVR.SQC program is identical to the SQLTP1SV.SQC program developed in Chapter 34. In fact, we just copied many of the procedures. So, what is it that makes CLUBSVR.SQC special? Here's the list of what's value-added and new:

- **The transaction dispatcher:** This new piece of code provided by the **dispatch_transaction()** function is a switch that invokes the appropriate transaction handler procedure. The switch dispatches a handler procedure based on the "transaction id" field value it reads from the incoming request message. TP1 did not require a switch because its server was only capable of executing a single transaction: TP1.

- **Club Med-specific transactions:** The Club Med server executes the eight transactions described earlier in "The Club Med Transactions" on page 1024. These transactions are, of course, all new and specific to the club application. The SQL code for the *get_club_names* transaction is supplied in the listing. The code for the remaining transactions is on the program diskette.

- **The BLOB return mechanism:** The TP1 server did not return large objects to the client. This is an area where the Club Med server provides a value-added function.

The BLOB return mechanism is demonstrated in the **get_club_names**() listing. It's very simple:

1. Transactions that generate multirow responses create a client-specific response file. The server is responsible for naming the file and assigning unique names.
2. The transaction handler writes the results of a query into the response file one row at a time. This is done as part of the SQL cursor loop.
3. The formatting of the rows in the response file is based on a common format known to both the client and the server.
4. The transaction handler closes the response file when the last row is fetched.
5. The transaction handler returns the name of the response file to the client as part of the transaction reply message (see "The Club Med Transactions" on page 1024).
6. The client can access the response file using the LAN requester. The file can be directly manipulated or copied over the network.
7. The client is responsible for deleting the response file from the shared subdirectory.

Except for the three items described above, you should find no surprises in the code. We've left it all in one chunk because it requires no further explanation.

```
/****************************************************************************/
/*   PROGRAM NAME: CLUBSVR.SQC                                             */
/*                                                                        */
/*                                                                        */
/*   PROGRAM DESCRIPTION:  This program is run as a child task of the LAUNCHER*/
/*     program and executes the CLUB Server transactions using Named Pipes  */
/*     to communicate with a client.                                      */
/*                                                                        */
/****************************************************************************/
#include <process.h>               /* For exit()                  */
#include <string.h>                /* For printf                  */
#include <sys\types.h>             /* For time()                  */
#include <sys\timeb.h>             /* For time()                  */
#include <sys\stat.h>              /* For stat()                  */
#include <stdlib.h>                /* For atoi                    */
#include <stdio.h>                 /* For sprintf, printf         */
#include <io.h>                    /* For mktemp                  */

#define INCL_DOSPROCESS            /* for DosGetInfoBlocks         */
#define INCL_DOSNMPIPES            /* include named pipe api calls */
#define INCL_ERRORS                /* include error definitions    */
#include <os2.h>

#include <sqlca.h>                 /* sqlca                       */
#include <sql.h>                   /* error msg. retrieval        */
#include <sqlcodes.h>              /* SQL return code constants    */
#include <sqlenv.h>                /* environment functions and    */

#include "clubtxns.h"
#pragma stack16(8192)
```

Figure 45-4 (Part 1 of 8). CLUBSVR.SQC: The Transaction Server Program.

```
                        /*————————————————————*/
                        /* forward declarations of functions   */
                        /*————————————————————*/
VOID read_config(VOID);
VOID initialize_task(VOID);
VOID initialize_pipe(VOID);
VOID execute_task(VOID);

SHORT dispatch_transaction(VOID);
SHORT get_club_names(VOID);
SHORT get_club_graphics(VOID);
SHORT get_club_description(VOID);
SHORT get_club_prices(VOID);
SHORT find_all_reserv(VOID);
SHORT find_reservation(VOID);
SHORT add_reservation(VOID);
SHORT cancel_reservation(VOID);
SHORT generate_message_filename(VOID);
SHORT open_response_file(VOID);
SHORT open_message_file(PCHAR);
SHORT unknown_transaction(VOID);

VOID print_error(USHORT, PCHAR, PCHAR, USHORT);
VOID format_error(PCHAR msgbuf, LONG Error, PCHAR msg,
                  PCHAR file, USHORT line);
                        /*————————————————————*/
                        /* constant definitions                */
                        /*————————————————————*/
#define GOOD              0
#define FAILED           -1

                        /*————————————————————*/
                        /* variables                           */
                        /*————————————————————*/
CHAR    input_msgbuf[1024];       /* msg buffer for receiving txn    */
CHAR    txn_parms[512];           /* tranaction parms from input msg */
CHAR    output_msgbuf[1024];      /* msg buffer for sending resp.    */
CHAR    error_msgbuf[1024];       /* msg buffer for formating errors */
USHORT  rc;                       /* return code variable            */
CHAR    error_string[80];         /* error string container          */
SHORT   txn_id;                   /* transaction identifier          */
PCHAR   fn_template="FLXXXXXX";   /* template for generated file name */
CHAR    file_name[13];            /* generated file name             */
CHAR    response_file_name[13];   /* generated file name with ext    */
CHAR    message_file_name[13];    /* message file name               */
PTIB    ptib;                     /* for generating temp. file name  */
PPIB    ppib;                     /* for generating temp. file name  */
ULONG   process_id;               /* for generating temp. file name  */
USHORT  filenum;                  /* for generating temp. file name  */
FILE    *rsp_file;
FILE    *msg_file;


ULONG   pipe_handle;
CHAR    pipe_name[] = "\\PIPE\\CLUB";
ULONG   bytes_read;
ULONG   bytes_written;

struct sqlca sqlca;
```

Figure 45-4 (Part 2 of 8). CLUBSVR.SQC: The Transaction Server Program.

```
EXEC SQL WHENEVER SQLERROR CONTINUE;
EXEC SQL WHENEVER SQLWARNING CONTINUE;
EXEC SQL WHENEVER NOT FOUND CONTINUE;

                        /*————————————————————————*/
                        /* SQL Host variables        */
                        /*————————————————————————*/
EXEC SQL BEGIN DECLARE SECTION;
  char      club[33];
  char      country[33];
  char      activity[21];
  char      picture[21];
  char      description[21];
  char      adult_price[9];
  char      child_price[9];
  char      week_date[11];
  char      last_name[33];
  char      first_name[33];
  char      age[4];
  char      party_member[2];
  char      reserv_no[10];
  char      phone_no[21];
  char      address[33];
  char      city[33];
  char      state[3];
  char      zip[11];
  char      payment_method[10];
EXEC SQL END   DECLARE SECTION;

/*————————————————————————————————————————————————————————*/
/* Main routine.                                             */
/*————————————————————————————————————————————————————————*/
VOID main(USHORT argc, PCHAR argv[])
{
  initialize_task();               /* perform database connect etc. */

  initialize_pipe();               /* create Named Pipe             */

  execute_task();                  /* Loop executing TP1s           */

} /* end main */


/*————————————————————————————————————————————————————————*/
/* Perform onetime initializations for the task such as database connects. */
/*————————————————————————————————————————————————————————*/
VOID  initialize_task(VOID)
{
  /*————————————————————————————*/
  /* connect to the database, restart if */
  /*    necessary                        */
  /*————————————————————————————*/
  sqlestrd("CLUB", 'S', &sqlca);

  if (sqlca.sqlcode == SQLE_RC_DB_RESTART)
     sqlerest("CLUB", &sqlca);

  if (sqlca.sqlcode)
     { sprintf(error_string,"connnecting to the database, sqlca.sqlcode = %ld",
          sqlca.sqlcode);
```

Figure 45-4 (Part 3 of 8). CLUBSVR.SQC: The Transaction Server Program.

```
            print_error(0, error_string, __FILE__,__LINE__);
            exit(FAILED);
         }

      /*_____*/
      /* get PID for file name generation   */
      /*_____*/
      DosGetInfoBlocks(&ptib, &ppib);
      process_id = ppib->pib_ulpid;

      /*_____*/
      /* install database signal handler    */
      /*_____*/
      sqleisig(&sqlca);
      if (sqlca.sqlcode)
         { sprintf(error_string,"installing signal handler, sqlca.sqlcode = %ld",
                 sqlca.sqlcode);
           print_error(0, error_string, __FILE__,__LINE__);
           exit(FAILED);
         }

   } /* end initialize_task */

/*_____*/
/* Perform onetime initialization  for the the Named Pipe      */
/*_____*/
VOID  initialize_pipe(VOID)
{

   #define PIPE_OPENMODE     0x4002    /* no write-behind allowed, duplex  */
   #define PIPEMODE          0x0580    /* message pipe, 128  instances     */
   #define TIMEOUT           0L        /* wait forever timeout value       */

   rc = DosCreateNPipe(pipe_name,          /* PipeName                     */
                       &pipe_handle,        /* pipe handle returned         */
                       PIPE_OPENMODE,
                       PIPEMODE,
                       512,                 /* Output buffer size in bytes  */
                       512,                 /* Input  buffer size in bytes  */
                       TIMEOUT);
   if (rc)
      {print_error(rc,"Making a named pipe",__FILE__,__LINE__);
       exit(FAILED);
      }
} /* end initialize_pipes */

/*_____*/
/* Task routine. This routine continuously 1) waits for a remote request  */
/*    2) reads the incoming parameters,  3) invokes the transaction dispatcher*/
/*    4) sends back response  5) disconnects from client       */
/*_____*/
VOID execute_task(VOID)
{
   /*_____*/
   /* continuous loop                    */
   /*_____*/
   while (TRUE)
      {
        /*_____*/
        /* execute a transaction               */
        /*_____*/
```

Figure 45-4 (Part 4 of 8).   CLUBSVR.SQC: The Transaction Server Program.

```
      rc = DosConnectNPipe(pipe_handle);
      if (rc)
         {print_error(rc,"Connecting to pipe",__FILE__,__LINE__);
          exit(FAILED);
         }

      rc = DosRead(pipe_handle,
                   input_msgbuf,
                   sizeof(input_msgbuf),
                   &bytes_read);
      if (rc)
         {print_error(rc,"Reading from pipe",__FILE__,__LINE__);
          exit(FAILED);
         }

      if ( dispatch_transaction() )
         exit(FAILED);

      rc = DosWrite(pipe_handle,
                    output_msgbuf,
                    strlen(output_msgbuf) + 1,
                    &bytes_written);
      if (rc)
         {print_error(rc,"Writing to pipe",__FILE__,__LINE__);
          exit(FAILED);
         }

      rc = DosDisConnectNPipe(pipe_handle);
      if (rc)
         {print_error(rc,"Disconnecting from Pipe",__FILE__,__LINE__);
          exit(FAILED);
         }
   }/* end while */
} /* end execute_task */

/*_____*/
/* function to dispatch a transaction                           */
/*_____*/
SHORT dispatch_transaction(VOID)
{
  strcat(input_msgbuf, ";");
  sscanf(input_msgbuf, "TRANSACTION_ID=%d %[^;]", &txn_id, txn_parms);

  switch (txn_id)
  { case GET_CLUB_NAMES       : get_club_names();              break;
    case GET_CLUB_GRAPHICS    : get_club_graphics();           break;
    case GET_CLUB_DESCRIPTION : get_club_description();        break;
    case GET_CLUB_PRICES      : get_club_prices();             break;
    case FIND_ALL_RESERV      : find_all_reserv();             break;
    case FIND_RESERVATION     : find_reservation();            break;
    case ADD_RESERVATION      : add_reservation();             break;
    case CANCEL_RESERVATION   : cancel_reservation();          break;

    case GET_MESSAGE_FILENAME : generate_message_filename();   break;
    default                   : unknown_transaction();         break;
  } /* endswitch */

  return(GOOD);
} /* end dispatch_transaction */
```

Figure 45-4 (Part 5 of 8).   CLUBSVR.SQC: The Transaction Server Program.

```
/*_____*/
/* execute get_club_names      transaction            */
/*_____*/
SHORT get_club_names(VOID)
{
   if (open_response_file())
      return(FAILED);

   /*_____*/
   /* Select clubs and countries           */
   /*_____*/
   EXEC SQL DECLARE CLUB_SEL CURSOR FOR
            SELECT DISTINCT CLUB, COUNTRY
            FROM CLUBS
            ORDER BY COUNTRY;

   /*_____*/
   /* Open the cursor                      */
   /*_____*/
   EXEC SQL OPEN CLUB_SEL;
   if (SQLCODE)
      { format_error(output_msgbuf, SQLCODE,"opening cursor",__FILE__,__LINE__);
        return(FAILED);
      }

   /*_____*/
   /* Get row data                         */
   /*_____*/
   while (TRUE)
   { EXEC SQL FETCH CLUB_SEL
             INTO :club, :country;

     if ((SQLCODE!=0) && (SQLCODE != 100))
        { format_error(output_msgbuf,SQLCODE,"fetching data",__FILE__,__LINE__);
          return(FAILED);
        }

     if (SQLCODE == 100) break;

     /*_____*/
     /* Write row to response file           */
     /*_____*/
      if (!fprintf(rsp_file,"%32s  %32s\n", club, country))
         { format_error(output_msgbuf, 0L,"writing to response file",
                     __FILE__,__LINE__);
           return(FAILED);
         }
   } /* end while */

   /*_____*/
   /* Close the cursor                     */
   /*_____*/
   EXEC SQL CLOSE CLUB_SEL;
   if (SQLCODE)
      { format_error(output_msgbuf, SQLCODE,"closing cursor",__FILE__,__LINE__);
        return(FAILED);
      }

   /*_____*/
   /* Set the message, close response file*/
   /*_____*/
```

Figure 45-4 (Part 6 of 8). CLUBSVR.SQC: The Transaction Server Program.

```
    sprintf(output_msgbuf,
        "TXN_COMPLETION = SUCCESS RESPONSE_FILE = %s", response_file_name);
    fclose (rsp_file);
    rsp_file = NULL;
    return(GOOD);
}/* end get_club_names */


         See program diskette for the following functions:
SHORT get_club_graphics(VOID)            {  ...  }
SHORT get_club_description(VOID)         {  ...  }
SHORT get_club_prices(VOID)             {  ...  }
SHORT find_all_reserv(VOID)             {  ...  }
SHORT find_reservation(VOID)            {  ...  }
SHORT add_reservation(VOID)             {  ...  }
SHORT cancel_reservation(VOID)          {  ...  }
SHORT generate_message_filename(VOID)   {  ...  }
SHORT unknown_transaction(VOID)         {  ...  }



/*_____*/
/* open a response file                                                 */
/*_____*/
SHORT open_response_file(VOID)
{
  sprintf(response_file_name,"R%5.5d%2.2d.TMP", process_id, filenum % 99);
  if (NULL == (rsp_file = fopen(response_file_name,"w")))
     {format_error(output_msgbuf, (LONG)rsp_file,"opening response file",
                __FILE__,__LINE__);
      return(FAILED);
      }
  return(GOOD);
} /* end open_response_file */

/*_____*/
/* open a message file                                                  */
/*_____*/
SHORT open_message_file(PCHAR message_file_name)
{
  if (NULL == (msg_file = fopen(message_file_name,"r")))
     {format_error(output_msgbuf, (LONG)rsp_file,"opening message file",
                __FILE__,__LINE__);
      return(FAILED);
      }
  return(GOOD);
} /* end open_message_file */

/*_____*/
/* Error Format Routine                                                 */
/*_____*/
VOID format_error(PCHAR msgbuf, LONG Error, PCHAR msg,
                  PCHAR file, USHORT line)
{
  CHAR sql_msgbuf[256];

  if (rsp_file != NULL)
     { fclose (rsp_file);
```

Figure 45-4 (Part 7 of 8). CLUBSVR.SQC: The Transaction Server Program.

```
     rsp_file = NULL;
   }
 if (SQLCODE)
 { sqlaintp(sql_msgbuf,                          /* buffer for msg text */
           sizeof(sql_msgbuf),                   /* buffer size         */
           80,                                   /* line width          */
           &sqlca);                              /* SQLCA               */
 } /* endif */
 sprintf(msgbuf, "TXN_COMPLETION = FAILED RESPONSE_FILE = NONE\n"
                 "Error %ld detected while %s at line %d in file %s.\n%s\n",
                 Error, msg, line, file, sql_msgbuf);
} /* end format_error */

/*————————————————————————————————————————————————————*/
/* Error Display Routine                              */
/*————————————————————————————————————————————————————*/
VOID print_error(USHORT Error, PCHAR msg, PCHAR file, USHORT line)
{

 if (Error == 0)
    printf("Error detected while %s at line %d in file %s.\n",
           msg, line, file);
 else
    printf("Error %d detected while %s at line %d in file %s.\n",
           Error, msg, line, file);
} /* end print_error */
```

Figure 45-4 (Part 8 of 8).   CLUBSVR.SQC: The Transaction Server Program.

CONGRATULATIONS AND GOODBYE

This is where the Club Med Grand Finale all comes together. This is also where the book comes to an end. If you've made it this far, congratulations; it was a long journey. We hope you got out of it what you were looking for. The future is with "downsized" client/server applications that run on PC LANs. OS/2, in one form or another, provides most of the major components you will need to build mission-critical applications on PCs. We hope this lengthy introduction to client/server has shown you what elements are required to build such systems.

Now that you know what to look for, you can shop around for the pieces. The IBM solution is the *de facto* standard for extensions and is an excellent base for comparison shopping. Now that you've mastered SQL using the Database Manager and the examples in this book, you may decide to switch database engines to SQL Server, Oracle, or Gupta's SQLBase. For database front-end tools, you may prefer to use Borland, Sybase, Enfin/3, or Ingres tools. You may want to develop your own graphic interface using Gupta's SQLWindows, Choreographer, or Easel. Or, you may decide to go the Ellipse route (from Cooperative Solutions); they provide an environment that helps you create, manage, and deploy both your client and server applications. Client/Server is synonymous with "mix and match." Have fun!

Figure 45-5.   Bye-Bye

Index

A

Address Resolution Protocol (ARP)   114
Advanced Peer-to-Peer Network (APPN)
  96,177
AF_INET   434—435
AIX   184
Alerters   165
Alerts   107, 109, 132, 134, 136, 533
ALMCOPY   98
Andrew File System (AFS)   191
Anonymous Pipes   70
Apollo RPC   189
APPC   37—38, 46, 100—102, 156, 160, 182,
  393, 396, 479, 481—482, 484—488, 491,
  493, 543—544, 546, 549, 553
  Attach Manager   477, 493, 507
  Basic Conversations   479
  Blocking and Flushing   491
  Configuration Verbs   485
  Control Verbs   481
  Conversation   475
  Conversation States   491
  Conversation Verbs   482
  Logical Unit (LU)   474
  LU 6.2   177, 474
  Mapped Conversations   479
  Network Management Verbs   487
  Operator Verbs   484
  Parallel Conversations   478
  Parallel Sessions   474, 478
  Password   477, 489
  Peer-to-Peer Exchanges   490
  Peer-to-Peer Protocol   396
  Physical Unit (PU)   475
  PIP Data   489
  Protocol "Sniff"   553
  PU Type 2.1   475
  Security   488
  Session Limits   474

APPC *(Continued)*
  Sessions   477, 490
  SNA Session   474
  Synchronization Services   489
  Terminology   474
  Transaction   489
  Transaction Program (TP)   474
  Tutorial   471
  Two-phase Commit   102
  Verb Categories   479
  Verb Definition   476
  Verb, Invoking   507
  Verbs   481—482, 484—489, 491, 493
APPC Verbs
  ACTIVATE_DLC   484
  ACTIVATE_LOGICAL_LINKS   484
  ALLOCATE   481—482, 488, 493
  CNOS   484
  CONFIRM   482, 489, 491, 493
  CONFIRMED   482, 489, 493
  DEACTIVATE_CONVERSATION_GROUP
    484
  DEACTIVATE_DLC   484
  DEACTIVATE_LOGICAL_LINK   484
  DEACTIVATE_SESSION   485
  DEALLOCATE   482, 489, 491, 493—494
  DEFINE_COS   486
  DEFINE_LOCAL_LU   486
  DEFINE_LOGICAL_LINK   486
  DEFINE_LU_LU_PASSWORD   486
  DEFINE_MODE   486
  DEFINE_PARTNER_LU   486
  DEFINE_PARTNER_LU_LOCATION
    486
  DEFINE_TP   486
  DEFINE_USER_ID_PASSWORD   486
  DELETE_COS   486
  DELETE_LOCAL_LU   486
  DELETE_LOGICAL_LINK   486
  DELETE_LU_LU_PASSWORD   486
  DELETE_MODE   486
  DELETE_PARTNER_LU   486

B

C

3Com   133
802.2   100
80586   50

__FILE__   238, 310
__LINE__   238, 310
_beginthread   204, 281
_endthread   205

Order Your Programs Here!

As a convenience and learning aid you may order a diskette containing the current version of the sample programs in **"Client/Server Programming with OS/2 2.0."** The source files are shipped on an unsupported, as-is basis. Neither the Authors, Van Nostrand Reinhold, nor Computer Literacy Bookshops assume any liability with respect to the use, accuracy, or fitness of information contained within the diskettes.

Order Your Programs Here!

As a convenience and learning aid you may order a diskette containing the current version of the sample programs in **"Client/Server Programming with OS/2 2.0."** The source files are shipped on an unsupported, as-is basis. Neither the Authors, Van Nostrand Reinhold, nor Computer Literacy Bookshops assume any liability with respect to the use, accuracy, or fitness of information contained within the diskettes.

"Client/Server Programming with OS/2 2.0" Diskette Offer

Please Mail This Form & Payment to:

COMPUTER LITERACY BOOKSHOPS
2590 North First Sreet
San Jose, CA 95131 USA

Order Now By Credit Card	
TEL: (408) 435-0744	Mon-Fri: 9:00 AM-9:00 PM
FAX: (408) 435-1823	Sat-Sun: 10:00 AM-6:00 PM (Pacific Time)

To Request Ordering Information, Send Internet Message to:
info@clbooks.com

Ship This Order To: **Date:** _____

_____
NAME (FULL NAME, NO INITIALS PLEASE)

_____
COMPANY/MAIL STOP

_____
ADDRESS

_____
INTERNET ADDRESS

_____
CITY   STATE/PROVINCE   ZIP/POSTAL CODE

_____
COUNTRY   DAY PHONE (Required for Courier Delivery)

Method of Payment (use U.S. currency)

☐ Check Enclosed (Payable to Computer Literacy)

☐ Charge my credit card:

☐ VISA   ☐ Mastercard

☐ American Express   ☐ Diner's Club/Carte Blanche

Card#: _____

Expiration Date: _____

Signature: _____

Programs are stored in compressed, self-extracting files on one 3 1/2", 1.44 Mb diskette.

Quantity ____ @$34.95 $_____

CA ____ %   TAX $_____

Shipping $_____

TOTAL $_____

California Residents: Please add your county's sales tax.

Shipping & Handling Charges/Shipping Policies

US		Europe		Canada/Mexico		Asia	
Mail	$2.00	Airmail	$2.00	Mail	$2.00	Airmail	$3.00
UPS Ground	$3.75	Courier	$11.00	Courier	$11.00	Courier	$11.00
UPS 2-Day Air	$6.00						
UPS Overnight	$11.00						

Prices: All orders must be prepaid.

Shipping Time: All orders shipped no later than the next day.

TAKE $200 OFF

Our Documentation Services

We write documentation for software developers.

Our products include: user manuals, reference manuals, hands-on tutorials, keyboard templates and training materials.

Make your products easier to use with our professionally written and produced documentation (and take $200 off your first invoice over $1000). Call us at 1-800-676-4199 for more information.

For a free example of our products: our **OS/2 2.0 Workplace Shell and Windows 3.1 to OS/2 2.0 Upgrade Template**, mail this coupon with $4.00 for shipping and handling to:

Charles Hatvany and Associates, Inc.
25 Newport Street, Arlington, MA 02174

____ Please send me my free **OS/2 2.0 Workplace Shell and Windows 3.1 to OS/2 2.0 Upgrade Template**. I enclose $4.00 for shipping and handling.

____ Please send me more information about Charles Hatvany and Associates' Documentation Services.

Name: _____

Title: _____

Company: _____

Address: _____

City, State, Zip: _____

Phone: _____

Thank you for buying this VNR book.
Van Nostrand Reinhold, a world leader in publishing books on IBM topics, is proud to offer the first-ever series of books on the operating system of the future, OS/2 2.0.

VNR is committed to bringing you the information you need to take best advantage of OS/2 2.0's unique features. Please complete, fold, seal with tape and mail this card with your comments and suggestions about this book and we'll keep you advised of new books of interest to you.

Sincerely,

Van Nostrand Reinhold
Publishing for Professionals Since 1848

OS/2 is a Registered Trademark of IBM Corporation

Yes, I'd like to receive information on future OS/2 2.0 books from Van Nostrand Reinhold.

Name _____

Company _____

Address _____

City _____ State _____ ZIP _____

Phone ( ) _____

Where did you buy this book? ❏ Bookstore ❏ Mail ❏ IBM ❏ Other

What OS/2 topics would you like VNR to publish books on?

What other areas are you interested in books on?

❏ IBM Mainframe ❏ IBM Midrange ❏ IBM PC's ❏ Artificial Intelligence

❏ Automation in Manufacturing ❏ Computer Security ❏ Databases ❏ DEC, VAX, VMS ❏ MIS

❏ Networking and Communications ❏ Software Engineering ❏ UNIX

❏ Other _____

Please give us your comments about the book you purchased and any suggestions for future editions?

(Author/Title) _____

_____

_____

_____

_____

NO POSTAGE
NECESSARY
IF MAILED
IN THE
UNITED STATES

BUSINESS REPLY MAIL

FIRST CLASS MAIL   PERMIT NO. 704   NEW YORK, NY

POSTAGE WILL BE PAID BY ADDRESSEE

Van Nostrand Reinhold

Att: Computer Science Product Manager

115 Fifth Avenue

New York, NY 10003